D1091357

THE ANNUAL
OBITUARY 1980

THE ANNUAL
OBITUARY 1980

FIRST EDITION

EDITOR
ROLAND TURNER

ASSOCIATE EDITOR
JANET PODELL

ASSISTANT EDITORS
EDWARD TALLMAN
ANN WEISS

ST. MARTIN'S • NEW YORK

Simultaneously published by
MACMILLAN PRESS LTD.
London and Basingstoke

Companies and representatives throughout the world.

ISBN: 0 333 32502 8

This book is printed on long lasting, acid free paper. The signatures are
Smyth sewn with cotton thread.

CONTENTS

Editor's Note   page vii

Alphabetical Index of Entrants   ix

Index of Entrants by Professions   xii

Obituaries   1

Addendum   869

Index of Obituary Writers   877

Abbreviations Index   881

This first edition is dedicated
to the memory of

JOHN LENNON
1940-1980

In my life I've loved them all

EDITOR'S NOTE

The Annual Obituary 1980 is volume one in a series which will describe and evaluate the lives and achievements of notable people who have died.

When we first recognized the need for a new and international biographical reference series, we had little idea as to how we would organize each annual edition. However, in devising methods of entry selection, it became apparent that there were advantages to be gained from producing each volume as a collection of the year's major obituaries. Such an arrangement obviated the need to survey thousands of notable contemporaries for possible inclusion, as our choice could be made from the few hundred people whose deaths are reported in leading newspapers and journals. Also, by covering the complete life and works of all entrants at the time of death (rather than in the course of still-productive lives), extensive updating would never be required and each edition would remain valuable indefinitely; no volume would be superseded, or even partially duplicated, by a subsequent volume. Furthermore, we felt that by bringing together in one volume new essays on important people who have died during the year, the series might prove to be a useful historical document, likely to be of interest to casual enquirers and library browsers as well as to students and researchers.

We originally intended to include about 350 entries in the first edition, but it quickly became apparent that a book of that size would not provide adequate coverage of the world's notable people who died in 1980. We thus increased the number to 450 entries, basically comprising: (a) people of "major historical importance" in their field (including Sir Alfred Hitchcock, Aleksei Kosygin, John Lennon, Jean Piaget, Jean-Paul Sartre, the Shah of Iran, and Marshal Tito); (b) people who are "internationally prominent" in their profession or field of endeavor (about 300 entrants fall into this category); and (c) people whose positions or work have made them "nationally prominent." Bearing in mind the book's major areas of distribution, a high proportion of the nationally prominent people are from the United States, Canada, the United Kingdom, and other English-speaking countries. Deciding upon people's relative importance is, of course, an impossible task; but nevertheless, with valuable guidance from many experts and scholars, and assistance from the staffs of professional organizations and embassies, I hope we have come close to providing a comprehensive coverage of the interesting and notable people from all countries and all professions who died during the year.

The length of the obituaries—varying from a few hundred to several thousand words—is not a true indication of the importance we attach to the entrants. Our aim has simply been to cover *all* noteworthy points in a person's career, whatever the length, and to provide fuller information and evaluations than can be found in any other general biographical reference work or newspaper obituary. But our extensive research has not always given us the answers to all the important questions which have come up and while the responses from the deceased's family or colleagues to our letters of inquiry have helped us enormously, there is inevitably some variation in the scope of the information we provide. Some inconsistencies and information gaps cannot, unfortunately, be avoided, but I am confident that the experience we have gained from compiling this first edition will help us to minimize problems in future volumes.

To avoid encumbering the obituaries with minutiae, full biographical data and career details are collected in a "Who's Who" format and placed in a separate section which follows immediately after the essay. When applicable, entries also include suggestions for further reading, and in many cases photographs of the subjects are provided. We hope that the photographs serve as an interesting embellishment; but of course, their inclusion does increase the book's price, and we shall take note of the views of librarians and reviewers regarding the inclusion of illustrations in future volumes. We hope to keep intact the general organization and scope of *The Annual Obituary,* but we shall be more than happy to make changes which will enhance the book's usefulness. Already, a group of American Library Association members, who kindly met with us, have offered valuable advice, and as a result we are planning to expand the Further Reading lists to include titles of other reference works in which entrants appear.

The entries are arranged chronologically by death date so that much of the book can be compiled before the end of the year. An alphabetical index of entrants, and an index of entrants by profession, precede the main text. Future editions will also contain cumulative alphabetical and professions indexes. The book is completed by an index of obituary writers and a list of abbreviations used in the biographical data section of each entry.

The Addendum in this first edition comprises three entries which were not completed until it was too late to place them in chronological sequence. An obituary may occasionally be omitted, as some deaths are not immediately noted in newspapers; in such cases, the entry will appear in the Addendum of the next edition, as will any corrections and additions to existing entries or necessary updating of the Further Reading lists. Whenever revisions occur, the page numbers will be noted in the cumulative alphabetical index; thus, by the end of the decade, it is likely that some of the subjects will have several page references. If for any reason an entry has to be completely rewritten, subsequent indexes will list only the page number of the new obituary.

I am very grateful to the families, friends and associates of many of the entrants for their kindness in supplying hitherto unpublished information and photographs. The cooperation of numerous embassies and consulates in Washington D.C. and New York, and the generous assistance of libraries, institutions and professional bodies in many parts of the world has enabled us to provide much information which has previously been available only in widely scattered sources. I also wish to thank numerous colleagues at St. Martin's Press who have assisted in the compilation, design and production of this book. Particularly, I would like to mention Steve Goulden, Kathy Hecht, Ariane Hogg, Sandi Resnick, and Jeff Sherman, and Assistant Editors Ed Tallman and Ann Weiss. These members of the Reference Book Division, together with freelance writers Michael Deaves, Louise Forsyth and Ed Sklepowich, have been involved in many stages of the book's progress; their enthusiasm and diligence has been a constant source of encouragement. Special thanks are due to Janet Podell, my Associate Editor. Janet has played an important part in ensuring that the book is reliable and readable, and I consider myself extremely fortunate to have such a talented colleague.

Many significant individuals died in 1980 and with few exceptions the world mourns their departure. But *The Annual Obituary* is not an elegy for the departed; rather, it is a book about people who led remarkable lives. We hope you enjoy using it as much as we have enjoyed compiling it.

–Roland Turner

Photographs
Unless otherwise specified, photographs are reproduced by permission of Wide World Photos.

Alphabetical Index of Entrants

Harold Abramson *USA*, 585
Abū Salmā *Palestine*, 542
Mildred Adams *USA*, 666
Theodore Adams *USA*, 140
Joy Adamson *Austria*, 8
Sir Titus Aderemi I *Nigeria*, 388
Charles Adler, Jr. *USA*, 636
Herbert Agar *USA*, 720
Conrad Ahlers *Germany*, 790
Salah ad-Din al-Bitar *Syria*, 423
Chaudhri Mohamad
  Ali *Pakistan*, 739
Sheik Muhammad Ali
  Ja'abri *Jordan*, 315
Abd al-Karīm al-Karmi
  Palestine, 542
Yigal Allon *Israel*, 143
Mary O'Hara Alsop *USA*, 621
Andrei Amalrik *USSR*, 680
Giorgio Amendola *Italy*, 325
H.S. Amerasinghe *Sri Lanka*, 751
Alfred Andersch *Germany*, 116
Robert Ardrey *USA*, 31
Anthony J. Arkell *UK*, 132
Lord Armstrong *UK*, 411
Elliot Arnold *USA*, 298
Boris Aronson *USA*, 692
Ingri Parin d'Aulaire *USA*, 638
Tex Avery *USA*, 491
Sir Geoffrey H. Baker *UK*, 288
Lord Ballantrae *UK*, 731
Margaret Ballinger *South
  Africa*, 85
Don Banks *Australia*, 540
Lady Barnett *UK*, 630
William Baroody, Sr. *USA*, 446
Tom Barry *Ireland*, 397
Roland Barthes *France*, 203
Sir Edric Bastyan *UK*, 596
L.C. Bates *USA*, 481
Gregory Bateson *UK*, 400
Gregory Battcock *USA*, 832
Richard Baxter *USA*, 575
Sir Hugh Beadle *Rhodesia*, 775
Sir Cecil Beaton *UK*, 37
John Beecher *USA*, 292
Jan Bélehrádek
  Czechoslovakia, 289
Adrian Bell *UK*, 509
Patriarch Benedictos I *Greece*, 768
Ahmed Taibi Benhima
  Morocco, 833
Margot Bennett *UK*, 759
Samuel Berger *USA*, 95
Maurice Bévenot *UK*, 700
Barney Bigard *USA*, 376
S.T. Bindoff *UK*, 821
Salah ad-Din al-Bitar *Syria*, 423
Sir Kenneth Blackburne *UK*, 663
Paul Blanshard *USA*, 60
Richard Bonelli *USA*, 327
John Bonham *UK*, 577
George Borg Olivier *Malta*, 657

Maurice Boukstein *USA*, 702
Prince Boun Oum *Laos*, 170
Marcel Boussac *France*, 180
Edmund Bowen *UK*, 703
Robert Brackman *USA*, 415
Donald Brennan *USA*, 239
Lord (Russell) Brock *UK*, 498
Lynn Bronson *USA*, 345
Alexander Brook *USA*, 134
Manlio Brosio *Italy*, 163
Petr Brovka *USSR*, 189
Rachel F. Brown *USA*, 33
Dereck Bryceson *UK*, 616
Sir Edward Bullard *UK*, 215
E.H.S. Burhop *UK*, 47
G.M. Burnett *UK*, 503
Sir Alan Burns *UK*, 565
David Burpee *USA*, 366
Millar Burrows *USA*, 265
Sir Billy Butlin *UK*, 339
Henry Byrd *USA*, 65
Marcello Caetano *Portugal*, 646
Angus Campbell *USA*, 781
E.R. Campbell *Rhodesia*, 478
Patrick Campbell *UK*, 675
Hector Cámpora *Argentina*, 808
Richard Carline *UK*, 696
Francisco Sá Carneiro
  Portugal, 752
Rhys Carpenter *USA*, 6
Alejo Carpentier *Cuba*, 245
Sir Ferdinand Cavendish-
  Bentinck *UK*, 773
Sangad Chaloryoo *Thailand*, 717
Gower Champion *USA*, 485
Sheldon W. Cheney *USA*, 607
Vulko Chervenkov *Bulgaria*, 632
J.T. Christie *UK*, 519
Eliot C. Clark *USA*, 307
Harold Clurman *USA*, 529
Nevill Coghill *UK*, 667
Dame Margaret Cole *UK*, 285
Lord Coleraine *UK*, 689
John Collier *UK*, 222
Peter Collinson *UK*, 785
William Colmer *USA*, 536
Marc Connelly *USA*, 812
Howard N. Cook *USA*, 368
Sir Conrad Corfield *UK*, 590
Maurice Cornforth *UK*, 859
Dame Cicely Courtneidge *UK*, 249
Willis D. Crittenberger *USA*, 450
Edward Croft-Murray *UK*, 556
Sir Rupert Cross *UK*, 541
Sir Charles Curran *UK*, 18
Lil Dagover *Germany*, 67
Zhao Dan *China*, 609
Dorothy Day *USA*, 733
Dixie Dean *UK*, 147
Alberto Demichelli *Uruguay*, 618
Robert Lee Dennison *USA*, 165
Adolph Deutsch *USA*, 5
Viscount Dilhorne *UK*, 516

Alioune Diop *Senegal*, 269
C.H. Dobinson *UK*, 839
Harold W. Dodds *USA*, 643
Karl Dönitz *Germany*, 816
John Dollard *USA*, 599
Walter R. Dornberger
  Germany, 316
Helen Gahagen Douglas *USA*, 379
William O. Douglas *USA*, 40
Jessica Dragonette *USA*, 173
Jimmy Durante *USA*, 63
Roger Duvoisin *USA*, 384
Carl Ebert *Germany*, 302
George P. Elliott *USA*, 272
Sir Charles Ellis *UK*, 19
Baroness Emmet *UK*, 610
Fred Emney *UK*, 835
Milton H. Erickson *USA*, 193
Nihat Erim *Turkey*, 417
Lord Erskine *UK*, 777
Pierre Etchebaster *France*, 190
Bill Evans *USA*, 496
Diego Fabbri *Italy*, 870
Peter Farb *USA*, 224
Edelmiro Farrell *Argentina*, 660
Bernard Edward Fergusson
  UK, 731
Thomas K. Finletter *USA*, 247
John Fischetti *USA*, 697
Terence Fisher *UK*, 353
Joan Fleming *UK*, 691
Joseph Fontanet *France*, 74
James K. Foreman *UK*, 686
Jacobus J. Fouché *South
  Africa*, 571
Virgil Fox *USA*, 644
G.S. Fraser *UK*, 11
Elizabeth Friedman *USA*, 873
Erich Fromm *USA*, 175
Frances Fuller *USA*, 791
Waldemar J. Gallman *USA*, 383
Sanjay Gandhi *India*, 358
W. Horsley Gantt *USA*, 136
Reginald Gardiner *UK*, 404
Romain Gary *France*, 741
William Gaunt *UK*, 311
Maurice Genevoix *France*, 520
Ernö Gerö *Hungary*, 158
José Maria Gil-Robles *Spain*, 543
Jacky Gillot *UK*, 566
James Gilluly *USA*, 850
V.V. Giri *India*, 370
Lord Glenavy *UK*, 675
Sir Richard Glyn *UK*, 640
Lord Godber *UK*, 489
Frederick Goldie *UK*, 638
Lord Gordon-Walker *UK*, 743
P.E. Gorman *USA*, 499
Ivan Gosnjak *Yugoslavia*, 92
Alvin Gouldner *USA*, 782
Solomon Grayzel *USA*, 466
John Howard Griffin *USA*, 533
Hugh Griffith *UK*, 304

Sir Kenneth Grubb *UK*, 321
Victor Gruen *USA*, 105
Louis Guilloux *France*, 619
Philip Guston *USA*, 328
Sir Ludwig Guttman *UK*, 178
P. E. Haggerty *USA*, 587
Kay Hammond *UK*, 275
Tim Hardin *USA*, 851
Sir Harwood Harrison *UK*, 538
Arnold Haskell *UK*, 687
Eric Hass *USA*, 589
Mohammed Hatta *Indonesia*, 166
Roger Hawkins *Rhodesia*, 152
Robert E. Hayden *USA*, 128
Dick Haymes *USA*, 207
H.R. Hays *USA*, 612
Sir Philip Hendy *UK*, 514
Sir Alfred Hitchcock *UK*, 253
Charles B. Hoeven *USA*, 677
Gilbert Holliday *UK*, 784
Thea Holme *UK*, 755
Sir Stephen Holmes *UK*, 240
Elston Howard *USA*, 779
John Hubbard *UK*, 730
Thomas Hunt *UK*, 819
Ruby Hurley *USA*, 462
Joel Hurstfield *UK*, 735
Sultan I. Ibraimov *USSR*, 756
The Oni of Ife *Nigeria*, 388
Ras Imru *Ethiopia*, 477
Franz J. Ingelfinger *USA*, 195
Jose Iturbi *USA*, 381
Jaroslaw Iwaszkiewicz *Poland*, 150
Sheik Muhammad Ali
   Ja'abri *Jordan*, 315
Hattie Jacques *UK*, 594
David Janssen *USA*, 100
Gerald W. Johnson *USA*, 185
Howard Mumford Jones *USA*, 300
Dov Joseph *Israel*, 13
Puran Chand Joshi *India*, 678
René Journiac *France*, 84
Ida Kaminska *Poland/USA*, 309
Shotaro Kamiya *Japan*, 840
Simon Kapwepwe *Zambia*, 54
Abd al-Karīm al-Karmi
   Palestine, 542
Boris Kaufman *USA*, 373
Walter Kaufmann *USA*, 505
Helmut Käutner *Germany*, 241
William Keeton *USA*, 473
Robert Kellar *UK*, 604
Pearl Kendrick *USA*, 601
Douglas Kenney *USA*, 493
Mildred Adams Kenyon *USA*, 666
Sir Seretse Khama *Botswana*, 413
Yahya Khan *Pakistan*, 460
William Kienbusch *USA*, 187
Robert E. Kintner *USA*, 824
Virginia Kirkus *USA*, 537
Arthur Kleiner *USA*, 214
Sir Cyril Kleinwort *UK*, 522
Oskar Kokoschka *Austria*, 120
Andre Kostelanetz *USA*, 29
Aleksei N. Kosygin *USSR*, 793

Sir John Kotelawala *Sri
   Lanka*, 583
Imre Kovács *Hungary*, 652
Marianne Kris *USA*, 718
Louis Kronenberger *USA*, 260
Joseph Krumgold *USA*, 409
Stephen Kuffler *USA*, 615
Judy LaMarsh *Canada*, 650
Evelyn Lampman *USA*, 345
Noel Langley *USA*, 664
John Laurie *UK*, 360
Mikhail Lavrentyev *USSR*, 622
Camara Laye *Guinea*, 77
Jules Léger *Canada*, 708
John Lennon *UK*, 761
Jean Lesage *Canada*, 771
Sol Lesser *USA*, 568
Joël Le Theule *France*, 780
Sam Levene *USA*, 847
Sam Levenson *USA*, 494
Walpole Lewin *UK*, 50
Willard F. Libby *USA*, 524
Sir Laurence Lindo *Jamaica*, 291
Norman Lloyd *USA*, 449
Barbara Loden *USA*, 511
Professor Longhair *USA*, 65
James B. Longley *USA*, 471
Luigi Longo *Italy*, 624
Alice Roosevelt Longworth
   USA, 112
Clifford Lord *USA*, 634
Allard Lowenstein *USA*, 168
Eric Lyons *UK*, 125
Yakov Malik *USSR*, 93
Sir William Mallalieu *UK*, 161
Nadezhda Mandelstam *USSR*, 854
Olivia Manning *UK*, 426
A.P. Mantovani *UK*, 208
Arthur Marder *UK*, 836
Albert Margai *Sierra Leone*, 804
Marino Marini *Italy*, 454
Jessica Marmorston *USA*, 633
Maurice Martenot *France*, 602
Maria Martinez *USA*, 422
Rube Marquard *USA*, 318
Pyotr Masherov *USSR*, 591
Bernd Matthias *USA*, 651
John Mauchly *USA*, 15
Solomon McCombs *USA*, 699
John W. McCormack *USA*, 710
James McDonnell *USA*, 483
Sir John McEwen *Australia*, 704
Sir Roderick McLeod *UK*, 760
Marshall McLuhan *Canada*, 860
Steve McQueen *USA*, 670
Carey McWilliams *USA*, 377
George Meany *USA*, 21
Kay Medford *USA*, 225
Nikolai V. Melnikov *USSR*, 806
Kurt Mendelssohn *UK*, 557
David Mercer *UK*, 457
Sir John Methven *UK*, 244
Walter Midgley *UK*, 559
Lewis Milestone *USA*, 578
Henry Miller *USA*, 332

John D. B. Mitchell *UK*, 809
A.S. Mike Monroney *USA*, 103
Hans J. Morgenthau *USA*, 418
Frank V. Morley *USA*, 603
Paul Morrison *USA*, 856
Shalom Moskowitz *Israel*, 849
Sir Oswald Mosley *UK*, 746
Luis Muñoz Marín *Puerto
   Rico*, 261
Pietro Nenni *Italy*, 1
Lord Netherthorpe *UK*, 673
Emanuel Neumann *USA*, 648
Lillian Ngoyi *South Africa*, 160
Arthur C. Nielsen, Sr. *USA*, 319
John Jacob Niles *USA*, 148
Frank Norman *UK*, 826
Mary O'Hara *USA*, 621
Masayoshi Ohira *Japan*, 340
Arthur M. Okun *USA*, 181
Sir Geoffrey Oliver *UK*, 313
Sir Charles Orde *UK*, 336
Prince Boun Oum *Laos*, 170
Jesse Owens *USA*, 212
Rafael Paasio *Finland*, 172
Marcello Pagliero *Italy*, 767
Mohammed Reza Pahlevi *Iran*, 437
George Pal *USA*, 270
Justas Paleckis *Lithuania*, 119
Lord Pannell *UK*, 184
Vasilios Papadopoulos *Greece*, 768
Ingri Parin d'Aulaire *USA*, 638
Charles Parker *UK*, 769
I.M. Parsons *UK*, 658
Dimitrios Partsalides *Greece*, 357
Roy Pascal *UK*, 488
Gail Patrick *USA*, 403
William A. Patterson *USA*, 347
William L. Patterson *USA*, 154
Ernest A. Payne *UK*, 35
Lord Pearson *UK*, 69
M. Murray Peshkin *USA*, 474
Prince Peter of Greece &
   Denmark, *623*
Allan Petterson *Sweden*, 354
Jean Piaget *Switzerland*, 545
Sir George Pickering *UK*, 501
Sergio Pignedoli *Italy*, 349
Sir George Pirie *UK*, 45
Genevieve Pitot *USA*, 593
H.H. Plaskett *UK*, 57
Alexander Poniatoff *USA*, 641
Katherine Ann Porter *USA*, 560
Duke of Portland *UK*, 773
William Prager *Germany*, 274
George Raft *USA*, 722
John H. Randall, Jr. *USA*, 749
Shlomo Ravitz *Israel*, 849
Stanley F. Reed *USA*, 217
Ambrose Reeves *UK*, 823
Arnold Renshaw *UK*, 324
Paul Robert *France*, 464
Rachel Roberts *UK*, 728
Richard B. Roberts *USA*, 219
William Roberts *UK*, 43
William A. Robson *UK*, 296

Oscar A. Romero *El Salvador*, 192
C.P.M. Romme *Netherlands*, 628
Finn Ronne *Norway*, 26
Alan Ross *UK*, 573
Konstantin N. Rudnev *USSR*, 467
Muriel Rukeyser *USA*, 97
Sir Gordon Russell *UK*, 598
Lord St. Helens *UK*, 846
Shalom of Safed *Israel*, 869
Abū Salmā *Palestine*, 542
Geoffrey T. Sambell *Australia*, 811
Francisco Sá Carneiro
    Portugal, 752
Colonel (Harland) Sanders *USA*, 787
Alexandre Sanguinetti *France*, 606
Jean-Paul Sartre *France*, 231
Dore Schary *USA*, 406
Albert E. Scheflen *USA*, 468
Fabian von Schlabrendorff
    Germany, 508
O.D. Schreiner *South Africa*, 445
John Dick Scott *UK*, 157
Sir Alan Scott-Moncrieff *UK*, 725
Peter Sellers *UK*, 428
Shah of Iran *437*
Sir Geoffrey Shakespeare *UK*, 527
Shalom of Safed *Israel*, 869
Abdul Hamid Sharaf *Jordan*, 398
Bob Shawkey *USA*, 863
Henry Knox Sherrill *USA*, 294
Elizabeth Shoumatoff *USA*, 737
Ari A. Shternfeld *USSR*, 402
Ahmed Shukairy *Palestine*, 139
Jay Silverheels *USA*, 156
William Hood Simpson *USA*, 470

Alf Sjöberg *Sweden*, 237
A.J.M. Smith *Canada*, 706
Robert A. Smith *UK*, 306
Tony Smith *USA*, 841
C.P. Snow *UK*, 389
Anastasio Somoza *Nicaragua*, 552
Marian Spychalski *Poland*, 337
William Stein *USA*, 75
Sir Roger Stevens *UK*, 114
Donald Ogden Stewart *USA*, 452
Clyfford Still *USA*, 363
Milburn Stone *USA*, 343
Martin Sullivan *UK*, 513
Baroness Summerskill *UK*, 80
Walter Susskind *UK*, 197
Dame Lucy Sutherland *UK*, 479
Graham Sutherland *UK*, 108
Henrietta Swope *USA*, 724
Sir Roland Symonette *UK*, 162
Ali Akbar Tabatabai *Iran*, 425
William Talbot *USA*, 695
Jacob L. Talmon *Israel*, 351
Wladyslaw Tatarkiewicz
    Poland, 220
Maurice F. Tauber *USA*, 580
Edwin Way Teale *USA*, 629
Ton Duc Thang *Vietnam*, 210
Lord Thomas *UK*, 89
Sir Jules Thorn *UK*, 772
Josip Tito *Yugoslavia*, 277
Harold Tittman, Jr. *USA*, 857
William R. Tolbert *Liberia*, 229
Ton Duc Thang *Vietnam*, 210
Ben Travers *UK*, 807
Francis Tubbs *UK*, 815

Sir Mark Turner *UK*, 774
Kenneth Tynan *UK*, 433
Arland Ussher *UK*, 830
Egidio Vagnozzi *Italy*, 844
Martial Valin *France*, 570
Romolo Valli *Italy*, 72
J.H. Van Vleck *USA*, 654
Princess Viktoria
    (Luise) *Germany*, 788
Fabian von Schlabrendorff
    Germany, 508
Vladimir Vysotsky *USSR*, 432
Konrad Wachsmann *USA*, 726
Raoul Walsh *USA*, 865
Stella Walsh *USA*, 757
Baroness Ward *UK*, 252
Shields Warren *USA*, 395
Hugh Watt *New Zealand*, 82
Heinrich Wendel *West
    Germany*, 267
Jan Werich *Czechoslovakia*, 661
Mae West *USA*, 714
Irvin F. Westheimer *USA*, 858
Antonia White *UK*, 227
Alec Wilder *USA*, 828
John Wilkinson *UK*, 685
Paul R. Williams *USA*, 51
Sir Richard Williams *UK*, 87
Ethel Wilson *Canada*, 820
Robert Lee Wolff *USA*, 683
James Wright *USA*, 200
Sir Eric Wyndham White *UK*, 59
Mar Ignatius Yacoub III *Iraq*, 375
Collier Young *USA*, 838
Aleksandr Zimin *USSR*, 130

Index of Entrants by Professions

The Index is categorized under the following headings:

Actors, Actresses & Entertainers
Archaeologists
Architects & Planners
Anthropologists
Artists & Sculptors
Art Historians & Critics
Biologists & Zoologists
Business Executives & Industrialists
Cartoonists & Animators
Chemical Scientists
Children's Writers
Composers & Songwriters
Dancers & Choreographers
Designers & Craftspeople
Diplomats
Directors (Theater, Film, Television & Radio)
Dramatists, Screenwriters & Scriptwriters
Earth Scientists
Economists & Financial Specialists
Educationists & Educational Administrators
Engineers & Technologists
Ethnologists
Explorers
Farmers & Horticulturists
Heads of State, Presidents, Premiers & Governor-
  Generals
Historians
Human Rights Activists
Illustrators
International Affairs Advisors & Officials
Inventors

Journalists & Editors
Judges & Lawyers
Labor Leaders
Lexicographers
Librarians
Literary Scholars (including Critics & Translators)
Mathematicians
Medical Practitioners & Researchers
Military Officers & Strategists
Musical Performers & Conductors
Naturalists
Novelists & Short Story Writers
Performing Arts Reviewers & Critics
Philologists & Linguistics Scholars
Philosophers & Philosophy Scholars
Photographers & Cinematographers
Physicists
Poets
Politicians
Political Scientists
Producers (Theater, Film, Television & Radio)
Psychologists & Psychiatrists
Public & Government Administrators
Radio & Television Personalities
Religious Leaders & Theologians
Royalty & Socialites
Social & Political Activists
Sociologists (including writers and scholars in the
  general field of social science)
Space Scientists
Sports Figures

Actors, Actresses & Entertainers

Marc Connelly, 812
Dame Cicely Courtneidge, 249
Lil Dagover, 67
Zhao Dan, 609
Helen Gahagen Douglas, 379
Jimmy Durante, 63
Carl Ebert, 302
Fred Emney, 835
Frances Fuller, 791
Reginald Gardiner, 404
Hugh Griffith, 304
Kay Hammond, 275

Dick Haymes, 207
Thea Holme, 755
Hattie Jacques, 594
David Janssen, 100
Ida Kaminska, 309
John Laurie, 360
Sam Levene, 847
Sam Levenson, 494
Barbara Loden, 511
Kay Medford, 225
Steve McQueen, 670
Marcello Pagliero, 767

Gail Patrick, 403
George Raft, 722
Rachel Roberts, 728
Peter Sellers, 428
Jay Silverheels, 156
Milburn Stone, 343
Romolo Valli, 72
Vladimir Vysotsky, 432
Jan Werich, 661
Mae West, 714

Archaeologists

Anthony J. Arkell, 132

Millar Burrows, 265

Rhys Carpenter, 6

Architects & Planners

Victor Gruen, 105
Eric Lyons, 125

William A. Robson, 296
Konrad Wachsmann, 726

Paul R. Williams, 51

Anthropologists

Robert Ardrey, 31
Gregory Bateson, 400

Peter Farb, 224
Prince Peter of Greece &

Denmark, 623

Artists & Sculptors

Sir Cecil Beaton, 37
Robert Brackman, 415
Alexander Brook, 134
Richard Carline, 696
Eliot C. Clark, 307
Howard N. Cook, 368
William Gaunt, 311

Philip Guston, 328
William Kienbusch, 187
Oskar Kokoschka, 120
Marino Marini, 454
Solomon McCombs, 699
William Roberts, 43
Shalom of Safed, 869

Elizabeth Shoumatoff, 737
Tony Smith, 841
Clyfford Still, 363
Graham Sutherland, 108
William Talbot, 695

Art Historians & Critics

Gregory Battcock, 832
Richard Carline, 696
Sheldon W. Cheney, 607

Edward Croft-Murray, 556
William Gaunt, 311
Sir Philip Hendy, 514

Wladyslaw Tatarkiewicz, 220

Biologists & Zoologists

Jan Bélehrádek, 289
William Keeton, 473

Pearl Kendrick, 601

Stephen Kuffler, 615

Business Executives & Industrialists

Marcel Boussac, 180
David Burpee, 366
Sir Billy Butlin, 339
E.R. Campbell, 478
Lord Erskine, 777
Lord Godber, 489
P.E. Haggerty, 587
Shotaro Kamiya, 840
Robert E. Kintner, 824

Sir Cyril Kleinwort, 552
Sol Lesser, 568
James McDonnell, 483
Sir John Methven, 244
Lord Netherthorpe, 673
Arthur C. Nielsen, Sr., 319
I.M. Parsons, 638
William A. Patterson, 347
Alexander Poniatoff, 641

Colonel (Harland) Sanders, 787
Sir Geoffrey Shakespeare, 527
Sir Roland Symonette, 162
Lord Thomas, 89
Sir Jules Thorn, 772
Sir Mark Turner, 774
Irvin F. Westheimer, 858
Sir Eric Wyndham White, 59

Cartoonists & Animators

John Fischetti, 697

Chemical Scientists

Edmund Bowen, 703
Rachel F. Brown, 33
G.M. Burnett, 503

James K. Foreman, 686
Willard F. Libby, 524

Bernd Matthias, 651
William Stein, 75

Children's Writers

Roger Duvoisin, 384
Joseph Krumgold, 409

Evelyn Lampman, 345
Mary O'Hara, 621

Ingri Parin d'Aulaire, 638

Composers & Songwriters

Don Banks, 540
Henry Byrd, 65
Adolph Deutsch, 5
Tim Hardin, 851

Arthur Kleiner, 214
John Lennon, 761
John Jacob Niles, 148
Allan Pettersson, 354

Genevieve Pitot, 593
Vladimir Vysotsky, 432
Alec Wilder, 828

Dancers & Choreographers

Gower Champion, 485

Genevieve Pitot, 593

Designers & Craftspeople

Boris Aronson, 692
Sir Cecil Beaton, 37
Maria Martinez, 422

Paul Morrison, 856
Sir Gordon Russell, 598

Graham Sutherland, 108
Heinrich Wendel, 267

Diplomats

H.S. Amerasinghe, 751
Ahmed Benhima, 833
Samuel Berger, 95
Manlio Brosio, 163
E.R. Campbell, 478
Hector Cámpora, 808
Baroness Emmet, 616

Thomas K. Finletter, 247
Waldemar J. Gallman, 383
Gilbert Holliday, 784
Sir Stephen Holmes, 240
Ras Imru, 477
René Journiac, 84
Jules Léger, 708

Sir Laurence Lindo, 291
Yakov Malik, 93
Sir Charles Orde, 336
C.P.M. Romme, 628
Sir Roger Stevens, 114
Ali Akbar Tabatabai, 425
Harold Tittman, Jr., 857

Directors
(Theater, Film, Television & Radio)

Tex Avery, 491
Gower Champion, 485
Harold Clurman, 529
Peter Collinson, 785
Marc Connelly, 812
Carl Ebert, 302
Terence Fisher, 353

Sir Alfred Hitchcock, 253
Thea Holme, 755
Ida Kaminska, 309
Helmut Käutner, 241
Barbara Loden, 511
Lewis Milestone, 578

Marcello Pagliero, 767
George Pal, 270
Dore Schary, 406
Alf Sjöberg, 237
Raoul Walsh, 865
Jan Werich, 661

Dramatists, Screenwriters & Scriptwriters

Andrei Amalrik, 680
Alfred Andersch, 116
Robert Ardrey, 31
John Collier, 222
Marc Connelly, 812
Diego Fabbri, 870
Jaroslaw Iwaszkiewicz, 150

Helmut Käutner, 241
Douglas Kenney, 493
Oskar Kokoschka, 120
Joseph Krumgold, 409
Noel Langley, 664
David Mercer, 457

Frank Norman, 826
Jean-Paul Sartre, 231
Dore Schary, 406
Donald Ogden Stewart, 452
Ben Travers, 807
Jan Werich, 661

Earth Scientists

Sir Edward Bullard, 215   James Gilluly, 850

Economists & Financial Specialists

Lord Armstrong, 411   Arthur M. Okun, 181   Sir Eric Wyndham White, 59
William J. Baroody, Sr., 446

Educationists & Educational Administrators

G.M. Burnett, 503   Howard Mumford Jones, 300   Robert A. Smith, 306
J.T. Christie, 519   Clifford Lord, 634   Sir Roger Stevens, 414
C.H. Dobinson, 839   O.D. Schreiner, 445   Dame Lucy Sutherland, 479
Harold W. Dodds, 643

Engineers & Technologists

Charles Adler, Jr., 636   Nikolai Melnikov, 806   Konstantin Rudnev, 467
Walter R. Dornberger, 316   Alexander Poniatoff, 641   Ari A. Shternfeld, 402
John Mauchly, 75   William Prager, 274

Ethnologists

Gregory Bateson, 400   Prince Peter of Greece and   Denmark, 623

Explorers

Sir Kenneth Grubb, 321   Finn Ronne, 26

Farmers & Horticulturists

David Burpee, 366   Lord Netherthorpe, 673   Francis Tubbs, 815

Heads of State, Presidents, Premiers, and Governor-Generals

Sir Titus Aderemi I, 388   Edelmiro Farrell, 660   Luis Muñoz Marìn, 261
Chaudhri Mohamad Ali, 739   Jacobus J. Fouché, 571   Masayoshi Ohira, 340
Lord Ballantrae, 730   V.V. Giri, 370   Rafael Paasio, 172
Salah ad-din al-Bitar, 423   Mohammed Hatta, 166   Justas Paleckis, 119
Sir Kenneth Blackburne, 663   Sultan I. Ibraimov, 756   Shah of Iran, 437
George Borg Olivier, 657   Sir Seretse Khama, 413   Abdul Hamid Sharaf, 398
Prince Boun Oum, 170   Yahya Khan, 460   Anastasio Somoza, 552
Marcello Caetano, 646   Aleksei N. Kosygin, 793   Marian Spychalski, 337
Hector Cámpora, 808   Sir John Kotelawala, 583   Sir Roland Symonette, 162
Francisco Sá Carneiro, 752   Jules Léger, 708   Josip Tito, 277
Sangad Chaloryoo, 717   Jean Lesage, 771   William R. Tolbert, Jr., 229
Vulko Chervenkov, 632   Albert Margai, 804   Ton Duc Thang, 210
Alberto Demichelli, 618   Sir John McEwen, 704   Hugh Watt, 82
Nihat Erim, 417

Historians

Herbert Agar, 720   Joel Hurstfield, 735   Dame Lucy Sutherland, 479
Andrei Amalrik, 680   Gerald W. Johnson, 185   Jacob L. Talmon, 351
Anthony J. Arkell, 132   Howard Mumford Jones, 300   Wladyslaw Tatarkiewicz, 220
S.T. Bindoff, 821   Clifford Lord, 634   John Wilkinson, 685
Millar Burrows, 265   Arthur Marder, 836   Robert Lee Wolff, 683
Lord Gordon-Walker, 743   John H. Randall, Jr., 749   Aleksandr Zimin, 130
Solomon Grayzel, 466   James Dick Scott, 157

Human Rights Activists

Andrei Amalrik, 680
Margaret Ballinger, 85
L.C. Bates, 481
Dorothy Day, 733

John Howard Griffin, 533
Ruby Hurley, 462
Lillian Ngoyi, 160
Ambrose Reeves, 823

Oscar Romero, 192
Muriel Rukeyser, 97
O.D. Schreiner, 445
Baroness Summerskill, 80

Illustrators

Roger Duvoisin, 384

Ingri Parin d'Aulaire, 638

Edin Way Teale, 629

International Affairs Advisors and Officials

Donald Brennan, 239
Manlio Brosio, 163

René Journiac, 84

Sir Eric Wyndham White, 59

Inventors

Charles Adler, Jr., 636

Maurice Martenot, 602

John Mauchly, 15

Journalists & Editors

Mildred Adams, 666
Conrad Ahlers, 790
Elliot Arnold, 298
L.C. Bates, 481
Patrick Campbell, 675
Dorothy Day, 733

Alioune Diop, 269
Jacky Gillot, 566
John Howard Griffin, 533
Gerald W. Johnson, 185
Douglas Kenney, 493
Robert E. Kintner, 824

Virginia Kirkus, 537
Carey McWilliams, 377
Frank V. Morley, 603
Rafael Paasio, 172
I.M. Parsons, 658

Judges & Lawyers

Richard Baxter, 575
Sir Hugh Beadle, 775
Maurice Boukstein, 702
Marcello Caetano, 646
Sir Rupert Cross, 541
Viscount Dilhorne, 516
William O. Douglas, 40
Nihat Erim, 417

Jose Maria Gil-Robles, 543
Dov Joseph, 13
Judy LaMarsh, 650
Allard Lowenstein, 168
Sir John Methven, 244
John D.B. Mitchell, 809
William L. Patterson, 154

Lord Pearson, 69
Stanley F. Reed, 217
William A. Robson, 296
Francisco Sá Carneiro, 752
Fabian von Schlabrendorff, 508
O.D. Schreiner, 445
Sir Eric Wyndham White, 59

Labor Leaders

P.E. Gorman, 499
George Meany, 21

Lord Pannell, 184

Lord Pearson, 69

Lexicographers

Paul Robert, 464

Librarians

Maurice F. Tauber, 580

Literary Scholars
(including Critics & Translators)

Mildred Adams, 666
Herbert Agar, 720
Alfred Andersch, 116
Roland Barthes, 203
Sheldon W. Cheney, 607

Harold Clurman, 529
Nevill Coghill, 667
George P. Elliott, 272
G.S. Fraser, 11
Robert E. Hayden, 128

H.R. Hays, 612
Howard Mumford Jones, 300
Virginia Kirkus, 537
Louis Kronenberger, 260
Nadezhda Mandelstam, 854

Marshall McLuhan, 860   Jean-Paul Sartre, 231   Arland Ussher, 830
Henry Miller, 332   A.J.M. Smith, 706   Antonia White, 227
Frank V. Morley, 603   Kenneth Tynan, 433   James Wright, 200
Roy Pascal, 488

Mathematicians

Mikhail Lavrentyev, 622

Medical Practitioners & Researchers
(Also see Psychologists & Psychiatrists)

Harold Abramson, 585   Franz J. Ingelfinger, 195   M. Murray Peshkin, 474
Lord (Russell) Brock, 498   Robert Kellar, 604   Sir George Pickering, 501
Rachel F. Brown, 33   Pearl Kendrick, 601   Arnold Renshaw, 324
Milton H. Erickson, 193   Walpole Lewin, 50   Baroness Summerskill, 80
Sir Ludwig Guttman, 178   Jessica Marmorston, 633   Shields Warren, 395
Thomas Hunt, 819

Military Officers & Strategists

Yigal Allon, 143   Karl Dönitz, 816   Sir George Pirie, 45
Sir Geoffrey H. Baker, 288   Edelmiro Farrell, 660   Konstantin Rudnev, 467
Lord Ballantrae, 731   Thomas K. Finletter, 247   Sir Alan Scott-Moncrieff, 725
Tom Barry, 397   Ivan Gosnjak, 92   William Hood Simpson, 470
Sir Edric Bastyan, 596   Ras Imru, 477   Anastasio Somoza, 552
Donald Brennan, 239   Yahya Khan, 460   Marian Spychalski, 337
Manlio Brosio, 163   Luigi Longo, 624   Josip Tito, 277
Sangad Chaloryoo, 717   Pyotr Masherov, 591   Martial Valin, 570
Willis D. Crittenberger, 450 Sir Roderick McLeod, 760   Sir Richard Williams, 87
Robert Lee Dennison, 165   Sir Geoffrey Oliver, 313

Musical Performers & Conductors

Barney Bigard, 376   Tim Hardin, 851   Maurice Martenot, 602
Richard Bonelli, 327   Dick Haymes, 207   Kay Medford, 225
John Bonham, 577   Jose Iturbi, 381   Walter Midgley, 559
Henry Bird, 65   Arthur Kleiner, 214   John Jacob Niles, 148
Jessica Dragonette, 173   Andre Kostelanetz, 29   Shlomo Ravitz, 849
Jimmy Durante, 63   John Lennon, 761   Walter Susskind, 197
Bill Evans, 496   Norman Lloyd, 449   Vladimir Vysotsky, 432
Virgil Fox, 644   A.P. Mantovani, 208

Naturalists

Joy Adamson, 8   Peter Farb, 224   Edwin Way Teale, 629

Novelists & Short Story Writers

Alfred Andersch, 116   Romain Gary, 741   Camara Laye, 77
Robert Ardrey, 31   Maurice Genevoix, 520   Olivia Manning, 426
Elliot Arnold, 298   Jacky Gillot, 566   Henry Miller, 332
Adrian Bell, 509   John Howard Griffin, 533   Frank Norman, 826
Margot Bennett, 759   Louis Guilloux, 619   Katherine Anne Porter, 560
Alejo Carpentier, 245   H.R. Hays, 612   Jean-Paul Sartre, 231
Dame Margaret Cole, 285   Jaroslaw Iwaszkiewicz, 150   John Dick Scott, 157
John Collier, 222   Imre Kovács, 652   C.P. Snow, 389
George P. Elliott, 272   Louis Kronenberger, 260   Antonia White, 227
Joan Fleming, 691   Noel Langley, 664   Ethel Wilson, 820

Performing Arts Reviewers & Critics

Sheldon W. Cheney, 607
Harold Clurman, 529

Kenneth Tynan, 433

Arnold Haskell, 687

Philologists & Linguistics Scholars

Alan Ross, 573

Philosophers & Philosophy Scholars

Gregory Bateson, 400
Maurice Cornforth, 859
Erich Fromm, 175

Walter Kaufmann, 505
Jean Piaget, 545
John H. Randall, Jr., 749

Jean-Paul Sartre, 231
Wladyslaw Tatarkiewicz, 220

Photographers & Cinematographers

Sir Cecil Beaton, 37
John Howard Griffin, 533

Boris Kaufman, 373

Edwin Way Teale, 629

Physicists

Sir Edward Bullard, 215
E.H.S. Burhop, 47
Sir Charles Ellis, 19
John Hubbard, 730

Bernd Matthias, 651
John Mauchly, 15
Kurt Mendelssohn, 557
H.H. Plaskett, 57

Richard B. Roberts, 219
Robert A. Smith, 306
C.P. Snow, 389
John H. Van Vleck, 654

Poets

Abū Salmā, 542
John Beecher, 292
Petr Brovka, 189
George P. Elliott, 272

G.S. Fraser, 11
Robert E. Hayden, 128
H.R. Hays, 612
Jaroslaw Iwaszkiewicz, 150

Muriel Rukeyser, 97
A.J.M. Smith, 706
James Wright, 200

Politicians

Sir Titus Aderemi I, 388
Chaudhri Mohamad Ali, 739
Yigal Allon, 143
Giorgio Amendola, 325
Margaret Ballinger, 85
Ahmed Benhima, 833
Salah ad-din al-Bitar, 423
George Borg Olivier, 657
Prince Boun Oum, 170
Dereck Bryceson, 616
Marcello Caetano, 646
Hector Cámpora, 808
Francisco Sá Carneiro, 752
Sir Ferdinand Cavendish-Bentinck, 773
Sangad Chaloryoo, 717
Vulko Chervenkov, 632
Dame Margaret Cole, 285
Lord Coleraine, 689
William Colmer, 536
Alberto Demichelli, 618
Viscount Dilhorne, 516
Helen Gahagen Douglas, 379
Baroness Emmet, 610
Nihat Erim, 417
Edelmiro Farrell, 660

Joseph Fontanet, 74
Jacobus J. Fouché, 571
Sanjay Gandhi, 358
Ernö Gerö, 158
José Maria Gil-Robles, 543
V.V. Giri, 370
Sir Richard Glyn, 640
Lord Godber, 489
Lord Gordon-Walker, 743
Ivan Gosnjak, 92
Sir Harwood Harrison, 538
Eric Hass, 589
Mohammed Hatta, 166
Roger Hawkins, 152
Charles B. Hoeven, 677
Sultan I. Ibraimov, 756
Ras Imru, 477
Sheik Muhammed Ali Ja'abri, 315
Dov Joseph, 13
Puran Chand Joshi, 678
René Journiac, 84
Simon Kapwepwe, 54
Sir Seretse Khama, 413
Yahya Khan, 460
Aleksei N. Kosygin, 793
Sir John Kotelawala, 583

Judy LaMarsh, 650
Jean Lesage, 771
Joël Le Theule, 780
James B. Longley, 471
Luigi Longo, 624
Allard Lowenstein, 168
Sir William Mallalieu, 161
Albert Margai, 804
Pyotr Masherov, 591
John W. McCormack, 710
Sir John McEwen, 704
A.S. Mike Monroney, 103
Sir Oswald Mosley, 746
Luis Muñoz Marìn, 261
Pietro Nenni, 1
Emanuel Neumann, 648
Masayoshi Ohira, 340
Rafael Paasio, 172
Justas Paleckis, 119
Lord Pannell, 184
Dimitrios Partsalides, 357
William L. Patterson, 154
Duke of Portland, 773
William A. Robson, 296
C.P.M. Romme, 628
Francisco Sá Carneiro, 752

Alexandre Sanguinetti, 606
Lord St. Helens, 846
Shah of Iran, 437
Sir Geoffrey Shakespeare, 527
Abdul Hamid Sharaf, 398

Ahmed Shukairy, 139
Anastasio Somoza, 552
Marian Spychalski, 337
Baroness Summerskill, 80
Sir Roland Symonette, 162

Josip Tito, 277
William R. Tolbert, Jr., 229
Ton Duc Thang, 210
Baroness Ward, 252
Hugh Watt, 82

Political Scientists

Angus Campbell, 781

Hans J. Morgenthau, 418

Producers
(Theater, Film, Television & Radio)

Douglas Kenney, 493
Joseph Krumgold, 409
Sol Lesser, 568

Gail Patrick, 403
Dore Schary, 406
Romolo Valli, 72

Jan Werich, 661
Collier Young, 838

Psychologists & Psychiatrists

Harold Abramson, 585
John Dollard, 599
Milton H. Erickson, 193

Erich Fromm, 175
William Horsley Gantt, 136
Marianne Kris, 718

Jean Piaget, 545
Albert E. Scheflen, 468

Public & Government Administrators

H.S. Amerasinghe, 751
Lord Armstrong, 411
Sir Edric Bastyan, 596
Sir Kenneth Blackburne, 663
Manlio Brosio, 163
Dereck Bryceson, 616
Sir Alan Burns, 565
Sir Conrad Corfield, 590
Sir Charles Curran, 18

Sir Charles Ellis, 19
Lord Erskine, 777
Elizebeth Friedman, 873
Sir Stephen Holmes, 240
Pearl Kendrick, 601
Mikhail Lavrentyev, 622
Jules Léger, 708
Nikolai Melnikov, 806

Sir John Methven, 244
Lord Netherthorpe, 673
Lord Pearson, 69
Konstantin Rudnev, 467
Sir Alan Scott-Moncrieff, 725
C.P. Snow, 389
Harold Tittman, Jr., 857
Lord Thomas, 89

Radio & Television Personalities

Lady Barnett, 630
Patrick Campbell, 675

Jessica Dragonette, 173
Jacky Gillot, 566

Charles Parker, 769

Religious Leaders & Theologians

Theodore Adams, 140
Benedictos I, 768
Maurice Bévenot, 700
Millar Burrows, 265
Frederick Goldie, 638
Sir Kenneth Grubb, 321

Ernest A. Payne, 35
Sergio Pignedoli, 349
John H. Randall, Jr., 749
Ambrose Reeves, 823
Oscar A. Romero, 192
Geoffrey Sambell, 811

Henry Knox Sherrill, 294
Martin Sullivan, 513
Egidio Vagnozzi, 844
John Wilkinson, 685
Mar Ignatius Yacoub III, 375

Royalty & Socialites

Sir Titus Aderemi I, 388
Prince Boun Oum, 170
Alice Roosevelt Longworth, 112

Prince Peter of Greece &
    Denmark, 623

Shah of Iran, 437
Princess Viktoria (Luise), 788

Social & Political Activists

L.C. Bates, 481
Tom Barry, 397
Maurice Boukstein, 702
Dame Margaret Cole, 285
Dorothy Day, 733
Alioune Diop, 269
Eric Hass, 589
Ruby Hurley, 462

Imre Kovács, 652
Luigi Longo, 624
Allard Lowenstein, 168
Sir Oswald Mosley, 746
Emanuel Neumann, 648
Lillian Ngoyi, 160
William L. Patterson, 154

Ambrose Reeves, 824
Muriel Rukeyser, 97
Jean-Paul Sartre, 231
Fabian van Schlabrendorff, 508
Ahmed Shukairy, 139
Baroness Summerskill, 80
Irvin F. Westheimer, 858

Sociologists
(including writers and scholars in the general field of social science)

Mildred Adams, 666
Paul Blanshard, 60

Angus Campbell, 781
Erich Fromm, 175

Alvin Gouldner, 782
Marshall McLuhan, 860

Space Scientists

Walter R. Dornberger, 316
H.H. Plaskett, 57

Ari A. Shternfeld, 402

Henrietta Swope, 724

Sports Figures

Dixie Dean, 147
Pierre Etchebaster, 190
Elston Howard, 779

Rube Marquard, 318
Jesse Owens, 212

Bob Shawkey, 863
Stella Walsh, 757

THE ANNUAL
OBITUARY 1980

JANUARY

PIETRO NENNI
President, Socialist Party of Italy, and Deputy Prime Minister
Born Faenza, Emilia-Romagna, Italy, February 9th, 1891
Died Rome, Italy, January 1st, 1980

Pietro Nenni, statesman and leader of the Italian Socialist Party, was born into a peasant family in the northern province of Emilia-Romagna, a stronghold of Republican sentiment. Both parents died when he was seven; until he was 18 he lived in an orphanage. As a youth, he was increasingly attracted to political activity in the tradition of Mazzini, and in 1909 organized a strike in Carrara as part of an international protest against the execution of the Spanish anarchist Francisco Ferrer.

By 1911 Nenni was secretary of the trade union labor exchange in Forlì, where he led a general strike against Italy's Libyan War. He and Benito Mussolini, then the leading Socialist agitator in Romagna, were arrested and jailed for several months. Three years later, Nenni, now a journalist in Ancona, was arrested for his part in organizing "Red Week," a demonstration against the conservative government of Antonio Salandra.

When Italy entered World War I, Nenni enlisted in the Army and was wounded in action. On convalescent leave in 1917 he became the editor of the democratic newspaper *Il Giornale del Mattino* in Bologna; three years later he became editor-in-chief of *Il Secolo* in Milan.

The rapid growth of Mussolini's new fascist movement forced Nenni into a personal crisis that resulted in his joining the Partito Socialista Italiano (PSI), or Italian Socialist Party, in 1921, when he was 30 years old. The PSI was badly split over the issue of cooperation with non-Marxist parties, and had recently suffered the secession of two factions: the Leninists, opposed to collaboration, who had formed the Italian Communist Party (PCI), and the reformists, who advocated collaboration and had formed the Unitary Socialist Party (USP). Although Nenni, now managing editor of the PSI newspaper *Avanti!*, tried to articulate a middle course between the leftist and rightist factions in the Socialist ranks, the infighting between them constantly undercut the efficiency of the party.

Between 1923 and 1925 Nenni was arrested three times on charges of subversion. In 1925 he denounced the anti-proletarian program of the Fascists and called for a united leftist front against their regime. When this suggestion was rebuffed by the PSI leadership, Nenni resigned from *Avanti!* and became the publisher of *Il quarto stato* with Carlo Rosselli, a Resistance journalist who was later killed by the Fascists. When this journal, like all opposition journals, was suppressed by the Government in October 1926, Nenni went into exile in France, as did many of his compatriots on the left. His wife and children accompanied him.

In Paris, Nenni wrote for French left-wing newspapers and joined the *Concentrazione Antifascista*. From 1931 to 1939 he was secretary of the PSI and Paris director of *Nuovo Avanti*. During the Spanish Civil War, he served in Spain as political commissar of the Garibaldi Brigade.

When World War II broke out, Nenni attempted unsuccessfully to organize a Free Italian Legion. In February 1942 he was imprisoned in St.-Flour by the Vichy Government; the following year he was arrested by the Gestapo and taken to Germany, then transferred at Mussolini's request to the Island of Ponza in Italy, where the deposed Mussolini soon joined him.

Nenni, whose daughter Vittoria died in the Nazi death camp at Auschwitz, was released in August 1943 and became an organizer of the Resistance Movement. A year later he became Secretary-General of the PSI, a post he held for 19 years.

The shared adversity of the war years had convinced many Socialists of the need for cooperation with non-Marxist groups. They now joined six other anti-Fascist parties in the Committee of National Liberation (CNL), which countered neo-Fascist elements and formed occupation governments under Allied authority. In June 1945 Nenni entered the cabinet of Actionist Party leader Ferruccio Parri as Vice-Premier, Vice President of the Council of Ministers, High Commissioner for Sanctions against Fascism, and Minister for the Constituent Assembly, in which post he organized a public referendum on the establishment of a Republic and the election of national delegates to draft a new constitution. He continued to hold these positions in the first coalition government of Alcide de Gasperi, head of the Christian Democratic Party.

In June 1946, the Italian monarchy was abolished, by popular vote, in favor of a republic. In July, national elections made the PSI the second most powerful party in Italy, behind the Christian Democrats. Nenni was included in De Gasperi's second cabinet as Minister without Portfolio, then as Foreign Minister, negotiating with the Allied governments over the peace treaty with Italy and with Yugoslavia over possession of Trieste.

In the fall of 1946 the Communists, under Palmiro Togliatti, and Socialists announced their "unity of action pact." Under its terms, the two parties retained individual autonomy, but pooled their political strength to outvote the Christian Democrats on such issues as nationalization of industries and passage of pro-labor legislation. Nenni, long an enthusiastic supporter of the alliance, resigned his cabinet post in January 1947 when an anti-Communist faction in the PSI seceded in protest to become the Italian Socialist Worker's Party (later known as the Social Democratic Party). Subsequent elections produced a third De Gasperi government with no representation from the left at all.

Nenni was elected to the legislature as Deputy for Rome in 1948 and retained his seat for the next 15 years. Initially he was aligned with the Communist-led Peace Partisans movement, denounced the U.S. for attempting to divide the world into power blocs, and received the Stalin Peace Prize from the USSR for his opposition to Italy's membership in NATO.

Nenni's attitude towards Communism, however, had always been ambivalent. Before the war, he had published articles criticizing the dogmatic, undemocratic stance of the Soviet leadership, and had warned against its tendency to bureaucratic centralism. By 1953, realizing that the possibilities for social reform would be far stronger if the PSI were not relegated to a solely oppositional role, he repudiated the "unity of action pact" and actively sought an *apertura a sinistra* ("opening to the left") from the Christian Democrats and other centrist groups. His determination to break with the Communists crystallized after the Soviet invasion of Hungary in 1956; he returned the Stalin Peace Prize and donated its $24,000 award to the International Red Cross. Eventually he withdrew his opposition to NATO and became a supporter of European unity, establishing official links with the British Labour Party. "The Communist objective," he later said, "remains the conquest of power under the more or less totalitarian hegemony of their own party. . . . In countries they govern, every revisionist attempt to have a socialism with a human face has been crushed with violence and terror." (Despite the dissolution of the alliance, the Communists and Socialists continued to work together at the local level.)

A decade later, Nenni's initiative bore fruit with the formation of a four-party center-left coalition government headed by Christian Democrat Aldo Moro, in which Nenni, now President of the PSI, was deputy prime minister. It was the first time in 16 years that the Socialists had entered the government. The main achievement of the coalition was to return to regionalism in governmental administration; this, in Nenni's view, was the best way to train new political leaders, reduce bureaucracy, and open up new possibilities for social reform.

But his participation in the coalition proved costly to the inner solidarity of the PSI, which lost members both to the left and the right. A short-lived unification of the PSI and the Social Democrats, with Nenni as president, proved unsuccessful. Nenni served briefly as Minister for Foreign Affairs in the coalition government of Mariano Rumor in 1969, but resigned that post and the presidency of the PSI when the center-left coalition collapsed in July 1969.

Nenni's career began to draw to a close. Now in his eighties, he continued to write regularly for *Avanti!*, attended the Senate as Senator for Life, and was briefly considered for the Presidency; in 1970 he was a member of an ad hoc commission that met with the Vatican over the hotly contested issue of legalized divorce. He also worked on an autobiography, tentatively entitled *Witness to a Century*. Nenni died in Rome of a heart attack.

In a 1971 interview with journalist Oriana Fallaci, Nenni said: "My greatest victory was the Republic—no one wanted it with a commitment equal to mine. . . . I wanted . . . a system where the sociality of the means of production and exchange is combined with the greatest freedom for man. . . . Because I'm convinced that he, man, is always the decisive proof, and that only by changing man do you change society. In 65 years of participating in political struggle, my problem has always been that of improving myself as a man and of helping my comrades in arms to make the same effort."   J.P./L.F.

Son of Giuseppe N. and Angela (Castellani) N., peasants. Political pseudonyms: Pietro Emiliano; Ennio. Married Carmen Emiliani 1911 (d.1966). Children: Vittoria (d. Auschwitz WWII); Giuliana; Eva; Luciana. Mil. Service: Sgt. bombardier, Italian Army 1915–18.

Organizer of strike in Carrara 1909; Secty. of Labor Exchange, Forlì
1911; jailed for 7½ months for organizing protest against Libyan War
1911; Ed., Lucifero, Ancona 1911–14; leader in Red Week disorders
1914, arrested and sentenced by Court of Assizes of Aquila, granted
amnesty Jan. 1915; Ed., Il Giornale del Mattino, Bologna 1917, 1919;
founding member, Bologna *fascio* (interventionist group) 1919; Ed.-
in-chief, Il Secolo, Milan 1920; joined Partito Socialista Italiano
(Italian Socialist Party) 1921. With Avanti! (official newspaper of
P.S.I.): Paris Corresp. 1922; Ed. 1923–25, 1944–46; weekly contributor thereafter. Arrested three times 1923–25. Co-ed., Il quarto stato
1926. In exile in France 1926–43: corresp. for Paris newspapers
Quotidien, Populaire, Peuple; Secty., Concentrazione Antifascista
1927; Paris Dir., Nuovo Avanti, and Secty., P.S.I. 1931–39; Exec.,
Socialist Intnl, 1931–39. Concurrently in Spain 1936–38; Co-Founder
and Political Commissar, Garibaldi Brigade of Intnl. Brigade, Spanish
Civil War; Member, Cttee. for the Defense of Madrid. Joined Cttee.
for Union of Italian People 1941. Imprisoned by Vichy Govt. 1942;
arrested by Gestapo and taken to Germany; transferred to Island of
Ponza, Italy; released Aug. 1943. Leader of partisan resistance
movement 1943–45. With P.S.I.: Secty.-Gen. 1944–63; Pres. 1963–69;
Pres., Econ. Cttee. With Parri Cabinet 1945: Vice-Premier; V.P.,
Council of Ministers; Minister for Constituent Assembly; High Com-
mnr. for Sanctions Against Fascism. With first De Gasperi Cabinet
1945–46: Vice-Premier; V.P., Council of Ministers; Minister for
Constituent Assembly. With second De Gasperi Cabinet 1946–47:
Minister without Portfolio, then Minister for Foreign Affairs. Deputy
to Constituent Assembly 1946; Member, Chamber of Deputies, and
Pres., parliamentary group, I, II, III Legislatures 1948–63; Pres.,
Natl. Cttee. of Peace Partisans ca. 1948–49; V.P., World Council of
Peace ca. 1951; Ed., Mondo operaio, Rome, from 1954. Deputy
Prime Minister, four-party coalition govt. of Aldo Moro 1963–68; re-
elected Deputy for sixth time 1968; Minister for Foreign Affairs,
Rumor Cabinet 1968–69. Hons: Stalin Peace Prize 1952 (returned
1956); appointed Senator for Life 1970. *Author:* Lo spettro del
comunismo, 1914–1921, 1921; Storia di quattro anni (1919–1922),
1926, 4th ed. 1976; Six ans de guerre civile en Italie, 1930, German
trans. 1930, English trans. 1932, Italian trans. 1945; Histoire de la
Lutte de classes en Italie, 1930, Spanish trans. 1931; Le libérateur en
chemise rouge, 1930, published in Italy as Garibaldi, 1961; Il delitto
africano del Fascismo, 1936; Taccuino, 1942, 1955; Una battaglia
vinta: Documenti e testimonianzi, 1946; Pagine di diario, 1947; Il
cappio delle alleanze, 1949; La politica della distensione (ed. by S.
Bermani), 1952; Dal Patto Atlantico alla politica di distensione: Pace
e guerra nel Parlamento italiano; Lo Stato e la Chiesa fuiori del
concordato: scritti e discorsi, 1953; Diologo con la sinistra cattolica,
1954; Una legislatura fallita, 1953–58, 1958; Spagna (ed. by G. Dallò),
1958, 3rd ed. 1976, French trans. 1959, Spanish trans. 1964; Ren-
contres: Nenni, Bevan, Mendès-France, Février 1959, 1959; Vingt
Ans de fascisme (collection of three previously published works),
1960, Italian ed. by G. Dallò, 1964; Le prospettive del socialismo
dopo la destalinizzazione, 1962; Il diciannovismo (1919–1922) (ed. by
G. Gallò), 1962; La battaglia socialista per la svolta a sinistra nella
terza legislatura, 1958–63, 1963; Il socialismo nella democrazia: realtà
del presente, 1966; L'eredità della breccia di Porto Pia, 1971; I nodi
della politica estera italiana, 1974; Intervista sul socialismo italiano,
1977; La battaglia socialista contro il fascismo, 1922–1944, 1977;
Vento del Nord, 1978. Also author of many political pamphlets and
published speeches.
Further reading: Pietro Nenni by E. Bartalini, 1946.

ADOLPH DEUTSCH
Film composer and music arranger
Born London, England, October 20th, 1897
Died Palm Desert, California, U.S.A., January 1st, 1980

Adolph Deutsch, London-born film composer and arranger, began studying music at the age of five. As a schoolboy he studied composition and piano under Clara Wieck Schumann at the Royal Academy of Music. Brought to the United States at the age of 13 by an uncle, Deutsch settled in Buffalo, where he left high school to work in the automobile accessories department of the Ford Motor Company. He began to send his orchestral arrangements to various entertainment firms. An invitation from a Broadway publisher brought him to New York as a music arranger, though he continued to support himself with sales jobs for a time. During the next decade he worked for Paul Ash at the Chicago Oriental Theater in New York, learned film-score arranging at Paramount Productions on Long Island, scored and directed musical shows for George Gershwin and Irving Berlin, and did freelance arranging for radio programs. After three years at Paul Whiteman's Music Hall, he was hired in 1937 by Warner Brothers to compose scores for adventure and mystery films, including *They Drive by Night, The Maltese Falcon,* and *The Mask of Dmitrios.* In 1939 he assisted Max Steiner in the 12-week marathon session that produced the score for *Gone With the Wind.*

Deutsch left Warner Brothers in 1946, preferring to turn his talents to comedies and light romances. Two years later he was hired by MGM executive Arthur Freed and given the position of music director under John Green. The golden era of the MGM musical was already underway. Here, over a period of 14 years, Deutsch was able to refine his sonorous, richly textured style, winning Academy Awards for his work on *Oklahoma!, Seven Brides for Seven Brothers,* and *Annie Get Your Gun.* Deutsch also wrote a number of songs, instrumental works, and one symphonic piece, *Scottish Suite,* which was performed by the Philadelphia Orchestra and the New York Philharmonic.

Deutsch, one of the most articulate of Hollywood composers, said and wrote much about the problems of his craft. Producers, he complained, are apt to call in composers too late, especially with films that have not turned out well, and expect them to "save the bacon." In 1943 he founded the Screen Composers' Association to promote the rights of composers in such matters as contracts with studios and publishers, copyright laws, and royalty arrangements.

Deutsch was a frequent contributor to professional journals and wrote college textbooks on film music. His favorite hobby was tinkering with cars. "I get better ideas from adjusting my carburetor," he once said, "than I ever got from murders or avalanches." He died of heart failure at his California home.   J.P./S.J.

Married: (1) Hermina Selz; (2) Dianne Axzelle. Children: 1st marriage—Alan, b.1932. Brought to U.S.A. 1910. British at birth; naturalized American 1920. Educ: Royal Acad. Music, London 1906–10. Worked in automobiles accessories dept., Ford Motor Co., Buffalo. Music arranger with Ager, Yeller, and Bornstein, NYC ca. 1920; with Henry Busse and Arnold Johnson, NYC ca. 1925; with Paul Ash, Chicago Oriental Theater, NYC, and with Paramount Pictures, Long Island, N.Y. 1928–34; with Paul Whiteman's Music

Hall, NYC 1935–37. Composer and arranger, Warner Bros., Hollywood 1937–46; Music Dir., composer, and arranger, M-G-M Studios, Hollywood 1948–62. With Screen Composers' Assn.: Founder 1943, V.P., Pres.; Pres. emeritus 1955–80. Member, American Soc. Composers, Authors and Publishers 1940–80. Hons: LL.D., Univ. Wyoming 1975. Acad. Awards for Best Scoring of a Musical: (with Roger Edens) Annie Get Your Gun 1950; (with Saul Chaplin) Seven Brides for Seven Brothers 1954; (with Robert Russell Bennett and Jay Blackton) Oklahoma! 1955. Acad. Awards nomination for Best Scoring of a Musical or Best Film Background Score: Showboat 1951; The Band Wagon 1953; Deep in My Heart 1954; Some Like it Hot 1959; The Apartment 1960. *Composer: Film Scores*—Take Me Out to the Ball Game, 1949; Annie Get Your Gun, 1950; Pagan Love Song, 1950; Showboat, 1951; The Belle of New York, 1952; Million Dollar Mermaid, 1952; Torch Song, 1952; The Band Wagon, 1953; Seven Brides for Seven Brothers, 1954; Deep in My Heart, 1954; Oklahoma!, 1955. *Film Background Scores*—They Won't Forget, 1937; Cowboy from Brooklyn, 1938; Indianapolis Speedway, 1939; Three Cheers for the Irish, 1940; They Drive by Night, 1940; High Sierra, 1941; The Maltese Falcon, 1941; Across the Pacific, 1942; The Great Mr. Nobody, 1942; Action in the North Atlantic, 1943; Northern Pursuit, 1943; Uncertain Glory, 1944; The Mask of Dmitrios, 1944; Escape in the Desert, 1945; Three Strangers, 1946; Shadow of a Woman, 1946; Nobody Lives Forever, 1946; Ramrod, 1947; Whispering Smith, 1949; Litle Women, 1949; The Stratton Story, 1949; Intruder in the Dust, 1949; Stars in My Crown, 1950; Father of the Bride, 1950; Mrs. O'Malley and Mr. Mallone, 1950; Soldiers Three, 1951; Long, Long Trailer, 1954; Battle of Gettysburg, 1954; The Rack, 1956; Interrupted Melody, 1956; Tea and Sympathy, 1956; Funny Face, 1957; The Matchmakers, 1957; Les Girls, 1957; Some Like it Hot, 1959; The Apartment, 1960. *Songs and Instrumentals*—March of the United Nations; Margot; Lonely Room (Theme from The Apartment); Clarabelle; Three Sisters; Piano Echoes; Skyride; Stairways; March Eccentrique. *Symphonic Scores*—The Scottish Suite. *Author:* textbooks on film music. Articles in professional jrnls.

RHYS CARPENTER
Classical archaeologist
Born Cotuit, Massachusetts, U.S.A., August 5th, 1889
Died Devon, Pennsylvania, U.S.A., January 2nd, 1980.

Rhys Carpenter, whose research led to a new understanding of the ancient classical civilizations of the Mediterranean, was chairman of the Department of Classical Archaeology at Bryn Mawr College for more than 40 years.

A graduate of Columbia University and a Rhodes Scholar, Carpenter read history at Balliol College, Oxford, graduating with a B.A. degree in 1912. Upon his return to the United States he joined the faculty of Bryn Mawr College and founded its classical archaeology department (the only college in the nation offering an undergraduate course in the subject). Within five years, Carpenter, who earned his doctorate from Columbia University in 1916, had risen to academic seniority as a professor and was ready to pursue site work in the Mediterranean basin.

After conducting extensive research at the American Academy in Rome, Carpenter became director of the American School of Classical Studies in Athens, a post he held again between 1946 and 1948. During the 1940s he also served as Professor-in-Charge of the School of Classical Studies of the American Academy in Rome and as Sather Professor at the University of California. Throughout these years, he maintained close contact with the developing department in his home college.

Carpenter's scholarship was broadly interdisciplinary. He was an authority on the transmission of alphabets; an accomplished excavator, skilled in the identification of archaeological remains; and an expert on Greek and Roman history, art, and literature.

One of Carpenter's major discoveries was that of an ancient town on the Mediterranean coast of Spain. It took two years of painstaking excavation before he was prepared to announce the find in 1925. According to Carpenter, the town, called Hemeroskopeion ("watchtower"), had been built in the eighth century B.C. and used as a port until the decline of Greek civilization had resulted in its abandonment.

Not all Carpenter's theories won support. Particularly controversial was his suggestion that drought-induced relapses in civilized life in the Mediterranean basin correlated with northward shifts in the trade winds resulting from recessions of the polar ice cap. His opponents argued that sea-level changes around the shores of Greece might be better explained by sea-bed volcanic activity, and that polar ice cap variations were not substantial enough to broaden the trade wind zone.

In 1918 Carpenter was invited to serve as advisor to the U.S. Commission that negotiated peace terms in Paris at the end of World War One. As a specialist in the cultural geography of the Mediterranean area, he assisted in the resolution of territorial disputes between Albania and Greece.

Carpenter's long and distinguished literary career began with the publication of three books of poetry in the classical tradition. The first, a retelling in blank verse of the tragedy of Pelleas and Etarre, was praised by critics as a courageous challenge to Tennyson's treatment of the subject. Many of his works on Greek art and history have become standard textbooks for students.

Carpenter continued to write, travel, and lecture after his retirement in 1955. He died at the age of 90 after a long illness.   J.P./M.D.

Son of William Henry C. and Anna Morgan (Douglass) C. Married Eleanor Houston Hill 1918 (d.1976). No children. Educ: Columbia Univ., A.B. 1908, Ph.D. 1916; Balliol Coll., Oxford (Rhodes Scholarship), B.A. 1912, M.A. 1915. With Dept. Classical Archaeol., Bryn Mawr Coll., Pa.: Founder 1913; Instr, 1913–15; Assoc. 1915–16; Assoc. Prof. 1916–18; Prof. 1918–55; Prof. Emeritus 1955–80. Attached to the U.S. Commn. to Negotiate Peace at Paris 1918–19. Annual Prof. 1926–27 and Prof.-in-Charge, Classical Sch. 1939–40, American Acad. in Rome; Dir., American Sch. for Classical Studies, Athens 1927–33 and 1946–48; Sather Prof., Univ. Calif. 1944–45. Member: Hispanic Soc. of America; Pontifical Roman Acad. of

Archaeol.; Greek Archaeol. Soc.; German Archaeol. Inst.; Austrian Archaeol. Inst.; American Philosophical Soc. Hons: Gold Medal, American Inst. of Archaeol. 1969. *Author:* The Tragedy of Etarre, 1912; The Sunthief, and Other Poems, 1914; The Plainsman, and Other Poems, 1920; The Land Beyond Mexico, 1921; The Esthetic Basis of Greek Art of the 5th and 4th Centuries B.C., 1921, 2nd ed. 1959; The Greeks in Spain, 1925; The Sculpture of the Nike Temple Parapet, 1929; The Defense of Acrocorinth, 1936; Greek Sculpture: A Critical Review, 1960; Greek Art: A Study in the Evolution of Style, 1963; Beyond the Pillars of Heracles, 1966; The Architects of the Parthenon, 1970. *Published lectures:* The Humanistic Value of Archaeology (Harvard), 1933; Folk Tale, Fiction and Saga in the Homeric Epics (Sather), 1946; Discontinuity in Greek Civilization (J.H. Clark), 1966. Contributor to American Jrnl. of Archaeology and Natl. Geographic.

JOY ADAMSON
Writer on animal behavior, conservationist and painter
Born Troppau, Silesia, Austria (now Opava, Czechoslovakia),
January 20th, 1910
Died Shaba Game Reserve, Kenya, January 3rd, 1980

Joy Adamson, famous for her work with Elsa the lioness, was a naturalist, artist, writer, and scientist combined. Probably more than any other single individual, she was able, through her popular and widely translated books, to bring African wildlife and the need for its conservation to worldwide attention, launching international movements on its behalf.

Born into a wealthy family in the capital of Austrian Silesia and raised in Vienna, Joy Adamson (then Gessner) spent her holidays at her mother's family's estate outside of Troppau. Her first choice for a career was that of concert pianist. She had learned to play the piano before she could read or write and later earned a state diploma for pianists. When her hands proved too small for a professional career, she began to explore a variety of disciplines, including metalwork, poster and book jacket design, dressmaking, singing, art history, drawing, shorthand, typing, and woodsculpting. She assisted in the excavation of a prehistoric site and learned traditional methods of mixing pigment by watching the restoration of Quattrocento paintings. After studying psychoanalysis and visiting the dissecting room of the Anatomical Institute in Vienna, she decided to study medicine; she went back to school to work for her Matura (the Gynmasium diploma required for university entrance) but never sat for the exam.

In 1935 Gessner married Victor von Klarwill. Because he was Jewish and Austria was already within the Nazi orbit, he decided to move to Kenya, and sent her on an exploratory trip there in March 1937. She met her second husband, Peter Bally, on the voyage out. Shortly after von Klarwill joined her in Kenya, they were divorced.

Bally was a botanist exploring the plants of Kenya and surrounding areas. As a member of his expeditions to such sites as the Chyulu Hills and Mt. Kenya, Gessner started collecting and painting flora. Of her 700 paintings from this period, many were used as illustrations in seven books on East African flowers, trees, and shrubs, and are now in the possession of the National Museum (formerly the Corydon Museum) in Nairobi. In 1947 an exhibition of her botanical paintings won the Grenfell Gold Medal from the Royal Horticultural Society in London.

After her marriage to Bally ended in divorce, Gessner married George Adamson, a British citizen who was senior game warden in the North Frontier District of Kenya. Their life together was a continuous safari over 120,000 square miles of Kenyan wilderness. Mrs. Adamson now extended the range of her artistic subject matter to include fauna and tribespeople. The colonial government of Kenya commissioned her to paint and photograph 22 tribes in order to document their traditions before they were swept away by modernization. Over 600 paintings of tribespeople, made over the course of six years, were placed on permanent exhibition in the State House and National Museum in Nairobi. A selection of these paintings was published some 20 years later in the *Peoples of Kenya.*

George Adamson's responsibilities as game warden included the care of orphaned animals. In 1956, he brought home three small lion cubs whose mother he had been forced to shoot in self-defense. The two larger cubs were sent to a zoo, but the Adamsons adopted Elsa, a peaceable cub with a playful disposition. Mrs. Adamson, who claimed to enjoy a telepathic rapport with Elsa, made many sketches of her pet as aids to the observation and recording of her behavior, but soon set herself a much more difficult and important task: that of teaching Elsa to hunt and kill game in preparation for a return to the wild. She described her success in *Born Free,* a best-selling book that earned her international recognition. It was followed by two sequels, *Living Free* and *Forever Free,* retold for children in *Elsa* and *Elsa and Her Cubs.* These books were copiously illustrated with photographs and were generally applauded by critics, who found Mrs. Adamson's writing unpretentious and her approach untrammeled by sentimentality or anthropomorphism. The screen adaptation of *Born Free* was a popular success, though two sequels were less well-received. An American television series was later adapted from *Born Free.*

In 1964, Mrs. Adamson adopted an eight-month-old female cheetah, Pippa, who had been the house-trained pet of a British Army officer. For four and a half years she shared Pippa's life at Meru National Park, a preserve she and her husband had been instrumental in establishing. Her retraining of Pippa was described in *The Spotted Sphinx* and *Pippa's Challenge,* adapted for children in *Pippa the Cheetah and Her Cubs.*

Not all of her work in rehabilitating tamed animals for survival in the wild was successful. One lion who was returned to the wilderness mauled a child and later killed one of the Adamsons' servants and had to be put to death. Mrs. Adamson also studied various other wild animals, including hyraxes, leopards, baby elephants, colobus monkeys, impala does, Arabian oryxes, and young buffaloes.

In the 1960s, Mrs. Adamson became a leading spokesperson for the cause of wildlife preservation, beginning in 1962 when she launched the World Wildlife Fund during a US lecture tour sponsored by the Academy of Natural Sciences. She also founded the Elsa Wild Animal

Appeal, helped to establish animal preserves, and worked on behalf of a number of international organizations, to which she contributed the royalties from her Elsa books. She encouraged the public to boycott furs and jewelry made from animal parts. In 1970, after losing the use of her right hand in an automobile accident, Mrs. Adamson and her husband moved to a house overlooking a bird sanctuary on Lake Naivasha, some 75 miles from Nairobi, where she continued her activities.

On January 3, 1980, Joy Adamson was found dead near the Shaba Game Reserve in northern Kenya, a remote camp from which she had been studying the behavior of leopards. Initial reports claimed that she had been mauled by a lion. The autopsy indicated that death had resulted from head injuries. Three men, all former employees, were taken into custody. On February 2nd, one of these men, a 23-year-old herdsman named Paul Nakware Ekai, was charged with her murder.

J.P./L.F.

Born Friederike Victoria Gessner. Daughter of Victor G., architect and sr. civil servant, and Traute Friederike G. Married: (1) Victor von Klarwill 1935 (div.); (2) Peter Bally, botanist, 1938 (div.); (3) George Adamson, game warden, 1943. No children. Protestant. Emigrated to Kenya 1937. Austrian at birth; British citizen by 3rd marriage. Educ: Staatsprüfung in Piano, Vienna 1927; Gremuim (diploma) in dress-making 1928; studied sculpting with Prof. W. Frass, Vienna 1929–30; studied metalwork, Kunstgewerbschule, Vienna 1931–32; graduate pre-medical course 1933–35; Slade Sch. of Art, London 1945. Active as painter of flora in Kenya 1938–43; thereafter painter and sketcher of wild animals and tribal life; commissioned by Govt. of Kenya to paint tribes of Kenya in traditional garb 1944–52. Researcher on wild animals 1956–80 and author 1958–80. Founder, Elsa Wild Animal Appeal Intnl. for Wildlife Preservation, U.K. 1961, U.S. 1969, Canada 1971. Hons: Gold Grenfell Medal, Royal Horticultural Soc., London 1947; Award of Merit (Silver Medal), Czechoslovakia 1970; Joseph Wood Krutch Medal, Humane Soc., U.S.A. 1971; Cross of Honor for Science and Art, Austria 1976. *Author:* Born Free: A Lioness of Two Worlds, 1960, 1964, new ed. 1965, filmed 1966; Elsa: The True Story of a Lioness, 1961; Living Free: The Story of Elsa and Her Cubs, 1961, 1964, filmed 1971; Forever Free: Elsa's Pride, 1962, 1966, filmed 1971; Elsa and Her Cubs, 1965; The Story of Elsa, 1966; (also illustrator) The Peoples of Kenya, 1967; The Spotted Sphinx, 1969; Pippa the Cheetah and Her Cubs, 1970, filmed 1970; Pippa's Challenge, 1972; Joy Adamson's Africa, 1972, also filmstrip; The Searching Spirit: Joy Adamson's Autobiography, 1978 (filmed as Joy Adamson, 1978); works translated into German, French, Polish, Swahili, and 31 other languages; articles in English, German, African, and Austrian scholarly and popular jrnls. *Exhibitions:* Royal Horticultural Soc., 1947; London Tea Center, 1970; Tyron Gall., Nairobi 1972; Edinburgh 1976. *Collections:* National Mus., Nairobi; State House, Nairobi; Fort Jesus Mus., Mombasa.

G(EORGE) S(UTHERLAND) FRASER
Poet and literary critic
Born Glasgow, Scotland, November 8th, 1915
Died Leicester, England, January 3rd, 1980

G.S. Fraser, poet and literary critic, was born in Glasgow to a family of Highland origin and grew up in Aberdeen, where his father was town clerk and where he attended Byron's alma mater, the Aberdeen Grammar School. He was already a published poet when he entered St. Andrews University at the age of 16, and received his degree before he was 21. For two years he worked as a reporter on the *Aberdeen Press and Journal.* Called up by the army in 1939, Fraser served in the Black Watch and other units in the middle East, working first on military newspapers and magazines in Cairo and Asmara, then at the Ministry of Information in Cairo, where he struck up friendships with Lawrence Durrell and other visiting British authors. His first major book of poems, *Home Town Elegy,* was published during the war. The gentle, nostalgic poems in *Home Town Elegy* reflect Fraser's lifelong principle to

. . . . take sword up only for the human,
Not to revive the broken ghosts of Gael.

Writing from Egypt of his native Aberdeen, he remembers

. . . Bunny and Sheila and Joyce and Rosemary
Chattering on sofas or preparing tea,
With delicate voices and their small white hands.
This is the sorrow everyone understands
More than Rostov's artillery. . . .

As a young poet, Fraser was associated with the New Apocalypse movement, whose members repudiated the revolutionary passions of Auden's generation in favor of a quasi-religious devotion to human imagination, emotion, and creativity. It was, as Babette Deutsch has written, "a kind of ethical anarchism in which a leonine Christianity lay down with a lamblike Freudianism." Fraser's own work was more influenced by Yeats than by his fellow Apocalyptics, and the loosely organized movement soon died away.

Fraser married Eileen Lucy Andrew in 1946 and settled in London, where he continued to write poetry and took up a career as a freelance literary journalist, writing reviews for the *Times Literary Supplement* and the *New Statesman* and broadcasting the BBC Third Programme series "New Poetry." His Chelsea flat was the scene of many literary meetings, where he gave encouragement to would-be poets. A three-month tour of Uruguay, Argentina, and Chile on a cultural mission in 1946, and an 18-month stint in Japan as cultural advisor to the U.K. Liaison Mission in 1950–51, resulted in two travel books. More important, Fraser established himself as a trenchant literary critic with the publication in 1950 of *The Modern Writer and His World,* originally written as a guidebook for Japanese students who had lost touch with English literature during the war. For some years, he continued to write critical essays, translate works from the French, and edit anthologies.

In 1958 Fraser joined the University of Leicester as a lecturer, later a reader, of modern English literature. Although teaching slowed his critical output, he continued to produce reviews and essays. His development as a poet also suffered, but, he said, "teaching, especially the teaching of poetry, has became as true a vocation as writing poetry." Fraser continued to help young poets and was active in the Leicester Poetry Society. He taught until a year before his death.

As a critic Fraser was widely respected. The *Times Literary Supplement* review of his book *Vision and Rhetoric,* a collection of magazine articles, noted his "critical breadth and knowledgeability," his "gift of hitting off the essence of a writer or work with one brief, pregnant phrase." His poetry met with less approval; though capable of much lyrical power and tenderness, Fraser, in the eyes of many reviewers, failed to sustain his early intensity. Fraser himself cited the limitations that time and finances constantly placed on his creative work and suggested that his main contribution to literature lay elsewhere. "If I pride myself on anything in my career," he once said, "it is more on having been generally helpful to the profession of letters and particularly to the appreciation of poetry, than on the lasting value of anything I myself have accomplished in prose or verse."   J.P./S.P.

Son of George Sutherland F., town clerk, Aberdeen. Married Eileen Lucy Andrew 1946. Children: Two daughters, one son. Educ: Aberdeen Grammar Sch.; Univ. St. Andrews, Scotland, M.A. 1935. Mil. Service: British Army, Middle East 1939–45. Journalist, Aberdeen Press and Journal 1937–39; freelance journalist 1945–58; on cultural mission to South America 1946; Cultural Advisor to U.K. Liaison Mission in Japan 1950–51; Lectr. in English 1959–63 and Reader in Modern English Lit. 1964–79, Univ. Leicester; Visiting Prof., Rochester Univ., N.Y. 1963–64. Sometime poetry editor and regular reviewer for Times Literary Supplement and New Statesman; New Poetry broadcaster on B.B.C. Radio. Chmn., Leicester Poetry Soc. 1976; Member, Soc. of Authors. Hons: Hodder and Stoughton Bursary for ex-service writers 1946. *Books: Verse*—The Fatal Landscape and Other Poems, 1943; Home Town Elegy, 1944; The Traveller Has Regrets and Other Poems, 1948; Leaves Without a Tree, 1956; Conditions: Selected Recent Poetry, 1969. *Criticism*—Post-War Trends in English Literature, 1950; The Modern Writer and His World: Continuity and Innovation in Twentieth-Century English Literature, 1953, rev. ed. 1964; W.B. Yeats, 1954; Keith Douglas, 1956; Dylan Thomas, 1957; Vision and Rhetoric: Studies in Modern Poetry, 1959; Ezra Pound, 1960; Lawrence Durrell: A Critical Study, 1968; Lawrence Durrell, 1970; Metre, Rhythm, and Free Verse, 1970; (author of introduction) The Poetry of Louis MacNeice (by Donald B. Moore), 1972; P.H. Newby, 1975; Essays on Twentieth-Century Poets, 1977; Alexander Pope, 1978. *Editor*—(with J. Waller) Collected Poems of Keith Douglas, 1951, rev. ed. (with Waller and J.C. Hall) 1966; (with Ian Fletcher) Springtime: An Anthology of Young Poets and Writers, 1954; Poetry Now: An Anthology, 1956; Selected Poems of Robert Burns, 1960; Vaughan College Poems, 1963; (with others) British Writers and Their Work, Vol. 5, 1965; (with J. Waller and J.C. Hall) Alamein to Zem Zem (by Keith Douglas), 1966; (with others) Workshop 8, 1969; John Keats's Odes, 1971; (reviser) Selections from the Sacred Writings of the Sikhs (by Adi Granth), 1974; The Canterbury Tales (by Geoffrey Chaucer). *Translator*—The Dedicated Life in Poetry, and the Correspondence of Laurent de Cayeux (by Patrice de la Tour du Pin), 1948; The Mystery of Being (by Gabriel Marcel), 1950; Men Against Humanity (by Gabriel Marcel), 1952; Pascal: His Life and Works (by Jean Mesnard), 1952; (with E. de Mauny) Béla Bartók (by S. Moreux), 1953; (with others) Dante's

Inferno and Paradiso, 1966. *Travel*—Vision of Scotland, 1948; News from South America, 1949; Impressions of Japan and other Essays, 1952; (with E. Smith) Scotland, 1955. *Contributor* to New Statesman; Times Literary Supplement; Commentary; Poetry (Chicago); Poetry (London); Observer; Partisan Review; Listener; other lit. mags. Anthologized in Oxford Book of Scottish Verse; Oxford Book of 20th Century Verse; Modern Scottish Verse; Scottish Love Poems; Of Poetry and Power; Other anthologies.
Further reading: Poetry in Our Time by Babette Deutsch, 1963; Contemporary Poets of the English Language by James Vinson (ed.), 3rd ed. 1980.

DOV JOSEPH
Israeli cabinet minister and lawyer
Born Montreal, Canada, April 27th, 1899
Died Tel Aviv, Israel, January 6th, 1980

Courtesy Alma Shapir

A founder of the State of Israel, Dov Joseph held seven different ministerial posts in a political career which included the military governorship of Jerusalem under siege.

Son of an influential Canadian family, Joseph was raised by his grandfather from the age of four after his father died. As a young man he founded the Young Judea Movement in Canada and subsequently became its president. He broke off his law studies at McGill University in 1918 to enlist in the Jewish Legion in Palestine, returning at the end of the First World War to complete his studies. In 1921 he went back to Palestine and settled in Jerusalem, where he engaged in private law practice until 1948, meanwhile obtaining a Ph.D. in civil law from London University.

Joseph quickly established himself as a leading member of the Palestine Bar and became prominent in the work of the Jewish Agency (then an arm of the World Zionist Organization), serving successively as its legal adviser, a member of its executive committee, and its treasurer. He was closely associated with Moshe Sharatt, head of the Jewish Agency's Political Department, and took much of the responsibility for representing Palestinian Jewry to the British mandatory authorities.

In the early months of the Second World War, Joseph's offer of Jewish recruits to fight alongside the Allied armies was flatly refused by the British, but his predictions of German territorial advances and Allied insecurity in the Middle East soon proved to be accurate and his earlier offer of assistance was accepted. Subsequently he became chairman of the board which recruited Jews for the Allied armies. In 1946, however, Joseph was among those arrested and detained in Latrun when the British authorities decided to raid the Jewish Agency in reprisal for terrorist attacks by militant Jews.

As a member of the Political Committee of the World Zionist Organization, Joseph was sent to the United States in September 1947 to take part in last-minute efforts to obtain a favorable vote in United Nations discussions leading to the establishment of Israel and the partitioning of Jerusalem. On his return to Jerusalem three months later, Joseph was appointed co-chairman of the Jewish Emergency Committee, the body formed by the merger of the Jewish Agency and the Va'ad Leumi (National Council).

When the British Mandate ended in May 1948, Joseph became Military Governor of Jerusalem, coordinating resistance to the Arab forces which laid siege to the Jewish sector of the city and dealing with the collapse of essential services and supplies. Under Joseph's leadership the Jewish residents displayed great fortitude, though enemy mortar and sniper fire claimed many casualties and the Jewish Quarter of the Old City was eventually captured. Joseph's younger daughter Leila was killed in action in defense of the city.

Once the new state was established, Joseph was chosen by David Ben-Gurion, its first Prime Minister, as Minister of Supply and Rationing. Having faced the prospect of mass starvation earlier in Jerusalem, he was prepared to inaugurate rigorous austerity measures. He immediately imposed a tight and uncompromising program which rationed all essential commodities, controlled all wages, and reduced cash flow. These measures brought about a marked reduction in Israel's cost-of-living index between April 1949 and mid-1950, but the concomitant reduction in the quality of life earned Joseph the criticism of populace and politicians alike. Nevertheless, he continued with his policies, rationing all clothing and cutting back even further on food allowances through 1950–51. The economy dwindled as merchants ceased trading; public outrage led to mass street demonstrations against Joseph's austerity program. Rather than face continued government unpopularity, the Prime Minister provided Joseph with alternative ministerial responsibility. But his almost puritanical disposition was not welcomed by many of his younger political colleagues. Finally, differences with Prime Minister Levi Eshkol forced him into retirement in 1966.

After his retirement, Joseph continued to live in Jerusalem, following his lifelong recreational interests of reading and listening to classical music. His books include *The Faithful City,* his own account of the siege of Jerusalem, and *Nationality,* a treatise on the legal claims of Jews and Arabs in Palestine.   J.P./M.D.

Born Bernard Joseph (changed name on becoming citizen of newly-created State of Israel). Son of Yerachmiel J. and Sarah (Fineberg) J. Married Goldie O. Hoffman 1922. Children: Amiram; Alma Shapir; Leila (killed in action, Israeli War of Independence). Jewish. Emigrated to Palestine 1921. Educ: Univ. Laval, Que,; McGill Univ., Montreal, B.A., B.H.L. 1921; London Univ., Ph.D. civil law 1929. Mil. Service: Jewish Legion, Palestine 1918. Founder and Pres., Young Judea Movement, Canada 1919. Private law practice and member Palestine Bar 1921–48. With Jewish Agency for Palestine; Legal adviser, Political Dept. 1936–45; Member, Exec. Cttee. 1945–48; Treas. 1956–61; Member, Jewish Agency Missions to Great Britain, U.S.A., Canada, South Africa. Chmn., Voluntary Recruitment Bd. of Jerusalem during WWII; Member, Emergency Cttee., Jerusalem 1947–48; Mil. Gov., Jerusalem, during siege 1948–49; Member, Mapai Party, 1st, 2nd, 3rd Knesset, State of Israel 1949–60. Minister of Supply and Rationing 1949–50; Communications 1950–51; Trade 1951–52; Justice 1952 and 1961–65; State 1952–53; Development 1953–55; Health 1955. Gov., Bank Leumi-le-Israel, B.M.; Mekorot (natl. water co.); Zim (natl. shipping line). *Author:* Nationality: Its Nature and Problems, 1923; British Rule in Palestine, 1948; The Faithful City: The Siege of Jerusalem 1948, 1960; In Quest of Peace.

JOHN WILLIAM MAUCHLY
Physicist, research engineer and a developer of computers
Born Cincinnati, Ohio, U.S.A., August 30th, 1907
Died Abington, Pennsylvania, U.S.A., January 8th, 1980

Dr. John William Mauchly, a research scientist who originally envisioned and helped to construct the first electronic general-purpose digital computer, was one of the major innovators in the field of computer technology.

Mauchly was born in Cincinnati and grew up in Chevy Chase, Maryland. His father was a noted research physicist at the Department of Terrestrial Magnetism, Carnegie Institution. In 1925 John Mauchly won a state scholarship to the engineering college at Johns Hopkins University. After two years he transferred to the physics department, pursuing studies in theoretical and experimental physics.

He became involved with molecular spectroscopy in the early 1930s. The structure of the single atom had been discovered, but clustered atom structuring was not yet fully understood. A year after completing his doctoral dissertation—an analysis of the carbon monoxide molecule—Dr. Mauchly accepted a position at Ursinus College in Pennsylvania working as a one-man faculty in their physics department. While working on a weather analysis project, Mauchly recognized the need for a high-speed computer. Using parts and equipment he purchased himself, he experimented with ways to count electronically and built an analog computer (a machine which operates with numbers represented by directly measurable quantities such as voltages or rotations) to help him make harmonic analysis of weather data.

In the summer of 1941, Dr. Mauchly enrolled in a defense training course in electronics at the Moore School of Electrical Engineering at the University of Pennsylvania. There he met J. Presper Eckert, who, although having just received his bachelor's degree, had taken out a patent on a television scanning device. Combining Eckert's skill in electronics with Mauchly's expertise in mathematics, calculators and computing machines, they discussed the possibilities of building a computer which, like a radio, would use vacuum tubes. Eckert maintained that reliability problems could be avoided if radical improvements could be made to the design of the circuits.

Dr. Mauchly accepted a post as electrical engineering instructor at the Moore School, which was under contract to Army Ordnance to calculate ballistic tables for U.S. forces in North Africa. It had become apparent that much of the data compiled from peacetime practice was useless under foreign combat conditions. In August 1942 he requested permission from the School to build an electronic computer. The proposal was rejected, but a year later, an Army lieutenant assigned to expedite the production of ballistics data revived the proposal and the School received funding from the Aberdeen Ballistics Research Laboratory.

Within the scientific community doubts were expressed that, because of the number of vacuum tubes needed and the complexity of circuits involved, the machine would continuously break down. But Mauchly and Eckert estimated that one hour of daily operation by the machine would surpass the work performed in two months by the school's mechanical analyzer and teams of people using desk calculators. When work finished in 1946, ENIAC (Electronic Numerical Integrator and Calculator) weighed more than 30 tons, took up more than 15,000 square feet of floor space and contained 18,000 vacuum tubes. ENIAC could solve any problem whose factors had been translated into numerical values, performing 5,000 additions or about 300 multiplications a second, a thousand times faster than any calculator then in existence. The machine was programmed by the insertion of wires into plugboards similar to telephone switchboards, and input and output data were stored on punch cards. Contrary to expectations, ENIAC only broke down for a period of about one hour every other day.

Prior to completion of ENIAC, Mauchly, Eckert and mathematician John von Neumann had designed EDVAC (Electronic Discrete Variable Automatic Computer) which was planned to be the first machine capable of modifying its own store program. Using electronically alterable memory devices called "mercury delay lines" instead of ENIAC's plugboards and programming switches, EDVAC would contain only one or two thousand tubes and would easily be able to solve problems too complex for ENIAC.

Before ENIAC's completion and before EDVAC could be developed, a dispute over the patent rights to the computer caused Mauchly and Eckert to resign from the University in March 1946. The two men formed the Electronic Control Company—later the Eckert-Mauchly Computer Corporation—the first commercial organization devoted to the design and construction of automatic electronic digital computers. Assisted by research contracts from several large organizations, they developed models of an acoustic memory system, an advanced mathematics unit, and a magnetic tape device. This led to a contract with the Northrop Company for the development of a computer to guide missiles. The machine, BINAC (Binary Automatic Computer), was completed in 1949 and was the first computer to be programmed by internally stored instructions. One-tenth ENIAC's size, it has 25 times the memory. Joined now by Isaac Auerbach, Mauchly and Eckert entered a period of exceptional creativity. Only a lack of capital prohibited them from developing more than one computer at a time. Their next machine, UNIVAC I (Universal Automatic Computer), was the world's first large, general-purpose, commercially available computer. Completed for the U.S. Census Bureau in March 1951, UNIVAC I used an elaborate magnetic tape system for data input, could handle alphabetic as well as numeric symbols, and was suited to a wide variety of tasks. The key to both BINAC and UNIVAC was their large electronic memory, the "mercury tank register," a device invented by Mauchly and Eckert.

In 1950, the company was sold to Remington Rand, with Mauchly remaining as Director of UNIVAC Applications Research. Still interested in weather prediction, he produced in 1954 the first statistical confirmation that the moon affects precipitation. He left the company in 1959 to form Mauchly Associates, introducing in 1962 a "Critical Path" (CP) computer, which could provide optimum plans, schedules and sequences for complex projects which might involve large numbers of operators, materials, and activities.

John Mauchly's primary interest was always the application of computers and the development of their programming language. At a meeting of industrial engineers in 1962, he announced that he was working on a pocket-sized computer to replace another of his inventions, the suitcase-sized one. He founded Dynatrend—a computerized stock research firm—in 1967. Six years later he returned to the Sperry Corporation, where he remained as a consultant until his death at the age of seventy-two.   J.S.

Son of Sebastian Jacob M., research physicist, and Rachel Elizabeth M. Married: (1) Mary Augusta Walzl 1930 (d.1946); (2) Kathleen Rita McNulty 1948. Children: first marriage—James, Sidney; second marriage—Sara Elizabeth, Kathleen Ann, John William, Virginia, Eva. Roman Catholic. Educ: Johns Hopkins Sch. Engineering 1925–27 and Sch. Physics 1927–32, Ph.D. physics 1932. Phi Beta Kappa, Sigma Xi. Research Asst., Johns Hopkins Univ. 1932–33; Head, Dept. of Physics, Ursinus Coll., Collegeville, Pa. 1933–41; Assoc., Dept of Terrestrial Magnetism, Carnegie Inst., Washington, D.C. summers 1936–38; Instr. in Elec. Engineering 1941–43 and Asst. Prof. 1943–46, Univ. of Pennsylvania. Consultant, Naval Ordnance Lab., White Oaks, Md. 1944–45; established (with J.P. Eckert) Electronic Control Co. 1946; Pres., Eckert-Mauchly Computer Corp. 1947–51; Dir., Remington Rand Weather Project 1951–53. Dir., systems studies, Eckert-Mauchly Div., Remington Rand 1953; Dir., UNIVAC Applications Research Center, Remington Rand UNIVAC Div., Sperry Rand Corp. 1954–59; Pres. 1959–65 and Chmn. of the Bd. 1965–69, Mauchly Assocs; Visiting Prof. systems engineering, Carnegie Inst. of Technol., Pittsburgh, Pa. 1959–60; Pres., Dynatrend Inc., Springhouse, Pa. 1967–80; Pres., Marketrend Inc. 1970–80; Consultant, Sperry Rand 1973–80. Dir.: Pyrometer Corp.; Jonkers Corp.; Data Systems Corp.; Package Devices Inc.; Duovent Inc. Member: Franklin Inst.; American Geophysical Union; Inst. Mathematical Statistics; American Meteorological Soc.; Assn. Computing Machinery (Founder; V.P. 1947–48 and Pres. 1948–50); Soc. Industrial and Applied Mathematics (Founder; Trustee 1953–54; Pres. 1955–56); Natl. Acad. of Engineering; American Astronomical Soc.; American Physical Soc.; Soc. for the Advancement of Management. Hons: Recipient, Howard N. Potts Medal (with J.P. Eckert), Franklin Inst. 1949; John Scott Award 1961; Modern Pioneer Award, N.A.M. 1965; Harry Goode Award, American Fedn. Information Processing Socs. 1966; Award of Excellence, Gov.'s Cttee. of 100,000 Pennsylvanians 1968; Philadelphia Award 1972; Pender Award, Moore Sch., Univ. of Pennsylvania 1973; Pennsylvania Award; Emanuel R. Piore Award, Inst. of Electrical and Electronics Engineers, Inc. (with J.P. Eckert) 1978; LL.D. Univ. of Pennsylvania 1974; D.Sc. Ursinus Coll. 1977; Fellow, Inst. of Electrical and Electronics Engineers, and American Statistical Assn. *Publications*—Contributed articles to scientific jrnls.

and 1963 Industrial Engineering Handbook. Papers housed in Van Pelt Library, Univ. of Pennsylvania.

SIR CHARLES (JOHN) CURRAN
Director-General, British Broadcasting Corporation
Born Dublin, Ireland, October 13th, 1921
Died London, England, January 9th, 1980

Sir Charles Curran was the first British Broadcasting Corporation employee to work his way from junior trainee rank to its senior management post.

Son of an army schoolmaster who later turned to civilian teaching, Curran went to Magdalene College, Cambridge, on a scholarship in October 1939. After just one year he was called up and served the remainder of the Second World War in the Indian Army. He later returned to Cambridge and graduated in 1947 with First Class Honors.

Curran joined the staff of the BBC as a talks producer in 1947 after being rejected by the British Consular Service. He stayed with the BBC Home News Department for three years until a disagreement over the handling of editorial matter led him to resign. In 1950 he went to Canada to become assistant editor of the trade paper "Fishing News", gaining a knowledge of the country which was later to prove valuable.

A year later, Curran returned to the BBC as a report writer in its Monitoring Service and became the first beneficiary of the BBC's administrative training program, rising to the level of senior administrative assistant. By the late 1950s Curran was the BBC's representative in Canada, where his fluency in French was an asset. His success there resulted in promotion to senior administrator of the BBC's External Services. After four years in this post, Curran became Secretary of the BBC, serving both the Board of Governors and the Director-General. In 1967 he was promoted to Director of External Services, and two years later, at the age of 48, Curran succeeded Sir Hugh Greene as Director-General.

His appointment was unexpected; the chairman of the BBC Board of Governors, Lord Hill, later disclosed that Curran's nomination had met with some opposition because he was considered "colorless". Once installed, Curran found himself facing an array of difficulties, including labor unrest and public criticism over BBC policies. His first major crisis came with the screening of the television program *The Question of Ulster,* which brought together, for the first time on television, politicians of all the main parties in Northern Ireland. The Conservative Government of the time was critical of the BBC's handling of the issue and the end result was an ongoing public debate into the ethics of reporting terrorist activities—a debate which overshadowed the remainder of Curran's time as Director-General.

Another controversy erupted over *Yesterday's Men,* a political program that was sharply critical of many Labour politicians and ministers. The program was aired shortly before a General Election and provoked Labour Party accusations of bias. An inquiry was called for, but the capacity of the BBC Board of Governors to deal impartially with the problem was compromised by some of its members, who had viewed the program prior to its broadcast; Curran himself was held responsible for allowing it to be shown at all. Ultimately, an independent Complaints Commission was set up within the BBC to investigate incidents of this nature.

By contrast, Curran emerged relatively unscathed from the public row over reorganization of radio services and the future of the BBC's Third Programme. Curran's contemporaries attributed his success in this area to his greater understanding of radio than of television. Later he played a vital role in securing for the BBC a stable financial base. A broad vindication of his views on the ethics of radio and television journalism was offered by the Annan Report on Broadcasting in 1977.

During the last five years of his time with the BBC, Curran undertook the presidency of the European Broadcasting Union, becoming deeply involved with its many diplomatic, financial, technical, and legal problems. He was knighted in 1974. After his retirement in 1978 Curran became Managing Director and Chief Executive of Visnews, the television news agency. His memoir of the BBC, *A Seamless Robe,* was published in 1979.   J.P./M.D.

Son of Felix C., teacher, and Alicia Isabella (Bruce) C. Married Silvia Meyer, B.B.C. studio manager, 1949. One daughter. Roman Catholic. Educ: Wath-on-Dearne Grammar Sch., South Yorks.; Magdalene Coll., Cambridge (Scholarship and First Class Honors), B.A. 1947. Mil. Service: Indian Army 1941–45. Home Talks Producer, B.B.C., London 1947–50. Asst. Ed., Fishing News, Canada 1950–51. Rejoined B.B.C. 1951: Report Writer, Monitoring Service 1951–56; Canada Rep. 1956–59; Sr. Admin., External Services, London 1959–63; Secty. to B.B.C. Govs. 1963–67; Dir., External Broadcasting 1967–69; Dir.-Gen. 1969–77; Consultant on Intnl. Broadcasting 1977–78. Pres., European Broadcasting Union 1973–78; Managing Dir. and Chief Exec., Visnews 1978–80. Exec. Cttee. Member 1973–78 and Bd. Member 1978–80, British Council; Member, Tablet Trust 1976–80; Dir., Nationwide Bldg. Soc. 1978; Member, U.K. Marriage Research Centre; Member, United Oxford and Cambridge Univ. and Garrick Clubs. Hons: Knighted 1974; D.Litt., City Univ., London 1977; D.Litt., Open Univ., Britain 1978; Knight, Comdr. St. Silvester 1979; Fellow, British Inst. of Management. *Author:* A Seamless Robe (memoirs), 1979.

SIR CHARLES DRUMMOND ELLIS
Physicist and public administrator
Born London, England, August 11th, 1895
Died Cookham Dean, Berkshire, England, January 10th, 1980

Sir Charles Ellis began his distinguished scientific career in a prisoner-of-war camp in Germany. Over the next 50 years he applied his knowledge in a variety of fields ranging from coal and gas utilization to cigarette smoking. Ellis's career was characterized by meticulous attention to detail and by an insistence on high standards in a clearly defined and planned work program.

One of the foremost all-round sportsmen of his school years at Harrow—he was named Victor Ludorum in 1912 and 1913—Ellis graduated first in his class from the Royal Military Academy at Woolwich. But he was soon caught up in the turmoil of World War One, taken prisoner, and interned in Germany. This proved fortuitous, for it was during his imprisonment in the camp at Ruhleben that he met James Chadwick, discoverer of the neutron.

Chadwick had been doing postgraduate research under Hans Geiger when the war broke out; although he was interned at Ruhleben, he had been able to continue his researches using materials and books supplied to him by Lise Meitner, Max Planck, and Walther Nernst, and had set up a laboratory in a stable. He now introduced young Ellis to quantum theory and radioactivity. Ellis provided him with much-needed assistance for his experiments on the photochemical reaction of carbon dioxide and chlorine and on ionization in the oxidation of phosphorus.

At the end of the war Ellis went to Trinity College, Cambridge, to continue his studies. He gained his doctorate and took a university teaching post while collaborating with Chadwick and Ernest Rutherford in radiation research. This work led toward their publication of *Radiations from Radioactive Substances* (1930), which was to become a basic textbook for all students in the field. Ellis's own achievements earned him a Fellowship in the Royal Society in 1929.

In 1936, Ellis accepted the Wheatstone Chair of Physics at London University. This move, coupled with the outbreak of World War Two, heralded a shift and diversification in his career. His grasp of the basic physics of weaponry—not least of atomic physics—resulted in his appointment to the Army Council as scientific advisor. A similar appointment followed at the Ministry of Supply. Under his guidance the science of operational research was much advanced. At the conclusion of hostilities, his work gained recognition with the conferment of a knighthood.

Following the war, Ellis broadened his career. Always a physicist at heart, in his wartime service he had demonstrated a flair for higher administration. He became a scientific member of the National Coal Board and then scientific advisor to the Gas Council. In the latter post, he was responsible for reorganizing the whole of that industry's research efforts, as well as for planning and implementing a new range of research facilities.

Ellis's interest in the fuel industry was comprehensive and went far beyond the laboratory. For eight years he was a member of the Advisory Council of the Ministry of Fuel and Power. He served nine years as president of the British Coal Utilisation Research Association at a time when the coal industry was threatened by the development of nuclear power.

In 1955, the same year that he joined the gas industry, Ellis also accepted an invitation to become scientific advisor to the British-American Tobacco Company. Again Ellis was faced with the challenge of reorganization and innovation. Under his supervision, the tobacco industry in Britain, hitherto very much a craft industry, began to adopt scientific techniques. As a member of the Tobacco Research Council, Ellis was also instrumental in setting up a research program providing statistical analysis of bioassay experiments. He retained an active interest in the tobacco industry after his retirement in 1972.

M.D.

Son of Alfred Charles E. and Isabella (Carswell) E. Married Paula Warczcewska (Dantziger) 1925. No children. Educ: Harrow Sch., Middx.; Royal Mil. Acad., Woolwich; Trinity Coll., Cambridge, B.A. 1921, Ph.D. physics 1924. Mil. Service: Royal Engineers 1915; P.O.W. Germany. Fellow and Lectr., Trinity Coll. 1921–36, and Lectr., Dept. Physics 1926–36, Univ. Cambridge; Wheatstone Prof. of Physics, King's Coll., Univ. London 1936–46; External Prof. Physics at all Canadian univs. 1938–39. Scientific Advisor to the British Army Council 1943–46; Member, Advisory Council on Scientific Research and Tech. Devel. to the Ministry of Supply, London 1943–46. Dir., Finance Corp. for Industry 1945–69; Scientific Member, Nat. Coal Bd. 1946–55; Pres., British Coal Utilisation Research Assn. 1946–55; Member, Advisory Council to Ministry of Fuel and Power 1947–65; Sr. Scientific Advisor, Civil Defence, London Region 1947–65; Scientific Advisor 1955–66 and External Member 1966–80, Gas Council; Scientific Advisor, British-American Tobacco Co. Ltd. 1955–72; Scientific Advisor, Tobacco Research Council; Scientific Advisor, Battelle Memorial Inst. Gov., Harrow Sch.; Member, Ct. of Govs., Admin. Staff Coll., London. Hons: Fellow, Royal Soc., London 1929; knighted (K.B.E.) 1946. *Author:* (with Sir Ernest Rutherford and James Chadwick) Radiations from Radioactive Substances, 1930; papers on radioactivity in many professional jrnls.

GEORGE MEANY
U.S. Labor leader; President, AFL-CIO
Born New York City, U.S.A., August 16th, 1894
Died Washington, D.C., U.S.A., January 10th, 1980

Courtesy AFL/CIO News

George Meany presided over the evolution of American organized labor from a craft union movement with limited scope to a powerful force in national and international politics. As head of the AFL-CIO for nearly a quarter of a century, he molded the federation into an effective lobbying entity for liberal causes and an influential opponent of Communism.

Meany was born in 1894 to an Irish Catholic family in Harlem, the second of ten children, and grew up in the Port Morris section of the Bronx, where he attended public schools and played semi-professional baseball. In his working-class neighborhood, the union was an institution second only to the Church in influence; Meany's father, a plumber, was president of his union local. Meany left school to become a plumber's apprentice at the age of 16 and qualified as a journeyman and union member at 21; after the death of his father and older brother he was the sole support of his large family. In 1919 he married Eugenia McMahon, a militantly pro-union seamstress, with whom he had three daughters.

Three years later Meany was elected business agent of local 463, covering Manhattan and the Bronx. In 12 years in this post he earned a reputation as a tough, shrewd leader who resisted bribery attempts by contractors and fought off jurisdictional incursions by competing unions.

Between 1934 and 1939, Meany, now in his early 40s, was president of the New York State Federation of Labor, an umbrella organization dominated by the building trades and the largest state affiliate of the American Federation of Labor (AFL). Working in association with Gov. Herbert Lehman, Meany successfully lobbied for the passage of numerous pro-labor bills, some which became models for national legislation. These included the establishment of employer-financed unemployment insurance and a 48-hour work week for women. In 1935 he forced the Works Progress Administration in New York State to pay union-scale wages, producing an upward revision of the wage scale in the national W.P.A.

A lifelong friend of the Democratic Party, Meany never hesitated to alter his allegiance when it was in the interest of labor. In 1930 he helped organize the American Labor Party in an attempt to ensure Governor Franklin Delano Roosevelt's re-election by preventing defections to the Socialist Party. The next year he organized a committee to elect pro-labor Republican Fiorello LaGuardia to the mayoralty of New York City on the Fusion Party ticket.

In 1939 Meany was unanimously elected Secretary-Treasurer of the American Federation of Labor and began his rise to power as a national spokesman for organized workers. During World War Two President Roosevelt appointed him to the War Labor Board and the National Defense Labor Board; in 1945 and 1946 he led the AFL effort to protect wage standards and job security during the nation's conversion to a peacetime economy. Beginning in 1947, he was in the forefront of the fight against the Taft-Hartley Act, a bill designed to curb alleged unfair union practices. Meany called it a tool of "profit-greedy industrialists . . . attempting to destroy workers' organizations as the first step in their plan to control the economic life of America." Although he mounted the largest lobbying effort in AFL history, the bill was enacted over President Truman's veto.

One of the bill's provisions, requiring union officials to sign affidavits of non-Communist loyalty, became the focus of a bitter contest between Meany and United Mine Workers Leader John L. Lewis. Meany viewed the affidavits as a lever with which to pry out Communist influence, particularly from unions affiliated with the rival Congress of Industrial Organizations (CIO); Lewis viewed them as an infringement of civil rights and led his union out of the AFL after Meany insinuated that he was a Communist sympathizer. Over the years, Meany forced the AFL to break off relations with a number of organizations, including the International Federation of Free Trade Unions, of which he was an executive, to protest Communist infiltration.

To counter further Congressional attacks on labor, Meany founded Labor's League for Political Education, a branch of the AFL dedicated to electing pro-labor candidates. A major purpose of the League was to fight for the repeal of Section 14(b) of the Taft-Hartley Act, which permitted individual states to prohibit closed-union shops.

In November 1952, following the death of William Green, Meany was unanimously elected President of the AFL. He immediately reopened stalled negotiations with Walter Reuther, head of the CIO, on a proposed merger of the two major labor federations. Reuther's conditions for the merger included the setting up of organizational machinery to resolve jurisdictional disputes between competing craft and industrial unions and the expulsion of corrupt union officials. Soon after, Meany engineered the expulsion of the International Longshoremen's Association on charges of harboring racketeers and gangsters (the reformed union was later reinstated). A few years later he expelled the Teamsters Union after Congressional hearings exposed the corruption of its top officials, Dave Beck and Jimmy Hoffa. In December 1955 the two federations merged to become the AFL-CIO, and Meany began his 25-year tenure as president, with Reuther his second-in-command. The organization represented 12.4 million members, or 90 percent of organized labor, in 130 affiliate unions.

Temperamentally and ideologically, the two leaders were worlds apart. Reuther, a civil-rights activist and a critic of American foreign policy in Indochina, saw the labor movement as the vanguard of social reform. Meany, whom he called the "comfortable, complacent custodian of the status quo," was more concerned with protecting his constituents' economic interests, including union rights, higher wages, and better health and fringe benefits, and with safeguarding his authority from all challengers. Meany criticized Reuther for meeting with Soviet leaders Nikita Khrushchev and Anastos Mikoyan in 1959 and blocked Reuther's appointment to the U.N. delegation in 1961. After a final confrontation in 1968, Reuther withdrew his union, the United Auto Workers, from the AFL-CIO. He died in a plane crash two years later.

Additional criticism of Meany's position came from black workers, who were barred from several affiliate unions and were discriminated against in others. Despite his unwillingness to discipline these unions, and to adopt racial quotas in union apprentice programs, Meany lobbied on behalf of a provision for equal job opportunity in the Civil Rights Act of 1964. His distrust of non-traditional labor groups, including farmworkers and women, continued for decades.

Meany's relations with the six U.S. Presidents who held office during his years of leadership varied according to their stands on behalf of organized labor; he rejected all attempts to limit the prosperity of workers as a method of improving the general economic health of the nation. During the Korean War he served on the Advisory Board on Mobilization Policy and led protests against the Truman Administration's attempts to halt wage increases; during Dwight D. Eisenhower's presidency he spent much of his time lobbying to prevent a conservative Congress from strengthening the Taft-Hartley Act. He supported John F. Kennedy's bills on medicare and federal aid to education and Lyndon Johnson's Great Society programs. After initial cooperation with the Nixon Administration's economic restraint policies, Meany grew disgusted with its anti-labor bias, which he called "Robin Hood in reverse," and withdrew from the Nixon Pay Board amid the brickbats of a public feud. Jimmy Carter, he said, was the most conservative President since Calvin Coolidge.

Whatever his opinion of their economic policies, however, Meany fervently supported the efforts of all Presidents to make war on Communist nations, and placed his organizational resources in their service. In 1944 he joined with other labor leaders to found the Free

Trade Union Committee, which distributed funds and assistance to non-Communist unions in Europe and Japan. After Fidel Castro's revolution in Cuba, Meany set up the American Institute for Free Labor Development to do the same in Latin America. These groups, and the AFL's international labor department, were heavily subsidized by the CIA and other Government agencies and were responsible for the overthrow of leftist governments in Guatemala, British Guiana, and Brazil.

In the late 1960s, when domestic opposition to President Johnson's conduct of the war in Vietnam was increasing, Meany suppressed all criticism from the AFL-CIO leadership and arranged for the federation to provide assistance to US supply bases and equipment and training for South Vietnamese trade unions. He weakened the candidacy of anti-war Democrat George McGovern in 1972 by withholding the AFL-CIO's endorsement and roundly criticized all Presidential attempts at détente with the People's Republic of China and the USSR.

Despite the power he wielded in U.S. politics, Meany's authority in the AFL-CIO was not absolute. He did not control bargaining and strike activities or membership policies in the autonomous affiliate unions, nor could he always dictate policy to the 35-member executive council. A good deal of his time was spent reconciling the disparate interests represented in the federation and welding them into a united front, of which he was the spokesman and symbol. In his six decades as a labor leader he never called a strike.

A heavy-set, cigar-chomping man, Meany possessed a stentorian voice, a Bronx accent, and an acid wit, with which he lambasted many a public figure. In the last few years he suffered from leukemia and arthritis and was under constant criticism from younger labor leaders who thought his old-fashioned ideas a deterrent to progress. He retired in November 1979, eight months after the death of his wife, and was succeeded by Lane Kirkland, his hand-picked heir to the presidency.

Two months later, Meany died of cardiac arrest in Washington, D.C., 63 years to the day after he received his first union card. His funeral was attended by more than 1,000 people, including virtually every major American politician and union official. President Carter and Governor Carey of New York ordered flags flown at half-mast in his honor.   L.F./J.P.

Born William George Meany. Son of Michael Joseph M., plumber and pres. of union local 2, and Anne (Cullen) M. Married Eugenie A. McMahon, garment worker, 1919 (d.1979). Daughters: Regina Clare Mayer, b.1923; Eileen Lee, b.1925; Genevieve Lutz, b.1930. Roman Catholic. Educ: Public Sch. 109, Bronx, NYC; Morris High Sch., Bronx 1908–09; attended vocational sch., Harlem, NYC 1910–12. Played semi-professional baseball 1910–16. Messenger 1909; plumber's apprentice 1910–15; journeyman 1915–17; plumber 1917. Admitted to Local 2 of United Assn. of Plumbers and Steam Fitters of U.S. and Canada 1915. Member Exec. Bd. 1919 and Business Agent 1922–34, Local 463, United Assn. of Plumbers, NYC; Secty.-Treas., N.Y. Building Trades Council 1923. V.P. 1932–33 and Pres. 1934–39, N.Y. State Fedn. of Labor; Delegate 1923 and Member, later Chmn., Works Progress Admin. Cttee. 1933–35, NYC Central Trades and

Courtesy AFL/CIO News

Labor Council; Member, N.Y. State Industrial Council; Member, N.Y. State Advisory Council on Unemployment Insurance; Co-founder, German Labor Chest for aid to labor refugees from Nazism, N.Y. 1933. With American Fedn. of Labor, Washington, D.C.: Secty.-Treas. 1940–52; Rep. to President's Cttee. to Establish Wartime Labor Policy; Co-founder, Free Trade Union Cttee. 1944; Fraternal Delegate to British Trade Union Congress 1945; Founder and Dir., Labor's League for Political Educ. 1948; Acting Pres. 1952–53; Pres. 1953–55; ed. and contributor, American Federationist. With AFL-CIO: Pres. 1955–79; Founder 1961 and Chmn. Exec. Bd., American Inst. for Free Labor Devel.; Chmn. Exec. Bd., Asian-American Free Labor Inst. and African-American Labor Center; Chmn. Bd. of Trustees, AFL-CIO Labor Studies Center; Pres. Emeritus 1979–80. Appointed by Pres. Roosevelt to Natl. Mediation Bd. 1941; Natl. War Labor Bd. 1942–45; Advisory Cttee. to Pres. Roosevelt on Wartime Labor-Management Problems. Appointed by Pres. Truman to Advisory Council, Marshall Plan legislation 1947; Natl. Advisory Bd. on Mobilization Policy 1951; Natl. Contract Compliance Cttee. 1952; as U.S. Labor Delegate to American States, Conference of Intnl. Labor Org., Mexico City 1953. Co-founder 1949 and Member Exec. Bd. 1951, Intnl. Confedn. of Free Trade Unions; Delegate to U.N. General Assembly 1957, 1959. Appointed by Pres. Eisenhower to Advisory Bd., Foreign Operations Admin. Appointed by Pres. Nixon to Pay Bd. 1971–72. Member: Columbia Country, University, International clubs; Bd. of Govs., American Red Cross. Hons: Man-of-the-Year Award, Pa. Council of Public Employees 1945; Laetare Medallist, Univ. Notre Dame 1956; Philip Murray Award, Legal Defense and Educ. Fund, Natl. Assn. for Advancement of Colored People 1957; Equal Opportunity Day Award, Natl. Urban League 1959; Americanism Gold Medal, Veterans of Foreign Wars 1959; Cross of Merit with Star and Ribbon, Fed. Republic of Germany 1959; Americanism Award, Amvets, 1963; Presidential Medal of Freedom 1963; Grand Official of the Order of Merit, Italy, 1964; Freedom Award, Intnl. Rescue Cttee. 1965; John La Farge Award for Interracial Justice, Catholic Americans Council 1968; Knight Commander, Order of St. Gregory with Grand Cross, 1969; 1969 Freedom Award, Hungarian Freedom Fighters Fedn., U.S.A.; Patriots Award, Congressional Medal of Honor Soc. 1973; Democratic Heritage Award, American Jewish Cttee. 1973; Brotherhood Citation, National Conference of Christians and Jews, 1975; Medal of Appreciation, Italian Trade Unions, 1976; Medal, American Irish Historical Soc., 1976; World Series Medallion, No Greater Love, 1976; Eugene V. Debs Award, Social Democrats of the U.S.A., 1977; Theodor Herzl Award, Zionist Organization of America, 1978; United Way of America's Alexis de Tocqueville Soc. Award, 1979; Dr. of Laws and other hon. degrees and awards from colls. and univers; posthumously—Order of the Brilliant Star with Grand Cordon, Republic of China, 1980; Hubert Humphrey Award, Leadership Conference on Civil Rights, 1980. *Author: AFL and AFL-CIO publications*—"Free Labor Unites: after years of effort, I.C.F.T.U. is born," American Federationist, Jan. 1950; The Last Five Years: how American Federation of Labor fights communism around the world (pamphlet), 1951; Our Program for Social Security, 1954; By Intelligence and by Faith, an address, 1957; Power—For What?, 1959; "Labor's Role in a Free Society," American Federationist, Oct. 1966; (co-author) To Clear the Record, 1969; Labor and the Philadelphia Plan (based on an address to the Natl. Press Club), 1970; also many articles in American Federationist. *Other*—Recommended Report for

the Presidential Cttee. on the Cost of Living, by labor members
George Meany and R.J. Thomas, submitted Jan. 25, 1944; The
Challenge of International Communism, in Proceedings of the 49th
Annual Conference of the League for Industrial Democracy, How
Free is Free Enterprise?, 1954; What Organized Labor Expects of
Management (pamphlet), 1955; American and Soviet Economy,
Contrast and Comparison, 1958, Spanish trans. 1958; (co-author)
Government Wage-Price Guideposts in the American Economy,
1967; Resignation from the Pay Board (sound recording on cassette),
1972. *Published addresses and speeches:* Congress Must Choose:
Subsidies or Inflation (text of coast-to-coast radio talk over mutual
network, Nov. 18, 1945); Labor Looks at Capitalism (address deliv-
ered to the 50th anniversary world convocation of the Natl. Industrial
Conference Bd. in NYC, 1966); We Call All Men Brothers (address
delivered upon receipt of the Philip Murray Award from the Natl.
Assn. for the Advancement of Colored People Legal Defense and
Educ. Fund, 1957); The Shambles of Détente (address to AFL-CIO
Maritime Trade Dept., Apr. 8, 1975); others. *Published congressional
testimony:* The A.F. of L. Case for a Just Labor Law: statement by
George Meany on the revision of the Taft-Hartley law, presented
before the Senate Cttee. on Labor and Public Welfare, Apr. 27, 1953;
Testimony before the Subcttee. on Labor of the Senate Labor and
Public Welfare Cttee., May 8, 1956, on the Fair Labor Standards Act
and minimum wage; Statement on HR 4222 (Medicare Bill) before the
House Ways and Means Cttee., 1961; Statement before the House
Ways and Means Cttee. on Hosp. Insurance for the Aged through
Social Security, Jan. 20, 1964; The AFL-CIO case for repeal of 14(b),
based on testimony on May 25, 1965 to a House Labor Subcttee. in
support of HR 77 to repeal section 14(b) of the Taft-Hartley Act;
Testimony before Senate, U.S. Congress, Cttee. on Foreign Rela-
tions, Aug. 1, 1969, hearings on American Inst. for Free Labor Devel.
Interviews in Oral History Collections: Herbert H. Lehman project,
Butler Library, Columbia Univ., NYC; John F. Kennedy Library,
Boston, Mass.
Further reading: "Meany and Reuther: Uneasy Togetherness" by
A.H. Raskin, New York Times Magazine, May 5, 1959; "The Many-
Sided Mr. Meany" by John Corry, Harper's, March, 1970; Meany by
Joseph C. Goulden, 1972.

FINN RONNE
Antarctic explorer
Born Horten, Norway, December 20th, 1899
Died Bethesda, Maryland, U.S.A., January 12th, 1980

Finn Ronne, Antarctic explorer, mapped the last uncharted coastline
in the world and surveyed some 250,000 square miles of new territory.
In his nine visits to Antarctica, Ronne traveled a total of 3600 miles by
dog and ski sled, farther than anyone else has yet done.

Ronne was born to Antarctic exploration. His father, Martin
Richard Ronne, was himself a polar explorer who served as a
sailmaker on Roald Amundsen's voyage of discovery to the South
Pole and was a member of Admiral Richard E. Byrd's first Antarctic
expedition. Young Ronne was educated at schools in his home town
of Horten, Norway, where he excelled in alpine sports. After

graduating from Horten Technical College with a degree in mechanical engineering, Ronne stayed on to take courses in naval design and architecture and boiler construction, and was hired by an Oslo shipping line.

Ronne emigrated to the United States in 1923, working first for the Bethlehem Shipbuilding Company in New Jersey as a ship machinery and equipment designer, and later as a mechanical engineer with the Westinghouse Electric Corporation in Pittsburgh. He was naturalized in 1929.

Ronne's first chance to undertake polar exploration came in 1933, when he served in Byrd's second expedition as a radio operator, dog driver, sailor, skier, and surveyor. During this expedition Ronne reached the 83rd degree, South Latitude, and assisted in seismic work beyond the Queen Maud Mountains. There was a poignant moment when he entered an old encampment and found his own name, along with those of his eight sisters and brothers, on a leather tent strap, carved there by his father seven years before.

After another four years with Westinghouse, Ronne returned to Antarctica for more than a year as chief of staff and executive officer of Byrd's third expedition, which explored 1000 miles of coastline between Little America and Palmer Island. For Ronne, it proved to be a fruitful opportunity: in 84 days he and a companion delineated 450 miles of the coastline of Alexander Island.

When World War Two intervened in 1941, Ronne was commissioned a lieutenant in the US Naval Reserve, serving in the Maintenance Division of the Bureau of Ships and earning three military medals.

In January 1947 Ronne left once again for Antarctica at the head of a 23-member geographic and research expedition to the Palmer Peninsula, sponsored by the American Geographic Society. The group included his wife, Edith, and Jenny Darlington, both research scientists, the first women ever to set foot on the continent. Using three airplanes, two tractors, two dog-team parties, and a reconditioned Navy ship, the team mapped the remainder of the Weddell Sea coast, added 90 new place names to the map, recorded 700,000 square miles of territory with aerial-trimetrigon photographic techniques, and conducted research in geology, seismology, solar radiation, meteorology, terrestrial magnetism, seawater salinity, and tidal observations. The results of the 15-month exploration enabled Ronne to determine conclusively that the Antarctic was not two continents, as had been hypothesized, but one.

The expedition's achievements, accomplished on a modest budget and with a minimal number of personnel, were acclaimed by the international scientific community. However, there were reports of dissatisfaction from some participants, who objected to Ronne's aggressive, uncompromising manner.

On his return to the US, Ronne joined the staff of the US Testing Company as an advisor on the development of a climatological research laboratory. In 1957 he was appointed scientific and military leader of Ellsworth Base, one of the seven US bases established in the Antarctic as a contribution to International Geophysical Year. The appointment was made despite warnings that Ronne's temperamental style would disrupt morale at the base. Within a short time, reports critical of Ronne began arriving at IGY headquarters and at the

Pentagon, which was monitoring the US effort. At the end of 12 months, the US Navy sent in two psychiatrists and a psychologist, who found all 39 base members "united in hostility" to their leader, although, paradoxically, this appeared to have improved their performance. Ronne replied to the criticisms of his leadership in his 1961 book *Antarctic Command*.

The criticism did not deter Ronne from pursuing his vocation. He went back to Antarctica in 1958 as a guest member of an Argentine naval expedition. From 1962 to 1963 he outfitted a sealing ship and conducted scientific research in the Arctic. In 1971, on the 60th anniversary of the Amundsen expedition, Ronne and his wife were flown over the South Pole as guests of the US Department of Defense.

An accomplished linguist, Ronne lectured in five languages and served as a consultant to the US Navy through the US Department of Defense and the Central Intelligence Agency. In retirement, he retained his early physical agility, remaining active as a writer, broadcaster, and advisor on polar exploration and travel.   J.P./M.D.

Son of Martin Richard R., polar explorer, and Maren Gurine (Gulliksen) R. Married Edith Maslin, research scientist and writer, 1944. Daughter: Karen Tupex. Emigrated to U.S.A. 1923. Naturalized American 1929. Educ. Horten Tech. Coll., degree in mechanical engineering 1922, postgraduate courses in naval design and architecture and ship boiler construction 1923. Mil. Service: Commissioned Lt., U.S. Naval Reserve 1941–47. Naval Reservist 1947–61, Capt. 1956–58. Engineering Asst., Fred-Olsen Shipping Line, Oslo 1922–23; Draftsman and Designer, Bethlehem Shipbuilding Corp. (now Bethlehem Steel Corp.), Elizabeth, N.J. 1923; Mechanical Engineer, Westinghouse Electric Corp., Pittsburgh, Pa. 1923–39. Member, Second Byrd Antarctic Expedition 1933–35; Transportation Engineer, U.S. Dept. Interior, and Second-in-Command, E. Base, U.S. Antarctic Service Expedition 1939–41; U.S. Naval Arctic Operation, Nanook, Greenland, and Canadian Arctic 1946; Leader and Comdr., Ronne Antarctic Research Expedition, Stonington Island, Marguerite Bay, and Palmer Peninsula 1946–48; First U.S. Postmaster in Antarctica, Oleana Base 1946–48; Military Comdg. Officer and Scientific Leader, Ellsworth Station, Weddell Sea, Antarctica, Intnl. Geophysical Year 1957–58; Member, Argentine Naval Expedition to Antarctica 1958–59; Participant, U.S. Naval Flight to South Pole 1961; Leader, Svalbard Expedition 1962–63; on first American tourist cruise to Palmer Peninsula area 1966; Participant, U.S. Dept. Defense Flight to South Pole 1971. Consultant and Advisor, U.S. Dept. Defense 1948–62; Advisor, U.S. Testing Co. 1948; Consultant and Advisor, C.I.A. and U.S. Navy. Member: Trimetrigon Engineering Soc.; N.Y. Adventure Club; Gibson Island Club; Mason (Norsemen's Lodge). V.P., American Polar Soc. 1948; Bd. Member, Arctic Inst. 1949–52; Chmn., American Antarctic Assn. Inc. Hons: U.S. Congressional Medals for service in the Antarctic, 1935, 1943, 1948, 1958; U.S. Defense Medal 1945; American Area Campaign Medal 1945; WWII Victory Medal; Argentine Navy Decoration 1961; Citation of Merit, U.S. Explorers Club 1963; U.S. Legion of Merit Award 1964; Knight, Royal Order of St. Olav, Norway 1966; Elish-Kent-Kane Gold Medal, Geog. Soc. of Philadelphia 1966; Golden Apple Trophy 1967; Gold Medal, U.S. Explorers Club 1968; Fellow, American Geog. Soc. Hon. Life Memberships: American Geophysical Union; American Polar Soc.; U.S. Explorers Club; Arktisk Club, Norway.

Author: Antarctic Conquest, 1949; Antarctic Command, 1961; Hellhole of Antarctic, 1968; The Antarctic Husky, 1968; Antarctica Comes to Life, 1971; Giants of Polar Exploration, 1971; The Ronne Expedition to Antarctica, 1971; Adventure, 1971; The Call of the Ice, 1972; Antarctica My Destiny, 1980. Contributor to Encyc. Americana and Encyc. Britannica; major articles in Geog. Review, Scientific Monthly, Explorers' Jrnl.

ANDRÉ KOSTELANETZ
Conductor
Born St. Petersburg (Petrograd, now Leningrad), Russia,
December 22nd, 1901
Died Port-au-Prince, Haiti, January 13th, 1980

Conductor André Kostelanetz dedicated his career to bridging the gap between "serious" and popular music and to expanding the musical tastes of the American public through broadcasting, recordings, and innovative concert programming. He considered himself "fortunate to have lived at a time when radio and records have made it possible for more people to hear more music than has been heard since the beginning of time." Though Kostelanetz was criticized as a popularizer who would do anything to attract audiences, his musicianship was widely respected.

Kostelanetz was born in St. Petersburg in 1901, the son of wealthy, musically sophisticated parents (both amateur musicians) active in the cultural events of the city. He began studying the piano as a child and gave his first recital at five. At the age of 15 he was in the Caucasus, working as a rehearsal pianist and coach for an opera company made up of refugees from the Revolution. After a special audition for Alexander Glazunov he was accepted as a student in the St. Petersburg Conservatory of Music, later working as assistant conductor of the Imperial Grand Opera in Petrograd.

In 1922 his family decided to emigrate to America and stopped en route in Warsaw, where Kostelanetz first heard American popular music of the day. He was very enthusiastic about the "dynamism and melody" and was convinced that composers like "Gershwin, Porter, Rogers and Berlin can and should be treated as seriously as Beethoven or Brahms." In the United States he worked for several years as coach, chorus master, and general assistant to several small opera companies, eventually becoming accompanist for singers with the Chicago and Metropolitan Operas.

In 1928 Kostelanetz was asked to replace an indisposed conductor on a radio broadcast for the Atlantic Broadcasting Company, forerunner of the Columbia Broadcasting System. Thus began an alliance with C.B.S. that included one of the most popular radio programs of th 1930s. His shows were a tradition-breaking blend of classical and popular music, designed to be appreciated by the widest possible audience. With this in mind, Kostelanetz did not hesitate to edit the classics down to their melodic passages, omitting lengthy development of themes and inflating popular sections.

Kostelanetz soon became an authority on sound reproduction, using batteries of microphones and sophisticated engineering tricks to create a rich, distinctive ensemble sound. He also embarked on a recording career with C.B.S., becoming their best-selling artist on the Masterworks label, with total career sales amounting to more than 52 million copies. In 1936 he began to work part-time in California, where the "Kostelanetz sound" was influential in the development of contemporary film music. There he met coloratura soprano Lily Pons, whom he married in 1938. They often performed together and were an extremely popular combination, drawing huge crowds to their concert tours.

From time to time Kostelanetz appeared as guest conductor with such outstanding orchestras as the Berlin Philharmonic, the Philharmonia of London, and the symphonies of Chicago, Los Angeles, Cleveland, Boston, and Philadelphia. Aaron Copland, Jerome Kern, Ferde Grofé, Ezra Laderman, William Schuman, Alan Hovhannes, Virgil Thomson, and Paul Creston were among the many distinguished composers from whom he commissioned works.

During World war II Kostelanetz organized and conducted orchestras of service personnel in Europe, the Middle and Far East, and North Africa, receiving the Asiatic-Pacific campaign ribbon of the U.S. Army for his work.

In 1952 Kostelanetz began his association with the New York Philharmonic, which he conducted for 27 consecutive seasons, longer than any other conductor in its history. In 1954 he undertook the first series of Saturday night non-subscription concerts at the Philharmonic and in 1963 introduced the Promenade Concerts in Lincoln Center's Philharmonic (now Avery Fisher) Hall.

The Promenades were intended to appeal to the general public, especially to people who had never come to concert halls before. They featured refreshments, casual seating arrangements, and a combination of light and serious compositions that accompanied everything from dancers, mimes, and puppets to folksingers and films. Kostelanetz's distinctive approach worked and the "Proms" sold out each spring for 16 years.

Comfortable in eight languages, very much the old-world gentleman, Kostelanetz loved to travel, spending as much as half the year away from his home in New York and occasionally doing his own piloting. He died of a heart attack following pneumonia while on vacation in Port-au-Prince, Haiti.   J.P./S.P.

Son of Nachman K. and Rosalie (Dimscha) K. Married: (1) Lily Pons, singer, 1938 (div. 1958, d.1976); (2) Sara Gene Orcutt, medical technician, 1960(div. 1969). No children. Jewish. Emigrated to U.S. 1922. Naturalized American 1928. Educ: St. Petersburg Conservatory of Music. Mil. Service: Organized and conducted mil. orchestras for U.S. Army in N. Africa, Persian Gulf, Italian Theater, summer 1944; China, Burma, India, European Theaters, winter 1944–45. Asst. Conductor, Imperial Grand Opera, Petrograd 1921. Began association with Atlantic Broadcasting Co. (later C.B.S.) 1928: arranged and transcribed radio music; conducted symphony orch; hosted radio program; recorded. Began association with N.Y. Philharmonic Orch. 1952: inaugurated non-subscription concerts 1953; Artistic Dir. and Principal Conductor of Promenade Concerts 1963–79. Guest conductor with leading symphony orchs. in U.S., Canada, S. America, Europe; also conducted music for motion pictures. Hons: Medal of Merit, Radio Guide 1936, 1937; D.Mus., Albion Coll 1939; D.Mus., Cincinnati Conservatory of Music 1945; awarded U.S. Army Asiatic-Pacific campaign ribbon; Fame Award, radio eds. of U.S. and Canada (several times).

ROBERT ARDREY
Anthropologist, playwright, screenwriter, and novelist
Born Chicago, U.S.A., October 16th, 1908
Died Kalk Bay, Cape Province, South Africa, January 14th, 1980

Courtesy Ardrey estate

As a playwright, novelist, and screenwriter, Robert Ardrey was more critically praised than commercially successful. It was Ardrey's four highly controversial books on anthropology, explaining his theories on the continuities between animal behavior and human nature, which brought him acclaim and wide recognition.

Ardrey was born in Chicago and earned a Ph.D. from the University of Chicago in 1930. Originally a student of the natural and social sciences, he decided to put aside anthropology and zoology in favor of playwriting after taking a writing course taught by Thornton Wilder. During five years of apprenticeship to Wilder, he supported himself by working as a jazz pianist and civil service test writer. He also lectured on Pre-Columbian Indians at the Mayan exhibit of Chicago's Century of Progress Fair.

His first play, *Star Spangled*, produced by Arthur Hopkins, opened on Broadway on March 10th, 1936. Although Ardrey was praised for his sense of the ridiculous, his farce about Poles in Chicago was panned and closed after 23 performances. Wilder helped his protégé to obtain a Guggenheim Fellowship, which enabled Ardrey to spend 1937–38 touring the United States by bus and writing. In 1938 two of his plays, *How to Get Tough About It* and *Casey Jones,* opened in New York. Both were failures. "All of Mr. Ardrey's plays are long on character and short on sustained drama," wrote Brooks Atkinson in the *New York Times*. "He's a tantalizing scribbler—always on the verge."

Having sustained two simultaneous Broadway flops, Ardrey "became slightly famous and in great demand in Hollywood . . . and Samuel Goldwyn bought me." He worked at MGM Studios for only three months, then went to Nantucket to write *Thunder Rock,* an anti-Fascist, anti-isolationist allegory. Directed by Elia Kazan, with a cast that included Luther Adler, Morris Carnovsky, and Lee J. Cobb, the play opened on Broadway in 1939, closing after a three-week run. Ardrey felt that the American public, which had no direct experience of totalitarian regimes and was still several months away from war, could not yet accept his political position. Two days after the fall of France, the play, starring Michael Redgrave, opened in London and was a smash hit. *Thunder Rock* played in London for most of the war, and was popular in Central and Eastern Europe after the war. It was made into a successful British film and also into a BBC television drama.

During World War Two, Ardrey worked for the Office of War Information in New York City, meanwhile writing screenplays and his first novel, *Worlds Beginning*. The films were more successful than the book. In 1946 Ossie Davis and Ruby Dee starred in Ardrey's new play, *Jeb,* the story of a one-legged, decorated black veteran returning from the war with what he thinks is an asset—the ability to operate an adding machine—only to learn that in his Southern town jobs requiring this skill are restricted to whites. Discouraged by still another theatrical failure, Ardrey returned to Hollywood to write screenplays, including MGM's *The Three Musketeers* and *Madame Bovary*. His second novel, a thriller called *Brotherhood of Fear,* elicited some favorable reviews. In October 1954, his play *Sing Me No Lullaby* opened at the Phoenix Theatre in New York. The play concerned a brilliant mathematician whose Soviet sympathies as a student in the 1930s make him a doomed man in the McCarthy era. Despite its timeliness, it was not a success.

In 1955 Ardrey decided to abandon playwriting and accepted an assignment to write articles on Africa for "The Reporter." In South Africa he met Dr. Raymond A. Dart and studied the anthropologist's collection of bones and artifacts. Dart's theories on the violent nature of early humans rekindled Ardrey's interest in anthropology.

Ardrey was pursuing these theories at London's Museum of Natural History in 1956 when the Hungarian uprising broke out. He went to Vienna to talk with Hungarian refugees. These events resulted in a new play called *Shadow of Heroes: A Play in Five Acts from the Hungarian Passion*. It opened in London in 1958 and in New York in 1961. The reviews were mixed and the play was a failure in both cities. Ardrey returned to anthropology. His unsuccessful career as a playwright gave him "a growing dissatisfaction with contemporary understanding of human motivations."

During the next 15 years, Ardrey published four commercially successful books dealing with the nature of human beings. In *African Genesis* he theorized that *Homo sapiens* developed from predatory killer apes, and that human belligerence is due to an instinct to acquire status and defend territory. He also suggested that humans originated in Africa rather than Asia. Critics deplored his naiveté, claiming he was an amateur and that his book was simplistic and sensational. But the majority of reviewers, even those with reservations, admitted that *African Genesis* was a gripping book. His idea that violence is an unavoidable inheritance of humanity, that we act not in terms of present circumstances but because of our evolutionary past, was hotly debated in the scientific community.

In *The Territorial Imperative* Ardrey claimed that attachment to property is instinctive rather than acquired, and is not unique to human beings. Most reviewers liked Ardrey's exciting, enthusiastic style, but still warned readers against accepting all of his ideas. *The Social Contract* and *The Hunting Hypothesis* furnished new evidence for Ardrey's contention that the problems of modern civilization are rooted in the aggressive instincts of our primate ancestors. In his review of *The Social Contract* in "The New Republic," Robin Fox wrote that Ardrey "can no longer be dismissed with a sneer as a clever

journalist with one good idea for a receptive public. His display of
scholarship, powerful argument and sheer *chutzpah* in the face of
academic hostility requires our respect, and severest and most
responsible criticism."

Ardrey lived in Rome from 1963 to 1978, when he moved to Kalk
Bay, South Africa, a suburb of Cape Town. He died at home, of lung
cancer.   J.P./S.P.

Son of Robert Leslie A., editor and publisher, and Marie (Haswell)
A. Married: (1) Helen Johnson 1938 (div. 1960); (2) Berdine
Grunewald, actress and artist, 1960. Children: 1st marriage—Ross,
Daniel; 2nd marriage—Vanessa Jenkins (stepdaughter). Educ: Univ.
Chicago (Phi Beta Kappa), Ph.B. 1930. Mil. Service: Office of War
Information, NYC, WWII. Active 1936–80 as playwright, screenwri-
ter, novelist, author of books on anthropology, contributor of articles
to jrnls, and mags. Member: Authors Guild; Dramatists Guild;
Writers Guild of America; Screen Writers Guild. Hons: Guggenheim
Fellowship 1937–38; Sidney Howard Memorial Award (for Thunder
Rock), Playwrights Co. 1940; Theresa Helbrun Memorial Award (for
Shadow of Heroes), Theatre Guild 1961; Wilkie Brothers Foundn.
Grant 1963; Intnl. Forum for Neurological Org. Award 1970; Univ.
Chicago Award for Professional Achievement 1972; Annual Award,
United Steelworkers of America 1978; Fellow, Royal Soc. of Lit.,
London. *Author: Nonfiction*—African Genesis: A Personal Investiga-
tion into the Animal Origins and Nature of Man (illus. by his wife
Berdine Grunewald), 1961; The Territorial Imperative: A Personal
Inquiry into the Animal Origins of Property and Nations (illus.
Berdine Grunewald), 1966; The Social Contract: A Personal Inquiry
into the Evolutionary Sources of Order and Disorder (illus. Berdine
Grunewald), 1970; The Hunting Hypothesis, 1976. *Plays*—Star Span-
gled, 1936; How to Get Tough About It, 1938; Casey Jones, 1938;
Thunder Rock, 1939; Jeb, 1946; Sing Me No Lullaby, 1954; Shadow
of Heroes, 1961. *Screenplays*—They Knew What They Wanted, 1940;
The Lady Takes a Chance, 1943; The Green Years, 1945; The Three
Musketeers, 1947; The Secret Garden, 1949; Madame Bovary, 1948;
Quentin Durand, 1955; The Power and the Prize, 1956; The Wonder-
ful Country, 1959; The Four Horsemen of the Apocalypse, 1962;
Khartoum (nominee, Acad. Award for best screenplay), 1966.
Novels—Worlds Beginning, 1944; Brotherhood of Fear, 1952.
Further reading: Man and Agression by Ashley Montague (ed.), 1968.

RACHEL FULLER BROWN
Chemist
Born Springfield, Mass., U.S.A., November 23rd, 1898
Died Albany, N.Y., U.S.A., January 14th, 1980

Penicillin owes much of its reputation as a "wonder drug" to Rachel
Fuller Brown. In the first few years after its introduction in 1941, the
drug was a source of frustration to physicians. Its extraordinary
antibacterial properties killed the microorganisms controlling body
fungal growth—while a bad sore throat might be cured, an attack of
moniliasis, a mouth fungus, was likely to follow. Rachel Brown and

Elizabeth L. Hazen, a microbiologist in the New York State Department of Health, together produced nystatin in 1950, the first nontoxic antibiotic for fungal diseases. Initially used in treating individuals suffering from side effects of penicillin and other antibiotics, nystatin (named after New York State, where it was developed) was later used extensively as an antidote for molds on artwork, fruit, tree trunks, livestock fodder and other susceptible hosts.

Rachel Brown's interest in science developed at Mt. Holyoke in an introductory chemistry course taught by Dr. Emma Carr. Encouraged by Dr. Carr, Brown pursued graduate studies at the University of Chicago. She completed her master's degree in organic chemistry, but before her doctoral thesis could be accepted, she ran out of funds. Rachel Brown moved to Albany to support herself and her family, taking a job with the State Health Department—one of the few research positions available that did not require a Ph.D. (She completed the Ph.D. seven years later.)

At the State Health Department Brown first studied bacteria samples and diagnosed diseases. This led to experiments with vaccines, serums, antitoxins, and other chemical means of combatting germs. Pneumonia posed the greatest challenge because its causes and types were numerous and difficult to pinpoint. Brown became a specialist in the field, identifying over 40 different types of pneumonia and formulating successful antiserums for nearly all of them. She also conducted research on syphilis, and devised an efficient screening test which is still used to confirm a negative diagnosis.

During her 43 years in the State Health Department research division, Rachel Brown wrote extensively for a variety of medical journals. She earned considerable recognition for her contribution to scientific scholarship and received honors and awards for original research in biochemistry, including—with Dr. Hazen in 1975—the Pioneer Chemist Award from the American Institute of Chemists. They were the first women ever to receive the honor. The Brown-Hazen Fund and the New York City Research Corporation continue to give grants to needy students of medicine from the $13 million in royalties nystatin has earned since 1957.   A.B.P.

Daughter of George Hamilton B. and Annie Hubbard B. Unmarried. Episcopalian. Educ: Central High Sch., Springfield, Mass.; Mt. Holyoke Coll., S. Hadley, Mass., (Phi Beta Kappa, Sigma Xi), A.B. 1920; Univ. of Chicago, M.S. 1921, Ph.D. organic chemistry and bacteriology 1933. Taught chemistry and physics at Frances Shimer Sch., Chicago 1921–24; with N.Y. State Dept. of Health, Div. of Laboratories and Research, Albany, N.Y.: Asst. Chemist 1926–32; Asst. Biochemist 1932–36; Sr. Biochemist 1936–51; Assoc. Biochemist 1951–64; Assoc. Research Scientist (Biochemistry) 1964–68. Abstractor for Chemical Abstracts 1930–78. Sec., Advisory Cttee. for Brown-Hazen Fund 1951–78. *Hons:* Fellow, Amer. Assoc. for the Advancement of Science 1941; Squibb Award in Chemotherapy (joint with E.L. Hazen) 1955; Fellow, N.Y. Academy of Sciences 1957; Distinguished Service Award, N.Y. State Dept. of Health 1968; Hon. D.Sc., Hobart and William Smith Colls., Geneva, N.Y. 1969; Hon. D.Sc., Mt. Holyoke Coll. 1972; Rhoda Benham Award, Medical Mycological Soc. of the Americas (joint with E.L. Hazen) 1972; Pioneer Chemist Award, Amer. Inst. of Chemists (joint with E.L. Hazen, first women awardees) 1975. *Discoveries:* with Elizabeth L.

Hazen, nystatin, the first nontoxic antibiotic for fungal diseases 1950; antiserums for 40 different types of pneumonia 1926–41; screening test for detection of syphilis 1946–48. Wrote extensively on pneumonia, serodiagnosis of syphilis, nystatin and other antibiotics in the Amer. Jrnl. of Medical Sciences, Amer. Jrnl. of Clinical Pathology, Antibiotics & Chemotherapy, Nature, Jrnl. of Tropical Medicine and Hygiene, Glasgow Medical Jrnl. and others 1939–70.

ERNEST A(LEXANDER) PAYNE
President, World Council of Churches, and historian
Born London, England, February 19th, 1902
Died Oxford, England, January 14th, 1980

The Rev. Dr. Ernest A. Payne, a leader in the British and international ecumenical movements, was the first English Freechurchman to attain the presidency of the World Council of Churches.

Payne was born in London to Baptist parents. At King's College, London, he came under the strong spiritual guidance of W.R. Matthews, the future Dean of St. Paul's; he was also much influenced by the renowned Old Testament scholar Wheeler Robinson, his tutor (and later his colleague) at Regent's Park College, a Baptist institution. After postgraduate study at the Universities of Oxford and Marburg, Payne received ordination in 1928 and assumed the pastorate of the village of Bugbrooke in Northamptonshire. From 1932 to 1940 he worked for the Baptist Missionary Society before returning to Regent's Park College as a teacher of church history and the modern missions. Here he embarked on a prolific writing career which lasted well into his retirement. For six of his eight years at Regent's Park he also served as editor of the Baptist Quarterly. He joined the faculty of the University of Oxford in 1946.

In 1951, the Baptist Union of Great Britain and Ireland surprised many of its members by inviting the scholarly Payne to become its General Secretary, an influential office that had hitherto been offered only to individuals with a strong preaching background. Nevertheless, Payne's erudition suited him for the task at hand—that of bringing Baptists into the ecumenical movement, which was at that time achieving considerable prominence throughout the Christian Church. With his unexpected election to the vice-chairmanship of the Central Committee of the World Council of Churches in 1954, Payne quickly found himself at the center of the ecumenical dialogue. His new role provided him with the opportunity to observe the life and work of Christian denominations in many countries, notably in Europe, North and South America, Australia, and the Iron Curtain states.

Although Payne was a somewhat diffident speaker, his skillful handling of the day-to-day responsibilities of his office, his firm control of debate, and his intelligent approach to critical issues made him an unusually popular leader among representatives of all denominations. At the fourth assembly of the World Council of

Churches, held in Uppsala in 1968, he was elected to the presidency, succeeding Dr. Michael (later Lord) Ramsey, the Archbishop of Canterbury.

Payne's presidency was marked by a lively involvement in the ecumenical process. Unquestionably fair to all points of view, he directed the ongoing dialogue between the churches over doctrinal obstacles to ecumenism and focused attention on such issues as the ordination of women and the problems of christian churches in the Third World and in Communist nations.

Payne also steered his own church closer to the ecumenical debate, despite resistance from members who were wary of compromising the Baptist tradition of dissent from the Church of England. In his writings, Payne stressed his commitment to the tenets of the Baptist Church, crediting its adherents with an important role in the development of religious freedoms.

When Payne relinquished the presidency at the Nairobi assembly in 1975, he did not return to academic life, as had been expected, but went on to hold office as vice-president and president of the Baptist Union of Great Britain and Ireland.

Payne's work won him honors from the City of Paris in 1962 and appointment as a Companion of Honour in 1968. The British Council of Churches, whose executive committee he had chaired for nine years, created a special Honorary Presidency for him in 1978, as a mark of its regard for his lifelong services to ecumenism.   M.D.

Son of Alexander William P., accountant, and Mary Catherine P. Married Winifred Mary Davies 1930. Daughter: Elizabeth Ann Prain. Baptist. Educ: Hackney Downs Sec. Sch., London; King's Coll., London, B.A. 1921; Regent's Park Coll., London, B.D. 1925; St. Catherine's and Mansfield Coll., Oxford, B.Litt. 1927, M.A. 1944; Univ. Marburg, grad. studies 1927–28. Ordained to Baptist ministry 1928, first pastorate Bugbrooke, Northants., England 1928–32; Young People's Secty. and Ed., Baptist Missionary Soc., London 1932–40. Sr. Tutor, Regent's Park Coll., Oxford 1940–51; Ed., Baptist Quarterly 1944–50; Lectr, in Comparative Religion and Hist. of Modern Missions, Oxford 1946–51. With Baptist Union of Great Britain and Ireland: Gen. Secty. 1951–67; V.P. 1976–77; Pres. 1977–78. Vice-Chmn., Central Cttee. 1954–68 and Pres. 1968–75, World Council of Churches; Moderator, Free Church Fed. Council 1958–59. V.P. 1960–62 and Chmn., Exec. Cttee. 1962–71, British Council of Churches; V.P., Baptist World Alliance 1965–70. Examiner, Univs. Oxford, Wales, Edinburgh, and Bristol. Pres., Baptist Historical Soc.; V.P., United Soc. for Christian Lit.; Dir., Baptist Insurance Co. Ltd.; Member, Athenaeum, London. Hons: D.D., Univ. St. Andrews 1951; LL.D., McMaster Univ. 1961; Grande Médaille d'Argent de la Cité de Paris 1962; Companion of Honour, Great Britain 1968; Hon. Life Pres., British Council of Churches 1978. *Author:* The Saktas: An Introductory and Comparative Study, 1933; Freedom in Jamaica: Some Chapters in the Story of the Baptist Missionary Society, 1933; The First Generation: Early Leaders of the Baptist Missionary Society in England and India, 1936; Marianne Lewis and Elizabeth Sale: Pioneers of Missionary Work Among Women, 1937; The Great Succession: Leaders of the Baptist Missionary Society During the Nineteenth Century, 1938, 2nd ed. 1946; Henry Wyatt of Shansi 1895–1938, 1939, 2nd ed. 1946; The Church Awakes: The Story of the Modern Missionary Movement, 1942; (with K.M. Shuttleworth)

Missionaries All: A Pageant of British History, 1942; Before the Start: Steps Towards the Founding of the London Missionary Society, 1942; (ed.) Studies in History and Religion, 1942; The Free Church Tradition in the Life of England, 1944, new rev. ed. 1965; The Fellowship of Believers: Baptist Thought and Practice Yesterday and Today, 1944, enlarged ed. 1952; South-East from Serampore: More Chapters in the Story of the Baptist Missionary Society, 1945; Henry Wheeler Robinson, Scholar, Teacher, Principal: A Memoir, 1946; College Street Church Northampton 1697–1947, 1947; The Baptist Movement in the Reformation and Onwards, 1947; (trans. from German) The Teaching of the Church Regarding Baptism (by Karl Barth), 1948; The Bible in English, 1949; The Baptists of Berkshire: Through Three Centuries, 1951; The Excellent Mr. Burls, 1951; The Free Churches and Episcopacy, 1952; The Free Churches and the State, 1952; The Baptist Union and Its Headquarters: A Descriptive Record, 1953; James Henry Rushbrooke 1870–1947: A Baptist Great-heart, 1954; The Baptists of the World and Their Overseas Missions, 1955; The Growth of the World Church: The Story of the Modern Missionary Movement, 1955; The Meaning and Practice of Ordination Among Baptists, 1957; (with D.G. Moses) Why Integration? An Explanation of the Proposal before the World Council of Churches and the International Missionary Council, 1957; (trans. from German) Baptism and Church in the New Testament (by Johannes Schneider), 1957; The Baptist Union: A Short History, 1959; (compiler with S.F. Winward) Orders and Prayers for Church Worship: A Manual for Ministers, 2nd ed. 1962, U.S. ed. (with Winward and J.W. Cox) as Minister's Worship Manual: Orders and Prayers for Worship, 1969; Roger Williams 1603–1683, 1961; (with N.S. Moon) Baptists and 1622, 1962; Veteran Warrior: A Memoir of B. Grey Griffith, 1962; Baptists and Church Relations, 1964; Free Churchmen Unrepentant and Repentant, and Other Papers, 1965; Thomas Helwys and the First Baptist Church in England, 2nd ed. 1966; Some Recent Happenings in the Roman Church, 1966; Violence, Non-Violence and Human Rights, 1971; Thirty Years of the British Council of Churches 1942–1972, 1972; The Free Churches: Today's Challenges, 1973; Out of Great Tribulation: Baptists in the Soviet Union, 1974. *Contributor:* New Cambridge Modern Hist., vol. II: The Anabaptists, 1958; Twentieth Century Christianity, 1961; (introduction) An Inquiry into the Obligation of Christians to Use Means for the Conversion of the Heathens (by William Carey), 1961; From Uniformity to Unity 1662–1962, 1962; The Churches and Christian Unity, 1963; Preaching on Pentecost and Christian Unity, 1966; A Palette for a Portrait: Franklin Clark Fry, 1972; Intnl. Review of Missions; Congregational Quarterly; Jrnl. of Theological Studies; Dictionary of Natl. Biography. *Lectures published:* The Anabaptists of the 16th Century and Their Influence in the Modern World, 1949; The World Council of Churches 1948–1969, 1970.

SIR CECIL (WALTER HARDY) BEATON
Photographer, stage and film designer and artist
Born London, England, January 14th, 1904
Died Broadchalke, Salisbury, England, January 18th, 1980

Sir Cecil Beaton, first-born son to what he described as a "nice, ordinary, middleclass family" in London, became Britain's leading society photographer in a career spanning 35 years. His innovations in portraiture set the tone for a host of imitators, and his costume design influenced the fashions of Paris and New York.

Beaton attended Heath Mount Day School and St. Cyprian's, a preparatory school, before being sent to Harrow, where he first demonstrated his skill with the camera and the drawing block. As a student at St. John's College, Cambridge, his artistic bent proved stronger than his academic resolve. He embraced photography as a hobby and for half-a-crown a week rented himself a studio above a shop near the Cambridge Union Society, where his contemporaries were following their more scholastic pursuits. A study of George Rylands, one of the Cambridge stage doyens, resulted in Beaton's first credit in the society magazine "Vogue." He left Cambridge without a degree, but with a career in prospect.

On the advice of his father, Beaton joined the family business as a clerk, but ran into bookkeeping problems and was fired for ineptitude after little more than a year. Meanwhile, he had been studying the work of photographers of the period, including Francis Brugière, Baron de Meyer, George Hoyningen-Huene, and Curtis Moffatt, and had been cultivating socially prominent friends in order to build up a clientele for his stylish portraiture.

In 1926 Beaton first met the Sitwells, around whom much of the elegant society of the period revolved. From this point on, his career was assured. Edith Sitwell modeled for him and, with the aid of her brothers Osbert and Sacheverell, provided him with the necessary invitations to the high-life gatherings of the day. Within three years, Beaton was established as Britain's top society photographer.

Beaton now looked to the United States as a means of expanding his enterprise. In 1929 he made the first of many trips to New York, where he signed a contract with Condé Nast, the publisher, for the supply of fashion pictures for "Vogue." The financial proceeds from this venture enabled him to lease Ashcombe, an 18th-century country house on the edge of the Wiltshire Downs, which became his home for many years. Beaton decorated it in his own flamboyant style; his bed canopy was held aloft by "barley-sugar columns of brass."

A year after his first visit to New York, Beaton returned to mount an exhibition in Lady Mendl's interior deocrating establishment on 57th Street, specially loaned to him for the occasion. More contracts followed, including a lucrative one with Condé Nast.

Successful exhibitions at London's leading galleries, and the publication of his first book of photographs, now made Beaton the darling of British society. In 1935 he was commissioned by Mrs. Wallis Simpson to take the pre-wedding photographs for her marriage to King Edward VIII, later Duke of Windsor. His flattering portraits of the British royal family became famous throughout the world.

In the mid-1930s Beaton also launched a celebrated career as a designer for the stage, opera, and ballet. He won Oscars for his work on *My Fair Lady* in 1956 and for *Gigi* in 1958. When *My Fair Lady* was revived as a film in 1963, Beaton designed every detail of the costumes and sets, infusing the screen with his impeccably Edwardian sensibility.

During World War Two, Beaton worked for the Ministry of Information and became the official photographer of the Royal Air Force, covering all aspects of the land and air wars in Britain. His depictions of bomb victims and gutted buildings, particularly the Wren churches of London, were popular in wartime Britain and were used to drum up sympathy and support in the United States.

Throughout his career, Beaton kept up a steady flow of books, the early volumes comprising mainly collections of captioned photographs. His later works became more literary in content and included one play, *The Gainsborough Girls,* first performed at Brighton in 1951. It was not popular with the critics, who contrasted its "naiveté" with the sophistication of his other work for the stage.

Beaton's diaries, like his photogarphs, provide a vivid description and a historical record of Anglo-American café society between the two World Wars. More than half his memoirs of the 1940s deals with his pursuit of actress Greta Garbo, the only woman he claimed ever to have loved romantically.

Throughout his life, Beaton regarded himself as an Edwardian and retained the mannerisms befitting the period, although his broad-brimmed hats and vividly colored ties and scarves would not always have accorded with the style of an Edwardian gentleman.

Beaton received the C.B.E. in 1957 and was knighted five years later. Despite a stroke in 1974 which partially paralyzed his right arm and hand, he never lost his wit or zest for life, learning to paint and photograph with his left hand. He died of heart failure at Broadchalke, near Salisbury, four days after his 76th birthday.   J.P./M.D.

Son of Ernest Walter Hardy B., timber importer, and Esther (Etty) Sisson B. Unmarried. Educ: Heath Mount Day Sch.; St. Cyprian's Sch.; Harrow Sch., Middx.; St. John's Coll., Cambridge, no degree. Mil. Service: Photographer, Ministry of Information, London 1940–42; Official Photographer, R.A.F. 1942–46. Hons: Acad. Awards for costume design, My Fair Lady 1956, Gigi 1958; C.B.E. 1957; Légion d'Honneur 1960; knighted 1972. *Exhibitions: Photographs*—Cooling Gall., London 1930; Natl. Portrait Gall., London 1968–69; Michael Parkin Gall., London 1976. *Painting and stage designs*—Redfern Gall., London 1936, 1958, 1965; Sagittarius Gall., NYC 1956; Lefevre Gall., London 1966; Wright Hepburn Gall., London 1968. *Stage, scenic and costume designer:* Follow the Sun, London 1935; Lady Windermere's Fan, London and NYC 1946; Return of the Prodigal, London 1948; Charley's Aunt, London 1949; Cry of the Peacock, NYC 1950; The Second Mrs. Tanqueray, 1950; The Gainsborough Girls, 1951; The Grass Harp, 1952; Aren't We All, London 1953; Quadrille, London and NYC 1954; Portrait of a Lady, 1954; The Chalk Garden, 1955; The Little Glass Clock, 1956; My Fair Lady, London and NYC 1956; Look After Lulu, 1959; Saratoga, 1959; Dear Liar, 1960; Tenderloin, 1960; School for Scandal, Comédie Française, Paris 1962; Coco, 1969; Vanessa; Turandot. *Film costume designer:* Dangerous Moonlight, 1941; Beware of Pity, 1946; An Ideal Husband, 1948; Anna Karenina, 1948; Gigi, 1958; The Doctor's Dilemma, 1959; My Fair Lady, 1963; On a Clear Day You Can See Forever, 1970; also Black Vanities; Kipps; Pitt the Younger. *Photographic publications:* The Book of Beauty, 1930; Cecil Beaton's Scrapbook, 1937; Cecil Beaton's New York, 1938; My Royal Past, 1939, rev. ed. 1960; (with Peter Quennell) Time Exposure, 1941; Air of Glory, 1941; Winged Squadrons, 1942; Near East, 1943; British Photographers, 1944; Far East, 1945; Chinese Album, 1946; Time Exposure, 1946; Portrait of New York, 1949; Ashcombe, 1949; Ballet,

1951; Photobiography, 1951; (with Kenneth Tynan, q.v.) Persona Grata, 1953; The Glass of Fashion, 1954; It Gives Me Great Pleasure (in USA: I Take Great Pleasure), 1955; The Face of the World, 1957; Japanese, 1959; Quail in Aspic, 1962; Royal Portraits, 1963; Images, 1963; Cecil Beaton's Fair Lady, 1964; The Best of Beaton, 1968; My Bolivian Aunt, 1971; (with Gail Buckland) The Magic Image, 1975; *Diaries:* The Wandering Years, 1961; The Years Between, 1965; The Happy Years, 1972; The Strenuous Years, 1973; The Restless Years, 1976; The Parting Years, 1978. *Contributed* photographs and drawings to many published works, including History Under Fire (by James Pope-Hennessy), 1941; The Importance of Being Earnest (Folio Society edition), 1960; Bomber Command. *Author:* The Gainsborough Girls (play), first performed Brighton, England, 1951.
Further reading: Cecil Beaton: Stage and Film Designs by Charles Spencer, 1977; Beaton, edited with text by James Danziger, 1980.

WILLIAM O. DOUGLAS
Associate Justice of the United States Supreme Court, and author
Born Maine, Minnesota, U.S.A., October 16th, 1898
Died Washington, D.C., U.S.A., January 19th, 1980

William Orville Douglas, whose membership of the US Supreme Court spanned nearly four decades, was an outspoken champion of liberalism and a strict constructionist in his interpretation of the First Amendment as an absolute guarantee of free speech. On civil rights, equal protection under the law, freedom of speech and of the press, right to privacy, and on environmental protection measures, Douglas insisted that he drew his progressive opinions from the Constitution itself. He believed throughout his life that the Constitution was constructed to limit governmental interference in people's lives.

Douglas was born in 1898, the son of a Presbyterian "home missionary" in Maine, Minnesota. The family traveled west to California and Washington shortly after his birth, his father preaching in frontier churches along the way. When the elder Mr. Douglas died in 1904, his widow and three children settled in Yakima, Washington. At a young age Douglas contracted polio; in order to rebuild his strength, he took up a vigorous schedule of hiking and riding in the Cascade Mountains, which led to a lifetime involvement with the outdoors.

Douglas graduated valedictorian from Yakima High School and entered nearby Whitman College on a scholarship. He worked as a farm laborer in the wheat fields of eastern Washington during his summer vacations and learned firsthand of the laborers' maltreatment under the law. His co-workers were members of the IWW—International Workers of the World, known popularly as the "Wobblies"— and Douglas from that time forward was an ardent partisan of the 'underdog', gaining a populist's belief in the need to guard the powerless from exploitation by either government or big business.

In 1920 Douglas graduated Phi Beta Kappa from Whitman and spent the next two years teaching English, Latin, and public speaking at his hometown high school in Yakima. He was then accepted by Columbia University Law School and worked his way east as a freighthand; he supported his studies at Columbia by tutoring, researching case histories for correspondence-course law textbooks, and working at a settlement house for immigrant Italian children. He studied commercial law and legal sociology under Prof. Underhill Moore, managed to graduate second in his class despite the extracurricular work load, and served as editor of the *Columbia Law Review*. In 1925 he stepped into a position with Cravath, DeGersdorff, Swaine and Wood, a Wall Street firm with a large corporate clientele.

He was a success at Cravath but found he cared for neither corporate practice (he later referred to brokerage firms on Wall Street as "a cross between a casino and a private club") nor for city life. He returned briefly to a small law practice in Yakima until Columbia University offered him a position teaching law, which he accepted. The following year, 1928, he joined the faculty at Yale, where Dean Robert Maynard Hutchins recruited a brilliant young group of "legal realists." The interdependence of law and social reality upon which the legal realists based their thought was fundamental to Douglas's legal philosophy. He did not simply apply detached legal theory to questions of law, but also considered the practical effect any ruling might have. Between 1929 and 1932 Douglas collaborated with the US Department of Commerce on bankruptcy studies, gaining him national recognition as an expert on financial law, and designation as Sterling Professor of Law in 1932.

With this appointment Douglas caught the attention of Joseph P. Kennedy and President Franklin D. Roosevelt. FDR named him to the Securities and Exchange Commission—then headed by Kennedy—in 1934. The SEC had been set up to revamp the Stock Exchange following the crash of 1929, and Douglas was selected to study corporate reorganization for the SEC. He became a member in 1936 and was named its chairman in 1937. During his tenure the Commission regulated the sale of securities and the stock exchange assumed its present form.

Douglas became a member of Roosevelt's inner circle—his air of informality, his ability as an earthy raconteur, and his cut-throat expertise at poker made him a favorite of FDR. When a Supreme Court position fell vacant in 1939, Roosevelt wanted a New Dealer from a western state to replace the retiring Louis Brandeis. He leaned more towards Senator Lewis Schwellenback of Washington rather than to Douglas, who was criticized, ironically, as being a "tool of Wall Street" by some liberal members of the Senate. With the backing of Senators LaFollette and Borah, however, Douglas was named to the vacancy by a vote of 62-4, and retained his seat on the bench for the next thirty-seven years.

Throughout the 1930s and 40s Douglas was a staunch supporter of FDR and New Deal legislation. Indeed he and Justice Hugo Black were the only liberals on an extremely conservative Court, having been appointed by Roosevelt to offset the philosophical imbalance. It was a period in which Douglas recorded dissent after dissent and his incendiary liberalism soon gained him a political constituency. In 1944 Roosevelt submitted Douglas's name as a possible running mate to party leaders, but key liberals—notably I. F. Stone and Gilbert Harrison of *The New Republic*—opposed him on the grounds, once again, that he was a former Wall Street lawyer with close ties to big business. Four years later, when President Truman needed a running mate with strong liberal credentials, Douglas was offered the vice-presidency, but Douglas declined, possibly because he sensed a Republican victory and did not wish to leave the Court.

During the 1950s Douglas experienced the irrevocable animosity of Richard Nixon and other 'cold warriors' with his stay of execution for Ethel and Julius Rosenburg, an event which ignited the first of several impeachment attempts. Earl Warren's appointment as Chief Justice in 1954 altered the Court's political complexion. Douglas suddenly found himself a leading member of the nascent liberal majority.

The continued efforts of conservatives to rid the Court of Douglas stemmed from his uncompromising liberalism. Douglas had angered many by advocating recognition of the People's Republic of China in 1951. Vehement opposition by the Justice to American military involvement in Southeast Asia reached a peak in 1973 when he took advantage of a Court recess to rule that U.S. bombing of Cambodia was unconstitutional. Even Douglas's marriage at the age of 68 to a 23 year old cocktail waitress was sufficient to elicit cries of impeachment from Douglas's opponents. More serious accusations, however, stemmed from his association with the Parvin Foundation.

Albert Parvin was a Las Vegas hotelier with ties to organized crime, and the Parvin Foundation had named Douglas a life member and voted him a salary of $12,000 a year—a fee Douglas collected until he severed connections with the organization in 1969. The matter came to light shortly after Justice Abe Fortas had resigned from the court under a cloud of suspicion. Fortas had received $20,000 from the Wolfson Family Foundation and was charged with returning the funds to aid Wolfson in avoiding prison for questionable stock manipulations. Parallels between the two cases were uncomfortably close. In the end the question became whether or not Justice Douglas knew of the Parvin Foundation's entanglement—apparently he had not—and the thwarted impeachment drive was generally seen as part of President Nixon's strategy for building a conservative majority in the court.

Douglas continued to serve as a Justice of the Supreme Court into his seventies, although he was increasingly plagued with ill health and was fitted with a pacemaker in 1968. On New Year's Eve 1975, he suffered a stroke that left him confined to a wheelchair and he resigned his seat later that year. At his funeral on January 19, 1980 President Carter called him a "lion-like defender of individual liberty." Douglas was buried at Arlington National Cemetery.   K.C.

Son of William D., Presbyterian minister, and Julia Bickford D. Married: (1) Mildred Riddle 1923 (div. 1953); (2) Mercedes Hester Davidson 1954 (div. 1963); (3) Joan Carol Martin 1963 (div. 1966); (4) Cathleen Heffernan 1966. Children: 1st marriage—Mildred Riddle, William Orville. Presbyterian. Educ.: Yakima High Sch., Wash.; Whitman Coll., Walla Walla, Wash. (Phi Beta Kappa, Beta Theta Pi, Phi Alpha Delta, Delta Sigma Rho), B.A. 1920; Columbia Univ. Law Sch., LL.B. 1925. Mil. Service: Private, U.S. Army 1918. Instr., Yakima High Sch., Wash. 1920–22; admitted to N.Y. Bar 1926; Attorney-at-Law, Cravath, DeGersdorff, Swaine and Wood, N.Y.C. 1925–27; adjunct instr., Columbia Law Sch. 1925–26; pvt. law practice, Yakima, Wash. 1927–28; Yale Law Sch. faculty 1928–34, Sterling Prof. of Law 1932. Bankruptcy studies, Yale Inst. of Human

Relations and U.S. Dept. of Commerce 1929–32; Secty., Cttee. on Business of Fed. Cts., Natl. Commn. on Law Observance and Enforcement 1930–32. With Securities and Exchange Commn.: Dir., Protective Cttee. Study 1934–36; Commnr. 1936–39; Chmn. 1937–39. Assoc. Justice, U.S. Supreme Ct. 1939–75. Member: Royal Geog. Soc., London; Overseas Press Club, N.Y.C.; Himalayan Club, New Delhi; Mason. Hons: Yale Univ., M.A. 1932; Whitman Coll., LL.D. 1938; Wesleyan Univ., LL.D. 1940; Washington and Jefferson Coll., LL.D. 1942; William and Mary Coll., LL.D. 1943; Rollins Coll., LL.D. 1947; Natl. Univ., LL.D. 1949; Morris Morgenstern Award, Yeshiva Univ. 1950; New Sch. for Soc. Research, LL.D. 1952; Univ. Toledo, LL.D. 1956; Bucknell Univ., Dalhousie Univ., Univ. Nova Scotia, LL.D. 1958; Colby Coll., LL.D. 1961; Wayne Univ., L.H.D. 1964; Univ. N.M., W.Va. State Coll., Parsons Inst., Univ. So. Calif. at San Fernando Valley, LL.D. 1964; Fairleigh Dickinson Univ., Colgate Univ., LL.D. 1973; John Muir Award, Sierra Club 1975. *Author:* Democracy and Finance, 1940; Being an American, 1948; Of Men and Mountains, 1950; Strange Lands and Friendly People, 1951; Beyond the High Himalayas, 1952; North from Malaya, 1953; Almanac of Liberty, 1954; We The Judges, 1955; Russian Journey, 1956; The Right of People, Exploring the Himalaya, and West of the Indus, 1958; (ed.) The Mind and Faith of A. Powell Davis, 1959; America Challenged and My Wilderness—East to Katahdin, 1960; My Wilderness—The Pacific West and Muir of the Mountains, 1961; Democracy's Manifesto, 1962; Mr. Lincoln and the Negroes and The Anatomy of Liberty, 1963; Freedom of the Mind, 1964; Wilderness Bill of Rights, 1965; The Bible and the Schools, 1966; Farewell to Texas, 1967; Toward a Global Federalism, 1968; Points of Rebellion, 1969; International Dissent (and) Holocaust or Hemispheric Co-operation: Cross-Currents in Latin America, 1971; The Three Hundred Year War, 1972; Go East Young Man (autobiog.), 1974; The Court Years 1939–1975 (autobiog.), 1980. Contributed numerous articles to legal jrnls. and mags.' author of several legal casebooks. *Further reading:* Justices Douglas and Black: Political Liberalism and Judicial Activism by Roy Lee Meek, 1964; The Judicial Record of Justice William O. Douglas by Vern Countryman, 1974; William O. Douglas by Edwin P. Hoyt, 1979.

WILLIAM (PATRICK) ROBERTS
Painter
Born London, England, June 5th, 1895
Died London, England, January 20th, 1980

William Roberts, the distinguished painter of portraits and figure compositions, was born in London in 1895, the son of a carpenter. At the age of 15 he was apprenticed as a commercial artist with a London poster design and advertising firm, meanwhile taking evening courses at St. Martin's School of Art. A London County Council scholarship in drawing, and later a Slade Scholarship, enabled him to study for the next three years at the Slade School of Art, then a center for avant-garde movements, where he developed an abstract style based on the simplification of the human figure into tubular forms. (Of his introduction to Cubism at the Slade School, Roberts once wrote: "For myself, the 'angularities' of Picasso's *Guitarists* made me forsake for many a long day the succulent 'rotundities' of Ingres' *Odalisques*.") In 1913 he worked briefly at the Omega Workshops under Roger Fry, absorbing Fry's precepts on the free use of abstract forms in painting. Within the year, Wyndham Lewis, the radical defector from Omega, chose two of Roberts's paintings to hang in his Rebel Art Centre, and the young artist found himself a member of the emerging Vorticist Movement.

Roberts's connection to the group, however, was tenuous. The Vorticists, seeking to subvert the prevailing aesthetic of 19th-century romanticism, called for the rejection of representational realism in favor of pure form, unrelated to objective materials; Roberts's schematic figures and severely geometrical compositions complied well with this mechanistic ideal. His signature appeared on the 1914 Vorticist manifesto, he exhibited with the group, and his pictures were used as illustrations in the Vorticist magazine *BLAST*. But he lacked real dedication to the group's vanguard posture and Lewis eventually withdrew his patronage of the young man.

After serving in the Royal Field Artillery in 1916, Roberts became an official war artist during the First World War. Here his Vorticist techniques aided him in capturing the frenetic energy of machine-dominated battle scenes in such paintings as *Machine Gunners, Hoisting Camouflage,* and *Combat*. A greater concentration on facial expression and dramatic attitudes marked his 1918 painting of *The First Gas Attack at Ypres*, executed under the patronage of the Canadian War Memorials Fund.

This growing interest in the rendering of the immanent character brought a new balance to Roberts's work after the war. In *The Char, The Boat Pond, Sun Bathing,* and other paintings, Roberts took typical scenes of London street life and turned them into complex, classically designed compositions invested with a gritty Cockney humor. His forms were now less severely mechanistic than before, but no less thoughtfully constructed. Through his studies of gesture and personality, Roberts also acquired a high reputation as a portrait painter; among his commissions was the 1940 portrait of Major-General McNaughton, General Officer Commanding of the Canadian Forces. During World War II he served once again as official war artist.

Roberts exhibited with a number of groups, including the London Art Association, the New English Art Club, and the London Group, and received one-person shows at top London galleries. Collections of his work were acquired by the Imperial War Museum, the Contemporary Art Club, and the Tate Gallery, which presented a retrospective of his paintings in 1965.

Between 1956 and 1969 Roberts produced a series of polemical pamphlets on his own work. Although he disclaimed in these the significance of his Vorticist period, Roberts's entire corpus demonstrates a reconciliation of the Vorticists' extreme abstraction with the naturalism of a sensitive draftsman, a blend most clearly revealed in Roberts's eloquent painting of 1962, *The Vorticists at the Restaurant de la Tour Eiffel*.

Roberts began exhibiting at the Royal Academy in 1952 and was elected an associate in 1958 and a Royal Academician eight years

later, when he was 71. He continued to exhibit at the Royal Academy
until a year before his death in London at the age of 84.   J.P./A.S.

Son of Edward R., carpenter, and Emma C. R. Educ: St. Martin's
Sch. of Art, London 1909; Slade Sch. of Fine Art, London Univ.
(London County Council and Slade Scholarships) 1910–13; Omega
Workshops, London 1913. Mil. Service: Royal Field Artillery 1916;
Official War Artist 1917–18, 1939–45. Apprenticed to Sir Joseph
Causton Ltd., poster design/advertising firm 1909; active as painter,
portrait artist, watercolorist, London 1914–80; Member, Vorticist
Group, London 1914–15; elected Member, London Group 1915.
Visiting Teacher, Central Sch. of Art, London 1925–60; Teacher,
Oxford Tech. Sch. 1939–45. Member, London Artists' Assn. 1927–32;
New English Art Club; Contemporary Art Soc. Hons: Melvill Nettle-
ship Prize for Figure Composition and Prize for Figure Drawing 1913;
elected Assoc. of Royal Acad. 1958; Calouste Gulbenkian Foundn.
Award 1961; elected Royal Academician 1966. *Exhibitions: One-
person* (all London)—Chenil Galls. 1923; Cooling Galls. 1929, 1931;
Lefevre Gall. 1935, 1938; Redfern Gall. 1942; Leicester Galls. 1945,
1949, 1958; Tate Gall. (retrospective) 1965; d'Offay Couper Gall.
(retrospective) 1969; Hamet Gall. (retrospective) 1971. *Group*—New
English Art Club 1913; Rebel Art Centre, London 1914; Grafton
Group, Alpine Club Gall. 1914; Twentieth Century Art, Whitechapel
Art Gall., London 1914; London Group Exhib. 1915; Vorticist
Exhib., Dore Galls., London 1915; Vorticist Exhib., NYC 1917;
Group X Exhib., Mansard Gall., London 1920; London Artists' Assn.
1927; Royal Acad. 1952–80. *Collections:* Contemporary Art Soc.,
London; Imperial War Mus., London; Tate Gall., London; Natl. Gall
of Canada, Ottawa; private collections. *Other works:* The Legend of
Cú Chulainn (tempera wall painting), Fulham Girls' Club, London
1911; wall painting, Crosby Hall, London 1912; three paintings for
Eiffel Tower restaurant, Paris 1919; The History of the Omnibus,
poster, British Empire Exhib., Wembley, London 1924. *Illustrations:*
in *BLAST* No. 1, summer 1914; in *BLAST* No. 2, July 1915; to Seven
Pillars of Wisdom (by T.E. Lawrence), 1926. *Reproductions:* Sawing
Wood, in Studio, Dec. 1957; Canal Fishers, in Studio, Aug. 1958;
London Transport poster, in Graphis, May 1959. *Author:* The Vortex
Pamphlets, 1956–58; Abstract and Cubist Paintings and Drawings,
1957; Paintings 1917–58, 1960; Paintings and Drawings 1909–64, 1964.

AIR CHIEF MARSHAL SIR GEORGE (CLARK) PIRIE
Military officer and barrister
Born Pittenweem, Fife, Scotland, July 28th, 1896
Died London, England, January 21st, 1980

Air Chief Marshal Sir George Pirie was one of the founding members
of the British Royal Air Force. As one of its most senior officers
during the Second World War, he helped plan and direct its efforts in
two theaters of conflict.

Pirie's military career began when he left St. Andrews University in
1914 to volunteer for service in World War One. He was commissioned in the Scottish Rifles, where he remained for the duration of

the conflict. Pirie was awarded the Military Cross in August 1917 for gallantry while working with the artillery and was granted a permanent commission in 1919.

At this time the Royal Flying Corps, forerunner of the Royal Air Force, was being organized, and Pirie was among the young army officers selected for secondment into the new service. In 1921 he was awarded the Distinguished Flying Cross for his efforts during the relief of Diwaniyah in Iraq. When hostilities ceased, Pirie studied law at the newly founded RAF Staff College, earning his LL.D. in 1925.

But Pirie preferred the active life of the military service and rose through the junior officer ranks to join the staff of the Directorate of Operations and Intelligence at the British Air Ministry, where his legal training secured him a further promotion to Deputy Director. From 1937 to 1941 he served as Air Attaché at the British Embassy in Washington, D.C., advising US military planners on British air requirements.

Courtesy A.K. Pirie

Pirie was recalled to Britain in August 1941 and commanded the RAF in Northern Ireland for several weeks. He was then sent to the Middle East as Air Officer in Charge of Administration, responsible for building up and maintaining the strength of the RAF in the region. His success in this task led to his recall in April 1943 for a three-month appointment as the RAF's Director of War Organisation. In July 1943 and for the remainder of the war he occupied the more senior position of Director-General of Organisation. Two months before the surrender of Japan he again saw active service as Deputy Air Commander-in-Chief, South East Asia.

As the postwar Allied Air Commander-in-Chief of South East Asia, Pirie oversaw the demobilization programs of the RAF, administered the Government's unpopular demobilization payment scheme, and made recommendations concerning the phased reduction of British military presence and the relocation of headquarters bases for peacetime utilization. As Inspector-General of the RAF, appointed in 1948, he developed a program of housing construction to enable the families of armed forces personnel to accompany them on overseas assignments. Pirie was able to implement many of these recommendations as Member of the Air Council for Supply and Organisation from 1948 to 1950.

In 1949 Pirie was appointed Chief Air Marshal. During his last year of service he was Head of the Air Force Staff of the British Joint Services Mission to the United States. Pirie retired from the RAF in 1951 and received his second knighthood that same year.   M.D.

Son of Dr. G. Clark P. Married Dora Kennedy 1926. Children: One son, one daughter. Educ: Fettes Coll., Edinburgh; St. Andrews Univ., Scotland; Royal Air Force Staff Coll., England, LL.D. 1925. Mil. Service: commissioned from univ. into Royal Scottish Rifles 1914; served in WWI 1914–18; seconded Royal Flying Corps (later R.A.F.) 1920. Staff 1933–36 and Deputy Dir. 1936–37, Directorate of Operations and Intelligence, Air Ministry, London; Air Attaché, Washington, D.C. 1937–41; Comdr., R.A.F., N. Ireland 1941; Air Officer in charge of Admin., Middle East Command 1941–43; Dir., War Org. 1943 and Dir.-Gen. of Org. 1943–45, Air Ministry, London; Deputy Comdr.-in-Chief 1945–46 and Allied Air Comdr.-in-Chief 1946–47, Air Command, S.E. Asia; Inspector-Gen., R.A.F. 1948;

Member, Air Council for Supply and Org. 1948–50, London; appointed Air Chief Marshal 1949; Head, Air Force Staff, British Jt. Services Mission to the U.S., 1950–51; retired from R.A.F. 1951. Chmn., Air League of the British Empire 1955–58; Member, Royal Air Force Club. Hons: M.C. 1917; D.F.C. 1919; C.B.E. 1942; C.B. 1943; knighted (K.B.E.) 1946, (K.C.B.) 1951.

E(RIC) H(ENRY) S(TONELEY) BURHOP
Nuclear physicist
Born Hobart, Tasmania, January 31st, 1911
Died London, England, January 22nd, 1980

As a scientist Burhop's contributions to theoretical and experimental physics have assured him of distinction in the history of nuclear research. As a humanist his involvement with the causes of nuclear disarmament and world peace earned him, during the "red-baiting" politics prevalent in America in the 1950s, the opprobrious label "left-wing." To forge a reconciliation of his work in nuclear physics with his commitment to the humanitarian application of science, Burhop helped establish several organizations devoted to the promotion of greater international scientific cooperation.

The deeply moral strain in Burhop's character was shaped in his childhood home. Burhop was raised by compassionate, although doctrinally strict, Protestant parents, both of whom were Salvation Army officers. In elementary and high school, young Burhop displayed great aptitude for mathematics and science. He entered Melbourne University in 1928 intending to study engineering but transferred to physics after one academic year. On completion of his undergraduate program, Burhop enrolled in graduate school where he conducted a measurement of atomic inner shell ionization processes. Burhop's interest in the behavior of ionized atomic particles—especially those within the atomic inner shell which is the spherical domain of particles closest to the atomic nucleus—formed the basis of his career in nuclear physics.

From 1933 to 1935 Burhop undertook research at the Cavendish Laboratory in Cambridge, England, a leading center of nuclear studies. At Cambridge he produced the first definitive calculations of the behavior of ionized inner shell particles and of the Auger Effect—the transition of electrons within an atom from "discrete" to "continuous" energy states. During this period Burhop met H.S.W. Massey, a young physicist who was interested in atomic, nuclear, and space physics, and the two men began a lifelong collaboration.

Returning to Melbourne in 1935, Burhop initiated Australian research in neutron physics and was instrumental in the construction of that continent's first neutron accelerator. The war, however, disrupted opportunities for pure research and Burhop undertook work on optical munitions. In 1944 he joined Massey and the British research team which was working with American scientists at Berkeley, California on the electromagnetic separation of uranium isotopes, an investigation which contributed to the success of the Manhattan Project.

In the research at Berkeley, Burhop's expertise in both theoretical and experimental physics proved invaluable. The Berkeley group achieved significant results in the study of the collision behavior of atomic particles and the behavior of energy discharges in strong magnetic fields. Their study of collision physics during the war years enabled Burhop and Massey to write *Electronic and Ionic Impact Phenomena* (1952), the first broad survey of the subject and a profound influence on subsequent atomic research. In 1945, he joined Massey again, this time in the mathematics department at University College, London, and moved with him to the physics department in 1950.

Shortly after his arrival at University College, Burhop began to study the use of photographic emulsions for the tracking of ionized particles, a technique which had been pioneered by C.F. Powell and to which Burhop later made important contributions. He was also involved in the construction of a new type of circular electron accelerator, the microtron, and of an electronic lens for use in electron scattering experiments, a device which became essential to atomic research.

While working with C.F. Powell and G.P.S. Occhialine in 1959, Burhop established an organization to further international cooperation between physicists regardless of ideological affiliation, which still exists: the "European $K-$ Collaboration." Burhop believed international collaboration was rendered essential by the increasing magnitude and complexity of experimentation in high energy physics. Originally attended by physicists from western European nations, the group later expanded to include scientists from Warsaw pact countries as well.

Burhop himself led the group from 1959 to 1969, and, during that period, contributed significant scholarship to the interactions of atomic particles with nuclei. In 1967, as a result of observations of the capture of $K-$ particles (negatively charged inner shell particles) in emulsions, Burhop inferred the existence of a significant excess of neutrons in the extreme periphery of the nuclear surface. This was later confirmed experimentally by D.H. Davis and others, and has made possible the elaboration of new techniques in the study of nuclear structure.

At about this time, Burhop assumed leadership of the Bubble Chamber Group at University College, a position he held until 1975. The bubble chamber technique was developed for tracking the movements of charged atomic particles and Burhop subsequently organized several European bubble chambers and the European Nuclear Research Center (CERN) at Geneva. Through this program, the existence of weak neutral currents was established, providing strong experimental support for the Weinberg-Salam unified theory of weak atomic interactions.

Burhop also originated the "hybrid" technique in nuclear research. In this process, the wave functions of one experimental problem are combined to approximate the wave function of another, thereby permitting an assimilation of otherwise diffuse experimental techniques. In 1963 he suggested the combination of spark chambers with emulsions to locate rare neutrino interactions in the nuclear emulsion,

and to detect particles with extremely short lifetimes. The prac-
ticability of this method was experimentally demonstrated, but at that
time there was little theoretical interest. Ten years later, however, the
location of these particles and neutrino interactions had become a
critical subject and Burhop, leading a team drawn from seven
European laboratories, conducted a series of very successful experiments. Within a year, 37 neutrino interactions were discriminated,
and the first lifetime measurement was made of "charmed" particles.
Without the hybrid technique it would have required nearly 1,000
scanner-years to scan the large volume of emulsion used in these
experiments. A second experiment, carried out at CERN and employing the emulsion technique with the largest European bubble chamber, was even more successful, and the importance of the hybrid
technique was firmly established.

As a humanitarian, Burhop was active in anti-fascist movements in
the 1930s, and his participation in the Manhattan Project was
predicated upon official assurances that the bomb would not be used
destructively unless its power had been first demonstrated to the
enemy in an unpopulated area. The bombings of Hiroshima and
Nagasaki were viewed by Burhop as a betrayal of the entire scientific
community. In later years he worked assiduously for the abolition of
nuclear weapons.

Together with C.F. Powell, J. Rotblatt, and Bertrand Russell,
Burhop was a founding member of the Pugwash Conferences on
Science and World Affairs begun in 1957, which contributed greatly to
erecting the foundations of understanding in scientific affairs between
Eastern and Western bloc nations. Burhop played a key role
throughout, as he also did in the formulation of the Russell-Einstein
Appeal of 1955, a statement of protest by Nobel scientists condemning
non-peaceful applications of atomic power. Also in the cause of
international cooperation, Burhop helped establish the influential
World Federation of Scientific Workers in the early 1950s. Providing
guidance and leadership through many difficult periods of the Cold
War, he served the WFSW until the time of his death.   E.S.

Son of Henry B. and Bertha B., Salvation Army officers. Married
Winifred Stevens 1936. Children: two sons, one daughter. Educ:
Melbourne Univ., B.A. physics 1931, MSc 1933; Cambridge Univ.,
Ph.D. maths. 1937. 1851 Overseas Fellowship 1933–35; Research at
Cavendish Lab., Cambridge 1933–35; Research Physicist and Lectr.,
Melbourne Univ. 1935–45; Deputy Dir., Radio Research Lab.,
Melbourne Univ. 1942–44; Tech. Officer, DSIR Mission to Berkeley,
Calif. 1944–45. With Univ. Coll., London: Lectr. in Maths. 1945–49;
Reader in Maths. 1949–50; Reader in Physics 1950–60; Prof. of
Physics 1960–78. Pres., World Fedn. of Scientific Workers 1971.
Hons: F.R.S. 1963; Joliot-Curie Medal 1966; Lenin Peace Prize 1972;
Foreign Member, Acad. of Science, German Democratic Republic
1974. Hon. D.Sc., Open Univ. 1975. *Author:* The Challenge of
Atomic Energy, 1951; The Auger Effect, 1953; (with H.S.W. Massey)
Electronic and Ionic Impact Phenomena, 1953; (ed.) High Energy
Physics, Vol. I, II, 1967, Vols. III, IV, 1969, Vol. 5, 1972. Various
publications on atomic and nuclear physics.

WALPOLE (SINCLAIR) LEWIN
Neurosurgeon
Born London, England, August 20th, 1915
Died Cambridge, England, January 23rd, 1980

Walpole Lewin, one of the leading British neurosurgeons of his generation, combined professional practice with wide-ranging activity as an administrator in the field of local, national, and international medicine.

London-born, he attended University College and qualified as a doctor in University College Hospital, one of the capital's largest medicals schools. He remained there for his postgraduate medical training, serving as house physician, house surgeon, and surgical registrar. In 1942, the year he obtained his Mastership of Surgery, he was commissioned as an officer into the Royal Army Medical Corps, where he served in the Middle East, attaining the rank of Lieutenant-Colonel.

Upon his return to civilian practice five years later, Lewin moved into the neurosurgical specialty which had long been his particular interest. He became Clinical Lecturer in Neurosurgery at Oxford University and practiced at the Radcliffe Infirmary as an assistant neurological surgeon from 1949 to 1961, eventually specializing in brain damage arising from head injuries. He built up a reputation within the medical profession as one of Britain's leading authorities on the management of head injuries following road accidents. He was appointed Consultant Neurological Surgeon to the British Army in 1964, and was invited to give the Ruscoe Clarke Lecture at Birmingham University in 1967 and the Horsley Memorial Lecture in 1975.

In the wider sphere, Lewin took an active part in the local administration of hospitals and health services, particularly at Cambridge, where he served as Neurological Surgeon to Addenbrooke's Hospital from 1955 until his death. Lewin took a keen interest in the establishment by Cambridge University of a clinical school, where he took up an associate lectureship in 1976. He was a member of the Council of the Royal College of Surgeons for many years and twice served as its Vice-President. He also played a prominent part in the administration of the British Medical Association.

Internationally, Lewin was active with the World Medical Association and the British Commonwealth Medical Association. From 1974 to 1977 he was President of the Standing Committee of Doctors of the European Economic Community.

In 1978 Lewin was appointed a CBE. His professional and administrative services to medicine were acknowledged in 1979 with the award of the British Medical Association's Gold Medal.   M.D.

Son of Eric Sinclair L. Married Marion Cumming 1947 (d.1979). Children: one son, one daughter. Educ: Univ. Coll., London (First Entrance Exhibitioner 1934); Univ. Coll. Hosp., London (Magrath Clinical Scholar, Atkinson Morley Surgical Scholar), M.B., B.S., L.R.C.P., and Member, Royal Coll. of Surgeons 1939, M.A. 1942; Fellow, Univ. Coll., London; Fellow, Darwin Coll., Cambridge. Mil. Service: Lt.-Col., Royal Army Medical Corps, Officer Comdg. Surgical Div., Middle East 1942–47. With Univ. Coll. Hosp. 1939–42:

sometime house physician; house surgeon; casualty surgical officer; Harker Smith Surgical Registrar. First Asst., Nuffield Dept. Surgery, Oxford; Clinical Lectr. in Neurosurgery and Asst. Neurological Surgeon, Radcliffe Infirmary, Univ. Oxford 1949–61; Consultant Neurological Surgeon, Addenbrooke's Hosp., Cambridge 1955–80; Consultant Neurological Surgeon, British Army 1964–80; Assoc. Lectr. in Medicine, Univ. Cambridge 1976–80; Examiner in Surgery, Univ. Cambridge 1979–80. With Royal Coll. of Surgeons: Leverhulme Research Grant 1947; Hunterian Prof. 1948; Erasmus Wilson Demonstrator 1965; Council Member 1970–80; Council V.P. 1976–77, 1978–79. Member, Central Health Services Council 1966–76; Member 1966–74 and Chmn. 1968–71, Central Cttee., British Hosp. Medical Services; Member 1966–74 and Vice-Chmn. 1967–71, Jt. Consultants Cttee.; Member 1968–80 and Chmn. 1971–76, Council, British Medical Assn.; Member, Gen. Medical Council 1971–80; Delegate 1971–80 and Pres. 1974–77, Standing Cttee. of Doctors of E.E.C.; V.P., Commonwealth Medical Assn. 1972–80; Member, Scientific Advisory Council, Huntingdon Research Centre 1974–80; V.P., Intnl. Soc. of Psychiatric Surgery; Council Member, World Fedn. of Medical Educ.; Member, Intnl. Soc. of Surgeons. With Gen. Assembly of World Medical Assn.: Delegate 1971–80; Council Member 1974–80; Council Chmn. 1977–79. Corresp. Member: American Assn. of Neurological Surgeons; American Assn. of Neurological Surgery; Deutsche Gesellschaft für Neurochirurgie. Member, Athanaeum Club. Lectureships: Ruscoe Clarke Lectr., Birmingham 1967; Victor Horsley Memorial Lectr. 1975. Hons: Fellow, Royal Coll. of Surgeons 1940; M.A., Univ. Cambridge 1970; D.Sc., Univ. Hull 1974; C.B.E. 1978; Hon. V.P. 1979–80 and Gold Medal 1979, British Medical Assn.; Hon. Member, Brazil Medical Assn. Also Fellow: Assoc. of Surgeons; Royal Soc. Med.; Soc. of British Neurological Surgeons; Cambridge Philosophy Soc. *Author:* The Management of Head Injuries, 1966; neurosurgery sect., British Surgical Progress 1958. Also neurosurgical papers in British Medical Jrnl. and other professional jrnls.

PAUL REVERE WILLIAMS
Architect
Born Los Angeles, California, U.S.A., February 18th, 1894
Died Los Angeles, California, U.S.A., January 23rd, 1980

Paul Revere Williams, one of the first prominent black architects in the United States, broke the racial barrier that had formerly prevented non-whites from joining the profession. During a long career Williams designed many public buildings, hotels, and stores in the Los Angeles area, as well as some 2,000 private homes ranging from modest development housing to lavish, million-dollar mansions. His major projects, on which he served as an associate, include the County Court House, International Airport, and Federal Customs Building, all in Los Angeles, and the United Nations Building in Paris.

Williams was born in Los Angeles and was orphaned at the age of three. While attending Polytechnic High School he decided to become an architect and ignored the warnings of sympathetic instructors that his color might be a serious handicap. Williams worked his way through evening art classes and found a $15-per-week job as an apprentice draftsman. A favorite story of Williams's—and an example of his strong desire to succeed—concerns his first assignment as an apprentice. He took the assignment home, worked on it throughout the night, completed it by morning, and delivered it to his astonished boss upon his arrival at the office.

At the age of 19 Williams entered the Beaux Arts Institute of Design (now the National Institute for Architectural Education), where he won the Beaux Arts Medal in the course of three years of study. From 1916 to 1919 he attended the University of Southern California.

Williams eventually worked his way up to the position of chief draftsman and was accepted by the Society of Architects of Los Angeles. In 1922 he opened his own architectural firm. He was forced to accept small commissions at first, but overcame prejudice and won clients with a combination of talent and good salesmanship.

By the late 1940s, his commercial buildings and private residences were visible throughout Southern California, Nevada, and Arizona. He worked on the remodeling of the Beverly Hills Hotel and designed additions to the Ambassador and Beverly-Wilshire Hotels. His successful design of "a shop with a residential atmosphere" for the Beverly Hills branch of Saks Fifth Avenue was a factor in his winning hotel commissions. His Arrowhead Hot Springs Hotel near San Bernardino and the Tennis Club at Palm Springs were subjects of photographic essays in the major professional architectural magazines.

Williams's designs for memorials were also in demand. His marble and mosaic memorial to singer and actor Al Jolson at Hillside Memorial Park in Hollywood, dedicated in 1951, was Williams's conception of a modern Greek temple. In 1952 he was commissioned by the Disabled American Veterans' national convention to design the Grave of the Unknown Sailor at Pearl Harbor.

Williams was also a prolific and respected designer of homes, receiving commissions from such entertainment celebrities as Frank Sinatra, Cary Grant, Tyrone Power, Lon Chaney, Zasu Pitts, and Charles Cottrell (Andy of "Amos 'n' Andy"), as well as from business magnates E. L. Cord and William Paley. Although he specialized in providing Tudor elegance for his elite clients, Williams suited his style to the individual commission. "If I build the kind of house a client wants," he once said, "I'm a good architect."

In June 1953 the National Association for the Advancement of Colored People awarded Williams the Spingarn Medal, a prize given to blacks who have made an unusual contribution to the community (previous recipients included George Washington Carver, Marian Anderson, and Dr. Ralph Bunche). The Medal was given in recognition of his designs for modest homes for the average homeowner. In accepting the award, Williams suggested that the quality of home designs in black communities could help dispel segregationist pressures: "If we as a minority could become noted as the group which has the greatest percentage of homeowners, it would automatically erase

any stigma of second-class citizenship. . . . The thing our people
should do is abandon the old, decaying neighborhoods, buy cheap
acreage in the suburbs, and let the city grow out toward us. This will
increase our standard of citizenship and will make us taxpayers with a
voice in our community's affairs."

Williams was the first black member of the American Institute of
Architects and the recipient of three honors from that organization. In
1938 he received the Award of Merit from the Southern California
chapter for his work on the Music Corporation of America Building in
Beverly Hills. He was elected to the AIA's College of Fellows in 1957
and received a commendation from the Los Angeles chapter in 1973.

Three U.S. Presidents also admired his talents and called him to
government service. President Coolidge appointed him to the National Monument Committee, President Hoover engaged him to
direct plans for a Negro Memorial to be erected in Washington, D.C.,
and President Eisenhower appointed him to the Federal Housing
Advisory Commission.

Williams lived his entire life in California and died in Los Angeles
after a long illness. His funeral was held in the First African Methodist
Church in Los Angeles, a church which he designed.   J.P./M.D.

Son of Chester Stanley W. and Lila (Wright) W. Married Della M.
Givens 1917. Children: Marilyn Francis Hudson, b.1926; Norma
Lucille Harvey, b.1928. Methodist. Educ: Polytechnic High Sch., Los
Angeles; Beaux Arts Inst. of Design, NYC and L.A. 1913–16; Univ.
Southern Calif., L.A. 1916–19. Mil. Service: Architect, U.S. Navy,
WWII; Selective Service 1940–45. Certified architect 1915; designer
with John Austin, Architect; Pres., Paul R. Williams & Assoc.
1922–73. With American Inst. of Architects: Member, L.A. Chapter
1926–80; Chmn., Competition Cttee. 1954; Member, Materials Re-
search Cttee. 1955; Member, Civic Devel. Cttee.; Feature Ed.,
A.I.A. Bulletin. Presidential appointments: Natl. Memorial Commn.
(by President Coolidge) 1929–32; Natl. Housing Commn. (by Presi-
dent Eisenhower) 1953. Member: City Planning Commn. of L.A.
1920–28; City Housing Commn., L.A. 1933–41; Calif. Redevel.
Commn. 1947–49; Calif. Housing Commn. 1949–55; Special Study
Commn. on Correctional Facilties and Services, State of Calif. 1955;
Calif. Civil Rights Commn. Pres., L.A. Art Commn. 1953–65. Bd. of
Dirs.: YMCA 1936–54; Southern Calif. Heart Assn.; L.A. Chapter,
American Red Cross; Big Brothers of Greater L.A. Inc.; L.A. Area,
Travelers Aid Soc.; United Service Org. Member: L.A. and Calif.
State Chambers of Commerce; L.A. Urban League; Natl. Assn. for
the Advancement of Colored People; Masons. Consulting Architect,
Fisk Univ., Nashville, Tenn.; V.P. and Dir., Broadway Fed. Savings
& Loan Assn., L.A.; Chmn., Intnl. Opportunity Insurance Co.;
Trustee, Howard Univ., Washington, D.C.; Treas., Southwest Area,
March of Dimes Foundn. Hons: Citizens of L.A. Award 1938; Award
of Merit for Music Corp. of America Bldg., Beverly Hills, from
Southern Calif. Chapter, A.I.A. 1939; D.Sc., Lincoln Univ. 1941;
Omega Psi Phi Natl. Award 1941; Veterans of Foreign Wars Award of
Merit 1948; Distinguished Citizen Award, Natl. Conference of Chris-
tians and Jews 1951; D. Arch., Howard Univ. 1952; Springarn Medal,
N.A.A.C.P. 1953; Los Angeles Tribune Award 1954; Award for
Creative Planning, L.A. Chamber of Commerce 1955; D.F.A.,
Tuskegee Inst. 1956; Wisdom Mag. Award 1956; Fellow, A.I.A. 1957;

Commendation, L.A. Chapter, A.I.A. 1973. *Architect:* County of L.A. Court House (assoc.); U.C.L.A. fraternity, sorority houses; Fed. Customs Bld., L.A. (assoc.); Fed. Office Bldg., L.A. (assoc.); YMCA, Hollywood; W.J. Sloan & Haggerty's, Beverly Hills; Saks Fifth Avenue, Beverly Hills 1948; Arrowhead Hot Springs Hotel, San Bernardino, Calif.; Tennis Club, Palm Springs, Calif. (assoc.); West Coast Company Theatre; Nutibara Hotel, Colombia 1948, expansion 1954; Golden State Mutual Life Insurance Home Office, L.A. 1950; Al Jolson Memorial, Hollywood 1951; St. Nicholas Church, L.A.; Memorial, Pearl Harbor 1952; U.N. Bldg., Paris (assoc.); Imperial-Compton Housing Project, L.A. 1954; New Hope Baptist Church, L.A. 1954; L.A. County Gen. Hosp. Wing (with Adrian Wilson), 1954; El Mirador Hotel, Palm Springs; Royal Nevada Hotel (with John Replogle), Las Vegas 1955; Church of St. Viator, Las Vegas; Franz Hall and Botany Bldg., U.C.L.A. 1958; Music Corp. of America office bldgs., Beverly Hills and NYC; Jr. High Sch., Marina Del Rey, Calif. 1960; L.A. Intnl. Airport (with Charles A. Luckman, Welton Becket), 1961; Roosevelt Naval Base, San Diego; others. *Author:* Small Homes of Tomorrow, 1945; New Homes for Today, 1946; many mag. articles.

SIMON (MWANSA) KAPWEPWE
Vice President of Zambia and leader of nationalist movement
Born Chinsali, Northern Province, Northern Rhodesia (now Zambia), April 12, 1922
Died Northern Province, Zambia, January 26th, 1980

Simon Mwansa Kapwepwe, one of the pioneers of black political development in Northern Rhodesia, helped found the nationalist movement that resulted in the establishment of the State of Zambia in 1964. Tall and ascetic, he was a charismatic leader who combined socialist idealism with a pragmatic approach to African development.

Kapwepwe was born in 1922 to a family of the Bemba tribe at Chinsali in the Northern Province. His father, for many years a British South Africa Company policeman, was later Head Warder for the District Commissioner.

Two years after his birth, the country, which had long been administered by the British South Africa Company, became a protectorate of the British Crown. The European settlers who controlled the area's copper industry, fearful of Britain's growing commitment to majority rule in its African colonies, agitated for the establishment of a constitution that would allow the white minority to retain political power, and to that end sought an amalgamation of Northern Rhodesia with white-controlled Southern Rhodesia. This move was met with strenuous opposition from the Africans, who had begun to build their own political organization, later known as the Federation of African Welfare Societies, out of local trade and farmers' groups.

Kapwepwe trained for a career as a teacher at the Lubwa Mission School, where he became close friends with Kenneth Kaunda, two years his junior. Together with John Sokoni, another student, they discussed avenues of resistance to the colonial government and particularly to the proposed federation with Southern Rhodesia. After qualifying as a teacher in 1945, Kapwepwe was turned down for several teaching jobs, including one as an army instructor, because of his reputation as a political activist (one report on him noted that his politics were "still in the bad, and could ripen at any time"). He eventually found a post at Wusakile, near Kitwe, at the missionary school of the United Missions of the Copperbelt, where he witnessed the degrading and oppressive treatment accorded black African workers by their white employers. In 1948 he returned to Chinsali to set up an agricultural project and became a founding member of the Northern Rhodesia African Congress (NRAC), the successor to the Federation of African Welfare Societies.

From 1951 to 1955, Kapwepwe, who had married the daughter of a Chinsali mission teacher, studied journalism in India on a scholarship arranged by the NRAC (now known as the African National Congress, or ANC). During his absence, the Federation of Rhodesia and Nyasaland was established and was met by protests and sit-ins from the ANC. Kapwepwe returned to find the organization's leaders, Kaunda and Harry Nkumbula, imprisoned on a charge of possessing subversive literature; he assumed temporary leadership of the ANC, earned a reputation as a forceful politician and mesmerizing orator, and was rewarded with election as treasurer of the ANC and appointment as president of its Northern Province branch.

Nkumbula, the president of the ANC, now adopted a policy of moderation that, in the view of many ANC members, played into the hands of the white settlers. Kapwepwe also accused the flamboyant Nkumbula of misappropriation of party funds for personal gain. In 1958 Kapwepwe led a secession from the ANC and with Kaunda, Justin Chimba, Reuben Kamanga, and Munukuyumbwa Sipalo formed the militantly anti-Federation Zambian African National Congress (ZANC). Kaunda was elected president, and Kapwepwe, whose reputation as a radical made him unsuitable for that office, became treasurer, with Sipalo as Secretary General. (The adoption of the name Zambia—a contraction of Zambezia, the name by which Northern Rhodesia had once been known—was suggested by Kapwepwe.) The group led a boycott of the 1959 elections, which were held under regulations designed to minimize African voting power; in reply, the Government banned the ZANC and imprisoned and exiled its leaders, who became officers of the newly formed United National Indepence Party (UNIP) as soon as they were released.

In October 1960 the British Government's Monckton Commission report was issued; though inconclusive, it came out against the Federation and in favor of a new constitution guaranteeing African rights. The white settlers escalated their efforts to prevent such a constitution and the Africans escalated their mass demonstrations. At the end of 1961, Kapwepwe accompanied Kaunda to London for high-level discussions on the possibility of self-government for Northern Rhodesia.

In 1962, despite continued Government schemes to reduce their voting power, the Africans won a majority of seats in the Legislative Council, Kapwepwe's among them. The UNIP, swallowing old enmities, arranged a coalition with Nkumbula and the ANC to gain a majority over the white-controlled United Federal Party, and Kapwepwe was named Minister of Agriculture.

On the last day of 1963, the Federation of Rhodesia and Nyasaland was abolished and Northern Rhodesia was granted full internal self-government. The UNIP, now a majority party, took control of the Legislative Council and the Cabinet, with Kaunda as Prime Minister. Kapwepwe became Minister of Home Affairs and transferred to Foreign Affairs in September 1964.

One month later, Zambia became an independent republic of the British Commonwealth, with Kaunda as its first president. Within a year the new government was faced with a major crisis when Ian Smith, Prime Minister of Rhodesia (formerly Southern Rhodesia), illegally declared his country's independence from Britain in an attempt to thwart the British policy of transition to black majority rule. Kapwepwe called for armed intervention by Britain to put down the rebellion; Britain rejected the use of military force and instead persuaded the United Nations Security Council to impose mandatory economic sanctions on Rhodesia, whereupon Kapwepwe went to the UN to denounce its "humiliating appeasement of Britain's kith and kin." In the meantime, Zambia was required to accept economic aid from Britain, the United States, and other nations in order to avoid trade with Rhodesia, on which it depended for oil, consumer goods, and communications.

In August 1967 Kapwepwe led a successful campaign at the general conference of the UNIP to install a Bemba-based ethnic alliance in all the party's top posts. After a bitter inter-tribal struggle he became deputy leader of the party and Vice President of Zambia, defeating his one-time friend and colleague Reuben Kamanga. This victory enabled Kapwepwe to extend his ministerial responsibilities into economic affairs, including the imposition of an austerity budget to deal with the worldwide fall in the price of copper, Zambia's chief export. On a wider front, he was responsible for an ongoing campaign to safeguard Zambian culture through the use of tribal languages in schools and the preservation of traditional crafts and customs.

However, Kapwepwe's maneuvering had divided the ruling party, and this, coupled with Kaunda's efforts to end tribal infighting, led to moves to unseat him. As a test of his political strength he offered his resignation as Vice President and deputy party leader in August 1969. But this move failed to win him much support, and at Kaunda's request he withdrew his resignation, exchanging his Development and Finance portfolio for that of Culture. In January 1970 he became Minister of Provincial and Local Government; his efforts to dismantle the old colonial system in favor of a pattern of local administration won him widespread praise. He was succeeded in the vice-presidency by Mainza Chona in October 1970, but retained his ministerial portfolios for another year.

Then, in August 1971, he resigned from the government and a day later announced the establishment of a new opposition party, the United Progressive Party (UPP), whose aim was to work for "a socialist labor code and to stamp out all forms of capitalism, tribalism, and sectionalism." This move marked an irreconcilable breach between Kapwepwe and Kaunda, who now viewed his old friend's militancy as a threat. Despite support from many disillusioned members of the UNIP, including Justin Chimba and Harry Nkumbula, the party failed to prosper; when it contested government by-elections in December 1971, Kapwepwe was the only party candidate to win a seat. Throughout the autumn of 1971 UPP members were subjected to detention without trial ; still Kaunda forebore to punish his boyhood friend and ally. In April, however, he banned the UPP and imprisoned Kapwepwe and 122 of his followers for the remainder of the year. The day after their release, Kaunda declared the UNIP the only legal political party in Zambia.

Foiled in his attempt to stay active in politics, Kapwepwe turned his attention to farming in the Northern Province. But the Zambian authorities maintained a close watch on his activities and in February 1973 charged him with the illegal possession of two guns. He was found guilty and given a two-year suspended prison sentence. Kapwepwe then made one further bid to re-enter politics. On September 9th, 1977, he announced that he would rejoin the UNIP in the interests of "national unity." But the following year he failed to win the UNIP nomination for the presidency and his attempt to overturn the UNIP decision through an appeal to the Supreme Court was unsuccessful.

Kapwepwe died in the Northern Province of a stroke.   J.P./M.D.

Son of parents of the Bemba tribe; father a policeman. Married. Educ: Lubwa Mission Sch., qualified as teacher 1945; attended univs., Bombay, India (scholarship) 1951–55. Teacher, United Missions of the Copperbelt, Kitwe 1948; teacher, Chinsali 1949–50. Member, Chinsali Young Men's Farming Assn. 1949–51. With Northern Rhodesia African Congress (from 1953, African Natl. Congress): Founding Member 1948–58; temporary leader 1955; appointed Pres., Northern Province Branch 1955; Treas. 1956–58. Jt. Founder 1958 and Treas. 1958–60, Zambian African Natl. Congress; imprisoned with Z.A.N.C. leaders Mar.–Dec. 1959. With United Natl. Independent Party: Member 1960–71, 1977–80; Treas. 1960–70; Delegate to Fed. Review Conference, London 1961; elected to Zambian Legislative Council 1962–71; Minister of Agriculture 1962–64; Minister of Home Affairs 1964; Minister of Foreign Affairs 1964–67; Vice President of Zambia and deputy leader of party 1967–70; Minister of Development and Finance 1969; Minister of Culture 1969–71; Minister of Provincial and Local Govt. 1970–71; elected to Natl. Assembly 1971. Jt. founder and leader, United Progressive Party 1971; imprisoned 1972–73. Farmer, Northern Province 1973–80. *Author:* Tunyongandimi, 1959; Shalapo Chanichandala, 1960; Ubutungwa mu Jambo Jambo (political fiction), 1967.

H(ARRY) H(EMLEY) PLASKETT
Astrophysicist
Born Toronto, Canada, July 5th, 1893
Died Oxford, England, January 26th, 1980

H.H. Plaskett, solar physicist and Savilian Professor of Astronomy at Oxford for almost 30 years, was born into the field of astronomy. His father, Dr. John Stanley Plaskett, was Director of the Dominion Astrophysical Observatory at Victoria, B.C., and one of Canada's foremost observational astronomers.

The younger Plaskett, who was educated at the University of Toronto, volunteered for the Canadian Field Army and saw active service on the Flanders battlefield in France during 1917–18. At the end of the war, Plaskett spent a brief period with Professor Alfred Fowler in South Kensington before joining his father's observatory at the age of 26. Here he made his reputation as a keen observer and theoretician by his influential study of the largest and hottest O-type stars in connection with Saha's ionization theory of stellar spectra, which predicts the relative population of ions in solar atmospheres of varying temperatures and pressures. He was also at work on the development of techniques to measure the intensities of specific areas of stellar spectra, techniques which have been adopted as standard practice by astronomers.

Between 1928 and 1932 Plaskett was Professor of Astrophysics at Harvard University, where he worked on the evaluation of temperature gradients and other data from solar absorption lines.

In 1932 Plaskett returned to Britain to take up the Savilian Chair of Astronomy at the University of Oxford. Plaskett immediately involved himself in the life of the university, becoming a Fellow of New College and serving on many of the university's advisory bodies and on one of its central governing authorities, the Hebdomadal Council. Meanwhile, he continued his research on solar physics and in his early years at Oxford concentrated on building up the university's observatory as a world center of solar information. This he did by adding to the range and quality of its equipment and by diversifying its investigations from matters of theoretical interest to problems in astrophysics. Some of his researchers did pioneering work in the field of radiative transfer.

Plaskett, who was elected a Fellow of the Royal Society in 1936, employed his detailed knowledge of telescope design on the construction of two telescopes at Oxford, in 1935 and 1954. During his Presidency of the Royal Astronomical Society in the 1940s, he put forward a plan to provide all British astronomers with better research facilities through the construction of a new 100-inch telescope. Though the proposal was slow to win acceptance, it resulted in the construction of the Isaac Newton reflector telescope at the Royal Greenwich Observatory in 1967.

After serving in an anti-aircraft battery and an RAF research station during World War Two, Plaskett returned to Oxford to continue his studies of absorption spectra, to begin work on solar movement at the photospheric level, and to direct his students in their research on wavelength measurement, solar interferometry, chromospheric spectra, and sunspots. He was known as a demanding but encouraging teacher who trained a generation of British astronomers. Since 1960 he was professor emeritus; Plaskett's Star was named in his honor.

J.P./M.D.

Son of Dr. John Stanley P. and Rebecca Hope (Hemley) P. Married Edith Alice Smith 1921. Children: one son, one daughter. Educ: Ottawa Collegiate; Univ. Toronto, B.A. 1916. Mil. Service: Canadian Field Army, Flanders 1917–18; anti-aircraft battery, England 1939–40; tactical navigational research for U.K. Ministry of Aircraft Production 1940–44. Astronomer, Dominion Astrophysical Observatory, Victoria 1919–27; Prof. of Astrophysics, Harvard Univ. 1928–32; Savilian Prof. of Astronomy 1932–60, Savilian Prof. Emeritus 1960–80, and Fellow of New College 1932–80, Univ. Oxford. Pres., Royal Astronomical Soc., London 1945–47; served on Hebdomadal Council, Univ. Oxford. Hons: Elected Fellow, Royal Soc. 1936; LL.D., Univ. St. Andrews, Scotland 1961; Gold Medal, Royal Astronomical Soc., London 1963. Contributed papers on observational astrophysics to professional jrnls.

SIR ERIC WYNDHAM WHITE
Lawyer and economist; First Director-General, General Agreement on Tariffs and Trade
Born January 26th, 1913
Died Ferney-Voltaire, Ain, France, January 27th, 1980

Sir Eric Wyndham White, the British lawyer and economist who founded and headed the General Agreement on Tariffs and Trade (GATT) after the Second World War, was a lifelong advocate of international trade liberalization.

Wyndham White graduated from the London School of Economics with a First Class degree in law. But instead of settling for a career at the Bar, he chose economics as a more challenging proposition. After a brief period as a lecturer at the London School of Economics, during which time he attended Congresses of the International Chamber of Commerce in Berlin and Copenhagen as a member of the British delegations, Wyndham White joined the Ministry of Economic Warfare on the outbreak of World War Two.

His economic expertise marked him out for promotion and in 1942 he was sent to the British Embassy in Washington, where he laid the groundwork for his ensuing career in higher economics and international trade. He was later posted to the British Embassy in Paris. In 1945 he became Special Assistant to the European Director of the United Nations' Relief and Rehabilitation Administration. From that he moved to the task of establishing a secretariat to bring into being a new international trade organization—a development he had long advocated. GATT was formed in 1948 and Wyndham White became its first Executive Secretary. In 1965 he took over as its Director-General. Throughout his work for GATT, Wyndham White was at the forefront of world trade negotiation and his advice in the field of economics was sought by the governments of many countries and by the United Nations Organization. He was asked to lead many international trade conferences and rounds of negotiation, in particular the Dillon Round of the late 1940s which helped set the pattern of world trade following the disruption of World War Two. His leadership in the 1967 Kennedy Round was seen as a major factor in its success: 46 nations signed tariff-cutting agreements which increased trade liberalization in almost 76 percent of world commerce. The following year his efforts were officially recognized with the conferment of a British knighthood.

Wyndham White resigned from GATT in 1968 to move into private finance, joining the board of Investors Overseas Service, a giant mutual fund complex based in Geneva. When a financial crisis resulted in the ouster of founder and chairman Bernard Cornfeld, Wyndham White took over as president, chairman of the board, and chief executive officer, steering IOS through a proxy fight with Cornfeld over control of the organization. In 1972, after rescue operations failed, he supervised the liquidation of the group and later became a private investment consultant with the Canadian government.

Largely because of his work with GATT and IOS, Wyndham White made his home in Switzerland, although he retained close links with his homeland. His death at the age of 67 occurred as a result of a heart attack he suffered while swimming in a municipal pool at Ferney-Voltaire, a French village near Geneva.   J.P./M.D.

Son of Henry Wyndham W. and Helen (Peppiatt) W. Married Tina Gibson Thayer 1947 (div.). Daughters: Amy; Carolyn. Educ: Westminster City Sch.; London Sch. Econs., Univ. London, LL.B. (1st Class Hons.) 1935. Called to Bar, Middle Temple 1938. Member, British delegations, Intnl. Chamber of Commerce Congresses, Berlin 1937 and Copenhagen 1939; Asst. Lectr., London Sch. Econs. 1938–39; with Ministry of Econ. Warfare 1939–41; First Secty., British Embassy, Washington, D.C. 1942–45; Econ. Counsellor, British Embassy, Paris 1945–46; Special Asst. to European Dir., U.N. Relief and Rehabilitation Admin. 1945; Secty.-Gen., Emergency Econ. Cttee. for Europe 1946; Exec. Secty. to Preparatory Cttee. for Intnl. Trade Org., then Secty.-Gen. to U.N. Conference on Intnl. Trade and Employment, London, Geneva, and Havana 1946–48; Exec. Secty. 1948–65 and Dir.-Gen. 1965–68, Gen. Agreement on Tariffs and Trade. With Investors Overseas Service, Geneva: Member, Bd. of Dirs. 1968–72; named Pres., Chief Exec. Officer, and Chmn., Bd. of Dirs. 1970. Advisor to Canadian Govt. on multilateral trade orgs. 1978–79. Hons: Dr. *rerum publicarum*, Sch. Econs., Business and Public Admin., St. Gall, Switzerland 1963; Dr. Laws, Univ. Calif. at Los Angeles 1966; Dr. Laws., Dartmouth Coll. 1968; knighted (K.C.M.G.) 1968. *Author:* legal and economic articles and addresses.

PAUL (BEECHER) BLANSHARD
Writer and sociologist
Born Fredericksburg, Ohio, U.S.A., August 27th, 1892
Died St. Petersburg, Florida, U.S.A., January 27th, 1980

Paul Blanshard, like his distinguished twin brother—the Yale philosopher Brand Blanshard—was a man who seemed to thrive on controversy. He spent his life promoting causes and criticizing powerful organizations—most notably the Catholic Church.

Born in Fredericksburg, Ohio, the son of a Congregational minister, Blanshard's parents died when he was still very young. He and his brother were raised in considerable poverty, by their Methodist grandmother. Both brothers attended Detroit Central High School and went on to the University of Michigan. Paul Blanshard then pursued graduate studies at Harvard and Columbia Universities.

Blanshard transferred to Columbia's Union Theological Seminary, and was ordained a Congregationalist minister in 1917. He abandoned the calling in the following year, later saying: "I have come to the conclusion that Christianity is so full of fraud that any honest man should repudiate the whole shebang and espouse atheism."

Blanshard became increasingly involved with the Socialist Party and worked successively as Labor Organizer and Educational Director for the Amalgamated Clothing Workers in Rochester, New York. While there he wrote his first book, *An Outline of the British Labour Movement*. Blanshard then became Field Secretary for the League of Industrial Democracy, in New York City, a post he held for eight years. It was during this period that he wrote *What's The Matter With New York* (1932) with the socialist, Norman Thomas, for whom Blanshard had campaigned in the Presidential race of 1928. He began writing articles for liberal magazines, and after a brief stint as Associate Editor of "The Nation" magazine, Paul Blanshard worked for the City of New York, becoming Executive Director of the City Affairs Committee (1930–33). Blanshard severed his connections with the Socialist Party in 1933 to support Fiorello LaGuardia—a man he much admired—for Mayor of New York City. With the election of LaGuardia, Blanshard was appointed Commissioner of Investigations and Accounts. He became well-known for his investigations of holdovers from the previous administration, and by 1935 more than twenty officials had been expelled. Blanshard studied at night at Brooklyn Law School and received his degree in 1937. He resigned his position later that year and moved to a small farm he had inherited in Alabama to realize his dream of becoming a writer. He was not successful either as a poet or fiction writer and returned to New York where he practiced law until 1941 and also served as Director of the Society for the Prevention of Crime.

During World War II Blanshard worked in the State Department as an economic analyst and consultant to the Caribbean Commission. His third book, *Democracy and Empire in the Caribbean* was published in 1947. By that time Blanshard had moved to a small farm in Thetford Center, Vermont, where he began to write on Catholic policy. He later said: "My interest in the Catholic Church sprang partly from a burning moral conviction that birth control was and is one of the world's greatest necessities for the poor, and that the priests are imposing on their subjects a fundamentally immoral rule on that question."

To write his second book on Catholicism, Blanshard went to Rome for the Holy Year of 1950 as a representative of *The Nation*. His next book, *The Irish and Catholic Power—An American Interpretation*, written at the suggestion of an Irish Jesuit scholar, was commenced in Dublin, continued in London, and completed in Boston. In answering charges that his attacks on the Catholic Church were too caustic, Blanshard said; "When a church enters the arena of controversial social policy and attempts to control the judgment of its own people (and of other people) . . . it must be reckoned with as an organ of political and cultural power." For a time his writings in *The Nation* and his book *American Freedom and Catholic Power* were banned in New York public schools.

In all, Blanshard wrote 15 books, many of them dealing with aspects of religious policy. His autobiography, *Personal and Controversial* was published in 1973, and his last book, *Classics of Free Thought* in 1977.

He says in his autobiography: "In my zigzag career I have been transformed from Christian fundamentalist to humanist atheist, from stodgy Puritan to sexual rebel, from doctrinaire socialist to socialist pragmatist." And later: ". . . if this century ever bears a distinctive, descriptive label for its religious condition, the label should be 'hypocrisy'. We profess to believe not because we actually believe but because pretense is more socially acceptable . . . arrival at the port of atheism has brought me great psychological release . . . Now I can be honest about life, death and morals. I can reject openly all the semantic jugglery of over-belief. There is no longer up in the sky even the shadow of a vengeful Old Man telling me what to think . . . We who are pilgrims on the long journey to oblivion may love and serve our fellow pilgrims without any supernatural intervention . . . since God has never been anything more than a helpful psychological crutch created by the human imagination for its own comfort."

Paul Blanshard died in St. Petersburg, Florida. He is survived by his third wife, two sons by his first marriage, and his twin brother.   R.T.

Son of Francis George B. and Emily C. Married: (1) Julia Anderson 1915 (d. 1934); (2) Mary W. Hillyer 1935 (d. 1965); (3) Beatrice Enselman Mayer 1965. Children: 1st marriage—Paul Jr., b.1919; Rufus, b.1921. Atheist, formerly Unitarian, Congregationalist. Educ.: Univ. Michigan, Ann Arbor, A.B. 1914; Postgrad. studies Harvard Univ., Columbia Univ., and Union Theological Seminary, Brooklyn Law Sch., L.L.B. 1937. Mil. service: Econ. analyst and consultant, Caribbean Commn. of State Dept. 1942–46. Ordained minister, Congregationalist Church 1917; Pastor, First Church, Tampa, Florida 1917–18; Educational Dir., Amalgamated Clothing Workers, Rochester, N.Y. 1920–24; Field Secty., League for Industrial Democracy 1925–33; Assoc. Ed., "The Nation" 1928–29; Exec. Dir., City Affairs Committee, N.Y.C. 1939–41; Dir., New York Soc. for the Prevention of Crime 1941; writer 1946–80; Columnist, St. Petersburg Times, Fla. *Author:* An Outline of the British Labour Movement, 1923; (with Norman Thomas) What's the Matter with New York, 1932; New York (City) Dept. of Investigation and Accounts, Investigating City Government in the LaGuardia Administration, 1937; Democracy and Empire in the Caribbean, 1947; American Freedom and Catholic Power, 1949, 2nd ed. 1958; Communism, Democracy and Catholic Power, 1951, reprint 1972; The Irish and Catholic Power—An American Interpretation, 1953, reprint 1972; The Right to Read—The Battle Against Censorship, 1955; God and Man in Washington, 1960; Freedom and Catholic Power in Spain and Portugal, 1962; Religion and the Schools—The Great Controversy, 1963; Paul Blanshard on Vatican II, 1966; Personal and Controversial (autobiog.), 1973; Some of My Best Friends are Christians, 1974; Classics of Free Thought, 1977. Frequent contributor to mags. and journals including: Nation, New Republic, New York Times, World Tomorrow, and Readers' Digest.
Further reading: "American Freedom and Catholic Power" (review), Commonweal, June 17, 1949, and New Statesman, Sept. 3, 1949; Catholics and American Freedom, by J. O'Neill; Atlantic Monthly, May 1950 and Aug. 1951; Newsweek, May 21 and June 4, 1951.

JIMMY DURANTE
Comedian, actor, singer
Born New York City, U.S.A., February 10th, 1893
Died Santa Monica, California, U.S.A., January 29th, 1980

Jimmy Durante was one of the most beloved clowns in American entertainment history. Generations of fans from Prohibition days to the television era enjoyed his gentle humor, raspy-voiced nonsense songs, preposterous mangling of the English language, and zany stage antics. Among his comedy trademarks were a droopy felt hat and his beaked nose, which earned him the nickname "Schnozzola" and was immortalized as a noseprint in the cement outside Grauman's Chinese Theatre in Hollywood.

Born on Catherine Street on Manhattan's Lower East Side, James Francis Durante was the son of immigrant French-Italian parents. His formal education ended with grammar school, after which he went to work selling papers, washing dishes, running errands, and lathering faces in his father's barber shop. When he was 12 his father bought him a piano on which he taught himself to play ragtime. Within a few years he was playing for neighborhood social clubs for $2 a night. In 1910 he began his professional career playing piano from 9:00 P.M. to 6:00 A.M. for $25 a week at Diamond Tony's Saloon in Coney Island, where the audience included a colorful assortment of gangsters, pimps, and shady politicians. He continued to play clubs in Chinatown, the Bowery, and on Broadway, going to New Orleans in 1916 to put together a six-piece jazz band for Harlem's Club Alamo.

In January 1923 Durante and a partner, song-and-dance man Eddie Jackson, opened the Club Durant in a loft above a garage on West 55th Street in Manhattan. (Legend has it that Durante ran out of money for his sign and had to drop the final "e".) The two were soon joined by a third partner, Lou Clayton, a dancer, businessman, and big name in vaudeville, who built a successful comedy act around Durante and his prominent nose. (Although laughs about his "schnozzola" earned him a fortune, Durante admitted that he was never happy about the nose jokes.) The club, frequented by New York café society and Clayton's free-spending mobster friends, did a booming business for a year and a half, buying bootleg whisky at $4 a quart and selling it for $1 a drink until Prohibition agents padlocked the door in 1925. The partners opened another speakeasy on 51st Street and took in $4,000 on opening night.

When racketeers attempted to muscle in on their successful operation, Clayton persuaded Durante and Jackson to give up club management and tour as a vaudeville comedy act. The trio headed the bill at The Palace and broke the house record. At the Club Rendezvous they invented the now classic "wood act," in which they dragged dozens of wooden things on stage, including wooden Indians, a rowboat, even an outhouse.

The trio split up in 1931 when MGM brought Durante to Hollywood. Lou Clayton remained as his manager until his death in 1950. During the next 20 years Durante made over two dozen films and appeared on the New York stage in such hits as "Red, Hot, and Blue!," with Ethel Merman and Bob Hope, and "Jumbo," a circus extravaganza in the old Hippodrome.

Radio was a natural medium for the verbally manic comedian, who introduced his trademark song, the nonsensical "Inka Dinka Doo," when he was Eddie Cantor's replacement on a "Chase & Sanborn Hour" in 1933. He had a summer show in 1934 on NBC, but did not have a continuing radio program until 1943, when producer Phil Cohen teamed Durante and Garry Moore in "The Camel Comedy Caravan" as a replacement for the popular "Abbot and Costello Show" after Costello's heart attack. The show was prepared in a few weeks, debuted on an understandably frenetic note, but soon attracted its own enthusiastic audience. The cool and witty Moore made the perfect straight man for the frantic, bewildered, malaprop-spouting Durante. In one running routine, Moore would describe something ("I have a new job in the shoddy, shabby, and shady suburb in the Shropshire section of Massachusetts with a flashy, trashy, but fairly fashionable cash haberdashery") and Durante would repeat it, with devastating results. The partnership ended in 1947 and Durante had a solo show for three years until he left radio for television.

During the 1950s Durante hosted several TV variety shows, including NBC's comedy-variety "All Star Revue." From 1954 to 1957 he starred in "The Jimmy Durante Show" with his old friend Eddie Jackson. The setting was a small nightclub—the Club Durant—where he would conduct interviews and auditions and occasionally perform. However, Durante's improvisational style was more suited to live clubs than television. In the 1960s he played big clubs throughout the United States, bringing down the house with his vintage routines (such as "Umbriago") and trademark lines ("Goodnight, Mrs. Calabash, wherever you are").

In the 1960s and '70s, when comedy acts relied heavily on insult jokes and double-entendres, Durante's light-hearted clowning was a welcome relief to many audiences. Generous with his time as well as his humor, he gave benefit performances to aid the Damon Runyon Cancer Fund and was well-known in Hollywood circles for his warm, unpretentious treatment of colleagues and friends.

Durante's wife Jeanne, whom he had married in 1921, died of cancer in 1943. In 1960, after a 12-year engagement, Durante married Margie Little, an employee at the Copacabana Club. The couple adopted a baby girl, CeCe, in 1961, over the objections of adoption officials who maintained that the 68-year-old performer was too old. A sympathetic judge ended the controversy, saying, "I have heard this man sing 'Young at Heart.'"

Durante was partially paralyzed by a stroke in 1972 and spent his last years in a wheelchair, in frail health. He died of pneumonitis on January 29th, 1980, and was buried at Holy Cross Cemetery in Culver City, California.   J.P./S.P.

Born James Francis Durante. Son of Bartolomeo D., barber, and Rosea (Millino) D. Married: (1) Jeanne Olson, singer, 1921 (d.1943); (2) Marjorie Little, actress, model, 1960. Daughter: Cecilia Alicia, adopted 1961. Roman Catholic. Educ: public schools, 1900–10. Entertainer/pianist at Diamond Tony's Saloon, Coney Island, NYC 1910; Kenny Walsh's Club, NYC; Club Alamo, NYC 1916; Silver Slipper, NYC 1920; Club Durant, NYC 1923; Parody Club, NYC; Dover Club, NYC; Les Ambassadeurs, NYC 1928; The Rendezvous, NYC 1929; Copacabana, NYC 1943, 1949, 1956, 1957, 1957; Palumbo's, Philadelphia 1959–64; Desert Inn, Las Vegas; Blinstrubs,

Boston; Latin Casino, Camden, N.J.; Chez Paree, New Orleans. Appeared extensively in films 1928–63, also on radio and television. Member: Actors Equity Assn.; American Fedn. of Television and Radio Artists; American Guild of Variety Artists; American Soc. of Composers, Authors, and Publishers; Screen Actors Guild. Hons: Best TV Performer, Motion Picture Daily 3rd Annual Television Poll 1951; George Foster Peabody Award 1951; Citation of Merit, City of New York 1956; Special Page One Award 1962. *Performances: Stage*—Show Girl, 1928; The New Yorkers, 1930; Strike Me Pink, 1933; Friars Club Frolic, 1933; Jumbo, 1935; Red, Hot and Blue!, 1936; Stars in Your Eyes, 1939; Keep Off the Grass, 1940; Comedy act at the London Palladium 1936, 1952; others. *Films*—Roadhouse Nights, 1930; New Adventures of Get-Rich-Quick Wallingford, 1931; The Cuban Love Song, 1931; The Passionate Plumber, 1932; The Phantom President, 1932; Speak Easily, 1932; The Wet Parade, 1933; What? No Beer?, 1933; George White's Scandals, 1934; Palooka, 1934; Strictly Dynamite, 1934; Hollywood Party, 1934; Sally, Irene and Mary, 1938; Little Miss Broadway, 1938; Start Cheering, 1938; Melody Ranch, 1940; You're in the Army Now, 1941; The Man Who Came to Dinner, 1941; This Time for Keeps, 1942; Her Cardboard Lover, 1942; Two Girls and a Sailor, 1944; Music for Millions, 1944; The Ziegfeld Follies, 1946; Two Sisters From Boston, 1946; It Happened in Brooklyn, 1947; On an Island With You, 1948; The Great Rupert, 1950; The Milkman, 1950; Pepe, 1960; Billy Rose's Jumbo, 1962; It's a Mad Mad Mad Mad World, 1963; Blondie of the Follies; Broadway to Hollywood; Meet the Baron; She Learned About Sailors; Student Tour; Land Without Music; Carnival; Yellow Cab Man. *Radio*—Atlantic Spotlight; The Chase & Sanborn Hour, 1933; Rexall Show, 1944; The Camel Comedy Caravan (with Garry Moore), 1943–47; The Jimmy Durante Show, 1947–50. *Television*—All Star Revue, 1951; Texaco Star Theatre, 1955; Colgate Comedy Hour, 1953–54; Give My Regards to Broadway, 1959; Boy Meets Girl, 1961; The Jimmy Durante Show, 1954–57, 1959, 1961; Jimmy Durante Meets the Seven Lively Arts, 1965; Jimmy Durante Presents the Lennon Sisters, 1969; The Hollywood Palace. *Books*—(with Jack Kofoed) Night Clubs, 1931; The Candidate (humor), 1952; Schnozzle Durante's Song Book.
Further reading: Good Night Mrs. Calabash: The Secret Life of Jimmy Durante by William Cahn, 1963.

HENRY (ROELAND) BYRD
Pseudonym: Professor Longhair
Rock-and-roll pianist, singer, composer
Born Bogalusa, Louisiana, U.S.A., December 19th, 1918
Died New Orleans, Louisiana, U.S.A., January 30th, 1980

Henry Byrd was raised in music. He was the son of musicians who moved, when Byrd was an infant, from rural Louisiana to New Orelans, the birthplace of some of America's greatest musical idioms. Traditional forms—the blues of the descendants of black slaves, the folk songs of Cajuns and Creoles, the ceremonial music of native Indians, the dances imported by sailors from the West Indies and Latin America—flourished alongside their hybrids, such as brass-band funeral marches and the carnival music of Mardi Gras. Moreover, the city's indigenous ragtime music had achieved international popularity and jazz was entering its classic era, nurtured by such locals as Jelly Roll Morton and Louis Armstrong. This was the potpourri that Byrd shaped into rock-and-roll.

As a boy, Byrd earned tips by dancing on the streets outside New Orleans nightclubs. He met many important musicians, among them Tuts Washington, an early mentor who encouraged Byrd to learn to play an instrument. First he took up the drums, then the guitar, and then taught himself to play an old upright piano he found abandoned in an alley. From the start, his musical style was a blend of the sounds he had heard in the nightclubs and on the streets and docks, all of which he merged with his own unique rhythms.

During the 1930s Byrd danced professionally in New Orleans nightclubs while continuing to play and sing. In 1949 he began to work regularly as a musician and that year cut his first record, "Bald Head."

For the next five years Byrd, billed as "Professor Longhair," performed in the New Orleans area, singing and playing his own compositions, leading a band, and recording extensively. His innovative style—characterized by heavily syncopated dance rhythms, boogie-woogie bass lines in the left-hand and layered arpeggios in the right—had an immediate and lasting influence on the rock-and-roll then emerging in New Orleans. Adopting the Longhair style, Fats Domino, Huey "Piano" Smith, and Ernie K-Doe all won fame and fortune, while Byrd—although a legend among devotees—remained unknown to general audiences.

A stroke suffered in 1954 and a year's confinement in the hospital hurt Professor Longhair's chances for building a popular following. His poor health interfered with regular performances for the rest of his life, a problem compounded by financial mismanagement which denied him any royalties on his published compositions and recordings. He worked intermittently throughout the 1950s and 1960s, but even Longhair "standards" such as "Go To the Mardi Gras"—which became a theme-song of the annual carnival—and "Big Chief," a hit in 1964, brought him little in the way of financial gain. For a time in the late 1960s he earned money by sweeping the floors of the studio where he had recorded some of his most important work.

Byrd and his family were rescued from poverty when he was rediscovered by a talent agent for the New Orleans Jazz and Heritage Festival in 1971. His appearance at that year's Festival caught the attention of a new generation of rock-and-roll fans, a generation familiar with the music of Mac "Dr. John" Rebennack, Allen Toussaint, and Paul McCartney—all of whom had been strongly influenced by Professor Longhair. From then on, the Professor headlined the Festival every year until his death. National and European tours and appearances at the music festivals of Montreux, Nice, and Newport spread his fame even further. A collection of early recordings was released and he recorded three critically acclaimed—and modestly profitable—albums.

Prior to his death, Longhair had been engaged to tour with the

Clash, an influential group of English punk-rockers; and only four
nights before he died he played a 2:00 a.m.-to-dawn set at Tipitina's, a
New Orleans club that takes its name from one of the Professor's
songs.   K.B.

Son of James B. and Ella Mae B., musicians. Married Alice (maiden
name unknown) 1939. Seven children. Educ: primary sch., New
Orleans. Dancer and vaudeville entertainer, New Orleans 1930s and
40s; musician, New Orleans 1949–80. Asst. Col. in Civil Defense
Special Forces. *Recordings in print (1980):* Bald Head (first single),
1949; New Orleans Piano, 1973; Rock and Roll Gumbo, 1975; Live on
the Queen Mary, 1978; Crawfish Fiesta, 1980; featured on New
Orleans Jazz and Heritage Festival 1976, 1977. *Major concerts:* New
Orleans Jazz and Heritage Festival, annually 1971–79; Newport Jazz
and Folk Festival, 1973; Montreux International Jazz Festival, 1973;
Grande Parade du Jazz, Nice, 1978.

LIL DAGOVER
Actress
Born Madiven, Java (now Djawa), September 30th, 1897
Died Munich, Federal Republic of Germany, January 30th, 1980

Lil Dagover, actress for over fifty years on the German stage and
screen, was closely involved in the flourishing cinema of post-World
War One cinema. She played major roles in many of the movies which
have now become classics of the silent screen, such as *The Cabinet of
Dr. Caligari* and *Destiny,* and worked under most of the great German
directors, many of whom later moved to Hollywood.

She had begun to act while still in boarding school in Weimar and
fell in love with Fritz Daghofer, the dramatic actor, whom she later
married. Through him she was introduced to Robert Wiene, who later
cast her in *The Cabinet of Dr. Caligari,* an expressionist film produced
by Erich Pommer and considered by film historians to be a milestone
in German cinema.

Wiene recommended Lil Daghofer (who that year took the name
Dagover) to Fritz Lang, and she made her film debut as the lead in his
Harakiri (Madame Butterfly) in 1919. She also starred in several of his
other early films: *Die Spinnen (The Spiders),* and *Dr. Mabuse der
Spieler (Dr. Mabuse the Gambler).* She worked under Carl Froelich
when she played the title role in *Luise Millerin,* based on Schier's
Kabale und Liebe (Intrigue and Love). Under F.W. Murnau, she
starred in *Phantom* in 1922 and three years later played Elmira, co-
starring with Emil Jannings and Werner Kraus, in his *Tartuffe,* a film
adaptation of Molière's play. She made her stage debut under the
great regisseur and director Max Reinhardt, in Salzburg in 1925.

In 1926 Lil Dagover made two films in Sweden, one—*Hans engelska
fru (Discord)*—with Gustav Molander. She was in France in 1928–29
and made three films, including *Le Tourbillon de Paris* with Julien
Duvivier. Her talents and exotic looks brought her to the attention of

Hollywood, which she visited briefly in 1927–28. In 1931, Warner Brothers invited her as their candidate in the competition against Garbo and Dietrich, but had difficulty creating the appropriate vehicle for her. When *Woman from Monte Carlo* (co-starring Warren William and directed by Michael Curtiz) was finally released, it failed. Dagover returned to Germany, where she remained for the rest of her life.

In the 1930s Dagover was a favorite of the German screen and a prolific performer. She received uniformly good reviews which often commented on her "perennial youth," but by and large the films of this period and for the rest of her career were of insignificant artistic interest. Her most renowned films of these years were *The Kreutzer Sonata* and *The Congress Dances;* her directors included Detlef Sierck (Douglas Sirk), Veit Harlan, Hans Hinrich, Johannes Meyer, and Eric Charell. Throughout the Nazi era she continued to make films in Germany—but was no longer seen on the American or English screen until the mid-1970s, when she acted in a few films for Maximilian Schell and one for Hans-Jurgen Syberberg.

Lil Dagover, who spoke five languages and was widely read was not an actress of extraordinary ability, but rather one who always performed competently and with grace and dignity. Her exotic presence—her shoulders were once insured for $15,000—made her very much a part of the glamorous 30s and, when they ended, her own career waned. She published her memoirs in 1979.   L.F.

Born Maria Antonia Siegelinde Marta Liletts. Daughter of Adolf Ludwig Moritz Seubert, forester and Dutch government employee, and Marta Herf S. Married: (1) Fritz Daghofer, actor 1917 (div. 1919, d.1936); (2) George Witt, film producer 1936. Children: 1st marriage—one daughter. Educ: boarding schs. in Baden-Baden and Weimar, Germany, Lausanne, and Geneva. Lived in Germany since 1903. Film actress since 1919; also active on stage and television in Germany, Austria, Sweden, Switzerland, France, and Luxembourg. West Berlin Festival, 1954; Bad Herzfeld Festival, 1958. Hons: Staatsschauspieler (State Actress) 1937; Bundesfilmpreis (gold ribbon) 1962; Bambi Prize 1964; Grosses Bundesverdienstkreuz (Cross of Merit), Federal Republic of Germany 1967. *Performances: Films—* Harakiri, 1919; Das Cabinett des Dr. Caligari, 1919, released 1920; Die Spinnen (The Spiders:I—Das Brillantenschiff; II—Die Goldene See), 1920; Das Blut der Ahnen, 1920; Die Jagd nach dem Tode, 1920; Tiefland, 1920; Das Geheimnis von Bombay, 1920; Der Müde Tod (Destiny), 1921, released in U.S.A. as Between Two Worlds in 1923 and Beyond the Wall in 1928; Der Richter von Zalamea, 1921; Phantom, 1922; Luise Millerin (Kabale und Liebe), 1922; Dr. Mabuse, der Spieler (Dr. Mabuse the Gambler), 1922; Seine Frau, die Unbekannte, 1923; Komödie des Herzens, 1924; Tartüff (Tartuffe), 1925; Zur Chronik von Grieshuus (Chronicles of the Grey House or At the Grey House), 1925; Liebe Macht Blind (Love Makes Us Blind), 1925; Die Doppelgängerin, 1925; Der Demütige und die Sängerin, 1925; Der Geheime Kurier (Red and the Black), 1926; Die Bruder Schellenberg (Two Brothers), 1926; Der Veilchenfresser, 1926; Bara en Danserka (in Sweden), 1926; Hans engelska fru (in Sweden: Discord), 1926; Der Anwalt des Herzens, 1926; Ein Moderner Don Juan, 1926; Orient Express, 1926; Der Ungarische Rhapsodie (Hungarian Rhapsody), 1928; Monte Cristo (France), 1928; Le Tourbillon de Paris (in France), 1928; The Grand Passion (in France),

1929; Der Günstling von Schönbrunn, 1929; Spielereien einer Kaiserin, 1929; Die Ehe, 1929; Es Flüstert die Nacht, 1929; Melodie des Herzens (Melody of the Heart), 1929; Va Banque, 1930; Der Grosse Sehnsucht, 1930; Das Alte Lied, 1930; Der Weisse Teufel (The White Devil), 1929; Boykott, 1930; Es Gibt eine Frau, die Dich niemals vergisst, 1930; The Woman from Monte Carlo (in U.S.A.), 1931; Der Fall des Generalstabsoberst Redl (The Case of Colonel Redl), 1931; Elisabeth von Österreich (Elisabeth of Austria), 1931; Der Kongress Tanzt (Congress Dances), 1931; Das Schicksal einer schönen Frau (Die Abenteuer/Adventures of a Beautiful Woman, 1938; Johannisnacht, 1933; Barberini, Der Tanzerin von Sanssouci (The King's Dancer), 1933; Der Storch Hat Uns Getraut (Married by the Stork), 1933; Ich heirate meine Frau, 1934; Einer Frau, die Weiss, was sie will, 1934; Der Flüchtling von Chicago (The Fugitive from Chicago), 1934; Der höhere Befehl, 1935; Der Vogelhändler, 1935; Lady Lindermeres Fächer (Lady Windermere's Fan), 1935; Schlussakkord (The Final Chord), 1936; Fridericus, 1936; August der Starke, 1936; Das Mädchen Irene, 1936; Streit von den Knaben Jo (Strife over the Boy Jo), 1937; Das Schönheitspfästerchen (The Beauty Spot), 1937; Die Kreutzersonate, 1937; Dreiklang, 1938 (Triad); Maja zwischen 2 Ehen, 1938; Rätsel um Beate, 1938; Unwege zum Glück, 1939; Friedrich Schiller, 1940; Bismarck, 1940; Wien 1910, 1942; Kleine Residenz, 1942; Musik in Salzburg, 1944; Die Söhne des Herrn Gaspary, 1948; Man Spielt nicht mit der Liebe, 1949; Das Geheimnis von Bergsee, 1950; Es Kommt ein Tag, 1950; Von Teufel gejagt, 1950; Rote Rosen, rote Lippen, rober Wein, 1953; Königliche Hoheit, 1953; Schloss Hubertus; Der Fischer von Heiligensee (The Big Barrier), 1955; Die Barrings, 1955; Ich weiss, wofür ich lebe, 1955; Rosen im Herbst, 1955; Meine 16 Söhne, 1955; Kronprinz Rudolfs letzte Liebe, 1956; Verwegene Musikanten, 1956; Unter Palmen am blauen Meer, 1957; Bekenntnisse des Hochstaplets Felix Krull, 1957; Die Buddenbrooks (television movie), 1959; Die seltsame Gräfin, 1961; Karl May, 1974; Der Fussgänger (The Pedestrian), 1974; Tales from the Vienna Woods, 1974; Murder on the Bridge, 1975. *Plays—* Der grosse Welttheatre (The Great Theater of the World), debut, Salzburg Festival, 1925; The Prisoner, Berlin, 1926; Amphitryon 38, (Leda), Berlin, 1931; Don Juan's Raincoat, Berlin, 1933; Eine etwas sonderbare Dame (title role); Schloss in Schweden (Agatha); Dabale und Liebe (Lady Milford); Wintermärchen (Hermione); Mad Woman of Chaillot, Munich; Gigi (Alicia), Munich; others. *Books:* Ich war die Dame, Erinnergung (memoirs), 1979.
Further reading: See filmography in *Ich war die Dame* (1979).

BARON PEARSON OF MINNEDOSA AND KENSINGTON
Judge and civil arbitrator
Born Minnedosa, Manitoba, Canada, July 28th, 1899
Died London, England, January 31st, 1980

Lord Pearson, Lord of Appeal in Ordinary from 1965 to 1974, was Britain's leading industrial arbitrator. His expert knowledge of the law, ability to analyze issues, and unfailing courtesy and impartiality earned him the trust of all parties in a series of difficult labor disputes and enabled him to guide opposing sides to mutually agreeable solutions.

The second son of an influential Canadian family, Colin Hargreaves Pearson was given an English education at St. Paul's School, London. After a brief interlude on active service in World War One, he studied at the University of Oxford as a Classical Scholar and demonstrated a brilliance which might have pointed him to an academic career. But Pearson chose the legal profession and in 1924 was called to the Bar by the Inner Temple, where his scholarship was rewarded with an Exhibition. He served pupillage in chambers under the direction of F.T. Barrington-Ward, K.C. Later he entered the chambers of Sir William Jowitt, K.C. (subsequently Lord Chancellor) and built up a common law practice.

Pearson was appointed Junior (Common Law) Counsel to the Ministry of Works in 1930 and Recorder of Hythe in 1937. During the Second World War he also undertook duties in the Treasury Solicitor's Department in London. He became a Judge of the High Court in 1951 and served on a number of judicial bodies, including the Supreme Court Rules Committee.

In 1958 Pearson was appointed chairman of a committee set up to investigate better management of funds held in trust by British courts of justice. His recommendations on this complex issue were accepted by Parliament and incorporated into the Administration of Justice Act of 1965. He served for one year as president of the Restrictive Practices Court until his promotion to Lord Justice of Appeal in 1961.

By this time, Pearson's ability to preside over arbitral bodies and to achieve universally accepted results had become widely recognized. In July 1963 he began a ten-year period as chairman of the Law Reform Committee, in which post he undertook an investigation of the law of evidence in civil and criminal cases. His skill in arbitration was first put to a real test in 1964, when the Labour Government appointed him to head a Court of Inquiry into a deadlocked dispute in the power industry which was disrupting electricity service throughout Britain. Pearson's report evaluated the competing claims of the local electricity boards and the five trade unions opposing them and cleared the way for successful negotiations.

In 1966, a year after he had been created Life Peer, Lord Pearson found himself at the center of an angry dispute between ship owners and the National Union of Seamen which threatened to cripple the commercial life of the nation. His suggestions for reform of working conditions were greeted with approval by both sides. A year later, when the British Airline Pilots Association walked out of pay negotiations conducted by the Joint Council for Civil Air Transport on behalf of the two national airlines, Lord Pearson steered all parties back to the negotiating tables by proposing new methods for grievance resolution. His talents were again called upon in the 1968 steel industry dispute, the 1970 Dock Strike, and the 1971 and 1972 conflicts over teachers' remuneration.

From 1973 to 1978 Lord Pearson chaired the Royal Commission on Civil Liability and Personal Injury. The nearly unanimous report of the commission, published in March 1978, proposed that manufacturers of defective products—in particular, of pharmaceutical products—be held liable for resultant physical damage. At the time of

Lord Pearson's death, the commission's findings were the subject of international discussion.

In a tribute to Lord Pearson, his colleague Lord Diplock wrote in the *Times* (London): "It can be said of him that not only has he made many friends but what is perhaps more difficult I do not think he ever made an enemy."   J.P./M.D.

Born Colin Hargreaves Pearson. Son of Ernest William P. and Jessie (Borland) P. Married Sophie Grace Thomas 1931. Children: One son, one daughter. Educ: St. Paul's Sch., London; Balliol Coll., Oxford (Classical Scholar, Jenkyns Exhibitioner), B.A. 1922. Mil. Service: British Army 1918. Called to Bar, Inner Temple 1924; Yarborough Anderson Exhibitioner 1925; Reader 1973; Treas. 1974. Jr. Common Law Counsel to Ministry of Works 1930–49; Recorder of Hythe, Kent 1937–51; Temporary Member, Treasury Solicitor's Dept. 1939–45; appointed King's Counsel 1949; Judge of High Court, Queen's Bench Div. 1951–61; Judge 1957–61 and Pres. 1960–61, Restrictive Practices Court; Lord Justice of Appeal 1961–65; Lord of Appeal in Ordinary 1965–74. Member: Legal Cttee. on Medical Partnerships 1948; Supreme Court Rule Cttee. 1957–65; Exec. Council of the Inns of Court 1962–65; Senate of Inns of Court 1966–69. Chmn., Cttee. on Funds in Court 1958; Law Reform Cttee. 1963–73; Royal Commn. on Civil Liability and Compensation for Personal Injury 1973–78. Chmn., Courts of Inquiry: Electricity Supply Industry dispute 1964; Shipping Industry dispute 1966–67; Civil Air Transport Industry dispute 1967–68; Steel Industry dispute 1968; Dock Strike 1970. Chmn., Arbitral Body on Teachers' Remuneration 1971 and 1972. Member 1925–80 and Pres. 1960–63, Old Pauline Club; Pres., Inc. Assn. of Prepatory Schs. 1965–70; Visitor, Balliol Coll., Oxford 1965–74; Chmn., St. Paul's Sch. Bldg. Appeal 1966–80. With Bedford Coll., Univ. London: Council Member 1958–66; Vice Chmn. 1959–62; Chmn. 1962–63. Hons: C.B.E. 1946; knighted (K.B.E.) 1951; P.C. 1961; Life Peer 1965.

ROMOLO VALLI
Actor and producer
Born Reggio nell'Emilia, Italy, February 7th, 1925
Died Rome, Italy, February 1st, 1980

Romolo Valli was one of the best-known actors of the Italian stage and screen and a skilled impresario, producer, and manager. With Giorgio De Lullo, he co-founded the Compagnia dei Giovani, a repertory group widely considered the most vital development in postwar Italian theater.

Valli was born in Reggio nell'Emilia to a family of professionals (his father and brother were engineers; another brother was a physician). From 1945 to 1949 he studied law at the University of Parma. After earning his degree, he worked as a critic and journalist for local newspapers, but his growing love for the theater overshadowed any desire for a career as either lawyer or journalist. In 1949 he joined the Carrozzona theatre in Bolzano, a repertory company directed by Fantasio Piccoli, where he became familiar with all phases of production and made his acting debut. He was still writing articles and verses for local newspapers, but the theater soon took over his life, and for the next 30 years Valli never missed a season. He remained with Piccoli's group for three years, then worked for two years at the Piccolo Teatro in Milan with director Giorgio Strehler, touring South America and performing in works by Giovaninetti, Pirandello, and T.S. Eliot.

In 1954 Valli and Giorgio De Lullo, an actor and director, founded the Compagnia dei Giovani (The Young Players), sponsored by Alberto Cappelli. In its 16-year existence, the company became the most innovative, exciting repertory group in Rome, winning international praise. Valli and De Lullo were initially joined by actresses Rosella Falk and Anna Maria Guarnieri; in later seasons the roster included Tino Buazelli, Elsa Albani, Marcello Mastroianni, Paolo Stoppo, and Rina Morelli. Their repertory productions, including works by de Musset, Betti, Farquhar, Fabbri [q.v.], D'Annunzio, Biagi, Goldini, Henry James, and Shakespeare, were mounted without stinting on expense and were acted with consummate ability; the Compagnia dei Giovani never knew a fiasco and grossed some of the highest box-office receipts in contemporary Italian theater. Their greatest success was a production of Goodrich and Hackett's *The Diary of Anne Frank*, in which Valli won acclaim for his portrayal of Anne's father. The company toured in South America and played at the Festival Internazionali in Venice and Paris. Rising costs and high taxes imposed on theatrical productions by the government caused the dissolution of the company in 1971.

Valli also appeared in films and television programs, although these were always subordinate to his stage interests. He worked with Europe's top directors, including Joseph Losey, Bernardo Bertolucci, and Roman Polanski. Most recently he appeared in Costa-Gavras's *Claire de Femme,* portraying an aging vaudevillean. His film roles included the family priest in Luchino Visconti's *The Leopard (Il gattopardo),* the hotel manager in Visconti's *Death in Venice,* and the middle-class Jewish patriarch in Vittorio De Sica's *The Garden of the Finzi-Continis.*

In addition to his work as an actor, Valli was considered one of Italy's most versatile producers. In 1972 composer Giancarlo Menotti asked him to come to Spoleto to be artistic director of the Festival of Two Worlds. At the time, the Festival was almost completely financed by the United States. Valli, an able administrator and formidable fundraiser, eventually persuaded the Italian government to under-write the lion's share of the Festival's ever-increasing budget. Valli also revitalized the lagging theatrical side of the Festival, choosing a play rather than an opera to open the 1974 season. Valli himself starred that year in a much-praised performance of Molière's *Le Malade Imaginaire.*

Valli continued to administer the Festival until 1979, when he and his old friend Giorgio De Lullo assumed the joint directorship of the Teatro Eliseo and the Piccolo Eliseo in Rome. The partners had two brilliant seasons, producing works by Pirandello, Andreev, Giacosa, Kemp, Shakespeare, Goldini, and Molière. At the time of his death, Valli was starring in a production of *Prima del silenzio* by the Neopolitan playwright Guiseppe Patroni Griffi, directed by De Lullo. He was also appearing in an Italian version of a one-man show by John Gay based on the life and works of Oscar Wilde.

Valli was killed in an automobile accident on the Via Appia Antica in Rome while driving home in the early morning hours after a performance. His funeral mass, held in the Basilica dei Santi Apostoli in Rome, was celebrated by a friend, Cardinal Pignedoli, [q.v.] Valli was buried in his hometown of Reggio nel'Emilia.   J.P./S.P.

Unmarried. Roman Catholic. Educ: Università di Parma, law degree 1949. Actor and stagehand, Carrozzone di Bolzano theater company 1949–52; actor, Piccolo Teatro di Milano 1952–54; co-founder and actor, Compagnia dei Giovani, Rome 1954–71; Artistic Dir., Festival of Two Worlds, Spoleto, Italy 1971–79; Artistic Dir. (with Giorgio De Lullo), Teatro Eliseo and Piccolo Eliseo, Rome 1979–80. Hons: San Genesio (for The Diary of Anne Frank); Nastro d'Argento (for Una storia milanese); Grolla d'Oro (for Il gattopardo). *Performances: Plays*—Many appearances, including leading roles in the Greek and Roman classics and in works by Anouilh, Betti, Biagi, Chekhov, D'Annunzio, de Musset, T.S. Eliot, Fabbri, Farquhar, Giovaninetti, Gogol, Goldini, Henry James, Molière, Moravia, Pirandello, Praga, Sartre, and Shakespeare. Films—Jovanka e le altre; La ragazza con la valigia; Una storia milanese; Il gattopardo; Io la conoscevo bene; Barbarella; La grande guerra; Vento del sud; I piaceri del sabato notte; Il carro armato dell' 8 settembre; La viaccia; Un giorno da leoni; Boccaccio '70 (episode: Il lavoro); Peccati d'estate; Confetti al pepe; I fuorileggi del matrimonio; La vendetta della signora; I complessi; Come imparai ad amare le donne; La mandragola; Non stuzzicate la zanzara; Il marito e mio e l'ammazzo quando mi pare; La scoliera dei desideri; Il giardino dei Finzi-Contini; Death in Venice; Un borghese piccolo; Bobby Deerfield; 1900; Claire de Femme.

JOSEPH FONTANET
French Cabinet Minister and politician
Born Frontenex, Savoie, France, February 9th, 1921
Died Paris, France, February 2nd, 1980

Joseph Fontanet, who was murdered by gunshot in a Paris street, rose to political eminence in postwar France and held Cabinet offices on a number of occasions in the 1960s and 1970s.

He was the son of a Savoie industrialist and although brought up in the bourgeois tradition was regarded in his later years as a politician who never lost touch with any sections of his electorate. He read law at Lyons and Paris, but his progress towards a career in that subject was halted by World War Two. When France was invaded, Fontanet joined the Resistance in Spain and later served with the French forces in North Africa, Provence, Alsace, and Germany. His personal heroism earned him the Croix de Guerre and brought him to the notice of Charles de Gaulle. In 1945 he helped found the Mouvement Républicain Populaire (MRP) a Gaullist party formed from liberal Catholic movements.

After serving as director of the staff of the Secretary of State for Public Health and Population, Fontanet became Assistant Secretary-General of the MRP and a member of the Assembly of the French Union. He was elected Deputy from Savoie in 1956, but surrendered his seat two years later to take up the post of Secretary of State for Industry and Commerce in the cabinet of Michel Jean-Pierre Debre. In 1959 he was given additional duties as Secretary of State for Domestic Trade, winning a reputation for his efforts to halt inflation, and was appointed Minister of Public Health and Population in 1961. He quit the government of Georges Pompidou in 1962, along with four other MRP ministers, to protest de Gaulle's stand on European unity.

Between 1962 and 1969 Fontanet served as Secretary-General of the MRP and took up his old seat as Deputy from Savoie, joining the Progress and Modern Democracy party in 1968 and founding the Democracy and Progress group in 1969. He also served as General Councillor of Savoie and as mayor of the town of Saint-Martin-de-Belleville. He was named Minister of Labor, Employment, and Population by Jacques Chaban-Delmas in 1969 and Minister of National Education by Pierre Messmer in 1972 and 1973.

On the death of Georges Pompidou in 1974, Fontanet supported Chaban-Delmas for the presidency against the victorious Valéry Giscard d'Estaing. He lost an attempt to win a Parliamentary seat and retired from active politics.

In 1977, Fontanet founded a daily newspaper, *J'informe*, which lasted three months. The following year he turned to business administration, joining the Société d'études et de réalisations pour les équipements collectifs, part of the Crédit Mutuel, which supplied equipment for local government work.

His death by assassination left police with no clue as to the identity of the murderer and no apparent motive for the killing. Investigations indicated that Fontanet had lived a quiet, almost austere life unconnected with business dealings or extremist politics of the kind that would have made him a target for a killer.

He was shot outside his Paris home in the fashionable 16th *arrondissement* after returning late at night from giving a lecture, and he was found beside his vehicle by the sister and brother-in-law of

President Giscard d'Estaing, who were returning to their home nearby. Fontanet underwent major surgery to remove a bullet in his lung, 36 hours after the shooting. The only information he gave to police was that he had been shot by a car driver. Police discounted the attempts of six extremist political groups to claim responsibility; at this writing, they were investigating the possibility that the murder was a case of mistaken identity or the result of a dispute over a parking space.   J.P./M.D.

Son of Joseph F., industrialist, and Marthe (Blanchard) F. Married Hélène Pouliquen 1947. Children: Xavier; Chantal; Anne; Isabelle; Arnaud. Educ: Institution des Chartreux à Lyon; Faculté de Droit de Lyon; Faculté de Droit de Paris; D. en D., Diplômé de l'École des hautes études commerciales. Mil. Service: French Resistance 1940–43; French forces in N. Africa and Europe 1943–45. With Mouvement Républicain Populaire: Founding Member 1945; Asst. Secty.-Gen. 1951–56; Member, Assembly of the French union (as head of M.R.P.) 1952–55; Secty.-Gen. 1963–68. Dir. of Staff, Secty. of State for Industry and Commerce and Secty. of State for Domestic Trade, Debré cabinet 1959–61; Minister of Public Health and Population, Debré cabinet 1961–62, Pompidou cabinet 1962; Minister of Labor, Employment, and Population, Chaban-Delmas cabinet 1969–72; Minister of Natl. Educ., Messmer cabinets 1972–74. Deputy from Savoie 1956–58, 1962–69, 1973; Member, Natl. Assembly Cttee. on Culture, Family, and Social Affairs; joined Progress and Modern Democracy party in Natl. Assembly 1968; Founder and first V.P., Democracy and Progress movement 1969. Councillor, Canton of Moutiers-Tarentaise 1951–76; V.P. 1961–64 and Pres. 1964–76, Gen. Council of Savoie; V.P. of Admin. Council for Vanoise Natl. Park 1964–70; elected Municipal Councillor, Saint-Martin-de-Belleville 1965; elected Mayor, Saint-Martin-de-Belleville 1965 and 1971. Ed., J'informe 1977; Dir. of Devel., SEREC (Société d'études et de réalisations pour les équipements collectifs) 1978–80. Hons: Croix de guerre 1939–45; Chevalier, Légion d'honneur; Médaille des évadés. *Author:* Le Social et le Vivant, 1977.

WILLIAM (HOWARD) STEIN
Biochemist and Nobel prizewinner
Born New York City, U.S.A., June 25th, 1911
Died New York City, U.S.A., February 2nd, 1980

Dr. William H. Stein devoted a lifetime of research to the understanding of the structure and biological activities of proteins and to the development of quantitative chromatographic procedures for the separation of amino acids, the basic subunits of proteins.

Stein was born in New York City in 1911, the second of three children. His father was a businessman who retired early to devote himself full-time to social concerns, in particular to matters of community health; his mother was active in improving the lot of underprivileged children in New York City. Stein attributed his decision to pursue a career in medicine or science to the strong encouragement of his father.

He began his scientific career as a chemistry major at Harvard, graduating with a B.S. degree in 1933. After a year of graduate study at Harvard, he came to the Department of Biochemestry at Columbia University's College of Physicians and Surgeons, where he wrote his Ph.D. thesis on the composition of the protein elastin. Similar research was under way at the Rockefeller Institute for Medical Research, now Rockefeller University, where a research team under the direction of Dr. Max Bergmann, a noted German biochemist, was engaged in determining the exact arrangement of the constituents of proteins. Bergmann had made a considerable reputation for himself, both for the brilliance of his research and for his ability to attract the most talented scientists to his laboratory. In 1938, Stein became one of Bergmann's promising recruits. Stanford Moore joined the laboratory a year later, beginning a professional collaboration and friendship with Stein that lasted 40 years.

Their research was interrupted in the early 1940s when the Bergmann team turned to investigations of the chemical properties of mustard gases as their contribution to the war effort. Following Bergmann's death in 1944, Stein and Moore took over the laboratory's research and work continued on the analysis of the precise composition of proteins. It was known that protein molecules contained different kinds and amounts of amino acids in various orders of arrangement. Chromatographic methods of separating a particular protein into its constituent parts had been developed, but the testing process was laborious and slow. Stein and Moore spent many years collaborating on the development of procedures and special equipment which greatly improved the accuracy and speed of protein analysis. The automatic fraction collector and the automatic amino acid analyzer which they designed for this purpose are now marketed commercially and used in laboratories all over the world.

Beginning in the early 1950s, Stein and Moore set out to decipher the structure of the enzyme ribonuclease. At that time, the chemical structures of only a few proteins were known, and none of these were enzymes (proteins which act as catalysts in triggering or speeding up biological processes). By 1959, their improved technique of separation and analysis enabled Stein and Moore to determine the full sequence of the 124 amino acids which make up ribonuclease. This breakthrough laid the groundwork for the unraveling of the structures of other protein molecules by other researchers in the years that followed, and to the first synthesis of a naturally occurring enzyme in 1969. Knowledge of protein structure is fundamental to a complete understanding of the complex chemistry of living matter, and to advances in the prevention and treatment of certain diseases.

In 1972, Stein and Moore were awarded the Nobel Prize in Chemistry for their pioneering studies on the molecular structure and catalytic activity of pancreatic ribonuclease. They shared the honor with Dr. Christian Anfinsen, who had determined the physical conformation of the components of ribonuclease.

During the 1950s and 1960s Stein lectured widely and was a visiting professor at the University of Chicago and at Harvard University. His talents as a skillful communicator of scientific knowledge led to his appointment as Editor-in-Chief of the Journal of Biological Chemistry in 1968. The scope of his activities was restricted somewhat by the severe case of Guillain-Barré syndrome he contracted the following year, which left him almost totally paralyzed and confined to a wheelchair for the last ten years of his life. His intellectual acuity and enthusiasm continued undiminished, however, and he consulted with Moore on the course of their research until his death.

Within the scientific community, Stein was known not only for his accomplishments as a researcher, teacher, and writer, but also for a generosity of spirit which gave abundant recognition to his peers and consistent encouragement to his younger colleagues.   J.P./B.S.

Son of Fred M. S. and Beatrice (Borg) S. Married Phoebe L. Hockstader 1936. Children: William H.; David F.; Robert J. Jewish. Educ: Lincoln Sch. of Columbia Univ. Teachers Coll.; grad. Phillips Exeter Acad., N.H. 1929; Harvard Univ., B.S. 1933; graduate study, Harvard 1933–34; Coll. of Physicians and Surgeons, Columbia Univ., Ph.D. biochem. 1938. With Rockefeller Univ. (formerly Rockefeller Inst. for Medical Research), NYC: Asst., Chemistry 1938–42; Assoc. 1942–49; Assoc. Member 1949–52; Prof. of Biochem. and Member 1952–80. Visiting Prof., Univ. Chicago 1960; Phillips Lectr., Haverford Coll., Pa. 1962; Visiting Prof., Harvard Univ. 1964; Philip Shaffer Lectr., Washington Univ., St. Louis 1965. With American Soc. of Biol. Chem.: Chmn., Ed. Cttee. 1958–61; Assoc. Ed. 1964–68 and Ed.-in-Chief 1968–71, Jrnl. of Biol. Chem. Scientific Counselor, Inst. of Neurological Disease and Blindness, Natl. Inst. of Health 1961–66; Chmn., U.S. Natl. Cttee., Intnl. Union Biochem. 1965–68; Chmn., U.S. Natl. Cttee. for Biochem. 1968–69. Trustee, Montefiore Hosp., NYC 1948–74; Member, Medical Advisory Bd., Hebrew Univ.-Hadassah Medical Sch., Jerusalem 1957–70; Consultant, Quartermaster Corps, U.S. Army. Member: American Chem. Soc.; American Assn. for Adavancement of Science; Biochem. Soc., London; N.Y. Acad. Science; American Acad. Arts and Sciences; Harvey Soc., NYC. Hons: Fellow, American Swiss Foundn. 1956; elected to Natl. Acad. of Sciences 1960; (with Dr. Stanford Moore) Award in Chromatography and Electrophoresis, American Chem. Soc. 1964; (jointly) Theodore William Richards Medal, Northeast Section, American Chem. Soc. 1972; (jointly) Kaj-Linderstrøm-Lang Gold Medal and Prize, Copenhagen 1972; (with Dr. Christian Anfinsen and Dr. Stanford Moore) Nobel Prize in Chem. 1972; Award of Excellence Medal, Columbia Univ. Grad. Faculty and Alumni Assn. 1973; D.Sc., Columbia Univ. and Albert Einstein Coll. of Medicine, Yeshiva Univ. 1973; Fellow, American Acad. Arts and Sciences. *Major articles* (with Dr. Stanford Moore): "Chromatography," Scientific American, June 1951; "The Chemical Structure of Proteins," Scientific American, Feb. 1961; "Chemical Structures of Pancreatic Ribonuclease and Deoxyribonuclease," Science, May 4, 1973; articles in many other professional jrnls.

CAMARA LAYE
Novelist
Born Kouroussa, French Guinea (now Guinea), January 1st, 1928
Died Dakar, Senegal, February 4th, 1980

With his three published novels, Camara Laye established himself as one of the pre-eminent writers of the French-speaking *négritude* movement in African literature. Born in French Guinea (now Guinea) and educated in France, Laye wrote from a vision of the "timeless quality" of traditional African life, a vision made the more acute by his own painful sense of estrangement from that life. "It seems to me," he once said, "that that which distinguishes the much older Africa from Europe is the omnipresence of mystery. My ambition is to reveal mysticism in my memories. *Mystère* is inherent in our human condition."

Laye was born to Moslem parents of the Malinké tribe in the city of Kouroussa, where the influence of the ancient West African empires was deeply felt. His father and grandfather, who bore the family name of Kamara, were goldsmiths, his mother a goldsmith's daughter; their craft, traditionally associated with mystical and creative powers, was practiced in a household where animist beliefs still held sway, despite the encroachments of Western values. Laye attended local Islamic schools, then studied mechanics at a technical high school in the capital city of Conakry, where he graduated at the top of his class. A government engineering scholarship brought him to the Centre École Automobile near Paris, where he earned a Professional Certificate. He wished to pursue a baccalaureate degree, but the government cut off his funds; so Laye enrolled in evening courses in engineering at the Technical College for Aeronautics and Automobile Construction while earning a modest living as a mechanic at an automobile factory. During these unhappy years, Laye began to write down his memories of childhood as a defense against loneliness and homesickness. A friend encouraged him to show his work to a publisher, who brought out his autobiographical novel *L'enfant noir* in 1953. (It was published as *The Dark Child* in the US in 1954 and in England in 1955; a later edition was called *The African Child.*)

L'enfant noir evokes the traditional life of Laye's native village, where people live in a symbiotic harmony with nature under the guidance of the spirit world. Despite his attachment to this way of life, so vividly and lovingly rendered, the young protagonist is inevitably alienated from it by his Western education. The novel, for which he won the Prix Charles Veillon in 1954, was applauded by French critics as a major prose work of the *négritude* movement; detractors in the black African press, however, criticized it as a self-centered, idealistic work that pandered to the delusions of sophisticated French society.

The financial success of *L'enfant noir* enabled Laye to complete his second novel, *Le Regard du roi,* that same year. (An English edition, *The Radiance of the King,* was brought out in 1956.) This work, a symbolic allegory in a style influenced by Kafka, describes the humiliation and redemption of a bankrupt white gambler named Clarence as he wanders through the Sudan, stripped of his proud European identity by a self-sufficient black society that neither needs nor wants him. Broken by poverty and reduced to sexual slavery, Clarence abandons his body and soul to the mystical embrace of an African king, the embodiment of a black spiritual power unknown to the West. The book reinforced Laye's position as an outstanding figure in contemporary African literature.

In 1956, after a period as Attaché at the Ministry of Youth in Paris, Laye returned to Guinea to work as an engineer. After Guinea became an independent nation in 1958, Laye served on diplomatic missions to several African countries, including Liberia and Ghana, before his appointment as Director of the Centre de Recherches et d'Études in Conakry. But Laye, who had expected a restoration of traditional African culture in independent, black-ruled Guinea, was bitterly disappointed by the oppressive regime of President Sékou Touré. By 1960, his criticisms had earned him an unofficial sentence of house arrest. He was not permitted to go to the US in 1964 to receive emergency medical treatment for food poisoning.

During these years, Laye was sporadically engaged in writing a third novel, tentatively entitled *Return to One's Native Country*. After reading the manuscript, Touré told Laye to alter the text or accept exile from Guinea. Laye, his wife Marie, and their four children left the country in 1965; *Dramouss* (in English, *A Dream of Africa*) was published soon after. In this nightmarish story, Fatoman, the auto-biographical narrator, returns home after six years in Paris in time to witness the takeover of Guinea by a ruthless totalitarian government led by the savage Big Brute, who starves and persecutes his subjects. Fatoman comes to believe that the country can be rescued only by a coup and a return to traditional African values, including faith in the supernatural, whose powers are violently at work in Fatoman's own life.

After a stay in the Ivory Coast, the exiled Laye and his family were welcomed to Senegal by President Léopold Sédar Senghor, himself a French-language writer and one of the pioneer exponents of the *négritude* movement. Senghor arranged a post for Laye as a collector of Malinké folklore at the University of Dakar. *Le Maître de la Parole (The Master of the Word),* Laye's scholarly study of African oral historians, was published in 1978. However, the years of exile were hard on Laye, who suffered periods of mental instability. He refused to publish his work-in-progress, a continuation of *Dramouss* entitled *L'Exiles,* lest it disrupt relations between Senghor and Touré. His fears of Touré's continuing malice were painfully justified. In 1970 his wife returned to Guinea to visit her ailing mother and was seized and imprisoned as an enemy of the state.

Laye died in exile on February 4th, 1980. The announcement of his death was broadcast over Radio Senegal by President Senghor.   J.P.

Son of Kamara Komady, goldsmith, and Daman Sadan. Married Marie. Four children. Moslem. Educ: Collège Poiret (now Lycée Technique), Conakry, Guinea; Centre École Automobile, Argenteuil, France, Certificat d'aptitude professionelle de l'automobile; École Ampère, Paris; Conservatoire Nationale des Arts et Métiers, Paris; École Technique d'Aeronautique et de Construction Automobile, Paris, diploma 1956. Worked at Les Halles market and various part-time jobs; mechanic, Simca automobile factory, Paris c.1953; Attaché, Ministry of Youth, Paris 1955; Engineer, Guinea 1956–58; served in diplomatic posts to African nations 1958; Dir., Centre de Recherches et d'Études, Ministry of Information, Conakry 1958–60; Research Fellow in Islamic Studies, Institut Fondamental de l'Afrique Noire, Univ. Dakar, Senegal. Hons: Prix Charles Veillon 1954 (for L'enfant noir). *Author: Novels*—L'enfant noir, 1953 (trans. by James Kirkup, et.al. and published as The Dark Child, 1954, as The African Child, 1959); Le Regard du roi, 1954 (trans. by Kirkup as The Radiance of the King, 1956); Dramouss, 1966 (trans. by Kirkup as A Dream of Africa, 1968); L'Exiles, unpublished. *Story*—The Eyes of the Statue (trans. of French title) in Présence Africaine, No. 5, 1959. *Other*—Le Maître de la Parôle (scholarly study of African oral history traditions), 1978. *Major articles*—"The Black Man and Art" in African Arts, Autumn 1970. Contributed stories and articles to several African jrnls., including African Arts, Black Orpheus, and Paris-Dakar.

Further reading: Seven African Authors by Gerald Moore (ed.), 1962; "Alienation in the Novels of Camara Laye" by E. Selling, Pan-African Journal 4, 1971; An Introduction to the African Novel by Eustace Palmer, 1972.

BARONESS SUMMERSKILL OF KEN WOOD
British politician, Cabinet Minister, physician and womens' rights activist
Born London, England, April 19th, 1901
Died Highgate, London, England, February 4th, 1980

In her 23 years as a member of the House of Commons, Dr. Edith Summerskill was a forceful champion of health-care reform and women's rights. A tall, handsome woman who claimed Viking ancestry, she was known for her outspokenness, her candor, and her refusal to compromise.

She was born in 1901, the daughter of a physician who treated the poor of southeast London. By the age of 23, Summerskill was herself a licentiate of the Royal College of Physicians, specializing in gynecology. Together with her Welsh husband, Dr. E. Jeffrey Samuel, who had been a fellow student at Charing Cross Hospital, she began to practice in London's slum sections, where malnutrition and lack of hygiene were primary causes of disease.

Like her father, Dr. Summerskill believed that the national government has a responsibility to combat disease by eradicating the economic and social conditions that give rise to it. Dissatisfied with the progress made in this direction by the Socialist Medical Association, of which she was a vice president, she decided to enter politics as a member of the Labour Party, winning election to the Middlesex County Council in 1934.

In 1938, after twice standing for Parliament unsuccessfully, Dr. Summerskill won the seat for the London district of West Fulham, whose working-class women appreciated her efforts on behalf of maternity and child health care and her criticism of Prime Minister Neville Chamberlain's conciliatory policies towards Adolf Hitler. Her victory over the Conservative candidate was widely viewed as a signal of public distaste for Chamberlain's government. Dr. Summerskill then broke precedent by taking her seat in her maiden name. She continued to practice medicine until 1945 and to bring up her two young children while working vigorously for such principles as the right of wives to know their husbands' incomes.

With the outbreak of World War Two, Dr. Summerskill became a spokesman in Parliament for the contributions of women to the nation's war effort, including their employment and compensation on the home front and their conditions in the armed services. When the Minister of Health vacillated on the issue of effective regulations to control the wartime spread of venereal disease, she called him a "Victorian spinster reared in a country parsonage and sheltered from the facts of life." Most controversial was her demand that the newly founded Home Guard admit women to its ranks. To prove that women can fight, she set up the Women's Home Defence group, which trained hundreds of women in sniping techniques, street combat, homemade anti-tank weaponry, and other procedures for repelling an invading army. Dr. Summerskill herself shot seven bull's-eyes out of ten on the House of Commons rifle range. The Home Guard, acceding to her logic and to the shortage of civilian men, began to accept women in April 1943.

For five years following the end of the war, Dr. Summerskill served as Parliamentary Secretary to the Ministry of Food, helping to administer unpopular rationing programs for food and other commodities. During this period she had the satisfaction of witnessing the establishment of the National Health Service, for which she had long fought, and the passage of her bill requiring all milk sold for human consumption to be free from tuberculosis bacilli and other contaminants. In 1950, with her appointment as Minister of National Insurance, Dr. Summerskill became the first married woman to serve in a Cabinet. In this post she pioneered legislation on compensation for industrial injury and disease. After the fall of the Labour government in 1951, she became spokesman for health issues in the Opposition's Shadow Cabinet, campaigning vigorously for such reforms as equal pay for women workers, wages for homemakers, birth control, and the availability of anesthesia to all women in childbirth. On several occasions she introduced legislation to prohibit boxing, producing a human skull during one debate to illustrate the brain damage incurred by blows to the head.

Dr. Summerskill lost her West Fulham constituency in 1955 when the Parliamentary boundary lines were redrawn, but was immediately returned to Parliament for the constituency of Warrington in Cheshire. From 1954 to 1955 she was chairman of the Labour Party's National Executive Committee and national chairman of the Party.

In 1961, on the recommendation of Labour Party leader Hugh Gaitskell, who sought to strengthen Labour representation in the House of Lords, Dr. Summerskill was elevated to the peerage as Baroness Summerskill of Ken Wood and became the sixth woman to sit in the upper chamber. Breaking tradition yet again, she devoted her maiden speech to a controversial issue, attacking the Conservative government for its attempts to raise National Health Service charges and the American drug companies for their exploitation of the Service. Her ongoing battle to gain financial and legal security for women scored a victory in 1964 with the enactment of the Married Women's Property Act, and another in 1967 with the Matrimonial Homes Act, both of which entitled wives to a larger share of the jointly owned or occupied property of their marriages.

Lady Summerskill was the author of a number of books, including *Babies Without Tears* (a guide to childbearing and childrearing), *The Ignoble Art* (an attack on boxing), and *Letters To My Daughter,*

written to Shirley Summerskill, who, like her mother, is a physician
and member of Parliament.   J.P./M.D.

Born Edith (Clara) Summerskill. Daughter of William S., physician,
and Edith S. Married Dr. E. Jeffrey Samuel, physician, 1925.
Children: Michael Summerskill, barrister; Dr. the Hon. Shirley
Catherine Wynne Summerskill, Labour M.P. for Halifax and physi-
cian (b.1931). Educ: St. Paul's Girls' Sch., London; King's Coll.,
Univ. London; Charing Cross Hosp., London, M.D. 1924; Member,
Royal Coll. Surgeons, and Licentiate, Royal Coll. Physicians 1924.
Private medical practice, London 1924–45. With British Labour Party
1923–80: Member, Delegations to U.S.S.R. 1931, Spain 1937, U.S.A.
1938, People's Republic of China 1954; Member 1944–58 and Chmn.
1954–55, Natl. Exec. Cttee.; Natl. Chmn. 1954–55. Member: Wood
Green Urban District Council 1931–36; Wood Green Maternity and
Child Welfare Cttee. 1931–34. Member, Middx. County Council,
Green Lanes Div. of Tottenham 1934–41. Parliamentary candidate for
by-election, Putney, London 1934, and for gen. election, Bury, Lancs.
1935. As Member of Parliament (Labour) for W. Fulham, London
1938–55, and for Warrington, Cheshire 1955–61: Member, Women's
Consultative Cttee. to Ministry of Labour on Wartime Employment
of Women 1939; Member, Parliamentary Select Cttees. on Women's
Services 1942, and on Civilian War Injuries Compensation 1944;
Member, British Parliamentary Delegations, U.S., Australia, N.Z.,
Ceylon, Egypt, India 1944; Parliamentary Secty., Ministry of Food
1945–50; leader, Parliamentary delegation, U.N. Food and Agricul-
ture Org. Conference, Washington, D.C. 1946; Minister of Natl.
Insurance 1950–51; Member, Labour Parliamentary Cttee. (Shadow
Cabinet) 1951–57, 1958–61; Parliamentary Rep., Consultative Assem-
bly of Council of Europe, Strasbourg 1953. As Member, House of
Lords 1961–80: Member, Political Hons. Scrutiny Cttee. 1967–76.
Also Member, Parliamentary and Labour Party delegations to Palestine and Middle East. Founder, Women's Home Defence Movement 1939 (disbanded 1943). Pres., Married Women's Assn.; V.P.,
Socialist Medical Assn. Hons: P.C. 1949; created Life Peer 1961; C.H.
1966; LL.D., Univ. Newfoundland 1968. *Author:* Women, Fall In; a
Guide to Women's Work in Wartime (pamphlet), 1941; Babies
Without Tears, 1941; The Ignoble Art, 1956; Letters To My Daughter, 1958; A Woman's World, 1967. Also author of many mag.
articles, pamphlets, and reports.

HUGH WATT
Acting Prime Minister of New Zealand and Labour Party leader
Born Perth, Western Australia, March 19th, 1912
Died Wellington, New Zealand, February 4th, 1980

Hugh Watt, New Zealand's Acting Prime Minister for two months
during 1974, was closely associated with his country's Labour movement for more than thirty years.
    Born in Australia, Watt was brought to Auckland, New Zealand,

by his parents when he was two years old, and was educated in the colonial tradition, which attached a greater importance to acquired skills than to academic qualification. Following his graduation from technical college in 1929, Watt entered the engineering profession as an apprentice. An active member of the Engineer's Union, he opened his own sheetmetal and engineering business in 1947 and joined the Labour Party.

Six years later, in a parliamentary by-election, Watt won the Onehunga seat for Labour, a seat he held until 1975. After serving as chairman of the National Roads Board and the National Water and Soils Conservation Authority, he was appointed Minister of Works and Electricity from 1957 to 1960. Soon after, he became deputy leader of his party.

A close associate of Labour Party leader Norman Kirk from 1952, Watt earned a reputation as a politician who preferred action to diplomacy. In the early 1960s he became heavily involved in a prolonged political argument over proposals to raise the levels of Lake Manapouri and Lake Te Anau for the production of electricity. The New Zealand Scenery Preservation Society alleged that such a scheme would destroy the lakes' beaches, but Watt insisted there were no "beaches." Rather, he told critics, the "beaches" were marks left by the rise and fall in water levels. The proposals were eventually adopted.

In 1972, Watt became Deputy Prime Minister, serving on numerous parliamentary committees (including Foreign Affairs and Industry and Commerce) and as Convenor of the Works Development and Electrical Caucus Committees. When Norman Kirk, then Prime Minister, died in August 1974, Watt stepped in as Acting Prime Minister, but was succeeded a month later by Wallace Rowling, Minister of Finance.

In 1975, Watt was appointed New Zealand High Commissioner in the United Kingdom and Ambassador to Ireland, but was recalled in December when the Labour Party lost power. Upon his return to New Zealand he was appointed to the Accident Compensation Commission, a post which he held until his retirement in 1979.   J.P./M.D.

Married: (1) 1935; (2) Irene Frances Ray 1968. Children: two sons, two daughters. Emigrated to New Zealand 1914. Educ: Remuera Primary Sch.; Seddon Memorial Tech. Coll. 1929. Engineering apprentice; active in Engineer's Union from 1940s; founded Watt and Co. Ltd., sheetmetal and engineering business, Auckland 1947. With New Zealand Labour Party: joined 1947; Member, Exec. Cttee; Deputy Leader 1962–74. Member of Parliament for Onehunga 1953–75; Chmn., Natl. Roads Bd. and Natl. Water and Soils Conservation Authority, mid-1950s; Minister of Works and Minister of Electricity 1957–60; Deputy Prime Minister and Minister of Labour 1972–74, concurrently Member of several Parliamentary Cttees., including Industry and Commerce and Foreign Affairs, and Convenor of Works Devel. and Electrical Caucus Cttees; Acting Prime Minister Aug.-Sept. 1974. High Commnr. for New Zealand in the U.K. and Ambassador to Eire 1975–76; Commnr., New Zealand Accident Compensation Commn. 1976–79. Member, Auckland Harbour Bd. Hons: appointed Privy Councillor (P.C.) 1974.

RENÉ JOURNIAC
French diplomat
Born Saint-Martin-Vésubie, France, May 11th, 1921
Died Cameroon, February 6th, 1980

René Journiac was French President Valéry Giscard d'Estaing's principle advisor for African affairs and played a leading role in French policy in Africa during the 1960s and 1970s.

Journiac was born in 1921 in the southern Alps. He studied law and political economy at the University of Aix-en-Provence and government at l'École nationale de la France d'outre-mer.

In 1947 he began his diplomatic career as a legal advisor in Cameroon and thereafter held a series of posts in French West Africa, returning to France in 1955 to work in the French Ministry of Overseas Territories. In 1960 Journiac became head of the French Secretariat to the French-speaking African community, a post which enabled him to establish personal contact with the leaders of the newly independent former French colonies. From 1962 to 1966 he served as political advisor on African affairs to Prime Minister Georges Pompidou and in 1966 was named deputy to Jacques Foccart, Secretary General of African Affairs.

President Giscard d'Estaing abolished the General Secretariat of African Affairs in 1974 and appointed Journiac to replace Foccart. While Journiac was given the title of technical advisor for African affairs, no one doubted his power, authority, and access to the French President.

As the French government's principle specialist, Journiac designed a policy aimed at maintaining political stability, encouraging economic growth, and checking Communist penetration in the former French colonies. Journiac was also involved in all the principle French negotiations in Africa of the period, in 1975 arranging the release of Françoise Claustre, the French ethnologist held hostage by the Tubu rebels in Chad. Shortly thereafter, he obtained the release of French citizens held captive by Mauritanian guerrillas. In 1977 he was involved in the logistical support provided by France for Zairian troops fighting Katangan gendarmes in Shaba Province, and in 1978 he oversaw the French military intervention in that province when the Katangans mounted a more serious invasion from neighboring Angola. Journiac's last mission took place in 1979 when he attempted to persuade the Central African Empire's emperor, Bokassa I, to abdicate. When Bokassa refused to do so, Journiac helped to engineer the dictator's overthrow and subsequent exile to the Ivory Coast.

In addition to his diplomatic duties, Journiac also held several posts in the French judiciary system in Paris. He died in an air crash while traveling from Chad to Gabon.   J.P.

Son of Robert J. and Madeleine (Matton) J. Married Marie-Thérèse de Laroque. Educ: Univ. Aix-en-Provence, law and political economy; licensed, l'École nationale de la France d'outre-mer. With French govt.: Deputy to Cameroon 1947–49; Judge, Yaounde County 1949–51; Public Prosecutor, Garoua 1951 and Grand Bassam 1952–55; in French Ministry of Overseas Territories 1955–60; head of French Secretariat to the African community 1960–62; tech. advisor, cabinet of Georges Pompidou 1962–66, to Secty. Gen. for African Affairs 1967–74, and to Valéry Giscard d'Estaing 1974–80. With French judiciary: Deputy Gen. 1955 and 1963; Consul Gen. 1958, to Appellate Ct. of Paris 1966, and for Ct. of Appeals 1975; advisor to the govt. for judicial affairs 1978–80. Hons: Officer, Legion of Honor; Croix de Guerre 1939–45.

(VIOLET) MARGARET (LIVINGSTONE) BALLINGER
South African politician and writer
Born Glasgow, Scotland, January 11th, 1894
Died Cape Province, South Africa, February 7th, 1980

Margaret Ballinger, who in the early 1900s established herself as an authority on the life and history of the peoples of southern Africa, was for nearly 23 years an outspoken member of the South African Parliament. As a representative of black Africans, she directed much of her work both in national politics and in her private life toward improving African living conditions and ending racialism.

Born Margaret Hodgson—known as Peggy to her friends and family—her early Glaswegian upbringing was in the strict tradition of Scottish Presbyterianism. When she was ten, her parents decided to emigrate to South Africa and she began her secondary education at a Roman Catholic school in Port Elizabeth. Her academic abilities soon became evident and on graduating from the University College of Rhodes in 1913 she won a Queen Victoria Scholarship which took her through to Somerville College, Oxford. She read history throughout her student days at university and on return to South Africa she was appointed to a lectureship in the Department of History at the University of the Witwatersrand.

In 1928 her future husband, William Ballinger made his first visit to South Africa. He went from his native Scotland, to study African trade unions and then decided to remain and assist with their organization. Prior to their marriage both found a common interest in the social, economic and political advancement of the African people and together they undertook pioneering research into the Protectorates, publishing what scholars later came to regard as important works on Basutoland and Bechuanaland. In 1934 they married but since university regulations did not at that time permit married women to hold permanent posts, Mrs. Ballinger resigned in 1935. She decided to work with her husband for African political advancement.

Mrs. Ballinger's chance came with the passing of the 1936 Representation of the Natives Act which made provision for African voters to elect white representatives to Parliament and for an electoral college of men to elect Senators. In subsequent polling, Mrs. Ballinger won one of the four Parliamentary seats. Her constituency contained some two million Africans and when she was later joined in government by her husband, who was elected a Senator for the Orange Free State, the pair between them represented almost as many adults as made up the then entire white population of the country.

Right from her maiden speech in 1938, Mrs. Ballinger was regarded as a major political force who was always in command of her facts. She maintained a long battle against what she saw as the "complacent cruelties of the Government of Jan Smuts," at a time when popular African resistance to racist policies was muted in comparison with what it became thirty years later. Mrs. Ballinger also found herself in a position of great unpopularity within the urban white community of South Africa, which regarded any criticism of the Smuts Government as untoward. Nevertheless Mrs. Ballinger continued with her opposition to measures which she believed were racially discriminatory, attacks on civil liberties and those which failed to consolidate the economic and social sectors of policies governing black Africans. But from 1948 her task was made more difficult through the implementation of apartheid policies and although she saw herself on the losing side she continued to argue the African's case until the abolition of their right to be represented in Parliament and the Senate. With her parliamentary career thus terminated, Mrs. Ballinger undertook first a lecture tour of Australia and then accepted an invitation from Nuffield College, Oxford, to become an Associate Fellow while writing about her political life and experiences.

Meanwhile, Mrs. Ballinger had helped promote the foundation of the South African Liberal Party in 1953 and went on to become its first President. It began as a small pressure group and under Mrs. Ballinger's guidance was transformed into a political party within five months. Her resignation from the presidency was, she said at the time, for "personal reasons," though she made no secret of her opposition to the party's adoption of universal suffrage policy. She advocated qualified franchise as a first step towards African advancement and in this and similar respects acquired the reputation of being to the political right of mainstream party opinion. Nevertheless she remained a true Liberal and fully committed to the party, though on more than one occasion outspokenly condemned its more aggressive political tactics including its boycott campaign against South African goods.

Mrs. Ballinger's concern for black Africans went beyond the bounds of her political career. She founded the Margaret Ballinger Home for Crippled and Convalescent African Children and remained actively connected with its management for many years until enforcement of the Group Areas Act necessitated its closure. Though continually dogged by the South African Government's apartheid policy, Mrs. Ballinger diversified her activities. She was an active member of the South African Institute of Race Relations and worked for black advancement through her many connections with South African universities. When her husband died in the late 1970s she established five scholarships for African university students in his memory. She sought, meanwhile, to advance the status of African women through her work on the country's Nursing Council and on the South African National Council of Women. Her services were subsequently acknowledged with the award of Honorary Degrees from the Universities of Rhodes and Cape Town and the conferment of the Royal African Society Medal marking her dedication to the cause of the African people.

Mrs. Ballinger's major publication recalling her political career, which was written partly during her stay at Nuffield College, Oxford, and later at her home in South Africa, appeared in 1970 under the title of *From Union to Apartheid: A Trek to Isolation.* It was widely acclaimed by critics and politicians in Britain and the United States. The *Library Journal* described it as a work of "first importance" for its dispassionate documentation of the "planned dehumanisation of eight million people." The *New Statesman* viewed it as "an invaluable source for historians of South Africa," while the *Times Literary Supplement* said it would stand as a permanent reminder of the limits of what white spokesmen could achieve on behalf of black South Africans.   J.P./M.D.

Born Margaret Hodgson. Daughter of John H. and Lillias (Burt) H. Emigrated to South Africa 1904. Married William George Ballinger, politician, 1934. No children. Educ: Holy Rosary Convent, Port Elizabeth, South Africa; Huguenot Coll., Wellington; Univ. Coll. Rhodes (later Rhodes Univ.), Grahamstown, B.A. 1913; Somerville Coll., Univ. Oxford (scholarship) M.A. 1917; Assoc. Fellow, Nuffield Coll., Oxford 1961. Lectr. in hist. and econ., Univ. Coll. Rhodes 1918–19; Lectr. in hist. and econ. hist., Univ. Witwatersrand, Johannesburg 1920–34. Native Rep. for Cape Eastern Circle, Union Parliament of South Africa 1937–60 (elected 1937, 1948; returned unopposed 1942, 1954). With South Africa Liberal Party: Founding Member 1953; First Pres. 1953–55; Chmn., Cape Div. 1963–68. Pres., South African Assn. of Univ. Women 1932–33; Dyason Memorial Lectr., Inst. Intnl. Affairs, Australia 1960; Councillor, Univ. Cape Town 1966–72. Member: Workers' Educational Assn.; Assn. of European and African Women; South African Nursing Council; Council of the South African Inst. of Race Relations; South African National Council on Women. Founder, Margaret Ballinger Home for Crippled and Convalescent African Children. Hons: Royal African Soc. Medal 1961; LL.D., Univ. Cape Town 1962; LL.D., Rhodes Univ. 1964. *Author:* (with W.G. Ballinger; under name Margaret Hodgson) Basutoland, 1931; All Union Politics Are Native Affairs, 1944; From Union to Apartheid: A Trek to Isolation, 1970; Influence of Holland on Africa; Britain in South Africa. Contributor to European Civilisation, Its Origin and Development (by Edward Eyre), 1939.

AIR MARSHAL SIR RICHARD WILLIAMS
Chief of Air Staff, Royal Australian Air Force
Born Moonta, South Australia, Australia, August 3rd, 1890
Died North Balwyn, Victoria, Australia, February 7th, 1980

As a founding father of the Royal Australian Air Force, Air Marshal Sir Richard Williams outfitted the fledgling service with its first aircraft and equipment.

Williams was born in Moonta, South Australia, and was trained as a service pilot at the Central Flying School at Point Cook. After serving in the Australian Army, he joined the Australian Flying Corps (AFC) and in 1917 became flight commander of its No. 1 Squadron in the Middle East; a year later he was also given the command of the 40th (Army) Wing of the British Royal Air Force. For a few months he commanded the RAF's Palestine Brigade. He was awarded the D.S.O. in 1917 and the O.B.E. in 1919.

After the war, the Australian Government decided to phase out the AFC and to establish the Royal Australian Air Force as a separate branch of the armed forces and the operational arm of the Department of Air. Williams, now a staff officer of the AFC, was placed in charge of organizing and supplying the new service. In 1919 he spent eight months at Australian Imperial Forces headquarters in London, where he selected more than £1 million worth of aircraft equipment donated by the British Government.

With the official founding of the RAAF in 1921, Williams was appointed Chief of Air Staff and a member of the Australian Council for Defence. During the inter-war years he attended RAF staff college and Imperial College of Defence courses in Britain, declaring that it was his aim to keep the RAAF abreast of European developments.

When the Second World War broke out in 1939, Williams returned to Britain on exchange duties and for a year held the senior Air Administration post in the RAF Coastal Command, handling aerial reconnaissance over the entire British coastline. Williams increased the number of night and day patrols and stepped up liaison between air and ground watches. In 1940 he went home to Australia to assist in the organization of the Empire Air Training Scheme, which prepared air personnel for active service, and to build up the strength of the RAAF in readiness for the war effort in Europe and Asia.

In 1941, Williams returned to London as Air Officer Commanding RAAF headquarters there, then moved to Washington, D.C. for four years as the RAAF's representative. In 1946, recognizing the need to bring in fresh ideas as the RAAF moved into the jet age, Williams gave the task of re-equipping the RAAF to a younger man and began a ten-year period as Australia's Director-General of Civil Aviation. After his retirement in 1956, Williams wrote an autobiography, *These are the Facts,* which, not coincidentally, was also a history of the RAAF. Williams was knighted in 1954.   J.P./M.D.

Son of Richard W. Married: (1) Constance Esther Griffiths 1915 (d.); (2) Lois Victoria Cross 1950. No children. Educ: public sch., Moonta; grad. Central Flying Sch., Point Cook 1914; courses at R.A.F. Staff Colls., Camberley and Andover, and at Imperial Coll. of Defence. Mil. Service: Australian Army 1912–16; joined Australian Flying Corps (A.F.C.) 1916; Flight Comdr., A.F.C. No. 1 Squadron, Middle East 1917–18; simultaneously comdr. 40th (Army) Wing, R.A.F. 1918; commanded Palestine Brigade, R.A.F. 1918–19; despatches. Staff Officer, A.F.C. 1919–21. With R.A.A.F.: Wing Comdr. 1921; Chief of Air Staff 1921–38; on exchange duties as Air Officer-in-Charge of Admin., R.A.F. Coastal Command, Britain 1939–40; Air Member, Org. and Equipment 1940–41; Air Officer Comdg. Overseas Headquarters, London 1941–42; Rep., Jt. Staff Mission, Washington, D.C. 1942–46. Dir.-Gen., Civil Aviation, Australia 1946–56. Former member, Australian Council for Defence. Hons: D.S.O. 1917; O.B.E. 1919; Order of El Nahda of the Hedjaz 1920; C.B.E. 1927;

C.B. 1935; knighted (K.B.E.) 1954. *Author:* These are the Facts (autobiography), 1977.

BARON THOMAS OF REMENHAM
Civil airline administrator and industrialist
Born Ruabon, Wales, March 2nd, 1897
Died Slough, Berkshire, England, February 8th, 1980

Lord Thomas, a British pioneer of military aviation during World War One, became one of his country's leading industrialists and civil airline administrators in the 1950s and 1960s. Although he had no university education, Thomas rose from an engineering traineeship to management of one of the largest British car manufacturing combines of the 1930s. Later in his career—which spanned nearly 50 years—Thomas turned his attention to a wide variety of industrial and commercial enterprises.

Miles Thomas was born in Wales to a family of modest means and started out in the Birmingham engineering works of Bellis and Morcom Ltd. Almost immediately, however, he was caught up in World War One; after fighting in the German East Africa Campaign with the British Armoured Car Squadron in 1915, Thomas was commissioned to officer rank in the Royal Flying Corps. He was sent to Egypt, began stunt flying, and was made an aerial combat instructor at Heliopolis. Thomas's ensuing service with the British Royal Air Force in Mesopotamia, Persia, and southern Russia won him the Distinguished Flying Cross in 1918. He turned down the offer of a permanent commission in the RAF and, after a brief association with F.P. Raynham in air racing, he decided to combine his already extensive knowledge of engineering techniques with a flair for journalism by working for motoring journals, first as a reporter and then as an editor. It was at this time that he published his work advocating the use of multi-wheel and tracked vehicles for military use, a treatise based on his research and observations on World War One battlefields. Although at this early stage Thomas's career seemed to center on problems of ground transport he nevertheless retained an active interest in flying, taking part in many of the major aeronautical events of the 1920s. In addition to his interest in journalism, Thomas was also fascinated by radio as a means of mass communication—and, later, by television.

Thomas's published account of a press showing of automobiles produced by Morris Motors Ltd. attracted the attention of the head of the company, William R. Morris, and resulted in Thomas joining the Morris staff as an adviser on sales promotion. Two years later, in 1926, he helped found the Morris-Oxford Press and in all remained with the Morris company and its associates and subsidiaries for 23 years, holding a succession of executive positions.

The group was converted to munitions production during World War Two and in 1940, at the age of 43, he became managing director and vice-chairman in charge of its 63 factories. In all, his large aircraft repair organization put 88,000 war planes back into the Allied effort and did much work on tank production. In 1941, Thomas became chairman of the cruiser tank production group and, the following year, led a tank engine mission to the United States to discuss production and development. Thomas's wartime efforts earned him a knighthood.

After the war, as a means of reviving the country's industry and economy, Lord Thomas pressed for tax incentives to aid the production of medium-sized cars for home and overseas sales. His policies proved correct: by the end of 1946 Britain was closer to its pre-war car output than was the United States. Inflation intervened the next year, however, and Thomas again called on the British government to change the taxation system—this time to encourage production of larger cars as a means of retaining export gains.

That same year, Thomas became chairman of the Southern Rhodesian Development Co-ordinating Commission, established to aid industrial and commercial development in the former British colony. For three years Thomas also served as director of the Colonial Development Corporation, aimed at promoting economic growth in the British colonies, seeking ways to mine Africa's vast mineral resources in order to build up British dollar credits.

Thomas joined BOAC in April 1948 as deputy chairman, succeeding Lord Knolly to the chairmanship a year later. Although he arrived at a time when most of the replacements for BOAC's war-exhausted fleet had been made, Thomas fully endorsed the idea of faster jet aircraft and set about making the operation commercially viable by imposing rigorous commercial standards upon the organization. When BOAC's annual loss was close to seven million pounds, he cut the number of employees from 23,000 to 18,000 in less than a year.

With the arrival in 1952 of the Comet fleet of aircraft, Thomas exercised his journalistic and media talents to attract passengers to jet travel. His campaign was an early success: the first Comets going to Africa, India, and the Far East were easily filled. For a year they flew capacity loads around the world—until one crashed, followed by a second and a third. Modifications were made after the second crash and Lord Thomas demonstrated his own faith in the aircraft by traveling in one himself. When a third crashed, however, the British Government took the aircraft out of service and held a long, meticulous investigation into the cause of the disaster. Lord Thomas retained his faith in the Comet throughout—BOAC did not cancel its production orders for newer versions of the aircraft—maintaining that his company was pioneering in jet travel for the benefit of Britain and the world. BOAC revenue was cut following the crashes, however, and the company was involved in heavy expenditures at a time when costs generally were rising.

Although he steered the corporation back towards profitability, its continued need for government assistance resulted in friction with the Minister of Transport and Thomas at length resigned from BOAC altogether.

He joined the board of Monsanto Chemicals Ltd. in 1955 and a year later became chairman, retiring at the age of 67. Thomas also took up directorships in commerce, retaining his connection with aviation through the chairmanship of Britannia Airways Ltd. In 1965 he moved into a completely new field, succeeding Lord Mackintosh of Halifax as chairman of the National Savings Committee of Great Britain, over which he presided for seven years.

Lord Thomas was a bold and innovative thinker. As early as 1951, when he led the International Air Transport Association—a non-governmental organization of 70 airlines—he had predicted the future rapid growth of commercial civil aviation, maintaining its viability lay in faster aircraft and increasing numbers of passengers attracted by low rates, predictions which have proved correct.   M.D.

Born William Miles Webster Thomas. Son of William Henry T. and Mary Elizabeth (Webster) T. Married Hylda Nora Church 1924. Children: Michael; Sheila. Educ: Bromsgrove Sch., Worcs. 1910–14; Premium Pupil (engineering), Bellis and Morcom, Birmingham. Mil. service: British Armoured Car Squadron, East Africa 1914–15; commnd. to Royal Flying Corps, Egypt 1915; stunt flying and aerial fighting instr., Heliopolis 1916; flying missions for British Royal Air Force, Mesopotamia, Persia, southern Russia 1917–19. Reporter, Motor; ed., Light Car 1919–24. With Morris Motors Ltd.: sales promotion 1924-26; founder, Morris-Oxford Press 1926; Dir. and Gen. Sales Mgr. 1927-34; Dir. and Gen. Mgr., Morris Commercial Cars Ltd., Birmingham 1934–35; Dir. and Gen. Mgr., Wolseley Motors Ltd., Birmingham 1935–37; Managing Dir., Wolseley Motors Ltd. 1937–40; Vice-Chmn. and Managing Dir., Morris Motors Ltd. and its subsidiaries—Wolseley Motors Ltd., Morris Commerical Cars Ltd., M.G. Car Co. Ltd., Riley Motor Co. Ltd., Morris Industries (Exports) Ltd., S.V. Carburetor Co. Ltd., and Mechanisations and Aero Ltd., 1940–47. Chmn., Cruiser Tank Production Group and Member, Advisory Panel on Tank Production to British Govt. 1941–45; Leader, British Tank Engine Mission to the U.S. 1942–43; Chmn., Southern Rhodesian Devel. Co-ordinating Commn. 1947–55; Dir., Colonial Devel. Corp. 1948–51. Pres: Soc. of Motor Manufacturers 1947–48; Advertising Assocs. 1949–53; Intnl. Air Transport Assn. 1951–52; Neumo Ltd. Deputy Chmn. 1948–49 and Chmn. 1949–56, British Overseas Airways Corp. (B.O.A.C.); Chmn., Monsanto Chemicals Ltd. 1956–63; Pres. 1965–72 and Chmn. 1965–70, Natl. Savings Cttee. of Great Britain; Chmn., Devel. Corp. for Wales 1958–67, and Welsh Advisory Cttee. for Civil Aviation 1961–66; Deputy Chmn., P. Leiner and Sons Ltd. 1961–71; Chmn. 1964–70 and Pres. 1971–72, Carbon Electric Holdings; Chmn., Britannia Airways Ltd., and Chesham Amalgamations and Investments Ltd.; Vice-Chmn., Welsh Econ. Planning Council 1965–66. Member: Oxfordshire Council, Order of St. John 1947; B.B.C. Gen. Advisory Council 1952–56; British Productivity Council 1957–62 (Chmn. 1959); Ct. of Govs., Birmingham Univ. (Life); Soc. of Motor Manufacturers and Traders; Soc. of Aeronautical Engineers; Royal Armoured Corps Charities Trust (former Chmn.); English and Allied Employers' Natl. Fedn.; Horton Gen. Hosp. Mgmt. Cttee.; Inst. of Motor Trade. Directorships: Sun Insurance Office Ltd.; Dowty Group Ltd.; Thomson Org.; Thomson Travel Ltd. Hons: D.F.C. 1918; knighted 1943; Life Peer 1971; Comdr., Cedar of Lebanon; Fellow, Inst. of Mechanical Engineers; Fellow, Royal Aeronautical Soc. *Author:* Development and Use of Multi-Wheel Vehicles for Cross-Country and Military Purposes, 1924; Out on a Wing (autobiography), 1964.

Numerous articles in professional jrnls. B.B.C. radio and television
contributions 1934-64.

IVAN GOSNJAK
Yugoslav Defense Minister
Born Pankrac, Yugoslavia, 1909
Died Belgrade, Yugoslavia, February 9th, 1980

General Ivan Gosnjak was a principal architect of Marshal Josip Tito's
[q.v.] foreign policy for almost two decades. As Secretary of State for
Defense from 1953 until 1967, he was a powerful voice within military
circles. Gosnjak's influence began in 1948 with the Yugoslav defiance
of Moscow and ended in 1968 with the Soviet invasion of Czechoslovakia when he was quietly purged from office.

Ivan Gosnjak's ideology was formed early. As a young carpenter in
industrially undeveloped Yugoslavia, he was introduced to radical
politics through involvement in the trade union movement. An
organizer, Gosnjak headed an illegal trade union in Sisak, and having
acquired a rudimentary understanding of the communist theory of
proletarian revolution, he joined the then-illegal Communist Party in
1933. Two years later, Gosnjak travelled to the Soviet Union, where
he studied the basic texts of Marx, Engels, and Lenin and observed
Moscow's attempts to institutionalize the October Revolution.

In 1937 the politically educated Gosnjak sought to wed theory and
practice by joining the anti-Franco forces in the Spanish Civil War. He
remained in Spain until 1939 when he was deported and interned in a
concentration camp in France. In 1941 Gosnjak escaped and returned
to Yugoslavia, enlisting with Tito's partisan units, the war's most
effective resistance forces. Gosnjak eventually became Commander of
the Croatian headquarters.

When Tito seized power in 1946, he swiftly eliminated political
opposition by appointing to key positions fellow Communists who
were strong willed, ideologically committed, and loyal to the new
Premier. Gosnjak was installed as commander of the army in Zagreb,
served as a member of Parliament and, from 1948 to 1953, was Deputy
Defense Minister. As Yugoslav Secretary of State for Defense in the
mid 1950s, Gosnjak helped direct foreign policy when that country
first began to receive substantial economic and military assistance
from the United States and initiated expansion of trade with Western
Europe. After the death of Stalin, relations between Yugoslavia and
the USSR improved and, despite some liberalization of domestic
institutions, Yugoslav foreign policy remained largely pro-Soviet.

During the spring and summer of 1968, however, Tito gave his
support to the Czechoslovakian reformers and condemned the Soviet
invasion. Gosnjak was toppled from military power at Tito's behest
after official reports charged him and other generals with failure to
prepare for defense of their borders against the possibility of Soviet
attack. Gosnjak, now persona non grata because of a reputed
friendship with several Soviet generals, survived formal ouster from

the army's party organization by only one vote. He was still in official disfavor at the time of his death in Belgrade.   A.C.

Educ: Grammar Sch., Pankrac. Carpenter and local trade union leader 1925; joined Communist Party 1933; studied in U.S.S.R. 1935–37; fought with Spanish Republican Army 1937–39; interned in concentration camp in France 1939–41, escaped; with Natl. Liberation Army, Yugoslavia 1942–45; Comdr., 1st Croatian Corps; Comdr. Gen., Croatian Army Headquarters; Comdr., Zagreb Army 1945; M.P. 1945–63; Deputy Minister of Defense 1948–53; member, Fed. Executive Council and Secty. of State for Defense 1953–67; member, Praesidium of Central Cttee. of the Communist League of Yugoslavia; member, Council of the Fedn. Hons: Orders of Freedom and Natl. Hero; natl. decorations from Spain, France, Greece, U.S.S.R., Czechoslovakia, Romania, Poland, Albania, Egypt, and Ethiopia.

YAKOV (ALEKSANDROVICH) MALIK
Soviet Ambassador to the United Nations and Deputy Foreign Minister
Born Kharkov, Ukraine, December 6th, 1906
Died Moscow, U.S.S.R., February 11th, 1980

Yakov Malik, twice Soviet ambassador to the United Nations, was born in the industrial city of Kharkov in the Ukraine. First trained as an economist, he entered the University of Moscow school for the diplomatic corps in 1935 and joined the Ministry of Foreign Affairs two years later as its deputy press chief in Moscow. In 1939 he was posted to Tokyo as counselor to the Soviet Embassy, took over the ambassadorship in 1942, and returned to Moscow in 1945 after notifying Emperor Hirohito of the Soviet Union's declaration of war against Japan. During the next three years he served in the Foreign Ministry as an expert on Far Eastern affairs.

Malik's rise to international prominence began in 1948, when he replaced Andrei Gromyko as Soviet Ambassador to the United Nations. Malik arrived in New York exuding bonhomie and offering reporters Russian cigarettes. But this surface geniality soon gave way to the dour, abrasive style that became his trademark. In his maiden speech, he denounced the Netherlands's military presence in Indonesia and the activities of the UN Good Offices Committee there. His second major speech was devoted to attacks on the United States, for allegedly undermining the new State of Israel, and on Count Folke Bernadotte, head of the U.N. mediating team in the area, for siding with Great Britain against the Jewish population.

During 1949 Malik continued his blistering attacks against the Western powers and played a major role in negotiating an end to the Berlin blockade. In early 1950 he began a six-month boycott of the Security Council to protest the seating of Nationalist China. While he was away, the Security Council, under US instigation, authorized the deployment of UN troops to oppose the invasion of South Korea by the Communist government of North Korea, a vote Malik would have been certain to veto. Realizing his mistake, Malik, now chairman of the Council, took his revenge in a program of harassment against his colleagues and obstruction of UN deliberations. In 1951, however, as the tide of battle began to turn against the North Koreans, Malik proposed a truce during a UN radio broadcast. The proposal was accepted and eventually led to an armistice. Malik spent most of his time during the Korean War years criticizing the actions of the UN and US troops; in particular, he accused them of using germ warfare, though he vetoed a US proposal to have the International Red Cross investigate the charges.

In 1953 Malik returned to Moscow as First Deputy Foreign Minister, replacing Gromyko, who had been named Ambassador to Britain. But the death of Josef Stalin that year resulted in a shake-up of the diplomatic corps; Gromyko was recalled to Moscow, and Malik replaced him once again. He stayed in London for seven years and spent much of his time addressing businessmen's associations. Beginning in 1960, he was back in Moscow's foreign office as Deputy Foreign Minister.

Malik's second term as Ambassador to the UN began in 1968. This time his main target was Israel, which he accused of being an "expansionist" power. After 1971, however, he tended to train his rhetorical guns on the newly admitted state of Communist China, whose anti-Soviet foreign policy he labeled "reckless" and whose UN ambassador, Huang Hua, he once compared to a "hunchback for whom the only cure is the grave." He frequently crossed swords with Daniel Patrick Moynihan, the US ambassador, and walked out of a General Assembly session in 1975 after Moynihan quoted the call of Soviet physicist and dissident Andrei Sakharov for a world-wide amnesty for political prisoners.

Malik was an archetypal Soviet diplomat—conservative in dress and behavior, faithful to the orthodox party line laid down by Stalin. He spoke fluent English, French, and Japanese. On many of his diplomatic missions he was accompanied by his wife, Valentina, and their daughter Svetlana, who suffered from a polio-like disease; two sons remained at school in Moscow.

In 1976 Malik and his wife were injured when their limousine collided with a private automobile in Glen Cove, N.Y., a Long Island suburb. Malik returned to Moscow for medical treatment, but never completely recovered from the accident. He continued to work in the Ministry of Foreign Affairs until his death.   J.P.

Married Valentina. Children: Yuri; Yevgeny; Svetlana (b. 1943). Educ: Kharkov Inst. of Natl. Econs., grad. 1930; Inst. of Diplomatic and Consular Service, Univ. Moscow, grad. 1937. Economist, Ukraine 1930–35. Joined Diplomatic Service, Ministry of Foreign Affairs 1937. Sr. Consultant, then Asst. Chief, Press Dept., People's Commissariat of Foreign Affairs, Moscow 1937–39; Counselor, Soviet Embassy, Tokyo 1939–42; Ambassador to Japan, Tokyo 1942–45; Political Advisor to U.S.S.R. Rep. on Allied Council for Japan 1946; Deputy Foreign Minister for Far Eastern Affairs 1946; Deputy Minister of Foreign Affairs, Moscow 1946–53, 1960–80; Ambassador to Great Britain, London 1953–60; attained rank of Ambassador

Extraordinary and Plenipotentiary. As Permanent Rep. of U.S.S.R. to U.N. 1948–52 and 1968–76: Permanent U.S.S.R. rep. to U.N. Security Council 1948–52; Member, U.N. Org. Disarmament Commn., NYC 1952; Member, U.N. Sub-Cttee. on Disarmament, London; Member, U.N. Atomic Energy Commn. Joined Communist Party of Soviet Union 1938; Member, Central Cttee. 1952–61. Attended Moscow Foreign Ministers Conference 1945; Member, Soviet Delegation, San Francisco Conference to discuss peace treaty with Japan 1951; Member, Soviet Delegation to London Foreign Ministers Conference 1954; Member, Soviet Delegation to Geneva Foreign Ministers Conference 1959; attended Nigerian independence celebrations 1960; accompanied Leonid Brezhnev on tour of India 1961; visited Zambia, India, Iraq, Kenya, Uganda, Algeria 1965–66. Hons: Order of Lenin 1944, 1945; medal for valorous services in War of 1941–45; Order of Red Banner of Labor (twice, one in 1966); Order of October Revolution; other decorations.

SAMUEL D(AVID) BERGER
U.S. Ambassador to South Korea and Deputy Ambassador to South Vietnam
Born Gloversville, New York. U.S.A., December 6th, 1911
Died Washington, D.C., U.S.A., February 12th, 1980

Samuel D. Berger, a labor economist and career diplomat, served as Ambassador to South Korea in the post-Korean War years and as deputy Ambassador to South Vietnam during the late 1960s. He earned a reputation as a top-flight professional who worked hard to restore the economic and administrative stability to societies demolished by war.

Berger was born in Gloversville, New York, to Orthodox Jewish parents. At the age of 14 he was working as an office boy for four dollars a week at the Gloversville *Morning Herald*. Here he got his first taste of labor negotiating when he tried to convince the shop foreman to accept him as an apprentice at triple the normal salary. He continued to work on the newspaper staff until his departure for the University of Wisconsin, where he studied labor economics and philosophy under the guidance of Professor Selig Perlman, a leading scholar of the labor movement.

In 1938 Berger went to England for a year to study the British labor movement at the London School of Economics. He returned to England four years later as labor advisor to the special US Lend-Lease Mission under W. Averell Harriman. In 1945 he joined the staff of the US Embassy in London as the first labor attaché in the service of the State Department. When Conservative Party rule in Britain was ended by the Labour Party in 1945, the US diplomatic staff was able to draw on Berger's expertise as they forged contacts with the new administration.

Berger spent the years from 1950 to 1953 in Washington, then went to Tokyo as labor counselor to the US Embassy. He was reassigned to

New Zealand after a disagreement with Vice President Richard Nixon, who insisted that Berger underestimated the degree to which the Japanese labor movement was Communist-inspired. From 1958 to 1961 he was deputy chief of the embassy in Athens and helped disengage the Greek labor movement from Communist control.

In 1961 Berger was appointed Ambassador to South Korea, where he helped to repair the economic and political damage wrought by the Korean civil war. His main tasks included negotiating with the regime of General Park Chung Hee for a restoration of civilian rule, establishing a solid economic base for future growth, and encouraging the resumption of diplomatic relations between South Korea and its former occupier, Japan. Berger's cool demeanor earned him the nickname of "Silent Sam" from the Korean press.

After leaving Korea in 1964, Berger worked briefly as deputy commandant for foreign affairs at the National War College in Washington, D.C. and as Deputy Assistant Secretary of State for Far Eastern Affairs. In 1968, at the height of domestic and international furor over the Vietnam War, Berger was appointed deputy to U.S. Ambassador Ellsworth Bunker in Saigon. Although his position was a difficult one, Berger served with his customary professionalism. He later revealed his disenchantment with US policy in Vietnam and disclosed that, in his opinion, the US had given up realistic hopes for a military victory by the time of his arrival.

Berger returned to Washington in 1972 and worked as an official of the Foreign Service Institute until his retirement in 1974. He died of cancer on February 12, 1980.   J.P./L.C.S.

Son of Harry I.B. and Bess (Cohen) B. Married: (1) Margaret Fowler, economist, 1937 (d. 1967); (2) Elizabeth Lee (Bonner) Pressey, 1969. No children. Jewish. Educ: Univ. Wisc., Madison, Ph.B. 1932; graduate studies, Univ. Wisc. 1935–38; London Sch. Econs. (Social Science Research Council Fellowship) 1938–39. Mil. Service: Capt., U.S. Army 1944–45. Researcher in job opportunities, Rochester, N.Y. 1933–34; Dir. of Research, Natl. Refugee Service, NYC 1939–40; Job Market Analyst, Fed. Security Agency 1940–41; Labor Advisor to Special U.S. Lend-Lease Mission to Great Britain 1942–44; First Secty., U.S. Embassy, London 1945–50; on detail to White House staff from State Dept. 1950–51; Special Asst. to Dir. for Mutual Security 1951–53; Counselor, U.S. Embassy Tokyo, 1953–54; Deputy Chief, U.S. Embassy, Wellington, N.Z. 1954–58; Deputy Chief, U.S. Embassy, Athens 1958–61; Ambassador, South Korea 1961–64; Deputy Commandant for Foreign Affairs, Natl. War Coll., Washington, D.C. 1964–65; Deputy Asst. Secty. of State for Far Eastern Affairs 1965–68; Deputy to U.S. Ambassador in South Vietnam 1972; official of Foreign Service Inst., Washington, D.C. 1972–74.

MURIEL RUKEYSER
Poet and social activist
Born New York City, U.S.A., December 15th, 1913
Died New York City, U.S.A., February 12th, 1980

Courtesy William L. Rukeyser

The life of Muriel Rukeyser, like her poetry, has often been perceived as a series of uncomfortable paradoxes. She is remembered by her friends as tender and sympathetic, but her poetry was often criticized as aggressive and artless; choosing to find hope in a harsh age, she was condemned as groundlessly cheeful and captivated by an unexamined liberal piety. A relentless experimenter in new poetic forms, she was often dismissed as a treader of tired poetic ground, and having tried out more roles and vocations than women of her generation were normally allowed, she lived long enough to be criticized by latter-day feminists.

A lifelong believer in social justice and in the kinds of practical political dissent it takes to help achieve that justice, Rukeyser was a first-hand observer of many of the most prominent injustices and social calamities of the century. In 1933 she traveled to Alabama to witness the Scottsboro trials; in 1936 she went to West Virginia to observe the suffering of tunnel workers afflicted with silicosis; and in the last decade of her life she traveled to Hanoi to protest American involvement in Vietnam and went to South Korea to oppose that government's harassment of the radical Catholic poet, Kim Chi-Ha.

Having received her early education in New York, Rukeyser attended Vassar College, where she wrote on the staff of the "Student Review," and Columbia University for two summer sessions; she also enrolled in the Roosevelt School of Aviation in order to learn the mechanics of flying, a process celebrated in her first volume of poetry, *Theory of Flight* (1935), published when she was 22. She later taught at several universities, but regarded teaching—and tenure—as traps for a poet. She was a prolific writer and translator, producing books of poetry, scripts, a play and a novel, a biography of a scientist, and children's literature. The culmination of her career, in recognition of her 45 years as a publishing poet and as proof of her growing acceptability to the literary establishment, was the publication of *The Collected Poems* in the year preceding her death.

Rukeyser's poetry has been called impressive for its sheer bulk, sensitivity, and experimental quality. Throughout her long career, she was able to balance concreteness and precision of detail with a visionary, prophetic quality. The first poem in *Theory of Flight,* "Poem Out of Childhood," demonstrates the forcefulness of her poetic personality, her belief in the intensity of poetry, and the ability to balance contrasting experiences:

Breathe-in experience, breathe-out poetry:
Not Angles, angels : and the magnificent past
shot deep illuminations into high-school.
I opened the door into the concert-hall
and a rush of triumphant violins answered me
while the syphilitic woman turned her mouldered face
intruding upon Brahms.

In her first book, Rukeyser announced her arrival with a style hailed (and derided) by critics for its "toughness" and "intensity."

From the beginning, Rukeyser's poetry has been notable for its social and psychological awareness. In one of her most famous lines, she embraces political causes at the expense of literary niceties: "Not Sappho, Sacco." During the Vietnam conflict, she proclaimed her radical pacifism in these familiar-sounding lines from the 60s:

Wherever
we protest
we will go planting . . .

As with the social sensitivity and certain tendency to sprawl, the visionary quality of Rukeyser's poetry can partly be traced to the influence of Walt Whitman. Toward the end of her career, Rukeyser explained, "What I care about in Whitman is the extreme fight to keep the skin together, the extreme contradiction . . . . The violence, shamefulness, willingness are in myself." These lines from her hymn to aviation, "Theory of Flight," are indebted to Whitman's universalism:

A spark occurs, igniting America, opening India,
finding the Northwest Passage, Cipango spice,
causing the mixture to burn, expanding the gases
which push the piston away on the power stroke.

The critic, Joseph Warren Beach, objected to "the confident self-assurance of the young woman taking on the Whitman mantle of prophecy," while another, Laurence Liebermann, complained that "Her mystical vision is so dominant in the mentality of some poems, the writing becomes inscrutable."

Another feature of Rukeyser's career was her continuous experimentation. Her earliest poetry showed the influence of T. S. Eliot, the terseness of whose verse acted as a corrective to the prolixity of the Whitman side of Rukeyser's poetic personality. The opening line of "Effort at Speech Between Two People" echoes Eliot at his most abrupt: "Speak to me. Take my hand. What are you now?" A later line in the same poem alludes to Eliot's "Prufrock": "I have liked lamps in evening corners, and quiet poems." Late in her career, Rukeyser could evoke the limpid lyricism of W. B. Yeats, as in "Song: The Star in the Nets of Heaven":

The star in the nets of heaven blazed past your breastbone,
Willing to shine among the nets of your growth,
The nets of your love,
The bonds of your dreams.

The increasing economy of Rukeyser's verse belied the charge of prolixity and unliterary earnestness that dogged her throughout her career. She handled a wide range of forms and topics, from love poems and satires to political narratives and prophetic musings about the new technology.

Louise Kertesz, in the first full-length study of Rukeyser's poetry, contends that "there had not been anything in American literature like *U.S. 1,*" Rukeyser's second collection of poetry. In something of a reversal of John Dos Passos's strategy of incorporating verse-like sections into a novel, Rukeyser may have been the first poet successfully to insert committee transcripts into a poem. Her study of the mistreatment of workers and the ravages of disease among tunnel workers in West Virginia in the 30s, "The Book of the Dead," allowed Rukeyser to show compassion and indignation while experimenting with a provocative new verse form.

Throughout her life Rukeyser challenged the conventional limitations placed upon women. She was jailed briefly for associating with blacks during the Scottsboro trial in Alabama in the 30s and jailed again in the 60s for participating in anti-war activities. As a single parent, she raised her son alone. Women "are brought up to be retarded," she said; "we have to unlearn those things." Yet throughout her career she endured the barbs of other feminists who found her poetry defective when measured by the standard of "female lyricism." Other critics have felt that her toughness, frankness, and choice of traditionally masculine subjects (such as mining and aviation) make the adjective "feminine" difficult to apply to Rukeyser's poetry.

At the same time, the frankness and tenderness of her poems about human sexuality have an immediate, strong appeal. In "Anemone" she writes:

My eyes are closing, my eyes are opening.
You are looking into me with your waking look.

My mouth is closing, my mouth is opening.
You are waiting with your red promises.

My sex is closing, my sex is opening.
You are singing and opening, the way in.

My life is closing, my life is opening.
You are here.

In an age when poetry is expected to be ironic and antagonistic, Rukeyser was straightforward, erotic, vulnerable, and candid about her needs and problems, because she felt the poet should be a healer and consoler.

It is the optimism and open-heartedness that earned Rukeyser more than the occasionally unfavorable review. She opposed tradition when, in "Theory of Flight," she incorporated the flat, precise prose of science and technology into her poetry and chose emphatically not to yearn for a pre-industrial, spiritual past, as Eliot had done. Even one of her most astute early critics, M. L. Rosenthal, called "unearned triumphant conclusion" a persistent flaw in her poetry. When relentless irony and cultural despair were the fashion, Rukeyser was not given fair, unbiased criticism.

Rukeyser served as president of American PEN (the league of poets and writers) in 1975–76, and she won several prestigious awards, such as a Guggenheim Fellowship, the Shelley Memorial Award, and the Copernicus Award. Having suffered two earlier strokes, Muriel Rukeyser died on February 12, 1980, at the age of 66.   B.N.

Daughter of Lawrence R. and Myra Lyons R. Married Glyn Collins (div.). Daughter: Laurie. Son: William Laurie. Educ: Fieldston Sch. 1919–30; Vassar Coll., Poughkeepsie, N.Y., and Columbia Univ. (summer session) 1931, 1933. Briefly attended Roosevelt Aviation Sch. With U.S. Office of War Information, WWII. Ed.: Student Review, New Theatre, Housatonic, and Decision. Teacher, Sarah Lawrence Coll., Bronxville, N.Y. 1946, 1956–57. Clark Lectr., Scripps Coll., Claremont, Calif. 1968. V.P., House of Photography, NYC 1946–60. Member: Bd. of Dirs.,

Teachers-Writers Collaborative, NYC; Natl. Acad. of Arts and Letters; Natl. Inst. of Arts and Letters; Soc. of American Historians; Hist of Science Soc.; League of American Writers; Writers and Artists' Cttee.; Medical Bureau to Aid Spanish Democracy; American Assoc. of Univ. Profs. Pres., P.E.N. American Center 1975–76. Worked with: Americans for Amnesty; Natl. Council for Universal and Unconditional Amnesty; U.S. Cttee. for Justice in Latin America. Hons: Yale Series of Younger Poets Award 1935; Oscar Blumenthal Prize 1940; Harriet Monroe Award 1941; Natl. Inst. of Arts and Letters Award and American Acad. of Arts and Letters Award 1942; Guggenheim Fellowship 1943; Levinson Prize 1947; Hon. D.Litt., Rutgers Univ., 1961; Eunice Tietjens Memorial Prize 1962; Fellow, American Council of Learned Socs. 1963; Swedish Acad. translation award 1967; Copernicus Award, Acad. of American Poets 1977; Shelley Memorial Award, Poetry Soc. 1977; Colleague, Cathedral of St. John the Divine; poem in new Reform Jewish Prayerbook. *Books: Poetry*—Theory of Flight, 1935; U.S. 1, and Mediterranean, 1938; A Turning Wind: Poems, 1939; The Soul and Body of John Brown, 1940; Wake Island, 1942; Beast in View, 1944; The Children's Orchard, 1947; The Green Wave, 1948; Orpheus, 1949; Elegies, 1949; Selected Poems, 1951; Body of Waking, 1958; Waterlily Fire: Poems 1932–1962; The Outer Banks, 1967; The Speed of Darkness, 1968; 29 Poems, 1970; Breaking Open, 1973; The Gates, 1976; Collected Poems, 1979. *Children's books*—Come Back Paul, 1955; I Go Out, 1961; Bubbles, 1967; Mazes, 1970. *Other*—Willard Gibbs (biog.), 1942; The Life of Poetry, 1949; One Life (biog. of Wendell Willkie), 1957; The Color of the Day (play), 1961; The Orgy (novel), 1965; Poetry, and Unverifiable Fact: The Clark Lectures, 1968; The Traces of Thomas Hariot, 1971. Translator—(with others) Selected Poems of Octavio Paz, 1963 and revised ed. 1973; Sun Stone (by Octavio Paz), 1963; (with Leif Sjoberg) Selected Poems of Gunnar Ekelof, 1967; Three Poems of Gunnar Ekelof, 1967; Uncle Eddie's Moustache (by Bertolt Brecht), 1974. *Further reading:* The Poetic Vision of Muriel Rukeyser by Louise Kertesz, 1980.

DAVID JANSSEN
Film and television actor
Born Naponee, Nebraska, U.S.A., March 27th, 1930
Died Malibu, California, U.S.A., February 13th, 1980

In a late sixties British radio talk, a journalist who had recently travelled extensively in Spain, described his somewhat strange experience near Malaga: Approaching a village by car on a summer evening, he was surprised to find the place deserted, but he could hear a man's voice, muffled by the distance, shouting over a loudspeaker system. As he drove on the voice became louder and more distinct. Soon he arrived in the village square where the atmosphere was electric. The entire population of the village appeared to be crowded in the taverns watching, as if transfixed, the televisions set up above the bars. The visitor's first thought was that Franco had been assassinated. But he quickly discovered that the man commanding the rapt attention of every villager was neither Franco nor any other world

figure, but a tacitiurn American actor, dubbed into Spanish, and being pursued, as ever, by the police in yet another cliff-hanging episode of *The Fugitive.*

Born in Nebraska, David Harold Meyer's father was a banker, and his mother a former "Ziegfeld Follies" girl and Miss Nebraska. David's parents divorced while he was still very young and he moved with his mother and her new husband, Eugene Janssen, to California.

David, who had assumed his stepfather's last name, turned to acting when a torn knee ligament forced him to decline offers of athletic scholarships to college. He had already acquired some acting experience, having appeared on stage at the age of nine. He made his first movie, *It's A Pleasure* with Sonja Henie the ice-skating star, at the age of fifteen, and a year later he appeared as Johnny Weismuller's kid brother in *Swampfire.*

On commencing his career, Janssen worked with small theater groups in Los Angeles and played summer stock in Maine. He then went to New York and took a number of jobs while auditioning for stage plays. He secured a dancing part in a short-lived Mike Todd musical, then returned to California. Janssen was taken on by 20th Century Fox, but they soon dropped him, allegedly because of his resemblance to Clark Gable.

At the age of 21, Janssen signed-up with Universal Studios and while making minor film appearances, took various drama courses. After two years's interruption for military service, he returned to Universal and remained there until 1956, appearing in 32 films, mainly of the B-feature "hit and run" variety. Janssen's first break came in 1957 when he was selected for the title role in the television series, *Richard Diamond, Private Detective.* His portrayal of a tough private-eye—who, though impetuous and a law-breaker was also upright and true—appealed to audience across America. During the series' three-year run, Janssen appeared in a few stage plays. He returned to feature films in 1960, playing the star role of Bill on *Hell to Eternity,* for which he received the Motion Picture Exhibitor's Annual and the title "Number One New Film Star."

In 1963, after a few more films, Janssen catapulted to fame in ABC's smash-hit television series, *The Fugitive.* The series, produced by Quinn Martin, and loosely based on a famous crime of that time (the Sam Sheppard murder case), won Janssen three Emmy nominations. He played the part of Dr. Richard Kimble, a tough, gravel-voiced physician, suspected of murdering his wife, and constantly on the run from police lieutenant Philip Gerard. Was there really a 'one-armed man' and if so, could he prove the Fugitive's innocence? Could a relentlessly pursued loner triumph over the organized forces of the law and go free? Would justice prevail, or, heaven forbid, was the good doctor really guilty? At its best, the show had some of the tension and poignancy of Victor Hugo's masterpiece, *Les Miserables.* When the second half of the 118th and final episode of "The Fuge" aired in 1967, an estimated 30 million Americans tuned in for the answers. The 45.9 average audience rating was the highest-rated episode of a series ever transmitted.

After *The Fugitive*'s four-season run, Janssen starred as a journalist in two 1969 movies, *The Green Berets* with John Wayne and Jim Hutton, and *The Shoes of the Fisherman* with Oskar Werner and Anthony Quinn. He also appeared in three 1970 movies and played

the title role in *Macho Callahan* in 1971. That same year, Janssen
returned to television to play Ohara in *Ohara, U.S. Treasury* which
ran for one season. From 1974 to 1976, Janssen appeared as Harry
Orwell, a downbeat ex-police detective, in the popular ABC television series *Harry O*. In 1976 he played the part of a talented novelist
in the movie *Once Is Not Enough,* and a year later starred in *A
Sensitive and Passionate Man,* a television movie for which he also
wrote the title song.

Janssen, who had performed in more than 100 feature and television films, began to voice his criticism of movie-making trends,
believing that tight budgets and new, unprofessional directors were to
blame for the abundance of second-rate movies in the late sixties.
Abandoning feature films, Janssen turned his attentions toward
television mini-series translations of novels, and in 1978 appeared in
The Word (CBS) and James Michener's *Centennial* (NBC).

David Janssen, who made a fortune from his television involve-
ments and from Los Angeles real estate, was married to his first wife
for ten years. Seven years after their divorce, he remarried. He died in
Los Angeles of a heart attack at the age of 49. Two days before his
death he had started filming a re-enactment of the life of the leper-
priest, Father Damien.   R.T.

Born David Harold Meyer. Son of Harold Meyer, (banker), and
Berniece Graf (Mrs. Eugene Janssen). Married: (1) Ellie Graham,
artist and designer, 1958 (div. 1968); (2) Dani Greco, 1975. No
children. Educ.: Fairfax High Sch., Hollywood. Mil. Service: U.S.
Army Special Services, Calif. 1952–54. Briefly with 20th Century Fox,
then with Universal Pictures, Hollywood 1951–56; feature and televi-
sion film actor 1957–80; also songwriter. Member: American Fedn. of
Television and Radio Artists; Acad. of Motion Picture Arts and
Sciences; Acad. of Television Arts and Sciences; American Soc. of
Composers, Authors, and Publishers; American Guild of Variety
Artists; Screen Actors Guild; Artists Equity Assn.; Friars Club.
Hons.: TV Guide Award; TV-Radio Mirror Award, 1964; voted Man
of the Year on TV by Radio-TV daily, 1964; Emmy nominations for
The Fugitive, Acad. of Television Arts and Sciences, 1964 and 1966;
Special Editor's Award, Photoplay mag., 1965; Golden Globe,
Hollywood Foreign Press Assn., 1965; Gold Camera Award as most
popular star in South America, Ecran mag., Santiago 1966; Western
Heritage Wrangler Award. *Performances: Film*—It's A Pleasure,
1945; Swampfire, 1946; Never Say Goodbye, 1946; Chief Crazy
Horse, 1955; To Hell and Back, 1955; Francis in the Navy, 1955; The
Girl He Left Behind, 1956; Away All Boats, 1956; Lafayette Esca-
drille, 1958; Hell To Eternity, 1960; Dondi, 1961; Ring of Fire, 1961;
King of the Roaring Twenties, 1961; Twenty Plus Two, 1961; Man-
Trap, 1961; Belle Sommers, 1962; My Six Loves, 1963; Warning Shot,
1967; The Green Berets, 1968; The Shoes of the Fisherman, 1968;
Generation, 1969; Where It's At, 1969; Marooned, 1969; Macho
Callahan (title role), 1970; Once Is Not Enough, 1975; Covert Action,
1978. *Television series (star)*—Richard Diamond, Private Detective
(title role), 1957; The Fugitive (title role), 1963, 64, 65, 66; Ohara,
U.S. Treasury (Ohara), 1971; Harry O (title role), 1974. *Television
episode appearances*—Lux Vido Theatre, 1956; Zane Grey Theatre,
1957, 58, 59; You Are There, 1957; The Millionaire, 1958; Adventures In Paradise, 1961; Checkmate, 1962; Target Corruptors, 1962;
G.E. Theatre, 1962; Naked City, 1962, 63; Follow the Sun, 1962;

Cain's Hundred, 1962; Mystery Theatre, 1962; Route 66, 1962;
Eleventh Hour, 1962; Dick Powell Theatre, 1963; Cannon, 1973;
Police Story, 1977; Nowhere to Run, 1978. *Telefeatures*—Night Chase,
1970; Ohara, U.S. Treasury (later a series), 1971; The Longest Night,
1972; Moon of the Wolf, 1972; Birds of Prey, 1973; Harry O (later a
series), 1973; Hijack, 1973; Pioneer Woman, 1973; Smile, Jenny,
You're Dead (featured Harry O, later a series); Fer de Lance, 1976;
Joys (a special), 1976; A Sensitive Passionate Man, 1977; Centennial,
1978; The Word, 1978; Inchon, 1980. *Songwriter:* A Sensitive Passionate Man, 1977; 7 other songs.

A(LMER) S(TILLWELL) MIKE MONRONEY
U.S. Senator
Born Oklahoma City, Oklahoma, U.S.A., March 2nd, 1902
Died Rockville, Maryland, U.S.A., February 13th, 1980

Almer Stillman Monroney, Democratic Congressman and Senator
from Oklahoma, was born in Oklahoma City in 1902 and nicknamed
"Mike" by his father.

After graduating in 1924 from the University of Oklahoma, where
he was elected Phi Beta Kappa, Monroney joined the *Oklahoma
News* as a reporter and political writer. A 1927 interview with Charles
Lindbergh sparked the young journalist's interest in aviation.
However, his father's illness made it necessary for him to take over
the family retail furniture business in 1928.

After an unsuccessful try the previous year, Monroney, his name
now legally changed to A.S. Mike Monroney, won the Congressional
seat for Oklahoma's fifth district. He was propelled into public
attention when he co-sponsored resolutions culminating in the Congressional Reorganization Act of 1946. "We are trying to do this
[legislative] work," Monroney said, "sitting on an old-fashioned
bookkeeper's stool with a slant-top desk, a Civil War ledger, and a
quill pen." The act led to the first major overhaul of Congress in over
50 years.

Although Monroney later claimed that the act was only 50 percent
effective, it simplified some legislative functions, reduced the number
of committees in both houses, provided for the appointment of staff
experts to assist committee members, and required lobbyists to
register. The *New York World-Telegram* predicted in an editorial that
the bill's passage would be remembered as the outstanding event of
the 79th Congress, and *Collier's* magazine awarded Monroney its
Congressman of the Year Award for his part in it.

Throughout his political career, the soft-spoken, folksy Monroney
enjoyed a good relationship with the press. *Time* magazine once called
the tall Oklahoman "friendly as an Airedale pup."

In 1950, after six terms in the House, Monroney began the first of
three terms in the Senate, where he became an active supporter and
reformer of military and civil aviation. He sponsored legislation in
1956 that resulted in the establishment of the Federal Aviation
Agency, for which he earned the nickname "Mr. Aviation." Later he

served as chairman of the Aviation Subcommittee of the Senate Commerce Committee and supported the efforts of the Kennedy Administration to reorganize and upgrade the efficiency of the Civil Aeronautics Board. He also supported congressional funding for the development of the supersonic transport and for improvements in air safety.

In 1965 Monroney again took up the cause of congressional reform as co-chairman of the Joint Committee on the Organization of Congress. The Committee's recommendations, however, were way-laid in the House Rules Committee. In that year Monroney also became a member of the Senate Select Committee on Standards and Conduct and chairman of the Post Office and Civil Service Committee.

Monroney gained national attention as an angry critic of Senator Joseph McCarthy and as an early supporter of Democratic Presidential candidate Adlai E. Stevenson, who reportedly nearly invited Monroney to be his running mate in 1952.

A moderate liberal, Monroney supported most of the social reform programs of the Kennedy and Johnson Administrations and backed U.S. policy in Vietnam. In Monroney's 1968 bid for re-election, the opposition portrayed him as a member of the élite Eastern Liberal establishment who had lost touch with his native state. At the time, the once-solidly Democratic neighboring southern states were swing-ing toward the Republicans, and although Monroney had succeeded in getting much federal money appropriated to Oklahoma, the electorate seemed willing to believe the charges from the right; he was defeated by Republican Henry L. Bellmon. Monroney and his wife continued to live near Washington, where he served as an aviator-transport consultant. When Monroney died of an aneurysm and pneumonia, Gov. George Nigh of Oklahoma ordered state flags flown at half-mast in his memory. Part of his ashes were scattered on the grounds of the Mike Monroney Aeronautic Center, an FAA training facility in Oklahoma City.   J.P./L.C.S.

Born Almer Stillwell Monroney (changed name to A.S. Mike Monroney upon entering politics). Son of Almer Ellis Stillwell M., furniture merchant, and Mary (Wood) M. Married Mary Ellen Mellon 1932. Son: Michael. Episcopalian. Educ: Univ. Oklahoma (Phi Beta Kappa), B.A. 1924. Reporter and political writer, Oklahoma News, Okla. City 1924–28; dir. of retail furniture business, Okla. City 1928–38. U.S. Rep. (Democrat, 5th Okla. District) 1939–51: Vice-Chmn., Jt. Cttee. on Org. of Congress: Member, Banking and Commerce Cttee. U.S. Senator (Democrat, Okla.) 1951–69: Chmn., Aviation Subcttee., Interstate and Foreign Commerce Cttee. Member, Senate Select Cttee. on Standards and Conduct; Co-chmn., Congressional Jt. Cttee. on Org. of Congress; Chmn., P.O. and Civil Service Cttee. 1965–68; Senate Floor Mgr. 1966 and 1968. Aviation-transportation consultant 1968–74 and intermittently thereafter. Campaign advisor for Democratic Nat. Cttee. Chmn. Robert E. Hannegan's 1946 congressional campaign. Delegate, Democratic Natl. Convention 1968. Pres., Okla. City Retail Furniture Assn.; Pres., Okla. City Rotary Club; Pres., Okla. City Retailers Assn. Member, Bd. of Drs., Midland Mortgage Co., Calif. Hons.: Sigma Delta Chi; Phi Gamma Delta; Collier's Congressional Award 1945; Wright Brothers Memorial, Natl. Aeronautics Assn. 1961. Hon. degree:

Colgate Univ., 1948; Fed. Aeronautics Admin. training center in Okla. City named Mike Monroney Aeronautic Center in his honor.

VICTOR GRUEN
Architect and town planner
Born Vienna, Austria, July 13th, 1903
Died Vienna, Austria, February 14th, 1980

Victor Gruen, best known for designing the first suburban shopping mall, considered himself an "environmental planner" whose projects integrated many buildings into a pleasing and functional complex. For 17 years he headed one of the leading US architectural firms, which has done important work in urban revitalization and suburban development.

Gruen studied architecture with Peter Behrens in Vienna while working as a technician for the firm of Melcher and Steiner. In 1932 he opened his own architectural office in Vienna, but was restricted by the Depression largely to designing small stores and apartment interiors. He was also active in these years as a playwright and actor for a Viennese cabaret.

The German annexation of Austria in 1938 forced Gruen to flee to the US with little more than his books and drawing table. After helping plan some of the smaller pavilions of the 1939 New York World's Fair, he began to design retail stores in New York City. Among his early projects were the Lederer Shop and the Altmann and Kuehne Candy Store, both on Fifth Avenue. In 1949 he established his own architectural practice in Los Angeles. This expanded so rapidly that in 1951 he joined with two other architects and a civil engineer to form Victor Gruen Associates. By 1958 the firm had six U.S. offices, 32 associate architects and 200 employees.

Gruen's first major project was the Northland Center just outside Detroit, the nation's first suburban shopping mall. Completed in 1954, the complex consisted of 80 stores covering 160 acres. It was unique at the time in keeping the central mall entirely free of motor traffic, which was relegated to surrounding access roads and parking areas. Gruen intended the development as a true community center, with an auditorium and other facilities for public use. He elaborated on this concept in the Southdale Shopping Center, which opened outside Minneapolis in 1956. Here the mall was not only traffic-free but also enclosed and air-conditioned, a multi-story courtyard with fountains, gardens and hanging lamps.

The Northland and Southdale projects became prototypes for countless suburban shopping centers which sprang up throughout the US and soon spread to Western Europe. But Gruen had strong objections to the form his innovation took in the hands of real estate developers. "I refuse to pay alimony for those bastard developments," he insisted. In contrast to Gruen's original conception, many suburban shopping centers were built in remote areas accessible only to automobiles; and most contained only retail stores rather than the combination of facilities that Gruen had intended. In this way they reinforced what Gruen regarded as the two most objectionable features of modern metropolitan areas: functional specialization and the predominance of the automobile. Isolated developments used for a single purpose, he believed, separate social classes and occupations; shopping centers, educational centers, office, entertainment and geriatric centers keep groups away from one another and encourage the fragmentation of modern life. Mushrooming freeways and parking areas reinforce the problem by dividing human space into checker-board squares separated by vast stretches of concrete. In contrast to this trend, Gruen envisioned the emergence of multi-purpose centers characterized by "compactness, intensity of public life and a small-grained pattern in which all types of human activities are intermingled in close proximity."

Though he wishfully predicted that shopping centers would soon become "a thing of the past," Gruen realized that the new developments were contributing to the decline of central cities by drawing businesses and people into the suburbs. To counteract this trend, he and his firm undertook a number of urban redevelopment projects designed to make the city core safer and more attractive. Derived from the original shopping center idea, these plans consisted essentially of turning all or part of the central business district into a pedestrian area free of automobile traffic. Streets became landscaped malls served only by public transportation; automobiles were to be left in underground garages or parking areas built along the periphery of the central city. The first such plan, proposed in 1955 for Fort Worth, Texas, was rejected due to opposition from businessmen and a strong lobby of garage and parking lot owners. But the concept was later implemented in Fresno, California, Rochester, New York, Urbana, Illinois and other cities. The Fort Worth proposal also exerted strong influence on the work of other city planners in the US, Europe and Australia.

Even after his retirement from Victor Gruen Associates in 1968, Gruen continued to promote his vision of an integrated center featuring a "small-grained mixture of all urban functions." During the 1970s he helped formulate urban redevelopment projects for Vienna and other European cities. In all his work he gave primary attention to the entire environment which he created. The design of individual buildings was secondary to him and was not considered innovative by other architects. Gruen is remembered for trying to restore the unity and grace of urban life, broken apart by modern technology and profit-seeking developers.   S.L.G.

Born Viktor Grünbaum (changed name during WWII). Son of Dr. Adolf G. (lawyer) and Elisabeth Levy G. Married: (1) Lizzie Kardos 1930 (div. 1941); (2) Elsie Krummeck 1941 (div. 1951): (3) Lazette van Hauten 1952 (d. 1962); (4) Kemija Salihefendic 1963. Children: Michael; Margaret. Jewish. Emigrated to U.S.A. 1938. Austrian at birth; naturalized American 1943. Educ: Technology Inst. Vienna, 1923–32; Acad. of Arts, Vienna 1924–25. With Melcher and Steiner, Vienna 1923–32: Technician; Designer; Supervisor; Coordinator. Organizer, author and actor in "Politsche Kabarett," Vienna 1926–32; private practice, Vienna 1932–38; Designer: IVEL Corp. N.Y.C. and in office of Norman Bel Geddes, N.Y.C. 1938; Organizer and

Central Square, Midtown Plaza, Rochester, N.Y.—designed by Victor Gruen Courtesy St. James Editorial

Producer, Viennese Theater Group, N.Y.C. 1938–40; design partnership (with Elsie Krummeck), Grünbaum and Krummeck, N.Y.C. and Los Angeles 1940–48; private practice, Los Angeles 1948–51; Founder and Chief Architect: Victor Gruen Assocs., Los Angeles, N.Y.C., Washington, D.C. and Tehran 1951–68; and Victor Gruen International, Vienna, Paris and Los Angeles 1963–72. President, Victor Gruen Center for Environmental Planning, Los Angeles 1968–80; Chief Architect, Victor Gruen AG, Switzerland, Vienna and Paris 1969–80; President, Zentrum für Umweltplanung, Vienna 1973-80; Planning and Architectural Consultant: Préfecture de la Région Parisienne, France; Université Catholique de Louvain, Belgium; City of Vienna; Scandinavian countries; Italy; Switzerland; Fed. Republic of Germany; Spain. Lectr., U.S.A. and Europe. Fellow, American Inst. of Architects; Affiliate Member, American Inst. of Planners; Charter Member, Yale Arts Assoc.; Member: Architectural League of N.Y.; Faculty Club, U.C.L.A.; Citizens; Planning and Housing Council of N.Y.; Architectural Guild. Hons: Hon. Award, American Inst. of Arch., S. Calif. chapter 1949, 1950; Ave. of the Americas Assoc. Award 1952; A.IA. Natl. Award of Merit 1954; Gold Medal, A.I.A. Detroit chapter 1955; Progressive Architecture Design Awards 1956, 1957, 1958, 1959, 1963; 3 S. Calif. A.I.A. Merit Awards 1957; A.I.A. and U.S. Dept. of State Awards 1958; Gold Medal, A.I.A. Memphis chapter 1958; special medallion, "Architect of the People," Rice Univ., Houston 1963; 3 A.I.A. Citations for Excellence in Community Architecture 1965; Mich. Soc. of Architects Award of Merit 1966; Calif. Governor's Design Award 1966; Significant Artistic Achievement Award, City of Vienna 1972; Arts D., Peppardine Univ., Los Angeles 1976; Gold Medal, Republic of Austria 1978; Gold Medal award from City and Province of Vienna 1979. *Architect:* Lederer Shop, N.Y.C. 1939; 12 stores for Barton's Bonbonnerie, N.Y.C. 1939-51; Altmann and Kuehne Candy Store, N.Y.C. 1940; Northland Center, Detroit 1954; master plan for 5,000 acres, Palos Verdes, Calif. 1954; Dayton Dept. Store, Rochester, Minn. 1954; revitalization plan for Fort Worth, Tex. (project) 1955; Southdale Shopping Center, Minneapolis 1956–67; various office bldgs. for the Tishman Co. 1957–65; Wilshire Terrace Apt. House, Los Angeles 1958; revitalization plan for city core of Kalamazoo, Mich. 1958; 2,500 apts., Charles River Park, Boston 1958; commercial, recreational and civic center project, Redondo Beach, Calif. 1958–64; Southdale Medical Bldg., Minneapolis 1958–65; World's Fair plan (project), Washington, D.C. 1959; City, County and Fed. Civic Center, Syracuse, N.Y. 1959; Museum of Arts and Sciences, Evansville, Ind. 1960; Cherry Hill Center, Camden, N.J. 1960; Winrock Center, Little Rock, Ark. 1960; 27 acre commercial, residential and institutional complex at Newark, N.J. 1960; master plan for Welfare Model Town, N.Y.C. 1960; 9 dept. stores for May Co. in Calif 1960–66; Midtown Plaza, Rochester, N.Y. 1962; Randhurst Shopping Center, Mt. Prospect, Chicago 1962; Doheny Towers Apt. Bldg., Los Angeles 1962; Marina del Rey, Los Angeles 1962; redevelopment study of 27 acres, The Rocks, Sydney 1962; 12 block redevelopment project in center of Urbana, Ill. 1962; square block central area multi-functional development in Salt Lake City, Utah 1963; Wilshire Comstock Apt. Bldg., Los Angeles 1963; Calif. Mart, Los Angeles 1963-66; Leo Baeck Temple, Los Angeles 1964; new satellite town (in development), Valencia, Calif. 1965; Sea World (marine exhibit), San Diego 1966; bus. sector revitalization plan (in process), Boston 1966; Fox Plaza, San Francisco 1966; city core revitalization plan, Fresno, Calif. 1968; city master plan for Tehran (project) 1968; harbor and city core revitalization plan for Antwerp (project) 1969; University City plan (in process), Louvain-la-Neuve, Belgium 1971; city core revitalization plan (in process), Vienna 1971; city core plans for 7 satellite cities in Paris region 1972. *Exhibitions:* 1955–68: Natl. Gallery, Washington, D.C.; World's Fair, Brussels; U.S. Information Service, Washington, D.C.; Architectural League of N.Y.; 8th Pan-American Congress of Architects, Mexico City; American Inst. of Architects exhibition in Moscow; Berlin Intl. Bldg. Exhibition; American Embassy, Paris; Brooklyn Museum, N.Y. *Author:* How to Live with Your Architect, 1949; Shopping Towns USA (with Larry Smith), 1960; Stadsfornyelse i Forenta Staterna, '1963; Heart of our Cities, 1964; The Ideal City (with others), 1964; The People's Architect (with others), 1964; New Cities USA, 1966; Who Designs America? (with others), 1966; The Downfall and Rebirth of City Cores on both sides of the Atlantic, 1972; Centers for the Urban Environment, 1973; Das Überleben der Städte, 1973; Die Alte Schuhschachtel, 1973; Die Lebenswerte Stadt, 1975; Ist Fortschritt ein Verbrechen?, 1975; numerous articles in architectural journals throughout the world. *Further reading:* Urban Pattern: City Planning and Design by Arthur B. Gallion, 1950; Cities in the Motor Age by Wilfred Owen, 1959; Architecture and the Esthetics of Plenty by James Marston Fitch, 1961.

GRAHAM (VIVIAN) SUTHERLAND
Painter, designer, and engraver
Born London, England, August 24th, 1903
Died Hempstead, London, England, February 17th, 1980

Capturing the essential nature of a landscape, a tree, or a human face was the aim of painter Graham Sutherland, whose works combined continental Surrealism with British neo-Romanticism in a blend that became the model for many younger artists.

Sutherland, the son of a municipal lawyer, was born in London in 1903 and grew up at Merton Park in Surrey and at Rustington in Sussex. At the age of nine he entered boarding school at Sutton, where he developed an interest in Greek and Latin. His holidays were spent at Swanage, Dorset, where he wandered through the countryside, becoming more and more sensitive to the forms and colors of the rustic landscape.

After four unhappy years as a Classics student at Epsom College, Sutherland, now 15, was sent to serve as an apprentice in the engineering branch of the Midland Railway works at Derby under the eye of an uncle, meanwhile continuing the hobby of drawing which he had begun at school. A year later he enrolled in Goldsmiths' College of Art, where he remained for six years, learning the crafts of etching and engraving. His first one-person shows, held at London's XXI Gallery in 1925 and 1928, displayed etchings of landscapes in a mystical, romantic style reminiscent of William Blake and Samuel Palmer.

Leaving Goldsmiths' College in 1925, he set out to earn his living as an independent graphic artist and teacher; he was elected an associate member of the Royal Society of Painter-Etchers and Engravers in 1926 (the Society expelled him seven years later after a quarrel) and the following year joined the faculty of the Chelsea School of Art. When the market for etchings, previously strong, collapsed with the onset of the Depression, Sutherland turned to painting. Now a teacher of composition and book illustration at Chelsea, he accepted commissions to design posters for the Orient Line, the London Passenger Transport Board, the Shell-Mex Company, and the Post Office. He also designed ceramics, china, wallpapers, rugs, and fabrics for other concerns. In 1938 he held his first exhibition of paintings at the Rosenberg and Helft Galleries.

These early paintings were for the most part inspired by the artist's frequent trips to Pembrokeshire in Wales, whose rough landscapes he transformed into a series of convoluted, evocative forms, often in a Surrealist mode. "It was in this country that I began to learn painting," he wrote in a letter. "It seemed impossible here for me to sit down and make finished paintings 'from Nature.' Indeed, there were no ready-made subjects to paint. The spaces and concentrations of this clearly constructed land were stuff for storing in the mind. Their essence was intellectual and emotional. . . . I found that I could express what I felt only by paraphrasing what I saw. . . . I did not feel that my imagination was in conflict with the real, but that reality was a dispersed and disintegrated form of imagination."

Sutherland brought his idea of paraphrase—the dislocation and reconstitution of particular forms through the artist's perception—to the dramatic paintings of wrecked buildings and debris which he executed as official war artist during World War Two. Towards the end of the war, Sutherland, who had converted to Catholicism in 1926, received an invitation to paint *The Agony in the Garden* for St. Matthew's Church in Northampton. After negotiation, he received permission to paint instead a *Crucifixion,* which he rendered in a savagely expressionistic style fraught with the torment of the war years. Throughout the postwar years he found a personal idiom in the imagery of thorn trees, whose spikes and gnarls were transformed by him into distorted symbols of suffering. Many of his thorn tree paintings contained forms suggestive of anthropomorphic presences hidden in the landscape.

Beginning in 1945, Sutherland mounted frequent exhibitions and retrospectives throughout Europe and in North and South America. In 1947 he visited the south of France for the first time. This put him in closer contact with the works of his contemporaries, particularly Picasso and Matisse. He and his wife Kathleen, whom he met during his student days, bought a French home in Menton in 1954; their English home since 1945 was in Trottiscliffe, Kent.

In the 1950s, Sutherland undertook several large-scale works. The most noteworthy was a design for a tapestry, *Christ in Glory in the Tetramorph,* commissioned by the Dean and Chapter of Coventry Cathedral, newly rebuilt after its destruction by bombs during the war. This icon-like work measures 72 by 40 feet and takes up the entire east wall of the Cathedral. A large mural, *The Origins of the Land,* commissioned for the Festival of Britain in 1951, was later presented to the Tate Gallery (for which Sutherland served as a Trustee from 1948 to 1954).

A challenge by the writer Somerset Maugham to paint his portrait in 1949 opened the way to a new career for Sutherland in portraiture. Although seemingly a departure from his earlier work, this new endeavor was, in fact, a continuation, for in his depictions of organic objects Sutherland had always sought to capture their moods, their characters, their essential lines, in the manner of a portraitist. "It is a question," he said, "of bringing out the anonymous personality of these things; at the same time they must bear the mould of their ancestry." Though he occasionally painted figures from everyday life, such as Cornish tin miners during the war, Sutherland usually accepted commissions from the famous and powerful, including Dr. Konrad Adenauer, Edward Sackville-West, Lord Kenneth Clark, and Helena Rubinstein. In an interview, he said: "I do find it immensely fascinating (though not exclusively so) to deal with people who have had pressures put upon them or who have had the character necessary to direct great enterprises. There are psychological overtones in such people which it is absorbing to try and render."

Sutherland's method in painting portraits was to sketch voluminously from life, allowing the subject unconsciously to reveal his or her character through habitual gestures and expressions, while experimenting with different perspectives and conditions of light. The sitter's own choice of pose largely determined the arrangement of the composition, which Sutherland constructed with the precision of an engineer. This assimilatory process produced portraits that captured the personalities as much as the physical likenesses of the sitters, some of whom were none too flattered by the results.

The most controversial of all Sutherland's portraits was that of Sir Winston Churchill, commissioned by a Parliamentary committee to mark the former Prime Minister's 80th birthday. Unveiled on November 20th 1954, the life-sized portrait showed Churchill seated on a dais in his typical House of Commons attire (striped trousers, black coat and waistcoat, and bow tie), with a typically pugnacious expression. Though some critics approved it as an outstanding character study, Churchill spoke of it as "a remarkable example of modern art" which made him look "half-witted." On his instructions, the portrait was never publicly displayed. Some years after Churchill's death, his wife revealed that she had burned the canvas and frame in compliance with his wishes. Sutherland commented that, while he bore no rancor, the destruction was "without question an act of vandalism."

Sutherland was awarded the Order of Merit in 1960. Since 1973 he was engaged in setting up and administering the Graham Sutherland Gallery, now known as the Graham and Kathleen Sutherland Foundation, at Picton Castle in Pembrokeshire, where his paintings can be seen in the original setting that inspired them.   J.P./M.D.

Son of Graham H.V.S., civil servant and lawyer, and Elsie S. Married Kathleen Frances Barry 1927. Children: one son (d. in infancy). Roman Catholic (Protestant to 1926). Educ: boarding sch., Sutton, Surrey 1912–14; Epsom Coll., Surrey 1914–18; Goldsmiths' Coll. of Art, Univ. London, 1921–26. Mil. Service: Official War Artist 1940–45. Apprentice, Engineering Branch, Midland Railway, Derby 1919–20; Art teacher, Kingston-upon-Thames, Surrey 1927; teacher of engraving 1928–32 and of composition and book illus. 1932–39, Chelsea Sch. of Art, London; painter and designer 1931–80. Assoc.

Upper half of design for the *Coventry Tapestry* created by Graham Sutherland

Member, Royal Soc. of Painter-Etchers and Engravers 1925–33; Trustee, Tate Gall., London 1948–54; Trustee, Graham Sutherland Gall. (Graham and Kathleen Sutherland Foundn.), Picton Castle Trust, Pembs. 1976–80. Member, Athenaeum and Curzon clubs. Hons: Japanese Foreign Secty.'s Prize, Tokyo 1957; O.M. 1960; D.Litt., Oxford 1962; D.Litt., Leicester Univ. 1965; Menton Freedom Medal and Citoyen d'honneur, City of Menton, France 1968; Member, Natl. Inst. Arts and Letters, Britain 1972; Fellow, American Acad. Arts and Letters 1972; Guest of Honor and First Prize, Menton Biennale, France 1972; Commandeur des Arts et des Lettres, France 1973; Fellow, Accademia di San Luca, Rome 1973; Shakespeare Prize, Hamburg 1974; Pres., Menton Biennale, 1974; D.Litt., Cardiff Univ. 1979; Prize, Mus. of Modern Art, São Paulo. British Pavilion, N.Y. World's Fair 1939 (toured U.S.A., S. America, France); Natl. Gall., London 1940; Britain at War, Mus. of Modern Art, NYC 1941; (with Paul Nash, Henry Moore, and John Piper) Redfern Gall., London 1944; (with Bacon, Hodgkins, Moore, and Smith) Lefevre Gall., London 1945; Musée d'Art Moderne, Paris 1946; 40 Years of Modern Art, 1907–1947, Inst. of Contemporary Arts, London 1948; (with Marc Chagall) Hanover Gall., London 1950; Carnegie Intnl., Pittsburgh 1950, 1952, 1958; First Anthology of British Painting, 1925–50, New Burlington Gall., London 1951; (with Moore) Inst. of Contemporary Arts, Boston 1953; (with Moore) Phillips Gall., Washington, D.C. 1954; Documenta I, Mus. Fredericianum, Kassel, W. Germany 1955; British Painting 1700–1900. Pushkin Mus., Moscow, and Hermitage Mus., Leningrad 1960; British Art Today, Mus. of Art, San Francisco 1962 (toured U.S.A.); (with Francis Bacon) Gall. il Centro, Naples 1963; Art in the Church, Univ. Centre, Northampton, England 1968; British Drawing 1939-49, Scottish Natl. Gall., Edinburgh 1969; IXe Biennale Intnl. d'Art, Menton 1972. At Marlborough Fine Art, London: Moore/Picasso/Sutherland, 1970; Contemporary British Painters and Sculptors, 1973; XX Century Drawings and Watercolours, 1974. *Retrospectives:* (with Moore and Piper) Temple Newsam Gall., Leeds 1941; Inst. of Contemporary Arts, London 1951, 1953; British Pavilion, XXVI Biennale, Venice 1952 (toured France, Netherlands, Switzerland, Britain); Musée d'Art Moderne, Paris 1952; Tate Gall., London 1953; Stedelijk Mus., Amsterdam 1953; Kunsthaus, Zurich 1953; British Sect., *Exhibitions: One-person*—XXI Gall., London 1925, 1928; Rosenberg and Helft Gall., London 1938; Leicester Gall., London 1940; Buchholz Gall., NYC 1946, 1948; Roland Browse and Delbanco Gall., London 1947, 1960; Lefevre Gall., London 1947; Hanover Gall., London 1948, 1952; Redfern Gall., London 1952, 1958, 1959, 1964; Valentin Gall., NYC 1953; Arts Council of Great Britain, London 1953; Akademie der Bildenden Kunste, Vienna 1954 (toured Austria, W. Germany); Museu de Arte Moderna, São Paulo 1955; Kunstkabinett, Frankfurt 1957; Hoffman Galerie, Hamburg 1957; Belfast Mus. and Art Gall., N. Ireland 1959; Rosenberg Gall., NYC 1959, 1964; Galeria Galatea, Turin and Milan 1961; Marlborough Fine Art Gall., London 1962, 1968, 1973, 1974; Welsh Arts Council, Cardiff 1963; Gall. Fanti di Spade, Rome 1963; Galatea-Galleria d'Arte Contemporanea, Turin 1963; Prebendal House of Llandaff Cathedral, Wales 1963; Hags Gemeentemus., The Hague 1965; Haus am Waldsee, Berlin 1965; Wallraf-Richartz-Mus., Cologne 1965; Albrecht Durer Gesellschaft, Nurenberg 1969; Kestner Gesellschaft, Hanover 1969; Gall. il Fauno, Turin 1969, 1972; Palais d'Europe, Menton 1969; Gall. Narciso, Turin 1972; Marlborough Galerie, Zurich 1972; Bergamini Gall., Milan 1972; 2RC Gall., Milan 1979. *Selected group shows*—Royal Acad. 1923; Musée des Arts Decoratifs, Paris 1927; Exhib. of British Art in

Industry, Royal Acad. 1935; Intnl. Surrealist Exhib., New Burlington Gall., London 1936; Contemporary British Art, Third São Paulo Biennale 1954; Roland Browse and Delbanco Gall., London 1956; Arthur Jeffress Gall., London 1959; Berlin 1959; New London Gall. 1962; Gall. Civica d'Arte Moderna, Turin 1965; Haus der Kunst, Munich 1965, 1967 (toured W. Germany, Netherlands); Kunsthalle, Basle 1966; Marlborough Fine Arts, London 1966, 1977, 1979, Milan 1973; Natl. Portrait Gall., London 1977; Palazzo Reale, Milan 1979. *Collections:* Tate Gall., British Mus., and Victoria and Albert Mus., all London; Mus. of Modern Art, NYC; Musée de l'Art Moderne, Paris; many other public and private collections. *Other works:* The Crucifixion (painting), Church of St. Matthew, Northampton, England 1946; tapestry, Edinburgh Tapestry Co., 1949; The Origins of the Land (mural), Festival of Britain 1951; Christ in Glory in the Tetramorph (tapestry), Coventry Cathedral 1962; paintings in Chapel of St. Mary Magdalen, Chichester, and in St. Aiden's Church, Acton. *Books:* A Bestiary (lithograph series), 1968; Sutherland Sketchbook, 1974. *Major articles:* "A Trend in English Draughtsmanship," Signature 1936; "Welsh Sketch Book," Horizon, April 1942 (reprinted in Sutherland in Wales, 1976); "Thoughts on Painting," The Listener, Sept. 6, 1951. *Interviews and Discussions:* "The Living Image: Art and Life" (radio discussion between V.S. Prichett, Lord Kenneth Clark, Henry Moore, and Sutherland), The Listener, Nov. 13, 1941; reprinted in Henry Moore on Sculpture, 1966; "Modern Art Explained by Modern Artists, Part I," The Artist, March 1944; statement in Eight European Artists (ed. by Felix H. Man), 1954; Sutherland: Christ in Glory in the Tetramorph (ed. by Andrew Révai), 1964; Conversations with Painters (by Noel Barber), 1964. *Further reading:* Graham Sutherland by Edward Sackville-West, 1943; The Imagery of Graham Sutherland by Robert Melville, 1950; The Work of Graham Sutherland by Douglas Cooper, 1961.

ALICE (LEE) ROOSEVELT LONGWORTH
Socialite
Born New York City, U.S.A., February 12th, 1884
Died Washington, D.C., U.S.A., February 20th, 1980

Alice Roosevelt Longworth, the daughter of President Theodore Roosevelt and his first wife, Alice Lee, was once called "the closest thing we [Americans] have to royalty." Her biting wit and her influence in Republican Party politics made her a domineering figure in Washington society for eighty years.

She was born at her parents' Manhattan townhouse in 1884. Her father, then a State Assemblyman, rushed home from Albany at the news of the birth to find his wife dying of Bright's disease in one bedroom and his mother dying of typhoid fever in another. The griefstricken Roosevelt, hardly able to look at his infant daughter, gave her into the care of his sister Anna for the next three years.

When Roosevelt married Edith Kermit Carow in 1887, young Alice went to live with them at Sagamore Hill, the family estate at Oyster Bay, Long Island. Roosevelt's second wife bore him four sons and another daughter. As a child Alice was thought to be suffering from a hereditary congenital bone disease and was required to wear steel leg

braces by day and a steel device on her feet at night. She was educated at home by private tutors; gifted with a prodigious memory, she could recite whole poems and chapters of the Bible.

In 1901 Roosevelt was elected Vice President for President William McKinley's second term. Before the family had completed its move to Washington, however, McKinley was killed by an assassin and Roosevelt found himself suddenly President—an event that brought mixed shock and delight to his elder daughter, who had been "making magics" to provoke just such an occurrence.

Alice was 17 when she entered the White House, a handsome, headstrong young woman who quickly won the attention of the tabloid press. Forbidden by her father to smoke cigarettes in public, she reportedly took to the White House roof instead, and on one occasion switched to cigars. She kept a pet snake, hobnobbed with European aristocrats and the American *nouveau riche,* and drove around in her automobile without a chaperone. "I can do one of two things," her father told a family friend; "I can be President of the United States, or I can control Alice. I cannot possibly do both." The young socialite was nicknamed "Princess Alice" and her favorite color "Alice blue."

In 1906 Alice married Nicholas Longworth, a Congressional Representative from Ohio who was 14 years her senior. Their White House wedding was the social event of the season. For their wedding trip, they took a round-the-world tour, receiving expensive gifts from governments eager to court favor with the bride's father.

The Longworth mansion in Washington soon became the scene of all-night poker parties and gatherings of conservative politicians, who quickly felt the influence of Mrs. Longworth's "snob power." Opposition to the League of Nations and the World Court were among her favorite causes, most of which she inherited from her father. She frequently attended Senate debates, campaigned for favored candidates, and went to Republican conventions.

In 1924, when she was 41, Mrs. Longworth gave birth to a daughter, Paulina. Longworth was elected Speaker of the House a few months later. He died of pneumonia in 1931.

The 1932 election to the presidency of Democrat Franklin Delano Roosevelt, her fifth cousin once removed, was a bitter blow to Mrs. Longworth, who had vainly nursed dynastic ambitions for her half-brother Teddy Jr. She retaliated with a shower of barbed comments and venomous parodies at Washington dinner parties, directing the worst of her scorn against the First Lady, Eleanor Roosevelt, her first cousin and childhood friend. (Her acid wit was never an entirely partisan weapon, however. Of Republican Presidents Warren Harding and Calvin Coolidge, she called the first "just a slob," and said that the second "looked as if he had been weaned on a pickle.")

During the Depression and Second World War years, Mrs. Longworth attacked the New Deal and Democratic policies in columns written for the *Ladies Home Journal* and other magazines. With the return of the Republicans to the White House under Dwight Eisenhower, her salon again became a central meeting place for the powerful and power-seeking. Though opposed to their liberal policies, she made friends with the Kennedy brothers and admired Lyndon Johnson enough to vote for him, but voiced her delight when Richard Nixon was elected in 1968.

Mrs. Longworth's daughter Paulina, who had married Alexander McCormick Sturm, was a religious woman who devoted herself to charitable volunteer work. When she died suddenly in 1957, Mrs. Longworth, then 73, obtained custody of Paulina's daughter Joanna, whom she raised.

In recent years, Mrs. Longworth, whose wide-brimmed hats became something of a trademark, continued her aristocratic life in the Longworth mansion, reading voluminously, receiving visitors, and giving and attending dinner parties. (At one such party she boldly wound a live boa constrictor around her neck.) Still vigorous in her nineties, she was afflicted with glaucoma and cancer; two mastectomies made her, in her words, "the topless wonder of Massachusetts Avenue."

She died at the age of 96 of bronchial pneumonia. At her request, no funeral was held.   M.D.

Daughter of Theodore Roosevelt, 26th President of the United States, and Alice Hathaway (Lee). Married Nicholas Longworth, Speaker, U.S. House of Representatives, 1906 (d. 1931). Daughter: Paulina Sturm, b. 1925 (d. 1957). Educ: private tutors. Member: Bd. of Counselors, Women's Div., Republican Natl. Cttee. 1932; Ohio Delegation, Republican Natl. Convention 1936, 1940, 1944; Natl. Cttee. on Food for the Five Small Democracies 1940. Political columnist, Ladies Home Jrnl. and other mags. and newspapers. *Books:* Crowded Hours (memoirs), 1934; (with Theodore Roosevelt, Jr.) The Desk Drawer Anthology: Poems for the American People, 1937.

SIR ROGER (BENTHAM) STEVENS
British Diplomat and Vice-Chancellor of Leeds University
Born Lewes, Sussex, England, June 8th, 1906
Died Thursley, Surrey, England, February 20th, 1980

Sir Roger Stevens was a career diplomat whose service as ambassador to Persia in the 1950s, and overseer of British consulates in the Mideast and Africa, earned him a knighthood and a G.C.M.G. Stevens was regarded at the Foreign Office as a "new frontiers" man for his liberal views on emerging third world governments; he later guided Leeds University through a turbulent period, holding the position of Vice-Chancellor from 1963–70. His book, *The Land of the Great Sophy,* gained him a wide audience with students of Iranian history and of British diplomatic history as well.

Roger Bentham Stevens was born in 1906, the son of a justice of the peace in Lewes, Sussex. He was sent to Wellington College in Berkshire, a private school specializing in training for the military and other forms of civil service. He went on to Queens College, Oxford, receiving his degree in 1928. Stevens applied to the Consular Service in his last year at university and during the next ten years served in

Buenos Aires, New York, and Antwerp as a minor consular official. He returned briefly to Britain in 1939 and worked in the Ministry of Information. Three years later he took a consular post in Denver, Colorado.

Stevens's skilled articulation of the need for strong ties between America and Britain, nations he characterized as bulwarks of the democratic tradition, appealed to Americans during the second world war. Realizing Stevens's potential value to British diplomacy, Lord Halifax, the Ambassador, summoned him to Washington D.C., where he became secretary of the British Civil Secretariat in 1944. His rise through the ranks of the Foreign Office was then assured, and he moved quickly from his position as head of the economic relations department to Assistant Under-Secretary of State in London, Ambassador to Sweden, and, finally, to the post of British envoy to Tehran.

Relations with Persia had only recently been reestablished and a major oil crisis loomed at the time of Stevens's arrival in 1954. His skill as a negotiator led to a compromise among contentious petroleum interests and strengthened overall relations between the two countries. When he returned to London in 1958, Stevens was promoted to the post of Deputy Under-Secretary in the Foreign Office. Both the Mideast and African portfolios were now his responsibility, and for the next five years he traveled extensively, devoting much of his attention to political structures emerging in Central Africa.

Stevens left the Foreign Office in 1963 to take up the Vice-Chancellorship of Leeds University—the first outsider to be so appointed in the university's history. The diplomatic skills Stevens had developed in successfully representing a western industrial power to third world nations were severely tested by the student political activism of the 1960s. Dissident students and faculty members at Leeds demanded that the university reverse its traditional aloofness from participation in local and international politics. Although Stevens was frequently hard put to effect a durable compromise between those offering a radical critique of the university and those seeking to preserve its political independence, he helped draft a new constitution which redefined the roles to be played by the state, the students, and a diverse faculty in the governance of Leeds University. The constitution was installed in 1971, a year after Stevens's retirement from the vice-chancellorship.

In the 1970s, Stevens remained active in several national and international posts, including the Committee of Minerals Planning Control (1972–74), the Board of Directors of the British Bank of the Middle East to 1977, and the United Nations Administrative Tribunal (1972–80).   A.B.P.

Son of F. Bentham S. and Cordelia Wheeler S. Married: (1) Constance Hallam Hipwell 1931 (d. 1976); (2) Jane Irving Chandler 1977. One son. Educ: Wellington Coll., Berkshire 1924; Queens Coll., Oxford, B.A. 1928. Joined British Consular Service 1928; Served in Buenos Aires, N.Y., Antwerp 1928–39; Ministry of Information, London 1939–42; Consul in Denver 1942–44; Secty., British Civil Secretariat, Washington D.C. 1944–46; Head of Econ. Relations Dept., Foreign Office, London 1946–48; Asst. Under Secty. of State,

Foreign Office 1948–51; Ambassador to Sweden 1951–54; Ambassador to Persia (now Iran) 1954–58; Deputy Under-Secty., Mideast and African Portfolios, Foreign Office 1958–63; Advisor to First Secty. of State on Central Africa 1962. Appointed Vice-Chancellor, Leeds Univ. 1963–70. Chmn.: Yorkshire and Humberside Econ. Planning Council 1965–70; Cttee. on Minerals Planning Control 1972–74. Dir., British Bank of the Middle East 1964–77. Member: U.N. Admin. Tribunal 1972–80; Panel of Inquiry into Greater London Devel. Plan 1970–72; Travellers' (Club), London. Hons: C.M.A., 1947; knighted (K.C.M.G.) 1954; G.C.M.G. 1964; Hon. Fellow, Queens Coll., Oxford 1966. *Author:* The Land of the Great Sophy, 1962 (rev. ed. 1971).

ALFRED (HELMUT) ANDERSCH
Writer and radio broadcaster
Born Munich, Germany, February 4th, 1914
Died Berzona, Ticino, Switzerland, February 21st, 1980

Alfred Andersch, one of the major avant-garde literary figures in West Germany after the second world war, was a prolific writer in a variety of forms—including radio plays, short stories, novels, travel narratives and essays. He also translated a novel and an opera into German, wrote many magazine articles, and published poems and drawings. Andersch's central concern was individual freedom and the assumption of responsibility for the moral and political dilemmas posed by the modern world.

The origin of this motif lay in his own experiences. His father, an army officer, had enthusiastically supported General Ludendorff's anti-Semitic, pro-Nazi politics and participated in Hitler's abortive 1923 putsch. In total rejection of his father's political beliefs, Andersch became a Communist (KPD) youth organizer in Bavaria, and in 1933 he was arrested and interned for six months in Dachau concentration camp. Ironically, his father protected him from further harassment, but the young Andersch continued to protest against his country by going into "inner exile". He said: "My answer to the total state is total introversion."

For the rest of the 1930's Andersch worked as an advertising specialist in Munich and Hamburg. Drafted into the German army, he deserted in 1944 and was interned for a year in America prisoner of war camps in Louisiana and Rhode Island. After the war Andersch worked as an editorial assistant for *Neue Zeitung* in Munich and in 1947 edited the literary magazine *Der Ruf* with H.W. Richter; the magazine was banned the following year by the American military government. He and Richter then formed Gruppe 47, an association of writers which included Heinrich Boll, Gunter Grass, and Siegfried Lenz. Without formal political identification, the literary group acted as a forum for criticism of contemporary conditions and values.

Two years after he married his second wife in 1950 (she bore him three children), Andersch published a controversial defense of his desertion from the German army—*Kirschen des Freiheit (Cherries of*

Freedom). As an act of freedom and protest, he saw his desertion as a turning point in his life. The book was widely acclaimed. By this time Andersch had become known in the vanguard literary movement as a most effective critic of the conservatism of post-war Germany.

In the mid-1950's Andersch founded the literary bi-monthly *Texte und Zeichen* and published works by a variety of formerly exiled writers and intellectuals including Golo Mann and the neo-Marxist philosopher Theodor Adorno. As Andersch's success as a writer and radio broadcaster grew, he became increasingly disillusioned with Adenauer's Germany and left the country permanently in 1958—a year after he published his first novel, *Sansibar*—to live in Switzerland.

In *Sansibar* Andersch described the persecution and escape of anti-Nazi Germans from a small Baltic fishing village. Using stream-of-consciousness techniques, he devoted chapters to each of the major characters; the novel was an instant success and was translated into many languages. Andersch's second novel *Die Rote* (1960), published in English as *The Redhead*—superficially a suspense tale about the impulsive flight to Venice of a German businessman's wife and her dalliances with a wealthy homosexual and with a former Gestapo officer—describes the disillusionment with communism that Andersch himself experienced. *Die Rote* contained italicized internal monologues to link the narration of past and present events. A similar technique was used in *Efraim* (1967), written in the first person from the protagonist's 'notes'. The novel recounts the story of a London journalist who travels to Berlin to find someone who disappeared during the second world war. Described as "a spiritual odyssey of a modern wandering Jew," the book examined mid-life identity crisis in an atmosphere of existential nihilism. Andersch's fourth and last novel, *Winterspelt* (1974) portrays the soul-searching of a German commander facing American troops.

Andersch's novels and short stories were praised for their "Faulknerian" prose and innovative narrative techniques. His characterizations of people driven to action were skillfully realized and critics generally agreed that his writing was insightful, often possessing a lyrical and evocative quality.

Central to Andersch's writing is his belief that political, moral, and metaphysical self-awareness is crucial, not only for the individual but also for the society in which he lives; and the person who flees totalitarian oppression is, by deserting evil, a pilgrim.   L.F./R.T.

Son of Alfred A., WW I army officer, and Hedwig (Watzek) A. Married: (1)— (2) Gisela Dichgans (painter, photographer, book illustrator) 1950. Children: 2nd marriage—Michael; Martin; Annette. Lived in Switzerland 1958–80. Naturalized Swiss citizen 1973. Educ: Wittelsbacher Gymnasium, Munich. Mil. Service: Wehrmacht 1940–41; temporary discharge 1941; redrafted 1943; German Army in Italy 1943–44; deserted, June 1944; P.O.W. in U.S.A. 1944–45. Trained as bookseller, Munich 1928–30; unemployed 1931–33; youth organizer and leader, K.P.D. (Communist Party of Germany) 1932; arrested and interned for six months in Dachau concentration camp 1933; released under Gestapo Aufsicht (surveillance); worked as advertising specialist in industry, Munich and Hamburg 1933–40. Editorial asst. to Erich Kästner, *Neue Zeitung,* Munich 1945–46; co-founder and co-ed., *Der Ruf,* literary jrnl., Munich 1946–47; co-founder, Gruppe 47 1947; radio broadcaster and ed. of literary evening programs, Stuttgart, Frankfurt/M, and Hamburg 1948–60, including founder and dir., Abend (Evening) Studio, Frankfurt 1948–50; feature (film) ed., Hamburg and Frankfurt 1951–53; founder, co-dir., ed., Radio-essay, Stuttgart 1955–58. Ed., *Studio Frankfurt,* literary jrnl. 1952–54; co-founder, ed., *Texte und Zeichen,* literary bi-monthly 1955–57; contributor to *Frankfurter Allgemeine Zeitung* and *Merker;* leader of expedition into Arctic for German television 1965. Member: Gruppe 47; Communità Europea degli Scrittori 1961; Bayerischen Akademie der schönen Kunste, Munich 1968; PEN Zentrum 1967; Deutsche Akademie für Sprache und Dichtkunst 1970. Hons: Immermann-Fördererpreis 1957; Literaturpreis des Verbandes der duetschen Kritiker (German critics' prize) 1958; Förderungspreis, Stadt Düsseldorf (Advancement Prize, City of Düsseldorf) for *Sansibar* 1958; Schleussner-Schüller Preis, for *Aktion ohne Fahnen* 1959; Prix Charles Veillon and Nelly Sachs Prize, Stadt Dortmund (City of Dortmund) for *Efraim* 1968; Literaturpreis, Bayerischen Akademie der Schönen Kunste (Literary prize, Bavarian Acad. of Fine Arts) 1975–76; Bundesfilmprämie, for the film *Die Brandung von Hossegor. Books: Novels*—Sansibar: Oder, Der letzte Grune, 1957 (trans. as Flight to Afar, 1958); Die Rote, 1960 (trans. as The Redhead, 1961, filmed 1962); Efraim, 1967, (trans. as Efraim's Book, 1970); Winterspelt, 1974 (trans. 1978, also filmed). *Short story collections*—Piazza San Gaetano: Suite, 1957; Geister und Leute, Zehn Geschichten, 1958, other eds. 1961 and 1974 (trans. as The Night of the Giraffe and Other Stories, 1964; selections published in Evergreen Review, 1961); Ein Liebhaber des Halbschattens; drei Erzählungen, 1963 and 1974 (selections published in Un Amateur de demi-taintes, trans. 1967); Mein Verschwinden in Providence, neun neue Erzählungen, 1971 (trans. as My Disappearance in Providence and Other Stories, 1978); Tochter, Erzählung, 1970; Gesammelte Erzählungen, 1971 (collected stories). *Essays*—Deutsche Literatur in der Entscheidung, ein Beitrag zur Analyse der literarischen situation, 1948; Die Blindheit des Kunstwerks und andere Aufsätze, 1965; Norden, Süden, rechts und links, Von Reisen und Büchern, 1951-1971, 1972; Ein neuer Scheiterhaufen für alter Ketzer. Kritiken und Rezensionen, 1979. *Travel narratives*—Die bitteren Wasser von Lappland, ein Reisetagebuch, mit Stimmen von Touristen und von Urgebilder der Natur, 1953; Paris ist eine ernste Stadt, 1961; Wanderungen im Norden, mit 32 Farbtäfeln nach Aufnahmen von Gisela Andersch, 1962, fifth ed. 1970; Kie Arktis seiner Landschaft (fragments of a novel), 1964; Aus einem römanischen Winter, 1966; Hohe Breitengrade, oder Nachtrichten von der Grenze, mit 48 Farbtäfeln nach Aufnahmen von Gisela Andersch, 1969. *Radio plays*—Strahlende Melancholie, 1953; Der Bürde des weissen Mannes. Brennpunkt Indo-China, letzt crise des Kolonialen Zeitalters, 1953; Der Wunder an der Marne, 1955; Die Feuerinsel oder die Heimkehr des Kapitän Tizzoni, 1955; Die letzten von Schwarzen Mann, 1956; Synnöves Halsband (radio essay), 1958; Aktion ohne Fahnen (adaptation of Sansibar), 1958; Fahrenflucht, 1958, reprinted in Fahrenflucht (4) Hörspiele, 1965, and in Deutsche Lektüre, ed. by P.G. Krauss, 1969; co-author, Biologie und Tennis, 1958; Der Tod der James Dean, eine Funkmontage (text by John Dos Passos and others), 1960; Der Albino, 1960; Von Ratten und Evangelisten, 1960; In der Nacht der Giraffe (based on his short story), 1960; Russisches Roulette, 1961; Hörspiele (includes four radio plays: Fahrenflucht, In der Nacht der Giraffe, Der Tod der James Dean, Russisches Roulette), 1973; Neue Hörspiele: Die Brandung von Hossegor. TapetenWechsel.

Radfahrer sucht Wohnung, 1979. *Autobiographical*—Die Kirschen der Freiheit, Ein Bericht, 1952 (trans. as The Cherries of Freedom, 1978). *Editor*—Europäische Avantgarde (anthology), 1949; Offenes Tagebuch, by Elio Vittorini, 1959; Die andere Achse: Italienisch resistenza und geistiges Deutschland, by Lavinia Jollos-Mazzucchetti, 1964; Von der Notwendigkeit der Kunst, by Ernst Fischer, 1967. *Translator*—Looking for the Bluebird (Ein Musikant spinnt sein) by Joseph Wechsberg, 1949; Intoleranza (opera) by Luigi Nono, 1962. *Other*—Haakons Hosentaschen (film), 1966; Die Entwaffnung (television play), 1968; Giorgio Bassani, oder Vom Sinn des Erzahlens, 1969; Artikel 3 (poem), 1976; Einige Zeichnungen (drawings), 1977; Emport euch der Himmel ist Blau, Gedichte und Nachdictungen aus dreissig Jahren, 1946–1977 (poems), 1977; Öffentlicher Brief an einen sowjetischen Schriftsteller, das Überholte betreffend; Reportagen und Aufsätze, 1977; co-author, BRD-Sowjetunion. Offenheit gegen Offenheit. Meinungen, Kontroversen, Dialoge, 1978; Weltreise auf deutsche Art; eine Geschichte, 1977; Bericht, Roman, Erzählungen, selected works (includes bibliography), 1965; Ein Auftrag für Lord Glouster (includes bibliography), 1968; Mein Lesebuch, oder Lehrbuch des Beschreibungen, 1978; Das Alfred-Andersch Lesebuch, selections 1946–1979, (with chronology, bibliography, and afterword), 1979. Contributor to numerous anthologies, journals, and reviews. *Further reading:* "The Night of the Giraffe and other Stories" (review) by Marvin Mudrick, Hudson Review, Spring, 1965.

JUSTAS (IGNOVICH) PALECKIS
Lithuanian Premier
Born Telsiai, Lithuania, January 10th, 1899
Died Verkovny, Soviet Lithuania, February 21st, 1980

Justas Ignovich Paleckis left school at 16 and worked as a translator and general laborer. By the age of 20 he was writing poetry which extolled the virtues of his homeland and its people. Before becoming a full-time journalist in 1927, Paleckis taught elementary school, attended Kaunas University for two years, and served as Director of the Lithuanian Wire and Telegraph Agency. From 1927 to 1939, while working as a magazine and newspaper journalist, Paleckis's evolving interest in Communist ideology led him to write political tracts for the underground Baltic Communist movement. At the outbreak of World War Two, Paleckis was imprisoned by the nationalist government of Lithuania which knew of his identification with Communism and wished to suppress potential collaboration with either Germans or Russians.

After the fall of France in June 1940, the Soviets invaded Lithuania and deported many of the country's leaders to Siberia. Paleckis was selected to serve as premier but exercised no real political power. The general perception of Paleckis as a moderate Marxist allowed Moscow to give the impression of having no designs on the Balkan state. In fact, the Soviets simply disguised their intentions by instructing Paleckis to hold a referendum which would demonstrate widespread popular support for Lithuanian annexation by the USSR. Paleckis obediently rigged the vote.

When the Germans conquered Lithuania in 1941, Paleckis organized resistance forces and assisted the Soviet Army's conquest of Lithuania in 1944. He was subsequently named Chairman of the Presidium of the Supreme Soviet of Lithuania. The pinnacle of Paleckis's career was his election in 1952 to the Central Committee of the USSR as a Candidate Member. Throughout the late 1950s and early 1960s, he spent much of his time travelling to foreign capitals as a member of the Interparliamentary Union. Some observers have viewed his membership of the Union as an attempt to lend an air of legitimacy to Soviet rule in Lithuania.   T.P.

Alternate spelling: Paletskis. Educ: Kaunas Univ., Lithuania 1926–28. Elementary sch. teacher 1923–26; Dir., Lithuanian Wire Service 1926–27; journalist 1927–39; Lithuanian Premier from 1940; member, Communist Party of the U.S.S.R. 1940–80; Chmn., Presidium of the Lithuanian Supreme Soviet 1940–67; member, Central Cttee. of the Lithuanian Communist Party 1940–80; Deputy Chmn., Presidium of the Supreme Soviet of the U.S.S.R. 1941–66; Candidate Member, Central Cttee. of the Communist Party of the U.S.S.R. 1952–60; member, interparliamentary Union 1955–69; Chmn., Nationalities of the U.S.S.R. 1966–70; First deputy chmn., U.S.S.R. Parliamentary Group 1966–76. Hons: Four Orders of Lenin; Order of the Patriotic War, class 1. *Author:* The Last Tsar, 1937–38.

OSKAR KOKOSCHKA
Painter, playwright and poet
Born Pöchlarn, Austria, March 1st, 1886
Died Montreux, Switzerland, February 22nd, 1980

A major artist of the twentieth century, Oskar Kokoschka was also a prolific writer and a controversial dramatist. Caught up in the terror of two world wars he was forced to spend much of his adult life in exile— vigorously expressing through his art and writing his humanistic beliefs and his deep concern for victims of war and totalitarianism.

Oskar Kokoschka was born of artisan parents in the Austrian town of Pöchlarn on the river Danube. His father, a jeweler, was ruined by the economic crisis of 1889 and when Oskar was three the family moved to a new suburb of Vienna where his father found work as a traveling salesman. At about the time Oskar started school in Vienna, he had his first experience of tragedy; his eldest brother died.

Kokoschka won a scholarship to the Arts and Crafts School (Kunstgewerbeschule) in Vienna when he was 18 and studied drawing, design and crafts. His talents were quickly recognized by his teacher Carl Otto Czeschka and he was entrusted with the running of one of the preparatory drawing classes. Unlike many of the faculty who were Secessionists and concerned themselves entirely with the decorative arts, Kokoschka was interested in the human form and encouraged his students to make quick "action" sketches of child models. The commissions he received from the Vienna Crafts Studio (Wiener Werkstatte) were all for decorative work, but Kokoschka often introduced the human form into his designs. On his own he managed to master the techniques of oil painting and produced a few canvases, mainly portraits. His work was noticed by the Viennese architect Adolf Loos who like Kokoschka opposed the already degenerating decorative trend. In 1908 the two men met and Loos began to secure commissions for the young artist and introduced him to sympathetic artists and writers. Kokoschka who painted a portrait of Loos at that time later described their friendship as "decisive not only for my career but also for my life."

His career under way, Kokoschka concentrated first on landscapes, employing in his work many of the principles and techniques of Impressionism. He was not only concerned with the depiction of the natural appearance and mood of landscape but also with the projection of himself. Dreams and fantasies played an important role in Kokoschka's early works. Like Freud, dreams represented for him not only release, but intimated the "inner life". This inner element constituted the "fourth dimension" of his paintings, based on "the essential nature of vision, which is creative." In 1912 he wrote: " . . . things end up with no existence beyond my inner vision of them. Their spirit is sucked up by that vision as oil in a lamp is drawn up by the wick in order to nourish the flame."

Kokoschka started to write plays and although they appeared to echo the emerging style of the German Expressionist dramatists, Kokoschka denied that his earlier plays had anything to do with their rejection of society and plans for improvements of the world. A storm of protest broke when his play *Mörder Hoffnung der Frauen (Murderer, Hope of Women)* was performed in 1909. No less offensive than his play to the sensibilities of the cultured Viennese were his artistic illustrations prepared to announce and embellish the performance. The bold lines of the artwork reflected the savage and destructive love of the play's two characters. The critics were less than enthusiastic and the popular press berated him.

At the age of 24, Kokoschka went to Berlin for a year. His first one-man show was held at the Paul Cassirer gallery there and he worked for Herwath Walden who ran the Der Sturm gallery and the art journal of the same name. During his stay in Berlin Kokoschka began to paint portraits again. Returning to Vienna in 1911, he took up his old teaching post at the Kunstgewerbeschule but his plays scandalized the conservative Viennese and the school, pressured by the Ministry of Culture and Instruction, withdrew his stipend. That same year Kokoschka fell in love with Alma Mahler, widow of the Austrian composer, and doyenne of the Vienna artworld. Kokoschka later referred to this relationship as the "most unquiet time" of his life and depicted the involvement in one of his finest paintings, appropriately entitled *The Tempest* (1914) in which the large, free, almost monochromatic brushstrokes vividly express the turbulence of their affair.

His earlier portraits of the period were painted in narrow tense strokes of color and Kokoschka exaggerated certain character traits of his sitters to express his feelings about them. To eliminate the distance between himself and his subjects he would engage them in conversations, believing that animated informality would allow a sudden revelation of spirit. Kokoschka recalled this period saying "my early black portraits arise in Vienna before the world war; the people lived in security yet they were all afraid. I felt this through their cultivated form of living which is still derived from the baroque; I painted them in their anxiety and pain." Critics agreed that Kokoschka's portraits unmasked the spiritual vacuum behind the glitter of early 20th century Vienna. As Kokoschka's portrait style evolved, he painted with bolder, looser strokes of more varied color and his forms became more heavily outlined.

The Harbor of Marseilles II, 1925, by Oscar Kokoschka
Courtesy City Art Museum of St. Louis

At the outbreak of World War One, Kokoschka enlisted in the Austrian army, ending his relationship with Alma Mahler. He served as a cavalry officer on the Russian and Italian fronts (1915–17) but after being badly wounded he was hospitalized, first in Vienna and then in Dresden. In 1918 while still recuperating in Dresden, he wrote and produced three plays which reflect his increasing concern with politics and the horrors of war. Like many of his contemporaries, Kokoschka had welcomed revolution as the means of achieving a more humanitarian world. The Bolshevik takeover of the Russian Revolution led Kokoschka to believe that regimes created by armed revolt were often more horrendous than the ones they destroyed. His "Dresden Manifesto" (1920) sharply protested the inhumanity of totalitarian politics. Kokoschka settled quietly in Dresden, becoming a professor of fine art at the Akademie in 1919. His paintings which again included many landscapes were less sombre than before and he was influenced by the brighter, lighter work of the Brucke artists, then active in eastern Germany. In 1924 he left Dresden and for seven years journeyed through Europe and around the Mediterranean. The vivid paintings of this period, most notably his views of Prague and the Alps, demonstrate his great talents as a landscape painter.

Kokoschka returned to Vienna in 1931 and ending a ten year apolitical period, he accepted a commission to portray children at a Viennese orphanage. The painting, focussing on the children happily playing, demonstrated the humanitarian concern of the socialist city council which had provided the orphanage, and served as an ironic contrast to the reactionary policies of the Austrian government. The assassination of Chancellor Dollfuss by Nazi infiltrators in 1934 drove Kokoschka to Prague. He was commissioned to paint a portrait of Tomas Masaryk, the philosopher and president of the Czechoslovakian republic. Both men admired the social concerns of the 17th century theologian Comenius and Kokoschka painted him in the background of Masaryk's portrait. In 1937, the year in which a Kokoschka exhibition was mounted in Vienna, the Nazis removed all "degenerate art"—including all of Kokoschka's works—from Germany's museums. Kokoschka responded by producing his *Self Portrait of a Degenerate Artist*. That same year he painted a moving poster of children suffering because of the Spanish Civil War.

While in Prague, Kokoschka met Olda Palkovska and when the Munich Pact was signed in 1938, sealing Czechoslovakia's political fate, Kokoschka fled to England with her. They were married in 1941 and, almost penniless, Kokoschka had to work in watercolor. He executed a group of anti-Fascist paintings which expressed his anguish of the human misery caused by World War Two. When the war ended, Kokoschka's works were exhibited throughout Europe and in the United States, and for the first time in his life he did not have to worry about financial problems. He continued to paint landscapes and portraits and commenced two important mythological trilogies—*Prometheus Saga* and *Thermopylae*, the latter completed after he left England in 1953. Kokoschka began to increase his output of lithographs and designed tapestries and stage sets. In a 1956 poster for aid to Hungarian refugees, he portrayed a mother with her dead child. Major portraits after this time include one of the British publisher Sir Stanley Unwin (1959) and a self portrait with his wife Olda (1963-64).

Kokoschka's later paintings are grander, brighter and less compulsively animated than his early works but the intensity remains. A landscape painter of extraordinary distinction, it is his portrait masterpieces and his symbolic expressions of war-torn Europe and mankind's eternal torments which best demonstrate the visionary quality of his work and show us the depth of his compassion and psychological insight. The art critic G.S. Whittet wrote in 1975 that Kokoschka "was probably the last painter of modern history capable of carrying into paint the externalized figuration of internal anguish and frustration."   R.T.

Married: Olda (Palkovska) 1941. No children. Emigrated to England 1938. Czech citizen 1934; British citizen 1947. Educ: schs. in Vienna; Kunstgewerbeschule, Vienna 1904–09. Mil. service: Austrian army cavalry officer 1914–18; official War Artist on Isonzo 1915–16. Instr., Kunstgewerbeschule 1905–09; Designer, Wiener Werkstätte 1908; Joined staff of *Der Sturm* 1910; Prof., Akademie auf der Bruhlshen Terrasse, Dresden 1919–24; Instr. of Painting, Boston Mus. Sch. 1949; Guest Instr. in Painting, Minneapolis Sch. of Art 1952; Founder, Lectr., Intnl. Summer Acad. of Fine Arts, Salzburg 1953–62. Member Prussian Acad. of Art. Hons: Hon. Citizen of Vienna 1946, Pöchlarn 1951, and Salzburg; Hon. Member of Acad. of Fine Arts, Munich 1950; Order of Merit, West Germany 1956; O.B.E. 1959; Erasmus Prize (with Marc Chagall) 1960; Rome Prize 1960; Hon. D.Litt., Oxford Univ. 1963; Hon. Academician, Royal Acad., London 1970; Lichtwark Prize, Hamburg. *Exhibitions: One-person*—Paul Cassirer Galerie, Berlin 1910, 1918, 1923, 1925, 1927; Folkwang Mus., Essen 1910; Galerie Der Sturm, Berlin 1916; Galerie Lang, Darmstadt 1920; Galerie von Garvens, Hanover 1921; Galerie Caspari, Munich 1921; Kunstlervereinigung, Dresden 1921; Galerie Richter, Dresden 1921; Galerie Gurlitt, Berlin 1921; Graphisches Kabinett Erfuth, Dresden 1922; Kunstsalon Wolfsberg, Zurich 1923; Galerie Goldschmidt-Wallerstein, Berlin 1924; Galerie Goltz, Munich 1924; Neue Galerie, Vienna 1924; Kestner Gesellschaft, Hanover 1925; Galerie Arnold, Dresden 1925; Kunsthandlung Goldschmidt, Frankfurt 1926; Galerie Caspari, Munich 1926; Gemeente Mus., Amsterdam (toured Netherlands) 1927; Kunsthaus, Zurich 1927; Kunsthaus Schaller, Stuttgart 1927; Leicester Galls., London 1928; Kunsthaus Hermann Abels, Cologne 1929; Kunsthalle, Mannheim 1931; Galerie Georges Petit, Paris 1931; Galerie Feigl, Prague 1933; Osterreichisches Mus. fur Kunste und Industrie, Vienna 1937; Buchholz Gall., N.Y. 1938, 1941; Genootschap Kunstliefde, Utrecht; Gall. St. Etienne, N.Y. 1940, 1943, 1949, 1954; Arts Club, Chicago 1941; City Art Mus., St. Louis, Missouri 1942; Kunsthalle, Basel 1947; Stedelijk Mus., Amsterdam 1947; Kunsthaus, Zurich 1947; Inst. of Contemporary Art, Boston (toured U.S.A.) 1948; Feigl Gall., N.Y. 1949; Phillips Gall., Washington D.C. 1949; Haus der Kunst, Munich (toured Hamburg, Mannheim) 1950; Neue Galerie, Linz 1951; Wallraf-Richartz Mus., Cologne 1951; Schloss Charlottenburg, Berlin 1951; Inst. of Contem-

porary Arts, London 1952; Frankfurter Kunstkabinett, Frankfurt
1953; Kunstnernes Hus, Oslo 1953; São Paulo Bienal 1953; Mus. of
Art, Santa Barbara, Calif. and Calif. Palace, San Francisco 1954;
Museu de Arte Moderna, Rio de Janiero 1954; Kunstverein, Freiburg
1954; Galerie Welz, Salzburg 1954; Residenz, Salzburg 1955; Natl.
Gall., Prague 1956; Kunsthalle, Bremen 1956; Gropper Galls.,
Cambridge, Mass. 1956; Marlborough Fine Art, London 1960, 1967,
1976; Tate Gall., London 1962, 1969, 1974, 1976; Davison Art
Center, Middletown, Conn. 1964; Wurttembergisher Kunstverein,
Stuttgart 1966; Marlborough-Gerson Gall., N.Y. 1966; Badisher
Kunstverein, Karlsruhe 1966; Kunstsalm Wolfsberg, Zurich 1969;
Serge Sabarsky Gall., N.Y. 1971; Galerie Wilhelm Grossbennig,
Dusseldorf 1974; Kunsthaus, Hamburg 1975; Victoria and Albert
Mus., London 1976; Haus der Kunst, Munich 1976. *Group*—Intl.
Kunstschau, Vienna 1908, 1909; Neue Sezession, Munich 1914; Marc,
Campendonk, Kokoschka, Galerie Der Sturm, Berlin 1915; Galerie
Dada, Zurich 1917; XIII Biennale di Venezia, Venice 1922, 1932;
Intl. Kunstausstellung, Dresden 1926; Vom Abbild zum Sinnbild,
Galerie Stadel, Frankfurt 1931; Intl. Exhib., Carnegie Inst., Pitts-
burgh 1933; Exhib. of Degenerate Art, Munich (Nazi Exhib., toured
Germany) 1937; Modern German Art, Mus. of Fine Arts, Springfield,
Mass. 1939; Der Sturm, Kunstmus., Bern 1944; Dkimt, Schiele,
Kokoschka, Neue Galerie, Vienna 1945; XXIV Biennale di Venezia,
Venice 1948, 1952; Deutsche Kunst-Meisterwerke des 20 Jahrhun-
derts, Kunstmus., Lucerne 1953; Documenta I, Kassel, West Ger-
many 1955; Art in Revolt: Germany 1905–1925, Marlborough Fine
Art, London 1959; European Art: 1912, Wallraf-Richartz Mus.,
Cologne 1962; L'Art en Europe Autour de 1918, Ancienne Douane,
Strasbourg 1968; Gemaelde Bildwerke und Zeichnungen des 20
Jahrhunderts, Nationalgalerie, Berlin 1969. *Collections*—Stedelijk
Mus., Amsterdam; Stedelijk van Abbemus., Eindhoven, Nether-
lands; Mus. Boymans-van Beuningen, Rotterdam; Staatliche Museen,
Berlin, East Germany; Nationalgalerie, Berlin; Kunsthalle, Bremen;
Wallraf-Richartz Mus., Cologne; Mus. am Ostwall, Dortmund, West
Germany; Leopold-Hoesch Mus., Duren, West Germany;
Kunstmus., Dusseldorf; Folkwang Mus., Essen, West Germany;
Kunsthalle, Hamburg; Stadtisches Galerie, Hanover; Staatliche
Kunsthalle, Karlsruhe, West Germany; Stadtische Kunsthalle, Mann-
heim, West Germany; Bayerische Staatsgemaelde Sammlungen,
Munich; Von der Heydt Mus., Wuppertal, West Germany;
Staatsgalerie, Stuttgart, West Germany; Musées Royaux des Beaux-
Arts, Brussels; Musée des Beaux-Arts, Liege, Belgium; Neue Galerie,
Linz, Austria; Salzburger Festspielfond, Salzburg, Austria;
Kunsthistorisches Mus., Vienna; Oesterreichisches Mus. für An-
gewandte Kunst, Vienna; Albertina, Vienna; Scottish Natl. Gall. of
Modern Art, Edinburgh; Tate Gall., London; Narodni Galerie v
Praze, Prague; Moderna Museet, Stockholm; Kunstmus., Winterthur,
Switzerland; Kunstmus., Basel; Kunsthaus, Zurich; Albright-Knox
Art Gall., Buffalo, N.Y.; Fogg Art Mus., Harvard Univ., Cambridge,
Mass.; Inst. of Arts, Detroit, Mich.; Speed Art Mus., Louisville, Ky.;
Walker Art Inst., Minneapolis, Minn.; Mus. of Modern Art, N.Y.;
Allen Memorial Art Mus., Oberlin, Ohio; Art Mus., Portland, Ore.;
Providence Mus. of Art, R.I.; City Art Mus., St. Louis, Mo.; San
Francisco Mus. of Art; Phillips Gall., Washington D.C.; Art Inst.,
Chicago; Nelson Gall., Atkins Mus., Kansas City, Mo. *Illustrator*—
Tubutsch by Ehrenstein, 1912; Die Chinesische Mauer by Karl Kraus,
1914; Lob des hoben Verstandes by von Dirsztay, 1917; Mein Lied by
Ehrenstein, 1931; Erzählung by Ann Eliza Reed, 1952; Entwurfe für
die Gesamtausstattung zu W.A. Mozarts Zauberflöte with B.

Paumgartner and W. Furtwangler, 1955. *Stage design*—Die Zauberflöte, Salzburg Festival, 1955; Burgtheater, Vienna 1960, 1961. *Author: Plays*—Mörder, Hoffnung der Frauen, 1907; Sphinx und Strohman, 1908; Der brennende Dornbusch, 1911; Hiob, 1911; Orpheus und Eurydike, 1916; Comenicus, 1935; *Poetry*—Die Träumende Knaben, 1908; Dramen und Bilder, 1913. *Books*—Der Expressionismus Edvard Munchs, 1953; Thermopylae: Ein Triptychon, 1955; Spur in Treibsand (short stories), 1956 (English trans. Sea Ringed with Visions, 1962); Mein Leben (autobiog.), 1971; London Views, British Landscapes, 1972; Saul and David, 1973. Contributed to jrnls., mags., and newspapers. *Further reading:* Kokoschka: Life and Work by E. Hoffman, 1947; Oskar Kokoschka: The Work of the Painter by Hans M. Wingler, 1958; Oskar Kokoschka by Bernhard Bultmann, 1961; Oskar Kokoschka: The Artist and his Time by Josef P. Hodin, 1966; Kokoschka by Ludwig Goldscheider (written in collaboration with the artist), 1967; Fin-de-Siècle Vienna by Carl Schorske, 1980.

ERIC (ALFRED) LYONS
Architect and town planner
Born London, England, October 2nd, 1912
Died Hampton Court, Surrey, England, February 22nd, 1980

Courtesy Richard Lyons

Eric Lyons—whose concepts in urban residential development reshaped British architecture after World War Two—was in practice for nearly 30 years, winning international recognition and 18 British awards.

Lyons studied architecture at the Regent Street Polytechnic in London and began his career as an assistant to various London architects, continuing his study of architecture by attending evening classes. Among his early employers were Walter Gropius and Maxwell Fry, and from 1945 to 1950, Lyons was in partnership with a former student-friend, Geoffrey Townsend, who later became a developer. This early friendship and business association proved invaluable in later years when, as one of Lyons's clients, Townsend allowed him the freedom to develop his ideas. Recalling the architect-client period of their association, Lyons commented later: "I had the enormous benefit of the confidence of a client who gave me an extraordinarily free hand, which I believe to be almost the most important factor."

When Townsend decided to become a developer and the partnership was dissolved, Lyons continued to practice alone as a private consultant architect until 1963, when he formed a partnership with Ivor Cunningham—one which was to continue until Lyons's death. During the late 1950s and early 1960s, Lyons worked on many housing and flat designs for Span Developments Ltd., at a time when private speculative home-building was being criticized for its banal, unimaginative architectural style. He immediately set a new standard of design, layout, and landscaping, and although reactions from local government planning authorities were at first disapproving, Lyons quickly established himself. He fought many long battles with government bureaucracies and on one of his housing estates at Blackheath he erected a sculpture of an architect being crushed by a concrete plinth—his way of depicting the oppressive forces of municipal planning boards.

Lyons's Span housing developments were constructed in many towns and villages in Britain—terraces of houses or flats two to three stories high built with traditional materials rather than with concrete. That each unit had its own private garden, with larger communal gardens inside the development, was based on Lyons's own belief that residents of high-density housing should be given a feeling of openness. He experimented with various forms of courtyards and differing relations between private and shared land, preserving existing foliage and adding to it. Lyons explained: "There has always been a tendency for landscape architecture to be the cream on the pudding. I don't see it that way. Hideous buildings don't always matter. But I think man must maintain contact with nature—that is really the only sort of philosophy I have."

His Span developments pioneered a new way of life for residents of estates, who found themselves sharing responsibility for communal areas. Their common land was subject to rules: no washing to be hung on garden lines, cars severely restricted—even the color of waste-disposal containers was regulated.

Housing development by Eric Lyons
Templemere, Weybridge, Surrey
1964 Courtesy St. James Editorial

Lyons's developments were often small, against the 1950s and '60s trend toward larger and larger housing estates. Lyons later said: "I believe in small buildings. I think good architecture comes from small groups working closely together. I married a small wife. Even if I don't totally believe that you can nourish life in such simple terms, it is still a check against megalomania."

Even when faced with an enormous project—a village for 2,500 people in World's End, Chelsea, London—Lyons still constructed a residential area that was also a social environment. Much of his work, in particular that for Span and at World's End, derives its openness from the inspiration of Cambridge college architecture, which he admired for its system of communities surrounding courtyards.

In the 1970s, one of his greatest regrets was not being awarded the commission to design Cambridge's new £17 million Robinson College. Although he did win the international architecture competition in 1972 for Vilamoura, the Portuguese holiday resort, his busy professional involvement did not allow him to enter as many competitions as he might otherwise have done. He believed, however, that they were a valuable training ground: "Competitions are not only to find winners. They throw up also-rans, names not before known, or little known."

Lyons's election to the Presidency of the Royal Institute of British Architects in 1975 came at a time when new architecture in Britain was under severe criticism for its poor taste and lack of inspiration. Architects, rather than the commercial developers, were being blamed for the sprawl of buildings. The choice of a self-confessed autocrat who had always insisted that good architecture could only be produced free of governmental restraints on planning policy was viewed with concern by the traditionalist faction within the R.I.B.A. For many independent architects, however, Lyons's defiance of restrictions and his insistence on what he saw as professionalism made him something of a hero. He had repeatedly won prizes for buildings categorically condemned by local government because they violated planning regulations. "There is a tendency" he said, "to contain the architect, guide him, control him, make sure he doesn't make any mistakes. This is a modern disease and it is why we are not getting the best out of our architects. This process is guaranteed to get rid of the bumps, and one of my obsessions is that bumps matter. They are the sign of man, whereas flatness is the sign of the machine." During the two years of his presidency, Lyons cut costs by reducing bureaucracy, hoping to ensure that professional matters of design and architecture would come first. Under his guidance the R.I.B.A. was not, he said, to become a "trade union." Although criticized by some of his membership for this stand, Lyons knew that the majority of the 27,000 members supported him.

While often criticized for his innovations, Lyons always regarded his style as having evolved naturally from the village greens and the Bloomsbury squares of 18th-century England.   M.D.

Son of Benjamin L., toy designer, and Caroline L. Married Catherine Joyce Townsend 1944. Children: Richard, architect; Jane; Antony; Naomi. Educ: Regent Street Polytechnic, London 1936. Asst. architect, Walter Gropius and Maxwell Fry, London 1936–37; and others. Partnership with G. Paulson Townsend, London 1945–50; private practice, London 1950–63; partnership with Ivor Cunningham 1963–80. With R.I.B.A.: Council Member 1960–63; V.P. 1967–68; Sr. V.P. 1974; Pres. 1975–77. Chmn., A.C.A. 1973. Hons: O.B.E. 1959; Civic Trust Award 1961 (two), 1962, 1964, 1965, 1967; Ministry of Housing and Local Govt. Medal 1961 (three), 1963, 1964 (three), 1965, 1966, 1967, 1968; Distinction in Town Planning 1961; R.I.B.A. Eastern Region Architecture Award 1966; C.B.E. 1979; Fellow, R.I.B.A., F.S.I.A.D.; Hon. Fellow, American Inst. Architects; Member, Académie d'Architecture, France; *Architect:* Box Corner (flats), Twickenham 1951; Onslow Ct. (flats), Richmond 1952; Cavendish Ct. (flats), Richmond 1954; The Priory (flats), Blackheath; Parkleys (flats), Richmond 1955; The Hall (flats), Blackheath 1956; Soviet Trade Delegation (flats), Highgate 1957; The Cedars (housing), Teddington 1958; Applecourt (flats), Cambridge; Corner Green (housing) and Hallgate (flats), Blackheath; Howard House (housing), Bognor Regis 1959; Fieldend (housing), Twickenham; Hallgate (housing), Blackheath; Highsett (flats), Cambridge; Parkgate (flats), Hove 1960; Lansdowne Hill (flats and housing), Southampton; married soldiers' quarters, Pirbright; Pitcairn House (housing), Hackney; The Hamlet (housing), Bognor Regis 1962; Spangate (flats), Southrow (flats), and The Lane (housing), Blackheath; The Paddox (housing), Oxford 1963; Blackheath Park (housing), Blackheath; Albion Primary Sch., Bermondsey; Friar's Primary Sch., Southwark; Highsett II (housing and flats), Cambridge; Rayners Road (housing), Putney; Templemere (housing), Weybridge 1964; World's End redevel. (housing), Chelsea 1964–78; Brackley (housing); Castle Green (housing), Weybridge; Castle House (housing), Southampton; Hallgate (housing), Blackheath; Highsett (housing), Cambridge 1965; New Ash Green (new village), Kent 1965–70; Cedar Chase (housing), Taplow; Offices, Hampton Hill; Harlow New Town (housing), Essex; Weymede (housing), Byfleet 1966; Dryden House (flats), Cambridge; Grasmere (housing), Byfleet; Parkend (housing), Blackheath 1967; Westfield (housing), Ashtead 1969; married soldiers' quarters, Pirbright; Mayford (housing), Camden; New Ash Green Primary Sch., Kent 1971; Vilamoura holiday resort, Portugal; Walsingham Lodge (housing), Barnes 1972; Plan for central area, housing and shops, Vilamoura, Portugal 1973; Plan for center redevel., Chertsey, Wates House (univ. accommodation), Guildford 1974; Plan for new village, Aqueduct Green, Telford; Caledonian Estate (housing), Islington; Westbourne Neighbourhood (housing, community service facilities), Islington 1977; Holm Walk (housing), Blackheath 1978; Delhi and Outram Streets (housing), Islington; Fieldend (housing), Telford; Mallard Place (housing), Twickenham 1979. *Major articles:* "Rebuilding Britain," Twentieth Century, London, summer 1962; "Too Often We Justify Our Ineptitudes by Moral Postures," R.I.B.A. Jrnl., London, May 1968. Further reading: "Out of the Strong . . . ," The Architect (London), Feb.-Mar., 1975; "Rus in Urbe," The Architects' Journal (London), Jul. 9, 1975.

ROBERT (EARL) HAYDEN
Poet and teacher
Born Detroit, Michigan, U.S.A., August 4th, 1913
Died Ann Arbor, Michigan, U.S.A., February 25th, 1980

Robert Earl Hayden was a dedicated teacher of English literature and one of America's most underrated contemporary poets. In the last decade of his career, Hayden began to receive significant critical attention; and, in 1976, he was appointed the Library of Congress's consultant for poetry.

Hayden was born in 1913 in Detroit, Michigan, where he attended Wayne State University. After receiving his B.A. in English, he worked for the Federal Writers' Project in 1936 as a researcher in Negro history and folklore. Four years later Hayden began writing music and drama criticism for the *Michigan Chronicle,* a position he held until enrolling at the University of Michigan at Ann Arbor for graduate study. Hayden received his M.A. in 1944 and joined the faculty of Fisk University, a predominantly black school in Nashville, Tennessee in 1946. He remained there as Professor of English until 1968, when he returned to the University of Michigan as a visiting professor and writer-in-residence. A year later he was offered a permanent appointment as Professor of English at Ann Arbor, a position he held until his death.

Hayden's themes were drawn from the Afro-American experience of slavery and discrimination. He wrote extensively of black history and Negro folklore, evincing, in his early work, local color and urban black dialect. *A Ballad of Remembrance,* for which he won the grand prize for poetry in English at the first World Festival of Negro Arts at Dakar, Senegal in 1966, marked Hayden's progression toward more complex poetic forms. Two of the book's longer poems depict rebellion within total domination. "Middle Passage" chronicles the seizure of the slave galley *Amistad* by its captives, and "Runagate Runagate" celebrates Harriet Tubman, the abolitionist who helped hundreds of slaves escape to freedom.

While the subjugation of a whole race was the frequent concern of Hayden's poetry, his thoughtful tone belied the subjectivity of one whose knowledge of suffering derived more from abstract contemplation than concrete experience. Indeed, Hayden's allusive language owed less to the neo-African rhythms of Claude McKay, Sterling Brown, and Langston Hughes than to the cerebrations of Eliot and Pound. The concluding verses of "Those Winter Sundays" (from *Angle of Ascent,* 1975) compress into nine brief lines the complex feelings of a man, now poet and professor, for his working-class father:

I'd wake and hear the cold splintering, breaking
When the rooms were warm, he'd call,
and slowly I would rise and dress,
fearing the chronic angers of that house,

Speaking indifferently to him,
who had driven out the cold
and polished my good shoes as well.
What did I know, what did I know
of love's austere and lonely offices?

A critic who was sympathetic to the tensions of the black artist in an era of radical self-consciousness observed, "his fundamental impulse has always seemed not to be black, but to write as the spirit moved him. If it moved him racially, well and good, if not, well and good also." Regarding a tendency of the dominant culture to colonize ethnic writers who are politically engaged, Hayden cautioned black writers against taking residence "in a kind of literary ghetto;" and, likewise, urged critics not to house them there. Speaking of his own literary project, Hayden once said that he was a poet who happened to be black, writing verse as "a form of prayer—a prayer for illumination, perfection."

In the 1960s, Hayden's refusal to voice the cant and explosive rage that had become fashionable—and much expected of black writers— did little to enlarge his audience. Several black intellectuals castigated him for a "literary inwardness", with one critic charging that his aesthetic standards sounded "suspiciously like a poetic version of integration." Hayden's response was to affirm the glimpse of the universal that is afforded by a stress on the particular: "I believe the best art . . . is on the side of life. And the best poets are those concerned with the complicated matters of life, the things it's hard to get a handle on." In reducing such complexities to "racial utterance," he argued, one's art would suffer.

Publication of *Words in the Mourning Time* in 1971, and its nomination for a National Book Award, earned Hayden recognition as a major American poet. Other awards followed, but, ironically, there remained the residue of what critic Arna Bontemps had earlier termed Hayden's "Negro thing": with each honor, it was unfailingly mentioned that the previous recipients had all been white. Julius Lester celebrated Hayden's triumph in the *New York Times Book Review,* noting that his lionization came two decades late "primarily because he is black." R.C.

Married 1941. Children: Maia Tedla. Ba'hai faith. Educ: Wayne State Univ., B.A.; Univ. of Mich., Ann Arbor, M.A. 1944. Researcher, Federal Writers' Project 1936–40; music and drama critic, *Michigan Chronicle* 1940–42; teaching fellow, English, Univ. of Mich. 1944–46; Prof. of English, Fisk Univ., Nashville, Tenn. 1946–68; Univ. of

Mich.: Visiting Prof. 1968; Prof. of English and Writer-in-Residence 1969–80. Bingham Prof., Univ. of Louisville, Louisville, Spring 1969; Visiting Poet, Univ. of Wash., Seattle, Summer 1969; Visiting Prof., Univ. of Conn., Storrs, Conn. and Denison Univ., Granville, Ohio 1971; staff member, Bread Loaf Writers' Conference, Middlebury, Vt. 1972. Member of Board and poetry ed., *World Order* (B'hai mag.); P.E.N., Authors' League of America; Phi Kappa Phi (Mich. chapter). Hons: Jules and Avery Hopwood Prizes for Poetry from Univ. of Mich. 1938 and 1942; Julius Rosenwald Fellowship in creative writing 1947; Ford Foundn. Fellow 1954–55; Grand Prize for Poetry, First World Festival of Negro Arts, Dakar, Senegal 1966; Mayor's Bronze Medal for Distinguished Achievement by a Detroit native 1969; Russell Loines Award from Natl. Inst. of Arts and Letters 1970; Natl. Book Award nominee 1972; Fellow, Acad. of American Poets 1975; Poetry Consultant, Library of Congress 1976; Distinguished Citizen Award from Detroit Women's Club of the United Negro Coll. Fund 1977; hon. degrees from, among others, Brown Univ., Grand Valley State Coll., Benedict Coll., and Wayne State Univ. *Works: Poetry*—Heart Shape in the Dust, 1940; The Lion and the Archer, 1948; Figures of Time: Poems, 1955; A Ballad of Remembrance, 1962; Selected Poems, 1966; Words in the Mourning Time, 1971; The Night Blooming Cereus, 1972; Angel of Descent: New and Selected Poems, 1975; American Journal, 1979. *Ed.*— Kaleidoscope: Poems by American Negro Poets, 1967; Afro-American Literature: An Introduction (with David R. Burrows and Frederick R. Lapides), 1971; "Modern American Poetry" in The United States in Literature, 1972. *Other*—How I Write/I (with Judson Philips and Lawson Carter), 1972. *Recordings*—Today's Poets (Vol. IV), Scholastic Records, and others. *Films*—(with Derek Walcott) reading his work: Middle Passage and Beyond, for Natl. Educational Television at WETA, Washington, D.C. 1968. *Further reading:* Black on White: A Critical Survey of Writing by American Negroes by David Littlejohn, 1966; Modern Black Poets by Donald B. Gibson (ed.), 1973.

ALEKSANDR (ALEKSANDROVICH) ZIMIN
Historian
Born Moscow, U.S.S.R., February 22nd, 1920
Died Moscow, U.S.S.R., February 25th, 1980

Aleksandr A. Zimin was regarded by historians, both within the U.S.S.R. and in the West, as a leading authority on medieval Russian history. Zimin's scholarship encompassed Russian social history from the ninth to the seventeenth centuries, but he specialized in the late medieval period, particularly the 16th-century reign of Czar Ivan the Terrible. Tracts by Zimin on the reigns of Vasily II (reigned 1389–1425), Ivan III (1462–1505), and Vasily III (1505–33) were also widely acclaimed. In 1963 Zimin astounded the international academic community when he challenged the authenticity of the *Tale of Igor's Campaign,* a work attributed to twelfth century authorship but which he believed was written six centuries later. The findings aroused such controversy in the Soviet Union that only small segments of Zimin's massive study were allowed to be published. *The Tale of*

Igor's Campaign (translated into English by Vladimir Nabokov as *The Song of Igor's Campaign: An Epic of the Twelfth Century)*, is a folk tale that has been long enshrined in Russian culture. Allegedly, Igor was a courageous Russian prince who disobeyed the orders of his lord during a campaign against Asiatic invaders. Although he was defeated by the "barbarous hordes," Igor was eventually forgiven. Zimin's exposure of the myths concerning Igor's valor, the wisdom and benevolence of his leaders, and, by extension, the infinite mercy of Mother Russia was viewed with extreme displeasure by Soviet officials.

The decision to suppress large portions of the textological study, a source of great dismay to Zimin, was fed by several impulses. The idea that an epic masterpiece was not produced by medieval culture, but invented centuries later, offended a deeply rooted and persistent Russian cultural inferiority complex. Indeed, there were meanings within the subtext of *Igor's Song* which could be fashioned to validate Communist rule. According to this interpretation, the protagonist signified the intrinsic courage of the Russian people as well as their need for guidance; and the strength and kindness of the lord ratified the infallible authority of party leadership. Moreover, evidence of such a Russian "nature" as early as the twelfth century furnished support for the Soviet ideologists' view of history as an organic movement toward the communist ideal.

Sasha Zimin graduated in history and philosophy from the University of Central Asia in Tashkent in 1942 and became Senior Research Associate at the Institute of History for the Academy of Sciences of the U.S.S.R. in Moscow nine years later. He received a doctorate in historical sciences in 1959 and was elevated to the rank of professor at the Institute in 1970. As the author and editor of literary works, historical studies, and legal documents, Zimin's output was prodigious. Several of his works remain unpublished: *Russia on the Eve of the Time of Troubles, Russia at the Time of Ivan III, Russkaya pravda* (the medieval Russian law code), and *The Composition of the Boyar Duma.* Zimin died in Moscow after a protracted illness, leaving behind a number of unfinished works which include a study of the mid-fifteenth century feudal war.   E.T.

Married. Two children. Educ: Univ. of Central Asia, Tashkent 1942; Inst. of Hist. of the Acad. of Sciences of the U.S.S.R., Doctorate in hist. 1959. Sr. research assoc., Inst. of Hist., U.S.S.R. Acad. of Sciences 1951; Dept. Chmn., Archeographic Commn. and Dept. of Historical Sciences, U.S.S.R. Acad. of Sciences; Member, Ed. Bd. "Istoricheskiye zapiski" (Historical Notes) 1962–80. *Author:* The History of Moscow, vol. 1, 1952; Memorials of the Law of Feudal Divided Russia, 1953; The Structure of the Departmental Systems in Russia, 1954; Essays on the History of the U.S.S.R.: The Feudal Period, from the Late 15th to the Early 17th Century, 1955; A History of the Military Reforms of the 1550s, 1956; Guba Records of the 16th Century from the Museum Collection, 1956; Documents of the Zemsky Sobor of 1612–13, 1957; Sobornoe Ulozhenie Tsaria Alekseia Mikhailovicha 1644 goda, 1957; Compositions of Court Institutions of the Russian State in the late 15th and 16th centuries, 1958; I.S. Peresvetov i ego souvremenniki (I.S. Peresvetov and his Contemporaries: Outline History of Russian Socio-Political Thought in the mid-16th Century), 1958; Composition of the Boyars Duma in the 15th and 16th Centuries, 1959; Metodika izdaniia drevnerusskilch aktov, 1959; Poslaniia Iosifa Volotskogo, 1959; Russian Geographical Gazetteers of the 17th Century, 1959; Reformy Ivana Groznogo (The Reforms of Ivan the Terrible: Outline of Socio-Economic and Political History of Russia in the mid-16th Century), 1960; Russkie letopisi i khronografy kontsa XV-XVI v.v. Uchebnoe posobie (Russian Chronicles and Chronographs of the Late 15th and 16th Centuries), 1960; Transformations of the State Apparatus in the Years of the Oprichnina, 1961; Legislative Monuments of the Russian State from the end of the 15th to the Beginning of the 17th Centuries, A Textbook, 1961; The Formation of the Historical Views of V.O. Klyuchevsky in the 1860s, 1961; The Song of Shchelkane and the Emergence of the Historical Ballad Genre, 1963; Oprichnina Ivana Groznogo (The Oprichnina of Ivan the Terrible), 1964; Serfs in Ancient Russia, 1965; (co-author) An Outline History of Historical Science in the U.S.S.R., vol. IV, 1966; (co-author and ed.) A History of the U.S.S.R. from Ancient Times up to the Present, vol. II, 1966; Rossi ia na poroge novogo vremeni, 1972; Kholopy na Rusi (Serfdom in Russia), 1973. *Editor:* Kniga klivchei i Dolgovaia kniga, 1948; (joint ed.) Tysiachnaia kniga, 1950; Mezhdunarodnye sviazi Rossii, 1961; Khrostomatiia po istorii SSSR: Shestnadtsatyĭ-semnadtsatyĭ velca, 1962; Vologodskoe knizhnoe izd-vo, 1963.

ANTHONY (JOHN) ARKELL
Archeologist, historian and priest
Born Hinxhill, Kent, England, July 29th, 1898
Died Chelmsford, Essex, England, February 26th, 1980

The Reverend Anthony Arkell, the first Commissioner for Archeology and Anthropology in the Sudan, was a formidable opponent of slavery which had continued into the 20th century in that country. Through Arkell's work and influence it was brought to an end, his efforts recognized with the award of an M.B.E.

Arkell was born at Hinxhill Rectory in Kent, the son of a Church of England clergyman. A childhood interest in natural history in general, and snails in particular, introduced Arkell to archeology. He embarked on his Oxford education with a classics scholarship to Queen's College, but his studies were cut short by the First World War. He qualified as a pilot in the Royal Flying Corps and was awarded the Military Cross for his part in shooting down of a German bomber. He remained with the R.F.C. through its transition into the Royal Air Force, and in 1920 was demobilized.

Arkell was recommended for the post of Assistant District Commissioner in the Darfur Province of British-ruled Sudan. After being offered the post, Arkell later realized how he had to consult an atlas to discover the whereabouts of the Sudan.

Courtesy E. Burgess

Following his three years in the Darfur Province, Arkell moved to the Kosti (White Nile) Province and it was there, in 1928, that Britain officially recognized his personal crusade against slave-trading. Although such trade was formally illegal, it nevertheless continued between Ethiopia and the Sudan, the victims usually being small girls or boys. The clandestine operation of the traders, coupled with the victims' instinctive distrust of British authority, combined to hamper Arkell's efforts; but he persevered and the traders were eventually imprisoned. Children who had been sold into slavery were found and liberated and Arkell helped establish a village and several camps for their resettlement. The former slaves called themselves the "Sons and Daughters of Arkell." In 1932 Arkell was appointed Acting Deputy Governor of Darfur, and in the five years during which he held the post, he wrote a history of the province for which Oxford University awarded him the doctorate in literature (D.Litt.) degree.

From 1938 to 1948 Arkell was Commissioner for Archeology and Anthropology to the Sudan Government, with the aim of establishing the Khartoum Museum. Arkell had deepened his knowledge in the subjects through his work as a District Commissioner, particularly while at Sennar, but war again intervened and for four years (1940–44) he assumed strategic duties with the Sudan Government as its Chief Transport Officer. When the Allied Forces were established in North Africa, Arkell returned to his archeological pursuits. He began digging the mesolithic site of early Khartoum and in 1948 was appointed Archeological Adviser to the Sudan Government. In 1949 he worked on the neolithic site of Shaheinab on the west bank of the Nile, believed to date from 4000 B.C. Arkell's excavation produced a large quantity of ancient pottery and other objects, but he found himself embroiled in drawn-out disputes over the archeological validity of his findings; in particular, the assessment he made of their age was questioned. He held to his theories, however, and lived to see their corroboration.

One of his more controversial theories concerned the prehistoric origin of the art of clay pottery in that part of the world. He contended that the wavy line patterns on some pots pointed to an accidental discovery that clay could be fashioned and fired. This, he suggested, came about when baskets which had been lined with clay to prevent grain from falling through were inadvertently burned. Despite the controversy attending his views, Arkell established himself as one of the world's leading African pre-historians and the father of Sudanese prehistory.

In 1948, Arkell returned to England to become a lecturer in Egyptology at University College, London, and Curator of the Flinders Petrie Museum. The museum contained one of the most important teaching collections of prehistoric and early Egyptian items—at that time crated, and it was Arkell's job for the next 14 years to unpack, sort, identify, display, and catalogue the collection. The job lasted until his formal retirement in 1963.

Arkell maintained, until 1953, his connection with the Sudanese Government. Upon relinquishing that, he became London University Reader in Egyptology and later presented a unique collection of East African beads to the Oxford Pitt Rivers Museum. Arkell continued to demonstrate his active interest in Africa and in 1957 he joined the British Ennedi Expedition on its overland crossing of the Sahara Desert.

Arkell was also a prolific writer and contributed widely to historical journals. Author of six books, his major work was the *History of the Sudan from the Earliest Times to 1821* which dealt with the relations between Sudan and Egypt, and traced the fortunes both of the Christian kingdoms which survived in the Sudan for 800 years and of the Islamic dynasties until Ismail Pasha's conquest. In Britain the work was well received, but the *American History Review* thought that it suffered from lack of detail.

Arkell decided late in life to become a priest, and while still Curator of the Flinders Petrie Museum, studied theology at Cuddesdon College, Oxford. He was ordained deacon in 1960, became a Curate in Great Missenden, and the following year was admitted into the Anglican priesthood. In 1963 he gave up his Curatorship of the Flinders Petrie Museum to become Vicar of Cuddington with Dinton in the Oxford Diocese. Early fears among his parishioners that he would manifest a highly academic posture were dispelled, and he remained at Cuddington until his retirement in 1971. Arkell disclaimed any difficulties in making the transition from scholar to parish priest, saying: "God is everywhere and there is more God in the desert than anywhere else."   M.D./R.T.

Son of the Reverend John Norris A., Church of England clergyman, and Eleanor Jessy (Bunting) A. Married: (1) Dorothy Davidson (d. 1945); (2) Joan Margaret Burnell 1950. Children: 1st marriage— one son and one daughter. Educ.: Bradfield Coll. (private secondary sch.) and Queen's Coll., Oxford (Jodrell Scholar in Classics), studies terminated by WWI; award D.Litt., Oxford for history of Darfur Province, Sudan in late '30s; Cuddesdon Coll., Oxford (theology) 1960. Mil. Service: Royal Flying Corps 916–18; R.A.F. 1918–19. Joined Sudan Political Service 1920; Asst. District Commnr., Darfur Province 1921–24; Acting Reserve, Dar Masalit 1925–26; District Commnr., Kosti (White Nile) Province 1926–29, and Sennar (Blue Nile) Province 1929–32; Acting Deputy Gov., Darfur Province 1932–37; Commnr. for Archeology and Anthropology, Sudan Govt. 1938–48; Chief Transport Officer, Sudan Govt. 1940–44; Archeological Adviser to Sudan Govt. 1948–53. With London Univ.: Lectr. in Egyptology, Univ. Coll. 1948–53; Curator of Flinders Petrie Mus. of Egyptian Antiquities, Univ. Coll. 1948–63; Reader in Egyptian Archeology 1953–63. Member, British Ennedi Expedition 1957. Ordained deacon 1960, and priest 1961; Curate, Great Missenden 1960–63, Vicar, Cuddington with Dinton 1963–71, Diocese of Oxford. Member: Philosophical Soc. of Sudan 1947 (First Pres.; Hon. Life Member 1949); German Archeological Inst. 1953; Council, Soc. of Antiquaries 1956–57; Cttee., Egypt Exploration Soc. Hons: M.C. 1918; Order of the Nile, 4th Class (Egypt) 1931; M.B.E. 1928; Fellow, Soc. of Antiquaries. *Author:* Early Khartoum, 1949; The Old Stone Age in the Anglo-Egyptian Sudan, 1949; Shaheinab, 1953; The History of the Sudan from Earliest Times to 1821, 1955, 2nd rev. ed. 1961, reprinted 1966; Wanyanga, 1964; The Prehistory of the Nile Valley, 1975. Ed., Sudan Notes and Records, 1945–48; contributor to Encyclopaedia Britannica; numerous articles in historical jrnls.

ALEXANDER BROOK
Painter
Born Brooklyn, New York, U.S.A., July 14th, 1898
Died Sag Harbor, New York, U.S.A., February 26th, 1980

Alexander Brook, popular portrait and landscape painter of the pre-World War Two years, was born to Russian immigrants in Brooklyn in

Georgia Jungle, by Alexander Brook

1898. The youngest of six children, Brook was bedridden with polio at the age of 12 and took up painting to amuse himself, coached by a neighbor with a Van Dyck beard and a frock coat, who convinced him to become an artist. When he was 17 Brook won a scholarship to the Art Students League in New York, where he came under the guiding influence of Kenneth Hayes Miller.

In 1920 Brook married Peggy Bacon, later famous as a caricaturist and satirical illustrator and writer. His first significant exhibition in New York, a joint show with his wife in 1923, was a critical and popular success. That same year, Brook became assistant director of the Whitney Studio Club, one of the predecessor organizations of the Whitney Museum, and gave Edward Hopper and Reginald Marsh their first one-man shows. For several years he also taught on an irregular basis, chiefly at the Art Students League, and wrote a series of articles on contemporary artists for "The Arts," a magazine sponsored by Gertrude Vanderbilt Whitney.

By 1929 Brook had achieved enough prominence as a painter to be given a retrospective exhibition at the Art Institute of Chicago. His place in the art establishment, and his financial security, were fixed when he won the second prize and a purchase prize at the 1930 Carnegie International, the most prestigious American salon exhibition. The jury that year included Henri Matisse; the first prize was won by Pablo Picasso.

Brook then embarked on his career as a portraitist and in the late 1930s began to paint landscapes and portraits in poverty-stricken rural areas, particularly around Savannah, Georgia, where he lived for several years. One of these paintings, *Georgia Jungle,* won first prize at the 1939 Carnegie International.

At the height of his prominence, in the early and mid-1940s, Brook was as well-known to the general public as he was to art professionals, and he prospered as a painter of studio still-lifes and portraits of society ladies and movie stars: An illustrated article about him appeared in "Life" magazine; his work was used in cosmetic advertisements; and his painting of an American soldier who survived Bataan appeared on War Bonds posters in post offices across the United States.

With the rise of the New York School and the demise of the mainstream art establishment, Brook's career went into eclipse, though he retained his admirers. His best work, done in the 1920s, showed genuine gifts of design and an obvious enjoyment of the sensual qualities of paint, but his temperament was more suited to the conventions of American postimpressionism than to the uncompromising modernism of the Abstract Expressionists. He once said: "I find that my life, like my painting, can be realized on the back porch."

Brook died of a heart attack at his home in Sag Harbor, where he had been living in retirement.   J.P/D.S.

Son of Onufri Gregory B. and Eudoxia (Gelescu) B. Married: (1) Peggy Bacon, artist 1920 (div. 1940); (2) Libby Berger 1940 (div.); (3) Gina Knee artist, 1944. Children: 1st marriage—Belinda, Alexander Bacon. Educ: Art Students League, NYC 1915–19. Occasional teaching jobs 1920–29; Asst. Dir., Whitney Studio Club 1924–27. Active as painter and portraitist 1920–80. Member, Natl. Inst. Arts and Letters. Hons.: Logan Medal and purchase, Annual Exhib. American Art, Art

Inst. Chicago 1929; 2nd prize, Lehman Award and purchase, Carnegie Intl., Carnegie Inst., Pittsburgh 1930; Temple Gold Medal, Annual Exhib., Pa. Acad. Fine Arts, Philadelphia 1931; Guggenheim Fellowship in painting 1931; 1st prize, Los Angeles County Mus. 1934; Gold Medal, American Sect., Intnl. Exposition, Paris 1937; Medal of Award, San Francisco Mus. Art 1938; 1st prize, Carnegie Intl. 1939; Beck Gold Medal, Annual Exhib., Pa. Acad. Fine Arts 1948; 2nd prize, Natl. Acad. Design, 1957, 1960. *Exhibitions: One-person—* ACA Gall.; Art Inst. Chicago 1929; Curt Valentine Gall., NYC 1930; Downtown Gall., NYC 1934, 1937; Dayton Art Inst., Dayton, Ohio 1942; Frank Rehn Gall., NYC 1947, 1960; M. Knoedler & Co., NYC 1952; Larcada Gall., NYC 1969, 1972, 1974. *Group—*(with Peggy Bacon) Joseph Brummer Gall., NYC 1923; Univ. Rochester, N.Y. 1937; Brooklyn Mus.; Carnegie Inst., Pittsburgh; Metropolitan Mus., NYC: Toledo Mus., Ohio; Albright Gall., Buffalo; Art Inst. Chicago; Newark Mus., N.J. *Collections:* Metropolitan Mus., NYC: Art Inst. Chicago; Corcoran Gall., Washington, D.C.; Mus. Fine Arts, Boston; San Francisco Mus.; Carnegie Inst., Pittsburgh; Nelson Gall.; Kansas City, Mo.; Wadsworth Atheneum, Hartford, Conn.; Newark Mus., N.J.; Toledo Mus., Ohio; Univ. Mich., Ann Arbor; DeYoung Mus., San Francisco; Albright-Knox Gall., Buffalo; Art Mus., St. Louis; IBM Corp. *Author:* Alexander Brook, American Artists Group, NYC 1945 (monograph). *Major articles:* "The Purity of Provincetown," The Arts, NYC, July 1923; "Henri de Toulouse-Lautrec," The Arts, Sept. 1923; "Henry Lee McFee," The Arts, Nov. 1923; "Yasuo Kuniyoshi," The Arts, Jan. 1924; "Hermine David," The Arts, March 1924; "Andrew Dasburg," The Arts, July 1924; "Over the Spectacles—On Art Critics," Creative Art, NYC, June 1928; "Robert Chanler," Creative Art, April 1929; "Alexander Brook, Painter," Creative Art, Oct. 1929. Contributed memoir of Juliana Force to Juliana Force and American Art, A Memorial Exhibition, (ed. by Flora Whitney Miller) Whitney Mus. American Art, 1949.

W(ILLIAM ANDREW) HORSLEY GANTT
Psychiatrist and behaviorist researcher
Born Wingina, Virginia, October 24th, 1892
Died Baltimore, Maryland, February 26th, 1980

Dr. W. Horsley Gantt was one of the pioneers of behavioral psychology in the United States and an authority on the work of his teacher, Ivan Pavlov.

Born in Wingina, Virginia, in 1892, Gantt obtained his B.S. from the University of North Carolina at Chapel Hill and went on to the University of Virginia Medical School, graduating in 1920. He completed his internships at University Hospital in Baltimore.

In 1922 Gantt volunteered to serve as medical chief for the Petrograd Unit of President Hoover's American Relief Administration following World War One. After postgraduate training at University College, London, he returned to Petrograd (now Leningrad) for five years. There he conducted research on brain physiology and psychology in the laboratories of Ivan Pavlov, the Russian scientist who laid the groundwork for behaviorism with

pioneering experiments in which he conditioned dogs to salivate at the sound of a bell.

In 1928 Gantt published *A Medical Review of Soviet Russia,* a massive study of that nation's health conditions and system of medical treatment. He also became the first to translate the complete works of Pavlov, as well as other Soviet psychiatric writing.

Returning to the U.S. in 1929, Gantt founded the Pavlovian Laboratory at Johns Hopkins University, where he conducted research on the neurophysiology of humans and animals. Enlarging on Pavlov's experiment, he taught dogs to distingush between the sounds of two bells (one indicating a forthcoming food reward, the other not). By manipulating the expectations of these conditioned dogs, he succeeded in inducing manic behavior and asthma in them, proving that nervous illnesses could have environmental as well as psychological causes.

According to P.L. Broadhurst, Gantt's theoretical views "employ two fundamental concepts: 'schizokinesis' and 'autokinesis'". The first of these, Broadhurst says, implies that conditioned responses of the cardiac system form more quickly and are more enduring than those of the muscular system. Gantt's studies further showed that heart rate and blood pressure are subject to conditioning by exercise; his findings helped to initiate the nationwide interest in jogging and other health-oriented sports.

Autokinesis, the second concept cited by Broadhurst, implies that an organism can continue to develop responses even when the original stimulus for them is gone. Gantt followed up this idea with research into the effects of hormones and nerve impulses on bodily organs.

Gantt's emphasis on environmental factors as causes of mental disorders brought him into conflict with conventional Freudian theory, which holds that neurotic and psychotic behaviors grow out of traumatic experiences and sexual conflicts in childhood. In 1955 he organized a society for psychiatrists who shared his criticism of Freud, called the Pavlovian Society of North America, of which he was the first president.

In assessing Gantt's work, Broadhurst faulted him for expressing his theories in a form "too imprecise to provide testable deductions" and said that his research was too often "observational or even anecdotal in character." Nonetheless, Gantt received the Lasker Award for his work on mental diseases in 1940, the American Heart Association Award for his research on hypertension in 1950, and the Ira Van Giesen Award from Columbia University in 1974.

In 1958, Gantt left the Pavlovian Laboratory at Johns Hopkins to become chief scientist at the Veterans Administration Hospital at Perry Point, Maryland. He continued to lecture at Johns Hopkins until a few weeks before his death from cancer.   J.P./C.L.

Son of Thomas Perkins G. and Anna Maria Perkins (Horsley) G. Married: (1) Mary Gould Richardson 1934 (d. 1964); (2) Anna Rebecca Esler 1965. Children: 1st marriage—William Andrew Horsley II, b. 1936; Emily Birk Kahn. Educ: Univ. N.C., Chapel Hill, B.S. 1917; Univ. Va., Charlottesville, M.D. 1920. Internships: Union Memorial Hosp., Baltimore 1919–20; Church Home Hosp., Baltimore 1920–21; Univ. Hosp., Baltimore 1921–22. Postgraduate studies, Univ. Coll. Hosp. and Medical Sch., London 1923–24; brain anatomy

research, Kaiser Wilhelm Inst. für Hirnforschung, Berlin-Buch 1933.
Instr. in Anatomy, Va. 1917–18; Medical Chief, Petrograd Unit,
American Relief Admin. 1922–23; collaborator with Ivan Pavlov,
Research Inst. of Experimental Medicine, Petrograd 1924–29. With
Johns Hopkins Univ. Medical Sch. and Hosp., Baltimore: Psychiatric
Researcher, Phipps Psychiatric Clinic 1929–32; Founder and Dir.,
Pavlovian Lab. 1932–58; Hosp. Psychiatrist from 1930; Assoc. Prof. of
Psychiatry 1932–58; Dir. Emeritus, Pavlovian Lab., and Assoc. Prof.
Emeritus, 1958–80. Appointed consultant, U.S. Veterans Admin.
1949; Visiting Prof. of Pharmacology, Univ. P.R. 1954–55; Lectr.,
U.S.S.R. Acad. of Science 1957; Sr. Scientist, Pavlovian Research
Lab., Veterans Admin. Hosp., Perry Point, Md. 1959–78; Prof.,
Clinical Psychiatry Dept., Sch. of Medicine, Univ. Md. 1973–76;
Prof., Univ. Louisville 1976. Former Ed.-in-Chief, Pavlovian Jrnl.
Biol. Science. Former Ed.: Pavlovian Jrnl. Research; Conditioned
Reflex Jrnl.; Soviet Neurology and Psychiatry. With Foreign Policy
Assn.: Secty. 1935–44; Chmn. 1944–46; Exec. Bd. Member 1945–50.
Vice-Chmn., Russian War Relief, Baltimore 1942–46; Founder and
Pres. 1955–65, Pavlovian Soc. of N. America; V.P. 1958 and Pres.
1959, Soc. Biol. Psychiatry; Pres., American Psychopathological
Assn. 1960–61; Delegate, 2nd Intnl. Conference on Unity of Sciences,
Tokyo 1973. Former Pres., Collegium Internationale Activitatas
Nervosae Superioris sect. of World Psychiatric Assn.; Exec. Bd.
Member, MEDICO Advisory Bd. to CARE; Chmn., Neuropsychia-
try Sect., and Secty., Baltimore Medical Soc. Member: American
Acad. Neurology; American Assn. for Advancement of Science;
American Assn. for Advancement of Tension Control; American
Neurological Assn.; American Physiological Soc.; American Psychi-
atric Assn.; American Psychosomatic Soc.; American Soc. Phar-
macology and Experimental Therapeutics; Fulton Neurological Soc.;
Intnl. Brain Research Org.; Collegium Intnl. Neuro-Psychophar-
macologicum; Collegium Intnl. Psychosomatic Medicine; N.Y. Acad.
Science; Psychosomatic Soc.; Royal Soc. Medicine; Sigma Xi; Soc. for
Neuroscience. Member: 14th West Hamilton St. Club, Baltimore;
Princeton Club, NYC. Hons: Lasker Award 1946; American Heart
Assn. Award 1950; Gold Medal, Soc. Biol. Psychiatry 1971; Ira Van
Giesen Award, N.Y. Psychiatric Inst., Columbia Univ. 1974. Hon.
Member: Argentine Assn. Biol. Psychiatrists; Czech Medical Soc.;
Collegium Internationale Activitatas Nervosae Superioris; Purjinke
Acad. Medicine. Life Member, Southern Medical Assn.; Fellow,
American Coll. Psychiatrists; Fellow, American Medical Assn.; Life
Fellow, American Psychiatric Assn. *Author:* A Medical Review of
Soviet Russia 1928; Russian Medicine, 1937; Experimental Basis for
Neurotic Behavior 1944; Adaption and Preventive Psychiatry, 1955;
Physiological Psychiatry, 1958; Russian Physiology in the Atomic
Age. *Editor:* American Lectures in Objective Psychiatry Series, 1955;
Bykov's Cerebral Cortex and Internal Organs, 1957; Physiological
Bases of Psychiatry, 1958; Pavlovian Approach to Psychopathology,
1970; Soviet Neurology and Psychiatry. *Editor and Translator:* The
Nature of Human Conflicts (by Aleksandr Luria), 1932; Lectures on
Conditioned Reflexes (by Ivan Pavlov), Vol. I, 1928, Vol. II, 1941.
Author of many scientific papers and frequent contributor to profes-
sional jrnls. *Further reading:* "Abnormal Animal Behavior" in Pavlo-
vian Approach to Psychopathology by W. Horsley Gantt (ed.), 1970;
Drugs and the inheritance of behavior: A survey of comparative
psychopharmacogenetics by P.L. Broadhurst, 1978.

AHMED SHUKAIRY
Founder and First President of the Palestine Liberation Organization
Born Acre, Palestine, 1908
Died Amman, Jordan, February 26th, 1980

Ahmed Shukairy was born in 1908 in Acre, Palestine, then a province of the Ottoman Empire. The son of a Moslem religious leader, he studied at the American University in Beirut and received his Doctor of Laws degree from the Jerusalem Law School. From 1945 to 1948 he was chairman of the Jerusalem bar and headed the Arab Offices in Jerusalem and Washington.

In May 1948, the British evacuated Palestine in accordance with the UN partition plan, and Shukairy, who had recently returned to the country, was forced to flee during the Arab League's unsuccessful invasion of the new Israeli sector. He subsequently represented Saudi Arabia at the United Nations and later headed the Syrian delegation to the UN and served as assistant secretary-general of the Arab League.

During the 1950s, Shukairy founded the Palestine Liberation Organization (PLO), one of several small groups dedicated to Palestinian nationalism. The organization remained virtually unknown until 1964, when it gained official support from seven Arab nations at a meeting of the Palestine National Congress. The group's charter, which Shukairy helped to write, called for the end of the Jewish state of Israel and its replacement with a Palestinian state in which only those Jews who had emigrated before 1948 would be allowed to remain. Shukairy became the first president of the PLO and commander of its combat branch, the Palestine Liberation Army.

From its birth, the PLO was a pawn in the complex rivalries among the leaders of the Arab nations. Shukairy's main backing came from Gamal Abdel Nasser, president of Egypt, who allowed the PLO to use the Gaza Strip as a base for commando raids until Israeli reprisals forced him to rescind his offer. More support for guerrilla operations came from the radical army officers who took power in Syria after the 1966 coup. Nasser then enlisted Shukairy's assistance in his campaign to overthrow the monarchy of Saudi Arabia; at his request, the PLO leader instigated riots against the Saudis's ally, King Hussein of Jordan. These riots took place in Palestinian settlements on the West Bank of the Jordan River, an area that had once been part of Palestine but had been annexed by Hussein's grandfather during the 1948 war. Shukairy challenged Hussein's claim to represent the Palestinian people and assailed his refusal to allow the PLO to operate freely in Jordanian territory. He also tried to have Tunisia expelled from the Arab League after its president, Habib Bourguiba, urged direct talks between Arab and Israeli leaders. Jordan, Tunisia, and Saudi Arabia responded with conspiracies against Shukairy, who was wounded in an assassination attempt in February 1967.

In a 1966 interview, Shukairy accused Jordan of using "terror tactics" against the PLO and declared that the United States, through the CIA, controlled the Jordanian government. He also said that PLO members were receiving military training in North Vietnam and in the People's Republic of China.

During 1967, Shukairy's rhetoric became increasingly strident. In one of his speeches, he called on the Arabs to "drive the Jews into the sea." At a press conference just before the Six-Day War, he told reporters that "those [Jews] who survive will remain in Palestine. I estimate that none of them will survive."

The failure of the massive Arab attack in June 1967 hastened the end of Shukairy's career, already threatened by internal friction within the PLO. Shukairy's reliance on a hand-picked bureaucracy and heavy dependence on Egyptian support had cost him the allegiance of a group of dissidents who demanded a redistribution of authority and an increase in guerrilla activities. These dissidents now accused him of failing to coordinate the commando groups during the war and of alienating Western public opinion with his volatile remarks.

At the Khartoum Conference of Arab heads of state in September 1967, Shukairy insisted that all members break diplomatic relations with the US, expropriate American businesses, and continue their oil embargo against Israel's allies. A set of P.L.O.-sponsored proposals, including refusals to recognize Israel's borders and to conduct negotiations with Israel, was rejected by the conference. Finally Shukairy walked out after a dispute with King Hussein concerning Jordan's acceptance of U.N. Security Council Resolution 242, which calls for Israel to withdraw from territories gained in the 1967 war in exchange for recognition of its right to exist. Three months later, a majority of the PLO's ten-member Executive Committee asked Shukairy to step down.

After his resignation, Shukairy lived mostly in Lebanon. In late 1979, when he became ill, King Hussein invited him to come to Jordan for medical treatment at Amman University Hospital, where he died of a brain tumor.   J.P.

Also transliterated Ahmad ash-Shuqayri or Shukeiri. Son of a Moslem religious leader. Educ: M.A., American Univ. of Beirut; Dr. of Laws, Jerusalem Law Sch. Chmn. of Jerusalem bar 1945–49; head of Arab Office in Jerusalem 1946; head of Arab Office in Washington, D.C. 1947; Pres., Palestinian Delegation to U.N. 1948; Permanent Rep. to U.N., Saudi Arabian Delegation ca. 1948–49; Rep. of Syria before U.N. Trusteeship Council, Geneva 1949; Member, Syrian Delegation to U.N. 1950. With Palestine Liberation Org.: Founder and Pres. 1964–67; also Comdr., Palestine Liberation Army. Former Palestine Delegate and Asst. Secty.-Gen., Arab League. *Further Reading:* The Politics of Palestinian Nationalism by W. Quandt, F. Jabber, and A.M. Lesch, 1973.

THEODORE (FLOYD) ADAMS
President, Baptist World Alliance, pastor, and author
Born Palmyra, New York, U.S.A., September 26th, 1898
Died Richmond, Virginia, U.S.A., February 27th, 1980

The Reverend Theodore (Ted) Adams, who for five years was the spiritual leader of nearly 20 million Baptists all over the world, became the first American Protestant clergyman to administer com-

munion to Soviet worshippers since the 1917 Bolshevik Revolution.

Adams made an early commitment to his faith; talking about it in later life, he observed that it had hardly ever occurred to him that he should do anything else but enter the Baptist ministry. When he was five years old his family moved to his father's second pastorate in the small town of McMinnville, Oregon. Adams afterwards told of listening to an evangelist preacher invited to speak by his father. "He finished and asked for true believers to come forward. Without even knowing I was doing it, I stood up and I saw my father standing there waiting. It was only three or four steps up there, but even as a six-year-old, I thought to myself that they were terribly important steps. If I had waited 50 years more, I could not have made a truer commitment than I made on that day as a child." As a teenager, he found himself in industrial Hammond, Indiana, where his father had accepted another pastorate. It was there as a high school student that Adams finally made the choice of entering the Baptist ministry.

On graduation from high school, Adams decided to wait a year in order to go to college with his younger brother, Earl. He took his mother's advice and spent the year in Chicago learning chiropractic. It was a skill he never forgot and it always amused his congregations when his family spoke of him as a "neck-snapper and vertebrae-cracker—the best in the Baptist ministry." Adams and his brother—Earl Adams later became an official of the US National Council of Churches—both graduated Phi Beta Kappa from Denison University, Ohio, and Ted Adams went immediately to the Colgate-Rochester Divinity School where his father had studied for the ministry. After ordination he took a position with the Cleveland Heights Baptist Church and, before moving on to Toledo, married Evelyn Parkes.

When Adams moved to Richmond, Virginia in 1936 he found the First Baptist Church in a state of financial decline, but under his skillful guidance, building debts were quickly paid off and the church, where he served as pastor for 32 years, became one of the most generous financial donors in the Baptist world.

Adams was also deeply committed to the worldwide Baptist movement, and from 1947 to 1951 he served as Vice-President of the Baptist World Alliance, having been closely associated with its work over many years. At the London meeting of the Alliance in 1955, he was elected President. In the ensuing months he and three other US Baptist ministers visited the Soviet Union at the invitation of the All Union Council of Evangelical Christians-Baptists, a body then representing half a million Russian Baptists. During their two-week stay, Adams became the first American Protestant clergyman since the Russian Revolution to celebrate communion for a Soviet congregation. Nearly 2,500 people took part in the service, held in a Moscow Baptist Church.

Aside from his pastoral duties and the Baptist World Alliance, Adams involved himself in education, holding a Visiting Professorship at Southeastern Baptist Seminary in Wake Forest, North Carolina. At the same time he took a leading part in administrative duties for both church and secular bodies, in particular those dealing with missionary work. His efforts and achievements were acknowledged with numerous citations, a Christian knighthood from Liberia, and ten honorary degrees from universities and colleges.

Adams wrote four books, and his tendency to extol, rather
didactically, the moral superiority of a Christian lifestyle was questioned by reviewers. In 1964 his major work, *Tell Me How?* in which
he delineated correct Christian living, received a cool reception. The
Christian Century's reviewer thought that Adams had failed to answer
his own question, providing instead advice on why life should be lived
according to Christian precepts. The critic added: "He is a preacher
with a mission who will appeal to readers who like to quote scripture
and verse when punctuating their arguments with Biblical confirmation."   M.D.

Son of Floyd Holden A., Baptist minister, and Evelyn (Parkes) A.
Married Esther Josephine Jillson 1925. Children: Betsy Ann (Mrs.
Frank K. Thompson); Theodore F. Jr.; John Jillson. Educ: Denison
Univ. (Phi Beta Kappa), B.A. 1921; Colgate-Rochester Divinity Sch.,
B.D. 1924. Ordained Baptist minister 1924. Pastor: Cleveland, Ohio
1924–27; Toledo, Ohio 1927–36; First Baptist Church, Richmond, Va.
1936–68, Pastor Emeritus 1968–80. V.P., Baptist Young People's
Union of America 1925–26; Pres., Ohio Baptist Young People's
Union 1925–27; Member, Bd. of Promotion, Ohio Baptist Convention
1928–35. With Baptist World Alliance: Exec. Cttee. 1934–78; V.P.
1947–50; Pres. 1955-60; Admin. Cttee. 1960–78. Member, Foreign
Mission Bd., Southern Baptist Convention 1940–50, 1961–67; Visiting
Prof., Southeastern Baptist Seminary, Wake Forest, N.C. 1968–78;
Regional Devel. Counsellor (Va. and northern states), Baptist Church
1978–80. Trustee: Va. Baptist Children's Home 1936–57 (Pres. Bd. of
Trustees 1936–53); Southern Baptist Hosp. 1950–53; Council on
Religion and Intnl. Affairs 1951–71, 1973–78; Richmond Memorial
Hosp. (also Chmn.); Va. Union Univ.; Univ. Richmond. Member:
Bd. Dirs., Rockefeller Bros. Theological Fellowship Program
1961–70; Bd. Dirs., Co-operative for American Relief Everywhere
(C.A.R.E.) (V.P. 1960–70); Va. Inst. Pastoral Care. Hons: D.D.,
Univ. Richmond 1938, Denison Univ. 1940, Coll. of William and
Mary 1940, Baylor Univ. 1958, Washington and Lee Univ. 1958,
Stetson Univ. 1959, McMaster Univ. 1962, and Wake Forest Univ.
1968; L.H.D., Hampden-Sydney Coll. 1959; Upper Room Citation
1960; LL.D., Keuka Coll. 1964; Natl. Brotherhood Citation, Conference of Christians and Jews 1964; Knight, Order of African
Redemption, Liberia 1968. *Author:* Making Your Marriage Succeed,
1953; Making the Most of What Life Brings, 1957; Tell Me How?,
1964; Baptists Around the World, 1967. *Contributor:* The Living
Christ in the Life of Today, 1941; Faith of our Fathers Living Still,
1941; (G.P. Butler, ed.) Best Sermons of 1944, 1944; (G.P. Butler,
ed.) Best Sermons of 1945, 1945; (Garland Evans Hopkins, ed.) The
Mighty Beginnings, 1956; (Foy Valentine, ed.) Christian Faith in
Action, 1956; (H.C. Brown, ed.) Southern Baptist Preaching, 1959;
(G. Allen West Jr., ed.) Christ for the World, 1963; (J.S. Childers,
ed.) A Way Home, 1964. Articles in religious jrnls.

YIGAL ALLON
Israeli general and cabinet minister
Born Kfar Tabor, Lower Galilee, Palestine (now Israel), October 10th, 1918
Died Afulah, Israel, February 29th, 1980

Israeli cabinet member Yigal Allon, leader of the Palmach commando corps and a hero of the War for Independence, was born in 1918 in the Galilean agricultural settlement of Kfar Tabor, founded by his parents in Ottoman-ruled Palestine. The family of his mother, who died when he was six, had lived in the Palestinian town of Safed since the Middle Ages. His father, Reuven Paicovitch, a crusty, self-reliant veteran of World War I, emigrated from Russia in the 1880s and organized Kfar Tabor's first defense force, earning the respect of local Arabs for his firm resistance to harassment. Yigal, who had four brothers and a sister, learned to speak Arabic and to appreciate Arab culture, at the home of Hassan Abdoni, one of his father's friends. Nonetheless, Kfar Tabor, like most of the Jewish frontier settlements, was under constant threat of attack, and its young people were taught military tactics.

Yigal retained his father's surname of Paicovitch until 1948, when he and all generals in the Israel Defense Force adopted Hebrew names. "Allon" is the Hebrew word for "oak."

Allon was educated at Kfar Tabor and attended the nearby Kadoorie Agricultural School. He had twice been admitted to a more prestigious secondary school, but was denied a scholarship because of his father's political differences with the quasi-governmental financial aid administration. At Kadoorie, Allon joined ha-Kibbutz ha-Me'uchad (United Kibbutz), a socialist movement dedicated to the establishment of collective workers' settlements, operated on egalitarian principles, as the foundation of Israel's political life. After graduating in 1937 he became a founding member of Kibbutz Ginossar, a farming and manufacturing community on the western shore of the Sea of Galilee. For the next two years he served as a sergeant in the Jewish Settlement Police, a peace-keeping force sponsored by Britain, which had governed Palestine since 1919 under a League of Nations mandate. In 1938 he married Ruth Apisdorf, a refugee from Nazi Germany, with whom he had two children.

At the age of 18, Allon, while still a student, joined the Haganah, a clandestine Jewish self-defense force organized by Achdut ha-Avodah (Zionist Socialist Workers' Party, the political arm of ha-Kibbutz ha-Me'uchad). He and another young activist, Moshe Dayan, studied commando tactics under Haganah leader Yitzchak Sadeh, who chose them to head the newly founded Palmach commando corps in 1941. Allon, with Dayan, led two companies of volunteers behind enemy lines in Syria and Lebanon to reconnoiter Vichy French positions on the eve of the Allied invasion and carried out sabotage and intelligence missions for the British Army in 1942. By 1945, Allon, now Commander-in-Chief of the Palmach, was directing his main efforts against the restrictive immigration quotas imposed by the British at Arab insistence. His Operation Aliyah Bet succeeded in smuggling tens of thousands of Holocaust survivors past the British blockade.

When the British withdrew from Palestine under a UN partition plan in May 1948, five Arab states invaded the Israeli sector. The 29-year-old Allon distinguished himself in major campaigns on all three

fronts. His capture of Safed early in the war disrupted the Arab plan of attack, which depended on an invasion from the north. Called to Jerusalem to help break the Arab siege, he organized a frontal assault on enemy positions near the stronghold of Latrun. Later, his brigades captured a crucial transport and communications center at Lod-Ramleh.

In Operation Ten Plagues, the final campaign of the war, Allon's forces attacked through the Negev along an ancient Roman road and trapped the main bdy of the Egyptian army in the Sinai peninsula. His headlong advance was finally halted by Prime Minister David Ben-Gurion, who ordered him to withdraw after Great Britain threatened to come to Egypt's defense.

With the war over, General Allon was expected to become the army's chief of staff; however, he resigned in protest when Ben-Gurion, for political reasons, reduced the Palmach's standing in the armed forces. His place was taken by Moshe Dayan, whose subsequent fame as a military commander contributed to his strength as a political rival of Allon.

Allon took advantage of this hiatus in his career to study economics, political science, military history, and philosophy at the Hebrew University in Jerusalem, in preparation for a career in politics. In 1954 he was elected to the Knesset as a member of Achdut ha-Avodah, helping the party to break off its alliance with a pro-Soviet Marxist coalition. Except for the academic year 1960–61, when he took up a research fellowship in African-Asian affairs at Oxford University, Allon continued to sit in the Knesset until his death.

The first of Allon's four cabinet positions was that of Minister of Labor, assigned to him by Ben-Gurion in 1961. From 1968 to 1977 he was Deputy Prime Minister, simultaneously serving as Minister of Immigrant Absorption (until 1970), Minister of Education and Culture (until 1974), and Minister of Foreign Affairs. Allon came close to being named Defense Minister on the eve of the Six-Day War in June 1967, but was passed over in favor of Dayan.

That war left Israel in possession of territory captured from three of the attacking Arab nations. The question of what to do with these territories was hotly debated among the Israeli leadership. Before the war, Allon had taken a hard-line stance, saying "We prefer secure borders that are not agreed to, to agreed borders that are not secure." Now, however, Israel's capture of the West Bank area threatened to add well over half a million Palestinian Arabs to Israel's population, a development which would threaten both the Jewish, democratic character of the nation and the Arabs' own sense of honor and culture, with which Allon had been familiar since childhood. Changing his stance, he proposed that Israel only retain areas of strategic importance, such as the Golan Heights in Syria. The West Bank should be returned to Jordanian sovereignty, with Israel maintaining a belt of paramilitary settlements along its eastern edge, the thinly populated Jordan Valley, to ensure the security of its natural eastern defense boundary. The Allon Plan would thus provide "maximum security for the State of Israel with a minimum of Arab population." Though this moderate program was supported by the mainstream labor groups in Israel, it was rejected by Jordan's King Hussein and by the United States; nor did it ever receive formal Israeli government endorsement. In later years, Allon went so far as to urge acceptance of a Palestinian nation in the West Bank, in a federation with Jordan, as long as the Jordan River security line was still in force.

The death of Prime Minister Levi Eshkol made Allon acting Prime Minister for three weeks in early 1969. He expected to be confirmed in this office, but the party chose Golda Meir instead. Meir was succeeded in June 1974 by Yitzchak Rabin, whose primary mission was to repair the damage to security and morale wrought by the Yom Kippur War of 1973. Much of this responsibility fell on Allon, now Foreign Minister, who was given the delicate task of negotiating with US Secretary of State Henry Kissinger during his attempts to mediate a Middle East settlement. At issue was the status of the formerly Egyptian Sinai peninsula, occupied by Israel since 1967. Allon and Rabin expressed their willingness to give up the Sinai and its strategic advantages—including the complex Distant Early Warning system and the Abu Rudeis oil field—in exchange for such practical political concessions as the passage of Israeli cargoes through the Suez Canal and other guarantees of non-belligerency. When these terms were rejected by Egypt's President Sadat, Kissinger pressed Israel to give up the Sinai with no more recompense than a pledge of American support. Allon refused to capitulate, despite pressure from Kissinger and President Gerald Ford.

Labor was voted out of power in 1977, and Allon lost his cabinet positions, though he kept his seat in the Knesset. His political base, the kibbutz movement, had merged with two other groups in 1968 to form the Israel Labor Party; by that time, Dayan was a leader of one of the other factions and enjoyed a stature as military hero that rivaled Allon's, so that neither man could form an alliance broad enough to dominate the party. When he died, Allon had begun another campaign for the party leadership.

Allon was the author of several books on military history and strategy in Hebrew, English, and Arabic. His second book, *Massakh Shel Khol (Curtain of Sand)*, described his "thesis of the anticipatory counterattack," according to which any threat of enemy attack is met by a pre-emptive strike—a strategy which helped secure Israel's quick victory in the Six-Day War. His most recent work was a memoir, *My Father's House*, published in 1976.

For most of his adult life Allon lived at Kibbutz Ginossar; as a cabinet member, he returned there from Jerusalem on weekends, contributing his share to the agricultural, industrial, and domestic life of the commune and playing host to visiting statesmen. On the day before his death, he entertained Kamal Hassan Ali, the Egyptian defense minister. Soon after, he was stricken with chest pains and died of a heart attack at a hospital near his birthplace. He was buried at the kibbutz.   J.P./C.J.

Born Yigal Paicovitch (changed name during Israeli War for Independence, 1948). Pseudonym as a guerrilla; Jephthah. Son of Reuven Yosef P. and Chayah Etil (Schwartz) P., farmers and co-founders of Kfar Tabor. Married Ruth Apisdorf 1938. Children: Nurit, b. ca. 1951; Iftach, b. ca. 1954. Jewish. Subject of Ottoman Empire from birth until British mandate of Palestine 1919; Israeli since 1948. Educ: village sch., Kfar Tabor; Kadoorie Agricultural Sch., Mt. Tabor, grad. 1937; Hebrew Univ., Jerusalem, ca. 1950–54; Research Fellow, African-Asian Affairs, St. Anthony's Coll., Oxford 1960–61. Mil. service: Sgt., Jewish Settlement Police 1937–39. With Haganah 1936–38: Comdr., field units, Galilee 1939; Dir. and Instr., officers' sch. With Palmach commando unit of Haganah: Co-founder 1941; Comdr., 1st Company 1941–43; Comdr., special underground activity for British Army in Syria and Lebanon 1942; Deputy Comdr. 1943–45; Comdr.-in-Chief 1945–49. Co-organizer and Comdr., Operation Aliyah Bet 1945–58; Comdr. of major campaigns and Gen. Comdg. Officer, Southern Front, War of Independence 1948; Brig. Gen. (reserves), Israel Defense Force 1948–50; military mission, France and Sahara Desert 1949. Founding Member, Kibbutz Ginossar, Galilee 1937–80. Member, Knesset 1954–60, 1961–80: Minister of Labor 1961–68; Deputy Prime Minister 1968–77; Acting Prime Minister, Feb.-Mar. 1969; Minister of Immigrant Absorption 1968–70; Minister of Educ. and Culture 1970–74; Minister of Foreign Affairs 1974–77. Member, Military Advisory Cttee. to Prime Minister Levi Eshkol during Six-Day War 1967; Member, Advisory Cttee. to Prime Minister Golda Meir during Yom Kippur War 1973; Member, Cabinet Defense Cttee. and Econ. Affairs Cttee. Member since 1936 and Exec. Cttee. Member, ha-Kibbutz ha-Me'uchad (United Kibbutz Movement); Member and Secty.-Gen., Achdut ha-Avodah (Zionist Socialist Workers' Party). Council Member: Histadrut; Mapam; Israel Labor Party. Delegate, 20th Zionist Congress. *Author:* Ma'arkhot Palmakh (The Story of Palmach), 1951; Massakh Shel Khol (Curtain of Sand), 1959; The Making of Israel's Army, 1970; Shield of David; The Story of Israel's Armed Forces, 1970; Thalath Hurub Wa-Salem Wahad (Three Wars and One Peace), 1970; My Father's House (autobiography), 1976; Arabs and Israelis Between War and Peace. Contributor to Intnl. Affairs and other mags. and jrnls.

Further reading: Seven Fallen Pillars by J. Kimche, 1950; Both Sides of the Hill by J. and D. Kimche, 1960.

MARCH

DIXIE DEAN
England International and Association football player
Born Birkenhead, Cheshire, England, 1907
Died Liverpool, England, March 1st, 1980

William Ralph Dean—known to millions of British soccer fans as "Dixie"—was England's most celebrated center forward in the late 1920s and early 1930s. Dean rose to fame from obscurity and then, after his retirement from soccer, quickly faded from public attention.

The son of a railway engine driver, Dean was born in Birkenhead in 1907. His love of football was announced at the age of eight when the working-class lad declared that someday he would play for Everton, a professional soccer team. Impressed with his early display of athletic prowess, Dean's teachers allowed him to attend, voluntarily, an institution for juvenile delinquents having an exceptional sports program. After leaving school Dean's prospects for a career in professional football were dim and, following a circumscribed working-class pattern, he took employment similar to his father. While working with the Wirral Railway, Dean played for several amateur soccer teams and his abilities soon caught the attention of professional scouts. Invited to join the Tranmere Rovers in 1923, Dean appeared in 27 matches in the 1924–25 season—and scored 27 goals. Dean suddenly found himself in demand and many English Football League First Division clubs offered him contracts; permitted then to make good his childhood oath, Dixie joined the Everton club in 1925.

Dixie Dean played center forward with Everton from 1925 until 1938 and not even serious injury—he sustained a severe skull fracture in a 1926 motorcycle accident—could prevent him from becoming soccer's premier goal-scorer. In the 1927–28 season alone, Dean set no less than four league records, including: most goals in a season (60); most goals in a single match (5); most hat-tricks in a season (5); and, most matches in which he scored twice (14). Dean's leadership abilities and instinctive grasp of tactics made him more than just a great scorer. When Everton's poor record plunged the team into the Football League's second division, it was Dixie's skill and unofficial on-the-field coaching which ignited the club's renaissance, a comeback which culminated in the 1932 League championship.

By 1938 Dean's athletic prime was well behind him. In a desperate scramble for money, the Everton club transferred him to the Notts. County team; an unhappy move for Dean, and one that portended the end of his career. Dean suffered regularly from injuries in the 1939 season and he decided to quit. An attempted comeback during the World War Two years failed; the ex-superstar was by then a journeyman, shuttled ignominiously from team to team. In retirement Dean worked first as the proprietor of a public house in Chester and, later, as a private security officer. At the time of his death, Dean's

record of 60 goals in a single season and his career total of 37 hat-trick
scores remained unexcelled.   M.D.

Son of Thomas J.D., railway engine driver. Married 1931. Children:
three sons; one daughter. Educ: Birkenhead (to age 14). Apprentice
fitter, Wirral Railway 1921; football player, Birkenhead area teams
1920–22 and Wirral Railway team 1922. Player and member: Tranmere Rovers Football Club 1923–25; Everton Football Club 1925–38;
England Intnl. team 1927–32 (16 appearances); Notts County Football
Club 1938–39; Sligo Football Club, Ireland. From 1946, public house
landlord, Chester; later security officer.
Further reading: Centre Forwards, the Great Ones by Laurie Mumford, 1971.

JOHN JACOB NILES
Composer, folklorist, and folk singer
Born Louisville, Kentucky, U.S.A., April 28, 1892
Died Lexington, Kentucky, U.S.A., March 1st, 1980

John Jacob Niles, a pioneer in the preservation and revival of
American folk music, was born in Louisville, Kentucky, in 1892. He
was taught music theory by his mother, a pianist and church organist.
His father, a farmer, a carpenter, square-dance caller, and ballad
singer, encouraged him to build his own dulcimers. As a high-school
student, John Jacob Niles taught himself a system of musical notation;
after graduation he traveled through Southern Appalachia as a
surveyor, collecting songs from that region's vigorous oral tradition.
Within a year he had begun giving public performances in local
churches.

He continued his collecting work as an enlisted ferry pilot in the Air
Corps during World War I, taking down soldiers' songs until a plane
crash left him partially paralyzed. He walked with crutches or a cane
for the next seven years. After his discharge he studied music at
institutions in Lyons, Paris, and London, then spent two years at the
Cincinnati Conservatory of Music, where he began to organize his
now vast collection of songs.

Moving to New York, he supported his budding concert career with
work as a rose gardener, a groomer of Ziegfeld Follies horses, and a
master of ceremonies at a nightclub, then toured the U.S. and Europe
with contralto Marion Kerby in a program of traditional songs. He
picked up more folk material in the Southern Mountains, where he
served as a guide to traveling photographer Doris Ulmann. Not

Courtesy Mrs. John Jacob Niles

content to record the songs alone, he wrote down proverbs, riddles,
and superstitions culled from "farmers, preachers, handymen, old
grannies, moonshiners . . . and even jailbirds," as one critic noted. By
the end of the 1930s he had gathered one of the most extensive private
song collections in the world, had published 11 song books, and had
issued the first of many recordings. His concert performances numbered more than 50 each year. He had also begun to compose his own
ballads and carols in a folk idiom so perfectly realized that most
listeners could not distinguish his songs from the authentic products of
oral tradition. Among these songs were "Black is the Color of My

True Love's Hair," "I Wonder as I Wander," and "Go 'Way from My Window."

From 1940 onwards Niles continued his work of bringing folk music to people who had lost touch with it, entertaining those who already appreciated it, and inspiring others to learn and perform. His concerts at New York's Town Hall drew capacity audiences. More often, he performed at churches, schools, and college auditoriums, singing in the regional dialects in which he learned his songs. His high, intense voice, accompanied by his sensitive dulcimer playing, prompted one critic to compare him to an "itinerant preacher," another to an "ancient minstrel;" rural audiences were often moved to extremes of sadness and pleasure by his renditions of familiar ballads. Albums of his work were issued on several lables, including Camden, Tradition, and his own Boone-Tolliver label; new song collections continued to appear.

Between 1940 and 1950, Niles was engaged in the composition of *Lamentations,* an oratorio based on the Biblical account of the Jews' captivity in Babylon, with allegorical connections to the problems faced by democratic nations in an increasingly totalitarian, and specifically Communist, world. Other long works included *Rhapsody for the Merry Month of May* and *Mary the Rose,* both cantatas. His most recent work was the Niles-Merton Song Cycle (1981), a musical setting of 22 poems of Thomas Merton, Trappist monk and mystic.

Niles, a prolific writer of sonnets, also wrote a number of narrative works, including *One Man's War,* an account of the Laffayette Escadrille combat unit. He collaborated on a children's book with his wife Rena, with whom he had two sons.

He died at Boot Hill Farm, his home in Clark County, Kentucky.

                                                                              J.P.

Son of John Thomas N., farmer, carpenter, and sheriff, and Lula Sarah (Reisch) N., pianist and organist. Married Rena Lipetz, writer and editor, 1936. Sons: Thomas Michael Tolliver; John Edward. Episcopalian. Educ: DuPont Manual High Sch., Louisville, grad. 1909; Univ. de Lyons, France 1919; Schola Cantorum, Paris 1919; Univ. of London 1919; Cincinnati Conservatory of Music 1920–23. Mil. service: 1st Lt., U.S. Army Air Corps 1917–19; served with Italian, French, Belgian, English units; awarded War Crosses from Italy and Belgium; service citation from U.S. Army. Surveyor ca. 1909–10. Collector of American folk songs and composer of songs in the folk idiom; over 1,000 arrangements of folk songs published individually. Performed concerts throughout U.S., Europe, and Canada since 1927; recorded on RCA Victor, Tradition-Everest, Camden, and Folkways labels, and on his own label, Boone-Tolliver; participant in John Jacob Niles's Salute to the Hills, radio series broadcast by Univ. Ky. 1937–40. Teacher of short courses at Harvard Univ., Juilliard Sch. of Music, Curtis Inst., Eastman Sch. of Music, Univ. Mo. at Kans. City. Member, American Soc. Composers, Authors and Publishers; American Fedn. of Television and Radio Artists; American Folklore Soc.; Ky. Folklore Soc.; American Dialect Soc.; Iroquois Hunt Club. Hons: Mus.D., Cincinnati Conservatory of Music 1949; citation, Natl. Fedn. Music Clubs 1967; D. Litt.; Transylvania Univ. 1969; D. Fine Arts, Episcopal Theological Seminary 1970; D.Hum., Univ. Louisville 1971; D. Litt., Univ. Ky. 1973. *Books: Collections of folk songs and folk-idiom compositions—* Impressions of a Negro Camp Meeting: Eight Traditional Tunes,

1925; Singing Soldiers, 1927, reissued 1968; Seven Kentucky Mountain Songs, 1929; (with Douglas S. Moore and A.A. Wallgren) Songs My Mother Never Taught Me, 1929; Seven Negro Exaltations, 1929; Songs of the Hill-Folk, 1934; Ten Christmas Carols from the Southern Appalachian Mountains, 1935; More Songs of the Hill-Folk, 1936; Ballads, Carols, and Tragic Legends from the Southern Appalachian Mountains, 1937; Ballads, Love-Songs, and Tragid Legends from the Southern Appalachian Mountains, 1938; The Singing Campus, 1941; The Anglo-American Ballad Study Book, 1945; The Anglo-American Carol Study Book, 1948; The Shape-Note Study Book, 1950; John Jacob Niles Suite (compiled by Weldon Hart), 1952; The Ballad Book of John Jacob Niles, 1961; (with Helen Louise Smith) Folk Ballads for Young Actors, 1962; (with Smith) Folk Carols for Young Actors, 1962; John Jacob Niles Song Book for Guitar, 1963. *Other*—(with Hall) One Man's War, 1929; One Woman's War, 1930; (with wife, Rena Niles) Mr. Poof's Discovery (children's book), 1947; Rhymes for A. Wince (children's book), 1971; introduction to Appalachian Photographs of Doris Ulmann (Jonathan Williams), 1971. Author of over 250 sonnets; articles published in Scribner's Mag. *Compositions:* Lamentation (oratorio), 1950; Mary the Rose (Christmas cantata), 1955; Rhapsody for the Merry Month of May (cantata), 1955; Concerto for Piano and Orchestra in F-minor, 1957; The Little Family (Easter carol), 1962; Moses and Pharaoh's Daughter, 1962; Reward, 1963; Symphony No. 1, 1963; The Niles-Merton Song Cycle, 1972; Melodies from an October Song-Book; Courting Time (song cycle); Winter Lullaby; others. Best-known songs include I Wonder as I Wander; Go 'Way from my Window; Black is the Color of my True Love's Hair; The Rovin' Gambler; Venezuala. *Recordings:* Early American Ballads, 1939; Early American Carols and Folk Songs, 1940; American Folk Lore, 1941, reissued 1954; John Jacob Niles: 50th Anniversary Album, 1957; I Wonder as I Wander, 1958; An Evening with John Jacob Niles, 1960; John Jacob Niles Sings Folk Songs, 1964; John Jacob Niles: Folk Balladeer, 1965; The Best of John Jacob Niles, 1967; The Ballads of John Jacob Niles.

JAROSLAW IWASZKIEWICZ
Poet, novelist, essayist, playwright and biographer
Born Kalnik, Kieven Ukraine, February 20th, 1894
Died Warsaw, Poland, March 2nd, 1980

Jaroslaw Iwaszkiewicz, whose career as a major Polish writer spanned more than 60 years and whose works include novels, plays, poetry, critical essays, and biographies of musicians, wrote with a deep sense of Poland and its culture. At a state reception in his honor, he said; "Above all, I feel a Pole, I have deep roots in this land, I am present in the country and I want always to testify to this presence."

After graduating from the University of Kiev, Iwaszkiewicz and his family moved to Warsaw in 1918 because of political upheaval in the Ukraine. He became associated with a group of influential young Polish poets who sought the creation of new literary forms to express the uniqueness of contemporary Polish experience. Their readings in a Warsaw cafe—lyrical poetry written in the colloquial idiom—were enthusiastically received by the public. They became known as the

ourtesy Iwaszkiewicz estate

"Skamander" poets and, in 1920, published the *Skamander* newsletter of which Iwaszkiewicz was a co-founder. During this artistic revival he published his first book of poetry, *Oktostychy (Verses,* 1919), which experimented with metrics and assonance. This was followed in 1922 by *Dionizje (Dionysiacs),* another book of experimental poems which employed techniques such as unexpected rhythm breaks. Some critics have seen the influence of Oscar Wilde's aestheticism in Iwaskiewicz's early poetry. His later poetry reflected a sense of human isolation, the effusions of his early work being replaced by a steadier, more compassionate humanism.

To the larger public, however, Iwaszkiewicz was known primarily as a novelist and short story writer. Acknowledged as a master of the short-story, he was praised for vivid and succinct writing; "The Girls from Wilko," which was made into a film and nominated for an Academy Award, is representative of his highly compact literary style. *The Fame and the Glory,* an epic trilogy written between 1956 and 1962, follows the changes undergone by the Polish people from 1914 to 1939. The protagonists are Ukrainian Poles uprooted by the October Revolution, attempting to re-order their lives in Poland and other countries devastated by the war. The book (which has been compared to Sartre's [q.v.] *Roads to Freedom)* depicts the individual as a victim of history who grasps at even chance events to be delivered from an empty, meaningless life. A would-be poet, traveling through Europe to seek a renewal of faith in life and humanity, finds only torment and uncertainty; another character composes music with no faith in its permanence. The trilogy climaxes with the Warsaw uprising. Although most of the characters are unable to escape the verdict of history, the survivors must accept the challenge of seeking new forms of meaning.

A politically active man, Iwaszkiewicz contributed to the preservation and development of postwar Polish culture. As president of the Polish Writer's Union he called on authors to create conditions that would further the nation's socialist culture, which he believed was the only hope for peace in a country torn apart by two world wars. He said: "It is through culture that a nation realizes its existence. Through culture the individual becomes aware of his importance in that corporate unity which is called a nation; through culture a nation becomes aware of its importance in the world. It has become the lot of our generation, our times, to be a link between the old and the new . . ."

Iwaszkiewicz received many honors during his lifetime, including the Lenin Prize in 1970 and the Gold Medal for Fighters for Peace (U.S.S.R.) in 1979. At the time of his death on March 2nd, he was on the list of candidates for election to the Polish parliament.   A.W.

Pseudonym: Eleuter. Son of Boleslaw I., clerk in a sugar factory and Maria I. Married Anna Lilpop 1922. Children: Maria; Teresa. Educ: at home; Kiev Univ., law studies 1918. Emigrated to Poland 1918. Secty. Polish Embassies, Copenhagen 1932–35 and Brussels 1935. Ed.: Zycie Literackie 1945–46; Nowiny Literackie 1947–48; Two-rczósc 1955–64 and 1970–80. Pres., Union of Polish Writers 1945–48 and 1959–80; Secty. to Marshal of Seym (Polish parliament) 1922–25; Deputy in Seym since 1952; active as a writer in Warsaw since 1919. Member, World Council of Peace since 1950; Chmn., Defenders of Peace, Polish Cttee. 1952–58; Foreign member, Serbian Acad. of

Science 1971; Member presidium All-Polish Cttee. of Natl. Unity Front since 1971; Corresp. Member, Acad. of Arts, German Democratic Republic 1974; Pres., Polish Center of Securities and Exchange Commn; Chmn., Soc. for Polish-Italian Friendship. Hons: L. Reynal Prize 1937; Order of Banner of Labor, 1st class 1949; Prize of Minister of Culture and Art, 1st class 1963, 1977; Order of Builders of People's Poland 1964; Frederic Joliot-Curie Gold Medal 1969; Lenin Prize 1970; Hon. doctorate, Warsaw 1971; Grand Cross Order of Polonia Restituta 1974; Order of Friendship of Nations U.S.S.R. 1974; Hon. Gold Medal for Fighters for Peace U.S.S.R. 1979. *Books: Verse—* Oktostychy, 1919; Dionizje (Dionysiacs), 1922; Powrót do Europy (Return to Europe), 1931; Late 1932 (Summer 1932), 1933; Ody olimpijskie (Olympic Odes), 1948; Ciemne Ścieźki (Dark Paths), 1957; Senie i elegie (Xena and elegies), 1970; Spiewnik wloski (Italian Songbook),1974; Album Tatrańskie, 1976; Mapa Pogody, 1977. *Short Story Collections—*Panny z Wilka (The Girls from Wilko), 1933; Mlyn nad Ultrata (Mill on the Ultrata), 1936; Nowa milość (New Love), 1946; Matka Joanna od Aniolow (Mother Joan of the Angels), 1946; Nowele wloskie (Italian stories), 1946; Tatarak, 1960; Opowiadania muzyczne (Musical stories), 1971; Ogrody (Gardens), 1974. *Novels—* Ksieźyc wschodzi (The Moon Rises), 1925; Zmowa meźcyzn (Conspiracy of Men), 1930; Hilary, syn buchaltera (Hilary, son of a bookkeeper), 1932; Czerwone tarcae (Red Shields), 1934; Pasje bledomierskie (Bledomierski Passions), 1938; Ślawa i chwala (The Fame and the Glory), Vol. I, 1956, Vol. II, 1958, Vol. III, 1962; Kochankowie z Marony (Lovers from Marona), 1961. *Plays—*Lato w Nohant (Summer in Nohant), 1937; Maskarada (Masquerade), 1939; Wesele pana Balzaka (Mr. Balzac's Wedding), 1959; Kosmogonia (Cosmogony), 1967. *Biographies—*Fryderyk Chopin, 1938, 1953, 1966; Jan Sebastian Bach, 1951. *Reminiscences—*Petersburg, 1976; Spotkania z Śzymanowskim (Meetings with Szymanowski), 1976. *Prose—*Zarudzie, 1977; Podfozedo Wloch (Voyages in Italy), 1977; Podróże do Polski (Voyages in Poland), 1978; Szkice o Literaturze Skandynawskiej (Essays on Scandinavian Literature), 1977. Translated numerous works into Polish from English, Danish, French, Spanish, Russian, and Italian.

ROGER (TANCRED ROBERT) HAWKINS
Rhodesian Cabinet Minister and politician
Born Letchworth, Hertfordshire, England, April 25th, 1915
Died Selukwe, Rhodesia, (Zimbabwe), March 3rd, 1980

Roger Hawkins, for many years a prominent figure in the political party which led colonial Rhodesia to unilaterally declare independence from Britain in 1965, became head of his country's security operations aims at preventing a coup by guerrilla-led insurgency forces.

Hawkins's English family decided to emigrate to the southern African colony in 1926. Hawkins continued his early schooling in Rhodesia and returned to England for secondary and university education. This completed in 1936, he went back to Rhodesia and began a commercial career. With the outbreak of World War Two, he was commissioned into the First Battalion of the Northern Rhodesia

Regiment in 1940, participating in the British East Africa campaign before being sent to jungle warfare in Burma.

After the war, Hawkins returned to Rhodesia and resumed his career, becoming increasingly involved in politics. He helped to found the Rhodesian Front Party and subsequently decided to seek a seat in Parliament. The opportunity arose in 1964 when he was returned unopposed for the Charter constituency. He remained in Parliament, latterly representing the Swelo constituency, until failing health forced him to resign in 1978.

Hawkins was a close friend of the Rhodesian Front Party leader, Ian Smith, whose Unilateral Declaration of Independence (UDI) for the self-governing colony in November 1965 he helped plan and promote. When the United Nations Organization backed a trade embargo against Rhodesia after the UDI, Hawkins's knowledge of commerce and the country's mining industry made his role in the cabinet one of vital importance.

In April 1970, Hawkins was appointed Minister of Transport and Power, also taking ministerial responsibility for Roads and Road Traffic and for Posts. He concentrated on Rhodesia's need for an internal transport system and, in 1972, produced a major paper in economics relating the need for adequate transportation to Rhodesian exports. He also forecast the obsolescence of Rhodesian rail rolling stock and predicted its need for replacement by 1980. Despite the British Government's efforts to maintain trade sanctions against Rhodesia, Hawkins managed to secure delivery of 95 new locomotives in 1973.

At the height of the bush war against Africa nationalist guerilla groups, Hawkins accepted an invitation to head the country's security services as Minister of Combined Operations. He relinquished all other portfolios and was regarded by the white community of Rhodesia as one of the most successful anti-terrorist tacticians the country had known since the Unilateral Declaration of Independence.

M.D.

Son of Harry Bradford Tancred H. Emigrated to Rhodesia 1926. Educ: Barton Grange Sch., Bulawayo; Bedford Modern Sch., England; King's Coll., Univ. London, B.A. 1936. Mil. Service: Northern Rhodesia Regiment, E. Africa, Burma 1940–46. Rhodesian M.P., Charter Constituency 1964–74 and Gwelo 1974–78; Minister for Transport and Power, Roads and Traffic, Posts, 1970–77, and for Combined Operations (security) 1977–78. Member, Exec. Cttee., Rhodesian Chamber of Mines 1964–66; Past Chmn., Rhodesian Mining Fedn. Various offices with Gwanda and S. Western Districts Regional Development and Publicity Assn., and with Gwanda Town Management Bd. Hons: Independence Commemorative Decoration (I.C.D.), Rhodesia 1965; Grand Officer, Legion of Merit (G.L.M.), Rhodesia 1976. *Author:* "Transport in Relation to Exports," Rhodesian Jrnl. of Econs. Salisbury, Dec. 1972.

WILLIAM L(ORENZO) PATTERSON
American communist leader and attorney
Born San Francisco, California, U.S.A., August 27th, 1891
(autobiography) or August 29th, 1890 (other sources)
Died Bronx, New York, U.S.A., March 5th, 1980

William L. Patterson, a leader in the American Communist Party, was born in San Francisco in 1890 or 1891. (The actual date is unknown, owing to the destruction of municipal birth records in the earthquake of 1906.) His mother had been born a slave on a Virginia cotton plantation. His father, a British West Indian, was a strict Seventh Day Adventist who left the family to become a missionary.

Patterson's mother barely managed to support her children on her earnings as a domestic, and the family was evicted from several homes for lack of rent. Despite their poverty, Patterson resolutely pursued his education, working his way through school as a paperboy, racetrack hand, elevator operator, and dishwasher and cook on freighters, and graduating from Hastings College of Law in 1919. As a student, he was attracted to radical political activism as a means of combatting rampant bigotry that threatened the lives and economic stability of American blacks. He was jailed for five days after publicly urging blacks not to fight in the "white man's war." After failing the California bar examination (probably on grounds of poor character, as a punishment for his political involvement), he considered settling in Liberia, but moved to New York City, where he was admitted to the bar in 1924.

Patterson arrived in New York in the midst of the Harlem Renaissance; he became a founding partner in a Harlem law firm, made friends with actor and activist Paul Robeson, and was briefly married to a fashion designer. He was also exposed to communist ideas, and within a few years his outlook had changed markedly. The oppression of blacks, which he had formerly attributed to white racism, now appeared to him as merely one element of a deeper world-wide phenomenon: the oppression of workers by the ruling classes. Racism against blacks, he decided, could be eliminated only through a restructuring of capitalist society. In 1926 he was arrested in Boston during a demonstration against the sentencing of two immigrant Italian anarchists, Nicola Sacco and Bartolomeo Vanzetti, on trumped-up murder charges. When they were executed in 1927, Patterson left his law practice and enrolled in the Communist Party Workers School, which sent him to study in the Soviet Union. He found the USSR to be "a democracy with a new kind of content," where collective effort had apparently created a society free of racial, religious, or class prejudice. While there, he met and married his second wife. They chose to be amicably divorced when Patterson returned to the United States.

After his return, Patterson was elected to the Cental Committee of the American Communist Party, was the party's candidate for the mayoralty of New York in 1932, wrote for and managed its newspapers, and became national executive secretary of two Communist organizations, the International Labor Defense (ILD) and its successor, the Civil Rights Congress (CRC). In 1950 he was cited for contempt by a House committee investigating his communist affiliations. A three-month prison sentence, passed against him for his refusal to turn over a list of CRC contributors to the Internal Revenue Service, was reversed on appeal.

Patterson was active in many campaigns on behalf of black defendants convicted of capital crimes in biased trials. The most famous of these was the Scottsboro Boys case of the 1930s, in which nine black youths were accused of raping two white prostitutes on a train. Despite the evident perjury of the plaintiffs, who were persuaded to make false charges by the Alabama state police, eight of the defendants were condemned to death. Throughout the long appeals process, the ILD and the NAACP quarreled over tactics. A number of black critics accused the Communist Party of exploiting this and similar cases for its own financial and ideological profit, and of intentionally frustrating the defense efforts of non-communist organizations in order to radicalize American popular opinion.

In 1951, Patterson and Paul Robeson presented a petition to the United Nations, charging that the U.S. had violated the U.N.'s Convention for the Prevention and Punishment of Genocide by killing blacks through executions, lynchings, and systematic terrorism, and by "deliberately inflicting on the group conditions of life calculated to bring about its physical destruction." The General Assembly did not respond to the petition. It was republished in 1970 with a broad spectrum of signatories, including Ralph Abernathy, Ossie Davis, Shirley Chisholm, and Huey Newton.

Patterson's death followed a prolonged illness. A foundation that bears his name awards grants to those who "advance the people's struggles."   J.P.

Son of James Edward P., ship's cook, ship's steward, dentist, and Seventh Day Adventist missionary, and Mary P., domestic. Married: (1) Minnie Summer, fashion designer and dressmaker, 1926 (div.); (2) Vera Gorohovskaya 1928 (div.); (3) Louise Thompson 1940. Children: 2nd marriage—Lola Smirnova, engineer; Anna Carnegie, newspaper correspondent for Tass; 3rd marriage—Mary Louise Gilmer, physician, b. 1943. Agnostic. Educ: Tamalpais High Sch., Calif., grad. 1911; Hastings Coll. of Law, Univ. Calif., San Francisco, B.A. 1919; Communist Party Workers sch., NYC 1927; Univ. of the Toiling People of the Far East, Moscow 1927–30. Admitted to N.Y. bar 1924. Founding partner, Dyett, Hall and Patterson law firm, NYC 1923–27. Joined American Communist Party 1927: Member, Central Cttee.; nominee for Mayor of NYC 1932; Assoc. Ed., Daily Record, Chicago 1938–40; writer, Daily World, Community Daily Worker, and The Worker. Natl. Exec. Secty., Intnl. Labor Defense 1931–49; Natl. Exec. Secty., Civil Rights Congress from 1949. Dir., miners and metalworkers sch., Pittsburgh 1931; Founder, Abraham Lincoln Sch. (coll.), Chicago 1940 (closed 1943). Observer, 2nd Congress, League Against Imperialism, Frankfurt-am-Main 1929; participant, World Conference Against Racism and Anti-Semitism, Paris 1930; planner, First Intnl. Negro Workers Congress 1930. Chmn., N.A.A.C.P. branch, Oakland 1919; Member, Intnl. Org. to Help Workers, Moscow; Member, Intnl. Negro Worker Cttee., Hamburg. Hons: Lenin Anniversary Medal, U.S.S.R. 1971; Paul Robeson Memorial Medal, Acad. of Arts of German Democratic Republic 1978. *Author:* (ed.) We Charge Genocide: The Crime of Government Against the Negro People, 1951, reprinted 1970; The Man Who Cried Genocide (autobiography), 1971. Contributor to New Time, African Communist, New World Review, Negro Worker, Marxist Review. *Interviews:* L'Humanité, 1951; Action, 1951.

JAY SILVERHEELS
Film and television actor
Born Six Nations Indian Reservation, Ontario, Canada, ca. 1919
Died Woodland Hills, California, U.S.A., March 5th, 1980

Jay Silverheels, a Mohawk Indian of the Iroquois Nation, and an accomplished sportsman, portrayed American Indians to cinema and television audiences in an acting career that spanned 35 years.

Silverheels was born on the Six Nations Indian Reservation in Ontario, Canada, and was brought up in the traditions of his tribe. He first came to Hollywood in 1933 as a member of a touring professional lacrosse team and later achieved a reputation as a professional boxer, meantime securing occasional bit parts in movies. He appeared with Tyrone Power in *Captain from Castille* in 1947. During the 1950s, he made a specialty of playing the Bendonkohe Apache Indian chief Geronimo, whom he portrayed in *Broken Arrow, Battle at Apache Pass,* and *Walk the Proud Land.*

Silverheels became best known for his television role as Tonto, the faithful Indian sidekick of the Lone Ranger. Both characters were invented by Fran Striker for a radio show of the 1930s. Silverheels played Tonto in all 221 episodes of the television series, which ran from 1949 to 1957 and is still in syndicated reruns. He and Clayton Moore, as the masked man who fired silver bullets, also appeared in two feature films that grew out of the series. Silverheels's other film credits included roles in *True Grit, Key Largo, The Will Rogers Story,* and *The Man Who Loved Cat Dancing.*

Marriage to an Italian did nothing to weaken Silverheels's ties to his Indian background. He described his four children as "Indalian." All were raised in the strict Mohawk traditions of honesty, respect for elders, and respect for the natural environment as the universal provider. When his children complained about the inaccurate, often malicious representation of American Indians in films and television, Silverheels responded with his own philosophy: "Let me remind you that the people who write these things don't know the truth. But don't be angry. Remember our Indian proverb: 'Let me never condemn my brother until I have walked sun-up to sun-down in his moccasins.' Be slow to judge; respect the traditions and practices of others. Never be afraid to tell the truth; obey the laws wherever you live; show courtesy to all fellow human beings and tenderness to animals. What has endured is good and will be made better as we move, generation after generation towards perfection."

In the early 1960s, Silverheels founded the Indian Actors Workshop in Hollywood as a means of helping aspiring Indian actors into the profession. In August 1979, he became the first American Indian to have a star set for him in Hollywood's Walk of Fame along Hollywood Boulevard.

After his retirement from the screen, Silverheels continued as an enthusiastic sportsman. In 1974 he obtained a harness racing license and became a familiar figure at tracks across the United States. His death at the Motion Picture and Television Country House in California was caused by complications arising from pneumonia. M.D.

Son of Mohawk (Iroquois) parents. Married Mary Di Roma 1946. Children: Marilyn, teacher; Pamela; Karen; Jay Anthony. Emigrated to U.S.A. 1933. Educ: Six Nations Indian Reservation, Ontario.

Professional lacrosse player 1936, subsequently professional boxer. Actor, films 1938–73 and television 1949–65. Professional harness racer 1974–77. Founder, Indian Actors Workshop, Hollywood 1963. Hons: Star, Hollywood's Walk of Fame 1979. *Performances: Films—* The Prairie, Captain from Castille, 1947; Key Largo, Unconquered, Fury at Furnace Creek, Singing Spurs, Yellow Sky, 1948; Laramie, Lust for Gold, Sand, Trail of the Yukon, The Cowboy and the Indians, 1949; Broken Arrow, 1950; Red Mountain, 1951; Battle at Apache Pass, Brave Warrior, 1952; The Pathfinder, Jack McCall, Desperado, The Nebraskan, War Arrow, 1953; Saskatchewan, or O'Rourke of the Royal Mounted, Drums Across the River, The Black Dakotas, Four Guns to the Border, 1954; Masterson of Kansas, The Vanishing American, The Lone Ranger, 1955; Walk the Proud Land, 1956; Return to Warbow, The Lone Ranger and the Lost City of Gold, 1958; Alias Jesse James, 1959; Indian Paint, 1966; True Grit, 1969; The Phynx, 1970; One Little Indian, The Man Who Loved Cat Dancing, Santee, 1973; The Will Rogers Story. *Television—*The Lone Ranger, 1949–57; Geronimo's Revenge, 1964.

JOHN DICK SCOTT
Novelist and war historian
Born Lanarkshire, Scotland, February 26th, 1917
Died Tregaron, Wales, March 10th, 1980

One of the many aspiring writers of the World War Two generation, John Dick Scott, who was also an historian and an editor, emerged as a popular novelist in the late 1940s and 50s. Scott's first literary efforts at the University of Edinburgh, where he studied history, showed promise in both fiction and non-fiction genres. His career, however, was delayed by the war and he accepted a Civil Service appointment with the Ministry of Aircraft production in London. He was later commissioned by the government to work on the official history of the war.

Able to write full-time after 1945, Scott's first novel was published two years later. Set in France, *The Cellar* was a suspense story about an English fighter pilot hero who hides in a cellar with two other fugitives—a laconic, battle-hardened Scottish soldier and a young woman ambulance driver—to escape the Nazis. In *The Margin*, published two years later, Scott contrasted, schematically, a dreary-but-secure life in the Civil Service with the fragile glamour of the film world. *The End of an Old Song* (1953) depicted the steady erosion of a Scottish family's traditions and sense of heritage in the modern world. While Scott's themes were familiar, critics applauded his ability to construct suspenseful plots. However, Scott's last novel, *The Pretty Penny* (1963), an action-packed adventure story of gun-running in Africa which deplored moral and political corruption, was coolly received. To critics, the book was "solidly entertaining" but failed to explore thoughtfully its themes.

In an historical vein Scott published *The Administration of War Production* (1956), part of the British government's *Official History of the Second World War,* and *Life in Britain* (1956), an analysis of social mores, public institutions, and the inner workings of Britain's "Welfare State" in the postwar period. Reviewers faulted Scott for a shallow examination of trade unionism and the class divisions in British society. Scott's lifelong interest in the history of armaments and engineering was reflected in three later volumes: *The Siemens Brothers 1859–1958* (1958); *Vickers: A History* (1964); and *The Design and Development of Weapons* (with M.M. Postan and D. Hay, 1965).

In 1953 Scott accepted an invitation to become literary editor of the *Spectator,* a post he held for three years. He moved to Washington, D.C. in 1963 where he edited *Finance and Development,* a World Bank publication, for eleven years. Scott returned to Britain in 1974 and subsequently retired in Wales. M.D.

Son of Alexander S. (O.B.E.) and Margaret Gourlay (Allardice) S. Married Helen Elisabeth Whittaker 1941. Two sons. Educ: Stewart's Coll., Edinburgh; Univ. Edinburgh A.M., Hons. history 1939. Asst. Principal, Ministry of Aircraft Production, London 1940–44; historian, British Cabinet Office, London 1944; novelist, historian and freelance writer since 1945; Literary Ed., Spectator, London 1953–56; Ed., Finance and Development, Washington 1963–74. *Author: Novels* —The Cellar, 1947, as But if for a Song, 1948; The Margin, 1949; The Way to Glory or The Last Night of the Holidays, 1952; The End of an Old Song, 1954; The Pretty Penny, 1963. *Other*—(with Richard Hughes) The Administration of War Production, 1956; Life in Britain, 1956; The Siemens Brothers, 1858–1958: An Essay in the History of Industry, 1958; Look at Post Offices, 1962; Vickers: A History, 1963; (with Michael Postan and D. Hay) Mystic, 1964; Design and Development of Weapons, 1964; (contributor) Studies of Overseas Supply, eds. Hessel Hall and Christopher Wrigley, 1956.

ERNÖ GERÖ
First Secretary, Hungarian Communist Party
Born Budapest, Hungary, August 17th, 1898
Died Budapest, Hungary, March 12th, 1980

Ernö Gerö attained international prominence in 1956 as the Hungarian leader who called in Russian soldiers to suppress the broad–based uprising in his country. He was born into an assimilated Hungarian Jewish merchant family named Singer and although his earliest career interest was medicine, he turned to political journalism after joining the Communist Party in 1918. It was a time of great social and political upheaval: the Austro-Hungarian empire had collapsed with the Allied victory in World War One; the Bolsheviks seized power in Russia, and many young men like Singer identified Communism with the inexorable logic of history. He became increasingly involved with the Communist movement and was a youth leader during the short-lived regime of Béla Kun, but his activities resulted in a 14-year prison sentence after the fall of the Hungarian Soviet Republic in 1919. Singer adopted the name Gerö a year later.

Gerö won release when the Hungarian government offered the USSR left wing partisans being held in its jails in exchange for army officers imprisoned by the Soviets. In 1924 he settled in the Soviet Union to become a professional revolutionist. Between the World

Wars he became a senior agent of the Comintern, dutifully carrying— sometimes illegally—Moscow's orders to many countries. From 1936 to 1938 he fought in Spain but the Fascist victory forced a return to the Soviet Union, where he remained until 1944.

When the Soviet army entered Hungary in 1944, Gerö was with them and he played a leading role in the establishment of a new government at Budapest. In 1945 he became Minister of Transport and, three years later, assumed control of Hungary's economy as Minister of Finance. By 1950 Gerö had been installed as Minister of State as well as Minister of Foreign Trade. Throughout his administrative career, Gerö sought expansion of heavy industry to make Hungary the "country of iron and steel" within the Communist bloc. In short, Gerö, who had served continuously in the Hungarian politburo, was a powerful man. He was known as a shrewd political infighter and an inflexible Stalinist: to protest Premier Josip Tito's [q.v.] repudiation of Soviet orthodoxy, Gerö returned the war medals Yugoslavia had awarded him. Moreover, he waged an aggressive campaign against Cardinal Josef Mindzenty, who had been imprisoned for opposition to the secularization of Catholic schools, and during the late 1940s, Gerö blocked Jewish emigration to Israel.

In 1955 Hungarian Premier Mátyás Rákosi elevated Gerö to the post of Deputy Premier, but in Moscow, where Krushchev had come to power and anti-Stalinist sentiment was growing, events were under way which would end in dismissal of the Hungarian leaders. The Soviets moved to conciliate Tito—a strategy endorsed by Gerö—with the elimination of Rákosi, a Stalinist hard-liner whose very presence in Hungary was an affront to the Yugoslavian leader. Rákosi was forced to step down in July 1956 and, as Gerö succeeded him, the hopes of Hungarians supporting liberalization of domestic institutions soared. On October 23 students and workers poured spontaneously into the streets of Budapest seeking redress of past injustices. Gerö foolishly responded with a speech harshly denouncing the protestors, government troops fired randomly into the crowd, and a peaceful situation quickly became revolutionary. The following day Gerö was replaced by János Kádár and on November 4, Russian tanks brutally crushed the revolt. For a time Gerö was believed to have been killed during a period of street fighting but it was later established that Russian troops had provided him with safe conduct into the Soviet Union.

For four years the Hungarian government refused Gerö permission to enter the country. In 1960 he was allowed to return by promising to take no part in public or political life. He lived quietly in retirement but was formally expelled from the Hungarian Communist Party in 1962 for suspected reprisals against labor leaders during the 1956 uprising.   E.T.

Born Ernö Singer (changed name 1920). Emigrated to Germany 1919; returned to Hungary 1921; lived in U.S.S.R. 1924–44 and 1956–60; Hungary 1944–56 and 1960–80. Educ: medical studies, Budapest 1915–17 (no degree). Mil. Service: with Communist forces, Spanish Civil War 1936–38; with U.S.S.R. Army, Hungary 1944–45. With Hungarian Communist Party 1918–62: Member, Central Cttee. 1946–56; First Secty. Jul.–Oct. 1956. Comintern agent, U.S.S.R., 1924–44. Minister of Transport, Hungary 1945; Finance 1948; State

and Foreign Trade 1950; Deputy Prime Minister 1955–56; Prime
Minister 1956. Hons: Order of Republic, Yugoslav medals 1945
(returned 1949); Kossuth Prize 1949.

LILLIAN NGOYI
Black African nationalist
Born Pretoria, Transvaal, September 24th, 1911
Died Soweto, South Africa, March 12th, 1980

Lillian (Masediba) Ngoyi was a leading black African nationalist who
held high office in several organizations in South Africa. Since 1964
she had been a "banned person," which meant that her movements
and personal contacts were restricted and newspapers could not quote
her. Charismatic leadership and tireless dedication to the rights of
blacks earned her the title of "the mother of the black resistance."

Lillian Ngoyi was born in Pretoria in 1911. Her father, a Bapedi
from Sekhukhuneland, worked in a platinum mine. She had hoped to
be a teacher but was forced to abandon her education to help support
the family. After working as a domestic servant for three months in
1935—a position she found intolerable—she became a nurse. In 1934
she married John Ngoyi, a van driver, with whom she had three
children; the couple later separated. From 1945 to 1956 she worked as
a machinist in a clothing factory.

Her position as an official in the Garment Workers' Union (Native
Branch) was the start of a life dedicated to humanitarianism. In 1952
she joined the African National Congress (A.N.C.) and held executive positions—including National President and Transvaal Provincial
President of the A.N.C. Women's League—until the organization was
prohibited in 1960. Lillian Ngoyi served a short prison sentence in
1953 after taking part in the Congress Defense Campaign against the
race laws. In 1954 she became the only woman elected to the National
Executive of the African National Congress and in 1956 was made
National President of the newly organized Federation of South
African Women. She was an elected delegate to the World Mothers'
Conference in Lausanne, Switzerland, in 1955, having left South
Africa without a passport in order to attend.

On August 9, 1956, Lillian Ngoyi led 20,000 women in Pretoria to
the Union Building offices of then Prime Minister J.G. Strijdom,
protesting the extension to women of the "pass laws" controlling the
movement of blacks. She was arrested and tried for treason, and
finally acquitted five years later. She was arrested again during the
State of Emergency in 1960 and spent five months in solitary
confinement, without trial, in Pretoria Prison.

In 1963 Lillian Ngoyi was one of the first people to be held under a
90-day detention law, spending 71 days in prison in Johannesburg
without charge or trial. She was confined to the township of Orlando
from 1963–68. She was arrested and "banned" in 1964.

Lillian Ngoyi died at her home in the suburban black township of
Soweto.   S.P.

Daughter of Isaac Mmankhatteng and Annie Modipadi (Mphahlele)
Matabane. Married John Ngoyi 1934 (d.). Children: Edith Mosime;

161 SIR WILLIAM MALLALIEU

Memory Chauke; Eggart. Educ: Kilnerton Instn. 1925–27. Nurse, City Mine Hosp. 1928–30; garment factory machinist 1945–56. With African Natl. Congress: Member of Transvaal Exec. 1954–60; Natl. Pres. and Transvaal Provincial Pres., A.N.C. Women's League 1956–60. With Fedn. of S. African Women: Member, Natl. Exec. 1954–64; Natl. Pres. 1956–64. Delegate to World Mothers' Conference, Lausanne 1955.

SIR (JOSEPH PERCIVAL) WILLIAM MALLALIEU
British Cabinet Minister, politician and author
Born Delph, Yorkshire, England, June 18th, 1908
Died Aylesbury, Buckinghamshire, England, March 13th, 1980

Sir William Mallalieu, who served in successive British Labour Governments and held three ministerial appointments in a parliamentary career of more than three decades, was born into a family of Yorkshire Liberals. His father, County Alderman Frank Mallalieu, saw long service in local government as a member of the West Riding County Council and for a time served in national government as Liberal M.P. for Colne Valley. Mallalieu, like his elder brother Edward Lancelot, joined the British Labour Party and followed his brother into the House of Commons as a northern constituency Labour M.P.

From Cheltenham College he went on to Trinity College, Oxford, and was elected president of the Oxford Union Society, the university's main debating club, in 1930. Mallalieu studied at the University of Chicago for two years on a Commonwealth Scholarship. On his return to Britain he worked for several Fleet Street newspapers as a journalist. In 1936 he became Parliamentary Labour candidate for Huddersfield, but World War Two intervened and Mallalieu joined the Royal Navy, with active service aboard escort vessels in Arctic convoys to Russia. He gained the rank of Lieutenant, later describing the experience in his book, *Very Ordinary Seaman.*

After the war, Mallalieu entered the 1945 General Election campaign, winning the Huddersfield seat from the National Liberal Member, Sir William Mabane. During his first term in the House of Commons, he rose from the back benches to be Parliamentary Private Secretary to the Minister of Food. At the same time he established himself as a popular figure in Huddersfield so that when the parliamentary constituency boundaries were altered before the 1950 General Election, he was able to retain his seat.

In Harold Wilson's Labour Government of 1964, Mallalieu was appointed Parliamentary Under-Secretary of State for Defence with responsibility for the Royal Navy, and in February 1966 was appointed Minister of Defence (Navy). He was made Minister of State for the Board of Trade in 1967, and a year later was given the post of Minister of Technology.

Throughout his career Mallalieu maintained a steadfast commitment to political reform. Choosing to act on principle rather than submit blindly to party loyalty on important issues, Mallalieu's independence often earned the opposition of his colleagues in Parliament. In 1942 he published *Passed to You, Please,* a humorously critical treatment of Britain's wartime bureaucracy that nonetheless earned the wrath of the *London Times* which mistakenly labeled the book a "Marxist tract." Mallalieu retained the support of his East Huddersfield constituency until the General Election of 1979, when he retired.   M.D.

Son of County Alderman Frank W.M., Liberal M.P. Married Harriet Rita Riddle Tinn 1945. Children: one son; one daughter. Educ: Dragon Sch., Oxford; Cheltenham Coll.; Trinity Coll., Oxford, B.A. 1929; Commonwealth Fellow, Univ. Chicago 1930–32. Mil. Service: Royal Navy, Arctic Ocean 1942–45. Journalist, London 1933–41; Parliamentary candidate, Huddersfield (Labour) 1936–45; M.P., Huddersfield 1945–50 and E. Huddersfield 1950–79; Parliamentary Private Secty. to Under-Secty. of State for Air 1945–49; Parliamentary Private Secty. to Minister of Food 1946–49; Under-Secty. of State for Defence (Royal Navy) 1964–66; Minister of Defence (Royal Navy) 1966–67; Minister of State, Bd. of Trade 1967–68; Minister of Technology 1968–69. Pres., Oxford Union Soc. 1930; Member, management cttees.: Royal Natl. Lifeboat Instn. 1959–63 and Royal Hosp. Sch., Holbrook 1947–66. Hons: knighted 1979. *Author:* Rats, 1941; Passed to You, Please!, 1942; Very Ordinary Seaman, 1944; Sporting Days, 1955; Extraordinary Seaman, 1957; Very Ordinary Sportsman, 1957.

SIR ROLAND (THEODORE) SYMONETTE
Bahamian Prime Minister and business executive
Born Nassau, Bahama Islands, December 16th, 1898
Died Nassau, Bahama Islands, March 13th, 1980

Sir Roland Symonette, first Prime Minister of the Bahamas after Britain granted the islands domestic autonomy in 1964, came from an upper-middle-class family in Nassau. His efforts to attract foreign investment to the emergent nation were controversial and his United Bahamian Party was swept from power by the Black Progressive Party. He then served for ten years as Leader of the Opposition, during which time the islands gained full independence within the Commonwealth.

Symonette entered the islands' political life when he was a teenager. Elected to the Bahamian House of Assembly in 1925, he served there until 1977. He was a member of the Executive Council of the Bahamas from 1949 until internal self-government was granted and held the position of Leader of Government in the House of Assembly from 1955 to 1967.

As a financier with controlling interests in shipyards and extensive land-development enterprises, Symonette brought to government a practical understanding of the Bahamian economy. His efforts to improve it, particularly when independence was within sight, were, however, the subject of frequent criticism. He and Sir Stafford Sands, a former Bahamian Finance Minister, were leaders of the "Bay Street Boys," a conservative minority seeking to open the islands to foreign investment and establish gambling casinos. For a time, when the islands were almost completely dependent on U.S. tourist dollars, the black majority claimed to be receiving neither a representative voice in government nor a fair share of the wealth generated by the casinos. Critical articles appeared in the *Wall Street Journal* stating that the islands' gambling policies encouraged infiltration by U.S. racketeers. The Symonette administration's defeat in the 1967 election was attributed to its fiscal policies. Nevertheless, Symonette remained popular in the islands: renowned for acts of public and private charity, he was affectionately known throughout the Bahamas as "Pop." Symonette's efforts to re-organize the United Bahamian Party continued until shortly before his death. He had been knighted in 1959.

M.D.

Married twice; (2) Margaret Frances Thurlew 1945. Children: 1st marriage—two sons, one daughter; 2nd marriage—two sons (one son d.). Educ: Current Eleuthera Day Sch., Bahamas, to age 15. Financier, industrial contractor, land developer and shipyard owner, Bahama Islands since 1923. As a politician: Member: 1925–67 and Leader 1955–67, Bahamas House of Assembly; Member of Bahamas Exec. Council 1949–64; Prime Minister of the Bahamas 1964–67; Leader of the Opposition (United Bahamian Party) 1967–77. Hons: knighted 1959.

MANLIO (GIOVANNI) BROSIO
Secretary-General, North Atlantic Treaty Organization, and Ambassador
Born Turin, Italy, July 10th, 1897
Died Turin, Italy, March 14th, 1980

Courtesy Brosio estate

Manlio Brosio, whose diplomatic career in postwar Europe culminated in his Secretary-Generalship of NATO, was born in Turin in 1897 and studied law at Turin University. During the First World War he served as an artillery officer with the Italian Alpine Corps, was briefly held prisoner in Austria, and won the Silver Medal and the Cross of Valor. After receiving his degree in 1920, he opened a corporate law practice in Turin.

Interested in politics since his student days, Brosio soon became an administrator and writer for the Turin Rivoluzione Liberale, where he was much influenced by the Liberal writers Benedetto Croce, Luigi Einaudi, and Piero Gobetti. When Mussolini and the Fascists took over the government in 1942, Brosio temporarily withdrew from politics, although he lent covert assistance to liberal anti-Fascist groups.

During the Nazi occupation of Italy, Brosio joined the underground National Committee of Liberation, quitting his private practice altogether. He became Secretary of the Liberal Party in 1944 and participated in a series of postwar cabinets, serving as Minister without Portfolio under Bonomi, as Vice President of the Council of Ministers under Parri, and as Minister of War under De Gasperi.

In 1947 he began a distinguished diplomatic career as Ambassador to the U.S.S.R., where he negotiated peace treaties, war reparations claims, and prisoner exchanges, and concluded the first Italo-Soviet commercial agreement. During his five years in Moscow he became Dean of the Diplomatic Corps and an authority on Josef Stalin and the political processes of the Kremlin. Asked by a British politician for his opinion on Stalin's probable succeessor, Brosio replied, "I should like to be standing in Red Square watching the windows of the Kremlin to see who is going to be thrown out first."

As Ambassador to Great Britain from 1952 to 1954, Brosio was faced with the difficult task of negotiating the political status of the Free Territory of Trieste, occupied in part by the U.S. and Britain and claimed by both Italy and Yugoslavia. The result of his efforts was the Memorandum of Understanding, signed in October 1954, by which Italy was granted sovereignty of the city and Yugoslavia was guaranteed free access to its port.

Brosio's appointments as Ambassador to the U.S. from 1955 to 1961 under Presidents Eisenhower and Kennedy, and as Ambassador to France from 1961 to 1964 under President de Gaulle, prepared him for his seven-year tenure as Secretary-General of NATO, where he served until 1971. Although he contributed to the evolution of the policy of detente, he took a firm stand against proposed reductions in NATO's troop levels and strike capabilities without corresponding reductions in Soviet strength, especially after the Soviet invasion of Czechoslovakia in 1968. He also supervised the relocation of NATO headquarters to Belgium and assisted in the settlement of the rivalry between two Western allies, Greece and Turkey, over possession of the island of Cyprus.

Brosio, whose dry wit was as much appreciated by his colleagues as his ability to derive a consensus from conflicting views, made a point of studying the language and culture of his host countries, learning Russian and English simultaneously while on duty in Moscow and becoming something of a chess adept. He was described as an Americanophile during his stay in the U.S. and as a Francophile while in France. *Le Monde* called him "little interested in squabbles of ideologies, a clever negotiator, multilingual, benefiting from a favorable prejudice from all the NATO delegations."

After returning to Italy in 1971, Brosio spent four years as Liberal Senator from Turin. Ill health forced his retirement in 1976.   J.P.

Son of Edoardo B., judge, and Fortunata (Curadelli) B. Married Clotilde Brosio, his cousin, 1936. No children. Educ: Turin Univ., D.Jur. 1920. Mil. Service: Artillery Officer, Alpine Corps 1915–18; P.O.W., Austria 1918; Silver Medal and Cross of Valor, Italy 1918. Private law practice, Turin 1920–42. Member 1919–26 and Gen. Secty. 1922–25, Rivoluzione Liberale, Turin; publications ed. and writer, Opposition Cttee. Against Fascism 1924–26; Member, Natl. Cttee. of Liberation, Rome 1943–44. Secty., Liberal Party 1944–45. Minister without Portfolio in Bonomi cabinet 1944; V.P., Council of Ministers in Parri cabinet 1945; Minister of War in De Gasperi cabinet 1945–46. Italian Ambassador to Russia 1947–51, latterly Dean of Moscow Diplomatic Corps; Ambassador to Great Britain 1952–54; Ambassador to the U.S. 1955–61; Ambassador to France 1961–64. Secty.-Gen., NATO 1964–71. Senator (Liberal), Turin 1972–76. Hons: Freedom Medal, U.S.A. 1971. *Author:* Juridical articles in Foro Italiano and other professional jrnls.; also articles in La Stampa and other newspapers.

ROBERT LEE DENNISON
Admiral, United States Navy
Born Warren, Pennsylvania, U.S.A., April 13th, 1901
Died Bethesda, Maryland, U.S.A., March 14th, 1980

Robert Lee Dennison, Atlantic Fleet Commander of the U.S. Navy and Supreme Allied Commander of the Atlantic forces for NATO, was a U.S. naval officer for forty years. In 1961 he supervised the successful naval blockade of Cuba during the missile crisis.

After graduating from the United States Naval Academy in 1923, Dennison spent the next twelve years shuttling between land and sea assignments in order to complete his postgraduate education. While serving on the battleship Arkansas, he also managed to obtain a master's degree in diesel engineering. In 1925 Dennison was assigned to submarine service and, ten years later, assumed command of the U.S.S. Ortolan, a rescue vessel. That same year he received a doctorate in engineering.

Dennison was a member of the staff of the Commander-in-Chief of the Asiatic Fleet when Japan staged a surprise attack on Pearl Harbor. During the war Dennison received rapid promotions and decorations for bravery. He was awarded the Army Distinguished Unit Emblem for his service in defense of the Philippines and in 1942, he was appointed Chief of Staff to the Commander of the Allied Naval Forces in East Australia. He later became Chief of Staff to the Commander of the Amphibious Fleet in the Pacific, and participated in the recapture of the Aleutian Islands of Attu and Kiska in the summer of 1943. Because Attu was recovered without the loss of ships or naval personnel, Dennison was awarded the Legion of Merit.

In 1948 President Truman appointed Dennison as his naval aide. Dennison held the position until the end of Truman's term in 1952 and was subsequently promoted to the rank of Rear Admiral. In 1956 President Eisenhower nominated Dennison for the rank of Vice-Admiral. For the next three years Dennison commanded the United States Pacific Fleet, was a member of the Joint Strategic Plans Committee of the Joint Chiefs of Staff, and served as Commander-in-Chief of Naval Forces for the eastern Atlantic and Mediterranean region. Dennison became a full Admiral in 1959 and one year later, served in the dual NATO and United States Atlantic Commander posts. It was during these years that the Bay of Pigs invasion and the Cuban missile crisis occurred; upon the discovery of Russian missiles in Cuba in 1961 he was charged with the responsibility of carrying out a blockade of the islands. Shortly before Dennison's retirement in 1963 President Kennedy praised his "exceptionally meritorious service in duties of great responsibility."

Admiral Dennison was named a Vice-President of Copley Press, Inc.—a newspaper chain in Illinois and Southern California—upon his retirement from the Navy. He died at the National Naval Medical Center in Bethesda, Maryland.   L.G.

Son of Ludovici Waters D. and Laura Florence (Lee) D. Married Mildred Fenton Mooney Neely 1937. Children: Lee (daughter); Robert Lee. Educ: U.S. Naval Acad., B.S. 1923; Pa. State Coll., M.S. 1930; Johns Hopkins, Baltimore, D.Eng. 1935. Mil. Service: Comdr. ensign U.S.N. 1923, advanced through grades to Admiral 1954; served with Atlantic, Pacific and Asiatic fleets, Comdr.: U.S.S. Ortolan 1935–37; U.S.S. Cuttlefish 1937–38; U.S.S. John D. Ford

1940–41; U.S.S. Missouri 1947–48; Chief of Staff of Comdr. Submarines, E. Australia; Comdr., Allied Naval Forces, E. Australia 1942; Chief of Staff Amphibious Forces, U.S. Pacific Fleet 1942–43; Chief of Staff to Comdr., Ninth Amphibious Forces 1943; Member, Jt. War Plans Cttee., Jt. Chiefs of Staff 1944–45; Asst. Chief of Naval Operations for Political-Mil. Affairs 1945–47; Naval Aide to Pres. Truman 1948–53; Comdr., Cruiser Div. Four, U.S. Atlantic Fleet 1953–54; Dir., Strategic Plans Div., Asst. Chief Naval Operations for Plans and Policy, Office of Naval Operations 1954–56, 1958; Member, Jt. Strategic Plans Cttee., Jt. Chiefs of Staff and Comdr., First Fleet, U.S. Pacific Fleet 1956–58; Comdr.-in-Chief U.S. Naval Forces, Eastern Atlantic and Mediterranean 1959–60. Supreme Allied Comdr. Atlantic, NATO 1960–63. V.P., Copley Press, Inc. 1963–73. Member, Sigma Xi. Clubs: N.Y. Yacht; Metropolitan; Chevy Chase; Army-Navy (Washington); Ends of the Earth; American (London). Hons: Decorated Distinguished Service Medal; Legion of Merit; Gold Star in lieu of 2nd Legion of Merit; American Defense Award; Asiatic Pacific Area, Two Stars; Philippine Defence with Star: Navy Unit Commendation (U.S.S. Pennsylvania); Navy Occupation Service Medal (European Clasp), Natl. Def. Service medal; Army Distinguished Unit Citation (Philippines), American area; World War II Victory (U.S.); Order of British Empire; Grand Officer, Order Naval Merit (Brazil); Order of the Crown (Belgium); Legion of Honor (France). *Author:* The Stength and Flexibility of Corrugated and Creased-Bend Piping (doctoral thesis), reprinted from Jrnl. of the American Soc. of Naval Engineers, vol. 47, #.3, 1935.

MOHAMMED HATTA
Vice President and Prime Minister of Indonesia
Born Bukittinggi, Sumatra, Indonesia, August 12th, 1902
Died Jakarta, Indonesia, March 14th, 1980

Mohammed Hatta, a leading figure in the Indonesian independence movement, served in the first post-independence governments after he and President Sukarno jointly declared the country a republic in 1945.

Hatta, who came from a family of Moslem religious leaders, was born in western Sumatra, in what was then the Netherlands Indies, and became involved in the independence movement at an early age. Like many young Indonesians, he went to Holland to study, earning his doctorate in economics from the University of Rotterdam, where he became head of the militant Indonesian Students Association in 1926. In 1927 he met Jawaharlal Nehru, a leader of the independence movement in India and later first Prime Minister, at the first congress of the League Against Colonial Oppression; the two became close friends. Later that year, Hatta was jailed by the Dutch for several months on charges of spreading revolutionary propaganda.

When Hatta returned to the Netherlands Indies in 1932, he found the independence movement in a state of collapse as a consequence of the three-year imprisonment of its leader, Sukarno. To bolster it, Hatta and a colleague, Sutan Sjahrir, founded the Pendidikan Nasional Indonesia, an educational club and political party organized in semi-autonomous cadres that could function even in the absence of the group's officials.

Within two years, a crackdown by the colonial authorities had resulted in the arrest and exile of most of its leaders. Hatta was exiled first to Digul, then to the Moluccan Islands. He and the other political prisoners were freed by the Japanese Army after its capture of the Indies archipelago in 1942, during the Second World War, and were invited to administer the country during its period of military occupation. Although the Japanese trained a native defense force and consented to the existence of nationalist organizations, they were, on the whole, more concerned to exploit the available manpower through forced-labor programs. As their military fortunes declined, they attempted to secure Indonesian support with promises of future independence. Such a promise was made to Sukarno and Hatta in August 1945 by Marshal Terauchi in Saigon. The plan, which was opposed by Indonesian nationalists, collapsed when Japan surrendered to the Allies on terms that included the return of Indonesia to the Dutch. On August 17, the two leaders declared the country an independent nation, with Sukarno as its president and Hatta its vice president.

This action met with immediate military opposition from Britain, which was supervising the transfer of conquered territories to the Allies, and from the Netherlands, which was not prepared to give up its colony. In the ensuing guerrilla war, Hatta saw combat in his home province of western Sumatra. Pressure from the United States persuaded the Dutch to relinquish Indonesia in 1949.

Hatta served as the nation's Prime Minister for the first nine months following the transfer of sovereignty, then returned to the vice presidency. A succession of unstable governments followed, none of them able to deal adequately with the nation's severe economic and administrative problems. Hatta's relations with Sukarno became increasingly strained as the president moved to replace Indonesia's constitutional democracy with a "Guided Democracy" under his own authority.

When Hatta resigned in 1956 to protest Communist participation in Sukarno's cabinet, a group of dissident Army veterans, whom Hatta had supported, began a rebellion in western Sumatra that spread to other provinces. In 1958 these dissidents attempted to establish an alternative government with Hatta at its head, but were quickly suppressed by the armed forces. Hatta, who had been teaching at universities in Jogjakarta and Bandung, was deprived of his positions by the Government in 1960 and forced into seclusion. He spent his time writing articles in favor of a political structure based on Islamic tradition, Indonesian communalism, and European democratic socialism.

Following the downfall of Sukarno in 1967, Hatta returned to lecturing and served as consultant to a commission investigating corruption in Indonesia. His *Portrait of a Patriot* was published in 1976. In 1978 the government of President Suharto reported the failure of an attempted coup which would have made Hatta the nation's leader.   J.P.

Moslem. Educ: Rotterdam Sch. of Econs., Ph.D. ca. 1926. Chmn., Perhimpunan Indonesia (Indonesian Students Assn.) 1926. Arrested by Dutch 1927; tried and released 1928. Co-founder of Pendidikan Nasional Indonesia party 1932. Arrested and jailed by Dutch 1934;

exiled to Digul 1935; later exiled to Moluccan Islands; released by
Japanese 1942; leader in Japanese occupation govt. 1942–45. V.P.,
Republic of Indonesia 1945–49 and 1950–56; Prime Minister Dec.
1949–Aug. 1950; Minister of Defense 1949; Minister of Foreign
Affairs 1949–50. Prof. Gadjah Mada Univ., Jogjakarta, and Army
Command and Staff Coll., Bandung, ca. 1956–60; in forced seclusion
1960–70; returned to teaching 1970. Advisor, Commn. on Natl.
Corruption 1970. Writer on politics and econs. *Author:* Portrait of a
Patriot: Selected Writings, 1976.
Further reading: Nationalism and Revolution in Indonesia by George
Kahin, 1952.

ALLARD (KENNETH) LOWENSTEIN
Political activist, attorney, and Congressman
Born Newark, N.J., U.S.A., January 16th, 1929
Died New York City, U.S.A., March 14th, 1980

Though he served only one term in the United States Congress,
lifelong activist Allard K. Lowenstein exercised an influence upon
American political life out of all proportion to the offices he held or
the notoriety he achieved. A steadfast liberal—Lowenstein's vision
was that of the social democrat and not the radical ideologue—with a
gift for organizing and inspiring young people, Lowenstein was a
participant in many of the major struggles of the 1950s and 60s,
serving as an aide to Adlai Stevenson, an advisor to Martin Luther
King, and a motivating force behind the 1968 Presidential "peace"
candidacy of U.S. Senator Eugene McCarthy.

The son of a prominent physician-turned-restaurateur, Lowenstein
followed political affairs from an early age—his childhood heroes were
Eleanor Roosevelt and socialist Norman Thomas—espousing the
cause of the anti-Franco army during the Spanish Civil War and
championing the Allied forces in World War Two. "I felt we should
have been fighting Hitler earlier and wanted very much to get into it,"
he said, recalling his attempt, at the age of 16, to run away from home
to enlist in the U.S. Army. His sympathy for the downtrodden was
also evident early. "I wore glasses and I was funny looking," he said
of his childhood. "I was picked on and left out a lot. Maybe because of
that I always identified with ugly girls at dancing school, with blacks in
the back of the bus, with anybody that was in some way hurt or
excluded . . ."

Spurning an Ivy League education, young Lowenstein attended the
University of North Carolina, largely because he wanted to compete
on its wrestling team. As a student politician, he worked with
President Frank Graham to integrate the Chapel Hill campus and,
when Graham was elected to the U.S. Senate with Lowenstein serving
as special assistant, he received his first taste of national politics. In
1951, while attending law school at Yale, Lowenstein assumed the
presidency of the National Student Association; holding power within
the organization for the next two decades, he used it as a base for
recruiting students into political campaigns. When illegal C.I.A.
infiltration of the student association was exposed in 1967, some of
Lowenstein's opponents in the New Left smeared him as a govern-

ment agent. The groundless accusation was dismissed by Lowenstein
who said that he "was the one they hid it all from."

Interested in international as well as domestic affairs, he toured
South-West Africa in 1959 investigating racial oppression. To focus
world attention upon South Africa's abuse of the United Nation's
charter, he smuggled a black student out of that country. The
incident—which involved great physical risk—resulted in his book,
Brutal Mandate. In the early 1960s Lowenstein's attention turned to
the civil-rights movement in the American South. He helped to
organize volunteers and functioned as an advisor to the National
Southern Christian Leadership Conference and the Student Non-
violent Coordinating Committee but eventually broke with the movement when S.N.C.C. turned toward black power advocacy and came
to distrust the "interference" of white liberals whom Lowenstein
epitomized.

Contending that American military involvement in Vietnam was
"morally, politically, and economically indefensible," Lowenstein
launched in the summer of 1967 the "Dump Johnson" movement
which drove a political colossus from the White House. Lowenstein
tirelessly criss-crossed the nation, exhorted dissident students and
party professionals to oppose Johnson and said that, "when a
President is both wrong and unpopular, to refuse to oppose him is a
moral abdication and a political stupidity." Although many Democrats took up the cause, Lowenstein did not yet have a candidate
willing to challenge Johnson in the primaries. As vice-chairman of the
Americans for Democratic Action (ADA)—whose membership includes the mandarins of the liberal intellectual "establishment"—he
did, however, have the attention of the most prominent anti-war
congressmen. Lowenstein approached Senators Robert F. Kennedy
and George McGovern urging them to run, but they refused;
McGovern referred him to Senator Eugene McCarthy who declared
his candidacy in November, and by March Lyndon Johnson had
announced he would not seek re-election.

While organizing the "peace" forces for the 1968 Democratic
convention, Lowenstein ran for Congress from a Long Island district,
defeating his conservative Republican opponent. During his term in
the House of Representatives, he worked to reform its seniority
system and contributed to a nonpartisan effort with California
Republican Pete McCloskey to combat "widespread despair and
cynicism" through a voter registration drive aimed at newly enfran-
chised Americans. He was defeated in the 1970 election when the New
York State Legislature re-drew his district's boundaries. Despite
several attempts to be re-elected from Congressional districts in
Brooklyn and Long Island, Lowenstein never again held public office.
He was, however, an active participant on the Democratic National
Committee and, from 1971 to 1973 he was chairman of the A.D.A.
where, again, he worked to involve young voters in the political
system.

Energetic and sometimes impatient with the slow processes of
political change, Lowenstein could be abrasive and, in 1971, was
included in President Nixon's "enemies" list (he boasted that he was
"number 7"). Unconsciously idiosyncratic in his personal habits,
Lowenstein admitted to being a "talker," operated out of phone
booths and guest rooms, traveling only at night and working in his

sock-feet and rumpled clothes. Yet, "of all the partisans I have known, from the furthest steppes of the spectrum," William F. Buckley Jr, a political adversary, has written, "his was the most undistracted concern, not for humanity—though he was conversant with big-think idiom—but with human beings."

With cruel irony, Lowenstein was shot to death in his law office in New York City at the age of 51, a victim, police said, of a disturbed young man who had been attracted to political life in his college days by Lowenstein himself. Lowenstein's burial at Arlington National Cemetery, alongside the graves of Robert and President John F. Kennedy, attests to his stature in American political history.   A.C.

Son of Gabriel Abraham L., physician and restaurateur, and Augusta Goldberg. Married Jennifer Lyman 1966 (div. ca. 1972). Children: Frank Graham; Thomas Kennedy; Katherine Eleanor. Educ: Horace Mann Sch., Bronx, N.Y. 1945; Univ. N.C., Chapel Hill, B.A. 1949; Yale Univ., LL.B. 1954. Special Asst. to Senator Frank K. Graham 1949; admitted to N.Y. bar 1958; Foreign Policy Advisor to Senator Hubert H. Humphrey 1959; Asst. Dean of Law Sch., Stanford Univ. 1961. Faculty member, various times 1962–74: N.C. State Univ.; City Coll., N.Y.C.; Yale Sch. of Urban Studies; Univ. of Mass.; New Sch. for Social Research, N.Y.C. Member, 91st Congress, 5th District, N.Y. 1968–70; Visiting Fellow, John F. Kennedy Sch. of Govt., Harvard Univ. 1971, and Ezra Stiles Coll., Yale Univ.; Advisor to Gov. Edmund G. Brown, Jr. of Calif. 1975; U.S. Rep. to U.N. Commn. on Human Rights 1977; U.S. Rep. to U.N. Trusteeship Council 1977; U.S. Ambassador to U.N. for special political affairs 1977–78. Chmn., Students for Stevenson 1952 and Americans for Democratic Action 1971–73; Co-chmn., Conference of Concerned Democrats 1967; Member, Democratic Natl. Cttee. 1972–76. *Author:* Brutal Mandate, 1962.
Further reading: An American Melodrama: The Presidential Campaign of 1968 by Lewis Chester et al, 1969.

PRINCE BOUN OUM
Prime Minister of Laos
Born Champassak, Laos, December 11th, 1911
Died Paris, France, March 17th, 1980

Prince Bon Oum of Champassak was the conservative, pro-Western Prime Minister of Laos from late 1960 until 1962 when the Geneva Conference restored the neutralist regime of Prince Souvanna Phouma. Prince Boun Oum's brief period of rule occured at a time of growing tension between the United States and the USSR over the Laotian situation.

Prince Boun Oum was born into the royal line of the house of Champassak, a province in southern Laos on the Mekong River. During the period of French rule over Indochina, Champassak was a kingdom and young Prince Boun Oum belonged to one of the few aristocratic families in Laos. After graduating from a lycée in Saigon, he studied briefly in Paris. But Boun Oum was an unenthusiastic

student and preferred the pleasures of royal life in Champassak. He was considered an accomplished hunter and sportsman and in the 1930s and early 40s he managed the family's royal estates.

In 1945 the Japanese drove France from Indochina and, although independence was granted to Laos, the Japanese occupied the area. Resistance to the occupation was led by the royal northern house of Luang Prabang and by Prince Boun Oum in the south. In 1946 the French re-occupied Indochina and, later that year, formally recognized the unity of Laos and the autonomy of its provinces. A constitutional monarchy, headed by the king of Luang Prabang, was established and Prince Boun Oum, with some reluctance, renounced his sovereignty over the southern kingdom so that Champassak could merge with a newly unified Laos. Luang Prabang had greater power even though the southern provinces were richer and more populous. But in return for his support and as a reward for his successful guerrilla campaigns against the Japanese, Boun Oum was given a lifetime appointment as Inspector-General of the Laotian Kingdom.

In 1949 Boun Oum participated in the Franco-Laotian convention which allowed Laos a limited degree of autonomy within the French Union. From 1949 until 1950 Boun Oum served as Prime Minister; however all significant power was held by the French. When the 1954 Geneva Conference ended the Indochina War, Laos was established as a fully independent, neutral state and Prince Souvanna Phouma was installed as prime minister. Throughout the 1950s, however, the strength of the Pathet Lao forces (a Laos opposition group supported by North Viet Nam) had been growing. When the Pathet Lao made a strong showing in the 1958 general elections, rightist forces (whose leadership included General Phoumi Nosavan and Prince Boun Oum) responded by overthrowing Phouma's neutralist regime. Hostilities between the conservatives and the Pathet Lao continued through 1959 until General Nosavan seized the capital (Vientiane) in December and returned Boun Oum to the Prime Ministership. The new regime was immediately recognized by the United States.

Prince Boun Oum's grip on the country was weak. Ardently pro-Western, he received considerable U.S. aid but the coup which brought him to power caused Phouma's neutralist forces to join forces with the Pathet Lao. The ensuing hostilities were inconclusive and the rightists held on to Vientiane; efforts to arrange peace talks between the three factions failed. However, when President Kennedy endorsed the idea of a neutral Laos, the Geneva Conference was reconvened and a cease-fire accomplished. By late 1961 the Conference had settled all important disagreements except for one; Prince Boun Oum and General Nosavan balked at the concept of a coalition government. When the State Department threatened to suspend payment of the $3 million grants awarded monthly to the Vientiane government, Boun Oum modified his position, but still refused to support a neutralist coalition. In May 1962, however, the Pathet Lao broke the cease-fire and took control of almost two-thirds of the country; Boun Oum was then forced to accept a coalition government dominated by the neutralists.

Prince Boun Oum never again held real power in Laos. He stepped down as Minister of Religion in 1972 because of mounting Pathet Lao opposition and in 1974, he moved to Thailand. When the Pathet Lao gained control over Laos in 1975, Boun Oum emigrated to Paris. E.T.

Married Nang Bouaphanh 1942. Seven sons; three daughters. Educ: Lycée Chasseloup Laubet, Saigon; private study Paris. Managed Champassak royal estates 1930s to early 40s. Led guerrilla resistance to Japanese occupation in southern Laos, WWII; Pres., Laotian Delegation for Franco-Laotian Co-operation 1946–47; renounced sovereignty of Champassak and appointed Inspector-Gen. (for life) of Laotian Kingdom 1947; Pres., Natl. Assembly delegations for negotiating Laotian limited autonomy 1949; Prime Minister of Laos (under French dominance) 1949–50; a leader of conservative faction after establishment of independence in 1954; with Gen. Nosavan overthrew neutralist govt. 1959; Minister of Defense 1960; Prime Minister 1960–62; served in coalition govt. 1962–72, as Minister of Religion 1961, 62; moved to Thailand 1974, and to Paris 1975.
Further reading: Laos: Buffer State or Battleground by Hugh Toye, 1968.

(KUSTAA) RAFAEL PAASIO
Prime Minister of Finland and journalist
Born Uskela, Finland, June 6th, 1903
Died Turku, Finland, March 17th, 1980

Rafael Paasio, a printer and journalist actively involved in politics from his youth, twice served as Prime Minister of Finland during the late 1960s and early 1970s. Born and educated in Uskela, Paasio joined a printing works after leaving school at the age of 15 and was apprenticed to a typographer. Early in the 1920s he became associated with the Social Democratic Party and held a number of administrative posts until 1942, when he became editor-in-chief of the Social Democratic newspaper *Tarun Paivalehti* and acquired a national reputation as a political journalist.

Paasio began his career as a politician in 1945, when he was elected to the municipal council of the town of Turku. Three years later he was elected to the Finnish Parliament, whose Foreign Affairs Committee he chaired from 1949 to 1966. In 1962 he stood unsuccessfully for the presidency of Finland; the following year he succeeded Vaino Tanner as chairman of the Social Democratic Party, which had been out of power since 1954 as a result of pressure exerted by the Soviet Union, Finland's neighbor to the east.

In the spring of 1966 Paasio presided over the Social Democrats' return to power as part of a four-party coalition that included the Communists. (It was the first time that the Communists had participated in a government since 1948, when they were implicated in an attempted coup.) Paasio, a mild-mannered, conciliatory man, was chosen to head the coalition as Prime Minister. In reply to criticisms that he had accepted Communists into the government as a ploy to win popularity with the Soviets, Paasio noted that Communists with governmental responsibility were less likely to engage in subversion and to incite costly strikes.

In November 1966 Paasio visited Moscow to brief Soviet Premier Aleksei Kosygin [q.v.] on his plans for the leadership of the Social Democrats and to guarantee the continued neutrality of Finland. He emerged with favorable trade and cultural agreements.

The task of stabilizing the country's economy took longer than he and his coalition partners had expected and involved months of negotiations that culminated in the imposition of heavy new taxes, unpopular with the electorate and with the coalition's Communist and Left Wing Socialist members. Paasio resigned in 1968 after two years in power. From February to September of 1972 he tried to hold together a minority Social Democratic government, but domestic political problems and the combined pressure of the opposition parties forced his resignation after six months in office. He retired from the party and from Parliament in 1975 but continued to take an interest in politics as long as his health allowed.

Paasio was Speaker of the Parliament in 1966 and again from 1969 to 1972. His elder son, Perti, is also a member of Parliament.   J.P.

Son of Urho P. Married Meeri. Children: two sons (elder, Perti, M.P.) and one daughter. Educ: sch. in Uskela to age 15. Apprentice typographer ca. 1919; later printer. Journalist from 1920s; political writer 1930s; Ed.-in-Chief, Tarun Paivalehti 1942–66. Member, municipal council, Turku 1945–75. Member, Social Democratic Party from 1920s; held numerous administrative posts until 1942; candidate for Pres. of Finland 1962; pres. of party 1963–75. As M.P. 1948–75: Chmn., Cttee. for Foreign Affairs 1949–66; Speaker 1966 and 1969–72, Prime Minister 1966–68 and Feb.-Sept. 1972.

JESSICA (VALENTINA) DRAGONETTE
Soprano
Born Calcutta, India, February 14th, ca. 1910
Died New York City, U.S.A., March 18th, 1980

Jessica Dragonette, whose silvery soprano voice made her one of the most popular stars of early radio, was born in Calcutta to American parents who died when she was six. Separated from her brothers and sisters, she grew up in a Catholic orphanage in Lansdowne, Pennsylvania, and studied music at Georgian Court College. At her audition for Estelle Liebling, who became her coach, she sang a Puccini aria. "You are little and blonde," remarked Liebling; "you should sing the things that suit you better and will preserve that velvet-pansy quality you have."

Liebling referred her student to Max Reinhardt, who cast her as the voice of the angel in a New York production of Humperdinck's *The Miracle.* After performing lead roles in *The Student Prince* and *Grand Street Follies,* she made her radio debut in 1926 over New York's station WEAF. Later that year, she was the first commercial artist to sign an exclusive contract with the newly-founded National Broadcasting Company.

Her radio career was launched in 1928 with the role of the heroine in *The Coca-Cola Hour,* a popular singing-acting cliffhanger. After a season singing operettas for the *Philco Theater Memories* series, she switched to the concert format of *The Cities Service Hour.* "They hang her picture over the radio so they can pretend she is actually there when she sings," wrote a reviewer. "They call her the Jenny Lind of the Air; the girl with the dimple in her voice." She was also called "the Garbo of the radio" for the care with which she guarded her private life; even her age remained a lifelong secret.

During the eight years she sang for Cities Service, Dragonette memorized two new songs a day, never repeating a song twice in six months. At the peak of her career, she was singing to an estimated 66 million people weekly. Her adoring listeners voted her Queen of Radio in 1935 and every year thereafter until 1942.

In 1937 her contract was terminated by NBC. The network and the sponsor claimed that she had asked for an exorbitant salary increase and that the public wanted new talent. The public, however, threatened to retaliate with a boycott of NBC and of all radio programs, and she was soon signed by CBS. In her 1951 autobiography *Faith is a Song,* she described her "appalling disillusionment" over the episode and the "Machiavellian mischief" practiced on her by advertising agency and network executives.

On CBS, Dragonette began an operetta series that closed after nine months. She then embarked on a long, successful concert tour of the U.S. and Canada, performing as a soloist with symphony orchestras. 150,000 fans flocked to see her at Grant Park in Chicago, and a crowd of fifteen thousand braved a blizzard and taxi strike to hear her in Minneapolis. In Honolulu her concert was one of a three-part series with opera stars Kirsten Flagstad and Lawrence Tibbett. Her repertoire ranged over five languages and included arias, lieder, works by contemporary American composers such as Gershwin, old English airs, operetta pieces, and popular favorites. Said one reviewer, "Her songs were an eerie incantation, a spell, an other-worldly invocation of beauty—warm, fleeting, mysterious, and altogether alluring."

Two years after her departure, NBC hosted a "Dragonette Salute," but, she wrote, "the magic of former days had gone stale." At CBS she began a six-year stint on *Saturday Night Serenade.* During the Second World War she traveled widely to entertain servicemen and to take part in War Bond rallies, receiving medals from the Army and Navy and an appointment as honorary colonel from the Air Force for her efforts.

After her 1947 marriage to New York businessman Nicholas Turner, Dragonette rarely performed. She died of a heart attack. J.G.

Daughter of American parents; father a bridge engineer. Married Nicholas Meredith Turner, businessman, 1947. No children. Roman Catholic. Educ: Catholic schs., Lansdowne, Pa.; Georgian Court Coll., Lakewood, N.J., grad. 1923; coached in singing by Estelle Liebling. Singer in NYC stage productions 1920s; singer in network radio series 1926–47; concert and recital artist 1934–47. Hons: American Legion plaque 1935; Queen of Radio, Radio Guide Listener polls 1935–42; Stars of Stars, Radio Guide poll 1938; Best Female Singer of the Country, Movie-Radio Guide Contest 1942; Pro Pontifice et Ecclesia Cross, Vatican 1942; Hon. Col., U.S. Air Force 1942; Wings from U.S. Army and Navy; U.S. Treasury Dept. Silver Medal; medal of Knot of Order of Isabella the Catholic, Spain 1948; Lady of Grand Cross of Equestrian Order of Knights and Ladies of Holy Sepulchre of Jerusalem, Vatican 1955; inducted into Crow Tribe as Princess Singing Bird. *Performances: Stage*—The Miracle, NYC 1924; The Student Prince (Kathie), NYC ca. 1925; Grand Street Follies, NYC ca. 1925. *Radio*—Debut, WEAF, NYC 926. Featured singer: Coca-Cola Hour

(Vivian), 1928; Philco Theater Memories, 1928–29, Cities Service Hour, 1929–37; Palmolive Beauty Box Theatre, 1937; Saturday Night Serenade, 1939–45; Ford Summer Hour, 1940; G.M. Family Party; Show Boat; others. Participant in first broadcast to Adm. Richard Byrd at S. Pole 1929 and in first broadcast from NBC's Radio City studios 1932. *Concerts and recitals*—Songs of the Middle Ages, Brooklyn Acad. Music 1934; *tour,* U.S.A., Hawaii, Canada 1937–38, including appearances as soloist with symphony orchs. of Chicago, Milwaukee, Minneapolis, NYC, others. Sang for President Roosevelt at White House 1936; sang annually at Arlington Natl. Cemetery 1933–44. *Recordings*—The Ave Maria, 1950; With Love, Jessica Dragonette, 1977. *Films*—The Big Broadcast of 1936; Gulliver's Travels, 1939. *Television*—appeared in experimental telecast 1928. *Author:* Faith is a Song: The Odyssey of an American Artist (autobiography), 1951; Your Voice and You (on speech improvement).
Further reading: The Mighty Music Box by Tom Delong, 1980.

ERICH FROMM
Psychoanalyst, writer and social philosopher
Born Frankfurt Am Main, Germany, March 23rd, 1900
Died Muralto, Switzerland, March 18th, 1980

Courtesy Dr. Rainer Funk

Of the many intellectuals who fled Hitler's Germany in the 1930s, Erich Fromm was among the most renowned. An early disciple of Freudianism, Fromm leavened his social psychology with insights gleaned from the writings of the young Marx. Consisting of more than 40 books and articles, his work appealed to both academicians and the general public. Fromm examined the rise of fascism and the dehumanization of man in modern society to reveal the moral contours of human nature.

Although his first articles appeared in *Imago,* Freud's in-house publishing organ, Fromm's vision was informed by a radical humanism. He affirmed the idea of a human "essence" and stressed at all times man's potential for love, happiness, and freedom. This ethical conception of nature led Fromm to abandon such tenets of Freudian orthodoxy as the libido theory and the Oedipus complex. Believing Freud to have mistakenly identified these concepts with the universal human condition, he argued that they were produced within the social context of particular historical periods. Fromm's emphasis upon the environment in which character is formed derived from his appreciation of the Marxist framework for analyzing society. The integration of Freudian and Marxist perspectives—in clinical practice as well as philosophical theory—enabled Fromm to study the alienation of man by his own material creations.

As a psychoanalyst, Fromm was considered among the most prominent of the neo-Freudians. This school called attention to the cultural determinants of personality more emphatically than earlier Freudians had. Fromm, however, dissociated himself from the revisionists, claiming that even they did not sufficiently emphasize social factors. He developed a unique method of treatment in which the analyst would directly confront the patient as both therapist and empathic human being. "There is nothing human which is alien to us," Fromm said of his "humanistic technique." "Everything is in me: I am a little child, I am a grown-up, I'm a murderer, and I'm a saint, I'm narcissistic, and I'm destructive. There is nothing in the patient which I do not have in me."

Erich Fromm was born at the turn-of-the-century into a middle-class German-Jewish family. Raised in an orthodox home, Fromm was drawn, during adolescence, to the messianic elements in Jewish thought. He later said, "I was moved by the prophetic writings . . . [and] the vision of universal peace and harmony between nations." Although Fromm eschewed religion (after having been psycho-analyzed in 1962) he later acknowledged its decisive influence upon his thought and explained that Marxism had simply provided him with a secular translation of religious messianism.

The extreme nationalism and mass hysteria engendered by World War One alerted Fromm to "the irrationalities of human behavior" at an early age. With the aim of comprehending the psychological bases of social disorder, he studied psychology, philosophy, and sociology at the University of Heidelberg and received his doctorate at the age of 22. Further training was obtained at the Berlin Psychoanalytic Institute where he studied with some prominent Freudians as Theodor Reich and Hanns Sachs. Fromm's clinical practice began in 1931 and, during this period, he married Freida Reichman with whom he helped establish the Frankfurt Psychoanalytic Institute.

While teaching at the University of Frankfurt, Fromm joined the school's Institute for Social Research, whose faculty included Herbert Marcuse and Max Horkheimer. The Institute hoped to incorporate psychoanalysis into its neo-Marxist philosophy, a project to which Fromm greatly contributed. With his assistance, a massive study of workers' attitudes towards authority was undertaken.

Fromm's interpretation of their findings, first published in the Institute's critical journal, formed the basis of his most important book, *Escape From Freedom* (1941). In opposition to the conventional understanding of the Oedipus complex as a permanent aspect of human experience, Fromm insisted that it was characteristic only of stern patriarchal societies; the complex, he said, resulted largely from the son's traditional role as inheritor of the father's property. Fromm then proceeded to develop a character typology based upon oral, anal and genital modes. He identified anal repression with the "spirit of capitalism" and defined the bourgeois personality as puritanical, orderly, and possessive. The genital personality type, however, was equated with freedom and fellow-feeling, traits wholeheartedly en-dorsed by Fromm. Throughout his study, the family was cited as the agent through which society transmits values to the individual.

In 1933 Fromm was invited to lecture at the Chicago Psychoanalytic Institute and, rather than return to Nazi Germany, he obtained American citizenship the following year. While teaching and lecturing at several American colleges, Fomm continued his association with the Institute for Social Research which had moved to Columbia University. During the 1930s he also enriched his perspective with Zen Buddhism and studies of matriarchal cultures which replaced au-thoritarian norms with tenderness and compassion. These concerns were reflected in *Man for Himself* (1947), in which he diagnosed neurosis as a moral problem, and *Psychoanalysis and Religion* (1950).

His colleagues at the Institute for Social Research, however, believed the existence of fascism in Europe and subtle forms of domination in Western democracies rendered Fromm's optimism untenable. Moreover, they charged him with diluting revolutionary elements in Freudian theory and, after 1950, Fromm's connection with the Institute was severed.

The 1950s and 60s were productive years for Fromm. In his popular book, *The Art of Loving* (1956), he challenged Freud's notion of love as a zone of unremitting conflict and irrationality that was inextricably tied to sex. For Fromm, love was a feeling of universal brotherhood while the sexual instinct was only "one manifestation of the need for love and union." Escalation of cold war hostilities led him to write *The Sane Society* (1955) in which he linked man's alienation to a soulless, consumer-oriented world. Active in the peace movement, Fromm helped establish the National Committee for a Sane Nuclear Policy in 1957, and also joined the Socialist Party, U.S.A.

Fromm's ideas filtered from universities and book-filled apartments in New York and London to permeate the entire culture. By 1965 *Escape from Freedom* had reached 25 printings and *The Sane Society* and *The Art of Loving,* also best sellers, were required texts in many high schools; this enormous popularity led some observers to announce the existence of a "Fromm cult." Having analyzed the development of freedom, Fromm had shown how the dehumanizing tendencies of modern industrial society could make the individual turn from independence to embrace totalitarianism. Still, his outlook remained hopeful and he insisted that humanity could create a new world based on love, communion, and freedom; the spirit of the 1960s was clearly reflected in this attitude.

In *Beyond the Chains of Illusion: My Encounter with Marx and Freud* (1962) and *The Greatness and Limitations of Freud's Thought* (1980), Fromm continued to explore the principal influences upon his work. A controversial thinker, he was alternately praised and condemned for disregarding the traditional boundaries of philosophy, history, sociology, and psychoanalysis. To clarify his complex relationship to Freudian theory, Fromm said: "I have never left Freudianism unless one identifies Freud with his libido theory . . . I consider the basic achievement of Freud to be his concept of the unconscious, its manifestations in neurosis, dreams, etc., resistance, and his dynamic concept of character. The concepts have remained for me of basic importance in all my work . . . I never gave up psychoanalysis. I have never wanted to form a school of my own."   R.W.

Son of Naphtali F., wine merchant, and Rosa (Krause) F. Married (1) Frieda Reichmann 1926, psychoanalyst (div.); (2) Henny Gurland 1944 (d. 1952); (3) Annis Freeman 1953. Jewish atheist. Emigrated to U.S. 1934; naturalized American 1934. Educ: Univ. Heidelberg, D.Ph. 1922; Univ. Munich, Postgrad. psychoanalysis 1926; Berlin Psychoanalytic Inst. 1931. Private practice in psychotherapy 1925–1965; Lectr., Inst. Social Research, Univ. Frankfurt 1929–32; Member and Lectr., Intnl. Inst. Social Research 1938–54; Guest lectr. Columbia Univ., NYC 1940–41; Lectr., American Inst. Psychoanalysis 1941–42; Member faculty, Bennington Coll., Vt. 1941–49; Terry Lectr., Yale Univ., New Haven 1948–49; Co-founder and member faculty, William Alanson White Inst. Psychoanalysis, New York since

1946; Chmn., Faculty and Chmn., Training Cttee. 1945–50; Prof., psychiatry, Autonomous Univ. Mexico 1949–65; Dir., Mexican Psychoanalytic Inst. 1955–65; Prof., psychology, Mich. State Univ., East Lansing 1957–61; Adjunct Prof.. psychology, New York Univ. 1962–1968. Founder, Mexican Psychoanalytic Inst. 1955; Co-founder, Natl. Cttee. Sane Nuclear Policy 1957; Member, American Socialist Party 1957–66. Hons: Trustee, William Alanson White Inst. since 1945; Hon. Prof., Natl. Autonomous Univ. Mexico since 1965; (Hon.) Mexican Natl. Acad. Medicine; Diplomate in clinical psychology, Am. Psychol. Assn.; Fellow N.Y. Acad. Science, Member, American Acad. Arts and Sciences and Washington Psychoanalytic Soc. *Author:* Escape from Freedom, 1941; Man for Himself, 1947; Psychoanalysis and Religion, 1950; The Forgotten Language: An Introduction to the Understanding of Dreams, Fairy Tales, and Myths, 1951; The Sane Society, 1955; The Art of Loving, 1956; Sigmund Freud's Mission: An Analysis of his Personality and Influence, 1959; Zen Buddhism and Psychoanalysis (with D.T. Suzuki and R. deMartino), 1960; May Man Prevail? An Inquiry into the Facts and Fictions of Foreign Policy, 1961; (ed.) Der Friede: Idee and Verwirklichung; The Search for Peace, 1961 (bi-lingual vol.); Marx's Concept of Man, 1961; Beyond the Chains of Illusion: My Encounter with Marx and Freud, 1962; The Dogma of Christ, and Other Essays on Religion, Psychology and Culture, 1963; The Heart of Man: Its Genius for Good and Evil, 1964; (ed.) Socialist Humanism; An International Symposium, 1965; You Shall Be As Gods; A Radical Interpretation of the Old Testament and its Tradition, 1966; The Revolution of Hope, 1968; (ed. with R. Xirau) The Nature of Man, 1969; Social Character in a Mexican Village (with M. Maccoby), 1970; The Crisis of Psychoanalysis, 1970; The Anatomy of Human Destructiveness, 1973; To Have or To Be, 1976; The Well Being of Man in Society, 1978; The Greatness and Limitatons of Freud's Thought, 1980.
Further reading: Escape from Authority: The Perspectives of Erich Fromm by John H. Schaar, 1961; In the Name of Life: Essays in Honor of Erich Fromm by Bernard Landis and Edward S. Tauber (eds.), 1971; The Dialectical Imagination by Martin Jay, 1973.

SIR LUDWIG GUTTMANN
Neurologist; Founder-President, International Medical Society of Paraplegia
Born Tost, Silesia, Germany, July 3rd, 1899
Died Aylesbury, Buckinghamshire, England, March 18th, 1980

Sir Ludwig Guttmann, a German-born neurologist who devoted himself to the treatment and rehabilitation of paraplegics, helped establish the international "Wheelchair Olympics." His new approach to the problems of physical handicap particularly in the aftermath of World War Two, resulted in many thousands of disabled people leading fuller lives.

Ludwig Guttmann was raised in a coal-mining community in Silesia. During World War One he worked as an orderly in a hospital near the front lines, an experience which made him aware of the inadequacies of neurosurgical techniques. Guttman received his medical degree at the University of Freiburg in 1924 and immediately took an assistantship with Professor Ott Foerster, a pioneer of new neurosurgical methods at the University of Hamburg.

Guttman's career was interrupted by the rise of fascism in Germany. He was dismissed from his post at the University and became Director of the Jewish Hospital in Breslau. As Nazi persecution intensified he began to admit healthy Jews and saved them from concentration camps by teaching them to feign neurological disorder so well that Nazi doctors were deceived. In 1939 Guttmann moved his family to Oxford where he had been offered a position in the University's Department of Surgery by Sir Hugh Cairns.

At Oxford Guttman studied the central nervous system and the proper care of patients with spinal-cord injuries. In February 1944 he was placed in charge of a newly-opened unit for spinal-injury patients at the Stoke Mandeville Hospital and Guttmann introduced the most modern surgical techniques and employed, to an unprecedented degree, calisthentics and athletic games as therapy for the severely disabled. His radical methods resulted in the annual international "Wheelchair Olympics" for paraplegics. The first annual Stoke Mandeville Games for the Paralysed took place in 1948 and within four years achieved an international reputation. In 1956 it was recognized by the International Olympic Committee with the award of the Fearnley Cup to its organizers.

Guttmann trained doctors from around the world in his rehabilitation techniques for paraplegics. He lectured in more than 30 countries and helped establish special treatment centers. Two of them—in Spain and Germany—bear his name and in Holland, a street has been dedicated to him for helping the Dutch welfare services organize their rehabilitation programs for war victims. In 1961 Guttmann formed the International Medical Society of Paraplegia, serving as the first elected president and editor of its official journal.

Guttmann's efforts on behalf of the disabled brought him world recognition. Germany acknowledged Guttmann in 1957, making him Professor Ordinarius and backdating the honor to 1942, under the war restitution law. Guttmann was also honored by England; he was elected into Fellowship of the Royal Society and knighted in 1966, the year of his retirement.   M.D.

Son of Bernard G. and Dorothea G. Married Else Samuel 1927 (d. 1973). Children: Dennis (doctor); Eva. Jewish. Emigrated to Britain 1939; naturalized British 1948. Educ: Gymnasium, Konigshutte, Silesia; Univ. Breslau, Germany (now Wroclaw, Poland); Univ. Freiburg, M.D. 1924; also Univ. Wurzburg. Asst. 1923–28 and Assoc. 1930–33, Neurological and Neurosurgical Dept., Wenzel Hancke Hosp., Breslau; Neurosurgeon, Psychiatric Dept., Univ. Hamburg-Friedrichsberg 1928–29; Dir., Dept. Neurology and Neurosurgery, Jewish Hospital, Breslau 1933–39; Research Asst., Dept. of Surgery, Oxford 1939–44; Fellow, Balliol Coll., Oxford 1934–44; Dir. 1944–46 and Consultant Emeritus since 1966, Natl. Spinal Injuries Center, Stoke Mandeville; Albee Memorial Lectr., Kessler Inst., N.J. 1952; Visiting Prof. 1954 and Prof. Emeritus since 1954; Univ. Cologne; Ed., International Journal of Paraplegia 1963–66; Dir., Stoke Mandeville Sports Stadium for the Paralysed and other Disabled since 1969. Member, British Assn. of Neurologists and British Physiological Assn. 1947; Founder, Stoke Mandeville Games 1948; Consultant to Duchess of Gloucester House, Dept. of Social Security 1950. Pres:

British Sports Assn. for the Disabled 1962; Intnl. Sports Assn. for the Disabled 1966; and Intnl. Medical Soc. of Paraplegia 1971–79. V.P., Star and Garter Home for Ex-Servicemen, Richmond; Member, Chasely Home for Ex-Servicemen, Eastbourne. Hons: O.B.E. 1950; Comdr. de l'Ordre Oeuvre Humanitaire, France 1952; Rehabilitation Prize, World Veteran's Fedn. 1954; Order of St. John of Jerusalem 1957; Gold Medal for Verdiensten, Holland 1958; C.B.E. 1960; F.R.C.S.; Hon. D.Chir., Durham Univ.; Commendature dell'ordine Al Merito, Italy 1961; Hon. Freeman, Borough of Aylesbury, Bucks., England; F.R.C.P.; Officer, Order Oranje-Nassau, Holland; Grand Cross of Merit, Germany 1962; Comdr. Ordre de Leopold II, Belgium 1963; ordre du Merite, Combattante, France 1963; Order of the Rising Sun, Japan 1964; knighted 1966; Hon. LL.D., Univ. Dublin 1969; Order of Merit, Bavaria 1971; Golden Star, Order of Merit, Germany 1972; Olympic Gold Medal of Labour, Belgium 1972; Gold Medal, Dept. of Culture, Finland 1975; F.R.S. 1976. Also, Medaille d'Or du Sport et Jeunesse, France; F.R.C.P., Canada; F.R.S.M.; Hon. D.Med. Chir, Basle, Switzerland; Hon. D.Sc., Liverpool Univ., F.R.S.A. *Author:* Vol. VII Handbuch der Neurologie, Germany, 1936; Surgical Practice, Vols. 2 and 6, 1948; Survery vol. of Official British Medical History of Second World War, 1953; Modern Trends in Diseases of the Vertebral Column, 1959; (ed.) Neuro-Traumatology, Vol. II, 1971; Spinal Cord Injuries: Comprehensive Management and Research, 1973.

MARCEL BOUSSAC
French industrialist
Born Chateauroux, Indre, France, April 17th, 1889
Died Montargis, Loiret, France, March 21st, 1980

Marcel Boussac—French industrialist, racehorse owner, trainer, and breeder—was a self-made millionaire by the age of 30 and his fortune was estimated to be among the largest in France. Although his enterprises made him one of the most powerful businessmen in the country, Boussac's entire empire was eventually sold to cover debts.

Boussac, the son of a draper, was born in Chateauroux and received a basic education until he began to work in his father's shop at age of 16. Boussac gained sufficient experience to open his own drapery business in Paris in 1909 and purchased his first Rolls Royce just before the outbreak of World War One. At about this time Boussac began to buy large stocks of surplus cotton cloth which was used by the French and British Governments to cover airplane wings. After the war he converted the cloth into fashionable clothing; having turned a sizeable profit, he began to invest in textile mills in the Vosges, Alsace, and Normandy.

Boussac also invested in race-horses after the war and he built up a bloodstock which included some of the century's greatest stallions and brood-mares. With the first win coming in a 1920 race at Longchamp in the Grand Criterium, Boussac's horses also prevailed at several French and English classics (including six victories in the Prix de l'Arc de Triomphe and 11 in the Prix du Jockey Club). At one time Boussac owned more than 320 horses and one of his many famous stallions, Galcador, won the English Derby in 1950.

As Boussac grew wealthier he expanded into different sectors of the French economy. By the outbreak of World War Two he not only imported cloth and raw textile materials, but also owned the factories in which these products were dyed, painted, and woven. Boussac, known as the "Cotton King of France," was also interested in fashion design and the marketing of finished clothes. In 1946 he provided the financial backing for Christian Dior which launched the House of Dior as one of the most exclusive fashion marketers in Europe.

In 1951 Boussac, whose investments included banking and real estate, obtained majority shares in Paris's ultra-conservative newspaper, *L'Aurore,* and in the only French horse-racing daily, *Paris-Turf.* In 1952, as the owner of 65 French companies and factories, he had an annual sales turnover of $150 million. His business empire employed almost 30,000 people (8,000 of whom lived in accommodations provided by Boussac); he also introduced incentive schemes, provided free holiday camps for his workers, and arranged free child-care facilities for mothers working in his factories.

The decline of his business interests began in the late 1950s when the opening of French tariff barriers allowed cheap importation of both raw materials and finished goods. In 1968 Boussac sold many of his textile mills and the Dior perfume industry; in 1970 he was forced to liquidate his entire holdings and the Agache-Willot group bought the Boussac Saint-Frères Company for $175 million. Boussac was guaranteed two million French francs a year for the remainder of his life and was allowed to retain the use of his homes in Paris, Deauville, and the Loiret.   M.D.

Son of Louis B., draper, and Primitive Jeanne (Mette) B., poet. Married Margarita Deceuninck, singer (pseudonym Fanny Heldy) 1939 (d. 1973). Daughter: Colette (Mme. Andre Aupetit). Educ: Lycée de Chateauroux. Joined father in business, Chateauroux 1905; opened drapery shop, Paris 1909; Dir., Managing Dir., Dir.-Gen. of 65 textile processing companies and factories in France 1917–78; racehorse owner, Normandy, Versailles, Chantilly 1919–78; founder and Proprietor, Christian Dior 1946–68; major shareholder L'Aurore and Paris-Turf 1951–78; Chmn. and Dir.-Gen. 1963–70 and Pres. 1970–74, Comptoir de l'Industrie Cotonnière; Pres. and Dir.-Gen., Société des parfums Christian Dior 1970–72. Pres., Société d'encouragement (French horse racing) 1959–74; and Fédération nationale des sociétés de courses de France 1962–74.

ARTHUR M(ELVIN) OKUN
Economist
Born Jersey City, New Jersey, U.S.A., November 29th, 1928
Died Washington, D.C., U.S.A., March 23rd, 1980

The American economist Arthur Okun, whose "Okun's Law" brought a higher degree of accuracy to the forecasting of economic trends in the 1960s, combined technical expertise with a concern for the social effects of governmental economic policies, many of which he helped to formulate. The son of a candy and tobacco dealer, Okun was born in Jersey City in 1928 and attended public schools. After graduating Phi Beta Kappa and with the highest scholastic average in his class from Columbia College in 1949, he was named to *Life* magazine's list of promising young leaders. He earned his doctorate in economics from Columbia University in 1956 and became assistant professor at Yale University, where he had been teaching since 1952.

At Yale, Okun came under the strong influence of his colleague James Tobin, a "new economist" working in the tradition of British economic theorist John Maynard Keynes. (American Keynesians maintain that the federal government should regulate the nation's economy, slowing it by means of tax hikes and decreased government spending during periods of inflation, stimulating it through tax cuts and increased spending during periods of recession.) In 1962, at Tobin's invitation, Okun took a leave of absence from Yale to join the staff of the Council of Economic Advisers (C.E.A.) where he devised innovative methods for determining future trends in the gross national product (G.N.P.), a figure representing the total value of goods and services produced in the United States. Detecting a "growth gap" between potential and actual production of some $51 billion, he recommended a series of tax cuts, later enacted by Presidents Kennedy and Johnson, to boost the economy.

Okun also developed the formula which bears his name to describe the relationship of the G.N.P. to the rate of national unemployment, a ratio of 3.2 to 1. According to the formula, when unemployment is high, an increase of 3.2 percent in the G.N.P. will result in an increase of 1 percent in unemployment; a 3.2 decline in the G.N.P. will have the opposite effect. "Okun's Law" proved accurate until the 1970s, when it ceased to apply under the prevailing conditions of "stagflation"—a combination of unemployment, inflation, and lack of growth.

In 1964, Okun, after a year as director of graduate studies in economics at Yale, left teaching to accept an appointment to the C.E.A. from President Johnson. (At 39, he was the youngest appointee ever to serve on the Council.) Gardner Ackley, the former chairman of the C.E.A., called Okun "the best empirical economist I know, with surpassing skills as a forecaster." He was among the first economists to recognize the inflationary trend begun by the escalation of the Vietnam War, which placed a huge burden of new expenditures on a government already heavily committed to domestic spending. President Johnson, unwilling to lose public support for the war by imposing the taxes necessary to pay for it, allowed the U.S. Treasury to incur a massive deficit. To keep the C.E.A., and the public, ignorant of the situation, the Administration routinely concealed statistics on its military expenditures. In 1965, repeated protests from the Council members about this lack of information brought a response from Secretary of Defense Robert McNamara in the form of a forecast of military spending for fiscal year 1967, which presented estimates ranging from $7 billion to $17 billion. The study was marked "For Internal Use Only," to which Okun added in the margin, "But not to be swallowed."

Okun, who became chairman of the C.E.A. in 1968, sought to alleviate some of the pressure on the economy by successfully lobbying in Congress for the enactment of a ten percent tax surcharge. He was also an advocate of "jawboning," the practice of direct government discussions with large corporations to persuade them to keep their prices down, and of voluntary wage and price guidelines encouraged through tax incentives.

When President Nixon took office in 1969, Okun left the C.E.A. to become a Senior Fellow at the Brookings Institution, where he studied the effects of economic policies on the population's living standards. His 1975 book *Equality and Efficiency: The Big Tradeoff* analyzed the discrepancy between the nation's political ideal of equal opportunity and the severe social stratification created by its economic institutions. Along with a colleague, George Perry, he founded and edited a journal, *Brookings Papers on Economic Activity*. The Carter Administration's proposal to insure workers who accept non-inflationary wage settlements against rising prices was an outgrowth of his work on wage and price restraint.

Throughout the 1970s, Okun served as consultant to federal agencies, banks, investment firms, and businesses. He was an advisor to the campaign staffs of Democratic presidential candidate George McGovern in 1972 and, until his death, of President Carter and Senator Edward Kennedy in the 1980 presidential race.

Okun, who was married and had three sons, died of a heart attack. The Brookings Institution announced plans for posthumous publication of his last book, a study of stagflation.   J.P.

Son of Louis O., candy and tobacco wholesaler. and Rose (Cantor) O. Married Suzanne Grossman 1951. Sons: Lewis E., psychologist, b. 1954; Matthew J., b. 1957; Steven J., b. 1960. Jewish. Educ: Passaic High Sch., N.J.; Columbia Univ. (Phi Beta Kappa), A.B. 1949, Ph.D. in econ. 1956. With Econ. Dept., Yale Univ.: Instr. 1952–56; Asst. Prof. 1956–60; Assoc. Prof. 1960–63; Prof. and Dir. of Grad. Studies in Econ. 1963–64; Ed., Yale Econ. Essays 1963–64. Staff Member, Cowles Foundn. for Research in Econ., New Haven 1956–64. With Council of Econ. Advisers, Washington, D.C.: Staff Economist (on leave from Yale Univ.) 1961–62; Member 1964–68; Chmn. 1968–69. Co-founder 1972 and co-ed. 1972–80, Brookings Papers on Econ. Activity. Godkin Lectr., Harvard Univ. 1974; McGraw-Hill Lectr., Columbia Univ. 1978. Member: Advisory Bd., Challenge Mag. since 1972; Panel of Econ. Advisers, Congressional Budget Office, Washington, D.C. since 1975; Econ. Advisory Bd., U.S. Dept. of Commerce 1977–79; Counsel Cttee. on Social Sciences Policy, Yale Univ. since 1978; Time Mag. Bd. of Economists. Trustee, Jt. Council on Econ. Educ. since 1971; Dir., Intnl. Management and Devel. Inst. since 1976; Member, Visiting Cttee., Harvard Bd. of Overseers since 1977; Dir., Dean Witter Reynolds InterCapital, San Francisco; Dir. and Consultant, American Security Bank, Washington, D.C. Advisor to pres. election campaigns of Sen. George McGovern 1972 and of President Carter and Sen. Edward Kennedy 1980. Consultant: Donaldson, Lufkin & Jenrette, NYC since 1969; U.S. Dept. of the Treasury 1975; Stein, Rowe, Farnham, Chicago since 1977; Federal Reserve Bd., Washington, D.C.; Greenwich Research Assocs.; American Telephone and Telegraph; Gen. Electric Co. V.P., American Econ. Assn. 1972; Special Assoc. Member of the Conference of Business Economists since 1972; Member, Natl. Assn. of Business Economists since 1979; Member, American Statistical Assn. Hons: Albert Asher Green Prize for highest scholastic average in class, Columbia Coll. 1949; named to list of recent coll. grads. most likely to succeed, Life Mag. 1949; M.A., Yale Univ. 1963; Alumni Medal for Excellence, Columbia Univ. 1968; Fellow, Brookings Instn. since 1970; McKinsey Foundn. Book Award 1970; Frank E. Seidman

Distinguished Award in Political Econ., Southwestern Univ. at Memphis 1979; Fellow, American Acad. of Arts and Sciences; Fellow, Econometric Assn. *Author:* (ed.) The Battle Against Unemployment: An Introduction to a Current Issue of Public Policy, 1965, 2nd ed. 1972; The Political Economy of Propserity, 1970; (co-author) Inflation: The Problems it Creates and the Policies it Requires, 1970; Equality and Efficiency: The Big Tradeoff, 1975; (tentative title) Prices and Quantities in Cyclical Fluctuations, to be published posthumously. Frequent contributor to professional jrnls.

BARON PANNELL OF THE CITY OF LEEDS
Minister of Public Buildings and Works and trade unionist
Born London, England, September 10th, 1902
Died London, England, March 23rd, 1980

Lord Pannel, a lifelong member of the British Labour Party and a Member of Parliament for 25 years, helped devise a legal formula by which inherited peerages can be renounced by people who prefer to remain commoners. The arrangement was designed mainly to enable active politicians in the House of Commons to continue their careers instead of being forced out by elevation to the peerage.

He was born Thomas Charles Pannell in London in 1902 and gained an appetite for politics in the embryonic Labour Party, which he joined at the age of 16 as a member of the Amalgamated Engineering Union. His first elective office was a seven-year tenure on the Walthamstow Borough Council beginning in 1929. From 1938 to 1955 he sat on the Erith Borough Council, for many years holding the chairmanship of its Finance and General Purposes Committee. During the Second World War he coordinated the efforts of Erith's residents to cope with blitz attacks on their homes, becoming one of the borough's most popular figures. After the war he was elected Mayor for one year.

In 1946, Pannell, now an alderman, joined the Kent County Council, becoming deputy leader of the Labour Group. Three years later he won a Parliamentary by-election as a Labour candidate for West Leeds, a seat he continued to hold until his retirement in 1974. As a back-bencher in the House of Commons, he served on many Government Select and other committees investigating aspects of law, administration, and the conduct of the Houses of Parliament. Most notably, he served on the committee which considered the case of Anthony Wedgwood Benn, who wished to renounce his inherited peerage as Viscount Stansgate in order to remain in the House of Commons rather than join, as his peerage required, the House of Lords. The committee recommended a procedure by which peers could divest themselves of their titles. It was later enacted into law and invoked by the Earl of Home, who chose to renounce his earldom in order to become (as Sir Alec Douglas-Home) Prime Minister in 1963. From 1953 to 1964 Pannell was Secretary of the Trade Union Group of the Parliamentary Labour Party, playing a prominent role in the formulation of policies on employment and the social services.

Pannell constantly sought to abolish regulations for which he saw no purpose, pressing for many years to end the arbitrary rule exercised by the Lord Chamberlain over the House of Commons. In the end he won his point and was able to effect the change personally during his tenure as Minister of Public Buildings and Works in the mid-1960s. He also served as a delegate to a number of international parliamentary conferences. He was made a Life Peer in 1974, the year of his retirement, and continued to take part in House of Lords debates until shortly before his death.

Born Thomas Charles Pannell. Son of James William P. and Mary Jane P. Married Lilian Maud Frailing 1929. Children: one daughter. Educ: schs. in London to age 15. Member and admin., Amalgamated Engineering Union from 1918; joined Labour Party 1918; former chmn., Dartford Divisional Labour Party. As Member, Walthamstow Borough Council 1929–36: Chief Whip, Labour Group; Chmn., Rating and Valuation Cttee.; Member, Municipal Entertainments Cttee. As Member, Erith Borough Council 1938–55: Leader of Council and Chmn. of Finance and Gen. Purposes Cttee. 1938–49; chmn. responsible for post-blitz services 1939–45; Alderman 1944–55; Mayor 1945–46. Chmn. 1944–55, N.W. Kent Divisional Exec. for Educ.; Deputy Leader, Labour Group, Kent County Council 1946–49. As M.P. (Labour), W. Leeds 1949–74: Member, House of Commons Select Cttees. on Accomodation 1953–54, Procedure 1958–59, Law of Privilege 1967; Member, Jt. Select Cttee., Lords and Commons, on House of Lords Reform 1962; Member, Cttee. of Privileges 1968–74. Minister of Public Bldgs. and Works 1964–66. Parliamentary Delegate, Inter-Parliamentary Unions: Berne 1951; Belgium 1952; NATO Conference of Parliamentarians 1955, 1956, 1957; Poland 1958; W. Germany 1960; Singapore (leader) 1966; N.Z. Commonwealth Parliamentary Assn. 1971; U.A.R. (leader) 1973. Delegate, Atlantic Congress 1959; British Delegate, Commonwealth Parliamentary Assn. Conference, Ottawa 1966. V.P., Assn. Municipal Corps. Hons: Hon. Secty., Trade Union Group, Parliamentary Labour Party 1953–64; P.C. 1964; Life Peer 1974; LL.D., Leeds Univ. 1975.

GERALD (WHITE) JOHNSON
Journalist, historian, and author
Born Riverton, North Carolina, U.S.A., August 6th, 1890
Died Baltimore, Maryland, U.S.A., March 23rd, 1980

Gerald Johnson, a lifelong career journalist and newspaper reporter, published more than 30 books over a period of five decades. He was also an educator, current-affairs commentator, and achieved a world-wide reputation as an American historian, particularly as a biographer of several U.S. presidents.

Raised in North Carolina by devout Southern Baptist parents of Scottish descent, Johnson received his bachelor's degree from Wake Forest. Having failed to successfully establish his own weekly newspaper, *The Davidsonian,* in Thomasville, North Carolina, he joined the Lexington *Dispatch* in 1910 as a reporter. In 1913 he moved to Greensboro, North Carolina to work as a reporter and music critic for the *Daily News,* but his career was interrupted by World War One and

service with the 321st Infantry, 81st Division. From 1917 to 1919 he served with the American Expeditionary Force in France.

After the war he returned to the *Daily News* in Greensboro and in 1924 accepted an offer from the University of North Carolina to become Professor of Journalism. There he became involved in the controversy over the teaching of Darwin's theory of evolution in the University. Johnson said later that his appointment had been made to provide journalistic support for those fighting for the right to continue teaching Darwinism. The university won, and Johnson remained on the faculty at North Carolina until 1926, when he accepted a position with the Baltimore *Sun.*

For seventeen years Johnson wrote everything from news stories to editorials for both the morning and evening newspapers. Although he ended his formal connection with the *Sun* in 1943 in order to bcome a free-lance writer, he continued to contribute book reviews, observations on American life and politics, and letters.

Johnson's literary career had begun in 1925 with the publication of *Story of Man's Work,* an economic history of liberal capitalism written with William Hayward. Deeply interested in the presidency, Johnson wrote in 1927 a treatise on one of his president-heroes, Andrew Jackson; similar works on Woodrow Wilson and Franklin D. Roosevelt followed. A liberal Democrat, he became speech-writer for Adlai Stevenson during the 1952 and 1956 presidential campaigns.

Johnson was a versatile writer and, under the pseudonym Charles North, he wrote mystery novels. His three-volume history, *America: A History for Peter,* written for children, received good reviews and was considered an excellent survey for anyone of any age seeking an introduction to the subject. Johnson also wrote for many magazines and literary journals and became a contributing editor of *The New Republic* in 1954. His frequent appearances on Baltimore television from 1952 to 1954 as a commentator on current affairs earned him the Peabody Award.

Johnson's accomplishments were acknowledged in 1970 when Govenor Marvin Mandel of Maryland proclaimed the author's 80th birthday "Gerald White Johnson" Day throughout the state.   M.D.

Son of Archibald J., Baptist newspaper ed., and Flora Caroline (McNeill) J. Married Kathryn Dulsinea Hayward 1922. Children: Mrs. Frederick Allen Sliger; Mrs. Leonard van den Honert. Educ: Wake Forest Coll., N.C., B.A. 1911; also Univ. Toulouse, France. Mil. Service: Infantry, American Expeditionary Force, France 1917–1919. Founder, Davidsonian newspaper, Thomasville, N.C. 1910; Reporter, Dispatch, Lexington, N.C. 1911–13 and Daily News, Greensboro, N.C. 1913–17, 1919–24; Prof. of Journalism, Univ. N.C. 1924–26; Leader Writer, Evening Sun, Baltimore 1926–39 and The Sun, Baltimore 1939–43; freelance writer since 1943; television commentator WAAM-TV, Baltimore 1952–54; Contributing Ed., The New Republic since 1954. Hons: D. Litt., Wake Forest Coll., N.C. 1928; LL.D. Coll. of Charleston, S.C. 1935 and Univ. N.C. 1937; D.C.L. Univ. S.C. 1942; DuPont Commentators' Award 1953; Sidney Hillman Foundn. Award 1954; George Foster Peabody Award 1954; Gold Medal, State of N.C. 1964; Andrew White Medal, Loyola Coll., Baltimore 1969; Litt.D., Goucher Coll., Baltimore 1969; Mt. Royal, Baltimore, Improvement Assn. Award 1976; Enoch Pratt Library, Baltimore, Citation 1978; also hon. doctorates, Towson State and

Johns Hopkins Univs., Baltimore. *Author:* (with W.R. Hayward) The Story of Man's Work, 1925; What is News?, 1926; The Undefeated, 1927; Andrew Jackson: An Epic in Homespun, 1927; Randolph of Roanoke—A Political Fantastic, 1929; (under pseudonym Charles North) By Reason of Strength (novel), 1930, and Number 36 (novel), 1933; The Secession of the Southern States, 1933; The Wasted Land; A Little Night Music; (with Frank Kent, H.L. Mencken and Hamilton Owens) The Sun Papers of Baltimore, 1937; America's Silver Age, 1939; Roosevelt: Dictator or Democrat?, 1941; American Heroes and Hero-Worship, 1943; Woodrow Wilson, 1944; An Honorable Titan, 1946; First Captain, the Story of John Paul Jones, 1947; Liberal's Progress, 1948; Our English Heritage, 1949; Incredible Tale, the Odyssey of the Average American in the Last Half Century, 1950; This American People, 1951; Pattern for Liberty: The Making of a Southern Industrialist, 1952; Mount Vernon, 1953; Lunatic Fringe, 1957; Peril and Promise: The Lines are Drawn, 1958; America—A History for Peter (three vols.), 1959–60; The Man Who Feels Left Behind, 1960; Hod-Carrier, 1964; Communism: An American's View; Franklin D. Roosevelt, 1967; The Imperial Republic, 1972; America-Watching, 1976. Also articles in Harper's, Atlantic Monthly, The New Republic, and Virginia Quarterly Review.

WILLIAM (AUSTIN) KIENBUSCH
Artist
Born New York City, U.S.A., April 13th, 1914
Died New York City, U.S.A., March 23rd, 1980

The reputation of the painter William Kienbusch rests upon his lyric renderings of the Maine coast which reveal his much admired "sense of place." Born into a wealthy New York City family which appreciated art, Kienbusch received encouragement and support in his artistic career. His father took him every week to the Metropolitan Museum and gave him, when he was 12, a book about modern art which he later recalled as "having a decided influence" on him. His interest in art developed further while he was at Hotchkiss, a preparatory school in Connecticut, where his painting teacher, Robert Osborn, became "a sort of hero." At Princeton, Kienbusch studied art history and wrote his senior thesis on American art, the first Princeton student ever to do so.

From the time of his graduation until his entry into the U.S. Army in World War Two, Kienbusch concentrated on developing as an artist. Although his presence in Paris during the Spanish Civil War encouraged an interest in politics and his extended contact the following year with some Pennsylvania coal miners sharpened his social conscience, his material as an artist lay elsewhere. During his university years he had been impressed with the work of the landscape painter John Marin; in the summers of 1940 and 1941, he went to the same spot in Maine where Marin had painted, an experience which he later said was decisive for him. By 1946 Kienbusch was painting in a notably personal style. In the following year he was taken on by New York's Kraushaar Gallery with which he remained the rest of his life. After his first one-man show in 1949, his life followed a regular pattern of summers in Maine and winters in New York, where he taught as well as painted.

Although Kienbusch was inspired by the landscape of Maine and influenced by Marin and other landscape painters such as Marsden Hartley and Arthur Dove, his interest in abstract expressionism was almost equally strong. During most of his career he attempted to reconcile and combine these seemingly antithetical forms and through them reveal the spirit or "inner reality" of his subject. Although Kienbusch was not an innovator—"Less spectacular and audacious than a good many of his contemporaries," as one critic said in 1975— he was "nonetheless an artist who worked out of an evident devotion to authentic feeling, and (who) has made something quiet and beautiful out of his loyalty to a local tradition."

In his last few years Kienbusch was unable to paint because he had suffered a stroke; instead he worked in oil pastels. Although small in scale and produced in short working sessions, these pieces are among his best, revealing more directly than in his earlier work Kienbusch's loving attachment to the objects of his lifelong contemplation.   D.S.

Son of Carl Otto von K. and Mildred (Pressinger) K. Unmarried. Educ: Hotchkiss Sch.; Princeton Univ. (Phi Beta Kappa), B.A. 1936; Art Students League, N.Y.C. 1936–37; Colo. Springs Fine Arts Center (with Henry Varnum Poor) 1937; Colarossi's, and privately with Abraham Rattner, Paris 1937–38; American Artists Sch. (with Anton Refregier) and privately with Mervin Jules, N.Y.C. 1939–40; New Sch. (with Stuart Davis), N.Y.C. 1941–42. Mil. service: Sgt., U.S. Army 1942–46 (taught camouflage and compiled target charts for bombing raids in Japan). Painter, N.Y. and Me., 1946–80; taught at Brooklyn Mus. Art Sch., N.Y.C. 1948–69. Hons: 1st Prize, Drawing, Brooklyn Artists Biennial, Brooklyn Mus. 1952; Prize for Drawing, Metropolitan Mus., N.Y.C. 1952; 1st Purchase Prize, Watercolor, Columbia Mus. of Art, S.C.; Guggenheim Fellowship 1958; 1st Prize, Watercolor, N.Y. State Exposition 1958; Prize, Provincetown Arts Festival 1958; 1st Purchase Prize, Watercolor, Summer Art Festival, Portland, Me.; Ford Foundn. Purchase Award 1961; 1st Prize, Watercolor, Boston Arts Festival 1961; Artist-in-Residence, Univ. of Me., Orono 1968; Grant, Childe Hassam Fund, Natl. Inst. of Arts and Letters 1970; Purchase Award, American Acad. of Arts and Letters 1978. *Exhibitions: One-person*—Univ. of Me., Orono, 1956; Cornell Univ., Ithaca, N.Y., 1958; Princeton Univ., 1962; Kraushaar Gall., N.Y.C., 1949, '52, '56, '59, '62, '65, '69, '72, '75, '78. *Two-person*—Carnegie Inst., Pittsburgh (retrospective), 1954; Art Center, Ft. Worth, Tex., 1964. *Group* (partial list)—Whitney Mus., N.Y.C. ("New Decade," 1955; "Nature in Abstraction," 1958; Whitney Annuals, 1953, '56, '59, '61, '65; "Between the Fairs—25 Years of American Art," 1964; "The Friends Collect," 1964; "Art of the United States, 1610–1966," 1966); American Fedn. of Art Traveling Exhibs. ("Collector's Choice," 1956; "Brussels World's Fair," 1958; "Maine Artists," 1964–66; "Masters of American Watercolor," Corcoran Exhib., Washington, D.C., 1960–62; "Sixth International," Tokyo, 1962–63; "N.Y. World's Fair," 1965); Albright–Knox Gall., Buffalo, N.Y.; Baltimore Mus., Md.; Brooklyn Mus.; Carnegie Inst., Pittsburgh; Art Inst., Chicago; Cincinnati Mus., Ohio; Cleveland Mus., Ohio; Colby Coll. Art Gall., Waterville, Me.; Corcoran Gall., Washington, D.C.; DeCordova Mus., Lincoln, Mass.; Des Moines Art Center, Iowa; Detroit Inst. of Arts; Houston Mus. of Art; Krannert Art Mus., Univ. of Ill., Urbana; Joslyn Art Inst., Omaha,

Nebr.; Los Angeles County Mus.; McNay Art Inst., San Antonio, Tex.; Metropolitan Mus., N.Y.C.; Univ. of Mich., Ann Arbor; Mus. of Modern Art, N.Y.C.; Montclair Mus., Montclair, N.J.; Univ. of Nebr., Lincoln; New Sch. for Social Research, N.Y.C.; Pa. Acad. of Fine Arts, Philadelphia (Annuals 1952, '53, '58, '59, '62, '65, '67); Philadelphia Mus.; R.I. Sch. of Design, Providence; San Francisco Mus. of Art; City Art Mus., St. Louis, Mo.; Santa Barbara Mus., Calif.; Toledo Mus., Ohio; Va. Mus., Richmond. *Collections:* Albright–Knox Gall., Buffalo, N.Y.; Atlanta Univ., Ga.; Bowdoin Coll., Bowdoin, Me.; Boston Mus. of Fine Arts; Brooklyn Mus.; Carnegie Inst., Pittsburgh; Chrysler Art Mus., Norfolk, Va.; Colby Coll., Waterville, Me.; Colo. Springs Fine Arts Center; Columbia Mus. of Art, S.C.; Currier Gall. of Art, Manchester, N.H.; Dartmouth Coll., Hanover, N.H.; Univ. of Del., Newark; Des Moines Art Center, Iowa; Detroit Inst. of Arts; Ft. Worth Art Center, Tex.; Mus. of Fine Arts, Houston; Lehigh Univ., Bethlehem, Pa.; Univ. of Me., Orono; Metropolitan Mus., N.Y.C.; Univ. of Mich., Ann Arbor; Minn. Mus. of Art, St. Paul; Univ. of Minn., Minneapolis; Montclair Art Mus., N.J.; Montreal Mus. of Art; Munson–Williams–Proctor Inst., Utica, N.Y.; Mus. of Modern Art, N.Y.C.; Wichita Art. Mus., Kans.; Natl. Coll. of Fine Arts, Washington, D.C.; Univ. of Nebr., Lincoln; Nelson Gall., Kansas City, Mo.; Newark Mus., N.J.; New Britain Mus. of Art, Conn.; Pa. Acad. of Fine Arts, Philadelphia; Philadelphia Mus. of Art; Portland Mus. of Art, Me.; Santa Barbara Mus., Calif.; Princeton Univ. Art.Mus.; Sara Roby Foundn., N.Y.C.; Memorial Art Gall., Rochester, N.Y.; Speed Mus., Louisville, KY.; Toledo Mus. of Art, Ohio; Art Gall. of Toronto; Uniontown Friends of Art, Pa.; Va. Mus. of Fine Arts, Richmond; Wadsworth Atheneum, Hartford, Conn,; Whitney Mus., N.Y.C.; Williams Coll., Williamstown, Mass.; Neuberger Mus., Purchase, N.Y.
Further reading: Maine and its Role in American Art 1740–1963 by Elizabeth F. Wilder (ed.), 1963.

PETR (PYATRUS USTINOVICH) BROVKA
Soviet author
Born Putilkovichi, now Vitebsk Region of Byelorussian S.S.R., June 25th, 1905
Died U.S.S.R., March 24th, 1980

Petr Brovka, prominent Soviet writer and public figure, was known as the People's Poet of Byelorussia. Committed early in life to the ideals of the Russian Revolution, Brovka, published his first poems (ca. 1926) in the newspaper *Chyrvonaya Polachyna* of which he was managing secretary.

Brovka's early work—several collections of poetry and a novel published in the early 1930s—glorified the Revolution and romanticized the nascent socialist order. His style was lyrical; working within the framework of social realism he managed to avoid a maudlin portrayal of the "new human nature" which Brovka believed had been suddenly "liberated" from the "burden of history" of Communism. Two acclaimed works of this period are the heroic narrative poem of the Civil War and the Revolution, *Praz gory i step* (Through

Mountains and Steppes), published in 1932, and the lyrical narrative poem *1914,* which appeared in 1935.

The experience of World War Two, in which he worked with the partisan press at the front lines, motivated Brovka to write even more explicitly about his love for the people. He celebrated patriotism, the heroic exploits of the "common folk," and the strong character of the Russian people. After the war his poems were concerned with the good will of the Soviet people and their desire for international peace. In 1947 Brovka received the State Prize of the USSR for his patriotic collection *Sustrecha* (Meeting).

Brovka's later literary works were thematically ambitious and experimental in form. In works such as *Dalioka ad domy* (Far Away from Home), published in 1960, he extended the Communist dream to all of humanity. In addition to his poetry, he also wrote philosophic works, librettos, and translated Mayakovsky, Prokoviev, and Lord Byron, and others into Belyorussian. He also supervised compilation of the first Byelorussian Soviet Encyclopedia, and served as its editor-in-chief after 1967.

Brovka worked in various capacities for the government and received many honors in recognition of his services. He died at the age of 74 and was buried at Minsk.   D.D.

Educ: Byelorussian State Univ. 1931. Mil. Service: frontline and partisan press, Soviet Army, WWII. Managing Secty., Chyrvonaya Polachyna; Ed.-in-Chief, Polymia (Flame) 1945–48; Chmn. of the Bd., Byelorussian S.S.R. Writers' Union 1948–1967; Ed.-in-Chief, first Byelorussian Soviet Encyclopedia since 1967. Member, CPSU since 1940; Member, Central Cttee. of Communist Party of Byelorussia since 1952; Academician, Acad. of Sciences of the Byelorussian S.S.R. since 1966; Deputy, Supreme Soviet of U.S.S.R.; Secty. of the Bd., Byelorussian Writers' Union. Hons: State Prize of U.S.S.R. 1947, 1951; Ja. Kolas Prize for Literature 1957; Lenin Prize 1962; People's Poet of the Byelorussian S.S.R. 1962; three Orders of Lenin; Order of the October Revolution; Order of the Friendship of the Peoples; Hero of Socialist Labour. *Books: Poetry*—Gady yak Shtorm (Years as a Storm), 1930; Pramova faktami (Statement Based on Facts), 1930; Tsekhjavyia budni (Weekdays in the Workshop), 1931; Praz gory i step (Through Mountains and Steppes), 1932; 1914, 1935; Prykhod heroya (The Hero's Arrival), 1935; Viasna Radzimy (The Homeland's Spring), 1937; Sustrecha (Meeting), 1947; Doroga zhizni (The Road of Life), 1950; Dalioka ad domy (Far Away from Home), 1960; A dni idut . . . (But the Days Pass . . .), 1961; Vsegda s Leninym (Always with Lenin), 1967; Sredi krasnykh riabin (Among Red Rowanberries), 1967; Isbrannye proizvedeniia (Selected Works) vols. 1–2, 1969. *Novel*—Kalandry (The Calendars), 1931.

PIERRE ETCHEBASTER
World champion in court tennis
Born St. Jean-de-Luz, France, May 3rd, 1894
Died St. Jean-de-Luz, France, March 24th, 1980

Pierre Etchebaster, for more than a quarter of a century the unbeaten world champion of court tennis, was born and brought up in St. Jean-de-Luz in the Basque country of France, the homeland of racquet

sports. His paternal grandfather was the owner of Le Trinquet, a small hotel, restaurant, and sports area near St. Jean-de-Luz, where Etchebaster developed his abundant natural appetite. He first perfected his skill in a variant of jai alai called *pelota*. At the age of 16 he went to Valdivia, Chile, to work in an uncle's store; at 20 he was called back to France and earned two citations of the Croix-de-Guerre during four years of active service as a machine gunner.

After the war Etchebaster returned to St. Jean-de-Luz to work in the family bakery, soon taking the French championships of the Basque teams of *chistera* and *pala* (both variants of jai alai) and *mains nues* (handball). In 1922 he was invited by couturier Jacques Worth, then court tennis champion of France, to learn the sport at the Jeu de Paume Club of Paris. (Court tennis, in which a small, hard ball is played off the sides of an enclosed court and across a net with a heavy, gut-strung racquet, is the ancestor of all modern racquet sports.) Within two years Etchebaster had become the new national champion; by 1928 he had won the first of his 26 world championships. He was never afterwards beaten and relinquished his title only when he retired at the age of 60. No athlete in any sport has yet been able to match his record.

Etchebaster's swift, rhythmic play, powerful serve, graceful footwork, and unshakeable endurance gave him the mastery of challengers many years younger than himself, including Ogden Phipps and Alastair Martin. Long, gruelling rallies were his forte. He took the U.S. Open title from Jock Souter soon after he joined the New York Racquet and Tennis Club as its senior professional in 1928. The closest he ever came to defeat was his last defense of the world championship in 1954, when the 60-year-old athlete posted a hard-fought victory over the British Open champion, J. Dean, by seven sets to four. The title was in the balance on the last day of the three-day match, but Etchebaster's legendary reserve of energy secured him the title for the 26th consecutive year.

After retiring from the New York Racquet and Tennis Club and from competition, Etchebaster joined the staff of industrialist and financier John Hay Whitney as a teaching professional and played exhibition matches in the U.S. and Europe. He also collaborated with George Plimpton on a memoir, *Pierre's Book,* published in 1971. In 1975 he and his wife Jeanne, who had two children, returned to St. Jean-de-Luz, where they had maintained a second home throughout their years in New York.   J.P.

Son of Jean-Louis E., baker. Married Jeanne. Children: one son, one daughter. Educ: lycée, St. Jean-de-Luz to age 15. Mil. Service: machine gunner, French Army 1914–18; two citations of Croix-de-Guerre. Store asst., Valdivia, Chile 1910–14; asst., family bakery, St. Jean-de-Luz 1918–22. French championships 1918–22 in chistera, pala, mains nues (ball games). Court tennis player since 1922; French Champion 1924; World Champion 1928–54; U.S. Court Tennis Open Champion. Professional court tennis player and instr.: Jeu de Paume, Paris 1923–28; N.Y. Racquet and Tennis Club, 1928–54; staff of John Hay Whitney, U.S.A. 1954–75. In retirement, France 1975–80. *Author:* (with George Plimpton) Pierre's Book, 1971.

OSCAR ARNULFO ROMERO
Archibishop of San Salvador and advocate of human rights
Born Ciudad Barrios, El Salvador, August 15th, 1917
Died San Salvador, El Salvador, March 24th, 1980

Oscar Arnulfo Romero, Archbishop of El Salvador, was the most outspoken of Latin America's Roman Catholic clergy, many of whom have become increasingly committed to working actively for social reform. The son of a railway worker, Romero was apprenticed to a carpenter in his home town of Ciudad Barrios, then went to secondary school in San Miguel and spent two years at the minor seminary of the Claretians. He continued his theological studies in Rome and returned to his native country after receiving ordination in 1942. In 1970 he was named assistant bishop of the capital city of San Salvador; four years later he became titular bishop of the diocese of San Miguel. In 1977 the Vatican appointed Msgr. Romero to the Archbishopric of San Salvador, replacing Msgr. Luis Chavez y Gonzalez.

At the time of his appointment, Msgr. Romero was viewed as a conservative prelate, one not likely to concern himself with the volatile social and political issues that have provoked an ongoing bloodbath in his small Central American nation. Sixty percent of the country's arable land is owned by a handful of wealthy families; the remainder of El Salvador's population of almost five million consists largely of poverty-stricken peasants and laborers. Campaigns of terrorist violence, mounted by right-wing paramilitary groups and the Marxist organizations which oppose them, resulted in the deaths of more than 900 people in the first three months of 1980 alone.

Neither the military government nor the Catholic activist movement expected the shy, soft-spoken Archbishop to do more than administer Church affairs. However, the murder of a Jesuit friend, by right-wing assassins outraged Archbishop Romero. Increasingly, in radio broadcasts and sermons, he denounced political violence and called for needed social changes, including redistribution of wealth, land reform, and justice and equality for the poor. His stance brought him a huge public following as well as a series of death threats from extremist factions. In 1979, a group of 118 British Members of Parliament and 23 U.S. Congressmen nominated him for the Nobel Peace Prize.

When dictator Carlos Humberto Romero (no relation) was overthrown in the autumn of 1979, Archbishop Romero gave his qualified support to the military-civilian junta that came to power. But he soon grew disillusioned with its inability to carry out promised reforms; a few days before his death, he accused the junta of continued repression. Although his opposition to political violence extended to leftists, he had reluctantly come to believe that they represented the only possibility for change. In February he wrote an open letter to President Carter, begging him not to send continued military aid to the junta. "We are fed up with weapons and bullets," he said, urging President Carter to use the funds instead to feed thousands of hungry Salvadorans. His position was borne out a month later by an ecumenical fact-finding group, which reported that U.S. military aid to El Salvador was viewed there "as a clear sign of U.S. support for the repression and would undermine the long-range interests of the United States." Nevertheless, a House subcommittee approved the Carter Administration's request for $5.7 million in military aid for the junta.

On the morning of March 24, Archbishop Romero celebrated mass in memory of the mother of Jorge Pinto, a well-known opposition journalist, in the chapel of the Hospital of Divine Providence, an institution founded by the Archbishop to care for terminally ill cancer patients. He gave a ten-minute sermon on the need to end political violence, saying "Let the wave of murders in this country stop." As he was elevating the host, a middle-aged man in civilian clothes (accompanied, according to some reports, by three other similarly-dressed men) stepped from a hiding place inside the door of the church and fired a .22 caliber pistol at close range, striking the Archbishop in the heart and lung. The gunmen fled in a car.

The junta banned all publication and broadcasting of the details of the murder, but declared three days of public mourning. Although the assassins were not identified, El Salvador officials and the general public attributed the killing to rightists. Romero's funeral mass was held in the Metropolitan Cathedral in San Salvador, with more than 30,000 mourners crowded in the plaza in front of the cathedral. Gunfire broke out between leftist demonstrators and National Guard troops; 26 people were shot or crushed to death in the resulting stampede and some 200 injured. In subsequent days, leftist groups set off 30 bombs in the capital, and government troops shot and hacked to death nine civilians near Archbishop Romero's home town of Ciudad Barrios.   M.S.

Born Oscar Arnulfo Romero y Galdamez. Son of Santos R., railway employee, and Guadalupe de Jesus Galdamez. Roman Catholic. Educ: elementary sch., Ciudad Barrios; sec. sch., San Miguel; minor seminary of the Claretians; theological study in Rome. Ordained to the priesthood, Rome 1942; named Asst. Bishop of San Salvador 1970; named Bishop of the Diocese of San Miguel 1974; named Archbishop of San Salvador by the Vatican 1977. Hons: D.H.L., Georgetown Univ. 1978; nominated for Nobel Peace Prize 1979; Peace Prize, Ecumenical Action, Sweden 1980.

MILTON H(YLAND) ERICKSON
Psychiatrist and hypno-therapist
Born Aurum, Nevada, U.S.A., December 5th, 1901
Died Phoenix, Arizona, U.S.A., March 25th, 1980

Milton Hyland Erickson, for many years one of America's leading hypnotists, devoted much of his career to establishing hypnosis for therapeutic uses. Departing radically from the Freudian school of psychoanalysis, Erickson developed a form of therapy which used hypnotic techniques to identify problems and prescribe treatment.

At the age of seventeen Erickson was stricken with poliomyelitis and paralyzed in all but eye movement. Slowly, with intense concentration, he taught his body to move again. During the long process, Erickson observed the non-verbal language—which often contradicted the words—of those around him. Being additionally handicapped by tone-deafness and virtual color blindness enabled Erickson to focus exclusively on body language, without being distracted by color and tonal variations. (By simply observing an audience, Erickson could evaluate a musical performance.) He later attributed his academic success to these early studies of body language.

At the University of Wisconsin, Erickson was introduced to professional hypnotic practice and began his first experiments. After receiving his M.D. in 1928, he worked first at Colorado General Hospital and then as a special psychiatric intern to the Colorado Psychopathic Hospital. This led to an appointment with the State Hospital for Mental Diseases in Howard, Rhode Island and in 1931 Erickson became junior psychiatrist at the State Hospital in Worcester, Massachusetts. Shortly thereafter he was promoted to senior rank and by the following year, Erickson was the hospital's chief psychiatrist. From 1934 to 1948 Erickson worked at the Wayne County General Hospital and Infirmary in Michigan and, before turning to private practice in 1949, was Clinical Director of the Arizona State Hospital in Phoenix for a brief period.

Specializing in hypnotic psychotherapy, clinical hypnosis research and general psychiatry, Erickson treated patients from around the world. To induce a trance-like state in his patients, he used natural, spontaneous conversations. He was frequently consulted by scientists and other doctors, among them anthropologist Margaret Mead; and during the 1950s Erickson collaborated with Aldous Huxley to investigate states of consciousness and pursue hypnotic research. During his career, Erickson was estimated to have hypnotized more than 30,000 people.

The author of more than 140 scholarly articles, Erickson refused to theorize; too little is known about hypnotism, he said, to reduce it to a single theory. His techniques, however have been described by Dr. Jay Haley—Erickson's student and colleague for 17 years—in *Uncommon Therapy*. Although Erickson was regarded as an inordinately successful therapist by both the medical profession and his patients, critics claimed that his reputation, based largely on anecdotes and work that was not substantiated by the long-term observations necessary for scientific acceptance, was perhaps undeserved.   M.D.

Son of Albert E., cattle-herder, miner, and farmer, and Clara Florence E. Married: (1) Helen Hutton 1925 (div. 1935); (2) Elizabeth Euphemia Moore 1936. Children: 1st marriage—Albert; Lance; Carol Ann Deerington; 2nd marriage—Elizabeth Alice; Allan Hyland; Robert Bruce; Rosanna Lucy Klein; Kristina Karen, doctor. Educ: Univ. Wisc., B.A. 1927; M.A. 1928; M.D. psychiatry 1928. Intern, Colo. Gen. Hosp., Denver 1928–29; Special Psychiatric Intern, Colo. Psychopathic Hosp., Denver 1929; Asst., Physician, State Hosp. for Mental Diseases, Howard, R.I. 1929–30. With Worcester State Hosp., Mass.: Jr. Psychiatrist 1931; Sr. Psychiatrist 1931–32; Chief Psychiatrist 1932–34. Dir., Psychiatric Research and Training, Wayne County Gen. Hosp. and Infirmary, Eloise, Mich. 1934–48. With Wayne State Univ. Coll. of Medicine, Mich.: Instr., Pyschology Dept. 1936–40; Asst. Prof. 1940–44; Assoc. Prof. 1944–48; Prof., Grad. Sch. 1942–48. Clinical Dir., Arizona State Hosp., Phoenix and Visiting Prof., Clinical Psychology, Mich. State Coll., East Lansing (later Mich. State Univ.) 1948; private practice, Phoenix since 1949. Assoc. Ed., Diseases of the Nervous System 1940–55; Ed., American Journal of Clinical Hypnosis 1958–68. Founder-Dir., Research and Educ. Foundn. for the Study of Hypnosis; Founder and Pres. 1957–59, American Soc. of Clinical Hypnosis (life member). Member: Soc. for Experimental and Clinical Hypnosis; American Psychiatric Assn.;

American Psychological Assn.; American Assn. for the Advancement of Science; American Psychopathological Assn.; American Acad. for Psychosomatic Medicine; British Soc. of Medical Hypnotists; Nihon Saimin Kenkyukai of Japan; Sociedad Argentine de Hipnosis Medica e Hipnoalisis. Hons: Benjamin Franklin Gold Medal of the Intnl. Soc. of Hypnosis 1976. Co-Author: (with Linn F. Cooper) Time Distortion in Hypnosis, 1954; (with E.L. and S.I. Rossi) Hypnotic Realities, 1976; also, Practical Application of Medical and Dental Hypnosis. *Major articles:* "A Study of an Experimental Neurosis Hypnotically Induced in a Case of Ejaculatic Praecox," British Journal of Medical Psychology, 1935; (with Elizabeth M. Erickson) "Concerning the Nature and Character of Post-Hypnotic Behavior," Jrnl. General Psychology, Jan. 1941; "Hypnotic Investigation of Psychosomatic Phenomena," Psychsomatic Medicine, Jan. 1943; "The Method Employed to Formulate a Complex Story for the Induction of an Experimental Neurosis in a Hypnotic Subject," Jrnl. of General Psychology, 1944; "Special Techniques of Brief Hypnotherapy," Jrnl. of Clinical and Experimental Hypnosis, Apr. 1954; "Interspersal Techniques for Symptom Correction and Pain Control," American Journal of Clinical Hypnosis, Apr. 1966; (with E.L. Rossi) "Two-level Communication," American Journal of Clinic Hypnosis, Jan. 1976; others. *Contributor:* Encyclopaedia Britannica; Collier's Encyclopaedia; others.
Further reading: Uncommon Therapy by Jay Haley, 1973; Patterns of the Hypnotic Techniques of Milton H. Erickson M.D. by Richard Bendler and John Grinder, 1975.

FRANZ JOSEPH INGELFINGER
Physician and editor
Born Dresden, Germany, August 20th, 1910
Died Cambridge, Mass., U.S.A., March 25th, 1980

Franz Joseph Ingelfinger achieved distinction in a number of medical fields, and as a noted gastroenterologist, he conducted valuable, often original research on the esophagus, intestines, and liver. In addition, Ingelfinger was editor of the *New England Journal of Medicine* for a ten-year period during which time it became a lively journal of international reputation.

As a young man Ingelfinger announced to his family that "every ten years I want to do something different." Although he did not always limit himself to ten-year-interludes, Ingelfinger fulfilled his ambition. Beginning his medical career with an internship in the Harvard Service at Boston University City Hospital, he moved on, with the award of several fellowships, to other hospitals in the Boston area, and worked briefly at the University of Pennsylvania School of Medicine in Philadelphia. For many years he carried a heavy patient load at several Boston hospitals while also teaching at Boston University's School of Medicine (he later taught at Harvard and Tufts). His student protégés (known on the Boston University campus as "fingerlings") credit him with transforming gastroenterology from a practice of largely personal observations and often haphazard experiments into a field with a far more solid scientific basis. Ingelfinger published extensively with both scholarly journals and popular magazines.

During the period of his editorship, Ingelfinger considerably enlivened the *New England Journal of Medicine*. By 1967 the journal had fallen into a pattern of publishing articles which were "old news" to both the medical community and the general reading public. Under Ingelfinger's aegis, the journal's "archival role" became secondary; social and ethical problems affecting medical practice and society were emphasized, and an expanded correspondence section encouraged debate on articles and ideas. In 1970 the journal imposed "Ingelfinger's Rule" which forbade publication in the Journal of any article whose contents had been printed in another source—including newspapers. Responding to contributors who believed the practice to be harshly prohibitive, Ingelfinger said, "Why should people want to read my journal if they know that most of what is in it (has) appeared already in *Medical World News* or *Medical Tribune?*" Articles ranging from former *Saturday Review* editor Norman Cousin's first draft of the best-selling *Anatomy of an Illness* to a thoughtful series on drug abuse flooded in at an unprecedented rate; sales increased by seventy percent and European editions were launched.

Ingelfinger once confided during an interview that he thrived on "challenge and controversy" in medicine. Willing to take risks with his body, he often tried out on himself many experiments on the esophagus and intestines which involved the placement of tubes through the nose and throat. His work on arthritis, drugs, bowel disorders, and the liver brought him further renown in the medical profession in his later years. In 1977 Dr. Ingelfinger conducted a self-diagnosis and found that he was suffering from cancer of the esophagus—an area of internal medicine in which he was expert. That same year he relinquished his editorship of the journal.   A.B.P.

Son of Joseph I., physician and Eleanor (Holden) I., teacher. Married Sarah Shurcliff, furniture designer, 1941. Children: Joseph Abbot, b. 1942, physician; Alice Harris, b. 1945. No practicing religion. Brought to U.S. from Germany 1922; naturalized 1931. Educ: Phillips Acad., Andover, Mass. 1928; Yale Univ. (Phi Beta Kappa), B.A. 1932; Harvard Medical Sch. (Alpha Omega Alpha, Beta Theta Pi, Nu Sigma Nu), M.D. 1936. With Boston City Hosp.: Intern, Harvard Service 1937–38; Resident and Fellow, Thorndike Memorial Lab. 1938–39. Asst., medicine, Harvard Medical Sch. 1938; Fellow, gastroenterology, Univ. of Pa. Sch. of Medicine, Philadelphia 1939–40. With Boston Univ. Sch. of Medicine: Instr., internal medicine 1940–42; Asst. Prof. 1942–45; Assoc. Prof. 1945–58; Prof. 1958–61; First Conrad Wesselhoeft Prof. 1961–67; Clinical Prof. 1967–77; Prof. Emeritus since 1977. Visiting Physician, Chief Gastrointestinal Clinic 1940–67 and Member, Consulting Staff 1967–76, Boston Univ. Hosp. With R.D. Evans Memorial Hosp. Boston: Asst. 1940–42; Assoc. 1942–45; Staff Member 1945–67. Visiting Physician, Mass. Memorial Hosp. 1945–67; Staff Assoc., gastroenterology, New England Center Hosp. 1957–71; Member, Ed. Bd, 1961–67 and Ed. 1967–77, New England Journal of Medicine, Boston; Visiting Lectr., Harvard Medical Sch. since 1977; Visiting Lectr., Tufts Univ., Medford, Mass. Trustee, Boston Medical Library 1952–58, 1961–65. Consultant, gastroenterology: Boston Veterans Admin. Hosp. 1952–73; Lemuel Shattuck Hosp. 1955–71; Robert B. Brigham Hosp. 1960–71; Beth Israel Hosp. since 1977. Dir.: Postgrad. Medical Inst., Boston 1953–61; Medical Foundn. Inc. 1960–64; Fifth and Sixth Medical Services, Boston City Hosp. 1961–67. Various offices 1959–61 and

Pres., American Gastroenterological Assn. 1961–62; Natl. Advisory
Council, Natl. Inst. Arthritis and Metabolic Diseases 1961–65; Ad-
visory Cttee., Medical Research and Development Command, U.S.
Army 1963–67; Natl. Consultant to Surgeon Gen., U.S. Air Force
1966–70; Member, Selection Cttee, Medical Literature Analysis and
Retrieval Systems, Natl. Library Medicine 1967–73; Consultant,
Advisory Panel System, Bureau of Drugs 1970–75 and Chmn.,
Adverse Drug Effects Panel, Office of Technology Assessment,
Federal Drug Admin. 1976; Trustee, New England Medical Center,
Boston since 1976; Member 1970–76 and Chmn. 1974–75, Advisory
Cttee. on Medical Science, American Medical Assn; Chmn., Ed.,
Bd., Gastroenterology 1964–68; Member, American Bd. Gastroen-
terology 1966–68; Councilor 1960–64 and Member, Amory Prize
Cttee, 1963–69; Chmn., Research Cttee., Mass Chapter, Arthritis
Foundn. Fellow: American Acad. of Arts and Sciences; Royal Coll.
Physicans. Master, American Coll. Physicians; Inst. of Social Ethics
and Life Sciences. Member: American Soc. Clinical Investigation;
Assn. American Physicians; American Assn. Study Liver Diseases.
Ed. Bd., Disease-a-Month and Interurban Clinical Club. Hons:
Friedenwald Medal, American Gastroenterology Assn. 1969; Hon. D.
Sc., Boston Univ. Sch. of Medicine 1973; Distinguished Teacher
Award, American Coll. Physicians 1975; Abraham Flexner Award,
Assn. American Medical Colls. 1976; Distinguished Service Award,
American Medical Assn. 1977; Meritorius Award, Council Biological
Education 1978; Kober Award, Assn. American Physicians 1979;
Hon. D. Sc., Yale Univ. 1979, and from many other colls. and univs.
Diplomate, American Bd. Internal Medicine and American Bd.
Gastroenterology. *Books:* Editor—Internal Medicine, 1973; Contro-
versy in Internal Medicine, 1975. Wrote and edited over 300 articles
for jrnls., textbooks and mags.; co-ed. of ca. 250 articles for medical
publs.

(JAN) WALTER SUSSKIND
Conductor and pianist
Born Prague, Czechoslovakia, May 1st, 1913
Died Berkeley, California, U.S.A., March 25th, 1980

Walter Susskind, who built the St. Louis Symphony Orchestra into a
first-class ensemble during his seven years as its conductor and music
director, was born in Prague in 1913. His mother, a concert pianist,
recognized his talent early on but refused to allow him to take lessons
until he was nine, lest he become an unhappy child prodigy. As a
youth, he attended a regular secondary school as well as the State
Conservatory, where he studied conducting with George Szell and
composition with Josef Suk and Alois Hába. He gave his first public
concert at the age of 17 and at 20 was hired as assistant conductor and
coach at Prague's German Opera House, where he conducted works
by Verdi, Puccini, and Wagner.

When anti-Nazi sentiment in Czechoslovakia forced the closing of
the opera house in 1936, Susskind embarked on a 26-nation recital
tour. In Amsterdam he learned of the German invasion of Prague and
applied for British citizenship; once in England, he formed a trio with
two other refugees and went on tour. (All three players volunteered to

join a Czech military force organized in England in 1940, but were asked to play for troops and civilians instead.)

Following a season as conductor at London's Strand Theatre in 1941, Susskind was hired to conduct the Royal Carl Rosa Opera Company. A series of guest appearances with the Liverpool Philharmonic in 1945 led to engagements with the London Symphony, London Philharmonic, and BBC Orchestras and to tours of Germany (with the Sadler's Wells Opera Company of London) and Australia.

In 1946, the year he attained British citizenship, Susskind became director of the Scottish Orchestra, presiding over its re-organization as the Scottish National. After seven years he took over the Victoria Symphony Orchestra in Melbourne, Australia. By a coincidence, both the Victoria and the Scottish had formerly been led by George Szell, his teacher at the Prague Conservatory.

Courtesy Mrs. Janis Susskind

Susskind's directorship of the Toronto Symphony lasted from 1956 to 1968; he also spent seven summers as conductor and faculty music director of the Aspen Music Festival in Colorado. In 1968, having acquired an international reputation as a molder of orchestras, he was invited to take over the leadership of the St. Louis Symphony, the second oldest orchestra in the U.S., which was struggling to overcome the mediocrity into which it had fallen. With the strong backing of the symphony board, Susskind rebuilt the group, recruiting dozens of recent graduates from the prestigious Eastern conservatories and training them with an affection and sensitivity unusual in his profession. By 1974, the orchestra had won a solid reputation for excellence, and Susskind a reputation for erratic brilliance. "As a conductor," wrote one critic, "he has his ups and downs, apparently originating in the moods of a complex character. He has the musical capacity for greatness, and many of his performances fulfill the promise. Many others have a coarseness of detail, a feeling of having been outlined in broad stokes, that speak not of ineptitude but of an artist too much in a hurry, too little involved." Most critics praised his intelligent pacing, strong rhythmic sense, and robust yet aristocratic touch. Susskind's sponsorship of the 24-year-old Leonard Slatkin, whom he hired as his assistant conductor, was in keeping with his customary support of young musicians, on whose behalf he had founded the National Youth Orchestras of Great Britain and Canada.

After seven years at St. Louis, Susskind resigned to devote himself to guest conducting, saying "I need more time to look into my inner self, to continue the search for the true soul of music and its innermost meaning." There were also reports of dissatisfaciton on the part of the board over his colorful dress and five marriages. During the next three years he performed with symphonies in Tokyo, London, Johannesburg, and New Zealand, among many others.

In 1978 he accepted the temporary post of musical advisor to the Cincinnati Symphony Orchestra after the death of its leader, Thomas Schippers. Within a year he had fallen ill of the same rare form of lung cancer that had claimed Schipper's life.

Susskind made over 200 recordings, including works by Mahler and Shostakovich, for whom he had a particular affection. (Among his own compositions, which included orchestra works and operas, was a piece written in memory of Shostakovich.) He continued to play the piano throughout his career, often conducting concertos from the keyboard (very much an Old World art), and accompanied such masters as Heifetz, Schnabel, and Menuhin. His son Peter is also a conductor and instrumentalist.   J.G.

Son of Bruno S. and Gertrude (Seger) S., pianist. Married: (1) Eleanor Warren, cellist, 1943 (div.); (2) Jean Letcher (div.); (3) Diane Hartman (div.); (4) Jane Seymour, cellist, 1970 (div.); (5) Janis Tomfohrde 1973. Son: 1st marriage—Peter, conductor and clarinetist, b. 1944. Emigrated to England 1939; naturalized British citizen 1946. Educ: local schs. and piano teachers in Prague; grad. State Conservatory, Prague 1931; grad. German Acad. Music, Prague 1931. Piano debut, Prague 1930; Asst. Conductor and Coach, German Opera, Prague 1934–38; conducting debut, Prague 1938; pianist, London Czech Trio 1939–42; Principal Conductor, Strand Theatre, London 1941–43 and Royal Carl Rosa Opera Co., London 1943–45; Principal Guest Conductor, Sadler's Wells Opera Co., London and tour of Germany 1945–47; Guest Conductor, Australian Broadcasting Comm., and Principal Guest Conductor, Glyndebourne Opera, First Edinburgh Festival; Principal Conductor, Scottish Natl. Orch. 1946–52; Founder, Natl. Youth Orch. of Great Britain ca. 1950; Principal Conductor, Victoria Symphony Orch., Melbourne 1954–56; Music Dir., Toronto Symphony Orch. 1956–65; Conductor and Faculty Music Dir., Aspen Music Festival, Colo. 1958–65; Founder and Music Dir., Natl. Youth Orch. of Canada 1960; NYC piano debut with Beaux Arts Quartet 1963; Music Dir. and Principal Conductor, St. Louis Symphony Orch. 1968–75; Music. Dir. and Conductor, Miss. River Festival, St. Louis Symphony summer series 1969–75; Principal Conductor, Intl. Festival of Youth Orchs., Switzerland 1970–71; Music Advisor and Principal Guest Conductor, Cincinnati Symphony Orch. 1978–80. Lectr., Washington Univ., St. Louis, and Univ. So. Ill., Edwardsville, ca. 1968–75; Dir., American Inst. Orchestral Conducting. Hons: Hum. D., Univ. Southern Illinois 1969; D.F.A., Washington Univ. 1975. Guest Conductor with NYC Opera since 1941, Berlin Philharmonic, Concertgebouw Orch. of Amsterdam, Israel Philharmonic, Cleveland Orch., Philadelphia Orch., and many others. Conductor on more than 200 recordings with London Symphony Orch., Toronto Symphony, St. Louis Symphony Orch., many others. *Selected recordings:* Bartok, Bluebeard's Castle; Dvořák, Concerto for violincello, Op. 104; Dvořák, Concerto for piano; Handel, Messiah; Holst, Planets; Liszt, Hungarian Fantasia for piano and orch.; Mahler, Das Lied von der Erde; Mozart, Concertos No. 20 and 24 for piano; Rachmaninoff, Concerto No. 3 for piano; Rachmaninoff, Rhapsody on Theme of Paganini; Sibelius, Violin Concerto; Smetana, Má Vlast; Strauss, Also sprach Zarathustra; Tchaikovsky, Concerto No. 2 for piano; Wolf, Italian Serenade; works of Falla, Prokofiev, Ravel, and others. *Compositions:* works for orch., string quartet, piano, violin, tympani, other instruments; songs, cantatas; operas; film scores; memorial work for Dmitri Shostakovich. *Further reading:* International Gallery of Conductors by Donald Brook, 1951.

JAMES (ARLINGTON) WRIGHT
Poet, translator, and teacher
Born Martin's Ferry, Ohio, U.S.A., December 13th, 1927
Died Bronx, New York City, U.S.A., March 25th, 1980

James Wright was one of America's most influential poets in the late 1960s and 1970s. Originally a writer of ironic and meticulously crafted "academic" poetry made popular by the New Criticism, Wright became an innovator, recognized for originality of style, for great compassion, for honest expression of emotion and the courage to deal with it, and for the ability to transform mundane experience into images of great beauty that evoke powerful feelings.

Courtesy Jill Krementz

James Wright came from a working-class background. His home, Martin's Ferry, Ohio, is not unlike a score of other grim, industrial towns crowded along the Ohio River, and his father, who never received an education beyond the eighth grade, worked there fifty years for the Hazel-Atlas Glass Company. In high school Wright's facility with language earned praise from his teachers and, following a two-year peacetime stint in the Army, he enrolled at Kenyon College, supported by the G.I. Bill. At Kenyon he studied under John Crowe Ransom, the celebrated dean of "academic" poetry and the New Criticism. An exceptional student, Wright won a Fulbright scholarship for study at the University of Vienna where he began to read George Trakl. Trakl's expressionistic poetry, so different from Ransom's strict formalism, used imagery drawn from the unconscious; Wright later acknowledged Trakl's influence on his poetry.

Returning to the States in 1954, Wright enrolled in the graduate program at the University of Washington where Theodore Roethke, a leading American formalist poet in the 1950s, became his mentor. The work of both Roethke and Ransom epitomized the "well-made poem," a form which stressed careful craftsmanship, ambiguity, nuance, and tone. Indeed, Wright's early poetry, like that of his contemporaries—Donald Hall, Galway Kinnell, W.S. Merwin, and Lewis Simpson—was shaped by this tradition; and as with all of these poets, Wright found the form restrictive and departed from it in the early 1960s.

Wright's first two collections—*The Green Wall* (1957, winner of the prestigious Yale Series of Younger Poets Award) and *Saint Judas* (1959)—were carefully constructed out of meter and rhyme, made use of precise diction, and were stated in quiet, even tones. These competently executed poems contained little that was new or distinctive. However, an original voice occasionally broke through, a voice encouraged by the poems of Trakl, Edwin Arlington Robinson, and Robert Frost (poets who were relatively ignored and somewhat unfashionable during the reign of New Criticism) and grounded in Wright's home area, the Ohio River valley. "A Note Left in Jimmy Leonard's Shack" shows how a keenly-observed sense of place can compensate for the monotony of a fixed form:

Near the dry river's water-marks we found
Your brother Minnegan
Flopped like a fish against the muddy ground.
Beany, the kid whose yellow hair turns green,
Told me to find you, even in the rain,
And tell you he was drowned.

Having returned to the midwest from Washington, Wright's style began to change radically. During these so-called "Minnesota years" (when Wright taught alternately at the University of Minnesota and Macalester College) he became close friends with the poet Robert Bly, who encouraged him to read the South American poets Pablo Neruda and César Vallejo. (Bly and Wright later translated Neruda, Vallejo, and Georg Trakl.) Publication of *The Branch Will Not Break* in 1963 established Wright as a unique voice in American poetry and revealed his development of the "subjective image," a form described by poet-critic Stephen Stepanchev as that in which "the image . . . arises from the unconscious of the past and generates powerful emotions beyond the reach of logic or analysis."

Composed in free verse, the poems of this collection frequently mix objective and subjective imagery, and develop in a seemingly casual manner:

> To my right,
> In a field of sunlight between two pines,
> The droppings of last year's horses
> Blaze up into golden stones.
> I lean back, as the evening darkens and comes on.
> A chicken hawk floats over, looking for home.
> I have wasted my life.
> —from "Lying in a Hammock at William Duffy's Farm in Pine
> Island, Minnesota."

A haunting sadness, verging on despair, pervades many of the poems. In "Having Lost My Sons, I Confront the Wreckage of the Moon: Christmas, 1960," which alludes to the breakup of Wright's marriage when his first wife left Minnesota with his two sons, he concludes:

> Dead riches, dead hands, the moon
> Darkens,
> And I am lost in the beautiful white ruins
> Of America.

But sometimes a joyousness breaks through, as in "The Blessing" in which he speaks of playing with two ponies at twilight:

> Suddenly I realize
> That if I stepped out of my body I would break
> Into blossom.

Occasionally both moods are expressed in the same poem, as in one of his most famous poems, "Autumn Begins in Martin's Ferry, Ohio," with its poignant final image of the high school football players:

> Therefore
> Their sons grow suicidally beautiful
> At the beginning of October
> And gallop terribly against each other's bodies.

The Branch Will Not Break also contains several political poems, rare in American poetry, but common to the work of Neruda and other foreign poets who had influenced Wright. The success of such pieces as "Two Poems About President Hardin," "Eisenhower's Visit to Franco (1959)" and "In Memory of a Spanish Poet" depends on the use of the subjective image which prevents them from becoming didactic, polemical or propagandistic.

Wright's fourth book, *Shall We Gather at the River,* was published in 1968. Although this book contains many fine poems, it is not as strong a collection as its predecessor, and the poet is more occupied with inward concerns. Many poems are connected with places in Ohio, Minnesota, and North Dakota, but these locations seem to exist in name only and the imagery fails to convey a "sense" of place. Personal problems, such as drinking, poverty, and loneliness, make up the subjects of poems like "Inscription in the Tank" and "In Terror of Hospital Bills." The mood of darkness can be seen in "The River Down Home:"

Outside my window, now, Minneapolis
Drowns, dark.
It is dark.
I have no life.

One poem that does convey a strong sense of place and striking imagery is "In Response to a Rumor That the Oldest Whorehouse in Wheeling, West Virginia, Has Been Condemned." Perhaps the finest poem in the book is "Outside Fargo, North Dakota." Here Wright communicates both the outer and inner worlds of his experience:

Beyond town, three heavy white horses
Wade all the way to their shoulders
In a silo shadow.

Collected Poems, for which Wright won the Pulitzer Prize, appeared in 1971. This volume contains all of his previously published books—although some poems from *The Green Wall* are omitted—many of Wright's published translations, and a final section containing thirty-one "New Poems." Although most of the new poems were inspired by Wright's native region, there was a turning away from pure subjectivity to a more open, objective image. As such, they seem at times very much like prose. Wright's agony—deeper than in his earlier work—is expressed in some of these poems. Occasionally his anguish boils over in a torrent of self denigration and despair at life's futility. At his worst, Wright wallows in the pain and then his poetry seems slack and self indulgent.

The title of Wright's next book, *Two Citizens* (1973) refers to the poet and his second wife. Most of the poems are written from the point of view of an American traveling in Europe, and many are nostalgic, centered on memories of the poet's youth in Ohio. As Wright said of the trip, "I discovered America there." Although *Two Citizens* lacks the energy of Wright's previous books, there are some strong poems which make the collection worthwhile. The poems commemorating the death of Charles Coffin, one of Wright's professors at Kenyon, are deeply moving. "Voices Between Waking and Sleeping in the Mountains" is a powerful love poem. *To a Blossoming Pear Tree* (1977), Wright's last book, contained fifteen prose poems (previously published as *Movements of the Italian Summer,* 1976) and numerous other pieces which were written in his free-form style. The collection received a mixed reaction from critics, however, and Hugh Kenner, in a *New York Times* review, called the book "unexpectedly weak."

Critic Alfred Kazin described Wright's death in a Bronx hospital as "slow strangulation by throat cancer." He was 52 and had been teaching since 1966 at Hunter College in New York City. Wright once said of his poetry: "I have written about the things I am deeply concerned with . . . I try and speak of the beauty and again of the ugliness in the lives of the poor and neglected."   E.T./R.T.

Son of a factory worker. Married: (1) Liberty Kardulis; (2) Edith
Anne Runk 1967. Children: 1st marriage—Franz Paul, Marshall John.
Educ: grad. Shreve High Sch. 1946; Kenyon Coll., Gambier, Ohio,
B.A. 1952; Univ. of Vienna (Fulbright Scholarship) 1952–53; Univ. of
Wash., Seattle, M.A. 1954, Ph.D. 1959. Mil. Service: U.S Army
1946–48. Teacher of English: Univ. of Minn., Minneapolis 1957–63;
Macalester Coll., St. Paul, Minn. 1963–65; Hunter Coll., N.Y.C.
since 1966. Member, American Acad. of Arts and Letters 1974. Hons:
Eunice Tietjens Memorial Prize 1955; Yale Series of Younger Poets
award 1957; Kenyon Review Fellowship 1958; Natl. Inst. of Arts and
Letters grant 1959; Robert Frost Prize 1962; Guggenheim Fellowship
1964, 1978; Oscar Blumenthal Prize 1968; Brandeis Univ. Creative
Arts award 1970; Acad. of American Poets Fellowship 1971; Melville
Cane award 1972; Pulitzer Prize 1972. *Books: Poetry*—The Green
Wall, 1957; Saint Judas, 1959; (with Robert Bly and William Duffy)
The Lion's Tail and Eyes: Poems Written Out of Laziness and Silence,
1962; The Branch Will Not Break, 1963; Shall We Gather at the
River?, 1968; Collected Poems, 1971; Salt Mines and Such, 1971; Two
Citizens, 1974; Moments of the Italian Summer, 1976; Old Book-
sellers and Other Poems, 1976; To a Blossoming Pear Tree, 1977.
Translations—(with Robert Bly) Twenty Poems of Georg Trakl, 1961;
(with Robert Bly and John Knoepfle) Twenty Poems of Cesar Vallejo,
1962; The Rider on the White Horse (by Theodor Storm), 1964; (with
Robert Bly) Twenty Poems of Pablo Neruda, 1968; (also ed.) Poems
(by Herman Hesse), 1970; (with Robert Bly and John Knoepfle)
Neruda and Vallejo: Selected Poems, 1971; Wandering: Notes and
Sketches (by Herman Hesse), 1972. *Recordings:* (with others) Today's
Poets 3; The Poetry and Voice of James Wright, 1977.
Further reading: Critical study by Robert Coles, American Poetry
Review, 1974.

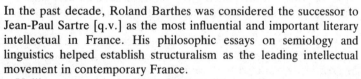

ROLAND (GÉRARD) BARTHES
Writer and essayist
Born Cherbourg, Manche, France, November 12th, 1915
Died Paris, France, March 26th, 1980

Courtesy Thomas Victor

In the past decade, Roland Barthes was considered the successor to
Jean-Paul Sartre [q.v.] as the most influential and important literary
intellectual in France. His philosophic essays on semiology and
linguistics helped establish structuralism as the leading intellectual
movement in contemporary France.

Unlike many critical writers, Barthes did not adhere to a particular
school or theoretical doctrine; instead, he gleaned ideas from one
system after another, and used them to illuminate the literary and
cultural phenomena of his time. To relate the evolution of prose styles
to socio-economic conditions, he appropriated the language of
Hegelian Marxism and Sartrean existentialism. To unmask the "mythologies"—or hidden assumptions—behind the artifacts of popular
culture, Barthes synthesized concepts from the neo-Marxist critique of
ideology (an analysis of the beliefs which shape the outlook of a
society's dominant classes); he also used ideas from semiology (the
study of signs and symbols in society), and from structuralism (an
interpretation of the myths generated by a society's passage from a

state of nature to a state of culture). Barthes created from these disparate ideas a constant stream of insights, sometimes forgettable, more often thought-provoking and felicitous.

Despite his reputation, Barthes was unable to secure a permanent teaching post until he was in his mid-40s; a tubercular condition had prevented him from receiving the French equivalent of a doctorate. It also prevented him from serving in the armed forces or the Resistance movement during the Second World War alongside others of his generation. As if to emphasize his position as a social outsider, Barthes was left-handed, homosexual, and of Protestant birth in a predominantly Catholic nation. Fatherless from infancy, he regretted not having experienced a typical Freudian childhood; he once wrote of himself that "he felt more than excluded: *detached:* forever assigned the place of the *witness,* whose discourse can only be, of course, subject to codes of detachment; either narrative, or explicative, or challenging, or ironic: never *lyrical,* never homogeneous with the pathos outside of which he must seek his place."

Barthes was born to a middle-class family in Cherbourg in 1915. A year later, his father, a naval officer, was killed in battle during the First World War; the family moved to the home of Roland's paternal grandparents in Bayonne, where his mother went to work as a bookbinder to support her two sons. Of his childhood, Barthes wrote: "Not an unhappy youth, thanks to the affection which surrounded me, but an awkward one, because of its solitude and material constraint." Despite financial insecurity, the home was an artistic one; Barthes could play the piano and write music before he knew how to read.

When the family moved to Paris in 1924, Barthes entered the Lycée Montaigne, then the Lycée Louis-le-Grand, and distinguished himself as a student of literature and philosophy. An attack of pulmonary tuberculosis prevented him from attending the École normale supérieure to study for the *agrégation* degree; instead, he read French literature and the classics at the Sorbonne, where he founded a dramatic group, the Groupe de Théâtre Antique. In 1939, having earned a degree in classical letters and been declared exempt from military service, he embarked on a teaching career, later obtaining an advanced degree in Greek tragedy. He spent the war years in hospitals and sanatoria, recovering from a second attack of tuberculosis and studying grammar and philology. After 1948 he alternated between teaching, research in sociology and lexicology, and writing.

Le Degré zéro de l'écriture (Writing Degree Zero), a collection of essays published in 1953, immediately established its author as France's foremost critic of modernist literature. Expanding on the Marxist views profered by Sartre, Barthes attributed the demise of traditional French realism to the breakdown of the bourgeois values to which it gave expression. Classic French literary style, he contended, was a product of the ascendancy of bourgeois ideals in 17th-century society; the dissolution of that society in class antagonism was aptly and necessarily reflected in the proliferation of personal writing styles and experimental fictions. He applauded such "new novelists" as Nathalie Sarraute and Alain Robbe-Grillet for writing in a colorless "degree zero" or "transparent" style that rendered events in pure and objective terms, conveying neither ideological judgment nor authorial bias, and avoiding the artifices of the so-called realists.

Similarly, he required of literary criticism that it abstain from its

usual judgments on the value of a literary work and the intentions of
the author and address itself instead to an analysis of the text as a sign
system, a network of symbols whose conjoined, interlocking associations form the meaning of the work as a whole. His application of this
technique to a Balzac novella (in *S/Z*, 1970) and, in a Freudian mode,
to the plays of Racine *(Sur Racine,* 1965), drew an outraged response
from more traditional scholars such as Raymond Picard of the
Sorbonne, who accused Barthes of gratuitously inventing pseudo-
scientific, dogmatic theories.

Barthes derived the same "thrill of meaning," the sudden, illuminating perception of underlying connections, from his interpretations of the "extralinguistic languages" employed in such
phenomena of mass culture as the sport of tag wrestling, the faces of
film stars, children's toys, advice to the lovelorn columns, and the
rhetoric of the Rev. Billy Graham. Each such phenomenon constituted a set of symbolic representations called "signifiers," which
Barthes deciphered as one does a dream, revealing the "signified"
meanings contained therein, and explicating the beliefs and illusions
of the society that created them. These "brilliant essay-epiphanies,"
as critic Susan Sontag called them, were collected in *Mythologies*
(1957). In the book's final section, "Myth Today," Barthes argued
that advanced technological societies engulf their citizens in an
unremitting flow of media-generated images which disguise bourgeois
values as universal truths. The staleness and oppressiveness of
bourgeois thinking, and of popular opinion in general, was abhorrent
to him; he invented a term for it, *la doxa,* and made it the focus of a
lifelong rebellion.

For many years Barthes considered himself a leftist; in 1956 he and
Edgar Morin founded *Arguments,* the only Marxist journal in France
that refused to follow—in fact, vehemently repudiated—orthodox
Soviet doctrine during the Cold War years. *Arguments* folded in 1962.
Gradually Barthes dissociated himself from political commitment,
having recognized that the left had a *doxa* of its own.

In 1960, Barthes joined the faculty of the École pratique des Hautes
Études in Paris; from 1962 to 1976, he was Director of Studies of the
school's sixth section. During these years he published a textbook,
Éléments de Sémiologie; Système de la Mode, an analysis of the visual
and verbal language of fashion magazines; *L'Empire des signes,* on
Japan; *Sade/Fourier/Loyola* and *Le Plaisir du texte,* two discussions of
the pleasures and passions to be found in the acts of writing and
reading; and several collections of critical essays. His prose style was
rich with intelligence, wit, and fluid imagination though at times it
degenerated into baroque abstractions. Often he chose to construct
his writings as a series of short fragments, well suited to the self-
contained, aphoristic character of his insights.

Since 1976, when he became Professor of Literary Semiology at the
Collège de France, Barthes published another five books, including
Roland Barthes by Roland Barthes, a work of imaginative autobiography, and *Fragments d'un discours amoureux (A Lover's Discourse),* a
meditation on a failed love affair that sold 60,000 copies in France
within a few months of publication. In 1979 he announced his
intention to write a novel. His influence, in the meantime, had spread
to England and the United States, where semiology and structuralism
were enjoying the beginnings of a vogue.

On February 25th, Barthes was struck by a van as he was crossing a Paris street. He died of his injuries a month later. Hill and Wang, the U.S. publisher of his works in English translation, will posthumously issue four more volumes of his writings.   E.T./J.P.

Son of Louis B., naval officer, and Henriette (Binger) B., bookbinder. Unmarried. Rejected Protestant religion. Educ.: elementary sch., Lycée de Bayonne 1916–24; Lycée Montaigne, Paris 1924–30; Lycée Louis–le–Grand, Paris, baccalaureates 1933, 1934; Univ. Paris (Sorbonne), license in classical letters 1939, diplômé d'études supérieures in Greek tragedy 1941, license in grammar and philology 1943. Exempted from mil. service on grounds of ill health. Reader at Debreczen, Hungary 1937; Prof. of Lit. and rectoral delegate, third and fourth forms, Lycée de Biarritz 1939–40; Prof. and rectoral delegate, Lycées Voltaire and Carnot, Paris 1940–41; Asst. Librarian, then Prof., Institut français, Bucharest 1948–49; Reader, Univ. of Bucharest 1948–49; Reader, Univ. Alexandria 1949–50; with Instruction Branch, Direction général des affaires culturelles, Ministry of Foreign Affairs, Paris 1950–52; Officer of Instruction and researcher in lexicography 1952–54 and Research Attaché in Sociology 1955–59, Centre Natl. de la recherche scientifique, Paris; Chmn. 1960–62 and Dir. of Studies and Prof. of the sociology of signs, symbols, and collective representations 1962–76, VI sect., Social and Econ. Sciences, École pratique des hautes études, Paris; Visiting Prof., John Hopkins Univ., Baltimore 1967–68; Prof. of Literary Semiology, Collège de France, Paris 1976–80. Founder, Groupe de Théâtre Antique, Univ. Paris ca. 1936; Co-founder, Théâtre populaire (jrnl.) 1953; Co-founder, Arguments (neo-Marxist jrnl.) 1956. Member of Jury, Prix Medicis since 1973. Hons.: Chevalier des Palmes académiques; elected member of Collège de France 1975. *Author:* Le Degré zéro de l'écriture, 1953 (trans. as Writing Degree Zero, 1967); Michelet par lui-même, 1954; Mythologies, 1957 (trans. as Mythologies, 1972); Sur Racine, 1963 (trans. as On Racine, 1964); Essais Critiques, 1964 (trans. as Critical Essays, 1972); La Tour Eiffel, 1964 (trans. as the Eiffel Tower, 1978); Eléments de sémiologies, 1965 (trans. as Elements of Semiology, 1967); Critique et Verite, 1966; Système de la mode, 1967; L'Empire des signes, 1970; S/Z, 1970 (trans. as S/Z, 1975); Sade/Fourier/Loyola, 1971 (trans. as Sade/Fourier/Loyola, 1976); Nouveaux Essais Critiques, 1972 (trans. as New Critical Essays, 1980); Le Plaisir du texte, 1973 (trans. as The Pleasure of the Text, 1976); Erte, 1975; Roland Barthes par Roland Barthes, 1975 (trans. as Roland Barthes by Roland Barthes, 1977); Et la Chine?, 1976; Fragments d'un discours amoreux, 1977 (trans. as A Lover's Discourse, 1978); Image/Music/Text, 1978; A Barthes Reader, 1980; La Claire Chambre, 1980. *Major Articles:* "Criticism as Language," in Times Lit. Supplement, Sept. 27, 1963; "Science versus Literature," in Times Lit. Supplement, Sept. 28, 1967; "Structuralist activity: diseases of costume," in Partisan Review, Winter 1967; "To Write: An Intransitive Verb?," in The Languages of Criticism and the Sciences of Man (ed. by R. Macksey and E. Donata), 1970. Frequent contributor to Combat, Esprit, Lettres Nouvelles, France Observateur, Tel Quel, Communications, La Quinzaine litteraire, others. Interviews: L'Express, May 31, 1970; Les Lettres Françaises, Feb. 9, 1972; Gulliver, March 1973; Le Figaro, Sept. 27, 1974.
Further reading: Nouvelle critique ou nouvelle imposture by Raymond Picard, 1965; Preface to the American ed. of Writing Degree Zero by Susan Sontag, 1968; Structuralist Poetics by Jonathan Culler, 1975; Roland Barthes: A Conservative Estimate by Philip Thody, 1977; Under the Sign of Saturn by Susan Sontag, 1980.

DICK HAYMES
Big Band singer; actor and performer
Born Buenos Aires, Argentina, September 13th, 1916
Died Los Angeles, California, U.S.A., March 28th, 1980

Dick Haymes was born in Buenos Aires, the son of a cattle rancher of Scottish descent. When his parents separated, Haymes and his brother were taken to New York by their mother, singer-actress Marguerite Wilson. Her career took them on trips to many parts of the world. Haymes received his early education in Lausanne, Switzerland, and when the family settled in Connecticut he continued his education in nearby New York. At the age of 15 he started to sing with a New Jersey amateur band. He went on to Peekskill Military Academy, New York, and then attended Loyola University in Montreal. An "all-rounder," Haymes was fluent in French and Spanish, held a pilot's license, was an expert fencer, a champion swimmer, and a deep-sea fishing guide.

From the age of 17 to 21, he lived in Hollywood, writing songs and appearing as a bit-player in westerns. In 1938, Haymes was hired to sing in Harry James' band. He also sang with the bands of Carl Hoff, Freddie Morton, and Orrin Tucker. In 1942, he worked at "La Martinique," a New York nightclub, and this led to an appearance in the film *DuBarry Was A Lady* with Benny Goodman's band the following year.

The increasingly popular Dick Haymes, often referred to as "Mr. Charm," appeared as a soloist with various Big Bands, including those of Tommy Dorsey and Bunny Berrigan. He succeeded Frank Sinatra, to whom he was frequently compared, in both the Dorsey and Harry James bands, and he performed on stage at New York's Paramount Theater. He also starred in his own nationally-syndicated radio show, *Here's To Romance*.

In the forties and early fifties, at the height of his career, Haymes made 35 movies, appearing with Betty Grable in *Diamond Horseshoe*, with Jeanne Craig in *State Fair* (both 1945), and with Ava Gardner in *One Touch of Venus* in 1948. His hit songs, which earned him a total of 9 Gold Records, included: *It Might As Well Be Spring, It Had To Be You, Little White Lies, You'll Never Know*, and *It's A Grand Night For Singing*. His high baritone voice, variously described as "creamy," "light," and "warm," suited well his often-sentimental songs.

In 1953, ending his third marriage—to Nora Eddington, a former wife of Errol Flynn—Haymes joined his wife-to-be, Rita Hayworth, who was filming *Miss Sadie Thompson* in Hawaii. As an Argentinian, Haymes had earlier claimed exemption from the U.S. military draft, and when he tried to re-enter the American mainland from Hawaii, which still had 'U.S. territory' status, he was ordered to be deported on the grounds that aliens who had claimed draft exemption and who had left the U.S.A. could be barred from returning. Haymes successfully appealed a federal court ruling that Hawaii was not a foreign country. Miss Hayworth, who had vowed to "stick by him to the end," divorced him shortly thereafter.

In the late fifties, Haymes' career declined and he suffered long bouts of alcoholism. By 1960, with alimony and tax claims against him, and debts to a studio and a record company, he was forced into bankruptcy. In 1963, Haymes married his seventh wife, an English model, and in the same year he began to rebuild his career, appearing in nightclubs in England, Ireland, South Africa and Australia. He became an Irish citizen in 1965.

His last album, *Dick Haymes—Then and Now* was recorded by the English Mercury label in 1971. He was seen on television in the U.S. on the *David Frost Show,* the *Tennessee Ernie Ford Show,* and on the television special, *Fabulous Forties.* In 1973 he appeared in Las Vegas nightclubs, and from then until his death he combined concert dates with acting parts on television. He died of lung cancer in Los Angeles at the age of 61.   R.T.

Born Richard Benjamin Haymes. Son of Benjamin H., cattle rancher, and Marguerite Wilson H., singer. Married: (1) Edith Harper 1939 (marriage annulled 1939); (2) Joanne Marshal Dru, actress, 1941 (div. 1949); (3) Nora Eddington 1949 (div. 1953); (4) Rita Hayworth, actress, 1953 (div. 1955); (5) Fran Makris, singer, 1956 (div. 1957); (6) Fran Jeffries 1957 (div. 1962); (7) Wendy Smith, model, 1963. Children: 2nd marriage—Richard Jr., b. 1942, singer; Helen, b. 1944; Barbara, b. 1947; 6th marriage—Stephanie, b. 1959; 7th marriage— Sean, b. 1966; Samantha, b. 1969. Brought to U.S.A. 1918; later naturalized. Became Irish citizen 1965. Educ: privately in Lausanne, Switzerland; Irving Prep. School, N.Y.C.; Loyola Univ., Montreal. Claimed exemption from mil. service. Popular singer of Big Band era, 1943–53; radio announcer; appeared in 35 movies, 1944–51; television and nightclub performer, 1970–80. Member, Actors' Equity. *Recordings*—It Might As Well Be Spring, It Had To Be You, Little White Lies, You'll Never Know, It's A Grand Night For Singing, others. *Films*—Command Performance, 1931; Du Barry Was A Lady, 1943; Hey Rookie, 1944; Irish Eyes Are Smiling, 1944; Four Jills In a Jeep, 1944; State Fair, 1945; Diamond Horseshoe, 1945; Do You Love Me?, 1946; Carnival in Costa Rica, 1947; The Shocking Miss Pilgrim, 1947; Up In Central Park, 1948; St. Benny The Dip, 1951; One Touch of Venus, 1950; All Ashore, 1953; Cruisin' Down the River, 1953.

(ANNUNZIO PAOLO) MANTOVANI
Conductor
Born Venice, Italy, November 15th, 1905
Died Tunbridge Wells, Kent, England, March 29th, 1980

Annunzio Paolo Mantovani—known simply as Mantovani—was a conductor whose lush, string-filled orchestrations of "easy listening" pieces won him a vast audience. His high ratio of strings in an orchestra (usually three to one)—encouraging such descriptions as cascading violins, "tumbling strings," and "a Niagara Falls of fiddles"—created the highly popular "Mantovani sound" that made him one of the best-selling recording artists and successful concert attractions of the past 30 years.

Mantovani was born Annunzio Paolo in Venice (he took his mother's maiden name when he began his performing career at 16), the son of Benedetto Paolo, concertmaster under Toscanini with La Scala Opera orchestra in Milan. When Mantovani was four, his father took the family to London, where La Scala had an engagement at Covent Garden. England became their home from then on. Although it was hoped by the family that Mantovani would become an engineer, and he was sent back to Italy for study, he was far more interested in music. His father had given him his early training on the violin, and as a teen-ager he began playing the instrument in a restaurant in Birmingham, England, and in London concert halls. Soon he was leading the salon orchestra of the Hotel Metropole in London and in 1927 began recording for the British Broadcasting Company. In 1932 he formed the Tipica Orchestra and toured the British Isles. He married in 1934 and became a naturalized British subject a year later. During the 1940s he had a successful career playing romantic "mood music" and was a well-known figure in light entertainment. Mantovani was musical director of several stage shows, including Noel Coward's "Sigh No More" in 1945.

In 1951 his hit recording of "Charmaine" dramatically changed his career. London Records, the American arm of the English Decca label, asked Mantovani to record an LP of waltzes. "London Records didn't specify that the waltzes should be played with strings," he recalled. "But I had always had an ambition to have an orchestra with plenty of strings. I wondered what I could do to make an impression in America when they have the finest orchestras over there. So I said, 'You must give me a big string section.' . . . I wanted to get a classic sound with plenty of violas and cellos . . . . I wanted an effect of an overlapping sound, as though we were playing in a cathedral."

Mantovani got his strings and "Charmaine" caught the attention of a Cleveland disc jockey who helped make it a hit. Issued as a single, the record quickly sold over a million copies, and became his "signature" song. After that his recordings and personal concert appearances were phenomenally popular. He was the first musician to sell over a million stereophonic records in the US, and a dozen of his albums are Golden Records (250,000 copies sold). His public was enthusiastic—on a two-month tour of the states in 1963 all but two of 54 concerts were sold out in advance—and Mantovani felt it was because "our kind of music . . . provides melodies you can hum." He once said in the 1960s, "Perhaps 25 percent of the people like the classics and about 25 percent like the Beatles. I aim to please the 50 percent in the middle."

Mantovani had been ill for several years and died in a nursing home in Tunbridge Wells, Kent, near London.   s.p.

Born Annunzio Paolo (took mother's maiden name, Mantovani 1921). Son of Benedetto P., violinist. Married Winifred Kathleen 1934 (d. 1971). Children: Kenneth Paul, electrical engineer; Paula Irene. Brought to England 1909. Naturalized British 1935. Educ: Trinity Coll. Music, London. Violinist, conductor, arranger. Orch. leader, Hotel Metropole, London; recorded for BBC 1927; formed Orch. Tipica 1932. *Recordings:* (Mantovani Orchestra)—Waltzes of Irving Berlin, 1957; An Album of Ballet Melodies, 1957; Favorite Melodies from Opera, 1957; An Album of Christmas Music, 1958; Mantovani Plays the World's Favorite Love Songs, 1958; Film Encores, 1958; Candlelight, 1958; Continental Encores, 1959; Four Pastoral Moods, 1959; Mantovani Magic, 1959; Concert Encores, No. 1, 1959; World's Favorite Love Songs, No. 1, 1959; Music by Jerome Kern, Cole Porter, Frederic Loew, 1959; Concert Encores, 1959; Film Encores, No. 2, 1959; The Best of Sigmund Romberg, 1960; American Scene, 1960; More Mantovani Film Encores, 1960; Concert Encores, 1960; Gems Forever, 1960; Mantovani Concert Spectacular, 1961; Songs to Remember, 1961; Operettic Memories, 1961; "Exodus" and Other

Themes, 1961; Italia Mia, 1961; Broadway Encores, 1962; Theatre-
land Encores, 1962; Four Fabulous Film Themes, 1962; Songs of
Praise, 1962; Great Films–Great Themes, 1962; Latin Rendezvous,
1963; A Song For Christmas, 1964; The Twelve Days of Christmas,
1964; Mantovani/Manhattan, 1964; The Great Film Hits (vol. 5),
1964; Folk Songs Around the World, 1964; Incomparable Mantovani,
1965; Ole Mantovani, 1965; Peyton Place, 1965; Mantovani Magic,
1965; Mr. Music . . . Mantovani, 1966; Mantovani's Golden Hits,
1967; Mantovani Sound, 1967; Old and New Fangled Tangos, 1967;
Mantovani/Hollywood, 1967; Mantovani Touch, 1968; Mantovani
Sampler, 1968; World of Mantovani, Vol. 2, 1969; Mantovani Scene,
1969; . . . Memories, 1969; Gypsy!, 1970; Mantovani Today, 1970;
Mantovani's Magic Touch, 1971; Mantovani Presents His Concert
Successes, 1971; From Mantovani With Love, 1971; To Lovers
Everywhere, 1972; An Evening With Mantovani, 1973; Mantovani
Plays All-Time Romantic Hits, 1975; Musical Moments with Man-
tovani, 1975; More Mantovani Golden Hits, 1976; The Greatest Gift
is Love, 1976; American Encores, 1977; Mantovani Favorites, 1977;
Mantovani in Concert, 1978; Faraway Places, 1978; Mantovani in
Vienna, 1978; For Lovers Everywhere, 1978; Theater Favorites, 1980;
Film Favorites, 1980. *Collections*—Hail Variety!, (Mantovani New
Music), 1960; Kingsize Sound of Hifi/Phase 4 Stereo, (Mantovani &
Cast), 1966; others.

TON DUC THANG
Communist leader; President of the Socialist Republic of Vietnam
Born Long Xuyen Province, Vietnam, August 20th, 1888
Died Hanoi, Vietnam, March 30th, 1980

At the time of his death the 91 year old Ton Duc Thang was the
world's oldest communist head of state. He was involved in Vietnamese independence movements from a very young age, and held
several high positions in the revolutionary movement which brought a
communist government to power in North Vietnam in 1954 and which
overthrew the government of South Vietnam in 1975. Ton assumed
the largely ceremonial office of President in 1969 following the death
of Ho Chi Minh, and although inactive in recent years because of ill-
health, as the country's figurehead he helped to stabilize the communist regime after South Vietnam's collapse.

Ton, born in Long Xuyen Province in the Mekong Delta in 1888,
was educated at a local French school and at Saigon's French high
school where he graduated in 1910. After two years as a schoolteacher
he had to flee Vietnam because of his anti-colonial activities. He went
into hiding in France and subsequently enlisted in the French Navy. In
1919 with a French sailor Andre Marty, Ton organized a mutiny on
the French heavy cruiser Waldeck-Rousseau on the Black Sea, to
protest the intervention of Western powers in the Russian Civil War.
Their attempt to turn the warship over to the Bolsheviks was crushed
and Ton was dishonorably discharged. Ton's action was one of the
earliest illustrations of how Vietnamese sympathy to communist ideas
had begun to take hold.

After working in an automobile factory in Paris, Ton returned in
1920 to Saigon. Five years later he joined the Vietnam Revolutionary

Youth Society founded by Ho Chi Minh, and instigated strikes against French intervention in revolutionary China. Ton was arrested by the French Colonial authorities in 1929 and sentenced to 20 years hard labor. The following year while imprisoned on an island off the coast of South Vietnam, he joined the Communist Party of Indochina. Ton regained his freedom 16 years later in 1945 when a Viet Minh uprising swept out the Wartime French administration (under Japanese command) and placed Ho Chi Minh's party in power in the north.

Ton became President of the Permanent Committee of the new government's National Assembly, a position which gave him considerable power. In 1946, in his new role of President of the National Popular Front Association (Lien Viet), he became leader of French resistance in Indochina. After the Geneva Conference of 1954, which effectively divided Vietnam into two countries—a Communist-dominated North and a U.S.-supported South—Ho Chi Minh's Lien Viet forces were reorganized under the name Mat-Tran To-Quoc (Fatherland Front) and Ton became its president. The following year the Fatherland Front also assumed the responsibilities of the Viet Minh (League for Independence). Under Ton the Front hoped to persuade South Vietnam to join the "Fatherland" and form a single Communist country.

In 1960 Ton was appointed Vice President of the Democratic Republic of Vietnam (North Vietnam); he became President nine years later when Ho Chi Minh died. Throughout the 1960s Ton organized the DRV's support of the Viet Cong (pro-communist forces in the South) which led to U.S. intervention and the Vietnam War of 1965–75. When the South Vietnamese government finally collapsed in 1975 it was replaced by a communist-dominated regime. The following year the two Vietnams were reunited and Ton was elected the first president of the Socialist Republic of Vietnam.

Ton Duc Thang was buried in an elaborate ceremony; according to the official Hanoi radio "hundreds of thousands of mourners lined the roadways" from Hanoi to the national cemetery five miles away. R.T.

Educ: French high sch., Saigon, grad. 1910. Mil. Service: French Navy 1912–1919. Schoolteacher 1910–1912; mechanic ca. 1919–1925; joined Revolutionary League of Vietnamese Youth 1925; imprisoned by French 1929–45; Pres., Permanent Cttee. of the Natl. Assembly and Natl. Popular Front Assoc (Lien Viet) 1946, reorganized in 1954 as the Fatherland Front (Mat-Tran To-Quoc). V.P. 1960–69 and Pres. 1969–76, Democratic Republic of Vietnam; Pres. and Chmn., Natl. Defense Council, Socialist Republic of Vietnam since 1976. Joined Communist Party of Indochina 1930; Member, Congress of Working People's Party of Vietnam 1951, 1960; Leader, Delegation of Natl. Assembly to U.S.S.R. 1956; Chmn., Vietnamese-Soviet Friendship Soc. Hons: Lenin Peace Prize 1967; Order of Suhbaatar (Mongolia) 1978; U.S.S.R. Order of the October Revolution 1978.

JESSE OWENS
Olympic track and field champion and public relations speaker
Born Danville, Alabama, U.S.A., September 12th, 1913
Died Tucson, Arizona, U.S.A., March 31st, 1980

Jesse Owen's achievements at the 1936 Olympic Games in Berlin, and his legendary snub from Adolf Hitler, have become identifying features of one of the most remarkable careers in the history of international track and field competition. He was born James Cleveland Owens in 1913, the son of rural Alabama sharecroppers one generation away from slavery, and spent his early childhood picking cotton along with his ten brothers and sisters. The crop failed when he was nine, and the family was forced to move north in search of work. They settled in Cleveland, Ohio, where "J.C.," as he was then called, helped out by shining shoes in his spare time.

Trained from the age of 13 by a school sports coach who noticed his abilities, Owens first entered the record books as a high school student in 1933, when he equalled the mark of 9.4 seconds for the 100-yard dash. At Ohio State University he supported himself by working nights as an elevator operator and earned the title "The Ebony Antelope" for the lithe, floating grace with which he broke one record after another. On May 25th, 1935, at a Big Ten meet at the University of Michigan's Ann Arbor campus, Owens shattered five world records (in the long jump, 220-yard low hurdles, 220-yard high hurdles, 220-yard dash, and 200-meter dash) and tied a sixth (the 100-yard dash) within the space of 45 minutes, even though he was suffering from a painful back injury sustained the week before. His score in the long jump (then called the broad jump) remained unbroken for the next 25 years.

Larry Snyder, Owens's coach at college and at the Olympics, attributed his strength to "a high tension nervous system" that primed his bloodstream with adrenalin. His seemingly effortless running style was the result of superb breath control. "In the sprints," Owens explained, "I stick with the field, breathing naturally, until 30 yards from the finish. Then I take one big breath, hold it, tense all my abdominal muscles and set sail. I do the same thing in the broad jump. About 13 yards from the takeoff, I get that big breath and then I don't let it out until I'm safely in the pit."

The 1936 Olympiad was hosted in Berlin by the Nazis, who were determined to make the Games a showcase for the supposed physical superiority of the so-called Aryan race. The Nazi-controlled press confidently predicted success for German athletes and reserved some of its most acerbic criticism for the ten black members of the U.S. track and field squad. A proposed boycott of the Games was voted down by U.S. Olympic officials.

To the chagrin of the Nazis, eight of the fourteen gold medals garnered by the U.S. in track and field were won by black athletes, and of these eight, fully half were won by Jesse Owens. He took the 100-meter dash, set new Olympic records in the 200-meter dash and the broad jump, and set the winning pace on the first leg of the 400-meter relay.

Ironically, Owens and his black teammate Ralph Metcalfe, another gold medallist, were not originally slated to run in the relay. They reluctantly stepped in at the last minute after U.S. Olympic officials, pandering to Nazi sensibilities, withdrew two Jewish athletes, Marty Glickman and Sam Stoller, from the race.

Although he was the acknowledged hero of the Games, Owens was pointedly not congratulated by Hitler. Nor did he receive congratulations from President Franklin Roosevelt after his return to the U.S., where second-class citizenship for black people was still the norm. "When I came back," Owens said later, "after all those stories about Hitler and his snub, I came back to my native country, and I couldn't ride in the front of the bus. I had to go to the back door. I couldn't live where I wanted. Now what's the difference?"

Owens took a job as a playground janitor, then gave up his amateur status to run exhibition races against dogs, horses, motorcycles, and trucks, and to barnstorm with the Harlem Globetrotters basketball team. After serving in a variety of executive positions and as a disc jockey, he opened his own public relations and marketing firm in the early 1960s and became a sought-after speaker, logging some 200,000 miles each year on the banquet and fund-raising circuit as a representative of corporate clients and charitable organizations. All his speeches, delivered in sweeping, evangelistic tones, stressed traditional virtues of sportsmanship, patriotism, and Olympic glory. (In part, his oratorical style was a product of college speech classes in which he had overcome a childhood stutter.)

In his later years, Owens was put forth by U.S. Olympic officials as an example to militant black athletes during their proposed boycott of the 1968 Games. Chided for being an Uncle Tom, Owens criticized black militancy in his 1970 book *Blackthink*, then softened his stance two years later in *I Have Changed*.

In 1972 Owens was honored with a victory lap at the Olympic Games in Munich, where he received the hearty applause of a German audience. Official U.S. recognition was not extended until 1976, when President Ford awarded him the Presidential Medal of Freedom; three years later he accepted the Living Legends award from President Carter. An organization of sportswriters voted him the outstanding athlete of the first half of the 20th century.

Owens, a heavy smoker, died of lung cancer. He and his wife had three daughters.   S.T./J.P.

Born James Cleveland Owens. Son of Henry O. and Emma O., sharecroppers. Married Ruth Solomon 1930. Daughters: Gloria; Beverly; Marlene. Baptist. Educ: E. Tech. High Sch., Cleveland; Ohio State Univ., A.B. 1937. Member, U.S. Olympic Track Team, Berlin 1936; afterwards professional runner. Promoter of baseball and basketball teams 1937–46; with Office of Civilian Defense, Philadelphia 1940–42; Dir., Negro Personnel, Ford Motor Co. 1942–46; exec., Leo Rose Sporting Goods Co. 1946–52; disc jockey, Chicago 1952–64; Pres., Jesse Owens and Assoc., Chicago, then Phoenix, since early 1960s. With Boys Club of Chicago 1949–55, Secty., Ill. Athletic Commn. 1952–55; with Ill. Youth Commn. 1952–60. Bd. Member: Boys Ranch of Ariz.; Boys Town, Nebr.; Memorial Hosp., Phoenix; Natl. Conference of Christians and Jews. Hons: Four gold medals, 1936 Olympic Games; Theodore Roosevelt Award for Scholastics and Athletics, Natl. Collegiate Athletic Assn. 1974; Presidential Medal of Freedom 1976; Living Legends Award 1979; voted outstanding athlete of the first half of the 20th century; Charter Member, Track and Field Hall of Fame; Member, Black Hall of Fame. *Author:* Blackthink, 1970; I Have Changed, 1972.

ARTHUR KLEINER
Pianist, composer, and conductor
Born Vienna, Austria, March 20th, 1903
Died Hopkins, Minnesota, U.S.A., April 1st, 1980

Self described as "an old museum piece," pianist Arthur Kleiner was for many years an accompanist of silent film classics. Also a composer, conductor, and historian of silent films, Kleiner's musical education began at the age of 11 when he studied piano, organ, harmony, counterpoint, and music history at Vienna's State Academy for Music and Dramatic Arts. After graduating in 1921, Kleiner became the accompanist for major European modern dance troupes until joining the Dalcroze School of Music in 1925 as pianist, composer, and conductor. He remained with the school for 13 years and, during this period, performed on Radio Vienna. Kleiner's work attracted the attention of Max Reinhardt, director of the well-known Seminar for Actors in Vienna, who invited Kleiner to teach at his school in 1931.

Kleiner emigrated to the United States in 1938 and found work as a rehearsal accompanist for choreographer George Balanchine. The following year, Iris Barry, the first Curator of the Film Department at New York City's Museum of Modern Art, sought the versatile musician to play for the museum's screenings; a three-month position became a career lasting almost three decades.

As Musical Director of the Museum Kleiner would often accompany two films a day. Working with a stop-watch and pencil, he needed to see film only once before scoring it—he simply "felt" the music that followed. When the original score for a film could not be found (as was the case for *Potemkin,* the first film score Kleiner composed at the museum) he carefully researched the music of the period, insisting that "everything must be historically correct."

In addition to a demanding schedule at the Museum, Kleiner composed scores for sound movies and plays as well as for television and radio programs. His oeuvre includes an award-winning score for *Anna Lucasta* (1945), a play commissioned by the writer William Morris; John van Druten's *I am a Camera* (1953); and James Agee's film, *The Mantle of Protection* (1955). In 1959 Kleiner recorded *Musical Moods from Silent Films* and during the 1960s and 70s performed at several film festivals. Kleiner was also a devoted researcher of early film music manuscripts, and at the time of his death, owned more than 500 scores, including over 50 original works for such movies as *Intolerance* and *Birth of a Nation* and 249 more than he had composed himself.   E.A.S.

Married. Children: Jeffrey, b. 1955; Erik, b. 1958. Emigrated to U.S. 1938. Naturalized American. Educ.: State Acad. for Music and Dramatic Arts, Vienna 1914–21; Univ. Vienna. Concert pianist and organist 1920–38; accompanist and composer for dance troupes in Europe 1921–28; Pianist and Conductor, Dalcroze Sch., Hellerau-Laxenburg 1925–38; Prof., Max Reinhardt Seminar for Actors, Vienna 1931–38; Musical Dir., Mus. of Modern Art, NYC 1939–67;

Solo Pianist, Conductor, and Composer, Agnes de Mille Dance
Theater (nationwide tour) 1953–54; solo pianist for major television
networks 1957–63. Film Accompanist: N.Y. Film Festival, Lincoln
Center, N.Y.C. 1965–69, 1973, 1976; Univ. Minnesota Film Society;
Univ. Texas, Austin; and American Film Inst., Washington D.C.
1967–72; and Walker Art Center, Minneapolis 1968–80. Lectr. and
performer: Univ. N.Y., Albany; and Amer. Film Inst., Washington
D.C. 1967–72; Z.D.F. Television, Berlin; and Northwest Film Study
Center, Portland, Oregon 1977; Amer. Film Inst., Film Cruise 1978;
Berlin Intnl. Film Festival 1979; Mus. of 20th Century, Vienna 1980;
Turin Film Music Festival; Montreal Intnl. Film Festival; Giornate Di
Francoforte A Milano, Milan; Film Music Symposium, Lugano; Three
Silent Film Festivals, Bonn; and others. Hons: award, William Morris
Agency (for music to play "Anna Lucasta) 1945; National Endow-
ment for the Arts 1974; Medal of Honour in Gold, Austrian Republic
(for distinguished service as film historian and musician) 1976; Society
for Cinephiles 1977; The Blue Crystal Obelisk, Photokina Cologne
1978; FilmBand in Gold, German Ministry of Interior 1979.

SIR EDWARD (CRISP) BULLARD
Geophysicist
Born Norwich, Norfolk, England, September 21st, 1907
Died La Jolla, California, U.S.A., April 3rd, 1980

urtesy Lady Ursula Bullard

Sir Edward Bullard, a founder of the science of marine geophysics,
was born to a family in the brewery business in Norwich, England.
After attending Repton School without distinction, he graduated from
Clare College, Cambridge, with a first class honours degree in physics,
and joined the atom-splitting team at the Cavendish Laboratory under
Lord Rutherford. A chance job with a geological surveying crew led
to a combined Ph.D. thesis in physics and geology.

Bullard, appointed Demonstrator in Geodesy at Cambridge, soon
began a series of pioneering experiments in geophysics. On an
expedition to the Eastern Africa Rift Valley, he developed a method
of measuring variations in gravity using an invariant pendulum. He
conducted seismic researches into the geologic structure of East
Anglia and supervised the first underwater explorations of the
European continental shelf, where oil deposits were later found. "We
showed the existence of a deep sedimentary basin instead of the hard
rocks that people had thought of for so long," recalled Bullard. "And
if you are going to find oil, a sedimentary basin is just the sort of place
to start looking. After the war, of course, the major oil companies got
in on the act and the pure scientists rather moved out. But there is no
doubt that our work paved the way for the oil companies."

During the Second World War, Bullard worked on problems in
submarine warfare, devising methods of ship demagnetization and
minesweeping. Towards the end of the war he served as Assistant
Director of Naval Operational Research in the British Admiralty and
participated in an Allied investigation of German V-weapons.

In 1945 Bullard was appointed head of Cambridge's Department of
Geodesy and Geophysics; three years later he moved to Canada to
take the chair of Geophysics at Toronto University. During the

summer months he worked at the Scripps Institute of Oceanography in California, developing techniques for measuring the flow of heat from the earth's core through the floor of the ocean. Based on these researches, he concluded that the molten core acts as a self-exciting dynamo, generating a fluctuating magnetic field.

From 1950 to 1957, Bullard served as director of the National Physics Laboratory in Middlesex, then returned to Cambridge to resume his old post as head of the Department of Geodesy and Geophysics. Under his leadership, the staff conducted several major projects, including studies of electromagnetic induction within the earth, measurement of stress within the planet's crust using probes in earthquake zones, a geological history of the Eastern Mediterranean, and the development of potassium-argon dating to determine the ages of rocks.

The theory of continental drift, according to which the present continents were originally conjoined in a single land mass, owed much of its early formulation to work done by Bullard. Highly controversial when it was first proposed, the theory has since been borne out by studies of the movement of the tectonic plates on which the continents rest.

Bullard retired from Cambridge in 1974 to accept a full-time chair at the San Diego campus of the University of California, with which he had long been associated. At the request of the U.S. Government, he served as a consultant to nuclear energy researchers, helping to design a reactor that consumes much of its own radioactive waste. He continued to travel and lecture and to pursue his long-standing interest in the history of science, particularly in the life and work of the astronomer Halley.

Bullard, who was knighted in 1953, was the recipient of many awards, including the 1968 Vetlesen Prize (the equivalent of a Nobel). His last paper, on which he had been working for some 25 years, was a study of changes in direction of the magnetic North Pole as recorded by observers in London from 1570 to 1975, including some observations made by King Charles II. It was completed, with the help of a collaborator, ten hours before his death from lung cancer.

Bullard was twice married and had four daughters.   J.P.

Son of Edward John B., brewer, and Eleanor Howes (Crisp) B. Married: (1) Margaret Ellen Thomas 1931 (div. 1974); (2) Ursula Margery (Cooke) Curnow 1974. Daughters: 1st marriage—Belinda; Emily; Henrietta; Polly. Educ: Repton Sch.; Clare Coll., Cambridge, B.A. (First Class Hons.) 1929, Ph.D. atomic physics and geol. 1932, Sc.D. geol. 1948; Fellow, Clare Coll. 1943–48, 1957–60; Fellow, Gonville and Caius Colls., Cambridge 1956–57; Fellow, Churchill Coll, Cambridge 1960–80. Mil. Service: Experimental Officer, H.M.S. Vernon and British Admiralty 1939–45; Asst. Dir., Naval Operational Research 1944–45; member, Allied cttee. investigating V-weapons. With Cambridge Univ.: Demonstrator in Geodesy 1931–35; Reader in Experimental Geophysics and Chmn., Dept. of Geodesy and Geophysics 1945–48, 1960–64; Asst. Dir. Research in Geodesy 1956–60; Prof. of Geophysics 1964–74. Prof. of Physics 1948–49 and Centennial Prof. 1967, Univ. Toronto; Dir., Natl. Physical Laboratory, Middx., 1950–55; Prof. 1963–79 and prof. emeritus 1979–80, Univ. Calif. at San Diego; Hitchcock Prof., Univ. Calif. at Berkeley 1975–80; Member, Inst. of Geophysics and Planetary Physics, Scripps

Inst. of Oceanography, La Jolla, Calif. since 1975; Visiting Prof., Univ. Alaska 1978. Member, British Natural Environment Research Council 1965–68, 1970–72; member, cttees. in Ministry of Defense; consultant to U.S. Govt. on nuclear reactor design ca. 1975. Dir., I.B.M. (U.K.) 1964–75; former dir., Bullard and Sons, Norwich. Foreign Correspondent Member, Geol. Soc. America 1952; Foreign Member, American Phil. Soc. 1969; Member, Cambridge Phil Soc. Hons: From Royal Soc.—Sedgwick Prize 1936; Smithson Research Fellow 1936–43; elected Fellow 1941; Hughes Medal 1953; Bakerian Lectr. 1967; Royal Medal 1975. K.B.E. 1953; Foreign Hon. Member, American Acad. Arts and Sciences 1954; Chree Medal 1956 and Hon. Member, Physics Soc., London; Day Medal, Geol. Soc. America 1959; Foreign Assoc., Natl. Acad. Science, U.S. 1959; Agassiz Medal and Gold Medal, Royal Astronomical Soc. 1965; Wollaston Medal, Geol. Soc. London 1967; Vetlesen Prize 1968; Bowie Medal 1975 and Ewing Medal 1978, American Geophysical Union. Contributor to many professional jrnls.

STANLEY (FORMAN) REED
Supreme Court Justice
Born Minerva, Kentucky, U.S.A., December 31st, 1884
Died Huntington, New York, U.S.A., April 3rd, 1980

Justice Stanley Reed, the second Supreme Court appointee of President Franklin Roosevelt, helped move a conservative Court toward ratification of liberal New Deal legislation. Although Reed's support for governmental intervention in the economy matched the liberalism of fellow Justices Douglas [q.v.] and Black, he did not always agree with their social libertarianism: during the 1950s Justice Reed was reluctant to extend Bill of Rights guarantees to American Communist Party members.

Stanley Reed was a lineal descendant of Kentucky's founding family. His father was a courtly, well-to-do physician and Stanley himself was to acquire the southern aristocrat's genteel and quietly sophisticated manner. He obtained bachelor's degrees from Kentucky Wesleyan University in 1902 and from Yale in 1906. Although Reed studied law at the University of Virginia, Columbia, and the Sorbonne, in Paris, he did not receive a degree from any of these schools; instead, he apprenticed with a local law firm (a customary practice at that time) in the small town of Maysville, Kentucky before being admitted to the state Bar in 1910. Reed enthusiastically took up local politics and was elected to the Kentucky General Assembly in 1912 where he sponsored progressive legislation such as child labor laws and workmen's compensation bills. Reed left the General Assembly four years later to serve with the U.S. Army during World War One as a 1st lieutenant in the Army Intelligence Division.

Reed resumed private law practice after the war and many of his clients were large co-operatives which handled dairy products, wool, lamb, and, particularly tobacco. This experience led to his appointment in 1929 by President Herbert Hoover as general counsel of the Federal Farm Board, a co-operative which marketed U.S. agricultural surplus abroad. In 1932 President Roosevelt named him general counsel for the newly created Reconstruction Finance Corporation, a position which, over the following years, brought him before a wary Supreme Court to defend such cornerstones of the New Deal as the National Industrial Recovery Act, the Agricultural Adjustment Act, and legislation favoring the Tennessee Valley Authority. For his support of New Deal programs, Reed was sent to the high Court in 1938 where he consistently supported the actions of successive Democratic administrations; he voted to uphold federal economic and social welfare laws and dissented from the majority when President Truman's seizure of the steel industry was ruled unconstitutional.

While Reed's belief in judicial restraint led to a liberal record on economic questions, it also prompted him to adopt a conservative posture on some civil libertarian issues during the McCarthy period. Thus he voted to uphold almost all government loyalty oaths and security investigations. He ruled, for example, in favor of the non-Communist oath of the Taft-Hartley Act in 1950 and for the conviction of American Communist Party leaders under the Smith Act of 1951. In 1955 Reed took exception to the Court's decision that the Civil Service Commission's Loyalty Review Board had illegally ordered the dismissal of a Public Health Service employee. Reed again dissented when the majority held in 1956 that government employees could be summarily dismissed as security risks only if they held sensitive positions.

On questions of free speech, Reed was more liberal and his voting record again coincided with that of Douglas and Black. He voted in two 1951 cases to strike down state laws requiring persons to secure permits for speaking in public parks or streets on the grounds that they gave too much discretionary power to the officials granting the licenses. On issues involving the rights of the accused, Reed was generally conservative and reluctant to overturn any conviction based upon the defendant's confession unless there was incontrovertible evidence that it had been given involuntarily

Justice Reed was viewed as a defender of civil rights and his consistent support of racial integration often earned him the wrath of conservatives. In 1946 Reed drafted the majority opinion which outlawed segregated seating on interstate buses. Three years later he wrote the opinion which, by striking down an Alabama "literacy" statute, outlawed primary elections in which only whites could vote. In the historic 1954 Brown vs. the Board of Education case, Reed voted with the majority to rule that racial segregation of schools was unconstitutional.

Reed retired from the Court in 1957. He had been the author of more than 300 opinions and although he was never ideologically doctrinaire, his positions largely supported New Deal policies. He was chosen by President Eisenhower to direct the newly formed Civil Rights Commission in 1957 but Reed declined, believing that his appointment might "lower respect for the impartiality of the Federal Judiciary." Reed continued to sit on various federal appellate courts and the U.S. Court of Claims on a part-time basis for many years. T.P.

Son of John R., physician, and Frances (Forman) R. Married Winifred Elgin 1908. Children: John and Stanley, both lawyers. Educ: Ky. Wesleyan Coll., B.A. 1902; Yale Univ., B.A. 1906; studied law at Univ. Va., Columbia Univ., Univ. of Paris. Mil. Service: First Lieut.

Army Intelligence Div., WWI. Private law practice 1910–29; Member, Ky. Gen. Assembly 1912–16; Gen. Counsel, Fed. Farm Bd. 1929–32; Gen. Counsel, Reconstruction Finance Corp. 1932–35; U.S. Solicitor Gen. 1935–38; Chmn., Pres. Comm. on Civil Serv. Improvement 1939–41; Assoc. Justice, Supreme Court 1938–57. Member: American Law Inst.; Soc. of Colonial Wars; Sons of the American Revolution; Fed. Bd. of Hospitalization; Dir., Commodity Credit Corp.; Trustee, Export-Import Bank; Exec. Comm., Red Cross. Hons: LL.D.: Yale Univ. 1938; Ky. Wesleyan Coll. 1941; Columbia Univ. 1940; Univ. of Ky. 1940; Univ. of Louisville, 1947.

RICHARD (BROOKE) ROBERTS
American biophysicist
Born Titusville, Pennsylvania, U.S.A., December 7th, 1910
Died Washington, D.C., U.S.A., April 4th, 1980

Richard Roberts, who helped to advance weaponry science during his 40-year career in nuclear physics and microbiology, was one of the American physicists who confirmed discovery of uranium fission. Roberts spent most of his professional life at the Carnegie Institution in Washington, where he studied microbiology and the biosynthesis of molecules and ribosomes. He also served on advisory boards with Princeton University and the University of Virginia.

Roberts joined the Carnegie Institute immediately after leaving Princeton University, where he had earned his undergraduate, master's, and doctoral degrees. His early nuclear physics studies took him into the field of weaponry when the Second World War began. He was instrumental in the discovery and development of an important aid to the allied war effort—the proximity fuse which detonates bombs when a sensor detects a specified target. In addition, Roberts confirmed the emission of neutrons from uranium fissions and was the principal contributor to the discovery of delayed neutrons (they were later used as the basis for atomic reactors). He also made the first observations of radioactivity from Be7, one of the particles emitted by radioactive isotopes. His work was officially recognized in 1947 when President Truman awarded him the Medal of Merit.

After the war Roberts turned from pure physics to microbiology because of his interest in biological warfare. He identified the chemical mechanism involved in living cell division and duplication, and in 1955 published his discoveries in *Studies of Biosynthesis in Escherichia coli,* which has become a standard microbiology textbook. Roberts used his understanding of radioactive particles to develop radioactive dyes for labeling and monitoring biological substances. In studies of the placenta conducted with Dr. Lewis B. Flexner, he recorded the transfer of radioactive sodium from the maternal to the fetal circulatory system.

Roberts died in Washington, D.C. at the age of 69.   M.P.

Son or Erastus Titus R. and Helen (Chambers) R. Married: (1) 1935; (2) Josephine Taggart 1967. Children: 1st marriage—Richard Furness; Helen Juliette; Edward Thomas. Educ: Princeton Univ., B.A. 1932;

M.A. (Queen Fellow) 1933; Ph.D. physics 1937. With Carnegie
Instn., Washington D.C.: Research Fellow in nuclear physics
1937–39; Assoc. Physicist 1939–43; Staff Member, Dept. of Terrestrial
Magnetism 1947–53 and 1963–75; Chmn., Biophysics section 1953–63.
With Natl. Defense Research Cttee., Office of Research and Devel.
1940–46; Physicist, Applied Physics Lab., Johns Hopkins Univ.
1943–46; Member, Cttee. Biological Warfare Research and Devel.
Bd. 1948–51; Consultant, Weapons Systems Evaluation Group 1950;
Member, and Pres. 1964–65, Biophysics Soc.; Member and former
Chmn., and V.P. of Zoological Section 1966, American Assn. for the
Advancement of Science; Member, Advisory Bds.: Princeton Univ.;
Univ. of Virginia; Arms Control and Disarmament Agency. Member:
Natl. Acad. of Sciences; Physical Soc.; Biochem. Soc. of Great
Britain; British Soc. of Microbiology. Hons: Medal of Merit 1947.
Author: Studies of Biosynthesis in Escherichia coli, 1955; Microsomal
Particles and Protein Synthesis, 1957. *Ed.:* Biophysical Soc. 1st
Symposium, 1958; Studies of Macromolecular Synthesis, 1964.

WLADYSLAW TATARKIEWICZ
Professor of philosophy and art history
Born Warsaw, Poland, April 3rd, 1886
Died Warsaw, Poland, April 4th, 1980

According to American philopher Max Reiser, "the emergence of
Wladyslaw Tatarkiewicz as a historian of philosophy and of aesthetics
is one of the most remarkable events in the history of philosophy in
Poland." Born and brought up in Warsaw, Tatarkiewicz was expelled
from that city's university for participating in an anti-czarist demonstration during the abortive 1905 Revolution, but returned to teach
philosophy there in 1915, having earned his doctorate at Marburg.
After brief terms at the universities of Wilno (Vilna) and Poznan
(Posen) during the re-organization period that followed the restoration of Polish independence in 1919, he once again returned to the
faculty at Warsaw, where he remained until his retirement in 1962.

Tatarkiewicz combined a native fluency in Polish and German with
a classical education in Latin and Greek and an acquired knowledge of
French, Italian, and Spanish, giving him a multi-cultural perspective
of unusual breadth. All his writings, which included numerous books
and more than 300 articles, were noted for their elegant and precise
prose style; reviewers noted his "omnivorous learning" and his "rare
talent for pinpointing the essential."

In 1931, Tatarkiewicz published a two-volume *History of Philosophy* (completed by a third volume in 1950). Its lucid explanation of
philosophical schools, and its pioneering demonstration of the connections between the philosophical thought of an era and its social,
economic, political, and religious atmosphere, soon made it a standard textbook in all Polish universities; its eighth edition, published in
1978, sold out 40,000 copies.

During Poland's occupation by the Nazis, Tatarkiewicz, then head
of the University and Secondary School Teachers Association, actively participated in the Underground University, holding illegal
philosophy seminars in his home despite the risk of summary execu-

tion if he and his students were caught. The manuscript of his *Analysis of Happiness,* written during this time, was hidden from the Germans and published after the war. In it, he contrasted the development of two concepts of happiness: its ancient definition as the possession of the highest material or spiritual goods, an objective value invoked by Plato and the Stoics and, in different guises, by the hedonists, Epicureans, Christians, and utilitarians; and its modern, subjective definition as a generalized satisfaction with life, a 19th-century idea with roots in Democritus.

The three-volume *History of Aesthetics,* completed when Tatarkiewicz was 81, surveyed the evolution of aesthetic theory in the West from the pre-Socratic age in Greece through the year 1700, when it became an independent discipline within philosophy. In addition to deriving explicit aesthetic ideas from philosophical texts, he attempted to deduce implicit ideas as well, through the interpretation of artistic works and from the statements and activities of artists, and the art-consuming public. Both sets of ideas were placed in their historical contexts, producing, for each era, a cultural as well as an intellectual history. Particularly valuable for fellow scholars were his discussion of medieval aesthetics, a neglected field, and his inclusion of selected texts in their original languages with modern translations. The work, translated into English, French, German, Russian, Italian, Rumanian, and Serbo-Croation, brought its author worldwide acclaim, though his methods and results were criticized as speculative. The reviewer in the *Journal of the History of Ideas* said ". . . he is very much concerned with those profound changes in cultural perspective, religious climate, and the social organization of artistic activities, that have a bearing on the way people have looked at the arts and thought seriously about their meaning and value. . . . a substantial achievement."

Rather than undertake a fourth volume, Tatarkiewicz continued his study of aesthetic theory with a history of six basic concepts, published in 1975. His *Notes to an Autobiography* was issued a year later.

Tatarkiewicz lectured at universities and academies in many countries. One student who attended his class at the University of California at Berkeley in 1967 remarked that he struck his audience as a "remarkable scholar but almost childlike in his continuing delight at everything he saw."   L.F./J.P.

Son of Ksawery T. and Maria (Brzezinska) T. Married Teresa Potworowka, writer 1919. Children: one son. Roman Catholic. Russian citizen 1910, then Polish. Educ: Gymnasium Warsaw, Reife 1903; Warsaw Univ.; Riga Univ.; Univ. of Zurich; Univ. of Paris; Berlin Univ.; Marburg Univ., Dr. Phil. 1910. Chmn., Dept. Philosophy, Warsaw Univ. 1915–19; Prof., Philosophy, Jan Kazimierz Univ., Wilno 1919–21. At Univ. of Poznan: Prof., Aesthetics and Modern Art 1921–23; Prof., Philosophy 1923–62; Prof. Emeritus 1962. Chief, Assn. of the Teachers of the Univs. and Secondary Schs. 1933–45; Visiting Prof. at univs. in Great Britain, France, Germany, the U.S. and other countries; Ed., Przegladu Filozoficzny (Philosophical Review, Polish Quarterly) ca. 1923–50; Member, ed. advisory bd., Révue Intnl. de Philosophie, Brussels since 1938; Ed., Estetyka (annual jrnl. of aesthetics) 1960–63; Ed. consultant, Jrnl. of Aesthetics and Art Hist. Member: Polska Akademia Umiejetnosci (Polish Acad. of Learning) 1930–51; Institut Intnl. de Philosophie since 1930; Polska Akademia Nauk since 1956; Serbian Acad. of Sciences 1972.

Hon. member, Comité Intnl. de l'Histoire de l'Art since 1930. Hons: Comdrs. Cross, Order of Polonia Restituta 1938, with star 1958; State Prize 1966; Officer 1939 and Comdr. 1978, Legion d'Honneur, France; Hon. doctorate, Catholic Univ. and Lublin Univ.; other hon. doctorates. *Author:* Die Disposition der Aristotelischen Prinzipien, 1910 (Dr. Phil. dissertation, trans. into Polish 1978); "Uber die naturliche Weltansicht" in Philosphische Abhandlungen, Hermann Cohen zum 70sten Geburtstag, 1912; O bezwzglodnosci dobra (On Good and Evil, 1919 and Rzady artystyczne Stanislawa Augusta, 1919; Piec studiow o Lazienkach Stanislawa Augusta, 1925; Historia filozofii, 2 vols., 1931 (Nineteenth Century Philosophy, 1973); Les Trois morales d'Aristote, 1932; Skupienie i marzenie (Concentration and Dreaming), 1935; Ethical bases of reparations, 1945; O szczesciu, 1947 (Analysis of Happiness, 1976); Zarys dziejow filozofii w. Polsce, 1948 (Outline of the History of Philosophy in Poland to W. W. II, ca. 1949, 1960); Droga do filozofii, 1948; Historia filozofii, Vol. 3, 1950 (Twentieth Century Philosophy 1900–1950, 1973); Skupienie i marzenie, studia z zak resu estetyki (addresses and essays), 1951; Dominik Merlini, 1955; Lazienki warszawski, 1957; Historia estetyki, Vols. I and II, 1960; O sztuce polskiej xvii i xviii wieku: architektura, rzezba (History of Polish architecture and sculpture in the 17th and 18th centuries, with French summary), 1966; Historia estetyke, Vol. III, 1967 (Modern Aesthetics, Vol. III, 1974); Lazienki krolewskie i ich osobliwoscii (on Lazienki castle, with English, German and French summary), 1967; L'estetica romantica del 1600, 1968; L'esthetique italienne de la Renaissance, 1969; (compiler) Jakiej filozofii Polacy potrzebuja; Wyboru dokonat i wstepem poprzedzit, 1970; Pisma zebrane, 1971; Droga do filozofii i inne rozprawy filozoficzne (Way to Philosophy and other Papers), 1971; Droga przez estethke, 1972; Dzieje szesciv pojec: sztuka, piekno, forma, tworczoso, odtworczosc, przezycie estetyczne, 1975; O doskonatosci (On Perfection), 1976; Zapiski do autobiograpfii (Notes to an Autobiography), 1976; Parega, 1978; (co-author with wife) Wspomnienia, 1979; over 300 articles in Polish, European and American jrnls.
Further reading: Wladyslaw Taterkiewicz by Marek Jaworski, 1975; "Tatarkiewicz and the History of Aesthetics" by Bohdan Oziemidok and Jean G. Harrell, Journal of the History of Philosophy, April 1976; "Tatarkiewicz' History of Aesthetics" by Monroe C. Beardsley, Journal of the History of Ideas, September, 1976.

JOHN COLLIER
Fiction and screenplay writer
Born London, England, May 3rd, 1901
Died Pacific Palisades, California, U.S.A., April 6th, 1980

The British writer John Collier, whose fictions display a lighthearted taste for the satiric and the macabre, was born in London to a middle-class family (an uncle, Vincent Collier, was also a writer) and privately educated. He began writing poems at the age of 19 and was poetry editor of the magazine *Time and Tide* from 1926 to 1935, during which time he lived on a farm in Hampshire. His first novel, *His Monkey Wife,* which featured a chimpanzee as the heroine, was published in 1930 and was soon followed by *Full Circle: A Tale* (published in England under the title *Tom's A-Cold),* an unsettling fantasy about the resurgence of savagery in war-torn England of the 1990s. A third novel, *Defy the Foul Fiend,* was published in 1934. By 1935 he had published five collections of short stories, with another six yet to come.

In 1952 Collier received an Edgar Award (in memory of Edgar Allen Poe) from the Mystery Writers of America for *Fancies and Goodnights,* a collection of short fiction. Here, as in most of his work, Collier took his readers on brief excursions into a wittily distorted world, a world more diverting than threatening, where genies, supernatural beasts, and demonic plants work their wills on the unsuspecting characters.

Anthony Burgess, who edited the *John Collier Reader* (1972), called Collier "very much a writer of the 20s and notable for lightly carried erudition, literary allusiveness, and quiet wit" who had a "capacity for horror masked mostly by an urbanity and elegance of style very beguiling but not well appreciated in the post-Hemingway era." In this respect he has most often been compared with the British fantasist Saki.

Collier came to Hollywood in 1935 to write screenplays for RKO; his credits include *I Am a Camera* (1955) and collaborative work on *Deception* (1946), *The African Queen* (1951), and *The War Lord* (1965). "Evening Primrose," a fantasy about a poet living a secret life in a department store, was directed by John Houseman for ABC-TV's *Stage 67,* with lyrics by Stephen Sondheim. Collier's 1973 adaptation of John Milton's *Paradise Lost,* subtitled a "screenplay for cinema of the mind," was described by a critic for *Time* magazine as "a symbiotic work of literary art, fast-paced, clever, well-crafted and full of knowledge and delight."

Collier also collaborated on an "informal history" of post-World War One Britain and edited the works of John Aubrey, the 17th-century biographer and writer. He was twice married and had one son.   J.P.

Son of John George C. Married: (1) Shirley Lee Palmer 1936 (div. 1943); (2) Margaret Elizabeth Eke 1945. Son: 2nd marriage—John. Educ: private. Novelist, short story writer, poet since 1920; film and television scriptwriter, U.S. since 1935. Poetry Ed., Time and Tide, London 1926–35. Hons: Four poetry awards, This Quarter 1922; Edgar Award, Mystery Writers of America (for Fancies and Good-nights) 1952. *Books: Novels*—His Monkey Wife, or, Married to a Chimp, 1930; Full Circle: A Tale, 1933 (in U.K. as Tom's A-Cold: A Tale); Defy the Foul Fiend, or, The Misadventures of a Heart, 1934. *Short story collections*—No Traveller Returns, 1931; Epistle to a Friend, 1931; Green Thoughts, 1932; The Devil and All, 1934; Variation on a Theme, 1935; Witch's Money, 1940; Presenting Moonshine: Stories, 1941; A Touch of Nutmeg and More Unlikely Stories, 1943; Fancies and Goodnights, 1951; Pictures in the Fire, 1958; Of Demons and Darkness, 1965. *Uncollected short stories*—"The Love Connoisseur," Ellery Queen's 14th Mystery Annual, 1959; "Meeting of Relations," The Best from Fantasy and Science Fiction, 1960; "Man Overboard," The Best from Fantasy and Science Fiction, 1961. *Plays*—Wet Saturday, 1971; His Monkey Wife, 1971; Milton's Paradise Lost: Screenplay for Cinema of the Mind, 1973. *Film scripts*—(with Gladys Unger and Mortimer Offner) Sylvia Scarlett, 1936; (with Akos Tolnay and Marcia De Silva) Elephant Boy, 1937; (with Anthony Veiller and William H. Wright) Her Cardboard Lover,

1942; (with Joseph Than) Deception, 1946; Roseanna McCoy, 1949; (with James Agee and others) The African Queen, 1951; (with others) The Story of Three Loves, 1953; I Am a Camera, 1955; (with Millard Kaufman) The War Lord, 1965. *Television script*—Evening Primrose, on ABC-TV's Stage 67, 1967. *Poems*—Gemini, 1931. *Other*—(ed.) Scandals and Incredulities by John Aubrey, 1931; (with Iain Lang) Just the Other Day: An Informal History of Britain since the War, 1932; The John Collier Reader (ed. by Anthony Burgess), 1972.

PETER FARB
Author, naturalist and anthropologist
Born New York City, U.S.A., July 25th, 1929
Died Boston, Massachusetts, U.S.A., April 8th, 1980

Peter Farb, whose best-selling books on natural history, science and linguistics have been translated into more than 15 languages, achieved prominence as a crusading conservationist in the 1960s and 70s.

After taking his B.A. degree from Vanderbilt University, Farb moved to New York where he studied English literature and anthropology for one year at Columbia University. Although Farb's first work, *Living Earth* (1954), was poorly received (a *New York Times* reviewer said that "the author plunges fearlessly into subjects beyond his depth"), he continued to publish books and articles at a prodigious rate, and developed his writing and intellectual abilities. With the publication in 1963 of *Ecology* and *Face of North America*—a natural history of the continent—Farb's reputation and popularity soared. President Kennedy sent copies of *Face of North America* to 100 foreign dignitaries and Stewart Udall, U.S. Secretary of the Interior, described Farb as "one of the finest conservation spokesmen of our period." Speaking of his commitment to the preservation of the North American continent's natural beauty, Farb once wrote:

> The true impact of landscape upon the beholder is not the present scene alone. Rather, understanding lies in knowledge of the many forces—climate, vegetation, soil, geologic change—that have molded the scene. A swamp I know, a place of brooding, lonely beauty, attracts many people simply because of the sensory impression it offers. But there are other people who can read this landscape. They see in the surrounding ridges and the soil that this swamp is a legacy of the last ice sheet, some ten thousand years ago. They see, too, unmistakable signs of the swamp's future: that it is destined to become dry land, which in its own way will nurture yet another community of living things.

Man's Rise to Civilization (1968) and *Humankind* (1978) were among Farb's most widely read books. The former was a history of North American Indians from the primeval to the modern industrial period and the latter examined, in a lucid prose style, recent scientific discoveries about the human species. Farb's only novel, *Yankee Doodle* (1970), about social problems of an industrial society, was unsuccessful and Farb thereafter concentrated on his scientific writings. *Word Play: What Happens When People Talk* (1974)—which included chapters on the nature of verbal transactions between psychoanalyst and patient, a survey of black dialect, and an analysis of Noam Chomsky's linguistic theories—was well received by the critics.

Farb died of leukemia at the age of fifty-one. Even though he had written more than twenty books and fifty major articles, many critics believed he was just reaching the peak of his intellectual powers. A new book, *Consuming Passions: The Anthropology of Eating* was in press at the time of his death and a collaborative effort with Irven DeVore, *The Human Experience: A Textbook of Anthropology,* was in an advanced state of preparation.   M.D.

Son of Solomon F. and Cecelia (Peters) F. Married Oriole Horch, museum dir. and painter 1953. Children: Mark Daniel; Thomas Forest. Educ: Vanderbilt Univ., Columbia (Phi Beta Kappa, Omicron Delta Kappa), B.A. magna cum laude 1950; postgrad. study, Columbia Univ. 1950–51. Feature Ed., Argosy mag., NYC, 1950–52; freelance writer since 1953. Ed.-in-chief, Panorama 1960–61; Curator, American Indian Cultures, Riverside Mus., NYC. 1964–71; Consultant, Smithsonian Instn. 1966–71; Visiting Lectr. in English, Yale Univ. 1971–72; Fellow, Calhoun Coll. 1971–75; Judge, U.S. Natl. Book Awards Cttee. 1971; Trustee, Univ. Mass. Libraries since 1976. Member: Allergy and Asthma Foundn. of America (Bd. of Dirs. 1970–73); American Anthropological Assn.; N.Y.C. Entymological Soc. (also Secty.); P.E.N. Club. Hons: Fellow, American Assn. for the Advancement of Science; Fellow, Soc. of American Historians. *Author:* Living Earth, 1959; The Story of Butterflies and other Insects, 1959; The Insect World, 1960; The Story of Dams, 1961; The Forest, 1961; 2nd. ed. 1978; (jt. ed.) Prose by Professionals, 1961; The Insects, 1962; 2nd. ed. 1977; The Story of Life, 1962; Ecology, 1963; rev. ed. 1970; Face of North America: The Natural History of a Continent (Book-of-the-Month Club, Outdoor Lif Book Club, A.L.A. Notable Book selection, Pres. Kennedy Intl. White House Library selection), 1963, young readers' ed. 1964; The Forest Reader, 1964; The Land and Wildlife of North America, 1964, 2nd. ed. 1978 (with John Hay) The Atlantic Shore, 1966; The Land, Wildlife and Peoples of the Bible, 1967; Man's Rise to Civilization as shown by the Indians of North America from Primeval Times to the Coming of the Industrial State (Book-of-the-Month Club, Book Find Club, Library of Science, History Book Club of London selection), 1968, 2nd. rev. ed. 1978; Yankee Doodle, 1970; Word Play: What Happens when People Talk (Book Find Club, Modern Psychology Book Club, Library of Behavioral Sciences selection), 1974; The Human Equation, 1977; Humankind, 1978. *In press* (at time of death)—Consuming Passions: The Anthropology of Eating. *In preparation* (at time of death)—(with Irven DeVore) The Human Experience: A Textbook of Anthropology. Contributor of maj. articles to Better Homes and Gardens, Reader's Digest, Saturday Review, Today's Health, Horizon, American Heritage, Natural History, Audubon, and other U.S. natl. and intnl. mags.

KAY MEDFORD
Actress
Born New York City, U.S.A., September 14th, 1920
Died New York City, U.S.A., April 10th, 1980

Kay Medford, actress, singer, and comedienne, was born Kathleen Patricia Regan in New York City and attended public and Catholic schools in Manhattan. Both her parents died when she was 15. As a teenager, Kay, whose mother and brother were theater performers, got small parts in summer stock productions. After graduating from high school, she shared an apartment with three roommates in Greenwich Village, supporting herself as a waitress, magician's assistant, and hat-check girl until film director Mervyn Leroy invited her to come to Hollywood. She was signed to the starlet treatment and made her film debut in *The War Against Mrs. Hadley* in 1942. After World War Two she interrupted her film career to direct G.I. shows in Japan and Hawaii and to tour in a nightclub act in England, Spain, and Los Angeles.

Medford's first appearance on Broadway was as Madame Cherry in the musical *Paint Your Wagon* in 1951. Two years later she found a showcase for her comic talents in *John Murry Anderson's Almanac,* a revue in which she understudied Hermione Gingold. Her skills as a mimic were shown to advantage in another revue, *Almost Crazy,* in which she portrayed Bette Davis, Louella Parsons, Barbara Stanwyck, Greta Garbo, Edith Piaf, and Johnny Ray. Audiences and critics liked her wry manner and her distinctive voice, variously described as "an idling eight cylinder" and "a busted brass gong."

Her favorite stage role was the part of Ladie in the 1954 comedy *Lullaby.* One reviewer noted that "Kay Medford has come into her own" as the hard-boiled but tender-hearted cigarette girl in a cheap nightclub who marries a middle-aged man (played by Jack Warden), only to have his overprotective mother (Mary Boland) appear at their honeymoon hotel to check up on them. That year she also played opposite Vincent Price in a sex farce, *Black-Eyed Susan.* The play received poor reviews, but Medford was praised for her charm and comic sense. She was later featured in City Center revivals of *Pal Joey* and *Carousel.*

Garson Kanin gave her the role of the Jewish mother in *A Hole in The Head* (1957), the first of her portrayals of memorable mothers. In *Bye Bye Birdie* (1960), she drew laughs and a New York Drama Critics Award as the deadpan, poisonously doting mother of Dick Van Dyke. For her performance as Rosie Brice, Barbra Streisand's wise-cracking stoical mother in *Funny Girl* (1964), she received a Tony Award and the Variety Poll Award. She re-created Mrs. Brice in the film version eight years later.

Kay Medford once remarked: "Just think, I started out by playing sexpots, nymphos, prostitutes, gun molls with wet lips and cigarettes dangling, then madame and now mothers. Sure, there's plenty of action in these mamma roles, but I've never even been a bride." But she did appear as a wife in *Don't Drink the Water,* co-starring with Lou Jacobi in a comedy about a vacationing American couple arrested as spies behind the Iron Curtain.

Although she said that she found the stage more rewarding than the screen, Kay Medford appeared in many films, notably *Butterfield 8, The Rat Race,* and *A Face in the Crowd.* She had been a frequent television performer since 1947, appearing as a regular on The Dean Martin Show during the 1970–71 season and as a guest star in many other series.

Kay Medford had started filming *Honky Tonk Freeway* with British director John Schlesinger shortly before her death.   J.P.

Born Kathleen Patricia Regan. Daughter of James R., laborer, and Mary (Kelly) R., actress. Unmarried. Roman Catholic. Educ: public and Catholic schs., NYC; grad. Morris High Sch. Directed G.I. shows in Japan and Hawaii after WWII; toured England, Spain, Los Angeles in cabaret act 1950. Member: Actors Equity Assn.; Screen Actors Guild; American Fedn. of Television and Radio Artists. Hons: Theatre World Award, Outstanding Newcomer 1954; N.Y. Drama Critics Award (for Bye Bye Birdie) 1960; Variety Poll Award (for Funny Girl) 1963–64; Tony Award (for Funny Girl) 1964; Straw Hat Award, Best Actress (for Light Up the Sky) 1971. *Performances: Plays*—Candida, NYC 1948; Paint Your Wagon, NYC 1951; John Murray Anderson's Almanac (revue), NYC 1953; Maya, NYC 1953; The Little Clay Cart, NYC 1953; Lullaby, NYC 1954; Black-Eyed Susan, NYC 1954; Put Them All Together, Somerset, Mass. 1954; Almost Crazy (revue), NYC 1955; Wake Up, Darling, NYC 1956; Mr. Wonderful, NYC 1956; A Hole in the Head, NYC 1957; Carousel, NYC 1957, Brussels 1959; A Handful of Fire, NYC 1958; The Poker Game, N.Y. 1960; Bye Bye Birdie (Mae Peterson), NYC 1960, toured 1961–62; The Counting House, NYC 1962; The Heroine, NYC 1963; Pal Joey, NYC 1963; The Tender Hell, 1963; Funny Girl (Mrs. Brice), NYC 1964, London 1966; Don't Drink the Water, NYC 1966; Barefoot in the Park, toured 1974; Light Up the Sky, toured 1975. *Films*—The War Against Mrs. Hadley, 1942; Swing Shift Masie, 1943; Adventure, 1945; Guilty Bystander, 1950; A Face in the Crowd, 1957; Jamboree, 1958; Butterfield 8, 1960; The Rat Race, 1960; Two Tickets to Paris, 1962; Ensign Pulver, 1964; A Fine Madness, 1966; The Busy Body, 1967; Funny Girl (Mrs. Brice), 1968; Angel in My Pocket, 1969; Lola, 1973. *Television*—Omnibus; Philco TV Theatre; U.S. Steel Hour; Suspense; Studio One; The Dean Martin Show 1970–71; various situation comedy and dramatic series.

ANTONIA WHITE
Novelist and translator
Born London, England, March 31st, 1899
Died London, England, April 10th, 1980

As a translator, novelist, and short-story writer, the literary reputation of Antonia White rests upon her four highly autobiographical novels, *Frost in May* (1933) and the Clara Batchelor trilogy which was published between 1950 and 1955. White's first two novels, which deal with a young woman's ambivalence toward the dominant authority figures in her life—the Catholic Church and her father—have earned comparison to the early writings of James Joyce.

Antonia White became a Catholic at the age of seven when her father, the Senior Classics Master at St. Paul's School in London, renounced his Protestant faith to join the Roman Catholic church. Two years later Antonia went to the Convent of the Sacred Heart, Roehampton, where, at the age of 14 she began a novel which she hoped to present to her father as a gift. Although the book was an innocent love story, the nuns confiscated the manuscript and expelled her from the school. Antonia's father was humiliated by the incident and found it hard to forgive his daughter. These events formed the basis of White's novel, *Frost in May,* which she began at the age of 16 but did not publish until she was over 30—when her father was dead and her Catholic faith had lapsed. In the meantime Antonia's first marriage had been annulled, a second marriage had also ended, and she had suffered a mental breakdown followed by a two-year convalescence in a public asylum.

Of White's four novels only *Frost in May* was commercially successful. The story closely resembles her experiences at the Convent of the Sacred Heart and is narrated in a cooly detached tone that virtually eliminates the subjective experience of the young heroine who is expelled from a strict Catholic school. After *Frost in May* White did not publish another novel until 1950 when the first of her Clara Batchelor books appeared. *The Lost Traveller* which again tells the story of a guilt-ridden young woman who believes she has failed her stern father both as a daughter and as a Catholic, was followed by *The Sugar House* (1952), the story of the dissolution of a young couple's marriage. The trilogy was completed in 1955 with the publication of *Beyond the Glass* which describes Clara's descent into madness.

Although White had reconverted to Catholicism and undergone four years of Freudian analysis during World War Two, these novels develop what critic Samuel Hynes calls the theme of the "closed heart." Indeed, there is no place for happiness or redemption in White's fictional universe. The destruction of love and the disintegration of the married couple's "sugar house" in the second novel seem inevitable; although Clara regains her sanity at the end of *Beyond the Glass,* she is unable to love or trust others. Like *Frost in May* the trilogy is narrated by a coldly objective voice. While this technique allowed the author to distance herself from painfully autobiographical subjects, it also eliminated dramatic structure from the novels; tragic moments of death, madness, and renunciation of love are, for example, presented with the same icy precision as a walk in the park on a bright morning might be described. Referring to the bleakness of her books, White once said, "The hardest article of faith for me to swallow is that God loves human beings."

Antonia White translated more than 30 French works, including many novels by Colette; her translation of Guy de Maupassant's *Une Vie* was awarded the Denyse Clairouin Prize in 1950. *The Hound and the Falcon* (1966), a collection of letters exchanged between Antonia White and a Catholic correspondent, details her journey from apostasy to reconciliation with the Church. White also wrote short stories, a play, two books for children and contributed articles to *La Vie Intellectuelle,* the French Dominican review.   E.T.

Daughter of Cecil George B., sch. teacher, and Christine Julia (White) B. Married: (1) 1920 (div. 1924); (2) 1924 (div. 1929); (3) H.T. Hopkinson, journalist 1930 (div. 1938). Two daughters: Susan Chitty, writer; Lyndall. Educ: Convent of the Sacred Heart, Roehampton 1908–14; St. Paul's Girls' Sch., London 1914–16; Acad. of Dramatic Art 1919–20. Teacher, governess, Civil Servant, and mag. story writer 1916–19; actress 1920–21; copywriter, W.S. Crawford Ltd. 1924–31; Asst. Ed., Life and Letters, London 1928–29; freelance journalist 1931–34; Copywriter, J. Walter Thompson, London 1934–35; Theater Critic, Time and Tide, London 1934; teacher and writer, London Theatre Studio 1935–36; Fashion Ed., Daily Mirror, London 1935–37 and Sunday Pictorial 1937–39; Writer, B.B.C., London 1940–43; Trans., Political Intelligence Dept., French Sect., British Foreign Office, London 1943–45; novelist, freelance writer, critic, and trans. 1945–79; visiting lectr. in English, St. Mary's Coll.,

Notre Dame, South Bend, Ind. 1959. Hons: Denyse Clairouin Prize
for trans. 1950; F.R.S.L. 1957. *Books: Novels*—Frost in May, 1933;
The Lost Traveller, 1950; The Sugar House, 1952; Beyond the Glass,
1955. *Short story collection*—Strangers (including verse), 1954.
Uncollected short story—"Surprise Visit," 1965. *Play*—Three in a
Room, 1947. *Children's stories*—Minka and Curdy, 1957; Life with
Minka and Curdy, 1970. *Other*—The Hound and the Falcon: The
Story of a Re-Conversion to the Catholic Faith, 1965. *Translations*—
A Woman's Life (Guy de Maupassant), 1949; Reflections on Life
(Alexis Carrel), 1952; Pathway to Heaven (Henry Bourdeaux), 1952;
The Cat (Colette), 1953; Sea of Troubles (Margeurite Duras), 1953; A
German Officer (Serge Groussard), 1955; The Wind Bloweth Where
it Listeth (Paul-André Lesort), 1956; I Am Fifteen and I Do Not Want
to Die (Christine Arnoth), 1956; Claridine at School (Colette), 1957;
Those Who Wait (Christine Arnoth), 1957; The Branding Iron (Paul-
André Lesort), 1958; It Is Not So Easy to Live (Christine Arnoth),
1958; The Stories of Colette, 1958; Claudine in Paris (Colette), 1958;
Thou Shalt Love (Jean-Marc Montguerre), 1958; The Swing (Fanny
Rouget), 1958; The Charlatan (Christine Arnoth), 1959; Children in
Love (Claire France), 1959; Tortoises (Loys Masson), 1959; I Will Not
Serve (Evelyn Mahyere), 1960; Claudine Married (Colette), 1960; Till
The Shadow Passes (Julie Storm), 1960; The Serpent's Bite (Christine
Arnoth), 1961; Claudine and Annie (Colette), 1962; The Whale's
Tooth (Le Notaire des Noirs: Loys Masson), 1962; The Trial of
Charles de Gaulle (Haute Cour: H. Fabre-Luce), 1963; The Shackle
(Colette), 1964; The Captive Cardinal (Christine Arnoth), 1964; The
Innocent Libertine (Colette), 1968; The Candle (Thérèse de Sainte
Phalle), 1968; Memoirs of the Chevalier d'Eon, 1970; The Glass Cage
(Georges Simenon), 1973; The Novels of Smollet (Paul-Gabriel
Boucé), 1974; History of Charles XII (Voltaire), 1976. *Contributor:*
articles in La Vie Intellectuelle (the French Dominican review).
Further reading: "Reputations: Antonia White" by Samuel Hynes,
Times Literary Supplement, July 3, 1969; Susan Chitty, Harper-
Queen, June 1974.

WILLIAM R(ICHARD) TOLBERT, JR.
President of Liberia
Born Bensonville, Liberia, May 13th, 1913
Died Monrovia, Liberia, April 12th, 1980

The assassination of William Tolbert, President of Liberia since 1971,
came as a shock to observers who thought the country one of the most
politically stable on the African continent. The nation was founded in
1847 by freed American slaves. By the mid-20th century, the de-
scendents of these founders formed a wealthy elite, representing only
five percent of the population, in whose hands most of the political
power was concentrated. Tolbert was born into this elite group in
1913. His father, a former slave from South Carolina, had emigrated
in the 1880s and had become a prosperous rice and coffee grower
whose wives bore him some 70 children.

Young Tolbert was educated in Christian institutions and graduated
with a B.A. degree from Liberia College (now Liberia University),
becoming a typist in the government's Treasury Department in 1935.
A year later he was promoted to disbursing officer and remained in

the post until 1943, when he was elected to the House of Representatives as a member of the True Whig Party, the only legal party in the country. In 1951 he was chosen by President William V.S. Tubman to serve as Vice President, a position he held for the next 20 years.

This largely ceremonial office gave Tolbert the time to pursue another career in the Baptist Church, in which he was an ordained minister. He supported missionary activities and during the 1960s was Vice President and then President of the Baptist World Alliance. He and his wife Victoria had six daughters and two sons, one of whom married the daughter of President Tubman.

When Tubman died in 1971 after 28 years of autocratic rule, Tolbert took his place, attending the investiture in an open-necked white suit rather than the top hat and morning coat affected by his predecessor. The spirit of modernization claimed by Tolbert for his presidency proved, however, to be more symbolic than actual, and the division between the rich and poor in Liberian society persisted despite his efforts at modest reform.

Tolbert attempted to place the nation's agricultural economy on a more secure footing by encouraging farmers to gear their crops to market trends rather than to tribal needs. He asked the merchant community, made up mostly of Lebanese and Indians, to provide training and financial support to native Liberians, and requested foreign corporations with branches in Liberia to hire more local workers. A system of unemployment compensation was also enacted. The curbs on civil liberties of the Tubman years were eased, including the freeing of political prisoners, the lifting of press censorship, and the abolition of a requirement that civil servants annually pay one month's salary to the True Whig Party; nonetheless, all candidates for public office were still selected by the Party, making elections little more than an empty process of ratification.

Tolbert also launched a campaign against corruption and nepotism in the government, most of whose officials held extensive business interests they found it necessary to protect. To set an example, he sold the presidential yacht, whose upkeep cost the Treasury some $250,000 yearly, and replaced his Cadillac limousine with a Volkswagen. But critics saw little evidence of change.

Tolbert's foreign policies were based on his desire to prove Liberia free of U.S. control while maintaining close ties with U.S. corporations, particularly with the Firestone Tire and Rubber Company, whose presence is crucial to the country's economic survival. He saw Liberia as a leader among modern African states and cast himself in the role of peacemaker, negotiating a reconciliation between Presidents Leopold S. Senghor of Senegal and Felix Houphouet-Boigny of the Ivory Coast and their former enemy, President Sékou Touré of Guinea. In discussions with Prime Minister Vorster of South Africa in 1975, Tolbert secured assurances that South Africa would eventually grant independence to South-West Africa, now known as Namibia. He continued to press for further concessions from South Africa as chairman of the Organization of African Unity, whose summit meeting he hosted in his capital city of Monrovia in July 1979.

Despite these successes, Tolbert's administration was increasingly plagued by domestic unrest. Many promised reforms in education, health care, government, and redistribution of income had not materialized, and demonstrations by dissatisfied citizens became increasingly common.

The troubles came to a head in April 1979, when a crowd of protesters was fired on by police and militiamen acting on Tolbert's orders. At least 74 people were shot to death; mass rioting followed. In January 1980, Tolbert, on the advice of an investigating commission, agreed to the formation of an opposition group, the People's Progress Party, but by March many of its leaders had been imprisoned for treason. In April the human-rights group Amnesty International charged that the True Whig Party had authorized rewards of up to $2,000 for the capture, "dead or alive," of the opposition's remaining leaders.

On April 12, a group of army officers calling themselves the Army Redemptive Council, under the leadership of one Sergeant Doe, broke into the executive mansion, assassinated Tolbert, and mutilated his body. Within 24 hours they had taken control of all transportation and communications in the capital. Public executions by firing squad of high-ranking government officials began shortly afterwards; among the victims were several members of Tolbert's family, including one of his sons.

Under constitutional law, Tolbert would have left office in 1983. J.P.

Son of William T., coffee and rice grower, and Charlotte (Hoff) T. Married Victoria David 1936. Children: Wokie Rose, fashion designer; Wilhelmina, physician; Willy Mae, businesswoman; three other daughters; two sons, one adopted. Baptist. Educ: Episcopalian high sch.; Liberia Coll., B.A. 1934. With Liberian Treasury Dept.: Typist 1935; Disbursing Officer 1936–43. Member, House of Reps. (True Whig Party) 1943–51; chosen V.P. of Liberia 1951–71; Senate V.P. 1951–55 and Pres. 1955; Pres. of Liberia since 1971. Pres., Org. of African Unity since 1979. Ordained Minister of Baptist Church; African V.P. 1960–65 and Pres. 1965–70, Baptist World Alliance; Chief Advisor, All-African Missionaries' Evangelistic Union 1973; Pres., Liberian Baptist Missionary and Educational Convention. Chmn., Bd., of Dirs.: Bank of Liberia; Mesurado Corp.; Liberia Univ. Hons: D.C.L., Liberia Univ. 1952; D.D., Liberia Univ. 1966; Hon. member, American Intnl. Acad.; Grand Master Emeritus, Masons of Liberia; numerous Liberian and foreign decorations.

JEAN-PAUL SARTRE
Philosopher, writer, political activist
Born Paris, France, June 21st, 1905
Died Paris, France, April 15th, 1980

An oeuvre of more than 50 volumes, including fiction, drama, philosophy, criticism, psychoanalytic biography, and political journalism, established Jean-Paul Sartre as one of the most versatile and original thinkers of post-war Europe. Espousing a radical concept of human freedom that evolved into a revolutionary political philosophy, Sartre brought to his work a dedication and vigor that have earned him comparisons with Rousseau and Zola.

Sartre's world view took shape during the 1930s, when the rise of Fascism focused his attention, with desperate emphasis, on the nature of the freedom of the individual. He saw this freedom as a conscious choice made by the individual in the face of the absurd, a creation of contingent values in a world devoid of absolute values. Such choice follows the anguished realization that "existence precedes essence," that the individual exists only in relation to other people, and that the individual "is alone, abandoned on earth in the midst of his infinite responsibilities, without help, with no other destiny than the one he forges for himself on earth." The "authentic" human being, said Sartre, does not turn away from this situation, but seeks to transcend it through action, understanding that he is "condemned to be free."

This vastly influential philosophy, called "existentialism" by the writer Gabriel Marcel, formed the basis for a huge body of writings by Sartre, in a variety of genres, all directed to its explication, its development, and its dramatization in the lives of fictional characters. Indeed, Sartre's own life was an exercise in the implications of his ideas.

Sartre's disassociation from bourgeois values began in his child-hood. His father, a naval officer, died shortly after his birth, and he was raised in the Parisian home of his maternal grandfather, Charles Schweitzer, an uncle of missionary physician Albert Schweitzer. This grandfather, an "Empire-bred republican," doted on young Jean-Paul and encouraged him to play the role of prodigy and future writer. Sartre obliged by rejecting God at the age of seven. In his memoir *The Words,* he recalled his grandparental home as a "hothouse" of bourgeois hypocrisy which, happily, left him with no encumbering super-ego. He spent a difficult adolescence at La Rochelle with his weak-willed mother and her second husband, a naval engineer, whose authority he resented.

Between 1924 and 1929, Sartre attended the prestigious École Normale Superieure at the University of Paris, where he grew dissatisfied with the inability of Cartesian and Kantian idealism to adequately represent the reality of human material presence. After failing his examinations for the *agrégation* (a degree slightly higher than a Ph.D.) in 1928, he studied with his fellow student Simone de Beauvoir; in the 1929 competitive examinations, he took first place, she second. Although the two refused, on principle, ever to marry, they built an emotional and professional partnership that lasted a lifetime.

After completing his military service in the Meteorological Corps, Sartre went as a teaching fellow to the Institut Français in Berlin, where he discovered the phenomenology of Edmund Husserl and Martin Heidegger. During the next four years, as professor of philosophy at various *lycées* in France, he began to incorporate phenomenology into his philosophy of existentialism.

Sartre delineated his controversial ideas in several books and articles before setting them into dramatic form in the novel *Nausea,* the study of a man stricken with anxiety at the suffocating horror of his own, and the world's, existence. (To some extent, the book reflects a mescaline-induced depression Sartre had suffered three years earlier.) It was a critical success and was soon followed by *The Wall,* a collection of short stories.

Sartre's political attitudes, until now largely quiescent, were gal-vanized by the Nazi invasion of France. He was mobilized with the 70th Division in 1939, captured on the Maginot Line before he saw combat, and interned for nine months in Stalag XIII D at Trèves, a prisoner-of-war camp, where he taught phenomenology to interned priests and wrote and produced a Christmas play, *Bariona.* After his escape the following year he returned to Paris and became active in the underground resistance movement, briefly heading a group of resistance intellectuals called "Socialism and Freedom."

In April 1943 Sartre published *Being and Nothingness,* a major work on the consciousness that was largely ignored. In June, his play *The Flies* was publicly performed; although it was cast as a reworking of the Orestes myth to fool the German censor, it conveyed an unmistakable message of resistance to Parisian audiences. A year later he staged *No Exit,* a dramatic inquiry into the possibilities of freedom for three characters locked in the same room with each other for eternity. Sartre's ventures into playwrighting demonstrated his emerging concern, a legacy of his war experiences, with human actions and their consequences; no longer content to describe the experience of "being," he now attempted to reconcile "being and doing." The war had "revealed history to him" and from this point on Sartre moved steadily leftward.

When the war ended, intellectual fashions caught up with existentialism, and Sartre suddenly found himself a celebrity. Inevitably, the vogue led to vulgar distortions in which Sartre's penetrating concepts were reduced to harmless, superficial slogans. Right-wing factions attacked him as a nihilist, a philosopher of "filth, excrement and despair," the Stalinist left characterized his thought as a passive individualism that masked the philosophical crisis of a dying class. Sartre later reflected, "Fame for me was hatred."

Consistent with his new stance as a man of action, Sartre now developed an increasing commitment to politics, urging France to steer a neutral course between the USSR and the United States and to forge a "third way" between liberal capitalism and Stalinist Communism. Sartre himself assumed the task of speaking "in favor of the freedom of the person *and* the socialist revolution," as founder and editor of *Les Temps modernes,* a monthly critical review that addressed politics, philosophy, and art. (The original editorial board included Simone de Beauvoir, the philosopher Maurice Merleau-Ponty, and the political writer Raymond Aron.) Though its content was decidedly leftist, *Les Temps modernes* scrupulously maintained its political independence and was influential in the post-war years. In 1950, when Sartre was edging closer to an alliance with the Communist Party, the journal nonetheless published proof of the existence of forced labor camps in the USSR.

During this period Sartre's tone became more stridently moralistic. In *What is Literature?* (1947), he maintained that "literature is in essence a taking of positions," challenging writers to become "engaged" in social conflicts and thereby take responsibility for the struggle of "bringing liberty to men." For a time, he was at pains to refute the Communist version of this struggle, arguing that dialectical materialism forfeited human values by eliminating human consciousness from the historical process. After 1948, however, Sartre refrained from harsh criticism of the French Communist Party in order to avoid giving ammunition to the "other side." Also in that year he became a founding member of the Rassemblement Democratique Révolutionaire, a group which sought to rally the support of independent leftists and workers for a political program committed to democracy and anti-Stalinism.

Throughout the 1940s and 50s, Sartre continued to turn out plays, pamphlets, radio broadcasts, critical essays, and three volumes of a novel entitled *Roads to Freedom*. In 1952 he published *Saint Genet, Actor and Martyr,* his most extensive work since *Being and Nothingness*. Genet was a novelist and playwright whose homosexuality, criminal record, and literary celebrations of murder and social degradation estranged him from proper French society. Sartre saw him as an exemplary man, an embodiment of "authenticity," who earned his freedom by breaking through socially enforced roles to establish his own morality. By revealing the social and economic basis of the values which the bourgeois world invoked to scorn Genet, Sartre began the integration of psychoanalysis and Marxism into his thought.

The collapse of the RDR movement in 1949 left Sartre in a political limbo from which he escaped in 1952 by effecting a rapprochement with the Communist Party. This move came in the wake of right-wing attempts to discredit the idea of class struggle, an idea to which Sartre was committed; it was also a gesture of sympathy with the Soviet Union, which Sartre then regarded as the protector of peace in the world of the Cold War. Although he did not officially join the Party— the fiercely independent Sartre never joined any political parties—the affiliation caused the rupture of several long-standing friendships, including those with Albert Camus, a liberal humanist and staunch anti-Communist, and Maurice Merleau-Ponty, who found Sartre's embrace of Soviet policy intolerable.

Sartre's brief period of fellow-traveling ended unequivocally in 1956: "The French Communist Party supported the (Soviet) invasion of Hungary, so I broke with it." He continued to enjoy close ties to the Italian Communists, "a party of tough, free men," and was a friend and admirer of its leader, Palmiro Togliatti. (From 1953 on, Sartre spent nearly all his summer holidays in Italy.)

Sartre's support of the Algerian National Liberation Front in its war of independence against French colonialism brought him into difficulties with the French government. As a metaphor for French "crimes" in Algeria, Sartre presented, in his play *The Condemned of Altona* (1960), the torment of a former Nazi who dreads the judgment of history. He tried in vain to provoke his own arrest as a gesture of opposition to the war; the authorities refused to jail him, for, as Charles de Gaulle said, "Sartre too, is France." However, issues of *Les Temps modernes* were increasingly subject to confiscation by the police, French army veterans called for Sartre's execution, and right-wing terrorists succeeded in exploding two plastic bombs in his Paris apartment.

In the midst of these political efforts, Sartre published the massive *Critique of Dialectical Reason,* a reconciliation of existentialism and Marxism in which he sought to produce an "historical anthropology," that would correlate the lived experience of the individual with the dynamic of history. Simone de Beauvoir, in *The Force of Circumstance,* describes the determined frenzy which possessed Sartre during its composition: "He did not work as he usually did, pausing to think and make corrections, tearing up pages and starting them over again. For hours on end he rushed on from page to page without re-reading what he'd written, as if he had been swept up by the ideas that his pen, even at that speed, could not catch up with." The *Critique* was followed by his autobiography, *The Words,* published in 1963.

In October 1964, Sartre was eating lentil soup in a Paris restaurant when he was informed that he had been awarded the Nobel Prize for Literature. In a letter of refusal to the Swedish Academy, Sartre explained that acceptance of the award would compromise his independence as a political activist (whose freedom to take sides must not be trammeled by any suggestion of bourgeois approval) and as a writer (whose authority must be earned rather than conferred by an institution.) Nor did the prize money tempt him greatly; Sartre, in his determination to be a free man, eschewed even such possessions as furniture.

Despite a decline in his health, Sartre maintained a hectic schedule of writing, traveling, lecturing, and attending international conferences on political and cultural issues. Throughout the 1960s he was occupied in writing *The Idiot of the Family,* a four-volume biography of Gustave Flaubert, using a dual Marxist and Freudian perspective to analyze in exhaustive detail the sources and nuances of the novelist's work. He interrupted these labors to support the student uprisings of May 1968 and to take part in violent demonstrations against the U.S. war in Vietnam. When the government banned *La Cause du peuple,* a Maoist newspaper, Sartre offered the cover of his prestige by allowing his name to be listed on its masthead. In keeping with his recently adopted Maoist insistence that the intellectual become engaged in practical political activities, he openly distributed the paper on Left Bank streets, for which he was duly arrested. "From 1940 to 1968," Sartre remarked, "I was a left-wing intellectual and from 1968 on I became an intellectual leftist. The difference is one of action."

In 1973, Sartre, now 68 years old, began to go blind. Simone de Beauvoir, his companion since his student days, read to him and kept him informed of world events. One of his last public acts was to sign, along with other French intellectuals, a statement condemning the Soviet invasion of Afghanistan and urging support for the United States boycott of the Moscow Olympic games.

On March 20, 1980, Sartre was admitted to Broussais Hospital in Paris. He died there on April 15 from pulmonary edema. A silent escort of 25,000 people escorted his body from the hospital to the Montparnasse Cemetery where he was provisionally interred. He was cremated without ceremony at Père Lachaise Cemetery.   E.T.

Born Jean-Paul-Charles-Aymard S. Son of Jean-Baptiste S., naval officer, and Anne-Marie (Schweitzer) S. Daughter: Arlette el Kaïm-Sartre (adopted as an adult 1965). Atheist. Educ: Lycée Montaigne, Paris 1912–13; Lycée Henry IV, Paris 1915, 1920–22; Lycée de la Rochelle 1917–20; Lycée Louis-le-Grand, Paris 1922–24; agrégé de philosophie, École Normale Supérieure, Paris 1929. Mil. Service: Sgt., Meteorological Corps, French Army 1929–31; Pvt., 70th Div., French Army 1939–40; prisoner of war 1940–41, escaped; active in the Resistance 1941–44. Prof. of phil., Lycée du Havre 1931–33, 1934–36; Teaching Fellow, Institut Français, Berlin 1933–34; Prof., Lycée de Laon 1936–37; Prof., Lycée Pasteur de Neuilly-sur-Seine 1937–39; Prof., Lycée Condorcet, Paris 1941–44. Film scriptwriter, Maison Pathe 1943. Special U.S. corresp. for Combat and Le Figaro 1945. Founder and ed., Les Tempes modernes (jrnl.), Paris 1944–80. Philosopher, playwright, novelist, essayist, ed., lect., political activist and critic of lit., art, and film since 1944. Co-founder, Liberation news agency 1971. Nominal ed of leftist jrnls: La Cause du Peuple and Tout 1970–74; Révolution 1971–74; Libération 1973–74; La France

Sauvage 1973–80. Founding Member, "Socialism and Liberty" group of Resistance intellectuals 1941. Member from 1943, elected Gov. Bd. Member 1953, Comité National des écrivains (Natl. Writers Cttee.); Member from 1943, Comité National du Théâtre (Natl. Theater Cttee.); Exec. Bd. Member, Rassemblement Democratique Révolutionaire 1948–49; Member, Peace Movement, since 1950s; participant, Special Session of World Peace Council, Berlin 1954; V.P., France-USSR Assn. 1954–56; elected Member, Intnl. Inst. of Phil. (Unesco) 1961; V.P., Congress of European Writers' Community 1962; Member 1966–71 and Exec. Pres., 1st session, Stockholm 1967, Intnl. War Crimes Tribunal of Bertrand Russell Foundn.; Member, American Acad. Arts and Sciences. Hons: French Popular Novel Prize (for La Nausee) 1940; Légion d'honneur 1945 (refused); N.Y. Drama Critics Award for best foreign play of the season (for Huis clos) 1947; French Grand Novel Prize (for La Nausée) 1950; Omega Prize, Italy for total body of work 1960; Nobel Prize for Lit. 1964 (refused); Fellow, Modern Language Assn. of America. *Major Works: Philosophy*— Esquisse d'une Théorie des Émotions, 1939 (The Emotions: Outline of a Theory, U.S. 1948; Sketch for a Theory of the Emotions, U.K. 1962); L'Imaginaire, 1940 (Psychology of the Imagination, U.S. 1948, U.K. 1949); L'Être et le Néant: Essai d'ontologie phenomenologique, 1943 (Being and Nothingness: An Essay on Phenomenological Ontology, U.S. 1956, U.S. 1957); L'Existentialisme est une humanisme, 1946 (Existentialism, U.S. 1947; Existentialism and Humanism, U.K. 1948); Questions de méthode 1957, (Search for a Method, U.S. 1963; Problem of Method, U.K. 1964); Critique de la raison dialectique 1960. *Novels*—La Nausée, 1938 (Nausea, U.S. 1949; The Diary of Antoine Roquentin, U.K. 1949); Les Chemins de la liberté (Roads to Freedom): Vol. I, L'Âge de raison, 1945 (The Age of Reason, U.K. 1947, U.S. 1959); Vol. II, Le Sursis, 1945 (The Reprieve, U.S. and U.K. 1947); Vol. III, La Mort dans L'ame, 1949 (Iron in the Soul, U.K. 1950; Troubled Sleep, U.S. 1951); Vol. IV, La Dernière Chance, unfinished, unpublished. *Plays*—Les Mouches, 1943 (The Flies, U.K., 1946, U.S. 1947); Huis clos, 1945 (In Camera, U.K. 1946; No Exit, U.S. 1947; stage version Vicious Circle 1946; French film 1954; Argentine film 1962; television version 1965; recording 1965); Morts sans sépulture 1946 (The Victors, U.S. 1949; Men Without Shadows, U.K. 1949); La Putain respectueuse, 1946 (The Respectful Prostitute, U.S. 1949; The Respectable Prostitute, U.K. 1949; film 1952; LP recording 1968; musical comedy 1967); Les Mains sales, 1948 (Dirty Hands, U.S. 1949; Crime Passionel, U.K. 1949; U.S. stage version Red Gloves 1948; film 1951); Le Diable et le Bon Dieu, 1951 (Lucifer and the Lord, U.K. 1953; The Devil and the Good Lord, U.S. 1960); Nedrassov, 1956 (U.K. 1956, U.S. 1960); Les Séquestrés d'Altona, 1960 (Loser Wins, U.K. 1960; The Condemned of Altona, U.S. 1961; Italo-French film 1963); Bariona, ou le fils de tonnere (written 1940), 1962 (Bariona, or the Son of Thunder, U.S. 1970); (adapter) Kean (by Alexandre Dumas père), 1954 (Kean, or Disorder and Genius, U.K. 1954, U.S. 1960; Italian film 1957); (adapter) Les Troyennes (by Euripedes), 1965 (The Trojan Women, U.K. 1967, U.S. 1969). *Short Story Collection*—Le Mur, 1939 (The Wall and Other Stories, U.S. 1948; Intimacy and Other Stories, U.K. 1952; film of story Le Mur, 1967). *Literary Criticism*—Baudelaire, 1947 (U.K. 1949, U.S. 1950); Qu'est-ce que la littérature?, 1964 (What is Literature?, U.S. 1949, U.K. 1950); Orphée Noir, 1948 (Black Orpheus, U.K. 1963, U.S. 1971); Saint Genet, Comedien et Martyr 1952 (Saint Genet, Actor and Martyr, U.S. 1963, U.K. 1964); L'Idiot de la famille: Gustave Flaubert de 1821 à 1857, Vols. I and II, 1971; Vol. III, 1972. *Essays and Articles*—Reflexions sur la question juive,

1946 (Anti-Semite and Jew, U.S. 1948, Portrait of an Anti-Semite, U.K. 1948); (ed. and commentator) L'affaire Henri Martin, 1953. Many essays and articles collected in Situations I, 1947; Situations II, 1948; Situations III, 1949; Situations IV: Portraits, 1964; Situations V: Colonialisme et néo-colonialisme, 1964; Situations VI: Problèmes du Marxisme, 2, 1965; Situations VIII: Autour de 68, 1972; Situations IX: Mélanges, 1972; Situations X, 1976. Many translated in Literary and Philosophical Essays (U.S., 1955). *Film scripts*—Les Jeux sont faits, film 1947 (The Chips are Down, U.S. 1948, U.K. 1951); Les Faux nez, 1947; L'Engrenage, 1948 (In the Mesh, U.K. 1954); Freud, film 1952 (withdrew name from credits); (adapter) Les Sorcières de Salem (from The Crucible by Arthur Miller), film 1957. *Autobiography*—Les Mots, 1964 (Words, U.K. and U.S. 1964).

Further reading: The Adventures of the Dialectic by Maurice Merleau-Ponty, 1955; The Prime of Life by Simone de Beauvoir, 1960; Sartre: The Origins of a Style by Frederic Jameson, 1961; Force of Circumstance by Simone de Beauvoir, 1963; Sartre's Ontology: A Study of Being and Nothingness in the Light of Hegel's Logic by Klaus Hartmann, 1966; The Obstructed Path by H. Stuart Hughes, 1968; Marxism and the Existentialists by Raymond Aron, 1969; Sartre by Hazel Barnes, 1972; The Writings of Jean-Paul Sartre Vol. I: A Bibliographical Life compiled by Michel Cartat and Michel Rybalka, trans. by Richard C. McCleary, 1974; Existential Marxism in Postwar France by Mark Poster, 1975.

ALF (SVEN ERIK) SJÖBERG
Theater and film director
Born Stockholm, Sweden, June 21st, 1903
Died Stockholm, Sweden, April 17th, 1980

Courtesy Karl G Kristoffersson

Alf Sjöberg was the most important film director in Sweden in the era after Stiller and Sjöstrom, the pioneers of silent film. He was also an outstanding director and producer of works for the stage. Unlike the trite, complacent Swedish films between the world wars, Sjöberg's films had profound themes—the consequences of cowardice and love, the defense of ideals, the struggle to survive in a hostile environment—and experimented with expressionist techniques to bring these themes to life. Rapid cuts, bold compositions, shadowy lighting, a mobile camera, and the heavy use of symbols were typical elements of his visual language. Critics appreciated his polished craftsmanship and deft handling of actors.

Sjöberg was born in Stockholm in 1903 and studied at that city's Royal Dramatic Theater School, where Greta Garbo was a fellow student. In 1929 he made a silent film, *Den Starkaste (The Strongest)*, a story of jealousy among seal hunters above the Arctic Circle. His use of montage, borrowed from Sergei Eisenstein, gave the film a documentary flavor, and his concentration on landscape and naturalistic acting helped to diminish the influence of stage conventions on Swedish cinema.

During the 1930s, Sjöberg stayed away from the studios, which were turning out light, escapist entertainment, and traveled through Europe studying theater productions, becoming director of Stock-

holm's Royal Dramatic Theater. In 1940 he returned to films with
Med livet som insats (They Staked Their Lives), a pacifist work about a
band of resistance fighters in an occupied country that reflected the
concern of the Swedes over the rise of Nazi Germany and the dilemma
of their own neutrality. Two years later he directed *Himlaspelet (Road
to Heaven)*, a movie version of a morality play by Rune Lundström,
who played a major role in it. This drama, which used images from
religious folk art to re-create the spiritual atmosphere of medieval
Sweden, is considered one of the finest examples of pre-1950 Scandinavian filmmaking. Here, as in most of his work, Sjöberg won praise
for his convincing evocation of an historical era.

Hets (Frenzy), made in 1944 from a script by Ingmar Bergman, then
a young film student, was a tale of the mental suffering inflicted on a
schoolboy by the sadistic teacher who competes with him for the
affection of a prostitute. Its international success encouraged young
Swedes to revitalize their national cinema, but the result, for a time,
was a number of despair-ridden, hypersensitive imitations which
lacked the psychological nuances of Sjöberg's work. He collaborated
again with Bergman in 1956 on *Sista paret ut (The Last Pair Out)*.

Sjöberg's 1952 film *Miss Julie*, which he adapted from the play by
August Strindberg, won the Grand Prix at the Cannes International
Film Festival and received praise for its technical experimentation,
including the integration of past and present action within the same
frame. Later Sjöberg directed film versions of two other Strindberg
plays, *Erik the Fourteenth* (as *Karin Månsdoter*) and *Fadern (The
Father)*. *Barabbas*, a Sjöberg film of striking visual effect, was written
by Sweden's Nobel Prize-winning author Pär Lagerkvist, several of
whose stage plays Sjöberg directed.

Throughout his career, Sjöberg continued to work in the theater; he
was particularly noted for his productions of plays by Shakespeare,
Ibsen, Brecht, and modern Swedish writers. At the time of his death,
he was rehearsing a play by Molière. He died of injuries suffered in a
car accident.   S.P.

Son of C.E.S. and Elisabet (Wickberg) S. Married: (1) Märta
Ekström, actress, 1930 (div. 1934); (2) Elsa Ahlsell 1935. Children:
one daughter; one son. Educ: Royal Dramatic Theatre Sch., Stockholm 1923–25; also studied acting abroad. Actor 1925–29 and Head
Dir. since 1931, Royal Dramatic Theatre, Stockholm; film director
since 1929; play and film producer since 1930; with Swedish radio
1952–54. Hons: Litteris et Artibus (Royal Medal for outstanding
contribution to Swedish culture) 1951; Grand Prix, Cannes Intnl. Film
Festival (for Miss Julie) 1952; St. Erik-Medaljen; Hon. Dr. Phil.
Director: Plays—Den Starkaste (The Strongest), 1929; Med livet som
insats (They Staked Their Lives), 1940; Den Blomstertid (Flowering
Time), 1940; Hem fran Babylon (Home From Babylon), 1941;
Himlaspelet (The Road to Heaven), 1942; Kungajakt (The Royal
Hunt), 1944; Hets (Frenzy), 1944; Resan bort (Journey Out), 1945;
Iris och löjtnantshjärta (Iris and the Lieutenant), 1946; Bara en mor
(Only a Mother), 1949; Fröken Julie (Miss Julie), 1951; Barabbas,
1953; Karin Månsdotter, 1954; Vildfågler (Wild Birds), 1955; Sista
paret ut (Last Pair Out), 1956; Domaren (The Judge), 1960; Ön (The
Island), 1966; Fadern (The Father), 1969. Also screenwriter on most
of his films.

DONALD G(EORGE) BRENNAN
President of the Hudson Institute
Born Waterbury, Connecticut, U.S.A., April 9th, 1926
Died Irvington, New York, U.S.A., April 18th, 1980

A specialist in national security problems, Donald G. Brennan served as President and later as Director of National Security Studies of the Hudson Institute, a "think tank" dedicated to research on military matters and policy issues relating to energy and economics.

Born in Waterbury, Connecticut in 1926, Brennan joined the U.S. Army in 1944. After discharge in 1947, he worked as a radio engineer for station WWCO in his home-town until 1949. He then joined the Crystal Research Laboratory in Hartford as a staff member and simultaneously taught at the Ward School of Electronics at the University of Hartford. From 1953 through 1959, while studying mathematics at the Massachusetts Institute of Technology, Brennan worked as a researcher with the university's Lincoln Laboratory. Receiving his doctoral degree in 1959, Brennan remained at M.I.T. as a research associate for two years. His professional interests included radio engineering, probability theory, classical and abstract harmonic analysis, functional analysis, fluctuation phenomena, and the statistical theory of communication.

During 1957 Brennan developed an interest in arms control and became the organizer of a group that led to the 1958 Summer Study of Arms Control held in Cambridge, Massachusetts, under the sponsorship of the American Academy of Arts and Sciences. Anticipating an acceleration of the arms race between the U.S. and the Soviet Union, Brennan, in the late 50s, called for an international agreement to control the use of "outer space." At the national level, he saw the need for an agency whose primary responsibility would be the reduction of cold war tensions and long-term military hazards and suggested the creation of a study center analogous to the RAND Corporation. This notion became a reality with the founding of the Hudson Institute by Herman Kahn in 1961.

From its beginning Brennan was part of the group of scholars associated with the Hudson Institute and, in 1962, he left M.I.T. to become president of the organization. Brennan saw the Institute as a ground-breaker through its systematic analyses of military and strategic affairs and felt that the group's research efforts removed emotional biases, thus providing a clearer understanding of the choices available and actions possible for international policymakers. He firmly denied the critics' position that military intellectuals inculcate militarism.

In 1964 Brennan resigned from his position as president of the Hudson Institute and became its Director of National Security Studies, a post he held until his death. His particular areas of expertise included arms control, alliance relationships with Europe and advanced military policy, especially policy involving tactical and strategic nuclear forces. During the 1960s Brennan was a consultant for numerous government agencies and frequently appeared before Congress to testify on defense issues such as the ABM system, which he supported.

Although he generally favored arms limitation and the nuclear test ban treaty, Brennan did oppose President Carter's SALT treaties because he felt they did nothing to improve US security.

Shortly before his death, an apparent suicide, Brennan had accepted an invitation to join presidential candidate Ronald Reagan's defense advisory committee.   S.S.

Son of George J.B. and Jessie B. Married: (1) . . . ; (2) Katie Sheldon 1969. No children. Educ: Mass. Inst. Technology, B.S. 1955, Ph.D. (Gerard Swope Fellow) maths. 1959. Mil. Service: U.S. Army 1944–47. Chief Engineer, radio station WWCO, Waterbury, Conn. 1947–49; Staff Member, Crystal Research Lab., Hartford, Conn.; Instr., Ward Sch. of Electronics, Univ. Hartford 1949–51. Staff Member 1953–59 and Group Leader 1959–62, Lincoln Lab., Mass. Inst. Technology 1959–61. Pres. 1962–64 and Dir. of Natl. Security Studies since 1964, Hudson Inst., Croton-on-Hudson, N.Y. Consultant: U.S. Dept. of Defense; U.S. State Dept.; Arms Control and Disarmament Agency; Atomic Energy Commn.; Energy Research Development Agency; U.S. Dept of Energy; Exec. Office of the Pres. Occasional lectr. on natl. security subjects, U.S.A., Canada, and Europe. Under American Acad. of Arts and Sciences: organizer, Summer Study on Arms Control, Cambridge, Mass. 1958; organizer and co-dir., Summer Study on Arms Control 1960. Chmn., Cttee. on Intnl. Studies of Arms Control 1961–62. Member: Pres.'s Natl. Citizens' Commn., Intnl. Co-operation Year 1965; Sigma Xi; American Mathematical Soc.; Council on Foreign Relations; Intnl. Inst. for Strategic Studies; Republican Natl. Cttee. Advisory Council on Natl. Security and Intnl. Affairs; Editorial Bd., Intnl. Security; Bd. of Dirs., Cttee. on the Present Danger; Bd. of Dir., World Trading and Shipping Corp. Hons: Fellow, American Assn. for the Advancement of Science. *Ed. and co-author:* Arms Control, special issue, Daedulus, Fall 1960; Arms Control, Disarmament, and National Security, 1961; Why ABM?, 1969. Contributed to both mags. and professional jrnls.

SIR STEPHEN (LEWIS) HOLMES
British High Commissioner in Australia and civil servant
Born Ealing, London, England, July 5th, 1896
Died Hastings, East Sussex, England, April 20th, 1980

Sir Stephen Holmes, whose experience in foreign trading led to his appointment as British High Commissioner in Australia, was a member of Britain's Diplomatic and Foreign Service for more than thirty-five years.

After attending Westminster School in London, Holmes was commissioned Second Lieutenant in the Special Reserve of the Royal Garrison Artillery, and within a year was posted overseas to the battlefronts of France and Belgium. By the end of the war, during which he received the Military Cross, Holmes had attained the rank of Acting Major.

Following his graduation from Christ Church College in Oxford, Holmes joined the British Colonial Service. After two years at the Imperial Defence College, Holmes was posted to Canada where for three years he was Senior Secretary at the British High Commission. He then moved to the Dominions Office and during World War Two, represented that office in Washington. From 1944 to 1946 Holmes was Deputy High Commissioner for the United Kingdom in Canada.

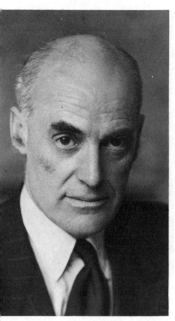

Courtesy Sir Stephen Lewis Holmes estate

Returning to Britain, Holmes became involved with the administration of overseas trade. During his first appointment as Under Secretary with the Board of Trade, he served on many British delegations to overseas trade and tariff conferences. Holmes received a Knighthood in 1950; the following year he was appointed Deputy Under Secretary of State at the Commonwealth Relations Office. Holmes was able to apply his earlier experience in international trade to help some of the newly emerging independent Commonwealth countries. He was named British High Commissioner in Australia in 1952, a time of domestic crisis in the country's import and tariff policies. During his tenure Holmes suggested ways to control imports without seriously affecting the goodwill of Australia's foreign trading partners. He retired from government service in 1957, less than a year after returning from Australia.   M.D.

Son of Basil H. and Isabella H. Married Noreen Charlotte Trench 1922. Children: two sons (one d.); one daughter. Educ: Westminster Public Sch.; Christ Church Coll. Oxford, B.A. 1921. Mil. Service: Royal Regiment of Gunners 1915, active service in France and Belgium 1916-19 (M.C.). Entered Colonial Office 1919; Principal Asst., Dominions Office 1928; at Imperial Defence Coll. 1934–36; Sr. Secty., British High Commn. in Canada 1936-39; Asst. Secty 1939–43 and Rep. in Washington, D.C. 1943–44, Dominions Office; U.K. Deputy High Commnr. in Canada 1944–46; Under-Secty. and 2nd. Secty. 1947–51, Board of Trade; Deputy Under-Secty. of State, Commonwealth Relations Office 1951–52; U.K. High Commissioner in Australia 1952–56. Hons: C.M.G. 1942; K.C.M.G. 1950; Master of Leathersellers' Co., London 1967–68.

HELMUT KÄUTNER
Director, screenwriter, and actor
Born Düsseldorf, Germany, March 25th, 1908
Died Castellina, Italy, April 20th, 1980

During the long period of artistic decline which afflicted the German cinema between 1933 and the rise of the New Wave directors in the early 1970s, Helmut Käutner stood out as one of the few German filmmakers of distinction. Though his earlier films—including some of his best work—were made under the Third Reich, he kept them largely free of Nazi propaganda, either implicit or overt, and in 1945 was widely expected to head the revival of the post-war German cinema.

Käutner, born in Düsseldorf in 1908, studied art history, philosophy and dramatic art at Munich; from 1931 to 1935 he worked as actor, scriptwriter and producer for the Munich student cabaret *Die Vier Nachrichter* (The Four Reporters), of which he was one of the co-founders. In 1934 he married the actress Erica Balqué, who subsequently worked with him on several of his films.

In 1936, Käutner moved into mainstream theater, working as an actor in Leipzig, subsequently in Munich, and—from 1938—in Berlin. His career in the theater, as actor, director, producer and designer, continued alongside his film work, and in fact outlasted it; Käutner was active in the theater until 1977, seven years after directing his last film.

He began writing film scripts in 1938, and directed his first picture the next year. He later remarked: "Actually I was not really interested in the cinema. Politically I was left-wing. . . I really wanted to go on working in the theater. It was painful for me to see how rigorously scripts were often changed in the studio." By shooting his own scripts, Käutner hoped for greater control.

Ironically, his first film ran into trouble with the authorities. *Kitty und die Weltkonferenz* (Kitty and the World Conference), a musical comedy with a lightly satirical political background, opened in Berlin just after the outbreak of war in Europe. The portrayal of one of the characters, a British diplomat, was found too sympathetic, and Goebbels had the film banned; it was not shown again under the Third Reich.

For the rest of the war, Käutner prudently avoided overt political comment by concentrating on romantic subjects, often set in the past, and dealing largely with the private lives of his characters. This approach was epitomized by *Romanze in Moll* (Romance in a Minor Key), 1943, a delicate and subtle account (based on a Maupassant short story) of a doomed love affair. The film won him a Critics' Prize in neutral Sweden, but was attacked by Goebbels as "defeatist."

Courtesy National Film Archive/British Film Institute

During the last months of the war, as the bombs fell and the armies closed in on Berlin, Käutner made *Unter den Brücken* (Under the Bridges), 1945, a quiet almost idyllic story set among the barge-people on the river Havel. This was his own favorite among his films and, with *Romanze in Moll,* probably his finest; strongly influenced by the humanists 'poetic realism' of Renoir and Carné, it can be interpreted as a plea for the rights of individuals to find their own happiness, free from regimentation.

Käutner's post-war work, though generally stylish and intelligent, and standing out from the predominantly vapid German films of the period, never quite fulfilled the promise of his early accomplishments. Among his stronger films were those in which he attempted to come to terms with the experience of the Nazi period: *In Jenen Tagen* (In Those Days), 1947; *Die letzte Brücke* (The Last Bridge), 1954; and *Des Teufels General* (The Devil's General), 1955. The latter was based on a play by Carl Zuckmayer, as were three more of Käutner's films, most notably *Der Hauptmann von Köpenick* (The Captain of Kopenick), 1956. For all these, as for most of his films, Käutner wrote his own scripts.

In 1957 he went to Hollywood, where he directed two unremarkable films for Universal Studios. Returning to Germany, he worked mainly on literary adaptations, at first for the cinema, then increasingly for television. His television work was never less than sound and skillful; after 1964 he made only one more cinema film. During the 1970s, Käutner continued to direct for television and the theater, as well as to act in works by other directors. In 1978 However, ill-health forced him to retire. His last years were spent at his home in Tuscany.   P.K.

Son of a merchant. Married Erica Balqué, actress. Educ: Sch. of Fine Arts, Düsseldorf; Univ. of Munich; Acad. of Arts, Cologne. Co-founder, writer, and dir., student cabaret Die Vier Nachrichter ("The Four Reporters"), Munich 1933–35; actor and dir. in theaters in Leipzig, Munich, and Berlin 1936–38. Became film dir. 1939; head of his own film company, Camera-Film Produktion 1947–49; dir. for television since 1965. Member, Akademie der Kunste, Berlin. Hons: Federal Film Prize: for directing Die letzte Brücke 1954; for directing Der Hauptmann von Köpenick 1957; for long and outstanding activity in the German cinema 1973. First Prize, Cannes Film Festival (for Die letzte Brücke) 1954; Kunstpreis Stadt Berlin 1956; Adolf Grimme Prize 1968; Great Fed. Distinguished Service Cross 1973. *Director: Films*—Kitty und die Weltkonferenz (also scriptwriter), 1939; Die acht Entfesselten, 1939; Frau nack Mass (also scriptwriter), 1940; Kleider machen Leute (also scriptwriter), 1940; Auf Wiedersehen, Franziska (also co-scriptwriter), 1941; Anuschka (also co-scriptwriter), 1941; Wir machen Musik (also scriptwriter), 1942; Romanze in Moll (also co-scriptwriter), 1942; Grosse Freiheit Nr. 7 (also scriptwriter), 1944; Unter den Brücken (also co-scriptwriter), 1945; In jenen Tagen (also co-scriptwriter), 1947; Der Apfel ist ab (also co-scriptwriter and actor), 1948; Königskinder (also co-scriptwriter), 1949; Epilog (also co-scriptwriter), 1950; Weisse Schatten (also co-scriptwriter), 1951; Käpt'n Bay–Bay, 1952; Die letzte Brücke (also co-scriptwriter), 1953; Bildnis einer Unbekannten, 1954; Ludwig II, 1954; Des Teufels General (also co-scriptwriter), 1954; Himmel ohne Sterne (also co-scriptwriter), 1955; Ein Mädchen aus Flandern (also co-scriptwriter), 1955; Griff nach den Sternen, 1955; Der Hauptmann von Köpenick (also co-scriptwriter), 1956; Die Zuercher Verlobung (also co-scriptwriter), 1957; Monpti (also co-scriptwriter), 1957; The Restless Years, 1957; Schinderhannes (also co-scriptwriter), 1958; A Stranger in my Arms, 1958; Der Rest ist Schweigen (also co-scriptwriter), 1959; Die Gans von Sedan (also co-scriptwriter), 1959; Schwarzer Kies (also co-scriptwriter), 1960; Das Glass Wasser (also scriptwriter), 1960; Der Traum von Lieschen Müller (also co-scriptwriter), 1961; Die Rote (also co-scriptwriter), 1962; Das Haus in Montevideo (also co-scriptwriter), 1963; Laububengeschichten, 1964; Die Feuerzangenbowle (also scriptwriter), 1970. *Television*—Romulus der Grosse (play), 1965; Die Flasche (play; also scriptwriter), 1965; Robin Hood, der edle Räuber (film), 1966; Leben wie die Fuersten (play), 1966; Die spanische Puppe (play; also scriptwriter), 1967; Stella (play; also scriptwriter), 1967; Valentin Katajews chirurgische Eingriffe in das Seelenleben des Dr. Igor Igorowitsch (play), 1967; Bel Ami (play; also scriptwriter), 1967; Tagebuch eines Frauenmoerders (play), 1969; Christoph Kolumbus oder die Entdeckung Amerikas (play; also co-scriptwriter), 1969; Einladung ins Schloss (play), 1970; Anonymer Anruf (film), 1970; Die gefaelschte Goettin (play; also co-scriptwriter), 1971; Die seltsamen Abenteuer des Geheimen Kanzleisekretaers Tusmann (play), 1971; Ornifle oder der erzuernte Himmel (play), 1972; Die preussische Heirat (play; also scriptwriter), 1974; Stiftungsfest (film), 1974; Margarethe in Aix (play), 1975; Mulligans Rückkehr (film), 1977. *Opera*—König Pausole; Der Prinz von Homburg, Hamburg State Opera. *Theater*—plays by Anouilh, Wilder, Arthur Miller, and Ustinov in Hamburg, Bochum, Berlin. *Co-scriptwriter:* Film ohne Titel, 1948; Nachts auf den Strassen, 1951; Franziska, 1958; Schneider Wibbel; Salonwagen E417; Die Stimme aus dem Aether; Marguerite: 3. *Other:* Zu jung für die Liese (supervisor and actor), 1962; Kreuzer emden (actor).

SIR (MALCOLM) JOHN METHVEN
Industrialist and administrator; Director-General, Confederation of
British Industry
Born London, England, February 14th, 1926
Died London, England, April 23rd, 1980

Sir John Methven was Director-General of the Confederation of British Industry (C.B.I.) during a critical period of economic and political instability. At the time of his appointment, the Confederation lacked the confidence of its member-industries and Methven was credited with strengthening a weak organization.

The son of a founder of the Royal Canadian Air Force, Methven attended Mill Hill School in London and studied law at Cambridge. Admitted solicitor in 1952, Methven subsequently worked with the Birmingham Corporation for five years. In 1957 Methven was asked to join Imperial Chemical Industries by his close friend Lord Fleck who was then its chairman. Initially working as a legal assistant in the company's Metals Division, Methven soon became head of the Central Purchasing Division and eventually assumed the Deputy Chairmanship of I.C.I.'s large Mond Inorganic Chemicals Division. In 1973 Methven was appointed Director-General of the Office of Fair Trading, the government agency serving as a watchdog over company mergers, corporate monopolization, business ethics, and consumer affairs. Methven quickly became known as a strong advocate of consumers' rights and in 1976, he was appointed Director-General of C.B.I.

Courtesy Confederation of British Industry

The Confederation, industrial management's representative body in government negotiations, theoretically held equal status with the Trade Union Congress, but many industries believed that C.B.I. failed to negotiate its interests as effectively as the T.U.C. bargained for its union membership. Dissatisfaction within C.B.I. was so strong that Britain's largest engineering group threatened to lead a number of other industries out of the organization.

Methven proved to be a conciliator. By offering C.B.I. membership to smaller businesses, he achieved a wider representation of commercial interests and insisted that heads of nationalized industries be allowed to retain their membership on Confederation boards on an equal basis with private industry executives. To insure that public debate of economic policies would be informed by an unbiased understanding of management decisions, all Confederation conferences were held publicly. Contending that even sophisticated marketing techniques could not accurately predict future economic trends, Methven strenuously opposed long-term planning projects by major industries. Because Methven had, throughout his career, consistently advocated increased participation by workers in factory decision-making processes, he was able to open channels of communication between the unions and management far more effectively than any previous C.B.I. head.

Methven was knighted in 1978 in recognition of his open and efficient style of management. He died suddenly of a heart-attack.

M.D.

Son of Lt.-Col. M.D. M., C.B.E. and H.M. M. Married: (1) Margaret Field Nicholas 1952; (2) Karen Jane Caldwell 1977. Children: 1st marriage—three daughters. Educ: Mill Hill Sch., London; Gonville and Caius Coll., Cambridge; (Tapp Exhibitioner in law) M.A.,

L.L.B. 1949; postgrad. study in law (Tapp Scholar) 1950; admitted solicitor 1952. Solicitor, Birmingham Municipal Corp. 1952–57. With Imperial Chemical Industries: Legal Asst., Metals Div. 1957; Asst. and Sr. Asst., Legal Dept. 1957-68; Head, Central Purchasing Div. 1968–70; Deputy Chmn., Mond Inorganic Chemicals Div. 1970–73. Dir.-Gen., Office of Fair Trading 1973–76; Dir.-Gen., Confederation of British Industry 1976-80. Member: Monopolies Commn. 1972; Natl. Economic Development Council 1976; also, Natl. Industrial Democracy Cttee.; British Industry 1500 Club (pres.); Custodian Trustee; Natl. Assn. of Citizens' Advice Bureaux (V.P.); Inst. of Trading Standards Admin. Hons: knighted 1978.

ALEJO CARPENTIER
Novelist and musicologist
Born Havana, Cuba, December 26th, 1904
Died Paris, France, April 24th, 1980

The Cuban novelist Alejo Carpentier, whose contribution to Latin American and international literature is comparable to that of Miguel Asturias and Jorge Luis Borges, wrote about the Caribbean with a combination of New World wonder and European realpolitik. Born of Franco-Russian parentage in Havana in 1904, Carpentier led the kind of uprooted existence, filled with periods of imprisonment, flight, and voluntary exile, that has come to be characteristic of the Latin American intellectual in the twentieth century. Although a firm believer in revolution, despite what he realized were its frequent failures and tendency to reproduce the conditions which had made it necessary, Carpentier never subscribed to standard socialist realism, not even after he returned to his native Cuba under the Castro regime. Instead, his explorations of the Caribbean are embellished with musical and architectural details that have at times been considered excessive.

After studying music and architecture at the University of Havana, Carpentier held several journalistic and editorial positions, including (from 1924–28) editor-in-chief of the influential magazine, *Carteles*. In 1928 Carpentier went into voluntary exile for eleven years in Paris where his first novel, *Ecué-yamba-O* was published (1932); begun during seven months of imprisonment under the Machado regime, it dealt with Afro-Cuban characters and situations. He also directed a spoken arts program, wrote an opera with Edgar Varèse, and edited the literary review *Iman*.

Involvement with the surrealist movement and its journal, *Révolution Surréaliste,* which expounded the doctrine of "only in the marvelous is beauty," greatly influenced Carpentier's aesthetics. As a vigorous, imaginative alternative to the flat realism then in vogue among the writers of the *nativismo* movement, Carpentier developed the concept of the *"real maravilloso."* This almost visionary "marvelous reality" was meant to convey the rich and impenetrable mysteries of Carpentier's Caribbean world which is described in this passage from *Explosion in a Cathedral* (translated by John Sturrock):

. . .Amidst a growing economy of zoological forms, the coral forests preserved the earliest baroque of Creation, its first luxuriance and extravagance, hiding their treasures where, in order to see them, the young man had to imitate the fish he had once been, before he was shaped by the womb—regretting the gills and tail which would have enabled him to choose these gorgeous landscapes as his permanent dwelling-place. In these coral forests Esteban saw a tangible image, a ready-and yet so inaccessible—configuration, of a Paradise Lost, where the trees, barely named as yet by the torpid, hesitant tongue of the Man-child, would be endowed with the apparent immortality of this sumptuous flora, this ostensory, this burning bush, where autumn and spring could be detected only in a variation in the colours, or a slight shifting of the shadows.

In 1939 Carpentier returned to Cuba, where he wrote and directed radio programs for three years before being appointed Professor of the History of Music at the Conservatorio Nacional, a post he held from 1941 to 1943. On a trip to Haiti in 1943 Carpentier discovered an appropriate vehicle for his concept of the real maravilloso in the fantastic reign of the nineteenth-century monarch, Henri Christophe. *El reino de este mundo (The Kingdom of This World),* published in 1941, transformed Christophe's history into something more closely resembling myth. Ornate, stylized scenes revealed Carpentier's interest in architecture and the book reflected his unwavering optimism about revolution. As Carpentier wrote elsewhere: "Men may fail, but ideas continue to make headway until the time comes for them to be fully realized."

During another long period of exile from 1945 to 1959, this time in Venezuela, Carpentier managed a radio station in Caracas and held a teaching position at the Central University there. *Los pasos perdidos (The Lost Steps),* published in 1953, was the story of a bored Cuban musicologist who journeys from New York City to the Venezuelan rain forest in quest of primitive musical instruments and his own lost self. Although some critics considered the style too elaborate and the musical analogies strained, the novel received an award for the best foreign book in France.

Among his other works are a history of Cuban music, *La Musica en Cuba* (1946), a novella about the persecution of a student during the Machado dictatorship; *El acoso (Manhunt),* which appeared in 1956; *Guerra del tiempo (The War of Time),* a collection of short stories published in 1958; *El recurso del metodo* (1974), another novel about the Machado regime; and *Concierto barroco* (1974), a fantasy that displayed his fascination with music. One of his most important works, *El Siglo de las luces (Explosion in a Cathedral),* was published in 1963. Although it dealt with the period of the French Revolution, it was less an historical novel than a fusion of the real and the fantastic which enabled Carpentier to explore the cyclical nature of time and revolution.

Carpentier was cultural attaché to Cuba's embassy in Paris from 1967 until his death in 1980. At the time of his death in Paris at the age of 75, he was at work on a three-volume history of the Castro revolution.   E.S.

Son of Jorge Julian C., architect, and Lina Valmont C., teacher. Married Andrea Esteban. No children. Lived in Paris 1928–39; Caracas 1945–1959; Paris 1967–80. Educ: attended Univ. Havana, studied music and architecture. Commercial journalist, Havana

1921–24; Ed., Carteles Mag., Havana 1924–28; Ed., Iman Mag., Paris ca. 1930; Dir., Foniric Studios, Paris 1933–39; writer and producer, CMZ Radio, Havana 1939–41; Prof., Hist. of Music, Conservatorio Nacional, Havana 1941–43; Dir., radio station, Caracas ca. 1945; columnist, El Nacional Mag., Caracas; Prof., Central Univ. of Caracas ca. 1950; Dir., Cuban Publishing House, Havana 1960–67; Cultural attaché, Cuban Embassy, Paris since 1967. Member, Acad. del Folklore de Mexico. Hons: Prix du Meilleur Livre Etranger 1956; Cino del Duca Prize 1975; Prix Medici 1979. *Books: Novels*—Ecué-yamba-O, 1933; El reino de este mundo, 1949 (The Kingdom of This World, 1957); Los pasos perdidos, 1953 (The Lost Steps, 1956); El acoso, 1956 (Manhunt, 1959); El siglo de las luces, 1962 (Explosion in a Cathedral, 1963); Tientos y diferencias, 1964; El derecho de asilo, 1972; Los convidados de plata, 1972; El recurso del metodo, 1974; El concierto barroco, 1974. *Short story collections*—Guerra del tiempo, 1958 (The War of Time, 1970); Tres Relatos, 1967; El camino de Santiago, 1967. *Poetry*—Poemas de las Antillas, 1929. *Essays*—Literatura y conciencia politica en America Latina, 1969. *Other*—La musica en Cuba (the first history of Cuban music), 1946; La cuidad de las columnas (study of Havana architecture, with photographs by Paolo Gasparini), 1970.
Further reading: Into the Mainstream by Luis Harss and Barbara Dohmann, 1967.

THOMAS K(NIGHT) FINLETTER
Secretary of the U.S. Air Force and Ambassador to NATO
Born Philadelphia, U.S.A., November 11th, 1893
Died New York City, U.S.A., April 24th, 1980

Thomas K. Finletter, former Secretary of the U.S. Air Force and NATO representative, was the principal author of a 1948 report that persuaded the U.S. government to triple its military air strength. At the same time, he was in the forefront of the movements for disarmament, peace, and world government.

Finletter was born into a prominent Philadelphia family. His mother was a descendant of colonial settlers; his father and paternal grandfather were judges. After attending Philadelphia's Episcopal Academy, Finletter spent a year in Paris, then entered the University of Pennsylvania, earning his B.A. in 1915. His studies were interrupted by First World War artillery service in France, where he met Gretschen Blaine Damrosch (daughter of conductor Walter Damrosch), whom he married after his graduation from law school in 1920. The couple moved to New York City; Finletter joined the firm of Cravath and Henderson and his wife embarked on a writing career. Breaking family tradition, Finletter became a member of the Democratic Party after the Republicans blocked the formation of the League of Nations.

In 1926 Finletter joined the New York Law firm of Coudert Brothers and later became a partner. In 1941 he received his first public service appointment as Special Assistant to Secretary of State Cordell Hull. His primary duty was to outbid the Axis powers in their attempts to purchase supplies and materials from neutral nations; in one instance, he persuaded Spain and Portugal to rescind their planned sale of tungsten to Germany. Assigned to the Office of Foreign Economic Coordination in 1943, he was responsible for economic planning in the liberated areas of Europe.

In 1945 Finletter served as a consultant and press liaison with the U.S. delegation to the United Nations organizational conference at San Francisco. Two years later, he assisted in the founding of the United World Federalists, an organization dedicated to promoting world peace by means of a strong world government. Unlike many "One World" supporters, however, Finletter advocated a strong U.S. military establishment as a deterrent to war. "I believe," he once said, "that our moral position will be judged by the vigor with which we push our efforts to achieve peace. I believe we would be faithless to our duty to ourselves and to our friends and allies of the free world if we were not to have a military force which would make it very plain to all that it would be a mistake to break the peace."

In July 1947 President Truman appointed Finletter chairman of a five-member Air Policy Commission to review the state of U.S. military and civil aviation. The Commission's 1948 report, *Survival in the Air Age,* of which Finletter was the principal author, concluded that the Air Force would soon be incapable of meeting defense requirements unless aircraft production and budget allocations were drastically increased. The report also proposed more thorough testing of commercial aircraft.

A few months later, Finletter went to the United Kingdom as Chief Representative of the Economic Cooperation Administration (the Marshall Plan) to assist in England's postwar economic recovery. During the Korean War President Truman appointed Finletter Secretary of the Air Force. Finletter left Washington in 1953 and entered New York State politics as chairman of the Democratic State Platform Committee, making an unsuccessful attempt to win nomination for the Senate in 1958. In 1961 President Kennedy named him permanent representative to the North Atlantic Treaty Organization, a post he held until 1965.

Finletter was the author of books and articles on bankruptcy law, on U.S. political structure and policy, and on the world peace movement. He died of heart failure at a New York hospital.   S.J.

Son of Thomas Dickson F., judge, and Helen (Grill) F. Married: (1) Gretchen Blaine Damrosch 1920 (d. 1969); (2) Eileen Wechsler Geist 1973. Children: 1st marriage—Margot Mitchell; Lili O'Neill. Episcopalian. Educ: Episcopal Acad., Philadelphia; Univ. Pa., B.A. 1915, LL.B. 1920. Mil. Service: Capt., 312th Field Artillery, U.S. Army, France, WWI. Admitted to Pennsylvania Bar 1920, and New York Bar 1921. Attorney, Cravath and Henderson, NYC 1920–26; Attorney 1926–41 and Partner 1944–48, 1965–70, Coudert Bros. law firm, NYC; Lectr., Univ. of Pennsylvania Law Sch. 1931-41. Special Asst. to Secty. of State, Washington, D.C. 1941–44; Staff Member, Office of Advisor on Intnl. Econ. Affairs 1941–43; Exec. Dir., then Deputy Dir., Office of Foreign Econ. Coordination 1943–44. Consultant, U.S. Delegation to U.N. Conference on Intnl. Org., San Francisco 1945; Chmn., President's Air Policy Commn. 1947–48; Chief Rep. to U.K. Mission, Econ. Cooperation Admin. (Marshall Plan) 1949; Secty. of U.S. Air Force 1950–53; U.S. Ambassador to NATO, Paris 1961–65. Chmn., Finance Cttee. to Defend America,

NYC 1939–41; Chmn., Democratic (Party) State Platform Cttee., N.Y. 1954; Chmn., U.S. Hosp. Funding Advisory Cttee. 1955; Chmn., Cttee. to insure compliance with Baker-Metcalf law barring discrimination in federally insured housing, N.Y. 1955; Chmn., N.Y. Civil Defense Commn. 1958. Elected Bd. Chmn., Freedom House, NYC 1946; Co-Founder, United World Federalists 1947; elected Pres., Woodrow Wilson Foundn. 1948, and Bd. Member, Eleanor Roosevelt Memorial Foundn. 1966; Trustee, New Sch. for Social Research, and Foreign Service Educ. Foundn. Dir., Consolidated Laundries Corp., NYC 1928–41; Bd. Member, N.Y. Post 1939–41; Dir., American Machine and Metals Inc.; Secty., Coty Inc. and Coty Intnl. Inc. Member: American Bar Assn.; Intnl. Law Soc.; Delta Phi fraternity; Athenaeum Club, London; Knickerbocker, Century, and Downtown Clubs, NYC; Metropolitan Club, Washington, D.C. Hons: LL.D., Univ. Pa., Univ. Rochester, and Syracuse Univ. 1950; LL.D., Coll. of St. Joseph 1951, and Rutgers Univ. 1959. *Author:* Principles of Corporate Reorganization, 1937; Cases of Corporate Reorganization, 1938; Law of Bankruptcy Reorganization, 1939; Can Representative Government Do the Job?, 1945; (principal author) Survival in the Air Age, (report of President's Air Policy Commn.), 1948; Power and Policy, 1954; Foreign Policy: The Next Phase, 1958; Interim Report on the American Search for a Substitute for Isolation, 1968.

DAME CICELY COURTNEIDGE
British stage and film actress
Born Sydney, New South Wales, Australia, April 1st, 1893
Died London, England, April 26th, 1980

The life of Dame Cicely Courtneidge—daughter of an actor and director, married to an actor and director, actress herself—was inextricably bound to the theater. She was born in Sydney, Australia where her father, Robert Courtneidge, was performing in *Esmeralda,* a comic opera. In 1901, after Mr. Courtneidge had returned to England as director of the Prince's Theatre in Manchester, Cicely was cast as Peaseblossom in *A Midsummer Night's Dream,* her only Shakespearean role. She reappeared on the English stage in 1907 as Rosie Lucas in *Tom Jones,* a successful production which opened at the Prince's Theatre and later moved to London. Under her father's direction of the Shaftesbury Theatre, she was cast for the part of Chrysea in the *Arcadians,* a popular play that launched Ciceyly's career on the London stage. Indeed, she acquired the role more by chance than nepotism. The actress originally selected for the part abandoned the production to get married, and when the understudy proved unsuitable, Cicely eagerly accepted the challenge.

Determined to prevent his daughter from being spoiled by early triumphs on the stage, Courtneidge assumed strict control of Cicely's career. He cast her in his own productions, administered a niggardly weekly salary, and, when Cicely became engaged to actor Jack Hulbert, Courtneidge stubbornly withheld his consent to marriage for two years. The outbreak of World War One, however, brought a reversal of the Courtneidge's fortunes as several of their musical productions failed leaving father and daughter unemployed for several months. Finding work only in coarse music halls—a form of exile for ambitious young actresses—Cicely was encouraged by her father to exploit her talents as a male impersonator. Instead she decided to develop her comedic talent through short character sketches. Appearing first in music halls, she went on to star in a London revue with her husband. Dame Cicely later recalled this period as critical for her personal and professional growth as she acquired the self-reliance and confidence her father's domination had stifled.

In 1923 the husband and wife team were engaged by Edward Laurillard for "Little Revue Starts at Nine O'Clock" at the Little Theatre in London. They became enormously popular and hired an associate to promote and manage three subsequent revues, a venture which quickly ran them into debt. Now under the yoke of serious financial obligation, they reluctantly decided to split up the act— realizing, unhappily, that while Cicely was playing SRO at one theater, Jack could be filling the aisles at another.

During the 1930s boom in British cinema, the two performers were prosperously reunited. While appearing together in box-office successes such as *The Ghost Train* and *Jack's the Boy,* Cicely starred in numerous films without Jack and was invited to the United States in 1937 to make *The Imperfect Lady*. The couple returned to the London stage in 1939 for a joint appearance in *Under Your Hat.*

During World War Two Cicely toured frequently on behalf of servicemen. In addition to regular performances in London and the provincial English cities, she entertained Allied troops stationed in Britain, Europe, and the Mediterranean. The war also provided Cicely with an opportunity to show London audiences that her comic talents were not limited to revue burlesques. Appearing in *Under the Counter,* a "straight" comedy about the English black market, she was a hit. The play, directed by Hulbert did not, however, successfully transfer to the Broadway stage where its allusions to the privations of wartime life in England left American audiences cold. Dame Cicely later declared that her theatrical ambition had been to portray ordinary, "straightforward" women drawn from everyday life and then embellish that characterization with a dash of farce; she added, regretfully, that her opportunities in the so-called legitimate theater had been diminished by early identification with the revue form.

Following an Australian tour of *Under the Counter* in 1949, Courtneidge returned to England to appear in *Gay's the Word*. The play was written expressly for her by close friend Ivor Novello, and the theme song, "Vitality", became Cicely's trademark. In 1956 she returned to non-musical theater in Ronald Millar's *The Bride and the Bachelor*. When the production closed after nearly 600 performances in London, she won the role of Madam Arcati in Noel Coward's *Blithe Spirit* and, during this time, became popular in radio and television. In 1967 she played opposite her husband in *Dear Octopus,* a role she regarded as possibly her most outstanding in the legitimate theater.

Miss Courtneidge continued a highly active career on the stage well into her seventies and accepted cameo appearances in her eighties. In 1971 she celebrated her seventieth performing year with an 18 month run of *Move Over Mrs. Markham* and, in 1974, a revival of *Breath of Spring* brought her together on stage with her husband again (he died in 1978). The longevity of her career and the widespread acclaim

which she received was acknowledged in the award of the C.B.E. in 1951, and in 1972 she became the sixteenth actress to be named Dame of the British Empire for excellence in theatrical achievement.
E.T.

Daughter of Robert C., actor and theater director, and Rosaline May C. Married Jack Hulbert, actor 1916 (d. 1978). Children: one daughter. Educ: Australia and London to age 15; stage training under father's direction. First stage appearance, Manchester 1901; first London stage appearance, April 1907; appeared in variety from 1916. Film actress 1929–39 and 1962–68; also radio and television actress and personality. Hons: C.B.E. 1951; Dame (D.B.E.) 1972. *Performances: Plays*—A Midsummer Night's Dream (Peaseblossom), Manchester 1901; Tom Jones (Rose Lucas), Manchester and London 1907; The Arcadians (Chrysea), London 1909; The Arcadians (Eileen Cavanagh), London 1910; The Mousme (Miyo Ko San), London 1911; Princess Caprice (Princess Clementine), London 1912; The Pearl Girl (Lady Betty Biddulph), London 1913; The Cinema Star (Phyllis), London 1914; The Arcadians (Eileen Cavanagh), London 1915; A Lucky Escape (Mabel), London 1937; Under Your Hat (Kay Porter), London 1938–40; Full Swing, London 1942; Something in the Air (Terry Potter), London 1943; Under the Counter (Jo Fox), London 1945, New York 1947 and Australia 1949; Her Excellency (Lady Frances Maxwell), London 1949; Gay's the Word (Gay Daventry), touring and London 1950–51; The Joy of Living (Marion), Aberdeen and London 1955; Star Maker (Susie Green), Glasgow 1956; Bachelor Borne (Isabel Kilpatrick), Edinburgh 1956, retitled The Bride and the Bachelor (Isabel Kilpatrick), London 1956; Fool's Paradise (Jane Hayling), London 1959; The Bride Comes Back, or The Bride and the Bachelor (Isabel Kilpatrick), Liverpool and London 1960; Mother Goose (title role), London 1961; There's A Yank Close Behind Me 1963; High Spirits (Madame Arcati), London 1964; The Reluctant Peer, touring 1965; Dear Octopus (Dora Randolph), London 1967; Dear Charles (Denise Darvel), London 1968; Oh, Clarence, touring England and South Africa 1970; Move Over Mrs. Markham (Olive Smythe), London 1971; The Hollow (Lady Angkatell), touring 1973; Breath of Spring (Dame Beatrice Appleby), London 1974; Don't Utter a Note, London 1974; Once More with Music, touring 1976. *Revues*—Little Revue Starts at Nine O'Clock, London 1923; By-the-Way, London 1924, 1926 and New York 1925; The House that Jack Built, touring 1941; Over the Moon, London 1953; Fielding's Music Hall, London 1964. *Films*—The Ghost Train, Jack's the Boy, 1932; Soldiers of the King, 1933; Aunt Sally, 1934; Me and Marlborough, 1936; The Imperfect Lady (U.S.), 1937; Take My Tip, 1938; Under Your Hat, 1940; The L-Shaped Room, 1962; Those Magnificent Men in their Flying Machines, 1965; The Wrong Box, 1966; Also; Things are Looking Up, Imperfect Gentleman and others. *Author:* Cicely (Autobiog.), 1953.
Further reading: Great Movie Stars by David Shipman, 1970; Dames of the Theatre by Eric Johns, 1974.

BARONESS WARD OF NORTH TYNESIDE
British politician
Born London, England, 1894
Died London, England, April 26th, 1980

Baroness Ward of North Tyneside became one of the longest-serving women members of the British Parliament, holding a Conservative seat for 34 years in the House of Commons before she entered the House of Lords.

The daughter of an architect, Irene Ward spent her childhood in Newcastle-upon-Tyne. She left school at the age of 16 and, unlike many of her contemporaries in politics, did not have the benefit of a university education. This drew tribute from her Conservative colleague, Margaret Thatcher, who remarked in 1972 that Ward was "a doughty fighter without being a blue stocking." Once, during a period in opposition, she was accused of "behaving like a fishwife" by a Minister of Agriculture; her retort, "I represent a fishing constituency and I am proud of it," brought her instant acclaim.

After leaving school, Ward obtained a secretarial position in the office of a northern British industrial firm and also became an active member of the Northumberland Conservative Association. She stood for the Morpeth seat in 1924 and again in 1929. Although unsuccessful both times, she contested the Wallsend constituency two years later, defeating the first British woman cabinet minister, Margaret Bondfield.

In the early years of her Parliamentary career, Ward was a member of the British Government delegation to the League of Nations and, during World War Two, she served as a member of the Ministry of Labour Committee which called women to the Armed Services and other spheres of the war effort. She also made several foreign trips on government assignment to promote the British and Allied position in countries not directly involved in hostilities, such as Communist China.

Ward lost her seat in the 1945 General Election but in 1950 won against a sitting Labour Member in Tynemouth. As a Tyneside M.P., she worked strongly on behalf of shipyard, fishing and other industries. While her constant questioning of ministers on local Tyneside issues could irk her Parliamentary colleagues, it greatly enhanced her reputation within the constituency.

For work on behalf of hospital nurses and midwives Ward was named honorary vice-president of the Royal College of Nursing. Her interest in nursing was reflected in her book *FANY Invicta* which detailed the work of the First Aid Nursing Yeomanry. Nurses, she believed, had an equal claim to pay increases along with workers in industry. This led to a clash with her own party leadership in 1962, when the Minister of Health, Enoch Powell, held nurses to a 2.5 percent pay raise while other workers were given more. Ward also successfully introduced four Private Members' Bills into the House of Commons and saw them through to legislation, among them aid for the elderly.

Ward was at her most controversial in 1968 in her protests against the Prime Minister Harold Wilson's government. Together with other M.P.s, she rebelled against the heavy Parliamentary work load, which resulted in several House sessions that continued for nearly 24 hours at a time and a bitter attack on the "dictatorship of the Labour

Government," resulted in a five-day suspension from membership of the House. On one occasion, she sat in the Prime Minister's temporarily vacant seat and declined to move; she said she was peacefully demonstrating in support of pensioners' rights.

Ward was made a Dame of the British Empire in 1955 and became a Life Peer on her retirement from the House of Commons in 1974. She continued to take an active interest in debates concerning Tyneside until shortly before her death.   M.D.

Born Irene Mary Bewick Ward. Daughter of Alfred W., architect, and Elvina Mary W. Unmarried. Educ: Newcastle-upon-Tyne schs. to age 16; secretarial training. Parliamentary candidate (Conservative), Morpeth 1924, 1929 and Wallsend 1945; M.P. (Conservative), Wallsend 1931–45 and Tynemouth 1950–74; Justice of the Peace, Newcastle-upon-Tyne. Hons: C.B.E. 1939; D.B.E. 1955; Hon. Fellow, Lucy Cavendish Collegiate Soc., Univ. Cambridge 1972; Hon. Fellow, Royal Soc. of Arts 1972; C.H. 1973; Baroness 1974 (Life Peer); Member, British Govt. delegation to League of Nations and Ministry of Labour Cttee.; Hon. V.P., Royal Coll. of Nursing. *Author:* FANY Invicta, 1955.

SIR ALFRED (JOSEPH) HITCHCOCK
Film director and producer
Born Leytonstone, London, England, August 13th, 1899
Died Los Angeles, California, U.S.A., April 29th, 1980

For millions of filmgoers, Alfred Hitchcock was not just a film director; he was the only film director. People who never gave a thought to directors, and who never heard of the *auteur* theory, would go to see a Hitchcock movie on the strength of his name alone, regardless of who was in it or what it was about.

The simplest explanation of this achievement is that Hitchcock's audiences always knew what they would get. A "Hitchcock movie" meant, almost invariably, a macabre thriller, a perfectly calculated study in suspense that kept viewers in a delight of horrified anticipation. Throughout most of his long career, he rarely moved outside this genre; on the occasions when he did, the results indicated that his instinct was right in sticking to what he did best.

Most important, Hitchcock's thrillers were identifiably his in every detail. The economical pacing, the technical mastery, the atmosphere of mounting tension heightened by odd comic touches, above all the moral ambiguities of his plots and characters, were unmistakable hallmarks of his style. This degree of control was largely the result of his meticulours working methods: he planned the entire film beforehand, sketching out each frame and camera movement in advance, rejecting any hint of on-set improvisation, and shooting with a minimum of spare film. He once remarked with satisfaction: "I used to shoot . . . in such a way that no one else could put the pieces together properly; the only way they could be edited was to follow exactly what I had in mind." This airtight technique allowed Hitchcock to operate without too much interference from the Hollywood studio system, with its notorious disregard for the wishes and intentions of even major directors.

Hitchcock was born in 1899 in Leytonstone, a working-class suburb of East London, where his father kept a fruit, vegetable, and poultry shop. He was the youngest of three children in a Roman Catholic family. By his own account, young Alfred was a quiet, sensitive, and solitary child: "I played by myself, inventing my own games.," One such game was to travel over every route covered by the London Omnibus Company. At the age of eight he was sent to a boarding school run by the Jesuits, whose zeal for corporal punishment instilled in him a lifelong fear of authority and a preoccupation with guilt (though his father once called him "a little lamb without a spot").

When his father died in 1914, Hitchcock left school and studied engineering, then took a job as a technical clerk at the W.T. Henley Telegraph Company, a cable-manufacturing firm, where he stayed for six years, becoming a writer and illustrator in the advertising department.

Since boyhood, Hitchcock had been fascinated by the cinema. When Famous Players-Lasky (later Paramount Pictures) opened a studio in Islington, North London, in 1920, Hitchcock saw his chance: he designed a number of silent-film title-cards and took them to the studio head, who was impressed enough to hire him on the spot. Over the next two years, Hitchcock wrote and designed titles for several films, simultaneously serving the informal apprenticeship in all aspects of filmmaking which furnished the basis for his formidable technique. In those early days of the cinema, specialization was almost unknown; Hitchcock rose rapidly to script writer, art director, and assistant director.

He was soon eager to try directing, and in 1922 began an independent production, *Number Thirteen*. Despite its modest budget, it foundered through lack of funds after two reels had been shot. Soon after, Hitchcock was called in to finish another film when its original director fell ill.

By 1925, Famous Players-Lasky had pulled out of British production, and Islington had been taken over by an independent company founded by Michael Balcon. Balcon sent Hitchcock to Munich and Italy to direct his first film, *The Pleasure Garden*. Despite a series of production disasters, the film was reckoned a success, as was his second picture, *The Mountain Eagle,* the only Hitchcock film of which no print seems to have survived.

He thus returned to London as a young director of promise, and quickly brought the film world to attention with his first thriller, *The Lodger* (1926). Set in a claustrophobically fog-bound London, it starred Ivor Novello as a mysterious stranger who is suspected— wrongly, it turns out—of being Jack the Ripper. The film contains much that anticipates the later Hitchcock: the theme of innocence wrongly accused, technical ingenuity (the lodger's obsessive pacing in his upstairs room is revealed from below through a glass floor, and the first of the celebrated brief personal appearances. It was highly acclaimed, in Britain and abroad, and Hitchcock's name was made.

The same year, 1926, he married Alma Reville, who had served as his assistant and scriptwriter on several films, and who subsequently was to script several more. They had one daughter, Patricia, who acted in some of her father's films.

Six more films followed in the silent era; the best (and most evidently German-influenced) is generally agreed to be *The Ring* (1927), a prize-fighting drama. Hitchcock returned to the thriller form in *Blackmail* (1929), the first British talkie. The film was in fact only half a talkie, having been almost completed in silent form when the new talking sensation panicked its producers into re-shooting several scenes with dialogue, and dubbing over most of the rest. Hitchcock characteristically regarded these technical limitations as a challenge. *Blackmail* introduced one of his favorite devices, the climactic fall from a high place—in this case, the roof of the British Museum.

Hitchcock's next half-dozen pictures were a mixed bag. They included two filmed plays (O'Casey's *Juno and the Paycock* and Galsworthy's *The Skin Game);* a social satire, *Rich and Strange* (1932); and Hitchcock's least favorite movie, *Waltzes from Vienna,* a comedy musical about the elder and younger Johann Strauss. Even while he was making this disaster, Hitchcock's mind was on his next film, which was to launch him into his first great period.

The six films he made between 1934 and 1938—*The Man Who Knew Too Much, The Thirty-Nine Steps, The Secret Agent, Sabotage, Young and Innocent,* and *The Lady Vanishes*—all now rank as classics of British cinema. In these films Hitchcock mapped out clearly the territory of which he was to become undisputed master. The tongue-in-cheek black humor; the indifference to mere plausibility; the unconcealed delight in playing with his audience, timing each build-up (or calculated let-down) to perfection—all these, deployed with narrative mastery and increasing technical virtuosity, can be found in the culminating films of his British period. So, too, can the characteristic moral obsessions: the interchangeability of guilt and innocence; the abyss beneath the deceptive security of everyday life; the erotic appeal of evil; the arbitrary nature of retribution.

Not surprisingly, given his growing reputation, Hitchcock had received several invitations from Hollywood, and in 1938 he accepted an offer from producer David O. Selznick. There was some delay, though, before he could go, and he made one more picture in Britain. By coincidence, both this and his first Hollywood film were taken from novels by Daphne du Maurier. *Jamaica Inn* (1939), a smuggling melodrama, was unconvincing; he was never at his best with costume pictures, and couldn't (or couldn't be bothered to) control his star, Charles Laughton, who indulged himself in one of his most overblown performances.

By contrast, *Rebecca* (1940), though more romantic novelette than thriller, succeeded completely and made a star of Joan Fontaine. Hitchcock's Hollywood career was now securely launched; he directed one more unsuitable assignment, *Mr. and Mrs. Smith* (1941), an unremarkable domestic comedy, and thereafter chose his own subjects. He also gained increasing control over all aspects of his filmmaking although RKO imposed an incongruously happy ending on *Suspicion* (1941), since they felt it would harm Cary Grant's image to have him prove a villain). Selznick, who learned to trust Hitchcock's judgment as he trusted that of no other director, still meddled in the casting and plotting decisions, and often sold his services to

other producers as part of package deals. One such occasion was the
transfer of *Notorious* to RKO, with Selznick insisting that bottled
uranium was not a plausible "MacGuffin" (Hitchcock's word for the
object or secret, irrelevant in itself, on which the plot turns). The
F.B.I., curious to know why Hitchcock was interested in uranium (the
atomic bomb was still in the planning stage), kept him under
surveillance for three months.

The Hitchcock's settled in the Hollywood suburb of Bel Air; later
they bought a house to which Hitchcock added an enormous kitchen
with a walk-in freezer and wine cellar, to accommodate his enthusiasm
for gourmandizing. Eventually the family adopted U.S. citizenship.
Their move was made difficult by the outbreak of World War II and
the threat of bombing attacks to their families at home. On a visit to
Britain in 1944, Hitchcock directed *Bon Voyage* and *Aventure
Malgache*, two French-language films on the French Resistance, for
the British Ministry of Information.

Throughout the 1940s, Hitchcock dug deeper into the anxieties that
fueled his art, plumbing them with a refined black humor that gave
even his worst nightmares an undertone of comedy. Audiences
responded to these nightmares with an almost guilty fascination. The
fear of heights and enclosed places, of sexual menace, of being hunted
down or unjustly accused—these were part of a larger, universally
shared fear, the fear of helpless entanglement in a reality controlled
by some nameless, irrational authority. Critics have pointed out the
irony by which the anxiety-ridden Hitchcock, ever a victim of that
fear, won escape from it by transforming himself into a manipulator,
controlling the very heartbeats of his viewers with merciless suspense.
Through his brilliant use of technique—cross-cutting, suggestive
camera angles, nuances of shadow and light—he forced them to
sympathize with murderers, to become voyeurs and accomplices, and
to watch with mixed terror and eagerness as ordinary life fell apart to
reveal evil just below. Thus the heroine in *Shadow of a Doubt* (1943)
recognizes her beloved uncle as a compulsive murderer who must be
done away with; the passengers in *Lifeboat* (1943) are finally driven to
face, and give vent to, the homicidal savagery that is in them; the
government agent in *Notorious* (1946), played by Cary Grant,
compels the woman he desires and despises into another man's bed in
the name of duty. (The other man, played by Claude Rains, is, like
many Hitchcock villains, cultured, charming, and far more sympathetic than the hero.) Buried childhood guilt forms the crux of
Spellbound (1945), as it would later of *Marnie* and *Psycho; Saboteur*
(1942) revives the theme of the hunted man, used once in *The Thirty-
Nine Steps* and destined to return again in *North by Northwest*.

Some of Hitchcock's own obsessions were rooted in childhood
incidents, such as the time when, as a five-year-old, having committed
some minor wrong, he was sent by his father to the local police station
to be locked up in a cell for ten minutes. The adult Hitchcock retained
so prodigious a fear of the police that he hardly ever dared to drive,
and once had an attack of nerves after throwing a cigar butt from a car
window. Little wonder that he once suggested, for his own epitaph,
the inscription "You see what can happen to you if you aren't a good
boy."

Following a slump in the late 1940s, Hitchcock took off into the

second of his great periods. Among the films from *Strangers on a Train* (1951) to *Psycho* (1960) are at least half-a-dozen which, by any account, must rank among the finest he made. Not all the 50s films succeed: *I Confess* (1952), unique among his pictures in dealing explicitly with Catholicism, is oddly cold and unengaging. But otherwise the films of this decade are rarely less than good, and mostly superb. Part of the stimulus for this fresh attack of creative energy was the agreement Hitchcock negotiated to produce his own films, thus acquiring almost total control over them.

As might be expected in a director who started with silent films, Hitchcock always insisted on the primacy of images over words, on telling the story as far as possible in visual terms. From all his finest films, telling images stick in the mind. James Stewart, peering pruriently through his telephoto lens in *Rear Window* (1954); the cigarette revoltingly stubbed into a fried egg in *To Catch a Thief* (1955). One head unmoving among a tennis-watching crowd in *Strangers on a Train* (1951), or the fairground murder, distortedly reflected in a spectacle lens, as in a sick mind. Cary Grant fleeing the crop-spraying plane, or stumbling down vast stone presidential faces (Mt. Rushmore), in *North by Northwest* (1959). The nightmare plunge from the rooftops which leads into the dreamworld of *Vertigo* (1958). Most famous of all, the stabbing of Janet Leigh in *Psycho* (1960), a scene that has made the simple act of taking a shower a traumatic one for legions of moviegoers.

An exception to this visual opulence is *The Wrong Man* (1957). Soberly shot in black and white, in a downbeat, documentary style, it most directly expresses Hitchcock's central preoccupation of the helpless individual unjustly incarcerated.

Hitchcock had always relished technical challenges, and at this period seemed intent on setting them for himself. *Lifeboat* is shot entirely from within the confines of the cramped boat, effectively making the spectator one of the shipwrecked passengers, and conveying their claustrophobic situation. This worked well; *Rope* (1948) less so. Hitchcock chose to film this in what was, in effect, one long unbroken take, without cutting. The technique is fascinating to watch, but at the expense of the film; as he later acknowledged, Hitchcock had broken his own rule that technique should always serve the action.

On the sets of his films, Hitchcock was imperturbable, his dress and manners the essence of civility. Off the set, he was a practiced eccentric who fell asleep in public and indulged shamelessly in publicity stunts. He did not think highly of actors, especially Method actors, since their art was entirely subordinate to his manipulation (and was inclined to despise audiences as well, for much the same reason). Most of his actors were cast to type, with Hitchcock's instincts governing the choice; on those occasions when producers imposed contracted stars on him, the results were almost always a disappointment.

Hitchcock has sometimes been accused of misogyny; many of his films, especially those of the 50s, feature the impeccably groomed blonde (Grace Kelly is the classic example) whose cool surface hides a passionate sexuality, and who gets messed up, or worse. As Hitchcock was far from a misogynist in his personal life, the explanation may lie in his willingness to cater to popular tastes; torturing the heroine, then as now, is the surest way to arouse conflicting emotions in the psyches of the audience.

Serious film critics tended to regard Hitchcock merely as an entertainer, but in 1957 when French critics Claude Chabrol and Eric Rohmer published an almost worshipful book on him, Hitchcock became the object of increased critical attention. This evidently afforded him huge delight. To critics, as to journalists, he was unfailingly polite and informative; not for him the brusque put-down ("I make Westerns") of a John Ford. He would straight-facedly assent to whatever theories were propounded, even—or especially—if they were completely opposed to each other; rather than contradict, he preferred to side-track the conversation into one of his favorite self-deprecatory anecdotes.

In 1955 Hitchcock made a revolutionary move for a film director by getting involved in the production of a television series, *Alfred Hitchcock Presents.* This show and its successor, *The Alfred Hitchcock Hour,* ran for a combined total of ten years, presenting thrillers and horror stories with typical Hitchcockian wit. Hitchcock directed a score of episodes himself. He also prefaced each episode with his famous profile caricature and a macabre introduction, delivered with deadpan charm. The two shows spawned a Hitchcock industry, including *Alfred Hitchcock's Mystery Magazine,* some 50 anthologies of short stories with such titles as *Stories That Scared Even Me* and *Slay Ride,* and an Alfred Hitchcock fan club. Hitchcock also contributed an article on filmmaking to the Encyclopedia Britannica.

Between 1925 and 1960, Hitchcock directed 47 full-length films, well over one a year. The six films he completed in the last twenty years of his life are generally held to show something of a decline, although both *The Birds* (1963) and *Marnie* (1964), poorly received on release, look increasingly impressive on subsequent viewing, despite technical deficiencies. Few enthusiast, though, have been found for *Torn Curtain* (1966) or *Topaz* (1970); nor was *Frenzy* (1972) greatly liked. But his last film, *Family Plot* (1976), was more successful; an unusually light, even benign, movie, it wove elegant patterns around a plot of playful intricacy.

Hitchcock assiduously cultivated his public persona. The celebrated plump profile, the stage-Cockney accent, the solemnly impish humor, the predilection for good food and practical jokes—these were all elements of a lovingly polished act. Despite this, he was also a devoted husband and father, a dutiful Catholic, doggedly unpolitical, and as conscientious an example of moral rectitude as Hollywood was likely to lay eyes on.

Astonishingly, he never received an Oscar, although he was nominated five times. *Rebecca* was awarded one but, as Hitchcock pointed out with understandable pique, it went to Selznick as producer. A few months before his death, he was knighted by Queen Elizabeth. For the private man, the belatedness of such official recognition may be deplored; for the director it hardly seems to matter. His best films seem sure to last, entertaining and delighting future generations, and demonstrating that there is really no such thing as a minor genre, in the hands of a major artist.

Hitchcock had been suffering from arthritis and kidney failure for a number of years. He was at work on another film, *The Short Night*, when he died.   P.K.

Son of William H., fruit importer and poultry dealer, and Emma (Whelan) H. Married Alma Reville, scriptwriter and film editor, 1926. Daughter: Patricia O'Connell, actress, b. 1928. Roman Catholic. Emigrated to U.S.A. 1939; naturalized citizen 1955. Educ: St. Ignatius Coll., London 1908–14; Sch. of Engineering and Navigation, London ca. 1914; course in mechanical draftsmanship, Univ. London ca. 1917. Exempted from mil. service; enlisted in Volunteer Corps of Royal Engineers 1917; made films for British Ministry of Information 1944. With W.T. Henley Telegraph Co., London ca. 1914–20: techn. clerk; estimating clerk; writer, illus., and layout ed., advertising dept. With Famous Players-Lasky British Producers Ltd., Islington, London 1919-23: asst. dir., art dir., scriptwriter, production. Film director from 1925. Hons: Nominated for Oscars by Acad. Motion Picture Arts and Sciences 1940 (for Rebecca), 1944 (for Lifeboat), 1945 (for Spellbound), 1954 (for Rear Window), 1960 (for Psycho); Best Picture Award (given to producer David O. Selznick for Rebecca) 1940. Best Dir. Award, N.Y. Film Critics (for The Lady Vanishes), 1938; Milestone Award, Producer's Guild 1965; D.W. Griffith Award, Directors' Award 1968; D.F.A., Univ. Calif. at Santa Cruz 1968; Irving G. Thalberg Memorial Award, Acad. Motion Picture Arts and Sciences 1968; Officier 1968 and Commdr. 1976, Ordre des Arts et des Lettres, France; Chevalier, Légion d'honneur, Cinématèque Française 1971; D.Hum.L., Columbia Univ. 1972; C.B. de Mille Award, Foreign Press Assn., Hollywood 1972; Filmex Award 1976; Life Achievement Award, American Film Inst. 1978; K.B.E. 1980. *Silent Films: Asst. Dir., Art Dir., and Scriptwriter (or Co-scriptwriter)—* Woman to Woman, 1922; (also ed.) The White Shadow 1923; The Passionate Adventure 1924; The Prude's Fall 1925; The Blackguard 1925. *Director—*Number Thirteen (unfinished; also called Mrs. Peabody), 1922; Always Tell Your Wife (co-dir.), 1922; The Pleasure Garden, 1925; The Mountain Eagle (in U.S.A. as Fear O' God), 1926; (also co-scriptwriter) The Ring, 1927; (also scriptwriter and cameraman) The Farmer's Wife, 1928; (also adaptor) Champagne, 1928; The Manxman, 1929. *Sound Films: Director—*(also co-scriptwriter) Blackmail, 1929; (sequence dir.) Elstree Calling, 1930; (also co-scriptwriter) Juno and the Paycock, 1930; Murder, 1930; (also co-scriptwriter) The Skin Game, 1931; (also co-scriptwriter) Number Seventeen, 1932; (producer only) Lord Camber's Ladies, 1932; Waltzes from Vienna (in U.S.A. as Strauss's Great Waltz), 1933; The Man Who Knew Too Much, 1934; The Thirty-Nine Steps, 1935; The Secret Agent, 1936; Sabotage (in U.S.A. as A Woman Alone), 1937; The Lady Vanishes, 1938; Jamaica Inn, 1939; Rebecca, 1940; Foreign Correspondent, 1940; Mr. and Mrs. Smith, 1941; Suspicion, 1941; (also subject originator) Saboteur, 1942; Shadow of a Doubt, 1943; Lifeboat, 1943; Bon Voyage, 1944; Aventure Malgache, 1944; Spellbound, 1945; (also producer and subject originator) Notorious, 1946; The Paradine Case, 1947; (also co-producer) Rope, 1948; (also co-producer) Under Capricorn, 1949; (also co-producer) Stage Fright, 1950. *Director and Producer—*Strangers on a Train, 1951; I Confess, 1952; Dial M for Murder, 1954; Rear Window, 1954; To Catch a Thief, 1955; The Man Who Knew Too Much, 1955; The Trouble with Harry, 1956; The Wrong Man, 1957; Vertigo, 1958; North by Northwest, 1959; Psycho, 1960; The Birds, 1963; Marnie, 1964; Torn

Curtain, 1966; Topaz, 1970; Frenzy, 1972; Family Plot, 1976; The Short Night (unfinished), 1980. *Television Producer:* Alfred Hitchcock Presents, 1955-61; The Alfred Hitchcock Hour, 1963-65. *Publications:* numerous collections of stories under his nominal editorship; Alfred Hitchcock's Mystery Mag.; Alfred Hitchcock's Psycho (screenplay), 1974. Interview: Cahiers du Cinema (with Charles Bitsch and Francois Truffaut), Aug.-Sept. 1956.

Further reading: Hitchcock by Eric Rohmer and Claude Chabrol, 1957; Hitchcock by François Truffaut (in collaboration with Helen G. Scott), 1967; Hitchcock's Films by Robin Wood, 1969; Hitch: The Life and Time of Alfred Hitchcock by John Russell Taylor, 1978. The Strange Case of Alfred Hitchcock by Raymond Durgnat, 1974.

LOUIS KRONENBERGER
Author, critic, anthologist and teacher
Born Cincinnati, Ohio, U.S.A., December 9th, 1904
Died Boston, Massachusetts, U.S.A., April 30th, 1980

Born into a secularized German-Jewish family in Cincinnati, Ohio, in 1904, Louis Kronenberger began to write a weekly news magazine at the age of nine; and at thirteen he was writing poetry and submitting it to many magazines.

From 1921 to 1924 he studied at the University of Cincinnati and left without a degree to go to New York City carrying a letter of introduction to Arthur Sulzberger of *The New York Times.* He was given a clerical job in the paper's accounting department, but several weeks later began reviewing books for Brooks Atkinson, editor of the *Times* Book Section.

At the end of the summer, with four unsigned reviews to his credit, Kronenberger embarked upon a career as a freelance writer, supplementing his book review earnings by tutoring. His first break as a freelancer came at *Saturday Review* in the autumn of 1924 when the editor, Henry Seidel Canby, gave him a book to review. He soon won the confidence of the *Review*'s editors and before long was receiving assignments such as Mann's *Death in Venice.* He subsequently became a reader for Boni and Liveright, at that time the publishers of Dreiser, Anderson, O'Neill, Hemingway, and Faulkner.

The job at Boni and Liveright lasted until 1932, after which he supported himself reviewing books and editing an anthology of light verse for Bennet Cerf, who was then with the Modern Library Series. In May of 1933 he went to work for Alfred A. Knopf as a reader and editor, remaining with that house until 1935 when he left for England to begin research on the book that would appear in 1942 as *Kings and Desperate Men,* a study of eighteenth-century England.

He began his association with *Fortune* in 1936, preferring freelance work rather than a staff position. In January of 1938 he became *Time*'s staff drama critic. Although a regular position, it allowed him summers free to pursue his own work; thus began a career of 23 years and nearly 2000 reviews. He became noted for his aphoristic dismissals—"one of those comedies that would be positively brightened up by a little tragedy"—of plays he didn't like. Kronenberger once said that while a good review might be dashed off in twenty minutes, a negative one could take hours.

He continued his prolific literary output nearly to the time of his death, producing three novels and numerous anthologies of poetry and drama; translating the works of authors from La Rochefoucauld to Anouilh; writing history and biography, as well as teaching drama at Columbia, Harvard, Oxford, the University of Buffalo, Stanford, and Brandeis.
R.C.

Son of Louis K., merchant, and Mabel Newwitter K. Married Emmy L. Plaut 1940. Children: John; Elizabeth Wanklyn. Jewish. Educ: Univ. Cincinnati 1921–24 (no degree). Ed.: Boni and Liveright, N.Y.C. 1926–32; Modern Youth (mag.) 1932–33; Alfred A. Knopf 1933–35. Freelance contributor, Fortune 1936–38; drama critic, Time 1938–61 and PM 1940–48; Lectr., English Dept., Columbia Univ. 1950–51. With Brandeis Univ., Waltham, Mass.: Lectr. 1951–53; Prof., theater arts and librarian 1953–70. In 1959: A. Lawrence Lowell Visiting Prof., Harvard Univ.; Lectr., Oxford Univ.; Adjunct Prof., Columbia Univ. Lectr., Christian Gauss Seminar, Princeton Univ. 1961; Visiting Prof., English, Stanford Univ., 1963; Regents' Visiting Prof., Univ. Calif., Berkeley 1968. Fellow, American Acad. Arts and Sciences. Member: Natl. Inst. Arts and Letters; Authors League; Century Assn., N.Y.C.; St. Botolph, Boston; Atheneum Club, London. Hons: Guggenheim Fellow, 1969. *Books: Novels*—The Grand Manner, 1929; Grand Right and Left, 1952; A Month of Sundays, 1961. *Other*—Kings and Desperate Men, 1942; The Thread of Laughter, 1952; Company Manners, 1954; The Republic of Letters, 1955; Marlborough's Duchess, 1958; No Whippings, No Gold Watches (Memoirs), 1970. Contributed to: After the Genteel Tradition, 1937; Books That Changed Our Minds, 1939; The State of the Nation, 1965; also to Atlantic Monthly and other magazines. *Ed.*—An Anthology of Light Verse, 1934; An Eighteenth Century Miscellany, 1936; Maxims of La Rochefoucauld, 1937; Viking Portable Reader's Companion, 1945; The Pleasure of Their Company, 1946; The Portable Johnson and Boswell, 1947; Selected Works of Alexander Pope, 1948; Robinson Crusoe, 1948; Don Juan, 1949; Pride and Prejudice, 1950; Tom Jones, 1952; A Cavalcade of Comedy, 1953; GBS: A Survey, 1953; Best Plays Series, 1953-62; Sheridan, 1957; Plays of G.B. Shaw, 1958; Way of the World, 1959; Novelists on Novelists, 1962; Plays of Oscar Wilde, 1962; Sense and Sensibility, 1962; Emma, 1962; The Great World, 1963; She Stoops to Conquer, 1964; Hamlet, 1964; Quality: Its Image in the Arts, 1969; The Polished Surface, 1969; The Cutting Edge, 1970; Atlantic Brief Lives, 1971; Animal, Vegetable, Mineral, 1972; Mania for Magnificence, 1972; For W.H. Auden, 1972; The Extraordinary Mr. Wilkes, 1974; Biography of Oscar Wilde, 1976.

LUIS MUÑOZ MARÍN
First Elected Governor of Puerto Rico
Born San Juan, Puerto Rico, February 18th, 1898
Died San Juan, Puerto Rico, April 30th, 1980

Luis Muñoz Marín, the first elected governor of Puerto Rico and its charismatic leader for 24 years, was born in San Juan in 1898. A week earlier, Spain had granted the island colony its first measure of self-

government in almost 400 years, Muñoz Marín's father, Luis Muñoz Rivera, had been in the vanguard of the long and delicate negotiation process. Within two months, Puerto Rico had fallen to the United States in the Spanish-American War and was put under military occupation.

Muñoz Rivera took his family to New York and Washington, D.C., where he served as the island's Resident Commissioner in the House of Representatives from 1910 until his death in 1916. Young Luis, educated in American schools, grew up fluent in Spanish and English and acquired a keen understanding of American politics. After leaving Georgetown University Law School without a degree, he became a freelance poet, translator and journalist, publishing two volumes of Spanish prose in 1917 and editing the bilingual journal *La Revísta de Indias* for a year. With his wife Muna Lee, a poet from Mississippi, he became part of New York's radical literary circle; he translated the works of Sandburg and Whitman into Spanish and made Edwin Markham's famous hymn to the downtrodden, "Man With a Hoe," one of the most quoted poems in Latin America.

Throughout the 1920s, Muñoz Marín returned occasionally to Puerto Rico to dabble in politics, campaigning for the Socialists in 1920 and editing *La Democracia,* the newspaper his father had founded, in 1926. He returned to the island permanently in 1931, determined to work on behalf of the *jíbaros,* or peasants, whose lives had been devastated by the collapse of the sugar industry during the Depression. Tens of thousands of illiterate and unemployed *jíbaros* were crowded into urban slums where dysentery and tuberculosis were epidemic. The various political parties were less concerned to help these refugees and to assist the failing economy than to argue over the merits of statehood versus independence.

Muñoz Marín joined the Liberal Party and won election as Senator-at-Large. His connections with U.S. New Deal officials helped him secure millions of dollars in aid to the unemployed and soon made him the most influential political figure in the island. Unfortunately, as junior senator in a minority party, Muñoz Marín had come too far too fast. His rise excited jealousies within the party hierarchy, and he was expelled by his father's old colleague, Antonio Barceló, in 1937. Most observers considered his political career finished.

Muñoz Marín, however, began building a grass-roots political machine, the Partido Popular Democrático (Popular Democratic Party, or PPD). Its slogan, "Bread, Land, and Liberty," reflected the founder's priorities, while its symbol, a silhouette of the straw-hatted head of a *jíbaro,* clearly defined the constituency on which he hoped to build his following.

In preparation for the 1940 elections, Muñoz Marín and a group of party leaders traveled from village to village in the countryside, explaining their program of land reform and economic development to the *jíbaros* and urging them not to sell their votes for two dollars, as they were accustomed to doing. The result of this campaign was a narrow victory that gave the PPD control of the island's Senate (control of the House came two years later) and effectively routed the pro-statehood coalition of Socialists and Republicans. Muñoz Marín, so recently written off as a failure, took his seat as President of the Senate in 1941.

This dazzling display of charisma and organization, on a platform compatible with New Deal objectives, guaranteed him respectful treatment from Washington. For the next six years, he and Rexford G. Tugwell, the appointed governor of the island and a leading member of President Roosevelt's brain trust, worked together, in an often strained partnership, to implement the PPD's plans for a peaceful economic revolution. Muñoz Marín's ability to command the trust and obedience of the population, to control local politicians, and to inspire political activists was matched by Tugwell's ability to deploy skilled technicians and administrators.

Full-scale implementation was delayed during the Second World War by the scarcity of U.S. funds and the threat of German submarine activity in the Caribbean. In the meantime, the government set up a power authority to expand rural electrification and enforced a law limiting corporate land ownership to 500 acres. Land parcels taken from offending corporations were given to peasants as collective farms, some of which were used for the development of new export crops. The establishment in 1942 of the Puerto Rican Industrial Development Company (PRIDCO), a New Deal agency, enabled Muñoz Marín to set up factories for glass bottles and cardboard boxes to support the rum and sugar trades. When government capital and expertise began to run short, PRIDCO attracted private business interests by granting ten-year tax exemptions to new and expanding companies. Among the incoming industries were shoes, electronics, optical lenses, metallurgy, and petrochemicals.

This intensive campaign, dubbed "Operation Bootstrap" by Muñoz Marín (in Spanish it was *Jalda arriba,* or "uphill climb"), radically transformed the economy of Puerto Rico in less than a quarter of a century. By 1960, tens of thousands of new jobs had been created and the population was served by hospitals, schools, and housing projects.

In 1947, the Puerto Ricans, having been granted the right to choose their own governor, elected Muñoz Marín by a landslide. The question of Puerto Rico's political status was now re-opened. Muñoz Marín, originally an *independista,* had since come to believe that a permanent relationship with the U.S. was essential to the island's economic health. On the other hand, he opposed statehood on the grounds that integration with the mainstream of American culture would rob Puerto Rico of its distinctive Hispanic identity. He envisioned a third option, the Commonwealth, which would preserve the autonomy and self-respect of the country while enabling it to profit from the prosperity and stability of its neighbor.

His brainchild, the *Estado Libre Asociado de Puerto Rico,* came into being on July 25, 1952. Under the terms of its constitution, which was ratified by popular vote and approved by the U.S. Congress, the federal government retains its authority to conduct Puerto Rico's foreign relations, defense, currency, postal service, and customs; the island's inhabitants, who are U.S. citizens and subject to congressional laws and military conscription, pay no federal taxes on island-generated income and are eligible for federal grant-in-aid programs; however, their representation in Congress is limited to a Resident Commissioner who has a voice but no vote, and they cannot participate in presidential elections. "Having your cake and eating it too," wrote former Gov. Tugwell of the arrangement, "was not after all impossible, if you happened to have the requisite political genius."

Nonetheless, popular opinion in Puerto Rico continued to be

divided, with nationalists objecting to U.S. sovereignty and middle-class citizens urging that economic ties be cemented through statehood. Only the formidable influence of Muñoz Marín kept the population working together. Operation Bootstrap and Operation Commonwealth, he declared, were preludes to Operation Serenity, the creation of a humane social order that would be "efficient in production and at the same time wise and modest in consumption. . . . for the good of our souls and bodies."

Muñoz Marín was re-elected in 1960 despite opposition from the Roman Catholic Church, which objected to his advocacy of contraception to combat overpopulation and which disapproved of his personal life (he had divorced Muna Lee, with whom he had had two children, to marry Inéz Mendoze de Palacios, a schoolteacher and political activist who had borne him two children out of wedlock). He refused to run for a fifth term in 1964, preferring to occupy a seat as Senator-at-Large and to serve on a commission reviewing Puerto Rico's political status.

Without his unifying leadership, the PPD dissolved into rivalries, and in the 1968 elections fell from power for the first time since its legendary beginning 28 years earlier. Muñoz Marín, who had gone to live in Europe, returned to help the party regain control of the government in 1972. Six years later, the 80-year-old statesman, his health impaired by a stroke, came out of retirement to travel through the countryside campaigning against the pro-statehood movement.

Muñoz Marín died of heart failure and was buried in his father's home town of Barranquitas.   R.C./J.P.

Son of Luis Muñoz Rivera, statesman and newspaper ed., and Amalia Marín de Muñoz R. Married: (1) Muna Lee, writer and translator, 1919 (div. 1947); (2) Inéz María Mendoza de Palacios, teacher and political activist, 1947. Children: 1st marriage—Luis, b.1920; Muna, b.1925 (d.1978). With Inéz Mendoza out of wedlock—Viviana, b.1939; Victoria, b.1940. Roman Catholic. Educ: Georgetown Preparatory Sch.; other private schs.; left Georgetown Univ. Law Sch. without degree 1916. Secty. to Resident Commnr. for P.R., U.S. House of Reps., Washington, D.C. 1915–16. Freelance writer, translator, poet, critic, and journalist, NYC 1916–18, 1919–25, 1927–31. Ed., La Revísta de Indias, San Juan 1918–19; Ed. and Publisher, La Democracia, San Juan 1926; Special Rep. to U.S. from Economic Cttee. of P.R. Legislature, NYC and Washington, D.C. 1928–29. Member, Partido Liberal, and Senator-at-Large, P.R. Senate, 1932–37; founded Partido Popular Democrático, Barranquitas, P.R. 1938; Pres. of P.R. Senate 1941–48; first elected Gov. of P.R. 1948–64; Member, Constituent Assembly of P.R. 1951; proclaimed Estado Libre Asociado de P.R. (Commonwealth of P.R.) 1952; Senator-at-Large, P.R. Senate 1964–70; Member, Jt. U.S.-P.R. Commn. to investigate political status of P.R. 1967. Hons: Gran Cruz de la Orden Vasco Nuñez de Balboa, Panama 1954; LL.D., Univ. Kans. 1954; LL.D., Harvard Univ. 1955; Freedom House Award 1956; LL.D., Bates Coll. 1957; LL.D., Brandeis Univ. 1961; Murray-Green Award 1962; Cardozo Award, 1962; Knights of San Juan Citizen of the Year 1963. *Author:* Borrones (prose), 1917; Madre Haraposa (prose), 1917; (ed.) Obras Completas de Luis Muñoz Rivera, 1925; The Commonwealth of Puerto Rico: A House of Good Will, 1956. Major articles: "Development Through Democracy," in

Annals of American Acad. of Political and Social Science, vol.
CCLXXV, Jan. 1953. Contributed sect. on P.R. to symposium These
United States, 1925. Critical reviews, articles, prose, poetry published
in The Nation, Smart Set, American Mercury, New Republic,
Baltimore Sun, N.Y. Herald Tribune, other mags. and newspapers in
1920s. *Interview:* "We've Come a Long Way in a Peaceful Revolution," in U.S. News and World Report, Mar. 28, 1960.
Further reading: Poet in the Fortress: The Story of Luis Muñoz Marín
by Thomas Airken, Jr., 1964; Luis Muñoz Marín: A Concise Biography by Thomas G. Matthews, 1967.

MILLAR BURROWS
Religious scholar and authority on the Dead Sea Scrolls
**Born Wyoming (now part of Cincinnati), Ohio, U.S.A., October
26th, 1889**
Died Ann Arbor, Michigan, U.S.A., April 29th, 1980

Religious scholar Millar Burrows, who achieved public recognition for
his comprehensive studies of the Dead Sea Scrolls, was born in
Wyoming, Ohio in 1889. He moved with his family to Buffalo, New
York in 1907 and later attended Cornell University. Burrows then
entered Union Theological Seminary and received his B.A. degree in
1915; that same year, he was ordained into the ministry of the
Presbyterian Church.

After positions as a minister in Texas and rural survey supervisor for
the Interchurch World Movement, Burrows became pastor and
professor of the Bible at Tusculum College in Tennessee. After
obtaining his doctorate in religion from Yale in 1925, he joined the
faculty of Brown University where he soon rose to the departmental
chairmanship of Biblical Literature and History of Religions. In 1934
Burrows moved to Yale as Winkley Professor of Biblical Theology
and after 1950, concurrently chaired the graduate department of Near
Eastern Languages and Literature.

Well-known for his studies of archaeological excavations, Semitic
languages, and Near Eastern civilizations, Burrows taught and con-
ducted research abroad. He was Visiting Professor of Religion at the
American University of Beirut from 1930 to 1931 and Director of the
American School of Oriental Research at Jerusalem when the Dead
Sea Scrolls were taken there. These scrolls—ancient Hebrew manuscripts on leather rolls contained in linen cloths—were discovered by
Bedouin shepherds in 1947 in caves on the western shore of the Dead
Sea. Because of apparent discrepancies between the scrolls and
traditional sources of Christian belief, the scrolls created much
interest and some controversy. These ancient documents helped
clarify the relation between early Christian practice and Jewish
religious traditions and enabled scholars to piece together a more
accurate history of Palestine from the fourth century B.C. to the
second century A.D.

In *The Dead Sea Scrolls* (1955) and *More Light on the Dead Sea
Scrolls* (1958) Burrows provided translations of some of the ancient
documents and a detailed account of their history, including a

description of the Essene sect of ascetic Jews reputed to have written them. Burrows emphasized the need for continued study of the scrolls to assess their impact upon modern scriptural interpretation, but maintained that no major revisions of Christian faith would result.

Burrows wrote several other books on topics, such as great religious leaders *(Founders of Great Religions)*, the significance of archaeology for biblical studies *(What Mean these Stones?)*, and the issue of Arab refugees from Israel *(Palestine is Our Business)*. Burrows was a member and president of American Middle East Relief, Inc., which provided relief and rehabilitation for approximately one million Palestinian Arabs who have been relocated to surrounding Arab-speaking countries.   S.R.

Son of Edwin Jones B., businessman, and Katharine Douglas (Millar) B. Married Irene Bell Gladding 1915 (d.1967). Son: Edwin Gladding. Congregationalist. Educ: Lafayette High Sch., grad. 1908; Cornell Univ., Ithaca (Phi Beta Kappa), B.A. 1912; Union Theological Seminary, N.Y.C., B.D. 1915; Yale Univ., New Haven, Conn., Ph.D. 1925. Ordained to ministry, Presbyterian Church 1915; Pastor, rural church, Tex. 1915–19; Rural Survey Supervisor for Tex., Interchurch World Movement 1919–20. Coll. Pastor and Prof. of Bible, Tusculum Coll., Greeneville, Tenn. 1920–23. With Brown Univ., Providence, R.I.: Asst. Prof., Biblical Lit. and Hist. of Religions 1925–29; Assoc. Prof. 1929–32; Prof. and Dept. Chmn. 1932–34. Visiting Prof. of Religion, American Univ. of Beirut, Lebanon 1930–31; Dir., American Sch. of Oriental Research, Jerusalem 1931–32 and 1947–48. Winkley Prof. of Biblical Theology, Yale Univ. Divinity Sch. 1934–58; Dept. Chmn., Near Eastern Langs. and Lits. 1950–58 and Prof. Emeritus 1958–80, Yale Grad. Sch. Trustee since 1934 (Life Trustee since 1971) and Pres. 1934–48, American Schs. of Oriental Research. Member since 1938 and Vice-Chmn. 1954–63, Standard Bible Cttee. Member and Pres. 1954, Soc. of Biblical Lit. and Exegesis. Member and Pres. 1954–56, American Middle East Relief Inc. Member: American Acad. of Arts and Sciences; American Acad. of Religion; American Oriental Soc.; Natl. Assn. of Biblical Instrs.; Natl. Council of Religion in Higher Educ. Hons: Fellow, American Acad. of Arts and Sciences 1949; Hon. D.D., Oberlin Coll., Ohio 1960. D.D.: Yale Univ. and Brown Univ. 1961. *Author:* (Jt. Ed. with Charles Foster Kent) Proverbs and Didactic Poems, 1927; Founders of Great Religions, 1931; The Basis of Israelite Marriage, 1938; Bible Religion, 1938; What Mean These Stones?, 1941; Outline of Biblical Theology, 1946; Palestine is Our Business, 1949; (Ed.) The Dead Sea Scrolls of St. Mark's Monastery, 1950–51; The Dead Sea Scrolls, 1955; More Light on the Dead Sea Scrolls, 1958; Diligently Compared—The Revised Standard Version and the King James Version of the Old Testament, 1964; Jesus in the First Three Gospels, 1977. Contributed numerous articles to professional jrnls., including Jrnl. of Biblical Lit., Bulletin of the American Schs. of Oriental Research, Annual of the American Schs. of Oriental Research, Jrnl. of the American Oriental Soc., Jrnl. of Religion, Jewish Quarterly Review, Christian Century, Jrnl. of the Palestine Oriental Soc.

HEINRICH (ERNST) WENDEL
Production and set designer
Born Bremen, Germany, March 9th, 1915
Died Düsseldorf, West Germany (Federal Republic of Germany),
May, 1980

Heinrich Wendel, whose innovative stage designs contributed greatly to the renaissance of classical ballet in postwar Germany, was born in 1916 in Bremen, where his father was a violinist with the Philharmonic. After studying art in Berlin and Hamburg and serving an apprenticeship, he worked in opera houses and theaters in Nuremberg, Wiesbaden, Göttingen, and Wuppertal, moving to the Wurttemberg state theaters in Stuttgart in 1945.

At the Wuppertal Opera House, which he joined as head of stage design in 1953, Wendel entered into a long and productive collaboration with Erich Walter, chief choreographer of the theater's ballet company. Together they created an elegant neo-classical style known as the Wuppertal School, which featured a striking integration of choregraphic and scenic forms. The unified effect thus achieved won them international acclaim. Their affection for renaissance and baroque composers did not prevent them from staging ballets to music by Bartok. Schönberg, Förtner, and Henze, and they often incorporated elements of mime and modern dance into their essentially classical forms and movements.

In 1964, the team of Wendel, Walter, and their director Georg Reinhardt moved to the more prestigious Deutschen Oper am Reihn in Düsseldorf at the invitation of its head, Grischa Barfuss, their former employer in Wuppertal. Here Wendel concentrated more exclusively on designs for opera, collaborating with musical artists such as Herbert von Karajan, Götz Friedrich, and Oscar Fritz Schuh, and exploring ever more imaginative ways of putting spatial abstractions to dramatic use. In his renowned production of Monteverdi's *L'Incoronazione de Poppea* in 1965, he combined ingenious lighting techniques with slide projections of scenery models to create the illusion of solid structures on stage. To complement the abstruse philosophical dialogues of Schönberg's *Moses und Aaron* (1968), he fashioned an endlessly diminishing archway. He used photographic collages in his set for Zimmerman's *The Soldiers* and mirror constructions in Stravinsky's *Le Sacre du Printemps* and Dallapiccola's *Ulisse*. Other noteworthy productions included Britten's *Death in Venice*, Berg's *Wozzeck*, Weber's *Der Freischütz*, Reimann's *Lear*, and three world premieres, including Penderecki's *St. Luke's Passion*.

Wendel, who considered himself a "spiritual artist," studied philosophy, mythology, archaeology, art history, physics, and astronomy, and frequently gave public lectures on these subjects. He was also a painter and organist. He continued to work at Düsseldorf until his death.   L.F.

Son of Ernst W., violinist, conductor, composer, and professor, and Ilse Wolde W. Unmarried. Educ: Berliner Kunstakademie; Hamburger Kunsthochschule; apprentice in Hamburg, Berlin, and Bremen 1933. Debut, Stendhal, Germany (now German Democratic Republic). Head stage designer: City Theatre, Wuppertal 1941–43; Nuremberg 1943–44; Wurttemberg State Theaters, Stuttgart 1945–48; State Theater in Wiesbaden and Deutsche Theatre in Göttingen, ca. 1948–53; City Theater and Opera House, Wuppertal 1953–63. Chief Set Designer and Production Designer, Deutsche Oper am Rein, Düsseldorf-Duisburg since 1964. Guest Designer: Staatsoper, Vienna; Städischen Oper, Berlin; Deutsche Oper, Berlin; Salzburg Festival; La Scala, Milan; Stuttgart Festival; Vienna Festival; and for productions in Buenos Aires, Brussels, Saarbrucken, and Amsterdam. Cofounder, Wuppertal Ballet and Krefeld Ballet Assn. Member of Bd., Assn. for the Advancement of the Dancing Arts. Public lectr. on hist. of art, theatre arts, philosophy, astronomy, and physics; exhibited paintings and stage designs; stage designs published in books and mags. *Designs: Operas*—Job (Dallapiccola), Wuppertal, 1956 and La Scala, 1969; Die Zauberflöte (Mozart), Wuppertal, 1957; Die Welt auf dem Monde, (J. Haydn), Salzburg Festival, 1959; La Finta semplice (Mozart), Salzburg Festival, 1960; Cardillac (Hindemith), Wuppertal, 1960; La Favola d'Orfeo (L'Orfeo, Monteverdi), Wuppertal, 1961 and Salzburg Festival, 1971; Don Juan (Gluck), Wuppertal, 1962; Doktor Faust (Busoni), Wuppertal, 1962; Palestrina (Pfitzner), Städischen Oper, Berlin, 1962; Tannhäuser (Wagner), Staatsoper, Vienna, 1963; L'incoronazione de Poppea (Monteverdi), Düsseldorf, 1965; Ritratto di Don Chisciotte (Petrassi), world premiere, La Scala, 1967; Moses und Aaron (Schoenberg), Düsseldorf, 1968; Marchen von der schönen Lilie (Klebe), world premiere, Schwetzingen, 1969; St. Luke's Passion (Penderecki), Düsseldorf, world premiere, 1969; Die Soldaten (Zimmerman), Düsseldorf, 1971; also Bluebeard's Castle (Bartok); Wozzeck (Berg); Death in Venice (Britten); Arlecchino (Busoni); Rappresentazione (Cavalieri); Prigioniero, Ulisse (Dallapiccola); Orfeo ed Euridice (Gluck); Saul (Handel); From the House of the Dead (Janacek); Clemenza de Tito, Idomeneo, Don Giovanni (Mozart); Boris Godunov (Mussorgsky); Lear (Aribert Reimann); Gluckliche Hand (Schoenberg); Rake's Progress (Stravinsky); Otello, Un Ballo in Maschera (Verdi); Der Fliegende Hollander, Lohengrin, Parsifal, Tristan und Isolde (Wagner); Der Freischutz (Weber). *Ballets*—Jacques Pudding (Henze), 1954; Musik für Saiteninstrumente Schlagzeug und Celeste (Bartok), 1955; Pelleas und Melisande (Schoenberg), 1955, 1969; Marsyas (Dallapiccola), 1956; Die Weisse Rose (Wolfgang Förtner), 1956, 1964; Der Feuervogel (Stravinsky), 1957, 1964; Der wunderbare Mandarin (Bartok), 1958; Ariadne (Monteverdi), 1958; Orpheus Britannicus Suite (Purcell), 1959; Persephone (Stravinsky), 1960; Verklärte Nacht (Schoenberg), 1961; Die Planeten (G. Holst), Staatsoper, Vienna, 1961; Der Zweikampf (Monteverdi), 1962; Ondine (Undine, H.W. Henze), 1962; Delphische Suite (A. Jolivet), 1963; Der Tod und das Mädchen (Schubert), 1964; Orkester Suite #3 in D-Dur (Bach), 1964; Petruschka (Stravinsky); Der Kuss der Fee (Stravinsky), 1966; Concert Champêtre (Poulenc), 1966; La Danviselle e élue (Debussy), 1966; Des Geschöpte des Prometheus (Beethoven), 1966; Cinderella (Prokofiev), 1967; Swanensee (Tschaikowsky), 1967; Concerto for Jazz Band and Symphony Orchestra (Rolf Liebermann), 1968; Le Sacre du Printemps (Stravinsky), 1970; Giselle (A. Adam), 1971; Romeo and Juliet (Prokofiev), also Boulevard Solitude (Henze); Flamingos (Fortner); Apollon Musagète; Jeu de Cartes.

ALIOUNE DIOP
Editor, political activist, and author
Born Saint-Louis, Senegal, January 10th, 1910
Died Paris, France, May 2nd, 1980

Alioune Diop was one of Africa's most influential thinkers and writers. For more than 30 years as editor of *Présence Africaine,* the oldest and most widely read journal of African cultural affairs, he participated in the struggle to free *le monde noir* from its colonial cultural heritage; he wrote countless editorials, sponsored leading African writers, and organized international celebrations of black culture.

Born in 1910 in Senegal, the son of a post-office worker, Diop trained as a teacher, studying first at the Lycée Faidherbe in his native city of Saint-Louis, then in Algiers as an undergraduate, and finally at the Sorbonne where he read classical literature. He taught French, Greek and Latin at a Paris lycée for a brief period before returning to Senegal to serve as *chef de cabinet* of the government.

In 1947 Diop returned to Paris as a socialist senator to the *conseil de la République* and became involved with the growing network of intellectuals who were opposed to French colonialism. During a meeting that year with Aimé Césaire, Richard Wright, Jean-Paul Sartre [q.v.], Albert Camus, André Gide and others, it was agreed that Diop would edit a new review focusing on the debate between Africa and the West. *Présence Africaine* was named, said Sartre, to connote a *présence,* "not like that of a child in a family circle, but like that of remorse and hope."

Présence Africaine quickly became a forum for debating political conflict in French West Africa. A remarkable feature of the journal— and perhaps the source of its credibility and success—was the wide range of opinion it published. Communists argued with liberals and black Americans with Africans; aside from a demand for independence from colonial powers and a recognition of the African cultural inheritance of all black people, there was no party line. Although published in French (until 1960 when an English edition appeared) the influence of *Présence Africaine* was felt throughout Africa, America and the Caribbean. Among the contributors have been political leaders such as Julius Nyerere and Eric Williams; poets David Diop, Leroi Jones, Léopold Sedar Senghor and Sekou Toure; and the African writers John Pepper Clark, Wole Soyinka, Chinua Achebe and Ezekiel Mphahele. Through the publishing house he founded in the late 1940s, Diop helped many writers publish their first books.

The journal's increasing prominence led Diop's close friend, Léopold Senghor, to organize International Congresses in 1956 and 1959. The Society for African Culture evolved from the first Congress and, founded by Diop, it was committed to promoting *négritude,* a movement emphasizing the African roots of black culture. After the 1959 Congress, however, many writers and intellectuals who had been associated with *négritude* came to deplore its ethnocentrism and apotheosis of the past. While *Présence Africaine* continued to celebrate African culture, the journal became increasingly political and in 1962 published excerpts from Frantz Fanon's *Les Damnes de la terre (The Wretched of the Earth),* which sought to justify the ethics of revolutionary violence.

In the 1960s and 70s Diop, a devout Roman Catholic all his life,

criticized the church as an irrevocably "occidental" institution which
had failed to understand the cultural bases of political unrest in French
West Africa. Despite the failure of the Mali Federation (a brief
unification of the independent territories of the French Sudan and
Senegal which ended when the latter country seceded), and continuing strife between the nations of French West Africa, Diop
remained hopeful that viable political solutions could be found.
R.W.

Son of post office employee. Married. Daughter: Marie-Aida Diop
Bah. Roman Catholic. Educ: Lycée Faidherbe, St.-Louis, Senegal;
Univ. Algiers, B.A.; post grad. study at Sorbonne. Asst. teacher, St.-
Louis 1932–35; chef de cabinet, Senegalese govt. 1946; socialist
senator to conseil de la République 1947; Ed., Présence Africaine
1947–80; founded publishing house Présence Africaine late 1940s.
Organized First Intnl. Congress of Negro Writers and Artists, Paris
1956; Secty. Intnl. Congress of Negro Writers and Artists, Rome
1959; founded Societé Africaine de Culture 1956; organized Assn. of
World Festival of Negro Arts, Dakar 1966; Pres., Assn. of World
Festival of Negro Arts, Lagos 1975. *Articles:* Niam n'goura or
Présence Africaine's raison d'être, 1947; Malentendus, 1949; Inno-
cence et résponsibilité, 1951; L'Artiste n'est pas seul au monde, 1951;
On ne fabrique pas un peuple, 1952; De l'expansion du travail, 1952;
Colonialisme et nationalisme culturels; Réfuges de l'amour propre
impérial, 1956; L'occident chrétien et nous, 1956; Discours d'ouverture au premier congrès international des peuples écrivains et artistes
noirs, 1956; Impressions de voyage, 1959; Tunis: The African People's
Conference, 1960; Solidarité du culturel et du politique, 1962;
Postface: Un hommage africaine à Jean XXIII, 1965; Discours au
congrès international des Africanistes sur la recherche scientifique au
service de l'Afrique, 1968; Discours d'ouverture de la table ronde sur
"élite et peuple dans l'Afrique d'aujourd'hui," 1970.

GEORGE PAL
Film director
Born Cegled, Hungary, February 1st, 1908
Died Beverly Hills, California, U.S.A., May 2nd, 1980

George Pal had two separate—and consecutive—careers in the
cinema. During the 1930s and 40s, he created a long series of
animated films, in which he raised the technique of stop-action
puppet-animation to a level of sophistication never approached before
(and rarely equalled since). Then, around 1950, he turned to producing, and sometimes also directing, science-fiction and fantasy films
remarkable for the impact and imaginative range of their special
effects.

Pal was born in Cegled, Hungary, into a theatrical family. He
studied architecture at the Budapest Academy of Arts, in the process
developing his talents for drawing and carpentry, before taking a job
with Hunnia Films designing title cards and posters. Simultaneously
he was exploring methods of animation, building on what he could
learn at second-hand about Hollywood cartoon techniques. In 1931 he
moved to Berlin, working for a time at UFA, where he became head

of the cartoon department, before setting up his own studio. His first
stop-action film was a cigarette commercial; bored with drawing
endless cigarettes, Pal hit on the idea of filming the cigarettes
themselves, moving them like a series of drawings.

In 1933 Pal left Germany, moving first to Prague, then to Paris, and
finally to Holland, where he set up a studio producing animated
commercials for Dutch, British and American companies. His work of
this period exhibits an apparently effortless fluency of technique, with
no trace of the jerkiness which marred earlier attempts at puppet-
animation.

In 1939, Pal was offered both British citizenship, and a visa for the
U.S.A.; he opted for America. On arrival he signed a contract with
Paramount, and set up a studio in Hollywood; between 1940 and 1947
he produced over forty 'Puppetoon' films, and in 1943 received a
special Academy Award (the first of his six Oscars) for his animation
techniques.

Paramount gradually lost interest in the relatively costly and time-
taking Puppetoons, and Pal turned to feature films, as an independent
producer. His first production, *The Great Rupert* (1949), was an
innocuous family comedy, starring Jimmy Durante [q.v.] and an
animated squirrel; but his next picture marked a totally new departure, both for him and for Hollywood. Until then, 'science-fiction'
movies generally involved variations on the *King Kong* formula:
assorted monsters carrying off screaming blondes. *Destination Moon*
(1950) has a good claim to be the first serious science-fiction film since
Things to Come in 1936; Pal followed its success with another
pioneering production, *When Worlds Collide* (1951). Both films are
distinguished by impressive special effects, and let down by poor
acting, creaky scripts and (by today's standards) a somewhat naive
approach to their subjects. No allowances, though, need be made for
War of the Worlds (1953), perhaps Pal's finest film. Based on the H.G.
Wells novel, it features a Martian invasion whose visual effects, even
today, still look highly convincing.

All three films won Oscars for their special effects. Pal had by now
returned to Paramount, and produced three further films for them.
The third, *The Conquest of Space* (1955), was an ambitious project,
ruined by studio interference. Pal, frustrated and disappointed, once
more left Paramount, and made his next six films (all but the last of
which he directed as well as produced) for MGM. The first, shot in
MGM's English studios, was *tom thumb* (1958), another Oscar-
winner.

Pal was always at his best with a strong story-line to follow, and
once again H.G. Wells furnished one. *The Time Machine* (1959),
though less overtly spectacular in its effects, ranks with *War of the
Worlds* in Pal's output, and won him his sixth and final Oscar.

The films from 1960 onwards were largely disappointing; *The
Wonderful World of the Brothers Grimm* (1962), perhaps the best of
them, was marred by the cumbersome Cinerama process. Recurrent
conflicts with the studio, and poor box-office returns, led to Pal's
eventual departure from MGM. For the last ten years of his life, he
was once again an independent producer. Of numerous projects, only
one reached realization: *Doc Savage, The Man of Bronze* (1975), a
sadly unfunny attempt at a 30s-style super-hero spoof.

It may be that the slightly facile optimism which weakens many of

Pal's films also exacerbated his problems with the Hollywood studios. A less good-natured man might perhaps have prevented too much studio interference, and stood more chance of making the films he wanted. The quality of Pal's output is highly variable, but that in no way detracts from his status as a pioneer, and master-technician of the cinema.

P.K.

Emigrated to U.S. 1940. Educ: Budapest Acad of Arts. Designer, Hunnia Films, Hungary late 1920s; Dir., Cartoon Dept., U.F.A. film studio, Berlin 1931. During 1930s: free-lance cartoonist, Berlin; Producer, Puppetoons, Horlicks, London; independent advertising filmmaker, Eindhoven, Holland; Dir., puppet short films, Phillips Co., Holland; also independent producer and cartoonist in Prague and Paris. With Paramount Pictures Corp., Calif. 1940–47 and ca. 1952–55; Dir., educational films, Shell Oil Co., Calif. 1946; independent producer, various times 1948–58; Producer and Dir., Metro Goldwyn Mayer (MGM), Calif. 1958–70; independent producer since 1970. Hons: Acad. Awards for special effects—Destination Moon 1950; When Worlds Collide 1951; War of the Worlds 1953; tom thumb 1958; The Time Machine 1960. Acad. Award for technical innovations in producing animated pictures 1943; Nebula Award, Science Fiction Writers of America 1976. *Films (as director): Advertising films include* —On Parade, 1936; What Ho! She Bumps, 1937; Sky Pirates, 1938. *Puppetoon series* include—Jasper goes Hunting, 1944; Jasper's Close Shave (The Barber of Seville), 1945. *Features*—The Great Rupert, 1949; Destination Moon, 1950; When Worlds Collide, 1951; War of the Worlds, 1953; Conquest of Space, 1955; tom thumb, 1958; The Time Machine, 1960; (co-dir. Harry Levin) The Wonderful World of the Brothers Grimm, 1962; (co-dir. Byron Haskin) The Power, 1967; Doc Savage, Man of Bronze, 1974; Houdini; Naked Jungle; Atlantis, the Lost Continent; Seven Faces of Dr. Lao.

GEORGE (PAUL) ELLIOTT
Novelist, essayist, poet and short story writer
Born Knightstown, Indiana, U.S.A., June 16th, 1918
Died New York, New York, U.S.A., May 3rd, 1980

George Elliott, who achieved literary prominence during the late 1950s, wrote lyric and narrative poetry, novels, short stories and essays. Although not a "religious" writer, an underlying faith in God and an affirmation of life and love are typical themes in Elliott's work.

Inspired by Coleridge's "Rime of the Ancient Mariner," Elliott decided to become a writer at the age of 12. After graduating from high school in 1934 and intermittently during his university attendance, Elliott held a variety of jobs including farmworker, service station attendant, chauffeur, high school teacher and real estate broker. He received a B.A. in English in 1939 and a master's degree in 1941, both from the University of California, Berkeley. Exempted from active service, Elliott worked as a wage rate analyst during the war and then taught literature at various colleges until 1963 when he became Professor of English at Syracuse University; he remained at Syracuse until his death.

In Elliott's first novel, *Parktilden Village* (1958), a "value-free" social scientist slowly begins to realize that the inner lives of individuals are not reducible to statistics. Reviewing the book, critic Norman Podhoretz praised the author's "judicious detachment" and the "absence of portentous solemnity." The hero of Elliott's second novel, *David Knudsen* (1962), is a man who confronts the moral implications of his father's co-invention of the atomic bomb dropped on Hiroshima. One reviewer called the book "a brooding vision of a godless culture."

Elliott deliberately avoided didactic themes that would impose rigid structures on his novels. In an essay he referred to his literary style as a "lucid and cool" narrative which, by a detached tone and omission of emotional rhetoric, forces the reader to think and visualize the story for himself. But his technique did not always succeed; critics charged that his fourth novel, *Muriel* (1972), had lost the intuitive fictional touch present in his earlier novels.

Elliott's poetry, essays, and short stories, however, are considered more innovative than the novels. During the 1950s and 60s many of Elliott's poems were published in magazines and journals. *Fever and Chills*, a long narrative poem, was published in 1961; followed by *Fourteen Poems* (1964) and *From the Berkeley Hills* (1969), a collection of poetry praised as "demanding and rewarding." In later essays and short stories, Elliott explored his religious beliefs—he had earlier rejected his father's Quakerism—and came to define spiritual awareness as an acceptance of life's unfathomable mysteries.

Elliott received several awards, including a Guggenheim Fellowship in 1961 and a grant from the National Institute of Arts and Letters in 1969.   M.D.

Son of Paul Revere E. and Nita (Gregory) E. Married Mary Emma Jeffress, editor 1941. Daughter: Nora Catherine b. 1943. Educ: Riverside Jr. Coll., Calif. 1934; Univ. Calif. at Berkeley, B.A. 1939, M.A. 1941. Wage rate analyst, U.S. War Labor Bd., W.W.II; Instr. and Asst. Prof. of English, St. Mary's Coll. of Calif., Moraga 1947–55, 1962–63; Asst. Prof., Cornell Univ., Ithaca 1955–56 and Barnard Coll., N.Y.C. 1957–60; Lectr. in English, Univ. of Iowa, Iowa City 1960–61 and Univ. Calif. at Berkeley 1962–63; Prof. of English, Syracuse Univ., N.Y. since 1963. Member: Corp. Yaddo Foundn. since 1980; P.E.N.; American Assn. of Univ. Profs. Hons: Albert Bender Grant 1951; Fund for Advancement of Educ. Fellowship 1953; Hudson Review Fellowship in Fiction 1956–57; Guggenheim Fellowship 1961, 1970; D.H. Lawrence Fellowship, Univ. N.M. and Ind. Authors' Day Award 1962; Ford Fellowship for theater writing 1965–66; U.S. Natl. Inst. Arts and Letters Grant 1969; Hon. D.H.L., St. Lawrence Univ. 1971. *Books: Novels*—Parktilden Village, 1958; David Knudsen, 1962; In the World, 1965; Muriel, 1972. *Short Story collections*—Among the Dangs: Ten Short Stories, 1962; An Hour of Last Things and Other Stories, 1968. Uncollected short stories—"Tourist and Pilgrim" Harper's, 1968; "Mikki for a Couple of Months," Esquire, 1969; "Femina Sapiens," Esquire, 1970; "A Fable," Kayak, 1974. *Poetry*—Fever and Chills, 1961; Fourteen Poems, 1964; From the Berkeley Hills, 1969. *Nonfiction*—A Piece of Lettuce: Personal Essays on Books, Beliefs, American Places and Growing Up in a Strange Country, 1964; Conversions: Literature and Modernist Deviation, 1971; (ed.) Fifteen Modern American Poets,

1956; Types of Prose Fiction, 1964. Also contributor to The Nation,
Hudson Review, Poetry, Epoch and other jrnls.
George Elliott:
Further reading: "Beyond Nihilism: The Fiction of George P. Elliot"
by Blanche H. Gelfant, in Hollins Critic (Hollins College, Virginia)
viii, 5, 1969.

WILLIAM PRAGER
Professor of engineering and applied mathematics
Born Karlsruhe, Germany, May 23rd, 1903
Died Zurich, Switzerland, May 3rd, 1980

William Prager was a leading authority on the plastic deformation of
metals, and as Professor of Applied Mechanics at Brown University,
he helped make that school a leading center for the study of the
mechanics of solids.

Prager attended the prestigious Institute of Technology at
Darmstadt where he graduated in civil and mechanical engineering.
At the age of 29 he became the youngest full professor in Germany; he
was also the first teacher to be dismissed from the Institute of
Technology at Karlsruhe by the nazis; he consequently accepted an
offer from Istanbul University to become Professor of Theoretical
Mechanics. At the newly re-organized University, Prager helped
develop the school's science and mathematics curricula, served as
education advisor to the government, and was a founder of the *Révue
de la Faculté des Sciences.* As German-Jewish emigrés in Turkey,
Prager and his family began to fear that the war could force their
return to Germany. Fortunately, Albert Einstein, aware of Prager's
standing in the German scientific community, recommended him to
Brown University. Prager arrived in the United States in 1941, shortly
before the bombing of Pearl Harbor.

Prager became Professor of Applied Mechanics at Brown and head
of the University's newly created Program of Advanced Instruction
and Research in Applied Mechanics; in 1946 he was selected Chairman of the new graduate program in applied mechanics. As a scientist
his pioneering studies of the plastic deformation of metals made new
theories of plasticity applicable to military ballistics, technological
processes such as metal-rolling, and structural design in engineering.

Prager took a leave of absence from Brown to work for the IBM
Research Laboratory at Zurich from 1963 until 1965. He then taught
applied mechanics at the University of California, San Diego and
returned to Brown in 1968 as Professor of Engineering and Applied
Mechanics and University Professor. Prager retired in 1973 and
moved to Switzerland.   M.D.

Son of Wilhelm P. and Helen P. Married Gertrude Ann Heyer 1925.
Son: Stephen, Prof. of physics and chemistry, b. 1928. Emigrated
U.S. 1941. Educ: Inst. Technology, Darmstadt, Engineering Diploma
1925; Dr. Eng. (civil) 1926. Instr., Mechanics, Inst. Technology,
Darmstadt 1927–29; Acting Dir., Inst. Applied Mechanics, Univ.
Göttingen 1929–33; Structural Inspector, Airsport League, Berlin

1929–33; Science Advisor, Fieseler Aircraft Co., Kassel 1933; Prof., Technical Mechanics, Technische Hochschule, Karlsruhe 1933–34; Prof., Theoretical Mechanics, Univ. Istanbul 1934–41; Founder and Managing Ed., Révue de la Faculté des Sciences de l'Université d'Istanbul 1935–41. With Brown Univ., Providence, R.I.: Prof. of Applied Mechanics 1941–65 (leave of absence 1963–65); Chmn., Grad. Div. of Applied Mathematics 1946–53; Chmn., Physical Science Council 1953–59; L. Herbert Ballou Univ. Prof. 1959-63; Prof., Engineering and Applied Mathematics 1968–73; Prof. Emeritus 1973. Managing Ed., Quarterly of Applied Mathematics 1943–65; Consultant, I.B.M. Research Lab., Zurich 1963–65; Prof., Applied Mechanics, Univ. Calif (San Diego) 1965–68; Technical Ed., Jrnl. of Applied Mechanics 1969–72; Ed., Computer Methods in Applied Mechanics and Engineering since 1972. Member: U.S. Natl. Acad. of Science; Natl. Acad. of Engineering; Soc. Industrial and Applied Mathematics; American Mathematical Soc; Natl. Acad. of Science (Poland); Groupe Française de Rhéologie; Groupe pour l'Avancement des Méthodes Numériques de l'Ingénieur, Acad. des Sciences de l'Institut de France: American Soc. Mechanical Engineers. Hons: Worcester Reed Warner Medal, American Soc. Mechanical Engineers 1957; Theodore Von Karman Award, American Soc. Civil Engineers 1960; Panetti Prize, Turin Acad. of Science 1963; Timoshenko Medal, American Soc. Mechanical Engineers 1966; Adamson Memorial Lectr., Univ. of Manchester 1978. Hon. doctorates: Univ. Liege (Belgium) 1962; Univ. Poitiers (France) 1963; Case Inst. of Technology 1963; Politeconico de Milano 1964; Univ. Waterloo (Canada), Univ. Stuttgart, Technical Univ., Hanover 1969; Brown Univ., R.I. 1973; Univ. Manchester 1974; Univ. Brussels 1975. Hon. Fellow, American Acad. of Arts and Sciences and American Soc. Civil Engineers. *Author:* (with K. Hohenemser) Dynamik der Stabwerke, 1933; Mécanique des solides isotropes, 1937; Tersimi Hendese, 1937; (with F. Gursan) Mihanik, 1941; (with P.G. Hodge) The Theory of Perfectly Plastic Solids, 1951; Probleme der Plastizitaetstheorie, 1955; An Introduction to Plasticity, 1959; Introduction to Mechanics of Continua, 1961; (ed.) Applications of Digital Computers, 1963; Introduction to Basic Fortran Programming and Numerical Methods, 1971; Introduction to APL, 1971; others. *Contributor:* (with Gustav Kuerti) Theories of Flight, 1945. Articles in many professional jrnls.

KAY HAMMOND
Stage and film actress
Born London, England, February 18th, 1909
Died Brighton, England, May 4th, 1980

Kay Hammond was raised in a theatrical family. Her father was the actor Sir Guy Standing and her mother the actress Dorothy Hammond. In 1946 Kay married John Clements (later Sir John Clements) and they became one of the great theatrical teams of the British stage.

Kay Hammond studied at the Royal Academy of Dramatic Art and, by 1927, had begun her career playing minor roles on the London stage. Her repertoire expanded rapidly and in 1931 her performance as a Cockney in a farce produced by Leslie Henson singled her out for mention by the critics as one of the most promising comedy actresses of the period. Her career on the London stage was established and at the same time she began to accept film parts, one of her early successes being *A Night in Montmartre* in 1931.

Her first leading part on the stage came five years later at the Criterion Theatre, when she played Diana Lake in Terence Rattigan's *French Without Tears*. The success of the production—the play ran for two years—was largely attributed to Kay Hammond's performance. She was in *Sugar Plum* in 1939 and, during World War Two, Noel Coward's *Blythe Spirit* and *Private Lives*. *Blythe Spirit* was filmed in 1945, the year her first marriage was dissolved.

She reappeared in Dryden's *Marriage a la Mode* with her new husband, John Selby Clements, in 1946 and three years later played Mrs. Sullen in *The Beaux Stratagem,* the part of Dame Edith Evans had excelled in twenty years earlier. During the play's 15 month run she and her husband took part in a popular BBC weekly radio discussion program, *We Beg to Differ.*

Revivals of *Man and Superman* and *The Happy Marriage* followed in 1951 and 1952 and then *Pygmalion* at the St. James' in 1953 and 1954, in which Miss Hammond took the part of Eliza. In her husband's production of *The Way of the World* at the Saville Theatre, Kay Hammond played the part of Millamant. In 1957 at the Piccadilly Theatre, Kay Hammond played Queen of the Amazons in Levy's *The Rape of the Belt,* opposite her husband, and two years later achieved noteworthy success in *The Marriage-go-Round.* In 1961 she made the film, *Fine Golden Hours.*   M.D.

Born Dorothy Katharine Standing. Daughter of Sir Guy S., actor, and Lady Dorothy S. (stage name Dorothy Hammond). Married: (1) Ronald George Leon (later 3rd baronet) 1932 (div. 1945); (2) John Selby Clements (K.B.E. 1968) 1946. Children: 1st marriage—two sons. Educ: The Lodge, Banstead, Surrey; Royal Acad. of Dramatic Art. *Performances: Plays*—on London stage: Nine till Six (Beatrice), 1930; Can the Leopard. . . ? (Daphne Hibberd), 1931; My Hat (Emmie), 1932; Woman Kind (Elsa Frost), 1933; Three-Cornered Moon (Elizabeth Rimplegar), 1934; Youth at the Helm (Dorothy Wilson), 1935; Bees on the Boatdeck (the Hon. Ursula Maddings), 1936; French Without Tears (Diana Lake), 1936–38; Sugar Plum (Adeline Rawlinson), 1939; Blythe Spirit (Elvira) 1941–44; Private Lives (Amanda), 1944–45; The Kingmaker (Lady Elizabeth Grey) and Marriage a la Mode (Melantha), 1946; The Beaux Stratagem (Mrs. Sullen), 1949; Man and Superman (Ann), 1951; The Happy Marriage, 1952; Pygmalion (Eliza), 1953–54; The Little Glass Clock, 1954–55; The Rivals (Lydia Languish) and The Way of the World (Millamant), 1956; The Rape of the Belt (Queen of the Amazons), 1957; Gilt and Gingerbread and The Marriage-go-Round, 1959; others. *Films*— Children of Chance, 1930; A Night in Montmartre, 1931; Almost a Divorce, Out of the Blue, A Night Like This, Sally Bishop, 1932; Yes Madam, Sleeping Car, Bitter Sweet, 1933; Two on a Doorstep, 1936; Jeannie, 1941; Blythe Spirit, 1945; Call of the Blood, 1948; Fine Golden Hours, 1961; others.

MARSHAL TITO
Communist freedom fighter and President of Yugoslavia
Born Kumrovec, Austria-Hungary, May 7th, 1892
Died Ljbuljana, Yugoslavia, May 4th, 1980

Tito, who commanded the Yugoslavian partisans—the most successful resistance movement in nazi-occupied Europe during World War Two—became his country's leader and held that position until his death 35 years later. Disliking many aspects of Soviet communism and Western capitalism, he forged an independent brand of Yugoslav communism—often known as Titoism—and championed the independence of socialist states throughout the world. One of the twentieth century's toughest revolutionaries and one of its most enduring political figures, he was the last survivor of the generation of leaders which included Eisenhower, Churchill, De Gaulle, Nehru, Stalin, and Mao Tse-Tung.

Tito was born Josip Broz in the village of Kumrovec in Zagorje on the borders of Croatia and Slovenia, both at that time under Austro-Hungarian rule. The seventh of 15 children, eight of whom died in infancy, he was born into a Roman Catholic peasant family. His father, Franjo Broz, was a Croatian peasant and his mother, Marija, the daughter of a Slovenian landowner. Josip attended the local school—where there was only one teacher for 350 children—until he was 12. For a while he tended cattle for his uncle, then in 1907 he left home to work in the nearby town of Sisak as a waiter; but he soon took up his father's trade, becoming apprenticed to a locksmith and metalworker. Fluent in both Croatian and German, Josip worked as a wandering journeyman, traveling to Kamnik, Zagreb, Ljubljana, Trieste, Mannheim, Pilsen, and Munich as a mechanic and metalworker. Wherever Josip went, he took an interest in local trade union activities and when he was 18, he joined the Croatian Social Democratic Party.

While working as a skilled mechanic and test driver at the Daimler Benz factory in Weiner Neustadt near Vienna in 1913, Josip Broz was conscripted into the Austro-Hungarian Imperial Army and served in the 25th regiment in Zagreb. When war broke out the following year, he fought as a non-commissioned officer against the Serbs on the Russian front. Never an admirer of the imperial regime, Broz was accused in 1914 of stirring opposition to the war and was jailed in Petrovardin. But in the following January the charges were dropped (later in the war he was decorated for bravery) and he went with his regiment to the Carpathian front where he commanded a scouting platoon. Broz was almost killed by a Cossack's lance after he had been transferred to the Bukovina front. Captured by Circassian troops of the Imperial Russian "Savage Division," he was imprisoned in a Russian hospital in the foothills of the Ural Mountains and then sent to work as a mechanic in the Volga region and Siberia, becoming fluent in Russian. Broz was released following the abdication of Czar Nicholas II in 1917, and now a supporter of the Russian Revolution, he took a train to Petrograd and fought in the streets with Lenin's Bolsheviks, helping them in their first unsuccessful attempt to overthrow the democratic provisional government. Broz was arrested as a fugitive prisoner of war, imprisoned briefly, and then sent back to Siberia. But when the Communists took power in October of that year (1917), he joined the Red Guard to fight in the Russian Civil War.

Broz served in Omsk, then fleeing the White Russian forces, sought refuge with tribesmen in Kazakh and Kirgiz. Later he returned to Omsk, and married Pelagea Byelusnova, a 16-year old Russian girl, and went with her to Petrograd.

In 1920 when Josip Broz was 28, he returned to his native land as a Moscow agent. A monarchy, the kingdom of Serbs, Croats and Slovenes, had been formed out of Serbia and of some the ruins of the Austro-Hungarian empire. The former prince regent, Alexander, had become king, and a coalition government was trying with difficulty to rule the new country. Broz found work as a flour mill mechanic near Bjelovar to the east of Zagreb and joined the Communist Party of Yugoslavia (CPY). However, the following year, after the murder of the Minister of the Interior by a young Bosnian communist, the communist members of parliament were removed from office and the CPY was outlawed. Broz who had moved to Kraljevica, to take up work in the shipyards, was arrested in 1923 on suspicion of being a communist and briefly detained. He was again arrested in 1927 and this time was placed on probation for seven months. Josip and Pelagea lived in poverty during these years and three of their four children died.

In April 1927, Broz, still a loyal Soviet supporter, became a member of the CPY's Zagreb Committee—which supported an Open Letter from the Comintern opposing factions within the CPY. Following Stalin's victory over Trotsky in Moscow, Broz was named a deputy of the Politburo of the CPY Central Committee and leader of both the Croatian and Slovenian committees. Six months later his clandestine political activities led to his being arrested yet again. He denied his right to tribunal judgment and received a five-year sentence, which he served at Lepoglava and Maribor. Soon after Broz commenced his prison term, the government collapsed; all authority was vested in the crown and the country became officially known as Yugoslavia. In prison, Broz met the writer and painter, Mosha Pijade, who later became Yugoslavia's chief ideologist and theoretician. During this time, Broz's wife divorced him and returned to Russia.

In 1934, the year in which Broz was released, King Alexander was assassinated and under the terms of his will, a temporary regency administration was established until his son, a schoolboy, attained his majority. Broz, who had been restricted to his native village, found it necessary to use false names in order to travel. Becoming a full member of the CPY Central Committee and then of the Politburo of that Committee, Broz traveled to Paris, Vienna and Prague. He also went to Moscow for a year and worked in the Balkan section of the Committee International (Comintern). At about this time, Josip Broz adopted the name Tito which had been one of his underground code-names. His colleagues in Moscow, Stalin included, knew him as "Comrade Walter." In the summer of 1936, he was named Organizational Secretary of the CPY Politburo. The CPY narrowly avoided dissolution in 1937 when Stalin commenced a purge of leading Yugoslav communists; about 800 "dissidents" were liquidated. The Comintern appointed Tito provisional Secretary-General of the CPY and he returned to Yugoslavia to reorganize the still-outlawed party, bringing into the leadership young tough-minded revolutionaries such as Milovan Djilas, Aleksandar Ranković, and Edward Kardelj. One of Tito's first acts was to send Yugoslavian volunteer fighters to

support the Republicans in the Spanish Civil War; their combat experience was later to prove very useful to Yugoslavia. Secretly in October 1940, 105 of these 6,000 CPY members convened in Zagreb for the Fifth Conference. Tito's position as Secretary-General, which Moscow had imposed, was ratified.

In March 1941, Prince Paul (the Yugoslav regent) and his ministers reluctantly agreed to accept the Axis agreement which had been signed by Germany, Italy and Japan, and which effectively paved the way for further nazi encroachment. Two days later, some Yugoslavian army officers performed a coup d'état; they placed the 17-year old King Peter II on the throne and voided Yugoslavia's adherence to the Axis pact. On April 6, Germany invaded Yugoslavia and on Stalin's orders, Tito did nothing, except to denounce the "Serb ruling class" for bringing about Yugoslavia's defeat. The German-Soviet non-aggression pact of 1939, which profited both nations territorially, superseded all other interests; and Tito's party had little cause to come to the aid of the imperialist state which had outlawed and persecuted them. But non-communist local military groups, the "Chetniks" (western journalists' name for *cetnici*) formed guerrilla forces and openly revolted against the invaders. However, they were no match for the nazis; on April 17, Yugoslavia capitulated. The royal government went into exile and the country was divided up between the aggressors. In June, some Serbian peasants rose against the Croatian Ustashe (pro-German terrorists) but they were unable to liberate their area. That same month, Hitler, no longer in need of his powerful Soviet friend, attacked the USSR.

At a hastily-called Central Committee meeting, Tito was appointed Military Commander, and under the famous slogan, "Death to Fascism, Freedom to the People!" he issued a call to arms, promising the people that when the imperialists were smashed, there could be "brotherhood and equality" for all. The call was dramatic and the response enthusiastic and effective. In little more than two months, about half the country had been liberated. Tito's fighters became known as the Partisans, and they set up headquarters in the western Serbian town of Užice. Tito created a revolutionary government for the liberated areas but excluded the Chetniks who had freed parts of Serbia and Montenegro. Some parts of the country were dominated by other groups: in Croatia an "independent state" was set up by the pro-nazi Ustashe led by the fanatic Ante Pavelic; a section of Serbia was controlled by the nazi-collaborator Milan Nedic; and there were other more extreme para-military groups in various places. Moscow's immediate fear was that Tito might gain control of the whole country and of the government in exile, and such communist domination they believed would erode Western support for both Yugoslavia and themselves. While many Chetniks and even some of the fascist collaborators and supporters were joining the Partisans, responding to Tito's dramatic appeal for a unified struggle, the royal government in exile together with the Soviet and British allies, continued to support the Chetniks. It was the Chetnik resistance which received world attention, and initially much to Tito's chagrin, his successful guerrilla raids were often attributed to the Chetniks and their leader, Colonel Draja Mihailovích. The first signal of Tito's anger with the Soviets came when he cabled Stalin: "If you cannot help us, do not hinder us."

Toward the end of November 1941, the Germans recalled units from Greece and the Russian front and launched an attack on Tito's Užice headquarters. Weakened by fighting with the Chetniks and the Ustashe, Užice was taken and many Partisans died. Tito himself was almost captured battling through the German lines. Despite this major setback the ranks of the Partisans swelled. Many Yugoslavs preferred his clear-cut aggressive strategy to the Chetnik approach of lying low and building up strength for a more opportune moment, such as the arrival of allied forces. In December, Tito set up brigades comprised of small, highly-mobile guerrilla shock units. Gradually the allies began to learn about the Partisans; there was much speculation as to the identity of the clandestine Tito. Meanwhile, differences between the Partisans, the Chetniks, and other groups continued unabated. In 1942, Tito stated: "Our people are enduring terrible sufferings and misery; hungry, naked, bare-footed, exposed to the bestial terror of the Chetniks, the Ustashe, and the invaders." Early in 1943, more than ten German units, aided by Italian and quisling units, attacked the Partisans in Neretva and Sutjeska. The wounded Partisans struggled across the wintry mountains and smashed through all of the invaders' lines. In the process, thousands of Partisans died, and thousands more, Tito included, were wounded. But against all the odds, they had dealt a very severe blow to the nazis.

When Italy capitulated in September 1943, and then changed sides, the Partisans were greatly strengthened by the arms and equipment surrendered by the ten Italian divisions. Without informing Moscow, Tito reconvened the Anti-Fascist Council of the National Liberation Committee of Yugoslavia (Partisan's Parliament) and the country was declared a federal community of equal peoples. Tito became head of the new provisional government and had himself named "Marshal of Yugoslavia". His Chetnik enemies began to disintegrate when Roosevelt, Churchill, and Stalin officially recognized the Partisans at the Teheran Conference. The allies parachuted personnel into Yugoslavia to liaise with Tito's forces and administer aids and supplies. The Germans continued to attack and when they sent a parachute and tank force into Bosnia in May 1944, Tito was once again almost captured. Stalin and Churchill, hoping to reconcile the emigré government and Tito's revolutionary government, agreed on a "50-50" plan which gave equal status to both. But Tito, who met Churchill in August and Stalin in September, managed to prevent any such scheme from being effected. (Although for a while, following the Yalta Conference of February 1945, Tito admitted two non-communists into his cabinet in order to gain full allied recognition.) Aided by some Yugoslav nazis, the Germans fought on until May 15, 1945, when they finally admitted defeat. Six months later, Tito's communists won a resounding victory; the monarchy was abolished, and the following year a new constitution was signed. King Peter II never returned to Yugoslavia.

With eleven percent of its population wiped out, Yugoslavia had to rebuild its war-torn cities, industries, and railroads, and revive its neglected farmlands. Although the country was preoccupied with the task in hand, the bitterness created by the recent nazi atrocities and of Yugoslav killing Yugoslav, was slow to disappear. Believing that there could be "no compromise with the past", Tito—the new Prime Minister and a Minister of Defense—began a brutal regime, harsher by far than the imperial one it replaced. Under his colleague

Ranković, Tito set up a crack security police force, the dreaded UDBA, which viciously and methodically pursued all those who had opposed the communist-led war effort. Archbishop Stepinac, who had supported the briefly independent state of Croatia was sentenced to a long term of imprisonment; the Chetnik commander Mihailovich and his officers were tried as traitors and killed; many others were shot without trial. The first Constitution imposed rigorous central government control of each of the republics, and industry, commerce and banking were nationalized. Attempts to collectivize agriculture were later abandoned because of peasant resistance. Tito's international reputation plummeted: Catholics throughout the world loathed him because of his treatment of Stepinac, and the western powers, already annoyed by Yugoslavia's occupation of Trieste (1945), were infuriated by Tito's support of the communists in the Greek Civil War. When his army shot down two U.S. transport planes taking a short-cut over Slovenia in 1946, killing five Americans, the U.S. and her allies were outraged.

Tito also had to contend with Soviet fury at his determination to follow an independent line. He had turned to them after the war for development assistance; a feud started when it became clear that Moscow would only fund the establishment of light industry in Yugoslavia. The Soviets wished to centralize heavy industry in their own country while making use of Yugoslavia's resources. Soviet manipulation angered many Yugoslavs; still nursing their war wounds, they were in no mood to be bullied by another super-power, and applauded their leader when he berated the Soviet Union for its policy of "unconditional subordination of small socialist countries to one large socialist country," which "puts a brake on the further development of socialism in the world." Relations with the USSR deteriorated further when Stalin became incensed by plans of Tito and Bulgaria's Dimitrov to form a Balkan Federation; as well, Stalin was suspicious of Yugoslavia's designs on Albania, whose Partisan movement was closely linked with Tito. In June 1948, Stalin expelled the "Tito clique" from the Cominform (Communist Information Bureau, successor to the Comintern) for "boundless ambition, arrogance and conceit." This first crack in the massive edifice of communism stunned the world. The loyalties of many Communist Party members in Yugoslavia were divided and over a period of time about 100,000 party regulars lost their jobs. A Soviet invasion seemed likely at first, but Yugoslavia's emerging nationalistic pride and Tito's war-hero mystique rallied much of the population to his support. The country's large, battle-experienced, loyal military, together with its valuable war bases and the rugged terrain which aided local guerrillas, all served to discourage a Soviet attack. Yugoslavia set up a "re-education" camp at Goli Otok under the UDBA, to which 12,000 to 15,000 pro-Stalin Yugoslavs were sent to "repent." Undoubtedly one of the regime's worst excesses, Tito banned any discussion of it. According to his former close friend and Partisan comrade, Milovan Djilas, the abused and humiliated prisoners had to wear 'traitor' placards and publicly confess their non-political sins; those who were unrepentant had their heads stuffed into buckets of human excrement; some were lynched.

Weakened by the Soviet economic blockade, Tito turned to the west. Fearing the spread of Soviet communism, the western nations reluctantly came to his aid. America contributed more than one billion dollars; in return, Tito sealed the Yugoslav-Greek border (1953) thus ending the Greek Civil War. Although Tito carefully avoided any formal alliance with the capitalist nations, he began to adopt a more liberal stance, stating in 1951 that "the role of the state is gradually decreasing." But Tito always defended his ruthless measures of the past, saying they had to be enacted to "curb certain passions, certain forces that might try to impede the course of revolutionary changes." The centralized economy was slowly dismantled to create a system of worker-controlled enterprises which relied upon "free market" incentives to determine production levels in the factories. At the same time, the role of the CPY diminished. The Constitution was replaced by a new one in June 1953, six months after Tito had become President of Yugoslavia. The sovereignty of the major republics (Serbia, Croatia, Bosnia and Hercegovnia, Slovenia, Macedonia, and Montenegro) was made official; their relationship with the federation was defined as being "between two essentially equal and mutually independent and interlinked social and political communities." But Tito's reforms were too timid for some. When Djilas and others in the leadership pushed for greater liberal reform, Tito demonstrated his staunch adherence to Soviet-style communism by firing them. Djilas was imprisoned for his increasingly anti-communist pronouncements.

Stalin died in March 1953, and as Tito had anticipated, the new Soviet leader acknowledged Yugoslavia's right to take its own road to socialism. An official Soviet delegation headed by Khrushchev and Bulganin visited Belgrade in 1955 to formally reject Stalin's policies and acquiesce on the point of Yugoslavia's independent foreign policy. But the new cordiality was short-lived. In 1956 Tito angrily denounced the Russian invasion of Hungary and protested the Soviet execution of the former Hungarian Prime Minister, Imre Nagy. In 1957 he refused to relinquish an independent foreign policy for the sake of communist unity and "proletarian internationalism," and this drew sharp criticism from the Chinese (the Sino-Soviet conflict had not yet flared into the open) as well as the Russians. Relations between Moscow and Belgrade continued on an erratic course. There was warmth in 1963 when Khrushchev revisited Yugoslavia and praised Tito's employee self-management councils in plants and factories, and frigidity in 1968 when Russia sent tanks into the streets of Prague to crush the liberal movement in Czechoslovakia. The Soviet action, said Tito, "violated the sovereignty of a socialist country and dealt a grave blow to socialist and progressive forces all around the world." The periodic threats of Soviet invasion in Romania and Yugoslavia forced Tito to strengthen his army and to keep his territorial defenses on constant war alert. Moscow was in no doubt that an attack would be mightily resisted by the Yugoslav people. But Tito did not deliberately antagonize the Soviets; fearful of their ambitions in the country after his death, he wanted, if possible, to restore the friendship. The opportunity came in 1971 when the Soviet party leader Brezhnev (Khrushchev "retired" in October 1964) visited Belgrade and signed a non-interference pact with Tito. The following year Tito visited Moscow, returning home with the Order of Lenin. However, the possibility remained that, after his death, Russia might be tempted on some pretext to install a Soviet-oriented Yugoslavian government. Tito tried to insure that an orderly transi-

tion of power could occur after his death by instituting a rotating, collective leadership system in the party and in the government. Tito's worries were well-founded: in the spring of 1974, a group of pro-Soviet Yugoslavs tried unsuccessfully to set up an underground Soviet-dominated communist party. From then on, Tito viewed the USSR with more suspicion than ever. One of his last political acts was to protest the Soviet invasion of Afghanistan in December 1979.

At home throughout the 1950s and 60s, liberalization hesitatingly continued. With the 1953 Constitution in full effect, the influence of all the ethnic groups began to be felt. Further major reforms came in 1965 when Tito adopted a policy of "Market socialism," abandoning the stifling and inefficient Soviet-style economic system. These long needed reforms substantially increased living standards. While the party still dominated political life, considerable cultural freedom was tolerated. Many leading figures in the arts were openly non-Marxist and as more and more Yugoslavs were allowed to work in western Europe, cultural and scientific communications widened, and currency brought home from the booming western countries gave a further boost to the Yugoslav economy. When Tito was made President for life in 1974, a new constitution was adopted. Elected representatives were required to continue their regular jobs and perform their public duties in their own time. In this way Tito hoped to check the rise of the "technocratic and bureaucratic class" which his people feared.

However, Tito rigorously protected his own position. He had already ousted his heir apparent Djilas and in 1965 he got rid of Ranković because of his opposition to the decentralization policies; at the same time, he greatly reduced the power of the UDBA. Tito was also very careful not to let the various uprisings in his country get out of hand. While major rioting among the Albanian minority in 1969 did lead to some significant concessions, the 1971 armed revolt in Croatia resulted in a period of harsh repression during which much of the Croatian party leadership was purged. A rebellion in Serbia precipitated a crackdown against "liberal" officials and intellectuals.

Tito perceived that association with the non-alignment movement might keep his country from coming adrift on its sometimes stormy course between east and west. With Nasser of Egypt and Nehru of India, he convened a conference of 25 "positively neutral" states on his private Adriatic island in 1956. A declaration was issued condemning colonialism, super-power aggression, and racism, and supporting the Algerian uprising. In 1961, Tito hosted the Belgrade conference, the first summit conference of Third World leaders and during the 60s, he traveled in many parts of Africa, Asia, and Latin America to promote the causes of non-aligned and Third World nations. He visited the United States four times: in October 1960; in 1963 when he met with President Kennedy shortly before his assassination; in 1971 to meet with President Nixon; and in 1978 for talks with President Carter. The year before he met with Carter, Tito went to Peking where the Soviet-wary Chinese enthusiastically welcomed their comrade. A year before his death, Tito traveled to Havana to help prevent the Soviet-oriented Cubans from pushing the non-aligned countries into the Moscow camp. His tireless efforts on behalf of the non-aligned and Third World nations earned him world respect as an elder statesman.

In the early years of his leadership, Tito had lived a fairly modest life in Belgrade but he had gradually acquired a taste for luxury and assumed an opulence which exceeded that of the monarchy he replaced. In addition to Brioni (his private island), he became the owner of 17 castles and hunting-lodges. Always clean-shaven and immaculately dressed, his uniforms were edged with gold; as he grew older, he dyed his hair and used a sun-lamp to maintain a tan. He insisted that his staff dress in a formal style, even when they accompanied him to hunts in the forest. While Tito's vanity and pomp and his ready humor were almost legendary, other details of his private life remained somewhat vague. After his first wife divorced him (their son Zharko, a former Red Army soldier, later joined his father), Tito lived with, and it is thought, married a Slovenian revolutionary named Herta Has who bore him a son, Miso. Tito left her in 1952 and when he was 60, married 28-year old Jovanka Budisavljević, a former Partisan. She was his constant companion until their marriage ended mysteriously in 1977. It was rumored that Jovanka was involved in a political intrigue with Serbian generals; this was never confirmed, and it was not known if they were ever formally divorced. Also unconfirmed were reports that Tito had taken up with a masseuse, or more recently with an opera singer nearly fifty years his junior.

Tito was gravely ill for the last 15 weeks of his life and died in a Ljubljana clinic on May 5th. Leaders from all over the world gathered in Yugoslavia for his funeral. He was variously eulogized as a tenacious and courageous freedom fighter, the savior of his country, the father of the non-aligned nations, and a giant of the twentieth century. Even his enemies would generally agree with those assessments, but some would quickly add that he was for a time a brutal despot. Historians will undoubtedly remain divided in their appraisal of Tito; some will maintain that a man of deeper vision and humanity could have unified Yugoslavia without resorting to the terror tactics of a secret police force; others will believe that only an experienced communist warrior like Tito could deliver his people from imperialism and nazism, and steer them clear of Soviet domination. He was never—and never pretended to be—Yugoslavia's greatest political thinker; he left much of the ideology, and the planning, to others. Tito was essentially a man of action; but that, combined with his great courage and his will to survive, might not have been enough to make him the towering personality of his country for several decades. His success owes much to his great skill as a diplomat, and above all, to his lifelong pragmatism.   R.T.

Born Josip Broz (changed name 1934). Son of Franjo B. and Marija Javersek B. Married: (1) Pelagea Byelusnova 1918 (div. ca. 1930); (2) lived with, and possibly married, Herta Has, Partisan fighter ca. 1939–52; (3) Jovanka Budisavljević Partisan fighter 1952 (separated 1977). Children: 1st marriage—Zharko; 3 d.; by Herta Has—Miso. Educ: primary sch. from age 7 to 12. Mil. Service: soldier in Austro-Hungarian Army 1913–15; war prisoner in Russia 1915–17; fought in Red Army 1917–20. Wandering journeyman as metalworker and mechanic ca. 1909–13; joined Croatian Social Democratic Party 1910; returned home from Red Army and joined Communist Party of Yugoslavia (CPY) 1920; became Secty. of Regional Cttee., Trade Union of Metal Workers and Fedn. of Leather and Manufacturing

Workers of Croatia 1924; Secty., Zagreb Metal Workers Union, and Member, CPY Zagreb Cttee. 1927; Deputy of CPY Politburo 1928; imprisoned for illegal political activities 1929-34; became Member, CPY Central Cttee. and Politburo 1934; worked in Comintern, Moscow ca. 1935; Organizational Secty. of Politburo 1936; appointed Secty.-Gen. of CPY 1937; Comdr.-in-Chief of Yugoslav Natl. Liberation Army (leader of Partisan Movement) 1941–45; elected Marshal of Yugoslav Army, and Pres. of Natl. Liberation Cttee. 1943; Prime Minister and Defense Minister 1945–53; elected Pres. of Yugoslav Govt. 1945; Pres. of Natl. Front 1945–53; appointed Pres. of Yugoslav Republic 1953; Gen.-Secty., CPY Secretariat 1953–66; Supreme Comdr. of Armed Forces 1953; Chmn. of League of Communists from 1966; Life Pres. of Yugoslav Republic from 1974; also Life Pres., League of Communists. Hons: Grand Star of Yugoslavia; 3 orders of Natl. Hero; Hero of Socialist Work; Order of Liberty; Great Cordon of Yugoslav Flag; Partisan Star with Golden Wreath; Order of Lenin; Hon. G.C.B. (U.K.) 1972; Nehru Award for Intnl. Understanding 1974; U.S.S.R. Order of the October Revolution 1977; hon. doctorate, Warsaw Univ. 1977; many other domestic and foreign awards.
Further reading: Tito and Goliath by H.F. Armstrong, 1951; Tito Speaks by Vladimir Dedijer, 1952; Josip Broz Tito—Prilozi za Biografiju by Vladimir Dedijer, 1953; Disputed Barricade: The Life and Times of Josip Broz-Tito by Fitzroy MacLean, 1957; Titoism in Action: The Reforms in Yugoslavia After 1948 by F.W. Neal, 1958; Tito by Phyllis Auty, 1970; Tito by Milovan Djilas, 1980.

DAME MARGARET COLE
Political activist, writer, teacher, and editor
Born Cambridge, England, May 6th, 1893
Died London, England, May 7th, 1980

Margaret Cole and her husband G.D.H. Cole were leading members of the Guild Socialist Movement and the Fabian Society. They were also co-authors of a number of well-received detective novels, and both were noted political writers and analysts. Margaret was born into a family with a long tradition of political involvement. Her paternal grandfather, John Postgate, was a noted Victorian reformer whose campaign for the regulation and improvement of retail foodstuffs laid the groundwork for the 1875 Sale of Food and Drugs Act. Her father, a Cambridge University don, pioneered the "direct method" of teaching Latin which encouraged students to use the language in everyday discourse. Dame Margaret later attributed the formation of her political beliefs to the privileged social class and family from which she came. Her adolescence, she said, had been "middle class," but, "belonging to a professional academic group in which there was an atmosphere of comparative equality" instilled an egalitarianism which evolved into socialist political convictions.

Margaret disliked the strictly enforced rules of conduct at Roedean School and found the experience oppressive. However, at Girton College in Cambridge she quickly established herself as an outstanding student. The progressive ideas of the school's intellectual community appealed to her and she took up the cause of "non-dogmatic, idealistic English Socialism of the early nineteenth century." The Socialists urged ". . .world government, the abolition of all authority not based on reason, and of all inequality based on prejudice or privilege of any kind . . . and an immense increase of human welfare and material resources achieved by (an) all-wise, non-profit-making organization of economic life."

After graduation Margaret taught classics for two years at St. Paul's Girls' School in London, a position which provided little outlet for her political zeal. When her brother was imprisoned for refusing to serve with the army during World War One, Margaret's commitment to socialism deepened and she became associated with the Fabian Society's Research Department. The research group was controlled by Guild Socialists who, advocating worker control of factories, were more radical than the Fabians (led by Beatrice and Sidney Webb) who favored collective ownership of industries by the state. In 1916 Margaret met G.D.H. Cole who had propounded Guild Socialist doctrine in his 1913 book *The World of Labour;* they were married two years later. Ideological conflict between the two groups intensified and the couple were among the Guild Socialists' leadership when they broke away from the Fabians to form the Labour Research Department. After 1920, much to the Coles' dismay, the L.R.D. was increasingly influenced by the British Communist Party. They abandoned the organization in 1925 and moved to Oxford where Mr. Cole had obtained a Readership in Economics. Effecting a rapprochement with the Webbs, the Coles rejoined the Fabian Society in the late 1920s.

Margaret and Professor Cole gathered around them "bright young men" who would later become prominent in the British Labour Party government; among them were Hugh Gaitskell and Michael Stewart. The 1926 General Strike, precipitated by government efforts to reduce miners' wages, united the British Left and the Coles organized the Oxford Strike Committee which they staffed with undergraduates. In her autobiography, *Growing Up Into Revolution* (1949), Margaret Cole charged the government with deliberate provocation of the strike and lamented its ultimate failure as a "tragedy."

During the 1930s Margaret Cole's influence grew. Committed to providing educational opportunities for the disadvantaged, she administered tutorial classes for the Worker's Education Association (the working-class educational movement became the focus of a lifelong concern). With her husband she founded the Society for Socialist Inquiry and Propaganda and the new Fabian Research Bureau which helped revive the socialist cause after the collapse of Britain's second Labour Government in 1931. Under Margaret's guidance the Bureau collected much of the data, particularly that concerning salary rates in industry, upon which key legislation enacted by the 1945–53 Labour Government was based.

Margaret Cole and her husband wrote more than thirty critically acclaimed detective novels as well as two important political studies, *The Intelligent Man's Review of Europe To-Day* (1933) and *The Condition of Britain* (1937). Her books on British politics, *The Story of Fabian Socialism* (1961), *Beatrice and Sidney Webb* (1955), *The Life of G.D.H. Cole* (1971) and the two volumes of Beatrice Webb's diaries which she edited are considered vital documents in the history of Guild and Fabian socialism.

In 1963 Margaret Cole became President of the Fabian Society. A forceful political figure, she continued to fight for educational reform and in 1970, she was made Dame of the British Empire.   E.T.

Born Margaret Isabel Postgate. Daughter of John Percival Postgate, Latin scholar, and Edith P. Married G(eorge) D(ouglas) H(oward) Cole, economist and socialist organizer 1918 (d. 1959). Children: Janet Elizabeth Margaret, b. 1921; Ann Rachel, b. 1922; Humphrey John Douglas, economist, b. 1928. Educ: Roedean Sch., Brighton; Girton Coll., Cambridge, B.A. (First Class Hons. classics) 1914. Jr. Classics Mistress, St. Paul's Girls' Sch., London 1914–16; Asst. Secty., Fabian Research Dept. (later, Labour Research Dept.), London 1917–25; Tutor, Workers' Educ. Assn., London 1925–44; Lectr., tutorial classes, Univ. London 1925–49; Lectr., Univ. Cambridge 1941–44. Co-founder, Soc. for Socialist Inquiry and Propaganda 1930; Secty., New Fabian Research Bureau 1935–39. With Fabian Soc.: Hon. Secty. 1939–53; Vice-Chmn. 1954–55; Chmn. 1955–56; Pres. 1963–75. With London County Council: Member 1943–65 and Alderman 1952–65, Educ. Cttee.; Chmn. 1950–65 and Vice-Chmn. 1959–60, Further Educ. Sub-Cttee. With Inner London Educ. Authority: Member 1965–67; Vice-Chmn., Further and Higher Educ. Sub-Cttee. 1965–67. Chmn., Geffrye Mus. 1952–67; Chmn. 1961–72 and Vice-Chmn. 1972–75, Sidney Webb Coll, London; Chmn., Battersea Coll. of Educ. 1962–67. Hons: O.B.E. 1965; D.B.E. 1970; Hon. Fellow, London Sch. of Economics 1977; also Fellow, Royal Hist. Soc.
Author: The Control of Industry, 1921; An Introduction to World History for Classes and Study Circles, 1923; Local Government for Beginners, 1927; Books and the People, 1938; Women of Today, 1937; Marriage, Past and Present, 1938; (with R. Padley) Wartime Billeting, 1941; A Letter to a Student, 1942; Education for Democracy, 1942; The General Election of 1945 and After, 1945; Beatrice Webb: A Memoir, 1945; The Rate for the Job, 1946; The Social Services and the Webb Tradition, 1946; Makers of the Labour Movement, 1948; Growing up into Revolution, 1949; Miners and the Board, 1949; Robert Owen of New Lanark, 1953; Beatrice and Sidney Webb, 1955; Servant of the County, 1956; Plan for Industrial Pensions, 1956; The Story of Fabian Socialism, 1961; The Life of G.D.H. Cole, 1971. *Jt. author with G.D.H. Cole*—The Bolo Book, 1923; The Intelligent Man's Review of Europe Today, 1933; A Guide to Modern Politics, 1934; The Condition of Britain, 1937; also, The New Economic Revolution, and others. *Detective novels with D.G.H. Cole*—Death of a Millionaire, 1925; Murder at Crome House, 1927; Man from the River, 1928; Blatchington Tangle, 1928; Superintendent Wilson's Holiday, 1929; Poison in a Garden Suburb, 1929; Berkshire Mystery, 1930; Walking Corpse, 1931; Corpse in the Constable's Garden, 1931; Burglars in Bucks, 1932; Deadman's Watch, 1932; Death of a Star, 1932; Superintendent Wilson's Cases, 1933; Death in the Quarry, 1934; End of an Ancient Mariner, 1934; Murder in Four Parts, 1934; Big Business Murder, 1935; Brooklyn Murders, 1935; Doctor Tancred Begins: or, The Pendexter Saga, 1935; Lessons in Crime (short stories), 1935; Sleeping Death, 1936; Affair at Aliquid, 1936; Last Will and Testament: or, The Pendexter Saga, Second Canto, 1936; Brothers Sackville, 1937; Missing Aunt, 1938; Off with her Head!, 1939; Mrs. Warrender's Profession, 1939; Double Blackmail, 1939; Wilson and Some Others, 1940; Greek Tragedy, 1940; Murder at the Munition Works, 1940; Topers End, 1942; Knife in the Dark, 1942; Birthday Gifts and Other Stories, 1946;

Strychnine Tonic, and Other Stories, 1947; Fatal Beauty, 1948; Toys of Death, 1948; In Peril of His Life, 1948. *Editor*—(with G.D.H. Cole) Cobbett's Rural Rides in the Southern, Western and Eastern Counties of England, 1930; Twelve Studies in Soviet Russia, 1932; The Road to Success, 1936; Democratic Sweden, 1938; Our Soviet Ally, 1943; (with G.D.H. Cole) Opinions of William Cobbett, 1945; (with Barbara Drake) Our Partnership, 1948; The Webbs and Their Work, 1949; The Diaries of Beatrice Webb 1912–1924 (1952) and Vol. II, 1924–32 (1956); The Moonstone, 1953. Also contributed to newspapers, magazines and periodicals including London Evening Standard, New Statesman, Guardian, Listener, Socialist Commentary, Fabian Review, and New Society.

FIELD-MARSHAL SIR GEOFFREY (HARDING) BAKER
British Army Officer and Chief of General Staff
Born Muree, Pakistan, June 20th, 1912
Died Sussex, England, May 8th, 1980

Field-Marshal Sir Geoffrey Harding Baker, whose distinguished army career spanned over forty years, was born of a military family in Muree, Pakistan, in the period of the British Raj. His father was an officer in the Indian Army and Baker was sent to England for his education at Wellington College and the Royal Military Academy, where he was awarded the Sword of Honour for outstanding achievement.

Baker was commissioned into the Royal Artillery in 1932. Although he returned briefly to England with the Royal Horse Artillery, he was in India at the outbreak of World War Two. He accompanied his regiment to Egypt in 1939 and suffered the long desert marches into Eritrea in 1940–41. He was later awarded the Military Cross for his activities in the battle of Kern and the Abyssinian campaign.

In 1942 Baker returned to England as an instructor for the Middle East Staff College and served with the Eighth Army from 1942 to 1943. As Commanding Officer of the 127th Field Regiment, 51st Highland Division, he took part in the invasion of Sicily in 1943; he then returned to Britain and joined the Headquarters Staff of the 21st Army Group to assist with the liberation of France, where he remained until the end of the war. After serving as Director of the War Office in the postwar years, Baker was selected in 1955 to be Director of Operations and Chief of Staff to the Governor of Cyprus during a critical period filled with terrorist activities. Under his guidance the British army maintained law and order, preventing any major disturbances. Baker was rewarded for his work with the CMG in 1957.

In 1960, Baker, now a Major-General, became Chief of Staff in the Headquarters of the Army Southern Command and, a year later, he moved to the Supreme Headquarters of the Allied Powers, Europe, as Chief of Staff, Contingencies Planning—an important international appointment which demanded diplomatic skills. When Britain's armed services' administration was reorganized in 1964, bringing the Army, Royal Navy and Royal Air Force under the aegis of the

Ministry of Defence, Baker was made Vice-Chief of General Staff, a position he held until 1966 when he transferred to the Headquarters of the Army Southern Command as its General Office and Commander-in-Chief. Elevated to the rank of General the following year, Baker succeeded Field Marshal Sir James Cassells in 1968 as Chief of General Staff, Britain's highest Army post, and held the appointment until his 1971 retirement. The many honors conferred upon him included those of Aide-de-Camp to Queen Elizabeth II and Commander of the U.S. Legion of Merit.   M.D.

Son of Col. Cecil Norris B. and Ella Mary B. Married Valerie Lockhart 1946. Children: two sons and one daughter. Educ: Wellington Coll, London; Royal Military Acad., Woolwich (Sword of Honour) 1932. Commissioned into Royal Artillery 1932; 11th Field Brigade, India 1935; F. (Sphinx) Battery, Royal Horse Artillery, England 1937 and Egypt 1939. Training with Middle East Staff Coll., England 1940. Brigade Major, Royal Artillery, Fourth Indian Div., Western Desert and Eritrea 1940–41; Instr., Middle East Staff Coll, 1942; Gen. Staff Officer, H.Q. Eighth Army 1942–43; Comdg. Officer, 127th Field Regiment, 51st Highland Div., Sicily 1943; Brig., Gen. Staff, H.Q., 21st Army Group, North West Europe 1944–47; Deputy Dir., War Office, London 1947–50; Comdg. Officer, 3rd Regiment, Royal Horse Artillery 1950–52; Dir. of Operations, War Office, London 1952–54; Chief of Staff to Gov. of Cyprus 1955–57; Comdr., Royal Artillery, 7th Armoured and 5th Divs., British Army of the Rhine, Germany 1957–59; Asst. Chief of Staff, H.Q. Northern Army Group, Germany 1959–60; Chief of Staff, H.Q. Southern Command, London 1960–61; Chief of Staff, Contingencies Planning, SHAPE 1961–63; Vice-Chief of Gen. Staff, London 1963–66; Gen. Officer, Comdr. -in-Chief, H.Q. Southern Command 1966–68; Chief of Gen. Staff 1968–71; Field Marshal 1971. Other appointments include: Col. Commandant, Royal Artillery 1964–70; Royal Mil. Police 1968–71; and Royal Horse Artillery 1970. Dir., Grindlays Bank, London since 1972; Central London Region, Lloyds Bank since 1977; Consolidated Safeguards Ltd., since 1977; Cititel Consultancy since 1978. Pres., Officer's Assn. Army Benevolent Fund 1971; Council Member, Radley Coll, London 1973; V.P. Chmn. of Govt., Wellington Coll. 1976. Hons: M.C. 1941; O.B.E. 1943; C.B.E. 1946; Comdr., U.S. Legion of Merit 1946; C.B. 1955; C.M.G. 1957; K.C.B. 1964; G.C.B. 1968; A.D.C. to Queen Elizabeth II 1968-71; Master Gunner, St. James's Park, London 1970–76; Constable of the Tower of London 1980; also, Hon. Liveryman, Haberdashers' Co., London, and Hon. Freeman, City of London.

JAN BÉLEHRÁDEK
Biologist and author
Born Prague, Czechoslovakia, December 18th, 1896
Died London, England, May 8th, 1980

The scientific career of Dr. Jan Bélehrádek—interrupted on several occasions by political upheavals in his native Czechoslovakia—was consistently involved with the application of mathematics to biological science. For his work on the theory of the effects of heat on cell activity, Bélehrádek became well known in American and British academic circles and won the Légion d'Honneur for scientific achievement from the Universities of Paris and Marseilles.

Jan Bélehrádek was born in 1896 in Prague to a distinguished family. His father was an eminent educational reformer and close friend of the philosopher and President of Czechoslovakia, T.G. Marsaryk. (Jan Bélehrádek and Masaryk's son also became friends and after World War Two, they worked together to promote the formation of the United Nations.) A gifted student and scientist, Bélehrádek became Professor of Biology at Masaryk University in Brno at the age of 26 and Professor of General Biology at Charles University in Prague in his early thirties. A rector of Charles University from 1945 until 1948, Bélehrádek helped restore the institution, which had been devastated by the war, to its former prominence.

The work for which Bélehrádek achieved fame, *Temperature and Living Matter,* was published in 1934. A monograph that revised data compiled by Bélehrádek and other researchers during the 1920s, it comprehensively analyzed the interaction between temperature and various cell mechanisms. Studying the theory of temperature co-efficients, he discussed the application of mathematics to biology and his mathematical equation for temperature co-efficients won popular acceptance. When exceptions were later found, Bélehrádek quickly supplied new constants, but his earlier work had conclusively demonstrated the viability of his method. His book also analyzed changes in the morphology, elasticity, osmocitic resistance, electrical conductance, and bioelectrical potential that resulted from temperature modulations. Although Bélehrádek limited his study to cytochemical reactions (thereby ignoring the response of the whole body), he did devote special attention to the effects of extreme heating and chilling on entire organisms. A later book, *Man in Figures,* has become a popular study of physiology.

Bélehrádek's political troubles began with the signing of the Munich agreement in 1938. In open defiance of nazi domination of Czechoslovakia, he chaired the "We Shall Remain Faithful" Committee. For ridiculing nazi racial dogma and defending the rights of Jews, he was placed in the Terezin concentration camp, an ordeal he barely survived. The Communist takeover of Czechoslovakia in 1948 again brought Bélehrádek into conflict with the government. His introductory text, *General Biology,* was officially banned and labeled "anti-Marxist" and he was forced to relinquish his editorship of the journal *Science and Life.*

Shortly after Bélehrádek had fallen into official disfavor in Czechoslovakia, he secured a position with Unesco in France. In Paris he worked to organize the World Association of Universities until opposition by the Czech government forced him to abandon the post. A colleague at Unesco, Professor Julian Huxley, with whom Bélehrádek had collaborated on several papers during the 1920s and 30s, helped him emigrate to England. There, in Bélehrádek's later years, he campaigned against political repression as a founding member of the United Kingdom Committee for the Defense of the Unjustly Prosecuted. His son, Jan Bélehrádek, Jr., is a noted cancer researcher in France.   R.W.

Son of a Czechkslovakian educational reformer. Married. Son: Jan, cancer researcher. Educ: Schs. and Univ. in Czechoslovakia. Became Prof. of Biology, Masaryk Univ., Brno 1922; appointed Prof. of General Biology ca. 1927, and Rector 1945–48, Charles Univ., Prague. Interned in Terezin concentration camp ca. 1939. Staff Member, Unesco, Paris ca. 1949, active in formation of World Assn. of Univs. Later emigrated to England. Founding Member, U.K. Cttee. for the Defense of the Unjustly Prosecuted. *Major articles include:* Bioluminescence and biologic characteristics of *Armillarea mellea,* Mykologia, 1927; (with J.S. Huxley) Changes in oxygen consumption during metamorphosis induced by thyroid administration in the Axolotl, Jrnl. of Physiology, 1927; Gradual slowing of the heart at low temperature, Archives Internationale de Physiologie, 1928; (with J.S. Huxley and Francis Roy Curtis) Note on the relation between (a) external hydrogen ion concentration and (b) thallium salts, and the rate of amphibian metamorphosis, Biochemistry Journal, 1928; Retardation of biologic activity by cold is due to increased viscosity of protoplasm, Protoplasma, 1928; On the significance of temperature co-efficients, Protoplasma, 1929; The growth-stimulating action of a diet of fatigues muscles as a function of the extent of fatigue, Biologia Generalis, 1930; (with Jan Melchiar) The different actions of raised and normal temperatures on the survival of *Helodea canadansis Rich.,* Biologia Generalis, 1930; L'action de la température sur la marche et sur le degré de l'hémolyse par la digitonie et par l'oléate de sodium, Archives Internationale de Physiologie, 1932; (with J. Mladek) Richesse en eau du bioplasme et la grandeur du co-efficient thermique des oxidations, Protoplasma, 1934; Physiological aspects of hypothermia, Annual review of Physiology, 1957; Intermolecular aspects of the structural stability of protoplasm at temperature extremes, Intnl. Symposium on Cytoecology, 1963.

SIR (HENRY) LAURENCE LINDO
High Commissioner for Jamaica in London
Born Port Maria, Jamaica, August 13th, 1911
Died London, England, May 8th, 1980

Sir Laurence Lindo, Jamaica's first High Commissioner in London, was born in Port Maria, Jamaica in 1911 and educated at Jamaica College and Keble College, Oxford, where he was a Rhodes Scholar from 1931 to 1934. He began his career in the British Civil Service in 1935 as Inspector of Schools for Jamaica, and from 1939 to 1952 he served in the Colonial Secretariat. In 1952 Lindo was appointed Administrator of the island of Dominica, the first West Indian to hold the position. During his administration he improved the island's road network and introduced a ministerial form of government. He also served as Acting Governor of the Windward Islands in 1957 and again in 1959.

Lindo returned to Jamaica in 1960 as Governor's Secretary and helped to facilitate the transfer of power after three hundred years of colonial rule. In 1962, the year of Jamaican independence, he became the country's first High Commissioner in London. As High Commissioner he helped negotiate a loan and a grant of a million pounds each year from the British government to the newly independent country and was also involved in protecting Jamaican interests in the context

urtesy H.R. Lindo

of Britain's entry into the Common Market. Lindo was appointed ambassador to France in 1966 and in the following year was named ambassador to West Germany.

In addition to his duties as an international diplomat, Lindo worked with British authorities on ways to integrate the many Jamaicans who emigrated to England during the 1950s and 60s. Sir Laurence received many honors during his diplomatic career, including the Order of Jamaica (1957) and a knighthood in 1967.   T.P.

Son of Henry Alexander L. and Ethel Mary L. Married Holly Robertson Clacken 1943. Children: two daughters. Educ: Jamaica Coll.; Keble Coll., Oxford (Rhodes Scholar 1931). With British Civil Service: Inspector of Schools, Jamaica 1935-39; Asst. Information Officer 1939–43; Asst. Secty. 1945–50 and Principal Asst. Secty. 1950–52, Colonial Secretariat; Admin., Dominica, Windward Islands 1952–59; Acting Gov., Windward Islands 1957; 1959; Gov.'s Secty., Jamaica 1960–62; High Commissioner for Jamaica in U.K. 1962–73; Ambassador to France 1966–72; Ambassador to Fed. Republic of Germany 1967–70. Central Council of Royal Over-seas League 1975; Vice-Chmn. Bd. of Govs., Commonwealth Inst. Hons.: C.M.G. 1957; knighted 1967; O.J. 1973; G.C.V.O. 1974.

JOHN BEECHER
Poet and teacher
Born New York City, U.S.A., January 22nd, 1904
Died San Francisco, California, U.S.A., May 11th, 1980

Known best as a poet of protest, John Beecher infused his work with the Abolitionist fervor of his ancestors Henry Ward Beecher and Harriet Beecher Stowe. His poems, urging rebellion against the inequities of America's white capitalist society, chronicle the struggles of laborers, farmers, as well as blacks and whites fighting in the civil rights movement. Recurrent with themes of political liberty and oppression, Beecher's poetry is marked by spare, colloquial voices, speaking forth in angry narratives.

Beecher brought to his poems insights gleaned from diverse experiences, ranging from working in steel mills to teaching college. At sixteen, he worked 12-hour shifts in Alabama steel mills, where the harsh treatment of laborers remained deeply ingrained in his memory. During the Depression, Beecher oversaw New Deal programs in the South, providing aid to urban and rural poor, migrant workers, and to minorities discriminated against in jobs. Much later, he recast that experience into the collection of poems *To Live and Die in Dixie,* which includes the long narrative *In Egypt Land.* This poem describes a black sharecropper's revolt in Alabama, and shows the genesis of a farmer's union. For many readers the poem captures the anger that motivated the civil rights movement. Here, Beecher voices the particular rage of a black farmer who was lynched for trying to organize a union:

what kind of a Christmas and what kind of a country anyway
when you made ten bales of cotton

five thousand pounds of cotton
with your own hands
and your wife's hands
and all your children's hads
and then the Laws came to take your mules away
and drive your cows to sell in town
. . .and you couldn't even get commissary credit
for coffee molasses and sow-belly
and nobody in your house had shoes to wear
or any kind of fitting Sunday clothes
and no Christmas for nobody. . . .

While serving on the S.S. Booker T. Washington in World War II,
Beecher kept a journal, later published as *All Brave Sailors,* that
recorded the comradeship among the racially mixed crew. The subject
of race relations drew him to elaborate in the book the history of his
family, its orators, theologians, college founders, and rebels. Ralph
Ellison, reviewing the book in 1946, noted that, for Beecher, the ship
became "a concrete floating symbol of tranquil interracial brotherhood, crossing the seas on duty in a war of racial strife, but remaining
within itself undisturbed." Though Ellison found the book marred by
sentimentality, he was intrigued by the utopian moment in Beecher's
vision, a search for an ideal democracy, and how that quest has been
embodied by the Beecher family since the American Revolution.

In 1950, when Beecher refused to sign a loyalty oath—California's
Levering Act later declared unconstitutional—he was blacklisted for
nine years and lost his job as sociology professor at San Francisco
State College. Turning to ranching, he continued to write and
founded, with his wife, a private press to publish his own books. From
1959 he taught at various colleges, working also as editor, publisher,
and journalist for numerous publications. Throughout the 1960s he
covered social problems for the *San Francisco Chronicle* and
Ramparts. One of Beecher's most well-known poems from this time is
"Report to the Stockholders," detailing the miserable working conditions of steel workers and demanding support for labor unions. He
continued to write until his death in San Francisco on May 14, 1980 of
lung fibrosis. At that time he was working on his autobiography, and
had just completed *Tomorrow is a Day,* a study of the farm labor
movement in Minnesota and the Dakotas.   E.T.

Son of Leonard Thurlow B., steel company executive, and Isabel
Garghill B. Married Barbara Marie Scholz, artist and book designer
1955. Children: (by previous marriage) David; Leonard; Joan (Mrs.
T. Eichrodt); Michael; Thomas Edward. Free-thinker. Educ: Va. Mil.
Inst., Lexington 1919–20; Cornell Univ. 1921–24; Univ. of Ala., B.A.
1925; Harvard Univ. 1929–30; Univ. of Wisc., M.A. 1930; Univ. of
N.C., Chapel Hill 1933–34. Mil. Service: Officer and Ensign, S.S.
Booker T. Washington, first integrated unit in U.S. Merchant Marine
1943–45 (Combat Medal). Steel worker, 1920–21 and 1923–24, U.S.
Steel Corp., Birmingham, Ala; open hearth metallurgist 1928–29;
Instr., English, Dartmouth Coll. 1927; Advisor and Instr., English,
Experimental Coll., Univ. of Wisc. 1929–33; District Admin., Fed.
Emergency Relief Admin., N.C. 1934–35; Mgr. resettlement projects
and migrant camps, U.S. Dept. of Agriculture 1935–40; Asst. Ed. and
writer, Birmingham Age-Herald and News 1940–41; Regional Dir.,
Pres's. Cttee. on Fair Employment Practice 1941–43; Dir., Displaced

Persons Program, U.N. Relief and Rehabilitation Admin. Stuttgart
1945; Chief Ed., Natl. Inst. of Social Relations, Washington, D.C.
1945–46; Asst. Prof., sociology 1948-50 and since 1977, San Francisco
State Coll. (now Univ.); rancher and Fine Press Operator,
Sebastopol, Calif. 1951-58; Lectr., English, Ariz. State Univ., Tempe
1959-61; Assoc. Ed., Ramparts 1959-63; Poet in Residence, Univ.
Santa Clara, Calif. 1963-65; Visiting Prof., Miles Coll., Birmingham,
Ala. 1966-67. Poet in Residence: N. Shore Community Coll., Beverly,
Mass. 1969-71; St. John's Univ., Collegesville, Minn. 1970; Assump-
tion Coll., Worcester, Mass. 1971. Visiting Scholar, Duke Univ.
1973-75; nationwide poetry readings since 1963; correspondent and
writer, San Francisco Chronicle. Hons.: L.H.D., Ill. Coll., Jackson-
ville 1948; Ford Fellowship 1951; Fellow, Fund for the Advancement
of Education 1951–52; Western Books Exhib. Award 1960–61, 1963;
Fellow, Assn. American Colls. Arts Program 1969–72; Fellow, Natl.
Endowment for the Arts 1976–77. *Books: Poetry*—And I Will Be
Heard, 1940; Here I Stand, 1941; Land of the Free, 1956; Observe the
Time, 1956; Just Peanuts, 1957; Inquest, 1957; Moloch, 1957; In
Egypt Land, 1960; Homage to a Subversive, 1961; Phantom City,
1961; Report to the Stockholders and Other Poems, 1932-62, 1962;
Undesirables, 1962; Bestride the Narrow World, 1963; Conformity
Means Death, 1963; On Acquiring a Cistercian Breviary, 1963; Yours
in the Bonds, 1963; An Air That Kills, 1963; A Humble Petition to the
President of Harvard, 1963; To Live and Die in Dixie and Other
Poems, 1966; Hear the Wind Blow!, 1968; Collected Poems 1924–74;
Recording: To Live and Die in Dixie (Folkways), 1968. *Other*—All
Brave Sailors; The Story of the S.S. Booker T. Washington, 1945;
Tomorrow is a Day, 1980. Contributor to Harper's, The New
Republic, Nation, Social Forces, Negro Digest, Science and Society,
Coastlines, Fellowship, and other publications. Complete Works and
Papers, 1973 (microfilm edit.).
Further reading: "The Booker T." by Ralph Ellison, The .New
Republic, Feb. 18, 1946; "The Poetry of John Beecher" by Leslie
Woolf Hedley, Mainstream, Sept., 1962.

HENRY KNOX SHERRILL
Presiding Bishop of the U.S. Episcopal Church and President of the
World Council of Churches
Born Brooklyn, N.Y., U.S.A., November 6th, 1890
Died Boxford, Mass., U.S.A., May 11th, 1980

The career of Bishop Henry Knox Sherrill was characterized by his
conviction that Christianity should dwell at the center of human
affairs. In the years following World War Two, when church growth
was reaching record levels, Bishop Sherrill was an influential and
progressive church leader dedicated to promoting an ecumenical
Christian outlook.

Henry Knox Sherrill graduated from Yale in 1911 and subsequently
attended the Episcopal Theological School where he received a
bachelor of divinity degree in 1914. After graduating from seminary
he served as a curate in the historic Trinity Church in Boston until
1917 when he went to France as an Army chaplain. Upon returning to
the United States at the end of the war, Sherrill became rector at All
Saints Church in Brookline, Massachusetts; in 1923 he went back to

Trinity Church to serve as rector, the youngest man ever to hold the position.

From his early days at Trinity, Sherrill persuasively insisted that preaching alone would not build a solid parish and advocated an action-oriented ministry. He devoted much time to paying house calls and this outreaching attitude was reflected throughout his career. By the time he was installed as Bishop of Massachusetts in 1930, Sherrill had earned a reputation as a liberal, ecumenical churchman, opposed to national isolationism and intolerant of the prevailing conservatism in the Episcopal church.

After serving as Chairman of the General Commission on Army and Navy Chaplains during World War Two, Sherrill was unanimously elected as presiding bishop of the Episcopal Church. During his term he advocated a more flexible church stance on birth control and divorce and opposed racial discrimination. Also under his administration the Seabury Press was founded as the principal publishing arm of the Episcopal Church. When the Seabury Bookstore opened in New York, Sherrill insisted that the store carry current bestsellers and paperbacks as well as religious titles.

Sherrill's efforts to promote Christian unity and cooperation led to the founding of the National Council of Churches in 1949, an ecumenical organization of 29 church bodies. Sherrill was its first President from 1950 to 1952, and after he helped found the World Council of Churches a year later, he served as President (from 1954 until 1961). His ambition to establish an international, ecumenical organization had been realized. Church unity, he said, was the key to revitalizing Christianity and society; "A united Christian approach to world problems is essential. How can we expect other nations to cooperate when we evidence so little ability at cooperation ourselves?"

After retiring in 1961 the Bishop's involvement with the church councils continued. Sherrill contributed many articles and editorials to both Christian and secular publications and also published an autobiography, *Among Friends*, in 1962. At the time of his death he was the oldest bishop in the Episcopal Church.   A.W.

Son of Henry Williams S. and Maria Knox Mills S. Married Barbara Harris 1921. Children: Rev. Henry Williams, b. 1922; Bishop Edmund Knox (of Northern Brazil), b. 1925; Rev. Franklin Goldthwaite, b. 1928; Barbara Prue Wilson, b. 1933. Episcopalian. Educ: Brooklyn Polytechnic Prep. Sch. 1906; Hotchkiss Sch., Lakeville, Conn., 1907; Yale Univ., B.A. 1911; Episcopal Theological Sch., Cambridge, Mass., B.Div. 1914. Ordained Protestant Episcopal Deacon, Mass., B. Div. 1914; Priest, 1915. Mil. Service: Red Cross and U.S. Army Chaplain, Bar-sur-Aube, France, 1917-18; Chmn., Gen. Commn. of Army/Navy Chaplains 1941-45; Asst. Minister, Trinity Church, Boston, Mass., 1914–17; Rector, Church of our Savior, Brookline, Mass., 1919–23; Rector, Trinity Church, Boston 1923–30; Bishop of Mass. 1930–47; Presiding Bishop of U.S. Episcopal Church 1947–58; First Pres., Natl. Council of Churches of Christ in U.S.A. 1950–52; Pres., World Council of Churches 1954–61. Pres., Greater Boston Fedn. of Churches 1927-30; Member, Gov. of Mass. Commn. on Racial and Religious Understanding 1943-47; Pres., Truman's Commn. on Civil Rights 1947; Trustee and Chmn. Bd., Mass. Gen. Hosp.; Member, Lambeth Conferences 1948, 1958; Fellow, Corp. of Yale Univ. and American Acad. of Arts and Sciences; Trustee,

Boston Univ. Hons: Medal of Merit 1947; Hon. D.D. from Yale, Harvard, Princeton, Columbia, Trinity Coll., Univ. of Edinburgh, Oxford, and others; Hon. S.T.D., Gen. Theological Sem. 1947; Hon. LL.D., Boston Univ. 1930; Hon. D.C.I., Union College. *Author:* William Lawrence—Later Years of a Happy Life, 1943; The Church's Ministry in our Times (Lyman Beecher Lecture Series, Yale Univ.), 1949; Among Friends (autobiog.), 1962; contributed articles, sermons and editorials to church and other publications.

WILLIAM A(LEXANDER) ROBSON
British jurist, town planner and political scientist
Born North Finchley, London, England, July 14th, 1895
Died London, England, May 12, 1980

Professor William Alexander Robson, a leading international consultant on city planning, was one of Britain's foremost authorities on local government law. A Fabian socialist, he founded *The Political Quarterly* in 1930 and maintained his association with it for the remainder of his working life.

Robson's father was a dealer in pearls in Hatton Garden, London's jewel metal quarter, and it was between there and the family home in North Finchley—at that time still a rural suburb of London—that the young Robson divided his childhood. However, the death of his father forced Robson, at the age of fifteen, to leave school.

Robson found employment with the Graham White Aviation Company as a clerk, and he later became assistant manager. The First World War intervened and Robson was commissioned as a lieutenant in the Royal Flying Corps (later the Royal Air Force). Robson, already familiar with airplanes, was quickly trained as a fighter pilot and saw active service in France for the rest of the war. In 1916 his first book, *Air-craft in War and Peace,* was published in London. The book caught the interest of George Bernard Shaw who introduced Robson to Beatrice and Sidney Webb, founders of the Fabian society, who were deeply involved in the British labor movement. The Webbs decided that Robson deserved a complete education and used their influence to have him specially enrolled at the London School of Economics (which they had helped to found). Robson vindicated their assessment of his intellectual skills by attaining First Class Honors. He continued to study, researching for his Ph.D. in economics while simultaneously reading law.

Called to the Bar in 1922, Robson began his career in jurisprudence at the chambers of Sir Henry Slessor, who later became Solicitor-General to the first Labour Government in Britain and through whom Robson acquired his knowledge of government. Robson took a lectureship at the London School of Economics in 1926 and two years later published *Justice and Administrative Law,* which demonstrated that administrative law and tribunals provided an effective means of asserting public control over government—without substituting the rule of lawyers for that of civil servants. His study promoted the development of public law in Britain as well as other Western European democracies, where his scholarship was acknowledged by the award of many honorary degrees.

Robson's independence of thought and his strong opinions in the field of public law endeared him neither to the higher Civil Service nor to the legal profession. Similarly, his intervention in the re-organization of London's government through his founding of the greater London group at the London School of Economics upset many of his Labour Party colleagues who saw the change from London County Council to the greater London Council more as a conservative manipulation than as useful streamlining of administration. Nevertheless, the London Government Act of 1963 reflected much of the evidence supplied by Robson's group to the royal commission on London government—not least because the group had no vested interest in reform. Abroad, Robson's views on planning met with enthusiasm and he was employed as a city planning consultant in Nigeria, Turkey, Japan, and Lebanon.   M.D.

Son of Jack R., pearl dealer. Married Juliette Alvin 1929. Children: two sons; one daughter. Educ: London Sch. of Econs., B.Sc. econs. (First Class Hons.) 1922; Ph.D. 1924; LL.M. 1928. Mil. Service: Lt., R.F.C. and R.A.F., France 1914-19. Clerk 1910-12 and Asst. Mgr. 1912-14, Graham White Aviation Co., London. Called to Bar (Lincolns Inn) 1922. With London Sch. of Econs.: Lectr. 1926-33; Reader in Admin. Law 1933-46; Prof., Public Admin. 1947-62; Prof. Emeritus since 1962. With British Govt., London: Principal Asst., Mines Dept. 1940-42; Ministry of Fuel and Power 1942-43; Asst. Secty., Air Ministry 1943-45; Ministry of Civil Aviation 1945. With Political Quarterly: Founder 1930; Joint Ed. 1930-75; Chmn., Ed. Bd. since 1975. Also, Ed., Politics Section, Hutchinson Univ. Library. Consultant to Govts. of Lebanon, Nigeria, Turkey, Tokyo Metropolitan; also to Unicef; State Commn. for N.Y.C. Charter Reform; Marshall Inquiry on Greater London. Visiting Prof.: Univ. Chicago 1933; Univ. N. C. 1951; Univ. Patna, India, and other Indian univs., 1953; Univ. Calif., Berkeley 1957; Indian Inst. of Public Admin. 1960; Intnl. Christian Univ. of Tokyo 1969. Noranda Lectr., Expo 67, Montreal; Pres., Intnl. Political Science Assn. 1950-53; V.P., Royal Inst. of Public Admin.; (Political Studies Assn.) Founder and Chmn. Greater London Group, London Sch. of Econs. Member of Council, Town and Country Planning Assn.; (Departmental Cttee. on Admin. for Overseas Countries.) Hons: Docteur de l'Univ. Lille 1953; D. Litt., Univ. Durham, 1963; D.Soc.Sci., Birmingham, 1970; also hon. doctorates from univs. of Grenoble, Paris 1955, Algiers 1959, and Manchester 1964. Hon. Fellow, Joint Univ. Council and Public Admin., London Sch. of Econs. *Author:* Aircraft in War and Peace, 1916; From Patronage to Proficience in the Public Service, 1922; The Relation of Wealth to Welfare, 1924; (with C.R. Atlee) The Town Councillor, 1925; Justice and Administrative Law, 1928; The Law of Local Government Audit, 1930; The Development of Local Government, 1931; Civilisation and the Growth of Law, 1935; Modern Theories of Law, 1938; The Government and Misgovernment of London, 1939; The British System of Government, 1940; Planning and Performance, 1943; Population and the People, 1945; Problems of Nationalised Industry, 1952; The Teaching of Political Science (Unesco), 1954; The Civil Service in Britain and France, 1956; Nationalised Industry and Public Ownership, 1960; The Governors and the Governed, 1964; The Heart of Greater London, 1965; Local Government in Crisis, 1966; Politics and Government at Home and Abroad, 1967; Welfare State and Welfare Society, 1976, also, The War and Planning Outlook. *Contributor:* London Essays in Economics, 1927; (jt. ed.) A Century of Municipal Progress, 1935; (jt. ed.) The British Civil Servant, 1937; (jt. ed.) Public Enterprise, 1937; (ed.) Social Security, 1943; The British Government since 1918, 1950. *Editor:* Great Cities of the World, 1955; rev. ed. (with D.E. Regan), 1973; (with B.Crick) Protest and Discontent, 1970; The Political Quarterly in the Thirties, 1971; Man and the Social Sciences, 1972; (with B. Crick) Taxation Policy, 1973.

ELLIOTT ARNOLD
Novelist and journalist
Born New York City, U.S.A., September 13th, 1912
Died New York City, U.S.A., May 13th, 1980

In 25 books produced between 1934 and 1977, Elliott Arnold may have strayed far from his native Brooklyn for themes, but he never strayed too far from the facts, returning again and again to historical incidents and personalities for his fictional material. The practice was probably the legacy of an early career in journalism, begun at age 15 when he worked for the old *Brooklyn Daily Times* covering the police, courts, city hall, fires, murders, and executions at Sing Sing. After graduating from New York University in 1934, he worked at the *New York World Telegram* as reporter, rewrite man, and feature writer.

During this period Arnold published three novels—*Two Loves* (1934), *Personal Combat* (1936), and *Only the Young* (1939—all based on his experiences as a reporter and all generally acclaimed for their "hard-boiled" reportorial style. Although Alfred Kazin noted a disconcerting fondness for stereotyped situations in *Only the Young,* he nonetheless called Arnold a writer of promise. Despite these favorite reviews, however, Arnold's books were ignored by the public.

His first best-seller, *Commandos* (1942), an action-thriller about the British commando corps, was based on information narrated to Arnold by a member of the unit. The reviewer Iris Barry commended its technical detail and journalistic style, and several critics observed Hemingway's influence. A reviewer for *The Nation* said of *Commandos:* "Hemingway . . . still has nothing to fear from his disciples, but his influence has done a good deal to raise books like this above the common run of adventure fiction."

An Army Air Corps private when *Commandos* first appeared, Arnold was soon commissioned, sent to Intelligence school, and assigned to Army Air Commands, first in North Africa and then in Italy. His commanding general asked him to write a history of the Air Corps in the Mediterranean; *Mediterranean Sweep,* written with Richard Thruelsen, appeared in 1944. The Air Commander of the South Pacific then commandeered the services of Arnold and Donald Hough to write a similar history for that area; *Big Distance* appeared in 1945. That same year Arnold also published *Tomorrow Will Sing,* a war novel.

Arnold's lifelong enthusiasm for American Indian culture led him to Tucson in 1945 to research the Chiracahua Apache chief, Cochise. The result was a novel, *Blood Brother* (1947), about the relationship between Cochise and the U.S. Indian agent and scout Thomas

Jeffords. Arnold's sympathetic evaluation of the Indian cause was applauded; a pro-Indian stance had not yet become popular. In the *New York Times,* Hoffman Birney wrote: *"Blood Brother* will delight those who believe that all Indians were as noble as Hiawatha. As biography it is inaccurate; as history it is often distorted; as ethnology it is balderdash." A popular film version, *Broken Arrow,* was made in 1950, for which Arnold and Michael Blankfort received awards for their contributions to the screenplay. Pleased by the impact of the movie, Arnold said, "The picture was especially good, I thought, because it started a new kind of thinking in Hollywood. From then on Indians got a break and it was about time."

The commercial success of *Blood Brother* and other novels written during the 1950s enabled Arnold to support himself exclusively by writing. In addition to magazine articles and short fiction, he wrote for film and television, including work on scripts for a television series called *Cochise.* He also wrote juvenile fiction bringing his love for history to the many books he wrote in this genre. *White Falcon* (1958), based on the life of John Tanner, a white boy captured and raised by Indians in the late eighteenth century, won an award for the best juvenile fiction of the year. In 1967, Arnold's story of the smuggling operation that saved Danish Jewry in World War Two, *A Night of Watching,* won a Brotherhood Award from the National Conference of Christians and Jews. Two later novels—*Code of Conduct* (1970) and *The Camp Grant Massacre* (1976), a skeptical look at the history of U.S.-Indian relations—were book club selections and best sellers.

While recognized for writing well-researched and exciting novels, Arnold was sometimes criticized for allowing his plots to interfere with his communication of historical knowledge. Before falling ill in early 1980, Arnold was reportedly working with Marlon Brando on a motion picture project about American Indians.   R.C.

Son of Jack A. and Gertrude (Frank) A. Married: (1) Helen Emmons 1945 (div. 1957); (2) Julie Kennedy 1958 (div. 1961); (3) Jacqueline Harris Stephens 1961 (div. 1963); (4) Glynis Johns, actress 1964 (div. 1973); (5) Jeanne Shwam 1979. Children: 1st marriage—Thomas Guy; Mary Jean Evans. Educ: N.Y. Univ., B.A. 1934. Mil. Service: Capt. and Intelligence Officer, Mediterranean and South Pacific Theaters 1942–45; awarded Bronze Star. Reporter, Brooklyn Daily Times 1930–34; Reporter, Rewrite Man, and Feature Writer, N.Y. World Telegram 1934-42; Member, Ed. Staff, The American Indian since 1948. Freelance writer and novelist since 1945. Member, The Players, N.Y.C. Hons: Silver Medal, Commonwealth Club of Calif. (for Blood Brother) 1948, (for Flight from Ashiya) 1960, and (for A Night of Watching) 1967; (with Michael Blankfort) Screenwriters' Guild Prize (for Broken Arrow) 1951; William Allen White Children's Book Award for best juvenile fiction of the year (for White Falcon) 1958; Brotherhood Award, Natl. Conference of Christians and Jews (for A Night of Watching) 1967. *Books: Novels*—Two Loves, 1934; Personal Combat, 1936; Only the Young, 1939; Nose for News, 1941; Commandos, 1942 (also published as First Comes Courage, 1943); Tomorrow Will Sing, 1945; Blood Brother, 1947; Everybody Slept Here, 1948; Deep in My Heart (fictional biog. of Sigmund Romberg), 1949; Walk with the Devil, 1950; Time of the Gringo, 1953; Flight from Ashiya, 1959; A Night of Watching, 1967; Code of Conduct, 1970; Forests of the Night, 1971; Proving Ground, 1973; The Camp Grant

Massacre, 1976; Quicksand, 1977. *Juvenile books*—Finlandia: The
Life of Sibelius (biog.), 1941; Broken Arrow, 1951; White Falcon,
1958; Brave Jimmy Stone, 1960; A Kind of Secret Weapon, 1969;
Spirit of Cochise, 1972. *Screenplays*—(with Michael Blankfort) Broken Arrow, 1950; other screen and television scripts. *Nonfiction*—
(with Richard Thruelsen) Mediterranean Sweep, 1944; (with Dennis
Hough) Big Distance, 1945; Rescue!, 1956. Frequent contributor of
articles and short fiction to mags., including Story Mag., Cosmopolitan, Atlantic Monthly, Saturday Evening Post, and Reader's
Digest.

HOWARD MUMFORD JONES
Teacher, cultural historian, and author
Born Saginaw, Michigan, U.S.A., April 16th, 1892
Died Cambridge, Massachusetts, U.S.A., May 13th, 1980

As a scholar, educator, poet, and translator, Howard Mumford Jones
fought for academic freedom and an increased study of the arts and
humanities in American higher education. An historian of ideas, he
deeply believed that cultural pluralism was the foundation of a free
society.

Born in Saginaw, Michigan in 1892 and raised in La Crosse,
Wisconsin, Howard Mumford Jones received his B.A. degree from
the University of Wisconsin in 1914, and his M.A. in English from the
University of Chicago a year later. His first teaching position at the
University of Texas was followed by periods at the University of
North Carolina and the University of Michigan. In 1936 he accepted a
professorship with Harvard University, where he remained until his
retirement in 1962.

Jones received the Jusserand Medal in 1927 for *America* and *French
Culture,* in which he argued that social critics and historians must not
neglect the impact of non-English influences on American culture. At
Harvard he published numerous monographs and collections of his
lectures on the history of ideas in French, English, and American
literature, and seventeenth century American history. He also continued to write poetry, translate German, Italian, medieval Latin, and
many other languages, and to produce essays on educational theory.
A diverse writer, Jones's work was unified by commitment to the idea
that the humanities could enable Americans to reveal the democratic
ideals embodied by their nation—the first one in history, he declared,
to have been "created on philosophic assumptions."

In addition to writing, Jones was an important figure in the
academic community. He was Dean of Harvard's Graduate School of
Arts and Sciences for a year, President of the American Academy of
Arts and Sciences for seven years, Chairman of the American Council
of Learned Societies for four years, and President of the Modern
Language Association in 1965. As an educator he attempted to
"convey relatively complicated ideas to a general audience without
oversimplification and without condescension."

Jones's belief in national strength through cultural diversity and his
opposition to conformism—which he called "thought control"—led
him to take sharp public issue with McCarthyism. As editor of a 1949

volume, *Primer of Intellectual Liberty,* he denounced attempts to
suppress and penalize dissent, declaring that only through the open
conflict of ideas could truth be obtained. In 1950 he declined a visiting
professorship at the University of California to protest their requirement of a loyalty oath.

After his retirement at age seventy, Jones completed nine major
works in addition to an autobiography written at the age of eighty-
five. For one of these books, *O Strange New World,* he won a 1964
Pulitzer Prize for general non-fiction. In 1973 Jones was presented
with a Phi Beta Kappa award for distinguished service to the
humanities and at the time of his death, he had completed eight
chapters of a book, *The Old West: An Unconventional View.*   R.C.

Son of Frank Alexander J. and Josephine Whitman (Miles) J.
Married: (1) Clara Edgar McLure 1918; (2) Bessie Judith Zaban 1927.
Children: 1st marriage—Eleanor McLure Jones Ingersoll. Educ:
Univ. of Wisc., Madison, B.A. 1914; Univ. of Chicago, M.A. 1915.
Assoc. Prof., Comparative Lit., Univ. of Texas 1919–25; Assoc. Prof.
1925–27 and Prof., English Lit. 1927–30, Univ. of North Carolina;
Prof., English Lit., Univ. of Michigan 1930–36. With Harvard Univ.:
Prof. of English 1936–60; Dean, Grad. Sch. of Arts and Sciences
1943–44; Abbot Lawrence Lowell Prof. of Humanities 1960–62; Prof.
Emeritus since 1962. Ed., Harvard Library Bulletin 1966–68; Educa-
tional Consultant, Provost Marshall General's Office 1945; Paley
Visiting Prof., Hebrew Univ., Jerusalem 1964; Gov. Winthrop Rock-
efeller Distinguished Lectr., Univ. of Arkansas 1975. Member:
Massachusetts Hist. Soc.; Modern Lang. Assoc. (Pres. 1965); Colo-
nial Soc. of Mass.; Tex. Philosophical Soc.; Acad. of Arts and
Sciences (Pres. 1944–51); American Council of Learned Socs. (Chmn.
1955-59); American Philosophical Soc. Hons: Litt. D. from Harvard
Univ. 1936, Univ. of Colo. 1938, Western Reserve Univ. 1948, and
others; L.H.D. from Tulane Univ. 1938, Ohio State Univ. and
Hebrew Union Coll. 1962, and Northwestern Univ. 1966; LL.D. from
Colby Coll. 1962, Univ. of Utah 1966, and Univ. of Windsor 1969.
Pulitzer Prize, Gen. non-fiction (for O Strange New World) 1964;
Guggenheim Fellow 1964-65; Phi Beta Kappa Award and Medal for
Service to Humanities 1973. *Author:* A Little Book of Local Verse,
1915; The Shadow (Play), 1917; Gargoyles (poems), 1918; The King
in Hamlet, 1921; (with R.H. Griffith) A Bibliography of the Works
and Manuscripts of Byron, 1924; American and French Culture
(1750–1848), 1927; The Life of Moses Coit Tyler, 1933; The Harp
That Once-, 1937; They Say the Forties (poems), 1937; Ideas in
America, 1944; Education and World Tragedy, 1946; The Theory of
American Literature, 1948; The Bright Medusa, 1952; The Pursuit of
Happiness, 1953; The Frontier in American Fiction, 1956; American
Humanism, 1957; Reflections on Learning, 1958; One Great Society,
1959; O Strange New World, 1964; History and the Contemporary,
1964; Emerson on Education, 1966; Jeffersonianism and the Amer-
ican Novel, 1966; Belief and Disbelief in American Literature, 1967;
The Literature of Virginia in the Seventeenth Century, 1968; The Age
of Energy, 1971; Revolution and Romanticism, 1974; (with Bessie
Judith Zaban) The Many Voices of Boston, 1976; Howard Mumford
Jones: An Autobiography, 1979; Translator: Heinrich Heine, The
North Sea, 1918; (with P.S. Allen) The Romanesque Lyric, 1928.
Editor: The Poems of Edgar Allen Poe, 1929; (with D. MacMillan)
The Plays of the Restoration and Eighteenth Century, 1930; (with

F.F. Leisy) Major American Writers, 1936; (with R.M. Lovett) The College Reader, 1936; (with S.I. Hayakawa) Oliver Wendell Holmes, 1939; Primer of Intellectual Liberty, 1949; (with Richard H. Ludwig and Marvin Perry) Modern Minds, 1949; (with Walter B. Rideout) The Letters of Sherwood Anderson, 1953; (with Richard H. Ludwig) Guide to American Literature and Its Backgrounds Since 1890, 1959, Revs. 1964, 1972; (with I. Bernard Cohen) A Treasury of Scientific Prose, 1963.

CARL (ANTON CHARLES) EBERT
International stage and opera director
Born Berlin, Germany, February 20th, 1887
Died Santa Monica, California, U.S.A, May 14th, 1980

Professor Carl Ebert, who began his career as a stage actor and star in silent films in the early 1900s, achieved prominence as an international director of the opera. In an operatic career spanning more than fifty years, he performed with—and helped establish—many of the leading opera houses and companies of Western Europe, Turkey, the United States and Argentina.

Ebert began studying drama at the age of sixteen under Max Reinhardt, one of the most distinguished European directors and producers. Upon completing his studies Ebert was offered roles at the Berlin Deutsches Theater, and from there went on to make regular appearances at the Schauspielhaus in Frankfurt and at the Berlin Staatstheater. Early successes included portrayals of Leicester in Schiller's *Mary Stuart* and Faust, Petruchio, and Karl Moon in *Die Raüber*. In 1925 he founded the Berlin Hochschule for Musik in conjunction with the State Academy of Music, and two years later became General Director and producer of the Darmstadt State Theater where his interest in operatic production reached its fullest expression.

With the rise of nazism, Ebert decided to leave Germany in 1933 to accept his first commission with the Teatro Colon in Buenos Aires as guest producer. The following year he was invited to work with the Glyndenbourne Festival Opera in England. There he met Fritz Busch and Rudolf Bing (who had been his assistant in Berlin), both German emigrés. Together, through their work at Glyndenbourne, they helped revitalize the British operatic tradition and Ebert's production of *Figaro* in 1935 was regarded as a turning point for English opera. *The London Times* commented: "What (Ebert) accomplished at Glyndenbourne in collaboration with Fritz Busch as conductor was to give a living demonstration that opera was a form of art *sui generis* . . . and not . . . a vehicle for star singers against tattered scenery and rough-and-ready stage management." Ebert also established an annual Mozart Festival in Sussex, broadening its repertory to include Verdi and Donizetti.

In 1936 Ebert accepted the Turkish government's invitation to develop a national theater in Ankara, where he established both the Turkish State School for Opera and Drama, and the Turkish National Theater. He subsequently worked in Argentina and at the University of Southern California, Los Angeles, where he founded the Guild Opera Company. The university created a chair of opera in 1948 and Ebert was named first professor and head of the school's operatic studies. He returned to Glyndenbourne in 1951 as artistic director of the Festival Opera, where he worked with Vittorio Gui and other conductors until 1959.

Ebert was widely sought by those European countries seeking to rebuild their operatic companies after the war—particularly in Germany and Austria. He regarded as personal triumphs the re-opening of the Hamburg and Cologne opera houses in the early 1950s, and the Berlin Opera in 1954. He was also closely associated with the New York Metropolitan Opera in its first productions of Verdi's *Macbeth* and Mozart's *Così fan Tutte*.

He returned to Glyndenbourne again as guest producer in 1962 and 1963, producing *Der Rosenkavalier* as his farewell concert. Twice—in 1965 and 1967—he was featured as guest producer in a British television series portraying masters of the classical arts. His accomplishment was widely recognized in honors and awards given by many countries.   M.D.

Son of Wilhelm E. and Maria E. Married: (1) Lucie Splisgarth 1912 (div. 1923); (2) Gertrude Eck 1924. Children: 1st marriage—Peter, stage and opera dir., b. 1918; also one daughter d. 1946; 2nd marriage—Michael, psychotherapist; Renata, scriptwriter; Christina, poet. Educ: Friedrich Werder'sche Oberrealschule; Max Reinhardt's Sch. of Dramatic Art, Berlin 1904–14. Actor: Max Reinhardt's Deutsches Theater, Berlin 1909–14; Schauspielhaus, Frankfurt/Main 1915–22; Staatstheater, Berlin 1922–27; also silent film actor. Founder and Dir., Frankfurt (sch. of dramatic art) 1919 and Berlin Hochschule fur Musik (also prof.) 1925; Dir., German Actors' Union 1919–27; Gen. Intendant and producer, Landestheater, Darmstaadt 1927–31; Dir., Deutscher Buhnenverein 1927–33; Intendant, Stadtische Opera, Berlin 1931–33. Guest producer: Salzburg Festival, Vienna State Opera and Burgtheater, Arena Verona 1932–38; Maggio Musicale, Florence 1933–37; Teatro Colon, Buenos Aires 1933–36. Artistic Dir. and producer, Glyndebourne Festival Opera, England 1934–59; Advisor, theatrical matters to Turkish Ministry of Educ., Ankara 1936–47; Founder and Dir., Turkish Natl. Theater 1939–47; Producer, Edinburgh Festival 1947–55; Guest producer, Turkish State Opera 1947-59; Founder and Producer, Sussex Mozart Festival 1948–52; Chmn. and Prof., Opera Dept., Univ. S. Calif., Los Angeles 1948–54; Gen. Dir. 1950–54 and Artistic Dir. since 1954, Guild Opera Co., Los Angeles; Gen. Intendant and Producer, Stadtische Opera, Berlin 1954–61. Guest Producer: Deutsche Opera, Berlin 1961-67; Glyndebourne Festival 1962, 1963; Swiss Natl. Opera, Zurich 1963, 1965; Wexford Festival, Ireland 1965; B.B.C. Television, London (Master Classes) 1965, 1967; Cambridge Theatre, London (New London Opera Co.); La Scala, Milan; Royal Opera, Copenhagen; Metropolitan Opera, N.Y.C.; Paris Opera; State Opera, Vienna. Founder, Turkish State Sch. for Opera and Drama 1936. Hons: Hon. Mus.D., Univ. Edinburgh 1954; Hon. D.F.A., Univ. S. Calif. 1955; Ernst Reuter Plakette, City of Berlin 1957; Das Grosse Ehrenzeichen for services to Mozart compositions, Austria 1959; Hon. C.B.E., Britain 1960; Hon. Member, Deutsche Opera, Berlin 1961 and Landestheater, Darmstadt 1963; Bd. of Dirs., Opera Guild of S. Calif., Los Angeles 1965; Commendatore, Order of Merit, Italy 1966; Knight,

Dannebrog Order, Denmark; Das Grosse Verdienstkreuz mit Stern,
Germany; La Grande Médaille d'Argent de la Ville de Paris. Various
stage and film performances.

HUGH (EMRYS) GRIFFITH
Stage, film, radio and television actor
Born Marian Glas, Anglesey, Wales, May 30th, 1912
Died London, England, May 14th, 1980

Hugh Griffith, one of Britain's most prominent and versatile character
actors on stage, in films and on radio and television after World War
Two, first worked as a bank clerk in rural Wales. His real interest,
however, was the stage and in 1938, after extensive part-time acting
and study, he received a scholarship to the Royal Academy of
Dramatic Art in London. The following year Griffith won the
academy's Bancroft Gold Medal and made his debut on the London
stage in an acclaimed performance as Jimmy Farrell in *The Playboy of
the Western World*. An appearance that same year in *Julius Caesar* was
the beginning of his successful career in Shakespearian theater.

During World War Two Griffith fought with the Royal Welsh
Fusiliers in Burma and India. Returning to England after the war he
became involved with the Shakespeare Memorial Theatre Company at
Stratford-upon-Avon (later, the Royal Shakespeare Company at
Stratford and London) where his reputation as a Shakespearian actor
was firmly established. He played King Lear in Welsh—on radio as
well as on stage—and in English, and acted in other Shakespearian
roles to general acclaim. Although Griffith said that Lear was his
favorite role, critics preferred his performances as Falstaff which
brought out his flamboyant personality and captivating stage presence.

Griffith had noteworthy successes with the Royal Shakespeare
Company as Holofernes in *Love's Labour's Lost* and as Mephi-
stopheles in Marlowe's *Dr. Faustus*. He went on to play roles in
Stratford, London and on tour, as various as the Cardinal in *The
White Devil* and Christopher Mahon in *The Playboy of the Western
World*.

Griffith's New York debut came in 1951 when he appeared in
Anouilh's *Legend of Lovers* (in which he had appeared the previous
year in England under the title *Point of Departure);* his performance
as the father won him the Clarence Derwent Award. Back in England
he played the Bellman in Fry's *The Dark is Light Enough* and the
bitter General in Anouilh's *The Waltz of the Toreadors*, which ran for
a year in London and thereafter in New York. For his appearance as
the father in *Look Homeward Angel* in 1957 Griffith received a Tony
Award. He continued to give successful London performances including Count Cenci at the Old Vic in 1959 and the Royal Shakespeare
Company's 1962 production of Brecht's *The Caucasian Chalk Circle*.
In 1964 he joined the Company again for its Quatrocentenary
celebration and in 1972 undertook a European Shakespeare tour for
the British Council.

Griffith's film career began before World War Two (Neutral Port,
1939) but it was not until 1948 that he appeared in films again, notably

two detective films, *The Three Wierd Sisters* and *London Belongs to Me*. *The Last Days of Dolwyn,* a film about social conditions in 19th century Wales, was made the following year. From then on Griffith appeared regularly on the screen and, in all, made over fifty films. In *The Beggar's Opera* (1953) he appeared with Laurence Olivier and for his performance as Sheik Ildermin in *Ben Hur* (1959) he won an Academy Award for best supporting actor. He received an Academy Award nomination in 1963 for his portrayal of the bawdy Squire Western in *Tom Jones*. Later successes included *How to Steal a Million* (1966), *Oliver* (1968), *Start the Revolution Without Me* (1969) in which he played Louis XVI, and *The Last Remake of Beau Geste* (1977). His last film, *A Nightingale Sang in Berkeley Square* (with David Niven) was completed in 1979, a year before his death.

From the mid-1960s Griffith became as well-known as a radio and television performer both in Britain and in the United States, appearing in many of the roles he had played on stage and in films. He retired a year before his death.   M.D.

Son of William G. and Mary G. Married Adelgunde Margaret Beatrice von Dechend 1947. No children. Educ: Llangefni Grammar Sch., Anglesey; Royal Acad. Dramatic Art (Leverhulme Scholar) 1938–39. Mil. Service: 1st Battalion Royal Welsh Fusiliers, India and Burma 1940–46. Bank clerk, N. Wales 1929–37; Actor in Britain and U.S. 1939–79. Hons: Bancroft Gold Medal, Royal Acad. Dramatic Art 1939; Clarence Derwent Award, (Legend of Lovers) 1951; Tony Award nomination (Look Homeward Angel) 1957; Oscar (Ben Hur) 1959; Acad. Award nomination (Tom Jones) 1963; Hon. D.Litt., Univ. Wales 1965. *Performances: stage*—The Playboy of the Western World (Jimmy Farrell, Shaun Keogh), London 1939; Rhondda Roundabout (Rev. Dan Price), London 1939; Julius Caesar (Marullus, Popilius Lena, Lepidus), London 1939; The Venetian (Concini), London 1940; with Shakespeare Memorial Theatre Co., Stratford-upon-Avon & London in The Tempest (Trinculo), Love's Labour's Lost (Holofernes), Henry V (King of France), As You Like It (Touchstone), Dr. Faustus (Mephistopheles); Fatal Curiosity (Old Wilmot); The White Devil (Cardinal Monticelso), London 1947; The Respectable Prostitute (the Senator), Hammersmith 1947; A Comedy of Good and Evil (Rev. John Williams), London 1948; The Playboy of the Western World (Christopher Mahon), London 1948; Mandragola (Nicia), London 1949; with Swansea Festival, Wales 1949 in King Lear (Lear); touring Britain in The White Falcon (Cranmer) and Rosmersholm (Ulric Brendel) 1950; Point of Departure (the father), Hammersmith and London 1950; with Shakespeare Memorial Co., Stratford-upon-Avon 1951 in Richard II (Gaunt) and The Tempest (Caliban); Legend of Lovers (the father), N.Y. 1951; Escapade (Andrew Deeson), London 1953; The Dark is Light Enough (Bellman), Edinburgh and London 1954; The Waltz of the Toreadors (General St. Pé), London and N.Y. 1956; Look Homeward, Angel (W.O. Gant), N.Y. 1957; The Cenci (Count Cenci), London 1959; The Caucasian Chalk Circle (Azdak), London 1962; Andorra (the Teacher), N.Y. 1963; with Royal Shakespeare Co., Stratford-upon-Avon 1964 in Henry IV, Parts I and II (Falstaff); The Tempest (Prospero), Nottingham 1972; touring, Europe for British Council 1972. *Films*—Neutral Port, 1939; Three Weird Sisters, So Evil My Love, London Belongs to Me, The Last Days of Dolwyn, 1948; The Galloping Major and Gone to Earth, 1950; Laughter in Paradise,

1951; The Titfield Thunderbolt and The Beggar's Opera, 1953; The Sleeping Tiger, 1954; Passage Home, 1955; Lucky Jim, 1957; Ben Hur, 1959; The Day They Robbed The Bank of England, 1960; Exodus, 1961; The Counterfeit Traitor, Mutiny on the Bounty, The Inspector, Term of Trial, 1962; Tom Jones, 1963; The Bargee and Hide and Seek, 1964; The Amorous Adventures of Moll Flanders, 1965; How to Steal a Million and Danger Grows Wild, 1966; Oh Dad! Poor Dad! and A Sailor from Gibraltar, 1967; The Fixer, Oliver, and Dare I Weep, Dare I Mourn, 1968; The Chastity Belt and Start the Revolution Without Me, 1969; Wuthering Heights and Cry of the Banshee, 1970; The Abominable Dr. Phibes, Dr. Phibes Rises Again, Who Slew Auntie Roo? 1971; The Canterbury Tales, What! 1972; Take Me High, 1973; Luther, Craze, Legend of the Werewolf, 1974; The Final Programme, 1975; Loving Cousins and The Passover Plot, 1976; Casanova and Co., Joseph Andrews, The Last Remake of Beau Geste, 1977; The Hound of the Baskervilles, 1978; A Nightingale Sang in Berkeley Square, 1979; also The Gingerbread House; Lead Us Not into Temptation, and Brown Eye, Evil Eye. *Radio and television performances:* King Lear (Lear) in English and Welsh, 1949; The Walrus and the Carpenter series (Luther Flannery), 1965; The Proposal and Uncle Rollo, 1971; Clochemerle series, 1972; also, The Waltz of the Toreadors; Owen M.D.; The Joke; Legacy series; Grand Slam, The Citadel; Treasure Island; Dare I Weep, Dare I Mourn; and others, together with television showings of films.

ROBERT ALLAN SMITH
Physicist and Educator
Born Kelso, Scotland, May 14th, 1909
Died Kelso, Scotland, May 16th, 1980

Robert Allan Smith, under whose guidance Heriot-Watt University became one of Britain's leading scientific and technological universities, played a major part in the improvement of radio and telecommunications networks during World War Two. After graduating with First Class Honours in mathematics and natural philosophy from Edinburgh University, Smith went to Cambridge where he received his Ph.D. in mathematics in 1936. He then taught at St. Andrews University, Scotland and at the University of Reading in Berkshire, England.

Soon after the outbreak of World War Two, Smith joined the Telecommunications Research Establishment and assisted with the fundamental research which led to the installation of radar. He also contributed to the improvement of radio communications for wartime mobile units and designed highly accurate navigational aids. This experience provided much of the material for his *Radio Aids to Navigation,* published two years after the war. After the war, Telecommunications Research Establishment became the Royal Radar Establishment and Smith remained on its staff to study the properties of radio reception and transmission, semi-conductors, and infra-red detection. In 1947 he became head of the Physics Department. In 1960 Smith was honored by appointment as Commander, Order of the British Empire and the following year, he became Professor of Physics at Sheffield University. In 1962 he accepted an offer from the Massachusetts Institute of Technology to head their Center for Materials Science and Engineering.

Smith returned to England in 1968 when he was appointed Principal and Vice-Chancellor of Heriot-Watt University in Edinburgh. Under his guidance the university doubled its size and added many new faculty positions in the disciplines of science, engineering, economics, and social studies; moreover, the university offered its research facilities to the engineers who were extracting oil from the nearby North Sea. Smith retired from the administration of Heriot-Watt in 1974 and that year he was made a Commander of the Order of St. Olav of Norway. In 1976 Smith became President of the Royal Society of Edinburgh.   M.D.

Son of G.J.T. Smith. Married Doris M.L. Ward 1934. Children: one son; two daughters. Educ: Kelso High Sch.; Edinburgh Univ., M.A. (First Class Hons., maths. and natural philosophy) 1930; Cambridge, B.A.(First Class Hons., maths.) 1932 and Ph.D. (physics) 1936. Carnegie Research Fellow, St. Andrews Univ., Scotland 1935–38; Lectr., Reading Univ., England 1938–39. With Telecommunications Research Estab. (later, Royal Radar Estab., Malvern, England): Sr. Staff Member 1939–47 and Head of Physics Dept. 1946–61. Prof., Physics, Sheffield Univ. 1961–62; Prof., Physics and first Dir., Center for Materials Science and Engineering, Mass. Inst. Technology 1962–68; Principal and Vice-Chancellor, Heriot-Watt 1968–74. Hons: Mayhew Prize, Cambridge 1932; C.B.E. 1960; F.R.S. 1962; F.R.S.E. 1969 (Pres. 1976–79); Comdr., Order of St. Olav (Norway) 1974. Also: Fellow, American Acad. of Arts and Sciences; American Physics Soc.; British Inst. of Physics; British Physical Soc. *Author:* Radio Aids to Navigation, 1947; Aerials for Meter and Decimeter Wavelengths, 1949; The Physical Principles of Thermodynamics, 1952; The Detection and Measurement of Infra-Red Radiation, 1957; Semiconductors, 1959, 2nd. ed. 1978; The Wave Mechanics of Crystalline Solids, 1961.

ELIOT CANDEE CLARK
Landscape painter
Born New York, New York, U.S.A., March 27th, 1883
Died Charlottesville, Virginia, U.S.A., May 19th, 1980

Eliot Candee Clark, whose life spanned three generations of American art, was raised in an artistic milieu. A gifted child, he was introduced to the art world by Winslow Homer, George Innes and Frank Duveneck, all of whom were friends of his father Walter Clark, a noted sculptor and landscape painter. At the age of nine, Clark had two small water colors exhibited at the New York Water Color Club and, four years later, "A Hillside"—an oil landscape—was accepted by the National Academy of Design. In a trip across the United States, he and his father sketched the scenery and stopped to paint in Yellowstone National Park. Clark traveled extensively throughout his life, both in America and abroad, painting and sketching wherever he went.

In the early 1900s Clark met Matisse and Picasso while studying in

Paris with other American artists under the guidance of Claude Monet. For work exhibited in his first one-man show in 1912, he won the Third Hallgarten Prize, and in 1915, Woodrow Wilson brought the painting "Rolling Country." From 1916 to 1919, when landscape painting was much in vogue, and throughout the 1920s, Clark's work was widely exhibited in galleries and museums around the country.

Clark was influenced by luminism and tonalism, as exemplified in the work of Alexander Wyant and J. Francis Murphy—about each of whom Clark later wrote a biography. Clark's work displayed much diversity and his best studies encompassed both traditions. Rather than "conform to a single formula," Clark attempted to "record" his impressions, emphasizing receptivity towards nature. "The conception and treatment of the picture," he said, "should grow out of the subject rather than be imposed upon it."

In 1937 and 1938 Clark visited India and Tibet and his paintings from this time, many of which reflect an Eastern influence, were later exhibited in New York at the Iranian Institute and at the Asia Institute.

In addition to his biographies of fellow artists, Clark wrote what is considered the definitive history of the National Academy of Design, of which he served as president for three years. He also wrote frequently for art publications in the United States and Europe until the late 1950s. He retired at that time to Charlottesville, Virginia to paint, lecture, and write.   A.B.P.

Courtesy Mrs. Eliot Clark

Son of Walter C., sculptor and painter, and Jennie Woodruff C. Married: (1) Elizabeth Trowbridge Egleston 1922 (div.); (2) Margaret Winslow Fowler 1944. No children. Educ: Private tutor; N.Y.C. public schs.; studied Art Students' League, N.Y.C. under Walter Clark and John Twachtman, and in Europe 1904–6. Landscape painter and watercolorist N.Y.C. 1907–59; art critic and reviewer for Art in America and other art mags. 1914–27; American art rep. for Studio, London 1921–61. Teacher: Art Students' League, Savannah Art Club 1924–25; Univ. of Va., Charlottesville 1933, 1934; Roerich Mus., N.Y.C. 1940–43; Asia Inst., N.Y.C. Pres., American Water Color Soc. 1919–23 (Permanent Honorary Pres. 1963–80). Natl. Acad. of Design: Member 1917–80; Council 1945–48; Corresp. Sec. 1948–55; First V.P. 1955–56; Pres. 1956–59; Member Awards Jury 1962. Pres., Allied Artists of America 1948–52. Fellow and (ex-officio) Trustee, Metropolitan Mus. of Art, N.Y.C. 1956–59. Bd. Dirs.: City Center Art Gall. and Fine Arts Fedn., N.Y.C. Bd. Govs., Natl. Arts Club, N.Y.C. 1943–80. Chmn.: Commn. on Painting & Advertising, Fine Arts East and West Assn. Member: N.Y. Soc. of Painters (Chm. 1958); Intl. Inst. of Arts and Letters; India Inst; Kent Assn.; N.Y. Water Color Club; League of N.Y. Artists; Artists Fund Soc.; Conn. Acad of Fine Arts; Union Internationale des Beaux Arts et des Lettres; Century Assn.; Natl. Sculpture Soc. (hon.); Salmagundi Club (hon.). Hons: Third Hallgarten Prize, N.A.D. 1912; Ranger Fund Purchase Prize 1922; Edgar Davis Prize, San Antonio, Tex. 1929; Natl. Academician 1944; Burton Bush Prize, Allied Artists of America 1950; Certificate of Merit, Allied Artists of America 1972; Children's Purchase Fund, Muncie, Ind. One-man shows: Louis Katz Art Gall., N.Y.C. 1912; Paintings of India, Iranian Inst., N.Y.C. and Art of India, Asia Inst., N.Y.C. 1947; Retrospective, Univ. of Va. Mus. of Fine Arts, Charlottesville 1961–62, 1975. Exhibitions: N.Y.

Water Color Club 1892; N.A.D. 1899, 1912, and frequently after 1917; Pan-American Exposition, Buffalo, N.Y. 1916; Thirty Paintings by Three American Artists, Milwaukee Art Inst. 1919; Exhib. of Contemporary American Landscape, Reinhardt Gall., N.Y.C. 1919; Six American Painters, N.Y.C., Cincinatti, Youngstown (Ohio), Providence (R.I.) 1920–21; Rochester Arts Assn., Rochester, Minn. 1923; J.W. Young Art Gall., Chicago 1923; Fort Worth Mus. of Art 1928; Highland Park Soc. of Arts, Dallas 1931; American Water Color Soc; Art Inst., Chicago; City Art Mus., St. Louis; Carnegie Inst.; Pa. Acad. of Fine Arts; R.I. Sch. of Design; Metropolitan Mus. of Art, N.Y.C.; Md. Inst.; Muncie Inst., Muncie, Ind; Barbizon Gall., N.Y.C.: Corcoran Gall., Washington, D.C.: and others. *Permanent Collections:* Metropolitan Mus. of Art; N.A.D.; Natl. Arts Club; Dayton Art Inst., Dayton, Ohio; Muncie Art Assn., Muncie, Ind.; Witte Memorial Mus.; Fort Worth Art Assn.; and others. *Author:* Alexander Wyant, 1916; Sixty Paintings by Alexander H. Wyant, 1920; John Henry Twachtman, 1924; J. Francis Murphy, 1926; History of the National Academy of Design 1925–1953, 1954; Theodore Robinson (unpublished ms.); extensive writing for Sutdio, Art in America, Arts & Decoration, and others.

IDA KAMINSKA
Director, Jewish State Theater of Poland and actress
Born Odessa, Russia, September 4th, 1899
Died New York City, U.S.A., May 21st, 1980

Known as the "shining light of the Yiddish theater," Ida Kaminska devoted her entire career as an actress and theatrical director to developing and enriching Yiddish theater. Raised in a theatrical family, Kaminska made her first stage appearance in Warsaw at the age of four, playing opposite her mother in a comedy. The production was staged by her father's company, formed in the early 1900s and one of the first Eastern European companies to perform literary and classical works in Yiddish. Kaminska briefly considered a career in psychiatry but remained in theater after her successful performance in an operetta produced by her parents. Encouraged by her father, Kaminska became a director and for the next 65 years staged hundreds of productions in theater companies she had established.

From 1918 to 1921, Kaminska toured Russia in order to avoid the chaos of postwar Warsaw. Having returned to Poland, she developed a successful Yiddish theater company but the German invasion in 1939 forced her emigration to Soviet Russia. Although she and her family were initially welcomed in the U.S.S.R., her daughter and son-in-law were arrested during one of Stalin's postwar crackdowns on dissidents, artists, intellectuals and Jews and they spent five years in exile in Siberia.

In 1946 Kaminska returned to Poland with her husband and immediately began to reconstruct the Yiddish theater, an experience she considered the most meaningful in her life. She established, in Lodz, one of only two troupes to survive in the aftermath of World War Two (all other Yiddish theater groups had been decimated by the Holocaust). In 1949 the Polish government unified the troupes to form the Jewish State Theater of Poland. Supported by a full state subsidy and with Kaminska the director, it was by 1961, the only Jewish repertory theater in the world to have earned an international reputation. Kaminska continued to work in the tradition of her parents, bringing to the Yiddish stage both classical and Jewish plays—including many by Jacob Gordin—and contemporary works by Brecht, Ibsen, Dürrenmatt, Lope de Vega, Arthur Miller and Alejandro Casona which were translated into Yiddish. Her own performances included Brecht's Mother Courage, and the title roles in *Glick Hameln Demands Justice,* the story of a seventeenth century Jewish woman who demands justice when her husband is murdered by a German officer, and *Mirele Efros,* a determined matriarch who faces a scheming daughter-in-law.

Kaminska appeared in *The Shop on Main Street*—her first film in almost thirty years—which won the Academy Award for best foreign film in 1966. The film brought her international renown, both as an actress and as a symbol of the will to survive. In 1968 when the Polish government, in a wave of anti-Semitism following the 1967 Arab-Israeli War, accused her and her troupe of failing to denounce an alleged "Zionist" campaign against Poland, Kaminska was again forced to become an emigré. She and her family, all of whom were members of the acting troupe, moved to the United States. In New York she established a Yiddish repertory troupe which soon failed; a similar attempt in Israel several years later was also unsuccessful. Kaminska starred opposite Zero Mostel and Harry Belafonte in *The Angel Levine* (a film based on a Bernard Malamud novel) in 1970 and before her husband's death in 1978, she had hoped to tour with him in *The Gin Game,* which she had translated into Yiddish.

Ida Kaminska, who had seen genocide become the official policy of a modern nation toward its Jewish citizens and who had experienced the dispersion of Jewish culture from Eastern Europe, remained hopeful that the Yiddish theater could survive. Her last Yiddish-language role on the stage was in Peter Weiss's *The Investigation* in which she made a cameo appearance only a month before her death at the age of 80.   L.F.

Daughter of Avram Itzhak Kaminski (1867–1918), actor, theatrical producer, playwright, founder of Jewish Theater in Moscow, and Esther Rachel K. (1870–1925), actress. Married: (1) Zygmunt Turkow, actor, theatrical producer 1918, (div. 1931); (2) Meier Melman, impresario, actor, lawyer, journalist 1936 (d. 1978). Children: 1st marriage—Ruth Tarkow K., (Mrs. Karol Latowicz) b. 1919, actress, author; 2nd marriage—Victor Melman, b. 1941. Jewish. Fled from Poland to Soviet-occupied Poland in 1939, then to Kirghiz, U.S.S.R. 1941; Moscow 1944–1946; Poland 1946; emigrated to U.S.A. 1968 and to Israel 1975; returned to U.S.A. ca. 1977. Educ: Gymnasium Francke, Warsaw. Career: first stage appearance 1904; stage mgr. 1906; toured Russia with mother 1907; official stage debut, Warsaw 1916; Dir. and actress, Kaminski Theatre, Warsaw 1916–17 and E.R. Kaminska Theatre, Warsaw 1917–23; toured Russia with troupe 1918–21; played in Centralny Theatre, Warsaw 1921; Co-founder with first husband and Dir. Warsaw Jewish Art Theatre, Warsaw. On tour Poland and Western Europe 1923–31; appearances in Polish films 1924–36; Dir., Drama Theatre of Ida Kaminska (Ida Kaminska Ensemble), Warsaw ca. 1932–39; toured Vilna and Kovno, Lithuania,

organizing Jewish theatres 1936; Managing Dir., Jewish State Theatre of Western Ukraine (Lvov), Soviet-occupied Poland 1939–41; elected Deputy to City Council and twice as chmn. of professional theatre org.; dir. and actress, Jewish theatres in Frunze, Kirghiz, U.S.S.R. 1941–44; collaborated with Jewish Section, United Polish Patriotic League and propaganda work for Soviet govt. Moscow 1944–46; Founder and Dir., Jewish Theatre of Poland 1946–49; Dir., Jewish State Theatre of Poland, state-subsidized Yiddish co., Lodz and Warsaw 1949–68; resided in Lodz to 1955 and Warsaw to 1968. Worldwide tours with Jewish State Theatre: London 1948, Paris and Belgium 1956, East Berlin and Leipzig 1957, Israel 1958–60, Australia 1960, London 1961 and 1964, N.Y. 1967, S. America 1967; rep. Poland at Jewish cultural conference, Paris 1955; teacher, theatre studio, Warsaw 1965; dir. over 100 productions; appeared ca. 200 parts; trans. over 70 plays from the classical repertory into Yiddish; adapted novels and stories for the stage. Toured Israel 1968; settled in N.Y.C. 1969; founder, Jewish Repertory Theatre, N.Y.C. 1971; Dir. Yiddish Theatre Workshop, Queens Coll. N.Y.C. 1971; Yiddish repertory, Israel; Member: Assn. Theatre Writers; Polish Theatre and Film Actors Assn.; Hebrew Actors Union, N.Y.C.; affiliate, Actor's Equity. Hons: State Natl. Award, Poland (Polish Natl. Prize) 1955; Polish Cross of Merit; Officer's Cross of Polish Liberation; Polish Natl. Flag of Labor, 1st and 2nd classes; State Award for Acting, Czechoslovakia 1966; acting Award, Cannes Film Festival 1965; nominated for Acad. Award as Best Actress 1966; Citation, Natl. Council on Jewish Audio-Visual Materials 1969. Programs in her honor include: Warsaw 1967, 50th anniversary of her stage debut; Hanukkah Festival, Madison Square Garden 1969; Queens Coll.; Univ. of Judaism, Los Angeles, 1969. *Performances:* (Selected) *Plays* —The Mother (Siomke), Warsaw 1904; Akejdas Itzchok (The Binding of Isaac) 1916; The Soul of My People (Itzik, operetta); Uriel Acosta (Yehudis); Therese Raquin (title role); A Doll's House, (Nora); Glikl Hameln Demands Justice (title role); Frank V. (Madame Frank); Mirele Efros (title role); Meir Esofovitch (grandmother); Julius & Ethel (Ethel); The Jewish Wife; Program of Yiddish songs, poetry, scenes, Berlin, Munich and Frankfurt 1968; An Afternoon with Ida Kaminska, N.Y.C. and elsewhere in the metropolitan area 1969 and after; The Investigation, N.Y.C. 1980. *Films—* Without a Home; Vilna Legend; The Dybbuk; The Black Dress (all Yiddish films made in Poland); The Shop on Main Street (Rosalie Lautmanova) 1966; The Angel Levine (Fannie) 1970. *Television—*A production of Osip Mandelstam's Witness 1975. *Author:* Once There Was a King (play), 1928; Close the Bunkers (Cover the Shelters) (play) 1964; My Life, My Theatre (autobiography, ed. and trans. by Curt Leviant), 1973; articles in professional journals.
Further reading: I Don't Want to be Brave Anymore, 1978 and Mink Coat and Barbed Wire, 1979 by Ruth Turkow Kaminska.

WILLIAM GAUNT
Author and painter
Born Hull, Yorkshire, England, July 5th, 1900
Died London, Englan May 24th, 1980

Over the past forty years the reputation of the once-neglected artists of Victorian England—especially that of the Pre-Raphaelites and their circle—has risen steadily. For this, William Gaunt can claim a large share of the credit. Gaunt, a prominent art historian and critic, will be chiefly remembered as a writer; but he was also a more-than-competent artist.

The son of a designer and chromolithographer, Gaunt was born in Hull in 1900 and educated at Hull Grammar School. He served in the First World War before reading Modern History at Worcester College, Oxford. At this time he planned to make his career as an artist, and studied for a while at the Ruskin School of Drawing, and later at the Westminster School of Art—where he came under the influence of Bernard Meninsky, who taught figure drawing.

Simultaneously, he was actively embarking on a parallel career as writer and editor. He edited some special issues of *The Studio* magazine, and throughout his life contributed to most leading art journals. In 1946 he joined the *Evening Standard* as art critic, and from 1957 worked for *The Times* as special correspondent on art subjects.

But alongside his journalistic activities, Gaunt continued to work as an artist. In 1930 he produced his first book, *London Promenade*, a collection of drawings which earned him his first one-man show, at London's Redfern Gallery. He had further one-man shows and exhibitions during the 1930s and 40s, but until a major retrospective in 1975, shown at Colchester, London, and at the University Gallery in his home town of Hull, his work appeared mainly in book form. His last exhibition, in 1978, was of some London drawings and water colours.

Writing and editing gradually overtook Gaunt's career as an artist. In 1936 he had published *Bandits in a Landscape,* a study of Salvator Rosa and his school, which traced the romantic spirit in Old Masters. But it was the publication, in 1942, of *The Pre-Raphaelite Tragedy* which established Gaunt as a major writer on art. In this and two subsequent books, *The Aesthetic Adventure* (1945) and *Victorian Olympus* (1952), Gaunt placed the artistic movements of the Victorian era firmly in their social, historical and artistic contexts, rescuing these British artists and their ideas from relative obscurity and neglect. Never less than scholarly, but always readable and full of narrative interest, Gaunt's books provide useful introductions to their subjects for the general reader as well as the serious student of art.

In all, Gaunt wrote and edited some 30 books, including one novel, *The Lady in the Castle* (1956). Many of his books, especially the later ones, were general surveys of a school or period, such as *A Concise History of British Painting* (1964), and *Impressionism: A Visual History* (1970); but throughout his writing can be detected an interest in writers and poets who dealt in the fantastic. Hence his sympathy with the anarchic dream world of *The Surrealists* (1972), and with the idealized medieval landscapes of the Pre-Raphaelites.   T.F.

Son of William G., designer and lithographer, and Harriet (Spence) G. Married Mary Catherine O'Reilly (Connolly) 1935 (d. 1980). No children. Educ: Worcester Coll., Oxford, B.A. Hons. 1922; M.A. 1926; Ruskin Sch. of Drawing; Westminster Sch. of Art. Mil. Service; Durham Light Infantry, British Army 1918. Editorial Dir., Studio Publications 1926–39; Ed., Documentary war-time publications, Odhams Press, Ltd. 1939–45; Art Critic, Evening Standard 1945–47;

Museums Corresp., The Times (London) 1963–71. *Exhibitions* (all London) paintings and drawings, Redfern Gall. 1930; Leger Gall. 1930, 1932; Reid and Lefevre Galls. 1936; Walker Gall. 1947; retrospective, Colchester, Hull and London 1975; Michael Parkin Gall. 1978. *Publications:* English Rural Life in the Eighteenth Century, 1925; (ed.) The Etchings of Frank Brangwyn (catalogue), 1926; Rome, Past and Present, (ed. by C. Geoffrey Holme), 1926; (author of introduction) Etchings of Today (ed. by C.G. Holme), 1929; (self-illus.) London Promenade, 1930; Touring the Ancient World with a Camera (photos. by C.G. Holme), 1932; Bandits in a Landscape: A Study of Romantic Painting from Caravaggio to Delacroix, 1937; (ed. with Frank A. Mercer) Poster Progress, 1939; The Pre-Raphaelite Tragedy, 1942, reissued as The Pre-Raphaelite Dream, 1966; (with F.G. Roe) Etty and the Nude: The Art and Life of William Etty, 1943; British Painting from Hogarth's Day to Ours, 1945, revised ed. 1946; The Aesthetic Adventure, 1945; (author of introduction and notes) Hogarth 1697–1764, 1947; (ed. and author of intro.) Selected Writings of William Morris, 1948; The March of the Moderns, 1949; Victorian Olympus, 1952; (author of introduction) Renoir, 1952, 2nd ed. 1971; Chelsea, 1954; (ed.) The Teach Yourself History of Painting, 1954; (author of introduction and notes on illus.) London in Colour: A Collection of Colour Photographs by James Riddell, 1955; Arrows of Desire: A Study of William Blake and his Romantic World, 1956; (ed.) The Dutch School, 1956, (ed.) The Flemish School, 1956; Teach Yourself to Study Sculpture, 1957; (contributor) Eugene Boudin 1824–1898 (cat. of exhbn. held in London, Nov-Dec 1958), 1958; Kensington, 1958; The Observer's Book of Painting and Graphic Art, 1958; (author of intro. and notes on illust) Old Inns of England in Colour: A Collection of Colour Photographs, 1959; (author of introduction) Cellini: The Life of Benvenuto Cellini, 1960; London, 1961; (compiler) Everyman's Dictionary of Pictorial Art, 1962; (ed. and author of introduction) Vasari: The Lives of the Painters, Sculptors and Architects (revision of trans. by A.B. Hinds), 1963; A Concise History of English Painting, 1964; The Observer's Book of Modern Art, from Impressionism to the Present Day, 1964; Oxford; 1965; The Observer's Book of Sculpture, 1966; A Companion to Painting, 1967; Dante Gabriel Rossetti, 1967; A Guide to the Understanding of Painting, 1968; Flemish Cities: Bruges, Ghent, Antwerp, Brussels: Their History and Art, 1969; Impressionism: A Visual History, 1970; The Impressionists, 1970; Great Century of British Painting: From Hogarth to Turner, 1971; Turner, 1971; Wilham De Morgan, 1971; The Restless Century: Painting in Britain 1800–1900, 1972; The Surrealists, 1972. *Other:* The Lady in the Castle (novel), 1956; Contributor to Times Literary Supplement and to art. mags.

SIR GEOFFREY (NIGEL) OLIVER
British Admiral
Born London, England, January 22nd, 1898
Died West Sussex, England, May 26th, 1980

Admiral Sir Geoffrey Nigel Oliver, whose career spanned two world wars, first joined the British Royal Navy as a cadet in 1915. After battleship service during World War One, Oliver, who had specialized in naval gunnery, rose quickly through the ranks. In 1925, he went to the China Station in the cruiser Carlisle but returned to larger, more heavily armored ships in 1930, serving under Andrew Cunningham (later Admiral Lord Cunningham of Hyndehope) on the H.M.S. Rodney. When Cunningham went to the Mediterranean as Rear Admiral, 1st Destroyer Flotilla, Oliver served with him as commander of the Diana, and later the Veteran. After attaining the rank of captain in 1937, Oliver held a brief staff appointment with the Admiralty in London.

In 1940 Oliver served as commander of the newly-commissioned battle cruiser Hermione which was torpedoed by a German U-boat off Tobruk in July 1942. Oliver received the D.S.O. for this command and was nominated for the shore-based post of Director of Naval Ordnance, but Cunningham told the British Admiralty that Oliver was needed to assist with the first allied landings in North Africa and to organize British naval support for American Fifth Army in the Bizerta campaign.

In overseeing the landing of the British X Corps in the northern assault area at Salerno in September 1943, Oliver faced the most difficult test of his career. Although the Italians had surrendered, the British and American allied landing force encountered, unexpectedly, such heavy German opposition that General Mark Clark (commander of the U.S. Fifth Army) sought withdrawal from one assault area in order to concentrate troops in another. Oliver refused to agree with the retreat, maintaining that the progress of troops depended upon the ability of the allies to keep all landing beaches open and to continue unloading men, ammunition and supplies. Cunningham, who supported Oliver's position, commended his firmness and later wrote: "Any evacuation or partial evacuation from one or other of the narrow allied beach-heads would have resulted in . . . an allied defeat which would have completely offset the Italian surrender, and have been hailed by the Germans as a smashing victor." For his activities off the Italian coast, Oliver was awarded the C.B.

In the 1944 Normandy assault Oliver took charge of one of the beaches where the British J Force landed in June. Following the allied invasion of Europe, Oliver commanded a squadron of Escort Carriers which provided cover for the Malayan Peninsula assault. During this service he was promoted to Rear-Admiral.

Returning to London after the war, Oliver was Admiral (Air) until being appointed Assistant Chief of Naval Staff a year later. From 1948 he served as Admiral-President of the Royal Naval College at Greenwich for two years. For two more years he was Vice-Admiral and then British Commander-in-Chief, East Indies. Oliver was knighted in 1951 and promoted to full Admiral in 1952; from 1953 until his retirement in 1955 (when he received the G.B.E.), he held the senior British naval appointment of Commander-in-Chief, the Nore (the area near the English Channel and the North Sea).   M.D.

Son of Prof. Frederick W.O. Married Barbara Jones 1933. Children: two sons (one d.); one daughter (d.). Educ: Rugby Sch. With British Royal Navy: Cadet 1915; Midshipman and Sub.-Lt., H.M.S. Dreadnought 1916; H.M.S. Renown 1917-20; gunnery specialist from 1923; H.M.S. Carlisle, China Station 1925-27; H.M.S. Rodney 1930-32; Comdr., H.M.S. Diana and H.M.S. Veteran, 1st Destroyer Flotilla,

Mediterranean 1934–36; Admiralty staff, London 1937–40; Comdr., H.M.S. Hermione, Western Mediterranean, Malta, Madagascar, and Eastern Mediterranean 1940–42; Sr. Officer, Inshore Squadron, Northern Africa 1942–43; Comdr., British Assault Force, Salerno 1943; Comdr., Force J. Assault Force, Normandy 1944; 21st. Aircraft Carrier Squadron 1944–45; Admiral (Air) 1946; a Lord Commnr. of the Admiralty and Asst. Chief of Naval Staff 1947–48; Pres., Royal Naval Coll., Greenwich 1948–50; Comdr.-in-Chief, East Indies Station 1950–52; Comdr.-in-Chief, the Nore 1953 until retirement 1955. Appointed Captain 1937, Commodore (2nd class) 1942 and (1st class) 1944, Rear Admiral 1945, Vice Admiral 1949, and Admiral 1952. Hons: D.S.O. 1941 (Bars 1943, 1944); C.B. 1944; K.C.B. 1951; G.B.E. 1955.

SHEIK MUHAMMAD ALI JA'ABRI
Jordanian minister and Mayor of Hebron
Born Transjordan (now Jordan) 1900
Died Hebron, Israeli occupied territory, May 29th, 1980

Sheik Muhammad Ali Ja'abri was the Mayor of Hebron for 36 years and a leading Jordanian politician. He was educated at al-Azhar University in Cairo, where he studied Islamic law, and began his professional career as Chief Clerk in the religious Charei Court.

In 1940 he was appointed Mayor of Hebron by the British authorities and continued in that post after Transjordan became the independent state of Jordan in 1946. When Jordan annexed the West Bank during the 1948 Arab-Israeli War he joined King Abdullah's cabinet. After the June 1967 war when the Israelis drove the Jordanians from the West Bank, Ja'abri became known for his advocacy of moderate policies towards the Jews. Although firmly opposed to Jewish settlements in the occupied West Bank territory, he rejected terrorist activity and sought an open dialogue with Israeli authorities. As Mayor of occupied Hebron, his most immediate problem was Israel's establishment of a settlement at Qiryat Arba. He was unable to prevent its establishment and was defeated in the mayoral election of 1976 by Fahad Kawasmeh, a supporter of the Palestine Liberation Organization. Ja'abri's defeat was attributed, in part, to his close ties with King Hussein and indicated the increasing strength of the Palestine Liberation Organization on the West Bank.

T.P.

Married Zulfa Shukry Agha. Children: (known) one son. Educ: al-Azhar Univ., Cairo. Chief Clerk in the Charei Ct.; Pres., Al-Khalil Municipality; Mayor of Hebron 1940–76; Minister of Agriculture 1955; Minister of Justice 1955, 1958, and 1959–60; Minister of Education 1958. *Author:* Voice of Khalil.

WALTER R. DORNBERGER
Rocket engineer and administrator
Born Giessen, Germany, September 6th, 1895
Died Hamburg, West Germany, June 1980

Walter Dornberger's pioneering rocket development work in Germany and the U.S. paved the way for space flight. He is best known for heading the team of German scientists that built the V-2, the world's first mass-produced, liquid-fuel rocket.

The son of a pharmacist, Dornberger grew up and attended school in the western German town of Giessen. Though he hoped to become an architect, custom dictated that as his family's second son he choose a military career. He enlisted in the German Army in August 1914 and served during World War One as an artillery officer. Released from a French prisoner of war camp in 1920, Dornberger was accepted into the officer corps of the small German Army permitted by the Treaty of Versailles. He decided to enter one of the service's technical branches and in 1925 began to study mechanical engineering in Berlin.

Returning to active service as a captain in 1930, Dornberger was assigned to the ballistics branch of the Army Weapons Department. There he was put in charge of work on the military development of rockets, one of the few weapons permitted to Germany in unrestricted numbers by the Versailles treaty. Though initially skeptical about the military value of rockets, Dornberger established contact with various societies and individuals engaged in rocket research. He soon gained permission to set up a testing station at Kummersdorf near Berlin. Promoted to the rank of colonel, he worked there at the head of a small research staff that included the engineering student Wernher von Braun. By 1936 the group's expanding activities had outgrown the Kummersdorf site, and Army leaders authorized Dornberger to move his operation to the remote Baltic coastal town of Peenemünde. There he established a rocket research facility that for the duration of its existence was the world's largest.

Dornberger had charge of several projects at Kummersdorf and Peenemünde. The first weapon to be produced was a small, solid-fuel rocket with a thrust of up to 110 pounds and a range of several miles. Intended to supplement the Army's artillery, this device was used extensively on the Eastern front during World War Two. Dornberger also supervised development of the pilotless, jet-propelled "buzz-bomb" (later known as the V-1) until the project was transferred to another agency in 1940. But by far the most spectacular and important of Dornberger's efforts were the large, liquid-fuel rockets of the A (for Aggregate) series, which culminated in the missile known as the V-2.

The first successful test of an A rocket took place in December 1934 on Borkum Island in the North Sea. The A-4, which became the V-2, first flew on October 3rd, 1942. 47 feet long, the rocket had an initial weight of about 14 tons, including a one-ton warhead. Its alcohol and liquid oxygen-burning engine developed a thrust of 60,000 pounds, propelling the missile to a maximum altitude of 60 miles with a maximum range of 220 miles. Following an interview with Hitler in July 1943, Dornberger won top priority rating for the weapon's final development and production. But success only brought new problems. In August 1943 some 600 British bombers raided Peenemünde, causing heavy damage and killing over 700 of Dornberger's staff. Work on the V-2 continued, but Dornberger now had to contend with takeover attempts by other German agencies eager to expand their power. In July 1944 Heinrich Himmler's SS finally secured control over rocket development, and an SS general was installed as head of the V-2 project. The move effectively excluded Dornberger from decisions regarding the weapon's deployment and targeting. But he retained authority in matters of rocket research and production.

From mid-1944 to the end of the war, some 4,300 V-2s were fired against England and areas of northwestern Europe held by the Allies. Meanwhile Dornberger and his research staff began work on other projects, including a submarine-launched missile and a rocket capable of reaching the U.S. East Coast. As Russian forces approached Peenemünde in February 1945, Dornberger fled with most of his subordinates to the underground V-2 production facility at Nordhausen in the Harz Mountains. There he and some 130 rocket scientists surrendered, with their plans and equipment, to American troops. Dornberger, who ended the war as a lieutenant general, spent the next two years in a British prisoner of war camp before accepting an invitation to serve as a civilian missile consultant to the U.S. Air Force.

After emigrating to the U.S., Dornberger worked until 1950 at Wright-Patterson Air Force Base in Dayton, Ohio. When the government permitted former German missile experts to enter private industry, he moved to the Bell Aircraft Corporation, whose emphasis on manned space flight corresponded to his own priorities. One of Dornberger's proposals at Bell resulted in development of the X-15 manned rocket. He also helped design the Rascal air-to-surface missile and the Dyna-Soar, an early version of the space shuttle. Beginning in 1957 he held a series of administrative posts at Bell that involved coordinating the president's office with the company's laboratories and with outside organizations.

Dornberger retired in 1965 as vice president and chief scientist of Bell Aerosystems Company, a former Bell division taken over by Textron. He died while visiting friends in West Germany.   S.L.G.

Son of Herman D., pharmacist, and Hedwig (Roltsch) D. Married Alice Raeder 1932 (d. 1961). Emigrated to USA 1947. 2nd lt., German Army 1914–18; prisoner of war, Southern France 1918–20. Educ: Coll. of Geissen, Germany 1901–14; Berlin-Charlottenburg Technische Universität, B.A. 1927, M.A. 1930. With ballistics branch, German Army: (as capt.) Branch chief, German Bd. of Ordnance 1930–32 (as col.) Group and Div. Chief, Versuchsstelle (Experimental Station), Kummersdorf-West, Germany; (as maj.-gen. then lt.-gen.) Mil. and Technical Chief, Peenemünde, Germany 1936–44; Commnr., German Armed Forces for guided missile programs, Berlin 1944; prisoner of war, England 1945–47. Missile Consultant in Air Material Command, Wright-Patterson Air Force Base, Dayton, Ohio 1947–50. With Bell Aircraft Corp., Buffalo: Missile Design Consultant 1950–57; Technical Asst. to the Pres.

1957–59; V.P. 1959–60. V.P. and Chief Scientist, Bell Aerosystems Co. 1960–1965. Member, American Rocket Soc. Hons: Hon. D. Eng., Berlin-Charlottenburg Technische Universität 1935; Grand Award of the German Board of Ordnance 1943; American Rocket Soc. Astronautics Award 1959; Fellow, American Astronautical Soc.; Assoc. Fellow, Inst. of Aerospace Sciences; Knight Cross of the War; Merit Cross; Iron Cross.

(RICHARD WILLIAM) "RUBE" MARQUARD
Professional baseball player
Born Cleveland, Ohio, U.S.A., October 9th, 1889
Died Baltimore, Maryland, U.S.A., June 1st, 1980

Richard "Rube" Marquard's record of 19 consecutive victories during the 1912 season as a pitcher for the New York Giants stands unbroken to this day, and helped to earn him a niche in baseball's Hall of Fame. Marquard himself claimed his winning streak actually numbered 20 games. Whatever the inconsistencies between his reckoning and the judgment of official scorers, this left-handed pitcher enjoyed enormous success between 1908 and 1925.

Marquard's initial desire to play professional baseball was opposed by his father, Frederick Marquard, chief engineer in Cleveland, Ohio, who was determined that his son have an education and a more respectable occupation. However, at the age of 16 Richard hitchhiked and rode the rails to try out for the Waterloo club of the Iowa State League. Marquard's experiences in the bush leagues, which were typical of those of aspiring professional baseball players prior to World War One, reinforced his father's conviction that a baseball career was financially unstable when his son soon returned to Cleveland.

But Marquard continued to excel in the sandlot and semiprofessional circuits of Ohio and became affiliated with an ice cream company which paid him 25 dollars weekly for production work and for pitching on the firm's team. He was recruited by the local major-league team, the Cleveland Indians but declined their offer of $100 per month, preferring to play for the Indianapolis team of the American Association, a minor league club but one which promised to double his salary.

In 1907 Indianapolis optioned Marquard to Canton, a smaller minor-league club, but he was recalled after he recorded 23 victories his first year as a full-fledged professional. His brilliance during the 1908 season at Indianapolis attracted the attention of scouts from several major league teams. After he hurled a perfect game late in the season a bidding war for his services ensued, with Indianapolis selling his contract to the New York Giants for $11,000. The 18-year-old Marquard became the highest-priced player in the history of the sport.

After two undistinguished seasons with the Giants, in 1911 he compiled a 24–7 record and led the National League in both winning percentage and strikeouts. In 1912 he pitched at least 19 consecutive wins as part of a total record of 26 wins and 11 losses, Marquard contending he had been deprived of a victory during his winning streak in a game in which he appeared as a relief pitcher. No major-league pitcher has since equalled his record, whether the number of consecutive wins stands at 19 or at 20.

Marquard's achievements as a pitcher also included 23 victories in 1913: a 21 inning, complete-game victory in 1914; and a no-hitter in 1915. He appeared in three World Series with the Giants and in two with the Brooklyn Dodgers, to whom he was sold in 1915. He finished his major league career with the Cincinnati Redlegs and the Boston Braves, achieving a lifetime record of 204 wins and 179 losses.   s.t.

Son of Frederick M., engineer. Married: (1) Blossom Seeley, actress (div. 1920); (2) Naomi Wigley (d. 1954); (3) Jane Ottenheimer 1955. American Assn.: Indianapolis 1907. Natl. League: N.Y. Giants 1908; Brooklyn Dodgers 1915; Cincinnati Redlegs 1921; Boston Braves 1922. Hons: Baseball Hall of Fame 1971.
Further reading: The Glory of their Times by Lawrence S. Ritter, 1966.

ARTHUR C(HARLES) NIELSEN, SR.
Market research executive and founder of the "Nielsen ratings"
Born Chicago, Illinois, U.S.A., September 5th, 1897
Died Chicago, Illinois, U.S.A., June 1st, 1980

At the age of nine, Arthur C. Nielsen was keeping a double-entry book to record money earned and spent: his meticulousness and thoroughness were already apparent. He went on to study engineering at the University of Wisconsin, achieving the highest grade level in the history of the school and in 1918 graduating as class valedictorian. After brief service with the Naval Reserve until the close of World War One, he returned to Chicago, where he worked as an electrical engineer for the next four years.

In 1923, Nielsen organized the company that would one day make his name a household word, though the general public knew little of the man behind the institution. In its infancy, the A.C. Nielsen Company conducted performance surveys of industrial equipment and made product evaluation reports. After a shaky start, the company grew rapidly and became successful, but the depression reversed the company's fortune: to most manufacturers, the Nielsen service became an unaffordable luxury, and company revenue dropped below the level of the first year's income. Nielsen decided that the company must direct its energy toward other kinds of market measuring.

In 1933 Nielsen acquired a contract from a drug manufacturer to determine why its chief product was not selling. The resulting successful survey opened the eyes of other pharmaceutical companies. Soon, Nielsen had enough business in this market to establish the Food and Drug Index, a service that recorded the retail flow of specific products. Nielsen estimated national and local sales through a survey of carefully selected retail outlets; clients were provided with a record of market patterns and their fluctuations. With the aid of the Nielsen information, companies could determine their position and evaluate their performance in the marketplace in relation to the total market. *Business Week* termed Nielsen's pioneering efforts in market research "revolutionary." It was Nielsen's belief that, since the index increased the profits and productivity of his customers by showing them how to distribute their goods more effectively (even making it possible for them to lower the cost of those goods), he was contributing to a significant improvement of the standard of living.

As Nielsen added new commodities to his list of consumer purchase surveys, the Food and Drug Index evolved into the Retail Index. Today, this retail aspect of the Nielsen operation accounts for 90 percent of the company's revenue. Nevertheless, to the average person, *Nielsen* is identified with television and radio ratings system. This index often determines who or what is seen on American television. Having the power of life and death over network programming, one network executive referred to the "Nielsens" as the closest thing in modern times to a witch doctor.

The Nielsen media ratings service was first made available to clients in 1942, after four years of experimentation to develop a method and device that would record the programming choices of radio listeners in given locales. The Radio Index was expanded in 1948 to provide ratings "projectable to all U.S. homes." In 1950, the index was further expanded to include the rapidly growing television industry.

Networks and advertisers use the Nielsen television ratings chiefly to determine how many people watch any individual television show. The ratings have become the major factor in determining the prices networks charge for commercial time. In 1963, so much money and power hinged upon the Nielsen ratings that the company became the subject of a Congressional inquiry. The ratings index emerged from the inquiry stripped of its reputation for infallibility. Testimony by Congressional investigators revealed that names from the "top secret" list of viewers participating in the Nielsen survey sample were discoverable—hence, vulnerable to manipulation by interested parties. Near panic occurred in the broadcast industry, and there was speculation that Nielsen would discontinue its media ratings index. But the company acted rapidly to develop new techniques that would ensure the integrity of its sampling system. Within a short time, the Nielsen ratings were once again casting their magic spell.

Arthur C. Nielsen was a generous contributor to charitable organizations and institutions. In appreciation for his establishing 74 scholarships that allowed Scandinavian students to study business administration in the United States, Nielsen was knighted in 1961 by the king of Denmark. At the time of his death, Nielsen was chairman of the company he founded, a position he had held since 1957.   s.j.

Son of Rasmus and Harriet (Gunn) N., accountants. Married Gertrude B. Smith 1918. Children: Arthur C., Jr., b. 1919, Dir., A.C. Nielsen Co.; Margaret Ann Stiegele; Phillip Robert, b. 1929, V.P., A.C. Nielsen Co.; Barbara Harriet Whitcomb; Virginia Beatrice Upton. Educ: Morton High Sch., Cicero, Ill.; Univ. Wisc., B.S. summa cum laude 1918. Mil. service: Ensign, U.S. Naval Reserve 1918. Electric Engineer: Isko Co., Chicago 1919–20 and H.P. Gould Co., Chicago 1920–23. Pres. 1923–57 and Chmn. 1957–80, A.C. Nielsen Co. Established co. services: Retail Index Services; Media Research Services; Nielsen Clearing House; Petroleum Information Services; Nielsen Special Research Services; Neodata Services. Established A.C. Nielsen Co. offices in U.S.: Chicago, Evanston, and

Lincolnwood, Ill.; NYC; Hollywood, Menlo Park, and San Francisco, Calif.; Clinton and Mason City, Iowa; Green Bay and Fond du Lac, Wisc.; Denver and Boulder, Colo.; Lincoln, Nebr.; Dallas, El Paso, and Laredo, Tex.; Sarasota, Dunedin, and St. Petersburg, Fla.; Hackensack, N.J.; Atlanta, Ga.; Ft. Mitchell, Ky.; Westport, Conn. Established A.C. Nielsen offices abroad: Amsterdam; Brussels; Dublin and Limerick, Ireland; Frankfurt; Johannesburg; Lisbon; Lucerne; Madrid; Mexico City, Juarez, and Nuevo Laredo, Mexico; Milan; Oxford; Paris; São Paulo; Stockholm; Sydney; Tokyo; Osaka; Toronto, Montreal, St. John, and Calgary, Canada; Vienna; Wellington. Officer: DeMille Foundn., distribution cttee. of U.S. Council of the Intnl. Chamber of Commerce ca. 1950; Wisc. Alumni Research Foundn. Member: Tau Beta Pi; Eta Kappa Nu; Sigma Phi; West Side Tennis, Forest Hills, N.Y.; Univ., N.Y.C.; Indian Hill, Winnetka, Ill. Hons: Mich. Doubles Tennis Champion 1923; Silver Medal, Annual Advertisement Awards Cttee. 1936; for outstanding service, Chicago Federated Advertisement Club 1941; Winner of father-son and father-daughter Natl. Tennis Championships 1946; Paul D. Converse award, American Marketing Assn. 1951 and 1970; elected to Hall of Fame in distribution 1953; Knight in the Order of Dannebrog 1961; Parlin Memorial Award 1963; annual award, Intnl. Advertisement Assn. 1966; Marketing Man of the Year 1970; elected to the Natl. Lawn Tennis Hall of Fame 1971. *Major co. publications:* The Nielsen Researcher; Review of Retail Grocery Trends.
Further reading: article in the New York Times magazine, July 30, 1967.

SIR KENNETH (GEORGE) GRUBB
Church of England lay officer, missionary, and explorer
Born Oxton, Nottinghamshire, England, September 9th, 1900
Died Salisbury, Wiltshire, England, June 3rd, 1980

Sir Kenneth Grubb, who in his latter years was one of Britain's leading lay churchmen, began his career as an explorer and missionary. He demonstrated his deeply held beliefs through his concern for the religious well-being of the peoples of South America and for the Church in his homeland. Grubb documented both aspects of his life's work in his prolific writings over 40 years.

The son of a middle-class Nottinghamshire clergyman, Kenneth Grubb was educated at Marlborough College and served for the last year of the First World War in the Royal Navy. Advice and help from his family pointed him towards a missionary career in the Amazon basin, at that time still containing large tracts of unexplored territory. Grubb sailed to South America in 1923 and began his journeys of discovery into the interior of the continent, seeking out the native inhabitants and their customs. His ability to acquire languages facilitated dialogue with Indian tribes and the Spanish and Portuguese colonisers, and when Grubb found himself caught between warring Indians, he and his colleagues established themselves as successful mediators. Meanwhile, in surveying the religious condition of the people, he laid the foundations for the professional missionary societies of Europe, and in gathering information about a hitherto ill-documented part of the world, he earned an international reputation as an authority on South America.

It was the extent of his knowledge that led in 1928 to an invitation to join the Survey Application Trust, which had been set up to obtain religious data from all over the world. Grubb had, in addition, made studies of the Protestant minorities in Spain and Portugal and of the state of the churches and missions in South Africa. Thus, early in the Second World War he was asked to join the Ministry of Information in London as a specialist in the Latin American section, later being promoted to head of that section. Subsequently he became Controller of Foreign Publicity and then Controller of Overseas Publicity. Grubb's services were recognized in 1942 with a CMG.

At this point Grubb turned his attention to commerce, having been invited by a group of large firms specializing in Anglo-Latin American trade to advise on expansion of their operation. He organized the Hispanic and Luso-Brazilian Councils to further their trading interests and was their secretary-general from inception in 1946 through to 1953. Grubb, in 1944, was elected President of the Church Missionary Society and during the 25 years he held the office, he became regarded as a man with a knowledge of its entire operation. In 1946, Grubb was appointed first chairman of the Churches' permanent Commission on International Affairs, a post which he retained until 1968. This position involved him in work with both the World Council and the British Council of Churches and, in particular, with the ecumenical movement in his home country and abroad. He became a Church Commissioner in 1948 and was elected chairman of the Church Assembly's House of Laity in 1959, a post in which he stressed the Church's responsibility to aid Third World countries. From 1965 to 1973, Grubb was a Vice-President of the British Institute of Race Relations and from the late 1950s through the early 1960s he worked with an unofficial committee of the churches and the Institute of Strategic Studies on the moral implications of nuclear warfare, serving as the group's chairman for a time. Grubb, who had been knighted in 1953, was awarded the KCMG in 1970 upon his retirement from the House of Laity chairmanship.

A shy but often humorous man, his dispassionate approach to problems belied his great humanity and strong beliefs. Throughout his career he pursued his interest in literature, and wrote many books. His early works catalogued his explorations and for a number of years he edited the *World Christian Handbook*. Other major works include *Amazon and Andes* (1930), his *Parables from South America* (1932), and his autobiography dealing with his close association with the lay government of the Church of England, *Crypts of Power* (1971). M.D.

Son of Rev. H. Percy G., Church of England clergyman, and Margaret A. (Chrichton-Stuart) G. Married: (1) Eileen Sylvia Knight 1926 (d. 1932); (2) Nancy Mary Arundel 1935. Children: 2nd marriage—Martyn; Frederick; Richard; Margaret Jackson. Church of England. Educ: Marlborough Coll., Berks. Mil. Service: Royal Navy 1918. Missionary and explorer, South America 1923–28. Member from 1928 and Exec. Trustee since 1953, Survey Application Trust. Researcher and freelance writer 1928–39. With Ministry of Information, London: Head of Latin American Sect. 1939–41; Controller of Foreign Publicity 1941–42; Controller of Overseas Publicity 1942–46.

Secty.-Gen., Hispanic and Luso-Brazilian Councils 1946–54; U.K. delegate to UNESCO 1954; Publicity Consultant, Rank Org. 1955–59; U.K. Delegate to Atlantic Congress 1959. Pres.: Church Missionary Soc. 1944–69; Cheltenham Training Colls. 1948–79; Asia Christian Colls. Assn. 1969 (V.P. 1953, Chmn. 1959–69); also Grubb Inst. of Behavioural Studies and Argentina Diocesan Assn. V.P.: Inst. of Race Relations 1965–73; British Council of Churches 1965–68. Chmn.: Commn. of the Churches on Intnl. Affairs 1946–68; Royal Foundn. of St. Katharine 1957–77; House of Laity, Church Assembly 1959–70; Missionary and Ecumenical Council, Church Assembly 1964–67. Trustee, St. Peter's Coll., Oxford 1946–79; Church Commnr. 1948–73. Gov., Monkton Combe Sch. 1957–79. Member: World Council of Churches; British Council of Churches; Royal Inst. of Intnl. Affairs; Inst. of Strategic Studies (Chmn. 1958–63); British and Foreign Bible Soc. (also V.P.); United Soc. for Christian Lit. (also V.P.); Canning Club (also Vice-Chmn.); Authors' Club; Naval and Mil. Club. Hons: C.M.G. 1942; Hon. LL.D., Muhlenburg Coll., Allentown, Pa. 1951; knighted 1953; Hon. Fellow, St. Peter's Coll., Oxford 1961; K.C.M.G. 1970; also Life Member, Inst. of Linguists and American Geog. Soc. *Author:* The Lowland Indians of Amazonia: A Survey of the Location and Religious Condition of the Indians of Colombia, Venezuela, the Guianas, Ecuador, Peru, Brazil and Bolivia, 1927; Amazon and Andes, 1930; The West Coast Republics of South America, 1930; The Northern Republics of South America: Ecuador, Colombia and Venezuela, 1931; The Need for Non-Professional Missionaries, 1931; South America, the Land of the Future, 1931; Parables from South America, 1932; (with Erasmo Braga) The Republic of Brazil: A Survey of the Religious Situation, 1932; The Republics of South America, 1933; (trans. with E.R. Holden) The Significance of Portugal: A Survey of Evangelical Progress (by Eduardo Moreira), 1933; (with Carlos Garcia) Religion in the Republic of Spain, 1933; From Pacific to Atlantic: South American Studies, 1933; Time's Winged Chariot, 1934; Missions Rethought, 1934; (with G. Baez Camargo) Religion in the Republic of Mexico, 1935; An Advancing Church in Latin America, 1936; Evangelical Handbook of Latin America, 1937, vol. 2 1939; Religion in Central America, 1937; The Christian Handbook of South Africa, 1938; (contributor) Madras Series, 1939 (missionary reports); The Lowland Indians of Amazonia: Review of Ten Years Evangelical Progress to 1938, 1939; The Northern Republics of South America: Review of Ten Years Evangelical Progress to 1938, 1939; The West Coast Republics of South America: Review of Ten Years Evangelical Progress to 1938, 1939; (with M.A.C. Warren) Bridge Builders into a New Age, 1947; (ed. with Ernest John Bingle) World Christian Handbook, 1st ed. 1949, 2nd ed. 1953, 3rd ed. 1957; 4th ed. 1962, 5th ed. (with H. Wakelin Coxill) 1968; (ed. with Ernest John Bingle) A Digest of Christian Statistics Based on World Christian Handbook, 1952, 1953; Coexistence and the Conditions of Peace, 1957; A Layman Looks at the Church, 1964; Crypts of Power, 1971 (autobiog.).

ARNOLD RENSHAW
Physician and leader in forensic medicine
Born Rochdale, Lancashire, England, June 21st, 1885
Died Wilmslow, Cheshire, England, June 3rd, 1980

Arnold Renshaw came to be respected as an authority in two completely different fields. For the major part of his life Renshaw, as a physician and researcher, made important contributions to medicine, particularly the treatment of rheumatic disorders and in the field of forensic medicine in which he had the status of a pioneer. In his later years Renshaw became known as an art collector and an authority on English landscape paintings who brought to the judgment of paintings much of the discipline, impartiality, and attentiveness to detail that had become his hallmarks in medicine.

Renshaw, the son of a dental surgeon, was born in 1885 in Rochdale, Lancashire. After qualifying in dentistry in Manchester and earning his medical degree at London University, Renshaw served during World War One as a commissioned officer in the Royal Army Medical Corps. While in Belgium and France, he conducted a study of trench fever, later writing up his findings for the first paper he contributed to the medical press.

After the war he earned a Diploma in Public Health at Cambridge, with distinction in bacteriology, and returned to Manchester to specialize in pathology. He became Consultant Pathologist at Ancoats Hospital, Manchester, a position he held for many years.

A turning point in his medical career occurred in 1931 when the Chief Constable of Manchester asked him to use his knowledge of pathology to help investigate suspected murder cases in the area. Renshaw thus began his distinguished association with the relatively new field of forensic medicine, investigating many murder cases throughout the north of England with a scrupulous impartiality that often made his evidence as available for the defense as for the prosecution. In 1939 he published a paper in the *Medico-Legal and Criminological Review* on the "Investigation of Murder" which carefully described his methodology and the ways in which his medical knowledge was applied to questions of civil and criminal law. His paper included a wealth of pertinent examples from those of his investigations which had resulted in convictions.

In addition to his work in pathology and forensic medicine, Renshaw also conducted research into rheumatic disorders. In his private laboratory he developed an important intestinal extract that contained erepsin, an enzyme mixture that broke down proteins into simpler compounds and proved effective in the alleviation of rheumatic illnesses. Beginning in 1947 he published numerous articles on the value and use of this extract that was to improve considerably the treatment of rheumatic patients.

Renshaw's other area of interest and expertise was shared by his wife, a member of the prominent Rolfe family of Norfolk. Renshaw, who had been collecting paintings since the early years of his career, became devoted to the landscapes of the Norfolk area, especially to the works of Constable, the Norwich School, and later East Anglian artists such as Campbell Mellon. In 1969 he delivered a well-received lecture, later published, on his views on painting and art-collecting.

In 1963 the College of Pathologists (later Royal College) elected Renshaw one of its first Fellows. Renshaw died at his home at the age of 94.   M.D.

Married Barbara Rolfe. Three daughters. Educ: Qualified in dentistry. Manchester; M.D., London Univ.; Diploma in Public Health, Cambridge, distinction in bacteriology 1921. Mil. Service: First World War, commissioned in the Royal Army Medical Corps, served in Belgium and France. Consultant Pathologist, Ancoats Hosp., Manchester; began practice of forensic medicine, Manchester 1931; researched rheumatic disorders and developed new method of treatment. Member, Manchester Literary, Philosophical, and Medico-Legal Societies. Hons: Fellow, Royal Coll. of Pathologists 1963. *Articles:* "Investigation of Murder," in Medico-Legal and Criminological Review, 1939; others on trench fever and rheumatic illnesses and on art-collecting.

GIORGIO AMENDOLA
Italian Communist leader and Member of Parliament
Born Rome, Italy, November 21st., 1907
Died Rome, Italy, June 5th, 1980

tesy Amendola estate

A leading Italian Communist theoretician and member of the party's Steering and Central Committees, Giorgio Amendola was considered the most liberal of Communists, representing the moderate wing that aimed at a *via Italiana*. As a member of Parliament and the Communist Party of Italy (CPI) Central Committee, he attempted to unify all of Italy's left-wing parties on a new basis situated midway between Communism and Social Democracy.

Nicknamed *Il Grosso* for his large size, Amendola was the son of a famous liberal politician, Giovanni Amendola, who had also been a Minister, and who in 1926 was beaten to death by Fascists. Giorgio, a student at the time, was protected as a member of the anti-Fascist nobility; when he was arrested for militating against the early Mussolini regime, his father's friends obtained an immediate release and had his name removed from the police blotter. He received similar preferential treatment many times following his father's death. Although the Fascist regime sent him to the island of Ponza in 1932 for his political offenses, they did not force him to stand trial.

When Amendola sought part-time employment while attending the university and ex-Senator Luigi Albertini arranged to have him enter the Commercial Bank—adding that Giorgio would need Mussolini's approval as a precautionary measure—he refused the position. Instead he found employment as a clerk in Detken's antiquarian bookshop, where in 1929 he decided to join the Italian Communist Party. An aristocrat, he found it very difficult to talk to working-class people; whenever he attempted to befriend the workers, they spoke their local dialects to shut him out.

Amendola had been a confirmed anti-communist in his gymnasium days and only entered the CPI as a way of fighting the fascists. He had grown impatient with liberals and socialists who, it seemed to him, had given up the struggle against Mussolini. The CPI showed its presence in many ways even though it was forced to wage its war underground. Party members filled special courts for political offenses as well as most of the prisons and islands of confinement. Amendola felt certain, nonetheless, that the CPI could not only liberate Italy from the fascist dictatorship but eliminate the social and political causes underlying fascism itself. Thus began years of underground activity that landed him in prisons and in confinement on Ponza.

Despite his illustrious name, it took Amendola years to find a way of demonstrating his own political talents. At the outset he could only display his great physical courage; during World War Two, from a hiding place in the French Alps, Amendola helped to organize the anti-nazi partisans in Italy.

As commander of the Garibaldi Brigade, Amendola issued the order for the ambush of a German column at the Via Rasella in Rome in March 1944. The operation—successful in itself—brought an aftermath of bloody reprisals. For every German soldier that had been killed by the communist guerrillas, ten Italians were executed by the nazis in what came to be called the "Fosse Ardeatine Massacre." 335 Italians were killed, and after the war the relatives of several of the victims pressed charges against Amendola. He replied that he could not have let the communist partisans accept responsibility for the ambush since it was their duty to continue the fight against the Germans. He was never brought to trial.

Signor Giorgio Amendola's political career began in earnest just after the liberation when, in July 1945, he was appointed Under-Secretary to the President of the Council, a post retained through the first De Gasperi cabinet. Elected as a CPI deputy, Amendola was named to the "Commission of 75," which was responsible for drafting the new Italian Constitution. From 1948 on, he served as a member of the House and also sat on parliamentary commissions.

Among fellow communists in Europe, Amendola was considered a maverick. His individualism, self-confidence, and strong will could not be curbed; he liked to lead and was well-known for his commanding tone. With the coming of Maoist doctrine, he said, "I've shouted 'long live Stalin!' so many times that I can never again shout 'long live anybody!'" He became a critic of Soviet domination and was one of the communist leaders in Western Europe to strongly condemn the Soviet-led invasion of Czechoslovakia in 1968.

Amendola regarded himself as a communist within a capitalist country who was fighting for a socialism that would combine "respect for democratic and personal liberties . . . (with) de facto participation of the workers in the direction of social life." The Italian Communist Party's commitment to dialectical materialism made it difficult for Amendola to repudiate the Soviet system. Consequently, he refrained from harsh criticisms of other Communist nations because he feared that such statements would only give ammunition to capitalist ideologues. Amendola was often thwarted by doctrinaire forms of communism. When he sought creation of an independent, unified working-class party because the Social Democrats and the Communists had failed to achieve a radical transformation of society, he was severely reproached by Romana Ledda, a member of the Party's Central Committee. Ledda argued that Amendola's proposal amounted to "reformism" because it "separated . . . the revolution in the West from the world revolutionary processes."   M.S.

Son of Giovanni A., Liberal politician and Minister, and Eva Khun A. Married Germaine Lecocq 1934. Children: Ada Amendola Martino (d. 1976). Law degree. Mil. Service: Comdr., Garibaldi Brigade (anti-fascist partisans) 1943–45. Joined Italian Communist Party 1929; appointed Under-Secty. to Pres. of Council, Italy 1945; Member, Constituent Assembly from 1946; appointed to Commission of 75, for drafting Italian constitution; M.P. 1948–76; Member, Budget and Programming Commn. for State Shares 1948; Elected rep. of European parliament 1976; Member, Presidency of the Italian Communist Party Study Center for Economic Policy; member of various parliamentary commissions.

Further reading: Unity in Diversity: Italian Communism and the Communist World by Donald L.M. Blackmer, 1968.

RICHARD BONELLI
Operatic baritone
Born Port Byron, New York, U.S.A., February 6th, 1889
Died Los Angeles, California, U.S.A., June 7th, 1980

Richard Bonelli, a popular performer from the 1920s to the 1950s, enjoyed a singing career which encompassed light and grand opera and appearances in concerts and films and on radio and television. At the peak of his career, the critics praised Bonelli highly for his fine vocal sense and his imaginative interpretations of his roles.

Born Richard Bunn in 1889, Bonelli won an engineering scholarship to Syracuse University and was studying automotive engineering when he turned instead to a career of professional singing. He studied voice and toured twice abroad, making his Italian debut in Modena (1923). Before returning to the United States, he changed his name to Bonelli. From 1925 to 1931, he engaged in six seasons with the Chicago Civic Opera Company. In 1927 he appeared as Valentin in *Faust* over the first national radio hookup transmitted from the stage of an opera company, after which he was invited to join the Metropolitan Opera Company in New York.

Bonelli made his Met debut as Germont in *La Traviata* on November 29, 1932, to great acclaim. During his Met career, he appeared in 103 performances in New York and 35 on tour, singing 19 roles, mostly from the French-Italian repertoire but including Wolfram in *Tannhäuser*. He retired from the Company in 1945 at the age of 56, though carrying on his career as a recital artist with the San Francisco and Los Angeles Opera companies until the mid-1950s.

Bonelli was the featured singer in one of the earliest "talkies," a Fox Movietone short, and enjoyed wide radio exposure in the 30s and 40s. He also sang the role of Tonio in a pioneering telecast of *Pagliacci* on March 9, 1940.

Bonelli's last public appearance in New York was in 1966 when the Met first moved to its new quarters at Lincoln Center, at which he sang "Eri Tu" from *Un Ballo in Maschera*. Bonelli died at the age of 91 in Los Angeles.   R.C.

Born Richard Bunn. Son of Richard B. and Ida Homel B. Married: (1) Pauline Cornelys, singer 1917 (div. 1933); (2) Mona Modini Wood, writer and poet 1933. No children. Educ: Public schs., Syracuse, N.Y.; Syracuse Univ. Sch. of Engineering 1906–07; studied voice with Arthur Alexander, Los Angeles, Calif. 1907–08 and with Jean de

Reszke and William Vilonat, Paris 1909–15; Syracuse Univ., Mus. D. 1937. American debut, Brooklyn Acad. of Music 1915; sang with various small U.S. opera cos. and in Cuba 1915–19; European debut, Modena, Italy 1923; toured Germany with Mailland Opera Stagione 1923; engaged by Le Théâtre de la Gaiêté-Lyrique, Paris 1924; with Chicago Civic Opera Co. 1925–31; with Metropolitan Opera Co. 1932–45 and San Francisco Opera Co. 1932–35, 1937–40 and 1942; with Los Angeles Opera Co. 1948–56. Appointed voice instr. at Curtis Inst. 1941–43 and 1950–55; head of Voice Dept., Music Acad. of the West, Santa Barbara, Calif. 1947–50 (Chmn. of the Bd. 1948). Member, American Guild of Musicians and Artists (past V.P., past Gov.); American Fedn. of Radio and TV Artists; American Acad. of Teachers of Singing. *Major roles:* Valentin in Faust; Figaro in Il Barbiere di Siviglia; Germont in La Traviata; Marcello in La Bohème; Tonio in I Pagliacci; Amonasro in Aïda; Sharpless in Madame Butterfly; Manfredo in L'Amore dei Tre Re; Escamillo in Carmen; Barnaba in La Gioconda; Scarpia in Tosca; Ashton in Lucia de Lammermoor; Lescaut in Manon Lescaut; Wolfram in Tannhäuser; Count Luna in Il Trovatore; and Iago in Otello. Originated role of Wrestling Bradford in Howard Hansen's Merry Mount. *Other:* Sang in one of first talking films, a Fox Movietone short; sang in first opera (Faust) ever broadcast nationally from stage of an opera house, January 21, 1927; and in first televised broadcast (NBC) of an opera (Pagliacci), March 9, 1940. Voice featured in films Enter, Madame and There's Magic in Music, 1930s. Made frequent network radio appearances in 1930s and 1940s on shows sponsored by Chesterfield, Ford, General Motors, and Chase and Sanborn.

PHILIP GUSTON
Painter
Born Montreal, Quebec, Canada, June 27th, 1913
Died Woodstock, New York, U.S.A., June 7th, 1980

Few people ever felt indifferent toward Philip Guston and his work. His admirers believed that he took extraordinary risks in painting, moving successfully from large murals in the 1930s, through a representational phase on smaller canvases, on to an Abstract Expressionism with luminous, almost Impressionistic qualities, to his final, blunt cartoon scenes drawn with a heavy line and displaying a wry sense of political humor. Others felt his reputation was inflated and saw little merit in his surprising diversity. The *New York Times* art critic Hilton Kramer dismissed him as a colonizer, rather than a pioneer of New York abstract art. The recurring themes of tension and human frailty in his 50 years of painting were thought by some to be limited and overworked. "A paucity of ideas," one reviewer complained. But critics, gallery-goers, and art collectors were inevitably drawn to Philip Guston's work, whether or not they liked it or wanted it hanging on their walls. His paintings, in all their different manifestations, were too disturbing and personal to ignore.

His subtly shaded patches of color that dissolve into empty space and his waved lines on vacant canvas, both typical of his Abstract Expressionist period, are among his most well-known styles. Even his severest critics concede that his influence on younger artists and his

, 1961, by Philip Guston
esy Solomon R. Guggenheim Museum

contributions to what was known as the New York School were second only to Willem de Kooning's. For those interested primarily in light and the texture of brush strokes, Guston reigned supreme in a subset called the Abstract Impressionists. Guston never liked the comparisons to Claude Monet and other luminists, preferring to think of himself simply as a non-violent, painterly abstractionist.

He readily acknowledged the influences of Italian Renaissance masters Piero della Francesca, Paolo Uccello, and Andrea Mantegna. As a boy growing up in Los Angeles, he spent hours in the public library copying reproductions of frescoes and crumbling statues. In 1948–49 he went to Italy on a Guggenheim fellowship and a grant from the American Academy of Arts and Letters to see for himself the original Italian masterpieces. Another more modern Italian painter, surrealist Giorgio di Chirico, also left a mark on Guston's early painting style.

Guston had very little formal art training. Brought to California from Montreal by his parents at the age of six and encouraged by his mother to begin drawing, he briefly attended both the Los Angeles Manual Arts High School and the Otis Art Institute. He and Jackson Pollock were expelled from Manual Arts for distributing leaflets satirizing the English department. Otis "did nothing but push Frans Hals down my throat," according to Guston, so despite a generous scholarship he left. He worked in a factory and as a movie extra, and then went to Mexico where he carried banners for farm workers and began painting murals under the tutelage of famous Mexican muralist David Alfaro Siqueiros.

Guston returned to Los Angeles in 1935, allegedly fired with socialist zeal and anxious to bring art to the masses with large public murals. A job with the Works Progress Administration's (WPA) Federal Art Project was the only way he could afford to keep on painting, and he moved to New York a year later, where he worked for the WPA until 1940. At that point, with war approaching and the U.S. economy on the rise, he accepted his first of many university teaching offers and began concentrating on canvases.

His first successful oil was a reworking of one of his more famous murals, "Martial Memory," for the Queensbridge Housing Project. In the mural, small boys are jousting with each other, using the tops of garbage cans, saucepans and odd bits of wood and rope as their spears and foils. The painting depicts a more adult, withdrawn figure, obviously under stress. The small boys and the half-serious, half-mocking tensions surrounding them are the leitmotifs found again and again in Guston's work. In 1947 the figures appeared blindfolded or with gauze over their eyes. Shortly thereafter they became unrecognizable and abstract, but the new weighty shapes in their hermetic background conveyed the same alienation and fear. His controversial switch in 1970 to cartoon Ku Klux Klan figures smoking cigars and driving convertibles still retained the old themes of human combativeness and its ugly undercurrents.

Those who knew Guston claim the paintings were very much a part of him. During his two major transition periods in the late 1940s and 60s, he regularly destroyed everything he started, brooding for days over a shape or a pigment. He was slow to convert to abstract art and even less enthusiastic about the first wave of Pop Art and the new celbrity status of artists. He felt the work of Andy Warhol and others like him was "blasphemous—like feasting on pork after Yom Kippur services." But five years later, "I got sick and tired of all that purity," he told *Art News* in 1970. "I want to tell stories."

His new stories had a droll, deceptively familiar veneer. Matchbooks, clocks, shoes, a tea cup, anything lying around the studio was often included in his sly portraits of contemporary menace. The reverie effect of so many of his earlier paintings was gone completely in the new harsh lines and comic, wide-awake figures. These and his first representational efforts won prizes and are exhibited in a few American museums, but it is his dark, quivering, blocky masses and wispy threads in motion for which he will be remembered. His abstract paintings are still exhibited and collected all over the world, and will undoubtedly endure long after the art movement which inspired them.   A.B.P.

Married Musa McKim, painter 1937. Daughter: Musa Jane Kadish Mayer, b. 1943. Jewish. Brought to USA 1919. Educ: Manual Arts High Sch., Los Angeles; scholarship to Otis Art Inst., Los Angeles 1930. Traveled and worked as muralist in Mexico 1934; muralist for Works Progress Admin.'s Fed. Art Project in N.Y. 1936–40; taught at New York Studio Sch. as part of Fed. Arts Program 1936–40; Painting Instr., Univ. of Iowa, Iowa City 1941–45; Artist in Residence, Head of Painting Dept., Washington Univ., St. Louis, Mo. 1945–47; traveled in Italy, France, Spain, and England 1948–49; active in New York Abstract Expressionist Sch. of Painting 1949–70; taught at Univ. of Minn., Minneapolis 1950; Adjunct Prof., New York Univ. 1951–58; Painting Instr., Pratt Inst., N.Y. 1953–57; Guest Critic, Yale Univ. Summer Sch. 1961, 1963, 1970, 1971, 1973, 1974; Artist in Residence, Brandeis Univ., Waltham, Mass. Spring 1966 and Skidmore Coll., Saratoga Springs, N.Y. 1968; Guest Critic, Columbia Univ. Grad. Sch., N.Y. 1969–70 and 1972; Artist in Residence, American Acad. in Rome 1970–71; Prof., Boston Univ. 1973–75; retired and painting in Woodstock, N.Y. 1975–80. Member, Natl. Inst. of Arts and Letters, N.Y.; Bd. of Trustees, American Acad. in Rome since 1970. Hons: Popular Prize for Works Progress Admin. Bldg. outdoor mural at 1939–40 N.Y. World's Fair; Carnegie Inst. First Prize for Sentimental Moment 1945; Altman Prize, Natl. Acad. of Design, N.Y., for Holiday 1947; Guggenheim Foundn. Fellowship 1947, renewed 1968; Prix de Rome, American Acad. in Rome 1948; American Acad. of Arts and Letters grant 1948; Ford Foundn. grant 1949; Hon. D.F.A., Boston Univ. 1970; Distinguished Teaching Art Award, Coll. Art Assn. of America 1975; Creative Arts Award, Brandeis Univ. 1980. *Exhibitions: one person*—The Midtown Galls., NYC 1945; Sch. of the Mus. of Fine Arts, Boston 1947; Muson-Williams-Proctor Inst., Utica, N.Y. 1947; Univ. of Minn. 1950; Peridot Gall., NYC 1952; Charles Egan Gall., NYC 1953; Sidney Janis Gall., NYC 1956, 1958, 1960, 1961; V Bienal, São Paulo, (retrospective) 1959; XXX Biennale, Venice (retrospective) 1960; Guggenheim Mus., NYC (retrospective which toured Europe) 1962; Los Angeles County Art Mus. (retrospective) 1963; Jewish Mus., (NYC) 1966; Santa Barbara Mus. of Art, Calif. 1966, 1967; Rose Art Mus., Brandeis Univ. (retrospective) 1966; Gertrude Kasle Gall., Detroit 1969, 1973, 1974; Marlborough Gall., NYC 1970; Boston Univ. 1970, 1974; La Jolla Mus. of Modern Art, Calif. 1971; Metropolitan Mus. of Art, (NYC) 1973; David McKee Gall., NYC 1974; San Francisco Mus. of Modern Art (retrospective) 1980. *Group shows*—Stanley Rose Bookshop and Gall., Los Angeles 1931; Univ.

of Ill. 1944, 1961; Twelve Americans, Inst. of Modern Art, Boston 1946; Forty American Painters, 1940–50, Univ. of Minn. 1951; Abstract Painting and Sculpture in America, Mus. of Modern Art, NYC 1951; Abstract Expressionists, Baltimore Mus. of Art 1953; Younger American Painting, Guggenheim Mus. 1954; Modern Art in the U.S., Tate Gall., London 1956; Twelve Americans, Mus. of Modern Art (toured U.S.) 1956; IV Bienal, Museude Arte Moderna, São Paulo 1957; I Inter-American Paintings and Prints Biennial, Mexico City 1958; Nature in Abstraction, Whitney Mus. of American Art, NYC 1958; The New American Painting, Mus. of Modern Art (toured Europe) 1958–59; Modern American Painting, City Art Mus., St. Louis 1959; Eighteen Living American Artists, Whitney Mus. 1959; Philip Guston and Franz Kline, Dwan Gall., Los Angeles 1961; American Vanguard, Guggenheim Mus. (toured Europe) 1961–62; Paintings and Sculpture of a Decade—1954–64, Tate Gall. 1964; Carnegie Inst. 1964; New York Sch.: The First Generation, Los Angeles County Mus. 1965; Univ. of St. Thomas, Texas 1967; The New American Painting and Sculpture: The First Generation, Mus. of Modern Art 1969; N.Y. Painting and Sculpture: 1940–70, Metropolitan Mus. 1969–70; L'Art vivant americain, Fondation Maeght, St. Paul de Vence, France 1970; Immagine per la Citta, Palazzo dell'Accademia, Palazzo Reale, Genoa, Italy 1972; American Art at Mid-Century, Natl. Gall. of Art, Washington, D.C. 1973; Drawings by Five Abstract Expressionist Painters, Hayden Gall., Mass. Inst. of Tech., Boston 1975. *Collections*—Albright-Knox Art Gall., Buffalo; Allentown Art Mus., Pa.; Art Inst. of Chicago; Baltimore Mus. of Art; Bezalel Natl. Mus., Jerusalem; City Art Mus. of St. Louis; Cleveland Mus. of Art; Detroit Inst. of Fine Arts; Fogg Art Mus., Cambridge, Mass.; Guggenheim Mus.; Harvard Univ.; High Mus. of Art, Atlanta; Joseph Hirshorn Mus., Washington, D.C.; Krannert Art Mus., Univ. of Ill., Urbana; Los Angeles County Art Mus.; Metropolitan Mus.; Minneapolis Inst. of Arts; Mus. of Modern Art; Mus. of Art, Univ. of Iowa, Iowa City; Munson-Williams-Proctor Inst., Utica, N.Y.; Natl. Collection of Fine Arts, Smithsonian Instn. and Phillips Collection, Washington, D.C.; San Francisco Mus. of Art; S. Mall, State Capitol, Albany, N.Y.; Roy Neuberger Mus., Purchase, N.Y.; Tate Gall.; Univ. Art Mus. of Texas at Austin; Virginia Mus. of Fine Arts, Richmond; Washington Univ., St. Louis; Whitney Mus.; Worcester Art Mus., Mass.; Yale Univ., New Haven. *Other works*—Reconstruction and Well-Being of the Family, mural for Social Security Admin. Bldg. (now Dept. of Health and Human Services), Washington, D.C. 1938; mural for U.S. Post Office, Commerce, Ga. 1938; Martial Memory, mural for community bldg. of Queensbridge Housing Project, Queens, N.Y. 1938–40; Glass bar murals for steamships, Pres. Monroe, Pres. Van Buren, and Pres. Adams.

Further reading: "Philip Guston," by H.W. Janson, The Magazine of Art, Feb. 1947; Philip Guston by Dore Ashton, 1959; "Guston: A Long Voyage Home," by Irving Sandler, Art News, Dec., 1959; Philip Guston, interview with H.H. Arnason catalogue, 1962; The Unknown Shore by Dore Ashton, 1962; Yes, But . . . A Critical Study of Philip Guston by Dore Ashton, 1976.

HENRY (VALENTINE) MILLER
Novelist, essayist, and painter
Born New York City, U.S.A., December 26th, 1891
Died Pacific Palisades, California, U.S.A., June 7th, 1980

A controversial writer of autobiographical novels, most of them banned in Great Britain and America until the early 1960s because of their sexual frankness, Henry Miller was a major influence in world literature. Although he was initially read only by the literary elites of London, Paris, and New York, Miller became popular when his work was discovered by servicemen stationed in Paris after 1944. They smuggled contraband copies of his books into the English-speaking countries where, critic Kenneth Young said, "Miller's freedom of language and subject had a deep influence on the thousands of writers who benefitted from the literary emancipation from censorship."

Henry Valentine Miller was born of a second-generation German-American family in the Yorkville section of New York City. His father, a merchant who operated a modest tailor shop amid the fashionable stores of Fifth Avenue, moved the family in 1892 to Williamsburg, Brooklyn, where Henry and his mentally retarded sister were raised. In childhood, Miller learned German before English, absorbed the sounds of Yiddish and Polish which filled the Williamsburg streets, and quickly acquired a Brooklyn accent which—despite his later travels—he never lost. In *Black Spring* (1936), he wrote: "I was born in the street and raised in the street. In the street you learn what human beings really are. . . . What is not in the open street is false." A lifelong rebel, Miller regarded his family's Teutonic obsession with thrift, hard work, and straight-laced sexuality as an oppression which he defied "from the time [he] was able to talk."

Miller graduated from high school in 1909 and entered City College of New York but he found the academic atmosphere sterile and left after six weeks. After working for a cement company in Manhattan for two years, Miller's father gave him enough money to attend Cornell University. Instead, Miller said, "I took the money and disappeared with my mistress, a woman old enough to be my mother." He returned home a year later but soon grew restless and left again, traveling primarily in the western United States and working at odd jobs. By 1914 Miller was back in New York and employed by his ailing father in the family business. He also began to write and produced a long, never published essay on Nietzsche; but in 1917, after attempting to turn the shop over to the employees, Miller moved to Washington, D.C. where he worked three years as a clerk for several government agencies.

By 1920 Miller was a husband and father. While working as an employment manager for the Western Union Telegraph Company in New York City, he gathered material for his first (unpublished) fiction, *Clipped Wings,* a parody of the Horatio Alger myth. In 1924, having tired of both his wife and his job, Miller vowed that he would become a writer or starve in the effort to do so. He divorced his first wife and married June Smith, a dancer with literary ambitions, on whom he later based the seductive "Mona and Mara" of his autobiographical trilogy, *The Rosy Crucifixion.* Miller and his wife lived in poverty; he wrote pulp fiction for sex magazines and composed prose poems, called "Mezzotints" which June sold door to door in apartments and speakeasies. In 1927, however, Miller's life and art came together. Recalling his decision to transform himself into a fictional persona, Miller said: "One day . . . I was seized with this idea of planning the book of my life and I stayed up all night doing it. I planned everything that I've written to date in about 40 or 50 typewritten pages." (Miller's life, from childhood until he moved to France in 1930, is chronicled in *Tropic of Capricorn* [1939], *Black Spring,* and the three volumes which make up *The Rosy Crucifixion: Sexus* [1949], *Plexus* [1953], and *Nexus* [1959]. His adventures in Paris are described in the picaresque novel, *Tropic of Cancer.*)

In 1928 Miller's wife scraped together enough money for them to visit Europe. They returned to New York in early 1929 but, in France, Miller found an artistic freedom unknown to him in America where isolation had driven him to the brink of madness and suicide. Miller returned alone to Paris in 1930 and June obtained a divorce in Mexico four years later.

In Paris Miller lived as a bohemian. He worked at various jobs and, frequently destitute, turned to a circle of artist friends, which included Anaïs Nin, for sustenance. In 1931 he published his first serious fictional work, a short story entitled "Mademoiselle Claude," in the *New Review* and, by the end of 1932, *Tropic of Cancer,* sexually explicit and filled with obscenities, was completed. The manuscript was allegedly given to Jack Kahane, the founder of the Obelisk Press, by Ezra Pound with the statement, "Here's a dirty book worth reading." Kahane's edition appeared in 1934 with a dust jacket that warned bookseller's not to display the novel in shop windows.

The narrator and protagonist of *Tropic of Cancer* is Miller himself, a 40-year-old American expatriate living in Paris during the Depression. Miller's fictional world is populated by hustlers, drifters, and artists manqué who missed the glitter of Lost Generation Paris and, when Hemingway and Fitzgerald left, they were too poor to go home. *Tropic*'s heroes are sexual rogues who bed down with pliant secretaries in cheap hotels; as Nietzschean prophets, they forswore the hypocrisies of Western society to celebrate a "new man," the artist, whose task was "to overthrow existing values, to make of the chaos about him an order which is his own, to sow strife and ferment so that those who are dead may be restored to life." Structurally, *Tropic of Cancer* is an impressionistic, at times surrealistic, narrative consisting of 15 untitled chapters in which Miller's distinctive voice—at its best a blend of Joycean stream of consciousness and Whitmanesque exuberance—is finally realized.

During his years in Paris, Miller published two other fictional autobiographies, *Black Spring* and *Tropic of Capricorn.* However, these books were considered pornographic in America and only smuggled-in copies were available there. Thus, Miller's reputation in America far exceeded actual acquaintance with his work.

In 1939 Miller toured Greece with Lawrence Durrell, his friend and fellow novelist. Miller's visit inspired him to write *The Colossus of Maroussi* (1941), a meditation on Greek culture that contained some of his best writing. After the outbreak of World War Two, Miller returned to the United States and, in early 1940, he set off on a year-long tour of the country. His sociological account of these travels was published in 1945 as *The Air-Conditioned Nightmare,* an indictment of America's increasingly consumer-oriented culture.

With his European royalties cut off by the war, Miller, impoverished once again, resorted to publishing appeals for funds in journals such as *The New Republic*. In 1942 he moved to Beverly Glen, California, where he initially received food and lodging from friends; two years later, Miller was given a home at Big Sur near San Francisco. There he became the center of a colony of artists and bohemian admirers, many of whom were Beat generation writers emulating Miller's wandering, anarchistic lifestyle. He also took up painting and continued to write copiously. *Big Sur and the Oranges of Hieronymus Bosch* (1956) is Miller's account of these years.

In 1961, almost three decades after it had been written and published in Paris, *Tropic of Cancer* appeared in the United States. Published by Grove Press, *Tropic* became the subject of extensive litigation. In courtrooms across the country such critics as Harry T. Moore, Mark Schorer, and Aldous Huxley testified to the literary merit of Miller's works, and by 1964 the last legal barriers had been struck down. Over-the-counter purchase of these books was finally permitted and, their notoriety assured, they sold in the millions. Nevertheless, Miller had not achieved financial security until he was well past the age of 70.

Once reviled by middle-class philistines, Miller, in the 1970s, found himself violently denounced by yet another, quite different group—ideological feminists. In *Sexual Politics* (1970) Kate Millett called Miller "a compendium of American sexual neuroses." According to Millett, Miller and his confederates use women for sexual gratification and then "discard them as one might avail oneself of sanitary facilities—Kleenex or toilet paper." She charged that Miller was psychologically incapable of viewing women as other than sexual objects. In *The Prisoner of Sex* (1971), Norman Mailer accused Millett of having quoted Miller selectively, out of context and sometimes inaccurately, a tactic which painted a damaging, one-dimensional picture of a very complex man. He argued that Miller was capable of tenderness and affection as well as of violent passion, and that Miller's view of women resulted from his "utter adoration for the power and the glory and the grandeur of the female in the universe."

In the past two decades, Miller's literary reputation has declined. While Miller's dirty words, graphic episodes, and openness to all forms of experience were once liberating influences, his style of spontaneous writing suffers from an uncontrolled prolixity. Lacking the intellectual discipline of Proust or Joyce, Miller's torrent of words often overwhelms his ideas, his characters, and his best images. According to critic Denis Donoghue, "Reference to Whitman in this context is usual but irrelevant: Miller's theory of life is Darwinian." Thus, Miller's naturalism "leaves him helpless before the casual contents of his mind." Having obscured the distinction between fiction and autobiography, Miller, often at the expense of dramatic structure, indiscriminately records everything in his books and imaginatively transforms very little.

Also, Miller's sex scenes, once shockingly powerful, now seem dull and somewhat contrived. These erotic episodes, marathon bouts of sexual athleticism, were written with a sameness that led one critic to suggest that, for Miller, sex had no more meaning than urination.

Despite the diminution of his literary influence, Henry Miller was a writer of large, if idiosyncratic, talent. A cult figure among overseas G.I.s in the 1940s, rebellious Beats in the 50s, and civil libertarians in

the 60s, Miller's impact on American life was significant. "In his work
and in his career," writes Jeffrey Hart in *National Review*, "Miller was
an avatar of freedom . . . he was part of a cultural movement which
expanded the individual's options."   E.T./M.W.

Son of Henry M., merchant tailor, and Louise Neiting M. Married:
(1) Beatrice Sylvas Wickens, pianist 1917 (div. 1924); (2) June Edith
Smith 1924 (div. 1934); (3) Janina Martha Lepska 1944 (div. ca. 1952);
(4) Eve McClure, artist 1953 (div. 1962); (5) Hoki Takuda, cabaret
singer 1967 (div. 1969). Children: 1st marriage—Barbara, b. 1918; 3rd
marriage—Valentin, b. 1945; Tony, b. 1948. Free-thinker. Educ:
Eastern District High Sch., Brooklyn, grad. 1909; City Coll., NYC
1909–15. Clerk, Atlas Portland Cement Co., ca. 1910–11; ranch hand
1912–13; joined father's tailor shop 1914–17; clerk, War Dept. 1917;
sub-ed. catalogues, Bureau of Econ. Research 1917–18; Mgr, Western
Union Telegraph Co., NYC 1920–24; Freelance writer 1924–29;
proofreader, Chicago Tribune, Paris edition 1932; teacher, Lycée
Carnot, Dijon 1932; Editor, The Booster (later Delta) 1937–38;
Contributing ed., Volontés, Paris, and European ed., The Phoenix
1937–38. Active as a painter; exhib. of paintings London 1944 and Los
Angeles 1966. Member, Natl. Inst. of Arts and Letters 1958. Hons:
Formentor Prize Cttee. Citation 1961; Legion of Honor 1975. *Books:
Novels*—Tropic of Cancer, Paris, 1934 (U.S. 1961, U.K. 1963); Black
Spring, Paris 1936 (U.S. 1963, U.K. 1965); Tropic of Capricorn, Paris
1939 (U.S. 1961, U.K. 1964); Quiet Days in Clichy, Paris 1956 (U.S.
1965, U.K. 1966); The Rosy Crucifixion trilogy: Sexus, Paris 1949
(U.S. 1965, U.K. 1969), Plexus, Paris 1953 (U.K. 1963, U.S. 1965),
Nexus, Paris 1960 (U.K. 1963, U.S. 1965); *Correspondence*—(with
Michael Fraenkel) Hamlet, vol. I, 1939, 2nd ed. 1943, vol. II, 1941;
(with Hilaire Hiller and William Sarovan) Why Abstract? 1945; (with
Alfred Perles and Lawrence Durrell) Art and Outrage, 1961; Law-
rence Durrell and Henry Miller; A Private Correspondence (ed. by
George Wickes), 1963; Letters to Anaïs Nin, 1965; (with J.R. Child)
Collector's Quest: Correspondence (1947–65), 1968; Letters of Henry
Miller and Wallace Fowlie (1943–72), 1975. *Travel*—The Colossus of
Maroussi, 1941; The Air-Conditioned Nightmare, 1945; Remember to
Remember, 1947; Greece, 1964; First Impressions of Greece, 1973.
Literary Criticism—Patchen: Man of Anger and Light, 1946; Rim-
baud, Time of the Assassins, 1956; Books Tangent to Circle, Reviews,
1963; The World of Lawrence, A Passionate Appreciation, pub.
posth. 1980. *Autobiographical*—Aller Retour New York, Paris 1935
(U.S. 1945); Of, By and About Henry Miller, 1947; The Books in My
Life, 1952; My Life and Times, 1971; On Turning Eighty, 1972; Henry
Miller in Conversation with George Belmont, 1972; Henry Miller
from Brooklyn, 1974. *On Painting*—The Angel is My Water-Mark,
1944; Echolalia (Reproductions of Watercolors by Miller), 1945; The
Waters Reglitterized, 1950; To Paint Is to Love Again, 1960. *Plays*—
Scenario, a Film with Sound, 1937; Just Wild About Harry: A Melo-
Melo in 7 Scenes, 1963 (produced in Spoleto, Italy 1963). *Other*—
What Are You Going To Do About Alf?, Paris (privately printed),
U.S. 1944; Money and How It Gets That Way, Paris 1938, U.S. 1945;
Max and the White Phagocytes (stories), 1938; The Cosmological Eye
(essays), 1939; The World of Sex, 1940, rev. 1957; The Wisdom of the
Heart, 1941; Sunday after the War (stories and essays), 1944, 1947;
The Plight of the Creative Artist in the United States of America,
1944; Henry Miller Miscellanea, 1945; Obscenity and the Law of
Reflection, 1945; Maurizius Forever, 1946; Portrait of General Grant,
1947; Varda, the Master Builder, 1947; Nights of Love and Laughter,

1955; A Devil in Paradise; the story of Conrad Moruand, 1956;
Argument about Astrology, 1956; The Henry Miller Reader (ed. by
Lawrence Durrell), 1959; Intimate Henry Miller, 1959; Interview with
Henry Miller in Writers at Work/The Paris Interviews (2nd series) ed.
by George Plimpton, 1963; Henry Miller on Writing, 1964; Selected
Prose, 1965; Insomnia, or, the Devil at Large, 1970; Journey to an
Unknown Land, 1972; Nightmare Notebook, 1975.
Further reading: Miller: A Chronology and Bibliography by Bern
Porter, 1945; A Bibliography of Henry Miller, 1945–61 by Maxine
Renken, 1962; Henry Miller by Kingsley Widmer, 1963; The Mind
and Art of Henry Miller by W.A. Gordon, 1967; Sexual Politics by
Kate Millett, 1970; The Prisoner of Sex by Norman Mailer, 1971;
Miller: Three Decades of Criticism by Edward B. Mitchell (ed.), 1971;
Genius and Lust: A Journey through the Major Writings of Henry
Miller by Norman Mailer, 1976; Always Merry and Bright: The Life
of Henry Miller by Martin Jay, 1978.

SIR CHARLES ORDE
British Envoy to the Baltic nations and Ambassador to Chile
Born Nunnykirk, Morpeth, Northumberland, England, October 25th,
1884
Died Nunnykirk, Morpeth, Northumberland, England, June 7th,
1980

Sir Charles Orde was Britain's envoy in Latvia, Lithuania and Estonia
at a time when these Baltic nations—strategically important to the
West in the 1930s and early 40s—enjoyed a major trading relationship
with Britain. He served there until 1940 when the Soviet Union
dominated the area. During the rest of the Second World War years,
Sir Charles was Britain's ambassador in Chile.

Charles Orde was educated at Eton and King's College, Cambridge,
where he was an exhibitioner, graduating in 1907. In 1909 he
entered the British Foreign Office as a clerk and became a counsellor
in 1929.

His most noteworthy activity while at the foreign office was as
Secretary to the 1925 Arms Traffic Convention of the League of
Nations. The convention was designed as an extension and replacement of the 1919 convention of St. Germain. It concluded with
ratification of the anti-gas protocol forbidding the use of gas and
bacteria in warfare and took the first step towards a general system of
international agreement concerning arms trade. The trade agreements
were designed to check the danger that the uncontrolled import of
arms, including smaller revolvers, could spell for the importing
country.

In late 1937, Charles Orde left his post in the Foreign Office as head
of the Far Eastern Department and was appointed King's Envoy
Extraordinary and Minister Plenipotentiary to Riga, Tallinn and
Kovno—the respective capitals of Latvia, Estonia and Lithuania.
These Baltic nations were particularly important to the British, both
for economic and political reasons. 80 percent of Lithuania's trade was
with the British and while trade with Latvia and Estonia was less, the
volume never dipped below 50 percent of their total exports. They

produced dairy and agricultural products necessary to Britain while in return they provided a natural market for British finished goods. And politically the Baltic nations—situated between two increasingly aggressive powers, Nazi Germany and Soviet Russia—provided an outpost for observation. Latvia, Lithuania and Estonia maintained their independence until 1940 when the Soviets, freed from entanglements with the Finns, occupied all three countries. Soviet commissars were appointed as leaders of state and in June Orde left the Baltic arena, in a sense symbolizing the end of independence and self-determination for these small countries.

Following his knighthood, Sir Charles was appointed Ambassador Extraordinary and Plenipotentiary Designate to the Republic of Chile. The American diplomat Claude Bowers wrote in his memoirs, "Though we did not see eye to eye on rupture with the Axis or on the 300-mile safety zone in the Pacific, we worked generally in close cooperation throughout the war and well into the post-war period." Although Orde officially resigned in June 1945, he remained in South America as consultant and observer for the British. He died at his home in Northumberland at the age of 95.   S.J.

Son of William O., deputy Lt.-Col. Married Francis Fortune Davison 1914 (d. 1949). Two sons; two daughters. Educ: Eton Coll., Bucks.; King's Coll., Cambridge, B.A. First Class Tripos, Part I, Div. II, 1907. Clerk, British Foreign Office of Nations 1925; Counsellor, Head of Far Eastern Dept., British Foreign Office 1929–38; King's Envoy Extraordinary and Minister Plenipotentiary to Latvia, Estonia and Lithuania 1938–40; Ambassador Extraordinary and Plenipotentiary Designate to the Republic of Chile 1940–45. Hons: CMG 1931; KCMG 1940.

MARIAN SPYCHALSKI
Polish Head of State and Minister of Defense
Born Lodz, Poland, March 6th, 1906
Died Warsaw, Poland, June 7th, 1980

Marian Spychalski joined the Polish Communist Party (PCP) in 1926 and remained an active member until 1938, when Stalin's Comintern dissolved it because "it had been penetrated to the core by Trotskyite as well as Polish nationalistic subversive elements." In 1942, with Stalin's implicit consent, the Polish Worker's Party (PWP) was organized and Spychalski was a leading party cadre. As leader of the left-wing underground resistance movement in Poland and known as "Colonel Marek," he was received by Stalin in 1944 and chosen as Chief of Staff of the Polish High Command and Mayor of Warsaw.

The PWP, having few members with significant ties to Moscow, developed a platform stressing national patriotism and a certain measure of autonomy from Russian influence. They were nevertheless dedicated to the establishment of party rule. In 1948, however, the concept of a Polish road to socialism, which had been tolerated as helpful during the takeover period for tactical reasons, had now become dangerous in view of Tito's [q.v.] break with Moscow. A purge of less sympathetic members of the PWP took place. General Spychalski was replaced by the Russian General Rossokowsky in the Defense Ministry. In 1950, as the purge intensified, Spychalski was arrested and accused of supporting nationalist elements during the war, of having concealed his past from the party, and of allowing infiltration of the army by prewar career officers and intelligence agents. In 1951 Spychalski confessed at "show trials" that a group of Polish army officers had collaborated with the Gestapo.

The bloodless October Revolution of 1956—primarily nationalist as opposed to socio-economic in character and having blossomed with Khrushchev's 'thaw'—brought Gomulka back into power. Spychalski was released from prison and played an increasingly prominent role in the formulation and support of Gomulka's policies. With the return to a policy of rapid industrial growth and the subsequent need for tighter political controls, Spychalski's focus of opinion narrowed. In 1966 he attacked Cardinal Wyszynski and "politicians in cassocks" for celebrating the thousandth anniversary of Christianity.

As political infighting reached its peak in the wake of student demonstrations in April of 1968, Spychalski was appointed by Gomulka as Chairman of the Council of State. These days are referred to as the darkest days of Gomulka's regime and included increased suppression and censorship, support of the Czech invasion despite widespread pro-Dûbcek sentiments among the Poles, and a political purge of "liberals." Unlike 1956, however, it was economic factors that brought down Gomulka, with Spychalski close behind. Food price increases averaging 16–20 percent stimulated a wave of workers' strikes which eventually caused the government's collapse.

Joseph Fiszman, reflecting on the nature of Polish leadership in Gomulka's government, writes: ". . . they are nationalistic, conservative, status-quo oriented, culturally and esthetically narrow and committed to the system as an authority structure, a structure of power rather than one of beliefs and values which would set the world on fire."   S.J.

Son of Jósef S. and Franciszka (Léskiewicz) S. Married Barbara Skrzypczyk 1935. Two daughters. Educ: Warsaw Polytechnic. Mil. Service: Resistance leader, WWII, Poland. Member, Polish Communist Party 1926–38; Architect, Poznán and Warsaw 1928–39; organizer and Member, Polish Worker's Party 1942–48; Chief of Staff, Polish High Command and Mayor of Warsaw 1944–45; Vice Minister of Natl. Defense 1945–48; Deputy, Seym (Parliament) 1945–51; Minister for Reconstruction of Poland's Western Territories 1949; expelled from Polish Workers Party 1949; prison sentence 1950–56; Minister of Natl. Defense 1957–68; Deputy, Seym 1957–72; elected to Central Cttee. and Politburo 1959; Marshal of Poland 1963–80. Member, Politburo 1948–49, 1959–70 and Cttee. for Building a Monument to Warsaw Heroes of WWII 1956; Chmn., Council of State 1968–70; Chmn., All Poland Cttee. of Natl. Unity Front 1968–70; Member, Liaison Delegation of People's Council to Union of Polish Patriots in USSR WWII. Hons: Grand Prix, Paris Intnl. Exhib. 1937; Grunwald Cross 2nd Class 1945; Order of Banner of Labor 1959; Order of Builder's of People's Poland.

SIR BILLY BUTLIN
British entrepreneur and holiday camp pioneer
Born South Africa, September 29th, 1899
Died Jersey, Channel Islands, June 12th, 1980

Sir Billy Butlin, whose seaside camps helped to revolutionize the holiday habits of millions of Britons in the years following the Second World War, began his working life in poverty and died a multi-millionaire. He never lost sight of his humble beginnings and when his enterprise began to flourish, he became one of Britain's best-known charitable benefactors.

Butlin, son of a cycle shop keeper, was born in South Africa just before the turn of the century. He later recalled how his mother aroused his interest in the entertainment business through her stories of life in her native Gloucestershire where she sold her father's gingerbread at country fairs. At the age of ten, Billy found himself following in his mother's footsteps when he was taken for a family holiday in England and invited by his uncle to help out on the gingerbread stalls. Subsequently, the Butlin family moved to Canada and by the age of 14, Billy was working for Eaton's department store in Toronto. His family's travels had cost him his education—he received only about three years' formal schooling, he once estimated. In the department store Butlin worked as messenger, counter assistant and clerk. At the outbreak of the First World War, he lied about his age in order to enlist as a drummer boy in the Canadian Army. He saw active service in France and on return to Canada went back to Eaton's, accepting a job in the store's advertising department.

He had acquired a taste for adventure, however, and overcoming the opposition of his parents, he persuaded his mother to loan him enough money for a trip to England. At Montreal Butlin joined the crew of a cattle boat bound for Liverpool where he arrived in 1921. In order to save the fare, he walked the 150 miles to Bristol where he found his uncle, Marshall Hill, who had established himself as a traveling fun-fair showman and promoter. Billy worked for his uncle, maintaining the mechanical amusements, and eventually saved sufficient money to buy a hoopla stall. Later he branched out on his own, and by 1926 Butlin's amusements had achieved a country-wide reputation. An individual style characterized Butlin's business ventures throughout his life. His employees in their white coats marked with a large letter *B*, became familiar throughout the land as a symbol of entertainment.

But Butlin dreamed about ways of providing entertainment which was not at the mercy of Britain's changeable weather. Hundreds of thousands of people every year flocked to English coastal resorts for a hard-earned week's holiday only to endure rain. So Butlin purchased a potato field in the Lincolnshire seaside town of Skegness, and there, in 1935, he opened his first holiday camp. Providing accommodation and food affordable by low-income families, the camp incorporated in one sheltered area all the basic facilities and a variety of entertainments. The camp was an instant success. Built to accommodate 1,000 people, the size was doubled for the second year. Adhering to his motto, "Sell yourself big," Butlin opened his second holiday camp, at Clacton-on-Sea in Essex in 1937. His third, at Filey in Yorkshire, was incomplete at the outbreak of the Second World War.

Early in the war the camps were taken over by the government for use as military accommodation while Butlin joined the Ministry of Supply as Director-General of Hostels. Just two months after cessation of hostilities the major part of the Filey camp was completed, and Billy Butlin was back in business. In 1946 he was catering to some 4,000 holidaymakers a week at Filey, and by 1947 the Skegness and Clacton camps had been renovated and reopened and new camps started at Ayr in Scotland and Pwllheli, Gwynedd, Wales. In the years after the war when holiday money was in short supply, Butlin's inexpensive camps reached the peak of their popularity in the founder's original conception. Later, to meet changing holiday fashions, the Butlin camps sought not just the lower income groups wanting a basic holiday, but also those who could afford a higher standard of accommodation and more sophisticated entertainment. It was a timely adaptation and the Butlin camps continued through the 1970s to cater every year to many thousands of holidaymakers. Of his changing clientele, Butlin once said: ". . . now they've been abroad, they want a bit of Continental glamour . . . bedrooms in chalets and not so much organization."

Butlin himself retired from active management in 1968 and handed over to his son Robert. In 1972, the Rank Organization acquired a majority shareholding in both Butlin's Ltd. and Butlin Properties and Sir Billy was named President.

Outside his business ventures, and continuing long after his retirement, Sir Billy Butlin was a well-known benefactor, both to causes in the entertainment world and those outside it. He was knighted for his services to charity in 1966.   M.D.

Born William Edmund Butlin. Son of William B., engineer and shopkeeper, and Bertha B. Married Norah Faith Cheriton (div.; d. 1976). One son; three daughters. Emigrated from South Africa to Canada 1910, to England 1921. Educ: various schs. in Toronto and in Bristol, England. Mil. Service: Royal Canadian Army, France 1915–19. Messenger, clerk, shop asst., Toronto 1913–15; 1919–20. Asst., Marshall Hill's Amusements, S. and S.W. England 1921–26; founded his own fairground amusement business 1926; established first Butlin Holiday Camp, Skegness 1935; Founder Butlin's Ltd. and Butlin Properties Ltd. 1935: Chmn. and Jt. Managing Dir. 1935–68; Pres. since 1972. Member: Variety Club of Great Britain (served 3 times as Pres.); Vaudeville Golfing Soc. (also Pres.); Variety Club Intnl. (also C.P.). Hons: M.B.E. 1944; knighted 1964; Hon. Member: Worshipful Co. of Gardeners; Worshipful Co. Gold and Silver Wyre Drawers; Companion, Water Rats.

MASAYOSHI OHIRA
Prime Minister of Japan
Born Toyohama, Shikoku Island, Kagawa Prefecture, Japan, March 12th, 1910
Died Tokyo, Japan, June 12th, 1980

Masayoshi Ohira, who died in office as Prime Minister of Japan, was born to a poor farming family on the island of Shikoku in 1910. A convert to Christianity at an early age, he worked his way through

public school, becoming a marathon runner and a sumo-wrestling champion. After the death of his father, the 16-year-old Ohira was sent by his eldest brother to the elite Tokyo University of Commerce (now Hitotsubashi University), where he majored in economics, was active in the Salvation Army and the YMCA, and kept aloof from the ultranationalist fervor that pervaded Japan in the prewar years.

In 1936 Ohira began a long career at the Ministry of Finance, concluding with a term as private secretary to Minister Hayeto Ikeda. In 1952, at Ikeda's suggestion, he ran for election to the House of Representatives, the lower house of the Japanese Diet, from his native Kagawa Prefecture as a member of the Liberal Democratic Party (which, despite its name, is a conservative organization supported by big business interests). He retained the seat for the rest of his life.

Ohira's rise to prominence in the Liberal Democratic Party (LDP) began in 1960, when Ikeda, now Prime Minister, appointed him chief Cabinet secretary. Two years later Ikeda raised him to Minister of Foreign Affairs. Though he claimed to be an amateur in the field of foreign policy, he soon proved himself a formidable negotiator, arranging quick settlements of stalled Korean and Burmese reparations claims and affirming the nation's commitment to worldwide nuclear disarmament. Ikeda, acting on his advice, made concessions to the Socialist Party in the Diet to prevent the development of an overly powerful opposition. The economic growth that Japan experienced in the postwar years was largely a result of Ohira's work in establishing and maintaining close economic ties with the United States.

The shrewd, dignified Ohira occupied high-level posts in the LDP and served as Minister of International Trade and Industry in Eisaku Sato's cabinet before joining the cabinet of fellow LDP leader Kakuei Tanaka as Foreign Minister in 1972. He continued his policy of aligning Japan with the U.S. on most issues and engineered Japan's diplomatic reconciliation with the People's Republic of China, opening the way for a "peace and friendship" treaty and the rapid increase of trade between the two countries.

A crisis swept the LDP in 1974 when Tanaka was forced to resign following accusations that he had accepted a $42 million bribe from Lockheed Aircraft. Ohira and Takeo Fukuda, another leader in the faction-ridden LDP, agreed to unite behind a third leader, Takeo Miki, who became Prime Minister with their support. Ohira served in his cabinet as Minister of Finance. Miki, in turn, was replaced by Fukuda in 1976, and Ohira assumed the post of secretary-general of the LDP.

In 1978 Fukuda came up for re-election as chief of the party and was challenged by three faction leaders, including Ohira, who accused the incumbent of promoting nuclear armament and of inciting right-wing extremists to renewed militarism. The last-minute support of former Prime Minister Tanaka, who commanded a superior political machine, threw the victory to Ohira.

Once installed as Prime Minister, Ohira carefully balanced his cabinet with representatives of all five major LDP factions and announced a reduction in the planned domestic growth rate, the result of a decline in exports stemming from the depreciation of the U.S. dollar against the Japanese yen. His first major crisis in foreign policy was the threat by Vietnam to invade Cambodia over a border dispute in December 1978. Ohira responded by offering Nguyen Duy Trinh, Vietnam's Foreign Minister, an economic aid package that included grants of four billion yen (about $195 million), commodity loans worth ten billion yen, and the loan of 150,000 tons of rice, on condition that Vietnam negotiate a peaceful settlement. Vietnam invaded Cambodia later in the month, and the program was suspended. Deng Xiaoping, Deputy Premier of the People's Republic of China, suggested that Japan and China initiate joint diplomatic action on Cambodia's behalf, but Ohira, wary of incurring retaliation from the USSR, Vietnam's ally, declined to accept.

Prime Minister Ohira leading top party leaders of his Liberal Democratic Party in *Banzai* cheers

At a meeting with President Carter in May 1979, Ohira promised to correct a growing trade imbalance by expanding Japanese markets for U.S. exports and secured assurances from President Carter that U.S. troops would not be withdrawn from South Korea, Japan's western neighbor, until North Korea adopted a less threatening stance. In July he hosted the fifth annual economic summit meeting of the major industrial nations.

To shore up the LDP's power in the Diet, Ohira called general elections for the House of Representatives for June 1979, a year earlier than required. He was confident that the party would receive a comfortable majority. However, his proposals for tax increases to offset the national budget deficit alienated the electorate, and the LDP barely scraped by with the assistance of ten allied independents.

During the next eight months, Ohira's administration was beset by a series of corruption scandals involving high-ranking officials. Although Ohira himself was not under suspicion—his nonsmoking, nondrinking, book-loving habits contrasted strongly with those of many Japanese politicians—he was criticized for not taking more effective action against his implicated associates.

The holding of American hostages by the Khomeini regime in Iran resulted in further troubles for Ohira. Secretary of State Cyrus Vance criticized Japan for importing Iranian oil which the U.S. had refused to buy and for lending financial assistance to Teheran after U.S. banks froze Iranian assets. Ohira responded with a promise to lower oil purchase levels and to prohibit Japanese financial institutions from extending further credit to Iran, but cautioned the U.S. not to resort to force in ending the crisis. His efforts to secure additional supplies of oil from Mexico were not successful, and his popularity with Japanese voters was hurt by the nearly double-digit inflation rate caused by rising oil prices.

On May 17, a few days after Ohira attended the funeral of President Tito of Yugoslavia [q.v.], his government was suddenly toppled by the unexpected passage of a no-confidence motion in the Diet. This motion, one of many routinely introduced by the opposition Socialist Party and routinely voted down by the LDP majority, had passed because LDP faction leaders Fukuda and Miki ordered their followers to abstain rather than help Ohira. It was the first time that a Japanese Prime Minister was ousted by such a motion.

The defeated Ohira dissolved the House of Representatives and called general elections for June. Although he expected to continue as head of the LDP, and hence as the probable Prime Minister of the next government, his health was deteriorating, and LDP leaders began to look for a successor. On May 31 he was hospitalized for exhaustion; there were rumors that he had suffered a heart attack. He died two weeks later.

The LDP was returned to power with a solid majority in the June elections, with Zenko Suzuki taking office as Prime Minister. J.P./T.D.

Son of Toshikichi O. and Saku (Takuma) O., farmers. Married Shigeko Suzuki 1937. Children: Masaki; Hiroshi; Akira; Yoshiko. Christian. Educ: Takamatsu Commercial High Sch., grad. 1933; Tokyo Univ. of Commerce (now Hitotsubashi Univ.), degree in econs. 1936. With Ministry of Finance, Tokyo 1936–52: Supt., Yokohama Internal Revenue Office 1937–38; Private Secty. to Minister of Finance 1949–52. Member of the House of Representatives from Kagawa Prefecture since 1952; Chief Cabinet Secty. 1960–62; Minister of Foreign Affairs 1962–64, 1972–74; Minister of Intnl. Trade and Industry 1968–70; Minister of Finance 1974–76; Prime Minister 1978–80. With Liberal Democratic Party: Deputy Secty.-Gen. 1964; Chmn., Policy Bd. 1967–68; Secty.-Gen. 1976–79; Pres. since 1978. *Author:* Sugao no Daigishi (A Parliamentarian As He Is), 1954; Random Thoughts on Public Finance, 1956.
Further reading: Japan Today: People, Places, Power by William H. Forbis, 1975.

MILBURN STONE
Film, television, and stage actor
Born Burrton, Kansas, U.S.A., July 5th, 1904
Died La Jolla, California, U.S.A., June 12th, 1980

For 20 years Milburn Stone portrayed the gruff, arthritic Doc Adams on the television series *Gunsmoke,* and in a film career spanning more than 40 years, he appeared in more than 150 movies.

His father was a storekeeper in Burrton, Kansas and his mother a Kansas pioneer who had been brought up in a sod house. While Milburn was still a child, his father moved the family to Larned, Kansas, to obtain work. Dodge City (the eventual locale of *Gunsmoke)* was only 30 miles away, but the legendary past of the town had little influence on the young Stone. He was far more impressed by his uncle Joe Stone, one of the leading Broadway actors of the day, and Milburn never wavered from his desire to pursue an acting career.

Stone's formal education ended when he turned down a Congressional appointment to the U.S. Naval Academy and instead joined a repertory company that was touring the Midwest. He made his theatrical debut in Kansas, playing in a tent. In the late 1920s Stone left repertory for vaudeville. In 1930, he teamed up with another actor in a vaudeville act "Stone and Strain, songs, dances and snappy chatter." Two years later he made his first Broadway appearance, in Sinclair Lewis's *The Jayhawker,* a play set in Kansas during the Civil War. In the mid-1930s, Stone began to make a comfortable living in films, taking lead parts in many low-budget action productions, including some serials. He also gained feature roles in more expensive productions, typically playing a renegade or a villain, though often with a redeeming streak.

Despite his many film appearances, Stone failed to gain popular recognition until he created the character of the frock-coated Doc Adams on *Gunsmoke*. He played the irascible, compassionate physician of Dodge City, Kansas, from the series' inception in 1955 to its end in September 1975, winning an Emmy Award in 1968 for best supporting actor. Stone freely admitted that he patterned Doc on his own grandfather who had fought in the Civil War. The rustic Western character became so well-known to television viewers that before the series ended, Stone was quoted as saying: "Except for my immediate family, Milburn Stone no longer exists. To everyone else, I'm Doc. Good old Doc Adams. Getting so I have to restrain myself from making house calls."

Doc Adams's gruffness was not totally confined to the screen. Stone became the self-appointed, unofficial guardian of *Gunsmoke*, and he was not reluctant to take issue with anyone he thought was undermining the series. He openly criticized Dennis Weaver (who had created the role of the limping deputy, Chester) for his lateness and "high spirits" on the set; he argued that the appointment of a British producer, Philip Leacock, led to scripts being written by people with little understanding of the show and its milieu.

Stone never lost his love of the stage and a responsive audience. During the *Gunsmoke* years, he formed a song and comedy act with Ken Curtis, who played Festus on the series. The two toured extensively in the Midwest, performing at rodeos and state fairs. Curtis, one of Stone's closest friends and admirers, in 1965 said of the actor: "He is one of the most entertaining fellows I have ever been around. When he decides to do something, he doesn't pull any punches. You've got to admire him for it, because he really stands up and fights. He's one of the most honest guys I've ever met."

When the *Gunsmoke* series ended, Stone and his wife, Jane, moved to Rancho Santa Fe, north of San Diego, where he concentrated on raising prize livestock. He died of heart failure, nine years after he first underwent heart surgery.   M.D.

Son of John S., storekeeper. Married Jane S. One daughter. Educ: Larned, Kansas. Joined repertory in Kansas 1919; commenced vaudeville acts 1930; Broadway stage debut 1932. Film and television actor 1934–75. Hons: Emmy Award (as Doc Adams in CBS TV series, Gunsmoke) for best supporting actor 1968. *Films:* Ladies Crave Excitement, 1934; The Milky Way, China Clipper, The Princess Comes Across, The Three Mesquiteers, and Two in a Crowd, 1936; A Doctor's Diary, Atlantic Flight, Federal Bullets, Blazing Barriers, Swing It Professor, Youth on Parole, The Thirteenth Man, and The Man in Blue, 1937; Port of Missing Girls, Mr. Boggs Steps Out, Wives under Suspicion, Sinners in Paradise, Crime School, Paroled from the Big House, and California Frontiers, 1938; Mystery Plane, King of the Turf, Society Smugglers, Blind Alibi, Young Mr. Lincoln, Stunt Pilot, Tropic Fury, Sky Patrol, Danger Flight, Nick Carter Master Detective, Charlie McCarthy Master Detective, and Crashing Through, 1939; Chasing Trouble, Enemy Agent, An Angel From Texas, Framed, Colorado, The Great Plane Robbery, and Give Us Wings, 1940; The Phantom Cowboy, The Great Train Robbery, and Death Valley Outlaws, 1941; Reap the Wild Wind, Rubber Racketeers, Frisco Lil, and Police Bullets, 1942; Keep 'em Slugging, You Can't Beat the Law, Sherlock Holmes Faces Death, Captive Wild Woman,

Get Going, Corvette K-225, Gung Ho, and the Mad Ghoul, 1943; The
Imposter, Hi Good Lookin'!, Hat Check Honey, Moon Over Las
Vegas, Jungle Woman, Phantom Lady, Twilight on the Prairie, and
The Great Alaskan Mystery (serial), 1944; The Master Key (serial),
The Beautiful Cheat, The Daltons Ride Again, The Frozen Chest, I'll
Remember April, On Stage Everybody!, She Gets Her Man, Strange
Confession, and Swing Out Sister!, 1945; Danger Woman, Inside Job,
Little Miss Big, The Spider Woman Strikes Back, Notorious Gentle-
man, Strange Conquest, and Her Adventurous Night, 1946; Killer
Dill, Second Chance, The Michigan Kid, and Heading for Heaven,
1947; Train to Alcatraz, 1948; The Green Promise, Calamity Jane and
Sam Bass, Sky Dragon, and The Judge, 1949; No Man of Her Own,
The Fireball, Snow Dog, and Branded, 1950; Road Block, 1951; The
Atomic City and The Savage, 1952; The Sun Shines Bright, Arrowhead, and Pickup on South Street, 1953; The Siege of Red River,
1954; Black Tuesday, The Long Gray Line, White Feather, Smoke
Signal, and The Private War of Major Benson, 1955; Drango, 1957;
and others. *Plays:* The Jayhawker, New York, 1932; also Around the
Corner, and other. *Television:* Gunsmoke series (as Doc Adams)
1955–75; episode of Dragnet 1952, Front Row Center 1956, Climax
1957, and others.

EVELYN (SIBLEY) LAMPMAN
Writer of children's books and radio scripts
Born, Dallas, Oregon, U.S.A., April 18th, 1907
Died Portland, Oregon, U.S.A., June 13th 1980

Evelyn Sibley Lampman, a popular author for over 25 years, wrote 50
books for children ranging from adventure and fantasy to historical
and biographical fiction. Noted for her understanding portrayals of
the cultural and emotional problems of ethnic children—especially
American Indians—Lampman was also praised for presenting realistic
characters without recourse to old-fashioned sentimentality. Her
grandparents had made the westward trek to Oregon by covered
wagon and Evelyn, who decided to become an author in the first
grade, grew up familiar with the stories and traditions of American
pioneer life, a background that played an important role in many of
her stories.

Following her graduation from Oregon State University in 1929,
Lampman worked as a continuity writer at Radio KEX, a Portland
station, until her marriage in 1934 to wildlife editor Herbert Sheldon
Lampman. She returned to KEX in 1937 as Continuity Chief where
she remained for eight years. Her only non-juvenile work, *Of Mikes
and Men,* related her early experiences as a radio writer. In 1945
Lampman accepted a position at Radio KGW as Editorial Director,
writing and directing dramatized educational programs for Portland's
elementary schools; for her work there she received two Jean Hersholt
awards for script writing.

As Editorial Director Lampman discovered that she enjoyed
working with children. When her fourth-grade daughter complained
of not being able to find enough books at the library, Lampman
decided to write children's fiction. *Crazy Creek* was published in 1948
and the following year Lampman received an award from the

Committee on the Art of Democratic Living for her second book *Treasure Mountain*.

During the 1950s Lampman, often writing two books a year, alternated between using her own name and the pseudonym Lynn Bronson. In *The Bounces of Cynthiann'* (1950) Lampman realistically depicts self-reliance and interdependence in the orphaned Bounce children who are adopted by the town of Cynthianna. *Elder Brother* (1951) was Lampman's first story of an ethnic group; in it she related the difficulties experienced by a Chinese-American family when they adopt a boy from China. Lampman resigned from her post as Editorial Director in 1952 to become a full-time writer. Shortly thereafter her first fantasy adventure, *Captain Apple's Ghost* (1952) was published; another popular fantasy, *The Shy Stegosaurus of Cricket Creek* appeared in 1955. *Navajo Sister* (1956), in which an Indian girl begins to understand herself as she learns to adjust to the strangeness of a government school, is the first of Lampman's books to deal with the conflicts of Native Americans caught between two cultures. *Special Year* (1959) was a thoughtful exploration of the painful awakening of pre-adolescent girls to the gap between peer pressure and parental values.

Much of Lampman's work in the late 1960s and in the 70s reflects an historical interest; her best and most important books were published during this period. Three stories based on events in American Indian history display Lampman's sympathy for the American Indian plight. *The Tilted Sombrero* (1966) described the first Indian revolt against Spanish rule at the outbreak of the Mexican War of Independence; *Cayuse Courage* (1970)—for which Lampman received a Western Writers of America Golden Spur award—viewed the Whitman Massacre of 1848 through the eyes of a young Indian boy; and *White Captives* (1975), based on the story of Olive Oatman's capture by an Apache raiding party in the mid-1800s, showed that Lampman's understanding for the Indians did not exclude an appreciation of the white man's point of view.

In *Bargain Bride* (1977), her last book, Lampman departed from the ethnic theme to tell the story of Oregon's pioneer brides. Throughout her career as a children's writer, Lampman, who skillfully incorporated history, serious ideas and realistic characters into lively and often suspenseful stories, enjoyed popularity among a wide audience of children.

J.S.

Born Evelyn Sibley. Daughter of Joseph E. S. and Harriet Bronson S. Married Herbert Sheldon Lampman, wildlife editor 1934 (d. 1943). Children: Linda Sibley L. McIsaac, Anne Hathaway L. Knutson. Episcopalian. Educ: Oregon State Univ., Corvallis, B.S. 1929. Continuity writer 1929–34 and Continuity Chief 1937–45, KEX Radio Station, Portland; Education Dir., KGW Radio Station, Portland, 1945–52; Writer of children books, since 1948. Member Delta Delta Delta. Hons: two Jean Hersholt awards for radio script writing; Cttes on the Art of Democratic Living Award 1949; Dorothy Canfield Fisher Memorial Children's Book Award 1962; Western Writers of America Golden Spur Award 1968, 1970. *Children's Books:* Crazy Creek, 1948; Treasure Mountain, 1949; The Bounces of Cynthiann', 1950; (as Lynn Bronson) Timberland Adventure, 1950; Elder Brother, 1951; (as Lynn Bronson) Coyote Kid, 1951; Captain Apple's Ghost, 1952 (London, 1953); (as Lynn Bronson) Rogue's Valley,

1952; Tree Wagon, 1953; (as Lynn Bronson) The Runaway, 1953; The Witch Doctor's Son, 1954; The Shy Stegosaurus of Cricket Creek, 1955; Navaho Sister, 1956; (as Lynn Bronson) Darcy's Harvest, 1956; Rusty's Space Ship, 1957; (as Lynn Bronson) Popular Girl, 1957; Rock Hounds, 1958; Special Year, 1959; The City under the Back Steps, 1960 (London, 1962); Princess of Fort Vancouver, 1962; The Shy Stegosaurus at Indian Springs, 1962; Mrs. Updaisy, 1963; Temple of the Sun, 1964; Wheels West, 1965; The Tilted Sombrero, 1966; Half-Breed, 1967; The Bandit of Mok Hill, 1969; Cayuse Courage, 1970; Once upon Little Big Horn, 1971; The Year of the Small Shadow, 1971; Go Up on the Road, 1972; Rattlesnake Cave, 1974; White Captives, 1975; The Potlatch Family, 1976; Bargain Bride, 1977. *Other:* Of Mikes and Men; also wrote many radio scripts 1945–52.

WILLIAM A(LLAN) PATTERSON
Airline executive
Born Honolulu, Territory of Hawaii, U.S.A., October, 1899
Died Glenview, Illinois, U.S.A., June 13th, 1980

William Patterson, a pioneer of air travel, became his industry's leading spokesman. As an airline executive for most of his working life, he greatly contributed to the improvement of air-freight services and to the development of faster, more comfortable, and safer air travel.

Born in 1899, the son of a Honolulu sugar plantation foreman who died in 1906 of malaria, William Patterson was separated from his mother in 1912 when she went to San Francisco to attend business college. Left in the care of a strict military academy at the age of 13, Patterson managed—on his second attempt—to escape, rejoining his mother after talking his way aboard an old four-masted schooner bound for San Francisco.

In San Francisco he enrolled in grammar school and worked at a number of after-school jobs. His early career, including his 14 years at Wells Fargo (beginning as a 25-dollar-a-week office boy in 1914), reads like the story of Horatio Alger. Young, willing, good-natured, and constantly seeking to improve himself, his superiors soon noticed his talents. However, in 1927 he raised some eyebrows when he authorized a loan of $5,000 to the pioneer aviator Vern Gorst, of Pacific Air Transport, a west coast mail route. The branch's President advised Patterson to keep an eye on Gorst; flying machines were not acceptable investment risks.

Taking this advice to heart, Patterson became Gorst's unpaid financial counselor and in the process learned much about the fledgling air transport business—a knowledge which so impressed the man who bought out Gorst's P.A.T. operation that young Patterson was asked to join the new parent firm, Boeing Aircraft, as assistant to the President.

Philip Johnson, head of Boeing Aircraft and Boeing Air Transport, had quickly sized up Patterson as just the sort of man he needed to run West Coast operations while he took over the administration of the huge, Chicago-based operation that William Boeing was putting together—United Aircraft and Air Transport Company. Thus at age 30 Patterson became Executive Vice President and General Manager of Boeing Air Transport, a thriving concern with a 25-plane fleet and mail routes as far east as Chicago and Detroit. In 1931 he was brought to the Chicago headquarters and in 1934 was named President of United Airlines.

Patterson emerged as industry spokesman that same year, winning this distinction during February and March when President Roosevelt, charging collusion in the bidding for mail routes, abruptly canceled all government contracts with the commercial mail-carriers and ordered the Army Air Corps to take over this function. The immediate result was chaos for the Corps, which lost five pilots in the first week of service alone, and financial catastrophe for the nation's commercial aviation industry, which derived half of its revenues from government contracts. United was the largest company in the industry, and all others looked to it for guidance in this situation. Patterson gave it to them, declaring that United would operate as usual regardless of the loss of mail routes. Though this decision cost the company a million dollars, Patterson called it the best decision he ever made. By mid-March, Roosevelt admitted his error and restored the mail business to commercial concerns.

This not only established Patterson's preeminent position within the industry; it fostered in him a determination to eliminate industrial dependence on government patronage. Clearly that meant developing fast, safe, and comfortable passenger service, and it was to that task he so successfully turned his hand. By 1936 two out of every three dollars in United revenue came from passenger or freight services. He did this by emphasizing the passenger. He approved the first use of female flight attendants, introduced the first aircraft specially designed for passenger travel (the Douglas DC-4), was the first airline executive to commit his company to the purchase of jets, and oversaw the introduction of countless contributions to aircraft safety and comfort. He set the example and the industry followed.

In winning the confidence of the American traveler, Patterson early conceived of the airline company not as divided into labor and management but as partners, all of whom shared a stake in promoting the convenience and safety of air travel. Under the threat of a strike by underpaid and overworked pilots in 1934, Patterson sat down with flier representatives and came away from the meeting convinced that the pilots were mostly justified in their demands. He pledged himself to a new era in labor relations, in which satisfied employees became excellent advertisements for the industry as well as assets to the company.   R.C.

Son of William P. and Mary Castro P. Married Vera A. Witt 1924. Children: Patricia Ann Kennedy; William Allan, Jr. Educ: Mil. Acad., Honolulu; public grammar and high sch. (night), San Francisco. Various positions, office boy to loan officer, Wells Fargo Bank and Trust Co., San Francisco 1914–28; asst. to Pres., Boeing Airplane and Air Transport Co., Seattle, Wash. 1929–31; Pres., Boeing Air Transport, Pacific Air Transport, Natl. Air Transport and Varney Airlines, Chicago 1931–34. With United Airlines, Chicago: V.P. 1933; Pres. and Dir. 1934; Chmn. of Bd. 1963; Chmn. Emeritus 1966–80. Dir.: Insurance Co. of North America; Bell and Howell Co.; Westinghouse Electric Corp.; Gulf and Western Industries, Inc.;

Goodyear Tire and Rubber Co.; Harris Trust and Savings Bank of Chicago; Fund for Adult Education; Chicago Mus. of Science and Industry; Chicago Boys Club and Jr. Achievement. Trustee, Northwestern Univ., Evanston, Ill. and Passavant Memorial Hosp., Chicago. Member: Cttee. for Econ. Development; Newcomen Soc. of Engineers; Masons; Chicago Club; Execs. Club; Econ. Club; also Commonwealth, Tavern, Commercial, Bohemian, Pacific Union (San Francisco). Hons: Intnl. Council of Educators Communicator of the Year 1966; Aviation Writers Assn.'s Monsanto Safety Award; Flight Safety Foundn.'s Distinguished Service Award; Airline Medical Dirs. Assn. Aero Medical Award; Hon. Member, Aerospace Medical Assn.; Annual W.A. Patterson Aviation Prize, Chicago Assn. of Commerce and Industry.

Further reading: Pat Patterson by Frank J. Taylor, 1967.

SERGIO PIGNEDOLI
Cardinal of the Roman Catholic Church
Born Felina, Reggio Emilia, Italy, June 4th, 1910
Died Felina, Reggio Emilia, Italy, June 15th, 1980

Courtesy Pignedoli estate

Cardinal Sergio Pignedoli, a leading emissary of the Roman Catholic church, carried out many intricate missions in the 1960s and 70s and was often referred to as "the Vatican's Henry Kissinger." Regarded in his church as a "liberal" or "moderate," the cardinal was one of the major contenders for the papacy after the death of Pope Paul VI in 1978; he was a "papabile" when Paul's successor, Pope John Paul I died after only 34 days on the papal throne.

Sergio Pignedoli was born of poor parents in Reggio Emilia, Italy in 1910. He obtained his laureate in literature from Milan's Sacred Heart University, a licentiate in church history from the Gregorian University, and a laureate in canon law from the Lateran. Ordained in 1933, he served in several minor pastoral capacities before becoming a naval chaplain in 1940. The following year, Pignedoli earned the official displeasure of Mussolini, who had exhorted Italians to conduct a campaign of "hatred" against the British. Responding in an official student newspaper in Rome, Pignedoli wrote: "Hatred is one of the basest feelings and dishonors any uniform . . . Silence those who speak words of hatred. They bring shame to a country. Happily, you will hear very few of them." The newspaper was immediately seized and publication was banned for one month.

While serving as a chaplain in the Mediterranean during World War Two, allied forces sank his ship. Pignedoli was rescued and sent back to the Vatican for reassignment. There he met Monsignor Giovanni Martini (later Pope Paul VI), the Sub-Secretary of State under Pius XII, who recruited Pignedoli for his Vatican staff. It was the beginning of a long and mutually beneficial association.

After the war, Pignedoli remained attached to the Papal Curia and was named Chaplain to the Association of Italian Explorers and Vice Chaplain General of Italian Catholic Action. Appointed Secretary General to the Central Committee for Observances during the 1950 Holy Year, his services in that capacity were rewarded by an Archbishopric and commission as Pius XII's Nuncio first to Bolivia and then to Venezuela. He was recalled in 1955 when Montini, ousted as Secretary of State by Pius and denied a cardinal's cap, took up the Archbishopric of Milan and claimed Pignedoli as an auxiliary—a post the latter held for five years until Pius's successor John XXIII awarded Montini his promotion to the Sacred College.

At this juncture Pignedoli was appointed Apostolic Delegate to Central and West Africa, where one of his more important tasks was preparing the way for Montini's 1962 visit to Africa, the first ever by a European cardinal. It was an historic event and Pignedoli's contribution to its success was not to pass unnoticed.

Two years later Montini, now Pope Paul VI, named his old associate Apostolic Delegate to Canada but in 1966 recalled him for his most delicate assignment to date—representing Paul at an Extraordinary Assembly of Vietnam's Bishops to debate church policy and improve relations with the Buddhists in that war-torn country. Pignedoli discharged the mission smoothly and without incident.

Pignedoli's offices from this point on reflect his particular strengths and skills as a church ambassador. He served as Secretary of the Congregation of Missions and, after elevation to the rank of Cardinal, as head of the Secretariat for Non-Christians. He also sat in the College's Congregations for the Sacraments of Divine Worship, the Evangelicalization of Peoples, the Causes of Saints and Catholic Education, and as a member of the Secretariat for the Union of Christians. It was the dossier of a cardinal of possible papal caliber, although some of his colleagues reportedly doubted if he possessed the intellectual capacity for the job.

Father Pignedoli, the church's acknowledged Third World expert and its leading diplomat, headed the papal delegation to an historic Islamic-Christian conference in Tripoli (1976). The conference's concluding statement—which Pignedoli signed—contained a condemnation of Zionism and a demand for Israeli withdrawal from all occupied territories. A most embarrassing gaffe for the cardinal, he said later that he had been the victim of a poor or incomplete translation.

A personable, gregarious and candid man who loved traveling and had many pen-friends, he was also known for his great discretion in office. Although his rise within the church was greatly helped by his association with the somewhat conservative Pope Paul VI, he was known to be closer to the more progressive pope, John XXIII.   R.C.

Educ: Major Seminary, Reggio Emilia; Sacred Heart Univ., Milan, laureate in literature; Pontifica Universitas Gregoriana, Rome, licentiate in church history; Pontifica Universitas Lateranensis, Rome, laureate in canon law. Ordained priest in 1933; Vice-Rector of Major Seminary, Reggio Emilia 1933–36; Chaplain to students, Sacred Heart Univ., Milan 1936–40; Chaplain, Italian Navy 1940–43; attached to Curia, serving variously at the Secretariat of State, Vatican City, as Chaplain to the Assn. of Italian Explorers and Vice Chaplain-Gen. to Italian Catholic Action 1943–49; Secty. Gen. to the Central Cttee. for Observances of the 1950 Holy Year 1949–50; named titular archbishop (Iconium) 1951; Papal Nuncio to Bolivia 1951–54 and Venezuela 1954–55; auxiliary to Archbishop of Milan 1955–60; Apostolic Delegate to Central and West Africa 1960–64; Apostolic Delegate to Canada 1964–66; special mission to Vietnam Assembly of Bishops 1966; Secty. of Congregation for the Evangelicalization of Peoples

1967–73; raised to rank of Cardinal 1973 and awarded deaconate of San Giorgio; Pres., Secretariat of Non-Christians since 1973. Also member of Sacred Coll. of Cardinals, Congregations for the Sacraments of Divine Worship, the Causes of Saints and Catholic Education, and Secretariat for Christian Unity.
Further reading: The Inner Elite by Gary McEoin, 1977.

JACOB L(EIB) TALMON
Historian, author and teacher
Born Rypin, Poland, June 14th, 1916
Died Jerusalem, Israel, June 16th, 1980

Courtesy Irene Talmon

Jacob L. Talmon, Israeli intellectual historian, made his major scholarly contribution with a series of volumes tracing the rise of the modern totalitarian state from the late 18th to the mid-20th centuries. He did not, however, confine himself to academic explications of the history of ideas. Interested in the applications as well as the origins of modern state craft, he was recognized outside Israel as an eloquent defender of the Jewish state and culture; while at home, he acted as a frequent critic of what he perceived to be an increasingly inflexible and short-sighted policy toward the Arab world generally and Palestinians in particular. And always his arguments were based on a rational marshaling of his accrued stock of historical wisdom rather than upon simple patriotism or purely moral considerations, as both British historian Arnold Toynbee and Israeli Prime Minister Menachem Begin learned in their confrontations with him.

Talmon's family left Poland in 1934 and settled in Palestine as part of the Zionist vanguard during the inter-war years. Educated at the Hebrew University, he received his M.A. in 1939 and then left for further schooling in Europe, studying at the Sorbonne in Paris then moving to London where in 1943 he received his doctorate from the London School of Economics. He remained in England for the duration of the war, serving as Secretary to the Board of Deputies of British Jews, a relief agency, after which he returned to Israel to commence his academic career, beginning as an instructor in modern history at Hebrew University, Jerusalem, in 1949 and rising to the rank of full professor by 1960. Admired by students for his brilliance as a lecturer and debater, he was also at various times a scholar in residence at the prestigious Institute for Advanced Studies in Princeton and at St. Catherine's College, Oxford, as well as a visiting professor at Columbia University in New York City and at the Massachusetts Institute of Technology.

Underlying Talmon's international scholarly renown were two published volumes and one in manuscript at the time of his death in which he followed the evolution of "totalitarian democracy" from its origins in the French Revolution's ferment to its ultimate and disturbing manifestations in the 20th century. The first of these works, *The Origins of Totalitarian Democracy* (1952), established the thesis that the utopian impetus to the destruction of the old absolutist order beginning in France in 1789 resolved itself into two divergent philosophies of "democratic" government. One was the libertarian tradition which held man to be inherently good and perfectible; the other, a novel "messianic" authoritarianism bent on the establishment of a revolutionary new democratic order by brute, leveling force. In a subsequent work, *Political Messianism: The Romantic Phase* (1961), he concentrated upon the further fragmentation of Jacobite messianism into ideological (Communardism/Marxism) and nationalistic movements which led to the trans-European political upheaval of 1848. In a concluding volume, tentatively titled *The Myth of Nation and the Vision of Revolution: The Origins of Ideological Polarization in the Twentieth Century,* Talmon planned to bring his study of totalitarianism up to date, presumably tracing the messianic thread to the communist and fascist regimes established in the period between the wars. In a work related to this cycle, *Romanticism and Revolt* (1967), he investigated the roles of romanticism and major social and economic currents in philosophical and institutional developments between 1789 and 1848; while in a collection of essays, *The Unique and the Universal* (1966), he treated fascism and communism as polarities resulting from the clash of internationalism and national self-assertion in the modern era.

In addition to these scholarly achievements, Talmon was a frequently controversial commentator on the current political scene. A staunch Israeli patriot, he gained international attention by debating Arnold Toynbee in 1967 and mounting a skilled and articulate apologia for his nation and the principles of Zionism, which he restated in the volume *Israel Among Nations* (1970). Yet in Israel, he proved no less adept at criticizing the national government. Increasingly after the 1967 war, he found himself in opposition to official policy on the Palestinian issue. In numerous articles and lectures, he advocated compromise, including territorial concessions and recognition of the Palestinian right to self-determination. He argued firmly against occupation of West Bank territory, calling at one point for the resignation of the Begin government. "In the modern era," he wrote in the Jerusalem daily *Haaretz,* "it is not the territories of a country that pass down in heritage, but the consciousness and the will of the people who live in them. The true danger to Israel's existence lies in the continuation of the Sisyphean effort to subjugate the Palestinians." To Talmon, this was not an argument based on short-term political expediency, but on the entire sweep of nearly two centuries of western history.   R.C.

Son of Abraham T., businessman, and Ziporah T. Married Irene Anna Bugajer, physician 1961. Children: Daniella-Josephine; Maya-Anath. Jewish. Emigrated to Palestine 1934. Educ: Hebrew Univ. of Jersulam, M.A. 1939; attended Sorbonne, Univ. of Paris 1930–40; London Sch. of Economics and Political Science, Ph.D. 1943. Secty., Palestine Cttee. of the Bd. of Deputies of British Jews, London 1944–47; Instr. 1949–60 and Prof. modern history since 1960, Hebrew Univ. of Jerusalem; Visiting Fellow, Inst. for Advanced Study, Princeton, N.J. 1967–68 and St. Catherine's Coll., Oxford; Visiting Lectr., Massachusetts Inst. of Technology 1968–69; Visiting Prof., Columbia Univ., NYC; also lectr. at West European univs. Member, Netherlands Inst. for Advanced Study, Wassenaar and Israel Acad. of Sciences and Humanities. Hons: Israel Prize for Social Sciences and Law (for The Origins of Totalitarian Democracy) 1956; grant from Rockefeller Foundn. *Author:* The Origins of Totalitarian Democracy,

1952; The Nature of Jewish History: Its Universal Significance, 1957; Political Messianism: The Romantic Phase, 1960; The Unique and the Universal, 1965; Romanticism and Revolt: Europe 1915–1848, 1967; Israel Among the Nations, 1970; The Origins of Ideological Polarization in the Twentieth Century, unpublished. Contributor to Commentary, Midstream and Encounter.

TERENCE FISHER
Horror film director
Born London, England, 1904
Died Twickenham, Middlesex, England, June 18th, 1980

Courtesy Warner Brothers

The revival of Gothic horror movies which took place in the mid-1950s can be traced largely to one British company, Hammer Films. And, within Hammer's output, which varied disconcertingly from the effective to the inept, the most consistent achievement was the series of films directed by Terence Fisher.

It was mainly by chance that Fisher was chosen to direct the film that inaugurated Hammer's highly successful horror cycle—*The Curse of Frankenstein* (1956). He had been lined up for a costume film, *King Charles and the Roundheads;* when this project was cancelled, Hammer reassigned him to their forthcoming remake of the Frankenstein story. At first sight, it was a surprising choice; Fisher had not the least stylistic pretensions to expressionism or surrealism. But his workmanlike, matter-of-fact direction proved an apt counterbalance to the extravagance of his subject matter; where several of his successors attempted to match outrageous story-lines with equally flamboyant direction, and collapsed into bathos as a result, Fisher's straight-faced narrative approach lent the necessary minimum of credibility.

Terence Fisher was born in London in 1904. After a spell in the Merchant Navy, he worked for a time in the clothing trade; not until 1933 did he enter cinema, when he joined Michael Balcon at Gaumont-British as an assistant editor (or, as he later put it, "the oldest clapper boy in the business"). From 1936 he worked as editor on numerous films, for Warner's in the early 40s, later for Rank; his first directing assignment, *Colonel Bogey* (1948), was for the Rank subsidiary, Highbury Films. He made a number of films for Gainsborough, of which the best was *So Long at the Fair* (1950), a neatly-turned period thriller, before joining Hammer in 1952.

The huge—and largely unexpected—international success of *The Curse of Frankenstein* fixed the course of Fisher's career; all his subsequent films (he directed 48 in all) were made for Hammer, in the same highly-colored, neo-Gothic style. *Dracula* (1957) followed, and the first of several sequels to his initial success, *The Revenge of Frankenstein* (1957). Hammer were now enthusiastically recreating all the old Universal Studios subjects of the 1930s, including *The Hound of the Baskervilles* (1958) and *The Mummy* (1959); critical response, especially in Britain, ranged from the scandalised to the dismissive, but Fisher and (Hammer) could derive any consolation they needed from the box-office returns.

Fisher's later films included *The Phantom of the Opera* (1961), *The Devil Rides Out* (1967), two more Dracula subjects, and three more Frankensteins. The last of these, *Frankenstein and the Monster from Hell* (1972), was his final picture; ill-health prevented him from directing for the remaining eight years of his life.

Though he shared their subjects, Fisher's work owes nothing to the haunted, Germanic expressionism of such 30s horror-film directors as James Whale or Tod Browning; nor is he as stylistically imaginative as his near-contemporary Roger Corman. But, at their best, his films embody a robust, even stolid, narrative power which faithfully reflects the 19th century English Gothic-novel tradition from which they derive.   P.K.

Married; one daughter. Educ: Christ's Hospital, and H.M.S. Conway. Served with P&O Fleet as a Jr. officer ca. 1920–25; in clothing trade ca. 1925–30. Gaumont-British Studios: clapper boy (Falling for You) 1933, asst. ed. 1934, *Ed.:* Tudor Rose, 1936 (Robert Stevenson); On the Night of the Fire, 1939 (Brian Desmond Hurst); The Wicked Lady, 1945 (Leslie Arliss); Master of Bankdam, 1947 (Walter Forde). *Dir.:* Colonel Bogey 1947; To The Public Danger 1947; Song For Tomorrow 1948; Portrait From Life 1948; Marry Me 1948; The Astonished Heart (co-dir. with Anthony Darnsborough) 1949; So Long at the Fair (co-dir. with A. Darnsborough) 1949; Home to Danger 1950; The Last Page 1951; Wings of Danger 1951; Stolen Face 1951; Distant Trumpet 1951; Mantrap 1952; The Four-Sided Triangle 1952; Spaceways 1952; Blood Orange 1953; Face the Music 1953; Murder by Proxy 1953; The Stranger Comes Homes 1954; Mask of Bust 1954; Final Appointment 1954; The Flaw 1954; Children Galore 1954; Stolen Assignment 1955; The Last Man to Hang? 1955; Kill Me Tomorrow 1956; The Curse of Frankenstein 1956; Dracula 1957; The Revenge of Frankenstein 1957; The Hounds of the Baskervilles 1958; The Man Who Would Cheat Death 1958; The Mummy 1959; The Stranglers of Bombay 1959; The Two Faces of Dr. Jekyll 1959; The Brides of Dracula 1960; Sword of Sherwood Forest 1960; The Curse of the Werewolf 1960; The Phantom of the Opera 1961; Sherlock Holmes and the Deadly Necklace 1962; The Horror of it All 1963; The Gorgon 1963; The Earth Dies Screaming 1964; Dracula, Prince of Darkness 1965; Island of Terror 1965; Frankenstein Created Woman 1966; Night of the Big Heat 1967; The Devil Rides Out 1967; Frankenstein Must Be Destroyed 1972; Frankenstein and the Monster from Hell 1972. Television-drama anthology series "Douglas Fairbanks Presents", series "Robin Hood", "Dial 999".

ALLAN PETTERSSON
Composer and violist
Born Västra Ryd, Uppland, Sweden, September 19th, 1911
Died Stockholm, Sweden, June 21st, 1980

Allan Pettersson was an unusual, perhaps unique, figure on the Swedish musical scene. Unlike most of his contemporary composers, he was an expressionist in musical style, probably closest to Gustav Mahler; he was also a solitary individual who kept himself socially and professionally apart from the musical establishment and composers' cliques, even after he achieved recognition in the last 20 years of his life.

Pettersson was raised in Söder, the working-class slum of Stockholm, to which his family had moved when he was a year old. In spite of the ever-present poverty, the alcoholism of his father, and the cultural deprivation of the district, Pettersson at an early age began to work toward his goal of becoming a serious musician. He peddled picture postcards at the age of ten to scrape up the money to buy a violin; he taught himself to read music from a schoolbook. At the age of 19, he was accepted into the Royal Academy of Music, where he studied violin and viola with teachers such as Julius Ruthström and Henrik Melcher Melchers.

Although Pettersson encountered some prejudice because of his working-class origins, he nevertheless won the academy's highest student award, the Jenny Lind stipend, which allowed him to spend a year in Paris studying viola with Maurice Vieux. When he returned to Stockholm, he became a violist with the Stockholm Philharmonic. He remained there for the next 11 years, gaining a reputation as a slightly eccentric but first-class musician.

While playing with the Philharmonic, Pettersson continued to study composition with leading lights of Swedish music, including Karl-Birger Blomdahl. His professional life as a string player had a strong impact upon his compositions, which he had begun to write in 1934 while still a student at the Royal Academy. Most of his compositions of the next 15 years were on a small scale—chamber music pieces for a variety of instruments, sometimes including voice. In these compositions, a highly individualistic musical style began to emerge: expressive, evocative, lyrical, often romantic and intensely personal, with compelling asymmetrical rhythms and echoes of religious and spiritual anguish. It was this music, written for and about the "little man who goes unnoticed," in a style that sharply contrasted with the highly intellectual style of most 20th-century classical music, that marked him as a "proletarian composer." Pettersson maintained that he was the "Last, if not the only proletarian composer Sweden ever had."

Of his early compositions, several stand out. Pettersson himself considered his *Six Songs* of 1935 as among his best compositions. Many of his *Barefoot Songs,* written in 1943–45 to his own lyrics about the outcasts of society, became quite popular after an initial period of neglect, and he later used some of their themes in his symphonies. The Concerto No. 1 for string orchestra (1949) was selected in 1953 by a jury of conductors to be the sole Scandinavian entry for an international music festival at Cologne.

In 1951, believing that working as an instrumentalist was a hindrance to becoming a serious composer, Pettersson resigned his position with the Stockholm Philharmonic. He spent a year in Paris studying with three of the great modern composers, Honegger, Milhaud, and Leibowitz; the latter, who also taught Pierre Boulez, was the foremost exponent of the 12-tone school in France. Pettersson's *Seven Sonatas for Two Violins,* written during this year abroad, are considered to be among the most important chamber music works of the 1950s. After these were completed, he wrote mainly on a large scale: 13 symphonies, most of them cast in one movement; a violin concerto written for Ida Haendel, and two concertos for string orchestra, of which the "Mesto" movement of the third concerto became popular as a separate piece and won an award in 1968; and the *Vox Humana* for voices and orchestra, set to lyrics by working-class poets from Latin America. His Symphony No. 7, first performed in 1968 and later recorded by Antal Dorati, to whom the work was dedicated, marked a popular breakthrough in his career. It was a great success and was later used as a score by the Swedish Royal Ballet. The music critic of the *New Yorker,* reviewing the recording in 1975, called the symphony "entirely original . . . totally effective" and proclaimed Pettersson "one of the finest symphonists of today." Pettersson received increasing recognition from critics and audiences. Ironically, at the same time, he became an invalid due to chronic rheumatoid arthritis.

Pettersson often based his large-scale compositions on folk songs or religious hymns. Although he spoke of his own life as his "working material," he denied that he was a subjective composer. When he wrote, he said, his own personality disappeared; he sought the "heart's red square, where I meet mankind, where everybody always lives and where everyone is one." In his own estimation, he was a "voice in the wilderness . . . a voice that is threatened to be drowned in the noise of the times."   L.F.

Born Gustaf Allan Pettersson. Son of Carl P., blacksmith, and Ida Svensson P. Married Gudrun Gustafson 1943. No children. Educ: Royal Acad. of Music, Stockholm; private studies (as Jenny Lind stipend winner), Paris 1939–40; private studies in Stockholm and again in Paris 1951–52. Violist, Konsertforeningen (now Stockholm Philharmonic Orchestra) 1940–51. Bd. Member, Royal Acad. of Music, Stockholm. Hons: Expressens music prize for Fifth Symphony 1963; Christ Johnson-priset prize for Mesto 1968; Stockholm city hederspris for Sixth Symphony 1968; Grammis-priset for Seventh Symphony 1970; litteris et artibus (arts and letters award from the King) 1977; Prof. (title awarded by the state) 1979. *Compositions: Symphonies*— #1, 1951; #2, 1952–53 (first performance Swedish radio, May 9, 1954); #3, 1954–55 (Göteborg, Nov. 21, 1956); #4, 1958–59 (Stockholm, Jan. 21, 1961); #5, ca. 1960–62 (Stockholm, Nov. 8, 1963); #6, 1963–66 (Stockholm, Jan. 21, 1968); #7, 1966–67 (Stockholm, Oct. 13, 1968); #8, 1968–69 (Stockholm, Feb. 23, 1972); #9, 1970 (1971?) (Göteborg, Feb. 18, 1971); #10, ca. 1972 (Stockholm, Jan. 14, 1974); #11, 1973 (Bergen, Norway, Oct. 24, 1974); #12 (with chorus, subtitled De döda på torget, to poems by Pablo Neruda), 1974; #13, 1976, *Other compositions*—Two Elegies for violin and piano, 1934; Six Songs with piano, 1935; Fantasy for violin solo, 1936; Four Improvisations for string trio, 1936; Andante Expressivo for violin and piano, 1938; Romance for violin and piano, 1942; Lament for piano, 1945; 24 "Barefoot Songs" for voice and piano, 1943–45 (a suite for mixed chorus was drawn from these); Fugue for three woodwinds, 1948; Concerto for violin and string quartet, 1949; Concerto #1 for string orch., 1949–50 (Stockholm, 1952); Seven Sonatas for two violins, 1951–52; Concerto #2 for string orch., 1956 (Stockholm, Dec. 1, 1968); Concerto #3 for string orch., 1956–57 (Stockholm, Mar. 14, 1958); Symphonic Movement for orch., 1973; Vox Humana, 14 songs for soprano, alto, tenor, baritone, bass, chorus, and string orch., to texts by Latin American poets, 1974 (Stockholm, Mar. 19, 1976); Concerto for violin and orch. #2, 1977 (Stockholm, Jan. 1980). *Recordings*—Symphony #2, Swedish Radio Symphony Orch., conducted by Stig Westerberg (Swedish Soc. Discofil), 1966; Symphony #7, Stockholm Philharmonic Orch., conducted by Antal Dorati

(London), 1972; Barefoot Songs (Caprice), 1974; Six Songs, with
Margot Rödin, mezzo soprano, and Arnold Ostman, piano (Swedish
Soc. Discofil), 1975; Symphony #10, Swedish Radio Symphony
Orch., conducted by Antal Dorati (EMI Odeon), 1975; Concerto #1
for string orch., Swedish Radio Orch., conducted by Stig Westerberg
(Caprice), 1975, rereleased on album called Two Swedish Expression-
ists, 1977; Vox Humana—song cycle for soloists, choir and string
orch., Swedish Radio Orch., conducted by Stig Westerberg (BIS),
1976; Eight Barefoot Songs arranged for orch. and conducted by
Antal Dorati, Stockholm Philharmonic Orch. (HNN Records), 1977;
Symphony #12, conducted by Carl Rune Larsson (Caprice), 1978.
Author: "Konsert nr. 3 för Stråkorkester" (Concerto #3 for string
orch.), in Nutida Musik, I, 1957/58; "Den Konstnärliga lognen," in
Musiklivit, 28, 1958; Tjugofrya barfotasånger och andra dikter (Barefoot Songs and Other Poems), 1976 (includes discography).

DIMITRIOS PARTSALIDES
Greek Communist leader
Born Trabzon, Turkey, 1905
Died Athens, Greece, June 22nd, 1980

Dimitrios Partsalides, a leader of the Communist movement in
Greece, was born in the Turkish Black Sea port of Trabzon, from
which he emigrated in 1922 as a refugee from the Greek-Turkish War.
After attending high school in Salonika, he went to work in a tobacco
factory in Kavalla, where he joined the illegal Greek Communist
Party (Kommounistikón Kómma Ellados, or KKE). He was elected
mayor of Kavalla in 1930 and a member of Parliament in 1932.

When the Nazis invaded Greece in 1941, Partsalides became the
main organizer of the resistance group Ethnikón Apeleftherotikón
Métopon (National Liberation Front), which, by concealing its Communist affiliation, won the support of most of the population. In
addition to carrying out acts of sabotage against the Nazis, the EAM
and its military branch, ELAS, conducted armed attacks on rival
resistance groups in order to eliminate opposition to a Communist
takeover of the country when the occupation ended. The Germans
withdrew in October 1944, but the planned coup was called off under
orders from Soviet Premier Josef Stalin, whose recent peacekeeping
agreement with British Prime Minister Winston Churchill had brought
Greece under temporary British military protection.

The provisional government of George Papandreou now ordered
the KKE to surrender some of its guerrilla units for induction into a
new national army and to disband the rest. Unwilling to lose the
military advantage it had built up during the occupation, the KKE,
under pressure from Partsalides, George Siantos, and other hard-line
members of the party's Politburo, launched an armed uprising in
Athens that lasted five weeks and killed some 11,000 people. In
February 1945, after Churchill came to inform the rebels that they
could expect no support from the Soviet Union, Partsalides and other
KKE leaders signed the Varkiza Pact, which provided for the
dissolution of guerrilla forces and the legalization of the Communist
Party.

A few months later, at the Seventh Party Congress, Partsalides called for a "peaceful transition to socialism." Within a short time, however, the KKE had begun making plans for a full-scale revolution to counter growing right-wing sentiment in Greece and the possible restoration of the Greek monarchy. KKE leaders, wishing to avoid a test of their political strength, voted to boycott the March 1946 elections despite a warning from Soviet officials V. M. Molotov and A. A. Zhdanov, who told Partsalides in a Moscow conference that the Soviet government intended to recognize the outcome whether the KKE participated or not. The election was won by the Populist Party and the return of the monarchy was authorized by plebiscite soon afterwards.

With the assistance of the Communist governments in the neighboring Balkan countries, the KKE began a civil war known as the "Third Round." It lacked popular support, however, and lost ground steadily after President Tito of Yugoslavia [q.v.], who had repudiated Stalin's brand of orthodox communism, closed his country's frontier with Greece and suspended weapons shipments and military aid to the insurgents. When the war effort collapsed in August 1949, Partsalides, who had been appointed premier of the Communist "government in exile," fled to the Soviet Union, where he remained an active Politburo member.

After the USSR invaded Czechoslovakia in 1968, Partsalides, disenchanted, quit the pro-Moscow KKE to form the Communist Party of the Interior. In 1972 he returned to Greece to organize Communist resistance to the right-wing junta that had taken control in 1967. He was arrested and sentenced to life imprisonment, but was freed in 1973 under a general amnesty.   J.P./T.P.

Married and divorced. Emigrated to Greece as refugee of Greek-Turkish War 1922. Educ: high sch., Salonika. Worker, tobacco factory, Kavalla 1920s; Mayor of Kavalla 1930–32; M.P. (Communist) 1932. With Kommounistikón Kómma Ellados (Greek Communist Party): joined 1920s; leader, Ethnikón Apeleftherotikón Métopon (Natl. Liberation Front) 1941–49; Member since 1945 and Secty., Politburo; Premier, Communist self-proclaimed Interim Democratic Govt. during civil war 1949; Member, Politburo in exile 1956–68. Founder and Member since 1968, Greek Communist Party of the Interior. Sentenced to life imprisonment for illegally entering Greece 1972; granted amnesty 1973.

SANJAY GANDHI
Indian politician
Born New Delhi, India, December 14th, 1946
Died New Delhi, India, June 23rd, 1980

The sudden death of Sanjay Gandhi, son of India's Prime Minister Indira Gandhi, at the age of 33 cut short a tumultuous political career marked by extremes of popular hatred and adoration. Had he lived, Sanjay would, in all likelihood, have succeeded his mother as leader of the ruling Congress Party, thereby establishing within India's

democratic government a dynastic succession begun by his maternal grandfather, Jawaharlal Nehru, the nation's first Prime Minister.

Sanjay was the younger of two sons born to Mrs. Gandhi, a Hindu of Brahman descent, and Feroze Gandhi, a Parsi politician (no relation to Mahatma Gandhi). He attended a number of prestigious private schools without distinction and quit an apprenticeship at Rolls Royce after two years, preferring to indulge a passion for fast cars and high living. During the next few years he designed and built a compact car called the Maruti ("son of the wind god").

Within two years of his widowed mother's accession to the premiership, in 1969 Sanjay was awarded a government license to manufacture the Maruti on a mass basis, despite unresolved questions over the need for such cars in India's economy and the ethics of government involvement in private enterprise. Critics of the Prime Minister accused her of flagrant nepotism, alleging that Sanjay had acquired choice property for his factory through government intervention and that he had used his political influence to attract and reward investors. The company was a failure, with production never reaching more than a few hundred vehicles in six years.

Sanjay's rise to power began in June of 1975, after his mother was convicted of election-rigging. Rather than resign her office, the Prime Minister—acting, it is said, on her son's advice—proclaimed a state of national emergency and granted herself authoritarian powers to deal with it. Civil liberties and democratic political processes were suspended indefinitely, and some 10,000 members of the opposition were jailed.

Sanjay, who had been appointed head of the Congress Party's youth wing, embarked on a drastic program of modernization and enforced it with the aid of the police (which, like the press, was controlled by one of his personal friends). Its goals included slum clearance, family planning, tree planting, and the abolition of such Hindu customs as the caste system and the dowry.

The slum clearance project consisted largely of bulldozing, with little construction to replace lost housing. Squatters who resisted the efforts of the police to evict them were beaten and shot. According to a 1977 report on the destruction of a Delhi slum, "People were thrown out in the open without any protection against the ravages of weather and disease. Resistance took a toll of scores of human lives. . . . Sanjay Gandhi replied to his critics, 'The people have to be taught a lesson.'"

More controversial still was his campaign to reduce the birth rate, a major cause of mass poverty and hunger in India. The government's attempts to promote the use of contraceptives and to encourage voluntary sterilization through a system of economic incentives had accomplished little among a peasantry whose ancient religious tradition places great value on the birth of sons. Sanjay, impatient with these ineffectual methods, set monthly sterilization quotas; to fill them, young men and women were rounded up by the police and sterilized against their will. Hospital camps were set up in rural areas and civil servants were ordered to undergo the operation or lose their jobs.

These excesses were largely responsible for Mrs. Gandhi's defeat in the 1977 elections, when a conservative coalition succeeded in ousting the Congress Party for the first time in 30 years. A special court system was set up to try the Gandhis and their associates for abuses of power. Sanjay was sentenced to a two-year prison term for destroying a film that ridiculed his mother and was further charged with criminal conspiracy and rioting and assault.

But observers who thought the Gandhis finished politically had underestimated their appeal to the Indian public, for whom the Gandhi mystique is perennially fascinating. In January 1980 Mrs. Gandhi was returned to office as Prime Minister and Sanjay was elected to Parliament along with some 150 hand-picked followers whose campaigns he had personally supervised and whose parliamentary votes he controlled. Overnight he became one of the most powerful leaders in the Congress Party and the heir to revived hopes for a family dynasty. All charges and convictions against him were dropped. His home in Delhi, which he shared with his wife and infant son, was constantly besieged by crowds of well-wishers and favor-seekers. In May he cemented his authority by masterminding an election campaign that gave the Congress Party control of eight state legislatures. Supporters in Uttar Pradesh begged Mrs. Gandhi to let him take over as chief minister of the state's troubled government. Many up-and-coming young politicians and businessmen viewed him admiringly as an aggressive modernizer who would not allow out-moded customs and ideologies to stand in his way.

On the morning of June 23, Sanjay, a member of the New Delhi Flying Club, went up in a small plane to practice stunts with his instructor, Subash Saxena. The plane crashed in a drainage canal near the official residence of the Prime Minister and both men were killed instantly.

Sanjay was cremated on the banks of the Yamuna River near a memorial to his grandfather, Prime Minister Nehru, while a huge crowd of mourners chanted "Sanjay Gandhi has become immortal," the traditional tribute to great leaders.   J.P./S.J.

Son of Feroze G., M.P., and Indira (Nehru) G., Prime Minister of India. Married Maneka Anand 1974. Son: Varun, b.1980. Hindu. Educ: Doon Sch., India, left 1956; other private schs.; St. Columbus Sch., India 1964. Apprentice, Rolls Royce Ltd., Crewe, England 1966–68. Managing Dir.: Maruti Ltd. 1972–77; Maruti Tech. Services Ltd. 1973–77; Maruti Heavy Vehicles Ltd. 1974–77. Member, Exec. Cttee., Youth Congress (branch of Natl. Congress Party) 1975–77; Member, All-India Congress Cttee. 1975–77. Major influence in Indian politics since 1975. Devised Five Point Programme of social reform during Emergency Rule 1975–77. Convicted for film destruction 1978; conviction overturned by Supreme Court 1980. Elected to Parliament 1980. Member, New Delhi Flying Club.

JOHN LAURIE
British actor
Born Dumfries, Scotland, March 25th, 1897
Died Chalfont St. Peter, Buckinghamshire, England, June 23rd, 1980

A leading British character actor in the 1930s and 40s, John Laurie was a performer with many talents. He appeared in more than 100 films, and on radio his distinctive delivery and accent made him a

Courtesy National Film Archive/British Film
Institute

popular narrator of the works of Robert Burns. His dour manner particularly suited him for some of the more melancholy Shakespearean roles, and made him a natural choice for the mortician's part in the highly popular television comedy series, *Dad's Army*.

Laurie, born in Dumfries, Scotland of a middle-class family, was educated at Dumfries Academy where he decided upon a career as an architect. When he returned from service in the trenches in France however, he realized his talent lay more in the direction of the stage. After taking a course in basic drama at London's Central School, Laurie made his stage debut in March 1921 at the Lyceum Theatre in Dumfries, playing John Shand in *What Every Woman Knows*. He appeared on the London stage for the first time in August 1922, performing the role of Pistol in the Old Vic's production of *The Merry Wives of Windsor*. This was the beginning of a long association with a wide range of Shakespearean plays. By 1928, after several seasons at Stratford-Upon-Avon, he became the Old Vic's leading man and quickly established himself as one of Britain's major Shakespearean actors.

From the early 1930s until the years immediately after the Second World War, Laurie consolidated his career, adding not only more Shakespearean roles to his repertoire—notably Richard III, Othello, Malvolio and Sicinius Velutus—but also distinguishing himself in a wide range of other parts. As an established British actor Laurie was invited to represent his country on tours in Europe, Asia, Australia, the USSR, and the United States.

His long film career, which was to include a number of Shakespearean classics, began in 1930 with his appearance in *Juno and the Paycock*. During the next four decades Laurie was constantly in demand as a film actor, and appeared in several notable films, including *The Thirty-Nine Steps* (1935), *The Ghost of St. Michael's* (1941), and *The Way Ahead* (1944), as well as the Laurence Olivier Shakespeare films.

At the time of his death, critics agreed that his role in the popular television series, *Dad's Army*, was one of his most significant comic parts, and despite his advanced years, was equal to his earlier Shakespearean performances.   M.D.

Son of William L. and Jessie Anne L. Married: (1) Florence Saunders, actress 1924 (d. 1926); (2) Oonah V. Todd-Naylor 1928. Children: 2nd marriage—Veronica Ann L. Educ: Dumfries Acad.; Central Sch. of Speech Training, London 1919. Mil. Service: Hon. Artillery Co., France 1916–18. Began stage acting, Dumfries, Scotland 1921; London debut 1922; NYC debut 1955; Began film acting 1930, radio broadcasting 1947, television acting 1965. Founder, Apollo Soc. *Performances: Plays*—What Every Woman Knows (John Shand), Dumfries 1921; The Merry Wives of Windsor (Pistol), London 1922; King John (Hubert); The Winter's Tale (Autolycus); Love's Labours Lost (Costard) and others with Stratford-Upon-Avon Festival Co. 1925; Quinney's (Cyrus P. Hunsaker), London 1925; Much Ado About Nothing (Conrade), Prince Fazil (Armand), and Macbeth (Lennox), London 1926; Tristan and Isolde (Tristan), Enchantment, Anti-Christ and the Simoun, London 1927; Hamlet (title role), Stratford-Upon-Avon 1927; King Henry V (Pistol), and Judith of Israel (Joel), London 1928; Love's Labours Lost (Armando), The Vikings at Helgeland (Sigurd), Macbeth and Hamlet (title roles), Adam's Opera (Adam) at Odd Vic Theatre, London 1928; Hamlet

(Claudius), Richard III (Lord Hastings), and The Passing of the Essenes (Paul of Tarsus), London 1930; The Improper Duchess (the Rev. Adam Macadam) and And So To Bed (Pelling), London 1931; Napolean (Prince Lucien and Col. Campbell), Twelfth Night (Feste), Alison's House (Richard Knowles), and All's Well That Ends Well (Parolles), London 1932; Crime on the Hill (Inspector Groves), London 1933; toured with Open Air Theatre in 1933; performing in Twelfth Night (Orsino), As You Like It (Oliver), and A Midsummer's Night's Dream (Lysander); Crime on Son of Man (Herr Huebertz), London 1933; The Tudor Wench (Sir Thomas Seymour), London 1933; Mrs. Siddons (John Philip Kemble), London 1933; The Rivals (Faulkland), London 1934; The Country Wife (Sparkish), London 1934; with Open Air Theatre, touring 1934: The Tempest (Alonzo); A Midsummer Night's Dream (Lysander), London 1934; Love is the Best Doctor (Clitandre), London 1934; The Duchess of Malfi (Ferdinand), London 1935; Henry IV (Douglas), London 1935; The White Devil (Flamineo), London 1935; with Open Air Theatre, touring 1935: Twelfth Night (Sir Andrew Aguecheek), As You Like It (Oliver), Comus, A Midsummer Night's Dream (Flute); Rosmersholm (Rosmer), London 1936; Hedda Gabler (Lovborg), London 1936; Bees on the Boatdeck (Gaster), London 1936; touring in South Africa, 1937: Late Night Final, Boy Meets Girl, The Case of the Frightened Lady; Surprise Item (McKay), London 1938; White Secrets (MacDonald), London 1938; with Stratford-Upon-Avon Festival Company, 1939: Othello, Richard III, Coriolanus (Sicinius Velutus); Mandragola (Nicia), London 1939; The Peaceful Inn (Hatlock), London 1940; Heartbreak House (Captain Shotover), London 1943; Hamlet (title role and director), Perth 1945; Sense and Sensibility (Colonel Brandon), London 1946; John Knox (title role), Glasgow 1947; The Human Touch (Professor Syme), London 1949; MacAdam and Eve, London 1950, Edinburgh 1951; Thieves' Carnival (Peterbono), London 1952; The Laird o'Grippy (title role), Edinburgh 1955; Tiger at the Gates (Demokos), London and New York 1955; touring India, Ceylon, 1958 in Shakespearean and other English classics; touring Australia, 1959 in King Lear (title role), The Merchant of Venice (Shylock), A Midsummer Night's Dream (Bottom), The Winter's Tale (Autolycus); The Lizard on the Rock (Arthur Cameron), London 1962; King Lear (Gloucester), London 1964, touring Europe, U.S.S.R., U.S.A. 1964 in the same production; The Cherry Orchard (Firs) and Macbeth (Duncan), Chichester 1966; The Hero of a Hundred Fights (William McGonagall), Perth 1968; Dad's Army (Private Fraser), London 1975. *Films*—Juno and the Paycock, 1930; Red Ensign, 1934; The Thirty-Nine Steps, 1935; Tudor Rose and As You Like It, 1936; Farewell Again, 1937; Edge of the World, 1938; Q Planes, 1939; Sailors Three, 1940; The Ghost of St. Michael's and Old Mother Riley Cleans Up, 1941; The Gentle Sex and Fanny by Gaslight, 1943; The Way Ahead and Henry V, 1944; I Know Where I'm Going and Caesar and Cleopatra, 1945; The Brothers and Uncle Silas, 1947; Bonnie Prince Charlie and Hamlet, 1948; Trio, 1950; Laughter in Paradise, 1951; The Fake, 1953; Hobson's Choice, 1954; The Back Knight, 1955; Campbell's Kingdom, 1957; Kidnapped, 1960; Siege of the Saxons, 1963; Mr. Ten Per Cent, 1966; Dad's Army and others. *Radio broadcasting*—The Man Born to be King (John the Baptist); Dad's Army (Private Fraser) and others. *Television appearances*—Dad's Army (series) and others.

CLYFFORD STILL
Painter
Born Grandin, North Dakota, U.S.A., November 30th, 1904
Died Baltimore, Maryland, U.S.A., June 23rd, 1980

Born and raised in the expanses of the Pacific Northwest, Clyfford Still nursed an idea of the artist as a pioneer, braving the wilderness of self-knowledge in search of truth and creating a new visual language, unpolluted by popular or traditional idioms, to express what was found there. The bitterness with which he denounced all social and cultural institutions made him seem a fanatic to some, a visionary to others.

Still was born in North Dakota in 1904 and grew up in Spokane, Washington, and on his family's farm in Bow Island, southern Alberta. He taught himself to paint and to play the piano between farm chores, "when my arms would be bloody to the elbows shocking wheat." In 1924 he traveled east to visit the museums and galleries of New York and found them filled with works "dedicated to aesthetic puerilities and cultural pretensions. . . . The manifestos and gestures of the cubists, the Fauves, the Dadaists, Surrealists, Futurists, or Expressionists were only evidence that the Black Mass was but a pathetic homage to that which it often presumed to mock and the Bauhaus herded them briskly into a cool, universal Buchenwald." After a single class at the Art Students' League he went home in disgust and enrolled at Spokane University but left after one semester, partly for lack of funds; a scholarship enabled him to come back and graduate in 1933. He took an M.A. from Washington State College on a teaching fellowship in 1935 and remained on the faculty for the next six years.

During this period Still immersed himself in the philosophy of Plato, Longinus, Croce, and Blake, and spent two summers at the artists' colony at Yaddo, working his way through the successive ideologies of 20th century art in order to rid himself of their influence. He refused to join the Federal Writers' Project, which employed many artists during the Depression, so as not to compromise his vehemently pure individualism. During the Second World War he drew blueprints for ships and aircraft in Oakland and San Francisco factories.

In 1943 Still made his debut in a one-person show at the San Francisco Museum of Art. His 21 paintings were in a distorted figurative style, often employing dualities of male and female, light and dark, in a surrealistic prairie landscape. In the fall of the year, he joined the faculty of the Richmond Professional Institute in Maryland.

The next three years saw the evolution of Still's mature style, an expressionism that modulated between the gestural abstraction of Jackson Pollock and the chromatic abstraction of Barnett Newman. His broad fields of color, torn open by dark patches or split by jagged lines, suggested a terrain of ravines and crevices, as if the viewer were suspended above an uninhabited planet still raw from its creation. Often he applied paint with a knife in slabs so thick that the "forms seemed gouged out of the palpable pigment with the elemental force of ice-age glaciers tearing out lakes and uprooting forests," according to critic Barbara Rose. Through his dramatic color contrasts and his deliberate use of "ugly" forms, "Still achieves an impact that forces the viewer into a more immediate confrontation with the work of art."

In 1946 Peggy Guggenheim offered Still a one-person show at her

Art of the Century Gallery in New York. Viewers noted an affinity between his paintings and those of Adolph Gottleib, Mark Rothko, and other members of the emerging "New York School." Still returned to New York a year later to exhibit at the Betty Parsons Gallery in a group show, "The Ideographic Picture," and to assist in the foundation of Subjects of the Artist, an art school on East Eighth Street. At the California School of Fine Arts, where he taught from 1945 to 1950, Still exerted a strong influence on younger artists, to whom he offered a viable alternative to cubism and an attractively independent moral stance. John Schueler has noted the powerful effect on himself and on other students of Still's admonition, "You can make a painting out of the truth." What Still demanded of himself and of all artists was a commitment to complete self-reliance and self-confrontation and a refusal to bend to the authority of any external entity. "The work had to be carried on in aloneness and with ruthless purpose," he later wrote. "I had learned as a youth the price one pays for a father, a master, a Yahweh, or his contemporary substitute—an institutional culture."

In 1950 Still moved to New York, where he taught briefly at Hunter and Brooklyn Colleges. His appearance in the Museum of Modern Art's "Fifteen Americans" show in 1952 was his last until 1959, when the Albright Gallery in Buffalo exhibited a 72-painting retrospective installed and catalogued by the artist himself. It was dedicated to "all those who would know the meaning and the responsibilities of freedom, intrinsic and absolute." A few years later he donated 31 paintings worth more than $1 million to the gallery. Another retrospective followed in 1963 at the University of Pennsylvania's Institute of Contemporary Art.

From the end of the 1950s, Still worked increasingly in large dimensions, sometimes occupying an entire wall with a single painting. He continued to use zones of color interacting on the canvas without reference to a horizon. "If anything can be drawn from Still's work beside the exaltation of expanses and the challenge of limitless space," says critic Henry Rand, "it is a song of praise of individual freedom fully cognizant of the lethal responsibility of decision. The right to failure and the specter of inhospitable vastness greets the viewer. The hardiness of survival and triumph are the implicit health and joy of these pictures."

Some viewers found in the huge scale and obscure but suggestive shapes of Still's paintings a religious overtone much like the pantheism of the British Romantics. Robert Rosenblum called Still a "master of the Abstract Sublime", adding, "Not the least awesome thing about Still's work is the paradox that the more elemental and monolithic it becomes, the more complex and mysterious are its effects."

Still earned himself a reputation for cantankerousness with his bombastic denunciations of everything and everyone connected with contemporary art and the European cultural tradition. Critics were "as completely ignorant of the whole of painting which they befouled and presumed to direct as they were inept in the art of writing"; galleries were "those sordid gift-shoppes" with "gas-chamber white walls." He also indulged in melodramatic posturing on his own behalf. The development of his painting style, he said, was "one of the great stories of all time. . . . one of the few truly liberating concepts man has ever known. . . . I had made it clear that a single stroke of paint,

backed by work and a mind that understood its potency and implications, could restore to man the freedom lost in twenty centuries of apology and devices for subjugation."

Still's antipathy to the commercial art world (or Moloch, as he called it) led him to break off relations with dealers and galleries and to sell his paintings privately. This arrangement was partly necessitated by his sense of each painting as a mystical vessel with a life of its own, whose acquisition by unscrupulous owners could be disastrous. In 1969, after a seven-year hiatus, he agreed to be included in group shows at the Metropolitan Museum of Art and the Museum of Modern Art and to hold a retrospective at the Marlborough-Gerson Gallery, which he had accepted as his new dealer. Most of his works remained at his house in Maryland, where he had moved in 1961 along with his wife and daughters.

In 1976 a permanent exhibition of Still's work was installed at the San Franciso Museum of Modern Art. Three years later he was honored with an unprecedented retrospective at the Metropolitan, which displayed 78 of his large-scale paintings—the most extensive exhibit it had ever mounted for a living artist. More than half a century had passed since Still had walked out of the Metropolitan in disgust as a young art student.

Still died of cancer a year later.   J.P./D.S.

Both parents farmers; father also an accountant. Married Patricia. Two daughters. Educ: Spokane Univ., Washington (art scholarship), B.A. 1933; Washington State Univ. at Pullman (teaching fellowship), M.A. 1935. Mil. Service: Draftsman, ship and aircraft factories, Oakland and San Francisco, Calif. 1941–43. Instr. 1935–40 and Asst. Prof. 1940–41, Washington State Univ.; Prof., Richmond Professional Inst. of the Coll. of William and Mary, Richmond, Va. 1943–45; teacher 1946–48, also founder and Dir. of Advanced Painting Group 1948–50, California Sch. of Fine Arts, San Francisco; co-founder, Subjects of the Artist teaching group, NYC 1948. Prof.: Hunter Coll., NYC 1952; Brooklyn Museum Sch., 1952; Brooklyn Coll., 1952–53; Univ. of Colorado at Boulder, 1960; Univ. of Pennsylvania 1963. Hons: Fellow, Trask Foundn. (Yaddo), Sarasota Springs, Wyo. 1934, 1935; Gold Medal Award of Merit for Painting, American Acad. of Arts and Letters, NYC 1972; Medal for Painting, Skowhegan Sch. for Painting and Sculpture, Maine 1975; elected to American Acad. of Arts and Letters 1978. Hon. D.F.A. from Maryland Inst. of Art 1967, North Dakota State Univ. 1972, San Francisco Art Inst. 1976, Univ. of Maryland 1980. *Exhibitions: One-person*—San Francisco Museum of Art, 1943; Art of This Century, NYC 1946; Calif. Palace of the Legion of Honor, San Francisco 1946; Betty Parsons Gall., NYC 1946, 1950, 1951; Metart Gall., San Francisco 1950; Albright Art Gall. (retrospective), Buffalo, N.Y. 1959; Inst. of Contemporary Art, Univ. of Pennsylvania, Philadelphia 1963; Albright-Knox Art Gall. (permanent installation), Buffalo 1966; Buffalo Fine Arts Acad., 1966; Marlborough-Gerson Gall., NYC 1969, 1970; San Francisco Museum of Art (permanent installation), 1976; Metropolitan Museum of Art (retrospective), 1979. *Selected Group Shows*—The Ideographic Picture, Betty Parsons Gall., NYC 1948; Fifteen Americans, Museum of Modern Art, NYC and tour 1952; The New American Painting, toured Europe 1958–59; Documenta II, Kassel, West Germany 1959; The New American Painting and Sculpture, Museum of Modern Art 1969; Metropolitan Museum of Art 1969. *Collections*—Albright-Knox Art Gall., Buffalo; Phillips Collection, Washington, D.C.; Whitney

Museum, NYC; Museum of Modern Art, NYC; Kunsthalle, Basel;
Tate Gall., London; Mr. and Mrs. Carter Burden, NYC; Mr. and
Mrs. Frederick Byers III, NYC; Mr. and Mrs. Young Merritt Smith,
Hillsborough, N.C.; others. *Author:* "Comment" in Albright-Knox
Gall. Notes, Summer 1960; "An Open Letter to an Art Critic,"
Artforum, Dec. 1963; statement in Clyfford Still catalogue, Inst. of
Contemporary Art, Univ. of Pennsylvania 1963; "Letter to the
Editor," Artforum, Feb. 1964; statements in Clyfford Sill catalogue,
Albright-Knox Art Gall. 1966 (reprinted in Barbara Rose, Readings
in American Art 1900–75, 1975); statement in Clyfford Still catalogue,
Metropolitan Museum of Art 1979.
Further reading: Art and Culture by Clement Greenberg, 1961; The
Triumph of American Painting by Irving Sandler, 1970; The New
York School: A Cultural Reckoning by Dore Ashton, 1973; A Period
of Exploration: San Francisco 1945–50 by Mary Fuller McChesney,
1973; The Genius of American Painting by John Wilmerding (ed.),
1973; American Art Since 1900 by Barbara Rose, 1975; Modern
Painting and the Northern Romantic Tradition by Robert Rosenblum,
1975; The New York School: The Painters and Sculptors of the Fifties
by Irving Sandler, 1978; "The Extremist Factor" by Nancy Marmer, in
Art in America, April 1980.

DAVID BURPEE
Horticulturist and businessman
Born Philadelphia, Pennsylvania, U.S.A., April 5th, 1893
Died Doylestown, Pennsylvania, U.S.A., June 24th, 1980

For 55 years, David Burpee headed the W. Atlee Burpee Company,
one of the largest mail-order seed companies in the world. Mr. Burpee
earned renown in America and abroad for developing and marketing
hundreds of varieties of flowers and vegetables.

Born in 1893 in Philadelphia, Burpee was exposed to the seed
business at an early age. His father, Washington Atlee Burpee, had in
1878 founded the W. Atlee Burpee Company as a small seedstore and
built it into a mail-order seed company by the time of David's birth.

Burpee attended Doylestown High School and Culver Military
Academy. In 1913 he entered the Cornell University School of Agriculture, but within a few months, he was called home due to his
father's illness. He joined his father as an assistant and in 1914 became
general manager of the business. In 1915, after his father's death, he
became company president.

During his long tenure as president, Burpee used his annual seed
catalogues to introduce home gardeners to the many hybrid flowers
and vegetables that had been developed at the company's experimental breeding centers—Fordhook Farms in Doylestown, Pennsylvania
and Floradale Farms in Lompoc, California. Some of the more
popular varieties were the red and gold hybrid marigold; the first
ruffled sweet peas; hybrid zinnias, larger than any others yet produced; Big Boy and Big Girl hybrid tomatoes, more productive and
disease-resistant than previous varieties; the hybrid zucchini squash;
and the Ambrosia hybrid melon.

A keen businessman and merchandiser, Burpee found that naming

Courtesy Burpee estate

a flower after a famous person increased its popularity. He so honored, among others, Pearl Buck, Mrs. Douglas MacArthur, and Helen Hayes. Mr. Burpee also provided money-back guarantees on his seeds, thus insuring the Burpee slogan, "Burpee Seeds Grow."

Burpee was widely esteemed for his research and contributions to the field of horticulture. In addition to honorary doctorates, he was awarded the Liberty Hyde Bailey Award (1978), the highest award the American Horticulture Society can give.

For years, the sweet pea was Burpee's most popular selling flower, but a root fungus greatly reduced its hardiness, and in 1920, Burpee decided to develop a white marigold as a replacement. By 1954, Burpee and his breeding staff had still not succeeded, so Burpee offered a $10,000 prize to the first person to produce the seeds for the marigold. In 1975, 55 years after the initial research had begun, Burpee presented a check to Mrs. Alice Vonk of Iowa.

From 1959, Burpee campaigned to have the marigold named the national flower, because, he said, "it is a symbol of the desire of the United States for peace and friendship with all the peoples of the world." His efforts failed. Burpee sold the business to the General Foods Corporation in 1970. Until his death, he remained active as a consultant in the breeding of hybrid varieties.   R.B.

Son of Washington Atlee B., seedsalesman, and Blanche (Simons) B. Married Lois Torrance 1938. Children: Jonathan; Blanche Elizabeth Dohan. Educ: Doylestown High Sch., Pa.; Culver Military Acad., Ind.; attended Cornell Univ. Sch. of Agriculture 1913. Joined father's seed bus., W. Atlee Burpee Co. 1914; Gen. Mgr. 1915; Chief Exec. Officer 1915–70; Dir. and Consultant 1970–77. Chmn. Bd., James Vick's Seeds, Inc.; Bd. Dirs., Welcome House, Doylestown, Pa; Pres. and Dir., Luther Burbank Seed Co.; Past Pres. and Dir., American Seed Trade Assn.; V.P. 1933–35 and Dir. 1960, Union League; V.P., Natl. Sweet Pea Soc. of Great Britain. Dir.: Market Street Natl. Bank, Philadelphia; Abington Memorial Hosp.; Natl. Council on Business Mail, Inc.; Poor Richard, Philadelphia. Member: Soc. War 1812; New England Soc.; English Speaking Union, Pa.; Soc. of New York; Natl. Jr. Vegetable Growers Assn.; American Horticultural Council; American Management Assn.; Friends of the Land; American Museum of Natural History; Colonial Soc., Pa.; Franklin Inst. of Philadelphia; Scottish Natl. Sweet Pea Soc.; Royal Horticultural Soc.; Newcomen Soc. North America; Natl. Audubon Soc.; Natl. Acad. of Sciences; Natl. Geography Soc.; World Affairs Council; Philadelphia Soc. Promoting Agriculture; Pennsylvania Forestry Assn.; Men's Garden Clubs of America; Quaker City Farmers Club; Delta Upsilon; Racquet, Philadelphia; Hillsboro, Fla. Life Member, Société Nationale d'Horticulture de France. Hons: American Horticultural Council Citation 1958; hon. D.Sc., Bucknell Univ. 1959 and Delaware Valley Coll. of Science and Agriculture 1972; Henry Eckford Memorial Medal, Natl. Sweet Pea Soc. of Great Britain 1963; Gold Seal, Natl. Council State Garden Clubs 1964; American Home Achievement Medal 1964; Gold Medal for outstanding contribution to horticulture, Men's Garden Club of Los Angeles 1974; Certificate of Appreciation, Men's Garden Club of Delaware Valley 1975; Liberty Hyde Bailey Award, American Horticultural Soc. 1978; hon. member, Delta Mu Delta and Alpha Zeta; hon. Life Pres., Canadian Soc. Philadelphia; hon. Dir., Delaware Valley Coll. of Science and Agriculture and Bucknell Univ.

HOWARD NORTON COOK
Muralist, painter, and printmaker
Born Springfield, Massachusetts, U.S.A., July 16th, 1901
Died Santa Fe, New Mexico, U.S.A., June 24th, 1980

During his formative years as an artist and those of his initial success during the late 1920s and 1930s, Howard Norton Cook refused the security of teaching positions and other offers for the sake of what he called the "larger creative effort." A man basically reticent whose recognition came because of the quality of his work rather than the careful crafting of a public image, Cook was, in the words of the critic Carl Zigrosser, "among the impartial observers, the objective reporters, the recording angels." Seldom a man to opt for the secure or the predictable, Cook pursued his art with a commitment to experimentation that can be traced from his early realistic murals to his later abstract collages.

Born in Springfield, Massachusetts in 1901, Cook spent his boyhood working on farms and in tobacco fields in the area. After graduating from high school he painted outdoor billboards and worked in local photo-engravers' and lithographers' shops, doing odd jobs of lettering and drawing lions' heads on tomato soup cans. From 1919 to 1921 he studied for three sessions with the Art Students' League in New York with the etcher, Joseph Pennell, and the painter, Andrew Dasburg, among others.

For five years, beginning in 1922, Cook led a precarious financial existence doing pen drawings and woodcut illustrations for *The Forum, Survey Graphic,* and *The Century.* During this period he was able, nonetheless, to make sketching trips to England, France, Central America, the Orient, North Africa, Turkey, and the West Coast. This period, which included a four-month job as a quartermaster on a coastal steamer through the Panama Canal, was, as Cook wrote in his autobiographical essay, *From Printmaking to Frescoes (1942)* his "early independent schooling" and also the time during which he made his first etching at Thomas Handforth's studio in Paris in 1925.

Upon his return to the United States Cook married the artist Barbara Latham whom he met while in Taos, New Mexico. In late 1926, after he had been commissioned by *The Forum* to illustrate Willa Cather's novel, *Death Comes for the Archbishop,* he spent a year and a half in the American Southwest gathering material and finding considerable inspiration in the region. His first prints in 1927, were considered superior to any ever done before of the area; he made more than a hundred and fifty others in different media from Texas to New England.

A Guggenheim Fellowship in 1932 was a turning point in his development as an artist. He and his wife were able to travel to Mexico to study the technnique of *buon fresco,* or "true fresco," one of the most permanent forms of wall decoration known. While in Mexico he painted his first frescoes and, inspired by the humanity of the Mexican people, executed a series of sensitive, dynamic studies such as the wood-engraving, *Cocoanut Palm,* and the etching, *Fiesta.* When his Guggenheim was renewed in 1936, Cook traveled throughout the American South and Southwest, pursuing his interest in what he called the "character and significance of humble working people." Resulting from this period were many portrait drawings, several prints, and material that became the basis of his later frescoes in Pittsburgh and San Antonio. Among the more accomplished of the prints were *River Baptism, Southern Mountaineer, Church Wagon,* and *Texas Longhorns.*

In the mid-thirties Cook received a series of mural commissions for Springfield, Pittsburgh, San Antonio, and Corpus Christi to which he devoted most of his time until the beginning of World War Two. These murals, which placed him among the relatively few mural painters in the United States, were praised for their monumental design and expert draftsmanship. In 1937 Cook received the gold medal of the Architectural League of New York; the jury said that Cook's murals were "distinguished by exceptional originality, free from derivative influence, and possessing a masterful organization and form." His essay, "From Printmaking to Frescoes," described in illuminating and personalized detail his work on the mural at the San Antonio post office. The essay, which contained technical data for the San Antonio frescoes as well as pictures of Cook at work and of various sections of the continuous historical work, concluded with patriotic sentiment; ". . . murals in public places can portray the meaning of democracy for which we are fighting, the hopes and ideals of our people, the ultimate desire for a fruitful brotherhood of mankind."

During World War Two Cook served in several non-combative capacities. The Office of Emergency Administration commissioned him to do war industry paintings in Norfolk, Virginia in 1942. He was a leader of a war art unit of the Corps of Engineers of the Army in the Pacific Theater in 1943 and a war correspondent for *Collier's Magazine* from 1943 to 1944.

Beginning in 1942 with a one-year guest professorship of art at the University of Texas, Cook began a three-decade assocation with academic institutions and art schools. However, he never became a permanent member of any faculty, preferring to hold artist-in-residence and guest professor positions so that he could continue with his own work.

Although Cook's reputation rests firmly on the realistic murals he painted in the new Federal Buildings during the late 1920s and 30s, he continued to do interesting experimental work for the rest of his career. Many of his collages during the 1950s are almost completely abstract. Among his numerous awards is one from the Mark Rothko Foundation in 1951.

Cook died in his Santa Fe, New Mexico home at the age of 78. D.B.

Son of Frank Chester C. and Annie Norton C. Married Barbara Latham, artist 1927. Educ: Art Students' League, NYC, 1919–1921. Mil. Service: Leader, War Art Unit, Corps of Engineers, U.S. Army, Pacific Theater 1943; war artist correspondent, Collier's Magazine 1943–44. Active as muralist, painter, and printmaker since 1925; Guest Prof., Dept. of Art., Univ. of Texas 1942–43; Guest Prof., Dept. of Art, Univ. of New Mexico, summers 1947, 1960; Guest Prof., Dept. of Art, Univ. of California at Berkeley 1948; Guest Instr., Colorado Springs Fine Arts Center 1949; teacher of painting 1945, 1950 and Guest Artist, Scripps Coll 1951; Guest Artist, Washington Univ., St. Louis 1954–55; Guest Artist, Highlands Univ., Highlands, N.M., summer 1957; Artist-in-residence, Roswell Mus.

and Art Center Roswell, N.M. 1967–68. Jury Member: U.S. Govt. Sect. Fine Arts, 1937; American art, Metropolitan Mus. of Art, NYC, 1951. Life member, Art Students' League, Natl. Acad. of Design and Taos Art Assn.; Member, Soc. of American Graphic Artists, NYC. Hons: Two Guggenheim Foundn. Fellowships 1932, 1936; Gold Medal for Mural Painting, Architectural league of N.Y. 1937; Purchase Prize, Metropolitan Mus. of Art 1942; Painting Purchase Award, Denver Art Mus. 1950; Mark Rothko Foundn. Award 1951; Fleisher Memorial Purchase Painting, Phil. 1952; Tupperware purchase award 1956; first award, oil painting, Tucson Art Assn. 1958; Purchase awards, drawing, Mus. of New Mexico, Dallas Mus. of Fine Arts, and the Natl. Acad. of Design 1958; Samuel F. B. Morse Gold Medal, Natl. Acad. of Design 1963; Governor's Award, N.M. 1979, and numerous others. *Commissions* (murals): Hotel Tasqueno, Taxco, N.M.; Law Library, Springfield, Mass.; Fedeal Court House, Pittsburgh, Pa.; U.S. Post Offices, Alamo Plaza, San Antonio, and Corpus Christi, Tex.; Mayo Clinic, Rochester, Minn. *Exhibitions: One-person*—(first) Denver Art Mus. 1928; Weyhe Gall., NYC 1929, 1931, 1934, 1937, 1941; Mus. of Fine Arts, Springfield, Mass. 1936; The Print Club, phila. 1937; Kennedy Gall., NYC 1942, 1944; National Gall., Washington, D.C. 1944; Rehn Galleries, NYC 1945, 1950; Mus. of Fine Arts, Dallas 1945, 1953; Minneapolis Art Inst. 1950; Grand Central Moderns, NYC 1951, 1953, 1956, 1960, 1964; San Diego 1952; Santa Barbara Mus. of Art 1952; de Young San Francisco 1952; Nelson Art Mus., Kansas City 1953 Joslyn Art Mus., Omaha 1953; G.W.V. Smith Art Mus., Springfield, Mass. 1954; Mus. of Fine Arts, Houston 1954; Dartmouth Coll. 1954; Montclair Art Mus., Montclair, N.J. 1954; Alexander Rabow Galleries, San Francisco 1956; Carnegie 1958; Raymond Burr Gall., Los Angeles 1962, 1963; Rosequist Galleries, Tuscon 1962; Mus. and Art Center, Roswell, N.M. 1968, 1976; Governor's Gall., Santa Fe, N.M. 1977. *Retrospective:* Roswell 1975, 1977; Prakapas Gall., NYC 1976; Bethesda Art Gall., Md. 1977, 1978. *Group:* Artists for Victory Exhibition, Metropolitan Mus. of Art, NYC 1942; 20th Century Drawings from the Permanent Collection, Whitney Mus. of American Art, NYC, 1975. *Collections:* Baltimore Mus. of Arts; Art Inst., Chicago; Mus. of Fine Arts, Dallas; Dartmouth Coll.; Denver Art Mus.; de Young, San Francisco; Harvard Univ.' Mus. of Modern Art, NYC; Metropolitan Mus. of Art, NYC; Minneapolis Art Inst.; Oklahoma; Joslyn Art Mus., Omaha, Neb.; Orlando; Philadelphia Mus. of Art; Univ. of Rochester; Mus. of Art, Santa Barbara, Calif.; Santa Fe, N.M.; Whitney Mus. of American Artists, NYC. *Author:* Sammi's Army (juvenile picture book for which he did illustrations), 1943; "Road from Prints to Frescoes," American Magazine of Art, 1942; "Making a Watercolor," American Artist Magazine, 1945.

V(ARAHAGIRI) V(ENKATA) GIRI
President of India
Born Berhampur, Orissa, India, August 10th, 1894
Died Madras, Tamil Nadu, India, June 24th, 1980

V.V. Giri, the fourth President of India, was the second of 12 children born to a middle-class Brahman family in Berhampur. He was introduced to politics by his father, a liberal lawyer active in the movement to end British rule over India. At the National University

of Ireland, where he earned a law degree, Giri became an anti-British revolutionary, joining a student anarchist society and making friends with the leaders of Sinn Fein, Ireland's independence movement. The British deported him in 1916 after he participated in the Easter Rebellion uprising against them.

Back home, Giri started a law practice and was elected to the Indian National Congress. Though not entirely a convert to the ethic of nonviolence espoused by Mohandas Gandhi, whom he had met in London in 1914, Giri joined Gandhi's freedom movement, engaging in acts of civil disobedience against the British authorities and drawing several brief terms of imprisonment, on one of which he led a hunger strike.

In 1927 Giri began a career as a trade union organizer, leading workers on the Bengal–Nagpur railway in a major strike that proved to be the genesis of the Indian labor movement. To win public support, Giri forbade violence and made sure that passenger train service was not disrupted. Local merchants donated cartloads of wheat flour and rice to the workers' families in response to his appeals and were reimbursed by them when the strike ended. Giri later served two terms as president of the All-India Trade Union Congress.

In 1934 Giri was elected to the Central Legislative Assembly, the forerunner of the present Parliament, where he campaigned in favor of shortening the 54-hour work week for coal miners and raising their minimum age of employment from 13 to 15. When the British instituted provincial autonomy in 1937, Giri won a seat in the Legislative Assembly of the state of Madras (now called Tamil Nadu) and was appointed the state's Minister of Labour, Industry, Commerce, and Cooperation.

After India gained its independence in 1947, Giri spent four years as High Commissioner to Ceylon, then was elected to the *Lok Sabha* ("House of the People," the Lower House of Parliament) as a member of the Congress Party. He also served for two years as Minister of Labour in the cabinet of India's first prime Minister, Jawaharlal Nehru. Between 1957 and 1967 he held successive state governorships in Uttar Pradesh, Kerala, and Mysore.

Giri was elected Vice President of India in 1967 and became acting president in May 1969, after the death of Zakir Husain. The prospect of new presidential elections provoked a furious power struggle within the Congress Party, which had failed to resolve the country's desperate economic and social problems despite a 20-year monopoly on the government. Prime Minister Indira Gandhi, Nehru's daughter and leader of the party's leftist faction, sought to win back the support of disillusioned voters by a program of socialist policies, including nationalization of industries and banks, land reform, and curtailment of the rights of individuals to amass wealth. The old-guard leadership of the party, a right-wing group known as the Syndicate, fought her on these issues and made the presidential election a test of strength, nominating a conservative candidate despite her expressed preference for Giri.

At Mrs. Gandhi's urging, Giri resigned his post as acting president to run as an independent. Although the public demonstrated its approval of the Prime Minister in mass rallies outside her home, few observers believed that she was politically strong enough to steal the victory from the party's official candidate. But 40 percent of the

Congress Party electors swung to Giri, and these votes, plus those of the Communists and other leftist groups, secured him the presidency on the second ballot. The Syndicate retaliated by expelling Mrs. Gandhi, but most of the party membership deserted it to join her New Congress Party.

Giri was a loyal supporter of Mrs. Gandhi during most of his term in office, though many of his proposals for social reform were ignored. He enforced her plan to nationalize the country's 14 largest commercial banks, which together controlled about 75 percent of its private banking deposits, and in 1970 announced the abolition of India's 2,000-year-old princely order of *maharajas,* whose 300 remaining members had been receiving government stipends since 1947 as compensation for merging their realms with the Indian Union. (This order was later overturned by the Supreme Court.) Exercising his right to dissolve state governments, Giri imposed temporary presidential rule on Andhra Pradesh in 1970 to stop a secession movement there and did the same in Gujarat in 1974 after riots broke out over rising prices.

By the end of his term, Giri had become an outspoken critic of the Prime Minister, whose concentration on political infighting at the expense of economic development betrayed, he felt, an underlying moral bankruptcy in the government and the nation. In a 1973 speech, he quoted Mahatma Gandhi on the seven social evils (politics without principle, wealth without work, pleasure without conscience, knowledge without character, commerce without morality, science without humanity, and worship without sacrifice), saying, "Today these sins are present in our society in a more virulent form. . . . Unless and until we take immediate steps to remove them, lock, stock, and barrel, we cannot survive as a nation."

Denied renomination in 1974, Giri retired to Bangalore and Madras with his wife, Saraswathi Bai, a linguist, with whom he had 11 children. He was the author of several books and pamphlets on labor and unemployment and founded the Labour Party of India a year before his death.   J.P.

Son of Jogaiah Pantula G., lawyer and politician. Married Saraswathi Bai, linguist 1917 (d. 1978). Children: seven daughters, four sons. Educ: Kallikota Coll., Berhampur; Natl. Univ. Ireland, Dublin, law degree ca. 1916. Mil. Service: Indian Corps, Red Cross, London, WWI. Admitted to Irish bar ca. 1916. Active in Sinn Fein and Easter Rebellion, Dublin 1916; deported to India by British Govt. 1916. Lawyer, Madras ca. 1916–21; elected to Indian Natl. Congress ca. 1921; active in Indian independence movement and several times imprisoned for acts of civil disobedience. Organizer, Bengal–Nagpur Railway Union 1927; Founder, Pres., and Gen. Secty. 1929–36, All-India Railwaymen's Union; Founding Member and Pres., All-India Trade Union Congress. Member, Central Legislative Assembly 1934–37; Convener, Natl. Planning Cttee. 1937; Member, Legislative Assembly of Madras State 1937–39; Minister of Labour, Madras 1946–47; High Commnr. (Ambassador) to Ceylon 1947–51. Elected to Lower House of Parliament from Pathapatnam, Madras 1952; Minister of Labour 1952–54; Gov. of Uttar Pradesh 1957–61; Gov. of Kerala 1961–65; Gov. of Mysore 1965–67; V.P. of India 1967–69; Acting Pres. May–July 1969; Pres. of India 1969–74. Founder, Indian Students Assn., Natl. Univ. Dublin ca. 1914–15; Delegate to Intnl.

Labor Org. Conference from All-India Trade Union Congress, Geneva 1927; Labour Rep., Second Round Table Conference, London 1931; Pres., Indian Conference of Social Work 1958–60; Founder, Labour Party of India 1979. Hons: D.Litt. from Banaras Hindu, Lucknow, and Andhra Univs.; LL.D. from Agra, Moscow, Sofia, and Bratislava Univs. *Author:* Labour Problems in Indian Industry, 1958; Problems of Public Administration, 1967; National Regeneration Problems and Prospects, 1969; Jobs for our Millions, 1970; The President Speaks, 1970; Industrial Relations; memoirs.
Further reading: A New History of India by Stanley Wolpert, 1977; India's Second Revolution: The Dimensions of Development by A. Veit, 1976.

BORIS KAUFMAN
Cinematographer
Born Bialystok, Poland, August 24th, 1906
Died New York City, U.S.A., June 24th, 1980

When the Hoboken, New Jersey, waterfront was revitalized with much fanfare in 1973, a famous film depicting the once grim and decaying Hoboken docks was included as part of the publicity. Boris Kaufman, who had shot *On the Waterfront* 20 years earlier on those docks and in the rotting warehouses nearby, may have been one of the few to note their passing with regret. His cinematography of the area won him an Oscar in 1955 and established him in the vanguard of creative film photographers for years to come. Best known for his experimental and often beautifully crafted work in black and white, Kaufman also made important contributions in Technicolor *(Splendor in the Grass,* 1961, is considered his best), and Pauline Kael, *The New Yorker* movie critic, credits him with helping to bring filmmaking of all sorts back to New York from the West Coast.

Boris Kaufman was born in 1906 in Bialystok, Poland. Both his older brothers, Dennis and Mikail, were actively involved in the first Soviet film efforts of the early 1920s, and Dennis in particular went on to become a famous movie-maker in his own right under the pseudonym Dziga Vertov. The Soviet Kino Pravda Documentary Group, which Vertov and several others launched, was the only formal cinematographic training young Kaufman ever received. When he was 23, Kaufman chose to emigrate to Paris with his parents, leaving his brothers behind in Russia. For the rest of his life he was silent about his Soviet family connections and seldom acknowledged the early Kino Pravda influences on his work.

Two far greater influences, he believed, were the legendary French director Jean Vigo and American documentarist Willard van Dyke. Kaufman first met Vigo in Paris in 1929. Working on films together over the next eight years, the two became extremely close and when Vigo died after a long illness in 1937 Kaufman confessed, "A light has gone out for me." Their most famous joint endeavor, *Zéro de Conduite,* is an early film classic. Vigo directed and Kaufman captured on film a haunting dream world of French schoolchildren at odds with a rigid academic system. As Vigo's health worsened, Kaufman tried his own hand at directing scenes in *L'Atalante, A Propos de Nice,* and

Taris. He never formally directed films again, but those who worked with him later always remarked on his intuition and his ability to quickly grasp a director's thoughts or mood.

W.S. van Dyke knew Kaufman after his brief stint in the French Army (1940–41), and the two collaborated on a number of films, which were French versions of American pictures, including *The Feminine Touch* (1941) and *I Married An Angel* (1942). After emigration to Canada in 1942 and short tenure with the Canadian National Film Board, Kaufman made several documentaries in New York with Willard van Dyke (including *Journey into Medicine*, 1947, and *The Tanglewood Story*, 1950). During this period Kaufman became far more technically accomplished, establishing with the help of van Dyke a solid enough reputation in New York so that Hollywood never tempted him away. Through van Dyke he met Elia Kazan, who at the time was looking for someone a little out of step with the Hollywood studios to transform the New Jersey waterfront into just the right backdrop for a powerful filmscript starring Marlon Brando.

In *On the Waterfront, Twelve Angry Men, Long Day's Journey Into Night,* and countless other films, Kaufman proved that creative self-expression and commercial success can be interwoven seamlessly, given time and enough leeway. He made few compromises in his work and refused to be hurried. Producers and directors usually allowed him these unheard-of luxuries for he was reliable, efficient, and often brilliant in tough location work.

He loved experimenting with different camera and lighting effects. One afternoon, filming in Hoboken, he noticed some old trash cans burning refuse nearby. The dark, smoky blur surrounding them intrigued him. Instead of removing them, he dragged them in closer to heighten the foreground action and help set the scene apart from others. In *Twelve Angry Men,* he tried progressively longer lenses in the courtroom scene to bring the walls in closer and add to the claustrophobic tension. Both the smoke and the longer lens are now common techniques for most filmmakers.

Like all cinematographers, Boris Kaufman was the eye that always remained invisible. Movie buffs and film students may remember his name and many credits in the years to come; others may only recall the vivid images he photographed and fixed indelibly on film.   A.B.P.

Son of Abraham K. Married Helen Halpern 1930. Son: André, b. 1931, artist. Emigrated from Poland to France 1928, to Canada 1942, and to U.S.A. 1943. Educ: the Sorbonne, Paris. Mil. Service: French Army 1940–41. Involved in brother Dziga Vertov's Soviet Kino Pravda Documentary Group 1920–28; cinematographer and dir. with Jean Vigo and other filmmakers in Paris and Nice 1929–39; photographed French versions of popular American films with W.S. van Dyke 1937–41; cinematographer for Canadian Natl. Film Bd. 1942–43; cinematographer for Office of War Information documentaries in N.Y. 1943–45; freelance cinematographer in N.Y. 1945–70; collaborated with Elia Kazan, Sidney Lumet and other leading American filmmakers during the 1950s. Hons: Acad. Award (cinematography) for On the Waterfront 1955; Billy Blitzer Award for Outstanding Contributions to the Motion Picture Industry 1975; Fellow, American Acad. of Arts and Sciences 1979. *Films:* La Marche des Machines and 24 Heures en 30 Minutes, 1928; A Propos de Nice

and Les Hales, 1929; Taris, Champion de Natation, 1931; Le Mile
avec Jules Ladounegue, 1932; Zéro de Conduit, Seine, Woman
against Woman, Rich Man-Poor Girl, and Vacation from Love, 1933;
L'Atalante, 1934; Lucrèce Borgia, 1935; Pèe Lampion, 1936; Fort
Dolores, 1937; Serenade, 1938; Honolulo, Lucky Night, Fast and
Furious, and Babes in Arms, 1939; The Man From Dakota, The Earl
of Chicago, And One Was Beautiful, Strike up the Band, and Little
Nelly, 1940; Ziegfeld Girl, Love Crazy, H.M. Pulham, Esquire, and
The Feminine Touch (French version, with W.S. van Dyke), 1941;
Calling Dr. Gillespie, Cairo, Journey for Margaret, and I Married An
Angel (French version, with W.S. van Dyke), 1942; I Dood It, 1943;
Better Tomorrow, Capital, and The Southwest, 1945; Journey into
Medicine (with Willard van Dyke), 1947; Terribly Talented, 1948;
The Tanglewood Story (with Willard van Dyke), 1950; The Garden of
Eden and On the Waterfront, 1954; Crowded Paradise, Baby Doll,
and Patterns, 1956; Twelve Angry Men, 1957; That Kind of Woman,
1959; The Fugitive Kind, 1960; Splendor in the Grass, 1961; Long
Day's Journey into Night, 1962; All the Way Home and Gone Are the
Days, 1963; The World of Henry Orient, 1964; Film (short film) and
The Pawnbroker, 1965; The Group, 1966; Bye, Bye, Braverman,
1967; Uptight and The Brotherhood, 1968; Tell Me That You Love
Me, Junie Moon, 1970.

MAR IGNATIUS YACOUB III
Patriarch of Antioch and All the East of the Syrian Orthodox Church
Born Bartali, Iraq, 1912
Died Damascus, Syria, ca. June 26th, 1980

Mar Ignatius Yacoub III, Patriarch of Antioch and All the East of the
Syrian Orthodox Church, was born in Iraq in 1912 to a Syriac-
speaking family. He studied theology and philosophy at St. Matthew's
Seminary in Mosul, Iraq, and took his monastic vows at Homs, Libya.
In 1932, after a year of teaching in Beirut, he became private secretary
to the patriarchal legate in India, where he was ordained two years
later. From 1934 to 1947 he served as dean of the theological faculty of
the seminary of St. Ignatius in Malabar, then returned to Mosul to
lecture in theology. In 1950 he was consecrated Bishop for the diocese
of Beirut and Lebanon; seven years later he was chosen by the Holy
Synod to succeed Mar Ignatius Ephream I as Patriarch of the Church.

Mar Ignatius Yacoub's 13-year patriarchate was devoted to resolving differences within the Church and to expanding its services to
members living outside its traditional centers. He established two new
dioceses in Western Europe to minister to Middle Eastern emigrants
and moved the patriarchal residence from Homs to Syria's capital city,
Damascus. In 1968 he founded the Syrian Orthodox Seminary of St.
Ephream at Atchaneh, Lebanon. Although he was temporarily
successful in resolving a 50-year schism in the Indian branch of the
Church, he was unable to prevent its recurrence in the late 1970s.

The Patriarch, who wrote a number of books in Syriac and Arabic,
also spoke English and the Indian language Malayalam. To many
Western scholars he served as an authority on Syriac language and
culture, particularly the musical tradition of the Orthodox Church. On

several occasions he spoke out against the Israeli presence in Arab Jerusalem and against the civil war in Lebanon. A committed ecumenist, he visited the Archbishop of Canterbury in 1979 and Pope John Paul II a short time before his death.   J.P.

Born to Syriac-speaking parents. Educ: St. Matthew's Seminary, Mosul, Iraq. Prof., Beirut 1931; took monastic vows in Homs, Libya; private secty. to patriarchal legate, India 1932–34; ordained deacon and priest, India 1934; Dean of Theological Faculty, St. Ephraem's Seminary, Mosul ca. 1947–50; consecrated Bishop of the Diocese of Beirut and Damascus 1950; elected Patriarch by Holy Synod 1957; moved patriarchal residence from Homs to Damascus 1958; founded Syrian Orthodox Seminary of St. Ephraem, Atchaneh, Lebanon 1968; founded two new dioceses in Western Europe. Author of works in Syrian and Arabic.

BARNEY BIGARD
Jazz clarinetist and composer
Born New Orleans, Louisiana, U.S.A., March 3rd, 1906
Died Culver City, California, U.S.A., June 27th, 1980

Barney Bigard was born and raised in New Orleans, one of a generation of New Orleans clarinetists prominent in the development of jazz, which included Sidney Bechet, Johnny Dodds, Omer Simeon, and Jimmy Noone. Bigard had little formal training, but under the influence of Lorenzo Tio and Alphonse Picou, whose roots were in formal European music rather than the Afro-American folk music from which jazz originated, he developed early-on a technical precision not heard in the playing of others of his generation. His music, however, was unequivocally jazz, drawing deeply on the blues and marked by the irregular rhythms peculiar to jazz. He was a skilled improvisationalist known for his long, swooping runs over the entire range of the clarinet, but he was especially famous for playing in the low register, where his tone took on a dark, liquid quality.

Courtesy Mrs. B. Bigard

He first played professionally in the early 1920s, when he was with the New Orleans bands of Octave Gaspard and Albert Nichols. In 1925 he moved to Chicago to join King Oliver's Creole Jazz Band, with whom he played for three years. In 1927 he accompanied King Oliver on a tour to New York, where he remained for most of the following thirty years. After a short spell with Luis Russell he joined the Duke Ellington Orchestra in what was to be the longest and most celebrated association of his career.

Bigard's smooth and elegant style was perfectly suited to the Ellington sound, and the bandleader made full use of his talents as an accompanist, a featured soloist, and a composer. Ellington wrote the 1936 "Clarinet Lament," probably the first jazz piece in the form of a concerto for orchestra and solo instrument, specifically for Bigard. In turn Bigard wrote "Clouds in My Heart," "Minuet in Blues," and "Mood Indigo," which became an enduringly popular standard of the Ellington repertoire. His years with Ellington produced a number of classic recordings, among them "Finesse," recorded in Paris in 1939 with Django Reinhardt, the renowned Gypsty guitarist, and "Jack the Bear" in 1940.

He left the Duke Ellington Orchestra in 1942 and played with the Freddie Slack Band for two years before putting together the Barney Bigard Sextet. Among the musicians who played in various stages of the Sextet were pianist Art Tatum and bassist Charles Mingus. Bigard was uncomfortable in the role of bandleader, however, and in 1947 he accepted Louis Armstrong's invitation to join his All-Stars.

It was during these post-war years that Armstrong rose to the height of his international popularity, and with the All-Stars Bigard toured Europe three times, played in Japan and Australia, and appeared in motion pictures and television shows.

In 1956 Bigard left Armstrong and moved to Los Angeles, where he formed another of his own ensembles, but in 1960 he briefly rejoined the Louis Armstrong All-Stars for their famous State Department good-will tour of Africa. Back in California, he kept active with free-lance concert dates and recording sessions. In 1969, at the age of 63, he began a new career as a lecturer, visiting colleges and universities across the country to address students of jazz history and participate in jazz seminars. He continued to perform throughout the 70s, touring Europe with British percussionist Barry Martin in 1974 and appearing at the New York-Newport Jazz Festival in 1974 and 1975, and at the 1979 Grand Parade du Jazz in Nice.   K.B.

Born Albany Barney Leon B. Son of Alexander B. and Emanuella (Marquez) B. Married: (1) Arthemise; (2) Dorothe Edgecombe 1942. Children: 1st marriage—Winifred; Marlene; Patricia; Barney. Educ: Straight Coll., New Orleans 1919–23. Active as musician from the early 1920s in New Orleans, Chicago, New York, Los Angeles and other cities. Performed with: Octave Gasper's band and Albert Nichols band, New Orleans, early 1920s; King Oliver's Creole Jazz Band, Chicago 1925–27; Duke Ellington Orchestra, N.Y. 1927–42; Freddie Slack Bank, N.Y. 1942–44. Leader, Barney Bigard Sextet, N.Y. 1944–47; performer with Louis Armstrong's All-Stars, N.Y. 1947–56, 1960. Also tours in Europe, Japan, Australia, and Africa; free-lance concerts; lectrs. on jazz history from 1969. Member, American Soc. of Composers, Authors and Publishers. Hons: Lamplighter Gold Award 1943, 1944, 1945; Esquire Silver Jazz Award 1945, 1946, 1948; Hot Club of France Award 1972; Natl. Acad. of Recording Arts and Sciences Award 1975; named to Newport Jazz Hall of Fame 1975. *Composer:* Mood Indigo; Clouds in my Heart; Rocking in Rhythm; Minuet in Blues; Steps Steps Up and Steps Steps Down; Stompy Jones; and others. Also numerous recordings for television, motion picture and major record companies.

CAREY McWILLIAMS
Author and editor
Born Steamboat Springs, Colorado, U.S.A., December 13th, 1905
Died New York City, U.S.A., June 27th, 1980

Carey McWilliams was born in Steamboat Springs, Colorado in 1905, the son of a prosperous cattle rancher and state political figure, and raised in a region he called "extravagantly beautiful, long isolated and sparsely settled." When his father died in 1921 and his mother moved to Los Angeles, young McWilliams was left behind to attend the

University of Denver as a scholarship student. A 16-year-old with a small allowance and a Ford sedan, he apparently could not manage this first taste of freedom; he was expelled from the university in the spring of 1922 as a result of a St. Patrick's Day spree.

After this incident he joined his mother in Los Angeles and took a clerical job with the *Los Angeles Times,* enrolled at the University of Southern California, and in 1927 received his LL.B. McWilliams watched the city of Los Angeles burgeon; experienced its new cosmopolitan meld of Orientals, Hispanics, blacks, and whites; observed the great dust bowl migrations filter into the farm labor camps from Salinas to Bakersfield; and marked the peculiar hedonism that affected everything from politics-as-usual to radical reform.

As a student, McWilliams turned his hand to journalism, serving as editor of the campus daily, *The Trojan,* and soon found himself contributing reviews and cultural commentaries to the *Los Angeles Times, San Diego Union,* and various California magazines. He continued this as an avocation even after becoming a member of a conservative, business-oriented law firm, but gradually his focus changed from the literary to the political. He was particularly stirred by a series of violent confrontations between migrant farm laborers and the state-supported California Farmers' Association between 1930 and 1934, and he set out on a journalistic investigation of the agricultural laborer's plight. Two books—*Factories in the Field* (1939) and *Ill Fares the Land* (1942)—came out of this experience, each written in the reformist tradition and setting forth with compassion the grim plight of the farm worker both in California and around the nation. The first of these was published at the same time as Steinbeck's classic *Grapes of Wrath,* adding to as well as benefiting from the novel's impact.

It was this immersion in the farm laborers' struggle that led him into Upton Sinclair's unsuccessful campaign for Governor in 1934, and in 1938 led to his being appointed head of the State Division of Housing and Immigration (DHI) by the New Deal Democrat elected to the State House in that year. Between 1938 and 1942, McWilliams busied himself to such an extent in defense of migrant laborers from grower abuse that Republican Earl Warren, elected governor in 1942, declared that his first official act would be the firing of the DHI chief.

Leaving office, McWilliams quickly found a new cause—the wartime "resettlement" (internment) of the large West Coast Japanese population—and again distilled his observations into two volumes, *Brothers Under the Skin* (1943) and *Prejudice* (1944). Both dealt with the strain of racism in American democracy, and used to great effect the extremism of Hitler's racial theories to underline his point.

In 1945 he was named contributing editor to *The Nation;* in 1951 associate editor, editorial director in 1952, and in 1955, editor-in-chief. As an organ of the non-communist left, the journal under McWilliams persevered in its convictions through the cold war era, opposing the House Committee on Un-American Activities and McCarthyism and supporting the labor and civil rights movements.

One of his last and most memorable crusades was his early and adamant opposition to American involvement in Vietnam. Editorializing against intervention as early as 1963, McWilliams kept up a steady, increasingly blunt attack against President Johnson and his advisors. By 1966 he had abandoned the Democratic administration, and that year, at a *Nation*-sponsored teach-in in Los Angeles he suggested to one of the participants, Senator Eugene McCarthy, that he enter some of the early 1968 primaries to test the depth of antiwar sentiment. Since he was not up for re-election that year, McCarthy agreed, and the "Dump Johnson" movement finally had (thanks to Carey McWilliams) a candidate around whom to rally.   R.C.

Son of Jerry McW., cattle rancher and politician, and Harriet Casley McW. Married: (1) Dorothy Hedrick 1930 (div.); (2) Iris Dornfeld 1941. Children: 1st marriage—Wilson Carey, political scientist, b. 1933; 2nd marriage—Jerry Ross, librarian, b. 1942. Educ: Wolfe Hall Mil. Acad. and Steamboat Springs High Sch., diploma 1921, Univ. of Colo., Denver 1921–22; Univ. of Southern California, Los Angeles, LL.B. 1927. Clerical employee, Los Angeles Times and freelance journalist 1922–27; admitted to Calif. Bar 1927; member Black, Hammack and McWilliams, Los Angeles 1927–38; Commnr., Div. of Housing and Immigration, State of Calif. 1938–42. With The Nation, NYC: joined as Contributing Ed. 1945; Assoc. Ed. 1951; Editorial Dir. 1952; Ed. 1955–75. *Author:* Ambrose Bierce: A Biography, 1929; Louis Adamic and Shadow America, 1935; Factories in the Field, 1939; Ill Fares the Land, 1942; Brothers Under the Skin, 1943; Prejudice, 1944; Southern California Country: An Island on the Land, 1946; A Mask for Privilege: Anti-Semitism in America, 1948; North from Mexico: The Spanish Speaking People of America, 1949; California: The Great Exception, 1949; Witch Hunt: The Revival of Heresy, 1950; Rocky Mountain Cities, 1950; (ed.) The California Revolution, 1968; The Education of Carey McWilliams (autobiog.), 1979.

HELEN GAHAGAN DOUGLAS
Actress, congresswoman and political activist
Born Boonton, New Jersey, U.S.A., November 25th, 1900
Died New York City, U.S.A., June 28th, 1980

Though prominent between the wars as an actress and singer, Helen Gahagan Douglas is best remembered for campaigning unsuccessfully against Richard Nixon in a 1950 senatorial race. The election, famous for the questionable tactics used against her, ended her political career—she had served three terms in the House of Representatives—while it launched her opponent on the path to national office.

The daughter of a wealthy builder and shipyard owner, Douglas grew up in New York City. As a girl she was drawn to the stage, an interest she pursued while studying at Barnard College. In 1922 she starred in her first Broadway play and left school to begin an acting career. Over the next 15 years she appeared in a number of successful plays and one film. Hoping to become a singer, she left the U.S. in 1928 for two years of voice lessons in Europe. She returned to New York to appear in the musical *Tonight or Never*. Co-starring with her was the actor Melvyn Douglas, whom she married in 1931.

The Great Depression and its consequences gradually interested Mrs. Douglas in politics. Travelling from New York to California shortly after her marriage, she was aroused by the plight of migratory workers seeking jobs. In 1937 she broke off a concert tour of Austria after encountering discrimination against her accompanist and husband, both Jewish. Following the birth of her second child in 1938, she became active in the California Democratic Party, one of the first entertainment figures to make the transition from show business to politics. She also visited Moscow as a delegate to the Soviet-American Women's Conference. In 1945 she won election to the House of Representatives from California's fourteenth district, which included Los Angeles.

In the House Douglas served on the Foreign Affairs Committee, where she sought to help preserve America's international ties in the face of isolationist sentiment that re-emerged after World War Two. Among the measures she supported were bills to aid Europe (the Marshall Plan) and developing countries (the Point IV program), Reciprocal Trade Agreements to encourage international commerce and the North Atlantic Treaty of 1949. She also served in 1946 on the U.S. delegation to the United Nations General Assembly. In domestic affairs she favored such liberal measures as extending minimum wage laws and protecting the civil rights of public figures accused of Communist sympathies. In 1946 she co-sponsored the McMahon-Douglas bill with the aim of keeping military representatives off the newly-formed Atomic Energy Commission.

Re-elected to the House in 1947 and 1949, Douglas decided to run for the Senate in 1950. She won the Democratic nomination in a difficult primary race against a conservative editor who branded her a "red-hot" leftist. Her opponent in the general election was Richard Nixon, a two-term representative who had established a strong anti-Communist reputation on the House Un-American Activities Committee. Douglas hoped to wage an issue-oriented campaign focusing on the control of offshore oil deposits, an important controversy in California. But this strategy had little chance of success in the xenophobic atmosphere produced by the Cold War and the outbreak of the Korean conflict in June 1950. Douglas's internationalism laid her open to charges of being "soft on Communism," and the Nixon campaign exploited this weakness to the fullest. Strongly supported by the influential *Los Angeles Times* and many conservative Democrats, Nixon repeatedly questioned his opponent's loyalty, common sense and morality. A broadsheet printed on pink paper identified Douglas's voting record with that of American Labor Party Representative Vito Marcantonio. Douglas had little opportunity to counter such charges because the press would not report her statements. Forced onto the defensive, she lost the election by a wide margin.

Douglas had given up her House seat to run for the Senate, and after her defeat she did not seek to re-enter public life. She returned with her husband to New York, where she made occasional stage appearances and supported liberal causes. Her biography of Eleanor Roosevelt, whom she greatly admired, was published in 1963. In June 1979, bedridden with cancer, she made her last political statement, urging Congress to support cancer research. At the time of her death, Douglas was at work on the section of her autobiography desribing her 1950 campaign against Nixon.   S.L.G.

Daughter of Walter Hamer G., construction businessman, and Lillian Rose (Mussen) G., amateur singer. Married Melvyn Douglas, actor 1931. Children: Peter, b. 1934; Mary Helen, b. 1938; Gregory

Hesselberg (stepson). Educ: Berkeley School for Girls, N.Y.; Barnard Coll. 1920–22. Actress in NYC 1922–34; studied voice in Europe 1928–30; Debut, Metropolitan Opera 1930; Sang at Salzburg Festival 1937 and at Carnegie Hall 1956. Active in Democratic Party from 1938; Member, Natl. Advisory Commn. Works Progress Admin. 1939; Delegate, Democratic Natl. Convention 1940; Democratic Natl. Cttee.-woman from Calif. 1940; Vice Chmn. and Chmn., Women's div. 1941–44; Democratic State Central Cttee., elected to 14th Congressional district, Calif. 1945–47, re-elected 1947–49 and 1949–51; U.S. delegate, U.N. General Assembly 1946. Active in support of Marshall Plan, Point IV Program, Reciprocal Trade Agreements, Aid to Korea. Served on Un-American Activities Cttee., Foreign Affairs Cttee. Co-author of McMahon-Douglas Bill. Defeated for U.S. Senate seat, Calif. 1950. Member, Natl. Women's Trade Union League. Hons: Woman of the Year, N.Y. Haddassah 1945; 1 of 12 Outstanding women of Year, Natl. Council Negro Women 1945; hon. Co-chmn., Women's Intnl. League for Peace and Freedom 1964. *Performances: Plays*—Shoot, 1922; Dreams for Sale, 1922; Young Woodley, 1925; Enchanted April, 1925; Trelawney of the Wells, 1926; Tonight or Never, 1930; Mary Queen of Scotland, 1934; First Lady, 1952. *Film*—She, 1935. *Author*—The Eleanor Roosevelt We Remember, 1963.

JOSE ITURBI
Pianist, conductor, composer
Born Valencia, Spain, November 28th, 1895
Died Los Angeles, California, U.S.A., June 28th, 1980

Jose Iturbi led a diverse and enterprising musical career. A celebrated and versatile keyboard performer from a very early age, he later became a noted conductor and appeared with leading orchestras throughout the world. Iturbi also appeared as a soloist in a number of film musicals, and in some of them popularized classical works. With his late sister Amparo, who also became a distinguished pianist, he gave a number of highly successful duo piano recitals.

Iturbi was born in Valencia, Spain, of Basque ancestry, the son of a local gas company employee who tuned pianos in his spare time. A musical prodigy, he began lessons as a very young child and at the age of five, commenced studies at the Escuela de Musica de Maria Jordan. Two years later he was giving lessons himself and earning money by playing in silent movie houses from noon until past midnight. For several years he studied at the conservatory in Valencia and privately in Barcelona with Joaquin Malats. A Valencia journalist, enthusiastic over the local boy's talent, raised money through a newspaper campaign, and Iturbi was sent to study at the Conservatoire de Musique in Paris. He graduated in 1913, winning the school's Grand Prix, and went to Zurich where he taught privately and played the piano at a fashionable hotel café. This led to his being hired by the Geneva Conservatory as Professor of Piano Virtuosity—a post once held by Franz Liszt—and he taught there for four years. He made his London debut in 1923, and during this period toured with composer Igor Stravinsky, introducing his "L'Histoire du Soldat" suite.

His first U.S. performance was in October 1929 playing Beethoven's

G Major Concerto with the Philadelphia Orchestra under Leopold Stokowski. He made his New York debut two months later with the New York Philharmonic. During the 1930s Iturbi performed with many orchestras throughout the world, including the Orquestra Iturbi in Mexico City, organized for him after he gave a successful series of concerts in 1933; he was the regular conductor of the Rochester Philharmonic from 1936 to 1944.

During World War Two he played at War Bond drives, and in the 1940s appeared in several films for M-G-M. His rendition of Chopin's music in *A Song to Remember* made the film biography of Chopin a hit of 1945 and the soundtrack a bestseller. Other films in which he appeared, playing the forties' ideal of the suave, Continental gentleman, were *Anchors Aweigh*, *Holiday In Mexico*, and *Three Daring Daughters*. Iturbi was often criticized by musicians for "going Hollywood." "When I walk onto the stage of a concert hall today," he said in a 1951 interview, "I have to prove that I can still play the piano."

Although Iturbi once refused to appear with Benny Goodman because he disapproved of including jazz and classical music on the same program, he in fact enjoyed jazz and swing, and admitted to playing boogie-woogie on the harpsichord. Morton Gould composed *Etude in Boogie-Woogie Style* especially for Iturbi, and it became a popular concert piece. Iturbi was fond of the compositions of his good friend George Gershwin and included some of his new works on Philharmonic programs.

Iturbi lived mainly in Southern California, enjoying a climate similar to that of his native Valencia. As a younger man he had been an avid motorcyclist, an amateur boxer, and had logged thousands of miles as a pilot, often flying himself from one engagement to another. He continued performing into his later years, and in a *New York Times* review of a performance by Iturbi at Avery Fisher Hall in New York City to celebrate his 80th birthday, a critic wrote: "Pieces such as the Mendelssohn Concerto in G Minor . . . require agile, accurate fingers, and these the pianist supplied in full measure. (Iturbi) carried off the technical end of the performance with aplomb—at moments he played as if he were half his age—but he stayed on the surface of the music and did not offer any mature insight. His habit of accenting the first note of a phrase became a disturbing mannerism . . . and he did not seem interested in shaping phrases with much nuance."   s.p.

Son of Ricardo I. and Teresa (Baguena) I. Married Maria Giner 1916 (d. 1927). Daughter: Maria Hero 1918 (d. 1946). Naturalized American 1941. Mil. Service: Major, Civil Air Patrol, WWII. Educ: Conservatorio de Música, Valencia 1903–05; Conservatoire de Musique, Paris, grad. with highest honors 1913. Café performer, Zurich; Prof. of Piano Virtuosity, Geneva Conservatory 1919–23; Musical Dir., Orquestra Iturbi, Mexico City 1933; Musical Dir., Rochester (N.Y.) Philharmonic Orchestra 1935–44; Musical and Artistic Dir., Valencia Symphony Orchestra 1956–; Musical Dir., Bridgeport (Conn.) Symphony Orchestra 1967–72; Performed with and conducted many of the major orchestras of the world. Member, Real Academia de Bellas Artes de San Fernando (Madrid) and Real Academia de Bellas Artes de San Carlos (Valencia). Hons: Chevalier, French Legion of Honor 1932; Grand Cross of Alphonso X the Wise 1947; Gold Medal of Labor (Spain) 1968; Pre-eminent Son of

Valencia 1971; Quevedo Gold Medal for Arts 1972; Grand Cross of Isabel the Catholic (Spain) 1975; Colossal of Rhodes Award (Valencia) 1975; Lincoln Center Medallion 1975; Comdr., French Legion of Honor 1976; FFF Award of Spanish Press 1976; Companion, Order of St. Michael (Greece); Order of St. George (Greece); Gold Medal, Circle of Bellas Artes (Madrid). *Compositions:* Fantasy (for piano and orchestra); Soliloquy (for orchestra); Spanish Dance (for piano); Cradle Song (for piano); Seguidillas (for orchestra).

WALDEMAR J(OHN) GALLMAN
U.S. Ambassador to Poland, South Africa, and Iraq
Born Wellsville, New York, U.S.A., April 27th, 1899
Died Washington, D.C., U.S.A., June 29th, 1980

Waldemar Gallman, a career diplomat and ambassador to three nations, was born in Wellsville, New York, in 1899 and studied law at Cornell and Georgetown Universities. He began his professional career in 1923 with an appointment as diplomatic secretary to the U.S. Embassy in Havana, Cuba. During the next 20 years he served on the staffs of the embassies in Costa Rica, Ecuador, Latvia, and Poland, as consul general in the free city of Danzig (now Gdańsk, Poland), and as assistant chief of the State Department's European Affairs Division. During the Second World War he was posted to the U.S. Embassy in London as first secretary and deputy chief of mission.

After 1948, Gallman served successively as ambassador to Poland, deputy commandant for foreign affairs at the National War College, ambassador to South Africa, and ambassador to Iraq. From 1958 to 1961 he was director general of the Foreign Service with the rank of Assistant Secretary of State.

After his retirement, Gallman assisted the governments of South Korea and South Vietnam in the establishment of diplomatic training programs and was an advisor to the Asia Foundation.

In 1964 Gallman published *Iraq Under General Nuri,* a study of the accomplishments of Nuri al-Said, the statesman who was fourteen times prime minister of Iraq and who was assassinated in a military coup while Gallman was ambassador. The book described Nuri's policies of domestic modernization (coupled with repressive control of the press, politics, the army, and the police), his efforts on behalf of Arab unity, and his attempts to counter the growing power of President Nasser of Egypt. It also discussed the failure of the United States to join the Baghdad Pact in support of Nuri and to give his pro-Western regime adequate military and economic help through the Military Assistance Understanding and the Technical Aid Program. According to Gallman, this failure was largely the fault of Secretary of State John Foster Dulles, whose crisis-oriented approach to foreign policy kept U.S. relations with Iraq in a state of neglect except during emergencies. Gallman ended the book with an account of the July 1958 coup, executed by two army brigades under the leadership of Colonel Abdul Karim Qasim, which resulted in the deaths of Nuri and the young King Faisal II and in the eventual removal of Iraq from the sphere of U.S. influence.

"Through my experience in Iraq and elsewhere," Gallman wrote, "I have come to feel that the only area where there is any degree of certainty that [U.S. aid] efforts will be productive is in the field of education, and even there mishaps occur. There is, though, a greater hope of something lasting resulting from our support of schools, scholarships, and the exchange of students, teachers, and research workers, than from efforts in the other fields I have been discussing [pacts, military aid, and economic aid]."

Gallman, who was married and had two sons, died of a heart attack.

T.P.

Son of John G. and Henrietta (Engelder) G. Married Marjorie Gerry 1925 (d. 1973). Sons: John; Philip. Unitarian. Educ: Cornell Univ., A.B. 1921; grad. studies, Cornell Univ. and Georgetown Univ. Law Sch. With U.S. Foreign Service 1923–34: Diplomatic Secty., U.S. Embassy, Havana; staff member, U.S. Embassy, San José, Costa Rica; staff member, U.S. Embassy, Quito, Ecuador; staff member, U.S. Embassy, Riga, Latvia; staff member, U.S. Embassy, Warsaw. U.S. Consul Gen., Danzig (now Gdańsk) 1935–38; Asst. Chief, Div. European Affairs, State Dept. 1938–42; First Secty. 1942–48 and Deputy Chief of Mission 1943–48, U.S. Embassy, London; Ambassador to Poland 1948–50; Deputy Commandant for Foreign Affairs, Natl. War Coll. 1950; Ambassador to South Africa 1951–53; Ambassador to Iraq 1954–58; Dir. Gen., Foreign Service, with rank of Asst. Secty. of State 1958 until retirement 1961. Consultant to Asia Foundn. and to the govts. of South Vietnam and South Korea. Member: Columbia Historical Soc.; Cosmos Club; All Souls Unitarian Church; DACOR (Diplomatic and Consular Officers, Retired). *Author:* Iraq under General Nuri: My Recollections of Nuri al-Said, 1954–58, 1964.

ROGER DUVOISIN
Illustrator and author for children
Born Geneva, Switzerland, August 28th, 1904
Died Morristown, New Jersey, U.S.A., June 30th, 1980

Over a period of some 45 years, Roger Duvoisin wrote and illustrated many books for juveniles. With his gentle, imaginative prose and deliciously witty illustrations, he created a whole menagerie of animal characters which continue to delight millions of children.

Duvoisin's artistic interests developed at an early age. He loved to draw and to read, and was particularly interested in animal fables and books about jungles and the American Plains. His artistic pursuits were encouraged by his mother and also by his godmother who was a distinguished enamelist, but his father wanted the young Duvoisin to become a chemist. However, it was eventually agreed that Roger could go to art school in Geneva. He also studied at the Geneva Conservatory of Music and continued to play the flute, clarinet and piano throughout his life.

After graduation, Roger was sent to work for an uncle, but missing his home, he returned to Geneva after only a few days. He then found work as a scenery painter for the Geneva Opera. In his spare time he produced illustrations and posters and took up pottery. This interest led to a managerial position with a ceramics firm in Fernay-Voltaire, a French village just across the border from Geneva. But his predecessor in the job made life difficult by continually breaking pots and misplacing orders; he even threatened to cut Duvoisin's throat.

Duvoisin quickly left the job and moved to Lyon to design textiles for a Lyon-Paris company. In Paris he met and married the Swiss-born Louise Fatio. Two years later, in 1927, with a four-year contract to work in the U.S. for the prestigious Mallinson Silk Company, Duvoisin and his wife moved to New York. However, the firm was bankrupted during the Depression, and Duvoisin decided to take a book he had written for his own children to Charles Scribner, a New York publisher. It was accepted and published as *A Little Boy Was Drawing* in 1932. With the success of this book and his next one, *Donkey, Donkey* (1933), he embarked on his career as a children's writer and illustrator, supplementing his royalties with illustrations for the *New Yorker* and other magazines. Duvoisin and his wife acquired American citizenshsip in 1938; that same year he published his fourth book—and first non-fiction work—*And There Was America,* which became a standard textbook for children. Duvoisin wrote 32 works of fiction for children, as well as three non-fiction works and two books in which he retold popular fairy tales.

Perhaps his most popular character is Petunia, a young goose who convinces her farmyard friends that because she possesses a book—which she keeps tucked under her wing—she is an expert and a scholar in all matters. Only after airing her knowledge disastrously on many occasions does she finally admit that she had better learn to read. Another of his animals, Jasmine the cow, has an exotic and highly individual taste in clothes. Finding a particularly fancy hat one day, Jasmine puts it on and parades around in it even though the sight of her makes her colleagues roll about with laughter in the barnyard.

In all, Duvoisin illustrated well over 120 books; he was constantly in demand as an illustrator for other authors' works, and in 1947 he began to collaborate with the children's writer, Alvin Tresselt; he received the prestigious Caldecott Medal for his illustrations in their first book, *White Snow, Bright Snow.* When his wife began to write children's stories in 1950, Duvoisin illustrated them. Their *Happy Lion* series recounts the adventures of a kind and gentle lion from the zoo, who thanks to his friendship with the zoo-keeper's son, is allowed to leave his cage at will. The warmth and quietly-stated moral themes of these stories have made the *Happy Lion* one of the most endearing characters in contemporary fiction for young children.

Duvoisin's illustrations combined an economy of form with bright, appealing colors. He would specify the placement of each illustration, as well as the book's typeface and binding, and would inspect the color separation acetates to insure high quality reproduction. Both as a writer and as an illustrator, through his wit and spirit of fun, he demonstrated a deep understanding and love for children. Writing in *Twentieth Century Children's Writers* (1978) Duvoisin said: "I love the lively curiosity children show . . . and the free way they have of expressing their reactions in their conversation, in their drawings and paintings, and even in their poems and letters. . . . It is good to observe that children are now more and more encouraged to express themselves, to create, and that they are taken more seriously. Because of this, making books for children is a more captivating form of art for the writer and illustrator."   H.S./R.T.

Son of Jacques Jonas D., architect, and Judith E. (More) D. Married Louise Fatio, writer 1925. Children: Roger Claire, neurologist; Jacques Alfred, architect. Protestant. Emigrated to USA 1927. Naturalized American 1938. Educ: Ecole Professionelle, Geneva 1915–17; Ecole des Arts et Metier, Ecole des Beaux Arts 1917–24, teaching diploma. Stage Designer (painted murals and scenery), Geneva Opera Co. 1922–24; Mgr., Ceramics firm, Fernay-Voltaire, France 1924–26; Textile Designer, Lyon and Paris 1927, and Mallinson Silk Co., NYC 1927–31; Visiting Prof., Parsons Sch. of Design, NYC 1942–50; freelance illustrator and author since 1932. Hons: Bronze Medal Paris Exhibition of Potteries of Fernay 1925; American Inst. of Graphic Art, Fifty Best Books of the Year annually from 1933–1938, 1939, and annually from 1945–50; American Library Assn., Nine Best Children's Books of the Year 1937; N.Y. Herald Tribune Award 1944, 1952; Ten Best Books 1952, 1954, 1955, 1956, Federal Republic of Germany, First Prize for Juvenile Fiction 1956; Soc. of Illustrators Award 1961; Bicentenary Award, Rutgers Univ. 1966; runner-up, Hans Christian Biennial Award 1968; Univ. of South Mississippi Award 1971; New York Acad. of Science Award for Nonfiction 1975; Univ. of Minnesota Kerlan Award 1976; Hon. Dr. of Let., Kean State Univ. *Exhibitions: Group Shows*—Art Alliance Gall., Phila. 1946; Mus. of Modern Art, NYC 1946; Durand Rue Gall., NYC 1949; Philadelphia Mus. Sch. of Art 1953; American Inst. of Arts, Graphic Art Exhibs., Best Books 1953, 1954, 1955, 1957, annually from 1958–60, 1961, 1962, 1965, 1966 and annually from 1965–68; Graphic Art in the USA, European tour 1963; Bratislava Biennale, Rutgers Univ. Museum of Art 1973. *Books: Illustrator and author*—A Little Boy was Drawing, 1932; Donkey-Donkey: The Troubles of a Silly Little Donkey, 1933; All Aboard, 1935; And There Was America (non-fiction), 1938; The Christmas Cake in Search of Its Owner, and The Three Sneezes and Other Swiss Tales, 1941; They Put Out To Sea: The Story of a Map (non-fiction), 1943; The Christmas Whale, 1945; Chanticleer, 1947; The Four Corners of the World (non-fiction), 1948; Petunia, 1950; Petunia and the Song, 1951; A for the Ark, and Petunia's Christmas, 1952; Easter Treat, 1954; One Thousand Christmas Beards, See Smith Toy Shop, Eat at Joes, 1955; The House of Four Seasons, 1956; Petunia Beware!, 1958; Day and Night, 1960; The Happy Hunter, and Veronica, 1961; Our Veronica Goes to Petunia's Farm, 1962; Lonely Veronica, and Spring Snow, 1963; Veronica's Smile, 1964; Petunia, I Love You, 1965; Two Lonely Ducks: A Counting Book, 1966; The Missing Milkman, 1967; What Is Right for Tulip, 1969; Veronica and the Birthday Present, 1971; The Crocodile in the Tree, 1972; Jasmine, 1973; Petunia's Treasure, 1975; Periwinkle, 1976; Crocus, 1977. *Illustrator only*—Mother Goose, ed. by William Rose Benet, 1936; Pied Piper of Hamlin by Robert Browning, 1936; Riema, Little Brown Girl of Java, 1937; Soomoon, Boy of Bali, 1938; Jo-Yo's Idea, by Kathleen Morrow Eliot, 1939; The Feast of the Lamps by W.H. Hudson, 1939; Rhamon, A Boy of Kashmir by Helwig Fischer, 1940; At Our House by John McCullough, 1943; A Child's Garden of Verses, 1944, and Travels with a Donkey, 1956 by Robert Louis Stevenson; Virgin With Butterflies by Tom Powers, 1945; The Life and Adventures of Robinson Crusoe by Daniel Defoe, 1946; Daddies: What They Do All Day, 1946, The Sitter Who Didn't Sit, 1949, by Helen Walker Puner;

White Snow, Bright Snow, 1947, Johnny Maple-Leaf, 1948, Sun Up, 1949, Follow the Wind, 1950, Hi, Mr. Robin, 1950, Autumn Harvest, 1951, Follow the Road, 1953, Wake Up Farm, 1955, Wake Up City, 1957, The Frog in the Well, 1958, Hide and Seek Fog, 1965, The World in the Candy Egg, 1967, It's Time Now!, 1969, and The Beaver Pond, 1970, all by Alvin Tresselt; The Christmas Forest, 1950, Anna the Horse, 1951, The Happy Lion, 1954, The Happy Lion in Africa, 1955, The Happy Lion Roars, 1957, A Doll for Marie, 1957, The Three Happy Lions, 1959, The Happy Lion's Quest, 1961, Red Bantam, 1963, The Happy Lion and the Bear, 1964, The Happy Lion's Vacation, 1967, The Happy Lion's Treasure, 1971, Hector Penguin, 1973, The Happy Lion's Rabbits, 1974, Marc and Pixie and the Walls in Mrs. Jones's Garden, 1975, and Hector and Christmas, 1976, all by Louise Fatio; The Camel Who Took a Walk, 1951 and Tigers Don't Bite, 1956, by Jack Tworkov; Chef's Holiday by Idwal Jones, 1952; Gian-Carlo Menotti's Amahl and the Night Visitors, 1952; The Night Before Christmas by Clement C. Moore, 1954; One Step, Two. . . , 1955, Not a Little Monkey, 1957, In My Garden, 1960, and The Poodle Who Barked at People, 1964, all by Charlotte Zolotow; The Sweet Pattotie Doll, 1957, Wobble the Witch Cat, 1958, Houn' Dog, 1959, The Nine Loves of Homer C. Cat, 1961, and The Hungry Leprechaun, 1962, all by Mary Calhoun; The Three Cornered Hat by Pedro Antonio de Alarcon, 1959; Angélique, 1960, Mr. and Mrs. Button's Wonderful Watchdogs, 1978, by Janice; Lisette, 1962, The Rain Puddle, 1965, and The Remarkable Egg, 1968, all by Adelaide Holl; Poems from France, ed. by William Jay Smith, 1967; The Old Bullfrog, 1968, and The Web in the Grass, 1972, by Berniece Freschet; Which Is the Best Place?, translated by Mirra Ginsburg, 1976; Whatever Happened to the Baxter Place? by Pat Ross, 1976; Heinz Hobnail and the Great Shoe Hunt by Anne Duvoisin, 1976.
Further reading: "Roger Duvoisin," by Henry Pitz, in American Artist, Dec., 1949; A Roger Duvoisin Bibliography by Irvin Kerlan, 1958; Books Are by People by Lee Hopkins, 1970.

SIR TITUS MARTINS ADESOJI TADENIAWO ADEREMI I
The Oni of Ife and Governor of Western Nigeria
Born Ile-Ife, Nigeria, November 21st, 1889
Died Ife, Oyo State, Nigeria, July 1980

Born into the Royal House of Ile-Ife, Aderemi I held various positions in the Traffic Section of the Nigerian Railways and in the Nigerian civil service before establishing himself as one of the leading produce and merchandise traders in western Nigeria. In September 1930 he was installed as the Oni (Paramount Ruler) of Ife, becoming spiritual head of the Yoruba tribe and custodian of the holy city of Ife and its relics. Aderemi ruled his kingdom in southwestern Nigeria until his death, during which time he reorganized the administration of schools, improved the transportation system and founded Oduduwa College, a secondary school for boys. Under his rule Ife became one of the most progressive kingdoms in Nigeria.

Between 1946 and 1963 Aderemi held a succession of legislative and commercial posts in the Nigerian government, including membership in the House of Representatives, Minister without Portfolio in the Central Government Council and President of the House of Chiefs of Western Nigeria. He also belonged to the Action Group, a political party organized in 1951 to work for Nigerian independence from Great Britain. Nevertheless, he did not favor immediate independence when the matter came up for decision in 1956, fearing that the country was not politically and economically prepared for freedom. He resigned from the Central Government Council on the day of the House debate over the independence resolution so that he could speak and vote as an ordinary House member. But he served as a delegate to the final conferences on the Nigerian Constitution in London during the late 1950s.

On July 8, 1960 Aderemi was appointed Governor of Western Nigeria, the first African to hold the position. Three years later he was removed from power, along with the entire Western Nigeria regional government, following disputes in the Western House of Assembly. Although charges of sedition were raised against many of the suspended officials, none were brought against the Oni, who in his final years withdrew from active involvement in Nigeria's increasingly complex political situation.   S.J.

Son of Oshundeyi and Adekunbi. Polygamous marriage, 1st in 1910. Many children. Roman Catholic. Educ: St. Phillip's Church Missionary Society Day Sch., Ile-Ife, Nigeria. Joined Traffic Sect. of Nigerian Railway Construction 1909; with Civil Service 1910–21; began private produce and motor transport bus. 1921; elected Oni of Ife 1930. Member: House of Assembly 1946–47; Legislative Council and Nigerian Cocoa Marketing Bd. 1947. Dir., Nigerian Produce Marketing Co. Ltd. 1947; Member, Nigerian House of Reps. and Central Minister without Portfolio 1951–56; Western House of Chiefs since 1951; Pres., House of Chiefs, Western Nigeria 1953–60; Gov., Western Region 1960–63; Chmn., Council of Obas and Chiefs,

Western Nigeria since 1966. Delegate, London-African Conference 1948; Delegate, Conference for revision of Nigerian Constitution, London 1953, 1957, 1958 and Lagos 1954. Member, Action Group Party 1951–63; Chief emissary, Nigerian delegation to the coronation 1953. Hons: CMG 1943; KBE 1950; P.C., Western Nigeria 1954; KCMG 1962; hon. LL.D., Univ. of Ife 1967.

C(HARLES) P(ERCY) SNOW
(Baron Snow of Leicester)
Novelist, physicist, and civil servant
Born Leicester, England, October 15th, 1905
Died London, England, July 1st, 1980

A physicist by education and an administrator by profession, C.P. Snow brought to his novels a perspective shared by few other contemporary writers of fiction: in the words of one critic, he "curiously views science as an imaginative art and makes literature into a category of social science." His novels, which explore the power structures of the bureaucratic world and the motives and moral dilemmas of those who control them, are as much appreciated in the Soviet Union as they are in the West. Despite his attempts to act as a goodwill ambassador between the hostile camps of science and the arts (or between the rational and the emotional, as he might have put it), he regarded science as the true intellectual adventure of the modern world; in literature, he was content to stay with the traditional modes and themes of the Victorians. Melvin Maddocks has aptly called him "the greatest living 19th-century novelist."

Snow was born in 1905 in the Midlands City of Leicester, where his father earned a meager living as a clerk in a shoe factory and as a church organist. By the time he was 18, Snow, the second of four sons, knew that he wanted to be a writer, but had made up his mind to follow a scientific career instead, thinking it the best route by which to break through the confines of working-class life and make his name known. Like Lewis Eliot, the semi-autobiographical figure of his major novels, he wanted "the power to make my own terms, to move through the world as one who owned it, to be waited on and to give largesse."

Having specialized in science at Alderman Newton's School, Snow stayed on as a laboratory assistant in order to study for one of the competitive scholarships offered by the University of Leicester. He proceeded to take First Class Honors in chemistry in 1927 and won a research grant that enabled him to continue for a master's degree in physics. Another research grant brought him to Christ's College, Cambridge, where, within two years, his work on the infrared spectroscopy of molecular structures earned him a doctorate and subsequent election as a Fellow of the College.

Three years of research followed under Lord Rutherford, who had recently discovered the existence of the atom. "Living in Cambridge," Snow wrote, "one could not help picking up the human, as well as the intellectual excitement in the air. . . . The tone of science was the tone of Rutherford: magniloquently boastful because the major discoveries were being made—creatively confident, generous, argumentative, lavish, and full of hope." This heady enthusiasm, contrasting so strongly with the misery suffered by the general population during the Depression (and which was reflected in the literature of that era), gave Snow a lasting impression of scientists as the unique possessors of optimism, the only intellectuals "with the future in their bones."

Snow's own career as a professional scientist proved brief, however. In 1933, a botched experiment convinced him that he was not good enough to make it to the top. "Like everyone, I wanted to be a success," he later said, "and I was not one in physics. I thought I could be as a writer." He had already made moves in that direction, completing an unpublished novel, *Youth Searching,* while an undergraduate, and more recently turning out a detective story, *Death Under Sail,* and a science fantasy, *New Lives for Old* (issued anonymously so that its prudent author might not arouse the envy of his laboratory colleagues). In 1934 he published *The Search,* a novel about an ambitious young crystallographer who makes an error on an experiment and is tempted to falsify the data in order to save his career. The friendly reception given the book by the critics and by such scientists as the American physicist I.I. Rabi, who praised its authenticity, encouraged Snow to quit research and devote himself to writing fiction.

A brief period of distress followed in which "everything, personal or creative, seemed to be going wrong." On New Year's Day of 1935, Snow was walking on an icy Marseilles street when he received a flash of inspiration: the complete outline and organization of a multi-volume novel sequence had, on the instant, taken shape in his mind. "As soon as this happened, I felt extraordinarily happy. I got the whole conception, I think, as far as that means anything, in a few minutes."

The sequence, which later came to be known by the title of its first volume, *Strangers and Brothers,* consists of eleven interrelated novels built around the experiences of Lewis Eliot, a lawyer, Cambridge don, and government official with a yen for power and prestige and a taste for the infighting necessary to achieve them. Sometimes narrating the progress of his own life, sometimes that of his myriad friends and colleagues, Eliot records the minute interplay, the chess-like moves and countermoves, by which the day-to-day politics of university and government life are carried on. It is "the resonance between what [Eliot] sees and what he feels," according to Snow, that gives the sequence its overall design.

The world described by Eliot is a polar one, governed by sets of dualities which his characters struggle, often in vain, to reconcile. These pairs—of which the most recurrent are power and responsibility, ambition and ethics, private suffering versus public performance, and the inborn traits of personality and intellect versus the imposed effects of class, education, and culture—are summed up in the personas of "the stranger" (the individual who is born and will die ineluctably alone) and "the brother" (the social being whose life is inextricably bound up with that of others). The balance between these opposing selves is differently constituted in each character and governs his or her choice of action within the quasi-historical circumstances set forth in the novels, choices that inevitably raise serious moral questions. But no moral judgments are made against the characters themselves, Snow's purpose being not to judge but purely to examine, with all the dispassionate fairness of the social scientist.

This concern with the moral development of people within their social milieus makes Snow the heir to such Victorian novelists as Anthony Trollope (on whom he wrote an essay in 1975) and John Galsworthy. Indeed, he regarded nearly all the innovations of twentieth century writers, particularly those of Woolf and Joyce, as barbaric, intellectually dishonest, and socially pernicious, the result of an overweening fascination with the dark side of the self. Though he admired the rich, all-encompassing consciousness at work in the novels of Proust, his own prose style was as flat, plain, and rigorously objective as the prose of a scientific report.

The first book of the series, published in 1940, concerned a charismatic young lawyer, a combination of idealist and sensualist, whose promising career is wrecked by a scandal. During its writing, and for the next five years, Snow was a tutor at Christ's College, as well as editor of *Discovery* magazine and the Cambridge Library of Modern Science. The next volume was delayed by the Second World War, during which Snow served on a Royal Society advisory subcommittee on the wartime deployment of university scientists. When this group was absorbed by the Ministry of Labour in 1942, Snow joined the Ministry as Director of Technical Personnel; his services in the allocation of a scientific manpower were acknowledged with the conference of a CBE in 1943.

The following year, Snow became Director of Scientific Personnel at the English Electric Company in London. His promotion to the Board of Directors in 1947 coincided with the publication of *The Light and The Dark,* the second volume of the *Strangers and Brothers* series (but third in the overall chronology, which differs from the order of composition), in which a brilliant but melancholy linguist finds in the Manichean heresies he is studying a reflection of his own struggle with good and evil. *Time of Hope,* about Eliot's own early life and disastrous marriage, came out two years later.

The publication of *The Masters* in 1951 brought Snow a larger audience than he had previously enjoyed. The most engaging of all his novels, it concerns the complex politicking between the 13 fellows of a Cambridge college, Eliot among them, as they meet to select the successor to the dying Master. Snow won the James Tait Black Memorial Prize in 1955 for *The Masters* and *The New Men,* which describes the rivalries among a team of scientists working on the development of the atomic bomb and their moral conflicts following the debacle at Hiroshima. The next volume was *Homecomings* (1956), a further narration of Eliot's personal life, including the suicide of his wife, and *The Conscience of the Rich* (1958), about the son of an aristocratic Anglo-Jewish family who rejects his parents, his class, and his ethnicity.

In 1959, Snow, who had been knighted two years before, sparked a furious controversy with *The Two Cultures and the Scientific Revolution,* originally delivered as the Rede Lectures at Cambridge. He noted with alarm the divergence of the literary and scientific communities in the West, and castigated modern writers for their angst-ridden pessimism about the human condition, their ignorance of science, and their reactionary distrust of the industrial revolution (which, he claimed, had improved living standards to an extent that far outweighed its disadvantages). The writers' excessive concern with emotion, he said, precluded an intellectual confrontation with complex and vastly important social issues and had led them to poison Western culture with hopelessness. Meanwhile, the action-oriented "men of science" were creating a technological Renaissance in which he urged the alienated "men of letters' to join.

A scathing reply to Snow was delivered two years later by the literary critic F.R. Leavis, who condemned him as the representative of a corrupting materialism bent on driving the imagination out of life and art. Snow, he said, was a contemptible thinker and writer, "as intellectually undistinguished as it is possible to be," with a prose style so boring and humorless that it might have been written by "a computer named Charlie" to which the author fed the chapter headings.

Many less intemperate critics have also expressed their dissatisfaction with Snow's narrow definition of the novel form and the sterility of his characters, whom (they say) he maneuvers like puppets through contrived situations that are the opposite of realistic. "He doesn't understand people," wrote Frederick R. Karl in *Contemporary English Novelists.* "Were he to confront the true nature of man, his 'naturalistic-realistic' approach would fail and we would see the 'very absurd world' he has so often deplored in modern fiction." According to LeRoy W. Smith, "Snow's bent is analytical and expository. He lacks the artistic capacity to transform his vision into art."

Snow's opinions occasioned another controversy in 1961, when he delivered the Godkin Lecture (later published as *Science and Government*) at Harvard University. In it, he described the court politics practiced by Prime Minister Winston Churchill during World War II and their tragic consequences for British servicemen, who were sacrificed to an unwise bombing strategy advocated by an overly powerful science advisor. This account raised the ire of Churchill's defenders but was widely admired for its demonstration of the dangers of excessive power in the hands of a single scientist immune from the criticism of his fellows.

Snow's first-hand understanding of the workings of power and of those who wield it and vie for it, whether in Whitehall, Cambridge, or an atomic research laboratory, was his main strength as a social critic and as a writer of fiction. His astute explication of "bureaucratic man" (women had little place in Snow's wood-paneled committee rooms) was responsible for the popular success of *The Affair* (1960), the story of an unpleasant young scientist with Marxist leanings who is unjustly convicted of scientific fraud. *Corridors of Power* (1964) described Eliot's participation in the cabinet of a conservative prime minister who tries in vain to stop the arms race. *The Sleep of Reason* (1969) and *Last Things* (1970) brought to an end the series that had taken Snow 35 years to complete. Subsequently he wrote three more novels with plots hinging on youth terrorism and murder. He was also the author of a series of one-act plays and the editor of an anthology of Russian fiction in collaboration with his wife, the novelist and critic Pamela Hansford Johnson, with whom he had one son.

In 1964 Snow achieved the summit of that public recognition to which he had aspired since childhood: he was named baron Snow of Leicester and appointed to represent the newly-formed Ministry of Technology in the House of Lords. He now entered on his final incarnation as a grand old man of British society, entertaining Nobel Prize Winners and distinguished foreign visitors, as well as his vast circle of friends, and issuing frequent warnings on such global problems as the inevitably disastrous arms race and the necessity of exporting the industrial revolution to undeveloped nations. In 1968 he wrote that the imminence of worldwide famine had brought him "nearer to despair . . . than ever in my life," adding, "I would not be happy to be my son's age now." Still he retained his conviction that technological expertise and moral sensitivity, if given the chance, could resolve even these desperate problems.

His final novel, *A Coat of Varnish*, was published in 1979, a year before his death in London.   R.C./J.P.

Born Charles Percy Snow; later Lord Snow, Baron of Leicester. Son of William Edward S., shoe factory clerk and organist, and Ada Sophia (Robinson) S. Married Pamela Hansford Johnson, novelist and critic, 1950. Son: Philip Charles Hansford, b. 1952. Educ: Alderman Newton's Sch., Leicester; Univ. Coll., Leicester (scholarship and research grant), B.Sc. (First Class Hons. in chemistry) 1927, M.Sc. 1928; Christ's Coll., Cambridge (research grant), Ph.D. in physics 1930 and Fellow 1930–50 (in residence 1930–40); Interim Fellow, Silliman Univ., Negros Oriental, Philippine Islands 1961; Chubb Fellow, Yale Univ. 1961. Mil. Service: Member, Royal Society Advisory Sub-Cttee. on Deployment of Scientific Resources 1939–42; Dir. of Tech. Personnel, Ministry of Labour 1942–45. Researcher in physics, Cambridge Univ. 1930–35; Tutor, Christ's Coll. 1935–45; Ed., Discovery (scientific mag.) 1938–40 and Cambridge Library of Modern Science 1938–early 1940s; British Civil Service Commnr., London 1945–60; Dir. of Scientific Personnel 1944–47 and Physicist-Dir. 1947–64, English Electric Co. Ltd., London; Dir., Educational Film Centre Ltd., London 1961–64; Parliamentary Under-Secretary, Ministry of Technology 1964–66. Rede Lectr., Cambridge Univ. 1959; Godkin Lectr., Harvard Univ. 1960; Regents Prof., Univ. of California at Berkeley 1960; Rector, St. Andrews Univ. 1962–64; John Findley Green Foundn. Lectr., Westminster Coll., Mo. 1968. Pres., Library Assn. 1961. Member: Arts Council of England 1971–74; Société Européene de Culture; Savile Club, London; Athenaeum Club, London; Garrick Club, London; Marylebone Cricket Club, London; Century Club, NYC. Hons: Crime Club Selection (Death under Sail) 1927; CBE for services to Ministry of Labour 1943; British Book Soc. Selection (The Masters) 1951; elected Fellow, Royal Society of Literature 1951; James Tait Black Memorial prize (for The Masters and The New Men) 1955; KBE 1957; British Book Soc. Selection and Book-of-the-Month Club Selection (The Affair) 1960; Life Peer 1964; Hon. Fellow, Christ's Coll., Cambridge since 1966; Extraordinary Fellow, Churchill Coll., Cambridge; Hon. Fellow, Morse Coll., Yale Univ.; Diamond Jubilee Medal, Catholic Univ. of America; Centennial English Medal, Pennsylvania Military Coll.; Resolution of Esteem, U.S. Congressional Cttee. on Science and Astronautics. Hon. Foreign Member: American Acad. of Arts and Letters. Hon. LL.D. from Univ. of Leicester 1959, Univ. of Liverpool 1960, St. Andrews Univ. 1962, Brooklyn Polytech. Inst. 1962, Univ. of Bridgeport 1966, Univ. of York 1967, Univ. of Toronto; Hon. D.Litt. from Dartmouth Coll. 1960, Bard Coll. 1962, Temple Univ. 1963, Syracuse Univ. 1963, Univ. of Pittsburgh 1964, Westminster Coll. 1968, New York Univ. 1976, Univ. of Louisville 1976, Pace Coll. 1977, Widener Coll. 1978, Union Coll. 1979, Ithaca Coll.; Hon.

D.H.L. from Kenyon Coll. 1961, Washington Univ. 1963, Univ. of
Michigan 1963, Alfred Univ., Akron Univ., Hebrew Union Coll.;
Hon. D.Sc., Pennsylvania Military Coll. 1966; Hon. Doctor of
Philological Sciences, Rostov State Univ., East Germany 1963.
Novels: Death Under Sail, 1932, rev. ed. 1959; New Lives for Old
(published anonymously), 1933; The Search, 1934, rev. ed. 1958; The
Malcontents, 1972; In Their Wisdom, 1974; A Coat of Varnish, 1979.
Novels in the Strangers and Brothers series: Strangers and Brothers,
1940 (retitled George Passant, 1970); The Light and the Dark, 1947;
Time of Hope, 1949; The Masters, 1951; The New Men, 1954;
Homecomings (in U.S. as Homecoming), 1956; The Conscience of the
Rich, 1958; The Affair, 1960; The Corridors of Power, 1964; The
Sleep of Reason, 1969; Last Things, 1970. *Plays:* View Over the Park,
1950; (with Pamela Hansford Johnson) The Supper Dance, Family
Party, Spare the Rod, To Murder Mrs. Mortimer, The Pigeon with
the Silver Foot, Her Best Foot Forward, 1951; A Time of Hope
(adapted by Arthur and Violet Ketels from novel), 1963; The Affair,
The New Men, The Masters (adapted by Ronald Millar from novels),
1964; (adapter, with Pamela Hansford Johnson) The Public Prosecu-
tor (by Georgi Djagarov), 1967; The Case in Question (adapted by
Ronald Millar from novel In Their Wisdom), 1975. *Other:* Richard
Aldington: An Appreciation, 1938; Writers and Readers of the Soviet
Union, 1943; The Two Cultures and the Scientific Revolution, 1959,
rev. as The Two Cultures: And a Second Look, 1963; Science and
Government, 1961; (ed., with Pamela Hansford Johnson) Winter's
Tales 7 (in U.S. as Stories from Modern Russia), 1961; The Moral Un-
Neutrality of Science, 1961; A Postscript to Science and Government,
1962; Magnanimity, 1962; C.P. Snow: A Spectrum; Science, Criticism, Fiction (ed. by Stanley Weintraub), 1963; intro. to A London
Childhood (by John Holloway), 1966; Variety of Men (biographical
portraits), 1967; The State of Siege, 1969; Public Affairs (collected
essays), 1971; Trollope: His Life and Art, 1975; The Realists (lit.
criticism), 1978. Author of many scientific papers, particularly on
infrared spectroscopy of molecular structures, and of many reviews
and essays; contributor to Sunday Times and other periodicals.
Further reading: "Structure and Style in the Novels of C.P. Snow," in
Review of English Literature, April, 1960; "C.P. Snow: Spokesman
of Two Communities," in Books With Men Behind Them by Edmund
Fuller, 1962; "Some Current Fads," in Postwar British Fiction: New
Accents and Attitudes by James Gindin, 1962; The World of C.P.
Snow by Robert Greacen, 1962; "A Brilliant Boy from the Mid-
lands," in Contemporaries by Alfred Kazin, 1962; Two Cultures? The
Significance of C.P. Snow by F.R. Leavis, 1962; "The Type to Which
the Whole Creation Moves? Further Thoughts on the Snow Saga," in
Encounter, XVIII, Feb., 1962; "The Achievement of C.P. Snow," in
Western Humanities Review, VI, Winter, 1962; "Science, Literature,
and Culture: A Comment on the Leavis-Snow Controversy," in
Commentary, XXXIII, June, 1962; C.P. Snow: The Politics of
Conscience by R. Frederick R. Karl, 1963; Cultures in Conflict:
Perspectives on the Snow-Leavis Controversy by David K. Cornelius
and Edwin St. Vincent, 1964; Science and the Shabby Curate of
Poetry by Martin Green, 1964; C.P. Snow by Robert Gorham Davis,
1965; C.P. Snow by Jerome Hale, 1965; The Reaction Against
Experiment in the English Novel, 1950–60 by Rubin Rabinovitz, 1967;
C.P. Snow: Scientific Humanist," in After the Trauma: Representa-
tive British Novelists since 1920 by Harvey Curtis Webster, 1970; C.P.
Snow by David Shusterman, 1975; The Novels of C.P. Snow: A
Critical Introduction by Ramanthan Suguna, 1978.

SHIELDS WARREN
Experimental pathologist
Born Cambridge, Massachusetts, U.S.A., February 26th, 1898
Died Cambridge, Massachusetts, U.S.A., July 1st, 1980

Shields Warren was an experimental pathologist who contributed greatly to current understanding of cancer and of the harmful and beneficial effects of radiation fallout at Hiroshima and Nagasaki.

Shields Warren's grandfather was the first President of Boston University and his father was the dean of the University's College of Liberal Arts. This family connection brought Shields there to study in 1914. He received his B.A. degree in 1918 and a year later entered Harvard Medical School where he obtained his M.D. in 1923.

In 1925 he accepted a position on the faculty of Harvard Medical School and continued to teach there until his death. He also became a staff pathologist at the New England Deaconess Hospital in 1927 and conducted research into the effects of cancer and radiation on tissue and cell structure. He became chief pathologist at the hospital in 1946.

Towards the end of the 1930s, Warren found evidence to support the theory that cancerous cells may be transmitted from one part of the body to another by the lymphatic system. This eventually led to the current surgical practice of removing specific lymph nodes after the elimination of nearby cancerous tissue. Later Warren found that cases of multiple malignancy occur more frequently than can be expected by chance alone. "It appears," he wrote, "that certain individuals or groups of individuals have a susceptibility or predisposition to the development of cancerous tissue." In the mid 1940s, with the assistance of Olive Gates, Warren developed the 'cervical smear' which is still used today to diagnose carcinoma of the cervix in women. He also developed an interest in the study of radiation induced cancers and of radiation effects upon cancerous tissue.

During World War Two, Warren served on the advisory board of the Army Institute of Pathology and after the war, he led the U.S. Atomic Casualty Committee in Japan. He concluded from his studies on the pattern of injuries and pathology of the casualties in Hiroshima and Nagasaki that the majority of injuries and deaths were the result of "radiation blast, not solid or water blast." Burns were largely of the 'flash type' and were observed to a distance of two-and-a-half miles from ground-zero. Lethal radiation effects, the study found, occurred rarely beyond one mile of ground-zero. Those beyond this mile radius, however, were exposed to ionizing radiation and experienced delayed pathological changes similar to those observed following overexposure to x-rays. These delayed changes manifested themselves after the second week when damage to the system which produces blood plasma and red blood cells resulted in leukemia and anemic responses.

Despite his first-hand knowledge of the effects of large scale nuclear radiation, Warren refused to join the thousands of scientists who called for a halt in nuclear-bombing tests. "Nuclear energy," he said, "is a force the world must reckon with and if we are to make use of atomic energy for peaceful purposes, we must learn how to control such hazards as are associated with Strontium 90 and other radioactive isotopes."

Warren also undertook a short study of atomic effects at Bikini Island in the Pacific. He continued his experiments in cancer and radiation at Deaconess Hospital, and developed various cytological techniques which enabled pathologists to improve their cell sections for analysis under the newly developed electron microscope. In the last five years of his life, Warren shifted his experimental emphasis to the connection between cancer and the endocrine system.   S.J.

Son of William M.W., dean at Boston Univ., and Sara W. Married Alice Springfield 1923. Children: A. Emile McLeod and Patricia Palmer. Educ: Boston Univ., B.A. 1918; Harvard Univ., M.D. 1923. Methodist. Mil. Service: Capt., U.S. Naval Reserve 1943–45; Consultant, U.S. Air Force 1948–62 and Veteran's Administration 1952–1980; Member, Science Advisory Bd., Armed Forces Inst. of Pathology 1952–1980 and Research Consulting Bd., U.S. Navy 1953–1980; Special Consultant, U.S. Dept. of Defense 1959–62; Sr. Statesman, Science Advisory Bd. U.S. Air Force 1961–62. With Harvard Medical Sch.: Instr. 1925–36; Asst. Prof. 1936–48; Prof. 1948–65; Prof. Emeritus from 1965. With New England Deaconness Hosp: Pathologist 1927–46; Chief Pathologist 1946–80; Dir., Cancer Research Center 1951–68 and Consultant 1968–80. With Mass Tumor Diagnosis Service: Dir. 1928–55 and Consultant 1955–71. Pathologist: Boston City Hosp 1923–25; Pondville State Hosp. 1923–48; New England Baptist Hosp. 1928–63; Huntington Memorial Hosp. 1938–42. Consultant: House of Good Samaritan, Boston 1927–43; Channing House, Boston 1935–58; Space Program Advisory Council, Cttee. for Life Sciences, NASA 1971–76. With U.S. Atomic Energy Commn.: Dir., Biology and Medicine 1947–52; Member Advisory Cttee. 1952–58; Consultant 1959–80. Special Advisor, Acting U.S. Representative to Second Intnl. Conference of Peaceful Uses of Atomic Energy, Geneva 1958. Member, Natl. Advisory Cancer Council 1946–50; U.S. Rep. on the U.N. Science Cttee. on Effects of Atomic Radiation 1955–63; Dir., Mallinckrodt Inc.; Corp. Chmn and Bd. of Trustees, Boston Univ. 1953–69; Member: American Assn. for Advancement of Science (V.P., 1948); American Assn. of Pathologists and Bacteriologists (V.P. 1947, Pres. 1948); American Assn. of Cancer Research (V.P. 1941, Pres. 1942–46); American Medical Assn.; American Acad. of Arts and Sciences; Phi Beta Kappa; American Philosophical Soc.; American Soc. of Experimental Pathology (past Pres.); Soc. of Experimental Biology and Medicine. With Natl. Acad. of Science: Member 1962–80; Member, Sub-Cttee. on Somatic Effects 1971–80. Hons: Ward Burdick Award, American Soc. of Clinical Pathology, 1949; William Proctor Award, Scientific Research Soc. of America 1952; Modern Medicine Award 1953; Banting Medal, American Diabetes Assn. 1953; Charles V. Chaplin Medal, Providence, R.I. 1958; Order of the Cross, Degree of Comdr., Brazil 1961; Albert Einstein Award 1962; Citation, Atomic Energy Commn. 1962; Enrico Fermi Award 1972; from Natl. Cancer Soc.: Medal 1950 and National Award 1968. D.S.: Boston Univ. 1959. Dr. Honoris Causa, Univ. of Brazil 1964; D.M.S., Brown Univ. 1969. *Author:* Chemistry of the Carbonyl Group: A Programmed Approach to Reaction Mechanism Chemistry; extensive articles in medical jrnls.

TOM BARRY
Military tactician and commander
Born Rosscarberry, County Cork, Ireland, July 1st, 1897
Died Cork, Ireland, July 2nd, 1980

Tom Barry, an outstanding military leader in the Irish War for Independence, contributed significantly to the development of scientific guerrilla warfare. The tactics and strategies which he formulated between 1919 and 1922 in the Irish rebellion against British rule have since become part of the training curriculum of American, British, and Chinese military officers. Barry, who described his theories and experiences in *Guerrilla Days in Ireland* (1949), felt that his greatest and most ironic tribute was the assignment of his book to future officers at Britain's Royal Military Academy at Sandhurst.

The irony of British recognition of Barry's military accomplishments is compounded by the fact that his career as a soldier began under England's aegis. At the age of 18 Barry joined the Royal Field Artillery at Ballincollig and served in Iraq during the First World War. He says in his book: "I went to see what war was like, to get a gun, to see new countries and to feel a grown man." News of the executions of Irish revolutionary leaders after the suppression of the 1916 Easter Week rebellion in Dublin prompted Barry to reconsider his loyalties. On receiving his demobilization orders in 1919, he returned to his native County Cork and promptly enlisted in a local unit of the Irish Republican Army (IRA). His colleagues, in recognition of his military experience and gift for organization, appointed him training officer, and then commandant, of the West Cork Number 3 Brigade.

By 1920, after extensive drill and training with his soldiers, Barry put his theories of warfare into practice. Recognizing the numerical superiority of the British forces, he organized his men into highly disciplined "flying columns" of eight to ten men who were familiar with local terrain and could advance and retreat rapidly. Barry stressed continuous movement of his meager forces, concentrating his troops for ambushes and quick strikes against British units. Such strategy was employed at the battle of Kilmichael in November of 1920, where Barry's volunteers wiped out a superior force of British Auxilliaries and Black and Tans and secured a substantial quantity of ammunition. According to Tom Jones, Secretary of the Cabinet, the Kilmichael ambush helped to convince British Prime Minister Lloyd George that the Irish military challenge was real and that the IRA was not merely a handful of unorganized assassins.

Barry's success at Crossbarry in March of 1921, occurred just as revolutionary forces in Ireland had sustained several defeats and as the British sought to enforce a partition of northern and southern Ireland. The defeat of the Essex Regiment and Auxilliaries obliged the British government to negotiate with the Irish insurgents.

After the open civil war subsided in 1922, Barry maintained an independent view on the question of British intervention. While retaining his strong sense of Irish nationalism, he expressed criticism of both the deValera government and the IRA. He was interned by the deValera administration in 1935 after criticizing its compromises with the British. The following year he was named IRA Chief of Staff, but Barry left the Army in 1938, protesting the IRA's bombing campaign in England. He continued to condemn the killing of civilians in bombing attacks in Northern Ireland and England, declaring in 1976, "I won't be associated with putting bombs in pubs."

Barry's military accomplishments were the most dramatic expressions of his ardent nationalism and allegiance to the cause of Irish Republicanism. At the fiftieth anniversary of the battle of Kilmichael in 1970, Barry reaffirmed his conviction that all 32 counties of Ireland should be united and that any force which inhibited unification should be considered an enemy of Ireland. Barry justified the use of counterforce to oppose British rule when he asked rhetorically whether "peaceful means obtain in the six counties" which are still part of Great Britain.

Barry's involvement in the movement for Irish independence led to his marriage in 1921 to Leslie Bean de Barra, an Irish nationalist and member of Cumann nam ban who participated in the seizure of Dublin's General Post Office in 1916. Mrs. Barry was the chairwoman of the Irish Red Cross for many years. Barry served as the General Superintendent of the Cork Harbour Commissioners between 1927 and 1965. He ran unsuccessfully for office in the City of Cork in 1946, but was honored in 1949 when he was selected to raise the tricolour over Cork City Hall upon the official declaration of the Irish Republic.

Irish Prime Minister Charles Haughey said in a statement after Tom Barry's death: "He has earned an honoured place in Irish history for all time."   s.t.

Married Leslie Bean de Barra, Irish nationalist fighter and Chairwoman of Irish Red Cross, 1921. Roman Catholic. Mil. Service: Volunteer, British Army 1915–19; training officer and commandant, Irish Republican Army 1919–38. Defeated British forces in decisive battles of Kilmichael (1920) and Crossbarry (1921) during war for Irish independence. General Supt., Cork Harbour Commnrs. 1927–65, Named IRA Chief of Staff 1936, resigned from Army 1938. Defeated in Cork municipal election 1946. *Author:* Guerrilla Days in Ireland, A Firsthand Account of the Black and Tan War (1919–1921), 1949.

ABDUL HAMID SHARAF
Prime Minister of Jordan
Born Baghdad, Iraq, July 8th, 1939
Died Amman, Jordan, July 3rd, 1980

Sharaf, a personal friend and close adviser of Jordan's King Hussein, held a number of important posts in the Jordanian government before being appointed Prime Minister in December 1979. Praised by Hussein as a "martyr" of the Palestinian cause, Sharaf had the unusual combination of diplomatic flair and an understanding of Arab revolutionary politics that proved indispensable in dealing with Jordan's problems. His skill in dealing with both Western governments and radical Arab leaders was highly valued by Hussein, who lamented that Sharaf's death came at a time when his country needed him most.

Born into the Hashemite nobility, Sharaf spent his early years in Istanbul, where his family fled when British authorities deported his father in 1941 for pro-Axis sympathies. After World War Two the family settled in the Jordanian capital of Amman at the invitation of King Abdullah, Hussein's grandfather. Following secondary school in

urtesy Leila Sharaf

Amman, Sharaf studied philosophy and economics at the American University in Beirut. There he became involved in politics, joining the newly-formed Arab Nationalist Movement founded in 1952 by the Palestinian radical George Habash. Sharaf left the party only in 1963, when Habash split with the Syrian government, then friendly to Jordan.

Sharaf's government career, which began in 1962 with a post in the Ministry of Foreign Affairs, led within a year to the directorship of the Jordanian Broadcasting Service. His performance attracted the attention of Hussein, who appointed Sharaf assistant head of the Royal Diwan (Cabinet) in 1964. After serving for two years as Minister of Information, Sharaf was named Jordanian ambassador to the U.S. in 1967. When Jordan lost the West Bank of the Jordan River in the Arab-Israeli war of that year, he was instrumental in persuading the U.S. government to press Israel to allow the return of thousands of Arab refugees. In 1972 Sharaf was appointed Jordan's permanent delegate to the United Nations, where he continued his efforts to secure Israeli withdrawal from the West Bank. Return of the occupied territories, he indicated, was the necessary precondition of a Jordanian diplomatic settlement with Israel.

In 1976 Sharaf returned to Jordan as chief of the Royal Cabinet, a post which gave him constant access to King Hussein. After Egyptian President Anwar Sadat's trip to Jerusalem in 1977, Sharaf advised Hussein to maintain a position of neutrality between Egypt and radical Arab states such as Iraq and Syria, which rejected any compromise with Israel. At this time Sharaf also intitiated negotiations with the Palestinian Liberation Organization, which had been expelled from Jordan in September 1970. In 1978–79, with the Iranian revolution and the failure of Israel and Egypt to settle the Palestinian question, he urged a Jordanian "tilt" toward the anti-Sadat camp.

In December 1979 Hussein named a new government in which Sharaf served concurrently as Prime Minister, Foreign Minister and Defense Minister. He had the dual mission of eliminating governmental inefficiency and corruption and seeking "a sounder foundation for Jordan's relations with the rest of the Arab world." Sharaf's appointment was viewed as a sign of Hussein's commitment to closer ties with the PLO and the "Baghdad group" of states opposed to a settlement with Israel.

Sharaf died in his sleep, apparently the victim of a heart attack. T.P.

Married Leila Najjar. Two sons. Educ: American Univ. in Beirut, B.A., M.A. 1962; Georgetown Univ., Washington, D.C., Ph.D. 1968. With Jordanian govt.: Chief of Arab and Palestine Affairs, Dept. of Foreign Ministry 1962–63; Dir., Jordanian Broadcasting Service 1963–64; Asst. Chief, Royal Cabinet 1964–65; Minister of Information 1965–67; Ambassador to the U.S. 1967–72 and to Canada 1969–72; Delegate to the U.N. General Assembly 1972–76; Chief, Royal Cabinet 1976–79; Prime Minister and Minister of Defense and Foreign Affairs since 1979.

GREGORY BATESON
Anthropologist, ethnologist and philosopher
Born Grantchester, near Cambridge, England, May 9th, 1904
Died San Francisco, California, U.S.A., July 4th, 1980

Like the better-known philosopher-scientists Marshall McLuhan [q.v.] and Buckminster Fuller, Gregory Bateson developed important analytical concepts for use in a number of distinct contexts. Among these concepts were "paralinguistics" or the science of non-verbal communication; "schismo-genesis," the mechanism of breakdown in intersystem (or individual human) relationships and its aftermath; and the "double bind" theory (a phenomenon of human communication which the *New Yorker* neatly described as "issuing a command and implying at the same time you will hate forever anyone who obeys the command"). Like his fellow luminaries, he also sought to develop new frames of philosophical reference for coming to grips with a complex and interdependent universe.

Gregory Bateson was the son of an eminent British zoologist and pioneer in the field of genetics, and grandson of a classical scholar and Master of a Cambridge College. He was nurtured in the traditions of Britain's intellectual elite—families like those of the Huxleys and Haldanes—in which tremendous and widely celebrated creativity was often accompanied by cross-grained rebelliousness. At the time of Gregory's birth in 1904, his father, William Bateson, was a fellow of St. John's College and already a leading figure in research into heredity. In 1910 the family moved to London where Gregory's father continued his research and devoted time to the defense of his increasingly radical theories, while also serving as a trustee of the British Museum of Natural History.

Raised in this rich atmosphere, young Gregory became a supreme rationalist and fifth generation atheist (his father read from the Bible every morning "lest we grow up to be *empty-headed* atheists"). Following in his father's footsteps, he took his bachelor's degree in Biology at St. John's College, Cambridge in 1925, after which he traveled to the Pacific to do morphological field work. In New Guinea in 1928 he met the American anthropologist Margaret Mead, who first introduced him to the less restrictive discipline of social anthropology. In 1936 she became his first wife, and that same year he published his first book, *Naeven,* a study of the Iatmul tribe.

In this work his cybernetical analyses of the dependence of ecological systems first took shape. It was clear that he would go far beyond the frontiers of anthropology, in which he had taken his M.A., also from St. John's in 1930. By making use of cybernetics—the science of communications and control throughout the entire ecology—in the interpretation of his findings about the Iatmul, he showed more a philosopher's penchant for raising questions about the nature of the universe than an empiricist's desire to answer them.

Bateson emigrated to the U.S. in 1942 and subsequently held a number of teaching positions. Prior to his year as visiting professor in anthropology at Harvard University, he served for three years as a regional specialist for the U.S. Office of Strategic Services in Washington, D.C. From 1949 until 1951 he was a research associate in psychiatry and communications at San Francisco's Langley-Porter Clinic, and he then spent 11 years conducting research into the ethnological aspects of alcoholism at the V.A. hospital in Palo Alto; at the same time he was a visiting professor in anthropology at Stanford University. In the early 1960s, Bateson worked as research director in ethnology at the Communications Research Institute and then headed the Biological Relations Division of the Oceanic Institute in Hawaii for eight years. Returning to the mainland in 1972, Bateson took up a new post as Professor of Anthropology and Ethnology at the University of California, Santa Cruz.

Bateson's second book, written with Margaret Mead (*Balinese Character*, 1943), was followed in 1950 with *Communication*, written with J. Ruesch. His collected essays appeared in 1972 under the title *Ecology of Mind*, and a year before his death he published *Mind and Nature: A Necessary Unity*. John Pfeiffer, writing in the *New York Times Book Review*, called *Mind and Nature* "an extraordinary testament . . . by one of the most creative investigators of our time." A more critical appraisal of the book came from A.M. O'Brien, who said: "Uncritically assumed philosophical presupposition, generally of the empiricist tradition, make the discussion somewhat problematic for the professional philosopher, while technical language makes it difficult reading for one unfamiliar with biology or cybernetics. Yet, *Mind and Nature* is a significant exercise of creative imagination. . . ."

Admitting to being more consciously elitist than most philosopher-scientists, Bateson never attempted to simplify his perceptions for his youthful, would-be disciples. Indeed, he could be irritatingly obscure, arguing that he addressed himself to the "top one per-cent." When Governor Jerry Brown appointed him to the University of California Board of Regents in 1976 to "shake things up," Bateson observed: "I prefer the top one-percent who may contribute to one stock of eternal varieties." As for the rest, "they will go into various sorts of activities which will perpetuate our way of life and, on the whole, perpetuate its pathologies, its greed, its hatred of nature and its hatred of the intellect."

Bateson was not an easily comprehended thinker; his meanings and suggestions were rarely accessible except to those with a willingness to "wrestle" (Bateson's favorite metaphor for the acquisition of knowledge) with their implications. He did not translate his ideas into words either with the ease or in the volume of Margaret Mead; yet psychiatrists, philosophers and linguists as well as social anthropologists, ethnologists and ecologists have had to consider seriously his theories of communication and his holistic conclusions about the nature of existence. That he did not achieve wider recognition is due in part to his mystical evocations of oriental philosophy, particularly Taoism, and his association with such avant-garde organizations as the Esalen Institute of Big Sur, California (which disturbed many establishment intellectuals) and in part to his obvious preference for the role of *agent provocateur* to that of popular leader.   R.T./R.C.

Son of William B., geneticist, and Beatrice Durham B. Married: (1) Margaret Mead, anthropologist, 1936 (div. 1950); (2) Elizabeth Sumner 1951 (div. 1958); (3) Lois Cammack 1961. Children: 1st marriage—Mary Catherine Kassarjian, anthropologist, b. 1938; 2nd marriage—John, b. 1951; 3rd marriage—Nora, b. 1968. Atheist. Emigrated to USA 1942. Naturalized American. Educ: Charterhouse Sch., London 1917–21; St. John's Coll., Cambridge, B.Sc., biology 1925, and M.A., anthropology 1930. Engaged in anthropological field

work 1927–28 (New Britain), 1928–33 and 1939 (New Guinea) and 1936–38 (Bali). Anthropological film analyst, Mus. of Modern Art, NYC 1942–43; Lectr., Naval Sch. of Govt. and Admin., Columbia Univ., NYC 1943–44; Visiting Prof., Anthropology, New School for Social Research, NYC 1946; Regional Specialist, U.S. Office of Strategic Services, Washington, D.C. 1944–47; Visiting Prof., Anthropology, Harvard Univ., Boston, 1947–48; Research Assoc. in psychiatry and communications, Langley-Porter Clinic, San Francisco 1949–51; Ethnologist/researcher on alcoholism, Veteran's Admin. Hosp., Palo Alto, Calif. and Visiting Prof., Anthropology, Stanford Univ., Palo Alto, 1951–62; Research Dir. in ethnology, Communications Research Inst. 1962–64; Chief, Biological Relations Div., Oceanic Inst., Waimanalo, Hawaii 1964–72; Prof. of Anthropology and Ethnology, Univ. of Calif., Santa Cruz 1972–78; Member, Univ. of Calif. Bd. of Regents 1976–78; Scholar in Residence, Esalen Inst., Big Sur, Calif. 1978–80. Member: Royal Anthropological Inst. (England); N.Y. Acad. of Science; American Ethnological Soc.; Inst. for Intercultural Studies; American Anthropological Assn. Fellow, American Assn. for the Advancement of Science. Hons: Guggenheim Fellow 1946–47; Freida Fromm-Reichmann Award for research in schizophrenia 1962; D.Sc., Northwestern Univ., Evanston, Ill. 1972. *Works:* Naeven 1936, rev. ed. 1958; (with Margaret Mead) Balinese Character, 1943; (with J. Ruesch) Communication, 1950; Ecology of Mind (collected essays; in U.K. as Steps to an Ecology of Mind), 1972; Mind and Nature: A Necessary Unity, 1979.
Further reading: review of Steps to an Ecology of the Mind, in New York Review of Books, Oct. 19, 1972; "Both Sides of the Necessary Paradox," in Harper's, Nov., 1973; Gregory Bateson: The Legacy of a Scientist by David Lipset, 1980.

ARI A. SHTERNFELD
Rocket expert
Born in Poland, ca. 1905
Died Moscow, U.S.S.R., July 5th, 1980

Ari Shternfeld was an early expert on rocketry and space flight. A Jew, Shternfeld was never admitted to the inner circle of Soviet science.

Shternfeld was born in Poland. His early years were divided between France and Poland where he conducted research on space flight. In 1933 Shternfeld wrote *An Introduction to Astronautics,* for which he received the Hirsch Prize for Astronautics in Paris, one of the first books on space flight and rocketry. He moved to the Soviet Union in 1935 and continued to write books and articles about space flight, including *Artificial Satellites of the Earth* and *Soviet Space Flight* (1959), which were published in the West.   E.T.

Jewish. Emigrated to USSR 1935. Educ: Nancy Univ., grad. 1927. Lectr: at meeting of Warsaw Astronomical Observatory; Sorbonne, Paris; French Acad. of Sciences. Member, Soviet Acad. of Sciences. Hons: Hirsch Prize for Astronautics (for An Introduction to Astronautics). *Author:* An Introduction to Astronautics, 1933 (Paris) and 1937 (Moscow); Artificial Satellites of the Earth; Soviet Space Flight, 1959; others.

GAIL PATRICK
Movie actress and television producer
Born Birmingham, Alabama, U.S.A., June 20th, 1911
Died Hollywood, California, U.S.A., July 6th, 1980

Gail Patrick, a popular Hollywood film actress in the 1930s and mid-40s, went on to a second career as an executive producer of the long-running *Perry Mason* television series.

In her youth, Margaret Lovelle Fitzpatrick intended to pursue a life in politics, with the goal—an ambitious one for a young woman in the 1920s—of becoming governor of Alabama. While studying law in evening classes at the University of Alabama, friends urged her to enter a screen test for Paramount Pictures. She won the "Panther Woman" contest, and a trip to Hollywood and more screen tests. Choosing Gail Patrick as a name that would better fit a movie marquee, she appeared in almost 60 films; her dark beauty and poise suiting her for numerous roles as "the other woman."

Gail Patrick appeared in a few distinguished films working with actors such as Sterling Holloway, Carole Lombard, and William Powell, but she wished to pursue a more "serious" career. "I never considered myself a star," she later said, "I was always a featured player." As early as 1937, not long after she had arrived in Hollywood, she predicted that by age 40 she would no longer want to make movies but would like to "star in an executive role." In fact, she retired from acting in 1947 at the age of 36, and for a while ran a children's clothing shop in Beverly Hills.

Her third husband, Cornwall Jackson, had been literary agent for mystery writer Erle Stanley Gardner, and Gail Patrick conceived the idea of producing a television series based on Gardner's Perry Mason character. She became executive producer—an unusual position for a woman in television's early years—of the *Perry Mason* show and maintained that position throughout the show's very successful nine-year run. Proud of the fact that there was never any on-screen violence in the program, she said "We're a whodunit. Our action takes place in court. We start with a body!"

Gail Patrick was active as a civic leader during both of her careers. As an actress she helped in the war bond effort and aided the Crippled Children's Clinic in her native Birmingham. Later she served as president of the Hollywood chapter of the Academy of Television Arts and Sciences. She defended commercial television and the right of the public to choose its own programming. A diabetic herself, she also served as chairperson of the American Diabetes Association. L.B.

Born Margaret Lovelle Fitzpatrick. Daughter of Lawrence F. and Lavelle (Smith) F. Married: (1) Robert Howard Cobb 1936 (div. 1941); (2) Lt. Arnold Dean White 1944; (3) Cornwall Jackson 1947 (div. 1969); (4) John E. Velde, Jr. Children: 3rd marriage—Thomas, Jr.; Jennifer (both adopted). Educ: Howard Coll., Birmingham, Ala., Bachelor of laws (with honors); attended classes, Univ. of Alabama Law Sch., Birmingham. Hollywood screen actress in 1930s and through the mid-40s; owner of children's clothing shop, Beverly Hills, Calif., ca. 1947; Exec. producer, Perry Mason series, CBS Television 1956–65. Pres., Hollywood Chapter, Natl. Acad. of Television Arts and Sciences 1961; natl. Chairperson, Christmas Seal Campaign 1970; Chairperson, American Diabetes Assn. 1975; made appearances in behalf of Crippled Children's Clinic in Birmingham, Ala. *Perfor-*

mances: Mysterious Rider, 1933; Doubting Thomas, 1935; Murder with Pictures, and My Man Godfrey, 1936; John Meade's Woman, 1937; My Favorite Wife, and Gallant Sons, 1940; Hitler's Children, 1943; Up in Mabel's Room, 1944; Claudia and David, and The Plainsmen and the Lady, 1946; Stagedoor; Death Takes a Holiday; and others.

REGINALD GARDINER
Actor
Born Wimbledon, Surrey, England, February 27th, 1903
Died Los Angeles, California, U.S.A., July 7th, 1980

Reginald Gardiner's career as a character actor and comedian spanned nearly five decades. He appeared in almost every entertainment medium: theater, films, television, and the night club stage. Gardiner, whose appearances with the Canadian comedienne Beatrice Lillie endeared him to New York theater audiences, is perhaps best remembered for the amiable, bumbling English gentlemen he portrayed in Hollywood movies and for his unusual imitations of such inanimate objects as lighthouses, French wallpaper, and marine machinery.

Born in Wimbledon near London, Gardiner showed an early flair for the stage, appearing in student theatricals. After a short-lived architectural apprenticeship, he gained admittance to the prestigious Royal Academy of Dramatic Art in London.

Soon after his graduation from the Academy in 1923, Gardiner made his London debut at the Haymarket Theatre as a walk-on in "The Prisoner of Zenda." He then joined the Repertory Players, a West End troupe, and appeared in almost 30 plays in London, his roles ranging from dramatic portrayals to parts in musicals and revues. During this busy period, Gardiner also played in 20 British films, beginning as an extra in Alfred Hitchcock's [q.v.] *The Lodger* in 1928.

Gardiner met Beatrice Lillie in 1933 in the revue *Oh, Please!* at London's Savoy Theatre. Lillie, her reputation as "the funniest woman in the world" firmly established, recognized a kindred comedic spirit in Gardiner and persuaded her employers, the Shuberts, to bring the young actor to New York to appear in her next revue *At Home Abroad.* "We regarded each other as rather funny in a deranged sort of way," said Lillie. "Who but an inspired loon could reduce an audience to helpless laughter by sounding exactly like a swinging door, empty shoes . . . or a fog settling over Flushing flats?" In 1936 the two appeared in another revue, *The Show Is On,* and in 1952 in *An Evening With Beatrice Lillie.* In his review of the latter, Brooks Atkinson, then theater critic for the New York *Times,* said, "By applying a trivial mind to profound mechanical achievements, he [Gardiner] fantastifies the machine age and devastates the audience." Gardiner's most famous imitation of this type, that of a passenger train, was recorded and is now a collector's item.

After Gardiner made his Hollywood film debut in 1936 in *Born to Dance,* an Eleanor Powell vehicle, a series of movies followed, including *The Great Dictator* (1940), *The Man Who Came to Dinner*

(1941), *A Yank in the RAF* (1941), *Back Street* (1961), and *Mr. Hobbs Takes a Vacation* (1962). In all, Gardiner appeared in more than 90 feature films.

Gardiner returned to the New York stage in 1964 in a revival of *My Fair Lady* at the New York City Center. John Canaday of the *New York Times* called his performance as Alfred Doolittle "wonderful, boozy, abominable, bug-ridden, [he's] an altogether reprehensible charmer."

During the 1950s Gardiner frequently appeared on television, most notably in "Burke's Law," "Hazel," "77 Sunset Strip," "The Ed Sullivan Show," and "I've Got a Secret." During the last few years of his life, Gardiner devoted much time to his hobbies of painting and fashioning figurines of characters from Arthurian legends. He died at the age of 77 in Los Angeles.   S.T.

Born William Reginald Gardiner. Son of Robert Edward G., actuary, and Henrietta Pennington G. Married: (1) Wyn Richmond, actress (div.); (2) Nadya Pretrova, model, 1942. Children: 2nd marriage—Peter. Emigrated to U.S. 1935. Educ: Shrewsbury Sch., Shropshire 1921; Royal Acad. Dramatic Art, London 1923. Active on London stage 1923–35; N.Y. stage debut 1935; appeared in over 30 Hollywood films 1936–65; night club appearances in N.Y. and London. Member, AEA; SAG; AFTRA. Hons: Henry Ainley Special Medal Award, Royal Acad. Dramatic Art 1923. *Performances: Plays*—The Prisoner of Zenda, London 1923; Old Heildeberg, London 1925; 9:45, London 1925; Down Hill (Captain Hunter), London 1926; Chance Acquaintance, London 1927; Blackmail (Jimmy Manning), London 1928; Our Little Wife (Tommy), London 1928; If We But Knew (Aubrey Tamarest), London 1928; The Tragic Muse (Basil), London 1928; A Damsel in Distress (Viscount Totleigh), London 1928; Baa, Baa, Black Sheep (Osbert), London 1929; The Middle Watch (Commander Baddeley), London 1929; Leave It to Psmith (Freddie Bosham), London 1930; Naughty Cinderella (Banton West), London 1931; The Lady Known As Lou (Sanchez), London 1931; Chance Acquaintance (Sebastian Beynes), London 1931; A Flat to Let (Tony), London 1931; Pleasure Cruise (Richard Hemming), London 1932; Over the Page, London 1932; Money for Jam (Peter Paul Lutz), London 1932; Mother of Pearl (John Sterling), London 1933; A Present from Margate (Freddie Carew), London 1933; Oh, Please!, London 1933; Indoor Fireworks (Teddy), London 1934; Hi-Diddle-Diddle, London 1934; Charlot's Char-a-Bang!, London 1935; At Home Abroad, N.Y. 1935; The Show Is On, N.Y. 1936; An Evening with Beatrice Lillie, N.Y. 1952; tour USA 1953–54; Little Glass Clock (Abbe Matignon), N.Y. 1956; My Fair Lady (Alfred Doolittle), N.Y. 1964. *Films*—The Lodger, 1928; Born To Dance, 1936; Damsel In Distress, 1937; Everybody Sing, 1938; Sweethearts, 1938; Marie Antoinette, 1938; The Girl Downstairs; The Doctor Takes A Wife, 1940; Dulcy, 1940; The Great Dictator, 1940; Sundown, 1941; Yank in the RAF, 1941; The Man Who Came to Dinner, 1941; My Life with Caroline, 1941; Captains of the Clouds, 1942; Immortal Sergeant, 1943; Claudia, 1943; Sweet Rosie O'Grady, 1943; The Horn Blows at Midnight, 1945; The Dolly Sisters, 1945; Molly and Me, 1945; Christmas in Connecticut, 1945; Cluny Brown, 1946; One More Tomorrow, 1946; Do You Love Me?, 1946; I Wonder Who's Kissing Her Now, 1947; Fury at Furnace Creek, 1948; That Wonderful Urge, 1948; Lady in Ermine, 1949; Wabash Avenue, 1950; Halls of Montezuma, 1950; Elopement, 1951; Androcles and the Lion, 1952; Black Widow, 1954;

Ain't Misbehavin', 1955; The Birds and the Bees, 1956; Rock-a-bye
Baby, 1958; Back Street, 1961; Mr. Hobbs Takes a Vacation, 1962;
What a Way to Go, 1964; Do Not Disturb, 1964; Sgt. Deadhead, the
Astronaut, 1965. *TV*—Mr. Belvedere, 1950s; The Pruitts of South-
hampton, 1966; guest appearances on Burke's Law; Hazel; Mr. Smith
Goes to Washington; 77 Sunset Strip; My Man Higgins; Behind
Closed Doors; the Ed Sullivan Show; I've Got a Secret; What's My
Line; Playhouse 90; Border Patrol; Adventures in Paradise; The
Millionaire; Alfred Hitchcock Presents; Laramie. *Night clubs*—Carl-
ton Hotel, London; Claridge's Hotel, London; Berkeley Hotel,
London; Montmarte Club, N.Y. 1935–36.
Further reading: Every Other Inch a Lady by Beatrice Lillie, 1972.

DORE SCHARY
Film producer, screenwriter and playwright
Born Newark, New Jersey, U.S.A., August 31st, 1905
Died New York City, U.S.A., July 7th, 1980

Dore Schary, who supervised the production of some 350 films and
wrote the scripts for 40 others during a quarter-century in Hollywood,
was almost as well-known for his active support of liberal causes as he
was for his movie-making. Although he produced some of the most
entertaining films in American cinema, including *Singin' in the Rain*
and *Seven Brides for Seven Brothers,* he preferred to use films and
plays as didactic instruments for raising the moral sensitivities of his
audiences and bringing social issues to their attention.

Schary was born in Newark, New Jersey, in 1905. His parents were
immigrant Jews from Eastern Europe who ran a kosher catering
business and hotel, where the family, a large, close-knit clan, staged
amateur theatrical productions for the entertainment of their guests.
At the age of 14 he quit school to work variously as a china buyer, a
haberdashery salesman, and a printer's devil for the Newark *Call,*
then returned to the *Call* as a reporter and feature writer after
finishing four years of high school in one. He joined a theater group at
the Newark YMHA and changed his name from Isidore to Dore
(pronounced Dor-ee). Over the next six years he acted in stock
companies, won bit parts in two Broadway shows, and wrote plays,
one of which caught the eye of Columbia Pictures producer Walter
Wanger, who offered "Miss Schary" a $100-per-week screenwriting
job.

Schary arrived in Hollywood in 1932 with "36 dollars, two clean
shirts and my wife" and wrote 11 scripts in one year, earning a
reputation as a reliable craftsman. He soon left Columbia to become a
freelance writer for the major studios. In 1938 he was hired by M-G-M
and won an Academy Award for the script of *Boys Town*. He also
wrote a play, *Too Many Heroes,* which ran on Broadway for two
weeks in 1937.

In 1941 M-G-M made Schary the head of its low-budget production
unit, where he turned out such critical and financial successes as
Bataan and *Lassie Come Home*. His talent for picking out solid
scripts, matching them with appropriate directors and players, and
sticking to a tight budget with no loss of quality soon made him one of

the industry's most sought-after executives. After a short stint with David O. Selznick's Vanguard Productions, he moved to RKO, where his first four movies (including *The Spiral Staircase* and *The Farmer's Daughter*) doubled the company's profits within a single year. This feat earned him a five-year contract as executive vice-president in charge of production. His next project was the groundbreaking *Crossfire*, Hollywood's first serious treatment of anti-Semitism. Subsequent films for RKO included *Mr. Blandings Builds His Dream House* and *The Boy with Green Hair*.

Schary was moving ahead with plans for more films dealing with ethnic and racial intolerance (a subject he had studied at first hand in his Newark neighborhood) when, in 1947, the House Un-American Activities Committee declared the movie industry a target of its anti-communist investigations. Called to testify before the committee, Schary iterated his belief that the exercise of a constitutionally protected right, such as the freedom to hold unpopular political views, should not disqualify a person from employment. The industry as a whole, however, quickly succumbed to pressure from the right wing. Ten screenwriters and directors who had received contempt citations from HUAC for refusing to deny or confirm their membership in the Communist Party were blacklisted by all the major studios, despite Schary's arguments; nor could he convince RKO to retain two employees accused of being "soft on communism." Left-wing groups expected him to resign in protest and vigorously criticized him when he chose to keep his job and press for change from inside the industry.

Within a year, however, Schary had left, not for political reasons but as a result of a clash with the eccentric billionaire Howard Hughes, who took control of RKO in 1948 and promptly called a halt to "message" films. The soft-spoken but fiercely independent Schary returned to M-G-M, where he produced some 250 movies in the next eight years, including such classics as *Singin' in the Rain, The Blackboard Jungle, An American in Paris,* and *Bad Day at Black Rock.* M-G-M films produced under his supervision received 31 Academy Award nominations in 1956 alone. But the studio heads, citing declining profits and Schary's increasing commitment to political activism, ousted him soon thereafter.

Schary now decided to revive his career as a playwright, interrupted in 1937. His first attempt in this direction was *Sunrise at Campobello*, a drama about Franklin Delano Roosevelt's struggle to overcome the crippling effects of polio. It ran for 556 performances on Broadway, won five Tony Awards, and was named Best Play of 1958. Schary adapted it for the screen in 1960.

Subsequent plays, several of which he produced and directed, included *The Highest Tree*, on the dangers of nuclear bomb testing; *The Devil's Advocate*, an adaptation of the Morris West novel about a dying priest; *Banderol*, the story of a power struggle in a film studio; *One by One*, on the lives of two paraplegics; and *Brightower*, about a writer driven to suicide by the demands of his public. None were commercial successes. His last play, *Herzl*, written with Amos Elon, closed after one performance. Critics pointed out that Schary, though he created strong characters and knew how to build an emotional scene, too often sacrificed dramatic structure and dialogue to his educational purpose, subordinating more purely theatrical elements to the preaching of his humanitarian ideals.

These ideals were the focus of Schary's life as a private citizen, the more so as he grew older. He actively supported Democratic candidates for the presidency, served on a number of government commissions on issues of social reform, and was national chairman of the Anti-Defamation League of B'nai B'rith. During the 1965 drought he organized a successful attempt by actors and writers to persuade New Yorkers to cut their water consumption. Mayor Lindsay appointed him New York City's first Commissioner of Cultural Affairs in 1970. He was a firm supporter of the civil rights movement, the "one world" movement, and the State of Israel.

In 1977, Schary was asked by members of the Academy of Motion Picture Arts and Sciences to join in a campaign against giving the Best Actress Award to nominee Vanessa Redgrave as a gesture of the film industry's disgust with her anti-Israeli activities. Although he said that he would not sit in the same room with Redgrave, Schary refused to participate in the boycott, saying, "We went through a period years ago in the industry when people were barred for their political opinions. It would be awful if we did it again."

In addition to writing plays since his departure from Hollywood, Schary ran an independent film and television production company, made documentaries on political subjects, directed the movie *Act One* from his own screenplay, and wrote two autobiographies. He and his wife had three children. He died of cancer.   R.C./J.P.

Born Isidore Schary. Son of Herman Hugo S. and Belle (Drachler) S., caterers. Married Miriam Svet, artist, 1932. Children: Jill Robinson, writer, b.1936; Joy Stashower, b.1938; Jeb, b.1940. Jewish. Educ: Central High Sch., Newark, N.J. Journalist with Newark Call, publicity dir., playwright 1926–32; also actor and drama coach with theater group, Newark YMHA, and actor with Cincinnati stock co. and other groups. Staff screenwriter, Columbia Pictures, Hollywood 1932–33; freelance screenwriter for major film studios, Hollywood 1933–37. With M-G-M Studios, Culver City, Calif.: Screenwriter 1938–41; Exec. Producer 1941–43; Exec. V.P. in Charge of Production and Studio Operations 1948–56. Producer, David O. Selznick's Vanguard Productions 1943–45; Exec. V.P. in Charge of Productions, RKO Studios, Hollywood 1945–48; independent theater and film producer and playwright since 1956; Dir., Schary, Productions and Schary Television Productions since 1959; Pres. and Chief. Exec., Telepremiere Intnl. and TheatreVision, Inc. Chmn., NYC commn. on water shortage 1965; Commnr. of Cultural Affairs, NYC 1970–71. Member: President's Cttee. on Employment of Handicapped; Advisory Council, U.S. Cttee. for the United Nations; Citizens' Crusade Against Poverty; Natl. Citizen's Cttee.; Natl. Advisory Commn. on Farm Labor; natl. Cttee. on Immigration. Pres., Dramatists Guild 1962; Natl. Chmn., Anti-Defamation League of B'nai B'rith 1963–69; Bd. member, Authors League. member: Theatre guild 1956–60; Screenwriters Guild; Screen Producers Guild; League of New York Theaters; Acad. of Motion Picture Arts and Sciences. Trustee, Eleanor Roosevelt Memorial Foundn.; Trustee, Brandeis Univ.; Bd. Member, Jewish Theological Seminary of America; patron, Univ. of Judaism; sponsor, New York Shakespeare Festival. Hons: Academy Award, Best Screenplay (for Boys Town) 1938; Golden Slipper Club Award for Humanitarianism (for Crossfire) 1947; One World Motion Picture Award (for Crossfire) 1948; Thomas Jefferson Award, Council Against Intolerance in America (for Crossfire) 1948; Hon. D.H.L.,

Coll. of Pacific and Wilberforce Univ. 1951; Tony Award (for Sunrise at Campobello) 1958; Natl. Assoc. of Independent Schools Award 1959; Hon. D.F.A., Lincoln Coll. 1960; Hon. Chmn. since 1969 and Haym Salomon Award 1980, Anti-Defamation League of B'nai B'rith; Hon. V.P., United World Federalists; Fellow, Eleanor Roosevelt Memorial Fund. *Screenplays:* Young and Beautiful, 1934; Let's Talk it Over, 1934; Murder in the Clouds, 1934; Chinatown Squad, 1935; Your Uncle Dudley, 1935; Silk Hat Kid, 1935; (with Harry Sauber) Her Master's Voice, 1936; Mind Your Own Business, 1936; Outcast, 1937; The Girl from Scotland Yard, 1937; Big City, 1937; Boys Town, 1938; Young Tom Edison, 1940; Edison the Man, 1940; Broadway Melody of 1940, 1940; Married Bachelor, 1941; Behind the News, 1941; It's a Big Country, 1952; Battle of Gettysburg, 1956; Lonelyhearts, 1959; Sunrise at Campobello, 1960; (with Sinclair Lewis) Storm in the West, 1963; Act One, 1963; others. *Plays:* Too Many Heroes, 1937; Sunrise at Campobello, 1958; The Highest Tree, 1959; The Devil's Advocate, 1961; Banderol, 1963; One by One, 1964; Brightower, 1970; Antiques, 1973; (with Amos Elon) Herzl, 1976. *Exec. Film Producer:* Joe Smith, American, 1942; Journey for Margaret, 1942; Bataan, 1943; Lassie Come Home, 1943; Lost Angel, 1943; I'll Be Seeing You, 1945; The Spiral Staircase, 1945; Till The End of Time, 1946; The Farmer's Daughter, 1947; The Bachelor and the Bobby-Soxer, 1947; Crossfire, 1947; Mr. Blandings Builds His Dream House, 1948; Intruder in the Dust, 1948; Berlin Express, 1948; The Boy with Green Hair, 1948; The Window, 1949; The Set-Up, 1949; Battleground, 1949; The Next Voice You Hear, 1950; Father of the Bride, 1950; Red Badge of Courage, 1951; An American in Paris, 1951; Singin' in the Rain, 1952; Plymouth Adventure, 1952; Ivanhoe, 1952; Dream Wife, 1953; Take the High Ground, 1953; Lili, 1953; Executive Suite, 1954; Seven Brides for Seven Brothers, 1954; Bad Day at Black Rock, 1954; Blackboard Jungle, 1955; Tea and Sympathy, 1956; The Swan, 1956; The Last Hunt, 1956; many others. *Director and Producer: Plays*—A Majority of One, 1959; The Highest Tree, 1959; The Unsinkable Molly Brown, 1960; The Devil's Advocate, 1961; Something About a Soldier, 1962; (director only) Banderol, 1963; Love and Kisses, 1963; One by One, 1964; The Zulu and the Zayda, 1965. *Film*—Act One, 1963. *Actor:* Four Walls (Jake), NYC 1928; The Last Mile (Reporter), NYC 1930; The M-G-M Story (teleplay), 1954. *Other:* Producer of film on hist. of Democratic Party, 1956; The Golden Streets, 1970; writer and producer, Israel: The Right to Be (documentary). *Author:* (with Charles Palmer) Case History of a Movie, 1950; For Special Occasions (autobiog.), 1962; Heyday (autobiog.), 1979.

JOSEPH (QUINCY) KRUMGOLD
Author, screenwriter, and film producer
Born Jersey City, New Jersey, U.S.A., April 9th, 1908
Died Hope, New Jersey, U.S.A., July 10th, 1980

Joseph Krumgold achieved prominence in two fields: as a writer and producer of B-movies and documentary films, and as an award-winning children's writer.

Born into a family strongly associated with movies—his father was a cinema owner and film distributor, his brother an organist for the great silent-movie houses in New York—Joseph decided at an early age that he wanted to make movies, and geared his education toward understanding the science as well as the art of filmmaking.

After graduating from New York University in 1928, Krumgold began a job as publicist for M-G-M in New York, during which time he wrote a script for Lon Chaney that was never produced. A year later, he went to Hollywood where "talkies" were beginning to be made, and wrote a variety of B-movies for RKO, Columbia, and other companies.

Krumgold soon involved himself in film production, but by 1940, he was dissatisfied with Hollywood as it did not allow him to make the kind of documentary feature that had begun to intrigue him. He returned to New York and with Henwar Rodakiewicz set up his own production company. Their first endeavor, *One Tenth of a Nation*, was an unsuccessful film about the education of Southern blacks. During the war, Krumgold wrote and produced propaganda documentaries for the Office of War Information, the best known of which was *The Autobiography of a Jeep*.

With the emergence of Israel, Krumgold became active for the Israeli cause. He spent six years (1946–52) in Israel as head of the production company, Palestine Films, and made 15 pictures. Some of these were used as fund raisers for Israel, and *The House in the Desert*, won a prize at the Venice Film Festival.

In 1952, Krumgold returned to the United States and created his own company, Krumgold Productions. Shortly thereafter, he was commissioned by the State Department to produce a documentary on rural America for people in Turkey and the Arab states. Choosing as his subject a shepherd's family (with which many of the film's viewers would readily identify), Krumgold spent a year with a Mexican-American rancher, filming the cycle of sheep-raising. This documentary, . . . *And Now Miguel,* focused on the strong Mexican-American traditions of the family and told the story of the son, Miguel, and his readiness to take on a man's responsibility—the traditional winter pasturing of the sheep in the mountains.

A publisher encouraged Krumgold in his desire to turn the story of Miguel into a book for children (he had already published a children's book, *Sweeney's Adventures,* in 1942). The task turned into months of writing and rewriting; Krumgold was quite surprised when . . . *And Now Miguel* won the Newbery Medal for the most distinguished book written for children in 1953. It has been translated into 15 languages.

Continuing to produce films, Krumgold heard about a boy whose values conflicted with those of the people in his small town. Krumgold turned this true story into a drama, *Onion John* (awarded the Newbery Medal, 1960) in which a young boy's search for identity forces him to choose between a misfit, Onion John, and his father. *Henry 3,* the third book in Krumgold's self-described trilogy, concerns a boy whose father is a successful executive in New York, but critics found its portrayal of men's and women's roles stereotyped—greedy businessmen became heroes when faced with real danger, while weak, fur-clad wives dissolved in hysterics.

Of his children's trilogy, he said: "The child is examined by the adult for his maturity and understanding. And—less obviously—the community is examined, its wisdom and values are measured with all innocence by the child. It is this fresh insight, the test we're put to by our young, that determines the shape of these stories."

Krumgold's fifth and last book for children, *The Most Terrible Turk,* was published in 1969. While his moving—but never sentimental—children's fiction is, in many ways, unusually fresh and intelligent, his portrayal of female characters is generally unsympathetic and shallow.

He died at the age of 72 at his home in Hope, New Jersey.   H.S.

Son of Henry K., motion picture exhibitor, and Lena (Gross) K. Married Helen Litwin 1947. Son: Adam, b. 1952. Jewish. Educ: New York Univ., B.A. 1928. Publicity writer, Metro-Goldwyn-Mayer, NYC 1928; film writer and producer, Paramount, RKO, Columbia, and Republic Studios, Hollywood 1929–40; producer and dir., Film Assocs., NYC and Office of War Information 1940–46; Pres., Palestine Films, Jerusalem and NYC 1946–52; owner, Krumgold Productions 1952–60; television dir., producer, and writer, CBS, NBC, WNET, and Westinghouse, N.Y., Rome, and Istanbul since 1960. Member: Screenwriters Guild; Authors League; Players, NYC; Pi Lambda Phi. Hons: American Library Assn. Newbery Medal 1954 and 1960; film prizes, Venice, Edinburgh, and Prague film festivals. *Author: Children's books*—Sweeney's Adventures (illus. Tibor Gergely), 1942; . . . And Now Miguel (illus. Jean Charlot), 1953; Onion John (illus. Symeon Shimin), 1959; Henry 3 (illus. Alvin Smith), 1967; The Most Terrible Turk (illus. Michael Hampshire), 1969. *Other*—Thanks to Murder (mystery), 1935; Where Do We Grow From Here: An Essay on Children's Literature, 1968; The Oxford Furnace, 1741–1925 (local hist.), 1976. *Screenplays*—(with Lee Loeb and Harold Bluchman) Blackmailer, 1936; (with others) Lady From Nowhere, 1936; (with Bruce Manning and Lionel Houser) Lone Wolf Returns, 1936; Adventure in Manhattan (orig. story only), 1936; (with Olive Cooper) Jim Hanvey—Detective (also assoc. producer), 1937; (with Olive Cooper and Karl Brown) Join the Marines, 1937; Speed to Burn (contributor), 1938; (with Olive Cooper) Lady Behave, 1938; Main Street Lawyer, 1939; The Phantom Submarine, 1940; (with others) The Crooked Road, 1940; Seven Miles from Alcatraz, 1942; (with Robert Riskin) Magic Town (also orig. author), 1947. *Documentary films*—(with Henwar Rodakiewicz) One Tenth of a Nation, 1940; Mr. Trull Finds Out, 1941; (with Henwar Rodakiewicz) Hidden Hunger (also dir. and orig. author), 1942; Autobiography of a Jeep, 1943; Dream No More (orig. author, screenwriter, and dir.), 1950; . . . And Now Miguel (orig. author, screenwriter, and dir.), 1953; House in the Desert; Israel Speaks; The Promise; Adventures in the Bronx; and others.

LORD ARMSTRONG OF SANDERSTEAD
British Civil Servant
Born Stirling, Scotland, March 3rd, 1915
Died London, England, July 12th, 1980

Lord Armstrong rose through the ranks of Britain's Treasury Department to serve as Joint Permanent Secretary in charge of economic and financial policy for six years; he went on to head the entire Civil Service under two administrations, and after his retirement from public service, became chairman of a major British bank and served in the House of Lords.

William Armstrong was born in Stirling, Scotland in 1915; both of his parents were Salvation Army officers. William won a scholarship from a London County Council secondary school to Exeter College, Oxford. Graduating with a degree in classics in 1938, Armstrong joined the Civil Service as an assistant principal at the Board of Education, becoming assistant secretary to the Board's president in 1940. Marked as a young man of promise from the outset, he was named private secretary to Edward Bridges, Secretary to the War Cabinet, in 1943. After the war, he was posted to the Treasury where he spent the rest of his civil service career. He served as principal private secretary to three Chancellors of the Exchequer—Stafford Cripps, Hugh Gaitskell, and Rab Butler—and it was in their service that Armstrong developed political sensitivities that were to become characteristic of his service. In 1953 he gained promotion to Under-secretary and did service in both the Overseas and Home Finance Divisions; and in 1958 was named Third Secretary and Treasury Officer of Accounts.

Courtesy Midland Bank

In 1962 a movement to reform the organization of the Treasury bureaucracy was set in motion by Selwyn Lloyd. Discontent with operations of the department had been growing within the Civil Service and in the government, largely because the realities of economic life—particularly the new post-war relationship between business and government—had been ignored, leading to inflexibilities of structure and usage. Armstrong played a major role in modernizing the department, helping to draw up a plan for the elimination of some outmoded divisions of labor and the institution of some long-needed ones. His work in this area was capped by his appointment, at the relatively young age of 47, as Joint Permanent Secretary of the Treasury. A period of instability followed the Common Market's rejection of Britain's application for entry, and the replacement shortly thereafter of the Conservative government by a precarious Labour majority meant that Armstrong found himself hard put to keep the Treasury Service functioning. That he did so is a tribute to his phlegmatic competence—particularly in the face of attacks on the Civil Service made by the Labour Party left.

Indeed, it was his ability and coolness under fire that made him the logical choice to succeed Lawrence Helsby when the latter retired as Head of the Home Civil Service in 1968. His tenure in this office was marked by continued upheaval, chiefly because of the economic (wage and price) policy established under the Heath Ministry of 1970–74. So close were his relations with the Conservative Prime Minister, in fact, that he became known as the "Deputy Prime Minister" and was attacked as a *bete noire* by Labour spokesmen and their trades union allies for his role in development and defense of the government's wage policy. With the Tories' fall in 1974, he retired from the service to a seat on the Board of the Midlands Bank Group, becoming its chairman in 1975. As chairman of the London Clearing Banks' Committee, he led the campaign against Labour's plans to nationalize the clearing banks. He was created a life peer in 1975.   M.D.

Son of William Armstrong, Salvation Army officer. Married Gwendolyn Enid Bennett 1941. Children: one son and one daughter. Educ: Bec Sch., Tooting, London and Exeter Coll., Oxford, classics degree 1938. Joined Civil Service 1938: Asst. Principal, Board of Educ.

1938–40; Asst. Private Secty. to Pres. of Board of Educ. 1940–43; Private Secty. to Secty. of War Cabinet 1943–46. With H.M. Treasury: Principal Private Secty. to Chancellor of the Exchequer 1949–53; Undersecty., Overseas Finance Div. 1953–57 and Home Finance Div. 1957–58; Third Secty. and Treasury Officer of Accounts 1958–62; Jt. Permanent Secty. of the Treasury in charge of economic and financial policy 1962–68; Permanent Secty., Civil Service Dept. and Head of Home Civil Service 1968 until retirement 1974. Chmn. of the Bd., Midland Bank 1975–80 and Midland and International banks Ltd. 1976–80; Deputy Chmn. 1976–78, and Chmn. 1978–80, Cttee. of London Clearing Banks. Visiting Fellow, Nuffield Coll., Oxford 1964–72. Pres., Manpower Society 1970–73; Governor, London Business Sch. 1970–74; Member, Council of Manchester Business Sch. 1970–74, and Council of Oxford Centre of Management Studies 1970–80; Trustee, Wellcome Trust 1974 and Civic Trust 1975. Hons: M.V.O. 1945; C.B. 1957; K.C.B. 1963; Hon. Fellow, Exeter Coll., Oxford 1963; G.C.B. 1968; D.C.L., Oxford 1971; P.C. 1973; D.Litt., City Univ. 1974, D. Univ., Open Univ. 1974; Hon. Liveryman, Salter's Co. 1974; D.Litt., Heriot-Watt 1975; hon. degrees from Cranfield Inst. of Technology and Sheffield Univ. 1975; created Life Peer 1975; Hon. Fellow, Imperial Coll. of Science and Technology.

SIR SERETSE KHAMA
First President of Botswana
Born Serowe, Bechuanaland (now Botswana), July 1st, 1921
Died Gaborone, Botswana, July 13th, 1980

During his 14 years as the first president of Botswana, Sir Seretse Khama led his southern African nation, once the British protectorate of Bechuanaland, to a position of political security under a democratic constitution, and proved himself an eloquent and patient moderator in the racial conflicts that continually threaten the stability of the region.

Khama, born in 1921, was the heir to the chieftainship of the powerful Bamangwato tribe, which constitutes more than three quarters of the country's population. Under the leadership of his grandfather, Khama "the Great," who ruled the tribe for over 50 years, the country had been made a protectorate of Great Britain. His father, Chief Sekgoma Khama II, died when Khama was four, and his uncle, Tshekedi, took over as temporary regent.

Khama, like several other black African leaders, was educated in secondary schools and at Fort Hare university in South Africa. He then took a law degree at Oxford University, where he met Ruth Williams, a white secretary at the Lloyds of London insurance company. They were married in 1948 despite the strenuous objections of Britain's Labour Government, which, according to some historians, did not want to offend the segregationist South Africans. The Anglican Church refused to perform the wedding. After a civil ceremony, the couple went to Bechuanaland, where the Bamangwato confirmed Khama as their chief. However, the regent, Tshekedi, disputed his right to the office and invited the British government to conduct an inquiry. On the advice of this tribunal, Khama, "whose absence from the Bechuanaland protectorate was essential to the peace and good order of the Ngwato reserve," was banished from his homeland. The Labour Government's offers of a yearly tax-free stipend in return for his renunciation of the chieftainship was refused. After a six-year exile with his family in London, he signed the declaration of renunciation and was allowed to return to Bechuanaland as a private citizen.

For the next six years, Khama was secretary to the tribal council and served on a number of advisory groups, where he worked on the terms of Bechuanaland's constitution in preparation for its eventual independence. He won election to the Legislative Assembly in 1961. The year after, he founded the multi-racial, moderate Bechuanaland Democratic Party, which swept to power in the protectorate's first elections, held in 1965. Khama, who became Prime Minister, conducted the final negotiations through which Bechuanaland relinquished its colonial status. He was knighted by Queen Elizabeth II in 1966, a few days before he took office as the first president of Botswana (a post to which he would be four times re-elected).

The new nation was among the 25 poorest in the world, with a largely illiterate population. Heavily dependent on cattle-raising, with about half its territory taken up by the Kalahari Desert, it was an unlikely candidate for agricultural development. A long drought worsened conditions still further. Sir Seretse, speaking to the 24th General Assembly of the United Nations in 1969, said that Botswana had "been entrusted with the responsibilities of upholding the universal values of democracy and non-racialism, of human dignity and equality in a part of the world where they are being distorted, turned upside down and even destroyed." His appeal for assistance was met with foreign aid and loan programs from Western nations and the establishment of closer ties with African states.

Most important for the country's long-term growth was Sir Seretse's decision to work with the South Africans, despite their white supremacist policies, in the development of Botswana's immense diamond, copper, and nickel deposits, discovered in 1969. Within the decade, operations by De Beers Consolidated Mines Ltd. made Botswana the world's fourth largest producer of diamonds, most of which are bought by South Africa. In addition, Botswana depends on its southern neighbor for the majority of its oil and other imports, and for the export of the its beef. About half its workers are employed in South African mines.

With the survival of Botswana so closely bound up with that of South Africa, Sir Seretse was careful not to jeopardize relations between the two countries, despite pressure from more militant black African states. Although he was consistent in his denunciation of apartheid and granted asylum to thousands of refugees from the 1976 Soweto riots, he refused to harbor guerrillas and discouraged economic sanctions against South Africa that might result in harm to his own country. He did, however, seek to expand capital investments from other sources, securing U.S. aid for the construction of a trade route to Zambia and founding a national bank. He also established diplomatic relations with the USSR and the People's Republic of China.

The civil war in Rhodesia (now Zimbabwe), with which Botswana shares a frontier, compelled Sir Seretse to exercise some of his most careful diplomacy to avoid taking sides in another racial conflict. He declined to allow guerrillas to use Botswana as a base of operations, but provided shelter for nearly 25,000 refugees and assisted Britain in negotiating a peaceful transition to black majority rule in its former coloney.

By the time of his death from pancreatic cancer, Sir Seretse, himself a millionaire cattle-rancher, had built up a multi-racial, multi-party democracy with many of the problems but none of the repressive policies that characterize most other emerging nations. The presidency was temporarily filled by Vice-President and Foreign Minister Quett Masire pending new elections. Observers noted that potential challenges to Botswana's future political stability might come from Sir Seretse's eldest son, Ian, a general in the army and chief of the Bamangwato, and from militant young opponents of the South African regime. S.J./J.P.

Son of Sekgoma K. II, Chief of Bamangwato tribe, and Tebogo K. Married Ruth Williams 1948. Children: Jacqueline; Ian, Deputy Chief of Botswana Defense Force and Chief of Bamangwato tribe; Tshekedi; Anthony. Christian. Educ: secondary schs. in South Africa; Fort Hare Univ., South Africa, B.A. 1944; Univ. of Witwatersrand, South Africa 1944–45; Balliol Coll., Oxford, B.A. 1947; legal studies, Inner Temple, London 1948. Confirmed successor to chieftainship of Bamangwato tribe 1949; banished from Bechuanaland by British authorities 1950–56; renounced claim to chieftainship 1956. Deputy Chmn., later Secty., Ngwato Tribal Council since 1957; Member, African Advisory Council 1958–59; Member, Jt. Advisory Council 1958–61; Member, African Council 1959–61; Member, Legislative Council, and Assoc. Member for Social Services and Labor, Exec. Council 1961–65, Member, Legislative Assembly 1961–66. Formed Bechuanaland Democratic Party (now Botswana Democratic Party) 1962. Prime Minister of Bechuanaland 1965–66; Pres., Republic of Botswana since 1966. Chancellor, Univ. of Botswana, Lesotho and Swaziland 1967–70; Founder, Natl. Bank of Botswana. Hons: OBE 1961; KBE 1966; Grand Comdr., Order of the Lion of Malawi 1967; Hon. Fellow, Balliol Coll., Oxford 1969; Nansen Medal, U.N. 1978; Royal Order of Sobhuza II Grand Counsellor, Swaziland 1978; Hon. D.Litt., City Univ. 1978. Hon. LL.D. from Fordham Univ., 1965; Univ. of Botswana, Lesotho and Swaziland 1965; Princeton Univ. 1976; Harvard Univ. 1978. *Major article:* Bostwana: A Developing Democracy in Southern Africa, 1970. Speech to U.N. General Assembly, Sept. 1969.
Further reading: Khama and Botswana by Anthony Dachs, 1971; A Short Political History of Botswana by Anthony Sillery, 1974.

ROBERT BRACKMAN
Portrait and still-life artist, teacher
Born Odessa, U.S.S.R., September 25th, 1898
Died New London, Connecticut, U.S.A., July 16th, 1980

Robert Brackman, a staunch proponent of realism in art and a highly popular portrait painter, reached the enviable position of being able to choose which of the many potential commissions each year he would accept. His portraits include notables in many fields, ranging from the singer Helen Morgan to Charles and Anne Lindbergh, John D. Rockefeller, Jr. and New York governor Herbert Lehman.

At the age of ten, he emigrated with his parents from Odessa to the United States. Showing strong artisitc talents during childhood, he began his formal training in New York City, under the supervision of artists Robert Henri and George Bellows, two well-known members of the "Ashcan" School. Brackman then studied at the National Academy of Design from 1919 to 1921, supporting himself by working as a photo-engraver and lithographer.

The most popular artistic styles at that time were expressionism and cubism, and Brackman learned the techniques of both, but he concentrated primarily on the realist style of painting. The works of these student-years show Picasso's influence on the artist, but Brackman soon moved away from imitation to develop his own restrained style of figure and still-life painting.

His first official recognition as an artist of note came in 1929, when he was awarded the Anonymous Prize of the Art Institute of Chicago. The following year Brackman held his first one-man show at the MacBeth Gallery in New York City; he frequently exhibited there during the next 14 years.

Brackman served as the faculty of the Art Students League for more than 40 years, and for two years, he was a member of the Brooklyn Museum School faculty. He also lectured at the Brooklyn Institute of Arts and Sciences and conducted summer art courses at his home in Mystic, Connecticut.

Failing health forced Brackman to retire in the mid-1970s but he continued to teach at the Lyme Art Academy and the Madison Art School, both in Connecticut. At the time of his death, Brackman's paintings were to be found in many prestigious public and private collections across the country, including the Brooklyn Museum, the Metropolitan Museum, Colonial Williamsburg, the U.S. Military Academy, and the State Department.   J.S.

Son of Moycee B. and Celia Miners B. Married: (1) . . .; (2) Frances Davis, 1936. Children: Roberta Frances, Celia Davis. Emigrated with parents to U.S.A. Russian at birth. Educ: with Robert Henri and George Bellows, ca. 1915; N.Y. Academy of Design, 1919–21. Photo-engraver and lithographer, 1919–21; still-life and portrait artist, 1920s–1980. Member of Faculty, Art Students League, NYC, 1934–75; leave of absence, 1975. Member of faculty, Brooklyn Museum School, 1936–38; Lectr., Brooklyn Inst. of Arts and Sciences, ca. 1940; teacher of own summer classes in art, Mystic, Conn., ca. 1940–80; Member of Faculty, American Art School, NYC, 1951–80; teacher, Lyme Art Academy, and Madison Art Sch., Conn., 1970s. Member: Allied Artists of America; Mystic Art Assn. (Pres., 1951–52); Natl. Acad. of Design, 1932–80; Audubon Soc. of Artists; American Water Color Soc.; Connecticut Acad.; Wilmington Acad.; New Haven Paint and Clay Club; Intl. Inst. of Arts and Letters; Royal Soc. of Arts, London. Hons: 1st prize, Anonymous Prize, Art Inst. of Chicago, 1929 and 1948; Thomas B. Clarke Prize, Natl. Acad. of Design, 1932; Saltus Gold Medal, Natl. Acad. of Design, 1941; First Award, Connecticut Acad. of Fine Arts, 1947; Hon. Mention, Carnegie Inst. of Paintings in U.S., 1949; Gold Medal, Natl. Arts Club, 1950; Gold Medal of Honor, Allied Artists of America, 1952 and 1956; 1st prize. Laguna Beach Art Festival, 1952; Carol H. Beck Gold Medal, Pennsylvania Acad. of Fine Arts, 1958; Salmagundi Club Award, 1961; Andrew Carnegie Prize, Natl. Acad. of Design, 1965; Membership, National Pastel Soc. Hall of Fame. *Exhibitions: One-*

man—MacBeth Gall., NYC, 1930, 31, 33, 34, 36, 40, 44; Grand Central Gall., NYC, 1946. *Group*—Natl. Acad of Design; Connecticut Acad. of Fine Arts; Pennsylvania Acad. of Fine Arts; Audubon Soc. of Artists; and others. *Commissions:* Helen Morgan (commn. by Flo Ziegfield); John D. Rockefeller, Jr. and other Rockefellers; Pres.-Emeritus of Yale Univ., Charles Seymour; former Gov. and Senator of N.Y., Herbert H. Lehman; Charles and Anne Lindbergh; Rabbi Stephen S. Wise; Henry L. Stimson, Secty. of War, W.W.II; A Portrait of Jenny (motion picture, 1950); and others. *Collections:* Toledo Mus. of Art, Ohio; Municipal Gall., Davenport, Iowa; Georgia Univ.; Brooks Memorial, Memphis, Tenn.; Houston Art Mus., Texas; Connecticut Mus., New Britain; Univ. of Connecticut; Rockford Art Assn., Ill.; Canajoharie Mus., N.Y.; Minneapolis Inst. of Arts; Wilmington Soc. of Arts; New Haven Library; High Mus., Atlanta, Ga.; Montclair Mus., N.J.; Newark Mus., N.J.; Metropolitan Mus. of Art, NYC; Pasadena Mus.; Honolulu Mus.; Rhode Island Sch. of Design; Brooklyn Mus.; Colonial Williamsburg; Connecticut Life Insurance Co.; Encyclopaedia Britannica; DuPont Co.; Harvard Club of N.Y.; Intnl. Business Machines; Milton Acad.; Princeton Univ.; U.S. Military Acad.; U.S. State Dept.; numerous other public and private collections.

NIHAT ERIM
Turkish politician and professor of law
Born Kandira, Kocael Province, Turkey, 1912
Died Istanbul, Turkey, July 19th, 1980

Prime Minister of Turkey for thirteen months in 1971–72, Nihat Erim led his country during a turbulent period of martial law, earning the animosity of his former colleagues on the political left when the military under his government cracked down on leftist students as well as extreme rightists.

Once a member of the left-of-center Republican People's Party, Erim became associated with the Turkish right after resigning from the RPP, coming to power as head of a cabinet of experts that took office as an alternative to a military coup. Erim's government went far to meet the demands of the military for widespread reform and strong measures against political terrorism. In an effort to restore law and order, Erim declared martial law, banning all student associations along with the right-wing National Order Party and the left-wing Turkish Labor Party. He also responded to pressure from U.S. narcotics officials by banning the cultivation of opium poppies. Though he envisioned sweeping domestic reforms, including limitation of land ownership and measures to modernize Turkish agriculture, Erim resigned from leadership after the National Assembly refused to grant him emergency powers to put down the mounting political violence to which, in time, he also fell victim.

Erim, a constitutional scholar, first came to prominence as a professor of international law. He served as a legal adviser in the Turkish foreign ministry, and became a member of the country's delegation to the San Francisco conference that drew up the United Nations charter in 1945. During the mid-1950s he was also Turkey's chief legal adviser in negotiations with Great Britain over the status of

Cyprus, a sore point in relations between Greece and Turkey. In 1959 Erim headed the committee that drafted the Cypriot constitution, which provided for the island's independence with a political system carefully balanced between the Greek majority and the Turkish minority. Although as Prime Minister Erim advocated improved relations with the Soviet Union, he reaffirmed Turkey's support for NATO and close ties to the U.S.

In the years before his death, Erim lived at his summer residence in the suburbs of Istanbul, working on his memoirs. He was assassinated at the age of 68, the clandestine Revolutionary Left taking responsibility for the murder. Former Prime Minister Bulent Ecevit, a strong opponent of the Erim government, nevertheless hailed him as a "statesman" whose assassination represented a "direct attack on parliamentary democracy in Turkey."   A.C.

Married Kamile. Educ: Lycée of Galatasary, Istanbul; Univ. of Istanbul Law Sch.; Univ. of Paris. Prof., Constitutional and Intnl. Law, Univ. of Ankara; Legal Advisor, Ministry of Foreign Affairs 1942; M.P. 1945–50; Ed., and Publisher of ULUS (organ of Republican Peoples' Party) 1950; Ed. and Publisher, Halkci; Turkish member, European Human Rights Commn.; Member, Natl. Assembly 1961–72; Member, Turkish Parliamentary Group, European Council 1961–70; Deputy Chmn., Republican Peoples' Party Natl. Assembly Group 1961–71; Prime Minister 1971–72; Member, Senate of the Republican Peoples' Party 1972–80. *Author:* several books on law.

HANS J(OACHIM) MORGENTHAU
Political scientist
Born Coburg, Germany, February 17th, 1904
Died New York City, U.S.A. July 19th, 1980

The conduct of American foreign relations since the 1950s has been much influenced by the views of Hans Morgenthau, a political scientist whose pragmatic and realistic approach to international and domestic issues was utilized by Secretary of State Henry Kissinger and other top-level officials of several Administrations. Although he sought to make foreign policy an instrument of rational problem-solving rather than a tool of idealistic crusades, by the end of his career he had become discouraged about the ability of the objective viewpoint to prevail over vested interests in the motivation of necessary social change.

Morgenthau was born in 1905 in Coburg, Germany, where he attended local elementary schools and the Humanistisches Gymnasium. As a seven-year-old he followed with interest the progress of the Tripolitan and First Balkan Wars, marking the changing fronts on a map with colored pins. During his adolescence he thought of becoming a writer or a poet, but was forbidden to study literature by his father, a practical-minded physician. After briefly studying philosophy at the universities of Berlin and Frankfurt, Morgenthau entered the University of Munich, from which he graduated with a law degree in 1927. During this period he came under the influence of the sociologist Max Weber, whose works provided him with a model of scholarly objectivity by a nonetheless passionately concerned observer, and of an historian who specialized in the analysis of the *realpolitik* practiced by German Chancellor Otto von Bismarck. He was awarded his doctorate two years later on the strength of a dissertation on the limitations of international law and in 1932 undertook postgraduate studies in Geneva

A grant from the Swiss Committee for the Aid of Refugee Scholars enabled Morgenthau, a Jew, to remain in Geneva after the Nazis came to power in Germany. He taught in Madrid for a year before emigrating to the United States in 1937 with his wife, with whom he had two children. During the next six years he served on the faculties of Brooklyn College and the University of Kansas City.

In 1943 Morenthau began a long association with the University of Chicago, whose Center for the Study of American Foreign and Military Policy he directed for 17 years. His first book in English, *Scientific Man vs. Power Politics*, was published in 1946. (Morgenthau spoke five languages fluently and had a reading knowledge of three others.) Two years later he published his major work, *Politics Among Nations,* a critical analysis of international relations that has been widely accepted as a college text. Arguing that "forces inherent in human nature" are responsible for the creation and evolution of social conditions, the author described as hopeless all utopian attempts to restructure societies along absolutist moral lines, and defined effective foreign policy as a constantly fluctuating compromise between conflicting interests. The task of the statesmen, he said, is to achieve a clear, rational perspective on the issues at stake and their relative importance and to act in accordance with the best interests of the nation, regardless of world opinion or ideological dogma, however widely held. This emphatically realistic posture (called "pessimistic" and "Machiavellian" by some critics) was continued in his 1951 book *In Defense of the National Interest,* which challenged the prevailing view of the United States as the moral policeman and economic benefactor of the world

Although Morgenthau deplored the anti-communist hysteria that swept the U.S. during the Cold War era, he was a steadfast supporter of military preparedness, both conventional and nuclear. During the Cuban Missile Crisis of 1962 he urged that the U.S. take whatever steps were necessary, including invasion, to deter Soviet initiatives in the Caribbean, warning that inaction would invite even more dangerous confrontations in the future. His views influenced policymaking in the U.S. Departments of State and Defense, where he served as a consultant. In 1963 he became the Michelson Distinguished Service Professor at the Univerity of Chicago

Morgenthau first came to the notice of the general public in the mid-1960s, when he predicted (correctly, it turned out) a disastrous outcome for the American attempt to intervene in Vietnam's civil war. That war, he said, was being fought in China's legitimate sphere of interest, and U.S. military assistance would not, in the end, prevent the installation of a government whose character reflected the actual balance of power in the region. Given the historic and ethnic enmities between the Vietnamese and the Chinese, the new Communist regime, if allowed to emerge naturally, would be an independent-minded one, similar to that established by Tito [q.v.] of Yugoslavia.

By going to the aid of the South, the U.S. was foolishly driving the North into the Chinese camp, thereby breaking two of Morgenthau's cardinal rules: Never allow a weak ally to make policy decisions for you, and never maneuver yourself into a situation from which retreat would be humiliating and advance too perilous

Morgenthau spelled out his position in *A New Foreign Policy for the United States* (1968). He was an early leader of Teach-In anti-war activities on university campuses and served as advisor to Eugene McCarthy during the 1968 presidential election, but began to withdraw from the peace movement after it became an instrument of dramatic social confrontation on the part of political radicals.

In *Truth and Power* a collection of essays published in 1970, Morgenthau wrote of the naive surprise with which he had come to realize that the government would continue to pursue its fatal course despite the objective, soundly reasoned arguments of scholars like himself, and that it would even attempt to discredit and suppress responsible critics in order to protect its own power. "It has become obvious," he wrote, "that the great issues of our day—the militarization of American life, the Vietnam War, race conflicts, poverty, the decay of the cities, the destruction of the natural environment—are not susceptible to rational solutions within the existing system of power relations. . . . Poverty on a large scale, like the decay of the cities and the ruination of the natural environment, is a result not of accidental misfortunates but of social and economic policies in whose continuation powerful social groups have a vested interest." With popular revolution a virtual impossibility (the necessary funds and technologies having been monopolized by the dominant groups), and with elected politicians incapable of effecting a redistribution of power, the only possibilities for American society that Morgenthau could envision were the dissolution of "the establishment" as a result of general alienation and loss of confidence; the voluntary acceptance of the status quo by its defeated critics, and their disappearance into conformity; or the imposition of a totalitarian system by which the status quo would preserve itself through repression.

Despite this disillusionment, Morgenthau continued his task of "speaking truth to power" whether or not the holders of power chose to listen. He assailed the U.S. support of fascist regimes, particularly the CIA's overthrow in 1974 of a freely elected Marxist government in Chile, and warned of the consequences of continuing "the economically ruinous and, in the end, biologically fatal nuclear arms race." He opposed the creation of a West Bank Palestinian state governed by the PLO and, as chairman of the Academic Committee on Soviet Jewry, campaigned on behalf of dissidents persecuted by the Soviet Government in violation of the Helsinki Accords

In early 1980 Morgenthau retired from the New School for Social Research, whose faculty he had joined in 1974 after six years as Leonard Davis Distinguished Professor at the City College of New York. His last book, *Science: Master or Servant?*, was published in 1971. He died following surgery for a perforated ulcer.   R.C./J.P.

Son of Ludwig M., physician, and Frieda (Bachmann) M. Married Irma Thormann 1935 (d.1979). Children: Matthew; Susanna. Jewish. Emigrated to U.S. 1937; naturalized American 1943. Educ: Humanistisches Gymnasium, Coburg, grad. 1923; Univs. of Berlin and

Frankfurt; Univ. of Munich, LL.B. magna cum laude 1927; Univ. of
Frankfurt, J.U.D. summa cum laude 1929; postgrad. studies, Gradu-
ate Inst. of International Studies, Geneva 1932; Member, Inst. for
Advanced Studies, Princeton, N.J. 1958–59. Admitted to German bar
1927; law practice, Munich and Wolfrathshausen 1927, Frankfurt
1928–30; Asst. to Law Faculty, Univ. of Frankfurt 1931–32; Acting
Pres., Labor Law Court, Frankfurt 1931–32; Instr. in German public
law 1932–33 and Instr. in public law and political science 1933–35,
Univ. of Geneva; Prof. of Intnl. Law, Inst. of International and
Economic Studies, and Lectr., Union of Spanish Societies for Interna-
tional Studies, Madrid 1935–36; Instr. in govt., Brooklyn Coll., NYC
1937–39; Asst. Prof. of Law, Hist., and Political Science, Univ. of
Kansas City, Missouri 1939–43; admitted to Missouri bar 1943. With
Dept. of Political Science, Univ. of Chicago: Visiting Assoc. Prof.
1943–45; Assoc. Prof. 1945–49; Prof. 1949–61; Prof. of Political
Science and Modern History 1961–63; Albert A. Michelson Dis-
tinguished Service Prof. 1963–68. Dir., Center for the Study of
American Foreign and Military Policy, Univ. of Chicago 1950–68;
Assoc., Washington Center for Foreign Policy Research 1948–60; Sr.
Research Fellow, Council on Foreign Relations 1966; Leonard Davis
Distinguished Prof., City Coll. of New York 1968–74; Univ. Prof. of
Political Science, New Sch. for Social Research, NYC 1974–80.
Visiting Prof.: Univ. of California at Berkeley 1949, 1961; Harvard
Univ. 1951, 1959–61; Northwestern Univ. 1954; Columbia Univ. and
Yale Univ. 1956–57; Univ. of Wyoming 1955, 1958. Faith and
Freedom Lectr., American Univ., Washington, D.C. 1961. Lectr.:
Armed Forces Staff Coll.; NATO Defense Coll.; Air Force War Coll.;
Army War Coll.; Naval War Coll.; Natl. War Coll. Consultant: U.S.
Dept of State 1949–51 and 1960s; U.S. Dept. of Defense 1961–65.
Temporary Chmn., Councils of the Gradualist Way to Peace, Univ. of
Chicago Chapter 1962; Chmn., Academic Cttee. on Soviet Jewry.
Member: Deutsche Gesellschaft für Voelkerrecht, Frankfurt; Interna-
tionale Vereinigung für Rechts- und Wirtschaftsphilosophie, Frank-
furt; American Philosophical Soc.; Intnl. Inst. of Philosophy of Law
and Legal Sociology; Intnl. Inst. of Ibero-American Studies; American Soc. of International Law; American Political Science Assn.;
Intnl. Political Science Assn.; Foreign Policy Assn.; American Acad.
of Arts and Sciences; American Acad. of Political and Social Science;
American Assn. of Univ. Professors; Johns Hopkins Soc. of Scholars;
PEN; Quadrangle Club, Chicago; Century Club, NYC. Hons:
awarded grant from Swiss Cttee. for Aid of Refugee Scholars 1933;
awarded grant from Rockefeller Foundn. through Emergency Cttee.
in Aid of Displaced Scholars 1939; awarded research grant from
American Philosophical Soc. 1940; Hon. Litt.D., Western Reserve
Univ. 1965; Hon. L.H.D., Hebrew Union Coll. 1975; Hon. Member,
Spanish Inst. of Political Science. Hon. LL.D. from Ripon Coll.,
1962; Alma Coll., 1965; Univ. of Denver, 1971; Clark Univ.. *Books:*
Die internationale Rechtspflege, ihr Wesen und ihre Grenzen (The
International Law, Its Nature and Its Limitations, dissertation), 1929;
La notion du "politique" et la théorie des différends internationaux,
1933; La Réalité des normes, en particulier des normes du droit
international, 1934; (ed.) Peace, Security, and the United Nations,
1946; Scientific Man vs. Power Politics, 1946; Politics Among Nations:
The Struggle for Power and Peace, 1948, rev. ed. 1973; (ed. with
Kenneth W. Thompson) Principles and Problems of International
Politics, 1950; (ed.) Germany and the Future of Europe, 1951; In
Defense of the National Interest: A Critical Examination of American
Foreign Policy, 1951 (in U.K. as American Foreign Policy: A Critical
Examination, 1952); Dilemmas of Politics, 1958; The Purpose of

American Politics, 1960; Politics in the Twentieth Century, 3 vols., 1962; The Crossroad Papers: A Look Into the American Future, 1965; A New Foreign Policy for the United States, 1969; Truth and Power (collected essays), 1970; Science: Master or Servant?, 1971. Contributed articles to H-Bomb, 1950; Encyclopedia Britannica; many professional jrnls., newspapers, and mags.
Further reading: "Intellectual Biography of Hans Morgenthau," in Society, Jan.-Feb., 1978.

MARIA MARTINEZ
Potter
Born San Ildefonso Pueblo, New Mexico, U.S.A., April 5th, 1887
Died San Ildefonso Pueblo, New Mexico, U.S.A., July 20th, 1980

Maria Martinez is considered to be the foremost Indian potter of this century. As a young child on the San Ildefonso Pueblo in New Mexico, a Tewa community near the Rio Grande, she showed great facility for the crafting of coiled pots and was trained by her aunts to assume the central role in the Pueblo's production of pots for ceremonial use and sale to tourists.

After her marriage to Julian Martinez in 1913, Maria developed the blackware style for which she is best known. Julian Martinez worked closely with Maria, and while he was employed at the archaeological investigations at Frijoles and Tyvonyi in 1909, the couple was approached by the director of the program, Dr. Edgar L. Hewett, concerning the reproduction of blackware ceramics from fragments of pots found during the excavations. After some experimentation and a period of interest in polychrome pottery, the Martinezes found that by firing the pots, made from particularly resilient local clays, in carefully regulated fires smothered in sheep or horse manure, carbonization was achieved. Extensive burnishing of the damp pots before firing resulted in highly reflective surfaces. Julian's designs of mythical figures and elemental forces painted with refractory clay slip remained as matte areas against the shiny black finish of the pots.

The first pots commissioned by Hewett were sold to John D. Rockefeller on a visit to the Pueblo in the 1920s. From this auspicious beginning grew a lucrative business and an international reputation based on Maria's refinements of traditional ceramic processes.

While a few of the pots were produced for use within the homes and ceremonies of the San Ildefonso Pueblo, many plates, pots, and decorative pieces were made expressly for sale to tourists as a major source of income for the Tewa. Maria Martinez actively promoted the commercial success of other local craftspersons, eschewing personal wealth and recognition, though she did receive awards from such groups as the AIA, the Indian Fire Council of 1934, and the University of Colorado. In 1954 she was awarded the Palmes Academique by the French Ministry of Education. She worked always in conjunction with other family members; following her husband's death in 1943 Maria's pots were decorated and fired by her sisters, sons, daughter-in-law, and until her own death in 1980, she worked closely with her great-granddaughter. Pots signed by Maria Martinez (often with anglicized versions of *Maria*, or with her Tewa name, Poveka) usually bear the name of the person who painted the pot as well.

Groups from the San Ildefonso Pueblo demonstrated the techniques of potting at several world's fairs, and in 1973, Maria and her great-granddaughter led workshops at the University of California's summer program, the Idyllwild School of Music and the Arts. Maria felt that pottery could not be taught by formal methods of instruction, but only by observation and participation in the craft. In maintaining this attitude she encouraged traditional forms of interaction between practiced artisans and younger atists. Prolonged contact with the white community, which had begun in the 19th century, precipitated a general breakdown of Tewa social and religious mores, due primarily to the introduction of alcohol and jobs outside the Pueblo. Maria Martinez's artistic and commercial abilities, developed in response to contemporary white American tastes for native American arts, are credited with strengthening the San Ildefonso Pueblo's social structure and ensuring its continued economic self-sufficiency.   A.S.

Daughter of Thomas Montoya and Reyes M. Married Julian Martinez, painter (d. 1943). Children: Adam; John; Popovi Da; Phillip. Catholic. Educ: St. Catherine's Indian Sch., Santa Fe, N.M. Active as potter in New Mexico from 1907. Demonstrated at: Century of Progress Exposition, Chicago 1934; Golden Gate Intl. Exposition 1939; St. Louis World's Fair. Instructor, Idyllwild Sch. for Music and the Arts, Univ. of Calif. 1973. Hons: Achievement Award, Ford Exposition Medal 1934; Outstanding Indian Woman, Indian Council Fire 1934; Hon. LL.D., St. Catherine's Indian Sch. 1953; Palmes Académique, French Ministry of Education 1954; Craftsmanship Award, American Inst. of Architects 1954; American Ceramic Soc. Award 1968; Hon. LL.D., Univ. of Colorado 1971. *Exhibitions:* Exposition of Indian Tribal Arts, 1931–33; Renwick Gall. of the National Collection of Fine Arts, Smithsonian Institution, Washington, D.C. 1978. *Collections:* American Mus. of Natural History, NYC; Denver Art Mus.; Fenn Gall., Santa Fe; Laboratory of Anthropology, Santa Fe; Mus. of the American Indian, NYC; Mus. of New Mexico, Santa Fe; Smithsonian Institution, Washington, D.C.; Southwest Mus., Los Angeles.
Further reading: Maria of San Ildefonso by Alice Marriott, 1946; The Pottery of San Ildefonso Pueblo by Kenneth Chapman, 1970; The Living Tradition of Martinez by Susan Peterson, 1978; Five Generations of Potters by Susan Peterson, 1978.

SALAH AD-DIN AL-BITAR
Prime minister of Syria and cofounder of the Baath party
Born Damascus, Syria, 1912
Died Paris, France, July 21st, 1980

A leading figure in the development of Arab nationalism, Salah ad-Din al-Bitar helped establish the Baath party, which today rules in Syria and Iraq. Though he once headed the Syrian government, factional conflict in his party forced him into exile, where he became a focus of opposition to Syria's President Hafez Assad.

After studying in Damascus and Paris, al-Bitar received a licentiate in political science at the Sorbonne in 1934. He then returned to Damascus to teach secondary school. His political perspective while in Paris had been Communist. But after returning to Syria, he found Marxist "materialism" incompatible with Arab nationalism, which became the lifelong focus of his political activity. Nevertheless, Communist ideology left a permanent imprint on al-Bitar; for the young teacher, notions of a revolutionary socialism and anticolonialism became closely tied with pan-Arab nationalism.

Pan-Arabism exerted a strong appeal in the Middle East following World War One. Resentful of French and British rule, Arab intellectuals sought some means of overcoming religious and social differences to recreate a strong, unified Arab state. With this political ideal central to their platform, al-Bitar and his former univeristy friend Michael Aflak founded the Baath (Renaissance) party in 1943. Al-Bitar was editor of the party newspaper. The party officially entered Syrian politics in 1947.

A change of government in 1952 sent al-Bitar into a brief exile in Lebanon. He returned less than a year later and united his party with Akram Hawrani's Arab Socialist Party. Hawrani's contacts with young Army officers led to a coup d'etat in 1954, beginning the rule of the Baath Socialist party, as the coalition was called.

In the new government, al-Bitar became the chief spokesman for Baathist ideology. At one point simultaneously minister of foreign affairs and head of the Syrian delegation to the U.N. General Assembly, al-Bitar set out to put his ideal of Arab unity into practice. His efforts led in 1958 to establishment of the United Arab Republic, a union between Syria and the Egyptian government of Gamal Abdel Nasser. Al-Bitar hoped to persuade other Arab nations to join the new state, which he served as Minister of Culture and National Guidance; but within a year he found himself distracted by internal difficulties. Nasser refused to provide the Baath leaders with some of the powers they desired; in December 1959, al-Bitar and most of his fellow Syrians resigned from their posts. This event was followed in 1961 by al-Bitar's participation in the publication of a Baath manifesto supporting secession from the UAR. Syria in fact seceded from the union in that year, and Nasser assumed the role of champion of Arab nationalism. Ironically, the Egyptian leader's ideology closely resembled that of the Baathists.

Al-Bitar later renounced the manifesto, and in 1963 a coup brought him to power as a prime minister and minister of foreign affairs. He sought to "atone for the crime of secession" by leading Syria back to the union. But Nasser proved difficult to convince a second time. He frequently recalled al-Bitar's initial support of secession and throughout unification talks proved himself the more astute diplomat. Al-Bitar and Aflak, often on the defensive, contradicted themselves throughout the talks. In the end, al-Bitar's efforts failed; unification with the Baathists meant little to Nasser, who offered his rivals only symbolic positions within the union.

Al-Bitar's subsequent political fortunes reflected the instability of Syrian politics. In November 1963 he lost the premiership in a general election, no doubt due partly to his failed efforts at unification with Egypt. But he remained on friendly terms with General Amin Hafiz, the new head of state, and was given the premiership for five months in 1964 and again in January 1966.

Despite his resentment of Nasser, al-Bitar could not completely discard the idea of an Arab union. This ideal was shared by Hafiz and other prominent officers. In February 1966, a dissident group of Baathists—most of them young and all opposed to a union with Nasser—staged a coup that drove out al-Bitar and Hafiz. Al-Bitar fled to Beirut following his expulsion from the Baath party. When the Lebanese civil war broke out, he moved to Paris. There, in 1979, he founded the fortnightly Arabic magazine, *Al-Ihya al-Arabi* (Arab Renaissance). The periodical was highly critical of the Syrian Baathists under President Hafez Assad.

In early 1980 al-Bitar helped establish a National Front of Exiled Syrians opposed to the Assad government. He also attended an Arab People's Conference sponsored in Baghdad by the Iraqi government, Syria's chief rival for influence in the region. On the morning of July 21, al-Bitar was fatally shot as he was about to enter his Paris office. Reports at the time linked his death and the deaths of various journalists covering Syrian politics to the Assad regime.   S.J.

Son of Kheir al-B. Muslim. Lived in Lebanon in 1952 and 1966–75 and in Paris since 1975. Educ: Univ. of Damascus; Univ. of Paris (Sorbonne), Lic. of Political Science 1934. Secondary sch. teacher, Damascus 1934–42; Cofounder, Baath Party 1943; founder 1943, Ed., and Publisher, Baath Party newspaper; elected to parliament, Deputy for Damascus 1954–56; Minister of Foreign Affairs, Syria 1956–58; head of Syrian delegation, U.N. General Assembly 1957; Minister of Culture and National Guidance, UAR 1958–59; Prime Minister, Syria 1963, 1964, and 1966; Minister of Foreign Affairs, Syria 1963; V.P., Council of Revolutionary Command, Syria 1963–64; expelled from party 1966; Founder and Ed., al-Ihya al-Arabi (Arab Renaissance), Paris since 1979.
Further reading: The Arab Cold War by Malcolm Kerr, 1968.

ALI AKBAR TABATABAI
Iranian diplomat
Born in Iran
Died, Washington, D.C., U.S.A., July 22nd, 1980

Ali Akbar Tabatabai, a former Iranian diplomat in the service of the Shah, was an outspoken leader of anti-Khomeini Iranian exiles living in the United States.

Born into a large and prominent Iranian family, Tabatabai first came to the U.S. in the early 1950s to study architecture and law at Howard University. He attended college part time while working at the Iranian embassy in Washington. Tabatabai graduated with a master's degree and returned to Iran in the early 1960s, working as the government's director-general of press and information in Teheran. In 1975 he returned to Washington as press attaché under Iranian Ambassador Ardeshir Zahedi. He later rose to become the embassy's press counselor.

Following the Shah's fall in early 1979, Tabatabai was ordered to return to Iran by officials of the revolutionary government. Fearing for his life, he asked for and received political asylum in the U.S. In April 1979 he began meeting with former officials of the Shah's

government, anti-Khomeini intellectuals and Iranian businessmen. On the basis of these talks, the Iranian Freedom Foundation (IFF) was formed in June. Though comprising only 10 members, it was by far the most prominent of the Iranian exile groups in the U.S. Tabatabai served as its president and chief organizer, since the other members were unwilling to expose themselves to possible retribution. He appeared frequently on radio and television shows and in early July 1980 organized a protest marsh in Los Angeles, the largest anti-Khomeini demonstration to date. At the time of his death he was arranging a second demonstration in downtown Washington. Though the IFF included supporters of the former Shah, Tabatabai did not favor a restoration of the Pahlavi dynasty. His activism was motivated mainly by animosity towards Moslem extremists, and he hoped to see the establishment of a "secular democracy" in Iran.

Like other members of the IFF, Tabatabai was aware of the risks he ran as a result of his public stand. He held himself aloof from other residents of his Bethesda, Maryland neighborhood, installed a burglar alarm system in his home and kept the curtains tightly drawn at all times. Tabatabai was fatally shot on his front doorstep by an unknown assailant posing as a postman with a special delivery letter.   S.L.G.

Married (div.). One daughter. Educ: Howard Univ., Washington, D.C., M.A. architecture. With Iranian govt.: Dir.-Gen. of press and information, early 1960s to mid-1970s; became press attaché then press counselor of the Iranian Embassy in Washington, D.C.; Founder 1979 and Pres. until death, Iran Freedom Foundn.

OLIVIA MANNING
Novelist
Born in Portsmouth, Hampshire, England ca. 1915
Died England, July 23rd, 1980

Olivia Manning's strength as a novelist was twofold: she had a cool, observant eye together with a delicacy of introspection and these attributes made her a shrewd commentator upon the relationship between public life and private passion, the outer, and the inner world. Her greatest achievement is considered to be *The Balkan Trilogy*, a study of European cultures as they shift and change under the pressures of the Second World War. This ambitious theme is handled with authority and skill—the author was drawing on personal experience—and is all the more powerful because it is examined in detail, in terms of a marriage. Guy and Harriet Pringle, a young English couple abroad, are caught up in events quite out of their control; they flee from Bucharest to Athens and to Cairo and their emotional life reflects the turbulence and uncertainty around them. The balance between survival and destruction is precarious and the tension thus created never slackens. Manning was a born storyteller; her own opinion of the novel form was that it seemed "perfectly adapted to the expression of our bewildered and self-conscious civilisation."

The early years of her career were difficult ones; she worked in a secretarial job, lived in London on very little money and wrote late every night. Her dedication was rewarded by the success of her first book *The Wind Changes*. Shortly after its publication she married Reggie Smith, then a lecturer for the British Council; their wartime travels together provided the material for her Balkan novels. *The Great Fortune* describes Roumania as it awaits the German invasion; Bucharest is a city of rumors and betrayals and the young Harriet, fresh from England, finds herself playing a party in a tragi-comedy, amused and yet appalled. It was no secret that the fictional Harriet and Guy Pringle were based on Olivia Manning's own marriage; her narrative relies on the contrast between the ebullient, compulsively sociable husband and the quieter, reflective wife. Their two natures are brought into focus by the menace of war. Guy's reaction to fear is continual activity while Harriet watches events in isolation, easily becoming ill. In *The Spoilt City* and *Friends and Heroes* the pair travel across Europe. Their adventures exploit Manning's excellent sense of place, and the characters they encounter, whether pathetic or bizarre, draw out the full force of her irony.

In later novels, the scope broadened geographically while the central characters remained constant; the Pringles, especially Harriet, take on the quality of old friends who are predictable, if occasionally irritating. *The Levant Trilogy* comprises *The Danger Tree*, *The Battle Lost and Won* and, her final work, *The Sum of Things*. Harriet's path takes her to Damascus; Guy, believing that the ship carrying her home has been torpedoed, is learning to live life without her. While the second trilogy did not attain the popularity of the first, it contains some memorable portraits of the English abroad, including a feather-brained Edwina Litte, the toast of wartime Cairo, and a young soldier Simon Boulderstone, badly wounded but aching to return to active service.

Olivia Manning's re-creation of history in her six major novels is unique; it is both detached and compassionate. Always highly esteemed by her fellow critics, the tone of Manning's writing has been compared to that of Christopher Isherwood. A prolific and varied writer, Manning wrote, in addition to novels, short stories, radio plays and articles for magazines and journals.   J.C.

Daughter of Oliver M., Comdr., Royal Navy, and Olivia M. Married Reginald Donald Smith, Prof., New Univ. of Ulster 1939. Educ: private schs. Press Officer, U.S. Embassy, Cairo 1942; Press. Asst., Public Information Office, 1943–44, and British Council 1944–45, Jerusalem; reviewer, Spectator 1949–50 and Sunday Times 1965–66, London. Hons: Tom-Gallon Trust Award 1949. *Books: Novels*—The Wind Changes, 1938; Artist among the Missing, 1949; School for Love, 1951; A Different Face, 1953; Doves of Venus, 1955; The Balkan Trilogy: The Great Fortune, 1960, The Spoilt City, 1962; Friends and Heroes, 1965; The Rain Forest, 1974; The Levant Trilogy: The Danger Tree, 1977, The Battle Lost and Won, 1978, The Sum of Things (published posthumously), 1980. *Short stories*—Growing Up, 1948; A Romantic Hero, 1966. *Plays*—The Play Room, 1970; The Little Ottleys (screenplay), 1964; The Card, 1964; Futility, 1973; adaptation for radio. *Other*—The Remarkable Expedition: The Story of Stanley's Rescue of Emim Pasha from Equatorial Africa (history), 1947; The Dreaming Shore (travel), 1950; My Husband Cartwright, 1956; Extraordinary Cats, 1967. Contributed to Horizon,

Windmill, Spectator, New Statesman, Punch, The Observer, Times Literary Supplement, Vogue, Harper's, The Queen, Saturday Book, Best Short Stories, and other mags. and jrnls.
Further reading: The Novel Today by Anthony Burgess, 1953; Tradition and Dream by Walter Allen, 1964; "Olivia Manning" by James Parkhill Rathbone, in Books and Bookmen, 1971; Continuance and Change: The Contemporary British Novel Sequence by Robert K. Morris, 1972.

PETER SELLERS
Film actor
Born Southsea, Hampshire, England, September 8th, 1925
Died London, England, July 24th, 1980

In his 30-year film career, the British comic actor Peter Sellers, a consummate mimic, brought to life a diverse set of characters ranging from an English duchess to an American hippie to a Nazi scientific madman, sometimes assuming multiple identities for a single film. His perfectly executed caricatures were confected from a shrewd blend of satire and pathos. "A Sellers film," wrote critic Janet Maslin, "always had its own brand of illogic, its own perfectly unreasonable world view. More than just movies, they were a state of mind." At the time of his death, he was arguably the most popular British film actor in the world.

Sellers was born in Southsea, England to a family of vaudeville performers, and grew up in provincial music halls, where his father played the piano and his mother acted and sang. His maternal grandmother had introduced the musical revue to Britain and was the first entrepreneur to use swimmers in stage shows; Sellers made his debut at the age of five in her show *Splash Me*. Although he was Jewish on his mother's side, tracing his ancestry to Prime Minister Benjamin Disraeli and the bareknuckle boxing champion Daniel Mendoza, he attended a Catholic school, St. Aloysius College, where he did poorly in everything but drawing. He spent his teens in nightclubs, playing drums in a dance band and learning the ukelele.

In 1943, when he turned 18, Sellers enlisted in the Royal Air Force. His poor eyesight disqualified him from aerial combat; instead, he served as an armorer in a Spitfire ground crew in Burma and India. By the end of the war his impersonations of Air Ministry officials at camp concerts had landed him a spot in an RAF entertainment show that toured the Middle East. He was discharged in 1946 and returned to London, where he joined the ranks of fledgling performers trying to find bookings. He worked as the entertainment director of a holiday camp, played small music halls, and did comic turns between strip-tease acts at the Windmill Theatre. Finally he won a spot on the BBC radio show *Show Time* by telephoning the program director and urging him, in the voices of two different radio stars, to hire a brilliant but unheralded comedian named Peter Sellers.

In 1951 Sellers teamed up with Spike Milligan and Harry Secombe in *The Goon Show,* a comedy series on BBC radio that ran for seven years and had an enormous influence on British and American film

Peter Sellers in *Being There*

and television humor. Sellers and his fellow Goons developed dozens of voices and characters for their satiric, surrealistic skits (the Goons climbing Mount Everest from the inside or from the top down and underwater) and achieved a sublime anarchism similar to that of the Marx Brothers. When television arrived, the Goons switched to a visual format with somewhat less success. Sellers appeared on a number of comedy programs, in performances at the Palladium, and as the lead in George Tabori's farce *Brouhahs* at the Aldwych Theatre.

In 1955, Sellers, who had been doing comic turns in movies for several years, got his first notable part as a hapless bank robber in *The Ladykillers,* which starred his screen mentor, Sir Alec Guinness. More praise greeted his subsequent roles as the drunken projectionist of a dilapidated movie house in *The Smallest Show on Earth,* a television star who botches the murder of his blackmailer in *The Naked Truth* (called *Your Past is Showing* in U.S. release), a foiled criminal in *Tom Thumb,* and as a duchess, a diplomat, and a policeman in *The Mouse that Roared,* a spoof of Cold War politics.

But the movie that established him internationally as a master of film comedy was *I'm All Right, Jack,* a satire on trade union and management politics in which he played a bellicose and incompetent communist shop steward named Fred Kite, who abuses his powwer and speaks in jargon. Sellers, who saw the character as something of a tragic figure, won a British Film Academy award for his performance in 1959. In the same year he won the Golden Gate Award at the San Francisco International Film Festival for his independent production of *The Running, Jumping, and Standing Still Film,* an 11-minute short in zany *Goon Show* style that was directed by the then unknown Richard Lester.

From then on, Sellers worked continually in film, seldom letting a year go by without at least one appearance. He played a timid accountant who plots the perfect crime in *The Battle of The Sexes* (based on James Thurber's *The Catbird Seat),* an East Indian doctor in George Bernard Shaw's *The Millionairess,* and the vicious leader of a car theft ring in *Never Let Go,* his only venture into melodrama. He also tried his hand at directing with *Mr. Topaze (I Like Money* in U.S. release).

The master of 20 British regional dialects and of a seemingly infinite number of foreign accents, Sellers built each character around his or her voice, a natural approach for someone who started in radio. Once the voice was established, he drew pictures until he found the right face, which he adopted as his own with the help of a makeup expert; then he developed the character's walk and stance. "And then it happens. I have the feeling that the film character enters my body as if I were a kind of medium. It's a little frightening." So adept was Sellers at transforming himself into other people that he often denied having a personality of his own. "Write any character you have in mind and I'll shape myself to what you have written," he said. "But don't write a part for me."

The director Stanley Kubrick chose him for the role of Clare Quilty, the mad nemesis of an even madder sex maniac, in the movie adaptation of Vladimir Nabokov's *Lolita* in 1962. Pauline Kael wrote: "An inspired Peter Sellers creates a new comic pattern—a crazy quilt of psychological, sociological commentary so 'hip' its surrealist. . . .

The rather frightening strength of his Quilty (who has enormous—almost sinister—reserves of energy) is peculiarly effective just because of his ordinary, 'normal' look. He does something that seems impossible: he makes unattractiveness magnetic."

Sellers and Kubrick worked together again in 1963 on *Dr. Strangelove, or: How I Learned to Stop Worrying and Love the Bomb,* in which he played a U.S. President Merkin Muffley, RAF Group Captain Lionel Mandrake, and the title character, a mad Nazi-American inventor with an artificial arm that has a mind of its own. (Andrew Sarris has pointed out that Kubrick originally intended Sellers to play a fourth role, that of Major "King" Kong, commander of the plane that drops the bomb, but that Sellers was replaced because of an injury. Had he completed the part, Kubrick would have achieved a "satiric symmetry" in which "everywhere you turn there is some version of Peter Sellers holding the fate of the world in his hands.") Both Kubrick and Sellers were nominated for Academy Awards.

Also in 1963, Sellers joined writer-director Blake Edwards for the first of the Inspector Clouseau films, *The Pink Panther,* followed a year later by a sequel, *A Shot in the Dark.* Clouseau, the only character Sellers carried from film to film, is an incompetent French detective with a uniquely Sellerian French accent and a gift for defeating, unawares, the most devious of villains. "He is like a Keaton character," said Sellers, "fearless, bold, and serenely confident that in the end he will triumph. . . . But if I had to define his outstanding trait in one word, it would be purity."

Sellers, who suffered a near-fatal heart attack that forced him to drop out of Billy Wilder's *Kiss me Stupid,* in 1964, went on to star in *The World of Henry Orient, The Wrong Box, What's New, Pussycat?, The Bobo, I Love You Alice B. Toklas,* and *The Magic Christian.* He was rescued from a string of mediocre films in the early 1970s by three more Inspector Clouseau films, *The Return of the Pink Panther* (1975), *The Pink Panther Strikes Again* (1976), and *The Revenge of the Pink Panther* (1978), the last two grossing nearly $200 million. Vincent Canby observed that Sellers "needed to collaborate with talents that matched his own. Only when he found such talents . . . did he soar."

Seller's romantic affairs and unhappy marriages kept his private life in the tabloid newspapers and made him the subject of unkind remarks in the memoirs of various actresses. He was an expert photographer, a collector of cars, and a strong believer in ghosts and reincarnation.

In 1979 Sellers reached new heights of comic subtlety and insight in *Being There,* based on the book by Jerzy Kosinski. His character, Chauncy Gardiner, with whom he felt a kind of mystical affinity, is a gentle idiot with no personality except what he derives from the television shows he constantly watches. According to Janet Maslin, "he rose beautifully to the challenge of bringing antic intelligence to an almost entirely passive role. Without the usual fireworks of a Sellers movie—without odd accents or multiple characterizations of anything wildly out of the ordinary—he managed to create the same atmosphere of serene lunacy that always distinguished his work."

Sellers was writing a final episode for Inspector Clouseau and awaiting the release of *The Fiendish Plot of Fu Manchu,* in which he

Peter Sellers as Inspector Clouseau

played both villain and detective, when he died of a second heart attack.   R.W./J.P.

Born Peter Richard Henry Sellers. Son of William S., pianist and music hall performer, and Agnes (Marks) S., actress and singer. Married: (1) Anne Howe, actress, 1951 (div. 1964); (2) Britt Ekland, actress, 1964 (div. 1969); (3) Miranda Quarry 1970 (div. 1974); (4) Lynne Frederick, actress, 1977. Children: 1st marriage—Michael, recording engineer, b. 1954; Sarah, b. 1957; 2nd marriage—Victoria, b. 1965. Jewish. Educ: St. Aloysius Coll., Highgate. Mil. Service: Corporal, RAF 1943/-46; armorer, Spitfire ground crew, Burma and India; official RAF entertainer with Ralph Reader's Gang Show, Middle East. Drummer in jazz band 1941/-43; entertainment dir. at holiday camp 1946/-47; vaudeville comedian 1949/-54; radio, television, and film comedian and actor since 1951. V.P., London Judo Soc.; Member, Marylebone Cricket Club. Hons: Best Actor Award, British Film Acad. 1959; Golden Gate Award for best fiction short, San Francisco Intl. Film Festival (for The Running, Jumping, and Standing Still Film), 1959; San Sebastian Award for Best British Actor 1962; Academy Award nomination for best actor 1963 (for Dr. Strangelove), 1979 (for Being There); CBE 1966; Best Actor Award, Teheran Film Festival 1973; Evening News Best Actor of the Year Award 1975. *Performances: Comedy acts*—performed in London music halls 1946/-48; debut at Windmill Theatre, London 1948; toured vaudeville circuit 1949/-56; Royal Command Variety Performance at Palladium, London 1954; three other performances at Palladium 1949/-54. *Radio*—Show Time; Ray's a Laugh; The Goon Show, 1952/-59. *Television*—A Show Called Fred; Son of Fred; The Idiot Weekly; Yes, It's the Cathode Ray Tube Show; The April 8th Show Seven Days Early. Guest appearances on Gently Bentley; Saturday Spectacular; Saturday Night at the Palladium; Saturday Showtime; Carols for Another Christmas. *Stage*—Brouhaha, London 1958. *Films* —Penny Points to Paradise, 1951; Down Among the Z Men, 1952; Orders Are Orders, 1954; John and Julie, 1955; The Ladykillers (Harry), 1955; The Smallest Show on Earth, 1957; The Naked Truth (in U.S. as Your Past is Showing), 1958; Tom Thumb, 1958; Up the Creek, 1958; Carlton-Browne of the F.O. (in U.S. as Man in a Cocked Hat), 1958; The Mouse that Roared, 1959; I'm All Right, Jack (Fred Kite), 1959; (producer, co-editor, co-cinematographer) The Running, Jumping, and Standing Still Film, 1959; The Battle of the Sexes, 1960; Two-Way Stretch, 1960; Never Let Go, 1961; The Millionairess, 1961; (also directed) Mr. Topaze (in U.S. as I Like Money), 1961; Only Two Can Play, 1962; Lolita (Clare Quilty), 1962; Waltz of the Toreadors, 1962; The Dock Brief (in U.S. as Trial and Error), 1963; Heavens Above, 1963; The Wrong Arm of the Law, 1963); Dr. Strangelove (Pres. Merkin Muffley, Capt. Lionel Mandrake, and Dr. Strangelove), 1963; The Pink Panther (Inspector Clouseau), 1963; The World of Henry Orient, 1964; A Shot in the Dark (Inspector Clouseau), 1964; What's New, Pussycat? (Fritz Fassbinder), 1965; The Wrong Box, 1966; After the Fox, 1966; Casino Royale, 1967; The Bobo, 1967; Woman Times Seven, 1967; The Party, 1968; I Love You Alice B. Toklas, 1968; The Magic Christian, 1969; Hoffman, 1970; There's A Girl in My Soup, 1970; Where Does it Hurt?, 1972; Alice's Adventures in Wonderland (The March Hare), 1972; The Optimists of Nine Elms, 1972; Soft Beds and Hard Battles, 1973; Ghost in the Noonday Sun, 1973; The Great McGonagall (Queen Victoria), 1974; The Return of the Pink Panther (Inspector Clouseau), 1975; Murder by Death (Sidney Wang), 1976; The Pink Panther Strikes Again

(Inspector Clouseau), 1976; The Prisoner of Zenda, 1978; The
Revenge of the Pink Panther (Inspector Clouseau), 1978; Being There
(Chauncey Gardiner), 1979; The Fiendish Plot of Fu Manchu, 1980.
Records: The Best of Sellers; Songs for Swingin' Sellers; others.
Author: (with Joe Hyam) Sellers' Market.
Further reading: The Mask Behind the Man by Peter Evans, 1968.

VLADIMIR (SEMYONOVICH) VYSOTSKY
Ballad singer and actor
Born in U.S.S.R., 1938
Died Moscow, U.S.S.R., July 25th, 1980

With his satirical ballads that told of Russian hypocrisy, Stalin's prison
camps, food lines and other Soviet ills, Vladimir Vysotsky endeared
himself to the Russian people. Although Vysotsky's performances,
especially in recent years, were often banned, his travel limited, and
some of his songs censored in his television appearances, he was
tolerated by the authorities, and Soviet officials were among the eager
collectors of his illegal songs.

Little is known of Vysotsky's background, and it seems, according
to his songs, that he never knew his parents. What is certain is that in
1932 when he was 14 years old, he spent a year in a "corrective
colony." All of his life, he wrote ballads and accompanied himself on
the guitar. Graduating with honors from the Moscow Art Theater
Drama School in 1964, Vysotsky, with a "rugged, handsome, expressive face," was a natural performer. He joined the newly formed
Comedy and Drama Theater (the Taganka), headed by Yuri
Lyubimov. The theater became famous for its unusual and iconoclas-
tic productions, often incurring admonitions from the government but
winning wide popular support.

Vysotsky played a variety of roles and his first major appearance
was as Yang Sun, the airman, in Brecht's *Good Woman of Setzuan.*
The opening scene of his *Hamlet* found Vysotsky alone on stage,
guitar in hand, singing the poem "Hamlet" from *Dr. Zhivago.*
Vysotsky also achieved wide popularity as a movie star, playing in a
number of Soviet films. Among his film roles was that of a detective
based on the widely read novels of Arkadi and Zhura Viner.

But it was as a ballad singer that Vysotsky achieved his great
popularity with the Soviet people. His songs, seldom harsh in their
criticisms as were those of the two other leading Soviet balladeers,
Bulat Okudzhava and Alexander Galich, were endowed with a true
Russian folk spirit. He often poked fun at Soviet officials, as in
"Ballad of a Currency Store," or gently criticized the privileges of
certain Soviets, as in "Notes." But he performed "Wolf Hunt," a song
about persecution with an unusual emotionalism; and the revue
"Watch Your Faces" at the Taganka in which the song featured was
closed by the Soviets after only three performances.

Vysotsky was only occasionally recorded by the official Soviet label,
Melodya. His songs found their way into Russian homes by an
underground recording and distribution system called *magnitizadt.* As
a star Soviet performer, Vysotsky reaped special privileges, such as his

own apartment in Moscow and a Mercedes sports car. These possessions, however, did not stop him from representing the restless Soviet
youth of the 1960s or from touching the Soviet people from every walk
of life. One Russian claimed that he was not against the totalitarian
system but "was simply saying that life here is often very hard; for a
Russian this is a wonderful thing to hear." The Russian poet Bella
Akhmadulina said that Vysotsky sang of "the grimy, gritty, poignant
things that are not supposed to exist in our society but that the people
live by."

Vysotsky died in his early forties of a heart attack after performing
one of his most famous roles, the lead in Brecht's *Galileo*. As 30,000
Russians jammed Taganka Square to mourn his death, there were
orders to disperse the crowds. A brief riot ensued, the mourners
crying in unison, "posor, posor!" (shame, shame!).   H.S.

Married: (1); (2); (3) Marina Vlady, actress. Educ: corrective colony
1952–52; Moscow Art Theatre Drama Sch., grad. with hons. 1964.
Joined Yuri Lyubimov's Comedy and Drama Theatre (the Taganka)
1965; actor, singer and movie star since 1965. *Songs*—The Psychiatric
Lyric; The Ballad of a Currency Store; The Wolf Hunt; Notes;
Metroplei, a collection of 15 ballads; Seryoshka Fomiah; many others.
Performances: Plays—The Good Woman of Setzuan (Yang Sun); Ten
Days That Shook the World; Antiworlds; Hark; Sergei Yessin (title
role); Life of Galileo (title role), 1967; Hamlet (title role), 1972;
Cherry Orchard (Lupakhin), 1977; Crime and Punishment
(Svidrigailov), 1979. *Films*—The Heights (Vysota), 1957; featured as
a detective in numerous films, and major appearances in many others.

KENNETH (PEACOCK) TYNAN
Drama critic and literary manager of the National Theatre of Britain
Born Birmingham, England, April 2nd, 1927
Died Santa Monica, California, U.S.A., July 26th, 1980

Kenneth Tynan, whose ambition as a youth was to become "Britain's
first postwar myth," made his mark instead as an acutely perceptive
drama critic and social commentator with a biting and elegant prose
style and a broad range of interests and sympathies. He was also one
of the prime movers in the creation of the British National Theatre
and its literary manager during its first decade. He once recalled
having set out to become "the best drama critic in the English
language," adding, "I probably achieved it for a while."

Tynan was born in Birmingham in 1927, the illegitimate son of Sir
Peter Peacock and Letitia Rose Tynan, a Lancashire woman of Irish
descent. His father, an affluent businessman who had started out as a
clerk, was at one time the mayor of Warrington, Lancashire, and had
hopes that his son would be a lawyer. His mother took him on theater
trips to London and to the Birmingham Repertory Company; by the
time he entered King Edward's School in Birmingham, he had
become addicted to all things theatrical. At the age of 16 he wrote a
review of a Stratford production of *Hamlet* that revealed "a great
dramatic critic in the making," according to the *London Times* critic
James Agate. His playful iconoclasm had already made itself felt at his

school, where he campaigned for liberalized abortion and homosexuality laws during a mock election and led a noisy protest against the headmaster.

Tynan continued his deliberate flouting of the rules as a scholarship student at Magdalen College, Oxford, where he affected purple doeskin suits, gold satin shirts, top hats, opera cloaks, and long hair. Fellow students burned him in effigy on Guy Fawkes Day; Tynan drove a car over the bonfire. In addition to serving as editor of the student newspaper *Cherwell* and the magazine *Avant-Garde,* as drama critic for the university magazine *Isis,* and as secretary of the Oxford Union Debating Society, he was president of the Experimental Theatre Club, for which he acted, directed, and wrote. After taking second class honors in 1948 he became director at a Lichfield repertory company, then directed *A Man of the World* in London and *Othello* on an Arts Council tour. By 1951 he had published a book of essays, *He That Plays the King,* with a foreword by Orson Welles, and was writing theater criticism for *The Spectator.*

In 1951 Tynan was invited by Sir Alec Guinness to play the Player King in his production of *Hamlet.* His performance was panned by a critic of the *London Evening Standard,* to whom Tynan replied in a letter to the editor so witty that it won him a place as the newspaper's drama critic. His study of Guinness was published in 1953, followed by *Persona Grata,* a book of biographical sketches with photographs by Cecil Beaton [q.v.]. He put in a few months at the *Daily Sketch* before joining the prestigious *Sunday Observer* in 1954 at the age of 27.

For the next nine years, with time out for two seasons at the *New Yorker,* Tynan used his enormous critical influence to "rouse tempers, goad, lacerate, raise whirlwinds" from the pages of the *Observer.* His prose style was vibrant, precise, erudite, and trenchantly witty. From an early enthusiasm for the theater of "fantasy and shock" he moved quickly to the Brecht-inspired realization that theater must be rooted in the political, social, and economic realities of the day; this made him an early champion of the "New Wave" of English realist playwrights, including John Osborne and Arnold Wesker, with whose "instinctive leftishness" he was much in sympathy. Of Osborne's *Look Back in Anger,* Tynan wrote: "One cannot imagine Jimmy Porter listening with a straight face to speeches about our inalienable right to flog Cypriot schoolboys. You could never mobilize him and his kind into a lynching mob, since the art he lives for, jazz, was invented by Negroes; and if you gave him a razor, he would do nothing with it but shave." He agreed with Sir Philip Sidney that art is "that which instructs through delight"; socialism, he wrote, "ought to mean more than progress for its own sake; it ought to mean progress towards pleasure." Likewise, he saw "healthful pleasure" as the purpose of both art and criticism, saying of drama critics: "What counts is not [their] opinion, but the art with which it is expressed. They differ from the novelist only in that they take as their subject-matter life rehearsed instead of life unrehearsed. . . . The true critic cares little for the here and now. . . . His real rendezvous is with posterity. His review is a letter addressed to the future. . . . It matters little if he leans towards "absolutism" or "relativism," towards G.B.S. or Hazlitt. He will find readers if, and only if, he writes clearly and gaily and truly; if he regards himself as a specially treated mirror recording a unique and unrepeatable event."

During his two years at the *New Yorker,* Tynan campaigned

successfully to have Lorraine Hansberry's *Raisin in the Sun* chosen by the New York Drama Critics Circle as the best play of 1958–59 and did the same for Jack Gelber's *The Connection* the year following. His merciless pen made him *persona non grata* with some segments of the American theater world (producer David Merrick wanted him banned from play openings) and his socialist opinions incurred the suspicion of the Senate internal security subcommittee, which questioned him in a closed hearing about his role in producing *We Dissent,* a British television program featuring the noncomformist views of such artists and intellectuals as Norman Thomas, Norman Mailer, and Allen Ginsberg. He returned to England in 1960, weary of Broadway's "light comedies and heavy musicals," and took up his old post as drama critic of the *Observer,* switching to film critic in 1964. He also headed the script editing department at Ealing Films, edited *Tempo,* a television program on the arts, and wrote *Bull Fever,* an appreciation of the sport of bullfighting.

For many years Tynan had crusaded for a subsidized national theater that would commission new plays and present the best of the international classical and contemporary stage without the interference of commercial interests. The plan was approved in 1963, and Tynan gave up reviewing to serve as literary manager. He remained with the National Theatre for the next ten eyars, exerting a strong influence on its choice of repertory and becoming the *eminence grise* to Sir Laurence Olivier, who was artistic director. When the National refused to produce Rolf Hochhuth's play *The Deputy* because it criticized Winston Churchill, Tynan co-produced it at the New Theatre, sparking a public debate that resulted in the termination of the Lord Chamberlain's right to censor British productions. Tynan later expressed an interest in "a theater devoted to the restaging of great trials" in which the audience would act as the jury. "And I don't just mean murder trials, but political trials, the Soviet purge trials, for example, the Eichmann trial, trials from all countries and periods."

In 1969, Tynan, a connoisseur of eroticism in the arts, expanded the limits of theatrical sex with *Oh! Calcutta!,* a "nude revue" for which he recruited skits from Samuel Beckett, Joe Orton, John Lennon [q.v.], Sam Shepard, Jules Feiffer, and himself, among others. Despite attacks by the critics, who dismissed it as "frivolous" and "a silly little diversion," the show enjoyed long runs in New York and London and was revived in New York in 1979.

In a 1970 interview for *Playboy Magazine* (never published), of which he had become associate editor in 1968, Tynan explained his appreciation for the "journalism of witness" practiced by Norman Mailer and Mary McCarthy as the outgrowth of recent events in Czechoslovakia, which had made him see the need for "private evidence" over "public theory." "In my own generation, in Europe, I saw that radical change *was* possible, and that socialism and freedom were compatible. . . . Prague, in 1965, 1966, and 1967, had the best theatre in Europe, the best cinema, it had marvellous poets, marvellous novelists. Out of socialism had come what one had always hoped would come, an incredible, enthusiastic, almost frenzied creativity. And then, when one saw *that* crushed by the Russians in 1968, it meant finally that the possibility of radical and total change, even in a very small country, was no longer to be considered. Because one or another of the great powers would step in and kill it."

During the 1960s and 70s Tynan published five collections of

journalistic and critical essays in which he lampooned the mediocre
while saluting the "High Definition Performer"—one who can "command the essence of one's talent to an audience with economy, grace,
no apparent effort, and absolute, hard-edged clarity of outline." His
list of such performers included actors Sir Laurence Olivier, Nicol
Williamson, and Marlene Dietrich, the bullfighter Antonio Ordoñez,
and film director Roman Polanski, with whom Tynan collaborated on
the script for the film version of *Macbeth*. Some writers have identified
this tendency to hero-worship as the greatest weakness of his criticism.
"Despite his power and reputation," according to the *London Times,*
"he seems in retrospect to have suffered an unhappy division between
his temperament, which drew him naturally to the flash and sparkle,
the big star performance, the most shamelessly, even mindlessly
theatrical of theatre, and his intellect, which forced on him the
sometimes painful duty of approving the drably worthy, the sober, the
politically correct."

Tynan, who was twice married and had three children, suffered
from pulmonary emphysema and moved in 1976 to the drier climate of
Southern California, where he wrote profiles of celebrities for the *New
Yorker.* Five of these profiles, of Sir Ralph Richardson, Tom
Stoppard, Johnny Carson, Mel Brooks, and Louise Brooks, were
collected in *Show People,* published a few months before his death.

J.P./A.C.

Born Kenneth Peacock; later adopted his mother's last name. Son of
Sir Peter Peacock, businessman, and Letitia Rose T. Married: (1)
Elaine Brimberg Dundy, actress and writer, 1951 (div. 1964); (2)
Kathleen Halton, writer, 1967. Children: 1st marriage—Tracy; 2nd
marriage—Roxana; Matthew. moved to California 1976. Educ: public
elementary schs., Birmingham; King Edward's Sch., Birmingham;
Magdalen College, Oxford, B.A. (Second Class Hons. in English)
1948. At Oxford: Ed., Cherwell (newspaper); Ed., Avant-Garde
(mag.); Drama critic, Isis (mag.); Secty., Oxford Univ. Debating
Soc.; Pres., Experimental Theatre Club. Dir., Lichfield repertory co.
1949; dir., London 1950; actor, London 1951. Drama critic: The
Spectator 1951–52; Evening Standard, London 1952–53; Daily Sketch,
London 1953–54; The New Yorker, NYC 1958–60. Drama critic
1954–58 and 1960–63, The Observer, London; concurrently Script
Ed., Ealing Films 1956–58, and Ed., Tempo (television program on
the arts) 1961–62. Literary Mgr. 1963–69 and Literary Consultant
1969–73, National Theatre of Britain; concurrently film critic, The
Observer, 1964–66. Chmn., International Drama Conference 1961;
Assoc. Ed., Playboy Mag. since 1968. Member: drama panel, British
Council. Hons: Fellow, Royal Soc. of Literature. *Author: Drama
Criticism*—He That Plays the King, 1950; Alec Guinness, 1953, 3rd
ed. 1961; Curtains, 1961; Tynan on Theatre, 1964; Tynan Left and
Right, 1967; The Sound of Two Hands Clapping, 1975; Show People:
Profiles in Entertainment, 1980. *Plays*—A Toy in Blood (adaptation
of Hamlet), ca. 1947–48; (ed.) Othello (by William Shakespeare;
National Theatre Production), 1966; (ed.) The Recruiting Officer (by
George Farquhar; National Theatre Production), 1965; (deviser and
co-author) Oh! Calcutta! An Entertainment with Music (revue), NYC
1969, London 1970; (deviser and co-author) Carte Blanche (revue),
Phoenix 1976. *Screenplays*—(with Harold Long) the Quest for Cor-
bett (radio play), 1960; (ed.) We Dissent (television program), 1960;
The Actors (television documentary), 1968; (with Roman Polanski)
Macbeth (by William Shakespeare; film adaptation) 1972. *Other*—
(with photographs by Cecil Beaton [q.v.]) Persona Grata, 1953;

(contributor) Declaration (ed. by Tom Maschler) 1959; Bull Fever, 1955; enlarged ed. 1966; (author of introduction) How to Talk Dirty and Influence People (by Lenny Bruce), 1966; (contributor) Perspectives on Pornography (ed. by Donald Hughes), 1970. *Theater: Director*—repertory plays in Lichfield, Staffordshire, 1949; Man of the World, London 1950; Othello, British Arts Council tour 1950. *Producer*—(co-producer) Soldiers (by Rolf Hochhuth), London 1968. *Actor*—Hamlet (The Player King), London 1951.
Further reading: articles in New Statesman, Oct. 13, 1961; New York Times Magazine, Jan. 9, 1966; Vogue, Nov. 1, 1958.

MOHAMMED REZA SHAH PAHLAVI
Shah of Iran
Born Teheran, Persia (now Iran), October 26th, 1919
Died Cairo, Egypt, July 27th, 1980

In 1971, Mohammed Reza Pahlavi, Shah of Iran, celebrated the 2,500th anniversary of kingly rule over Persia with a display of pomp and splendor worthy of a potentate of the ancient Middle East. By the end of the decade the monarchy had come to an abrupt end, driven out of existence by a political convulsion which had all the emotional fervor of a religious war. The Shah, self-proclaimed heir to Cyrus the Great, who thought himself called by God to restore Iran to its rightful place among the nations, had proved himself so odious a monarch that many of his subjects considered him more demon than man.

It was Iran's misfortune that the Shah possessed two selves that could never be reconciled. He was a progressive leader, an expert on oil production, oil revenues, and oil diplomacy, who pushed Iran relentlessly to raise itself from rural poverty to industrial and military superiority in the space of a generation. But he was too obsessed with his own power to share it with the Iranian people of whom he asked so much; his genuine desire to create a thriving capitalist society was counterbalanced by his mystical adherence to the idea of himself as a paternal king bearing complete responsibility for the welfare of his loyal subjects. Identifying himself with the nation, the Shah defined anyone who opposed his will as an enemy of Iran, deserving of extermination. "What the Shah has done, in effect," wrote one observer, "has been to encourage enormous economic change and some social change in order to prevent any basic political change." After a quarter-century of this national schizophrenia, the harassed Iranians chose the unknowns of an Islamic republic to the hated certainties of life under the Shah, displaying their newly-won power by holding a group of American citizens hostage in Teheran for 444 days.

This drama had its beginnings in a territorial rivalry between two foreign powers, imperial Britain and czarist Russia. Since the second half of the 18th century, when Britain expanded its colonial empire to the Indian subcontinent, Persia, along with neighboring Afghanistan, Turkestan, and Transcaspia, had served as a buffer zone preventing direct confrontations between the two powers. The discovery of huge oil deposits at the end of the 19th century intensified their rivalry over Persia and encouraged its division into Russian and British zones of influence, weakening the already bankrupt and corrupt Qajar monarchy.

In 1921 the Qajar shahs were overthrown by Reza Khan (later called Reza Shah), commander of the Russian-trained Cossack Bridgade, who had started his career as an illiterate mule driver. Four years later, with the approval of Parliament, he obtained dictatorial powers and crowned himself Shah, his dynasty to be known by the name of the ancient Persian language Pahlavi. Under his rule, Persia (renamed Iran in 1935) took its first steps toward modernization and established close ties with Germany, whose totalitarian government he admired.

Mohammed Reza Pahlavi, the eldest son of Reza Shah by his consort, Taj ol-Molouk, and his twin sister Ashraf were born in 1919. From the moment of his designation as Crown Prince in 1926, the boy underwent a rigorous training program intended to mold him into an emperor. A special military elementary school was set up in the Teheran palace and augmented with lessons from a French governess, athletics, and daily lectures from his father on the rights and duties of kingship. In 1931 he was sent to a day school in Lausanne, Switzerland, and a year later to the famous Le Rosey boarding school on Lake Geneva, from which he graduated in 1936. After two years at Teheran Military College he entered the army as a second lieutenant, still tutored daily by Reza Shah.

Despite the careful planning of his father, the Crown Prince unexpectedly developed a deep mystical bent. As a young child he had suffered frequent illnesses and accidents during which he saw visions of Islamic saints. At the age of five, according to his own account, he fell against a rock and was saved from injury by the Prophet Ali. These childhood visions, and the prescient dreams he had as an adult, convinced him that God had chosen him to lead Iran to greatness. "My life has gone forward under the sign of destiny," he told journalist Oriana Fallaci in 1973. "You can't rebel against destiny when you have a mission to accomplish. . . . One is either a king or one isn't. If one is a king, one must bear all the responsibilities and all the burdens of being a king, without giving in to the regrets or claims or sorrows of ordinary mortals."

In 1941 Britain and the Soviet Union, having temporarily allied themselves for the duration of World War II, jointly occupied Iran in order to secure their supply routes and prevent Germany from making military use of the country and its oil fields. Reza Shah was forced to abdicate in favor of his 21-year-old son and died in exile three years later.

Mohammed Reza Pahlavi thus ascended the Peacock Throne as the puppet of two governments whose rivalry had all but destroyed the country in the past. At the end of the war, the Soviet Union refused to withdraw its troops from the northwest province of Azerbaijan and instigated the formation of secessionist republics among several of Iran's ethnic minorities. Pressure from the United States and the United Nations persuaded the Soviets to leave in 1946, and the Shah rode into Azerbaijan at the head of the Imperial Army.

Political conflicts between ideological factions were rife during the first 12 years of the Shah's reign, with ministerial governments attempting to reduce the monarchy to the limited position spelled out for it in the 1906–11 Constitution. The idea of a strong king appealed to many Iranians, particularly those from tradition-bound rural villages, but in the main the Shah's power base was confined to conservative groups interested in preserving the economic status quo. The crisis came in 1952, when Britain, which had enjoyed vastly lucrative oil exploitation rights since 1901, refused to agree to an equitable profit-sharing commitment. Prime Minister Mohammed Mossadeq, backed by a majority of Iranians, took the revolutionary step of nationalizing the oil industry, and the British instituted a punishing international boycott. The Iranians, their economy at a standstill, turned for assistance to the U.S. (which had lately developed an interest in Iran both for its oil and for its strategic location on the Persian Gulf) but were rebuffed by President Eisenhower, who suspected the Mossadeq government of receiving communist support and was determined to replace it with a strong pro-Western monarchy. On August 19, 1953, Mossadeq was toppled by a coup planned and executed by the CIA with the complicity of Muslim clergymen and bribed demonstrators. Soon after, the Shah, who had fled to Rome to avoid arrest by Mossadeq, was restored to Iran as an absolute monarch.

Having narrowly escaped an ignominious exile, the Shah declared martial law, which was to last three years, and moved to consolidate his regime with the financial and technical help of the United States. The oil industry, the controlling factor in Iran's economy, was placed under the authority of a consortium of American and European companies. (Although such an arrangement was contrary to American anti-trust laws, President Eisenhower had ruled that the oil companies were important instruments of U.S. foreign policy in the battle against communism and hence immune from anti-trust prosecution by the Justice Department.) Between 1953 and 1957 alone the U.S. provided the Shah with nearly $367 million in aid, an unusually large sum for a non-NATO country, in addition to billions of dollars in military aid, private investment, and the services of military and business personnel.

In 1957 the Shah, with the assistance of the CIA, established a state intelligence and security organization, known by its initials SAVAK. It soon grew into a massive terrorist apparatus which imprisoned, tortured, and executed thousands of Iranians suspected of opposing the government. The Shah was particularly fearful that domestic subversion was being used against him by hostile regimes in Moscow and the radical Arab states.

Indeed, widespread popular resentment of the Shah was on the increase. Despite Iran's burgeoning oil revenues, the country continued to live under a feudal society governed by a corrupt bureaucracy and powerful local landowners, with an 85% illiteracy rate, no civil liberties, and epidemic poverty. In 1963, partly in response to pressure from the U.S. government, the Shah initiated his "White Revolution," a vastly ambitious program of political, social, and economic reforms ranging from the redistribution of land and the enfranchisement of women to a system of profit-sharing for industrial workers and the establishment of village courts staffed by the members of a youth corps.

This White Revolution, though it made some headway in the alleviation of Iran's social problems, provoked an outburst of opposition from the Shi'ite Muslim *mullahs,* a powerful presence in Iranian society since the 16th century, who resented the loss of their estates and the erosion of their traditional influence. Most outspoken among them was the Ayatollah Ruhollah Khomeini, who was exiled in June 1963.

The Shah, increasingly isolated from his subjects by a circle of high government officials, was the target of an assassination attempt by one of his Imperial Guards in 1965. He had narrowly missed serious injury in an earlier attempt at Teheran University in 1949, when a "presentiment" warned him that a gunman was about to open fire on him. These escapes, coupled with his survival of several plane crashes and accidents, served to intensify his sense of divine mission.

In 1967 the Shah staged a sumptuous coronation ceremony, officially crowning himself *Shahanshah* ("King of Kings") and *Aryamehr* ("Light of the Aryans"). His wife, Farah Diba, was crowned *Shahbanou,* and the eldest of their four children, Cyrus Reza, was proclaimed Crown Prince. (The Shah had previously been married to Princess Fawzieh of Egypt and to Soraya Esfandayiari Bakhtiari, but had, in turn, divorced them both, neither one having produced a male heir.) He followed this spectacle in 1971 with an even more extravagant ceremony celebrating two and a half millennia of monarchic rule in Persia. Held in Persepolis, the capital and burial place of the ancient Persian kings, it clearly identified the Shah with the glories of Darius and Xerxes and gave the world a glimpse of the *Tamaddon-e Bozorg* (Great Civilization) which the Shah envisioned for the future, when the once prostrate country would be a rich global power, culturally and technically sophisticated, and reliant on diversified industries rather than on limited oil supplies. The achievement of this goal by the late 1980s, according to the Shah's timetable, entailed massive industrialization of the country within a matter of decades and the complete rearrangement of its social and economic structures. With the U.S. no longer providing its former levels of aid, the Shah, who had discovered the political power of Iranian oil during the 1967 Six-Day War, determined to wring every possible dollar out of the industry in order to finance the Great Civilization before the supply ran out.

After skillfully consolidating his position during the Middle East War of 1973, he began a series of price hikes that raised Iran's oil revenues by some 300% in the course of the first year alone. Some of this money went to pay for Iran's social development programs, but the majority was spent on defense.

In 1974 the Shah made plans to double spending for economic development. More than $69 billion was allocated over the next three and one-half years to artificially hold down food prices, improve educational facilities, and modernize such industries as steel and petrochemicals. However, in 1976 it was announced that oil revenues were $3 billion less per month than planners had anticipated; reluctantly, the Shah decided to postpone many of his plans for revitalizing the Iranian economy. In 1977 the Shah was spending $9.4 billion per year on advanced weapons systems purchased from the U.S. and the Soviet Union (with which the Shah had established trade agreements despite his distrust of Marxism). This arms build-up enabled him to dispense military aid to Kurdish secessionists in Iraq and to regimes in Pakistan, Oman, and Somalia.

A profile of the Shah prepared by the CIA in 1975 called him "a brilliant but dangerous megalomaniac" whose insatiable urge for power stemmed from "his cruel father, his years as a pawn of the West, his undistinguished lineage, his fear of impotence." On the subject of energy, however, he was a lucid realist. Explaining to Oriana Fallaci in 1973 why he intended to raise the price of oil tenfold, he said, "You [Westerners] buy crude oil from us and then sell it back to us, refined into petrochemicals, at a hundred times what you paid for it. You make us pay more for everything, and it's only fair that from now on you should pay more for oil. . . . The need for oil is rising at an accelerated pace, the oil deposits are being exhausted, and you'll soon have to find new sources of energy. Atomic, solar, or something. There'll have to be many solutions; one won't be enough. For example, we'll even have to resort to turbines driven by the ocean tides. . . . Oh, when you talk about oil . . . the most important thing isn't the price, it's not Qaddafi's boycott, it's the fact that oil is not everlasting and that before we exhaust it we must invent new sources of energy."

Had the Shah been able to view his domestic situation with the same cool-headed pragmatism, he might have foreseen the surge of opposition brought on by the severe strains his rapid drive for modernization imposed on Iranian society. The lack of training programs for a poverty-stricken population still 60% illiterate, the concentration of wealth in the bank accounts of a Western-educated elite (which included many members of the royal family), the disruptive presence of thousands of foreign personnel—these, coupled with a 50% inflation rate, rampant corruption, mass migration of farmworkers to the cities, and institutionalized terror, contributed to a growing avalanche of frustration which the overly confident Shah deigned not to notice. The middle class, especially, was growing impatient with waiting for the promised benefits of modernization, while young Iranians, educated abroad by the tens of thousands, came back with idealistic dreams of democracy and socialism and were often drawn to the urban guerrilla groups that sprang up in the early 1970s. Nor could the political system, geared to centralized, one-man rule, provide a channel for the legitimate expression of these frustrations. Indeed, in 1975 the Shah banned all political parties but one and called on his subjects to support this party or risk punishment as traitors.

Asked to comply with President Carter's human rights campaign, the Shah in 1977 announced a handful of liberalizing measures, including the selective freeing of political prisoners and a curtailment of the activities of SAVAK. The President acknowledged these measures at a New Year's Eve gathering in Teheran in January 1978, during which he said: "Iran, because of the great leadership of the Shah, is an island of stability in one of the more troubled areas of the world. This is a great tribute to you, Your Majesty, and to the respect and the admiration and the love which your people give you."

Nine days after this display of friendship, 20 people were killed by police gunfire during an anti-government protest in the city of Qum, a center of Shi'ite Islam. A few weeks later, mourners demonstrating in Tabriz against the first shooting were themselves fired on. In August, 377 people were killed when arsonists set fire to a locked movie theater in Abadan, agents of the Shah were blamed, and protests followed. From his exile in Paris, the Ayatollah Khomeini had succeeded in mobilizing orthodox Muslims in an opposition movement that attracted supporters of every ideological stripe, including students, workers, intellectuals, and people from the middle class.

The Shah, who had originally ignored the demonstrations as the work of religious fanatics and communists backed by foreign powers, now realized the extent of the opposition and responded with gestures of appeasement, including the return of some civil liberties and the closing of casinos, cinemas, and nightclubs in deference to Shi'ite sensibilities. But these concessions were not enough. A strike by oil workers led to escalating rounds of riots, police violence, and more riots, including the burning of banks and airline offices.

In November, the Shah, concluding that his partial restoration of civil liberties had succeeded in whetting rather than assuaging the dissidents' appetites, moved to strengthen his position by instituting a military government and simultaneously promising to clean up his regime. Agents of SAVAK, in addition to shutting down universities and newspapers, arrested 12 high-ranking officials on charges of corruption, and an investigation was launched into the financial dealings of the royal family. The Carter administration had already assured the Shah that it supported whatever actions he deemed necessary and offered to sell him tear gas and riot batons. But it was too late; by the end of the year, although more than 3,000 people had died in the disturbances, the tide of hostility showed no signed of abating. Khomeini and other extremist leaders of the opposition turned down a proposal for a coalition government and ordered strikes and protests so massive that oil production virtually stopped, and with it Iran's economy.

Still the Shah refused to give up his absolute rule or even to consent to a limited constitutional monarchy, hoping, perhaps, to delay events until he could safely abdicate in favor of his eldest son. Possibly such an abdication had been his intention for years; he had known since 1973 that he had histiocytic lymphoma, a cancer of the lymph system.

In January 1979, the Carter administration, fearing that the instability of the Shah's regime might invite a coup d'état, applied pressure sufficient to persuade him to accept a constitutional monarchy. On the 16th of the month, a civilian government headed by the moderate opposition leader Dr. Shahpour Bakhtiar was approved by Parliament and took over the responsibility for ruling the country, and the Shah and his family flew to Cairo, ostensibly for an extended holiday. Most of his vast fortune, estimated at well over $1 billion, had already been transferred to foreign banks. He and his wife traveled to Morocco and the Bahamas before settling in a walled mansion in Cuernavaca, Mexico. Triumphant celebrations were held in the streets of Teheran at the news of his departure.

The Ayatollah Khomeini returned from 14 years of exile in Paris on February 1st. Within two weeks the Bakhtiar government had been overthrown and Khomeini acclaimed as the leader of an orthodox Islamic Republic controlled by the clergy. A purge of political and social offenders was promptly set in motion through a system of Islamic courts.

On October 22nd the Carter administration, encouraged by former Secretary of State Henry Kissinger and banker David Rockefeller, overruled its own advisors and permitted the Shah to enter a New York hospital for cancer treatment. On November 4th, a group of

young Iranian militants, with the approval of the Ayatollah Khomeini, attacked the U.S. Embassy in Teheran and took a group of staff members hostage, demanding, as the price of their release, the return of the Shah and his fortune and a public confession by the U.S. of complicity in his crimes. While the President was struggling to cope with this crisis, which was to have the gravest ramifications for his own political future, the Shah left a Texas military base for the Panamanian island of Contadura, where he stayed for three months before accepting an invitation of permanent residence from President Sadat of Egypt, virtually his sole remaining friend among the heads of state with whom he had dealt for 38 years. Soon afterward he underwent further surgery to remove his diseased spleen and part of his liver. In an interview with an Egyptian newspaper, the Shah predicted that Iran would eventually be taken over by Communists and noted bitterly that his supposed ally, the U.S., in urging him to give his subjects more democracy and modernization than they could absorb, had brought about his downfall.

By July 1980, a military attempt to rescue the hostages had failed and international economic sanctions against Iran were having little effect. In the confrontation between Iran and the U.S., which was vilified by the Muslim militants as the incarnation of evil, the Shah had ceased to play a crucial role, except in symbolic terms. His death on July 27th did not alter the stalemate in negotiations.

Nonetheless, the people of Iran were contemptuously jubilant. Grotesque cartoons of the Shah, with such captions as "The Shah has croaked," were posted on walls. Teheran radio called him "the bloodsucker of the century." The official Pars press agency said he was "the Pharaoh of our time," along with Presidents Carter, Sadat, and Hussein of Iraq and Prime Minister Begin of Israel, all of whom were flouting "the divine words of God."

Although the Shah had requested a simple Shi'ite Muslim funeral, President Sadat ordered that his burial in Cairo's Al-Rifai mosque be held with full military honors. The Shah was interred in the same tomb that had once held the body of his father. Few foreign nations sent representatives. Among the mourners were former U.S. President Richard Nixon, a close friend of the Shah, attending as a private citizen.   J.P.

Son of Reza Shah Pahlavi, founder of Pahlavi dynasty, and Her Imperial Majesty the Empress Mother of Iran Tadj ol-Molouk. Married: (1) Princess Fawzieh of Egypt 1939 (div. 1948); (2) Soraya Esfandayiari Bakhtiari 1951 (div. 1958); (3) Farah Diba, architecture student, 1959. Children: 1st marriage—Shahnaz, b. 1940; 3rd marriage—Cyrus Reza, b. 1960, proclaimed Crown Prince 1960; Maasoumeh Farahnaz, b. 1963; Ali Reza, b. 1966; Leila, b. 1970. Religion: Shi'ite Muslim. Educ: private tutors and governess; military sch. in Teheran palace, grad. 1931; private sch., Lausanne, Switzerland, 1931–32; Le Rosey boarding sch., Rolle, Switzerland, grad. 1936; Teheran Military Coll., grad. 1938; personally trained by father in kingship. Mil. Service: 2nd Lieutenant and Inspector, Imperial Iranian Army 1938–41. Named Crown Prince at father's coronation 1926; succeeded to the throne of Iran in 1941 after his father was compelled to abdicate by the USSR and Britain; regime beset by governmental crises and challenges 1941–53; led Imperial Iranian Army into Azerbaijan province in 1946 after USSR withdrew its occupation troops at the insistence of the U.N.; target of assassination attempts 1949 and 1965; identified by Pres. Eisenhower as a potential U.S. ally in the Middle East 1953; became absolute ruler of Iran in 1953 after the CIA deposed his chief rival, Prime Minister Mohammed Mossadeq; consolidated dictatorial rule with heavy financial, military, and technical support from the U.S. 1953–63; organized SAVAK intelligence and security org. with help from CIA 1957; joined Org. of Petroleum Exporting Countries 1960; initiated White Revolution program of social reform 1963; undertook an ambitious series of economic development programs, financed by oil revenues, with the goal of making Iran a global power by the end of the century; crowned himself His Imperial Majesty the Shahanshah Aryamehr at Teheran 1967; celebrated 2,500th anniversary of Persian monarchy at Persepolis 1971; encountered increasing opposition to his repressive regime beginning in early 1970s, culminating in mass riots in 1978; imposed martial law Nov. 1978 but could not prevent the paralysis of Iran's economy by mass protests and strikes; agreed to become constitutional monarch under civilian govt. headed by Shahpour Bakhtiar in Jan. 1979; left Iran Jan. 16, 1979; found himself in permanent exile after Bakhtiar govt. was overthrown in Feb. 1979 and replaced by an Islamic republic under Ayatollah Ruhollah Khomeini; his arrest and extradition and the return of his wealth demanded by orthodox Muslim militants in exchange for American hostages taken at the U.S. Embassy in Teheran in Nov. 1979; died in exile with the hostage issue still unresolved. Hons: Order of Merit, Germany; Order of Merit, Italy; Order of Isabel la Católica, Spain; Royal Victorian Order, U.K.; Order of Al Hussein Ben Ali, Jordan; Order of Pakistan; Order of Independence, Tunisia; Order of Omayyad Syria; Order of Poland Restored; Order of Saint Olav, Norway; Order of the Netherlands Lion; Order of the Great Star of Yugoslavia; Order of the White Rose, Finland; Order of the Nile, Egypt; 12 other foreign decorations. Hon. degrees from Univs. of Michigan, Columbia, Pennsylvania, California at Los Angeles, Chicago, Harvard, New York, Washington, Aligarh, Bangkok, Malaya, Madras, Punjab, Agra, Beirut, Rio de Janeiro, Bucharest, Sofia, Karlova, Warsaw, Peshawar, Istanbul, and Teheran. *Author:* Mission for My Country, 1961; The White Revolution, 1967; Towards the Great Civilization, 1978. Interviews: Interview with History (by Oriana Fallaci), 1977; "Nobody Can Overthrow Me—I Have the Power," in U.S. News and World Report, June 26, 1978.

Further reading: Reza Shah: Feldherr, Kaiser Reformer by E. Bey, 1956; The History of Modern Iran: An Interpretation by J.M. Upton, 1961; Mandate for Change, 1953–56 by D.D. Eisenhower, 1963; Triumph and Tragedy by W. Churchill, 1964; The Shah of Iran: A Political Biography by R. Sanghvi, 1968; Effects of the White Revolution on the Economic Development of Iran by M. Shamlon, 1969; The Economy of Iran, 1940–70; Iran: Economic Development under Dualistic Conditions by J. Amuzegar and M.A. Fekrat, 1971; A Bibliography by W.H. Bartsch, 1971; The Political Elite of Iran by M. Zonis, 1971; Intervention and Revolution: The United States in the Third World by R.J. Barnet, 1972; The Politics of Iran: Groups, Classes and Modernization by J.A. Bill, 1972; Politics and Oil: Moscow and the Middle East by L. Landis, 1973; Power Play: The Tumultuous World of Middle East Oil, 1890–1973 by L. Mosley, 1973; The Foreign Relations of Iran: A Developing State in a Zone of Great-Power Conflict by S. Chubin, 1974; Israel and Iran: Bilateral Relationships and Effect on the Indian Ocean Basin by R.B. Reppa, 1974; The Kingdom of Oil: The Middle East: Its People and Its Power by R. Vicker, 1974; Arab States of the Lower Gulf: People, Politics,

Petroleum by J.D. Anthony, 1975; Oil and Politics by H. Madelin, 1975; Iran's Foreign Policy, 1941–73: A Study of Foreign Policy in Modernizing Nations by R.K. Ramazani, 1975; The Shah: The Glittering Stars of Iran and its People by Edwin P. Hoyt, 1976; No Easy Choice: Political Participation in Developing Countries by S.P. Huntington, 1976; Iran: Past, Present and Future by J.W. Jacqz, 1976; Oil and Empire: British Policy and Mesopotamian Oil, 1900–20 by M. Kent, 1976; The Seven Sisters: The Great Oil Companies and the World They Shaped by A. Sampson, 1976; The Imperial Shah, An Informal Biography by G. de Villiers et. al., 1976; Iran: Past and Present by D.N. Wilber, 1976; Multinational Enterprises and Employment in Iran by F. Daftary and M. Borghey, 1977; The Shah by M. Lang, 1977; The Rise and Fall of the Shah by Amin Saikal, 1980.

O(LIVER) D(ENEYS) SCHREINER
Judge of Appeal and university chancellor
Born Cape Town, South Africa, December 29th, 1890
Died Johannesburg, South Africa, July 27th, 1980

O. D. Schreiner was a vigorous opponent of *apartheid,* a champion of African civil rights, and an eminent lawyer and judge. He served for 15 years as a South African Judge of Appeal, and shortly after his official retirement, presided over several important South African institutions.

Oliver came from a prestigious and talented Cape Colony family of Anglo-German descent. His father, William Schreiner, a strong advocate of justice for black Africans, became Prime Minister of the Colony at the outbreak of the South African War. He sought, unsuccessfully, to negotiate a peaceful settlement between the British and the Boers, and later served as South Africa's high commissioner in London. Oliver's mother was the sister of F.W. Reitz, President of the Orange Free State, and his father's sister, Olive Schreiner, was a remarkable crusader and author who wrote the much-admired *Story of an African Farm,* and a pioneering work of the Woman's Movement, *Woman and Labour* (1911).

Oliver Schreiner received his education in Cape Colony and then attended Trinity College, Cambridge, interrupting his studies during the First World War to serve as a captain in the Northamptonshire Regiment and the South Wales Borderers. He was badly wounded in action and was awarded the Military Cross. After receiving his bachelor's degree from Trinity in 1916, Schreiner was elected to a fellowship at the college. He returned to Cape Colony and was called to the Johannesburg bar in 1920. While practicing law, he also lectured in the subject at the University of the Witwatersrand. In the 1930s, Schreiner strongly supported South Africa's ties to the British Commonwealth, believing then that the Commonwealth "stands in a unique position to save the world from catastrophe."

In 1937, Schreiner was appointed to a judgeship in the Transvaal Division of the South African Supreme Court; eight years later he became Judge of Appeal in the Appellate Division in Bloemfontein, in which position he continued until his retirement in 1960 at the age of 70. Thereafter he was appointed President of the recently-created

Appeal Courts of Bechuanaland (now Botswana), Basutoland (now Lesotho) and Swaziland. In 1962 he returned to the University of the Witwatersrand as Chancellor, remaining as titular head of the rapidly-expanding institution until 1974.

O. D. Schreiner endeavored to impress upon his fellow white South Africans that equal education for people of all races, male and female, was both an humanitarian necessity and a sensible policy. He served as President of the South African Institute of Race Relations from 1962 until 1964, and in a presidential address, he said: "In effect the *apartheid* principle, operating through all forms of the colour bar, means that employers, including the government, are, by law or by the power of trade unionists armed with the vote, precluded from employing the best man for the work to be done, that the skilled and responsible work of the country is being done by persons chosen from only a fifth of the population, instead of from the whole, that there is a constant shortage of people to do such work, and that the whites, through being sheltered from the competition of the non-whites, are without the stimulus to hard work and self-improvement that they otherwise would have."

His keen knowledge of South African and English law was displayed at Cambridge in 1967 when he gave the 19th series of Hamlyn Lectures. O. D. Schreiner's humanitarian concerns were demonstrated in many practical ways, most notably through his long chairmanship of the Board of Management for the Alexandra Health Centre, which provides the population of a Johannesburg township with voluntary medical care.   S.T./R.T.

Son of William Phillip S., Prime Minister of Cape Colony, and South African High Commnr. in London. Married Edna Lambert Fincham 1919 (d. 1962). Three children. Educ: Rondebosch Boy's High Sch.; South Africa Coll. Sch.; South Africa Coll., B.A.; Trinity Coll., Cambridge, B.A. 1916, elected fellow 1916, M.A. Cantab. Mil. Service: Capt., Northamptonshire Regiment, and South Wales Borderers, WWI. Called to Johannesburg Bar 1920; practice of law 1920–38; appointed Lectr., faculty of Law, Univ. of the Witwatersrand 1922; Judge, Transvaal Div., Supreme Court 1938–45; Judge of Appeal, Bloemfontein Appellate Div., Supreme Court 1945 until retirement 1960; appointed Pres., Appeal Courts of Bechuanaland, Basutoland and Swaziland 1960. Councillor from 1938, and Chancellor 1962–74, Univ. of the Witwatersrand; Pres., South African Inst. of Race Relations 1962–64; Chmn., Bd. of Mgrs., Alexandra Health Centre, Johannesburg township; Hamlyn Lecturer on contribution of English law to South African law, and rule of law in South Africa, Cambridge 1967. Member, Rand Club. Hons: M.C., WWI; Hon. LL.Ds from Univ. of Cape Town, Univ. of the Witwatersrand, and Rhodes Univ.

WILLIAM J. BAROODY, SR.
President, American Enterprise Institute for Public Policy Research
Born Manchester, New Hampshire, U.S.A., January 29th, 1916
Died Alexandria, Virginia, U.S.A., July 28th, 1980

An influential political adviser to public officeholders, William J. Baroody is best known for his work as president of the American

Enterprise Institute, which he built into one of the most important conservative policy organizations in the U.S.

The son of a Lebanese stonecutter who emigrated to the U.S., Baroody grew up in New Hampshire. After graduating from St. Anselm's College in Manchester, he worked as a statistician for the New Hampshire Unemployment Compensation Agency while doing graduate work at the University of New Hampshire and the American University. During World War Two he directed the statistical division of the New Hampshire War Finance Committee then served for two years in the Naval Reserve. In 1946 Baroody moved to Washington, D.C., where he worked for the Veterans Administration and the U.S. Chamber of Commerce before joining the American Enterprise Association in 1954 as executive vice president.

The American Enterprise Association had been founded in 1943 to disseminate ideas favorable to free market capitalism. When Baroody began working for the organization, it was strongly identified with the business community, which provided most of its financial support. Baroody tried consistently to reduce this dependence by broadening both the range of issues studied by the association and the scope of opinion expressed within it. Under Baroody's influence the organization became less predictable in its recommendations, though still leaning towards the conservative side on most issues. Shortly after becoming president of the association in 1962, he persuaded the governing board to change its name to the American Enterprise Institute for Public Policy Research (AEI). Despite charges that the AEI had violated its tax-exempt status in 1964 by providing policy advice to Barry Goldwater's presidential campaign, the Internal Revenue Service concluded that it was a truly nonpartisan organization.

Baroody remained at the head of the AEI through 1978, presiding over a period of rapid growth. This began in 1970 with two innovations: the transfer of AEI's public relations work to a firm headed by one of Baroody's sons, and the introduction of a series of videotaped discussions of current issues. Increasing public recognition enabled the AEI to broaden its support; foundations provided about three-quarters of the institute's 1979 budget of $8 million, up from $85,000 in 1954. Well-known Democratic intellectuals, including sociologist Seymour Martin Lipset and political strategist Ben Wattenberg, also began to accept positions at the AEI. Particularly striking was the expansion of the organization's publishing activity, resulting in the creation of four new AEI-sponsored periodicals in 1979. Following the 1980 presidential election, the AEI was generally recognized as one of the most important potential sources of information and advice for the incoming Reagan administration.

In addition to his work for the AEI, Baroody was a confidant and adviser to such public figures as Richard Nixon, Gerald Ford, Barry Goldwater and Patrick Cardinal O'Boyle. An active member of the Melkite Catholic Church, he served on the U.S. Catholic Bishops' Advisory Council. He also sat on the board of Georgetown University's Center for Strategic and International Studies, another leading conservative "think tank."

After resigning as president of the AEI, Baroody directed the organization's development committee and remained active as an adviser. His son, William Jr., succeeded him as president.   A.C.

Son of Joseph Assad B. and Helen (Hasney) B. Married Nabeeha
Ashooh 1935. Children: Anne Mary Gallagher; William Joseph;
Joseph D.; Helene Payne; Michael E.; Maryfran Cummishey; Katherine Jane. Melkite Greek Catholic. Educ: St. Anselm's Coll.,
Manchester, N.H., B.A. 1936; postgrad. studies, Univ. of New
Hampshire 1937–38 and American Univ. 1938. Mil. Service: Lt.,
USNR 1944–45. Asst. Statistician 1937–40 and Supervisor of fiscal
research and legislative planning sections 1941–44, N.H. Unemploy-
ment Compensation Div.; Dir., Stats. Div., N.H. War Finance Cttee.
1943–44; Chief, Research and Statistics Div., Readjustment Allowance Service, Washington, D.C. 1946–49; Exec. Secty., Cttee. on
Economic Security 1950–53; Exec. V.P., American Enterprise Assn.
1954–62; Pres., American Enterprise Inst. for Public Policy Research
1962–78; Counsellor and Chmn., Development Cttee., American
Enterprise Inst. 1978–80. Member, Near East Trustee Inst. for Social
Science Research, Washington, D.C. 1957–80; Bd. overseers, Hoover
Instn., Stanford Univ. since 1960; Bd. of cons., National War Coll.
1973–75; U.S. Catholic Bishops' Advisory Council 1973–75; Advisory
Comm. U.S. Catholic Conference on Social Development and World
Peace, 1976–79; American Revolution Bicentennial Advisory Coun-
cil; Exec. Cttee., Georgetown Center for Strategic and Intnl. Studies;
Bd. of advisers, De Sales Graduate Sch. of Theology; Advisory
Council, Virginia Polytechnic Inst. and State Univ. at Blacksburg; Bd.
of dirs., Herbert Hoover Birthplace Foundn.; Bd. of dirs., Near East
Foundn.; Bd. of dirs., Georgetown Univ.; vs. com., Gerald R. Ford
Inst.; Bd. of dirs., Govt. Research Corp.; Chmn. of the bd.,
Woodrow Wilson Intnl. Center for Scholars; Trustee, Lehrman Inst.;
Trustee 1957–80, and treas., St. Anselm's Coll.; Trustee, Inst. for
Social Science Research, Washington, DC 1957–80.

NORMAN LLOYD
Composer, conductor and music theorist
Born Pottsville, Pennsylvania, U.S.A., November 8th, 1909
Died Greenwich, Connecticut, U.S.A., August 1st, 1980

Norman Lloyd demonstrated his talent in a number of musical fields, and through his song books, his musical encyclopedia, and his innovative teaching, communicated to a wide audience his deep enjoyment and appreciation of American music.

Born in Pottsville, Pennsylvania, Lloyd commenced his career as a pianist, accompanying silent movies. He studied piano with Abbey Whiteside and composition with Aaron Copland and Vincent Jones. During the 1930s he spent several summers at Bennington College in Vermont and composed modern dance works for Martha Graham and Hanya Hahn, and later for Doris Humphrey, Ignacio Sanchez Mehias and José Limón. While at Bennington he met a pianist, Ruth Rohrbacher, and married her.

After receiving his bachelor's degree (1932) and his master's degree (1936) from New York University, Lloyd taught there, and at Sarah Lawrence College in the Bronx where he also, for a time, conducted the chorus. He became Director of Education at the Juilliard School of Music in 1946 and joined the teaching faculty three years later, establishing the Literature and Materials of Music Program. This, cited as the "School's most famous innovation," developed the study of composition by in-depth classroom discussions of the scores rather than by traditional textbook-oriented methods. Lloyd helped his students develop a deeper musical understanding and appreciation by inviting composers to come to talk about their works. He also invited choreographers he had known at Bennington to join the Juilliard faculty and a dance department was formed.

Following his 17 influential years at Juilliard, Lloyd became Dean of the Conservatory of Music at Oberlin College (1963–65) and from there, went on to assume the directorship of the Rockefeller Foundation Arts Program, remaining as director until his retirement in 1972.

Norman Lloyd, who had much admired the ragtime pieces of Scott Joplin during the Depression, helped to revive interest in Joplin in the early 1970s, and persuaded Vera Lawrence to compile the popular *Complete Works of Scott Joplin*. Lloyd founded and directed the Riverside Singers in New York City, and helped to establish the Dance Theater at the University of North Carolina in 1970. He served on the faculties of numerous conservatories and schools of music.

Throughout his career, Norman Lloyd performed professionally, both as a pianist and as a conductor, and he was still composing until he became ill with leukemia. His works include some film scores, several compositions for modern dance, a band piece, and numerous orchestral and vocal works.   R.T.

Son of David L., businessman, and Annie Sarah (Holstein) L. Married Ruth Dorothy Rohrbacher 1933. Children: David; Alex.

Educ: New York Univ., B.A. 1932, M.A. 1936. Instr., Ernest Williams Band Sch., Brooklyn 1935–37; Lectr., New York Univ., 1936–45; Faculty Member, 1936–46 and Chorus Conductor 1945–49, Sarah Lawrence Coll.; Dir. of Educ. 1946–49 and Faculty Member 1949–63, Juilliard Sch. of Music, NYC; Dean, Oberlin Coll. Conservatory of Music, Ohio 1963–65; Dir., Arts Program, Rockefeller Foundn., NYC 1965–72. Sometime faculty member and visiting prof. at numerous music schs., colls. and conservatories; Member, Visiting Cttee., Humanities, Massachusetts Inst. of Technology 1973–75 and Visiting Cttee., Arts, Tufts Univ. 1976–80; Member and Consultant 1973–76, Natl. Assn. Schs. of Music; Consultant, Mary Flagler Cary Charity Trust 1974; Founder and Dir., Riverside Singers, NYC. Member; American Soc. of Composers, Authors and Publishers and Pi Kappa Lambda. *Compositions: Choreographical works*—for Martha Graham 1935, Hanya Holm 1937, Doris Humphrey 1941–46 and 1949, Ignacio Sanchez Mehias (Lament), and José Limón ("La Malinche") 1949. *Film scores*—Moment in Love, 1956; The Ancient Egyptian, 1962. *Orchestral works*—Restless Land, 1950; Nocturne for Voices, 1953; Three Pieces for Violin and Piano, 1957; Five Episodes and a Sonata, 1960; A Walt Whiteman Overture for Band, 1962; Three Scenes from Memory and Sonata for Piano, 1963; Episodes for Piano, 1964; Rememories for Wind Orchestra, 1974; also numerous scores for experimental and documentary films, for Office of War Information, Intnl. Film Foundn., Museum of Modern Art, Shirley Clarke-Haleyon Films. *Books:* (compiled with M. Boni) Fireside Book of Folk Songs, 1947; Fireside Book of American Songs, 1952; Fireside Book of Love Songs, 1954; Favorite Christmas Carols, 1957; Songs of the Gilded Age, 1960; (compiled with Arnold Fish) Fundamentals of Sight Singing, 1963; (compiled with Ruth D. Lloyd) Complete Sight Singer, 1963; Golden Encyclopedia of Music, 1968.

WILLIS D(ALE) CRITTENBERGER
Army officer and Commander of the Allied forces
Born Baltimore, Maryland, U.S.A., December 2nd, 1890
Died Chevy Chase, Maryland, U.S.A., August 4th, 1980

A career officer who helped create the armored formations of the U.S. Army, Lieutenant General Willis D. Crittenberger is best remembered as a World War Two commander in Italy, where he was a key figure in the Allied drive up the peninsula.

Crittenberger was educated at the Braden Preparatory School and West Point Military Academy from which he graduated as a lieutenant in the U.S. Army Cavalry. He was first assigned to a unit in Texas, where he saw action against the Mexican guerillas of Pancho Villa. In the early 1920s he returned to West Point as an instructor. After a variety of staff and field assignments, Crittenberger was posted in 1934 to Fort Knox, Kentucky, where plans were being formulated for the mechanization of the U.S. Cavalry. He played an important part in this process and in 1938 moved to the Office of the Chief of Cavalry in Washington, D.C. There he helped draw up the first table of organization for an Army armored division, which remained in effect with slight modifications through his retirement. In 1940 he became the first chief of staff of the newly-organized First Armored Division, based in Fort Knox.

Courtesy W.D. Crittenberger, Jr.

During the early years of World War Two, Crittenberger held stateside posts of increasing importance in the U.S. armored forces. The last of these was command of the Third Armored Corps, which he organized in 1942 and accompanied to England at the start of 1944. In March 1944 he was ordered to the Mediterranean theater as commander of the Fourth Corps, a multinational force composed of U.S., British, Italian, South African, Indian and Brazilian units. The Corps entered action south of Rome, originally assigned to distract German forces from the main Allied thrust on the eastern side of the peninsula. But Crittenberger soon discovered an unexpected weak spot in the German line, penetrated it and ordered an all-out advance. In a record-breaking 401 days of continuous combat, his troops pushed north past Rome, across the Arno River, through the Apennine Mountains and across the Po River. Units of the Fourth Corps finally occupied the Alpine passes to prevent German forces in Italy from retreating into their homeland. On April 29th, 1945 the German Ligurian Army surrendered to Crittenberger, beginning the collapse of enemy resistance in Italy. In the course of the campaign, Crittenberger's troops liberated 600 cities and towns and captured elements of 23 German divisions.

In October 1945 Crittenberger was transferred to the Caribbean Defense Command, where he became the first commander in chief of all U.S. military forces stationed in the area. He returned to the U.S. in 1948 and served on several international military bodies, including the Military Staff Committee of the United Nations and the Military Committee of the North Atlantic Treaty Organization. Following his retirement in 1952 he headed the Free Europe Committee, operator of Radio Free Europe, and served as civil defense adviser to New York's Mayor Robert Wagner.   S.L.G.

Son of Dale J.C. and Effie Alice Daniels C. Married Josephine Frost (Woodhull) ca. 1919 (d. 1978). Children: Willis Dale, Jr., Maj.-Gen., Regular Army, b. 1919; Townsend Woodhull, b. 1925 (d. 1945, WWII); Dale Jackson II, b. 1927 (d. 1969, Vietnam War). Educ: Braden Preparatory Sch., Highland Falls, N.Y.; U.S. Military Acad., grad 1913. Commissioned 2nd Lt. of Cavalry, U.S. Army 1913; with A Troop, 3rd Cavalry, Texas 1913–16; became Aide-de-Camp to Gen. James Parker, Texas 1916; returned to Mil. Acad. as instr. in horsemanship then in Dept. of Mil. Topography and Graphics, and Tactics 1920–23; Advanced Course, Cavalry Sch., Ft. Riley, Kans.; Command and General Staff Sch., Ft. Leavenworth, Kans., grad. 1925. From 1925–34: Instr., Cavalry Sch., Ft. Riley, Kans.; with War Dept. General Staff, Washington, D.C.; commanded 2nd Squadron, 8th Cavalry, Ft. Bliss, Texas; Asst. Chief of Staff for Intelligence (G-2) at HQ, Philippine Dept. At Ft. Knox, Ky. to mechanize the Cavalry 1934–38; joined Office of the Chief of Cavalry, Washington, D.C., 1938; Chief of Staff, 1st Armored Div., Ft. Knox 1940–41. Commanding Gen. during WWII: 2nd Armored Brigade, 2nd Armored Div., Ft. Benning, Ga., and II Armored Corps 1941–42; III Armored Corps, Camp Polk, La. 1942–43; XIX Corps, England 1943–44; IV Corps, Mediterranean Theater of Operations 1944–45. Commanding Gen., Caribbean Defense Command and Panama Canal Dept. 1945–47; Unified Comdr.-in-Chief, U.S. Forces in the Caribbean Command 1947–48; Chmn., Inter-American Defense Bd., Washington, D.C. 1948; U.S. Army Member and later Chmn., U.S. Delegation to the Mil. Staff Cttee. of the U.N. 1948–52; U.S. Deputy

Rep., Mil. Cttee. and Chmn., Standing Cttee., NATO, Washington, D.C. 1949; Commanding Gen., First Army, Governors Island, NYC 1950–52; retired 1952. Pres., Greater New York Fund, Inc., NYC 1952–55; Head, Free Europe Cttee., NYC 1956–59. Advisor to Mayor Wagner on Civil Defense for NYC. Pres: Assoc. of Grads., U.S. Military Acad.; N.Y. Alumni Chapter of Sigma Chi; Soldiers', Sailors' and Airmen's Club. V.P., U.S. Assoc. of Armor; Comdr., N.Y. Chapter of the Military Order of the World Wars; Member, Bd. of Mgrs., Governors Island Branch, YMCA of NYC and Bd. of Trustees, N.Y. Chapter, American Red Cross. Hons: Distinguished Service Medal (with Oak Leaf cluster); Bronze Star Medal (with Oak Leaf cluster); Legion of Honor, Grade of Comdr. (France); Croix de Guerre (France); Hon. Companion of the Mil. Div. of the Most Honourable Order of the Bath (Great Britain); Medalha de Guerra, Orden de Merito Militar (Brazil); Cruizeiro de Sul, Grand Officer (Brazil); Medalha de Campanha, Forca Expedicionaria Brasileira; Star of Abdon Calderon, 1st Class (Ecuador); Order of Avacucho, Grand Officer (Peru); Silver Star for Valor (Italy); Order of St. Maurice, St. Lazzaro, Grand Officer (Italy); Order of Malta (Italy); Order of Fasco Nunez de Balboa (Panama); Cross of Military Merit, 1st Class (Guatemala); Order of Merit of Bernardo O'Higgins, Grand Officer (Chile); Order of Liberator of San Martin, Grand Officer (Argentina); Orden Cruz de Bovaca (Colombia); Military Order (Mexico).

DONALD OGDEN STEWART
Screenwriter, playwright, humorist
Born Columbus, Ohio, U.S.A., November 30th, 1894
Died London, England, August 5th, 1980

A prolific screenwriter of the 1930s and 40s, Donald Ogden Stewart is praised for the sparkling dialogue he brought to limply-plotted movies featuring such stars as Fredric March, Norma Shearer, John Barrymore, Tallulah Bankhead, Spencer Tracy, and Katharine Hepburn. But before his success at M-G-M (where most of his movies were made), Stewart achieved literary acclaim in New York as a humorist and playwright.

Frustrated by efforts to prosper as a midwestern businessman, Stewart was determined to pursue literary ambitions cultivated at Exeter and Yale. He arrived in New York in 1921 and caught the attention of Edmund Wilson, then an editor at *Vanity Fair*. Wilson bought Stewart's parody of Theodore Dreiser and commissioned more humorous pieces. These were soon published as *A Parody Outline of History,* which recounts historical episodes in the styles of such popular writers as Sinclair Lewis, Scott Fitzgerald, Ring Lardner, and Edith Wharton. The book was immensely popular and another, *Perfect Behavior: A Parody Outline of Etiquette,* quickly followed. Established as a widely-read humorist, Stewart gained access to the Algonquin Round Table, New York's literary salon of the 1920s, and traded quips with such luminaries as Dorothy Parker, Robert Benchley, Edmund Wilson, and George S. Kaufman.

Stewart's third book, *Aunt Polly's History of Mankind,* was inspired by Voltaire's *Candide,* and satirized the complacent beliefs of a provincial midwestern matron. A departure from his nonsensical mode of crazy humor, the book did not sell and was ignored by the critics. Stewart had sought the transition from comic to serious writer and failed; he did not attempt again until the late 1930s when dissatisfied with the glamour of Hollywood. His later books of the 1920s were unabashed nonsense and very popular, though hardly readable today.

In 1929 Stewart quit writing for magazines and turned to plays and screenplays. His first play, *Rebound,* tells of two rich socialites from Long Island who marry on the rebound after suffering dismal love affairs. Called "slight but charming," it has many echoes from Philip Barry, whose comedies about the frivolous rich, *Holiday* and *The Philadelphia Story,* Stewart adapted for the screen with much success. Achieving fame on Broadway, Stewart joined many of his friends in Hollywood to begin a lucrative career.

From 1930 to 1942 Stewart worked primarily as an adaptor, shaping plays and novels into screenplays. For one critic, Stewart's adaptations, especially of plays, are "notable for both their fidelity and sensitivity to the original materials. When Stewart does change a line or add an additional scene, it is with an uncanny gift for writing in the precise style of the playwright."

In the late 1930s he made sporadic efforts at writing his own plays. While drafting a play in which a minor character was a communist, Stewart stumbled across John Strachey's *The Coming Struggle for Power* and the *Nature of the Capitalist Crisis.* These books he read with enthusiasm, recalling the anger that had compelled him to attack middle class hypocrisy in *Aunt Polly's Story of Mankind* over ten years earlier.

The Soviet Union was to Stewart "the country where the underdog had taken power into his own hands, and I wanted to be on the side of the underdog." He promised to write plays that would teach the lessons of socialism, regardless of his Hollywood contracts. Determined to fight fascists and nazis, and to uphold the rights of workers, Stewart became president of both the Hollywood Anti-Nazi League and League of American Writers. In these positions he helped raise funds for exiled authors and collected medical aid for Loyalist Spain. In 1940 he edited *Fighting Words,* a collection of papers sponsored by the League of American Writers, which denounced fascism and exhorted all writers to promote, through their works, social and economic justice for workers everywhere. Thomas Mann, Louis Aragon, Dorothy Parker, Dashiell Hammett, and Langston Hughes were among the contributors. Stewart attacked Hollywood producers for using films to defend democracy but failing to portray the advantages of labor unions.

These political causes did not apparently, enrich his writing; his "socialist" plays, produced in the 1940s and 50s, were thought turgid and didactic, appealing neither to audiences nor critics. Throughout the 1940s Stewart continued to produce popular screenplays, although his political activities eventually cost him his career and many friends in Hollywood. Blacklisted in 1950, he moved to England with his second wife, Ella Steffens, a political journalist and activist. He wrote little until publishing his autobiography in 1975; it found favor with many for its chapters on frivolous years in New York, Europe and Hollywood, although reviewers considered his account of the Red

Scare and his political conversion somewhat superficial. He died in
London of a heart attack.   E.T.

Son of Gilbert Holland D., lawyer and judge, and Clara Landon S.
Married: (1) Beatrice Ames 1926 (div. 1938); (2) Ella Winter Steffens,
writer 1939. Children: 1st marriage—Ames Ogden, b. 1928; Donald
Ogden, Jr., b. 1932. Free-thinker. Educ: High Sch., East Columbus,
Ohio; Phillips Exeter Acad., Exeter, N.H.; Yale Univ., B.A. 1916.
Mil. Service: Instr. in navigation, naval ordnance, and signals and
chief quartermaster, Naval Reserve Force 1917–1919. Engaged in
business 1920–21; writer of humorous essays for Vanity Fair, Smart
Set, Bookman, Harpers Bazaar, NYC 1921–29; actor on stage and in
films 1928–30; playwright and screenwriter 1928–50. Pres., League of
American Writers 1937–41; Pres., Hollywood Anti-Nazi League;
Member, Yale Club, Players Club, and Exec. Bd. of Screen Writers'
Guild. Hons: Acad. Award (Oscar) nomination for Laughter 1930–31;
Acad. Award for best screenplay, The Philadelphia Story 1940.
Books: Novels—Mr. and Mrs. Haddock Abroad, 1924; Mr. and Mrs.
Haddock in Paris, 1926. *Plays*—Rebound, 1928; Fine and Dandy
(musical), 1930; How I wonder, 1947; The Kidders, 1957; Honor
Bright, 1958; Emily Brady (unproduced). *Film appearances include:*
Holiday and Rebound, 1928; Not So Dumb, 1930. *Screenplays*—
(author or collaborator) Laughter, 1930; Smiling Through, 1932;
White Sister and Going Hollywood, 1933; The Barrets of Wimpole
Street, 1934; Another Language and No More Ladies, 1935; Prisoner
of Zenda, Holiday and Marie Antoinette, 1938; Night of Nights and
Love Affair, 1939; Kitty Foyle and The Philadelphia Story, 1940; That
Uncertain Feeling and A Woman's Face, 1941; Tales of Manhattan
and Keeper of the Flame, 1942; Forever and a Day, 1944; Without
Love, 1945; Life Without Father, 1947; Cass Timberlaine (based on
Sinclair Lewis's novel); Edward My Son, 1949; Malaya, 1950. *Humor
and Satire*—A Parody Outline of History, 1921; Perfect Behavior,
1922; Aunt Polly's Story of Mankind, 1923; The Crazy Fool, 1925;
Father William, 1929. *Other*—(ed.) Fighting Words (essays), 1940;
(contributor) Exeter Remembered, 1965; By a Stroke of Luck
(autobiog.), 1975.
Further reading: "The Many Voices of Donald Ogden Stewart" by
Gary Carey in Film Comment, winter, 1970–71.

MARINO MARINI
Sculptor, painter, and graphic artist
Born Pistoia, Italy, February 27th, 1901
Died Viareggio, Italy, August 6th, 1980

Marino Marini was born and raised in Pistoia, Tuscany—a region
renowned for its sculptors, such as Nicola and Giovanni Pisano of the
13th century, and the Florentine Renaissance masters Donatello,
Verrocchio, and Michelangelo. In the vanguard of modern Italian
sculpture, Marini always acknowledged the inspiration provided by his
Tuscan forbears.

Marini enrolled, at the age of 14, in the Academy of Fine Arts in
Florence, where he was a student of Domenico Trestacoste. After
leaving the Academy in 1919 he traveled extensively throughout
Europe studying medieval art and architecture. He lived for several

years in Paris, where he became acquainted with Pablo Picasso, Georges Braque, and Henri Matisse; the cubists' structural style later became evident in Marini's own work. The year after Marini returned to Italy, he took a teaching position at the Villa Reale Art School in Monza; he held that position from 1928 until 1940.

During those years he developed his own interest in sculpture. Before 1930 his work had been almost exclusively in painting and printmaking (he had exhibited in Paris, Milan, and Rome, as well as locally), in a style that has been described as "academic" and "archaic." His earliest sculptures were neo-classical female figures made of terra-cotta, but his torsos of pugilists and athletes from later in the decade were sturdier and more realistic, and his basic forms became simpler and heavier.

Marini's "Pomona," a female nude cast in 1941, was described as "a delightful synthesis of the ancient and modern, of the sensuously domestic and the monumental." This solid, substantial work heralded a distinctive style—frank, expressive and above all concerned with form, in which its meaning could be grasped "unencumbered by event."

Throughout his life, Marini developed and matured this style, but he never essentially changed it. He confined himself to a few classical subjects and treated these to extensive variations—as in his best-known horse and rider series. This subject-confinement might have become monotonous, even obsessive, but through a consistent theme, Marini elicited a broad range of expression: his *Rider* series of the late 1930s and early 1940s are majestic and restrained; his post-war *Riders* —horses straining forward and riders leaning back with arms open-wide—evoked joy and celebration; while the late 1950s *Miracle* series—horses rearing or collapsing and riders being thrown—suggest anarchy and terror.

Igor Stravinsky, Henry Miller [q.v.] Marc Chagall, Samuel Barber, and Marini's lifelong friend the painter Campigli, were among the great figures of contemporary culture whose portrait busts Marini sculpted. Passive but powerful, and boldly sculpted, the busts are neither as dramatic as the horses-and-riders nor as decorative as the early nudes; but of all his work it is his portraits which best illustrate human reality. Marini was less concerned with achieving a likeness than in capturing his subject's "spirit of humanity." Critics now suggest that his portraits, which did not attract the high acclaim of his riders or nudes, will be of most interest to future generations.

Exhibiting extensively throughout Europe during the 1940s (while retaining his sculpture professorship at Milan's Accademia Brera, which he had acquired in 1940), Marini's reputation grew. By the time of his New York one-man exhibition in 1950, he had become a sculptor of international renown. However, sculpture was never his only medium; his strong sense of design was demonstrated by his often highly geometric graphic illustrations, and by his relief facings on modern buildings in cities all over the world. Painting was always an essential part of his work; he continued to produce canvasses for exhibition, and incorporated painting into his sculptural process. He would make paintings of his subjects before sculpting them in clay and then casting them in terra-cotta, bronze, or wood. Applying dyes to the bronzes, and paint to the terra-cottas and woods, Marini gave many of his sculptures stripes of color to emphasize their expressive forms.

Marini retired from teaching at the Accademia Brera in 1970 but continued to work in Milan, where in 1974 the Marino Marini Museum was built to house the artist's own collection of 64 sculptures and numerous drawings, paintings, and prints, which he donated to the city.

Marini once said, "I should like to defend for humanity its form." In that, he succeeded brilliantly, and he must rank with Henry Moore and Alberto Giacometti as one of the most important sculptors to come to prominence after the Second World War.   R.T./K.B.

Son of Guido M., bank dir., and Bianca Bonacchi M. Married Mercedes Pedrazzini 1938. No children. Lived in Switzerland 1942–46. Educ: Accademia di Bella Art, Florence. Instr., Art Sch. Villa Reale, Monza 1929–40; Prof. of Sculpture, Accademia Brera, Milan 1940–70; active as sculptor, painter, and graphic artist in Italy since 1920. Hons: award from Accademia Fiorentina della Arti, Florence 1932; 1st Prize for Sculpture, Quadriennale di Roma 1935; Diplôme de Grand Prix, Exposition Internationale des Arts, Paris 1937; award from Academie Royale Flamingue, Brussels 1950; award from Akademisches Kollegium, Munich 1951; award from Kungliga Academian fur de fria Konsterna, Stockholm 1952; 1st Prize for Sculpture, Biennale di Venizia 1952; award from Intnl. Mark Twain Soc. and Intnl. Grand Prize, Accademia dei Lincei, Rome 1954; award from Accademia Nazionale di San Luca, Rome 1957, from Bayerische Akademie des Schonen Kunste, Munich 1958, and from Accademia Latinitati Excolendae, Rome 1959; Medaglia d'Oro di Benemerenza, Commune of Milan 1962; Gold Medal Riconosciemento of the City of Florence 1964; Cavaliere Gran Croce, Order of Merit of the Republic of Italy 1974. *Exhibitions: One Man*—Galleria Milano, Milan and Galleria Sabatello, Rome 1932; Galleria Barbaroux, Milan 1937; Galleria Genova, Genoa 1941; Galleria della Zodiaco, Rome 1942; Galleria del Cavallino, Venice 1943; Kunsthalle, Berne 1945; Gall. of Modern Art, Basle and Aktuaryus Gall., Zurich 1945; Galleria dell'Obelisco, Rome 1949; Buchholz Gall., NYC 1950; Hanover Gall., London 1951; Kestner Gesellschaft, Hanover 1951; Frank Perls Gall., Los Angeles 1951; Kunstverein, Hamburg 1952; Curt Valentin Gall., NYC 1953; Kunstmuseum, Gothenburg 1953; Svensk-Franska Konstgalleriet, Stockholm 1953; Statens Museum für Kunst, Copenhagen 1953; Nasjonalgelleriet, Oslo 1953; Art Museum, Cincinnati 1953; Artek Gall., Helsink 1954; Gérald Cramer Gall., Geneva 1954; Gutekunst and Klipstein, Berne 1954; Der Spiegel Gall., Cologne 1954; Gall. of Modern Art, Basle 1954; Gall. 16, Zurich 1954; Mus. Boymans-Van Beuningen, Rotterdam 1955; Kunstverein, Düsseldorf 1955; Berggruen Gall., Paris 1955; Martha Jackson Gall., NYC 1955; Hoffman Gall., Hamburg, 1955; Pierre Matisse Gall., NYC 1955; Hanover Gall., London 1956; The Contemporaries Gall., NYC and Vömel Gall., Düsseldorf 1957; Pierre Matisse Gall., NYC and Vallotton Gall., Lausanne 1958; Natl. Mus. of Modern Art, Tokyo 1960; Kunsthaus, Zurich (retrospective), and Vonderbank Gall., Francfurt-am-Main 1962; Toninelli Gall., Milan 1963; Kunsthalle, Munich 1964; Galleria Ciranna, Milan 1964; Gunther Franke Gall., Munich 1964; Musée Royal des Beaux-Arts, Antwerp and Philadelphia Mus. of Art 1965; Palazzo Venezia, Rome 1966; Kunsthalle, Darmstadt 1966; Mus. of Art, Phila. 1966; Pierre Matisse Gall., NYC 1967; Galleria Ciranna, Milan and Weintraub Gall., NYC 1968; Graphic Arts Gall., London 1969; Centro Studi Piero della Francesca, Milan and Contemporary Sculpture Center, Tokyo and Osaka 1972; Galleria d'Arte Moderna, Milan 1974; Galleria San

Fedele, Milan 1974; Gallerie Wilhelm Grosshennig, Düsseldorf 1974; Haus der Kunst, Munich and The Patrick Seale Gall., London 1976; Gall. Universe, Tokyo and The Fine Arts Soc., London 1977; Musee d'art moderne de la ville de Paris 1978. *Group*—Marini, Moore, Wotruba, Welz Gall., Salzburg 1952; Sculpture in the Twentieth Century, The Mus. of Modern Art, NYC 1953; Contemporary Italian Art, City Art Mus., St. Louis 1955; Intnl. Exhibition of Contemporary Sculpture, Musée Rodin, Paris 1956; Italian Sculpture in the XXth Century, Messina, Rome and Bologna 1957; Giacometti, Marini, Matisse, Moore, Hanover Gall., London 1958; Le Corbusier, Marino Marini, Palette Gall., Zurich 1958; Morandi, Tosi, Marino Marini, Campigli, Sironi, De Pisis, Gall. of Contemporary Art, Caracas 1958; Sculpture of the 20th Century, Grosvenor Gall., London and XX Century Italian Art in American Collections, Palazzo Reale, Milan 1960; Exhibition of Italian Contemporary Sculpture, Tokyo 1961; Examples of Suffering in Modern Art, Mathildenhöhe, Darmstadt 1963; Sculptures from the Milan Sch., Pirelli Cultural Center, Milan 1963; Sculptures from the Milan Sch., Pirelli Cultural Center, Milan 1963; Great Contemporary Sculptures, Vondelpark, Amsterdam 1965; Contemporary Italian Sculpture, Wellington and Auckland, N.Z. 1965; Contemporary Italian Art, Mus. of Modern Art, Mexico City 1966; Images of Man, Kunsthalle, Darmstadt 1968; Galleria Toninelli, Milan 1968; Italienische Druckgraphik der Gegenwart, Albrecht Dürer Gesellschaft, Nuremberg 1976; A Selection of Paintings and Sculpture, The Fine Art Soc., London 1977. Collections: Marino Marini Mus., Milan; Galleria d'Arte Moderna, Florence; Galleria Civica d'Arte Moderna, Milan; Galleria d'Arte Moderna, Trieste; Musée Royal des Beaux-Arts, Antwerp; Jeu de Paume, Paris; Kunstmuseum, Basel; Kunsthaus, Zurich; Musee Royaux des Beaux-Arts, Brussels; Nationalmusei, Gothenburg, Sweden; Neue Nationalgalerie, Berlin; Kunstmuseum, Hamburg and Dusseldorf; Tate Gall., London; Rijksmuseum Kroller-Muller, Otterlo, Netherlands; Boymans-van Beuningen Mus., Rotterdam; Albertina Acad., Vienna; Inst. of Fine Arts, Detroit; Blanden Memorial Art Gall., Ft. Dodge, Tex.; Wadsworth Atheneum, Hartford, Conn.; Mus. of Modern Art, NYC; Portland Mus. of Art, Oregon; Mus. of Art, San Francisco; Art Gall. of Ontario, Toronto. *Other works:* open air sculptures, Hamburg; Sculpture in the Open Air, Holland Park, London; Sculptures in Battersea Park, London; Open Air Sculpture, Middelheim Park, Antwerp; many others. *Publications:* has illustrated numerous books, series of lithographs and graphics since 1942.
Further reading: Marino Marini by Douglas Cooper, 1959; Marino Marini by Eduard Trier, 1961; The Sculpture of Marino Marini by Eduard Trier, 1961; The Hand and Eye of the Sculptor by Paul Waldo Schwarz, 1969; Complete Works of Marino Marini, edited by Patrick Waldburg, et. al., 1971; Marino Marini by Alberto Busignani, 1971.

DAVID MERCER
Playwright and screenwriter
Born Wakefield, Yorkshire, England, June 27th, 1928
Died Haifa, Israel, August 8th, 1980

The British playwright and scriptwriter David Mercer, whose film *Morgan!* developed a cult following among college students in the late 1960s, devoted nearly all his work to the theme of the individual in sometimes confused, sometimes vigorous, often lunatic rebellion against social and political authority. Like his friend and fellow playwright David Storey, Mercer was born in Wakefield, Yorkshire, to working-class parents. He was educated at King's College, Newcastle-upon-Tyne, then spent three years as a laboratory technician with the Royal Navy before earning his B.A. in fine art from Durham University. In 1961 he left a teaching job to become a full-time writer; in the next two decades he produced more than 20 television plays, ten stage plays, two radio plays, and three film scripts, plus the English dialogue for a fourth film.

Mercer began writing in a naturalistic style modeled on that of the social realist playwrights John Osborne and Arnold Wesker, but soon turned to an open, experimental style more suited to the exploration of the emotional and mental states of his troubled characters. Unlike other leftist playwrights of his generation, Mercer did not hold on to his Marxist convictions long enough to be disillusioned; his natural suspicion of all institutions and power structures prevented his investing much faith in political systems (he once described himself as "a communist without a party"). Rebellion, in his plays, is the proper reaction of the individual to the oppressive conformity imposed on him or her by an overly powerful institution, whether it be capitalism, fascism, orthodox psychiatry, mindless labor, or class interests. "To say that all [his characters] are involved in this struggle," notes John Russell Taylor, "does not necessarily mean that all of them consciously engage in it, and it certainly does not mean that they all win out in the end. Some seek comfort in anonymity, uniformity, some contrive to contract out of the struggle, some are shattered by it and destroyed. But behind the action of all Mercer's plays is a consciousness of individuality under attack, and which has to be fought for with all one's strength if it is to be preserved."

Until *Morgan!*, Mercer was best known for his television trilogies, *The Generations* (including *Where the Difference Begins, A Climate of Fear,* and *The Birth of a Private Man*) and *On the Eve of Publication* (including the title play, *the Cellar and the Almond Tree,* and *Emma's Time*). In his first work, a radio play called *The Governor's Lady* (1960), the English governor-general of an African colony reverts to savagery, dons a gorilla suit, and is shot dead in a tree. *Let's Murder Vivaldi,* selected as one of the best short plays of 1974, dealt with the bitter consequences of an adulterous relationship, while *Ride a Cock Horse,* voted the work of "the most promising dramatist" of 1965 by the *Evening Standard,* delved into the unhappiness of a self-indulgent novelist. Mercer's "real heroes," writes C.W.E. Bigby, "are men like Morgan *(A Suitable Case)* and the eponymous hero of *Flint,* men to whom 'life became baffling as soon as it became comprehensible' but who impose their idiosyncratic personalities on the world around them, striking out, albeit for the most part ineffectually, at those who wish to contain their energy and anarchism. As Morgan says, 'Violence has a kind of dignity in a baffled man.'"

With *Morgan!* (1966), Mercer gave the British and American youth culture of the 1960s one of its popular symbols in Morgan Delt, the mentally disturbed artist in a gorilla costume who pounds his chest to proclaim his disdain for the society that cannot accommodate him and the mental hospital that proposes to cure him. The film was directed by Karel Reisz from Mercer's adaptation of his own award-winning television play *A Suitable Case for Treatment* (1962). Pauline Kael wrote of it, *"Morgan!* is Ionesco's *Rhinoceros* turned inside out: the method of *Rhinoceros* may have been absurd but its meaning was the conventional liberal theme—the danger of people becoming conformist-animals. *Morgan!* is a modernized version of an earlier, romantic primitivist notion that people are conformists, animals are instinctively 'true' and happy and, of course, 'free'. . . . Those who made *Morgan!* probably not only share in the confusion of the material but, like the college audience, *accept* the confusion." According to Stuart Byron and Elisabeth Weis, *Morgan!* shares with *King of Hearts* and *One Flew Over the Cukoo's Nest* the idea that the psychiatrist is "the creator and enforcer of society's definition of sanity—a definition that leads to war, sexual repression, and the suppression of creativity."

Critical opinion on Mercer's work was divided. Many who liked his stylistic experiments, sense of dramatic form, and precise wit nonetheless reproached him for his tendency to rely on unwieldy monologues and stock characters. Much of his best work was written for television, since, as Ronald Hayman observes, "madness can more easily take possession of the screen than of the stage."

Mercer won a British Film Academy award for *Morgan!* in 1965 and the French Film Academy award for his screenplay for Alain Resnais's *Providence* in 1977. He died of a heart attack in Haifa, Israel, while on vacation there with his wife, an Israeli citizen. He had one daughter.

B.N./J.P.

Son of Edward M. and Helen (Steadman) M. Married: (1). . . (div.); (2) Dafna. Daughter: 1st marriage—Rebecca. Educ: King's Coll., Newcastle-upon-Tyne; Univ. of Durham, B.A. (hons.) 1953. Mil. Service: technician, pathological laboratory, Royal Navy 1945–48. Supply Teacher 1955–59; Teacher, Barrett Street Technical Coll. 1959–61; playwright and scriptwriter for television and films since 1962. Member: Screenwriters Guild. Hons: Screenwriters Guild Award for best television play 1962, (for A Suitable Case for Treatment), 1967, 1968; named most promising dramatist (for Ride a Cock Horse), London Evening Standard 1965; award for best screenplay, British Film Acad. (for Morgan!) 1965; César Award, French Film Acad. (for Providence) 1977. *Plays: Television*—The Generation: Three Television Plays, 1964 (trilogy includes Where the Difference Begins, televised 1961; A Climate of Fear, 1962; The Birth of a Private Man, 1963); Three Television Comedies, 1966 (includes A Suitable Case for Treatment, televised 1962; For Tea on Sunday, 1963; And Did Those Feet, 1965); The Parachute with Two More Television Plays, 1967 (includes In Two Minds, televised 1967; Let's Murder Vivaldi, 1968; The Parachute, 1968); On the Eve of Publication and Other Plays, 1970 (trilogy includes On the Eve of Publication, televised 1968; The Cellar and the Almond Tree, 1970; Emma's Time, 1970); The Bankrupt and Other Plays, 1974 (includes The Bankrupt, televised 1972; You and Me and Him, 1973; An Afternoon at the Festival, 1973; Find Me, 1974); Cousin Vladimir and Shooting the Chandelier, 1978; The Monster of Karlovy and Then and Now, 1979. Also, The Buried Man, 1963; A Way of Living, 1963; Barbara of the House of Grebe (from a story by Thomas Hardy), 1973; The Arcata Promise, 1974; Huggy Bear, 1976. *Radio*—The Governor's Lady, 1960; Folie à Deux, 1974. *Stage*—The Governor's Lady, London 1965 (in Best Short Plays of the World Theatre 1958–67); The Buried Man, Manchester 1962; Ride a Cock Horse, Nottingham and

London 1965, NYC 1979; Belcher's Luck, London 1966; White Poem, London 1970; Flint, Oxford 1970, London 1970, Buffalo, N.Y. 1974; After Haggerty, London 1970; Blood on the Table, London 1971; Let's Murder Vivaldi, London 1972 (in The Best Short Plays of 1974); In Two Minds, London 1973; Duck Song, London 1974. *Film Screenplays:* Morgan! A Suitable Case for Treatment, 1965; Ninety Degrees in the Shade (English dialogue), 1965; Family Life, 1970; Providence, 1977. *Short story:* The Long Crawl Through Time, in New Writers 3, 1965.
Further reading: The Second Wavy by John Russell Taylor, 1971; The Quality of Mercer: Bibliography of Writings by and about the Playwright David Mercer by Francis Jarman (ed.), 1974.

(AGHA MUHAMMAD) YAHYA KHAN
Military officer; President of Pakistan
Born Chakwal, Northwest Frontier Province, India, February 4th, 1917
Died Rawalpindi, Pakistan, August 8th, 1980

Respected as an upright military officer and convinced nationalist who was generally uninterested in personal political power, Pakistan's General A.M. Yahya Khan became chief of state in 1969 when the 11-year reign of President Mohammed Ayub Khan ended in an outburst of demonstrations and strikes. Pakistani military leaders viewed Yahya Khan as a proponent of national unity who could restore order without being guided, like Ayub, by personal ambition. But Yahya proved unable to resolve the country's many problems, above all the increasingly severe division between East and West Pakistan. Indeed, his efforts to forge a more democratic system of government served as a catalyst for the eventual secession of East Pakistan, separated from the western section by a thousand miles of Indian territory.

A lifelong military man, Yahya was born to a Pathan family of hereditary warriors. After graduating from Punjab University in 1936 with a B.A., he was selected for training at the Indian Military Academy at Dehra Dun. Commissioned as a lieutenant in 1938, he served in the British colonial army in the Northwest Frontier area of the Raj. With the outbreak of World War Two he was assigned to an Indian regiment attached to Field Marshal Bernard Montgomery's Eighth Army, seeing service in North Africa and Italy. Assigned for further training to the British Colonial Staff College at Quetta in 1945, he completed the course of study and was appointed to the College's instructional staff, the only non-British officer so employed.

Courtesy Fakhima Yahya

With the partition of India in 1947 and the creation of the Islamic nation of Pakistan, Yahya was promoted to lieutenant colonel and charged with the task of establishing the first national army staff college. By 1957 he had risen to major general—the youngest man of his rank—and was appointed chief of the Army's General Staff. Soon after the 1958 military coup that ousted President Iskander Mirza in favor of Ayub Khan, Yahya became known as the President's protegé; after serving as an infantry commander in the 1965 "September War" with India, he was named the Army's commander in chief. He remained a loyal follower of Ayub until the latter's resignation on

March 25th, 1969. As head of the state's armed forces, Yahya then took over the office of President of Pakistan.

As Yahya took power, the country was in violent reaction against more than a decade of autocratic rule, increasing economic concentrations, government corruption and, most important, a constitutional system which favored West Pakistan over the impoverished Bengali majority of East Pakistan. The new President immediately proclaimed martial law, banning all strikes and demonstrations. Yahya's Army colleagues initially approved of Yahya's actions, but he soon proved his independence. In mid-1970 he announced a new five-year economic plan that allotted 53 percent of state investment to East Pakistan. At the start of the year he also restored full political freedom and issued a "Legal Framework Order," seeking to prepare the way for constitutional and political change.

Convinced that much of the nation's discontent resulted from the unrepresentative nature of it sgovernment, Yahya decided that a return to civilian leadership would have to be accompanied by preparation of a new democratic constitution reflecting the political realities of the divided state. The "Legal Framework Order" accordingly provided for the direct popular election of a national constituent assembly in which representation was to be, for the first time, proportional. This meant that East Pakistan, with 60 percent of the nation's population, would control a majority of legislative seats. The policy of east-west parity established in the constitutions of 1956 and 1962 was abandoned as discriminatory and undemocratic.

Yahya's reform program reflected his desire to take the Army out of politics without eliminating its importance as a force for national unity. He put the plan into effect over the protests of many high-ranking officers, arguing that with the political situation so fragmented no party could possibly emerge as a dominant force; compromise, with the Army as honest broker, would become the order of the day. To Yahya, this parliamentary system promised to eliminate East Pakistani grievances, dilute the disproportionate strength of such West Pakistani interests as the landed aristocracy and the merchant-industrial classes, and avoid the kind of radical upheaval brought on by more repressive regimes such as Ayub's

Though he hoped to foster good will in both parts of the country, Yahya failed to appreciate the depth of sectional passions and the cleverness of the two politicians between whom he was ultimately trapped—Sheik Mujibur Rahman, the charismatic leader of the Bangla Desh movement, and Zulfikar Ali Bhutto, former foreign minister and founder of the socialist Pakistan People's Party. In the national election of December 1970, Rahman's Awami League captured 167 of the 169 assembly seats allotted to East Pakistan, making him the leader of the majority party and prime minister designate. Matters were further complicated by the success of Ali Bhutto's party in the West, where it won 81 of the 132 seats on a platform of socialist reform, Pakistani unity and closer ties with China. These results put Yahya's government in an extremely difficult position. With the overwhelming success of the Awami League in East Pakistan, Rahman's autonomy demands, once seemingly negotiable, hardened; while in the West Ali Bhutto had a base from which to press for a hard line against the separatists.

All hope for compromise within the framework of a united Pakistan collapsed when Yahya, hoping to forestall Rahman's accession to the prime ministry, postponed the seating of the new assembly. In response, the Bengalis seized administrative control of East Pakistan and demanded total independence from the West. With Ali Bhutto loudly urging the use of force, Yahya ordered the Army into East Pakistan in March 1971. The West Pakistani troops brutally suppressed the revolt and sent millions of Bengali refugees fleeing into India. The Awami League was banned, and Rahman was arrested and brought to West Pakistan for trial. But such measures only enflamed the secessionist movement and gave India ample cause for intervention. In November 1971, using the influx of Bengali refugees as a *casus belli*, Indian forces crossed into East Pakistan to secure the area's independence.

By late December, the invading Indians had routed the Pakistani Army, and Yahya's administration lay in ruins. On December 19th, 1971, he resigned as President, and the following day rebellious junior officers brought about the transfer of power to a civilian government headed by Ali Bhutto. Denouncing the nation's "fat and flabby generals" for the disaster, Bhutto immediately retired Yahya from the military and placed him under house arrest, where he remained for the next two and a half years before being released.

Yahya spent the rest of his life in retirement, living on a government pension.   R.C.

Son of Khan Bahadur Agha Saadat Ali K., Police Superintendent, Jhelum District. Married: Begum Fakhira Yahya 1944. Children: Agha Daadat Ali Khan; Yasmeen Yahya. Shiite Muslim. Educ: Government Coll., Lahore and Punjab Univ., B.A. 1936; Indian Military Acad., Dehra Dun, King's Cadet. Commissioned Lt. 1938; Army Staff Coll., Quetta 1945–46. 1st Lt., 2nd Battalion, Worcester Regiment, 1938, in Northwest Frontier; 3rd Battalion, Baluchi Regiment, British 8th Army 1939–45 in North Africa and Italy (as Maj.); student and staff instr., Staff Coll., Quetta 1945–47; named Chief, Pakistani Staff Coll., Quetta 1947 (as Lt.-Col.); Battalion Comdr. 1948–51; promoted to Brigadier Gen. and attached to Corps Headquarters Staff; promoted to Maj.-Gen., Chief, Army Gen. Staff 1957–62; Chmn., Fed. Capital Commn. 1959; Chmn., Capital Development Authority 1960; Commanding Gen., East Pakistan 1962–64; Comdr., Infantry Div. during war with India 1965 (Chhamb-Jaurian Valley campaign); promoted to Lt.-Gen. and appointed Deputy Comdr.-in-Chief of Army, Mar.-Sept. 1966; promoted to Gen. and appointed Army Comdr.-in-Chief September 1966-December 1971; Pres. of Pakistan March 1969-December 1971; placed under house arrest 1972; released 1977. Hons: Hilal-i-jurat (military) and Hilal-i-Pakistan and Sitara-i-Pakistan (civil).

RUBY HURLEY
Civil rights leader
Born Washington, D.C., U.S.A., November 9th, 1909
Died Atlanta, Georgia, U.S.A., August 9th, 1980

Ruby Hurley, who distinguished herself as a civil rights leader in the Deep South during the 1950s and 1960s, was born in Washington,

D.C. in 1909—the year in which the National Association for the Advancement of Colored People was founded. As director of the NAACP's southeast regional office, Mrs. Hurley was involved with some of the most widely celebrated campaigns of the civil rights struggle as well as some of its darkest tragedies. Although she did not gain the wide recognition that Martin Luther King, Roy Wilkins, and the Rev. Jesse Jackson did, her influence, expertise, and charismatic presence within the movement earned her the name "the queen of civil rights" from her associates.

After graduating from Miner State Teacher's College in Washington and attending the Robert H. Terrell Law School, she worked for a short time in a Washington bank and for the federal government. Her lifetime association with the NAACP began when she became a founding member of a group that reorganized the organization's chapter in Washington. In 1943 she was appointed Youth Secretary of the NAACP and organized more than 100 college chapters throughout the country. In 1951 she became coordinator of the NAACP's organizational drive in its new southeastern regional office in Birmingham, Alabama.

Ruby Hurley was a woman who knew the virtues of patience and moderation as well as those of immediate action. She was directly involved in the 1951 investigation of the bombing threats of an NAACP field secretary and his wife in Mins, Florida; in the monitoring of the 1955 trial of two white Mississippians accused of murdering Emmet Till, a black youth; and in the preparation of the case that resulted in the admission by the University of Alabama of its first black student, Autherine Lucy. It was the aftermath of this volatile case that brought about Alabama's temporary banning of the NAACP in 1956 and resulted in Mrs. Hurley's move to Atlanta, where she opened a new regional office.

Mrs. Hurley was also involved in the desegregation of the Universities of Georgia and Mississippi and instructed such key leaders of the civil rights movement as the Rev. Jesse Jackson and Vernon Jordan. The record she kept of incidents of violence against civil rights workers was instrumental in the drafting of the Civil Rights Bill of 1964.

Mrs. Hurley's personal credo—a combination of Christian faith and persistent activism—was best described in the parable she recounted for an interviewer in 1957. "It seems there was an old man who converted a rubbish patch into a thriving vegetable garden. One day a friend passed by and admired all the crops growing on the plot. 'My, the Lord sure has been good to you,' he told the old man. 'Yes, I guess he has,' was the reply, 'but you should have seen this place when the Lord was tending it all by himself.'"   R.C.

Daughter of Edward Ruffin and Alice Patterson R. Married. No children. Educ: Miner State Teacher's Coll., Washington D.C.; attended Robert H. Terrell Law Sch., Washington, D.C. Employed by Industrial Bank of Washington, D.C. and by federal govt. With NAACP: Natl. Youth Secty. 1943–51; Regional Coordinator, Southeast Region, Birmingham, Ala. 1951–52; Regional Dir., Southeast Region, Birmingham 1952–56 and Atlanta, Ga. since 1956. Active in YWCA. Member: Bd. of Trustees, North Georgia Conference of the United Methodist Church; Southern Interagency Conference of Methodists; Conference Bd. of Christian Social Concerns; Bd. of Church and Soc.; Cttee. on Peace and World Order. Life member, Bd. of Atlanta License Review; Pres.: Wesleyan Service Guild, and United Methodist Women; Coordinator, Christian Social Involvement Mission. Hons: Citizen of the Year, Birmingham Chapter of Omega Psi 1953; special distinction, Civil Rights, Natl. Council of Negro Women 1957; Woman of the Year, Utility Club 1968; Bronze Woman of the Year in Human Relations, Delta Chapter of Iota Phi Lambda 1972; Chicago Defender's Honor Roll of Democracy; Outstanding Service to Advance of World Understanding, Peace and Prosperity, Wilberforce Univ., Ohio; Dynamic Christian Leadership in Fight for Freedom, St. Mark's Methodist Church; First Medgar Evers Award, Capitol Press Club of Washington, D.C. From NAACP: Freedom Award, W. Coast Div., Berkeley, Calif.; Distinguished Service Award, Savannah State Coll. Chapter; award for Outstanding Contributions to Fight for Freedom, Region V; Quarter Century of Service Award, Fla. Conference; numerous other hons.

PAUL (CHARLES JULES) ROBERT
Philologist and lexicographer
Born Orleánsville, Algeria, October 19th, 1910
Died Mougins, France, August 11th, 1980

Paul Robert, who was well known for the French dictionaries that bear his name, was called the "Flaubert of dictionaries," and he followed in the tradition of the distinguished nineteenth century lexicographers Pierre Larousse and Paul-Emile Littré. Robert's French language dictionaries have become established as essential reference sources not only in France but throughout the world.

Although his lexicographic career did not begin until he was 35, Robert's interest in words developed while learning English as a young student. After obtaining a law degree in Algiers, Robert worked as an attorney in Paris. There he also began preparing his thesis—*Citruses of the World,* for which he later received a laureate from the French Academy of Agriculture—for an *agrégation* (a degree slightly higher than a Ph.D.) in political economy. While researching the thesis, Robert became dissatisfied with the limitations of his vocabulary and compiled long lists of words which he defined by analogy rather than by traditional definition. When he began writing the thesis, he grew even more discouraged. "I am painfully aware of lacking the means to express myself," he said; "I understand the torment of a Flaubert composing novels page by page." A perfectionist from his school days, he would not continue writing until he found the exact word. A phrase from La Bruyère haunted him: "For all the ways to express an idea, there is only one that is true."

Restless after completing his thesis, Robert read English literature. Again he compiled extensive word lists, this time more systematically. The problem with existing dictionaries, he said, was that because definitions offered a poor selection of words, they failed to allow an *association* of meanings and ideas. In 1945 Robert began working full-time to develop his word lists, entertaining hopes of producing an alphabetical dictionary that would classify words by analogy. (The alphabetical thesaurus had not yet been published.) He envisioned a work whose scope would extend beyond basic definitions, correct usages and occasional locutions to provide a "vast reserve of ordered knowledge."

After five years of painstaking work, which included not only the editorial tasks but production and financial management as well, Robert published the first installment of what was to become the six-volume *Dictionnaire alphabetique et analogique de la langue francaise*—from *a* to *africanisme* was 70 pages. The Académie Française, in a rare recognition of an unfinished work, awarded Robert Le Prix Saintour. This enabled him to secure financial support and in 1951 he established La Société de Nouveau Littré in order to publish his dictionary. Named after Paul-Emile Littré (whose four-volume *Dictionnaire de la langue française* was published from 1863 to 1878), La Société du Nouveau Littré reflected Robert's respect and admiration for the *Littré*, as it was called, yet also signified his desire to update and modernize the old dictionary.

In 1964, nineteen years after initially launching his "adventure," Robert recorded the word *zymotique* to complete the sixth volume of *Le Grand Robert*, as it came to be known. Four days later he commenced work on *Le Petit Robert*, a one-volume abridged version of the dictionary designed for general, individual use. Innovative in systematizing the dating of words, *Le Petit Robert*, published in 1967, set a precedent; all French dictionaries now indicate the first recorded usage of a word. Enthusiastic response to the abridged edition established *Le Robert (Grand* and *Petit)* as the standard dictionary of contemporary French usage.

Revision of *Le Petit Robert* began soon after its publication; according to Robert a good dictionary could survive from 15 to 20 years. Revising *Le Petit Robert* was a task less formidable than attempting to revise *Le Grand Robert* and also more pressing because of its popularity. The revised edition was published in 1977.

The success of *Robert* dictionaries assured Robert the financial security necessary for developing other dictionaries as well as for writing a two-volume autobiography. His autobiography is generally considered to be of little interest; however, a four-volume dictionary of proper names, a dictionary of primordial French and a bilingual French-English, English-French dictionary have all taken their places on the shelves next to *Le Petit Robert* and *Le Grand Robert*.   A.W.

Son of Joseph R., Pres. des Assemblées algériennes 1919–44, and Marguerite Gouin R. Married: (1) . . .; (2) Wanda-Hélène Duda-Ostrowska 1963. Children: 1st marriage—Philippe. Educ: Ecole des Roches, Verneuil-sur-Avre, Normandy, France; Faculté de droit d'Alger; Faculté de droit, Univ. of Paris, docteur en droit 1931; Diplôme, Ecole libre des sciences politiques, Paris. Mil. Service: Decoder during WWII. At Court of Appeals, Algiers and Pres., Assoc. générale des étudiants d'Alger 1931–33; lawyer in Paris ca. 1940–45; philologist and lexicographer since 1945; with Societé du Nouveau Littré: Founder 1951; Pres.-Dir. Gen. 1953–77 then Administrateur-Pres. Member, Conseil International de la langue française. Hons: Laureat de l'Académie d'agriculture 1947; Prix Saintour de l'Académie française 1950; Prix Vaugelas 1967; Medaille de vermeil de la ville de Paris 1975; Officier de la Légion d'honneur; Chevalier des Palmes académiques; Commdr. des Arts et des Lettres; Commdr. de l'ordre du Lion (Sénégal); Officier de l'ordre de Léopold

(Belgium). *Editor and compiler:* Dictionnaire alphabétique et analogique de la langue française (6 vols., Le Grand Robert), 1964, supplement (1 vol.), 1970; Le Petit Robert, 1967, rev. as Le Petit Robert I,
1978; Le Micro-Robert: Dictionnaire du français Primordial (2 vols.),
1971; Dictionnaire universel des noms propres (4 vols.), 1974; Le Petit
Robert II des noms propres (1 vol.), 1974; Robert et Collins, Dictionnaire français-anglais, anglais-français, 1979. *Other:* Divertissements
sur l'amour: Dialogue des grands écrivains, 1951; Aventures et
mésaventures d'un dictionnaire: La genèse d'une oeuvre, 1966; Au fils
des ans et des mots (autobiog. in 2 vols.), Les Semailles, 1979 and Le
Grain et le Chaume, 1980.

SOLOMON GRAYZEL
Editor and authority on Jewish history
Born Minsk, Byelorussia, March 1st, 1896
Died Englewood, New Jersey, U.S.A., August 12th, 1980

Solomon Grayzel was an authority on Jewish history who wrote
primarily about Jewish-Christian relations during the Middle Ages.
Born in Minsk, Grayzel was brought to the United States in 1908 at
the age of 12. After obtaining an undergraduate degree from the City
College of New York and an M.A. from Colombia University,
Grayzel was ordained by the Jewish Theological of America in 1921.
He subsequently became the first rabbi of the Congregation Beth-El
in Camden, New Jersey. Five years later, however, he resigned and
moved to Europe to study the history of European Jewry. In 1927
Grayzel completed his doctorate in history at Dropsie University in
Philadelphia where he joined the faculty of Gratz College. Grayzel
taught there and served as registrar until 1945 when he was elected
president of the Jewish Book Council. In 1966 Grayzel became
professor of history at Dropsie University. He retired in 1978.

Grayzel's first work, *The Church and the Jews in the 13th Century*
(1933)—an expanded version of his doctoral thesis—focused on the
forms of anti-Semitism which, encouraged by the Catholic Church,
became increasingly systematic with the consolidation of Christian
hegemony in 13th century Europe. Analyzing the measures taken by
the papacy to inhibit the spread of Judaism, Grayzel documented the
segregation of Jews from Christians, the elimination of Jews from
positions of political authority, and the denial of property rights to
Jews. Although his study was neither revisionist nor innovative,
scholars applauded Grayzel's thoroughly-researched book. His next
book, *History of the Jews* (1947), which traced Jewish history from the
Babylonian exile to the founding of the state of Israel, became a
popular introduction to Jewish history and achieved many printings.
His last book, *A History of the Contemporary Jews* (1960), dealt with
20th century Jewry, criticized postwar Germany for adopting an
allegedly lenient policy towards war criminals, and expressed an
uncritical enthusiasm for the state of Israel.

Grayzel published numerous articles in such publications as *The
Jewish Quarterly Review* and *Historia Judaica*. He also translated
several books from German into English and, for more than 30 years,
was editor of The Jewish Publication Society of America. At the time

of his death, Grayzel was working on another study of Christians and Jews in the Middle Ages. T.P.

Son of Dov–Behr G. and Eta Kashdan. Married Sophie Solomon 1932. Jewish. Brought to USA 1908. Educ: City Coll. of N.Y., B.A. 1917; Columbia Univ., M.A. 1920; Jewish Theological Seminary, ordained rabbi 1921; Dropsie Univ., Philadelphia, Ph.D. 1927. Conservative rabbi of Congregation Beth–El Synagogue, Camden, N.J. 1921–29; Prof. of Jewish Hist. and Gratz Coll., Philadelphia 1928–45; ed. of Jewish Publication Soc. of America 1939–66; Prof. of Jewish Hist., Dropsie Univ., Philadelphia 1966–78. Pres. Jewish Book Council 1945; Member of Jewish Hist. Soc. *Author:* The Church and the Jews in the 13th Century, 1933; History of the Jews, 1947; A History of the Contemporary Jews, 1960; How the Jewish Present Came Out of the Jewish Past; Jewish Books for Your Home. Contributed to mags. and jrnls. and translated several books from German into English.

KONSTANTIN (NIKILAEVICH) RUDNEV
Minister U.S.S.R
Born Tula, Russia, June 22nd, 1911
Died Moscow, U.S.S.R., August 13th, 1980

Konstantin Rudnev was an important figure during the Khrushchev era in efforts to modernize the Soviet scientific establishment. After graduating from the Tula Mechanics Institute, he advanced through a series of engineering positions to become head of a munitions factory in Tula at the outbreak of World War II. Tula was in the path of the German advance on Moscow, and Rudnev was commended by the Soviet government for supplying vital arms to the front. After the war, he served in the Armaments Ministry.

In 1961 Rudnev took over the chairmanship of the State Committee for the Coordination of Scientific Research. This appointment was part of a thorough reorganization of Soviet scientific activity, which Rudnev helped carry out under Premier Nikita Khrushchev's direction.

Scientific research during the Stalin era had suffered from over-centralization. The Academy of Sciences, based in Moscow, had gradually assumed responsibility for the applied sciences in industry and technology as well as the theoretical sciences. This created bureaucratic inefficiency as research establishments proliferated in the capital, miles away from the centers of their respective industries. Khrushchev, in an effort to decentralize scientific work and create research centers all over the Soviet Union, reduced the Academy to half its size and limited it to the theoretical sciences. Rudnev's duties as chairman of the State Committee focused on improving Soviet military and space technology. He placed great emphasis on automation and encouraged the development of advanced mathematical models which could be applied in many industries. Closely connected with this was a drive for the application of computer technology.

Reform of the scientific apparatus was not easy, however. Few would give up their positions in Moscow and go to the hinterlands as part of the decentralization plan. When faced with a choice, many actually preferred to remain in the capital at a less responsible job. As a result, although the number of agencies in the Academy of Sciences had been halved, its personnel declined only by some 25 percent. In an article in *Pravda,* Rudnev criticized this and admitted that he had to "coax" even members of his own staff to work according to the new principles. In 1962 Rudnev survived politically unscathed when an assistant department head of the State Committee was arrested as an American spy.

Soviet scientific policy again shifted in 1965, when newly-installed Premier Alexei Kosygin reinstated some of the scientists and technocrats demoted by Khrushchev. Closely identified with the old policy, Rudnev lost his position at the State Committee for the Coordination of Scientific Research. But his experience was still valued, and he became head of the Ministry of Instrumentation, Automation Means and Control Systems. In his new post, Rudnev strongly promoted the use of computers and mathematical models to forecast Soviet economic growth and so improve industrial planning. He also urged greater stress on the training of technicians able to operate automated systems.

Soviet leaders were aware of Rudnev's importance in the development of modern applied scientific research. Press announcements of his death praised his "great contribution to strengthening of the country's defensive might, the development of missiles and space technology and the advancement of Soviet instrument making." H.S.

Educ: Tula Mechanical Inst., grad. 1935. Electrical fitter and electrician, Bubriki Mine, Tula 1929–30; Designer and Chief Engineer, design section 1935–40 and Chief Engineer and Dir. of munitions plant, Tula 1940–47; Chmn., Exec. Bd. of Collegium of the Ministry of Armaments 1948–52 and Deputy Minister of Armaments 1952–53; Deputy Minister of Defense Technology 1953–58; Deputy Chmn. then Chmn. (with rank of Minister), State Cttee. for Defense Technology 1958–61; Deputy Chmn., Council of Ministers and Chmn., State Cttee. for the Coordination of Scientific Research 1961–65; Minister of Instrument-Making, Automation Equipment and Control Systems since 1965. Became Member 1941 and Member, Central Cttee. Communist Party of the Soviet Union 1961; Deputy Supreme Soviet 1962, 1966. Hons: Hero of Socialist Labor 1961; six Orders of Lenin; Order of the October Revolution; two Orders of the Red Banner of Labor; Order of the Patriotic War (2nd class); Hammer and Sickle Gold Medal; others.

ALBERT E(DWARD) SCHEFLEN
Psychiatrist and behavioral anthropologist
Born Camden, New Jersey, U.S.A., November 15th, 1920
Died Chester, Pennsylvania, U.S.A., August 14th, 1980

Dr. Albert E. Scheflen contributed significantly to scholarship and research in the field of human communications, and helped to define human communications as a complex set of interactions which produce non-verbal codes as well as linguistic forms of behavior.

Born in Camden, New Jersey, in 1920, Scheflen received his undergraduate education at Dickinson College and his medical training at the University of Pennsylvania Medical School. He served in the United States Navy as a shipboard medical officer and psychiatrist, and afterwards spent several years conducting research in neurophysiology and neuropathology. After training at the Philadelphia Psychoanalytic Institute during the early 1950s, he opened a private practice and also began to study psycholinguistics and semantics.

At about this time Scheflen and other researchers, questioning the value of subjective reports about what actually happened in psychotherapy sessions, began to explore the problems of psychotherapy research. However, they were unable to discover reliable statistical methods of observing and recording the psychotherapy process. In 1955 Scheflen and other scientists were invited by Dr. John Rosen to observe and report on his psychotherapy techniques for schizophrenic patients. Each trained observer interpreted the sessions differently and they were unable to arrive at a consensus conclusion about the experiments. In 1956 they began to film psychotherapy sessions and Scheflen quickly realized that film was a valuable aid for understanding human communication. Scheflen reported his observations in *A Psychotherapy of Schizophrenia: Direct Analysis* (1960).

In 1959 Scheflen and the anthropologist, Dr. Ray Birdwhistell, devised a project for studying communications in psychotherapy and in other forms of human interaction through the context analysis of films. Their methodology blended behaviorism with certain aspects of structural linguistics. Given this approach, they viewed human communications as a complex network of behavioral patterns which the individuals of a shared culture use as a code to convey meaning. Thus, gesticulation, facial movement, touch, interpersonal space, odor, and so forth, become ways of embellishing and altering verbal forms of communication. After having observed, filmed and written extensively about three psychotherapy sessions with a schizophrenic woman, Scheflen, in his preface to *Communicational Structure: Analysis of a Psychotherapy Transaction*, said, "The major effort of ten years of my career has been the analysis of this thirty minute transaction . . . ."

In his best-known book, *How Behavior Means*, Scheflen continued his study of the ways in which body movement and posture modify the meaning of words. The book, one in a series entitled *Social Change*, is representative of Scheflen's work in the last decade of his life. In the 1970s, Scheflen studied territorial and communicational behaviors in the ghettos of New York City. He had become increasingly concerned with social problems such as racism, over-population, pollution, and urban decay, and his work clarified the complex relationships between human communication theories and contemporary political structures. Scheflen wrote: "The armchair notion that behavior is simply an expression of individual motives or emotions keeps alive a suppressive and controlling social mechanism. It allows us to attribute social and economic problems to the perversity of various individuals, factions or ethnic groups. Then by blaming these people we can not only justify discrimination but avoid the necessity of taking any real measures to (solve) the problems."

During the last decade of his life Dr. Scheflen served as Professor of Psychiatry at Albert Einstein College of Medicine. He conducted research at the Bronx Psychiatric Center, and was a consultant at the

Harlem Valley Psychiatric Center and the Nathan Ackerman Family
Institute. J.C.

Educ: Dickinson Coll., N.J.; Univ. of Pennsylvania Medical Sch.,
M.D.; Philadelphia Psychoanalytic Inst. Mil. Service: U.S. Navy,
shipboard medical officer and psychiatrist. Opened private practice
early 1950s; conducted research and studied psycholinguistics, semantics, psychotherapy, communications and territorial behavior from
early 1950s; Prof. of psychiatry, Albert Einstein Coll. of Medicine
1970s. Consultant, Harlem Valley Psychiatric Center and Nathan
Ackerman Family Inst. *Author:* A Psychotherapy of Schizophrenia:
Direct Analysis, 1960; Communicational Structure: Analysis of a
Psychotherapy Transaction; How Behavior Means.

WILLIAM HOOD SIMPSON
Army Officer
Born Weatherford, Texas, U.S.A., May 19th, 1888
Died San Antonio, Texas, U.S.A., August 15th, 1980

A brilliant military tactician, General William Hood Simpson—
"Texas Bill" to his troops—commanded the Ninth Army on its drive
into the heart of Germany in World War Two, securing victory for the
Allies in the European campaign. One of the last surviving commanders of the war, Simpson's military career began with his participation
in General John J. Pershing's 1916 Punitive Expedition against the
revolutionary leader Pancho Villa in Mexico.

Simpson, the son of a Civil War veteran had set his mind on a
military career at the age of ten and, in 1909, he graduated from West
Point. Assistant Chief of Staff of the 33rd Division in France during
World War One, by 1944 Simpson rose to Lieutenant General and
Commander of the Fourth Army, then stationed at Ft. Sam Houston,
Texas. When the Fourth was renamed the Eighth and ordered to
Europe (where it became the Ninth to avoid confusion with the British
Eighth Army), Simpson seized the strategic port of Brest and began
the drive through France, Belgium and the Netherlands, and on to
Germany.

Gains were counted in yards rather than miles, and the Germans
bunched as much as 40 percent of their forces, including most of their
best troops, to resist the assault of the Ninth. On February 23rd, 1945,
the First and Ninth Armies nevertheless surged forward across the
flooded Ruhr valley and reached the Rhine just 60 hours later.
Simpson believed that his troops were then in a position to take
Berlin, but Supreme Allied Headquarters halted them at the Elbe,
leaving the job to the Red Army.

As commander of the Ninth, Simpson was responsible for 13
divisions and 341,000 troops. Stressing the "spiritual as well as mental
and physical preparation for the ordeal of battle," the Doughboy
General, as he was also known, was well-liked by his field officers and
troops, whose advice he sought on many aspects of strategy. Simpson
is said to have visited virtually every unit of the Ninth by jeep or
plane. Known for his thoroughness of preparation, he once required a
minimum of 40 complete plans for a single aspect of his assault on
Germany's western fortifications.

An entertaining raconteur, he became an accomplished public speaker and was in great demand after he became Vice President of a San Antonio bank upon retirement. Though he had already won a Distinguished Service Medal, Silver Star, Croix de Guerre and Legion of Honor, he formally received four-star rank in 1954 when Congress and President Eisenhower enacted special legislation on behalf of 11 generals whose promotions, because of "administrative delays and the press of World War Two," had been hindered.

Twenty years after retiring from military life in 1946, Simpson returned to public attention. He vigorously defended the Ninth Army after the military historian S.L.A. Marshall argued that, because of strong German resistance, American forces were in no shape to seize Berlin. In a rebuttal in the *New York Times Book Review* Simpson stated that German resistance had "completely lost cohesion," and that German units wanted to surrender to American rather than Russian troops. Had permission been given, Simpson said, the Ninth was prepared to press on to Berlin. General Dwight D. Eisenhower's decision was "accepted by all in good grace," he wrote, "albeit with a certain amount of disappointment."   A.C.

Son of Edward James S., Civil War veteran, and Elizabeth Amelia (Hood) S. Married: (1) Ruth Webber Krakauer (d. 1971); (2) Catherine Berman. Children: Mrs. Jerome S. Vincent. Educ: U.S. Military Acad., West Point, N.Y., grad 1909; Infantry Sch., War Dept., Ft. Benning, Ga. 1924; Command and General Staff Sch., Ft. Leavenworth, Kans 1925. 6th Infantry, Philippines 1910–12; Presidio, San Francisco 1912–14; Mexican Punitive Expedition 1916; Asst. Chief of Staff (as Capt. and later Maj. and Lt.-Col.), 33rd Div. 1917–18; Chief of Staff, 6th Div., Camp Grant, Ill. 1919; reverted to capt. and promoted to maj. 1920; Comdr., battalion of 12th Infantry, Md. 1925–27; Army War Coll. 1928; Gen Staff 1932; faculty, mil. science and tactics, Pomono Coll. 1932–26; Lt.-Col. 1934 and Col. 1936–40, Army War Coll.; Comdr., 9th Infantry, Ft. Sam Houston, Tex. 1940; Temporary Brig,-Gen., Asst. Comdr., 2nd Div., Ft. Sam Houston 1940; Comdr., Camp Wolters, Tex; Temporary Maj.-Gen. and Comdr, 35th Div., Camp Robinson, Ark.; in Calif. after U.S. entry into WWII; Comdr., 30th Div. and XII Corps, Ft. Jackson, S.C. 1942; Temporary Lt.-Gen., Fourth Army (later the Eighth and then the Ninth), San Jose, Calif. 1943 and Ft. Sam Houston 1944; Comdr., Ninth Army, France 1944–45; Comdr., 2nd Army, Memphis and Baltimore 1946. Became V.P., Alamo Natl. Bank of San Antonio, Tex. upon retirement in 1946. Hons: Silver Star 1918; Distinguished Service Medal; Croix de Guerre; Legion of Honor; knighted OBE.

JAMES B(ERNARD) LONGLEY
Governor of Maine and businessman
Born Lewiston, Maine, U.S.A., April 22nd, 1924
Died Lewiston, Maine, U.S.A., August 16th, 1980

James B. Longley of Maine, the only independent candidate elected governor of any state in four decades, prided himself on being a politician "who kept his word." He served as governor from 1975 until 1979.

Having established himself as a successful insurance broker and tax expert, Longley came to public attention as a member of the Maine Management and Cost Survey Commission, a state-authorized group of business leaders who recommended ways to streamline state government. Frustrated when his group's proposals, aimed at saving taxpayers $28 million per annum, were ignored or rejected, Longley resigned from the Democratic party and offered himself as an independent candidate for governor in 1974. Winning 40 percent of the votes, he astonished political observers by defeating both his Republican and Democratic opponents.

As governor of Maine, Longley faced a Democratic–controlled House and a Republican Senate. This legislative opposition made it difficult for him to make good on campaign pledges which included substantial reductions in the costs of state government, revitalizing Maine's sagging economy, and lowering state taxes. Vetoing more legislation than any governor in the state's history—49 bills in 1977 alone, 22 of which were overridden—Longley nevertheless won approval for much of his program. During his term, Longley reduced the number of state employees by 15 percent and, exercising strong control over state finances, he personally examined all applications for federal funds. He rejected many of these applications, including one for federal money to help disabled Vietnam veterans find employment; instead, Longley organized a program which sought to accomplish the same goal through volunteer efforts. Despite reductions in state spending, social services in the state remained well-funded and Longley's welfare commissioner was able to establish a health insurance program. During his final year in office Longley pushed through legislation to provide over $40 million in tax rebates.

Longley's single-minded pursuit of these goals was at times highly controversial. Early in his administration some newspaper reporters dubbed the new governor "El Wacko" and other critics objected to what they considered his high-minded methods. His willingness to set a personal example in reducing unnecessary public expenditures, however, was quite popular; he reduced the budget for the governor's mansion by $13,853 and declined the traditional inaugural ball.

By the end of his term Longley was enormously popular with the state's voters and he had won the respect of opponents in the legislature. As the 1978 election approached, polls showed that he could defeat any challenger by a two-to-one margin. Although countless newspaper editorials and letters urged him to seek re-election, Longley declined, having pledged to serve only one term. "Nothing we might accomplish in a second term would be as important as a clear demonstration that this governor continues to keep his word," he announced. Every gubernatorial candidate in the state sought his endorsement.

At the time of his death from cancer at the age of 56, Longley served as co-chairman of the National Taxpayers Union's drive for a constitutional amendment mandating a balanced federal budget. According to John Martin, the Democratic speaker of the house during Longley's administration, Longley's legacy was that, "he finally made people realize that whatever they get from government they have to pay for."   A.C.

Son of Bernard L. and Catherine (Wade) L. Married Helen Walsh. Children: James B.; Susan M.; Kathryn; Steven J.; Nancy. Mil.

Service: U.S. Army Air Force, WWII. Catholic. Educ: Bowdoin Coll., Maine 1947; American Coll. of Life Underwriters, CLU 1954; Univ. of Maine Law Sch., LL.B. 1957. Gen. agent, New England Mutual Life Insurance Co., Boston; Partner, Longley and Buckley; Pres., Longley Assoc.; Governor of Maine 1974–79. Member, Million Dollar Round Table and Maine and American Bar Assn; Co-Chmn., Natl. Taxpayers Union. Hons: Lucien Howe Prize, Bowdoin Coll. 1947; President's Trophy Award, New England Life, three-time winner.

WILLIAM (TINSLEY) KEETON
Zoologist and neurobiologist
Born Roanoke, Virginia, U.S.A., February 3rd, 1933
Died Ithaca, New York, U.S.A., August 17th, 1980

The experimental zoologist, William Keeton, identified new species of millipedes and conducted important research into homing pigeon behavior. His pioneering work led scientists to revise their conceptions of how birds select their course and orient themselves when flying.

Keeton received two bachelor's degrees from the University of Chicago and a master's from Virginia Polytechnic Institute. He went on to Cornell University where he obtained his doctorate in 1958. He then joined the Cornell faculty and during the next decade, further developed the investigations he had conducted for his dissertation, "A Taxonomic Study of the Family Spirobolidae." Through his research into natural evolutionary (phylogenetic) relationships within the millipede genus, he revised its classification and described three new species.

In 1966 Keeton published the first edition of *Biological Science,* an introductory college textbook which explained biological systems in the light of modern evolutionary theory. Areas where recent research had made great advances—such as photosynthesis, cellular ultrastructure, molecular genetics and embryological development—were given extensive coverage. Now in its third edition, the book is widely used both as a basic text and for general reference purposes.

Keeton released his first study on homing pigeon behavior in 1969. He demonstrated that while it is true untrained pigeons need the sun for orientation, a trained pigeon will find its way even on an overcast day—thereby suggesting that the birds develop other navigational means. Keeton's further research focused on pigeons' sensitivity to minute changes in the locale's magnetic field, and on the birds' sense of smell. During 1969 and 1970 he staged experiments in which magnets were attached to the heads of pigeons. The results were astonishing. Trained pigeons, previously exhibiting a homing ability even without the sun, suddenly became disoriented and many pigeons were lost. Keeton concluded that the pigeon's perception of the normal fluctuations in the earth's magnetic field was a part of the complex system by which it plotted its direction and kept on course. (Very recent experiments indicate that people may also possess a home-directional "instinct" aided by the earth's magnetic field.)

Assisted by his Cornell colleagues and co-worker Melvin Kreithen,

Keeton, now a full professor and Chairman of Cornell's Department of Neurobiology, directed research which showed that ultra-violet and polarized light, barometric pressure changes, and low-frequency sounds inaudible to humans, were seen, felt, and heard by birds. Researchers are now investigating the significance of these perceptions for a bird's orientation and navigation.

An internationally-known expert in his field, Dr. Keeton traveled to many states in his researches and lectured widely, both at home and abroad. He had contracted rheumatic fever at an early age which brought on a heart condition requiring two open-heart operations. He died of heart failure at the age of 47. His colleague, Dr. Thomas Eisner, described Keeton as "a major conceptual beacon for us here at Cornell."   R.T.

Son of William Ivie K. and Doris (Tinsley) K. Married Barbara Sue Borcutt 1958. Children: Lynn Sue; Nancy Lee; William Scott. Educ: Univ. of Chicago, B.A. 1952, B.S. 1954; Virginia Polytechnic Inst., M.S. 1956; Cornell Univ., Ithaca, N.Y., Ph.D. entomology 1958. Teacher's Asst., Virginia Polytechnic Inst. 1955–56; Instr., Radford Coll., Va. 1956. With Cornell Univ.: Schuyler Gage Fellow 1956–58; Asst. Prof. 1958–59; Assoc. Prof. 1959–69; Prof. 1969–76; Chmn., Dept of Neurobiology 1970–76; Liberty Hyde Prof. since 1977. Consultant, N.Y. Dept. of Education 1961–66. Guest Prof.: Max-Planck Inst. of Physiology, West Germany 1972–73; Inst. of Biology, Pisa 1977; Univ. of Konstanz, West Germany 1978–79. Pres., Periculum Corp., Ithaca, N.Y.; Member, Bd. of Dirs., Cornell Univ. Ornithology Lab. 1971–77; Council Member, American Assoc. for the Advancement of Science 1963–73. Member: American Entomological Soc.; Soc. of Systematic Zoology; American Ornithology Union; Wilson Ornithology Soc.; American Inst. of Biological Science; Soc. for Study of Evolution; American Soc. of Zoologists; British Ornithology Soc.; N.Y. Acad. of Sciences; Sigma Xi; Phi Kappa Phi; Phi Gamma Delta; Gamma Alpha. Fellow, American Assoc. for the Advancement of Science; Hon. Member, Alpha Zeta. *Author: Books* —Biological Science, 1966, 3rd ed. 1980; Elements of Biological Science, 1968, 2nd ed. 1973. Also many articles in his fields.

M(ORRIS) MURRAY PESHKIN
Pediatric allergist
Born New York City, U.S.A., May 23rd, 1892
Died New York City, U.S.A., August 17th, 1980

Several million children wheeze and cough from dust, pollen, and animal fur, but only a handful have chronic asthma so severe that it stunts their physical and emotional growth or even kills them. Murray Peshkin, a New York pediatrician who once suffered from asthma himself, spent the better part of his life focusing on the problems of these seemingly incurable patients. And though his famous treatment—parentectomy—remains controversial in many circles, he did much to legitimize the notion that severe asthma, like many other diseases, often has psychosomatic roots.

Parentectomy, which involves removing asthmatic children to healthier environments and away from their parents for up to two

years, was a term coined by Dr. Peshkin after many years as a pediatrician at the Children's Allergy Clinic of Mount Sinai Hospital in New York City. When Murray Peshkin graduated from Fordham Medical School in 1914, the connection between allergies and asthma was just gaining credence, but the idea that an asthmatic paroxysm might also be connected to the complicated relationship between mother and child seemed too far-fetched for most doctors of the period; psychotherapy in general enjoyed little support in the organized medical establishment.

But Dr. Peshkin noticed something odd about many of his patients: their asthma almost always improved after a few nights in the hospital and invariably worsened in even the most antiseptic of homes. With the encouragement and guidance of Viennese diphtheria specialist Dr. Bela Schick, director of Mount Sinai's pediatric department in the 1920s, Peshkin finally put together enough evidence to advocate parentectomy as a cure for what he called "intractable asthma."

His paper, first published in the *Journal of Diseases of Children* in the 1930s, blamed parents ("mostly mama") for either neglecting or smothering a child to such an extent that asthma became a psychological weapon. Dr. Peshkin's solution was, for the child, a "warm emotional climate with sympathetic mother and father figures," far from home, and for the adults, some fairly intensive therapy during the absence of their offspring.

Although Mount Sinai's allergist was becoming increasingly well-known, it was ten years before he had a chance to put his theories into practice, at a treatment center in Denver. The Jewish National Home for Asthmatic Children (later, the Children's Asthma Research Institute and Hospital) was known in medical clinics as "the home of last resort." Children who did not respond to shots or carefully controlled diets and who seemed unlikely ever to lead normal lives were sent to the Denver home; almost all of the several thousand children Dr. Peshkin treated during his 22-year tenure with the facility returned home after 18 to 24 months, healthy and energetic for the first time in their lives. More important, close to 85 percent suffered no relapses. While asthma cannot be fully cured, because the allergy never disappears entirely, Dr. Peshkin proved that with proper treatment the vast majority of asthmatics, even the intractable ones, can keep asthma attacks under control.

Before he left Denver in 1962 to form his own clinics and foundation in Ossining, New York, Peshkin was active in founding a number of important scientific bodies, including the American College of Allergists, the American Association for the Study of Allergy, and the American Academy of Psychosomatic Medicine. He was also associate editor of the *Journal of the Children's Asthma Research Institute and Hospital* in Denver in 1961–62 and when it became the *Journal of Asthma Research,* based in Baltimore, he continued as a regular contributor. In addition, he taught several courses at Yeshiva University and Mount Sinai's medical school during the late 1950s and 60s.

With the establishment of the Asthma Care Association of America in Ossining in 1965, Dr. Peshkin continued to pour his energies into allergy and asthma, but he also began taking more time off for his other interests, which included Jewish philanthropies, music, fishing, and the race track. In November 1979, he suffered a heart attack from which he never fully recovered.

Children remember Dr. Peshkin as gentle and sensitive; adults recall a tougher, more pugnacious man. Pallbearers were dismayed to discover at the end of Peshkin's burial service that the grave was not large enough for the coffin. The final blessing was delayed while new ground was broken. "That was just like Murray," one close former associate maintained, "never giving up without a fight."   A.B.P.

Son of Zelick P., stable and garage owner, and Goldie Feigen P. Married Lillian Rapaport 1921. No children. Jewish. Educ: attended City Coll. of New York; Long Island Coll. of Medicine (now part of State Univ. of New York) 1910–12; Fordham Univ. Sch. of Medicine, M.D. 1914. Mil. Service: 1st Lt., U.S. Army, Ft. Slocum, N.Y. 1917. Intern, St. Michael's Hosp., Newark, N.J. 1915. With Mt. Sinai Hosp., NYC: Asst. Pediatrician 1915–25; Chief, Children's Allergy Clinic 1926–52; Assoc. Pediatrician 1942–52; Consulting Allergist 1952–79. Attending Allergist, Jewish Memorial Hosp., NYC 1938–40; Chief Medical Consultant, Jewish Natl. Home for Asthmatic Children (now Children's Asthma Research Inst. and Hosp.), Denver 1940–62; Attending Allergist, Bronx Municipal Hosp. Center 1954–60. Clinical Prof., Dept. of Pediatrics and Allergy, Albert Einstein Coll. of Medicine, Yeshiva Univ. 1954–60; Emergency Clinic Prof., Dept. of Pediatrics, Mt. Sinai Hosp. Sch. of Medicine, City Univ. of New York 1967–68. Founder and Chief Medical Consultant, Asthmatic Children's Foundn. of New York, Ossining since 1963; Founder, Assn. of Convalescent Home and Hosps. for Asthmatic Children (now Assn. for the Care of Asthma) 1963; Founder, and Chief Medical Consultant since 1963, Asthmatic Children's Foundn. Residential Treatment Center, North Miami Beach, Fla. since 1963; Medical Consultant, Illinois Foundn. for Asthma 1963–64; Chief Medical Consultant, Women's Service for Asthma since 1964. Founder, and Pres. 1935–36, American Assn. for the Study of Allergy; Founder, and Pres. 1953–54, American Coll. of Allergists; Secty. and Trustee, Allergy Foundn. of America 1956–63; Pres., American Acad. of Psychosomatic Medicine, N.Y. 1963–64; Founder, Pres. 1965–80, and Pres. Emeritus May–Aug. 1980, Asthma Care Assn. of America; Founder, Collegium Internationale Allergolicum and Philanthropic Orgs. for Rehabilitation of Chronic Asthmatic Child. Assoc. Ed., Journal of the Children's Asthma Research Institute and Hospital (now Journal of Asthma Research) 1961–62. Member: Asthma Publication Soc.; American Coll. of Physicians; American Acad. of Allergy; N.Y. Allergy Soc.; American Geriatric Soc.; American Acad. of Compensation Medicine; American Assn. for the Advancement of Science; N.Y. Acad. of Science; Friar's Club; Rod and Gun Club; Mason. Hons: Metropolitan Areas Chapter of the Jewish Natl. Home for Asthmatic Children at Denver 1955; Humanitarian Award for Pioneer Accomplishment 1956; Henry Hyde Salter Clinical Award, Tokyo 1973; Distinguished Service Award, Mt. Sinai Hosp. 1980; American Coll. of Allergists awards, NYC mayoral award, Wagner admin.; Hon. Member, French Allergy Soc.; Hon. Pres., Music Lovers League Inc. and Soc. for the Aid of Crippled in Israel. Contributed regularly to Journal of Asthma Research, American Journal of Diseases of Children, Allergology, and other medical jrnls. Contributed chapters to Psychosomatic Approach to Problems and Treatment, 1938; Progress in Allergy, 1952; The Asthmatic Child; and other medical texts.
Further reading: "The Story of Parentectomy" by George Robinson in the Journal of Asthma Research, June, 1972.

RAS HAILE SELASSIE IMRU
Diplomat, military leader and provincial governor
Born Shoa, Ethiopia, 1892
Died Addis Ababa, Ethiopia, August 17th, 1980

Ras Imru, a cousin of the Emperor Haile Selassie, commanded the Ethiopian army when his country was invaded by Italian armed forces in 1935. He had also been a liberal and highly popular, governor of the Harrar, Wollo, and Gojjam Provinces.

Haile Selassie Imru was born of the noble Modja family in Shoa, and attended school with Ras Tafari, the future emperor. When Ras Tafari challenged the rule of Emperor Eyasu, he received the support of Imru, who was briefly imprisoned for participating in the revolt. In 1918 Imru was appointed provincial governor of Harrar and he then accepted the designation Ras, a title of nobility equivalent to a dukedom. Ras Imru became known as a progressive governor and helped establish an Ethiopian civil service system to counteract the feudal power of the local nobility. In 1930, his cousin became Emperor Haile Selassie.

When the Italian army invaded Ethiopia in late 1935, the Empire's military forces were unprepared for modern warfare. Imru's troops were untrained and equipped with obsolete weapons; at first the Italians advanced at will but Imru launched an attack on their northern flank which halted the invader's progress. When his forces scored a stunning victory at the Dembeguina Pass near Aksum, the Italians were impeded for three months. In early March, however, Imru's ragtag army was routed. The emperor, forced to flee, appointed Ras Imru regent. The Ethiopians rallied until December when the Italian military overran the capital at Gore. Ras Imru was held captive on Ponza Island, off the Italian coast, until 1942.

In the postwar period Imru clashed with Emperor Haile Selassie over the question of land reform. A socialist, he believed the emperor was moving too slowly in the redistribution of land. Because of Ras Imru's popularity, the emperor appointed him to an ambassadorial post in Washington, D.C., to neutralize his political efficacy. Ras Imru later served as ambassador to India and the Soviet Union.

In late 1960 Ras Imru participated in an abortive coup against Haile Selassie. After a brief period of imprisonment, Ras Imru was pardoned by the emperor. Ras Imru's son, Lij Mikhael, also an opponent of the authoritarian rule of Haile Selassie, became Prime Minister for a brief period in 1974.   I.J.

Alternative spellings: Immeru, Emmerou, Imrou. Son of Dedjazmatch Haile Selassie Abayana. Married Princess Rosemary Sigemariam. Children: Lij Mikhael, Prime Minister of Ethiopia July–Sept. 1974, b. 1930; Judith, served as Vice-Minister for Foreign Affairs; one other daughter. Educ: Menelik 11 Sch., Addis Ababa. Gov.: Harrar Province 1918–29; Wollo Province 1929–32; Gojjam Province 1932–35. Comdr.-in-Chief of Ethiopian Army 1935–36 and of all Ethiopian Forces 1936; captured by Italian armed forces 1936, imprisoned until 1942; Gov. Gen., Begemidir and Simen 1944; Minister to Washington 1946–49; Ambassador-at-large 1949–53; Ambassador to India 1954–60, and to USSR 1961. Author: Fitawrari Belay, 1961.
Further reading: The Ethiopian War by Angelo del Boca, 1969.

E(VAN) R(OY) CAMPBELL
High Commissioner for Southern Rhodesia (now Zimbabwe) in the
U.K., farmer and businessman
Born Johannesburg, South Africa, September 2nd, 1908
Died Salisbury, Zimbabwe, August 20th, 1980

Evan Roy Campbell was a farmer and banker, and briefly, a Rhodesian diplomat who held the key position of High Commissioner in London during a volatile period in his country's history.

Born in Johannesburg in 1908, Campbell graduated from St. Andrew's College, Grahamstown, and the Potchefstroom Agricultural College. In 1931 he emigrated to Southern Rhodesia, settling in Umvukwes. He became a tobacco farmer and moved to Inyazura in 1935. During the Second World War, he enlisted in the Rhodesian Regiment and was seconded to the King's African Rifles, serving in Abyssinia, Burma, and India. He achieved the rank of major in the East Africa Infantry Brigade, and when the war was over, he returned to tobacco farming in Imyazura and became a prominent business-man.

Campbell stood unsuccessfully for Sir Roy Welensky's United Federal Party as a candidate for the Federal Assembly in 1957; his opponent, Winston Field of the Dominion Party, later became Prime Minister. It was Field who brought Campbell to the forefront of Rhodesian politics by appointing him, in January 1964, as High Commissioner in London. Before Campbell's appointment, the Federation of Rhodesia and Nyasaland had been dissolved (1963) creating serious diplomatic problems between Salisbury and London. These problems were exacerbated by Rhodesia' pro-white racial policies, and the idea of the country breaking with the U.K. (it was at that time a self-governing colony within the Commonwealth) gained currency in Rhodesian political circles. However, Campbell was adamantly opposed to this idea, and found himself in a difficult situation, which only worsened when Ian Smith was elected Prime Minister of Rhodesia in April 1964. He nevertheless performed the duties required of him as envoy, and in May 1965, despite his own views on the subject, bluntly told Britain that if independence were not granted, Rhodesia might make a "unilateral declaration of independence" (UDI) before the year was out. He returned to Rhodesia in June 1965, and five months later, UDI became a reality.

Campbell was named Chairman of the Rhodesian Board of Stan-dard bank in the year of his return, and held other chairmanships and several directorships. Regarded as a shrewd and politically moderate man, Campbell retained a considerable influence among the white population of Rhodesia. He died four months after his country became the Republic of Zimbabwe.   R.T.

Married Norah May Vaughan 1934. One son; one daughter. Emigra-ted to Southern Rhodesia 1931. Educ: St. Andrew's Coll., Grahams-town, South Africa; Potchefstroom Agricultural Coll., South Africa. Mil. Service: Enlisted in Rhodesia Regiment 1940; seconded to King's African Rifles, serving in Abyssinia, Burma, and India; graduated Staff Coll., Quetta, Pakistan 1944; Gen. Staff Officer, East Africa Div.; Brigade Maj., East Africa Infantry Brigade. Started farming in Umvukwes, Southern Rhodesia 1931; farmed in Inyazura 1935–65; High Commissioner in Great Britain for Southern Rhodesia 1964–65; Gov., Peterhouse Sch. Chmn.: Rhodesian Bd., Standard Bank Ltd.

since 1965; Rhodesia Fertilizer Corp. Ltd; Albatros Fisons Fertilizers
Holdings Ltd.; Fisons Pest Control Ltd.; Murray and Roberts Rho-
desia Ltd.; Central African Branch of Inst. of Dirs.; Manica Freight
Services Ltd., Rhodesia; Standard Finance Ltd.; and other com-
panies. Dir.: Tanganda Tea Co.; Discount Co. of Rhodesia; Messina
Rhodesia Investments; Sable Chemical Industries; and other com-
panies. With Rhodesia Tobacco Assn.: Member 1946; V.P. 1947;
Pres. 1952–1958; Life V.P. Chmn., Makoni Branch and Member
Council, British Empire Service League, 1947; Chmn., Tobacco
Export Promotion Council 1958; Chmn., Gwebi Agricultural Coll.
Council 1963; Pres., First Intnl. Tobacco Congress; Life V.P.,
Manicaland Agricultural Show Soc. Member, Tobacco Marketing Bd.
1950. Hons: C.B.E. 1958; Farmers' Oscar for Outstanding Services to
agriculture; British Empire Service League meritorious service medal
1962.

DAME LUCY SUTHERLAND
Historian and Principal of Lady Margaret Hall, Oxford
Born Geelong, Victoria, Australia, June 21st, 1903
Died Oxford, England, August 20th, 1980

Lucy Stuart Sutherland was born in the small Australian seaport town
of Geelong, near Melbourne. Her mother's family had been prominent in eighteenth-century London, and her father was a mining
engineer of Scottish descent. When Lucy was very young her family
moved to Johannesburg, South Africa where she soon distinguished
herself in her studies at the Roedean School and the University of the
Witwatersrand, where she graduated with honors in 1925.

At age 22 Lucy Sutherland left South Africa with her new M.A. to
become a B.A. in Modern History at Somerville College, Oxford.
Perhaps her early and lasting affection for Oxford owed a great deal to
her tutors, Maude Clarke, and her successor, May McKisack, both
gifted medieval scholars. After only two years at Somerville, and
before her Final Examination, Sutherland was elected to an assistant
tutorship. There she spent the next 12 years in charge of students
reading philosophy, politics and economics. She was given much of
the credit for the high reputation of this school, for which she was also
examiner from 1937–40. Her career as a historian was already taking
shape. Her first article was about Burke ("the ablest man of the
eighteenth century").

Sutherland's first book, *A London Merchant (1695–1774),* published in 1933, was based on the papers and ledgers of one William
Braund, merchant, financier, shipowner and shipping insurer.

In Sutherland's hands, Braund's ventures illustrate the mobility of
eighteenth-century commerce as well as the adaptability of a typically
skillful and vigilant merchant, a man who knew how to profit from his
opportunities. Through Braund, Sutherland was able to show the
strength of the more or less anonymous individual as part of the larger
financial and legal system growing up in London.

In the mid-1930s Lucy Sutherland took a slight diversion from her
studies of the eighteenth century to edit and complete the last two
books of her former tutor, Maude Clarke. With the help of May

McKisack she published Clarke's *Medieval Representation and Consent* in 1936 and her collection of shorter pieces, *Fourteenth Century Studies* in 1937. And in 1938 she (with the aid of Helen Cam and Mary Coate) completed the late Ada E. Levett's *Studies in Manorial History*, which described the day-to-day workings of St. Albans Abbey in the thirteenth and fourteenth centuries.

After these projects Sutherland returned to her investigations of the economics and politics of the eighteenth century. In 1939 she began work on her classic study, *The East India Company in Eighteenth Century Politics*. Before it could be completed, however, World War Two broke out. Sutherland joined the Temporary Civil Service in 1941 as Principal, then Assistant Secretary at the Board of Trade, in the department allocating scarce iron and steel production. After the War she was appointed Chairman of the Lace Working Party, one of a number of government committees created at the Board of Trade to spur the resurrection of key British industries.

It was in 1945 that she left the Board of Trade to succeed Mary L.D. Grier as Principal of Lady Margaret Hall, Oxford. It was under Sutherland's tenure that Lady Margaret Hall was able to demonstrate that its standards and results were equal to those of the men's colleges.

During this period Sutherland did not abandon her commitment to government and public service. She served on the United Nations Relief and Rehabilitation Administration, the Royal Commission on Taxation of Profits and Income, and other Commissions. She was also elected a member of the Hebdomadal Council, Oxford's governing body, from 1953 to 1971.

As result of all this activity, her book on the East India Company did not appear until 1952. But in the judgment of the Times Literary Supplement it was worth waiting for: "a piece of historical research so thorough and comprehensive, so masterly and lucid in its presentation, that it must rank among the foremost works on the period." Earlier histories of 18th-century trade between England and the East Indies tended to focus on a few great figures and their exploits, but the history of the Company itself (its management, negotiations, internal struggles, relations with government and parliament, etc.) had never been attempted. Sutherland was able to put an otherwise disjointed sequence of events and personalities into perspective. The story of the Company at home and overseas is also the story of the development of capitalism in England and the government in India.

Sutherland spent the next few years dealing with the more prosaic problems of running a growing University College. Although she finally realized her dream of full status for women students there were still the problems of resources, finances, building programs, curricula and so on. Between 1952 and her retirement in 1971 she was able to complete only one other project, the second volume of Edmund Burke's *Correspondence*, published in 1960.

After her retirement she published a slim volume which united her two great passions in life, *The University at Oxford in the Eighteenth Century* (1973). Although this period of Oxford's history was not highly regarded, she managed to find satisfaction in the progress of students away from a "stultifying curriculum" and instead "to find out things for themselves."

She spent the last years of her retirement enjoying her favorite pleasures, reading and travelling. When in Oxford she was always available to her old colleagues for tea and conversation, which was prized for her vitality of intellect and good humor. Her last project was a volume to be titled *The City of London in Eighteenth Century Politics,* testament to her inexhaustable fascination with that period of British history.   M.M.

Daughter of Alexander Charles S., civil engineer and public servant, and Margaret Mabel Goddard. Unmarried. Church of England. Emigrated to South Africa c. 1905; to England 1925. British. Educ: Roedean Sch., South Africa; Univ. of Witwatersrand, South Africa (Herbert Ainsworth Scholar) M.A. (Distinction) 1925; Somerville Coll., Oxford, B.A. 1927; M.A. 1930. Fellow and tutor in Economics, Politics, and History at Somerville Coll., Oxford 1927–45; first Temporary Principal, then Temporary Asst. Secty., Board of Trade, Whitehall 1941–45; Chmn., Lace Working Party 1946; Principal, Lady Margaret Hall, Oxford 1945–71; Member: Cttee. of Enquiry into Distribution and Exhibition of Cinematograph Films 1949; Royal Commission on Taxation of Profits and Income 1951–55; Cttee. of Enquiry into grants for Students 1958; Hebdomadal Council, Oxford 1953–71. Pro-Vice Chancellor, Oxford Univ. 1960–69; Grants Cttee. 1963–68. Hons: C.B.E. 1947; D.B.E. 1969; Fellow Royal Society of Arts 1950; Fellow British Academy 1954; Hon. Litt.D. (Cantab.) 1963 and Kent 1967; Hon LL.D. Smith Coll. 1964; Hon. D.Litt. from Glasgow 1966 Keele 1968, and Belfast 1970; Hon. D.C.L. Oxon 1972; Foreign Hon. Member American Acad. of Arts and Sciences 1963. *Author:* A London Merchant (1695–1774), 1933; (edited with M. McKisack) Medieval Representation and Consent by M.V. Clarke, 1936, and Fourteenth Century Studies, by M.V. Clarke, 1937; (edited with H. Cam and M. Coate) Studies in Medieval History by A.E. Levett, 1938; The East India Company in Eighteenth Century Politics, 1952; (ed.) The Correspondence of Edmund Burke, vol. 2, 1960; The University of Oxford in the Eighteenth Century, 1973; contributions to the Times Literary Supplement, English Historical Review, Economics History Review, Economic History, Transactions of the Royal Historical Society, and others.

L(UCIUS) C(HRISTOPHER) BATES
Black civil rights leader
Born Indianola, Mississippi, U.S.A., 1901
Died Little Rock, Arkansas, U.S.A., August 22nd, 1980

A proud and determined man who spent most of his adult life fighting for black civil rights in the South, L.C. Bates and his wife Daisy led the effort in 1957 to desegregate Central High School in Little Rock, Arkansas. This historic case, which brought federal troops into the South, served notice that the U.S. government would enforce, albeit reluctantly, the 1954 school desegregation ruling of the Supreme Court. That the effort was forced to such a crisis is due in large part to the persistance of the NAACP and Lucius and Daisy Bates.

Lucius Christopher Bates was born in Indianola, Mississippi. His father, who was a powerful influence on his life, encouraged him to pursue a college education and to value himself as a black man. "Sacrifice a friend before you compromise a principle," his father told him.

L.C. left home to attend Wilberforce College in Oklahoma. There he majored in journalism, taking a job after graduation with a newspaper in Colorado, finally joining the staff of the *Kansas City Call* in Missouri. But after nearly 10 years with newspapers he was not advancing as quickly as he had hoped and, feeling that he had failed, abandoned journalism for insurance. It was while traveling on an agency assignment that he met his future wife, then living with her parents in Little Rock. In 1941 they married and soon thereafter, L.C. returned to journalism, this time as the co-publisher (with his wife) of a newspaper, the Arkansas *State Press.*

Despite its modest budget, *State Press* soon became one of the most influential publications in its field, the circulation reaching 10,000 in the first few months. While L.C. solicited for advertisers who wanted to reach its largely black readership, Daisy reported on the numerous cases of police brutality, the mistreatment of Northern black soldiers stationed at nearby Camp Robinson, housing problems, the unequal job opportunities and other issues ignored by the white newspapers in the city. In its editorials the newspaper argued strongly in favor of unions.

Controversial as these positions were, the paper did not suffer until it began to speak out for school integration. Segregationists attacked Mr. and Mrs. Bates and their newspaper in a campaign that was fostered by Governor Faubus of Arkansas, who branded them Communists. Circulation dropped from 20,000 to 6,000 as an economic boycott lost the newspaper most of its white advertisers. The Bates's home in an integrated neighborhood was stoned and bombed; crosses were burnt on the lawn; guns fired from cars passing in front of the house. Over $500 in damage was done to front windows alone. Neighbors who helped guard the property were arrested on charges of carrying concealed weapons.

The climax of violence came in the fall of 1957 when the NAACP, mapping its strategy with L.C.'s guidance, decided upon a confrontation. Nine children from the all-black Horace Mann School would enter the all-white Central High School. If they were prohibited—and Governor Faubus had called out the National Guard to make sure of it—the NAACP could then appeal for the protection of federal troops.

On September 25th, President Eisenhower ordered the 101st Airborne Division and 10,000 federalized National Guardsmen to escort the children through a mob of angry whites, past Governor Faubus, and through the school doors. It was the first time since Reconstruction that the federal troops had been dispatched to the South to protect the constitutional rights of black people.

One of the students, Ernie Green, who later became Assistant Secretary of Labor in the Carter administration said of L.C. Bates: "He was the one who could make us feel secure that what we were about had long-range implications." During the years following integration, the students often returned to the Bates home for encouragement.

The *State Press,* however, did not survive integration. When it folded in 1959, L.C. Bates became a field secretary for the NAACP. In 1965 he confronted his old enemy, Governor Faubus, and asked to be put in charge of hiring blacks for state agencies that used federal funds. Faubus agreed and Mr. Bates was allowed to hire only those blacks who had supported civil rights. "He plays politics; we know that," Bates said of Faubus. "But while he is playing politics we are getting some of the things that we've been fighting for."   R.W.

Son of a farmer. Wife—Daisy; married 1941. Adopted son: Christopher. Southern Baptist. Educ: Wilberforce College, Okla., B.A. in journalism. Newspaper reporter in Colorado for 3 years; on staff of *Kansas City Call,* Mo.; worked in advertising and promotion in Memphis, Tenn. In insurance 1936–40; publisher, with wife, of Arkansas *State Press* 1941–59; Field Secty. for NAACP 1961–80.

JAMES (SMITH) McDONNELL
Aerospace industry executive and founder of McDonnell Douglas Corporation
Born Denver, Colorado, U.S.A., April 9th, 1899
Died St. Louis, Missouri, U.S.A., August 22nd, 1980

Courtesy McDonnell Douglas

A pioneer in aerospace engineering whose career spanned the days of the flivver to the exploration of outer space, James Smith McDonnell founded one of the largest aerospace companies in the world, manufacturing commercial jetliners, military aircraft and missiles. At the time of McDonnell's death at the age of 81, the company had begun research into fusion energy and space technology.

The corporation that grew out of one McDonnell formed in 1939, reported forty years later more than $5 billion in sales, an order backlog of nearly $7 billion, and almost 83,000 employees.

Born in Denver, McDonnell attended schools in Little Rock, Arkansas, earning a B.S. with honors in physics from Princeton in 1921. Four years later he was one of four to receive graduate degrees in aeronautical engineering from Massachusetts Institute of Technology. To learn to fly, McDonnell joined the Army Air Service, receiving his wings in 1924.

In 1928 McDonnell formed a small company of his own to develop a flivver to enter the 1929 Guggenheim $100,000 Safe Aircraft Competition. He refused to bail out when his plane went down in a competitive flight over Long Island. Though McDonnell sustained minor injuries and his aircraft was destroyed, he was again flying in demonstration flights the following year, this time in an inexpensive monoplane he called the "Doodlebug" and planned to market. When the Depression wiped out financing for the scheme, McDonnell worked for the small but numerous aircraft plants of that era, learning all aspects of the business as designer, aeronautical engineer and pilot.

After five years with the Glenn L. Martin Company of Baltimore, McDonnell at the age of 40 launched his own company, the McDonnell Aircraft Corporation, with $165,000 in capital, including $10,000 from Laurance Rockefeller, a friend from college days. His objective, he said, was "to be of maximum service possible to the United States government in the design and manufacture of airplanes," a goal that anticipated his role in the development of the American defense industry.

A slight man, bespectacled and a perfectionist, he was staunchly committed to fighting totalitarianism, and believed it would be a hundred-year struggle. McDonnell lived by the notion that "peace must be waged—comprehensively and continuously—from a foundation of strength." McDonnell Aircraft boomed with the onset of World War II. Contracting with the Navy to develop the world's first jet fighter to operate from an aircraft carrier, McDonnell Aircraft also received government contracts for jet propulsion research. By 1980, the company had become the second largest military contractor in the country.

In the 1940s and 50s, McDonnell expanded his work in missiles engineering and space research, receiving a contract in 1959 to manufacture the country's first manned orbital spacecraft, commencing work which would lead to the Mercury space capsule even before the government allocated money for the space program.

In the mid-1960s, the company reported financial difficulties, resulting in its merger in 1967 with Douglas Aircraft, then a major manufacturer of commercial jetliners, the largest such merger in aerospace history. The following year the firm began work on the DC-10, an advanced, wide-body jet airliner requiring a commitment of more than a billion dollars in funds.

An internationalist in business as well as in politics, McDonnell was a strong supporter of the United Nations, finding nothing contradictory, he said, "about supporting preparedness as the surest safeguard against war and at the same time supporting the UN. To the contrary, these are complementary concepts" that mark "the surest road to peace." Nationwide chairman of the UN Association of the United States, McDonnell also served as director, in 1963, of the Atlantic Council, an organization of private businessmen and former government officials who support the goals of NATO. In July 1980, a three-man review committee investigating allegedly questionable payments made by McDonnell-Douglas to sell planes outside the U.S. from 1969 to 1978, found that the total value of questionable payments came to $21.6 million. The review committee issued a strong call for greater outside control of the company, which had then been under the chairmanship of "Old Mac" for 40 years.   A.C.

Son of James Smith M. and Susan Belle (Hunter) M. Married: (1) Mary Elizabeth Finney 1934 (d. 1949); (2) Priscilla Brush Forney 1956. Children: 1st marriage—James Smith III, Corporate V.P. Marketing, McDonnell Douglas Corp.; John Finney, Corporate Exec., V.P., McDonnell Douglas Corp.; 2nd marriage—George David; Susan Brush Boyd; Priscilla Young Canny. Educ: Princeton Univ. B.S. hons. 1921; Massachusetts Inst. of Technology, M.S. 1925. Mil. Service: Army Air Corps Flying Sch., San Antonio 1923–24. Aeronautical Engineering Pilot, Huff Daland Airplane Co., Ogdensburg, N.Y. 1924; Stress Analyst and Draftsman, Consolidated Aircraft Co., Buffalo and Asst. Chief Engineer, Stout Metal Airplane Co., Dearborn, Mich. 1925; Chief Engineer, Hamilton Aero Manufacturing Co., Milwaukee 1926–27; formed McDonnell & Assocs. 1928; V.P. Airtransport Engineering Corp. 1930–31; Engineer and Test Pilot, Great Lakes Aircraft Corp., Cleveland 1933–38; formed McDonnell Aircraft Corp., St. Louis 1939, President 1939–62 and Chmn. and Chief Exec. Officer 1962–67; Chmn. and Chief Exec. officer 1967–72 and Chmn. since 1972, McDonnell Douglas Corp., St. Louis. Dir., Atlantic Council of the U.S. since 1963; Natl. Chmn.,

U.S. Cttee. for the U.N. 1955–64; Bd. of Dirs. 1965–75 and Natl. Chmn. 1975–77, U.N. Assn. U.S.A.; Chmn., McDonnell Foundn.; Pres., McDonnell Aerospace Foundn.; Advisory Council Member, Center for Strategic and Intnl. Studies; Member, Civic Progress, Inc. and Population Crisis Commn. Hons: Hon. D, Eng. from Univ. of Missouri 1957 and Washington Univ. 1958; St. Louis Award 1959; Hon. LL.D. from Princeton Univ. 1960 and Univ. of Arkansas 1965; Daniel Guggenheim Medal 1963; Robert J. Collier Trophy 1966; Founders Medal, Natl. Acad. of Engineering 1967; Forrestal Award 1972; D.Sc., Clarkson Coll. 1976; Spirit of St. Louis Aviation Award; named to Natl. Aviation Hall of Fame; Hon. Fellow, American Inst. Aeronautics and Astronautics.

GOWER CHAMPION
Choreographer, stage director, dancer
Born Geneva, Illinois, U.S.A., June 22nd, 1921
Died New York City, U.S.A. August 24th, 1980

One of the most influential choreographers and directors in the American musical theater, Gower Champion staged some of Broadway's biggest successes, including *Bye Bye Birdie, Hello Dolly!*, and *I Do! I Do!*. Together with Jerome Robbins, he is credited with developing an integrated theatrical style that expresses thematic ideas through choreography and set designs.

Champion was born in Geneva, Illinois, and raised by his divorced mother in Los Angeles, where he studied dancing under Ed Belcher. When he was 15, he and a classmate, Jeanne Tyler, won an amateur dance contest and quit school to tour the fashionable nightclub circuit as "Gower and Jeanne, America's youngest dance team." They also appeared in three films before Champion left to serve in the Coast Guard during World War Two. After the war he found a new partner in Marge Belcher, the daughter of his dance teacher; they were married in 1947. Their exuberant, sophisticated dancing was showcased on television's *The Admiral Broadway Revue* in 1949. During the 1950s they appeared on every major television program and starred in *The Marge and Gower Champion Show*, a situation comedy in which they played themselves. They also appeared in several musical films, including the autobiographical *Everything I Have is Yours*, and jointly choreographed two Broadway shows.

Lend an Ear (1948) was Champion's first attempt at combining choreography and direction on the Broadway stage. Although it was a hit, he did not attempt another until 1960, when he choreographed and directed the very successful *Bye Bye Birdie*. A string of successes followed, including *Carnival* (1961), *Hello, Dolly!* (1964), and *I Do! I Do!* (1966), the first two for producer David Merrick.

Of *Hello, Dolly!*, Walter Kerr wrote: "Mr. Champion's dancers began by exploding through the floor, wrapping themselves around rafters, and vaulting over the roof beams. . . . The second act opened with the men out of their minds once more, waiters all in a most elegant restaurant, trapped and racing through a silverware concerto in which chairs floated about, shish-kebab skewers duelled one

another, and stacks of jellied dishes changed hands in the night. . . .
It was the beginning of a musical-comedy madness that threatened to
linger with you until your ears wore out."

Champion's collaborations with Merrick were always difficult, with
both men competing for final control over the production. During
rehearsals for *The Happy Time* (1968), according to an anecdote
recorded by William Goldman in *The Season*, someone telephoned
Champion at home to tell him that Merrick had arrived on the set.
Champion spent the day touring the Michigan countryside in a rented
car until the producer had departed. Later he explained that he had
already had two bleeding ulcers and did not want a third. After the
success of *Dolly!*, Merrick trusted Champion sufficiently to allow him
to use an unorthodox set consisting of still photographs projected on a
screen for *The Happy Time*, saying, "I don't understand the projections. It's a big gamble; we have little scenery now. But Gower on the
visual side is sensational, and I'm trusting that judgment." When
Merrick was displeased with Champion, who had a reputation for
being a dictator on the set, he called him a "Presbyterian Hitler."

In addition to his Broadway shows, Champion made a few ill-
starred forays into movie directing and tried his hand at directing
straight plays. His failure in this regard, like that of Jerome Robbins,
was attributed by a colleague to a fascination with spectacle rather
than drama. "In a musical they [Champion and Robbins] start with a
total picture in their minds and then all they do is put in the puppets.
In a play they have to work with actors; they have to draw out, not put
in, and neither of them can do that."

Champion had better results with musical programs for television
and was often called in as a "show doctor" to fix ailing Broadway
productions. In one of these, Liza Minnelli's *The Act*, he also stepped
in to take the male lead. His house in Hollywood Hills was designed
with an entire rehearsal hall on the first floor. He and his wife, with
whom he had two sons, were divorced in 1973; he later remarried.

Champion returned to Broadway with *Sugar* (1972), *Irene* (1973),
and the short-lived *Mack and Mabel* (1973) and *Rockabye Hamlet*
(1976). In 1980, after a long hiatus, he was brought in by Merrick to
choreograph and direct a stage adaptation of *42nd Street*, a 1933 Ruby
Keeler film about a young ingenue and her rise to stardom under the
glittering lights of Broadway. During rehearsals at Washington's
Kennedy Center, Champion learned that he had Waldenstrom's
disease, a rare form of blood cancer. The show opened in New York
on August 25th to enthusiastic acclaim; at the end of the final curtain
call, Merrick went onstage to announce to the shocked cast and
audience that Champion had died that afternoon.

John Beaufort's review in the *Christian Scence Monitor* said: *"42nd
Street* opens with a stage full of dancers tap-tap-tapping their hearts
out. The music and Mr. Champion's masterful choreographic use of it
are the heart of this wonderful entertainment. There are a silhouette
shadow dance, a fling at Greco art deco, and one of those floral
numbers in which the ladies of the ensemble wield posied hoops . . .
they are all part of the fun and games that make *42nd Street* not only a
boisterous entertainment but a kind of Champion retrospective."

                                                            J.P./A.C.

Son of John W. C., advertising exec., and Beatrice (Carlisle) C. Married: (1) Marjorie Celeste Belcher, dancer and actress, 1947 (div. 1973); (2) Carla. Sons: 1st marriage—Gregg; Blake. Presbyterian. Educ: Fairfax High Sch., Los Angeles 1933–36; Ernest Belcher's dance sch., Los Angeles. Mil. Service: Ordinary seaman, transport duty, U.S. Coast Guard WWII; toured with musical show Tars and Spars. Professional dancer and actor since 1936: with Jeanne Tyler as dance team Gower and Jeanne, toured nightclubs and appeared in films 1936–41; with wife Marge Belcher as dance team Gower and Bell, later as Marge and Gower Champion, toured nightclubs and appeared in films, television shows, and musicals 1941–60; also solo dancer and actor. Director and choreographer of musical theater productions since 1948; also producer, director, and choreographer of television programs, and film director. Member: Screen Directors Guild; screen Actors Guild; American Guild of Variety Artists; Actors Equity Assn. Hons: Tony Award for best dir. of a musical (for Lend an Ear) 1949; Tony Awards for best dir. of a musical and best choreographer 1961 (for Bye Bye Birdie), 1965 (for Hello, Dolly!), 1969 (for Happy Time); also nominated for best dir. 1967 (for I Do! I Do!), 1973 (for Irene). Donaldson Award for choreography (for Lend an Ear) 1949; New York Drama Critics Circle award for direction and choreography (for Carousel) 1961; Dance Mag. Award for choreography. *Dancer and actor (with Jeanne Tyler): Clubs*—Rainbow Room, NYC; Empire Room, NYC; Cocoanut Grove, Los Angeles; many others. *Films*—Streets of Paris, 1939; The Lady Comes Across, 1942; Count Me In, 1942. *Dancer and actor (with Marge Belcher Champion): Clubs*—Normandie Room, Montreal 1947; Persian Room, Plaza Hotel, NYC 1947; Mocamb, Hollywood 1949: Flamingo, Las Vegas 1949; many others. *Films*— Mr. Music, 1950; Showboat, 1951; Lovely to Look At, 1952; Everything I Have is Yours (autobiographical), 1952; Give a Girl a Break, 1953; Jupiter's Darling, 1955; (also choreographer) The Girl Most Likely, 1956. *Television*—The Admiral Broadway Revue, 1949; The Marge and Gower Champion Show, 1957; guest appearances on the Steve Allen, Perry Como, Ed Sullivan, Jack Benny, Dinah Shore, Eddie Fisher, and Sid Caesar shows and many others. *Stage*— (also dir. and choreographer) Three for Tonight (revue), 1955. *Dancer and actor, solo: Films*—Till the Clouds Roll By, 1946. *Television*—Gene Kelly Show, 1965; Merv Griffin Show, 1965–66; Today Show, 1965–66; New York, New York (special), 1966. *Stage*—The Act, NYC 1978 *Director and Choreographer: Stage*—(choreographer only, with Marge Champion) Small Wonder, 1948; (choreographer only, with Marge Champion) Make a Wish, 1951; Lend an Ear, NYC 1948; Bye Bye Birdie, NYC 1960, London 1961; Carnival, NYC 1961; Hello, Dolly!, NYC 1964, London 1965, Las Vegas nightclub version 1965; The Happy Time, NYC 1968; Prettybelle, 1971; Sugar, NYC 1972; Irene, NYC 1973; Mack and Mabel, NYC 1974; Lyrics by Ira Gershwin: Who Can Ask for Anything More, Los Angeles 1975; Rockabye Hamlet, NYC 1976; 42nd Street, NYC 1980. *Television*—Accent on Love; 55 Minutes from Broadway. *Director: Stage*—Hemingway and All Those People, Indianapolis 1958; My Mother, My Father and Me, NYC 1963; (also co-producer) Three Bags Full, NYC 1966; I Do! I Do!, NYC 1966; Los Angeles 1973; A Flea in Her Ear, NYC 1968. *Films*—My Six Loves, 1963; Bank Shot, 1974; others. *Television*—(also producer) Mary Martin at Eastertime, 1966; (also producer) Academy Awards show, 1969.
Further reading: The American Musical Theater by Lehman Engle,

1967; A Theater Divided: The Postwar American Stage by Martin Gottfried, 1967; The Season: A Candid Look at Broadway by William Goldman, 1969; Thirty Plays Hath November: Pain and Pleasure in the Contemporary Theater by Walter Kerr, 1969; The World of Musical Comedy by Stanley Green, 1974; Better Foot Forward: The History of American Musical Theatre by Ethan Mordden, 1976.

ROY PASCAL
Scholar and writer on German literature
Born Birmingham, England, February 28th, 1904
Died Birmingham, England, August 24th, 1980

Roy Pascal, a professor of German at Birmingham University, was noted for his books on the German Reformation, on the German novel, and particularly on the writers of the *Sturm und Drang* genre. According to Pascal, he decided in his childhood, to study German literature after reading a poem by Goethe.

Pascal was educated at King Edward School, Birmingham, and later studied at the Universities of Cambridge, Munich, and Berlin. He was named Fellow of Pembroke College, Cambridge and with the outbreak of World War Two, he became Professor of German at the University of Birmingham where he taught until 1965.

The German Sturm und Drang (1953) was Pascal's most important critical work. *Sturm und Drang*, literally translated as "storm and stress," was a literary movement of the late 18th century which exalted nature and defied the Enlightenment faith in rationalism. It had been denigrated by many scholars for its alleged subjectivism and melancholic attitude towards life. Pascal argued that the *Sturm und Drang* form gave rise neither to solipsism nor a withdrawal from life. The Goethean hero, Pascal said, was torn between the authentic, freely created values of the inner life and the implacable demands of the external world; such a conflict between self and society forced the hero to forge a unity between himself and his world. This reconciliation thus achieved, the hero had adjusted to the world without betraying the truth of his inner experience. Pascal furthermore cited *Sturm und Drang* as the precursor of both 19th century romanticism and realism. Critics agreed that Pascal's study made it impossible for scholars to identify *Sturm und Drang* with quietism.

In *From Naturalism to Expressionism: Design and Truth in Autobiography,* and *The Dual Voice,* Pascal analyzed the narrative voice by relating literary forms to the social conditions which shaped them. Pascal received numerous awards and honors. He was elected Chairman of the Conference of University Teachers of German in 1960, received honorary doctorates from the Universities of Birmingham and Warwick, won the Hamburg Shakespeare Prize, and the Goethe Medal.
                                                                                    R.S.

Courtesy Susan E. Turner

Son of C.S.P. and Mary (Edmonds) P. Married Feiga Polianovska 1931. Two daughters. Educ: King Edward Sch., Birmingham; Pembroke Coll., Cambridge (Scholar); further studies at Univs. of Berlin and Munich. Fellow 1929–34 and 1936–39, and Dir., Modern Lang. Studies 1936–39, Pembroke Coll.; Lectr. in German, Univ. of

Cambridge 1934–39; Prof. of German, Birmingham Univ. 1936–69. Pres., Assn. of Univ. Teachers 1944–45; Chmn., Conference of Univ. Teachers of German 1960–61. Hons: Goethe Medal 1965; Shakespeare Prize (Hamburg) 1969; Hon. LL.D., Birmingham Univ. 1974; Hon. Fellow, Pembroke Coll. 1976; Hon. D. Litt., Warwick 1979. *Author: Books*—Martin Luther: the Social Basis of the German Reformation, 1933; The Nazi Dictatorship, 1934; Shakespeare in Germany 1740–1815, 1937; Growth of Modern Germany, 1946; The German Revolution 1848, 1949; The German Sturm und Drang, 1953; The German Novel, 1956; Design and Truth in Autobiography, 1960; German Literature 1500–1700, 1967; From Naturalism to Expressionism, 1973; Culture and the Division of Labour, 1974; The Dual Voice, 1977. *Other*—(ed.) German Ideology by Marx and Engels, 1938; Goethe's Faust, in Essays on Goethe, 1949; Moeller van den Bruck, in The Third Reich, ed. Vermeil, 1955; Introduction to Nietzsche's Thus Spake Zarathustra, 1958; the Art of Autobiography, in Stil un Formprobleme in der Literatur, 1959; Realism, in Spätzeiten, ed. Kohlschmidt, 1962; Contributor to The German Mind and Outlook, 1944–45 and to presentation vols. for several scholars; articles in Modern Language Review; Goethe Society Publications; German Life and Letters.

LORD GODBER OF WILLINGTON
British politician and cabinet minister
Born Willington, Bedfordshire, England, March 17th, 1914
Died Willington, Bedfordshire, England, August 25th, 1980

Joseph Godber, for 28 years a Member of Parliament, was a leading figure in intricate negotiations for his country on two occasions—as chief of the British delegation to the Geneva disarmament conference in the early 1960s, and as Minister of Agriculture during the complex and volatile farming policy talks with members of the European Economic Community prior to Britain's admission to the EEC.

Joseph Bradshaw Godber was born into a successful horticultural and farming family in Bedfordshire. Educated at Bedford School, Joseph entered the family concern in 1932, at the age of 18. When he was 32, he was elected as a conservative member of the Bedfordshire County Council, and particularly concerned himself with the interests of the rural communities. He later became the conservative parliamentary candidate for the borough of Grantham in rural Lincolnshire, and in 1951, he won the seat. He continued to be re-elected as M.P. for Grantham until his retirement before the general election of 1979.

After four years as a backbencher, Godber was named Assistant Government Whip, and in 1957 he joined the Ministry of Agriculture as Joint Parliamentary Secretary, where the conservative government of Harold Macmillan could call upon his expertise in farming matters. This was followed by Foreign Office appointments, firstly as Under Secretary (1960–61) and then as Minister of State (1961–63). He headed the 1961 and 1962 British delegations to the U.N. General Assembly, and attended the U.N.-sponsored 18-power Geneva disarmament conference of 1962–63. As Britain's chief negotiator there, he found himself in frequent disagreement with Mr. Zorin, the Soviet delegate. But displaying diplomatic skill and ability as a compromiser,

Godber played a significant role in the shaping of the nuclear test ban treaty.

For the last four months of the Macmillan government, Godber served as Secretary of State for War, and when, in October 1963, Sir Alec Douglas-Home became Prime Minister, Joseph Godber was named Minister of Labour. He held that position until October 1964, when the labour party took office under the premiership of Harold Wilson. During the tory (conservative) years in opposition, Godber was his party's spokesman on agricultural affairs; and with the conservative victory in 1970, it was widely expected that Prime Minister Edward Heath would give Godber the agriculture portfolio. However Heath surprised observers by selecting James Prior for that position, and Godber was once again appointed Minister of State at the Foreign Office. But in 1972, with agriculture a critical issue, Godber became Minister of Agriculture so that his expertise in that area and his skills as a negotiator might ease Britain's entry into the EEC. Godber tried to persuade Community members to freeze food prices so that the economic burden of Britain's admission would be alleviated. The EEC negotiators—intent on maintaining strong protections for the generally less-efficient continental farmers—remained obdurate, and the British minister became the butt of considerable invective in the House of Commons; some of the harshest reprobation coming from anti-Common Market M.P.s within his own party. However, many political commentators at the time said that Godber staunchly fought for British interests and was a steady and effective expositor of the official conservative position in the House. With much of the EEC's agricultural policy disadvantageous to Britain, it nevertheless officially joined the Community, along with Ireland, on January 1st, 1973.

When the Heath government was defeated in 1974, Godber, while remaining in parliament, did not serve in the shadow (opposition) cabinet. Instead, he became chairman of the board of Sidney Banks Ltd. and a director of several other companies. In 1976 he assumed the chairmanship of Tricentrol Ltd. and was appointed chairman of the Retail Consortium. Upon his retirement from the House of Commons in 1979, he was made a life peer.   R.T.

Son of Isaac G. and B.M. Chapman G. Married Miriam Sanders 1936. Children: two sons. Educ: Bedford School. Entered family business 1938. County Councillor for Bedfordshire 1946–52. Elected M.P. for Grantham, Div. of Lincs. 1951: Asst. Party Whip 1955–57; Jt. Parliamentary Secty., Ministry of Agriculture, Fisheries and Food 1957–60; Parliamentary Under Secty. of State 1960–61 and Minister of State 1961–63, Foreign Office; Secty. of State for War, June–Oct. 1963; Minister of Labour 1963–64; Leader British Delegation to U.N. General Assembly 1960–61 and to Geneva Disarmament Conference 1962–63; Chief Opposition Spokesman on Agriculture 1965–70; Minister of State, Foreign Office 1970–72; Chief of British Delegation to Commonwealth Parliamentary Assn. 1970; Minister of Agriculture, Fisheries and Food 1972–74. Chmn: Sidney Banks, Ltd. 1974–80; Tricenterol Ltd. 1976–80. Dir: Booker McConnell Ltd. 1974–80; British Home Stores Ltd 1977–80. Consultant, Beecham's Foods 1974–80. Hons: P.C. 1963; created Life Peer 1979.

TEX AVERY
Motion picture cartoonist
Born Taylor, Texas, U.S.A., 1909
Died Burbank, California, U.S.A., August 27th, 1980

Tex Avery, a leading American animator and cartoonist for 30 years, was instrumental in the origination and development of a number of famous cartoon characters, including Daffy Duck, Elmer Fudd, and the inimitable carrot-chomping, wise-cracking, buck-toothed Bugs Bunny.

A lover of spoofs and visual puns, Tex Avery had a zany, almost surreal, sense of humor. One of his wilder creations was a car which, parodying the excesses of its immensely rich and slick owner, was so long that, like a train, it took many seconds to pass a fixed point. The rear bumper bore a sign: "Long, isn't it?" The rather flashy mouse who owned this elongated machine seduced his paramour (a once-gentle creature who became more and more like Mae West [q.v.] as the cartoon progressed) with a diamond of such magnificence that it was too brilliant for her mouse eyes to behold, and she had to view its loveliness through a welder's mask. As another inducement to matrimony, he delivered to her door the world's most exotic per-fume—in a daintily-decorated and gargantuan tanker. Her ex-beau, a pleasant mouse who had mortgaged himself to the hilt to buy her simple tokens of his eternal love, tied himself to the local railroad; but before a train could bear down upon him, the ecstatic newlyweds zoomed past in the monster car, drenching him with puddle water.

Tex, born Fred Bean Avery, was himself descended from a colorful character—Roy Bean, the famous "hanging judge." His only formal art training occurred during a summer course at the Art Institute of Chicago. Avery tried his hand at newspaper cartoons but without much success, then moved to California where he worked as an inker and painter, then as a director, for Walter Lantz in the cartoon department of Universal Studios.

From 1936 to 1942, he supervised cartoons for Leon Schlesinger, the producer of *Looney Tunes* and *Merrie Melodies* which were released through Warner Bros. Under Schlesinger, Avery teamed up with Chuck Jones, Bob Clampett and Bob Cannon. They established themselves away from the main studios in a cottage which became known as "Termite Terrace."

Although he bore little resemblance to the character famous today, Avery adapted Porky the Pig, already a popular character, for his own comics. He supervised the appearance of Daffy Duck in *Porky's Duck Hunt* (1937), and one of his characters, Egghead, evolved into Elmer Fudd. Avery's cartoons grew wilder and funnier, and under the influence of Frank Tashlin, another of Schlesinger's directors, more self-referential. *Thugs With Dirty Mugs* (1939), a spoof of Warner Bros. cop and robber movies, overflows with visual puns. A primitive version of Bugs Bunny appeared in *Porky's Hare Hunt* (1938), and over the next few years he turned into the brash mammal familiar to all. Avery, a Texan, was familiar with the use of "Doc" as a nickname, and the phrase "What's up, Doc?" was not uncommon in his youth. But uttered by his wily rabbit, it became an international catch-phrase. Many of Avery's cartoons were based on Texas folk humor and exaggeration. Under his supervision, the gags got more outrageous and surreal. After making the *Speaking of Animals* series for Paramount in 1942, Avery moved to Fred Quimby's cartoon unit at Metro-Goldwyn-Mayer. Here, as a director, he made fun of the sentimental Disney cartoons (*The Peachy Cobbler,* 1950) and invented Droopy Dog. Avery wrote his own versions of many fairy tales, and parodied sexual avarice in such films as *Red Hot Riding Hood* (1943), and *Uncle Tom's Cabaña* (1947).

Avery returned to work for Walter Lantz at Universal in 1954. Although the lush color and slick music of the M-G-M cartoons were missing, the gags were as furious and crazed as ever. At Lantz's behest, Avery created the penguin Chilly Willy, but he did not find his characterization very funny. A year later, after a salary dispute he left Universal and joined Cascade Studios where he did television commercials, including one for the bug-killer "Raid," in which sleazy looking insects were efficaciously annihilated; in another, Bugs Bunny became a leading advocate of Pre-Sweetened Kool Aid.

Avery, a short, bald, bespectacled man who looked like one of his cartoon characters, got away with some terrible puns in his time: in one of his sequences, hundreds of nibbling sheep roaming through pastureland are confronted by a sign: "Cattle Country. Keep Out. This Means Ewe."   J.K./R.T.

Born Fred Bean Avery. Educ: North Dallas High School. Honors: International Animated Film Society Annie Award, 1974. *Cartoons:Animator*—Ham and Eggs, 1933; Annie Moved Away; as supervisor, 1934; 1936: Golddiggers of '49, The Blow-Out, Plane Dippy, I'd Love to Take Orders from You, Miss Glory, I Love to Sing, Porky the Rainmaker, The Village Smithy, Milk and Money, Don't Look Now, Porky the Wrestler; 1937: Picador Porky, I Only Have Eyes for You, Porky's Duck Hunt, Uncle Tom's Bungalow, Ain't We Got Fun, Daffy Duck and Egghead, Egghead Rides Again, A Sunbonnet Blue; Porky's Garden, I Wanna Be a Sailor, The Sneezing Weasel, Little Red Walking Hen; 1938: The Penguin Parade, The Isle of Pingo Pongo; A Feud There Was, Johnny Smith and Poker-Huntas, Daffy Duck in Hollywood, Cinderella Meets a Fella, Ham-amateur Night, The Mice Will Play; 1939: A Day at the Zoo, Thugs With Dirty Mugs, Believe It or Else, Dangerous Dan McFoo, Detouring America, Land of the Midnight Fun, Fresh Fish, Screwball Football, The Early Worm Gets the Bird; 1940: A Wild Hare, The Bear's Tale, A Gander at Mother Goose, Circus Today, Ceiling Hero, Wacky Wild Life, Of Fox and Hounds, Porky's Duck Hunt, Holiday Highlights, Cross Country Detours; 1941: Tortoise Beats Hare, A Heckling Hare, Porky's Preview, Hollywood Steps Out, The Crackpot Quail, Haunted Mouse, Aviation Vacation, All This and Rabbit Stew, The Bug Parade, The Cagey Canary. *Director*—1942: Speaking of Animals Down on a Farm, Speaking of Animals In a Pet Shop, Speaking of Animals In a Zoo, The Early Bird Dood It, The Blitz Wolf; *1943:* Dumb-hounded, Red Hot Riding Hood, Who Killed Who? One Ham's Family, What's Buzzin' Buzzard?; *1944:* Batty Baseball, Happy Go Nutty, Big Heel-Watha, Screwball Squirrel; *1945:* Swingshift Cinderella, The Screwy Truant, The Shooting of Dan McGoo, Junior Turkey, Wild and Wolfy; *1946:* Henpecked Hoboes, Lonesome Lennie, Northwest Hounded Police, The Hick Chick; *1947:* King-size Canary, Red Hot Rangers, Uncle Tom's Cabaña, Slap-happy Lion, Hound Hunters; *1948:* What Price Fleadom, Lucky Ducky, The Cat That Hated People, Little Tinker, Porky's Duck Hunt, Half-pint Pygmy; *1949:* Bad Luck Blackie, Señor

Droopy, The House of Tomorrow, Doggone Tired, Wags to Riches, Little Rural Riding Hood, Outfoxed, Counterfeit Cat; *1950:* Ventriloquist Cat, The Cuckoo Clock, Garden Gopher, The Chump Champ, The Peachy Cobbler; *1951:* Droopy's Good Deed, Cock-a-Doodle Dog, Dare-Devil Droopy, Droopy's Double Trouble, The Car of Tomorrow, Symphony in Slang; *1953:* TV of Tomorrow, Three Li'l Pups, Little Johnny Jet, *1954:* Drag-along Droopy, Billy Boy, Homesteader Droopy, Farm of Tommorow, The Flea Circus, Dixieland Droopy; *1955:* Sh-h-h-h, I'm Cold, Chilly Willy in the Legend of Rockabye Point, Field and Scream, The First Bad Man, Cellbound, Millionaire Droopy, The Cat's Meow; *1956:* Crazy Mixed-Up Pup (and written by); *1958:* Polar Pests.
Further reading: Tex Avery, King of Cartoons by Joe Adamson, 1975.

DOUGLAS KENNEY
Magazine editor and humorist
Born Cleveland, Ohio, U.S.A., December 10th, 1947
Died Kauai Island, Hawaii, U.S.A., August 27th, 1980

Editor and humorist Douglas Kenney co-founded the magazine *National Lampoon*. He was also co-writer of the popular movie *Animal House*, and shortly before his death at the age of 32, he produced the film *Caddyshack*.

While an undergraduate student at Harvard, Kenney was an editor of its humor magazine, the *Harvard Lampoon*. Upon graduating in 1968, he pursued an idea he had nurtured for several years: to put together a slick national humor magazine on the Harvard model to be aimed at what Kenney called "the aging college student" audience which had outgrown *Mad* but was attracted neither to high-brow satirical alternatives nor to the underground sex and/or drug press.

With the help of a New York publicist who agreed to finance the project, the first issue of the *National Lampoon* went on sale in March 1970. Although the first six months brought no particular success, once the new magazine began to attract the attention of Kenney's projected market, circulation mounted rapidly. By 1973, he was presiding editor of what the publishing industry's monitoring agency called "the fastest growing magazine in America," with monthly sales of 685,000 issues and pre-tax profits of over one million dollars.

With the magazine an unqualified success, Kenney developed other *Lampoon* projects, including the Broadway review *Lemmings* (1974) and the 1978 film *Animal House,* based on a script co-authored by Kenney. Starring John Belushi of the *Lemmings* cast and "Saturday Night Live" television fame, the film (in which Kenney appeared as the character Stork) was a zany, nostalgic look at college fraternity life in the apolitical, sex-obsessed early sixties. The movie, which *Newsweek* called "a panty raid on respectability," not only broke box office records but inspired a host of spin-off projects, including prime-time "college frat" entries on all three networks during the 1978–79 season.

Kenney spent increasing amounts of time on outside projects, and finally left the *Lampoon* in 1979 to join Twentieth Century Fox. In 1980, he produced *Caddyshack* for that studio; and it was a reprise of the formula that had worked to such good effect in *Animal House*.

Douglas Kenney died in an accidental cliff fall while in Hawaii with his fiancée and comedian Chevy Chase, a star of *Caddyshack*.   R.C.

Son of Mr. and Mrs. Harry Kenney. Unmarried. Educ: Harvard Univ., A.B. 1968. Harvard Lampoon: staff 1966–68; Ed. 1968. Founder, and Senior Ed., 1970–79, The National Lampoon; Producer, Twentieth Century Fox studios since 1979. *Works:* (co-author) National Lampoon High School Yearbook; (with Chris Miller and Howard Ramis) script for Animal House, 1978; producer for Twentieth Century Fox, Caddyshack, 1980.

SAM(UEL) LEVENSON
Humorist and author
Born New York City, U.S.A., December 28th, 1911
Died Brooklyn, New York, U.S.A., August 27th, 1980

During the 1950s, Sam Levenson became a well-known television and radio humorist, and later, a popular writer. But he remained a most uncelebrity-like celebrity, specializing in a chatty, folksy, uncombative style of humor drawn from his poor but happy Lower East Side boyhood and his experiences as a Brooklyn high-school teacher during the depression. He was, as one interviewer noted, "everybody's Uncle Max."

The youngest of eight children of a Russian immigrant tailor and his wife, Levenson was motivated as a boy by a strong faith in advancement through education; he received a B.A. from Brooklyn College in 1934. In that year he began a 11-year stint as a teacher of Spanish in Brooklyn high schools. He studied Romance languages at Columbia University in his spare time and obtained his master's degree in 1938. Sam Levenson kept an index-card file of his daily observations, a practice he had been introduced to by one of his college teachers. His initial reason for doing so was based on the belief that experience is the best teacher, but it soon became apparent that the practice also had an entertainment value.

Courtesy Mrs. Esther Levenson

In the summer of 1940, Levenson was invited to serve as master of ceremonies for a group of teachers who had organized an orchestra to entertain in the Catskills. He took his card file along to provide material for between-numbers patter; his career as an entertainer was thus launched. In short order, he was supplementing his $38-a-week teaching salary with $50 to $60 in weekly earnings as a part-time entertainer at bar mitzvahs and club meetings.

In 1945, he decided to concentrate on show business and so applied for a five-year leave of absence from teaching. "I didn't want to throw it all out," he observed of his hedge against failure. Caution proved unnecessary. Spotted by one of the *Sullivan Show's* producers while doing a nightclub act in 1949, he was signed for a guest appearance. In subsequent appearances with Sullivan and on the *Jack Benny Show*

(CBS) in 1949–50, his soft-sell, conversational style proved so popular that he was given his own half-hour show by the network in 1951–52. During the 1950s, he was a frequent guest performer and panel show regular. His last major television assignment was as the morning replacement for the ailing Arthur Godfrey in 1959.

Increasingly disenchanted with television, in which he felt educational values were too much subordinated to entertainment, Levenson turned to writing during the 1960s and 70s, producing books much like his comedy routines—winsome recollections of life in a simpler era, spiced with acerbic comments on the modern scene, such as "Today the cats and dogs stand around and watch the kids."

Levenson pointedly refused to indulge in cutting satire or deprecatory humor, and stoutly defended his nostalgic approach. "There's a danger in perhaps glorifying the way we lived," he stated in a 1974 interview, "but there was a richness to it that's missing today." He also apologized for a tendency to laugh, openly and uproariously, at his own jokes (thereby violating one of comedy's cardinal rules) by reaching, typically, back into his own childhood: "It's because papa always told me, 'Never depend on strangers.'"   R.C.

Son of Hyman L., tailor, and Rebecca Fishman L. Married Esther Levine 1936. Children: Conrad, Emily. Jewish. Educ: N.Y. public schs.; Brooklyn Coll., B.A. 1934; Columbia Univ., M.A. 1938. Teacher, Abraham Lincoln High Sch., Brooklyn 1934–37; Samuel J. Tilden High Sch., Brooklyn 1937–46. Night club, radio, and television entertainer 1946–80. Appearances: Ed Sullivan Show, CBS-TV 1949–50; Jack Benny Show, CBS-TV 1950; star, Sam Levenson Show, CBS-TV 1951–52; Panelist, This Is Show Business 1951–54; Moderator, Two for the Money 1955–56; star, Sam Levenson Show, CBS-TV 1959. Guest appearances on The Match Game, To Tell the Truth, and various variety and panel shows, commercial and educational networks. Member: Bd. of Dirs., League Sch. for Seriously Disturbed Children; District Bd. of Govs., B'nai B'rith. Hons: Brooklyn Coll. Alumnus of the Year 1952; Brooklyn Coll. Alumni Association's Outstanding Achievement Award 1956; L.H.D., St. Francis Coll., Brooklyn 1973; D.H.L., Brooklyn Coll. 1976. *Works:* Everything But Money, 1966; Sex and the Single Child, 1969; In One Era and Out the Other, 1973; You Can Say That Again, Sam, 1975; A Time for Innocence, 1976; You Don't Have to Be in Who's Who to Know What's What, 1979.

BILL EVANS
Jazz pianist and composer
Born Plainfield, New Jersey, U.S.A., August 16th, 1929
Died New York City, U.S.A., September 1st, 1980

It has often been said that Bill Evans was the most important jazz pianist of the past quarter-century. Yet, even in a field rife with non-conformists, he was in many ways an anomaly among the musicians of the time. He was a craftsman when craft was often sacrificed to expression and favored quiet, introspective lyricism when the trend was toward high emotion and high volume. But—in the words of Miles Davis, with whom he recorded the landmark *Kind of Blue* album, "He played the piano the way it should be played."

His early musical training was not in jazz at all but in European classical music. He began studying the piano at the age of six, taking up the violin the next year and the flute at thirteen. Although as a teenager he played the piano in an amateur jazz band, its repertoire consisted of popular swing numbers of the previous decade rather than the bebop prominent in the 1940s. His four years at college in rural Louisiana and subsequent four years in the army further removed him from current developments in jazz. Consequently, Evans—almost alone among the musicians of his generation—was unaffected by the bebop revolution, although the influence of Art Tatum could be heard in the suspension of tempo and emphasis on harmonic structure of his later playing.

Although his familiarity with modern jazz was limited when he first came to New York for post-graduate study at the Mannes College of Music in 1955, he was given work by clarinetist Tony Scott almost immediately upon arriving in the city. Performing experience, stylistic maturity, and respect from the New York contemporary music community were soon acquired. In 1956 composer and theoretician George Russell, whose "Lydian Concept of Tonal Organization" had a profound effect on Evans's approach to harmony, wrote a concerto, "All About Rosie," for the young pianist. The following year Evans participated on Charles Mingus's *East Coasting* album and recorded one of his own.

He achieved wide and lasting prominence when, in 1958, Miles Davis, who was radically experimenting with jazz conventions, asked him to join his sextet. After six months of playing together, the Miles Davis Sextet—with Davis on trumpet, Evans on piano, John Coltrane on tenor saxophone, Julian "Cannonball" Adderly on alto saxophone, Paul Chambers on bass, and Jimmy Cobb on drums—recorded *King of Blue* which received immediate acclaim as well as being singled out by jazz critics twenty years later as the most important recording in jazz history. The five pieces comprising the album were conceived by Davis in the form of mere outlines of modes on which to improvise, and—according to the liner notes written by Evans—were presented to the participating musicians only when they were ready to record, thus making the performances almost purely spontaneous. In spite of the challenge of this sort of collective creation and the complexity of modal harmony, the resulting music was remarkably simple and coherent.

Evans left the Miles Davis Sextet less than a year after joining it to put together his own trio. Striving for the ideal of three like and equal voices, he did well in choosing for his partners bassist Scott LaFaro and drummer Paul Motian. The trio, although composed of what were traditionally regarded as three rhythm instruments, shared the functions of rhythm, harmony, and melody, interweaving a fabric of ever-changing colors, patterns, and textures. This notable collaboration was cut short in 1961 when LaFaro was killed in a car crash.

Evans continued over the following two decades to work with several trios that included drummers Jack DeJohnette, Marty Morell, and Joe LaBarbara, and bassists Chuck Israels, Eddie Gomez, and Marc Johnson, but he did not restrict himself to that format. He recorded one album, *Interplay*, with a quintet composed of guitarist Jim Hall, trumpeter Freddie Hubbard, bassist Percy Heath, and drummer Philly Joe Jones, and recorded solo albums and duet albums with Hall and Gomez. He joined pianist John Lewis and saxophonists Ornette Coleman and Eric Dolphy on *Jazz Abstractions,* an experiment at blending jazz with 20th-century European concert music. Perhaps his most interesting "ensemble" work was done on a 1963 album entitled *Conversations With Myself,* on which he used multi-track recording techniques to play three piano parts simultaneously.

Evans brought to all his music a subtle ingenuity borne as much of reason and reflection as of emotion. He was a pioneer not only of a new sound in jazz but also of a new attitude—one of restraint and introspections—and his example has inspired the best work of Herbie Hancock, Chick Corea, Keith Jarrett, and other pianists of the current generation.   K.B.

Wife: Nenette. Children: Maxine (adopted); Evan. Educ: Southeastern Louisiana Coll. 1946–50; Mannes Coll. of Music 1955. Served in U.S. Army 1950–54; active as musician and composer in N.Y. 1955–80. Hons: Grammy Award for best instrumentalist jazz performance with a small group—Conversations with Myself, 1963; Bill Evans at the Montreux Jazz Festival 1968; Alone 1970; The Bill Evans Album (also Grammy for best jazz soloist) 1971. Melody Maker Award, U.K. 1968; Edison Award, Scandinavia 1969; Swing Journal Award, Japan 1969. *Selected recordings* (by label): Fantasy—Alone Again; Crosscurrents; Intuition; Tony Bennett with Bill Evans; Montreux III; Since We Met; I Will Say Goodbye; Verve—Sessions, Chick Corea and Bill Evans; Trio-Duo; Milestone—Milestown Two-fer Giants; Second Trio; Spring Leaves; MCA—The Bass; Blues & The Abstract Truth; Encyclopedia of Jazz on Records, Vol. V; Columbia—Jazz Piano Anthology, Warner Bros.—Affinity; New Conversations; Prestige—Piano Giants; CTI—Montreux II; Bet—Idol of the Flies; IPV—Together Again.

BARON BROCK OF WIMBLEDON
Heart Surgeon
Born London, England, October 24th, 1903
Died Wimbledon, London, England, September 3rd, 1980

Lord Brock, one of the British pioneers of heart surgery, was a widely-respected authority on thoracic disorders whose early practice and researches were fundamental to both open heart surgery and heart transplantation. His work in the 1930s and 1940s in the United States and in Britain came to be regarded as the groundwork for the great advances in cardiac surgery during 1960s and 1970s. For three years in the 1960s he was president of the Royal College of Surgeons, and Britain honored him first with a knighthood and later, in 1965, with a life peerage. His international standing was reflected by the many honors he received from all over the world.

Russell Brock, as he continued to be known long after his life peerage was conferred in 1965, was born of an upper-middle-class family and schooled at Christ's Hospital. He trained at Guy's Hospital, winning a scholarship and qualifying with honors through London University. After attaining his Fellowship of the Royal College of Surgeons, Brock secured a Rockefeller Traveling Fellowship to the United States where in St. Louis, Missouri, he worked under the late Professor Evarts Graham. It was there, while assisting Professor Graham in his surgical practice, that Brock developed an interest in thoracic surgery and decided to make it his career.

From Missouri, Brock returned to England in 1932 to work at Guy's Hospital and while there he qualified as Master of Surgery which led on, in 1936, to surgeon appointments at two of the major London teaching hospitals, Guy's and Brompton. Meanwhile, Brock had made the study of heart valve constriction (mitral stenosis) his specialty, believing that surgical intervention would best relieve the condition. At that time a large and influential body of British medical opinion believed that no form of heart surgery could be seriously contemplated. But doctors in the United States held a different view more akin to Brock's own and this encouraged him to develop a repeatable operative procedure and techniques to relieve the condition. Brock's success coincided with that of his American counterparts who had been working independently on similar problems. Both Brock and the American doctors nevertheless achieved their success in blind operations—techniques to allow open heart surgery had not been developed. Brock remained deeply interested in cardiac surgery and lived to see the successful transplantation of hearts. But while he strongly supported this extension of the field he had pioneered, he remained deeply concerned about the emotional stress it placed on the patients and their families. In particular he favoured total anonymity in respect of donor and recipient.

Brock also achieved a reputation as an authority on surgical intervention in the lungs, and his books, *Anatomy of the Bronchial Tree* (1946) and *Lung Abscess* (1952) became standard reference texts. Earlier, in 1935, he won the Jacksonian Prize awarded by the Royal College of Surgeons for an essay on *New Growths of the Lung*. His scientific papers on both heart and lung surgery were published in professional journals throughout the world while his prodigious capacity for work—sometimes criticised by his colleagues who found it difficult to match his energy—enabled him to research and write the

Life and Work of Sir Astley Cooper (1952), his surgical predecessor at
Guy's Hospital.   M.D.

Born Russell Claude Brock, son of Herbert and Elvina B. Married:
(1) Germaine Louise Ladeveze 1927 (d. 1978); (2) Christia Palmer
Jones 1979. Children: 1st marriage—three daughters (one d.). Educ:
Christ's Hosp., London; M.R.C.S. and L.R.C.P. 1926; Guy's Hosp.
London (scholar) M.B., B.S. (London Univ., hons., medicine,
surgery, anatomy) 1927; F.R.C.S. 1928; M.S. (London Univ.) 1932.
Rockefeller Traveling Fellow, St. Louis, Mo., 1929–30. Demonstrator
in Pathology and Anatomy, Surgical Registrar, Tutor, Guy's Hosp.
1932–36. Consultant Thoracic Surgeon, London County Council (now
Greater London Council) 1935–46; Surgeon, Queen Mary's Hosp.,
Roehampton 1936–45, Guy's Hosp. 1936–68, and Brompton Hosp.
1936–68; Thoracic Surgeon and Regional Advisor in Thoracic Sur-
gery, Emergency Medical Service, London 1939–46; Exchange Prof.
of Surgery, Johns Hopkins Univ., Baltimore, Md. 1949. With Royal
Coll. of Surgeons: Member 1926; Fellow 1928; Hunterian Prof. 1938;
Council Member 1948–67; V.P. 1956–58; Hunterian Orator 1961;
Pres. 1963–66; Dir., Dept. of Surgical Sciences 1968–73. Research
Fellow, Assn. Surgeons of Great Britain 1932; Ed., Guy's Hosp.
Reports 1939–60; Pres.: Thoracic Soc. of Great Britain and Ireland
1952; Medical Soc. of London 1968. Public Lectr.: Lettsomian,
Medical Soc. of London 1952; Bradshaw, Royal Coll. of Surgeons
1957; Tudor Edwards Memorial 1963; Lister Orator 1967; Astley
Cooper Orator 1968. Hons. and prizes: Fellow, American Coll. of
Surgeons 1949; Hon. Member, American Assn. of Thoracic Surgeons
1950; Julius Mickle Prize, London Univ. 1950–51; Hon. Fellow,
Surgical Section, Royal Soc. of Medicine 1951; Hon. Fellow, Brazilian
Coll. of Surgeons 1952; Fothergillian Gold Medal, Medical Soc. of
London 1953; Leriche Medal, Intnl. Soc. of Surgery 1953; knighted
1954; Cameron Prize, Edinburgh Univ. 1954; Fothergillian Gold
Medal of Soc. of Apothecaries 1955; Gold Medal, West London
Medical-Chirurgie Soc. 1955; Fellow, Royal Australasian Coll. of
Surgeons 1958; Gardner Award 1960–61; Lannelongue Medal, Acad.
de Chirurgie 1963; Hon. M.D., Hamburg 1963; Fellow, Royal Coll. of
Physicians 1965; Hon. LL.D. Univ. Leeds 1965; Bronze Medal, City
of N.Y. 1965; life peer 1965; Lister Medal, Royal Coll. of Surgeons
1966; Fellow, Royal Coll. of Surgeons in Ireland 1966; Fellow, Royal
Coll. of Surgeons in Canada 1966; Fellow, Royal Coll. of Surgeons,
Edinburgh 1966; Hon. Sc.D. Cambridge Univ. 1968; Lettsonian
Medal 1971; Hon. M.D., Guelph 1971 and Munich 1972; Hon. fellow,
German Surgical Soc. 1972; Hon. Member AU-Union Soviet Soc. of
Surgeons 1974; also, Knight of St. John of Jerusalem. *Author:*
Anatomy of the Bronchial Tree, 1946; Life and Work of Astley
Cooper, 1952; Lung Abscess, 1952; Anatomy of Pulmonary Stenosis,
1957; also, articles in professional medical jrnls.

P(ATRICK) E(MMET) GORMAN
Union Leader
Born Louisville, Kentucky, U.S.A., November 27th, 1892
Died Chicago, Illinois, U.S.A., September 3rd, 1980

P.E. Gorman, head of the Amalgamated Meat Cutters and Butcher
Workmen of North America for 57 years, was the last survivor among

those labor leaders prominent during the era of Samuel Gompers. A man who championed the rights of women, minorities, and the handicapped, Gorman was a dramatic and charismatic figure familiar with the situation of the working person since he himself had started out at 19 as a hand trucker, moving beef and hog meat for 21 cents an hour, 55 hours a week.

Gorman, the son of a butcher, began his long union affiliation at the age of 21 when he was elected a full-time business agent of his union at the Cudahy Packing Company where his father also worked. Realizing that someone in this position needed a better education, Gorman, who had completed only the eighth grade, earned his high school diploma during two years of evening study and then his law degree from the University of Louisville Law School. He maintained a private law practice in Louisville from 1917 to 1920.

In 1920 Gorman, as a delegate to the Amalgamated Meat Cutters' convention in St. Louis, delivered a rousing speech to the 6000 members that brought about his immediate election as their vice-president. The ill health of the union president, John F. Hart, resulted in many duties falling to the newly-elected Gorman. Because of the recession of 1920–21, during which many workers lost their jobs and others had their pay reduced several times, the first years of his administration proved to be difficult. After the third reduction in pay, a strike was initiated by the employees in December 1920 which soon spread to over a hundred thousand workers throughout the nation. After the 13-week strike, during which 31 people died in violent circumstances, the union was in a state of almost complete confusion, its membership fewer than 7500.

Gorman, a clear-thinking realist and an unwavering optimist, met the challenge of rebuilding the devastated union. He firmly believed that, although it was impossible to conceive of a time when there would be no strikes, solutions to the inevitable problems would be found as long as there was open-minded communication between labor and management.

In 1923 Gorman was appointed president of the union, a position he held until 1942, during which no one attempted to run against him. As secretary-treasurer (and consequently chief executive officer) of the union from 1942 to 1976, Gorman, who identified himself politically as an independent, continued as the union's primary spokesperson, and in 1976 became chairman of the board. In 1979 he was made chairman emeritus of the board of the United Food and Commercial Workers' union, the largest affiliate of the American Federation of Labor and Congress of Industrial Organizations, formed by a merger the same year of the Meat Cutters and the Retail Clerks International Union.

Gorman was elected to the American Society of Composers, Authors, and Publishers, and to the Songwriters Hall of Fame. He was nominated for the Pope Paul VI Ecclesiastical Medal of Honor in 1973.   E.S.

Son of Maurice G. and Mary Ellen Dwyer G. Married: (1) Hattie Lee Dove 1914; (2) Dorothy Léchin. Roman Catholic. Educ: graduated Univ. of Louisville Law Sch. 1917. Hand trucker and butcher, Cudahy Packing Co., Louisville 1911–1920; Pres., Louisville Union Trades and Labor Assembly 1917–1919; law practice, Louisville 1917–1920; V.P., Ky. Fedn. of Labor 1918–1919. Amalgamated Meat Cutters and

Butcher Workmen of North America: Bus. Mgr. of Local 227, 1912–1920; special intnl. organizer 1917–1920; delegate to union convention, St. Louis 1920; V.P. 1920; Gen. V.P. 1923; Pres. 1923–42; Secty.-Treas. 1942–1976; Chmn. of the Bd. 1976–1979. Chmn. Emeritus, United Food and Commercial Workers (labor conglomerate formed by 1979 merger of Meat Cutters and the Retail Clerks Intnl. Union), since 1979. Pres., Eugene V. Debs Foundn.; Trustee, Roosevelt Univ., Chicago; Advisory Cttee., Harvard Univ. Trade Union Program. Member, American Society of Composers, Authors, and Publishers. Hons: designee, Pope Paul VI Ecclesiastical Medal of Honor 1973; humanitarian service award, Abraham Lincoln Centre 1975; chair established in his name, Weizman Inst. of Science, Rehovoth, Israel; elected to Songwriters Hall of Fame.

SIR GEORGE (WHITE) PICKERING
British physician and educator
Born Whalton, Northumberland, England, June 26th, 1904
Died Oxford, England, September 3rd, 1980

Sir George Pickering, Regius Professor of Medicine at Oxford from 1956 to 1968, made important contributions to clinical medicine and education. Pickering's research centered on the study of vascular disease and, specifically, on the causes of essential hypertension. As an educator, Pickering helped organize the Oxford Clinical Medical School into one of the leading clinics in England.

Pickering was born in Whalton, Northumberland in 1904. He completed his secondary education at Dulwich College in 1923, and obtained a Major Scholarship to Pembroke College, Cambridge. He finished with first class honours in parts I and II of the Natural Sciences Tripos.

In 1926, Pickering entered St. Thomas's Hospital, London for his clinical internship. On completion of this, he became a lecturer in cardiovascular pathology at University College Hospital, and in 1939 he was appointed to the Chair of Medicine at St. Mary's Hospital in London and remained there for 17 years until he became Regius Professor of Medicine at Oxford in 1956. Pickering also frequently traveled abroad, especially to the United States where he was popular as a guest lecturer and admired as a man of learning and scholarship.

Pickering's early research concentrated on headache, peptic ulcer, and fever, but his main contributions came later in the study of the arterial circulation. In 1955, Pickering published the results of his years of research in his important work *High Blood Pressure* (revised in 1968). Pickering's later research on the underlying causes of essential hypertension became controversial; he maintained that essential hypertension was largely due to heredity, the individual's mental attitude, and the stress imposed upon the individual by modern society. Contrary to the opinions of many of his colleagues, he denied that salt was a major determinant of essential hypertension since he had found that hypertensive patients ate and excreted the same amount of salt as other patients. Pickering thus concluded that patients with essential hypertension did not need to maintain a salt restricted diet. His two books on the subject are *The Nature of*

Essential Hypertension (1961), and *Hypertension: Causes, Consequences and Management* (1970).

When Pickering assumed the post of Regius Professor of Medicine at Oxford, he undertook several responsibilities. While maintaining his regular duties as a professor and physician, he also conducted a laboratory in essential hypertension and the mechanism of fever which attracted the leading students in England. By the time he retired in 1968, he had helped to build the Oxford Clinical School into an institution renowned for its excellent medical services and for the thorough, well-rounded education it provided medical students.

Sir George's concern and care for people, his odd mannerisms and personal charm all earned him a unique affection and respect among his colleagues, patients, and students. The Oxford Medical School Gazette aptly recalled "his tremor, his charateristic clearing of the throat, the imperfection of dress and sometimes of shaving technique, these things bring back the man vividly, and his hold over us." Sir George was admired for "the kindness, courtesy, and personal attention which he habitually brought to his patients . . . although students did not get the same respect . . . Woe betide the student who gave the history using technical terms rather than the patient's own words, thus perhaps missing important evidence."

Pickering often wrote on education and in his two works, *The Challenge to Education* (1967) and *The Quest for Excellence in Medical Education* (1978), as well as in numerous articles, Pickering argued against the tendency in medical schools to "require the student to assimilate a series of dicta, without inquiring into their validity." Pickering believed that the purpose of education was to stimulate and encourage the student to think for himself and to enable him to express his thoughts in clear and concise language. To counteract the overemphasis upon the sciences in medical schools, Pickering proposed the integration of the study of the sciences and humanities in order to benefit the student and to improve the quality of education.

Indeed, Pickering feared that the learned profession of medicine was becoming too much like a "technical trades union," and that doctors were becoming "technicians," thus lessening the quality of medical service. He felt that the decline in the clear and precise use of language in modern society had influenced the decline in learning and scholarship in the profession of medicine. The increasing use of technical jargon and acronyms, he observed, hindered rather than helped the doctor and patient to communicate with one another and tended to obscure the specific information of each individual case. The growth in the compartmentalization of medicine and thus, paradoxically, in the need for more specialized terms which neither the patient nor the doctor understood; the trends in medical education which emphasized a technical instead of humanistic attitude towards medicine; and, lastly, the increased use of unnecessary laboratory tests and equipment to diagnose patients in place of personal care were additional factors which Pickering thought had contributed to the depersonalization of the practice of medicine.

Pickering believed that the role of the doctor was "to make his patient's life more enjoyable as well as, if possible, longer." He insisted that medicine should maintain this humanistic attitude despite whatever changes occur in society and whatever the progress of scientific knowledge.   R.B.

Son of George P. and Ann P. Married: Mary Carola Seward 1930. Children: Thomas (physician); three daughters. Educ: Dulwich Coll.; Pembroke Coll., Cambridge (Scholar), First Class Hons., Natural Sciences Tripos, Part I 1925, Part II 1926; St. Thomas's Hosp., London (Scholar), M.B. 1930. Asst. in Dept. of Clinical Research and Lectr. in Cardiovascular Pathology, University Coll. Hosp., London; Herzstein Lectr., Stanford Univ. and Univ. of California 1938; Prof. of Medicine, Univ. of London and Dir. of Medical Clinic, St. Mary's Hosp., London 1939–56, on leave as Sims British Commonwealth Traveling Prof. 1949; frequent Visiting Prof. at several American and Canadian Univs.; Regius Prof. of Medicine at Oxford, Student of Christ Church, Master of God's House in Ewelme, and Physician to the United Oxford Hosp. 1956–68; a Pro-Vice-Chancellor, Oxford 1967–69; Master of Pembroke Coll., Oxford 1968–74. Pres., British Medical Assn. 1963–64; Trustee, Beit Memorial Fellowship Trust, Ciba Foundn., and Astor Foundn.; Emeritus Student 1969 and Hon. Student 1977, Christ Church, Oxford. Member: Univ. Grants Cttee. 1944–54; Medical Research Council and Clinical Research Bd. 1954–58; Hebdomadal Council at Oxford; Lord Chancellor's Cttee. on Legal Educ. 1967–71; Council for Scientific Policy 1968–71. Hons: Fellow of Royal Coll. of Physicians 1938; Fellow of Royal Soc. 1960; Knighted (K.B.D.) 1957; co-winner, Stouffer Prize 1970. Hon. Fellowships: Pembroke Coll., Cambridge 1959; Pembroke Coll., Oxford 1974; American Coll. of Physicians; Royal Coll. of Physicians, Edinburgh; Royal Coll. of Physicians, Ireland; American Medical Assn.; Academy of Medicine, Mexico; Royal Soc. of Uppsala; Royal Soc. of Medicine. Hon. Memberships: Assn. of American Physicians; American Gastroenterological Assn.; Australian Medical Assn.; Argentine Medical Assn.; Swedish Medical Soc.; Membre Correspondante Etranger, Soc. Medicine des Hôpitaux de Paris; Corresponding Member, Deutschen Gesellschaft fur Innere Medizin 1970; Czechoslovakian Medical Soc.; Hellenic Cardiac Soc.; Danish Soc. for Internal Medicine; Foreign Assoc., American Academy of Arts and Sciences; Royal Belgian Academy of Medicine; Foreign Assoc., American Natural Academy of Sciences 1970. *Author:* High Blood Pressure, 1955, 2nd ed. 1968; The Nature of Essential Hypertension, 1961; The Challenge to Education, 1967; Hypertension: Causes, Consequences and Management, 1970; Creative Malady, 1974; The Quest for Excellence in Medical Education, 1978; articles in many professional jrnls.

G(EORGE) M(URRAY) BURNETT
Polymer chemist and university administrator
Born Messina, South Africa, July 12th, 1921
Died Edinburgh, Scotland, September 4th, 1980

George Murray Burnett distinguished himself in two fields. His early career was devoted to chemical research and to the synthesis of the burgeoning body of knowledge on polymers, and he later became a university principal and vice-chancellor, expanding and diversifying academic programs during a time of economic constraint.

Born in South Africa of Scottish parents, Burnett was brought to Scotland by his mother when he was 16 in order to receive a Scottish education. When he graduated from the University of Aberdeen in 1943, he was recognized as the most outstanding chemistry student in his class. He began working with Professor (later Sir) Harry Melville, while a Department of Scientific and Industrial Research fellow at Aberdeen, and after obtaining his doctorate moved with Melville to the University of Birmingham, where Burnett combined advanced studies with a lectureship.

In 1954, Burnett gained his second doctorate and published *The Mechanism of Polymer Reactions,* one of the first comprehensive examinations of the processes of polymer chemistry. Burnett's efforts were significant among early attempts to understand how polymerization—the creation of complex molecules from smaller, like molecules—takes place. Polymerization, which is responsible for such materials as plastics, synthetic rubber and synthetic fabrics, was only partially understood up to the end of World War Two. While chemists, largely through trial and error, had gained an understanding of how some polymerization processes worked qualitatively—knowing which processes would result in certain products—they did not know the specific nature of the chemical reactions involved in polymerization. Burnett's most significant contribution, made possible by his detailed mathematical insight, was in furthering quantitative knowledge on the subject. Together with Melville, Burnett, worked toward the accurate determination of the rate coefficients for propagation, termination and chain transfer in photopolymerization.

Burnett's appointment in 1955 as Professor and Head of the Department of Chemistry at the University of Aberdeen was confirmation of his stature in the field. His involvement with the administration of the chemistry department proved successful, and led to positions of greater responsibility—three years as vice-principal and a temporary appointment as acting principal. Burnett also deepened and broadened his interest in the mechanism of chemical reactions by co-editing a four-volume series entitled *The Transfer and Storage of Energy by Molecules* in 1969 and 1970.

In 1974 Burnett became principal and vice-chancellor of Heroit-Watt University, where he was instrumental in developing new academic programs and improving faculty expertise despite a restrictive economic climate. Burnett stressed the importance of a balance between the vocational development and research functions of the university, and helped to implement cooperative programs between Heroit-Watt University and other universities and professional associations.   R.G.

Son of G., farmer. Married Anne Edith (Nan) Bow 1946. One son and three daughters. Brought to Scotland 1927. Scottish at birth. Educ: Robert Gordon's Coll., Aberdeen; Univ. of Aberdeen, B.Sc. 1943, Ph.D. 1947; Birmingham Univ., D.Sc. chemistry 1954. Lectr., Univ. of Birmingham 1949–54; with Univ. of Aberdeen: Prof. and Head, Department of Chemistry 1955–74, Vice-Principal 1966–69, Acting Principal; Prof., Principal and Vice-Chancellor, Heriot-Watt Univ., Edinburgh, 1974–80. Member, Science Bd., Science Research Council 1975–78; Member of Council, Open Univ. 1975–78; Chmn., Scottish Universities' Principals 1978–79 and Scottish National Cttee., English Speaking Union 1979–80; Secty., Council for Tertiary Educ. in Scotland 1979–80; Member, American Chemical Soc., and Faraday Soc.; Justice of the Peace, Aberdeen 1967–74. Hons: Fellow, Royal Soc. of Edinburgh 1957; Fellow, Royal Inst. of Chemistry 1961; Hon. LLD Strathclyde 1979. *Author:* Mechanism of Polymer Reactions,

1954; (ed. with Alastair M. Roth) Transfer and Storage of Energy by Molecules, vols. 1–2 1969, vols. 3–4 1970; more than 60 articles in various scientific journals.

WALTER (ARNOLD) KAUFMANN
Philosopher
Born Freiburg, Germany, July 1st, 1921
Died Princeton, New Jersey, U.S.A., September 4th, 1980

Walter Kaufmann, whose work rescued the reputation of Friedrich Nietzsche from its association with nazi ideology, was a German-born philosopher in the humanist tradition. A prolific writer, editor, and translator, he bypassed many of the technical issues considered important by professional philosophers and dealt instead with problems of personal freedom and ethical justification.

Kaufmann, the son of a lawyer, was born in Freiburg in 1921 and brought up in Berlin, where he received a classical education. In the prologue to his book *The Faith of a Heretic,* he explained that he was raised a Lutheran, finding himself unable to believe in the divinity of Jesus, renounced Christianity at the age of 11 and converted to Judaism. He learned later that all his grandparents had been Jewish and that his father, at the urging of his grandmother, had undergone baptism in order to make himself acceptable to German society. Following young Kaufmann's lead, his father and brother also returned to Judaism and the family became increasingly orthodox. "Judaism in Nazi Germany," he later wrote, "was not merely a matter of reading about the past. It was an existential experience that involved my whole being." After graduating from a Gymnasium in 1938, he visited Palestine and enrolled in Berlin's Lehranstalt für die Wissenschaft des Judentums, where he studied Jewish history and Talmud.

Kaufmann left Germany in February of 1939, when he was 17, to attend Williams College in Massachusetts. His father had just been released from a concentration camp. Although both parents escaped to England, one of his uncles was killed in a death camp and another was shot by the Gestapo.

At Williams, Kaufmann studied philosophy under William Pratt and took courses in history, comparative religion, and the philosophy and psychology of religion, gradually exchanging his own religious beliefs for rationalist humanism. He took his B.A. in 1941 with highest honors and won a scholarship to do graduate work in philosophy at Harvard. After serving with the U.S. Military Intelligence Service in Austria and Germany, he completed his dissertation on "Nietzsche's Theory of Values" in 1947, received his doctorate, and joined the faculty of Princeton University, which was to be his academic home for the rest of his life.

Kaufmann's first book, *Nietzsche: Philosopher, Psychologist, Antichrist,* was an expansion of his dissertation. The book, which introduced Nietzsche's work into American academic philosophy, dealt with the perennial problems that obsessed Nietzsche—nihilism, the morality of Christianity, cycles of hystory, and the will to power—and

located his thought in the critical tradition of Plato, Luther, Kant, and
Hegel. In addition, Kaufmann established authoritative texts of
writings corrupted by Nietzsche's sister. Kaufmann later translated
and edited the bulk of Nietzsche's work, much of which was included
in a 1954 volume called *The Portable Nietzsche,* an enormously
successful paperback and college textbook. In the introduction, he
debunked popular misconceptions of Nietzsche as an anti-Semite,
Social Darwinist, and apologist for nazism, saying, "No other German
writer of equal stature has been so thoroughly opposed to all proto-
nazism. . . . If some nazi writers cited him nevertheless, it was at the
price of incredible misquotation and exegetical acrobatics. . . . paren-
thetical statements were quotes as meaning the opposite of what they
plainly mean in context; and views he explicitly rejected were brazenly
attributed to him." Some recent scholars have complained that
Kaufmann, in his zeal to defend Nietzsche, chose to underplay
contradictory and unsavory elements in his work.

Critique of Religion and Philosophy appeared in 1958 and was
judged "a witty, learned, sometimes exasperating book" by reviewer
Arnulf Zweig, who noted that "hardly a school or party of current
philosophy and theology escapes reproof. . . . Kaufmann . . . rebukes
positivists for being insensitive to profound experience, and he notes
'messianic overtones' in both positivism and existentialism. . . ."
According to Philip Leon, "Kaufmann . . . is at his soundest when
. . . he protests against the objectification of God by religion and
theology," but undermines his own argument by "trying to unite two
mutually incompatible modes of thought and feeling, as so many
rationalists do who want to keep the valued emotions of traditional
religion while polemizing against everything else in it."

Kaufmann followed the *Critique* with a series of volumes on religion
and existentialism written in non-technical language for the educated
general readers. In *Tragedy and Philosophy* (1968), he studied the
exchange of influence between Greek philosophers and tragedians and
examined worked by Brecht, Sartre, and Styron for evidence of a new
tragic ideal. In *Without Guilt and Justice* (1973), he argued against
traditional norms of justice as decisive factors in the development of
individual ethics. In *The Future of the Humanities* (1977), he redefined
the mission of higher education as a communication of "vision," of a
critical spirit open to alternative points of view and to honest
reflection.

The Faith of a Heretic, published in 1961, was a coming-to-terms
with his own lapse from religious belief and his commitment to "the
will to honesty." "Man seems to play a very insignificant part in the
universe," he wrote, "and my part is negligible. The question
confronting me is . . . what I wish to make of my part. And what I
want to do and would advise others to do is to make the most of it: put
into it all you have got, and live, and, if possible, die with some
measure of nobility." In place of received tradition, he offered an
"ethic of virtues" consisting of love, courage, honesty, and a fusion of
humility and aspiration. He saw alienation from ossified systems of
belief as an occasion for enrichment of the individual's life, a
challenge to deepen one's understanding of oneself in relation to the
world.

In 1967, Kaufmann and R. J. Hollingdale published, in English, the
first critical edition in any language of Nietzsche's *The Will to Power,*

which they had pieced together from fragments in the philosopher's notebooks. Kaufmann also published translations of the work of the Jewish scholars Leo Baeck and Martin Buber, both of whom he had known in Germany, and of German poetry. Stephen Spender called his version of Goethe's 'Faust' "the best translation of Faust that I have read . . . First, his version has a rhythmic drive which is very close to Goethe's; second, he transmits a very important quality about the language of 'Faust': that it is packed with material of every kind—information, ideas, wit. These are all communicated with immense energy and a warmth of imagination, which . . . never succumbs to pedantry or showing off."

Religion in Four Dimensions, published in 1976, was a return to Kaufmann's early interest in comparative religion, especially the religions of the East. His discussion of ten major faiths focused less on their theological systems than on their differing effects on the lives of their adherents. Both this book and *What is Man?* were illustrated by the author's own expert photography.

Kaufmann, who was married and had two children, received Fulbright grants to teach at Heidelberg University and Hebrew University and served as a visiting professor at a number of institutions. In 1962 he was honored by the Princeton Undergraduate Council with an invitation to deliver a Witherspoon Lecture. He was named Stuart Professor of Philosophy in 1979. J.P./R.W.

Son of Bruno K., lawyer, and Edith (Seligsohn) K. Married Hazel Dennis 1942. Children: Dinah, b. 1944; David, b. 1947. Raised as a Lutheran by parents of Jewish origin; returned to Judaism as a child. Emigrated to U.S.A. 1939; naturalized 1944. Educ: gymnasium, grad. 1938; studied Jewish history and Talmud at Lehranstalt für die Wissenschaft des Judentuums, Berlin 1938; Williams Coll., Williamstown, Mass. (Phi Beta Kappa), B.A. 1941; Harvard Univ., M.A. 1942, Ph.D. in philosophy 1947; Resident Scholar, Villa Serbelloni, Italy, 1970, 1975. Mil. Service: U.S. Army Air Force and Military Intelligence Service, Austria and Germany 1944–46. With Philosophy Dept., Princeton Univ.: Instr. 1947–49; Asst. Prof. 1950–54; Praeceptor 1951–54; Assoc. Prof. 1954–61; Prof. 1962–78; Stuart Prof. of Philsophy since 1979. Visiting Prof.: Cornell Univ. 1952; Columbia Univ. 1955; Univ. of Washington, Seattle 1958; Univ. of Michigan, Ann Arbor 1959; New Sch. for Social Research, NYC 1960; Purdue Univ. 1966; Inst. of Philosophy, Hebrew Univ. 1975. Fulbright Research Prof., Heidelberg Univ., West Germany 1955–56; Fulbright Prof. 1962–63 and Phi Beta Kappa Visiting Scholar 1971–72, Hebrew Univ., Jerusalem; Visiting Fellow, History of Ideas Unit. Research Sch. of Social Sciences, Australian Natl. Univ., Canberra 1974. Member 1957–61 and Chmn. 1959–61, Advanced Screening Cttee., Philosophy and Religion Cttee. for Intnl. Exchange of Persons, Princeton Univ.; Co-founder and Bd. Chamn., InterFuture (student exchange program) 1970–71; Acting Dir., Christian Gauss Seminar in Criticism, Princeton Univ. 1967–68, 1972, 1975–76; Member, American Philosophical Assn. Hons: Intnl. Leo Baeck Prize 1961; Witherspoon Lectr., Princeton Univ. 1962. *Author:* Nietzsche: Philosopher, Psychologist, Antichrist, 1950, 4th ed. 1974; Critique of Religion and Philosophy, 1958; From Shakespeare to Existentialism, 1959, rev. ed. 1960 (in U.K. as The Owl and the Nightingale, 1960); The Faith of a Heretic, 1961; Cain and Other Poems (verse), 1962, 3rd ed. 1975; Hegel, 1965; Tragedy and Philosophy, 1968; Without Guilt and Justice, 1973; (also photographer) Religions in Four Dimensions:

Existential, Aesthetic, Historical, Comparative, 1976; Existentialism, Religion, and Death, 1976; The Future of the Humanities, 1977; (also photographer) What is Man?, 1978. *Translator and editor:* The Portable Nietzsche, 1954; Existentialism from Dostoevsky to Sartre, 1956, rev. ed. 1975; Judaism and Christianity: Essay by Leo Baeck, 1958; Philosophic Classics, 2 vols., 1961, 1968; Religion from Tolstoy to Camus, 1961, rev. ed. 1964; Goethe's Faust, 1961; 25 German Poets: A Bilingual Collection, 1962; Hegel: Texts and Commentary, 1965; (with R. J. Hollingdale) On the Genealogy of Morals (by Friedrich Nietzsche), 1966; Ecce Homo (by Nietzsche), 1966; The Birth of Tragedy (by Nietzsche), 1967; The Case of Wagner (by Nietzsche), 1967; (with R. J. Hollingdale) The Will to Power (by Nietzsche), 1968; The Basic Writings of Nietzsche, 1968; I and Thou (by Martin Buber), 1970; Hegel's Political Philosophy, 1970; The Gay Science (by Nietzsche), 1974; Beyond Good and Evil (by Nietzsche). *Contributor:* Toynbee and History (ed. by Ashley Montagu), 1956; The Philosophy of Karl Jaspers (ed. by P. A. Schilpp), 1957; The Meaning of Death (ed. by Hermann Feifel), 1959; preface to Europe and the Jews (by Malcolm Hay), 1960; Ideas in Cultural Perspective (ed. by Wiener and Noland), 1962; preface to The Present Age (by Søren Kierkegaard), 1962; Martin Buber (ed. by Schilpp and Friedman), 1963; Of Poetry and Power (ed. by Glikes and Schwaber), 1964; Art and Philosophy (ed. by Sidney Hook), 1966; Philosophy and Educational Development (ed. by George Barnett), 1966; numerous other volumes.
Further reading: review of Tragedy and Philosophy by George Lichtheim, in the New York Review of Books, July 15, 1965.

FABIAN VON SCHLABRENDORFF
Jurist and anti-nazi
Born Halle, Saxony, Germany, July 1st, 1907
Died Wiesbaden, Germany, September 4th, 1980

A general's son, a Prussian civil servant, a Wehrmacht staff officer, a liberal jurist and secret emissary, Fabian von Schlabrendorff was also the historian of the conspiracy against Hitler in which he played a key role.

Born in Halle, a Prussian enclave in Saxony, he found himself rescuing anti-nazi Conservatives from the hands of the Storm Troopers. Working in the Prussian Ministry of the Interior, Schlabrendorff was able to travel widely and noticed a stiffening in the opposition to the nazis by 1938. He soon became an important coordinator in the anti-nazi movement that revolved around Liepzig's Lord-Mayor, Carl Goerdeler. As a representative of this group, Schlabrendorff went to England shortly before the outbreak of war and spoke with Winston Churchill.

A lieutenant in the reserves, he was soon working closely with General Henning von Tresckow, Operations Chief for Army Group Center on the Eastern Front. Tresckow and his allies made several attempts on Hitler's life and Schlabrendorff was the key liaison between the plotters in Army Group Center and others in Berlin. In March 1943, Lieutenant Schlabrendorff had to retrieve a disguised bomb smuggled aboard the Führer's plane that had failed to explode. Not all the conspirators' failures were due to mechanical failures; the difficulties of persuading high-ranking officers to unite against Hitler prompted him to write later, "their lack of backbone gave us more trouble than the wanton brutality of the nazis."

Following the most famous attempt, the July 20th, 1944 bomb plot (Colonel Graf Claus von Stauffenberg exploded a bomb at a conference in East Prussia; Hitler escaped with minor injuries) Schlabrendorff like hundreds of other implicated suspects, was arrested and tortured. Ironically, the luck that had eluded their efforts seemed reserved for the thirty-seven year old Schlabrendorff: an Allied bomb killed the feared prosecuting judge, Roland Freisler, the day before his court appearance and the American advance delayed his summary execution at the Flossenbürg Concentration Camp where many of the plotters were murdered. Eventually, he was liberated by Allied troops in the Tyrol.

After the war, Fabian von Schlabrendorff returned to the practice of law in Frankfurt and Wiesbaden. He became a constitutional court judge in 1967 and served until his retirement in 1975 delivering judgments on a right-to-rebellion clause in the Federal Constitution and the Basic Treaty with East Germany. The author of several books about the military conspiracy against Hitler, Schlabrendorff earned from CIA Director Allen Dulles the tribute of being "one of the boldest and bravest of the anti-nazis."   L.R.

Son of Lt. Gen. Carl von S. and Ida Freiin von Stockmar S. Religion: Evangelical. Married: Luitgarde von Bismarck 1939. Six children. Educ: Leopoldinum Detmold Gymnasium; Univs. of Halle and Berlin. Mil. Service: Lieutenant in the Reserves; Aide to Chief of Operations, Army Group Center 1943–44. Lawyer with Prussian Ministry of the Interior during 1930s; law practice in Frankfurt and Wiesbaden in postwar years; named a Judge of the Constitutional Court 1967, retired 1975. *Author*—Offiziere gegen Hitler, 1946, as The Secret War Against Hitler, 1966. *Editor*—Eugen Gerstenmaier im Dritten Reich, 1965. Hons: Hon. Professorship, University of Gottingen.

ADRIAN (HANBURY) BELL
Novelist, essayist, crossword compiler and farmer
Born London, England, October 4th, 1901
Died Beccles, Suffolk, England, September 5th, 1980

City-born, Adrian Bell's great love of the English countryside and rural life is apparent in all of his works, which include 15 novels, five collections of essays, a volume of poems and an autobiography. A popular writer in the 1930s, 40s and 50s, Bell was also well-known as a regular contributor of crosswords to *The Times* (London).

Bell's father, Robert, a Scotsman, was a prominent journalist with the *Observer,* a London Sunday newspaper, and his mother, Frances, an Englishwoman, was known for her wit and artistic interests. As a youth Adrian read the classics, studied music and aspired to the life of the poet. During the years of World War One he was sent to Uppingham School, but he found the experience unpleasant and lost any desire for continued scholarship. He spent his 19th year at home, handicapped by migraine headaches, with no plans for himself other than a vague desire "to be a writer of some kind." He said later that during these years his father looked at him "as if I were a letter very difficult to answer to which a reply was overdue."

In 1920, his love of the countryside already acknowledged, Bell apprenticed for a year to an old-fashioned farmer near Newmarket, in Suffolk. His first book, *Corduroy,* published ten years later recounts the story of his apprenticeship. Though nominally a novel, it describes picturesquely and realistically his initiation into plowing, harrowing, sowing, reaping, threshing, milling, feeding and so on, as well as the diversions of rabbitting, pheasant-shooting, visits to agricultural shows and a day at the seaside. By the end of the year he had found a small parcel of land and persuaded his father to put up the money for a farm of his own.

Corduroy was received with unexpected popularity. His subtle observations on farming and rural pursuits as a way of life to be cherished, told with a gentle humor, had an immediate appeal to many who were beginning to find fault with industrial and urbanized life. Bell was able to combine in his writing the eyes of a city-bred poet with the brains of a practical farmer.

At the invitation of his father, Bell developed the first crossword puzzle for *The Times* which appeared on February 1st, 1930. Prior to this he had neither compiled nor solved one, but he took to the task with great enthusiasm, "wearing out a dictionary in the first year," and contributing regularly until his death.

Bell's second book, *Silver Ley,* published in 1931, described his first year as a farmer as he tried to make the most of his 50 acres. ("What a pity, when you've got a brain for other things," he reports a neighbor commenting.) In 1932 he published *The Cherry Tree,* in which he describes his marriage to Marjorie Gibson the previous year. She was town-bred like Adrian and met him as a result of her admiration for *Corduroy.*

Throughout the 1930s and early 1940s Bell published nearly a book per year. These novels, which often dealt with the changing problems of farming as new methods and technologies were introduced into a very traditional world, always remained personal and anecdotal. He admitted that the picturesque does not always make economic sense, but occasionally finds a nostalgia for the old ways in his writing.

After the Second World War, Bell moved to Beccles, a small town in the Waverly Valley, Suffolk. He began to publish weekly articles in the *Eastern Daily Press* under the title "Countryman's Notebook." Many of these affectionate musings have been collected in his books, *A Street in Suffolk, A Countryman's Notebook,* or often as set pieces in his later novels. His autobiography, *My Own Master,* appeared in 1961.

In his novel *Silver Ley,* Bell wrote: "My work was arduous, but my mind was easy. My hours were long, but I was master of them and did not have to live as a city man, tethered to nine-thirty a.m. like a goat to a tree. I got that first taste of that fierce and stubborn independence of the farmer which is both the wonder of others and their parrot cry against him when his trade is adverse."   M.M.

Son of Robert B., journalist, and Frances Hanbury B. Married
Marjorie Gibson 1931. Children: Martin, b. 1938 (journalist); two
daughters. Educ: Uppingham School, Norfolk. Apprenticed to a
Suffolk farmer 1920; since farmed in West and East Suffolk. Regular
contributor of crosswords to *The Times,* London, since 1930. Colum-
nist, Countryman's Notebook, Eastern Daily Press. *Books: Novels*—
Corduroy, 1930; Silver Ley, 1931; The Cherry Tree, 1932; Folly Field,
1933; Balcony, 1934; By-Road, 1937; Shepherd's Farm, 1939; Apple
Acre, 1942; Sunrise to Sunset, 1944; The Budding Morrow, 1947; The
Black Donkey, 1949; The Path by the Window, 1952; Music in the
Morning, 1954; A Young Man's Fancy, 1955; The Mill House, 1958;
Essays—Men and the Fields, 1939; A Suffolk Harvest, 1956; A Street
in Suffolk, 1964; *Other*—Poems, 1935; My Own Master (autobiog.),
1961; (editor) The Open Air, 1936.

BARBARA LODEN
Actress, writer, and film director
Born Asheville, North Carolina, U.S.A., July 8th, 1934
Died New York City, U.S.A., September 5th, 1980

urtesy Warner Brothers

In 1964, when Barbara Loden created the Marilyn Monroe role in
Arthur Miller's *After the Fall, Newsweek* marveled at her skill in
capturing the "carnality and pathos" of the late movie star. In 1970 as
"Wanda," the title character in a feature film she also wrote,
produced and directed, a critic wrote of her performance: "It is hard
to think of an actress who has allowed herself to be as dowdy as she is
in *Wanda."* A gifted actress, Miss Loden was invariably described off-
stage and off-screen as a well-scrubbed, girl-next-door beauty with a
lively independent mind. Rarer still in the often shallow world of show
business, she was a person who prized personal and artistic integrity
above commercial success, even if it meant long absences from the
public eye. "I don't want to feel I have to create a moneymaking
film," she declared in 1974, "just like I don't take an acting job I feel
shouldn't be done by anyone."

Born in 1934 in Asheville, North Carolina—a self-described "hill-
billy's" daughter—Loden grew up in the sort of impoverished Appalachian setting she would later evoke in *Wanda.* A rebellious girl,
she left her small town environment after graduation from high school
and went to New York City in search of "something glamorous." At
first the search, depending rather too much upon her good looks, led
her into glamor and pulp magazine modeling, night club dancing, and
TV walk-ons as the sexy butt of Ernie Kovac's slapstick humor.

A major change in the direction and quality of her career came in
1957 when she approached a casting director and begged him to give
her a job. She received a bit part in the play, *Compulsion,* and went
on to small roles in a series of plays and two films. During this period
she met Elia Kazan who, as director of Miller's *After the Fall,* cast her
in the role of "Maggie"—for which performance the heretofore
"unknown actress" won a Tony Award and citation as best actress by
the critics Outer Circle. With her run in *After the Fall* completed,
however, Loden retired from public view until the American release
of her film *Wanda* in 1971.

Reviewing Wanda, *New York Times* critic Roger Greenspun wrote: "It would be hard to imagine better or more tactful or more decently difficult work for a first film." Loden's film was completed on a budget of $115,000, shot in black and white 16MM film using hand-held cameras, and edited in a room in the back of the town house Loden shared with Kazan (whom she had married in 1967) and two young sons by a previous marriage. Loden presented her heroine—a poor and unintelligent woman fleeing a dead-end marriage and a drab environment—with subtlety and understanding. Without subordinating plot to character study, she crafted a film that made its point without the stridency of more polemical efforts. It was not, she told an interviewer, a film that advocated women's liberation so much as one which tried to show why women *should* be liberated. That she achieved this goal was evident in the comments not only of feminist critics like Marion Mead and Sharon Smith, but of cinema historian David Thompson who observed in Loden's work "a feeling for wayward, unordered lives [and] . . . an off-center unsentimental pathos."

The attention received by *Wanda* provided Loden with the chance to speak her mind on such issues as the "myth" of cinema technology, the artistically destructive "slickness" of the Hollywood product, and the image of women in film. Her "Wanda" was, she said, symbolic of millions of women living wasted, dependent existences because they had no other options—a situation encountered not only in the coal fields of Appalachia, but in the suburbs of New York and the foothills of Los Angeles. If there were more opportunities for women film-makers, Loden argued, there would be that many more possibilities of altering social values. She insisted that *Wanda* was not, however, an example of "new wave" revolt. "It's old wave. It's what they used to do. They took a camera and they went out and shot. Around that act this whole fantastic apparatus grew—the Hollywood albatross. They made a ship out of lead. It won't float anymore."

Loden died at the age of 46, a victim of cancer.   R.C.

Daughter of George T. L., barber, and Ruth Sadur L. Married: (1) Laurance Joachim, film producer (div.); (2) Elia Kazan, film and theatrical dir., 1967. Children: 1st marriage—Leo Alexander, b. 1961; Jon Marco, b.1963. Educ: L.H. Edwards High Sch., Asheville, N.C., grad. 1951. Model, chorus girl (Copa) and TV walk-on (Ernie Kovacs Show), NYC 1952–57. Member: Lincoln Center Repertory Co. 1960–64; American Fedn. of TV and Radio Artists. Hons: Tony Award and Outer Circle Award (for the role of Maggie in After the Fall) 1964; Intnl. Critics Prize for Best Film (for Wanda), Venice Film Festival 1970. *Performances: Plays*— Compulsion, 1957 (debut); Out of This World, 1957; Look After Lulu, 1959; The Long Dream, 1960; Forty-one in the Sack, 1960; After the Fall, 1964. *Films*—Wild River, 1960; Splendor in the Grass, 1962; Wanda (also producer, dir. and screenplay writer), 1971.

MARTIN (GLOSTER) SULLIVAN
Dean of St. Paul's Cathedral, London
Born Auckland, New Zealand, March 30th, 1910
Died Auckland, New Zealand, September 5th, 1980

The Very Reverend Martin Sullivan, Dean of St. Paul's Cathedral, London, from 1967 to 1977, was one of the best-known and most controversial Anglican churchmen of his generation. A pastoral man with a gift for communicating with children, he opened the staid ceremonies of the Cathedral to experimental change in order to attract young people to the faith.

Sullivan was born to a middle-class family in Auckland, New Zealand, and attended public schools there. After earning bachelor's and master's degrees from Auckland University College, he was ordained in 1934, becoming a parish priest. During the Second World War he served in Southeast Asia and Europe as chaplain of the Second New Zealand Expeditionary Force, and afterwards spent a year on the staff of St. Martins in the Fields, London. In 1951, following a curacy at Wellington, he became dean of Christchurch Cathedral. He returned to London in 1961 as rector of St. Mary in Bryanston Square and was named Archdeacon of London and Canon Residentiary of St. Paul's Cathedral in 1963. A powerful and moving preacher, he was called upon to read the lesson at the funeral of Sir Winston Churchill.

As chaplain to Wellington's Student Christian Movement and as principal of two schools in Christchurch, Sullivan had developed a warm rapport with young people. His attempts to involve them in the life of St. Paul's often drew criticism from more conservative clergymen, who were particularly incensed by his invitation to the cast of the rock musical *Hair!* to attend his celebration of the Eucharist. Such gestures, and his inaptitude for theolgical scholarship, provoked opposition to his appointment as Dean of the Cathedral in 1967. Late in 1968 he created another *cause célèbre* by organizing a national Festival of Youth at St. Paul's complete with popular singers and rock musicians, during which he made headlines by taking part in a simulated parachute jump outside the Cathedral along with other clergy. Canon Frank Colquhoun of London's Southwark Cathedral described the festival as an "ecclesiastical jamboree" and suggested that "such tomfoolery" had nothing to do with Christianity. Other critics in the Church and the press took Sullivan to task for remaining aloof from the activities of the diocese.

Despite his liberal attitude toward innovation in the worship service by young people, Sullivan was a traditionalist with regard to texts, holding to the Prayer Book liturgies and using the Authorized Version of the Bible.

Sullivan's forte was his oratory, both from the pulpit and in addresses to secular groups, where his lively wit and personal warmth won him standing ovations. Thanks largely to his enthusiasm and support, the Lord Mayor fund for restorations to the Cathedral amassed £3 million in two years. After playing a leading role in Queen Elizabeth's Silver Jubilee Thanksgiving service in 1977, Sullivan retired to New Zealand.

Sullivan, who was twice married, wrote a number of religious books with a pastoral outlook that enjoyed much popular appeal, particularly *On Calvary's Tree* (1957) and *Approach With Joy* (1961). His autobiographical *A Funny Thing Happened to Me on the Way to St. Paul's* appeared in 1968.   J.P./M.D.

Son of Denis S. Married: (1) Doris Cowen 1934 (d.1972); (2) Elizabeth Roberton 1973. No children. Church of England. Educ: Auckland Grammar Sch., N.Z.; Auckland Univ. Coll., B.A. 1931, M.A. 1932; St. John's Theological Coll. 1932. Mil. Service: Chaplain, 2nd N.Z. Expeditionary Force, Southeast Asia and Europe 1941–46. Ordained deacon 1932, priest 1934. Asst. Curate, St. Matthew's, Auckland 1932–34; Vicar, St. Columba, Grey Lynn, N.Z., and Te Awamutu, N.Z. 1936–46; Examining Chaplain to Bishop of Waikato, N.Z. 1937–46; on clergy staff of St. Martin's in the Fields, London 1945–46; Curate of St. Peter's, Wellington, N.Z. 1946–50; Chaplain to Student Christian Movement, Wellington 1946–49; Principal, Upper Dept., Christchurch Coll., Christchurch, N.Z. 1950–56; Principal, College House, Christchurch 1956–59. With Christchurch Cathedral: Dean 1951–62; Vicar-Gen. 1952–62; Commissary to Bishop 1962. Rector of St. Mary's, Bryanston Square, London 1961–63; Archdeacon of London and Canon Residentiary of St. Paul's Cathedral 1963–67; Examining Chaplain to Bishop of London 1963–67; Dean 1967–77 and Dean emeritus since 1977, St. Paul's Cathedral, London. Member, Guild of Freemen of the City of London since 1965; Freeman, Merchant Taylors' Company, London 1967; Dean of the Order of the British Empire 1967–77; Dean of the Order of St. Michael and St. George 1968–77; Freeman, Painter-Stainers Company, London 1974; Chaplain and Sub-Prelate of the Order of St. John 1968; Freeman, Glass Sellers Company, London 1976. Member, Council of Univ. of Canterbury, N.Z. 1953–62; Member, Court of Dirs., Royal Humane Soc. of New Zealand 1956–62; Member, Senate of Univ. of New Zealand 1961–62; Rep. of Vice-Chancellor of Univ. of Canterbury, Assn. of Univs. of the British Commonwealth 1962; Gov., St. Paul's Sch., London 1967–77; Gov., Haileybury Sch. 1971–75; Member, Central Council, Royal Overseas League. Hons: Hon. Litt. D., Univ. of Auckland 1976; KCVO 1979. Author: Children Listen, 1955; Listen Again, 1956; A World for Everyman, 1956; Draw Near With Faith, 1956; On Calvary's Tree, 1957; Approach with Joy, 1961; A Dean Speaks to New Zealand, 1962; A Funny Thing Happened to Me on the Way to St. Paul's, 1968; Watch How You go, 1975.

SIR PHILIP (AUSTISS) HENDY
Director, National Gallery, London, and art historian
Born Carlisle, Cumberland, England, September 27th, 1900
Died Oxford, England, September 6th, 1980

Sir Philip Hendy, Britain's National Gallery Director for twenty-one years and a noted art historian, was responsible for reclaiming and reorganizing the British national art collection following its protective dispersal outside London during the Second World War.

An acknowledged expert both with the Old Masters and more modern works, Hendy's scholarly and reserved disposition concealed an innate independence of thought and purpose which at times led him into controversy. His decision to have cleaned and restored several of the major works in the national collection—and in particu-

lar the way in which conservation was carried out—resulted in strong criticism while on another occasion, the theft of a Francisco Goya from the National Gallery called into question his judgment over security.

Born of an academic family background, Hendy attended Westminster School, and then went up to Oxford where during his undergraduate career at Christ Church College he developed his appreciation and knowledge of the fine arts. His first job was assistant to the keeper of the Wallace Collection in London. It was there that he produced one of his most popular catalogues, *Hours in the Wallace Collection,* published in 1926 and revised in 1928. It was this that resulted in an invitation from the Trustees of the Isabella Stewart Gardner Museum in Boston to compile a similar publication based on their collection. He produced a definitive work which remained a standard reference text for forty years until it was revised by Hendy himself. While in Boston, Hendy accepted the offer of a curatorship at the Museum of Fine Arts, and supervised redecoration and rehanging of the galleries, demonstrating his imaginative approach by creating specially sympathetic backgrounds and surrounds for many of the paintings in his charge. On his initiative the museum made several notable acquisitions during his stay, among them examples of Cézanne, Van Dyck and Tintoretto.

After three years in Boston, Hendy returned to Britain and became Director of the Leeds City Art Gallery. He remained at Leeds until the end of the Second World War while holding the visiting post of Slade Professor of Fine Art at Oxford. Following Sir Kenneth Clark's retirement from the National Gallery at the end of the war, Hendy was appointed director with the prime task of reassembling the nation's art collection.

The many priceless works of art were brought back from their secret hiding places, mainly in Wales, where they had been stowed to avoid bomb damage. Hendy ordered a number of paintings to be cleaned and this resulted in sharp criticism from a number of artists and scholars who contended that the paintings—among them Rubens' *Chapeau de Paille,* Rembrandt's *Woman Bathing,* and Velasquez's *Philip IV*—had been damaged by the process, while others maintained that the cleaning had been unnecessary. In 1947 Hendy mounted a special exhibition of the cleaned pictures together with photographic evidence of what had been done and a catalogue explanation. His quiet, reasoned approach was well received and his critics, if not completely won over, were at least placated. Hendy continued to pay special regard to conservation at the gallery and under his guidance its catalogue was much revised.

In 1961, Hendy again found himself at the center of controversy when Goya's portrait of the Duke of Wellington was stolen from the Gallery. Public criticism of the Gallery's security system, he felt, was a personal reflection on him and he offered to resign. But the Gallery trustees refused to blame Hendy and he remained director for a further six years. The theft did, however, lead to a substantial security improvement.

Hendy wrote and compiled a number of publications reflecting his own catholic tastes in art. His knighthood, conferred in 1950, recognized his services to art and in particular his efforts in restoring the National Gallery to its former prominence. Hendy maintained wide contacts in the world of art, in particular through the International Council of Museums over which he presided for a number of years. He was also called in as Artistic Advisor when Israel sought to build up its national fine art collection in Jerusalem.   M.D.

Son of Francis James Roberts H. (teacher) and Caroline Isobel H. (Potts). Married: (1) Kythé Ogilvy; (2) Cicely Martin. No children. Educ: Westminster Sch., London; Christ Church Coll., Oxford B.A. (fine arts) 1922; student of Italian painting, Florence 1927–30. Asst. to the Keeper, and Lectr., Wallace Coll., London 1923–27; Curator of Paintings, Mus. of Fine Arts, Boston, Mass. 1930–33; Dir., City Art Gall. and Temple Newsam Mansion, Leeds 1934–45; Slade Prof. of Fine Arts, Univ. Oxford 1936–46; Dir., Natl. Gall., London 1946–67. Art critic: *Daily Herald* 1923–26; *New Statesman* 1926–27; *London Mercury* 1934–36; *Britain Today* 1945–52. Pres.: Intnl. Council of Museums 1959–65; Intn;. Council of Museum Foundns. 1965–70. Artistic Advisor, Israel Museum, Jerusalem 1968–71. Hons: knighted 1950. *Author:* Hours in the Wallace Collection, 1926; The Wallace Collection: Catalogue of Paintings and Drawings, 1928; Isabella Stewart Gardner Museum (Boston): Catalogue of Paintings and Drawings, 1931 (rev. ed. 1974); Matthew Smith, 1944; Giovanni Bellini, 1945; Spanish Painting, 1946; The National Gallery, 1955; Masaccio (Unesco), 1957; Piero della Francesca and the Early Renaissance, 1968. *Contributor:* The Times (London); Burlington Magazine; Apollo; and others.

VISCOUNT DILHORNE OF GREEN'S NORTON
Lord Chancellor of Great Britain
Born Latimer, Buckinghamshire, England, August 1st, 1905
Died Harborough, Leicestershire, England, September 7th, 1980

Viscount Dilhorne, former British Attorney-General and Lord Chancellor, was a Conservative whose decisions as the Crown's chief law officer reflected his firm belief in the need for a strong system of "law and order." Dilhorne maintained that the "scales of justice" had been swayed too far in favor of the defendent and believed in eliminating "caution" (informing a suspect of his rights). He opposed the abolition of the death penalty, fought against liberalizing the laws against homosexuality and successfully strengthened the strict rules against abortion. Born Reginald Manningham-Buller, his blunt style and absolute refusal to be moved when he believed he was right caused some of his less charitable colleagues to dub him "Bulling-Manner".

Heir to a baronetcy, Dilhorne was in many ways typical of the English country squire. The Manningham-Bullers were part of the ruling élite of England and both of his grandfathers distinguished themselves in the army. His father, the third holder of the baronetcy, became a member of parliament. When the young Manningham-Buller married Lady Lindsay, daughter of the 27th Earl of Crawford (whose title went back to 1398), in 1930, it was a high society affair in which crowds of women waited hours in the rain in order to cheer the bride and groom. An avid sportsman and expert marksman, Manningham-Buller loved hunting and riding on his estate in Northamptonshire.

Educated at Eton and Oxford, Manningham-Buller was called to the bar (Inner Temple) in 1927 and maintained a private practice. During the Second World War he worked in the Judge Advocate-General's department and in 1943 he successfully ran as Conservative member of parliament for the Daventry Division of Northamptonshire. As part of the caretaker government of Winston Churchill, Manningham-Buller was Parliamentary Secretary to the Minister of Works for four months. In opposition after the war, he served his party as an expert on the complexities of the law and was active on a number of committees.

When the Conservatives were returned to power in 1951, Manningham-Buller was appointed Solicitor-General, and received the traditional knighthood for that position. He found himself prosecuting the sensational case of John Staffen, who was sentenced to death for murdering a five year old girl. He also prosecuted one of the early Russian spy cases, a precursor of several British scandals which were to rock his government and the whole country.

In 1954, Manningham-Buller was appointed Attorney-General, the senior law officer for the Crown, an appropriate position for a descendant of Edward Coke, the Attorney-General for Elizabeth I.

In 1957, Manningham-Buller prosecuted another sensational murder case in which Dr. John Bodkin Adams was accused of poisoning a patient. Adams was quickly acquitted after dramatic testimony introduced by the defense proved his innocence. The Attorney-General came under harsh criticism for his decision to prosecute but his explanations to parliament vindicated him totally. That same year it was discovered that the Home Office had illegally wiretapped a barrister about whom the Attorney-General had complained. The British viewed the wiretapping as a blatant invasion of privacy and faith in the Conservative government was shaken. Although Manningham-Buller was not finally held responsible for the incident, he was passed over the following year when the position of Lord Chief Justice had to be filled; it had been widely assumed that Manningham-Buller was next in line for the post.

In 1959, the Attorney-General refused to repeal the death sentences of two men who killed a policeman, maintaining his firm belief in the death penalty. Two years later, he prosecuted five persons, two of whom were British citizens in what became known as the "Portland Spy Ring" case. The group had passed anti-submarine plans to the Russians. The intricate case involved a Russian with a Canadian passport who was disguised as a U.S. Naval officer. Manningham-Buller's case was carefully prepared and his charge that the group had "clearly sold secrets of their country for money," was well documented.

In 1962, Prime Minister Harold Macmillan, in an effort to regain some of the popularity lost by his party, dropped several members of his cabinet and Manningham-Buller was named as Lord Chancellor, an appointment which was not well received. As Lord Chancellor, Dilhorne opposed any ex-official appointments of justices and encouraged magistrates to assume their full responsibilities or resign. While believing in the independence of magistrates, he deplored the disparities in the length of sentences given and devised machinery by which new magistrates were to undergo training.

Shortly after his appointment, Lord Dilhorne again found himself embroiled in a controversial case. It was found that the drug thalidomide caused birth defects and a debate arose about whether women who had unknowingly taken the harmful drug were entitled to an abortion. In a debate in the House of Lords with Lady Summerskill [q.v.], Dilhorne stated that the possibility that a child might be born deformed due to the effects of the drug was "not lawful grounds for abortion," and referred to the 1938 court ruling which stated that abortions could only be performed in order to save the mother's life. When pressed by Lady Summerskill, he conceded that "a jury might allow an abortion" if the childbirth might prove mentally and physically traumatic for the mother, but he would not admit that the existence of drugs like thalidomide made the 1938 ruling obsolete.

In 1963, Dilhorne headed the inquiry into the Profumo Scandal. John Profumo, then Secretary of State, was found to have lied when he had told the House of Commons that he had not been intimate with a woman (Christine Keeler) who was also at that time having relations with the deputy Soviet Naval attaché in London. Profumo's behavior, particularly his lie to parliament, caused public outrage and Macmillan's government came under very heavy fire for its seemingly casual handling of the scandal. Even though Dilhorne reported to the cabinet that he found "no breach of national security in connection with the scandal," the damage was done and Macmillan, in order to heal the wounds, expressed to his cabinet a desire to resign. Dilhorne had the thankless task of seeking advice from all the cabinet contenders as to which of them should become Macmillan's successor.

When the Earl of Home was chosen Prime Minister, most political analysts were surprised. The Conservatives had been trying to attract a young and middle class constituency, and Lord Home (who became Sir Alec Douglas-Home) appeared to represent the older more traditional element within the party. Dilhorne remained Lord Chancellor in Douglas-Home's new administration but the Conservatives were voted out in 1964, and the Lord Chancellor was made a viscount for "political and public service" in Douglas-Home's resignation honors list. For the next two years Dilhorne was deputy leader of the opposition, but in 1966, Conservative leader Heath realigned the shadow cabinet and dropped Lord Dilhorne from his post and from most party responsibilities. Lord Dilhorne was finally appointed Lord of Appeals in Ordinary in 1968, after being snubbed for nearly a year. A few weeks before his retirement at the age of 75, he ruled against the confidentiality of news sources by forcing Granada T.V. to disclose the identity of the "mole" at British Steel that had provided them with information for a program documenting a strike at the plant.

Lord Dilhorne's supporters argued that in many ways he was misunderstood by the public, with whom he never was popular, and who viewed his courage as obstinacy. His friends saw him as a kind man and a private person who never cultivated a public persona. But even people within his own party criticized his lack of imagination and heavily legalistic manner. His arguably laissez-faire attitude to English law suited well his more conservative colleagues, but reforming lawyers, and particularly human rights activists, became impatient with his judgments.

Whatever his faults might have been, Dilhorne was certainly sincere in his beliefs, and if he was saddened by Britain's abolition of the death penalty and the liberalization of laws on abortion and homosexuality, he was too much of a professional and a gentleman to display any public rancor. His family's motto is: "The Eagle Does Not Catch Flies."   R.T./H.S.

Born Reginald Edward Manningham-Buller. Son of Lt. Col. Sir Mervyn Manningham-Buller, 3rd Baronet, M.P., and Hon. Lilah Cavendish. Married Lady Mary Lillian Lindsay, 4th daughter of 27th Earl of Crawford and Balcarres, 1930. Children: Lord John Mervyn, b. 1932; Hon. Marian Cynthia Brendell, b. 1934; Hon. Elizabeth Lydia, b. 1948; Hon. Anne Constance, b. 1951. Church of England. Educ: Eton and Magdalen Coll., Oxford, B.A. 1926; called to bar of the Inner Temple 1927; King's Councillor (took silk) 1946; a Bencher 1951; Reader 1973. Mil. service: Major in Judge Advocate General's Dept, WWII. M.P. (Conservative) for Daventry Division of Northants. 1943–50, and for Southern Division of Northants. and Soke of Peterborough 1950–62; Member of the Rushcliffe Cttee. on Legal Aid 1944–45; Parliamentary Secty. to the Minister of Works 1945; Parliamentary Delegate to USSR 1945; Member of Anglo-American Cttee. on Palestine 1946; Chmn. of Paliament Legal Cttee.; Solicitor-Gen. 1951–54; Attorney-Gen. 1954–62; Lord Chancellor of Great Britain 1962–64; Recorder of Kingston-upon-Thames 1962; Deputy Leader of the Opposition 1964–66; Deputy Lt., Northants. 1967; Lord of Appeals in Ordinary 1969–80. Hons: Knighted 1951; Privy Councillor 1954; created 1st Visount Dilhorne of Green's Norton 1964; Hon. DCL, Southern Methodist Univ., Dallas; Hon LL.D. McGill Univ.

J(OHN) T(RAILL) CHRISTIE
Educator, Principal of Jesus College, Oxford
Born Chipping Ongar, Essex, England, October 19th, 1899
Died Great Henny, Suffolk, England, September 8th, 1980

John Traill Christie was Principal of Jesus College, Oxford, for seventeen years and enjoyed the almost unique distinction of having been headmaster at two of Britain's foremost Public Schools.

In September 1913, the young Christie won a scholarship to Winchester School where his great love of the Latin and Greek classics developed. In 1919 he went up to Trinity College, Oxford, as a scholar and there took firsts in Classical Honour Moderations and Greats. Christie's first teaching post was at Rugby School, then under the headmastership of W.W. Vaughan. He taught classics as a Sixth Form Master for five years and then returned to Oxford as a Fellow and Tutor of Magdalen College.

In 1932, at the remarkably early age of 33, Christie gained his first Public School headmastership, at Repton. Five years later he moved to the larger and prestigous Westminster School in London, to succeed A. Costley-White as headmaster. Soon thereafter, the Second World War forced the school's evacuation to hastily converted houses in Bromyard. Shortage of staff during the war caused Christie to break with the tradition that headmasters do not teach, and when the war ended, he continued his teaching, preferring the closer contact with his pupils and the classics which the classroom provided. Ill health caused Christie to resign from Westminster in 1949; but after a brief rest he returned to Oxford as Principal of Jesus College and remained there until his retirement in 1967, though for a further two years he taught at Westminster School.

Christie, a man of somewhat donnish temperament, found it difficult to reconcile his conservative and traditionalist approach to education with the changing values and movements for reform of the late 1960s and early 1970s. He made no secret of his opinion that senior officials of colleges, burdened with heavy administrative duties, could be more effectively employed dealing with academic matters. Nevertheless he made a congenial and able administrator and only on health grounds did he decline the Vice-Chancellorship of Oxford University which would have been given him in 1960.

In addition to his deep knowledge of the classics, Christie was widely read in English poetry and particularly admired the works of Shakespeare. When his health permitted, he much enjoyed the countryside and was an indefatigable walker.   M.D.

Son of Charles Henry C. (Justice of the Peace). Married: Lucie Catherine Le Fanu 1933. Two daughters. Educ: Winchester Sch. (scholar) 1913–18; Trinity Coll., Oxford B.A. (First Class Hons., classics) 1922. Sixth Form Master (classics), Rugby Sch. 1923–28. Fellow, tutor, Magdalen Coll., Oxford 1928–32. Headmaster, Repton Sch., 1932–37; Westminster Sch. 1937–49. Principal, Jesus Coll., Oxford 1950–67; Deputy Public Orator, Univ. Oxford 1957. Asst. Master (classics), Westminster Sch. 1967–69. Hons: Life Fellow, Jesus Coll., Oxford 1967. Articles in many professional education jrnls.

MAURICE (CHARLES LOUIS) GENEVOIX
Novelist
Born Decize, Nièvre, France, November 29th, 1890
Died Spain, September 8th, 1980

Maurice Genevoix was a popular First World War novelist and after the war he achieved distinction as a "regionalist," writing many novels set in rustic France. In later life he was active as Permanent Secretary of the Académie Française, and when well into his 80s became a radio and television personality.

Born in the Nièvre region, Genevoix spent much of his childhood exploring the countryside, particularly the Loire valley—the "land of eternal spring"—home of his mother's family. He was accepted to the École Normale Supérieure at the early age of 18, but his studies were interrupted by the First World War; he went to the front as a sub-lieutenant in the infantry. Severely wounded in 1915, Genevoix spent seven months convalescing and then returned to the École Normale for a short period. By 1918 when the armistice was signed, Genevoix had written three novels about his war experiences: *Sous Verdun*

(1916), *Nuits de Guerre* (1917) and *Au Seuil des Guitounes* (1918). He followed these in 1921 with *La Boue,* and two years later published *Les Eparges.* In 1950 these novels were collected under the title *Ceux de 14.*

Genevoix's documentary novels of the war evoke a sense of collective suffering and of the haunting closeness of death. Recording both the physical and psychological horror of war, Genevoix neither mystified nor romanticized it; but he did portray the romantic hope of the war-weary soldiers: "We marched silently, dreaming of impending peace. Having held it in our hearts for a brief moment, our eyes shone with the warm joy of returning home" *(Nuits de Guerre).*

Despite the many afflictions of war, Genevoix saw that it drew people closer; the soldiers rediscovered their natural brotherhood and respect for each other—feelings that had been almost forgotten in the impersonal and increasingly-selfish modern world. And near death, Genevoix experienced another instinctive feeling—his deep will to survive.

It was Genevoix's recognition of the damage wrought by the modern world, together with his strong attachments to rural life, which led him to become a "regionalist" writer. Seeing many aspects of industrialization and consumerism as environmentally and psychologically destructive, the regionalists believed that the countryside (particularly, for Genevoix, the forest, which he said had always haunted man's imagination and dreams) kept the rural man in touch with his instincts and intuitions, and thereby with his passion and humanity. In his first regionalist novel, *Rémi des Rauches* (1922), Genevoix explores the life of a simple fisherman who must evaluate and reorder his life when the banks of the Loire flood. *Raboliot,* which won the Prix Goncourt in 1925 and remains Genevoix's most widely-read novel, is the story of an incorrigible poacher: hunted by an antagonistic policeman, the poacher hides in the woods, living like an animal. But overwhelmed by his instinctive desire to see his family he is drawn back to the community and the trap that has been set for him.

Genevoix's many novels set in the Loire valley and the nearby Solonge do not espouse a morality or offer a deep philosophy; he was content, simply, to communicate his lifelong love of nature and the forest. Although his books were widely read, Genevoix was not a household name in France until the mid-1970s when he gave his series of talks on radio and television.

He was permanent secretary of the Académie Française from 1958 until his retirement in 1973 when he was appointed honorary secretary in perpetuity. During his lifetime, Genevoix traveled to Canada, Africa, Mexico and Central America, publishing books about his journeys. An avid painter—he almost chose painting as a career—he illustrated his own bestiaries.

Genevoix's penultimate book, *30,000 Jours,* a series of autobiographical sketches, appeared in 1980. Three days before his death, at the age of 89, he was reading page proofs for a volume on art history which was published posthumously.   A.W.

Son of Gabriel G., and Camille (Balichon) G. Married Suzanne Neyrolles 1943. Children: Françoise; Sylvie. Educ: Lycée Lakanal, Sceaux, France 1908–11; École Normale Supérieure 1911–14, 1915, diplôme d-Études Superiéures. Mil. Service: Sub-lt., 106 Reg. of the Infantry then Lt., 5th Compagnie 1914–15; wounded 1915 (Croix de Guerre; Médaille de Verdun). Pres., Conseil litteraire du Prince Pierre de Monaco; Pres. and founder, Memorial de Verdun; Pres., Assoc. des Écrivains Combattants. Member: Féderation du français universel; Défense de la langue française; Conseil international de la langue française; many other assocs. and cttees. Hons: Prix Goncourt (for Raboliot) 1925; Prix Osiris 1935; Grand Prix national des Letters (for body of work) 1970; Grand-Croix de la Légion d'Honneur; Grand-Croix de l'Ordre National du Mérite; Commandeur des Palmes académiques des arts et des lettres. *Books: Novels*—Sous Verdun, 1916; Nuits de Guerre, 1917; Au Seuil des Guitounes, 1918; Jeanne Robelin, 1920; La Boue, 1921; Rémi des Rauches, 1922; Les Éparges, 1923; La Joie, 1923; Euthymos, vainqueur olympique, 1924 (as Vaincre à Olympie, 1977); Raboliot, 1925; La Bôte a pêche, 1926; Les Mains vides, 1928; Cyrille, 1929; L'Assassin, 1930; Rrôu, 1931; Gai-l'Amour, 1931; Marcheloup, 1934; Tête baissée, 1935; Bernard, 1938; La Dernière harde, 1938; La Framboise et belle humeur, 1942; Eva Charlebois, 1944 (later as Je verrai, si tu veux, les pays de la neige); Sanglar, 1946 (as La Motte Rouge, 1979); L'Aventure est en nous, 1952; Fatou Cessé, 1954; Le Roman de Renard, 1958; Au cadran de mon clocher, 1960; La Loire, Agnès et les garçons, 1962; Beau-françois, 1965; La Forêt perdue, 1967; Un Jour, 1976; Lorelei, 1978. *Short stories, essays, and sketches*—L'Hirondelle qui fut le printemps, 1941; L'Écureuil du bois bourru, 1946; Jeux de Glaces (autobiog.), 1960; Les deux lutins, 1961; Derrière les collines, 1963. *Travel*—Canada, 1945; Afrique blanche, Afrique noire, 1949; Orlénais (a guide bleu), 1956; Routes de l'Aventure, 1959; Les Solognots de Sologne, 1977. *Nature*—Forêt voisine, 1932; Le Jardin dans l'île, 1935 (as Jardin sans murs, with Images pour un hardin sans murs, 1968); Images du Val de Loire, 1958; Chevalet de campagne, 1950; Tendre Bestiaire, 1969; Bestiaire enchanté, 1969; Bestiaire sans oubli, 1971; Maurice Genevoix illustre ses Bestiaires, 1973. *Juveniles*—Les Compagnons de l'Aubépin, 1936; Mon ami l'écureuil, 1957. *Other*—H.O.E. (reminiscences), 1931; Vlaminck (biog.), 1954; Vie et mort des français 1914–18, 1959; Une étoile entre toutes brillantes (in Ma Mère), 1969; Flaubert (in Le 41ème fauteuil), 1971; La Grèce de Caramanlis, 1972; La Mort de près (témoignage), 1972; La Per-pétuité, 1974; Trente mille jours (autobiog.), 1980; L'Enfant et le château, 1980.

SIR CYRIL (HUGH) KLEINWORT
Merchant banker
Born Haywards Heath, Sussex, England, August 17th, 1905
Died Upper Slaughter, Gloucestershire, England, September 8th, 1980

Sir Cyril Kleinwort, who was one of Britain's leading bankers in the 1960s and early 1960s and early 1970s, rose from a junior partnership in his family's banking business to head London's largest merchant bank.

Son of Sir Alexander Drake Kleinwort, the young Kleinwort was schooled privately before joining the family bank, Kleinwort and son, of which his father was chairman. He was offered no privilege and was required to learn the business of banking, investment and the operation of world money markets from the beginning. He later acknowledged that this fundamental grounding in basic principles and procedures was the main reason for the success of his career in finance.

The Kleinwort family bank merged in 1961 with another of the City's major banks, Benson Lonsdale, to form the holding company, Kleinwort Benson Lonsdale Ltd. Its main subsidiary then became Kleinwort Benson Ltd., the merchant bank, the first chairman of which was Kleinwort's brother Ernest. Meanwhile, his elder brother, Alexander had succeeded to the family baronetcy on the death of his father in 1935. Cyril Kleinwort followed his brother as chairman of the bank in 1966, retiring in 1971. In 1968 he also followed another brother, Ernest, as chairman of Kleinwort Benson Lonsdale; he retired from that post in 1977, but continued to serve on the board of directors until his death.

It was under Cyril Kleinwort's initiative and guidance that Kleinwort Benson, as a member of the London Accepting Houses Committee—the central group of the London merchant banks—expanded to become the largest merchant bank in the City with assets totalling more than £2,000 million at the time of Kleinwort's death.

Kleinwort served for sixteen years as joint vice-chairman of the British insurance giant, the Commercial Union Assurance Co. Ltd. Prior to 1968, he had interested himself in "invisible" exports, notably insurance, and had entered talks on the subject with both the Bank of England and the British National Export Council. Thus, in 1968 when the bank and the council decided to establish the national Committee on Invisible Exports, Kleinwort was a natural choice for chairman and was charged with suggesting and where possible implementing measures to encourage Britain's "invisible" export earnings. The committee's success was seen by financiers and noted by government, and in 1972, Kleinwort was appointed a member of the British Overseas Trade Board. Indeed his success in the field of commerce and overseas trade led to his appointment in 1971 as a member of the Advisory Committee for the Queen's Award to Industry—a post in which he was required to assess the efficiency and exporting achievement of commercial undertakings for official recognition.

Also in 1971, Kleinwort's achievements in British banking and commerce were acknowledged with a knighthood and appointment as one of Her Majesty's Lieutenants for the City of London.   M.D.

Son of Sir Alexander Drake K. (banker) and Etiennette Girard K. Married Elisabeth Kathleen Forde 1933. Three daughters. Educ: privately, London. Mil. service: Lt. Comdr., Royal Navy Volunteer Reserve, 1939–45. Partner, Kleinwort Sons and Co., London 1927–61; Chmn., North British and Mercantile Insurance Co. 1957–59 and Transatlantic Fund Inc., NYC 1959–61; Jr. Vice-Chmn., Commercial Union Assurance Co. Ltd., London 1959–75; Dir., 1961–80 and Chmn. 1968–77, Kleinwort, Benson, Lonsdale Ltd., holding co., London; Dir., Kleinwort Benson Investment Trust Ltd., 1961–77; Chmn., Kleinwort Benson Ltd., merchant bank, London 1966–71. Deputy Chmn., British Natl. Export Council 1968–72. Member: British Cttee. on Invisible Exports 1968–75; Advisory Cttee., Queen's Award to Industry 1971–75; Industrial Policy Group 1971–74; British Overseas Trade Bd. 1972–75. Hons: knighted 1971; Hon. D.Litt.,

City University, London 1973; Her Majesty's Lieutenant, City of London 1976–80. Contributed many articles to investment and other financial jrnls.

WILLARD F(RANK) LIBBY
Nuclear chemist
Born Grand Valley, Colorado, U.S.A., December 17th, 1908
Died Los Angeles, California, U.S.A., September 8th, 1980

In the past 20 years, the field of archaeology and geology have been revolutionized by the development of radiocarbon dating, a method of determining the age of organic materials by measuring the radioactivity of carbon atoms within them. The method was the brainchild of American chemist Willard F. Libby, who won the Nobel Prize for his work in 1960.

Courtesy Libby estate

Libby was born in Colorado, grew up on his parents' fruit ranch near Santa Rosa, California, and entered the University of California at Berkeley with the intention of becoming a mining engineer. Persuaded to switch to chemistry, he earned his bachelor's degree in 1931 and his doctorate two years later and became a member of the university faculty. In 1941 he interrupted the first of three Guggenheim Fellowships to serve on the Manhattan Project at Columbia University's division of war research, where he helped invent a gaseous-diffusion process for separating the isotopes of uranium, an essential step in the construction of the atomic bomb.

After the war Libby became a professor of chemistry at the University of Chicago's Institute for Nuclear Studies, where he and a group of students developed the radiocarbon dating technique (also known as the "atomic calendar"). Previous research had shown that cosmic ray particles are constantly bombarding the nuclei of atoms in the earth's upper atmosphere and knocking free their neutrons, which, in turn, collide with the nuclei of other atoms and become incorporated into them. The most frequent receptor of these neutrons is nitrogen-14, an istope of nitrogen found in abundance in the upper atmosphere, which then undergoes a change in atomic weight and becomes carbon-14, a radioactive isotope of carbon. Like ordinary carbon atoms, these radioactive atoms circulate through the atmosphere, form molecules of carbon dioxide, and enter living plants through the process of photosynthesis; the food chain eventually brings them into the tissues of animals as well, making them a part of all living matter.

According to Libby's calculations, there is an unchanging amount of radiocarbon (about 70 metric tons) in the world, with the formation of new carbon-14 atoms constantly offset by the decay of old ones. Each decaying radiocarbon atom casts off electrons (called beta particles) until it becomes a stable, non-radioactive carbon-12 atom. This process occurs at a steady rate that is measured in half-lives (e.g., the total amount of carbon-14 diminishes by exactly one-half during each period of 5,730 years). Since an organism ceases to ingest carbon-14 when it dies, a researcher, Libby reasoned, should be able to determine the organism's approximate date of death by measuring the amount of radiocarbon still remaining in its tissues or fibers. The older the object, the fewer beta particles it will emit.

Libby and his associates built an extremely sensitive Geiger counter to detect these emissions. The device was protected from interference by terrestrial and atmospheric radiation by an iron shield and a ring of secondary Geiger counters. The team then constructed a time scale by analyzing objects whose ages had already been determined by historical sources or by other scientific data. Among the first candidates for testing were the wood from a giant sequoia tree and a plank from the funerary boat of the Egyptian pharaoh Sesotris III. These experiments yielded a time scale reaching back nearly 70,000 years, with a margin of error of only 120 years.

Libby's findings, announced in 1949, immediately changed scientists' ideas of the past. Using his method, geologists established that the last Ice Age in North America took place 11,000 years ago rather than 25,000, as had previously been thought. Archaeologists used it to correlate the Babylonian, Mayan, and Christian calendars, to confirm the existence of basket-weaving tribes in North America some 9,000 years ago, and to date the Dead Sea Scrolls. The technique soon became an indispensable tool of research in several scientific fields, although some controversy still continues over its accuracy.

Libby's studies also shed light on the formation of tritium, an isotope of hydrogen produced by the collision of neutrons and nitrogen in the atmosphere. Tritium is used in the making of hydrogen bombs.

In 1954 Libby became the first chemist to serve on the Atomic Energy Commission, where he led President Eisenhower's Atoms for Peace project and studied the effects of radioactive fallout. An enthusiastic supporter of nuclear power and an apologist for nuclear weapons testing, he once said: "People have to learn to live with the facts of life, and part of the facts of life is fallout." During this period he also worked as a research associate in the Geophysical Laboratory of Washington's Carnegie Institute. In 1959 he resigned both positions to take a professorship at the University of California at Los Angeles, where he became director of the Institute of Geophysics and Planetary Physics. The following year he was awarded the Nobel Prize for his work on carbon-14. He was also the recipient of numerous other scientific prizes, including the Albert Einstein Medal and the Joseph Priestly Award.

Libby was a frequent appointee to federal and state bodies, including Governor Reagan's Air Resource Board and Earthquake Council in California, President Nixon's Task Force on Air Pollution, and the U.S.-Japanese Commission on Scientific Cooperation. Rumors that he would be named President Nixon's science advisor in 1968 drew protests from many of his colleagues who found his political conservatism too extreme.

Libby, known as "Wild Bill" to his friends, held directorships of several businesses, including Nuclear Systems, Inc., Research-Cottrell, Inc., and W.F. Libby Laboratories. He also served as consultant to the Esso Research and Engineering Company (now part of Exxon), the Rand Corporation, and other firms, and on the editorial boards of four scientific journals. In 1976 a workshop and symposium was held in his honor by the University of California at Los Angeles to mark his retirement.

Libby died of a blood clot in the lung, complicated by pneumonia. A second symposium in his honor is planned by the university.   s.m.

Son of Ora Edward L. and Eva May (Rivers) L., fruit farmers. Married: (1) Leonor Hickey 1940 (div. 1966); (2) Leona Woods Marshall, prof. of environmental engineering 1966. Children: 1st marriage—twins Janet and Susan, b. 1945. Protestant. Educ: Analytical Union High Sch., Sebastopol, Calif.; Univ. of California at Berkeley (Phi Beta Kappa), B.S. 1931, Ph.D. in chemistry 1933; Guggenheim Fellowships 1941, 1951, 1959. Mil. Service: Manhattan Project on development of atomic bomb, War Research Div., Columbia Univ. 1941–45. With Dept. of Chemistry, Univ. of California at Berkeley: Instr. 1933–38; Asst. Prof. 1938–45 (on leave for mil. service 1941–45); Assoc. Prof. 1945. Prof. of chemistry, Inst. for Nuclear Studies (now Enrico Fermi Inst. for Nuclear Studies) and Dept. of Chemistry, Univ. of Chicago 1945–59; Research Assoc., Geophysical Laboratory, Carnegie Instn. of Washington, D.C. 1954–59; Prof. of chemistry, Univ. of California at Berkeley 1959–76; Dir., Inst. of Geophysics and Planetary Physics, Univ. of California 1962–74; Special Visiting Prof. of chemistry, Univ. of South Florida, Tampa 1962–74; Special Visiting Prof. of chemistry, physics, astrophysics, and aero-engineering, Univ. of Colorado at Boulder 1967–70; Martha V. Filbert Distinguished Scholar Lectr., Univ. of Maryland 1971. With Atomic Energy Commn. (now Nuclear Regulatory Commn.): Member, Cttee. of Sr. Reviewers 1945–52; Member, Gen. Advisory Cttee. 1950–54, 1960–62; Member of AEC 1954–59; Member, Plowshare Advisory Cttee. 1959–72. Vice-Chmn., U.S. Delegation to 1st Intnl. Conference on Peaceful Uses of Atomic Energy, Geneva 1955; Member, Cttee. of Selection, Guggenheim Foundn. 1959–77; Member, Air Resources Bd., State of California 1967–72; Member, Visiting Cttee., Jet Propulsion Laboratory 1968–72; Member, Pres. Nixon's Task Force on Air Pollution 1969–70; Science Advisor, State of Idaho 1969–72; Member, U.S. Delegation to U.S.-Japan Cttee. on Scientific Cooperation 1970–73; Member, Governor's Earthquake Council, State of Calif. 1972–74. Member of Editorial Bd.: Science (jrnl.), 1962–70; Origins of Life (previously Space Life Sciences) since 1970; Environmental Geology since 1973; Science of the Total Environment since 1973. Member, Editorial Advisory Bd., Industrial Research 1967–73; Member, Academic Advisory Bd., Rank Corp. 1968–77. Pres. and Dir., The Isotope Foundn. 1960–77; Dir. and Chmn. of Bd., Scientific Research Instruments Corp. 1967–78. Dir.: Douglas Aircraft 1963–67; Hedge Fund of America 1968–74; Summit Capital Fund 1968–74; Nuclear Systems, Inc. since 1969; Research-Cottrell, Inc. since 1971; W.F. Libby Laboratories 1972–77. Consultant: Esso Research and Engineering (now Exxon) since 1946; Scientific Div., Douglas Aircraft 1962–67; Electro-Optical Systems 1963–66; Univ. of Denver 1966–69; Louisiana State Univ. since 1968; Rand Corp. since 1969; R & D Associates since 1971; Univ. of South Florida since 1972. Charter Member: Berkeley Fellows; Corresponding Fellow, British Acad.; Corresponding Member, Intnl. Acad. of Astronautics, Intnl. Astronautical Federation; Member: American Acad. of Arts and Sciences; American Assn. for Advancement of Science; American Chemical Soc.; American Geophysical Union; American Inst. of Aeronautics and Astronautics; American Inst. of Chemists; American Nuclear Soc.; American Philosophical Soc.; American Physical Soc.; Bolivian Soc. of Anthropology; California Catalysis Soc.; Catalysis Soc. of North America; Geochemical Soc.; Geological Soc. of America; Heidelberg Acad. of Sciences; Natl.

Acad. of Sciences; Newcomen Soc. in North America; Royal Swedish Acad. of Science; Southern California Acad. of Sciences; Alpha Chi Sigma; Phi Lambda Upsilon; Pi Mu Epsilon; Sigma Xi; Cosmos Club, Washington, D.C.; Explorer's Club; Century Assn.; Metropolitan Club, NYC; Hons: from American Chemical Soc.—Remsen Memorial Lectureship Award, Maryland Sect. 1955; American Chemical Soc. Award for Nuclear Applications in Chemistry 1956; Willard Gibbs Medal, Chicago Sect. 1958; Burton W. Logue Lectr., Tulsa Sect. 1977. Research Corp. Award 1952; Chandler Medal, Columbia Univ. 1954; City Coll. of New York Bicentennial Lecture Award 1956; Elliott Cresson Medal, Franklin Inst. 1957; Albert Einstein Medal, Strauss Memorial Fund 1959; Joseph Priestly Award, Dickinson Coll. 1959; Nobel Prize in Chemistry 1960; Arthur L. Day Medal, Geological Soc. of America 1961; California Alumnus of the Year, Univ. of California at Berkeley 1963; Gold Medal, American Inst. of Chemists 1970; Lehman Award, New York Acad. of Sciences 1971; Guedel Assn. Memorial Medallion 1971; Golden Key and Hon. Citizen, City of Baton Rouge, La. 1973; Symposium, The Orbit and Works of Willard Frank Libby, held at Univ. of Calif. at Los Angeles 1976; Centennial Medallion, Univ. of Colorado 1977. Hon. Sc.D. from Wesleyan Univ. 1955, Syracuse Univ. 1957, Trinity Coll., Dublin 1957, Carnegie Inst. of Technology 1959, Georgetown Univ. 1962, Manhattan Coll. 1963, Univ. of Newcastle upon Tyne 1965, Gustavus Adolphus Coll. 1970, Univ. of South Florida 1976, Univ. of Colorado 1977. *Author:* Radiocarbon Dating, 1952, 2nd ed. 1955. Numerous articles in scientific journals.

SIR GEOFFREY (HITHERSAY) SHAKESPEARE
Politician, journalist and businessman
Born Norwich, England, September 23rd, 1893
Died Chislehurst, Kent, England, September 8th, 1980

Sir Geoffrey Shakespeare pursued a diverse career spanning 60 years. Politically, he was the most active during the period between the two World Wars, and afterwards became a leading businessman. A popular figure, Sir Geoffrey was known for his wit, modesty and humanitarian concerns.

Geoffrey Hithersay Shakespeare was born in Norwich, England, on September 23, 1893. His father was a leading non-conformist and became secretary of the Baptist Union of Great Britain and Ireland. After receiving his *LLB* and *MA* degrees from Emmanuel College, Cambridge, Shakespeare began his law practice with a firm of City solicitors, until he was invited by Prime Minister David Lloyd George to become his private secretary in 1921. This appointment began a lifelong friendship between the two politicians.

During 1921 Geoffrey Shakespeare played a part in the settlement of the debate between the Britain and the Southern Irish Governments. Lloyd George sent Shakespeare to meet de Valera, parliamentary head of the Irish Republicans, and his delegation and invite them to negotiate with the British government at 10 Downing Street. The outcome of these negotiations was the end of the Anglo-Irish War (1919–1921), with the signing of the Irish Treaty at Westminster on

December 6th, 1921, by representatives of the British government and the Irish Assembly. Shakespeare himself traveled by destroyer through the night to deliver to the Irish leaders the draft of the proposals for the treaty, which had earlier been agreed upon by both governments. Under the terms of the treaty, Ireland was recognized as a dominion of the British Empire, with the same constitutional status possessed by the other British dominions. The new dominion included all of Ireland, but Northern Ireland, which had been established by the Government of Ireland act of 1920, was granted the right to declare itself independent, and did so immediately. With this declaration, Northern Ireland remained part of the United Kingdom, while Southern Ireland became the Irish Free State.

During the general government election of 1922, Shakespeare ran as the Liberal Party candidate for Wellingborough, Northamptonshire, and was elected to the House of Commons. But he served as an M.P. for only one year before losing his seat. He remained out of Parliament for the next six years, during which time he worked as a journalist becoming a political correspondent of the *Daily Chronicle*. In this position, with his first-hand knowledge of politics and experience at diplomacy, Shakespeare proved an able journalist. At one point, he was both lobby and diplomatic writer and achieved momentary fame when he surprisingly announced that the General Strike of 1926 was to be called off.

In 1929, Shakespeare resumed his career in politics by again being elected an M.P., this time for Norwich, a seat he held for 16 years. With the formation of the National Government in 1931, Shakespeare was appointed a Junior Lord of the Treasury and Chief Whip of the National Liberal Party. A year later he was promoted to Parliamentary Secretary at the Ministry of Health. In this position, Shakespeare played a major role in the national campaign against slums.

When Neville Chamberlain became Prime Minister in 1937, Shakespeare was appointed Parliamentary and Financial Secretary to the Admiralty. In this post, Shakespeare saw how militarily unprepared Britain was for a major conflict, and he could well understand Chamberlain's peace efforts in Munich with Hitler.

Perhaps Geoffrey Shakespeare's most rewarding political experience was as parliamentary under-secretary of state at the Dominions Office. Here, as Chairman of the Children's Overseas Reception Board his humanitarian concerns could be more fully expressed.

In 1942, under Winston Churchill, the British government established a War Cabinet, and Shakespeare, who received a baronetcy, returned to the back benches, where he remained until his defeat in the 1945 general election. That same year he was made a Privy Councillor. Sir Geoffrey then began a new career as an industrialist and administrator becoming Deputy Chairman of Abbey National Building Society and President of the Society of British Gas Industries. He also farmed in Hertfordshire.

His memoirs, *Let Candles be Brought In,* appeared in 1949.   s.m.

Son of Rev. John Howard S., Baptist minister and Amy Gertrude Goodman S. Married: (1) Aimée Constance Fisher 1926 (div. 1950); (2) Elizabeth Hare 1952. Children: 1st marriage—Judith Anne (d. 1939); William Geoffrey B. 1927. Protestant. Educ: Highgate School; Emmanuel Coll., Cambridge, M.A. and LL.B. 1922. President of the

Union. Mil. Service: Captain, 5th Batallion, Norfolk Regiment
1914–19, serving in Gallipoli, Egypt and in England. Private Secty. to
Prime Minister D. Lloyd George 1921–23; called to Bar 1922; M.P.
for Wellingborough Div. of Northants. 1922–23; journalist, *Daily
Chronicle,* and *Financial News* 1924–29; M.P. for Norwich 1929–45. A
Lord Commnr. of the Treasury, and Chief Whip, Liberal Nationals
1931–32; Parliamentary Secty., Ministry of Health 1932–36, and to
Board of Education 1936–37; Parliamentary and Financial Secty. to
Admiralty 1937–40; Parliamentary Secty. to Dept. of Overseas Trade
1940; Parliamentary Under-Secty. of State, Dominions Office, and
Chmn. of Children's Overseas Reception Bd. 1940–42. Deputy Chmn.
and Dir. Abbey National Building Soc., 1942–76; Pres., Soc. of
British Gas Industries, 1953–54; Chmn., Northern Star Insurance Co.
until 1968; Deputy Chmn., Bournemouth Water Co. until 1978;
Chmn., Industrial Co-Partnership Assn., 1958–68; Dir.: Associated
Portland Cement Co., and London Brick Co. Vice-Chmn. and
Member of Bd. of Govs., Westminster Hosp., London 1948–63;
Chmn., National Liberal Exec. 1950–51; Chmn., Industrial Co-
Partnershp Assn., 1958–68; Chmn. and Member of Bd. of Govs.,
Highgate Sch., London; elected a Knight of Mark Twain 1980. Hons:
Created Baronet of Lakenham, City of Norwich 1942, and Privy
Councillor 1945. *Author:* Let Candles Be Brought In (memoirs), 1949;
A Midsummer Morn's Awakening (play performed on CBS-TV,
U.S.A.); The Amorous Ghost (play), and others.

HAROLD (EDGAR) CLURMAN
Theater director, critic, and author
Born New York City, U.S.A., September 18th, 1901
Died New York City, U.S.A., September 9th, 1980

In 1929, Harold Clurman devised a dramatic dialogue in which "the
layman" declared: "If you will omit the evangelical tone, you may talk
to me about the theater." To this, "the theatre man" replied:
"Fanaticism is not only inevitable with us; it is almost indispensable."
"The theatre man" seems to have been articulating a philosophy that
was to apply to Harold Clurman for the five decades that followed.

By all accounts, Clurman was, simply and in the most benign sense,
a fanatic. One of his editors recalled: "Harold didn't—like the rest of
us—rise to an occasion; he was already up there, waiting for the
occasion to come up." A seminal thinker about the nature of theater,
a much praised director, and a highly respected teacher and critic, he
was wedded to his *métier.*

Clurman was born in 1901 on Manhattan's Lower East Side, the son
of an immigrant who had prospered as a physician. Harold, the
youngest of four brothers, was a paternal favorite, sharing with his
father a deep interest in art, music, and literature and a great love of
the theater.

After three years of Columbia University, young Clurman went to
Paris to complete his education. Sharing an apartment on the
boulevard Raspail with his friend Aaron Copland, he spent the years
1921–23 studying drama at the Sorbonne, winning his *diplôme* with a
thesis on *fin de siècle* French drama, and enjoying Paris during the
postwar years of artistic ferment. He returned home in 1924 and

deciding to devote himself to the theater, he worked as a bit-part actor, assistant stage manager, and script reader. During the period of 1924–31, Clurman gained a practical knowledge of the theater that helped to shape his theoretical vision, and he made a number of provocative acquaintances among young theater folk, including Lee Strasberg and Cheryl Crawford, who joined him in 1931 as co-founders and directors of the Group Theatre.

Undeniably the most influential force in 20th-century American theater, the Group—whose members included Stella and Luther Adler, Morris Carnovsky, Clifford Odets, Franchet Tone, and Lee J. Cobb—was more than a company of actors devoted to the production of new plays. It was an assault on the whole structure of American "commercial" theater, which—Clurman argued—tended to stifle adventurous themes and to restrict the scope of talented young playwrights, directors, and actors. A "for-profit" attitude reduced theatrical creativity to its lowest forms—melodrama, farce, the conventional musical, and the "leg show"—and prevented growth of the artistic aesthetic that Clurman saw as the root of all truly great theater.

Based on his European observations and his extensive historical knowledge, Clurman defined theater as "an art of direct communication grounded on shared social and moral values . . . a resource in civilization's human treasury." To exploit this resource, specific machinery, heretofore lacking, had to be built. The prototype was the Group Theatre, a permanent "body of craftsmen"—including actors, directors, designers, technicians, and administrative staff—who not only shared similar attitudes about theater but also agreed upon a unified, systematic approach to dramatic art. Plays, Clurman insisted, had to be understood as "artistic wholes" rather than as scripts subject to interpretation by acting, direction, and design; otherwise, the final product would be little more than a mechanical exercise. The permanent, communal, "no-star" structure of the company was one aspect of the Group's attempt to ensure this degree of understanding; the use of the Moscow Art Theatre system (also known as the Stanislavsky method) of acting was the other. A complex and (even today) easily misunderstood technique, the "method"—which Clurman had studied under Richard Boleslavsky in New York in 1927—was developed as a means of allowing an actor "to use himself more conscientiously as an instrument for the attainment of truth on stage." Still, at first even so thoughtful an actor as Morris Carnovsky dismissed it as "hocus-pocus." No wonder the theater traditionalists of the time treated the method, and the whole Group idea, with either amused forebearance or dignified ridicule.

While Strasberg drilled the company in intricacies of the Stanislavsky system and directed much successes as Paul Green's *The House of Connelly* and Sidney Kingsley's *Men in White* (in addition to such failures as Claire and Paul Sifton's *1931* and Maxwell Anderson's *Night Over Taos*), Cheryl Crawford (who Clurman thought gave the triumvirate's best impression of sanity) served as the Group's chief fund raiser and liaison with the rest of the theater world. Clurman's initial role was that of theorist and inspirator; he fired the imaginations of the 28 young players and salved the bruised egos so common in such an intense enterprise.

Clurman, who had become the closest friend and advisor of Clifford

Odets, made his directorial debut in 1935, with Odet's *Awake and Sing!*, the Group's first completely home-grown production. The play was a success. Over the next five years, he directed four more Odets vehicles—among them the perennially revived *Golden Boy*. Not all of these plays were successes; nevertheless Odets became recognized as the leading young American playwright of the 1930s, and Clurman's reputation as a director was assured. In 1937, Clurman assumed the position of executive director of the Group, establishing what was, in effect, a dictatorship. It was an effort to concentrate the energies of the company, beset as it was by the defections to Hollywood of such leading figures as Tone, Stella Adler, and John Garfield and by clashes between Strasberg and himself—a situation brought about and exacerbated by the Group's increasing critical recognition in combination with its continuing failure to achieve financial stability.

At times, Clurman admitted, he was himself almost overwhelmed by the lunacy of it all. One night in 1936, for example, he dreamed he had been committed to an insane asylum. "Aghast at my presence in such a place," he wrote, "I was told by way of consolation that Boleslavsky and Stanislavsky were inmates of long standing." Yet he kept the company together through ten "fervent years" (as he later titled the Group history). In the end, however, the Group simply could not sustain the cause of theater-as-art while operating in the dominant theater-as-commerce environment. In his *post mortem* on the Group, Clurman confessed that his idealism had never hidden from the fact that "in a very real sense we were fools. The point is, I believed in the value of our folly."

Clurman spent the years 1941–45 in Hollywood, during which time he directed one mediocre motion picture *(Deadline at Dawn*, script by Odets), married Stella Adler, and confirmed for himself an opinion he had once expressed to Columbia Pictures' Walter Wanger: "Pictures are an industry; theatre merely an art." Returning to New York and the stage in 1945, he directed Theodore Reeves's *The Beggars Are Coming to Town*, followed by Maxwell Anderson's *Truckline Café*. Over the next quarter-century, he was one of America's most active stage directors, with 30 more productions (including shows in Tel Aviv, London, and Tokyo). Among the most notable of these were Carson McCuller's *The Member of the Wedding* (1950), William Inge's *Bus Stop* (1955), Tennessee Williams's *Orpheus Descending* (1957), the posthumous premiere of Eugene O'Neill's *A Touch of the Poet* (1958), and Arthur Miller's *Incident at Vichy* (1964).

With his command of theater history and understanding of theatrical technique, Clurman was uniquely qualified as a critic, serving over the years on the staffs of the magazines *Tomorrow, The New Republic,* and *The Nation* and contributing pieces to the *New York Times* and the *London Observer*. As a judge of drama, he tried, after the manner of his ideal critic, George Bernard Shaw, to place each play he reviewed into a historical and cultural context and explain why it did or did not meet his standards. He admitted that holding a play to his notions of what it ought to be was "perhaps improper and certainly unfair," it was at least "constructive." The result was criticism that addressed itself to theater students and scholars rather than to audiences and backers. Collected in a volume, *Lies Like Truth,* Clurman's critical essays won the George Jean Nathan Award in 1959. During the last decade of his life, this sort of writing served as the chief outlet for Clurman's didactic temperament. Still, it could never supply satisfaction equal to his stage experience, as he tacitly admitted in quoting Tristan Bernard. "A critic," he reminded the suffering Leonard Bernstein, "is a virgin who wants to teach Don Juan how to make love."

As much acclaim as his direction, instruction, criticism, and writing brought him, Clurman never forgot that his most ambitious goal remained unachieved. America had no permanent national theater, substantially endowed, free from commercial restraints and dedicated to realizing the full, enriching potential of the dramatic form. But he believed that when a man stops thinking of himself as a failure, he becomes one. So in a world of "flops," Harold Clurman rejected the role of "crêpehanger or mourner," declaring "I disapprove of much, but I enjoy everything."   R.C.

Son of Samuel Michael C., physician, and Bertha Saphir C. Married: (1) Stella Adler, actress and teacher, 1943 (div. 1960); (2) Juleen Compton, actress, 1960 (div. 1962). No children. Jewish. Educ: attended Columbia Univ. 1919–21; Univ. of Paris (Sorbonne), *diplôme* 1923; studied with Jacques Copeau at Sch. of the Vieux-Colombier Theatre, Paris 1923–24 and with Richard Boleslavsky at the American Laboratory Theatre, NYC 1927. Extra, cast as The Saint, Greenwich Village Theatre 1924; with Theatre Guild, NYC: asst. stage magr. 1925; bit-part actor in productions of Caesar and Cleopatra, Goat Song, Juarez and Maximilian, and Spread Eagle 1925–27; stage mgr., The Garrick Gaieties 1926; script reader 1929–31. Founder, with Lee Strasberg and Cheryl Crawford, of the Group Theatre 1931–41: Managing Dir. 1931–37; stage dir. 1935–40; Exec. Dir. 1937–41. Producer and dir., 20th Century Fox, Paramount, and RKO studios, Hollywood 1941–45. Independent producer and stage dir. 1946–69. Drama critic for Tomorrow mag. 1946–52; The New Republic 1949–53; The Nation since 1953; and The London Observer (guest critic) 1959–63. Conducted private acting classes 1954–70; Andrew Mellon lectr. on theater, Carnegie-Mellon Univ. 1962–63; Prof. of theater, grad. div., Hunter Coll., NYC since 1967. Exec. consultant, Repertory Theatre of Lincoln Center, NYC since 1963; exec. bd. member and play selector for the Theatre Development Fund of NYC; exec. bd. member of Soc. of Stage Directors and Choreographers; Member, Players Club and Authors Club, NYC. Hons: Donaldson Award for direction (for The Member of the Wedding) 1950; George Jean Nathan Award (for book Lies Like Truth: Theatre Reviews and Essays) 1959; Chevalier, French Legion of Honor 1959; Litt.d., Bard Coll., Annandale-on-Hudson, N.Y. 1959; D.F.A., Carnegie-Mellon Univ., Ripon Coll., Wisc., and Boston Univ. 1963; Medal of Achievement, Brandeis Univ. 1976. *Director: Stage* (NYC unless noted)—Awake and Sing!, 1935; Paradise Lost, 1935; Golden Boy, 1937; Rocket to the Moon, 1938; Awake and Sing! (revival), 1938; The Gentle People, 1939; Night Music, 1940; The Russian People, 1943; The Beggars Are Coming to Town, 1945; Truckline Café, 1946; The Whole World Over, 1947; The Young and the Fair, 1948; Monserrat (Tel Aviv, Israel), 1949; The Member of the Wedding, 1950; The Bird Cage, 1950; The Autumn Garden, 1951; Desire Under the Elms, 1952; The Time of the Cuckoo, 1952; Mademoiselle Colombe, 1954; Bus Stop, 1955; Tiger at the Gates (London and NYC), 1955; Pipe Dream, 1955; The Waltz of the Toreadors (touring production and NYC), 1957–58; Orpheus Descending, 1957; The Day the Money Stopped, 1958; A Touch of the Poet, 1958; The Cold Wind and the Warm, 1958; Heartbreak House, 1959; Caesar and Cleopatra (Tel Aviv), 1959; Sweet Love Remember'd (closed in New Haven, Conn.), 1959; Jeanette, 1960; A Shot in the Dark, 1961; Judith (London), 1962; Incident at Vichy, 1964; Long Day's Journey into Night (Tokyo), 1965; Where's Daddy?, 1966; The Iceman Cometh (Tokyo), 1968; Uncle Vanya (Los Angeles), 1969. *Film*—Deadline at Dawn, 1946. *Producer: Stage*—(with Elia Kazan) Truckline Café, 1946; (with Elia Kazan, Walter H. Fried, and Herbert H. Harris) All My Sons, 1947. *Author:* The Fervent Years, 1945, rev. eds. 1955 and 1974; Lies Like Truth: Theatre Reviews and Essays, 1958; (ed.) Famous Plays of the 1930s, 1959; The Naked Image: Observations on Modern Theatre, 1966; On Directing, 1972; The Divine Pastime: Theatre Essays, 1974; All People Are Famous: Instead of an Autobiography, 1974; Ibsen, 1978. Frequent contributor to the New York Times mag., Harper's Bazaar, Theatre Arts, and Partisan Review.

JOHN HOWARD GRIFFIN
Writer and photographer
Born Dallas, Texas, U.S.A., June 16th, 1920
Ded Fort Worth, Texas, U.S.A., September 9th, 1980

A crusader against bigotry and racism, John Howard Griffin achieved international fame in 1961 with the publication of *Black Like Me*. Originally serialized in Sepia magazine under the title "Journey into Shame," the book records the author's reactions as he traveled through Louisiana, Mississippi, Alabama, and Georgia disguised as a black man, his skin darkened from hormone treatments. In many cities he looked for a job, presenting his credentials unchanged. Prospective employers interested in his qualifications lost interest when they discovered his color. Hitchhiking, riding in the rear of buses, and spending nights with rural black families, Griffin experienced the traditions that robbed blacks of civil and human rights. He wrote that "As a white, I had always been free to walk into a nearby door whenever hunger, thirst, or rest room needs made themselves felt. As a negro, I quickly learned what it meant not to be free to walk into such doors. . . . I began to see WHITE ONLY signs in a new way—as a cruel rebuff to nature and humanity. . . . This is not a matter of physical inconvenience. It goes far deeper. Life turns somber when a man is never for a moment free from his grinding concern of the purely animal aspects of his existence."

This blunt, vivid attack on bigotry, presented as journal entries, won him the Saturday Review Anisfield-Wolf Award, as well as hostility from his townspeople in Texas, who burned him in effigy. The book itself gained readership throughout the U.S.A. and Europe, and in Japan.

Griffin, while traveling in the south, was particularly shocked by racial discrimination in the Catholic church, and decried the irony that white racists often justify their actions with reference to Christianity and patriotism. Throughout his career he wrote about prejudice; he hoped his essays and lectures would foster understanding between people of differing cultures.

Griffin's initial exposure to complex issues of racism, religion, and culture came during his study and work in France. His plans to become a psychiatrist were cut short in 1939 when he joined the French Défense Passive, which smuggled Jews from Germany through France to England. Because the Défense was not always successful, he witnessed the anguish of many refugees sent back to Nazi Germany; that memory haunted him when he later investigated racial discrimination.

In 1942 he joined the U.S. Air Force and served in the Pacific for 39 months; his experiences there formed the basis for his second novel, *Nuni.* Suffering impaired vision from head wounds received in the war, Griffin returned to France to continue medical studies. With a prognosis of complete blindness, Griffin abandoned medicine and turned to music, studying at the Benedictine Abbey of Solesmes, reading also in philosophy, theology, and anthropology. Losing his sight entirely in 1947, Griffin returned to Texas, learned braille, and settled on his parents' ranch near Fort Worth, where he raised pure-bred cattle. Directed by the Discaleced Carmelite monks and the Basilian Fathers of Canada, he continued studies begun in France.

A few years later he wrote a memoir of his life in French monasteries. The book became a best selling autobiographical novel, *The Devil Rides Outside,* recording a young man's struggle between the spirit and the flesh, detailing the author's conversion to Roman Catholicism. For its frank sexual language, the book was banned in Detroit. After Griffin's publisher challenged Michigan's obscenity statute, the case eventually reached the U.S. Supreme Court, which in 1957 overturned a long standing precedent defining censorship and obscenity. Critics compared the first novel to the work of Graham Greene, though admitting it lacked Greene's polish.

Despite blindness and a two year illness of spinal malaria, Griffin completed in 1956 *Nuni,* the story of an English professor who, after a plane crash, is washed ashore to a Pacific island and captured by brutal tribesmen. Maxwell Geismar called *Nuni* the "true antecedent" of *Black Like Me* for treating the conflict bewtween a society and its victim in nightmarish vignettes.

In 1957 the blood clot that had obstructed his vision dissolved and his sight returned; Griffin saw his wife and children for the first time.

Recognized as a champion of civil rights after writing *Black Like Me,* Griffin was actively politically in the 1960s. He spoke in cities with racial unrest, attempting to promote communication between black and white leaders. During summers he lectured at the University of Peace in Huy, Belgium, an institution founded by Father Georges Dominique Pire, O.P., a Nobel Peace Prize laureate. He helped document and publicize the killings of blacks and bombing of black homes and churches in Alabama and Mississippi during the early 1960s. Disturbed by parallels he saw between anti-Semitism in Nazi Germany and bigotry in the U.S.A., Griffin spoke out against the Ku Klux Klan and Christian churches for promoting racism. Writing on Martin Luther King Jr., Griffin praised King's efforts to "place the Christ Ideal in firm opposition to segregationists who were persuaded that they themselves acted from the noblest Christian motives and who felt it wholly within the framework of Christianity to smear, terrorize, kill, or do anything else to protect the traditional Southern Christian system from anyone who sought to alter it."

Griffin published several books of photo-essays in the 1970s; the most notable were studies of Thomas Merton *(A Hidden Wholeness)* and Jacques Maritain *(Homage in Words and Pictures).* In Thomas Merton, Griffin found a writer sympathetic to his convictions regarding racism and Christianity. After completing *A Hidden Wholeness,* Griffin spent much of 1971 researching Merton's life in Gethsemani Abbey, near Bardstown, Kentucky. In 1973 he gave lectures, sponsored by the Thomas Merton Studies Center, on Merton, racism and creative writing at nearby Bellarmine College in Louisville.

He published in 1977 a second edition of *Black Like Me* and *A Time To Be Human,* a personal account of prejudice and racism in the U.S.A. At the time of his death he had several books in manuscript, including a novel, *Street of the Seven Angels;* an account of his blindness, *Scattered Shadows;* and a biography of Merton. He died in Fort Worth, of diabetes.   E.T.

Son of Jack Walter G. and Lena Mae Young G., concert pianist. Married Elizabeth Anne Holland 1953. Children: Susan Michele, John Howard, Gregory Parker, Amanda Clare Dominique. Roman Catholic. Educ: Paschal High School, Fort Worth, Tex.; Lycée Descartes, Tours, France, certificate of studies 1938; attended École de Médecine, Tours, France; audited classes at Univ. of Poitiers, France 1938–39; Conservatory of Fontainebleau, Abbey of Solesmes, France, certificates in piano and composition 1946; certificates from Benedictines and Dominicans, France; private studies in philosophy and theology 1949–54. Mil. service: Member, French Défense Passive, joined 1939; Private, discharged as Technical Sgt., U.S. Army Air Force 1942–45. Journalist and syndicated columnist, International News and King Features 1957–60; active as writer and lectr. on racism, world peace, religion, and censorship, in U.S.A. and Europe 1950–80; Dir., Fort Worth Foundation for Visually Handicapped Children, Fort Worth, Tex.; Assoc. Ed., Ramparts. Member: Authors Guild; American Society of Magazine Photographers; Royal Photographic Society of Great Britain; Texas Inst. of Letters. Hons.: Natl. Council of Negro Women's Award 1960; Saturday Review Anisfield-Wolf Award 1961; Christian Culture Award 1966; co-recipient Pope John XXIII Pacem in Terris Award 1964. *Books: Novels*—The Devil Rides Outside, 1952; Nuni, 1956. *Author*—Land of the High Sky, 1959; Black Like Me, 1961, 2nd ed. 1977; The Church and the Black Man, 1968; The John Howard Griffin Reader, 1968; A Hidden Wholeness: The Visual World of Thomas Merton, 1970; Twelve Photographic Portraits, 1973; A Time to Be Human, 1977. *Contributing author*—"Is This What It Means to See?," The Spirit of Man, W. Burnett, ed., 1968; "Dark Journey," The Angry Black, J. Williams, ed., 1962; "Martin Luther King," Thirteen for Christ, M. Harcourt, 1963; "Dialogue with Father August Thompson," Black White and Gray (21 Points of View on the Race Question), B. Daniel, ed., 1964; "The Intrinsic *Other,*" Building Peace, Father G. Pire, O.P., 1966; Thomas Merton Studies Center: Three Essays, with Thomas Merton, 1969; A Part of Space: Ten Texas Writers, 1969; Jacques Maritain: Homage in Words and Pictures, with Y. Simon, 1974. Contributed short stories to anthologies and periodicals. *Monograph*—A Report of the Crisis Situation Resulting from Efforts to Desegregate the School System, with T. Freedman, Anti-Defamation League of B'nai B'rith, 1956. *Major articles:* "The Living Chains of Blackness: Journey into the Mississippi Night," Southwest Review, Autumn, 1960; "Current Trends in Censorship," Southwest

Review, Summer, 1962; "On Either Side of Violence," Saturday
Review, Oct. 27, 1962; "Scattered Shadows," Ramparts, 1963;
"Martin Luther King's Movement," Sign, Aug., 1963; "Racist Sins of
Christians," Sign, Aug., 1963; "The Tip-Off," Ramparts, Autumn.
1964; "Maritain Charts a Course Through Change," Natl. Catholic
Reporter, Nov. 9, 1966.
Further reading: "Prospects of a Catholic Novel" by Eugene
McNamara, America, Aug. 17, 1957; American Moderns by Maxwell
Geismar, 1958.

WILLIAM (MEYERS) COLMER
Congressman, United States House of Representatives
Born Moss Point, Mississippi, U.S.A., February 11th, 1890
Died Pascagoula, Mississippi, U.S.A., September 10th, 1980

U.S. Representative William Colmer of Mississippi was a leading
Southern Democratic congressman whose 40-year career in the House
began with the New Deal and ended under President Nixon. Like
many Southerners of modest means who experienced the Depression,
Colmer entered politics as a liberal; he was first elected to Congress in
the 1932 Roosevelt landslide and consistently supported New Deal
programs. President Roosevelt rewarded him in 1939 by helping him
to become a member of the powerful House Rules Committee,
through which most bills had to pass before reaching the House floor.

Soon after, however, Colmer adopted a more conservative stance
which corresponded with the new mood of the South and his
Mississippi Gulf Coast district. His change of position helped consolidate the conservative Southern Democratic-Republican alliance which
dominated the Rules Committee until the 1960s. The alliance frequently blocked social legislation and the civil rights bills which began
to be introduced after the Supreme Court's 1954 desegregation ruling.
Colmer's segregationist views, out of step with his party's support of
civil rights causes, led him to support the independent presidential
candidacy of Senator Harry F. Byrd in 1960. The new President—
John Kennedy—urged House Speaker Sam Rayburn to purge Colmer
from the Rules Committee. But Rayburn, wishing to avoid controversy, agreed instead to add several liberals to the committee, thereby
creating an eight-to-seven liberal majority.

Colmer's career culminated in 1967 when he became the Rules
Committee chairman. Despite a nine-to-six liberal majority, Colmer
could occasionally maneuver a bill to death. In 1968, for example, he
delayed consideration of a gun control bill until its sponsor agreed to
oppose any attempts to add registration and licensing amendments to
the House floor. In 1970 he refused to schedule hearings on a bill that
would have increased the power of the Equal Employment Opportunity Commission to combat racial discrimination in industry and
unions. The same year he blocked the creation of an independent
consumer protection agency. Yet Colmer's position was weakened by
the congressional reforms which made committee chairmen less
powerful and by the generally liberal atmosphere of the time. In 1972,
at the age of 82, he decided not to run for re-election because of poor
health. He remained influential in Mississippi politics, however,

supporting President Nixon for re-election in 1972 and President Ford
in 1976.   T.P.

Son of Henry C. and Anna Meyers C. Married Ruth Miner 1917.
Children: William; James; Thomas. Educ: attended Millsaps Coll.,
Jackson, Miss. 1910–14. Mil. Service: U.S. Army 1918–19. Sch.
teacher 1914; admitted to Miss. bar 1917; County Attorney, Jackson
county, 1921–27; District Attorney, 2nd District of Miss. 1928–33;
Member, Congress, 5th Miss. District 1933–73; Chmn., House Rules
Cttee. 1967–73. Member, American Legion.

VIRGINIA KIRKUS
Book reviewer and author
Born Meadville, Pennsylvania, U.S.A., December 7th, 1893
Died Danbury, Connecticut, U.S.A., September 10th, 1980

Virginia Kirkus was the founder and president of Kirkus Reviews, a
book reviewing service that strongly influenced book buying and
selling in the United States. The reviews were honest, trustworthy,
and down-to-earth, "a check," Virginia Kirkus once said, "on the
natural enthusiasm of publishers' blurbs."

Virginia Kirkus was born in 1893, the daughter of an Episcopal
minister who later became rector of the American Church at Munich,
Germany. Soon after Virginia's birth, the family moved to
Wilmington, Delaware where Virginia spent most of her childhood.
She attended the Misses Hebbs School in Wilmington and the Hannah
More Academy at Reistertown, Maryland. After receiving her A.B.
in 1916 from Vassar College, Virginia Kirkus took some graduate
courses at Teacher's College of Columbia University.

From 1917 to 1920 Virginia Kirkus taught English and history
classes at Greenhill School in Wilmington, Delaware. She then moved
to New York City to pursue an editorial career. She became the
assistant fashion editor for a magazine called *Pictorial Review* and
later moved to *McCall's* as the "back of the book" editor. In 1926 she
became head of the children's book department at Harper & Brothers, a publishing company.

It was while she was running the children's book department at
Harper that Virginia Kirkus originated her book review service.
Rather than cut back on her department at Harper during the
Depression, she used her staff to review books in order to help
booksellers determine what books to order for their customers. In
1933 Virginia Kirkus left Harper to become president of Virginia
Kirkus Services, Inc. Although she started with only ten subscribers,
Virginia Kirkus soon built up a reputation in the book-buying and
book-selling world for her honesty and objectivity; she would read as
many as 700 books a year. In 1980 the Kirkus Service could claim over
4,600 subscribers, including librarians, authors, agents, booksellers,
and the publishing community.

The Kirkus reviews are written from the galley proofs of books
supplied by the publishers. Their aim, as Virginia Kirkus herself had
intended, is to be informal, colloquial and readable—never preten-

tious or literary. The Kirkus Service, now owned by *The New York Review of Books,* currently reviews 4,500 books a year.

In addition to Kirkus Reviews, Virginia Kirkus participated in other aspects of the world of books. During the Second World War she served on the Booksellers Authority in Washinton, D.C. and on the selection board for Armed Services Editions. She wrote a book about restoring the country house where she and her husband, Frank Glick, a department store executive whom she married in 1936, spent their weekends. She also wrote a book for children on gardening, which was published in 1956 and revised in 1976. In Connecticut she served as president of the Mark Twain Library in 1953–54 and was a member of Connecticut Governor's Commission on Rural Libraries from 1961 to 1964. She lectured on books and was a frequent contributor of articles to the *Saturday Review.*

In 1962 Virginia Kirkus sold Kirkus Reviews and retired to her Connecticut home where, in addition to her literary activities, she gardened, cooked, and collected antiques. She died in Connecticut at the age of 86.   J.N.

Daughter of Frederick Maurice K., Episcopal clergyman, and Isabella Clark K. Married Frank Glick, dept. store exec. 1936 (d.). No children. Educ: Misses Hebbs Sch., Wilmington, Del.; Hannah More Acad., Reistertown, Md.; B.A. Vassar Coll. 1916; graduate study, Teacher's Coll. of Columbia Univ., NYC 1917. English and history teacher, Greenhill Sch., Wilmington, Del. 1917–20; Asst. fashion ed., Pictorial Review, and back-of-the-book ed., McCall's, 1920–26; Head of children's book dept., Harper & Brothers, NYC 1926–32; Founder and Pres., Virginia Kirkus Service, Inc. 1933–62. During WWII served on Booksellers Authority, Washington D.C. and on selections bd. for Armed Services Editions. Pres., Mark Twain Library, Conn. 1953–54; Member, Conn. Governor's Commn. on Rural Libraries 1961–64; Member, American Library Assoc., P.E.N. (N.Y. bd. member 1962–65), League of Women Voters. *Author:* Everywoman's Guide to Health and Personal Beauty, 1922; A House for the Weekends, 1945; The First Book of Gardening, 1956, rev. ed. 1976. Frequent contributor of feature articles to Saturday Review.

SIR (JAMES) HARWOOD HARRISON
British politician
Born Bugbrooke, Northampton, England, June 6th, 1907
Died Woodbride, East Suffolk, England, September 11th, 1980

Harwood Harrison, whose parliamentary career as a Conservative member for the Eye division of Suffolk spanned the years 1951–79, was born into the home of a Church of England clergyman and educated at Northampton Grammar school. At Trinity College, Oxford, he took an honours degree in jurisprudence in 1928 and later returned to win his M.A. (1946).

While a member of the Ipswich Borough Council (1935–46), Harrison served in the Suffolk Regiment of the Territorial Army. He was promoted to Captain upon the outbreak of war and to Major a year later. Posted to the Far East, he was among the 60,000 British

Courtesy Harrison estate

and colonial troops captured when Singapore fell to the Japanese in February 1942. During 1943 he was put to work on the Burma Railway. After the war, he continued on active military service until 1951, when he transferred to the Territorial Army Reserve with the rank of colonel. He served in the Reserve Officer Corps until 1965.

Entering Parliament on his second attempt, as part of Churchill's postwar majority, Harrison soon became identified with future Prime Minister Harold Macmillan, then minister of Housing and Local Government, serving as his Parliamentary Private Secretary during 1953–54. He moved up to the party post of Assistant Whip in 1954 and served in the Ministry as a Lord Commissioner of the Treasury from 1956 to 1959 under Macmillan. From 1959–61 he was Comptroller of Her Majesty's Household, for which service he was created First Baronet of Bugbrooke in 1961.

As a member of Parliament he showed a special interest in automotive legislation, introducing and sponsoring the private member's bills which became the Road Transport Lighting (Rear Lights) Act of 1953 and the Road Traffic Act of 1964. Among his related political activities, he was active in the National Union of Conservative and Unionist Associations (Eastern Area), serving as vice chairman, chairman and president at various times; and in the Unionist Club as well, of which he was a member from 1966 to his death.

As a private citizen, Harrison was a landowner and chairman of a real estate concern, Cap Estate (St. Lucia) Ltd; he was also a director on the board of Chalwyns, Ltd., among other companies.   R.C.

Son of Rev. E.W.H., Church of England clergyman. Married Peggy Alberta Mary Stenhouse 1932. Children: Michael James Harwood, b. 1936; Joanna Kathleen Sanders, b. 1939. Church of England. Educ: Northampton Grammar Sch.; Trinity Coll., Oxford, B.A., Hons. 1928, M.A. 1946. Mil. Service: Commissioned Lt., 4th Battalion, Suffolk Reg., Territorial Army 1935; Capt. 1939; Major 1940; taken prisoner (Singapore) 1942; worked on Burma Railway 1943; Lt.-Col. and Commandant, 4th Suffolks 1947; breveted to Col. 1951; Territorial Army Reserve Officer 1951–65. M.P., Eye Div. of Suffolk (Conservative) 1951–79; Parliamentary Private Secty. to Harold MacMillan, then Minister of Housing and Local Govt. 1953–54; Asst. Party Whip 1954–56; a Lord Commnr. of the Treasury 1956–59; Comptroller of H.M. Household 1959–61. Presented and sponsored Road Transport Lighting (Rear Lights) Act of 1953 and Road Traffic Act of 1964. Vice Chmn. 1953–56, Chmn. 1956–59, and Pres. 1963–66, Natl. Union of Conservative and Unionist Assocs. (Eastern Area); Chmn. Unionist Club 1966–80; Member, Defense and External Affairs Subcttee. of Commons Expenditures Cttee. 1971–79; Treas. 1968, Vice Chmn. 1970 and Chmn. 1973–74, British Branch, Inter-Parliamentary Union. Chmn., Cap Estate (St. Lucia) Ltd.; Dir., Chalwyns Ltd. and other cos.; Pres., Ipswich District Far East POW Fellowship 1953. Hons: created first Baronet of Bugbrooke 1961.

DON BANKS
Composer and conductor
Born South Melbourne, Australia, October 25th, 1923
Died Sydney, Australia, September 12th, 1980

Don Banks was a leader of the modern movement in music in Great Britain and Australia. To achieve his unique style, Banks reconciled and combined elements drawn from jazz, classical, and electronic music.

The son of a professional jazz musician, Banks began his career as a jazz pianist and became interested in composing and arranging for jazz bands during the early 1940s. In 1947, he studied music composition with A.E.H. Nickson and Dorian Le Gallienne at the University of Melbourne Conservatory of Music. Banks moved to London in 1950 to continue his musical education with Matyas Seiber, and in 1953, having received an Italian Government scholarship, he moved to Florence to study with Luigi Dallapiccola.

Although Banks had written modernist works as a student and his music had been performed at London concerts and on radio, financial needs forced him, in the 1950s, to conduct arrangements of light, popular music and to compose scores for television and film. Ironically, it was Banks's "pop" music which brought him to the attention of the London classical music community.

By the early 1960s, he was established as a serious composer and had performed for the Cheltenham Festival, the Edinburgh Festival, the London Symphony Orchestra, the Calouste Gulbenkian Foundation, and the BBC. During this period, Banks developed his distinct musical style. In such pieces as *Horn Concerto, Violin Concerto,* and *Division for Orchestra,* British and Australian critics claimed he had successfully merged jazz, electronics, serial techniques, and classical forms to achieve a musical synthesis that was bright, lyrical, highly accessible and distinctively modern. Banks also wrote chamber music in the 1960s, including *Trio for Violin, Horn and Piano, Violin Sonata, Four Pieces for String Quartet,* and the *Sonata de Camera,* which was first performed at the 1961 Cheltenham Festival and dedicated to Matyas Seiber.

In the late 1960s and 1970s, Banks, who considered himself a member of the musical avant-garde, continued to experiment with the new tonalities made possible by electronic music; he also sought the integration of improvisational jazz with the traditional cadenzas played by classical soloists. He composed *Nexus for Symphony Orchestra and Jazz Quintet* and *Meeting Place for Chamber Orchestra, Jazz Group and Synthesizer* for jazz groups conducted by John Dankworth, and *Settings from Roget* and *Three Songs* for singer Cleo Laine. In 1972, Banks returned to Australia as Creative Arts Fellow at the Australian National University in Canberra. Although he returned regularly to London for performances and recording sessions, Banks spent considerable time campaigning for the introduction of modern music to the Australian continent. In 1973 he was appointed Chairman of the Music Board of the Australian Council of the Arts.   J.S.

Son of professional jazz musician. Jazz pianist, composer and arranger for jazz bands in early 1940s. Studied music composition, with A.E.H. Nickson and Dorian Le Gallienne, Univ. Melbourne Conservatory of Music 1947. Moved to London, studied with Matyas Seiber 1950. Moved to Florence, studied with Luigi Dallapiccola on Italian Govt.

scholarship 1953. Conducted arrangements of pop music, composed
television and film scores in 1950s. Creative Arts Fellow, Australian
National Univ., Canberra 1972; Chmn., Music Bd. of Australian
Council of the Arts 1973.*Commissioned performances:* Cheltenham
Festival, 1961; Edinburgh Festival, London Symphony Orchestra,
Calouste Gulbenkian Foundation, B.B.C. Orchestra, ca. 1960s;
A.B.C. Tasmanian Orchestra, 1977; The Kings' Singers, 1979; un-
finished project, London Sinfonietta, 1980; many other commissions.
Compositions: Horn Concerto; Violin Concerto; Division for Or-
chestra; Trio for Violin, Horn and Piano; Violin Sonata, Four Pieces
for String Quartet; Sonata de Camera; Nexus for Symphony Orchestra and Jazz Quintet; Meeting Place for Chamber Orchestra; Jazz
Group and Synthesizer; Settings from Roget; Three Songs; and many
others.

SIR (ALFRED) RUPERT (NEALE) CROSS
Professor of law and author of law textbooks
Born England, June 15th, 1912
Died England, September 12th, 1980

Sir Rupert Cross overcame the handicap of total blindness to become
not only an able academic, but a gifted teacher, author and authority
on criminal law and the law of evidence.

After becoming totally blind in early childhood, Cross was educated
at Worcester College for the Blind, and Worcester College, Oxford,
where he took degrees in modern history and jurisprudence. During
the war years he worked as a solicitor in a private London firm of
solicitors and it was probably this early experience of legal practice
which informed his lifelong sensitivity to the practical requirements of
law.

Cross's academic career began at the close of the Second World
War when he began working as a tutor in the Law Society's School,
(now College) of Law, assisting returning legal workers to re-enter
their profession by holding refresher courses. In 1948 Cross began
lecturing in law at Magdalen College—the start of a long and
distinguished career at Oxford. Cross received his doctorate in civil
law in 1958 and was appointed professor in the university in 1964.
Cross's rise to academic eminence was founded on his authorship of
many works on law, many of which became standard textbooks. He
retired in 1979.

Cross served on many legal committees, including the Law Reform
and Criminal Law Revision Committees; his attention to detail, and
the familiarity with legal cases and precedent which he showed in his
books, provided him with the background of knowledge against which
responsible decisions could be made. At the same time, his concern
with the wider range of practical matters, the contributions to be made
by other professionals such as penologists, social workers and psychologists, helped him to reach decisions which were both humane and
practical.

Sir Rupert, who had a reputation as a humorous and able teacher,
was an active committee-man and served on the Council of the Royal
National Institute for the Blind, showing by example that blindness

need not be a handicap. He received many honors during his life and was knighted in 1973.   G.D.

Son of Arthur George C., quantity surveyor, and Mary Elizabeth C. Married Aline Heather Chadwick 1937. No children. Educ: Worcester Coll. for the Blind; Worcester Coll., Oxford, B.A. Hons. 1933, M.A. 1937, D.C.L. 1958. Admitted solicitor 1939. Solicitor, private firm London 1939–45; Lectr., Law Soc. School of Law 1945–48; Fellow and Tutor, Magdalen Coll., Oxford 1948–64; Vinerian Prof. in English Law, Oxford 1964–79; Visiting Prof., Univ. of Adelaide 1962 and Sydney 1968. Member: Cttee. on Jury Service 1963–64; Criminal Law Reform Cttee. 1963–72; Diplock Cttee. on Legal Procedures 1972; Council of Royal Natl. Inst. for the Blind; also other cttees. concerned with criminal law and law of evidence reform. Hons: Elected Fellow, British Acad. 1976; Hon. Fellow, Worcester Coll. and Hon. Master of the Bench, Middle Temple 1972; knighted 1973; Hon. LL.D., Edinburgh Univ. 1973 and Leeds Univ. 1975; Hon. Fellow, Magdalen Coll. 1975. *Author:* Law of Wills, 1947; (with P.A. Jones) Introduction to Criminal Law, 1948; (with P.A. Jones) Cases on Criminal Law, 1949; Evidence, 1958; Precedent in English Law, 1961; (with Nancy Wilkins) An Outline of the Law of Evidence, 1964; The English Sentencing System, 1971; Punishment, Prison and the Public, 1971; Statutory Interpretation, 1976. Contributed to Law Quarterly Review; Modern Law Review; Criminal Law Review and other professional jrnls.

ABŪ SALMĀ
Pen-name of Abd al-Karīm al-Karmī
Poet, lawyer, and teacher
Born Tulkarm City, Palestine, 1906
Died Washington, D.C., U.S.A., September 13th, 1980

Abū Salmā (the pen-name means "Father of Peace"), a poet almost unknown in the West, became "Palestine's poet," and his themes were the dispossession, exile and promised return of the Palestinians to their homeland.

Abū Salmā, born Abd al-Karīm al-Karmī, was the son of a prominent official who became President of the Arab Academy, Chief Justice of the Jordanian government and head of the Majlis (consultative committee). As a boy Abū Salmā attended school in Tulkarm, then continued his elementary education in Damascus. After graduting from the Faculty of Law at the Jerusalem Law Institute, Abū Salmā worked as a teacher, and in broadcasting for Radio Palestine in Jerusalem. He subsequently became a lawyer in Haifa, and later returned to Damascus where he worked as a lawyer and teacher. He also became a judge of the Disciplinary Council and Director of the Guidance Department in the Syrian Ministry of Information. He moved to Chevy Chase, Maryland in the mid 1970s.

Abū Salmā believed that the *nakbi* (catastrophe) of 1948, made "orphans" of the Palestinians, who were forced to leave their country "with no hands to hold." They were "scarred by history which struck them like the shattering piece of a stupid bomb." He urged his people to always remember their land, where "patriots' blood, like tears, seeps into the earth; where grass and trees grow up as if from our bones." By remembering, the Palestinians might one day know *el awda* (the return). But he saw no hope of this without conflict. Those who wanted their freedom, he said, must be prepared to take up arms against the oppressors.

Writing in *Arab Perspectives,* Fawaz Turki says that there is "a jubilation, a roundedness, a celebration of the impulse to be free" in Abū Salmā's poetry, and believes that this is achieved by "a moral optimism, an aboriginal sense of history as every Palestinian's, every Arab's and every oppressed person's personal context."

Abū Salmā, whose four volumes of poetry are an inspiration to many of his people, died in exile and was buried in Washington, D.C. He had often expressed the hope of being buried in Palestine. In one poem he wrote: "my heart is on the Jaffa shore, proclaiming my purest dreams." Meanwhile, he acknowledged, "the irony of Palestine deepens."   R.T.

Son of al-Shaykh Sa'id al-Karmī, Chief Justice of Jordan, and Hasna Khalil Lahham. Married Ruquiyah Tawfiq Haqqi (Rokie) 1936. Son: Sa'id, b. 1937, physician. Muslim. Attended elementary schs. in Tulkarm and Damascus; graduated from Faculty of Law, Jerusalem Law Inst. Taught, and worked for Radio Palestine, Jerusalem; became a lawyer in Haifa; moved to Damascus and worked as lawyer and teacher; Member of Disciplinary Council (Judge) and Dir., Guidance Dept., Ministry of Information, Syria. Moved to U.S.A. mid 1970s. Elected Chmn., Union of Palestinian Writers 1980. Hon: Lotus Award of Afro-Asian Writers, 1978. *Vols. of poetry* (translated titles of works published in Arabic in the Middle East): The Homeless, 1964; Songs From Home, 1971; From Palestine, My Pen, 1971; Collected Works of Abū Salmā, 1971.
Further reading: "Abū Salmā: The Poet of National Anguish" by Fawaz Turki in *Arab Perspectives,* New York, Vol. 1, no. 8, Nov. 1980.

JOSÉ MARÍA GIL ROBLES
Leader of the Spanish Catholic Party and Minister of War
Born Spain, November 27th, 1898
Died Madrid, Spain, September 14th, 1980

José María Gil Robles was the leader of Spain's parliamentary right wing from 1933 until the beginning of the Spanish Civil War in 1936. In 1935, as Minister of War, he made the fateful decision to appoint Francisco Franco chief-of-staff of the army.

Gil Robles came from a prominent and actively Catholic family; his father was an eminent professor of law at Salamanca University. After receiving his law doctorate from Madrid University at the age of 22, the son studied comparative law at the Sorbonne and Heidelberg and joined the faculty at Salamanca in 1928. He also served as a lawyer for the Jesuits and for the Confederación Nacional Católica-Agraria, an organization of independent farming unions, whose secretary-general he became in 1931.

When the 200-year-old Bourbon monarchy was deposed in 1931 and

replaced by a socialist-dominated republic, Gil Robles, as deputy for
Salamanca in the Cortes, Spain's parliament, participated in debates
on the newly-drafted constitution and denounced its curtailments of
the Church's political, social, and educational powers. He also
defended in court a group of right-wing army officers who had been
involved in an attempted coup. At the invitation of a group of
Catholic journalists, he became the head of the new party, Acción
Popular, which merged with other Catholic groups to form the
Confederación Español de Derechas Autonómas (CEDA), or Spanish
Catholic Party. Many of its members supported the restoration of the
monarchy. This movement, formed for the purpose of defending
Catholicism, private property, and traditional social classes and
mores, soon began to take on the trappings of fascism: its members
adopted a nazi-style salute and anti-semitic slogans, wore brown-
shirted uniforms, and greeted Gil Robles with chants of "Jefe" (the
Spanish equivalent of "Führer" or "Duce"); Gil Robles himself paid a
visit to Hitler. Although he publicly repudiated Nazism and promised
his followers that their takeover of Spain would be gradual, not
violent, he was regarded as a fascist by the majority of workers and
leftists.

Courtesy Gil-Robles estate

The November 1933 general elections made CEDA the largest
parliamentary party in Spain. Gil Robles, though a likely candidate
for Prime Minister, refused to alienate his monarchist supporters by
declaring his loyalty to the Republic. Fearing that Gil Robles, once in
office, would establish a dictatorship like that of Catholic Prime
Minister Engelburt Dollfuss in Asturia, President Niceto Alcalá-
Zamora passed over him in favor of Alejandro Lerroux, head of the
centrist Radical Party, whom Gil Robles reluctantly agreed to
support. Accused by his more reactionary followers of selling out, he
soon forced a reorganization of the Lerroux cabinet under which
CEDA was granted three ministerial posts. This acquisition of power
by the Catholic right wing provoked an outburst of strikes and
political violence, already rampant in polarized Spain, culminating in
an uprising in the mining province of Asturias which was bloodily put
down. Gil Robles, while resisting rightist calls for a coup d'état,
brought down the government by rejecting a proposed commutation
of the death sentences given to the Austrian leaders.

While serving as Minister of War from May to December of 1935,
Gil Robles promoted to the post of chief of staff of the army General
Francisco Franco, who had led the attacks on the Asturian miners,
and joined him in purging the army of its liberal-republican officers.
When the leftist Popular Front came to power in the February 1936
elections, he attempted, in vain, to have martial law declared in order
to prevent an inevitable civil war.

On June 16th, Gil Robles, speaking in the Cortes, denounced the
most recent wave of political violence, saying, "A country can live
under a monarchy or a republic, with a parliamentary or a presidential
system, under communism or fascism. But it cannot live in anarchy.
Now, alas, Spain is in anarchy. And we are today present at the
funeral service of democracy." Less than a week later he narrowly
escaped assassination at the hands of socialists bent on avenging the
murder of a leftist assault guard by right-wing Falangists. They did
succeed in killing Calvo Sotelo, a Monarchist leader who had replaced
Gil Robles as spokesman for the right.

On July 18th, Franco entered Spain at the head of an insurgent rightist army and the civil war began. Expelled by the French Popular Front government from Biarritz, where he had been caught by the outbreak of the war, Gil Robles went to Lisbon, where he headed an arms-purchasing operation for the insurgents.

After Franco succeeded in establishing his totalitarian regime in Spain in 1938, Gil Robles remained in voluntary exile for another 15 years, in the hope that a more moderate government would evolve in which he could participate. He returned in 1953, became active in the legal defense of Spanish dissidents, and helped to organize the Christian Democratic movement, which was legalized in the late 1970s after Franco's death. From 1962 to 1964 he was exiled for suggesting that the European Economic Community bar Spain from membership until such time as it became a parliamentary democracy. When he retired in 1977, his son took over as co-leader of the movement's main sector, the Democratic Left. Gil Robles died in Madrid of heart failure.   J.P./T.P.

Son of a law professor. Married. One son, politician. Roman Catholic. Educ: Madrid Univ., doctorate in law 1920; studied comparative law at Univ. of Paris (Sorbonne) and Heidelberg Univ. Practicing lawyer; Prof. of Law, Univ. of Salamanca 1928; elected parliamentary deputy for Salamanca ca. 1930; Secty.-Gen., Confederación Nacional Católico-Agraria 1931; defended army officers who participated in rightist uprising ca. 1932; head of Acción Nacional, later Acción Popular, 1931–36; head of Confederación Española de Derechas Autonómas (CEDA; Spanish Catholic Party) 1933–36: Minister of War 1935–36; in voluntary exile during and after civil war 1936–53; active in legal defense of Spanish dissidents and development of Christian Democratic movement, Spain 1953–75; exiled 1962–64 for political opinions; head of Federación Democrática Popular 1975–77; head of Federación Democrática Cristiana 1977. *Author:* No Fué Posible la Paz (Peace was Impossible).
Further reading: The Spanish Civil War by Hugh Thomas, 1961; The Spanish Republic and the Civil War: 1931–1939 by Gabriel Jackson, 1965; An Oral History of the Spanish Civil War by Ronald Fraser, 1979.

JEAN PIAGET
Developmental psychologist
Born Neuchâtel, Switzerland, August 9th, 1896
Died Geneva, Switzerland, September 16th, 1980

Although Jean Piaget is widely considered the greatest psychologist since Freud, he regarded himself not as a psychologist but as a genetic epistemologist, bringing the perspectives of psychology, biology, and philosophy to bear on the central question of the nature of human knowledge. His original intention in studying the development of thought processes in children, the work for which he became famous, was to uncover the mental structures inherent in the human species as a whole. In the sixty years of research that followed, he debunked long-entrenched notions of childhood intelligence and revolutionized the approach of professional educators, particularly in America. "In light of Piaget's studies," wrote psychologist David Elkind, "the growth of knowledge could no longer be regarded as a simple learning process but had, instead, to be conceived as a giving up of erroneous ideas for more correct ones or as a transformation of these ideas into higher-level, more adequate conceptions. In short, these studies suggested that mental growth was not determined entirely by the unfolding of innate structures nor entirely by the influence of the environment but rather by the constant interaction of these two factors."

Piaget's model for this interaction was drawn from biology, in which he did his first research, and from philosophy, the main interest of his university days. Called equilibration, it is a dialectical process involving a constantly evolving set of reactions between the organism (the child) and its environment (the world). The two poles of this process are assimilation, the modification of an incoming stimulus to fit the organism's pre-existing structure, and accommodation, the modification of the structure to adapt to an incoming stimulus. Each new experience, whether sensory or conceptual, is assimilated by the child into her current conception of the world; when that conception is no longer adequate to make sense of her experiences, the child invents another, more complex conception, changing her own mental structures to accommodate the new information. The resulting equilibrium continues until further experiences intitiate a new phase of the process. (An example of equilibration is the child's evolving perception of moral authority. When very young, she perceives her parents as having ultimate and unquestionable authority, owing to their greater size and strength. Their flaws and inconsistencies are assimilated into this model until the evidence against their omnipotence becomes so great that the child is forced to reject the model and develop a new one, in which ultimate authority rests with some still higher body, such as government or God.) This discovery of dialectical mental processes in children was crucial for Piaget's investigations of epistemology, since it indicated that some form of logic exists even in infancy and that the growth of intelligence consists of a progressive refinement of cognitive ability from the simple making and revising of rules to the comprehension and invention of formal logical systems.

Piaget was born in 1896 to an old, established family in the Swiss canton of Neuchâtel. His mother, according to his own account, suffered from a "neurotic temperament" to which he reacted by taking refuge in the "private world and . . . non-fictitious world" of scientific study, in imitation of his father, a medieval historian. His first publication, written at the age of ten and printed in the local journal of natural history, was a one-page article on an albino sparrow he had observed in a park.

During the next four years Piaget spent his Saturday afternoons helping the director of Neuchâtel's museum of natural history to classify and augment the mollusk collection. By the time he was sixteen, he was regularly publishing articles in professional journals of malacology and had received an offer of a post as a museum curator. At about the same age he experienced a religious and intellectual crisis occasioned by his inability to reconcile the facts of biology with the dogmas of his mother's Protestantism. The dilemma was partially resolved when his godfather, Samuel Cornut, introduced him to Henri

Bergson's philosophy of "creative evolution." "The identification of God with life itself," he later wrote, "was an idea that stirred me almost to ecstasy because it now enabled me to see in biology the explanation of all things and of the mind itself. . . . The problem of knowing (properly called the epistemological problem) suddenly appeared to me in an entirely new perspective and as an absorbing topic of study. It made me decide to consecrate my life to the biological explanation of knowledge."

At the University of Neuchâtel, Piaget studied philosophy under Alan Reymond and wrote a philosophical novel, *Recherche*. After receiving his baccalaureate in 1915, he studied zoology, embryology, geology, physical chemistry, and group-theory mathematics, earning his doctorate in 1918 with a thesis on the mollusks of Valais. He spent the next three years at the University of Zurich and at the Sorbonne, where he administered intelligence tests to Parisian schoolchildren under the supervision of Theodore Simon in the laboratory of Alfred Binet. In the course of this work, he became intrigued by the wrong answers given by the children to the test questions. These errors appeared to exhibit underlying, and hitherto unsuspected, patterns of reasoning, very different from the logical processes of adults. To investigate them further, Piaget developed a technique known as the semiclinical interview. (In contrast to Freudian techniques of free association and dream analysis, which seek to reveal the emotions of the subject, and to behaviorist laboratory techniques, which seek to measure the actions and reactions of the subject, the semiclinical interview is intended to clarify the reasoning patterns of the subject through a guided conversation, preferably conducted in a comfortable and familiar setting and directed towards specific issues of comprehension.) Piaget decided to devote the next few years to studying the origins of intelligence in infants and children as a preparation for constructing an epistemological system based on biological principles. This system would utilize insights from all the sciences, which, he believed, are interdependent and have as their common feature the question of the acquisition and definition of knowledge.

The three articles that came out of his Sorbonne research brought Piaget the position of director of studies at the Institute J.J. Rousseau in Geneva, and, four years later, a professorship at the University of Neuchâtel. His first five books, published between 1924 and 1932, dealt with children's conceptions of natural objects, physical causality, and moral judgment. The interviews conducted by himself and his assistants with young schoolchildren showed them to be animists for whom the sun, the wind, dreams, and all natural objects are possessed of life and have a will of their own. In a typical case, the interviewer questioned a child about the activities of the moon. "What does the moon do when you are out walking? *It follows us.* . . . Why does it follow us? *To see where we are going.*"

These early volumes (intended by Piaget as preliminary observations, but misunderstood by his fellow psychologists as his final position) concentrated on language as the earliest expression of logic in children. "It was only later, by studying the patterns of intelligent behavior of the first two years, that I learned that for a complete understanding of the genesis of intellectual operations, manipulation and experience with objects had first to be considered." The birth of his children in 1925, 1927, and 1931 provided Piaget with ample material for the study of cognition in infants, in which task he was assisted by his wife and former student, Valentine Châtenay. These observations formed the basis of his theory of the sensorimotor period as the first stage of mental development, lasting from birth until approximately the age of two years, and comprising six substages, in the course of which the infant builds increasingly complex actions through equilibration. For example, the reflex act of arm movement brings the infant's thumb into accidental contact with her mouth; the reflex act of sucking makes the contact gratifying. Gradually, the child acquires the ability to bring the thumb to the mouth intentionally. Each such interaction with the environment, known as a schema in Piagetian terminology, is incorporated into the infant's cognitive repertoire, and, in combination with other schemas, produces progressively more complex patterns of response.

Only after they reach the age of eight or nine months, Piaget found, do infants comprehend that objects continue to exist even when they are hidden from view. Ideas of object permanence, causality, space, and time are developed through the process of equilibration; once learned, they form an integral part of the child's mental structure and cannot be un-learned. As a result of his sensorimotor studies, Piaget incorporated the manipulation of objects into his clinical interviews, which had previously been entirely verbal.

During the 1930s, Piaget, in addition to serving on the faculties of the universities of Geneva and Lausanne, and as co-director of the Institute J.J. Rousseau, became director of the International Bureau of Education, later to be affiliated with Unesco. His next phase of research, undertaken in collaboration with Bärbel Inhelder, Alina Szeminska, and others, concerned children's comprehension of physical quantities and numbers; later, following a suggestion by Albert Einstein, he investigated children's conceptions of time, speed, and movement. He also conducted a long-range study of perception in children to test the theories of the Gestalt school of psychology.

Based on these studies, Piaget posited the existence of a pre-operational stage of development, lasting approximately from the age of two to seven years, during which children acquire the ability to use symbols in place of seen and unseen objects, and a concrete-operational stage from approximately seven to twelve years, during which they master such logical operations as transitivity (if $A = B$ and $B = C$, then $A = C$), symmetry ("I am my brother's brother"), and seriation (the placement of objects in sequential order). Pre-operational children, Piaget believed, are intuitive, relying on perception rather than reason, and egocentric, i.e., unable to adopt another person's point of view. In his interviews, he would show a child a toy landscape and ask her to describe the scene from the perspective of a doll set within it. Most pre-operational subjects were unable to describe the scene from any but their own viewpoints. Children at the pre-operational stage also attribute their own motivations to others; when asked why Daddy goes to bed at eleven o'clock, such a child might answer, "Because his Daddy told him to."

The concrete-operational stage is characterized by mastery of conservation, the ability to attend to more than one dimension simultaneously. In one now-classic experiment, Piaget would pour the liquid contents of a short, stout breaker into a tall, thin beaker. Pre-operational children, observing the higher level of the liquid in thin beaker, invariably claimed that it contained more fluid; concrete-operational children, taking note of width as well as height, rightly concluded that the volume of liquid was identical in both beakers.

Piaget's work continued relatively undisturbed throughout the Second World War. In addition to his teaching duties at the Universities of Lausanne and Geneva, where he also directed the psychology laboratory and headed the Institute for Educational Sciences, he served for three years as president of the Swiss Society of Psychology and co-edited a number of professional journals. After the war he was appointed president of the Swiss Commission of Unesco and was elected a member of Unesco's executive council.

The final phase of Piaget's research concerned the development of formal operations in the adolescent and adult. At about the age of twelve, he said, the child becomes capable of hypothetical, abstract thinking. This capability quickly gives rise to elaborate systems and theories. "The intellectual egocentricity of the adolescent," he wrote, "is comparable to the egocentricity of the infant who assimilates the universe into his own corporal activity and to that of the young child who assimilates things into his own nascent thought (symbolic play, etc.). Adolescent egocentricity is manifested by belief in the omnipotence of reflection, as though the world should submit itself to idealistic schemes rather than to systems of reality. It is the metaphysical age par excellence. . . . Equilibration is attained when the adolescent understands that the proper function of reflection is not to contradict but to predict and interpret experience."

In 1950, Piaget, who had intended to devote a mere five years to the study of child development, returned at last to his original subject with the three-volume *Introduction to Genetic Epistemology*. A few years later, with the assistance of the Rockefeller Foundation, he founded the International Center for Genetic Epistemology at the University of Geneva. In addition to serving as its director, he continued to teach at the university and joined the faculty of the Sorbonne.

During the 1960s Piaget's theories finally gained wide acceptance in the United States, where the dominance of behaviorism in departments of psychology and the lack of English translations of his books had prevented them from becoming as well known as they had long been in Europe. In addition to producing a vast body of research on his theories, many American psychologists and educators have sought to derive from them methods of accelerating mental growth in children—a goal with which Piaget was not particularly sympathetic.

Although he resigned most of his academic positions in 1971, Piaget continued to conduct research in a variety of areas, including memory, education, and the biological foundations of intelligence. In 1978 he participated in a debate with linguist Noam Chomsky on the development of linguistic competence in children, with Chomsky claiming that such competence is innate, a product of the evolution of the human species, and Piaget arguing that it is acquired, the product of sensorimotor experiences and the self-regulating mental activities of the individual. Other critics of Piaget have noted his incorrect use of Boolean algebra to explicate his theories of logic and the occasional vagueness of his terminology. These criticisms, however, have not detracted from the general esteem in which he is held by psychologists and educators. In addition to founding the cognitive-developmental school of psychology, he refuted both the genetic determinism of the nativists and the environmental determinism of the behaviorists, demonstrating that human beings are not merely acted upon by inner and outer forces but are active participants in their own development.

Piaget died at the age of 84 in Geneva, where his customary meerschaum pipe and blue beret had been common sights for more than five decades. In the course of his career he published some forty volumes of research and more than 500 articles.   D.P./J.P.

Son of Arthur P., medieval historian. Married Valentine Châtenay, psychologist, 1923. Children: Jacqueline, b. 1925; Lucienne, b. 1927; Laurent, b. 1931. Protestant. Educ: Univ. of Neuchâtel, B.A. 1915, Dr.esSc. naturelles 1918; postgrad. studies in psychology and psychiatry, Univ. of Zurich 1918–19 and Univ. of Paris (Sorbonne) 1919–21. Released from mil. service 1916. With Univ. of Geneva: Privatdozent in child psychology 1921–29; Assoc. Prof. of History of Scientific Thought 1929–39; Dir., Inst. for Educational Sciences 1933–71; Prof. of Sociology 1939–52; Prof. of Experimental Psychology and Dir. of Psychology Laboratory 1940–71; Prof. emeritus since 1971; Founder and Dir., Intnl. Center for Genetic Epistemology since 1955. With Inst. J.J. Rousseau (affiliated with Univ. of Geneva since late 1920s): Dir. of Studies 1921–25; Prof. of Child Psychology 1921–29; Asst. Dir. 1929–32; Co.-Dir. since 1932. Prof. of Psychology, Philosophy, Sociology, and Philosophy of Science, Univ. of Neuchâtel 1925–29; Prof. of Experimental Psychology, Univ. of Lausanne 1936–51; Lectr., Collège de France 1942; Prof. of Developmental Psychology, Sorbonne 1952–63. Ed., Études d'épistemologie génétique since 1957. Co-Editor: Archives de Psychologie from 1930s; Revue Suisse de Psychologie, Geneva from early 1940s; Enfance, Paris; Acta Psychologica, Amsterdam; Methodos, Milan; Synthèse, Dordrecht, Holland; Dialectica, Neuchâtel and Paris; Linguistic Inquiry, Cambridge, Mass. Dir. 1929–67 and Asst. Dir.-Gen., Dept. of Education, Intnl. Office of Education (affiliated with Unesco since 1950s). With Unesco: Pres., Swiss Commn.; Member, Exec. Council; Chmn., Swiss Delegation, conferences; Rep. at Unesco meetings; ed., The Right to Education (pamphlet). Pres.: Swiss Soc. of Psychology, early 1940s; Intnl. Union of Scientific Psychologists 1954–57; Assn. de Psychologie scientifique de langue français. Member, 20 academic societies. Hons: elected Foreign Member, New York Acad. of Sciences 1966; elected Member, Natl. Acad. of Arts and Sciences 1966; Distinguished Service Contribution Award, American Psychological Assn. 1969; Erasmus Prize 1972; First Kittay Intnl. Award for Psychiatry 1973; Prize, Inst. de la Vie 1973; Balzan Prize 1979; others. Hon. doctorates from Harvard Univ. 1936, Sorbonne 1946, Univ. of Brussels 1949, Univ. of Rio de Janeiro 1949, Univ. of Chicago 1953, Cambridge Univ. 1960, Yale Univ. 1970, Temple Univ. 1971, Yeshiva Univ. 1973, Rockefeller Univ. 1975, others. *Books:* Le Langage et la pensée chez l'enfant, 1923 (The Language and Thought of the Child, 1926); Le Jugement et le raisonnement chez l'enfant, 1924 (Judgment and Reasoning in the Child, 1926); La Réprésentation du monde chez l'enfant, 1926 (The Child's Conception of the World, 1929); La Causalité physique chez l'enfant, 1927 (The Child's Conception of Physical Causality, 1928); Le Jugement moral chez l'enfant, 1932 (The Moral Judgment of the Child, 1932); La Naissance de l'intelligence chez l'enfant, 1936 (The Origins of Intelligence in the Child, 1952); La Construction du réel chez l'enfant, 1937 (The Child's Construction of Reality, 1954); Le Mécanisme du développement mental, et les lois du groupement des opérations, 1941; (With A. Szeminska) La Genèse du nombre chez l'enfant, 1941 (The Child's Conception of Number,

1952); (with B. Inhelder) Le Développement des quantités chez l'enfant, 1942 (The Child's Conception of Quantities, 1974); Classes, rélations, et nombres, 1942; La Formation du symbole chez l'enfant, 1945 (Play, Dreams, and Imitation in Childhood, 1951); Le Développement de la notion de temps chez l'enfant, 1946 (The Child's Conception of Time, 1969); Les Notions de mouvement et de vitesse chez l'enfant, 1946 (The Child's Conception of Movement and Speed, 1970); La Psychologie de l'intelligence, 1947 (The Psychology of Intelligence, 1950); (with B. Inhelder) La Réprésentation de l'éspace chez l'enfant, 1948 (The Child's Conception of Space, 1956); (with B. Inhelder and A. Szeminska) La Géometrie spontanée de l'enfant, 1948 (The Child's Conception of Geometry, 1960); Le Droit à l'éducation dans le monde actuel, 1949 (The Right to an Education in the Real World, in To Understand is to Invent: The Future of Education, 1973); Traité de logique, 1949; Introduction à l'épistemologie génétique, 3 vols. 1949–50; (with B. Inhelder) La Genèse de l'idée de hasard chez l'enfant, 1951 (The Origin of the Idea of Chance in the Child, 1975); Essai sur les transformations des opérations logiques, 1952; Logic and Psychology, 1952; Les rélations entre l'affectivité et l'intelligence dans le développement mental de l'enfant, 1954; (with B. Inhelder) De la logique de l'enfant à la logique de l'adolescent, 1955 (The Growth of Logical Thinking: From Childhood to Adolescence, 1958); La Genèse des structures logiques élémentaires, classifications et sériations, 1959 (English trans. 1964); Les Mécanismes perceptifs, 1961 (The Mechanisms of Perception, 1969); (ed., with Paul Fraisse) Traité de psychologie expérimentale, 1963–65 (Experimental Psychology: Its Scope and Method, Vol. 7, Intelligence, 1969); Six Études de psychologie, 1964 (Six Psychological Studies, 1967); (with B. Inhelder) The Early Growth of Logic in the Child, 1959 (English trans. 1964); Sagesse et illusion de la philosophie, 1965 (Insights and Illusions of Philosophy, 1971); Études sociologies, 1965; (with E. W. Beth) Épistemologie mathématique et psychologie, 1965 (Mathematical Epistemology and Psychology, 1966); (with B. Inhelder) Psychologie de l'enfant, 1966 (The Psychology of the Child, 1969); (with B. Inhelder) L'Image mental chez l'enfant, 1966 (Mental Imagery in the Child, 1971); Logique et connaissance scientifique, 1967; Biologie et connaissance, 1967 (Biology and Knowledge, 1971); (with B. Inhelder and H. Sinclair de Zwart) Mémoire et intelligence, 1968 (Memory and Intelligence, 1973); Épistemologie et psychologie de l'identité, 1968 (On the Development of Memory and Identity, 1968); Le Structuralisme, 1968 (Structuralism, 1970); Psychologie et pedagogie, 1969 (The Science of Education and the Psychology of the Child, 1970); L'Épistemologie génétique, 1970 (The Principles of Genetic Epistemology, 1972); Psychologie et Épistemologie, 1970 (Psychology and Epistemology, 1971); Où va l'éducation?, 1971 (Where is Education Going?, in To Understand is to Invent: The Future of Education, 1973); Épistemologie des sciences de l'homme, 1972; La transmission des mouvements, 1972; Problèmes de psychologie génétique, 1972 (The Child and Reality: Problems of Genetic Epistemology, 1973); La Formation de la notion de force, 1973; Main Trends in Interdisciplinary Research, 1970 (English trans. 1973); Adaptation vitale et psychologie de l'intelligence: selection organique et phénocopie, 1974; Récherches sur la contradiction, 1974; Réussir et comprendre, 1974 (Success and Understanding, 1978); La Prise de conscience, 1974 (The Grasp of Consciousness, 1976); Les explications causales (Understanding Causality, 1974); Le comportement, moteur de l'évolution, 1976 (Behavior and Evolution, 1978); L'équilibration des structures cognitives, 1976 (The Development of Thought: Equilbration of

Cognitive Structures, 1977). *Articles:* "Individual and Collective Problems in the Study of Thinking," in Annals of New York Acad. of Science, 91, 1960; Nécessité et Signification des récherches comparatives en psychologie génétique," in Intnl. Journal of Psychology, I, 1966; "Piaget's Theory," in Carmichael's Handbook of Child Psychology (ed. by P. H. Mussen), 1970; "Intellectual Evolution from Adolescence to Adulthood," in Human Development, 15 1972; "What is Psychology?", in American Psychologist, 33, 1978; some 500 other articles. *Other:* The Mission of the Idea (prose poem), 1915, and Récherche (novel), 1918, both in The Essential Piaget: An Interpretive Reference and Guide (ed. by H. E. Gruber and J. J. Vonche), 1977; Autobiography, in a History of Psychology in Autobiography (ed. by E. G. Boring), vol. 4, 1952.

Further reading: The Developmental Psychology of Jean Piaget by John H. Flavell, 1963; Piaget and Knowledge by Hans Furth, 1969; Piaget's Theory of Intellectual Development by Herbert Ginsburg and Sylvia Oppen, 1969; Piaget for Teachers by Hans Furth, 1970; Understanding Piaget by Mary Ann S. Pulaski, 1971; Jean Piaget: The Man and His Ideas by Richard I. Evans, 1973; Piaget, Education and Teaching by Douglas W. McNally, 1973; Piaget in the Classroom by Milton Schwebel, 1973; Piagetian Research: A Handbook of Recent Studies by S. Modgil (ed.), 1974; Catalogue des Archives Jean Piaget (in French and English), University of Geneva, 1975; Understanding Piaget by Rémy Droz, 1976; The Philosophy of Jean Piaget and its Educational Implications by Evelyn M. Neufeld, 1976; Pathway to Piaget: A Guide for Clinicians and Developmentalists by Hugh Rosen, 1977; Jean Piaget: Psychologist of the Real by Brian Rotman, 1977; Piaget's Theory of Intelligence by Charles J. Brainerd, 1978; Piaget: With Feeling by Philip A. Cowan, 1978; Piaget's Theory: A Psychological Critique by Geoffrey Brown, 1979; Jean Piaget by Margaret A. Boden, 1980; Conversations with Jean Piaget by Jean Claude Bringuier, 1980; Language and Learning: The Debate Between Jean Piaget and Noam Chomsky by Massimo Piatelli-Palmarini (ed.), 1980.

ANASTASIO SOMOZA (DEBAYLE)
President of Nicaragua and Commander in Chief of the National Guard
Born León, Nicaragua, December 5th, 1925
Died Asunción, Paraguay, September 17th, 1980

Anastasio Somoza Debayle, president of Nicaragua for 13 years, came to power in 1967 a few years after the assassination of his father, President Anastasio Somoza Garcia. Driven from office by a popular rebellion against his regime in 1979, he was himself killed by unknown assassins 14 months later. In all, the Somoza family ruled the country as a military dictatorship for nearly five decades, during which time they acquired a virtual monopoly on business and amassed an enormous fortune.

The Somoza regime was largely the creation of the United States government, which overthrew the dictator José Santos Zelaya in 1909 to protect American business interests. While the country was occupied by a force of Marines, the U.S. trained and armed a National Guard corps and entrusted it to the command of Anastasio Somoza

García, an affluent coffee planter who had been educated at an American business college and had served as an aide to Secretary of State Henry Stimson. In 1928 Somoza and the Guard took part in Marine military operations against guerrilla troops led by Augusto César Sandino, a young nationalist. When the Marines left the country in 1933, Sandino surrendered and was promptly executed on Somoza's orders. Somoza then staged a coup d'état with the assistance of the Guard, deposed President Juan Bautista Sacasa, his uncle, and made himself head of the country. In return for massive infusions of U.S. aid, most of which he expropriated to his own bank accounts, he allowed the CIA to use Nicaragua as a base of operations against the leftist governments of other Central American nations. President Franklin Delano Roosevelt once said of him, "He may be a son of a bitch, but he's *our* son of a bitch."

When Somoza García was assassinated in 1956, his place was taken by his older son, Luis, then by two representatives of the Somoza family, and finally by his younger son, Anastasio Somoza Debayle, who was elected to the presidency as head of the Partido Liberal Nacionalista in 1967. Born in León in 1925, Somoza Debayle had been groomed for the presidency since the age of seven; he was educated at the La Salle Military Academy in New York State and attended the U.S. Military Academy at West Point, after which he was made Inspector General of the Nicaraguan Army. It was said of him that he was the only cadet in the history of West Point to receive an army as a graduation present. By the time of his father's murder in 1956, Somoza had sped through the ranks to become chief of military staff, commander of the air force, and commander in chief of the National Guard. During the next decade, while the presidency was filled by Luis Somoza and his two successors, Anastasio Somoza made the Guard into the best military force in the region and allowed the U.S. to employ it in military actions in Cuba and the Dominican Republic. He won the presidency in an election tainted with violence and charges of fraud and took office for a five-year term.

Although Somoza tripled the gross national product by modernizing Nicaragua's agricultural system and increasing its industrial diversification, he suppressed civil liberties and devoted most of his efforts to enlarging his family's vast economic holdings, worth an estimated $500 million. In addition to the national airline, LANICA, and the national shipping line, MAMENIC, the family assets included a seaport, a bank, a newspaper, television and radio stations, hotels, cattle ranches, plantations, a sugar refinery, a brewery, an insurance company, a blood plasma export firm, factories for metal, fiberglass, textiles, and meat processing, and one-quarter of all the arable land in the country. Much of this wealth was derived from U.S. economic aid programs, which, by the late 1970s, had contributed an estimated $250,000,000 to Nicaragua since World War II. As a graduate of West Point, he had a close relationship with members of the American military establishment. The apparent stability of the country under Somoza's dictatorship, and his total control over the armed forces and the National Guard, made him a crucial ally to U.S. foreign policy planners, who found the country a convenient base from which to launch anti-communist activities in Central America.

Somoza maintained his hold on the governmental and military bureaucracies by appointing loyal friends and relatives to key posts. Officers in the National Guard were rewarded with special privileges, including separate stores, schools, and neighborhoods, and the opportunity to engage in smuggling, graft, and black-market operations. The vast majority of the country's population, most of whom are peasants and small farmers, continued to live in poverty and without adequate health care and education.

In May of 1972, a coalition of political leaders persuaded Somoza to resign from the presidency (though not from the command of the armed forces) in preparation for the election of a constitutional assembly to reorganize the government. The destruction of the capital city of Managua by an earthquake seven months later provided him with an excuse to resume executive powers and to declare martial law. Although the city was located on a geological fault and had been struck by major earthquakes twice before, it was rebuilt on the same site at the insistence of the Somoza family, which owned much of the real estate as well as cement and construction companies. Thousands of Managuans whose homes had not been rebuilt were still living in camps five years after the disaster.

In 1974 Somoza was re-elected to a second, six-year term in balloting that was denounced as fixed by a newly-formed opposition movement, the Union Democrática de Liberación. More violent opposition came from a guerrilla movement, the Frente Sandinista de Liberación Nacional (Sandinist National Liberation Front), which had been active since 1961. Named for Augusto César Sandino, the nationalist leader who had been executed by Somoza's father, the group operated from bases in neighboring Costa Rica and in Venezuela and was trained and armed, according to most reports, by Fidel Castro's Communist government in Cuba. The National Guard spent most of its time doing battle with the guerrillas and punishing peasant villages suspected of harboring them. Although the guerrillas had been all but eliminated by the late 1960s, by 1974 they had recovered enough to conduct a raid in which several of Somoza's friends and relatives were captured and held for ransom. Somoza declared martial law immediately afterward.

Popular opposition to Somoza intensified in 1977, when Archbishop Miguel Obrando Bravo denounced the National Guard for committing atrocities in its zeal to rout Sandinista sympathizers from the civilian population. His charges were confirmed by the human rights organization Amnesty International, which accused the Guard of having exterminated entire villages. Martial law was grudgingly lifted by Somoza in September 1977 after President Carter temporarily suspended arms shipments and economic aid in accordance with his human rights campaign.

The Sandinista rebels mounted a major attack in October of 1977 while Somoza was recovering from a heart atatck. They now had the support of Nicaragua's wealthy elite and middle class, both of which were being squeezed out of business by the Somoza family's near-monopoly on profit-making enterprises. The assassination of Pedro Joaquin Chamorro Cardenal, the publisher of an opposition newspaper, in January of 1978 further mobilized public opinion. Although Somoza's constitutional term of office was due to end in 1981, he was reported to be grooming his eldest son to continue the dynasty. A general strike was held in August to demand Somoza's resignation; Somoza responded by re-imposing martial law, and the fighting escalated into a bloody civil war.

By the spring of 1979, the increasingly victorious Sandinistas had secured enough territory and political legitimacy to set up a five-member provisional government of their own. Somoza and the Sandinista junta, together with representatives from the U.S., entered into a long round of negotiations that culminated in the dictator's resignation and his replacement by a Government of National Reconstruction. On July 17 Somoza flew to Miami, the bulk of his personal fortune (and the national treasury) having preceded him out of the country. Fearful of extradition, and angry at the U.S. for having transferred its support to the rebels ("I spit on the help of Carter the traitor"), he soon moved to the Bahamas but was expelled after two weeks. On his way to Paraguay to accept an offer of asylum from right-wing dictator Alfred Stroessner, Somoza crossed paths with another former American ally, the exiled Shah of Iran [q.v.], whose career resembled his own in a number of ways.

Somoza was riding in a limousine in the center of Asunción, Paraguay's capital city, on September 17, 1980, when the car was hit by blasts of machine-gun and bazooka fire. Somoza, his driver, and his bodyguard died in the attack. Leaders of the Nicaraguan government, though they expressed pleasure at the news, denied responsibility for the assassination and attributed it to "Paraguayan revolutionary forces." Other observers, noting that Somoza had become involved in an affair with the mistress of Stroessner's son-in-law, suggested that the killing had been done for personal rather than political reasons.

J.P./A.C.

Son of Anastasio Somoza García, dictator of Nicaragua, and Salvadora Debayle Sacasa. Married Hope Portocarrero 1950. Children: Anastasio, officer in the National Guard; Julio Nestor; Hope Carolina; Carla Ana; Roberto Eduardo. Educ: Instituto Pedagógico de Managua; La Salle Military Acad., Oakdale N.Y. 1936–42; U.S. Military Acad. at West Point 1942–46. With National Guard: Sub-Lt. 1941; 1st Lt. 1941; Capt. 1942; Maj. 1946; Col. 1948; Commander in Chief 1956–66, 1967–79. With Nicaraguan Army: Military Instr., 1st Presidential Battalion 1942; Inspector-Gen. 1946; Comdr., 1st and 5th Presidential battalions 1947; Chief of Operations 1947; Dir., Academia Militar 1948; Chief of Military Staff and Comdr. of Gen. Headquarters 1950; Asst. Dir. of Official Review 1952; Comdr., Air Force 1956; Brig. Gen. 1957; Maj. Gen. 1960; Div. Gen. 1964; Commander in Chief of Armed Forces 1967. Head of Partido Liberal Nacional; elected President of Nicaragua 1967; dissolved national congress 1971 and relinquished office 1972 preparatory to constitutional assembly; re-assumed exec. powers 1972; re-elected 1974. Pres. of Natl. Exec. Cttee. after earthquake 1972. Resigned 1979 after victory of Frente Sandinista Liberación Nacional (Sandinista National Liberation Front) in civil war; in exile in U.S., Bahamas, and Paraguay 1979–80. Hons: military and foreign decorations.

EDWARD CROFT-MURRAY
Art connoisseur and antiquary
Born Chichester, Sussex, England, September 1st, 1907
Died London, England, September 18th, 1980

During the course of five decades, Edward Croft-Murray, a noted specialist on drawings of the British School, was affiliated with the Department of Prints and Drawings of the British Museum. Serving first as a volunteer *attaché* in the Printroom, he was appointed Assistant Keeper in 1933. He returned to the museum in 1946 following his military service in World War II and was appointed Deputy Keeper in 1953. He then succeeded A. E. Popham as Keeper in 1954. It was from this post that he retired in 1973, though he continued to sit on the Appointments Board of the museum.

As a scholar, Mr. Croft-Murray's areas of specialty ranged from an encyclopaedic knowledge of English drawings and watercolors of the 16th to the first half of the 19th centuries, to a considerable knowledge of theatrical, operatic, and musical histories and personalities. He built up a remarkable collection of paintings and drawings of old musical instruments at his fine early Georgian house which had once belonged to Handel's impresario John James Heidegger.

Courtesy Croft-Murray estate

During the Second World War, he served in the Admiralty and in Military Intelligence, and later, 1943–46, with the rank of Major, in Austria and Italy in the Monuments and Fine Art Section of the Allied Control Commission.

Croft-Murray's scholarship was the result of meticulous research and observation among original archival material and a highly developed sense of period and taste. In 1960 he produced, in collaboration with Paul Hulton, the first volume of a full-scale catalogue of the British Museum's collection of British drawings. At the time of his death he was working alone on the nearly completed second volume, a project which had occupied him since his retirement in 1973. The particular care he gave to the biographical notices of individual artists of the British School makes it unlikely that his contribution will be supplanted as a basic source of information on English draughtsmen of the 17th and early 18th centuries.

His non-museum publications include *Venetian Drawings of the XVII and XVIII Centuries at Windsor Castle,* written with Sir Anthony Blunt and published in 1957, and his magnum opus, *The History of Decorative Painting in England from 1537 to 1837,* published in two volumes in 1962 and 1971. These texts are remarkable for their extraordinary thoroughness in their compilation of the data on the period and are considered the most comprehensive surveys of their kind. Mr. Croft-Murray also contributed papers to *Apollo, Burlington Magazine,* and the *British Museum Year Book.*

Something of an eccentric, Croft-Murray, "Teddy" to his friends, inaugurated his departmental exhibitions by performing on a pair of kettle drums. He could play the violin and occasionally wielded the baton. Handel and Purcell were his favorite composers, he disliked Brahms and there was a "right" and a "wrong" Beethoven.

Teddy Croft-Murray was never happier than when making excursions in England or abroad to collections, historical monuments, churches and ancient houses and would note down his precise observations in octavo-sized leather-bound notebooks. He was equally enthusiastic in his researches into musical history and in transcribing old scores to be played by the small band he brought together to perform 18th and early 19th century music on old instruments. He died of a heart attack on his way to a meeting of the Appointments Board of the British Museum.   A.E.

Son of Bernard C.-M. and Mary Amelia James. 1st marriage dissolved; 2nd marriage: Rosemary Jill Whitford-Hawkey 1960. Two daughters, one of each marriage. Educ: Lancing Coll.; Magdalen Coll., Oxford, B.A., French and Italian 1929, diploma with distinction in medieval and modern art 1930. Mil. Service: Admiralty 1939–40; Civilian Officer, Military Intelligence, War Office 1940–43; Major, Allied Control Comm., Monuments and Fine Arts Section, Italy and Austria 1943–46. Asst. Keeper 1933–40, 1946–53, Deputy Kepper 1953–54 and until retirement 1973, Dept. of Prints and Drawings, British Museum. Advisor on musical instruments to Messrs. Christie, London. Fellow, Soc. of Antiquaries. Member, Appointments Bd., British Mus.; Advisory Cttee., Cecil Higgins Art Gall., Bedford; Council for the Care of Churches; Cttee., Whitforth Art Gall., Manchester; Cttee., Benton Fletcher Collection (musical instruments), Fenton House, Hampstead; Musicians' Union; British Inst. Fund (representing Oxford Univ.); Architectural Advisory Panel of Westminster Abbey; Painter-Stainer's Co.; Walpole Soc. *Author:* (with Sir Anthony Blunt) Venetian Drawings of the XVII and XVIII Centuries at Windsor Castle, 1957; (with Paul Hulton) Catalogue of British Drawings in the British Museum, Vol. I, 1960 (Vol. II in progress); Decorative painting in England, 1537–1837, Vol. I, 1962, Vol. II, 1971.

KURT (ALFRED GEORG) MENDELSSOHN
Low temperature physicist
Born Berlin, Germany, January 7th, 1906
Died Oxford, England, September 18th, 1980

Dr. Kurt Mendelssohn, a pioneer in the field of low temperature research, conducted experiments which led to the discovery and understanding of liquid helium's properties of superfluidity and superconductivity. He was also a keen historian of science and technology and wrote accounts of the building of the pyramids, and of scientific and industrial developments in the western world.

Mendelssohn studied physics in his native Berlin under Max Planck, Walther Nernst, Erwin Schroedinger and Albert Einstein, and worked in a research group with Franz (later Sir Francis) Simon. On a visit to the Clarendon Laboratory at Oxford, he set up an apparatus with which, early in 1933, he cooled helium gas to a liquid—the first person in Britain to do so.

With Hitler's accession to power, Mendelssohn and his wife took up the invitation of Professor F.A. Lindemann (later Viscount Cherwell), another student of Nernst, and moved to England in March 1933. For a time Mendelssohn supported himself through grants.

In 1938, Mendelssohn and a research student, J.G. Daunt demonstrated that any surface on which liquid helium has been poured is covered by a layer of liquid film (between 50 and 100 atoms thick) which moves without friction, a phenomenon which is paralleled in superconductors where the current flows with no resistance. Investigating the analogous quality of superfluidity and superconductivity (their "frictionless state of aggregation"), Mendelssohn and his co-workers found that the superconducting electrons in a persistent current and the superfluid state of helium both had "zero entropy." In broad, simple terms this means that flow or conduct is unimpeded because the "super," low-temperature state releases all of the energy; whereas, in a "regular" thermodynamic system, a measure of the energy is retained and this causes friction which varies the speed and constancy of the flow. Dr. Mendelssohn explained his findings in two monographs, *Cryogenics* and *The Quest for Absolute Zero*. The identification and understanding of superfluid components and superconducting electrons has been significant in the field of atomic energy research and development.

Mendelssohn's first book outside the field of physics, *In China Now* (1969) is a description of his observations during his visits to the People's Republic as a visiting professor. In 1973 he published *The World of Walther Nernst*, an excellent account of Germany's pre-war scientific and industrial development and its sociological effects.

While on one of his many visiting professorships, Mendelssohn took time off to visit Egypt and became fascinated by the pyramids. He found it difficult to believe that the pyramids were simply monuments because, as he pointed out in his book *The Riddle of the Pyramids* (1974), there were more pyramids built than pharoahs to put in them, and often two or more pyramids were under construction at the same time. He formulated the currently unpopular theory that the pyramids were primarily built for political reasons—to forge an Egyptian unity.

In his last book, *The Secret of Western Domination* (1976), Mendelssohn argues that it is through the power of scientific knowledge rather than through any special aggressiveness or predisposition to exploit, that Europeans and their descendants in other countries, have dominated the modern world. He sees this superiority changing as Japan and, in the future, China, begin to make significant contributions to scientific knowledge and its applications.

Mendelssohn was elected a Fellow of the Royal Society in 1951 and in 1967 he was honored with the Society's Hughes Medal. The following year the Institute of Physics and the Physical Society awarded him the Simon Memorial Prize. He founded the journal *Cryogenics* and also the International Cryogenic Engineering Conferences. In the early 1970s he served as President of the A2 Commission of the International Institute of Refrigeration.   R.T.

Son of Ernst M.M. and Eliza Ruprecht M. Married Jutta Lina Charlottee Zarniko 1932. Children: Four daughters; one son. Jewish. British citizen. Educ: Goethe Sch., Berlin; Univ. of Berlin, M.A., D.Phil. 1930; Univ. of Oxford, M.A. Research and teaching posts, Univ. of Berlin 1929–31; taught at Technische Hochschule in Breslau 1931–32; emigrated to England, joined Clarendon Lab. at Oxford 1933 and became dir. of a research group in low temperature and solid state physics until retirement in 1973; Reader in Physics 1955–73 and Reader Emeritus since 1973; Univ. of Oxford; Professorial Fellow 1971–73 and Professorial Fellow Emeritus since 1973; Wolfson Coll., Oxford. Visiting Professorships: Rice Univ., Houston 1952; Purdue Univ., Lafayette, Ind. 1956; Tokyo Univ. 1960; Kumasi Univ., Ghana 1964; Tata Inst., Bombay 1969–70; Acad. Sinica, Peking 1966,

1970–71; Bulgarian Acad. of Sciences. Founder, and Ed. since 1960, Cryogenics jrnl.; Founder, Intnl. Cryogenic Engineering Confs.; Consultant, U.K. Atomic Energy Authority since 1973. Vice-Pres., Physical Soc. 1957–60; Chmn., Intnl. Cryogenic Engineering Cttee. since 1969; Pres., A2 Commn. of Intnl. Inst. of Refrigeration 1971–76. Hons: appointed Fellow of the Royal Society 1951; Hughes Medal, Royal Society 1967; Simon Memorial Prize, Inst. of Physics and Physical Soc. 1968. *Author:* What Is Atomic Energy?, 1946; Cryophysics, 1960; The Quest for Absolute Zero, 1966, 2nd ed. 1977; In China Now, 1969; The World of Walther Nernst, 1973; The Riddle of the Pyramids, 1974; The Secret of Western Domination, 1976; numerous contributions to Proceedings of the Royal Society, Proceedings of the Physical Society, Philosophical Mag., Nature, and other jrnls.

WALTER MIDGLEY
Operatic tenor
Born Bramley, Yorkshire, England, September 13th, 1914
Died Banstead, Surrey, England, September 18th, 1980

Walter Midgley entered the opera world in the late 1930s when operas were just beginning to be sung in English. However, the British opera companies could not, at that time, offer a beginner an extended period of training—a singer had to learn by performance. "Opera in English was still a sufficient novelty to make it a problem for the artist to risk," said David Webster, general administrator of the Covent Garden Opera Company, the company where Midgley made his debut as a principal tenor in 1946.

After studying the trombone at the Sheffield Academy of Music, Midgley became a shipping clerk for the Sheffield Steelworks, a large manufacturer, until the mid-1930s. Meanwhile, Joseph Lycett, a well-known bass of the time, encouraged him to study voice production. After graduating, he devoted all his spare time to music and eventually learned to play seven instruments. To gain experience, he took all the small offers of singing in choral societies and oratorios that he could find.

In 1938, he was discovered by tenor Frank Mullings who suggested that he try out for the Carl Rosa Opera Company in Brighton. He was immediately engaged for the chorus and minor roles. He remained until 1940 and also made guest appearances at the Sadler's Wells Opera Company. He was able to continue his musical studies during the Second World War when he was appointed by the British War Office as musical adviser to the military entertainment organization known as the Stars in Battle Dress.

After the war, he joined the Covent Garden Opera Company. He made his debut as a principal tenor when he sang the role of Rudolph in *La Bohème*. Soon, he was singing many of the leading roles in the company's repertoire.

In 1948, he left Covent Garden to undertake a world tour, giving recitals and broadcasts throughout Italy, India, New Zealand, and Australia. When he returned to England, he was a frequent guest artist at Covent Garden. He also appeared at the Glyndebourne

Festival and with the Welsh National Opera Company. Even through the 1970s, he was a popular opera singer on radio.

Midgley was known for his natural acting ability and versatility, and at its best, his voice was beautifully clear and possessed a lyrical quality. He believed that audiences liked the opera plots as much as the music. "Clear diction, coupled with true intonation in any language," was his chief rule for all singers. S.F.

Married Gladys Vernon. Children: Vernon, operatic tenor. Educ: Sheffield Acad. of Music. Mil. Service: Musical Adviser, British War Office, 1942–43. Chorus tenor, Carl Rosa Opera Co., Brighton, 1938–41; principal tenor, Covent Garden Opera, 1947–49; toured Italy, India, New Zealand, Australia, 1950–51; guest artist, Sadler's Wells, Covent Garden, Glyndebourne Festival, Welsh National Opera Company, Radio Theatre, 1955–80. *Major performances include:* La Bohème (Rudolph), Turnadot (Prince Calaf), Hugh the Drover, Werther (Massenet), Verdi's Macbeth (Macduff), Rigoletto (Duke of Mantua), La Tosca, Il Trovatore (Manico), Manon Lescaut (Des Grieux), Madame Butterfly.

KATHERINE ANNE PORTER
Short story writer and novelist
Born Indian Creek, Texas, U.S.A., May 15th, 1890
Died Silver Spring, Maryland, U.S.A., September 18th, 1980

The American writer Katherine Anne Porter made a lifework of the attainment of "perfect realism" in fiction. Her total output was small—of the many manuscripts she wrote, she published only some 20 stories, a handful of short novels and essays, and one long novel—but each work contained remarkable feats of perception and articulation. "My one aim," she said, "is to tell a straight story and give true testimony." Since her early childhood, writing was "the basic and absorbing occupation, the intact line of my life which directs my actions, determines my point of view, and profoundly affects my character and personality. . . . I did not choose this vocation, and if I had any say in the matter I would not have chosen it. . . . Yet for this vocation I was and am willing to live and die, and I consider very few other things of the slightest importance."

Her stories, most of them set in Mexico, Europe, or the rural, matriarchal American South of her childhood, explore a group of related themes: the transformation of the old social order into an uncertain new one, the self-delusions and self-betrayals practiced by individuals, the "majestic and terrible failure of the life of man in the Western World," and the possibility of living a responsible life in a  society that is becoming more and more technological, inhuman, perhaps totalitarian. "In the face of such shape and weight of present misfortunes," she wrote in 1944, "the voice of the individual artist may seem perhaps of no more consequence than the whirring of a cricket in the grass, but the arts do live continuously, and they live literally by faith; . . . they outlive governments and creeds and the societies, even the very civilizations that produced them. They cannot be destroyed altogether because they represent the substance of faith

Courtesy Jill Krementz

and the only reality. They are what we find again when the ruins are cleared away. And even the smallest and most incomplete offering at this time can be a proud act in defense of that faith." Her mission as an artist, indeed the mission of all true artists, she believed, was to detect meaning in the seeming chaos of existence.

She was born Katherine Anne Maria Veronica Callista Russell Porter in Indian Creek, Texas, in 1890, the fourth of five children born to Harrison and Mary Alice Porter. "We were brought up," she once wrote, "with a sense of our own history." Her maternal ancestors had come from Warwickshire, England, to colonial Virginia in 1648, her paternal ancestors to Pennsylvania in 1720. Jonathan Boone, Daniel Boone's brother, was her great-great-great grandfather; the short story writer William Sidney Porter, better known as O. Henry, was her father's second cousin. The family, which had once been "a good old family of solid wealth and property," moved to Texas with some of their freed slaves after the Civil War.

Porter's mother died when she was two, and the family went to live near Kyle, Texas, with Catherine Anne Porter, the formidable Grandmother who appears in many of her stories. "This summer country of my childhood," as she once called it, "was soft blackland farming country, full of fruits and flowers and birds," where were "the smells and flavors of roses and melons, and peach bloom and ripe peaches, of cape jessamine in hedges blooming like popcorn, and the sickly sweetness of chinaberry florets." The house had a good library where Katherine Anne, at the age of three, did her first reading and writing. By the time she was six she had written and sewed together a tiny novel about "the hermit of Halifax cave."

After her grandmother died, when she was 11, she was sent to convent schools in Texas and Louisiana. (Although her family was, apparently, Methodist, she was baptized a Roman Catholic at some point during her childhood; as she grew older she dissented from organized religion, and from most other emotional and intellectual orthodoxies as well.) At the age of 16 she ran away to get married; by 19 she was divorced and was earning a meager living as a newspaper writer, bit-part movie actress, and entertainer. In Denver, where she joined the staff of the *Rocky Mountain News,* she was nearly killed by a bout of influenza that turned her hair white; her lover, an Army soldier, caught the disease from her and died. (Twenty years later this loss would be worked into fiction as the short novel *Pale Horse, Pale Rider.)*

She then spent some time doing hack work and ghostwriting in New York's Greenwich Village, meanwhie writing and destroying her own stories "by the trunkful." At the suggestion of friends she traveled to Mexico to take part in the Obregon Revolution and stayed to help organize an 80,000-item exhibition of Aztec, Mayan, and Mexican art, the first show of such art to be seen in the United States. Returning to New York in the early 1920s, she published the short story "Maria Concepción" in *Century Magazine* and continued to support herself through book reviewing and journalism. She also became passionately involved in the defense of Nicola Sacco and Bartolomeo Vanzetti, the Italian-American anarchists who were tried and executed on trumped-up murder charges in Massachusetts.

Flowering Judas, her first collection of stories, was published in 1928 and was greatly praised by the reviewers for its expert handling of themes, its portraiture, and its crystalline prose style, perfected in 15 years of literary apprentice work. Her intention was to construct a fiction that "states no belief, gives no motives, airs no theories, but simply presents to the reader a situation, a place, and a character, and there it is; and the emotional content is present implicitly as the germ is in the wheat." Edmund Wilson was later to write that "she makes none of the melodramatic or ironic points that are the stock in trade of ordinary short story writers; she falls into none of the usual patterns and she does not show anyone's influence. She does not exploit her personality either inside or outside her work, and . . . writes English of a purity and precision almost unique in contemporary American fiction." This verbal control she attributed to her heritage as a Southerner. "We are in the direct, legitimate line; we are people based in English as our mother tongue, and we do not abuse it or misuse it, and when we speak a word, we know what it means."

Flowering Judas was chosen a Book-of-the-Month Club selection and earned its author a Guggenheim Fellowship for travel abroad. After some months in Mexico she sailed to Germany, where she met the "detestable and dangerous" leaders of the nazi regime, and lived in Switzerland and Paris, where she married Eugene Pressly, a member of the staff of the American consulate. In Paris she translated 17 French *chansons* that became *Katherine Anne Porter's Song-Book* and wrote a short novel, *Hacienda,* that was published in 1934. Divorced, she returned to the U.S. in 1938 and shortly afterwards married Albert Russel Erskine, a professor at Louisiana State University in Baton Rouge, from whom she was divorced in 1942.

By 1939 Porter had published the three short novels that confirmed her reputation as one of the best English-language fiction writers of the century. According to Robert Penn Warren, their insights sprang from the tension between emotional involvement and detached assessment on the part of their author, who "never confounds the shadowy and flickering shapes of the psychological situation with vagueness of structure and in the fiction itself, or permits the difficulty of making an ethical analysis to justify a confusion of form." Miranda, the heroine of *Old Mortality* and *Pale Horse, Pale River,* is an autobiographical figure who contends, in the first story, with the illusions and myths of her old Southern family, and in the second with the disease that kills her lover and brings her to the edge of death herself. *Noon Wine,* considered her best work by many critics, concerns the killing of a professional bounty hunter by a confused and fearful farmer afraid to lose his hard-working hired hand, who has turned out to be an escapee from an asylum for the criminally insane. Many years later, Porter, in an essay called "Noon Wine: The Sources," reconstructed the handful of disparate, barely-realized memories—a fragment of conversation, a harmonica tune, the scream of a murdered man—that had come together in her mind to form the story. This process of recollection and revision, the process by which all her tales were made, often took years, but once it was done the author needed only a few days to commit the finished work to paper "in a state of trancelike absorption," sustained by cold coffee and oranges.

Porter's translation of Fernández de Lizárdi's *The Itching Parrot* was published in 1942, and another volume of fiction, *The Leaning Tower and Other Stories,* in 1944. For the next 20 years, she was engaged in the writing of *Ship of Fools,* a massive novel that she began in journal form in the 1930s. The genesis of the novel, originally planned as a 25,000-word novella, was the sea voyage she took from Mexico to Germany in 1931, commingled in her mind with her reading of *Das Narrenschiff (The Fool-Ship),* a 15th century allegory of human folly by the German writer Sebastian Brant. Each year her publisher announced the book's imminent appearance—the editors of the 1942 volume *Twentieth Century Writers* confidently listed it as having been issued that year—but Porter refused to adhere to anyone's timetable but her own. Recurrent bouts of respiratory disease slowed her efforts, along with the necessity of earning a living. She maintained herself by teaching, lecturing, and reading her work at hundreds of colleges and writers' conferences, and by writing essays, which were collected in the 1952 volume *The Days Before.* She received grants from the Ford Foundation and the Yaddo writers' colony, and was a Fulbright Lecturer at the University of Liège, Belgium, and served as Fellow of Regional American Literature at the Library of Congress. In 1955 she was a delegate to the International Exposition of the Arts in Paris, and in 1960 and 1964 traveled to Mexico as a cultural representative of the State Department.

By the time *Ship of Fools* appeared in 1962 it was a pre-publication best seller, with the film rights long since sold for half a million dollars. (The movie version appeared in 1965.) The book describes the journey of a German ship, the S.S. *Vera,* from Veracruz to Bremerhaven in 1931. Among the passengers are a number of middle- and upper-class Germans, some of them avid racists; a thieving company of Spanish dancers, including two satanic and incestuous twin children; a drug-addicted and nymphomaniac Cuban countess, a pair of estranged American lovers, a resentful German Jew, and many more—in all, some 40 identifiable characters and a steerage full of poor Spanish workmen. In the course of the journey these strangers visit upon one another a series of degradations, torments, and unhappy passions that prefigure the coming nazi horrors and make the S.S. *Vera* a microcosm of human misery.

The publication of *Ship of Fools* was the literary event of the year and touched off a lasting controversy among the critics, who were moved to extremes of adulation and contempt. The majority regarded it as a Breughelesque picture of life in all its depravity and irony. Smith Kirkpatrick, writing in the *Sewanee Review,* called the novel "a lament for us all, a song artistically resolved, sung by a great artist of the insoluble condition of man." Mark Schorer, in a *New York Times* review entitled "We Are All on the Passenger List," wrote of "its magnificent lack of illusion about the human nature and especially the human sexual relationship," and compared it in greatness to George Eliot's *Middlemarch.*

There were also critics who found the book cold, queasy, dull, and morally banal, and the characters a collection of hopeless grotesques. Chief among these was *Commentary's* Theodore Solotaroff, who called the book "the most sour and morbid indictment of humans to appear in many years," the product of a "skewed and embittered" sensibility in "incessant quarrel with human nature." The vast popular success of the book, he argued, was a symptom of the same moral malaise that allowed journalists at the trial of Adolf Eichmann to assert that Eichmann's crimes were universal, that "we are all Eichmann."

After 1964, Porter, who had settled in College Park, Maryland,

worked on a biography of Cotton Mather that she had begun in 1927
and collected literary prizes, including the Pulitzer Prize and the
National Book Award, both for her *Collected Stories.* Her last book,
published in 1977, was *The Never-Ending Wrong,* an account of the
prosecution and death of Sacco and Vanzetti, in whose defense she
had been so active as a young woman. In that year she suffered a
stroke and was eventually confined to a nursing home, where she died
at the age of 90. "I have tossed a good many things considered
generally desirable over the windmill," she once said, "for that one
intangible thing that money cannot buy, and I find to my joy I was
right. There is no describing what my life has been because of my one
fixed desire to be a good artist, responsible to the last comma for what
I write."   J.P./M.W.

Born Katherine Anne Maria Veronica Callista Russell Porter. Daughter of Harrison Boone P., farmer, and Mary Alice (Jones) P. Married:
(1) . . . ca. 1906 (div. ca. 1909); (2) Eugene Dove Pressly, U.S.
Foreign Service consular aide, 1933 (div. 1938); (3) Albert Russel
Erskine, Jr., prof. of English 1938 (div. 1942). No children. Family
probably Methodist; christened Roman Catholic as child. Educ:
privately at home; convent schs. in Texas and Louisiana until 1906.
Fiction writer since childhood; first short story published 1922; also
essayist, biographer, translator, lecturer. Newspaper staff member
and movie extra, Chicago 1911; staff member, The Critic, Fort Worth,
Tex. 1917; reporter and arts critic, Rocky Mountain News, 1918–19;
ghostwriter and reviewer, NYC 1920; writer for trade jrnl., organizer
of Mexican art exhibition, and political activist, Mexico 1920–22;
actor, Fort Worth Little Theatre ca. 1921; hack writer and political
activist, NYC mid to late 1920s; lived in Mexico, Switzerland, Paris
1931–38. Lectr., reader, and teacher at some 200 univs., colls., and
writers' conferences in U.S. and Europe, including Olivet Coll., Mich.
1940; Lectr. in Writing, Stanford Univ., Calif. 1948–49; Guest Lectr.
in Lit., Univ. of Chicago 1951; Visiting Lectr. in Contemporary
Poetry, Univ. of Michigan 1953–54; Fulbright Lectr. in English Lit.,
Univ. of Liège, Belgium, 1954–55; Writer in Residence, Univ. of
Virginia 1958; Glasgow Prof., Washington and Lee Univ., Lexington,
Va. 1959; first Ewing Lectr., Univ. of California at Los Angeles 1960;
Regents' Lectr., Univ. of California at Riverside 1961; Univ. of
Maryland 1970s. U.S. Delegate, Intnl. Festival of the Arts, Paris 1952;
Member, Pres. Johnson's Commn. on Presidential Scholars 1964;
Lectr. in American Lit. under exchange grant from U.S. Dept. of
State, Mexico 1960, 1964. Co-V.P., Natl. Inst. of Arts and Letters
1950–52. Hons: Book-of-the-Month Club selection (Flowering Judas)
1930; Guggenheim Fellowship 1931, 1938; Book-of-the-Month Club
Award 1937; first annual Gold Medal, Soc. of Libraries of New York
Univ. (for Pale Horse, Pale Rider) 1940; elected Member, Natl.
Acad. of Arts and Letters 1943; Fellow in Regional American Lit.,
Library of Congress 1944; Ford Foundn. grant 1959–62; First Prize, O.
Henry Memorial Award (for short story Holiday) 1962; Emerson-
Thoreau Bronze Medal for Lit., American Acad. of Arts and Sciences
1962; Book-of-the-Month Club selection (Ship of Fools) 1962;
Pulitzer Prize and Natl. Book Award (for Collected Stories of
Katherine Anne Porter) 1966; Gold Medal, Natl. Inst. of Arts and
Letters 1967; elected member, American Acad. of Arts and Letters
1967; fellowship, Yaddo artists' colony, N.Y.; Hon. D. Litt from
Univ. of North Carolina Women's Coll. 1949, Smith Coll. 1958,
Maryville Coll. 1968, Wheaton Coll.; Hon. D.H.L. from Univ. of
Michigan 1954, Univ. of Maryland 1966, Maryland Inst. 1974; Hon.

D.F.A. from LaSalle Coll. 1962. *Novel:* Ship of Fools, 1962. *Short story collections and short novels:* Flowering Judas, 1930, augmented ed. as Flowering Judas and Other Stories, 1935; Hacienda: A Story of Mexico, 1934; Noon Wine, 1937; Pale Horse, Pale Rider: Three Short Novels, 1938; The Leaning Tower and Other Stries, 1944; The Collected Stories of Katherine Anne Porter, 1964, augmented ed. 1967. *Uncollected short stories:* "Christmas Story," in McCall's, Dec. 1967; "Spivvleton Mystery," in Ladies Home Journal, Aug. 1971. *Other:* (as M.T.F.) My Chinese Marriage, 1921; Outline of Mexican Popular Arts and Crafts, 1922; What Price Marriage, 1927; (trans. from French) Katherine Anne Porter's French Song-Book, 1933; (trans. from Spanish) The Itching Parrot (by Fernández de Lizárdi), 1942; preface to Fiesta in November (by Flores and Poore), 1942; The Days Before: Collected Essays and Occasional Writings, 1952; A Defence of Circe (essay), 1955; The Collected Essays and Occasional Writings of Katherine Anne Porter (augmented ed. of The Days Before), 1970; The Never-Ending Wrong (on Sacco-Vanzetti case), 1977; biography of Cotton Mather (unfinished). *Interviews:* "A Country and Some People I Love," in Harper's, Sept. 1965; in Writers at Work: The Paris Review Interviews, Second Series; others. Literary collection given to Univ. of Maryland at College Park.
Further reading: Classics and Commercials by Edmund Wilson, 1950; Images of Truth by Glenway Wescott, 1962; Katherine Anne Porter and the Art of Rejection by William L. Nance, 1964; Katherine Anne Porter by George Hendrick, 1965; A Bibliography of the Works of Katherine Anne Porter, and a Bibliography of the Criticism of the Works of Katherine Anne Porter by Louise Waldrup and Shirley Ann Bauer, 1969; Katherine Anne Porter: A Critical Symposium by Lodwick Charles Hartley and George Core (eds.), 1969; Katherine Anne Porter and Carson McCullers: A Reference Guide by Robert F. Kiernan, 1976; Katherine Anne Porter: A Collection of Critical Essays by Robert Penn Warren (ed.), 1978.

SIR ALAN (CUTHBERT) BURNS
Colonial administrator and author
Born Basseterre, St. Kitts, British West Indies, November 9th, 1887
Died London, England, September 19th, 1980

In five decades with Britain's Colonial Civil Service, Sir Alan Burns became known as an efficient and fair-minded administrator who carried out Colonial Office policy while retaining the respect of those placed in his charge. Towards the end of his career he was also a vigorous defender of the British colonial undertaking against the supporters of growing independence movements in Africa and Asia.

The son and grandson of colonial administrators, Burns served mainly in the British West Indies, Central America and western Africa. He gained a reputation in all his posts for ideas and policies that were progressive for their time. From 1929 to 1934 he served as chief secretary and deputy to the governor in Nigeria, where he sought to eliminate racial prejudice in the civil service by bringing educated young Africans into its ranks and by promoting social contact between the races through "dining clubs" and sports unions. Burns continued this policy as governor of the Gold Coast between 1941 and 1947, becoming one of the earliest official proponents of a greater role in

government for the indigenous population. Though he believed that
Africans were then incapable of managing a parliamentary democracy, he did appoint an African majority to the Gold Coast legislative
council, the first British administrator in Africa to take such action.

At the start of World War Two Burns returned briefly to London as
assistant under-secretary of state in the Colonial Office, where he
helped arrange the leasing of British bases in the Western Hemisphere
to the U.S. After leaving the Colonial Service in 1947, he served for
nine years as permanent British representative on the U.N. Trusteeship Council, where he defended his country's efforts to spread "the
principles of democracy and honest administration" in its colonies. He
had already begun to develop an articulate justification of British
colonial policy in a number of books, including histories of Nigeria
and the British West Indies and an autobiographical work, *Colonial
Civil Servant.* His *In Defence of Colonies,* published in 1957, summarized his political views and pointed out the inconsistency of those
who criticized the British colonial situation while ignoring far worse
conditions in countries not generally considered colonial powers. R.C.

Son of James B. (Treasurer). Married Kathleen Hardtman 1914 (d.
1970). Children: Helen Benedicta; Aileen Barbara. Roman Catholic.
Educ: St. Edmund's Coll., Ware, England 1900–05. Mil. Service:
Cameroon Expeditionary Force 1914–15; Egba Expedition, Nigeria
1918. Clerk, Treasury and Customs Dept., St. Kitts, Leeward Islands
1905–11; Justice of the Peace, St. Kitts, 1911; Supervisor of Customs,
Southern Nigeria 1912–15; attached to Central Secretariat, Nigeria
1915–24; Colonial Secty., Bahama Islands 1924–29 (Acting Gov. May-
Oct. 1924, Sept.-Nov. 1925, Sept. 1926–Mar. 1927, June-Sept. 1928);
member, Bahama House of Assembly 1925–28; Deputy Chief Secty.
to Gov., Nigeria 1929–34; Gov. and Comdr. in Chief, British
Honduras 1934–40; Asst. Undersecty. of State for Colonies, London
1940–41; Gov. and Comdr. in Chief, Gold Coast, West Africa
1941–47; Acting Gov., Nigeria 1942. Permanent U.K. Rep., Trusteeship Council of the U.N. 1947–56; Chmn., Cttee. of Inquiry into Land
and Population Problems, Fiji 1959–60. Member Atheneum Club.
Hons: Companion of St. Michael and St. George 1936; Knight, Order
of St. John of Jerusalem 1942; Knight, Grand Cross of St. Michael and
St. George 1946. *Author:* (compiler) Index to Laws of Leeward
Islands; Nigeria Handbook, 1923; Bridge for Beginners, 1924; History
of Nigeria, 1929 (rev. ed., 1978); Colour Prejudice, 1948; Colonial
Civil Servant, 1949; History of the British West Indies, 1954; In
Defense of Colonies, 1957; Fiji, 1963.

JACKY GILLOTT
Novelist, broadcaster, and journalist
Born Lytham St. Anne's, Lancashire, England, 1939
Died Somerset, England, September 19th, 1980

Jacky Gillot lived and worked through a period which saw better
opportunities for women and in which the plight of the working
mother was publicly debated for the first time. She was among the first
women to work in television news at a time when current affairs was
still an essentially male preserve, and as a novelist she highlighted the

lines of stress to be found in the nuclear family as her female protagonists outgrew the traditional role of housewife. Until her untimely death, Jacky Gillott successfully mixed her two careers with her role as a mother.

Born in 1939 in Lytham St. Anne's in Lancashire, Jacky Gillott first went into journalism on completion of an English degree at University College, London. She gained her indentures with the Sheffield Telegraph before moving, in 1962, to Radio Newsreel on the BBC World Service as a newsroom holiday relief typist. There she met her future husband John Percival, who was later to become a television producer, and they were married within five months. The birth of her two sons, in 1964 and 1965, hardly interfered with her work; she later claimed that she was broadcasting two days before and two days after the birth of her second son.

The characters in her novels, starting in 1968 with *Salvage,* were less fortunate than she in breaking out of the housebound wife mold. Domestic frustration, as critics pointed out at the time, was not an innovative theme, but her first book was well received.

In September 1968 Jacky Gillott started working full-time with Independent Television News (ITN); women news journalists were still a rarity, and although Joan Bakewell was becoming known as a TV arts presenter, it was another six years before television had its first woman news reader in Angela Rippon. In order to devote more time to writing, Miss Gillott reduced her work hours at ITN and five more novels appeared in the period 1971 to 1980. These subsequent works met with less enthusiasm. Critics generally felt that she tended to over-sympathize with her heroines' difficulties, and that she sometimes over-simplified their response to the achievement of a tentative emancipation. During this period Jacky Gillott also wrote a number of articles and book reviews for various publications including the *Times* and the *Sunday Times,* London. In addition to this freelance work, she took over the presentation of BBC radio's *Kaleidoscope* which, established in 1974, was the first daily arts programme on radio.   I.J.

Married John Percival, television producer, 1963. Children: Matthew, b. 1964; Daniel, b. 1965. Educ: University Coll. London, B.A. 1960. Trainee journalist, Sheffield Telegraph 1960–62; journalist, Radio Newsreel, BBC World Service 1962–68 and with Independent Television News (ITN) 1968; freelance reporter, ITN 1968–ca. 1971; freelance journalist, bookreviewer with various jrnls including Times and Sunday Times, London 1971–80; Presenter, Kaleidoscope, BBC Radio, ca. 1977–80. *Author:* Salvage, 1968; War Baby, 1971; For Better For Worse, 1971; A True Romance, 1975; Crying Out Loud, 1976; The Head Case, 1979; Intimate Relations, 1980.

SOL LESSER
Motion picture producer and theater operator
Born Spokane, Washington, U.S.A., February 17th, 1890
Died Hollywood, California, U.S.A., September 19th, 1980

Sol Lesser, a pioneer in the Hollywood film industry, developed a chain of motion picture theatres, instigated new methods of promoting films including previews and star appearances, and produced 117 feature movies. He was best known for his numerous Tarzan films starring Johnny Weismuller, but of all his films, he was most proud of *Our Town,* his adaptation of Thornton Wilder's play.

As a young boy, he sold ice creams in the nickelodeon his father opened up in San Francisco shortly after the earthquake in 1906. In 1922, three years after he moved to Los Angeles, Lesser began to produce his Jackie Coogan series of films. When he was 33, Lesser started the West Coast Theaters (later Fox West Coast Theaters) chain in Hollywood and co-founded First National Pictures. He became the last survivor of the group of movie producers responsible for Hollywood's ascendancy as the center of America's entertainment industry. At the age of 36 he sold his interest in the enterprise and embarked on a two-year round-the-world cruise. Finding the trip tedious after a few months, he returned home, purchasing a small Hollywood theater. That small venture grew into the Principal Theaters chain with locations throughout California. He also founded Stero Cine Corporation which, in competition with National Vision Corporation made 3-D movies requiring viewers to wear special Polaroid glasses. As a means of classifying movies for different audiences, Lesser designated certain theaters for particular kinds of movies. His idea has evolved into the present G, PG, R and X rating system.

Lesser's early film productions gained him recognition as a highly successful producer of movies with child stars. His *Oliver Twist* (1922) which introduced Jackie Coogan broke box office records; he discovered Margaret Montgomery, then dubbed "Baby Peggy," and introduced Bobby Breen in *Let's Sing Again* in 1936.

With his movie version of *Our Town* (made 1939, distributed 1940), Lesser took pains to obtain Wilder's approval for every proposed change. Wilder also suggested changes and wrote some of the additional dialogue. Unusual for that time, Lesser believed that a writer has the "inalienable right . . . to put pen on paper . . . without the interference of any other agent. True, a writer . . . may be given and accept advice or correction, but he is, nevertheless, the ultimate and only critic empowered to make changes in his own creation." The movie was a success with the critics but not at the box office.

As Lesser's career progressed, there were many other successes, the most significant one being *Stage Door Canteen* (made in 1942). From the profits of this movie, Lesser donated one-and-a-half million dollars to the American Theater Wing. In 1945 he formed Sol Lesser Productions. His 10 Tarzan films also proved to be highly successful at the box-office, and his 1951 movie of Thor Heyerdahl's popular *Kon-Tiki* book won him an Academy Award.

In 1961, he was awarded the Jean Hersholt Humanitarianism Award for his support of theatrical and film industry causes. Lesser was one of the organizers of the Writer's Club, a favorite cultural center and meeting place for Hollywood movie people, and he championed the idea of a Hollywood museum for the entertainment industry. In recent years, Sol Lesser taught cinematography at the University of Southern California (USC) and at the University of Redlands, California. At the age of 86 he was awarded USC's master's degree in film sciences for his thesis on a model curriculum for a film school; this marked Lesser as the oldest master's degree recipient in the school's history.

Lesser discounted predictions that films would be supplanted by other forms of entertainment. He believed that movies, like radio, had survived television and thought that the wide screen and the pursuit of more intellectual themes would help to keep the cinema, and Hollywood, thriving.

Sol Lesser died a year after his wife Fay; they had been married for 66 years.   R.T.

Son of L. and Julia L. Married Fay Grunauer, d. 1979. Children: Mrs. Marjorie Fasman; Julian. Jewish. Educ: schs. in San Francisco; Univ. of Southern California, master's in film sciences 1976. Established Golden Gate Film Exchange and All Star Feature/Distributors Exchange, consolidated with Miles Bros. and California Film Exchange 1914; established a Northern Californian circuit of theaters 1916; moved to Los Angeles 1919; with others organized West Coast Theaters, sold out interest 1926; associated with Inspiration Pictures 1930, resigned to become asst. to Joseph Schenck at United Theater Circuit; formed Principal Distributing Corp. 1933; joined RKO Radio as Exec.-in-Charge of Feature Productions 1941, resigned to form Sol Lesser Productions 1945 (Pres.); founded Standard Theaters 1947, Principal Theater Corp., American Principal Mgmt. Co., and Principal Securities Corp.; Prof. of Cinematography, Univ. of Southern California and Univ. of Redlands during 1970s. Member: Bd. of Dirs., Motion Picture and TV Relief Fund; Permanent Charities Cttee., Motion Picture Industry; Palm Springs Desert Museum. Founder Member: Los Angeles County Museum of Art; Los Angeles Music Center. Hons: Academy Award for best production, Kon-Tiki, 1951; Jean Hersholt Humanitarianism Award, Motion Picture Academy, 1960; Silver Platter, Sch. of Performing Arts, Univ. of Southern California, 1973; named Patriarch of Theater Industry, National Assn. of Theater Owners, 1976. *Films produced include:* My Boy, One Man in a Million, 1921; Oliver Twist, Trouble, Bing Bang Boom, 1922; Circus Days, Daddy, The Drug Traffic, 1923; Captain January, Helen's Babies, The Re-creation of Brian Kent, 1925; The Eyes of the World, 1930; Thunder Over Mexico, Tarzan the Fearless, 1933; Peck's Bad Boy, Return of the Chandu, 1934; The Dude Ranger, The Cowboy Millionaire, Hard Rock Harrigan, Thunder Mountain, Whispering Smith Speaks, 1935; O'Malley of the Mounted, The Border Patrolman, King of the Royal Mounted, Wild Brian Kent, The Mine with the Iron Door, Let's Sing Again, Rainbow on the River, 1936; Secret Valley, Dick Tracey (serial), The Californian, Western Gold, Make a Wish, 1937; Hawaii Calls, Breaking the Ice, Peck's Bad Boy with the Circus, 1938; Escape to Paradise, Fisherman's Wharf, Way Down South, Everything's on Ice, 1939; Our Town, 1940; That Uncertain Feeling, 1941; The Tuttles of Tahiti, 1942; Stage Door Canteen, Tarzan Triumphs, Tarzan's Desert Mystery, 1943; Three is a Family, 1944; Tarzan and the Amazons, 1945; The Red House, 1947; Kon Tiki, 1951; Under the Sea (documentary), 1952; Vice Squad, 1953; Quest for a Lost City, Tarzan's Hidden Jungle, 1955; Tarzan and the Lost Safari, 1957; Tarzan's Flight for Life, 1958.

MARTIAL (HENRY) VALIN
General, Free French Air Force
Born Limoges, Haute-Vienne, France, May 14th, 1898
Died Paris, France, September 19th, 1980

Like many professional soldiers in the French army of 1940, Martial Valin repudiated the Vichy government, which was collaborating with the German invaders, and joined the Free French forces under Charles de Gaulle. He served as Minister of War in de Gaulle's National Committee and as General of the Air Force.

A graduate of the military academy at Saint-Cyr, Valin earned the Croix de Guerre as an infantryman in Champagne during the German offensive of 1918. After the war he joined a cavalry unit as a subaltern and saw action in the Rif region of Morocco. In 1927 he volunteered for the newly-formed French Air Force. Trained as a night bomber-pilot, he became a squadron leader in 1936 and commanded the first reconnaissance mission over German lines in 1939, one of some 60 reconnaissance flights he made in the course of the war. He was serving on a military delegation in Brazil when the French government signed an armistice with Nazi Germany in June 1940.

Valin made his way to England, where General de Gaulle had announced the formation of the Free French forces, and was made chief of staff of the movement's Air Division. As de Gaulle's intermediary with the Allied commanders, he successfully negotiated for access to French troops in the Levant who were willing to fight despite the armistice, and persuaded the British to train and equip the Ile de France fighter squadron. He continued to make combat sorties over occupied France in defiance of a death sentence passed against him in absentia by the collaborationist Vichy government. As deputy chief of the Air Staff, he accompanied Generals Leclerc and de Gaulle when the Free French army entered Paris in August 1943.

When the war ended, Valin was promoted to Inspector-General of the Air Force and appointed to head the French delegation to the San Francisco conference on the organization of the United Nations. He was made a permanent member of the Air Force Council in 1951, the retirement regulations being waived for him in 1954 so that he could retain his generalship for life. Also in that year he published *Les Sans-culottes de l'Air,* a history of the Free French Air Force.

Valin, who was married and had two daughters, received a second Croix de Guerre, the Resistance Medal, and the Grand Cross of the Legion of Honor for his services during World War II. His foreign decorations included the Commander of the British Empire and the People's Friendship Order of the Soviet Union.   L.R.

Son of Georges V. and Louise (Durieux) V. Married Lucienne Sartorio 1927. Daughters: Monna Waché-Valin; Danielle. Educ: Bachelier, Lycée de Limoges; Saint-Cyr Military Acad. 1917–18. Mil. Service: Second Battle of the Marne 1918; 2nd Lt., Cavalry 1919; Lt. on cavalry campaigns in Levant and Morocco 1921; 2nd Spahi Regiment, Rif Campaign 1925, Volunteered for Air Corps 1927; Capt. 1929; Squadron Leader 1936; Major, 12th Air Brigade, then Major-Gen., Army of the Air, 1936; Comdr., 1/33 Squadron 1940; Lt. Col. 1940; Member, Military Mission to Brazil 1940–41. Deserted army to serve with de Gaulle's Free French forces 1940; Brigadier Gen. and Chief, Free French Air Force 1941; Comdr. of Air Force and Minister of Air in Natl. Cttee. 1941–44; condemned to death by

Vichy Govt. in absentia; Deputy Chief, Air Staff 1943; Gen. of Air Div. 1944; Chief of Air Staff 1944–46; Chief of Military Delegation to U.N. Organizing Conference, San Francisco 1946–47; Inspector-Gen. Air Force 1947–1955; Member of Air Council 1947–69; Gen. of Air Army 1950; Member 1951–55 and Permanent Member since 1954, Armed Forces Council. Hons: Croix de Guerre 1914–18 and 1939–45; Grand Cross of Legion of Honor; Compagnon de la Libération; Resistance Medal; Comdr., Legion of Merit; CBE and Comdr., Order of Bath, Britain; Grand Cross of the Order of Trujillo and Grand Cross of Merit Juan Pablo Duarte, Dominican Republic; Grand Cross of Aeronautic Merit, Brazil; People's Friendship Order, USSR. *Author:* Les sans-culottes de l'air: histoire du groupe Lorraine, 1954.

JACOBUS J(OHANNES) FOUCHÉ
South African politician and statesman
Born Wepener, Orange Free State, Union of South Africa, June 6th, 1898
Died Cape Town, South Africa, September 23rd, 1980

Jacobus J. Fouché, commonly known as Jim Fouché, was a prominent champion of Afrikaaner interests and held influential positions in South Africa's political hierarchy. He was administrator of his native Orange Free State for eight years and then served for seven years as Minister of Defense in the cabinet of Hendrik Verwoerd, an architect of the apartheid system. After that he held the lesser portfolio of Agricultural Technical Services and Water Affairs, and in 1968 he succeeded C. R. "Blackie" Swart as titular head of state. Fouché was the country's second president; prior to 1961, when South Africa withdrew from the Commonwealth, ceremonial authority was vested in the British monarch.

Fouché, the son of a prominent Afrikaaner landowner, was born in the Orange Free State of the Union of South Africa in 1898, a year before the Second Boer War broke out, which pitted the rebellious Afrikaaners against the British Empire. He attended Victoria College which, despite its name, was a hotbed of Afrikaaner nationalism and the alma mater of Jan Smuts and J.B.M. Hertzog, among others. Young Fouché soon became active in politics as a member of the Afrikaans Nationalist Party under the leadership of the old Boer War hero, General Hertzog. Indeed, Fouché's nationalist principles ultimately proved sterner than those of his leader; for, when Hertzog entered into a coalition in 1933 with Jan Smuts's Union Party on a platform of closer ties with the British Colonial administration, Fouché refused to go along, remaining with the uncompromising faction headed by Dr. D. F. Malan. In 1941 Fouché stood for Parliament on the Nationalist ticket and was elected, soon emerging as an influential spokesman for Afrikaaner interests and instrumental in the Nationalist's ultimate triumph in 1948. In 1951, he was named Administrator of the Orange Free State, serving until 1959 when he was awarded the portfolio for defense in the ministry of Hendrik Verwoerd.

His tenure as Defense Minister (1959–66) coincided with the

beginnings of South Africa's serious political isolation as a result of heightened global sensitivity to national liberation and the repression of indigenous populations by colonials. South Africa, with its apartheid policies and its increasingly harsh responses to the stirrings of black protest—most notably the Sharpeville Massacre of March, 1960, in which South African police killed 52 blacks and wounded 162 more during a protest against the government's recently instituted "pass" laws for blacks—became a major target of international condemnation. Besides trade restrictions framed by the United Nations, the country's two most important allies—the U.S. and Great Britain—were constrained to announce embargoes on arms shipments to the Verwoerd regime.

Under Fouché's direction, defense spending increased sixfold, the South African army emerged as one of the largest and best equipped of any nation of comparable size in the world, and the arms embargoes were offset by promoting an indigenous arms industry. Opponents of South Africa, he declared ominously in 1964, would be surprised if they knew just how well-armed the nation had become.

As defense spokesman, Fouché was a notable sword-rattler. In 1963, for example, on the eve of the start of the arms embargoes he warned the nations of Africa: "Stay where you are or there will be trouble." On another occasion, he announced that "white South Africans will defend their fatherland until the blood rises to their horses' bits." Yet in 1966 he was abruptly replaced in the defense post by P.W. Botha and shifted to the Ministry of Agriculture. It was clearly a demotion, the factors of Fouché's age and health notwithstanding, he was, within the context of the cabinet's policies, a leftwinger. Botha proved a more aggressive exponent of Verwoerd's increasingly rightist policies and further expanded South Africa's arsenal of weapons and defense systems.

In 1968, Fouché's years of service to the State were rewarded by election to the prestigious but largely ceremonial post of South African State President. During his term of office (1968–75) "Oom Jim" or Uncle Jim as he was known, continued to show his loyalty to the government by defending censorship and castigating outside "pressure groups" and "Communists" for attempting to sow internal discord; but he also was the Vorster ministry's chief spokesman when it wished to emphasize its "development" programs for tribal "homelands" or to announce the introduction of increased self-government for the "Bantustans," as these tribal preserves were known in the language of apartheid. In addition, Fouché was the first South African head of state to visit an independent black African nation when he went to Malawi in March, 1972, to return President Banda's visit the year before.   R.C.

Son of Jacobus Johannes F. and Maria Elizabeth Steynberg F. Married Letta Rhoda McDonald 1920. Son: Jacobus Johannes, diplomat, b. 1921. Educ: Victoria Coll., Stellenbosch. M.P. for Smithfield, Orange Free State (OFS) 1941–50 and for Bloemfontein West 1960–68; Administrator of Orange Free State OFS 1951–59; Minister of Defense, 1959–66, and for Agricultural Technical Services and Water Affairs, 1966–68, Govt. of South Africa; Pres. of the State, 1968–75. Hons: D.Phil. (honoris causa), Stellenbosch Univ. (formerly Victoria Coll.) 1966; Decoration for Meritorious Service 1971; Hon.

Member, South African Akademie vir Wetanskap en Kuns; Hon. Colonel, Regiment of President Steyn, Bloemfontein; Hon. Freeman of 15 cities and towns in South Africa.

ALAN (STRODE CAMPBELL) ROSS
Philologist and professor of linguistics
Born Brecon, Wales, February 1st, 1907
Died England, September 23rd, 1980

urtesy A.W.P. Ross

Alan Ross reached an audience—not always an approving one—far beyond the narrow confines of philological scholarship when, during the mid-1950s, he began to write articles and books on the speech patterns of the English aristocracy and the specific ways the lower classes could improve their status by changing their vocabulary, accent and word usage. But he had built a solid reputation as a philologist in academic circles long before this.

He was at first interested in astronomy, but soon switched to English language and literature after he commenced his studies at Balliol College, Oxford. Receiving a first class honours degree, Alan Ross rose steadily through the academic ranks, initially at Leeds University, and then, after a wartime stint at the Foreign Office, at Birmingham University, finally holding the newly created chair of linguistics there.

His first publication was a co-edition of a ninth-century Anglo-Saxon text, *The Dream of the Rood,* and three years later he published a work on the Lindisfarne Gospels, a beautifully illuminated 8th century manuscript combining Celtic and Germanic elements, produced by an Irish monastery in Saxon England. He later collaborated on the Urs Graf edition of the Gospels, and before his death was working on a commentary to them. His 1940 publication, *The Terfinnes and Boermas of Ohthere* included the original Anglo-Saxon text, and his Aldrediana of 1959 described Anglo-Saxon suffixes and prefixes. One of his most widely reprinted works was *The Essentials of Anglo-Saxon Grammar.* Anglo-Saxon language interested Ross throughout his life as did the Finno-Ugrian group and Indo-European languages in general. In all, he was fluent or knowlegeable in more than a dozen languages including Estonian, Lapp, and Tahitian. His scholarship in the field is reflected by his founding of a journal, *English Philological Studies.*

His one venture into general linguistics, *Etymology,* was not a great success. One reviewer praised him for his "hard work and insight" but said the book was "marred by inaccuracies, over-compression, occasional poor presentation, terminological infelicities . . . and the error . . . of pretentious technicality." Ross had intended the work for non-academics as well as for his professional colleagues, but seems to have failed in satisfying either audience, although the book did go into a paperback edition in 1965.

Much more successful was his work on the Pitcairnese language, which was praised for its "patient and unobstrusive erudition." The Pitcairnese language is of particular interest to philologists, since it was formed by the interaction of the English-speaking mutineers of the Bounty and the Tahitian-speaking natives of Pitcairn Island in the South Pacific during the late 18th and early 19th century. Ross had gone to Paris to study Tahitian, and particularly relished this project because the language's "actual birth can be witnessed and its history followed through to the present day."

Ross's work on the language used by the British upper classes first appeared in an article in 1954 in Germany and reached a wide English-speaking audience when he contributed a chapter in Nancy Mitford's *Noblesse Oblige.* He defined the delineation of accent, word choice, syntax, and pronunciation of the so-called upper class elite (essentially comprising those who had attended particular schools and universities such as those at Oxford and Cambridge) and called their usage "U." Everyone else was "non-U." The U and non-U movement came to be synonymous with "fashionable and non-fashionable" tastes and styles in general. But for a while, the most "fashionable" (and therefore "U") topic of conservation among Britons of all classes was—usually tongue-in-cheek—to identify the U and non-U aspects of their own speech and behavior as well as that of their friends, acquaintances and enemies.

In 1970, Ross published *How to Pronounce It,* in which he gave precise instructions for "correct" vowel sounds, and three years later, *Don't Say It,* a warning to English people seeking to raise their class station against using over-elegant euphemisms, Americanisms, and other "non-U" speech. Ross here also made distinctions between "lower-class" and "working class" speech patterns. The *Times Literary Supplement* called the work "splendid" (a "U" word if ever there was one) but said that "the mincing class consciousness of the enterprise gives cause for despondence. 'Hopefully' (a very "non-U" word) the book will be remaindered in a week."

After his retirement from Birmingham University in 1974, Alan Ross lived in Sussex, working on a commentary to the Lindesfarne Gospels. He was also writing a commentary on the gloss (marginal explanatory annotations) in the Durham Ritual, and editing a two-volume work on Indo-European numerals.

A tall, gawky individual devoted to philately, croquet and the game of patience, he was rather gentle and retiring, and was much liked at his university for his warm relationships with younger faculty and students.   L.F./R.T.

Son of Archibald Campbell Carne R., land agent, and Millicent Strode (Cobham) R. Married Elizabeth Stefanja Olszewska (lexicographer) 1932 (d. 1973). Children: Alan Waclaw Palmint. Educ: Lindisfarne, Blackheath; Naish House, Burnham-on-Sea; Malvern Coll.; Christ Coll., Brecon; Henry Skynner Scholar at Balliol Coll., Oxford, M.A. 1st class hons. in English Language and Literature, 1929. Asst. Lectr. 1929–35 and lectr. in English lang. 1936–40, Univ. of Leeds; seconded to Foreign Office 1940–45; with Univ. of Birmingham 1951–74: Lectr. in English Lang. 1946, Reader 1947; Prof. 1948–51; Prof. of linguistics 1951 until retirement 1974. Founder and Editor, English Philological Studies; Co-ed., Leeds Studies in English (I-VI). Participated in Lappland expedition under aegis of Royal Geographical Soc. Member: English Place-Name Soc.; Philological Soc.; Brecknock Soc.; Royal Commonwealth Soc.; Leeds Philosophical and Literary Soc.; Scottish Genealogy Soc.; Viking Soc. for Northern Research. Foreign corresponding member, Suomalais-

Ugrilainen Seura; Liveryman, Worshipful Company of Grocers; corresponding member, Société Finnoougrienne. Hons: M.A., Univ. of Birmingham 1949. *Author:* Studies in the Accidence of the Lindisfarne Gospels, 1937; The "Numeral Signs" of the Mohenjo-dara script (Memoirs of the Archeological Survey of India), 1938; The Terfinnes and Beormas of Ohthere, 1940; The Essentials of Anglo-Saxon Grammar, 1948, 1954, 1971, 1975, 1976; Tables for Old English Sound-Changes, 1951, 1976, 1977, reprinted with The Essentials of Anglo-Saxon Grammar, one vol. 1963; Ginger, a Loan-Word Study, 1952; (chapter contributor) Noblesse Oblige: An Enquiry into the Identifiable Characteristics of the English Aristocracy, ed. by Nancy Mitford, 1956, 1973; Etymology, with Special Reference to English, 1958, 1965; Aldrediana I: Three Suffixes, 1959; The Essentials of German Grammar, 1963; (co-author) Patience Napoleon, 1963; The Essentials of English Grammar, 1964; (co-author) The Pitcairnese Language, 1964; How to Pronounce It, 1970; Don't Say It; 1973. *Editor:* (co-ed.) The Dream of the Rood, 1934, 4th revised ed. 1956, 1963, 1966; (co-ed.) The Lindisfarne Gospels, (Urs Grat ed.) 1957–60; Arts v. Science: A Collection of Essays, 1967, 1968; What Are U, 1969; (co-ed.) The Durham Ritual, 1969. *Co-translator:* I.I. Reuzin, Models of Language, 1966. *Major articles:* "Linguistic class-indicators in present-day English" Neuphilologische Mitteilungen, 1954; Pize-ball, Proceeding of Leeds Philosophical and Literary Society, Literary and Historical Section, Vol. 13, Part 2, 1968; essay in U and Non-U Revisited, edited by Richard Buckle, 1968; contributed many articles to scholarly journals and popular press, including: Economic History Review, Acta Philologica Scandinavica; Englishe Studien; Jrnl. of Royal Statistical Soc.; Modern Lang. Review; Archivum Linguis-ticum; Biometrika; Finnish-ugrische Forschujgen; Indogermanische Forschungern; Geographical Journal; Journal of English and Ger-manic Philology; Mathematical Gazette; Moderna Sprak; Modern Language Notes; Neuphilologische Mitteilungen; Studia germanica; Zeitschrift fur vergleichende Sprachforschung; Saga-Book of Viking Soc.; Transactions of Philological Soc.; Nature; Folklore; Speculum; Times Literary Supplement; Holiday; Times (London); Observer; Guardian (Manchester and London); Washington Post; Encounter.

RICHARD (REEVE) BAXTER
Professor of international law and judge of the International Court of Justice
Born New York City, U.S.A., February 14th, 1921
Died September 25th, 1980

Judge Richard Baxter's career was devoted to international law; he was a noted scholar on the law of war and the law of international waterways. Elected a judge of the International Court of Justice at The Hague in February 1979, Baxter was also Manley Hudson Professor of Law at Harvard Law School and had served for many years as a U.S. government consultant and, for seven years, as a judge of the Permanent Court of Arbitration.

Born in New York City in 1921, Baxter received his A.B. degree in 1942 from Brown University. He joined the U.S. Army that year and six years later, when he received his LL.B. degree from Harvard, he was admitted to the Massachusetts Bar; but he remained with the army as an attorney until 1954 when he became a reserve officer with the rank of colonel. Baxter gained the diploma international law from Cambridge University, England, in 1951 and received his LL.M. degree from Georgetown University the following year.

Baxter joined the faculty of Harvard Law School in 1955 after a year as a research associate there; he became a full professor in 1959. During the year 1966–67 he was a visiting professor on the law faculty of Cambridge University. He joined the Permanent Court of Arbitration in 1968, serving until 1975. From 1970 until 1978 Baxter was editor-in-chief of the American Journal of International Law; he presided over the American Society of International Law from 1974 to 1976.

Judge Baxter's membership of the International Court of Justice was cut short by his death at the age of 59. He missed the Court's ruling in the case of *USA V. Iran* as he was undergoing hospital treatment. A firm believer in strict adherence to international law, Baxter felt that erring countries should be penalized by stiff sanctions. He said: "We must be mindful of the sound advice of a Canadian court, 'If you cannot resist an impulse in any other way we will hang a rope in front of your eyes and perhaps that will help.'"   M.S.

Son of Charles Minturn B. and Gladys Van Deventer B. Educ: Brown Univ., A.B. 1942; Harvard Univ., LL.B. 1948; Cambridge Univ., diploma in intnl. law 1951; Georgetown Univ., LL.M. 1952. Married Harriet Nell Latson 1943. Daughters: Alison Lawrence; Prudence Oliver. With U.S. Army: served as an attorney to rank of major 1942–54; Colonel, U.S. Army Reserves 1954–68. Admitted to Massachusetts bar 1948; attorney, Office of General Counsel, U.S. Secty. of Defense 1954; Research Assoc, 1954–55, Lectr. then Asst. Prof. 1955–59, and Manley Hudson Prof. of Law since 1959, Harvard Law Sch., Cambridge, Mass.; law consultant to U.S. govt. depts. and other bodies, various times 1955–78; Visiting Prof. of Law, Univ. of Cambridge 1966–67; Head of South House, Radcliffe Coll., 1968–70; Judge, Permanent Court of Arbitration, The Hague 1968–75; Judge, Intnl. Court of Justice, The Hague since 1979. Member Advisory Cttee., Intnl. Law Reports since 1962; Vice Pres., American Branch of Intnl. Law Assn. since 1963; Member, Massachusetts Commn. on Ocean Mgmt. 1968–71, and Commn. on Marine Boundaries and Resources 1969–71; Ed.-in-Chief, American Jrnl. of Intnl. Law 1970–78; Member of Advisory Panel on Intnl. Law 1970–75, Counselor on Intnl. Law for Office of Legal Adviser 1971–72, and Advisory Panel on Law of the Sea 1973–78, U.S. Dept. of State, Washington, D.C.; Member, Bd. of Advisors, Law and Population Prog., Fletcher Sch. of Law and Diplomacy of Tufts Univ. 1971–78; Alternate Rep. of U.S. Delegation to Conferences of Govt. Experts on Intnl. Humanitarian Law, and to Diplomatic Conference on Intnl. Humanitarian Law 1972–77; Member, Bd. of Syndics, Harvard Univ. Press 1973–77, 1978–79; Pres 1974–76 and Hon. Vice Pres. since 1976, American Soc. of Intnl. Law. Member: American Law Inst.; American Bar Assn.; Egyptian and Philippine Socs. of Intnl. Law; British Inst. of Intnl. and Comparative Law; American Acad. of Arts and Sciences; U.S. Council on Foreign Relations. Hon. Member, Indian Soc. of Intnl. Law; Corresponding Member, Canadian Council on Intnl. Law; Assoc., Inst. de droit intnl. Hons: Hon. Fellow, Jesus Coll., Univ. of Cambridge since 1976; LL.D. from Brown and Georgetown Univs. 1979. *Editor:* Documents on the St. Lawrence Seaway, 1960; The Law of International Waterways, 1964; (with Doris Carroll) The Panama

Canal, 1965; (with F.V. Garcia-Amador and Louis B. Sohn) Recent Codification of the Law of State Responsibility for Injuries to Aliens, 1974.

JOHN BONHAM
Rock musician
Born Kidderminster, Worcestershire, England, May 31st, 1948
Died Windsor, Berkshire, England, September 25th, 1980

John Bonham described himself as "a simple, straightahead drummer and I don't pretend to be anything better than I am." Modest words, perhaps, coming from a member of the world's most popular rock group during the 1970s, but words with which few—including his co-members in *Led Zeppelin*—seemed inclined to disagree. Of Bonham, the band's lead singer Robert Plant once remarked: "I couldn't be like that . . . spending money and living it up and drinking champagne all the time. You burn yourself out. But Bonzo's a good ingredient for us. He raves and we sit down and do the thinking."

Born in Kidderminster, Worcestershire in 1948, Bonham wanted to be a drummer from the age of five. His initial kit consisted of his "mum's pots and pans" and his first real drum, a battered snare, was acquired at age ten. But this devotion to his craft had to survive the counterpressures of his working-class background, his marriage at age 17 and a resultant shortage of money, and connection with such forgettable Midlands bands as *Terry Webb and the Spiders* and *Way of Life*. Although he repeatedly promised his wife he was going to give up music and settle down, it proved impossible. "Every night I'd come home," he later recalled, "and just sit down at the drums. I'd be miserable if I didn't."

His reputation as the loudest, strongest drummer in the North of England during the soft-pop dominated mid-60s led to the refusal of more than one club owner to book any band of which he was a member. Self-taught, Bonham always subordinated technique to feeling in his playing, as he built a thunderous wall of sound by ignoring almost entirely the cymbal sets and frequently abandoning the sticks in favor of a vigorous, bare-handed assault.

In fact, it was Bonham's primal approach that ultimately shaped the distinctive *Led Zeppelin* sound. When Jimmy Page, ex-*Yardbird* lead guitarist, decided to form a new band in 1968, Bonham was recommended to him by his prospective lead singer, Robert Plant, who had sung with the drummer in the group *Band of Joy*. After listening to Bonham play, Page, who admired equally Eric Clapton's hard-rocking and John McLaughlin's jazz-blues guitar styles, finally decided in favor of the sound that would eventually become known to the band's millions of fans as "heavy metal."

Bonham, however, became a submerged element in the band. Page's flamboyant lead guitar, Plant's lyrics and sexual charisma and, to a lesser extent, bassist Robert Paul Jones's general musical sophistication were all more obvious to both fans and critics. The drummer's job was to provide the band's music with its dinosaurian spine, a task Bonham performed happily but one which failed to gain him ranking with rock percussionists like Ginger Baker of the legendary *Cream* or the late Keith Moon of *The Who,* both of whom pioneered the use of the rock drumkit as a lead instrument.

However, John Bonham's share of the band's astonomical earnings enabled him to enjoy life in approved rock-musician fashion from his 20th year on—such as racing a 250 mph dragster down a quarter mile strip on his Worcestershire estate-farm, and drinking and brawling. At his 25th birthday party in Los Angeles, Bonham and ex-Beatle George Harrison threw the cake at each other in the hotel's ballroom. Recently a scheduled performance of *Led Zeppelin* in Germany was cancelled because of Bonham's physical exhaustion. John Bonham was found dead at the home of group member John Paul Jones. He was 32.   R.C.

Married Pat Phillips 1965. Children: Jason; one daughter. Drummer 1964–68: Terry Webb and the Spiders; Way of Life: Band of Joy; U.K. touring co. of singer Tim Rose. Drummer, Led Zeppelin from 1968. *Recordings:* Led Zeppelin I, 1969; Led Zeppelin II, 1970; Led Zeppelin III, 1971; fourth album, untitled, 1972; Houses of the Holy, 1974; Physical Graffiti, 1975; Presence, 1977; The Song Remains the Same, 1978; In Through the Out Door, 1980.
Further reading: Led Zeppelin: A Biography by Ritchie Yorke, 1976.

LEWIS MILESTONE
Film director
Born Odessa, Ukraine, September 30th, 1895
Died Los Angeles, California, U.S.A., September 25th, 1980

As a film direcor, Lewis Milestone could, with equal justification, be considered unusually fortunate, or unusually unlucky. Early in his career he directed a film, *All Quiet on the Western Front,* which was immediately hailed as a classic of the cinema—and which, despite its unevenness, still retains that status. On the strength of that one film— it might be said—he rarely thereafter lacked work throughout a not especially distinguished career. Or, viewed more sympathetically: through a chance combination of circumstances, he peaked too soon, and spent the rest of his career shadowed by expectations that he would repeat his early triumph—which he never did.

Milestone was born in Odessa (his family name was Milstein), and brought up in Kishinev, capital of Russian Moldavia. In 1912 he was sent to Mitweide, Saxony, to study engineering, which he did without much enthusiasm. At Christmas 1913 his father sent money for a trip home; Milestone used it instead for a passage to the USA with two friends. They arrived in Hoboken, New Jersey, with six dollars between them. Milestone eventually found work in a photographer's studio, before enlisting in the US Signal Corps in 1917. He ended up in Washington making Army training films; one of his co-workers was Josef von Sternberg.

After discharge from the Army, Milestone made his way to Hollywood, where he worked first as a cutter, then as assistant director, editor and scenarist. His first film as director was a crime comedy, *Seven Sinners* (1925); he wrote his own scenario in collaboration with another young tyro, Darryl Zanuck. He directed six further movies during the silent period, two of them for Howard Hughes, including a war picture, *Two Arabian Knights* (1927), for which he received his first Academy Award. His first sound film, a backstage melodrama, was *New York Nights* (1929); Milestone disliked the end result enough to want to take his name off it.

Partly on the strength of *Two Arabian Knights,* partly thanks to his agent, Myron Selznick (brother of David), Milestone was assigned to the film of Remarque's best-selling novel, *All Quiet on the Western Front* (1930). It was an immediate success, and Milestone received his second Academy Award and was internationally acclaimed as a major new director.

The timing was perfect. Midway between the two wars, before the rise of Hitler, was the ideal moment for an eloquent anti-war statement, seen sympathetically from a German standpoint. Today, the film looks surprisingly uneven. The battle sequences, filmed with the fast lateral tracking shots that were to become Milestone's stock-in-trade, still communicate with fierce immediacy; and several key images—the hero stuck in a shell-hole with a dead French soldier, the doomed hand reaching for a butterfly—remain vividly in the memory. But long stretches of the film lapse into sentimentality, or heavy melodrama.

Milestone's next film, *The Front Page* (1931), equally accomplished, was more consistent in quality. Taken from Hecht and MacArthur's wise-cracking press-room drama, it was executed with wit, pace, and an admirably fluid camera. The rest of his 1930s films, though, consisted mainly of routine assignments, mostly uninspired comedies which the director did little to rescue. Exceptions were *The General Died at Dawn* (1936), a stylish, atmospheric drama set in war-ravaged China; and a taut, adeptly-controlled version of Steinbeck's novella, *Of Mice and Men* (1939).

War films were again in vogue during and after World War Two, and Milestone made several; the best was *A Walk in the Sun* (1945), though *North Star* (1943), whose pro-Russian stance later caused embarrassment, contains some effective sequences. *The Strange Love of Martha Ivers* (1946), his sole excursion into *film noir,* conveyed a powerful sense of pervasive guilt and obsession.

He worked abroad for a time in the 1950s, making films in Australia, Britain and Italy, and also directed for television, a medium of which he had a low opinion. His last war film, *Pork Chop Hill* (1959), was set in Korea.

In 1962, Milestone took over from Carol Reed on the re-make of *Mutiny on the Bounty.* It was his last assignment, and not a happy one. Like Reed, he was unable to get on with the temperamental Marlon Brando, and by his own account spent his time reading the paper while Brando took over direction. On the final film, Milestone received sole directorial credit; it could have been assigned, with equal justification, to half-a-dozen others.

Milestone once said: "My approach, my style is governed by the story, not the story by my style. The story is the important thing and the director has no business intruding." This could be taken as an honest, workmanlike attitude. But it may also point to the lack of directorial commitment which underlies the long slow decline of Milestone's career.   P.K.

Born Lewis Milstein. Emigrated to USA 1913. Educ: Mitweide, Saxony, engineering studies 1912. Worked in photography studio ca. 1913–17; enlisted in U.S. Signal Corps 1917; made Army training films, Washington, D.C. In Hollywood: cutter; asst. dir.; ed.; scenarist. Director from 1925; directed films in Australia, Britain and Italy 1950s. Hons: Acad. Award for Two Arabian Knights 1927. *Director: Silent films*—Seven Sinners, 1925; The Caveman; 1926; The New Klondyke, 1926; Two Arabian Knights, 1927; The Garden of Eden, 1928; The Racket, 1928; The Betrayal, 1929. *Sound films*—New York Nights, 1929; All Quiet on the Western Front, 1930; The Front Page, 1931; Rain, 1932; Hallelujah, I'm a Bum, 1933; The Captain Hates the Sea, 1934; Paris in Spring, 1935; Anything Goes, 1936; The General Died at Dawn, 1936; The Night of Nights, 1939; Of Mice and Men, 1940; Lucky Partners, 1940; (co-dir., Joris Ivens) Our Russian Front (documentary), 1941; My Life with Caroline, 1941; Edge of Darkness, 1943; The North Star, 1943; The Purple Heart, 1944; A Walk in the Sun, 1946; The Strange Love of Martha Ivers (uncredited co-dirs., Byron Haskin and Kirk Douglas), 1946; Arch of Triumph, 1948; No Minor Vices, 1948; The Red Pony, 1949; Halls of Montezuma, 1951; Kangaroo, 1952; Les Miserables, 1952; Melba, 1953; They Who Dare (Great Britain), 1954 (in U.S., 1955); La vedova X (Italy), 1956, (in U.S. as The Widow, 1957); Pork Chop Hill, 1959; Ocean's 11, 1960; Mutiny on the Bounty (uncredited co-dir., Carol Reed), 1962. *Uncredited films*—Fine Manners (Richard Rosson), 1926; The Kid Brother (Ted Wilde), 1927; Tempest (Sam Taylor, uncredited co-dir., Victor Tourjansky), 1928; Hell's Angels (Howard Hughes, uncredited co-dirs., James Whale and Luther Reed), 1930; Guest in the House (John Brahm, uncredited co-dir., André de Toth), 1944; PT 109 (Leslie H. Martinson), 1963; La guerra segreta (Terence Young, Werner Klinger, Christian-Jaque, Carlo Lizzani: in U.S. as The Dirty Game, 1966), 1965.

MAURICE F(ALCOLM) TAUBER
Librarian and cataloging specialist
Born Norfolk, Virginia, U.S.A., February 14th, 1908
Died New York City, U.S.A., September 26th, 1980

Maurice F. Tauber's work in the development of cataloging and classification systems helped bring order to the vast tide of information that flows daily into American libraries. Born in Norfolk, Virginia, in 1908, he earned his first bachelor's degree, in English and sociology, from Temple University, took a second bachelor's degree in library science from Columbia University, and returned to Temple for a Master's degree in education. When he became a doctoral student in library science at the University of Chicago, he had already served for three years as head of the Temple University library's cataloging department.

At Chicago, Tauber studied under Louis Round Wilson, with whom he wrote a series of biographical sketches on prominent national and academic librarians in America and Europe. The series was written to demonstrate alternatives to the appointment of the poet Archibald MacLeish as Librarian of Congress. Tauber and Wilson also collaborated on *The University Library, Its Organization and Administration* (1945). Tauber later edited Wilson's papers and wrote his biography.

In 1944, Tauber left a position as chief of the Preparations Divisions of the University of Chicago libraries to become assistant director of technical services at the Columbia University libraries, where he reorganized an antiquated system of acquisition, cataloging, binding, and reproduction operations. He was soon acknowledged one of the foremost experts on cataloging, classification, and library management in the United States, and was asked to serve on numerous committees and advisory boards concerned with the improvement of information services. *Technical Services in Libraries,* his 1954 book, is considered the standard work in the field, and the rules for descriptive cataloging on which he worked in committee were approved for general use by the American Library Association.

Tauber conducted some 80 surveys of academic, public, and institutional libraries, using research techniques developed in the social sciences. In 1961, while in Australia on a Fulbright scholarship, he was invited by the Australian Advisory Council on Bibliographic Services, to survey the state of the nation's library resources. Among his other surveys were analyses of the holdings of Columbia University, Cornell University, and a section of the Library of Congress. Theodore C. Hines, Tauber's colleague at Columbia, wrote: "In surveys, Tauber often recommends sweeping, radical, and total changes in a library's procedures and ways of doing things—such as, for example, shifting the bulk of a library's cataloging operations to non-professional staff. . . . Yet Tauber's recommendations are almost always put into practice. This happens because they are so carefully presented, the background so meticulously gone over, the objections so careful anticipated, and the conclusions so inevitably drawn from the data."

In 1954, Tauber who had been teaching at the Columbia University School of Library Science for ten years, was made Melvil Dewey Professor of Library Science. His students have described him as a stimulating teacher, with a retentive memory and a Socratic, anecdotal style, generous with his time and encouragement and uncompromising in his insistence on impeccable research. He was the editor of a number of professional journals, including *College and Research Libraries,* and served as consultant to dictionaries and encyclopedias, in addition to chairing numerous conferences. In 1968 he participated in a global strategy discussion at the Naval War College in Newport, Rhode Island.

Tauber, who composed crossword puzzles in his spare time, was a prolific writer; his biobibliography, published in 1973, lists a total of more than 300 publications since 1934 (including monographs, surveys, book reviews, course outlines, and contributions to journals, conferences, and books). His collected papers have been donated to the Special Collections division of Columbia University's library.

Tauber was married and had two sons. In 1966 he established the Tauber-Begner Award in Technical Services, in memory of his wife and brother-in-law, for students at Columbia's School of Library Sciences.   J.P./D.S.

Son of A. Albert T. and Leona (Miller) T. Married Rose Anne Begner 1932 (d. 1964). Sons: Robert M.; Frederick J. Educ: Temple Univ., Philadelphia, B.S. 1930, M.Ed. 1939; Columbia Univ. Sch. of Library Service, B.S. 1934; Univ. of Chicago Library Sch. (Carnegie

Fellow), Ph.D. 1941. Asst. 1927–35 and Head of Catalog Dept.
1935–38, Temple Univ. Library. With Univ. of Chicago Library Sch.:
Research Asst. 1934–41; Instr. 1942–44; Asst. Prof. 1944. With Univ.
of Chicago Libraries: Chief of Catalog Dept. 1941–42; Chief of
Preparations Div. 1942–44. Asst. Dir. of Tech. Services, Columbia
Univ. Libraries 1944–47. With Columbia Univ. Sch. of Library
Service: Asst. Prof. 1944–46; Assoc. Prof. 1947–49; Prof. 1949–54;
Melvil Dewey Prof. of Library Science 1954–76; Dewey Prof. emeritus
since 1976. With College and Research Libraries (jrnl.): Asst. to
Managing Ed. 1944–46; Managing Ed. 1947–48; Ed. 1948–62. Mem-
ber, Bd. of Eds., Journal of Cataloging and Classification 1956;
Advisory Ed. 1957–61 and Editorial Advisor from 1962, Library
Resources and Technical Service (jrnl.); Assoc. Ed. 1957–62 and
Member of Editorial Bd. 1963–69, American Documentation (jrnl.);
Corresponding Ed. 1962–66, Journal of Higher Education; Advisory
Ed. and Consultant from 1963, Encyclopedia Americana; Member of
Editorial Bd. ASIS, Journal of the American Society for Information
Research 1970–72; Issue Ed., Library Trends (jrnl.), Vols. 2, 4, 10,
13. Member, Advisory Cttee. on Descriptive cataloging to Librarian
of Congress 1946–47; Member, Bd. of Dirs., Assn. of American
Library Schs. 1948–50; Member, Cttee. on Organization of Informa-
tion, American Documentation Inst. 1948–58; Member, Jt. Cttee. on
Education for Librarianship, Natl. Council of Library Assns. 1949–79;
Member, Advisory Cttee. for the Directorate of Information Sci-
ences, Air Force Office of Scientific Research 1962–63; Member of
Advisory Bd. since 1963, Encyclopedia International; Advisor and
Consultant since 1965, Grolier Universal Encyclopedia; Consultant,
American Heritage Dictionary of the English Language; Member of
Gen. Cttee., Anglo-American Cataloging Rules; Member of Advisory
Bd., The College and Adult Reading List of Books in Literature and
Fine Arts; Consultant, Random House Dictionary of the English
Language; Bd. of Advisors, Naval War Coll. Pres., Beta Phi Mu
1967–68; Pres., Div. of Cataloging and Classification, and Member,
American Library Assn.; Founding Member, Bd. of the American
Soc. of Indexers. Member: American Assn. of Univ. Professors; New
York State Library Assn.; New York Regional Group Catalogers.
Hons: Margaret Mann Award, 1953; Melvil Dewey Award and
Medal, American Library Assn. 1955; Fulbright Scholarship, Aus-
tralia 1961; Award, Assn. of Coll. and Research Libraries 1962;
Awards, Naval War Coll. 1967, 1968; Distinguished Service Award,
Findlay Coll. Library 1968; Citation for Establishment of Cooperative
Coll. Libraries Center, Atlanta 1969; First New York Technical
Services Librarian's Citation 1973. *Selected Works: Library Surveys*—
Australian Libraries; Columbia Univ.; Univ. of South Carolina;
Cornell Univ.; Jewish Theological Seminary; Library of Hawaii;
Canadian Dept. of Agriculture; Register and Catalogue Dept.,
Metropolitan Museum of Art; others. *Books*—(with Louis Round
Wilson) The University Library, 1945; (with others) Technical Ser-
vices in Libraries, 1954; Cataloging and Classification, 1960; (with
Edith Wise) Classification Systems, 1961; (ed., with R.E. Kingery)
Book Catalogs, 1963; Louis Round Wilson, Librarian and Admin-
istrator, 1967; (ed., with Irlene R. Stephens) Library Surveys, 1968;
(comp., with Hilda Feinberg) Book Catalogs, 1971; Library Binding
Manual, 3rd ed. 1972; others. Contributor of hundreds of articles,
essays, and book reviews to professional journals and conferences.
Interview: "Maurice Falcolm Tauber," in Librarians Speaking (ed. by
Guy R. Lyle), 1970.
Further reading: "Maurice F. Tauber" by Robert B. Downs, in
College and Research Libraries, May 1962; Maurice Falcolm Tauber:
A Bibliography, 1934–1973 by Marion G. Szigethy, 1974.

SIR JOHN (LIONEL) KOTELAWALA
Prime Minister of Ceylon (now Sri Lanka)
Born Colombo, Ceylon, April 4th, 1897
Died Colombo, Sri Lanka, September 28th, 1980

Sir John Kotelawala, the third prime minister of Ceylon, now Sri Lanka, played a prominent part in his country's political development before, during, and immediately after it gained independence from Great Britain in 1948. A fighter of the old colonialism under Britain, he fought the "new colonialism" of communism even more aggressively, calling it "nakedly totalitarian in intention and effect." He was one of the few Asian leaders who felt that colonialism in any form had to be opposed; but that the old colonialism, when correctly and frankly assessed, was not utterly undemocratic or completely indifferent to people's needs.

The son of a police inspector who committed suicide, Kotelawala received a British education under the watchful eye of his mother, to whom he gave great credit for his values and approach to life. Riots in 1915 forced him to leave school and go to Europe for five years. His vow to return and defend his country led him to become a soldier in 1922 in the Ceylon Light Infantry. His military training and love of sport helped him develop a team spirit and discipline—"The ability to face triumph and disaster with equanimity, which are so useful in fitting one for public life."

Entering politics in 1931, he represented his home district in the first State Council. He took on progressively more responsible positions in the colonial government, acting as Minister of Agriculture and Lands briefly in 1934 and becoming Minister of Communications and Works late the following year. During the Second World War, Kotelawala served on the War Council and afterwards he became Chairman of the Post-War Problems Committee. By 1947, the pressure for independence was growing within and outside Ceylon. Persistent efforts on the part of high Ceylonese officials had forced the British government in 1943 to propose reform to the Ceylon Constitution. One of these high officials was D.S. Senanayake, a relative of Kotelawala's. Senanayake's push for independence led, in 1948, to his election as first prime minister, and Kotelawala became Minister of Transport and Works. However, their party, the United National Party, which they helped to found in 1947, did not truly represent the people of Ceylon: it ignored the vastly impoverished and illiterate.

Several serious problems plagued the new state: Indo-Ceylon relations were strained because of the question of citizenship of the ethnic Indian Tamils, who made up more than 20% of Ceylon's population; and the economy, unable to support the country's people, suffered from high prices for rice, the food staple, and tumbling rubber prices, the main export. While Kotelawala was visiting Europe and the U.S. in 1952, Senanayake was killed in a riding accident. Kotelawala expected to be named premier, but Senanayake had, apparently, left instructions that his son, Dudley Senanayake, should succeed him. However the younger Senanayake was forced to resign as prime minister following a series of nationwide strikes which had led to a state of emergency. Kotelawala was the natural successor, and taking office in 1953, he was faced with a nation on the verge of revolution because of the government's decision to increase the price of rationed rice. To prevent increased violence, he promised "I shall have no truck with those who believe in revolutionary methods in politics and it will be one of my foremost duties to stamp out Communism in this country." A series of quiet measures and a Royal visit to Ceylon in 1954 quelled the immediate unrest. The other major problem of his administration, the stateless position of the Indian Tamils, whom worked in Ceylon's tea plantations remained unsolved, despite the joint efforts of himself and the opposition. Nehru steadfastly refused to recognize the Tamils as Indian nationals.

Kotelawala proposed a conference of South East Asian prime ministers in 1954, and the premiers of Burma, India, Indonesia and Pakistan attended, Kotelawala chaired the conference, whose resolution on the Indo-China War was placed before the Geneva Conference and helped lead to a measure of peace in the region. The conference, by setting up an association of Asian states filled the area's power vacuum; it also paved the way for the Bandung Conference, held in Indonesia in 1955, at which 29 African and Asian nations met to plan economic and cultural cooperation, and oppose colonialism. China, a nation Kotelawala derided ("We sell you rubber, you sell us rice. Ceylon has no other friendship or dealing with Communist China. Nor does she want it."), took a major role at the international meeting. Speaker after speaker denounced Western colonialism. Kotelawala differed, attacking instead the Soviet domination of its satellites. His view that communism was a form of imperialism upset his neighbors, embarrassed Nehru, shocked Chou En-Lai, but won support from the leaders of Iraq, Lebanon, Pakistan and Turkey and gained him world headlines. Eventually the conference adopted a resolution condemning colonialism "in all its manifestations." Its call for universal membership in the UN was later realized.

Kotelawala's achievements on the international level were important. At home, however, he and his party were facing nationwide rejection in the elections of 1956. This election has been described as a turning point in the history of Ceylon, in that the transfer of power from one group to another amounted to a social revolution. The adult franchise, granted in 1931, became fully effective for the first time, and finally the needs and interests of the rural population became paramount. Nationalistic feelings on religion and language swept the left wing People's United Front under Bandaranaike into office. Kotelawala and his people, reminders of British Colonial rule, were out for good. Upon his retirement, Kotelawala was made a Companion of Honor. In the preceding year he published his forthright book, *An Asian Prime Minister's Story*.

A rich man and a lavish host, Sir John gave his residence on the outskirts of Colombo to the Sri Lankan government to house a national defense academy.   H.W.

Son of John K., police inspector. Married; one daughter. Buddhist. Educ: Royal Coll., Colombo, Ceylon. Left sch. 1915; Christ's Coll., Cambridge, one year's study of agriculture. Member, Ceylon Light Infantry 1922–1933; retired as Col. 1939; promoted to Gen. 1980: elected Member of State Council 1931; Minister of Agriculture and Lands 1934; Minister of Communication and Works 1936–1953; Member, War Council 1939–1945; Leader, House of Representatives 1950–53; Prime Minister and Minister of Defense and External Affairs 1953–56. Hons: Knighted (KBE) 1948; appointed Privy Councillor 1954; Grand Cross, Legion of Honor, France 1954; Grand Cross,

Order of Merit, Italy 1954; Grand Cross, Order of White Elephant, Thailand 1955; C.H. 1956; LL.D., Univ. of Ceylon. *Author:* An Asian Prime Minister's Story, 1956.

HAROLD A(LEXANDER) ABRAMSON
Medical researcher, psychiatrist, and educator
Born New York City, U.S.A., November 27th, 1899
Died Cold Spring Harbor, New York, U.S.A., September 29th, 1980

Dr. Harold Abramson was a medical researcher who specialized in the investigation of psychological factors in asthma, eczema, and allergies. He came to national attention in 1975 when a Senate subcommittee opened an inquiry into the CIA's program of clandestine experiments with the hallucinogenic drug LSD, in which he had done research.

Abramson was born in New York City in 1899, served in World War One, and received his M.D. degree in 1923 from Columbia University's College of Physicians and Surgeons. After an internship at New York's Mt. Sinai Hospital, he was awarded fellowships to attend University College in London and the Kaiser Wilhelm Institute of Berlin. From 1928 to 1939 he taught on the medical faculties of Johns Hopkins, Harvard, Cornell, and Columbia Universities.

During the Second World War Abramson worked in the Technical Division of the Chemical Warfare Service on penicillin aerosol therapy of the lungs. He later joined the staff of Mt. Sinai Hospital as chief of the allergy clinic and became a resident psychiatrist at the Biology Laboratory at Cold Spring Harbor, Long Island. He founded a number of institutions dedicated to helping asthmatics, including the Asthmatic Children's Foundation and the Asthma Care Association, and was a founding editor of the Journal of Asthma Research. His work was used in the development of the theory of the Cronus-complex (a smotheringly close relationship between mother and child) as a contributing factor in severe cases of childhood asthma.

Abramson was one of the first researchers in the United States to study the potential medical applications of LSD, which he believed would prove useful in the treatment of schizophrenic patients. In the 1950s, as a consultant to the Department of the Army, he conducted experiments with the drug, in secrecy, on behalf of the CIA. On one occasion in 1953 he was called in to examine Dr. Frank Olson, an Army biochemist who had been fed a dose of LSD without his knowledge by two CIA agents. Olson developed psychotic delusions, and, on Abramson's advice, was taken for psychiatric care to New York City, where he committed suicide. Information about the incident was suppressed by the CIA for 22 years. In 1975, when the case came under investigation by a Senate subcommittee, Abramson sent a telegram describing his work and the foundations that had supported it. Olson's wife and three children later sued the CIA and won a settlement of $750,000.

Abramson, who was married twice and had three children, was the author and editor of a number of scholarly works, including *The Uses of LSD in Psychotherapy and Alcoholism* and *The Somatic and Psychiatric Treatment of Asthma*. At the time of his death, from cancer, he was director of psychiatric research at South Oaks Hospital in Amityville, Long Island.   L.R./J.P.

Son of F. Samuel A. and M. Rose (Richard) A. Married: (1) Barbara H. Smith 1933 (div.); (2) Virginia Tenney 1955. Children: 1st marriage—Alexandra Orhun; Harold A.; Barbara Vanderploeg; Howland W. Educ: Columbia Univ., B.A. 1920; Columbia Univ. Coll. of Physicians and Surgeons, M.D. 1923; Research Fellow, University Coll., London 1925–26; Fellow, Natl. Research Council, Kaiser Wilhelm Inst. for Physical Chemistry and Electrochemistry, Berlin 1926–27. Mil. Service: served in WWI; Tech. Div., Chem. Warfare Service, WWII; also Asst. Chief, then Chief, Def. Material; Lt. Col., Medical Corps Reserve. awarded Legion of Merit. Asst. in inorganic chemistry, Columbia Univ. 1918–20; intern, Mt. Sinai Hosp., NYC 1923–25; Instr. in medicine, Johns Hopkins Univ. 1928–29; Instr. in biochemical sciences, Harvard Univ. 1929–31; Assoc. in bacteriology and immunology, Cornell Univ. 1934–35; Asst. Prof of physiology, Columbia Univ. 1935–39; Chief, allergy clinic, Mt. Sinai Hosp., NYC; Research Psychiatrist, The Biology Laboratory, Cold Spring Harbor, N.Y. 1952–61; Dir. of Psychiatric Research, South Oaks Hosp., Amityville, N.Y. Consultant: in research psychiatry, State Hosp., Central Islip, N.Y. since 1956; Community Hosp., Glen Cove, N.Y. since 1958; Dept. of Army ca. 1950s. Founding Ed. and Ed.-in-Chief since 1962, Journal of Asthma Research; Member of Editorial Bd., Psychosomatic Medicine; Member of Editorial Bd., Annals of Allergy. Co-founded, Asthma Care Assn. of America 1954; Co-founder and V.P., Asthmatic Children's Found. 1962; Co-founder, Asthmatic Publications Soc. 1963. Trustee, Biology Laboratory, Cold Spring Harbor. Hons: Fellow of American Psychiatric Assn.; New York Acad. of Medicine; American Assn. for Advancement of Science; New York Acad. of Science; American Acad. of Allergists (also Distinguished Fellow); American Coll. of Chest Physicians. Pres., American Coll. of Allergists. Member: American Physiological Soc.; American Soc. of Biological Chemists; New York County Medical Soc.; Soc, for Experimental Biology and Medicine; Alpha Omega Alpha; Epsilon Chi. *Author:* Electrokinetic Phenomena, 1934; Electrophoresis of Proteins, 1942; Dimensional Analysis for Students of Medicine, 1950; The Patient Speaks, 1956; Psychological Problems in Father-Son Relationships, 1969. *Editor:* Problem of Consciousness, 5 vols., 1950–54; Somatic and Psychiatric Treatment of Asthma, 1952; Neuropharmacology, 5 vols.; The Use of LSD in Psychotherapy and Alcoholism, 1967; Clinical Applications of the Ultrasonic Nebulizer, 1968. Frequent contributor to professional journals.

OCTOBER

P(ATRICK) E(UGENE) HAGGERTY
Industrialist, engineer, and writer
Born Harvey, North Dakota, U.S.A., March 17th, 1914
Died Dallas, Texas, U.S.A., October 1st, 1980

P.E. Haggerty was the president, honorary chairman, and general director of Texas Instruments Inc., one of the world's largest manufacturers of electronics products. During Haggerty's tenure, Texas Instruments became the leading producer of silicon transistors, germanium radio transistors, and integrated circuits, which made possible the large-scale manufacture of miniature electronic calculators. Haggerty also wrote *The Productive Society* (1974) and contributed many articles to scientific and business journals. An influential member of the business community, he served as chairman of Rockefeller University's Board of Trustees, as an executive committee member of the Trilateral Commission, as director of the A.H. Belo Corporation, and as a member of the Chase Manhattan Bank's International Advisory Committee.

Born in a small North Dakota town, P.E. Haggerty studied electrical engineering at Marquette University. As an undergraduate he was employed part-time by Milwaukee's Badger Carton Company as an engineer. Haggerty graduated with a B.S. degree in 1936, and he established academic records that remain unequaled. He subsequently joined Badger Carton as production manager and became assistant general manager, overseeing all engineering and manufacturing phases of production in 1942, when he enlisted in the U.S. Navy Reserves. During World War Two, Haggerty, a lieutenant, served with the Bureau of Aeronautics in Washington, D.C., as head of its electronic production section. In 1945 Haggerty returned to civilian life as general manager of Geophysical Service Incorporated's (GSI) Engineering Research Laboratory and Production Branch in Dallas, Texas. Six years later, GSI was absorbed, as a subsidiary, into Texas Instruments, Inc. Haggerty served as executive Vice President and Director of Texas Instruments until 1958 when he became President; in 1966 he was elected Chairman, a post he held until his retirement 10 years later.

Haggerty moved the company into the production of transistors in the early 1950s. To Haggerty, the transistor, which had been invented in 1948, represented the future of technical development in the electronics field. In 1952 the Bell Telephone Laboratories placed the manufacture of transistors on the open market and, by 1954, Texas Instruments had become the first company to produce silicon transistors and germanium radio transistors on a commercial, industrially competitive basis. Silicon transistors helped improve the technology of satellites and rocket guidance systems while germanium transistors led to the development of the first pocket radio. Haggerty quickly initiated discussions with his company's technicians which led to the invention, in company laboratories, of the integrated circuit in 1958. This invention not only reduced the cost and size of electronic function equipment, it also increased reliability and scope. Mass production of integrated circuits has made electronic devices a common feature of modern society; applied first to military weapons systems, computers, and industrial management techniques, they are now popularly available in the form of hand-held "pocket" calculators.

In the 1960s, Haggerty organized the Objectives, Strategies, Tactics System (OST) which developed integrated circuitry for intercontinental ballistic missiles systems and complex radar techniques for tactical aircraft. In 1963 Texas Instruments produced and marketed a new method for digitally recording and processing information obtained from the seismic detection of oil. Three years later, the company developed the Advanced Scientific Computer, which is used to process, at high speeds, vast amounts of scientific data. Under Haggerty's leadership, Texas Instruments increased its overseas markets and, between 1958 and 1973, the company's annual sales of $92 million and its 25,000 employees grew to $1.3 billion and almost 75,000 employees in more than two dozen countries.   T.B.

Son of Michael Eugene H., telegrapher, and Lillian Evenson H. Married Beatrice Menne 1938. Children: Sheila Margaret; Kathleen Mary; Patrick Eugene; Teresa Ann; Michael Gamble. Catholic. Educ: Marquette Univ., Wisc., Bachelor of Electrical Engineering 1936. Mil. Service: Officer, and later head, Electronics Components Group, U.S. Navy Reserve Bureau of Aeronautics WWII. With Badger Carton Co., Milwaukee: Part-time cooperative student engineer 1935–36; Production Mgr, and later Asst. Gen. Mgr. 1936–42. Gen. Mgr. of Lab. and Manufacturing Div., Geophysical Service Inc., Dallas 1945–51. With Texas Instruments Inc., Dallas: Exec. V.P. and Dir. 1951–58; Pres. 1958–66; Chmn. of the Bd. and Chief Corporate Officer 1966–76; Retired Hon. Chmn. and Gen. Dir. from 1976. Dir. and member of Exec. Cttee., Community Chest of Greater Dallas 1959–60; Pres. 1962 and Co-Chmn. of merger Cttee 1963, Inst. of Radio Engineers; Member, President's Science Advisory Cttee. 1969–72; Member of Bd. of Govs., U.S. Postal Service 1971–73; Natl. fund Co-chmn. of campaigns for American Red Cross 1972–73; Chmn., Natl. Council of Educational Research 1973–74. With Rockefeller Univ: Trustee; Exec. Cttee. Member; Chmn. of Bd. of Trustees from 1975. Member, Nuclear Oversight Panel 1980; Member, Intnl. Advisory Cttee. of the Chase Manhattan Bank, NYC; Dir., A.H. Belo Corp., Dallas; Member of the Corp., Natl. Industrial Conference Bd., Owner, The Dallas Morning News; Life member and Vice-Chmn., Natl. Security Industrial Assoc.; Member, Bd. of Trustees, Univ. of Dallas; Life Member, Texas Acad. of Science; Exec. Cttee. Member, Trilateral Commn. Member: Soc. of Exploration Geophysicists; Natl. Acad. of Engineering; The Business Council; Navy League of the U.S.; American Assoc. for the Advance of Science. Hons: Distinguished Service Award, Univ. of Wisconsin 1964; Medal of Honor, Electronic Industries Assoc. 1967; Founders Award, Inst. of Electrical and Electronics Engineers (IEEE) 1968; Industrial Research Inst. Medalist 1969; Brotherhood Award, Natl. Conference of Christians and Jews 1970; John Fritz Medal, IEEE 1971; Medal of Achievement, Western Electronic Manufacturers Assoc. 1972; numerous hon. degrees 1959–74; Fellow, IEEE. *Author:* Management Philosophies and Practices of Texas Instruments Incorporated, 1965; The Productive Society, 1974; "Industrial Research and Development: in Science and the Evolution of Public Policy,

1973; "Individualized Instruction and Productivity in Education": in Individualized Instruction in Engineering Education, 1974; numerous company, professional and trade publication articles.

ERIC HASS
Editor, writer, and political activist
Born Lincoln, Nebraska, U.S.A., 1905
Died Santa Rosa, California, U.S.A., October 2nd, 1980

Committed to the ideals of both the U.S. Constitution and the philosophy of Karl Marx, Eric Hass was four times the presidential candidate of the Socialist Labor Party. Hass also ran for the U.S. Senate in Oregon and campaigned for the mayoralty of New York City on a platform that called for economic equality and worker-controlled industries, with management to be elected from within the unions themselves. Guided, he said, by Marx's advice to "doubt everything," Hass came into conflict in the 1960s with the party he had served for over 30 years as an organizer, editor, writer, and political candidate.

The son of German and Danish immigrants, Hass briefly attended the University of Nebraska but left school to become an itinerant laborer, working at such odd jobs as railroad brakeman, newspaper-man, waiter, and cook. Introduced to trade union militancy by the socialist writings of Daniel DeLeon, Hass, now committed to the "salvation of democracy" by worker control of industry, joined the Socialist Labor Party (SLP) in 1928. Four years later, he became a full-time organizer for the party and, in 1932, Hass moved to New York to become editor of *The Weekly People,* a position he held until 1968.

In the 1940s, Hass became the socialist party's oficial candidate for public office. He sought the New York City mayoralty three times in that decade, and he ran for the U.S. Senate in 1944 and in 1946. Occasionally, Hass was listed on the ballot as the candidate of the Industrial Government Party; this strategy was employed by the SLP to avoid identification with the then opprobrious label "socialist."

As party spokesman on national and international affairs, Hass was the presidential candidate of the SLP in each national election from 1952 to 1964. Hass campaigned, not to win nor even to draw votes from the Democrats and Republicans, but, as he put it, "to get people off dead center in their political thinking," and to address such issues as the Stalinist perversion of Marxism and the alienation of workers by automation in industry. Hass's greatest electoral success came in 1960 when his name was entered on the ballot in 14 states and he received 46,478 votes.

After 1964 Hass became increasingly disillusioned by leftist politics. To the militant blacks and radical students of the New Left, Hass was an anachronism, an "Old Left" ideologue who bore the scars of sectarian political disputes which dated back to the 1930s. Moreover, he disagreed with members of the New Left who advocated "tactical" violence; still, Hass did not attack these revolutionaries. Instead, he criticized his own party for adopting an "antagonistic attitude" toward radicals and also for having failed to provide these militants with a vision of society toward which they might democratically work. After years of ideological wrangling, the SLP's executive council expelled Hass in April, 1969, charging him with "disruptive contempt." Hass called the expulsion an example of "the intellectual stultification that is the logical consequence of the substitution of dogma for dialectics."

In the 1970s Hass worked as a librarian for the Trinity Parish in New York City and, as a freelance writer, he published several articles on such topics as conservation and gardening. He died after a heart attack in Santa Rosa, California, where he had retired in 1977. R.C.

Attended Univ. of Nebraska. Itinerant laborer ca. 1924–32; Organizer 1932–38 and ed., The Weekly People (party paper) 1938–68, Socialist Labor Party; Presidential candidate of Socialist Labor Party 1952, 1956, 1960, and 1964; candidate for City Council Pres., NYC, 1957; Mayoral candidate, NYC, 1941, 1945, 1949, U.S. Senate 1944 and 1946. Librarian, Trinity Parish, NYC, 1969–71. *Author:* John L. Lewis Exposed, 1936; Socialistic Industrial Unionism, 1940; The Americanism of Socialism, 1941; The Labor Draft, Step to Industrial Slavery, 1943; Socialism Answers Anti-Semitism, 1944; Stalinist Imperialism, 1946; Fascism is Still a Menace, 1948; Socialism: World Without Race Prejudice, 1949; The Socialist Labor Party and the Internationals, 1949; Militarism, Labor's Foe, 1955; Dave Beck, Labor Merchant, 1955; What Workers Should Know About Automation, 1956; The Reactionary Right, 1963; Capitalism, Breeder of Race Prejudice, 1964.

SIR CONRAD L. CORFIELD
British Civil Servant
Born Berkshire, England, August 15th, 1893
Died England, October 3rd, 1980

Sir Conrad Corfield, who began his twenty-seven year service with the government of India in 1920, was an advisor during the period of negotiations for Indian self-rule. He attended St. Lawrence College before World War One, during which he served in France as Captain of the First Cambridgeshire Regiment. Following the war, Corfield attended St. Catherine's College, Cambridge, and, while there, applied for a post with the Indian Foreign and Political Department; he was among the first candidates chosen to serve in the Indian Civil Service.

For 18 months, after receiving district training in the Punjab, Corfield served as Assistant Private Secretary to the Viceroy, at that time Lord Reading in Delhi. He subsequently returned to the Punjab for District work and, in 1925, was selected for service in the Foreign and Political Department of the Government of India. A series of appointments—Secretary to the Agent for the Government General in the Western Indian States, Assistant to the Political Agent in the Rapjunta States—led in 1931 to Corfield's installation as head of the Political Agency in Central India's Southern States and Malwa, and, later, as Secretary to the Resident in the Nizam's Dominions, Hyderbad. Corfield continued to advance through the Indian Civil

Courtesy Dr. H.M.C. Corfield

Service in the 1930s, and he returned to England in 1932 as Advisor for Rewa at the Indian Round-table Conference. From 1934 to 1938, Corfield was Joint Secretary of the Foreign and Political Department; he was awarded the Companion, Order of the Indian Empire in 1937.

Appointed Political Advisor to Lord Wavell, the Crown Representative, in 1945, Corfield was the official link between the Viceroy and the Chamber of Princes while plans for granting self-rule to India were underway. A supporter of the Chamber of Princes, Corfield was distressed by the absorption of Princedoms into the unified country of India under the incoming government of Jawaharlal Nehru. When Lord Mountbatten replaced Lord Wavell in early 1947, Corfield remained as Political advisor until the transfer of power had been completed in August of that year. He then returned to England where he was active in local education and political affairs. In 1975 Corfield published his memoirs, *The Princely India I Knew*.   J.S.

Son of Reverend Egerton C. Married: (1) Phyllis Bertha Pugh 1922 (d. 1932); (2) Sylvia Daunt 1961 (d. 1977). Children: 1st marriage— one son; one daughter. Educ: St. Lawrence Coll.; St. Catherine's Coll., Cambridge, grad. 1920. Mil. Service: Capt., 1st Cambridgeshire Reg., France WWI (M.C.). Entered Indian Civil Service 1920; Asst. Private Secty. to Viceroy, Delhi, 1921; Asst. Commnr. of the Punjab 1921–22; joined Foreign and Political Dept. of Govt. of India 1924; Secty. to Political Agent, the Rajputana States 1928; headed Political Agency in Southern States of Central India and Malwa 1921; Secty. to Resident in the Nizam's Dominions, Hyderabad 1931; Advisor to Delegation for Rewa, 3rd session of Indian Round-table Conference 1932; V.P. Rewa State Council 1933–34; Joint Secty., Political Dept., Simla 1934–38; Resident at Jaipur 1939–40; Officiating Resident for Rajputana 1939; Resident for the Punjab States 1941–45; Political Advisor to the Crown Rep. 1945–47; Gov. and V.P., St. Lawrence Coll., ca. 1950–80. Chmn. 1950–54 and Pres. 1954–62, Wokingham Div. Conservative Assoc.; Chmn., Wessex Area 1960–63; Chmn., Yately Industries for Disabled Girls 1954–64. Member: St. John Council for Berkshire 1944–62; St. Crispin's Sch., Wokingham 1954–67; Finchampstead and Parish Council 1955–61. Hons: CIE 1937; CSI 1942; KCIE 1945. *Author:* The Princely India I knew, 1975.

PYOTR (MIRONOVICH) MASHEROV
Soviet political leader and war hero
Born Shirki, Vityebsk, Byelorussia, U.S.S.R., February 26th, 1918
Died Moscow, U.S.S.R., October 4th, 1980

Pyotr Masherov, one of the youngest members of the Politburo, was a leading contender for the office of Premier of the Soviet Union and the position of General Secretary of the Soviet Communist Party. He was active in party, regional, and national politics for almost four decades.

Masherov, the son of Byelorussian peasants, was born in a rural village in 1918 during the Russian civil war. After graduating from a teachers' training college in 1939, he taught mathematics and physics at a secondary school until 1941, when Germany attacked the Soviet Union. Masherov subsequently went underground to become an organizer and leader of the resistance movement. During the period of nazi occupation, he commanded a Partisan detachment of guerillas, was appointed commissar of a Partisan brigade, and, having joined the Communist Party in 1943, became First Secretary of an underground Komsomol, or Young Communist League, regional committee. After the liberation in 1944 he was awarded the title "Hero of the Soviet Union" for his participation in the anti-nazi resistance.

Rather than return to teaching after the war, Masherov became involved in the Komsomol, often a training ground for potential party official. Masherov served as First Secretary of the Molodechno (Byelorussia) Regional Committee. He was later transferred to the Byelorussian capital, Minsk, to take a seat on the Komsomol Central Committee and in 1947, he became First Secretary, a position he held until 1954.

Masherov advanced from Communist youth league activities to responsibilities in the Byelorussian Communist Party apparatus. He steadily worked his way through the ranks, holding several positions with the Party's regional political organization, and rose to the position of Communist Party chief of the Byelorussian Soviet Socialist Republic, the third-largest republic in the USSR.

Masherov's prominence in the Byelorussian Communist Party led to his involvement in national government and central party affairs. Except for a brief period in the early 1960s, he had served since 1950 as a deputy to the Supreme Soviet, which convened annually in Moscow but exercised little real power. In 1964, however, Masherov had been chosen by the Kremlin to be Candidate Member, and two years later to be Full Member, of the Central Committee of the Communist Party of the Soviet Union, the important legislative body of the Soviet government. When, later that same year, he was named Candidate Member of the Politburo (formerly called the Presidium) of the Central Committee, he acceded to the highest branch of the USSR government. Masherov was elected by his fellow deputies in 1966 to the Presidium of the Supreme Soviet, which was authorized to act only when the entire body was not in session and held little more than symbolic authority.

As a Candidate Member, Masherov was granted a voice, but not a vote, in the Politburo. But he was nevertheless an influential member and played a key role in the formulation of Kremlin foreign policy particularly in détente with Western Europe. For helping to improve relations between member-nations of the Warsaw Pact, he was named "Hero of Socialist Labor," the Soviet Union's most prestigious civilian award.

As a war hero and a highly accessible leader, Masherov was popular with both the Byelorussian people and with his political colleagues. He was named to the Order of Lenin seven times and awarded the Gold Star Medal, the highest honor given to Soviet citizens. Western acquaintances described him as "intelligent," "affable," and "urbane." He impressed foreign diplomts with his ability to discuss international affairs knowledgeably and without reference to Soviet dogma.

During the early 1970s Western observers believed that Masherov was being groomed to succeed Alexei Kosygin [q.v.]; even inside the Kremlin rumors circulated that Masherov might be next in line to the ailing Premier. Masherov's influence began to decline, however, after the Communist Party Congress of 1976, which rejected many of the policies proposed by the relatively younger generation of party leaders. Despite his influence in the Politburo, Masherov was never made Full Member and it seems unlikely that he would have succeeded Leonid Brezhnev as General Secretary or Kosygin as Premier; his inability to advance further in the Politburo hierarchy denied that possibility.

The announcement of Masherov's death in an automobile accident, transmitted by the Soviet press agency Tass on behalf of the Central Committee of the Communist Party, expressed "profound regret" and praised him as "a man of vast erudition" who possessed "remarkable" qualities of leadership and organizational ability.   K.B.

Son of peasants. Educ: Kirov Pedagogical Inst., Vityebsk, grad. 1939. Secondary sch. teacher 1939–41. Joined Communist Party of the Soviet Union 1943; First Secty., Molodechno Regional Cttee., Byelorussian Komsomol 1944–46; Secty. 1946–47 and First Secty. 1947–54, Central Cttee., Byelorussian Komsomol; Deputy to Supreme Soviet of the USSR 1950–62 and from 1966. With Byelorussian Communist Party: Second Secty., Minsk Regional Cttee. 1954–55; First Secty., Brest Regional Cttee. 1955–59; Secty. 1959, Second Secty. 1959–65 and First Secty. from 1965, Central Cttee. Candidate member 1961–64 and Full Member from 1964, Communist Party of the Soviet Union; Deputy to Supreme Soviet, Byelorussian SSR from 1963; Member, Presidium of the Supreme Soviet of the USSR and Candidate Member, Politburo from 1966. Hons: Hero of the Soviet Union, Hero of Socialist Labor, Gold Star Medal, Orders of Lenin.

GENEVIEVE PITOT
Dance composer and musical arranger
Born New Orleans, Louisiana, U.S.A., May 20th, 1909
Died New Orleans, Louisiana, U.S.A., October 4th, 1980

Genevieve Pitot, a leading musical arranger and composer for the ballet and dance, was born in New Orleans of French descent. She studied classical piano with Alfred Cortot in Paris and first became involved with dance as a pianist for Martha Graham's classes in the early 1930s. In 1933 Pitot composed the music for *Candide* choreographed by Charles Weidman, and she subsequently wrote several scores for Helen Tamaris, including the *Walt Whitman Suite* (1934) and *How Long, Brethren* (1937). Choreographed for the Federal Theater Works Progress Administration project, *How Long, Brethren* was among the first black protest dances performed in America.

Through her association with Tamaris, Pitot became the first woman to compose music for the dance sequences of Broadway musicals. Pitot was noted for compositions which blended smoothly with the musical styles of other composers and for her ability to work closely with choreographers. During the late 1940s and early 50s she composed for several musicals scored by Cole Porter, including *Kiss Me, Kate* (1948), *Out of this World* (1950), *Can Can* (1953), and *Silk Stockings* (1955). *Can Can* also marked the beginning of her successful collaboration with Michael Kidd, the acclaimed choreographer, with

whom she worked on *Li'l Abner* (1956) and *Destry Rides Again*
(1959). Pitot also composed *This Property is Condemned* (1957),
Winesburg, Ohio (1956), and *Musical Comedy Ballet* (1961) for
choreographer Donald Saddler.

Because dance composers are listed in theater programs as ar-
rangers, not composers, Pitot compared her role to "that of a ghost
writer." The dance composer, she said, must avoid "the intrusion of
[her] musical personality on to the original composer's music." Pitot's
last stage work was performed with the New York City Light Opera
Company in 1965.   J.K.

Daughter of Henri Clement P. and Helena Marie (Chalaron) P.
Married Joseph Patrick Sullivan, stereo technician, 1941 (d. 1961).
Educ: studied classical piano with Alfred Cortot, Paris. Pianist for
Martha Graham ballet classes, early 1930s; composer from early
1930s. *Composer of ballet music:* Candide, 1933; Toward the Light,
1934; Walt Whitman Suite, 1934; How Long, Brethren, 1937; Ade-
lante, 1939; Floor Show, 1940; Roads to Hell, 1941; Liberty Song,
1941; As in a Dream, 1941; Bird of Paradise, 1955; This Property is
Condemned, 1957; Winesburg, Ohio, 1958; Musical Comedy Ballet,
1961. *Composer of dance music for musicals:* It's About Time (revue,
co-composer), 1942; Inside U.S.A., and Kiss Me, Kate, 1948; Miss
Liberty, and Touch and Go, 1949; Great to be Alive, Call Me
Madam, and Out of This World, 1950; Two on the Aisle, 1951; Two's
Company, 1952; Can-Can, 1953; By the Beautiful Sea, 1954; Silk
Stockings, 1955; Shrangi-La, and Li'l Abner, 1956; Livin' the Life,
1957; The Body Beautiful, 1958; Destry Rides Again, NYC and
Saratoga, 1959; Milk and Honey, 1961; La Belle, 1963; Cool Off!
Philadelphia, 1964; Kiss Me, Kate (revival), and Drat! The Cat!,
1965.

HATTIE JACQUES
Comedienne
Born Sandgate, Kent, England, February 7th, 1924
Died London, England, October 6th, 1980

Hattie Jacques was best known as a comedienne. Her large size
coupled to her little-girl-lost voice endeared her to audiences of
British light entertainment for over 30 years. Of her size she once said
"You're conditioned from childhood to people making jokes against
you. You have to learn to make them laugh with, rather than at you."
Seen by some as a ship in full sail her more subtle qualities of vocal
and facial expression were often not given due critical praise. As a
performer she was an inveterate member of comedy teams and a 'feed'
valued by many leading comedians on radio, stage, television and
film. She also sang, directed and wrote adaptations of pantomines.

National fame came early when Ted Kavanagh selected Jacques for
the part of Sophie Tuckshop, the greedy schoolgirl, in Tommy
Handly's radio series *Itma* in 1948, then from 1950 to 1954 she played
Agatha Dinglebody in Eric Sykes's *Educating Archie*. Her 30-year
association with Sykes was ended only by her sudden death. From
1959 the two appeared in the intermittent television series which was
eventually titled *Sykes* in which Jacques's out-size personality was

given full reign as Sykes's long-suffering sister. Some critics saw the series as rooted in the tradition of British Music Hall and in the *Daily Mail* in 1965, Monica Furlong wrote "Miss Jacques's acting has such wit, such a delicious habit of caricaturing itself that I could enjoy watching her at work with far worse lines than these." So entrenched was this series in the life of British light-entertainment, that in 1973 Stanley Reynolds wrote in *The Times* what many viewers felt, "We actually believe they are brother and sister."

Jacques's first stage appearance was two years before her radio work started. At the age of 20 she appeared in a Victorian Music Hall at the Players theatre, London. Again, this was the start of a long association and four years later, in 1948, in the same theatre she played the Fairy Queen in the Victorian pantomime *The Sleeping Beauty in the Wood*. Her Christmas-time appearances drew audiences from all over England and she often repeated her Fairy Queen role, which she once said was her favorite part. In 1951 Jacques played the Fairy Queen in *Riquet With The Tuft*, which she adapted with Joan Sterndale Bennett; she was Fairy Fragrant in *Cinderella* in 1953 and Fairy Antidota in 1954. The following year she directed, still for the Players Theatre, the revue *Twenty Minutes South* which transferred to the West End of London.

The *Carry On* series of films was the spine of another long-lasting association for Jacques. She starred in the first five films, starting in 1958, and after this joined the team whenever a part suited her personality. Over a period of 16 years she starred in 14 of the *Carry On* series. In all these films her ample size was put to full use, whether as the vast Captain Clark in *Carry On Sergeant* or as the buxom matron in several others. Gerald Thomas, who directed the series, employed his original performers for many years and Jacques appeared alongside such stars, dearly-loved by British film-goers, as Eric Barker, Dora Bryan, Fenella Fielding, Charles Hawtrey, Sid James, Bob Monkhouse and Kenneth Williams. Such critics saw the later films as mere repeats of the earlier ones: the same jokes in situational comedy, the double entendre and the bawdiness, though Jacques's true comic talents were sometimes singled out. John Coleman, in the *New Statesman* thought the cast of the 1971 *Carry On at Your Convenience* poor except for Jacques who was "engaged in a mesmerically funny colloquy with a budgerigar."

A few of her films gave her chance to show more of her real talents. In 1960 she played Nanette Parry in *Make Mine Mink*, an adaptation of Peter Coke's play *Breath of Spring,* and much earlier she had sung in David Lean's version of *Oliver Twist*. Yet all too often the roles were similar to those in the *Carry On* series.

Hattie Jacques's capabilities could have earned her a place in high-comedy on the stage but in later years she preferred to work mainly in film and television. She died suddenly of a heart-attack. The informal memorial service at St. Paul's, Covent Garden, London was in "a mood of joyous good humour," which is how the organizer thought she would have liked it.   A.G.S.

Born Josephine Edwina J. Daughter of Robin Rochester J. and Mary Adelaide (Thorn) J. Married John LeMesurier, actor, 1949 (div. 1965). Children: Robin, b. 1953; Kim. Educ: Godolphin and Latymer Upper Sch., London. Served as a Red Cross nurse, WWII. *Perfor-*

mances: Stage—singing Victorian songs in Music Hall, London 1944; The King Stag, tour 1947–48; The Sleeping Beauty in the Wood, London 1948; Beauty and the Beast, London 1949; Ali Baba (also co-adapted and wrote lyrics), London 1950; Riquet With The Tuft (also co-adapted), London 1951; Bells of St. Martins, London 1952; Cinderella (also adapted), London 1953; The Sleeping Beauty in the Wood, London 1954; Albertine by Moonlight, Ali Baba (also co-adapted), London 1956; Large as Life, London 1958; Riquet With the Tuft (2nd version, also co-adapted), London 1960. *Radio*—regularly featured in series: Itma, 1948; Educating Archie, 1950–54; Hancock's Half Hour, 1954; other appearances include: Frankie Howerd Show; Paradise Street. *Films*—Nicholas Nickelby, 1947; Oliver Twist, 1948; The Gay Lady (Trottie True in U.K.), The Spider and the Fly, 1949; Waterfront Woman (Waterfront in U.K.), Chance of a Lifetime, 1950; The Pickwick Papers, Scrooge, Vampire Over London (Mother Riley Meets the Vampire in U.K.), 1952; No Haunt for Gentlemen, 1953; As Long as They're Happy, The Adventures of Sadie (Our Girl Friday in U.K.), The Love Lottery, Up to His Neck, 1954; Carry On Sergeant, Square Peg, 1958; Carry On Nurse, Carry on Teacher, Follow A Star, Left Right and Centre, The Navy Lark, The Night We Dropped A Clanger, 1959; Carry On Constable, Make Mine Mink, School for Scoundrels, 1960; Carry On Regardless, In The Doghouse, 1961; The Punch and Judy Man, She'll Have to Go, 1962; Carry On Cabby, 1963; The Bobo, Bunny Lake is Missing, Carry On Doctor, 1967; Carry On Again Doctor, Carry On Camping, Crooks and Coronets, The Magic Christian, Monte Carlo or Bust!, 1969; Carry On Loving, 1970; Carry On At Your Convenience, 1971; Carry On Abroad, Carry On Matron, 1972; Carry On Dick, 1974; Three for All, 1975. *Television*—regular appearances in series: Sykes, 1959–80; Our House, 1960–61; Carry On, 1975; Miss Adventure; other appearances include: Blithe Spirit; Happy Holiday; Juke Box Jury; The Mikado, 1967; No, No, Nanette; Pickwick, 1969; Plunder; Saturday Spectacular; Two Mrs. Carrols; Variety Playhouse. *Directed: Stage*—The Players Minstrels, London 1954; Twenty Minutes South, London 1955. *Co-produced: Television*—Minstrel Show.

SIR EDRIC (MONTAGUE) BASTYAN
Army General and statesman
Born Ferndown, Dorset, England, April 3rd, 1905
Died North Adelaide, Australia, October 7th, 1980

A subaltern in Great Britain's peacetime army, Sir Edric Bastyan rose to senior officer rank during World War Two and he became a Lieutenant-General in 1957. Bastyan served as Governor of South Australia from 1961 to 1968 and as Governor of Tasmania from 1968 to 1974.

Bastyan was the son of a Lieutenant-General and, after attending Sandhurst, he was commissioned in 1923 as a second-lieutenant with the Sherwood Foresters. In England's peacetime army promotions came slowly, and it was 12 years before Bastyan was made captain of the West Yorkshire Regiment. After attending the Staff College, Bastyan was sent to Palestine, where he served from 1938 to 1939.

With the Wehrmacht's armored thrust into Poland in September, 1939, the war had begun auspiciously for the Germans. But by 1943,

Rommel's *Afrikakorps* was being hounded across the North African desert by the British Eighth Army in which Bastyan served as Chief Administrative Officer. Later, he participated in the Eighth Army's Italian campaign, but it was in South-East Asia that Bastyan faced his greatest wartime challenge.

The British and Indian forces in Burma had been fighting a long, arduous campaign against Japanese troops who had forced their retreat from Malaya and Singapore in 1942. In 1944 a new 14th Army was formed to drive the Japanese from the region and Bastyan was appointed its Chief Administrative Officer. His work was termed "outstanding" by his commanding officer, General William Slim, who turned 1942's defeat into victory in 1944.

By war's end, Major-General Bastyan was in charge of the administration of all Allied troops stationed in South-East Asia. After the war, he taught briefly at the Imperial Defense College before returning to Europe in 1946 as chief administrator for the British Army of the Rhine. In 1949, Bastyan was selected as a member of the committee that reviewed the army's administration and, for the next six years, his divisional command responsibilities alternated with special War Office duties. Bastyan returned to Asia in 1957 as commander of British troops in Hong Kong and he was subsequently promoted to Lieutenant-General.

Although he retired from the military in 1960, Bastyan continued to serve the Commonwealth as the Governor of South Australia. After the expiration of his term in 1968, he was invited to serve as the Governor of Tasmania. In retirement, Bastyan made Australia his home; he was a member of the Royal Australian Society of Arts and an exhibition of his drawings and paintings was given in 1974.   L.R.

Son of Lt.-Col. S.J.B. Married Victoria Eugenie Helen Bett 1944. One son. Educ: West Buckland Sch.; Royal Military Coll., Sandhurst, England. 2nd Lt. 1923 and with Sherwood Foresters 1923–35; Capt., West Yorks. Reg. 1935; Staff Coll. 1936–37; Royal Irish Fusiliers 1937; served in Palestine 1938–39. With British 8th Army: as Maj. in African and Italian campaigns 1940; Temporary Lt.-Col. 1941; Temporary Brig. 1942; Chief Admin. Officer 1943; Acting Maj.-Gen., 14th Army 1944. Maj.-Gen., Allied Land Forces, Southeast Asia Command 1944–45; Instr., Imperial Defense Coll. 1946; Chief Admin. Officer, British Army of the Rhine 1946–48; special duties, War Office 1949; Chief of Staff, Eastern Command 1949–50; Dir. of Staff Duties, War Office 1950–52; Comdr., 53rd Infantry Div. and Mid-West District 1952–55; Vice-Adjutant Gen. 1955–57 and Lt.-Gen. 1957, War Office; Comdr., British Forces, Hong Kong 1957–60; retired 1960. Gov. of South Australia 1961–68 and of Tasmania 1968–74. Member, Royal South Australian Soc. of Arts. Hons: CBE 1943; C.B. 1944; KBE 1957; Assoc. Knight of Justice, Order of St. John of Jerusalem 1961; KCMG 1962; KCVO 1963.

SIR (SYDNEY) GORDON RUSSELL
Industrial designer and furniture manufacturer
Born London, England, May 20th, 1892
Died, Chipping Campden, Gloucestershire, England, October 7th,
1980

Sir Gordon Russell, a leader in the industrial design and manufacture of furniture, managed to reconcile old-world traditions of the skilled artisan with modern esthetic standards. As demand for his furniture increased, Russell refused to reduce its quality to satisfy mass-market production techniques. He was a spokesman for the British furniture industry in his later years and served as Director of the Council on Industrial Design from 1947 until 1959.

Russell, the son of an innkeeper who also maintained a furniture repair shop, was raised in the Cotswolds where vestiges of pre-industrial artisan traditions continued on into the early 20th century and where the English Arts and Crafts movement flourished. After serving in the Worcestershire Regiment during World War One, Russell returned home to design and produce furniture in partnership with his father and brother. His first designs were hand-made and shorn of neo-classical decorations. To develop a market for his furniture, Russell mounted successful exhibits in London and Paris; when his products began to be purchased by such members of fashionable society as writer Lord Dunsany and actor Charles Laughton, success was assured.

In the 1920s and 30s, Russell expanded his business through the machine-production of well-made, stylishly designed furniture. He was involved in all phases of production—from original design to construction to final sale—and believed he could remain industrially competitive only by awakening both the general public and a new generation of manufacturers to the elements of good design. Russell urged manufacturers not to reproduce mechanically that which was meant to be designed by hand, and he criticized those who allowed esthetic standards to be dictated by mass market demand. Indeed, the Depression had eliminated Russell's most profitable markets but, rather than reduce the quality of his furniture or drastically inflate its price, he expanded his company to include the manufacture of radio cabinets.

During World War Two, Russell's company was sustained by the manufacture of such defense materials as ammunition boxes and airplane parts. Russell also entered government service as a member of the Board of Trade's Advisory Panel and oversaw the wartime production of "utility furniture." In 1947 he became director of the Council on Industrial Design and continued his campaign for the preservation of high standards in the furniture industry. He organized an exhibition of postwar arts and crafts for the 1951 Festival of Britain and in 1956, he established the Design Centre in London, a "national shop window" for well-designed consumer goods. After his retirement from the Council in 1959, he frequently worked as a consultant on industrial design.   R.C.

Son of Sydney B.R. and Elizabeth R. Married Constance Elizabeth Jane Vere 1921. Children: Michael, b. 1921; Robert, b. 1924; Oliver, b. 1926; Kate, b. 1928. Educ: Chipping Campden Grammar Sch. 1904–08. Mil. Service: Served with Worcester Reg. 1914–19 (M.C.

1917). Partner 1919–46 and Dir. and Chmn. 1970–76, Russell & Sons, The Lygon Arms, Ltd.; Designer and Managing Dir. 1926–40 and Chmn. and Dir. 1967–77, Gordon Russell, Ltd. With Council of Industrial Design: Member 1944–59; Dir. 1947–59; founded Design Centre, London 1956; Life Member since 1960. Member 1926 and Master 1962, Art Workers Guild; special assessor for Natl. Diploma in Design, Ministry of Educ. 1938–53; Member 1940 and Master of Faculty 1947–49, Royal Design Inst.; on Utility Furniture Advisory Panel, Bd. of Trade 1942; Chmn., Bd. of Trade Design Panel 1943–47; on Council, Royal Soc. of Art 1947–49 and 1951–55; served on Jury, Intnl. Low Cost Furniture Competition, Mus. of Modern Art, NYC 1948; on Arts Panel of Arts Council 1948–53; Member, Fine Arts Cttee. of British Council 1948–58; on Council of the Royal Coll. of Art 1948–51 and 1952–53; Member, Exec. Cttee., Festival of Britain 1951; on Council of Royal Sch. for Needlework 1951–68; Design Panelist, British Railways Bd. 1956–66; Pres., Design and Industries Assoc. 1959–62. Member: Arts Advisory Cttee. of Unesco Natl. Cttee. of U.K. 1960–66; Natl. Council for Diplomas in Art and Design 1961–68; Crafts Advisory Cttee. 1971–74. Hons: one gold, two silver medals, Paris Exhibitions (for furniture) 1925; First Fellow, Soc. of Industrial Arts 1945; CBE 1947; Fellow, Royal Soc. of Art 1949; first designer honored by Royal Coll. of Arts 1952, Senior Fellow 1960; Hon. Assoc. 1953 and Hon. Fellow 1965, Royal Inst. of British Architects; named to Swedish Royal Order of the Vasa 1954; Hon. Assoc., Inst. of Landscape Architects 1955; K.B. 1955; Hon. Member, Cttee, for Intnl. Exhibition of Architecture and Industrial Design, Sweden 1955; Commdr. Norwegian Royal Order of St. Olav 1957; Member, Higher Jury XIIth Milan Triennale Exhibition 1960; LL.D., Birmingham Univ. 1960; Gold Albert Medal, Royal Soc. of Art 1962; Ph.D., Royal Coll. of Art 1980. *Author:* The Story of Furniture, 1947; The Things we See: Furniture, 1948; Looking at Furniture, 1964; Designer's Trade (autobiog.), 1968; numerous articles, lectures, and broadcasts.

JOHN DOLLARD
Psychologist, teacher, and author
Born Menasha, Wisconsin, U.S.A., August 29th, 1900
Died New Haven, Connecticut, U.S.A., October 8th, 1980

John Dollard was the first American scholar to apply the insights of Freudian psychology to the social sciences. As a clinical researcher and professor at Yale University, he was known for his studies of personality formation, psychoanalytic and learning theory, and psychotherapeutic methodology. In the late 1930s he contributed to the understanding of the relationship between frustration and aggression and, during World War Two, he studied the nature of fear in battle. However, Dollard was best known for his pioneering study of race relations in the American South, *Caste and Class in a Southern Town* (1937).

Born in Menasha, Wisconsin in 1900, Dollard, after serving as a private in the United States Army in 1918, earned his undergraduate degree from the University of Wisconsin and his graduate degrees from the University of Chicago, with a thesis on *The Changing Functions of the American Family*. After working in an administrative

post at the University of Chicago, he spent a year in Germany on a
Social Science Council grant. When Dollard returned in 1932 he
accepted an appointment with the Institute of Human Relations at
Yale. At the Institute, he began to make use of individual "life
histories" in the study of personality development. A novel approach
at that time, he published a monograph on the subject in 1935.

Dollard subsequently decided to use these life histories as the basis
for a study of personality formation among negroes in the Deep
South. A Yale seminar on "The Impact of Culture on Personality,"
conducted jointly with Edwin Sapir, convinced Dollard that psychology's accepted notions of personality development had failed to take
into account the socio-cultural determinants of personality. Combining sociological method with Freudian terminology, Dollard investigated the structure of race relations and personality formation in
"Southerntown," his name for the research site. Published in 1937,
Caste and Class in a Southern Town had an immediate impact upon
the social science community. Explaining his dynamic, interdisciplinary approach, Dollard wrote: "The lives of white and negro people
are so dynamically joined and fixed in one system that neither can be
understood without the other."

The book was an unvarnished account of the Southern "caste
system" which Dollard described as the social mechanism erected by
white Southerners to replace the institution of slavery. Unlike the
class system, which allows for some upward mobility, the "caste
system," Dollard argued, was fixed and rigid, and based on forms of
intimidation, both subtle, as in the absence of honorific titles when
whites addressed blacks, and brutally overt, as in lynching. Dollard
also discussed interracial sex, the symbolic importance of rape (which
might include so slight an offense as a black man winking at a white
woman), the psycho-sexual emasculation of black men, and the "caste
system's" legitimation of sadism and authoritarian personality traits
among lower-middle class whites. *Caste and Class in a Southern Town*
was a controversial work. Although banned by the state of Georgia
and by the Union of South Africa, Dollard's study led social scientists
to view racism in America as a national, rather than strictly regional,
phenomenon.

Dollard's work on the relationship between frustration and aggression has had, perhaps, even greater impact. Although this study is not
usually associated with his name, *Frustration and Aggression* (1939)
was the result of a collaborative effort at the Institute of Human
Relations to which Dollard was the primary contributor. The idea that
frustration leads to aggression has become so commonplace in
psychology and sociology that, according to Daniel Patrick Moynihan,
it is generally forgotten that this human behavioral "law" was
unknown to social scientists before *Frustration and Aggression* was
published.

Dollard's study of fear in battle was undertaken during World War
Two when he worked as a consultant for the War Department. At the
time of his death, Dollard was conducting research on guilt as a
political phenomenon. He had been teaching at Yale University for
more than 35 years.   R.C.

Son of James D. and Ellen Brady D. Married: (1) Victoria Day 1930
(div. 1959); (2) Joan G. Palance 1961. Children: 1st marriage—Julie;

John Day; Victorine; Peter Day. Educ: Univ. of Wisconsin, Phi Beta
Kappa, B.A. 1922; Univ. of Chicago, M.A. 1930, Ph.D. 1931;
certified professional psychologist, American Psychological Assn.
1947. Mil. Service: private, U.S. Army 1918. Secty., Memorial Union
Building Cttee., Univ. of Wisconsin 1923–26; Asst. to the Pres., Univ.
of Chicago 1926–29; Social Science Research Council Fellow in social
psychology, Germany 1931–32. With Yale Univ.: Research Assoc.,
Inst. of Human Relations 1932–52; Prof. of psychology 1952–69; Prof.
emeritus from 1969. Consultant to Dept. of War 1942–45; Pres.,
Commn. on Mental Health, U.S. Public Health Service 1949–52.
Fellow. American Psychological Assn.; diplomat in social psychology,
American Assn. for the Advancement of Science; American Acad. of
Arts and Sciences; Western New England Psychoanalytic Soc.; Lawn
and Morey's Assn. (New Haven); Century, Coffee House, and Yale
(NYC); Cosmos (Washington, D.C.). Hons: M.A., Yale Univ. 1952;
Fellow, Berkeley Coll., Yale Univ. *Author:* The Changing Functions
of the American Family, 1931; Criteria for Life History, 1935; Caste
and Class in a Southern Town, 1937; (with C.S. Ford, C.I. Hovland,
R.T. Sollenberger, et al.) Frustration and Aggression, 1939; (with
Allison Davis) Children of Bondage: Personality Development of
Negro Youth in the Urban South, 1940; (with N.E. Miller) Social
Learning and Imitation, 1941; Victory Over Fear, 1942; (with Donald
Horton) Fear in Battle, 1944; (with N.E. Miller) Personality and
Psychotherapy, 1950; (with Frank Auld, Jr. and Alice White) Steps in
Psychotherapy, 1953; (with Frank Auld, Jr.) Scoring Human Motives,
1959.

PEARL KENDRICK
Microbiologist and Public Health Officer
Born Wheaton, Illinois, U.S.A. ca. 1890
Died Grand Rapids, Michigan, U.S.A., October 8th, 1980

Microbiologist Pearl Kendrick, a public health officer for the state of
Michigan, discovered a vaccine in 1939 that virtually eliminated
pertussis, or whooping cough. Previously the infection had been the
worst childhood disease in the U.S., killing some 6,000 children every
year through spasmodic coughing that hemorrhaged blood vessels in
the brain.

After attending college at Syracuse University and obtaining her
doctorate at Johns Hopkins University, Kendrick became chief of the
Western Michigan Branch Laboratory in Grand Rapids. Together
with Dr. Grace Eldering, she conducted a five-year study of whooping
cough which resulted in discovery of the vaccine. Partly funded by the
New Deal's Works Progress Administration, the two researchers
visited many poor households to collect specimens from sick children.
Kendrick later developed a method of combining the vaccines for
diphtheria, whooping cough and tetanus into a single shot, routinely
given today to children.   s.l.g.

Educ: Syracuse Univ.; John Hopkins Univ. Chief, Western Michi-
ganch Lab., Grand Rapids, and Public Health officer for state of
Mich. *Discoveries:* pertussis vaccine for whooping cough 1939; DPT
shot (combination of vaccines for diphtheria, pertussis and tetanus).

MAURICE MARTENOT
Musician, inventor, teacher and writer
Born Paris, France, October 14th, 1898
Died Paris, France, October 8th, 1980

An accomplished pianist, cellist, conductor, and an amateur electrical engineer, Maurice Martenot was the inventor of the Ondes Martenot, an electronic keyboard instrument that anticipated the synthesizer. A precocious piano student, Martenot, at the age of nine, made a successful concert tour with his sister, Ginette. Martenot subsequently studied piano and cello at the Paris Conservatoire and composition with André Gedalge.

Interested in the physics of sound waves, Martenot became a wireless instructor during World War One. In 1918, while demonstrating an apparatus for generating sound waves at various frequencies, Martenot, intrigued by the musical tones it produced, decided to use radio-electric science to invent an instrument capable of providing composers with an entirely new range of musical expression. For four years, Martenot, a musician and teacher by day, worked as an inventor by night. In 1922, he patented a model of the electronic instrument he later named the Ondes Musicales. Resembling a spinet, the five-octave Ondes Musicales—or Ondes Martenot, as it is popularly known—possessed a greater tonal versatility than such earlier electronic instruments as the Theremin.

For six years Martenot continued to refine and perfect the Ondes Martenot. In April, 1928, he exhibited the revised instrument to a gathering of artists and scientists at the Salle Gaveau in Paris. This exhibition led to public demonstrations of the Ondes Martenot at the Paris Opera and at the Salle Pleyel. Later that year, Martenot gave a command performance before President Gaston Doumergue and his Ministers at the Elysée Palace. Ginette Martenot later performed as Ondes Martenot soloist with several European orchestras and, in 1931, Martenot and his sister were invited to the United States by Leopold lStokowski, then conductor of the Philadelphia Symphony Orchestra. Martenot demonstrated his instrument's capacity to play different tones at concerts with Stokowski's Orchestra in Philadelphia and at Carnegie Hall in New York. Although American critics were less enthusiastic than European writers, they did appreciate the Ondes Martenot's unique sound and tonal diversity.

In 1931, Martenot published *Méthode pour l'enseignement des ondes musicales, instrument radio-électrique Martenot fait par Gaveau,* the first instructional text for an electronic instrument. Six years later, at the International Exhibition of Art and Techniques in Paris, Martenot and his sister organized "concert teams" of eight Ondes Martenots to perform pieces written by such noted modern composers as Florent Schmitt and Edgar Varèse. The Ondes Martenot, awarded the exhibition's Grand Prize, was hailed by some critics as the musical instrument of the future. Many solo, chamber, and orchestral scores have been written for the Ondes Martenot. Contemporary composers such as Boulez, Jolivet, Bussoti, and Prošev still employ the Ondes Martenot as an alternative to the human voice or conventional instruments. According to the London *Times,* the instrument is frequently used in Messiaen's *Turangalila-Symphonie* where its "soaring tones suggest a divine voice proclaiming a gospel of love."

Martenot taught at the Ecole Normale de Musique in Paris and was the founder and director of the Ecole d'Art Martenot in Neuilly. In

1947 he organized classes for the Ondes Martenot at the Paris Conservatoire, and in 1952 he published a second text on the instrument. Martenot also published treatises on musical education.

J.S.

Unmarried. Educ: Paris Conservatoire, studied piano, cello and composition. Mil. Service: conductor in Rhine Army. Concert pianist and wireless instr. 1918; cellist, conductor, teacher 1918–1922; inventor of Ondes Martenot, patented 1922, first demonstrated 1928; Prof., Ecole Normale de Musique, Paris, ca. 1920s; Founder 1947 and Dir., Ecole d'Art Martenot, Paris Conservatoire. Hons: Grand Prize of Intnl. Exhibition of Art and Techniques, Paris 1937. *Author:* Méthode pour l'enseignement des ondes musicales, instrument radio-électrique Martenot fait par Gaveau, 1931; second text on Ondes Martenot, 1952; Jeux musicaux, ca. 1940s; articles on musical educ. and electronic instruments.

FRANK V. MORLEY
Publisher, writer, and editor
Born Haverford, Pennsylvania, U.S.A., 1899
Died Buckinghamshire, England, October 8th, 1980

The youngest son of a prominent American mathematician, Frank Morley, a leading editor in both London and New York, planned to follow his father's career when he attended Oxford University as a Rhodes Scholar and obtained a doctorate in mathematics. Instead, he pursued a career in literature. Morley's two brothers, one of whom became an author and the other an editor of the *Washington Post,* also studied mathematics at Oxford.

A dedicated Anglophile, Morley, after leaving Oxford, moved to London rather than return to the United States. He joined the staff of the *Times Literary Supplement* in the early 1920s and subsequently became London Manager for the Century Company (Publishers) of New York. At the age of 30, Morley became a founding director of London's Faber and Faber and he remained with the publishing house for 10 years. Morley worked closely at Faber and Faber with several world-famous authors, including his friend and colleague, T.S. Eliot, with whom he shared an office. Morley's writing career was launched in 1936 with the publication of his novel, *The Wreck of the Active.*

Having accepted the Vice-Presidency of New York's Harcourt Brace and Company, Morley returned to the United States in 1939. He quickly rose to the position of chief editor and also continued to write. During World War Two, Morley served on the National War Labor Board in Washington, D.C., and published *My One Contribution to Chess* in 1945.

In 1947 Morley returned to England as director of Eyre and Spottswoode Publishers. Shocked by the sight of war-damaged England, he joined a group dedicated to raising funds for the restoration of literary and historical landmarks destroyed in the war.

Morley never returned to the United States. An enthusiastic patron of both young and established English writers, Morley was an influential member of London literary circles for the rest of his life. He was the author of nearly 20 books, many of them—*The Great North Road* (1961), *The Long Road,* and *Literary Britain: A Reader's Guide to its Writers and Landmarks* (1980), among others—were tributes to the culture of his adopted country.   J.S.

Son of a mathematician. Married Christina McLeod Innes ca. 1930s. Children: John; Hugh; Susanna; Peregrine. Educ: Univ. of Oxford (Rhodes scholarship), doctorate in mathematics ca. 1920. Mil. Service: Natl. War Labor Bd., Washington, D.C. WWII. Staff member, The Times Literary Supplement, ca. early 1920s; London Mgr., The Century Co. (Publishers), ca. mid-1920s; Founding Dir., Faber and Faber 1929; V.P. and Chief Ed., Harcourt Brace and Co., NYC 1939–47; Dir., Eyre and Spottswoode Publishers, London 1947. Member of landmark restoration group, England 1953. *Author:* The Wreck of the Active, 1936; My One Contribution to Chess, 1945; The Great North Road, 1961; The Long Road West, ca. 1960s; Literary Britain, a Reader's Guide to its Writers and Landmarks, 1980; numerous other books.

ROBERT (J.) KELLAR
Surgeon and professor of obstetrics and gynaecology
Born Great Britain, 1909
Died Edinburgh, Scotland, October 9th, 1980

Robert Kellar, a distinguished clinical scientist and surgeon, began his career at the University of Edinburgh, where he specialized in obstetrics and gynaecology. A brilliant student, Kellar, as an undergraduate, won many scholastic honors, including the Annandale Gold Medal for Clinical Surgery, the Wightman Prize for Clinical Medicine, the Murchison Prize for Medicine (shared), and the Buchanan Prize for Midwifery and Diseases of Women.

In 1932, Kellar, having completed his studies the previous year, served as House Officer and Tutor in Clinical Gynaecology, at the House Surgeon Outpatients Department and as Professor of Midwifery at the Royal Infirmary in Edinburgh. Two years later, Kellar became a Member of Edinburgh's Royal College of Physicians. Also that year, he received the Lister Prize for Surgery, the Leckie Mactier Research Fellowship, and the Freeland Barbour Fellowship in Obstetrics.

In 1935 Kellar moved to London to work with Professor F.J. Browne in the Obstetrical Unit of University College Hospital, London. Kellar was promoted in 1937 to the post of Reader in Obstetrics and Gynaecology at the British Post-Graduate Medical School, at the University of London. Throughout the 1930s, Kellar was involved in medical research; his study of masugie nephritis in rabbits developed into an investigation of hypertensive disorders during pregnancy.

Kellar's academic career was briefly interrupted by World War Two. While serving in the Royal Army Medical Corps as a Lieutenant Colonel, he established a surgical team in the North African theater. He later became head of the Surgical Division in Cairo and Advisor in Gynaecology to the Middle East Forces. Mentioned frequently in military despatches, Kellar was awarded a Master of the Order of the British Empire in 1943.

After the war, Kellar returned to Great Britain, where he was made a Fellow of the Royal College of Obstetricians and Gynaecologists and a Fellow of the Royal College of Physicians of Edinburgh. In 1946 Kellar was appointed to the Chair of Obstetrics and Gynaecology at the University of Edinburgh.

At Edinburgh, Kellar, in the 1940s, contributed to the science of maternal physiology through his work on cardiac output and peripheral blood flow; he also supported increased clinical research in pregnancy haemodynamics, urinary disorders, and endocrinology. Kellar helped establish one of the first cervical cytology programs and the M.R.C. Clinical Endocrinology Research Unit, a group which conducted important studies of sex steroids and the treatment of malformed gonads. An early proponent of family planning, Kellar allowed the subject to be taught in his department.

Well-known as a surgeon, clinical researcher, and teacher throughout the world, Kellar was honored in America by election to the James IV Association of Surgeons and the American Association of Obstetricians and Gynecologists. In 1968 he was appointed Commander of the Order of the British Empire.   J.S.

Son of James Dodds Ballantyne K. and Florence Maude (Conveney) K. Married Gertrude (d. 1980). Two sons; one daughter. Educ: Univ. of Edinburgh, M.B., Ch.B. 1931. Mil. Service: Lt.-Col., Royal Army Medical Corps, North Africa and Europe 1939–45. House Office and Tutor in Clinical Gynaecology, House Surgeon Outpatients Dept. and Prof. of Midwifery, Royal Infirmary, Edinburgh, ca. 1932; Asst. to Prof. F.J. Browne, Obstetrical Unit, Univ. Coll. Hosp., London 1935; Reader in Obstetrics and Gynaecology, British Post-Grad. Medical Sch., Univ. of London 1937; Head of surgical team, North Africa, ca. 1939; head of Surgical Division, Cairo and Advisor in Gynaecology to Middle East Forces, ca. 1939–45; Chmn., Obstetrics and Gynaecology, Univ. of Edinburgh 1946–80. Member: Royal Coll., Obstetrics and Gynaecology; Adrian Cttee.; Univ. Grants Cttee.; Gen. Medical Council; Overseas Registration Cttee.; James IV Assn. of Surgeons. Hons: Annandale Gold Medal for Clinical Surgery 1931; Wightman Prize for Clinical Medicine, 1931; Murchison Prize for Medicine 1931; Buchanan Prize for Midwifery and Diseases of Women 1931; Simpson Prize for Obstetrics 1932; Lister Prize for Surgery 1934; Freeland Barbour Fellowship in Obstetrics 1934; Leckie Mactier Research Fellow 1934–35; Fellow of the Royal Coll. of Surgeons of Edinburgh 1935; Beit Memorial Research Fellow 1935–37; MBE 1943; Fellow, Royal Coll. of Obstetricians and Gynecologists 1945; CBE 1968; Hon. Fellow, American Assn. of Obstetricians and Gynecologists.

ALEXANDRE (ANTOINE) SANGUINETTI
Politician
Born Cairo, Egypt, March 27th, 1913
Died Saint-Mande, France, October 9th, 1980

Alexandre Sanguinetti was a member of the French Chamber of Deputies from 1962 until the early 1970s and he served briefly in the cabinet of President Georges Pompidou. A prominent Gaullist politician, Sanguinetti urged France to steer an independent course in world politics and he aggressively opposed French alignment with either the United States or the Soviet Union.

Sanguinetti was born in Cairo where his father worked in the legal section of the Interior Ministry. Having studied law and literature at the Universities of Cairo, Angers, and Paris, he enlisted with the Free French forces following the Nazi occupation of France in 1940. Sanguinetti saw active duty in North Africa and lost his left leg while participating in the armed landings on Elba.

Although Sanguinetti's political career had begun in 1946 when he entered the Ministry of the National Economy, he came to national attention in the 1950s as an opponent of Algerian independence. He worked closely with Jacques Soustelle, the leader of the movement to maintain Algeria's colonial status, and, in 1956, Sanguinetti achieved political influence when he was elected Secretary-General of the French Veterans Association Action Committee. When Charles de Gaulle became President in 1958—Sanguinetti had repeatedly called for his return to power—Sanguinetti realized that Algerian independence was inevitable and he helped dismantle O.A.S., the French terrorist organization opposed to the liberation movement in Algeria.

In 1962 Sanguinetti was elected to the Chamber of Deputies. As Vice-President of the Assembly's Committee for National Defense, Sanguinetti supported the development of an extensive nuclear arms program. In 1966, he joined President Georges Pompidou's cabinet as Minister for Veterans and War Victims but he fell out with Pompidou and was dismissed from the post in early 1967. Sanguinetti was re-elected to the Assembly in 1968 and served as President of the National Defense and Armed Forces Commission until he lost his seat in 1973. However, Sanguinetti continued to hold power within the Gaullist party and, from October, 1973, until December, 1974, he was Secretary-General of the Union des Démocrates pour la République.

In the 1970s, Sanguinetti was a severe critic of President Valery Giscard d'Estaing's centrist policies. Regarding domestic affairs, he accused the French President of being too willing to compromise with the Socialists and Communists; on foreign policy, he charged that Giscard had moved France within the American zone of influence. In 1976, Sanguinetti urged the Gaullist Prime Minister Jacques Chirac to abandon his post so that he could challenge Giscard for the Presidency in 1981 from a completely independent position. However, when Chirac accepted Sanguinetti's advice and resigned, relations between the two Gaullists cooled, and, by 1980, Sanguinetti had switched his support to former Prime Minister Michel Debré.   T.P.

Son of Joseph S. and Lucie Pietri. Married. Children: Laetitia; Louis-Luc. Educ: Collège Stanislaus, Paris; Univs. of Cairo, Angers and Paris, degrees in law and literature. Mil. Service: Free French Forces, WWII (Médaille Militaire; Croix de guerre). Head of the Natl. Center

for Economic Information 1945–49; with Ministry of the Natl.
Economy 1946; Secty.-Gen. of French Veterans Assn. 1956–59; with
Ministry of Information 1959–61; Ministry of the Interior 1961–62;
Member, Chamber of Deputies 1962–67, 1968–73; V.P. 1962–66, and
Pres. 1968–73, Cttee. for Natl. Defense; Minister of Veterans Affairs
1966–67; Secty.-Gen. of the Gaullist Party 1973–74. Hons: Officer,
Légion d'honneur. *Author:* France et l'arme atomique; Une nouvelle
résistance, 1976; Une armée pour quoi faire; Sujets ou Citoyens:
Reformer la démocracie, 1977 J'ai mal à ma peau Gaulliste, 1978;
Lettre ouverte à mes compatriotes corses.

SHELDON (WARREN) CHENEY
Theater critic, art historian, writer
Born Berkeley, California, U.S.A., July 29th, 1886
Died Berkeley, California, U.S.A., October 10th, 1980

In the early 20th century, Sheldon Cheney was an enthusiastic
supporter of the modern movement in the drama. He believed in
freedom of artistic expression and, in 14 books, and more than 100
articles, he developed progressive ideas about art and its relation to
historical change. According to Professor Travis M. Bogard, Cheney
was "the first person to . . . define an esthetic for the theater in this
country. His work amounted to almost a manifesto for the American
theater, and his writing had such clarity that he continued to be a sort
of guru for two or three decades."

Cheney's father was a novelist, poet, reporter for the *San Francisco
Chronicle,* and an editor. Cheney enrolled in the liberal arts curriculum at the University of Calfornia, Berkeley, where his mother
worked as a placement director. In 1910 he began publishing drama
and art criticism in newspapers and magazines and, in 1913, he
attended Harvard University's graduate drama program before
returning to California where he studied at several art schools.

His first book, *The New Movement in the Theater,* appeared in 1914.
In it, Cheney argued for the development of a naturalistic theater in
America which would dispense with the expedients of commercial
stagecraft. The Broadway stage, Cheney said, produced "an unending
stream of musical comedies, and revues, and crook plays, and society
farces" which relied upon heavy-handed plots, artificial tension, and
gaudy manipulation of audience emotion.He also predicted that
progress in American drama would emerge from small, semi-professional theaters in which experimentation by serious literary dramatists
was encouraged. In the work of such European playwrights as Gerhart
Hauptman, J.M. Synge, and George Bernard Shaw, Cheney saw the
development of a new "intensive" drama which he hoped would be
taken up by American writers. Describing this movement, he wrote:
"The new drama usually is close to contemporary life in theme. It has
not an empty shell of dramatic story, like the farces and melodramas
of other days . . . the outward personal plot is illumined by an inward
social plot. The story is developed as typical of deep social truth."

In 1916 Cheney published *Art Theater* and founded *Theater Arts,* a
small review of the modern American theater movement which he

edited until 1921. Founded in Detroit as a quarterly publication, the magazine was moved in 1919 to New York City where it was published monthly. The journal had been established to promote American dramatic art and, highly influential, had a circulation of 60,000 when it ceased publication in 1964.

Through his work on *Theater Arts* and in his first two books, Cheney, by 1920, had set forth a new theory of the American theater which was later embraced by playwright Eugene O'Neill and the noted set designer, Robert Edmond Jones. His book *The Theater: 3000 Years of Drama, Acting, and Stagecraft* (1929) was regarded as the first major English-language history of the theater. During the 1920s, Cheney was also a playreader, press representative, and assistant director with Equity Players, now known as the Actor's Theater, in New York City. In 1926 he became director of the Independent Theater's Clearing House.

After the death of his first wife in 1934, Cheney married Martha Candler, a publicist and editor. They collaborated to write *Art and the Machine* (1936), a study of the revolutionary transformation of art in the industrial age. From 1935 through 1947, Cheney lectured on modern art at many universities and museums. His book, *A World History of Art* (1937) was the first important study of art history written in America by a proponent of modernism.

Cheney continued to write copiously until the death of his wife in 1975. He then moved from New Hope, Pennsylvania, to Berkeley where he edited his many notebooks and articles.   S.F.

Son of Lemuel Warren C., editor, writer, and businessman, and May Lucretia (Shepard) C., Univ. of Calif. exec. Married: (1) Maud Meurice Turner 1910 (d. 1934); (2) Martha Smithers Candler, editor and publicist 1934 (d. 1975). Children: 1st marriage—John Turner; Elizabeth; Michael Sheldon. Educ: Univ. of Calif., B.A. 1908; Harvard Univ., grad. work 1909. Mil. Service: War Camp Community Service 1918–19. Drama and art critic for various newspapers and mags. 1910–16; Founder 1916 and Ed. 1916–21, Theatre Arts Magazine, Detroit and NYC; freelance writer 1921–22 and 1926–75; playreader, press rep., Asst. Dir., Equity Players (now Actor's Theatre), 1922–25; mgr. for producer-dir. Augustin Duncan, 1925–26; dir., Independent Theatre's Clearing House, 1926; studied European theaters, 1926–30; lectr., Drama League Tour, 1930; conductor, Drama League Tour of Russian Theatres, 1931; lectr., univs. and museums, 1935–47. Member, Authors League of America, Soc. of American Historians. Hons: Fellow, Union College, 1937–40; Fellow, Royal Society of Arts, 1960. *Author:* The New Movement in the Theater, 1914; The Art Theater, 1916, 2nd ed. 1925; The Open-Air Theater, 1918; A Primer of Modern Art, 1924; Art and the Postage Stamp, 1926; Stage Decoration, 1927; The Theatre: 3,000 Years of Drama, Acting and Stagecraft, 1929, 2nd ed. 1952, 3rd ed. 1972; The New World Architecture, 1930; Expressionism in Art, 1934; Art and the Machine (with Martha Candler Cheney), 1936; A World History of Art, 1937; The Story of Modern Art, 1941; Men Who Have Walked With God, 1945; A New World History of Art, 1956; Sculpture of the World: A History, 1968; collected and edited Isadora Duncan's papers in The Art of Dance, 1928; frequent contributor to Encyclopedia Brittanica, The New Caravan, other encyclopedias. Frequent contributor to many art and drama magazines.

ZHAO DAN
Film and stage actor
Born Yangzhao, China, 1914
Died Peking, China, October 19th, 1980

Until recently, the rich and varied cinematic output of China remained largely unknown to the outside world. A retrospective season presented by London's National Film Theatre in October 1980 revealed, for the first time, what the world had been missing. Not least of these revelations was the range and achievement of Zhao Dan, generally held to be China's finest screen actor. Midway through the N.F.T. season, with over-neat irony, came the news of Zhao's death in a Peking hospital.

Zhao Dan was born Zhao Fengao in Yangzao; his father owned a cinema in Nantong, and Zhao's first screen appearance occurred at age 11. He began producing plays at 13, and went on to write stories and plays for a left-wing magazine; when the publication was censored by the Kuomintang Government, Zhao changed his given name to Dan ('red') as a political gesture. Moving to Shanghai in 1931, he attended the Technical College of Art, and graduated in 1934, by when he was acting regularly in films and plays. Among his stage roles was that of Helmer, the husband in Ibsen's *A Doll's House;* Nora was played by Lin Pang, later to become better known as Jiang Qing, second wife of Mao Tse-Tung.

During the 1930s Zhao appeared in over 30 films; the two most notable, which established his reputation as a major actor, were *Street Angel* and *Crossroads.* Both made in 1937, these films intriguingly blend Hollywood-influenced romantic comedy with a very Chinese appreciation of the underlying social and political realities, an ambiguity also apparent in Zhao's warmly likeable performance. When Shanghai fell to the Japanese later that year, he left the city and joined a touring company performing anti-Japanese plays. In 1939, straying into Sinjiang province, he was captured by a Kuomintang warlord, and imprisoned for four years.

Released in 1943, he returned to the stage, and when the war ended resumed his film career in Shanghai. (Around this time he also took up directing, making his first film in 1947; he was to direct four in all.) One of his finest performances occurs in *Crows and Sparrows* (1948), which he also co-scripted; the film conveys a warmth and immediacy comparable to the contemporary Italian neo-realist cinema, and features superb ensemble playing by the whole cast. Its openly satirical attitude to the Kuomintang led to the film being banned in mid-production; it was completed after the Communist victory.

Throughout the 1950s, Zhao's performances evidenced the ever-increasing breadth of his range, and insight of his interpretations. The authority, and unmannered simplicty of his characterizations are shown at their best in *Li Shizhen, the Great Pharmacologist* (1956), in which he portrayed the father of Chinese herbal medicine; the film evokes the period of the Ming Dynasty (16th century) with great subtlety and beauty. Also notable among Zhao's films in the 50s were *Soul of the Sea* (1957) and *The Opium War* (1959); the latter, in which he played a patriotic nobleman resisting British imperialism, was one of his few films to receive wide distribution outside China.

Zhao had acted in over sixty films when, at the height of his powers, he made *Red Crag* (1965). Set during the last stages of the Civil War in 1948, it deals with the brutal fate suffered by a Communist resistance group in Chonquin. Zhao plays the leader of the group; arrested and tortured, he spends most of the action in solitary confinement. The film tragically foreshadowed Zhao's fate, and was to be his last.

Red Crag was made on the eve of the Cultural Revolution, in which Zhao was among the first to be attacked. His earlier professional association with Jiang Qing told against him; Zhao was arrested, apparently on her personal orders, and imprisoned for five and a half years. During much of the time he was kept naked in solitary confinement, and was frequently tortured by the Red Guards. He survived, but greatly weakened and with his health ruined. Released in 1973, he rejoined the Shanghai Film Studio in 1976. His last years were spent teaching, directing for the stage, and writing his autobiography.

In 1980 Zhao was planning his return to the screen, when cancer of the pancreas was diagnosed. From his hospital bed, a few days before his death, he dictated an article for *The People's Daily,* attacking censorship and official control of the arts. "Literature and art are the business of writers and artists," he wrote. "If the Party controls them too tightly, there's no hope—they're finished."   P.K.

Born Zhao Fengâo. Changed name ca. 1930. Son of a cinema owner. Married twice. Children from both marriages and two adopted sons. Educ: Technical Coll. of Art, Shanghai 1931–34. First screen appearance 1925; began producing plays 1927; wrote stories and plays for left-wing mag.; stage and screen star from mid-1930s; imprisoned by Japanese warlord 1939–43 and by Jiang Qing 1967–73. *Performances: Stage*—A Doll's House; others. *Film*—Street Angel, 1937; Crossroads, 1937; (also co-scripted) Crows and Sparrows, 1948; Li Shizhen, the Great Pharmacologist, 1956; Soul of the Sea, 1957; The Opium War, 1959; Red Crag, 1965; many others. Author of two books.

BARONESS EMMET OF AMBERLEY
British M.P. and delegate to the United Nations
Born Cairo, Egypt, March 18th, 1899
Died Sussex, England, October 10th, 1980

Baroness Emmet of Amberley was the first Englishwoman to serve as a Full Delegate to the United Nations and the first Briton to represent her country in the U.N. while serving neither as a Government minister nor a member of parliament. An influential figure in the Conservative Party, Baroness Emmet served in parliament from 1955 to 1964. During her career, she supported the increased participation of women in politics and, concerned with the problems of child welfare, she sought eradication of the social conditions which perpetuate juvenile delinquency.

Evelyn Rennell was born in Cairo where her father, Baron Rennell, a career foreign service officer, served as secretary of the British legation. Evelyn attended French, Swiss, Swedish, and Italian schools before entering St. Margaret's School, Oxford, from which she graduated with honors in 1920. She received an M.A. degree from Oxford in 1924 and later studied at the London School of Economics.

During World War One, she worked as a secretary for her father when he was ambassador in Rome. When Baron Rennell resigned his post and returned to Great Britain in 1919, Evelyn was employed for several months as a social worker at the Toynbee Hall Settlement in London's East End.

In 1924, one year after her marriage to Thomas Addi Emmet, heir to Amberley Castle in Sussex, Mrs. Emmet was elected to the London County Council from the North Hackney constituency. She chaired several committees, most of which dealt with public health and the administration of hospital services. Emmet was defeated for re-election by an electoral swing to the left in 1933 and, when her husband died the following year, she moved with her four children to Amberley Castle. Emmet quickly returned to public service; from 1935 until 1944, she was chairman of the Children's Court and Matrimonial Court and, increasingly concerned with juvenile delinquency, she became chairman of the Approved School for girls at Shermanbury.

During World War Two, Emmet, having joined the Women's Voluntary Services as a Sussex County Organizer in 1938, supervised all war-related activities undertaken by women that were not subject to the authority of the Red Cross and the British Information service. In 1946, Emmet returned to politics as a member of the West Sussex County Council, where she served until 1952 when she was elected an Alderman. Named to the National Union Executive of the Conservative Party in 1948, Emmet combined her support for the Conservatives with her interest in women's affairs when she headed the Women's National Advisory Committee.

Emmet campaigned for Conservative candidates in the elections of 1951 and 1952, and she also chaired the 1952 Conservative Women's Conferences. Noted for her ability to interpret lucidly the complexities of British foreign policy, she was appointed Full Delegate to the United Nations in 1952 by Prime Minister Winston Churchill. Emmet served on the General Assembly's Social, Humanitarian, and Cultural Committee and, while living in New York, she studied the city's probationary and juvenile courts systems.

In 1955, Emmet was elected Conservative M.P. for the East Grinstead section of East Sussex, appointed chairman of the National Union of Conservatives, and presided over the Party's Annual Conference. In 1964, when she retired from parliament, Emmet was made a Life Peer, Baroness Emmet of Amberley. She continued to be active in public affairs, and in 1966 was appointed chairman of the Legal Aid Advisory Committee. Two years later, Baroness Emmet was elected Deputy Chairman of Committees in the House of Lords. From 1974 to 1977, she served as a member of the Select Committee on the EEC in the House of Lords.   L.F.

Daughter of Baron James Rennell, British diplomat and Ambassador to Rome, and Lilias (Guthrie) Rodd. Married Thomas Addis Emmet 1923 (d. 1934). Children: Gloria Lavinia Eileen, b. 1924; Christopher Anthony Robert, b. 1925; David Alastair Rennell, b. 1928; Penelope Ann Clare, b. 1932. Church of England. Educ: St. Margaret's Sch., Bushy; Lady Margaret Hall, Oxford, B.A. honors 1920, M.A., 1924; London Sch. of Economics. Social worker, Toynbee Hall Settlement, London 1919; Member, London County Council (for North Hackney) 1924–33; Justice of the Peace, Sussex 1936–71; Chmn., Children's

Court and Matrimonial Court 1935–44; Chmn., Child Guidance Cttee., Children's Cttee. of Further Educ.; Vice-Chmn., Educ. Cttee., Finance and General Purposes Cttee.; County Organizer, Woman's Volunteer Services 1939–45; Co-councillor of West Sussex 1944–52; Chmn., Sussex County Advisory Probation Cttee. 1945–51; Member, Home Office Probation Advisory Cttee. and Home Office Special Commn. 1950; Vice-Chmn., Conservative Women's Natl. Advisory Cttee. 1950; Chmn., Conservative Women's Natl. Advisory Cttee. 1951–54; U.K. Delegate to the U.N. 1952, 1953; West Sussex Alderman 1952–67; M.P. (Conservative), East Grinstead Div. (East Sussex) 1955–64; Chmn., Natl. Union of Conservatives 1955; Chmn., Lord Chancellor's Cttee. on Legal Aid 1966; Deputy Speaker and Chmn., Cttee. of House of Lords 1968; Member, Select Cttee. of House of Lords European Economic Commn. Cttee. 1974–77. Hons: created Life Baroness 1964. *Author:* Introduction to The Woman's Point of View, 1949; contributed to report on "The Cinema and the Child," 1950.

H(OFFMAN) R(EYNOLDS) HAYS
Poet, novelist, translator, and anthropologist and playwright
Born New York, U.S.A., March 25th, 1904
Died Southampton, New York, U.S.A., October 10th, 1980

A noted poet as well as an accomplished novelist, playwright, television dramatist, and popular anthopologist, H.R. Hays is best known for his faithful, often definitive, translations of South American writers such as Pablo Neruda, César Vallejo, and Jorge Borges. His anthology, *12 Spanish American Poets* (1942), introduced these writers to a North American audience. Hays also translated several plays and the selected poems of Bertolt Brecht. Although he published only four slender volumes of his own poems over a period of 40 years, Hays's uncollected verse is extensive.

Courtesy Mrs. H.R. Hays

Born in New York and educated at Cornell, Columbia, and the University of Liège, Belgium, he began to write poetry copiously during the late 1920s while working as an instructor in the English Department of City College in New York. *Strange City,* his first book of poems, appeared in 1929. Hays's artistic and intellectual growth took place in the politically charged, socialist-oriented atmosphere of literary New York in the 1930s and, during this period, as Director of the American Historical Theater for the Federal Theater Project, several of his plays were produced for the stage—one of them, *The Ballad of Davy Crockett* (1936) was later set to music by Kurt Weill. While political themes and an urgent, though never strident or shrilly polemical, tone pervades his early plays, all of Hays's work, in whatever genre, is concerned with social justice and the ironies of history.

After leaving the American Historical Theater in 1938, Hays divided his time between teaching, travel, and writing. In 1939, he visited Mexico and, for the next several years, studied the language and culture of Latin America. He subsequently published articles in *Poetry* on Neruda and Vallejo which formed the basis of the biographical notes on these poets in *Anthology of Contemporary Latin*

American Poetry (1942); edited by Dudley Fitts, Hays served as a translator and assistant editor. For his work on this book, Yale University Press chose him to translate and edit *12 Spanish American Poets.*

First published in 1943 but difficult to obtain until its re-issue in 1972, the book has been highly praised for the power and acuity with which Hays rendered such poets as Neruda and Vallejo. Moreover, as the influence of Latin American literature on American poetry became widespread in the 1960s and 70s, several poet-translators of Neruda and Vallejo such as Robert Bly and James Wright [q.v.] acknowledged their debt to the anthology. Bly once said that Hays had revealed Neruda's "wildness" to him and, speaking of the post-Robert Lowell generation of American poets, James Wright observed: "For us, Hays is the beginning of South America."

During the 1940s, Hays continued to visit Spanish-speaking countries and translate their literature. He made several trips to Cuba, returned dozens of times to Mexico, and, in 1947–48, he journeyed from Peru to New York. Two of Hays's novels reflect his love of South American culture: *Stranger on the Highway* (1943) is set in 16th century Mexico; and *The Envoys* (1953) sympathetically treats the revolutionary aspirations of the Peruvian people. A bitter indictment of U.S. foreign policy, *The Envoys* was among the first novelistic depictions of the "ugly American." Other translations by Hays of Spanish American writers include *The Stone Knife* (1947), a novel by his friend José Revueltas; *The Selected Poems of Jorge Carrera Andrade* (1972).

At the insistence of a mutual friend, Hanns Eisler, Hays became Bertolt Brecht's principal American translator in the 1940s. His translation of *The Trial of Lucullus: A Play for Radio* was published in 1943 and premiered as an oratorio by Roger Sessions in Berkely, California, four years later. *Selected Poems* of Bertolt Brecht also appeared in 1947, the year that Brecht left the United States—to avoid the consequences of his testimony before the House Committee on Un-American Activities—to live in East Germany.

In 1950, Hays obtained a teaching position in the Drama Department at Wagner College in Staten Island. There he became associated with a group of writers surrounding Fred Coe, who produced numerous teleplays in the early days of live television. During this period, Hays also began to write about myth and anthropology for the popular reading audience. He never aspired to scientific objectivity in this field and, in *Early Man and His Gods* (1963), Hays said: "The writer confesses to a prejudice against bloodshed and violence. The reader will therefore discover non-neutral language is employed in describing these acts of human behavior." *The Dangerous Sex: The Myth of Feminine Evil,* originally published in 1964 and re-issued eight years later when it was praised by writers in the Women's Movement, examined the forms of female subjugation in the works of such authors as Strindberg, O'Neill, and Melville. A biography of anthropologist Franz Boas was unfinished at the time of Hays's death.

In 1968, Hays's *Selected Poems: 1933–1967* was published. According to critic Ralph J. Miller, Jr., Hays's selected work reveals "a poetry that is subtley meditative, often calm, full of the closest observation of objects, the life of nature, and seasonal change." These lines are from one of Hays's early imagist poems:

The iris blades
Emerge
Sharp, green,
From old trash,
Warm with Secret Life.

Speaking of the work which had influenced his poetry, Hays said: "I don't use 'verse forms,' don't have characteristic subjects, [I] belong on the whole to the generation which developed out of imagism after William Carlos Williams, Pound, Eliot, etc. I suppose W.C. Williams, Latin American and French surrealism are the chief influence. My poetry adds up to an autobiography of my reactions to the world which I have found myself."

                                                              R.W.

Son of Hoffman Reynolds H. and Martha (Stark) H. Married Juliette Levine, interior designer 1935. Children: Daniel Henry, b. 1940; Penelope Martha Brown, b. 1942. Atheist. Educ: Cornell Univ., Ithaca, N.Y., B.A. 1925; Columbia Univ., NYC, M.A. 1928; Univ. of Liège, Belgium 1930–31. Instr. in English Dept., City Coll., NYC 1928–29 and at Univ. of Minnesota, St. Paul 1929–33, on leave to study in Belgium 1930–31; Dir., American Historical Theater, div. of Works Progress Admin. 1933–38; Co-ed. with Harold Rosenberg of New Act (mag.) 1933–34; trips to Mexico, Cuba and South America 1939–75; Asst. Ed., Anthology of Contemporary Latin American Poetry 1940–42; Teacher of Drama and Play writing, Wagner Coll., Staten Island, N.Y. and Dir., N.Y. Writer's Conference 1950–55; Assoc. Prof. of English 1955–59 and Acting Head of Drama Dept. 1960–63, Fairleigh Dickinson Univ., Rutherford, N.J.; Coordinator of Drama program, Southampton Coll., Long Island Univ., Southampton, N.Y. 1965–69; organizer of poetry readings, East Hampton Guild Hall, East Hampton, N.Y. 1975–80. *Books: Poetry*—Strange City, 1929; Selected Poems 1933–67, 1968; Inside My Own Skin, 1974; Portraits in Mixed Media, 1978. *Novels*—Stranger on the Highway, 1943; Lie Down in Darkness, 1944 (published in U.K., 1948); The Takers of the City, 1946 (published in U.K., 1947); *The Envoys*, 1953. *Translations*— 12 Spanish American Poets: An Anthology, 1943 (reissued 1972); The Trial of Lucullus: A Play for Radio, by Bertolt Brecht, 1943 (published in U.K., 1960); The Stone Knife, by José Revueltas, 1947; Selected Poems of Bertolt Brecht, 1947; The Selected Writings of Juan Ramón Jimenéz, 1957; The Selected Poems of Jorge Carrera Andrade, 1972; Selected Poems of César Vallejo, 1981. *Play*—Vincent Van Gogh, included in Best Television Plays 1950–51. *Other*—From Ape to Angel: An Informal History of Social Anthropology, 1958 (published in U.S., 1959); In the Beginnings: Early Man and His Gods, 1963; The Dangerous Sex: The Myth of Feminine Evil, 1964 (reissued 1972; published in U.K., 1966); Birds, Beasts, and Men: A Humanistic History of Zoology, 1972 (published in U.K. 1973). *Juvenile*—The Kingdom of Hawaii, 1964; Charley Sang a Song (with a son, Daniel Hays); Explorers of Man: Five Pioneers in Anthropology, 1971. *Play productions:* The Ballad of Davy Crockett, 1936, restaged with music by Kurt Weill and retitled One Man from Tennessee, 1938; Medicine Show, written with Oscar Saul with music by Hanns Eisler, 1940; translation of Mother Courage by Bertolt Brecht, 1941; Lie Down in Darkness, 1944; translation of The Rise of Arturo Ui by Bertolt Brecht, 1957. Poetry appeared in numerous anthologies 1926–80; over 25 dramas written for television 1950–55. Member of P.E.N. and Television Writer's Guild. Nonfiction Award from G.P. Putnam's Sons for In the Beginnings: Early Man and His Gods, 1963.

Further reading: "H.R. Hays Issue" of Voyages by Millen Brand and Allen Planz, Winter, 1969; "H.R. Hays and Spanish America" in Street, ii, 3, 1978.

STEPHEN KUFFLER
Neurobiologist and teacher
Born Tap, Hungary, August 24th, 1913
Died Woods Hole, Massachusetts, U.S.A., October 10th, 1980

Courtesy Harvard Medical School

Dr. Stephen W. Kuffler was noted for his contributions to the understanding of neuromuscular transmission and the nature of inhibition in the nervous system. Kuffler was born in Tap, Hungary, and received his medical degree from the University of Vienna in 1937. After working briefly as a medical assistant in pathology at Vienna's University Clinic, he moved to Australia where, for the next seven years, he studied the stimulation of muscles by nerve cells at the Kanematsu Institute of Pathology in Sydney. During World War Two, he conducted a study of nerve injuries sustained by soldiers during combat. With the assistance of such colleagues as Abner McGhee Harvey and Detlev Bronk, Kuffler emigrated in 1945 to the United States where he obtained a fellowship which enabled him to study with Ralph W. Gerard at the University of Chicago.

In 1947 Kuffler joined the newly formed Biomedical Engineering Division at Johns Hopkins University's Wilmer Institute as an associate professor. Having acquired improved laboratory equipment and recruited brilliant students from England, Europe, and America, he quickly transformed the Institute into a leading center of ophthalmological and neurophysiological research. In 1948, concluding the work he had begun at the Kanematsu, Kuffler demonstrated that, contrary to established scientific belief, signal transmission between nerve and muscle cells is accomplished by chemical messengers rather than by electrical transmission. With Samuel W. Talbot, Director of the Wilmer Institute, he also developed a multibeam ophthalmoscope, designed for the investigation of localized inhibition in stimulated cells. In 1956 Kuffler became a full Professor of Ophthalmic Physiology and Biophysics at Johns Hopkins.

In 1959 Kuffler moved to the Harvard University Medical School where he helped establish the Department of Neurobiology. He became Chairman of the Neurobiology Department in 1966 and held the post until 1974 when he was named the John Franklin Enders University Professor. He received in 1972 Columbia University's Louisa Gross Horwitz Prize for outstanding research in biology and, in 1976, he was on the Wakeman Award for neuroscientific research which had contributed to the understanding of paraplegia.   T.B.

Son of William K. and Elizabeth K. Married Phyllis Shewcroft 1943. Children: Suzanne; Damien; Julian; Eugenie. Emigrated to Australia 1938, to USA 1945. Naturalized American 1954. Educ: Univ. of Vienna, M.D. 1937. Asst., Medicine Pathology, Univ. Clinic, Vienna 1937–38; Member, Kanematsu Inst., Sydney Hosp., Australia 1938–45; Fellow, Natl. Research Council, Australia 1943–45; Seymour Coman Fellow, Dept. Physiology, Univ. of Chicago

1945–47; Asst. Prof., ophthalmology 1947–56 and Prof., ophthalmic physiology and biophysics 1956–59, Wilmer Inst., Johns Hopkins Univ. With Harvard Univ. Medical Sch: Prof., neurophysiology 1959–63; Robert Winthrop Prof of Neurophysiology 1964–74; Chmn., Dept. of Neurobiology 1966–74; John Franklin Enders Univ. Prof. 1974–80. Harvey Lectr. from 1959; Ferrier Lectr., Royal Soc. 1965; non-resident Fellow, Salk Inst., La Jolla, Calif. from 1966; Silliman Memorial Lectr., Yale Univ. 1971; Sherrington Lectr. 1972. Trustee, Marine Biological Lab., Woods Hole, Mass.; Member: American Physiological Soc.; Physiological Soc. of England; Natl. Acad. of Science; American Acad. of Arts and Science; Austrian Acad. of Sciences. Foreign Member, Royal Soc. and Royal Danish Acad. of Arts and Letters. Hons: John Simon Guggenheim Fellow 1956; Passano Award 1971; Louisa Gross Horwitz Prize 1972; Proctor Award in Ophthalmology 1973; Dickson Prize in Medicine, Univ. of Pittsburg 1973; Wakeman Award 1976; Armin von Tschermak-Seysenegg Prize, Austrian Acad. of Sciences 1977; several hon. degrees. *Author:* (with J.G. Nicholls) From Neuron to Brain, 1976; numerous articles in scientific jrnls.

DERECK (NOEL MACLEAN) BRYCESON
Tanzanian government official and politician
Born Hangchow, Chekiang, China, December 30th, 1922
Died Hanover, Germany, October 11th, 1980

A close friend and political associate of President Julius Nyerere, Dereck Bryceson served in the Tanzanian Parliament longer than any other white member. Bryceson was also one of the first white settlers to support Tanganyikan independence from Great Britain and, when Tanganyika merged with Zanzibar in 1964 to form Tanzania, he held several ministerial posts concurrently with his parliamentary seat.

Born in China of British parents, Bryceson attended St. Paul's School in London. With the outbreak of World War Two, he joined the R.A.F. and was severely wounded in 1942 when his fighter plane was shot down during a reconnaissance mission. After a medical discharge from the service, Bryceson studied agriculture at Trinity College, Cambridge, gaining a B.A. degree in 1946. He subsequently emigrated to Kenya and worked as a farmer for five years before moving to Tanganyika, where he purchased a large farm near Mt. Kilimanjaro.

Bryceson first entered politics in the mid-1950s as a leader of the Tanganyika National Society. In 1956 he met Julius Nyerere, the brilliant, Western-educated African nationalist leader. Bryceson had been initially put off by Nyerere's uncompromising nationalism but, after repeated discussions, the two men became friends and political allies. Indeed, Bryceson shared Nyerere's vision of a free, multi-racial African state, with a legislative system that would extend the right to hold public office to all citizens, regardless of their color. This shared idealism, however, was pragmatically anchored; both men recognized that a quasi-democratic arrangement ensured the political dominance of black Africans in a country with a relatively small white population.

In 1957, Bryceson was appointed Assistant Minister for Social Services by the colonial government, which was preparing to grant autonomy to the Tanganyikans. In elections held the following year, Bryceson resigned to support Nyerere's party, the Tanganyika African Nationalist Union (TANU) which had declared its support for non-Africans sympathetic to nationalist goals. Bryceson, who spoke fluent Swahili and received enthusiastic backing from TANU, was elected to a seat in the Legislative Council from the Northern Province. Thereafter, Bryceson was among the most popular candidates in the country; on two occasions, he defeated black African opponents by overwhelming pluralities.

In Tanganyika's first self-rule cabinet, headed by Nyerere in 1961, Bryceson served as Minister for Health and Labor. When he refused to support employment policies preferential to blacks, Bryceson angered the Tanganyikan Federation of Labor. The dispute was settled in Bryceson's favor by Nyerere who feared that a black "tyranny of the majority" might oppress a politically weak community of white settlers. In the following decade, Bryceson held several ministerial posts and, during his tenure as Minister for Agriculture from 1965 until 1972, he helped establish the Ujamaa co-operative village plan, which promoted social and economic development in Tanzania's rural areas. As Director of National Parks in 1972, Bryceson encouraged the preservation of wildlife and moved the departmental headquarters from the North to Dar-Es-Salaam.

A Member of Parliament since 1965, Bryceson represented three Dar-es-Salaam districts and he was a candidate for re-election at the time of his death from cancer. He had been married since 1972 to Jane Goodall, the renowned zoologist.   L.F.

Son of Kenneth B. and Norma (Henderson) B. Married (1) Bobblie Littleton (dissolved); (2) Jane Goodall, zoologist and ethnologist, 1972. Lived in Kenya 1947–51 and in Tanganyika (later Tanzania) 1951–80. Educ: St. Paul's Sch., London; Trinity Coll., Cambridge Univ., B.A. 1946. Mil. Service: RAF, 208 Squadron 1940–43. Farmer in Kenya 1947–51 and in Tanganyika 1951–60; co-founder, Tanganyika Natl. Soc. 1955; Asst. Minister for Social Services 1957–58; elected rep. from Northern Province to Legislative Council on Tanganyika African Natl. Union ticket 1958; Vice-Chmn., Elected Members' Org. 1958; deputy leader, Opposition 1958–59. With govt. of Tanganyika: Minister for Mines and Commerce 1959–60; Minister of Health and Labor 1960–62; Minister for Agriculture 1962–64. With govt. of Tanzania: Minister for Health 1964; M.P. for Dar-es-Salaam North 1965–80; Minister of Agriculture, forests and wildlife 1965; Minister of Agriculture, food and cooperatives 1965–72. Dir., Natl. Parks from 1972; Dir., Livestock Development Authority; City Councillor, Dar-es-Salaam. Member of several cttees. and bds.
Further reading: The Political Development of Tanganyika by J. Clagett Taylor, 1963.

(PEDRO) ALBERTO DEMICHELLI (LIZASO)
Uruguayan President and writer
Born Rocha, Uruguay, August 7th, 1896
Died Montevideo, Uruguay, October 12th, 1980

Alberto Demichelli briefly served as interim President of Uruguay in the summer of 1976. Demichelli was among several civilian political leaders who supported the military coup of June, 1973 which brought to power Juan Maria Bordaberry, the man whom Demichelli replaced three years later. Demichelli also published several books on politics, government, and South American history.

An attorney by profession, Pedro Alberto Demichelli Lizaso entered politics as a member of the liberal Colorado Party which represented the urban interests of Montevideo, Uruguay's capital and most important city. By the late 1920s, he was a leader of the party and, in 1930, he became Minister of Public Education, Minister of the Interior, and Vice-President in the cabinet of President Juan Pablo Terra. Opposed by a hostile majority in the Uruguayan Congress, Terra dissolved the parliamentary body in 1933 and declared himself the nation's sole political authority. Demichelli retained his posts until 1935 when he abandoned public service; he held no significant offices between 1935 and 1973.

The 1973 military coup was largely a reaction against the government's inability to suppress the urban guerrilla organization known as the Tupamaras. This revolutionary, Marxist-oriented group, formed in the early 1960s, had initiated a terrorist campaign which included numerous kidnappings and bank robberies. The Tupamaras had claimed responsibility for the 1970 murder of Daniel Mitrione, a U.S. foreign aid official who was alleged to have worked closely with the Uruguayan police, and the 1971 kidnapping of British Ambassador Geoffrey Jackson. Believing the restoration of civil order to assume precedence over constitutional rule, Demichelli and other civilian political figures supported the armed coup which brought Bordaberry to office and installed Demichelli as Vice-President of the country and President of the ruling Council of State.

The Council of State, which was established by the military to replace the legislature, quickly moved to ban political and union activities and impose censorship on the press. Effective power in the new arrangement, however, was held only by the military; Bordaberry and Demichelli were little more than figureheads. Thus, in June 1976, the army, which had been become dissatisfied with Bordaberry, ousted him and elevated the elderly Demichelli to the Presidency. After serving as caretaker for 80 days, he was replaced by Aparicio Mendez, the present Uruguayan chief of state.   T.P.

Married Sofia Alvarez Vignoli 1925. One son. Lawyer. From 1930–35: Minister of Public Educ.; Minister of the Interior; V.P. of Uruguay. Pres. of the Council of State and V.P. of Uruguay 1974–76; Pres. of Uruguay 1976. Hons: various hons. from Univ. of Montevideo and Univ. of Buenos Aires. *Author:* Los Entes Autonomes, 1925; Gobierno Local Autonomo, 1929; Lo Contencioso Administrativo, 1934; Formacion Constitucional Rioplatense: Origen Federal Argentino, 1966; Formacion Nacional Argentina, 1972.

LOUIS GUILLOUX
Novelist
Born Saint-Brieuc, Brittany, France, January 15th, 1899
Died Saint-Brieuc, Brittany, France, October 14th, 1980

Louis Guilloux was hailed by Albert Camus, André Gide, and André Malraux as the first politically engaged writer to portray honestly and without sentimentality the lives of common people. A committed socialist, Guilloux's political sympathies were unmistakably expressed in his novels; he examined the realities of working-class existence and chronicled the shattering impact of World War One upon French provincial life, contrasting the shared sense of community among workers with the stifling narrowness of the rural petit-bourgeoisie.

Guilloux was born in St.-Brieuc on the Brittany coast. He lived there and in other small Breton villages for most of his life and used the region in his fiction—as Joyce used Dublin—as a microcosm of the outside world. His father, a cobbler by profession, was the secretary of a socialist organization and Guilloux became active in leftist politics as a youth. In 1918, he moved to Paris and supported himself by various odd jobs until 1921 when he became a journalist; he abandoned the profession three years later to devote himself to writing.

His first book, *The House of the Common People,* a novelization of his impoverished childhood which depicted the struggles of a poor shoemaker and his family in the years preceding World War One, was published in 1927 and received the Blumenthal Prize. Guilloux was praised by Albert Camus for restoring to the common people "the only grandeur that they can never lose, that of truth." Two years later he co-edited (with Daniel Halévy) the letters of Pierre-Joseph Proudhon, the nineteenth century anarchist and father of French socialism.

Publication, in 1935, of *Bitter Victory (Le Sang Noir)* established Guilloux's international literary reputation. The novel, set in an isolated Breton village on a day in 1917, a critical year in the war, is the story of philosophy professor nicknamed Cripure—a contraction of the first and last syllable of Kant's *Critique de la Raison Pure*—who is in despair. Formerly an idealist and believer in humanity, Cripure has lost faith; his wife, whom he has always loved and with whom he had a son, has abandoned him, and the woman with whom he lives deceives him. Once a writer of optimistic philosophies, he is now preparing an *Anthology of Despair;* "My thesis," he says, "is completely negative. I destroy every idol and I no longer have a God at the altar." The brutalities of war also contribute to his hopelessness and Cripure, who has been called a precursor of Roquentin, the protagonist of Sartre's [q.v.] first novel, must confront the question of suicide.

In the mid-1930s, Guilloux was active in the fight against fascism. He served as secretary of the first congress of anti-fascist writers and visited Russia with André Gide; however, increasingly disenchanted with the course of Russian politics under Stalin, Guilloux rejected communist orthodoxy. Guilloux was also regional secretary of the Secours Populaires, which organized relief for Spanish Civil War refugees; *Salido* (1976) was the story of a refugee who wants to return to Spain and fight against the fascists. When Guilloux was forced to hide from the Gestapo in Toulouse for several years, the English-speaking world publicized their concern for his condition.

In his first postwar novel, *The Jigsaw Puzzle* (Le Jeu de patience, literally translated as *The game of patience,* 1949), Guilloux portrayed the history, from 1912 to the Liberation, of a small Breton town much like St.-Brieuc. A structurally complex novel in which the distinction between past and present and what is real and imagined is virtually obliterated, it is intentionally confusing. Although one critic described it as a game of patience for the reader, Guilloux nevertheless painted rich, vivid, and compassionate portraits of individual lives. Referring to his view of both aesthetics and life, he said, "There is only one reality, that of man." For *The Jigsaw Puzzle,* Guilloux received the prestigious Prix Renaudot in 1949.

A deep pessimism is evident in many of Guilloux's postwar novels; his hope for social revolt gave way to a bitter acceptance of the oppressiveness of everyday life. Camus once said, "I am a pessimist where man's fate is concerned but an optimist where man himself is concerned;" Guilloux, once possessed of a buoyant optimism, appeared to have lost faith in man as well.   A.W.

Son of Albert-Gaston G., cobbler and secty. of socialist group, and Philomène Marier S. Married Renée Tricoire 1924. Educ: scholarship student at lycée in St.-Brieuc; also studied in Rouen. Moved to Paris 1918; various occupations 1918–21; proofreader and translator for L'Excelsoir 1921 and L'Instransigeant 1921–24; professional writer since 1924. Secty., First Congress of Anti-Fascist Writers 1935; Regional Secty., Secours Populaires Français 1935–40; returned to Brittany after German occupation of France, tried to escape to England, fugitive from Gestapo, lived in hiding in Toulouse; interpreter for American Army in St.-Brieuc after Allied liberation. Hons: Prix Bluementhal (for La Maison du peuple) 1927; Prix Populist (for Le pain des rêves) 1942; Prix Theophraste-Renaudot (for Le jeu depatience) 1949; Grand Prix Natl. des Lettres 1967; Grand Prix de Littérature de l'Académie Française 1973; Officier des Arts et des Lettres. *Books: Novels*—La Maison du Peuple, 1927, new ed. with foreward by Albert Camus, 1953; Dossier Confidentiel, 1930; Hyménée, 1932; Angelina, 1934; Le Sang Noir, 1935, reprinted 1966, 1969, trans. as Bitter Victory by Samuel Putnam in U.S. 1936, in U.K. 1940; 1937 ed., introduction by Jean-Louis Bory, 1955 ed., introduction by André Malraux, new ed. with pages of the author's jrnls. and notebooks from 1933–63, 1964; Le Pain des rêves, 1942, 30th ed. 1948; Le Jeu de patience, 1949; Parpagnacco: ou, Le conjuration, 1954; Les batailles perdus, 1960; La confrontation, 1967; Salido, suivi de O.K. Joe!, 1976. *Short story collections*—Compagnons, 1931; German trans. Gefahrten: Erzahlung, 1950, adapted for television, 1967; Histoires de brigands, 1936. *Play*—Cripure; pièce en trois parties, 1962, produced by Marcel Marechal, Théâtre du Cathédral de Lyon, 1967. *Essays*—Coco perdu: essai de voix, 1978; Carnets (Notebooks 1921–44), 1978. *Translations*—La Nymphe au coeur fidele, 1928; Paturages du Ciel by John Steinbeck. *Television adaptations*—La folie Almayer and Heart of Darkness by Joseph Conrad, 1973; Les Thibault by Roger Martin du Gard. *Other*—(co-ed.) Lettres de Pierre-Joseph Proudhon, 1929; Souvenirs sur G. Palante, 1931; Le lecteur ecrit: choix de lettres receuillies par Louis Guilloux, 1932; Absent de Paris (memoirs), 1952; "Anti-preface," Helion, Retrospective 1926–69, 1969; La Bretagne que j'aime (text by Louis Guilloux, photographs by Charles le Quintrec), 1973; preface to Souvenirs de Bretagne, 1977. *Collections:* Louis Guilloux: Textes choisis et présentés par Edouard Prigent, 1970.
Further reading: The Intellectual Hero: Studies in the French Novel, 1886–1955 by Victor Brombert, 1961.

MARY O'HARA (ALSOP)
Children's author
Born Cape May Point, New Jersey, U.S.A., July 10th, 1885
Died Chevy Chase, Maryland, U.S.A., October 15th, 1980

Courtesy O'Hara estate

Best-known for her stories of a boy and his horse, and most notably the novel *My Friend Flicka* (1941), Mary O'Hara Alsop, who wrote under the name Mary O'Hara, won the hearts of readers everywhere with her enduring three-part saga of the McLaughlin family and their Wyoming ranch. Two of the books were sufficiently popular to merit adaptation to other media; *Green Grass of Wyoming* (1946), became a feature film, and *Flicka* served as the basis for both a film and a television series.

Mary O'Hara Alsop was born into an old American family with forebears that included William Penn and the theologian Jonathan Edwards. She was raised in Brooklyn, New York, attended finishing school in New England, and studied music and languages in Europe. In 1905, O'Hara married Kent Kane Parrot. The couple lived in California, where O'Hara wrote film scripts. The marriage ended in 1922, and O'Hara married Helge Sture-Vasa, with whom she went to live in Wyoming. That marriage, too, ended in divorce, and Mary O'Hara returned east, to Connecticut, to live. As a child she had developed interests in horses, writing, and music, and the years she spent on a ranch in Wyoming during her second marriage provided her with material for the McLaughlin-family novels.

Through the course of three books, Ken McLaughlin, the main character, matures from a boy of ten into a young man of seventeen. The novels are linked thematically by the McLaughlins' financial troubles and by the conflict between Ken and his strong-willed father, a West Point graduate who moved West with his artistic, Bryn Mawr-educated wife. The trilogy was praised by critics, who admired both its imagery—Marianne Hauser suggested that the reader could "smell the grass and feel the coolness of the wind"—and the sensitivity of its character portrayals: "Mary O'Hara," wrote Fred Erisman, a biographer, "makes the subtle antagonisms between the day-dreaming Ken and the determined Rob as much a part of the book as the genuine love that all three share. She deals, in fact, with all facets of life, . . . making the works accounts of believably fallible persons who are trying, at considerable cost to themselves, to live the life of their dreams."

In addition to her novels and screen adaptations, which included *The Prisoner of Zenda* and *Turn to the Right,* Mary O'Hara was a composer of works for piano and for chorus. She also wrote a play, *The Catch Colt,* for which she provided a musical score. O'Hara once told an interviewer that she "never really had any ambitions. I had always been writing, always composing. I just kept on doing what I had always done, and pretty soon somebody wanted to buy it." H.N.P.

Daughter of Reese Fell A., Episcopal priest, and Mary Lee (Spring) A. Married: (1) Kent Kane Parrot 1905 (div. 1922); (2) Helge Sture-Vasa 1922 (div. 1947). Children: Mary O'Hara; Kent Kane, Jr., retired U.S. Air Force col. Roman Catholic. Educ: Packer Inst., Brooklyn, studied foreign langs. and music in Europe. Active as film writer in Hollywood ca. 1905–20, novelist, playwright, and composer. *Books: Novels*—(as Mary O'Hara) My Friend Flicka, 1941; (as Mary O'Hara) Thunderhead, 1943; (as Mary O'Hara) Green Grass of Wyoming, 1947; The Son of Adam Wingate, 1952; Wyoming Summer, 1963. *Play*—The Catch Colt, 1964 (with music by the author; also novella, 1979). *Others*—(as Mary Sture-Vasa) Let Us Say Grace, 1930; Novel-in-the-Making, 1954; A Musical in the Making, 1966, *Compositions*—Esperan, 1943; May God Keep You, 1946; Wyoming Suite for Piano, 1946; Windharp; songs and other works for piano.

MIKHAIL ALEKSEYEVICH LAVRENTYEV
Mathematician, professor and administrator
Born Kazan, Tatar, Russian empire, November 6th, 1900
Died Moscow, U.S.S.R., October 15th, 1980

A distinguished mathematician and an exemplary Communist Party member, Mikhail Lavrentyev was appointed Hero of Socialist Labor, his nation's most prestigious civilian award. He was also a Candidate Member of the Communist Party's Central Committee and a Vice-President of the Soviet Union Academy of Sciences.

Lavrentyev, born almost seventeen years before the October Revolution, graduated in 1922 from Moscow University, where he subsequently taught until the German invasion during World War Two. A specialist in the theory of the functions of complex variables, Lavrentyev's first publication, *The Theory of Conformal Mappings* (1934), earned him directorship of the department of theoretical mathematics at the Mathematical Institute, a branch of the Soviet Union's Academy of Science. In 1939, with the publication of another theoretical study, he was named Director of the Mathematical Institute of the Ukrainian Academy of Sciences.

Lavrentyev also organized, and took part in, a scientific expedition which studied the break-up of ice on Dickson Island off the coast of northern Siberia and he accompanied another to the eastern end of the Soviet Union to determine the possible use of subterranean heat in the Kamchatka Peninsula. More recently, he had developed theories in the field of applied hydrodynamics and explosions, and conducted numerous applied computer studies.

A recipient of the Order of the Patriotic War, Lavrentyev joined the Communist Party in 1952 and was made a Candidate Member of the Party's Central Committee in 1961. During its convocations in 1958 and 1962, he served as a Deputy to the Supreme Soviet. A full member of the Soviet Union's Academy of Sciences in 1946, Lavrentyev served as its Vice-President in 1957; an honorary member of several foreign academies, he was also named Vice-President of the International Mathematical Union in 1966. The holder of five Orders of Lenin and two Stalin Prizes, and a titled professor in mathematics at Novosibrisk University, Lavrentyev directed the Siberian branches of the Academy of Sciences. His published studies included *Problems of Mechanics of Continuous Media* (1961) and *Methods of Calculations of Rail Chains by Electronic Computers* (1963).   L.R.

Educ: Moscow Univ., grad. 1922. Mil. Service: undesignated branch 1942–45 (Order of the Patriotic War). Prof. of Mathematics, Moscow Univ. 1931–41; Dir., Dept. of the Theory of Functions, Mathematical

Inst., USSR Acad. of Science 1934–39, made full Member of Acad. 1946; full Member 1939 and Dir., Inst. of Mechanics and Mathematics 1939–41, Ukranian Acad. of Science. With USSR Acad. of Science: Dir., Inst. of Precision Mechanisms and Computer Engineering 1950–53; Section Academician, Dept. of Physico-Mathematical Science 1954–57; Chmn., and Dir., Inst. of Hydrodynamics, Siberian Dept. since 1957. Member since 1952, and Candidate Member, Central Cttee. since 1961, Communist Party, Soviet union; V.P., USSR Acad. of Science 1957; Deputy, Supreme Soviet 1958, 1962; V.P., Intnl. Mathematics Union 1966–70; Member, Acads. of Science in Czechoslovakia 1966, Bulgaria, German Democratic Republic 1969, Poland 1970, France 171. Hons: Stalin Prize 1946, 1949; Lenin Prize 1958; Hero of Socialist Labor 1967; five Orders of Lenin; three Red Banners of Labor awards. *Author:* The Theory of Conformal Mappings, 1934; On Some Properties of Single Leaf Functions Applied to Theory of Jets; Fundamental Theorem of the Theory of Quasi-Conformal Depictions of Plane Areas, 1948; Problems of Mechanics of Continuous Media, 1961; Methods of Calculations of Rail Chains by Electronic Computers, 1963.

PRINCE PETER OF GREECE AND DENMARK
Anthropologist and Greek political figure
Born Paris, France, 1908
Died London, England, October 15th, 1980

Fourth in line to the Greek throne, Prince Peter of Greece and Denmark was a frequent critic of the royal Greek hierarchy. During the constitutional crisis of 1965, he called for the establishment of a "crowned democracy" in Greece and publicly announced his availability as a successor to his first cousin, King Constantine II. An ethnologist, Prince Peter published four anthropological studies.

Born in Paris, Prince Peter, the son of Prince George and Princess Marie Bonaparte, was the grandson of King George I and a cousin of Prince Phillip, the husband of Queen Elizabeth II. He studied political science and law at the University of Paris before obtaining a doctorate in anthropology at the London School of Economics with a thesis on Tibetan polyandry. (He had observed cultures in which women took more than one husband during an expedition to Tibet in 1937–39.) Having served as a private with the Royal Danish Foot Guards in 1932, Prince Peter was placed in charge of the allied liaison office in Athens when the Italians invaded Greece in 1940. When the German Army penetrated the Greek mainland in 1941, he moved with the Greek Royal Family to Crete and later participated in the Battle of Crete. During the war he took part in General Montgomery's desert campaign and, in 1945, he was stationed with Chiang Kai-Shek's headquarters in Chung King, China. Prince Peter finished his military service in 1947 having attained the rank of major; among several other decorations, he was awarded Britain's C.B. Prince Peter's marriage in 1941 to Irene Ovtchinnikov, a Russian commoner, and his failure to receive the King's consent, earned him the resentment of the Greek monarchy. His wife was ostracized by the royal court and, in 1947, Prince Peter was asked by King Paul to renounce his right of succession to the throne. When he refused, he was ordered to leave the country which was then wracked by civil war.

In the 1950s, Prince Peter conducted anthropological expeditions in India and Tibet. However, his father died in 1961 and he returned to Greece. He was offered a position with Athens University's anthropology department but the palace, which did not want him to remain in Greece, prevented the appointment. When King Paul died in 1964, bringing Prince Peter's cousin to the throne, the Prince used the situation as an opportunity to criticize the monarchy and its rules of succession. He accused Queen Frederika of being a "spendthrift" and he questioned the legality of a clause in the 1952 constitution which granted precedence in the line of succession to the daughters of kings over their male cousins. As long as King Constantine II had no son, the Prince reasoned, he was the legal heir. The royal court and the parliament ignored his arguments but, in 1965, King Constantine provoked a civil crisis when he challenged the authority of the Prime Minister. Prince Peter announced that he would support a democratic form of government and would accept the throne should his cousin be forced to abdicate. Three years later, a military dictatorship came to power, King Constantine's counter-coup failed, and the Greek monarchy was abolished in 1974.

Prince Peter died at the National Hospital for Nervous Diseases in London. He had been a member of the Royal Anthropological Institute and his valuable collection of Tibetan manuscripts were donated to the Royal Library in Copenhagen.   I.J.

Son of Prince George and Princess Marie Bonaparte. Married Irene Ovtchinnikov 1941. Lived in Kalimpong, India 1947–57, and in Copenhagen, Denmark, Paris, France, and London 1974–80. Educ: Univ. of Paris, baccalaureat; London Sch. of Economics, Ph.D., anthropology 1959. Mil. Service: Royal Danish Foot Guards 1932; transferred to Greek Army ca. 1934; Chief Liaison Officer 1940–41; active service with Freek Greek forces in Arabia 1942–43; attached to Military HQ of Chiang Kai-shek, Chungking, China; Maj., Greek Army 1947, demobilized 1947. Conducted expedition to Tibet 1937–39; barred from Greece by King Paul 1947; barred from India 1957; second visit 1950–52, and third visit 1978, to Tibet. Member, Royal Anthropological Inst. Hons: Grand Chancellor of the Danish Order of St. John; C.B.

LUIGI LONGO
Secretary General of Italian Communist Party, resistance leader and writer
Born Fubine Monferrato, Italy, March 15th, 1900
Died Rome, Italy, October 16th, 1980

Luigi Longo was a leading figure in Italian politics for almost six decades. As Deputy Secretary General of the Italian Communist Party (PCI) and—after party chief Palmiro Togliatti's death in 1964— as Secretary General, Longo worked for a distinctively Italian "road to socialism," though he remained loyal to the Soviet party line until the invasion of Czechoslovakia in 1968. After the Second World War

when the CPI was no longer an illegal organization, Longo was a member of the Italian parliament. He assumed the largely ceremonial office of President of the CPI in 1972.

Luigi Longo was born in the Piedmont region of Italy's industrial north. His parents owned a small farm on which they harvested grapes and, while Luigi was a child, they moved to Turin and opened a restaurant near the vast Fiat auto works. In 1915, Longo enrolled in the Turin Polytechnic where he studied engineering for three years before being drafted into the Italian Army during World War One. Assigned to the Officer's Training Corps in Parma, Longo attained the rank of commissioned officer. During his military service, Longo was introduced to Marxist theory and, when he returned to Turin in 1920, an area seething with revolutionary discontent, he was employed as an office worker in the Fiat factory. Longo joined a student socialist group and, shortly thereafter, was elected its secretary, a position which brought him into close contact with Palmiro Togliatti and the Marxist philosopher Antonio Gramsci.

In 1921, Gramsci, Togliatti and a group of radicals, which included Longo, seceded from the Italian Socialist Party (PSI) to form the Italian Communist Party (PCI). These dissidents rejected both the liberal reformism of the PSI leadership and the revolutionary romanticism of its rank and file members; instead, Togliatti, Gramsci, Longo, and their relatively small band of followers built a tightly organized, working-class party closely associated with Moscow. Having proved himself a gifted recruiter of disaffected socialists into the PCI, Longo was assigned to organize anti-fascist resistance groups in the Piedmont region as part of the communist campaign against Mussolini's bid for power. Party leaders were impressed with Longo and, as a measure of his growing prominence, they selected him in late 1922 to attend the Fourth Congress of the Communist International, the last congress over which Lenin was to preside.

Shortly after Mussolini became Premier in October, 1922, he outlawed the PCI while the Communist leaders were away in Moscow. When Longo and his confederates surreptitiously re-entered the country, they adopted pseudonyms—Longo was known as "Gallo" for the next 20 years—and the party went underground. During this period, Italian communists were brutally persecuted by Mussolini's black shirts; Longo himself was seriously injured in a beating administered by a gang of fascist thugs, and he was twice arrested and briefly imprisoned, in 1923 and 1924, for illegal political activities. By the late 1920s, the PCI was forced to move its headquarters to Paris, and Longo and Togliatti became increasingly dependent upon Stalin's support.

While living in exile in France, Switzerland, and Russia, Longo helped organized anti-fascist resistance activities in Italy and, from 1932 until 1934, he attended the Frunze Military Academy in Moscow, where he received instruction in tactical guerilla warfare. In 1935, he was a principal organizer of the Brussels congress which opposed the Italian invasion of Ethiopia and, also that year, he was named to the Comintern's Executive and Political Committees, thus achieving membership at the highest levels of the international Communist movement. With the outbreak of the Spanish Civil War in July, 1936, Longo traveled to Madrid and helped organize international brigades of anti-fascist volunteers who fought with the Loyalist forces. In late

1936, he assumed military command of the 2nd Brigade and, after being wounded in combat, was named inspector general of the international brigades, a position he held until the collapse of the Republican government in 1939.

Longo retreated to Paris, where he headed the Unione Popolaire Italiana, an organization of exiled Italians who participated in the popular front's struggle against fascism. However, when the French government authorized a dragnet raid of Communists shortly before the start of World War Two, Longo was arrested, locked up in a concentration camp, and handed over to the Italians in 1941. He was imprisoned on an island in the Tyrrhenian Sea until July, 1943, when Mussolini fell from power. Longo quickly made his way to Rome where he futilely attempted to foment a popular revolt against the city's German occupiers. He then moved north to serve as Command-ment-General of the Garibaldi Brigades, cadres of leftist guerilla fighters, and as Deputy Commander of the Volunteer Freedom Corps, a group of popular front partisans. These resistance units, along with others, fought so effectively in the Nazi-occupied regions that the Germans were forced to dispatch more than a quarter of their army to northern Italy. In April, 1945, a group of partisans serving under Longo captured Mussolini as he attempted to escape to Switzerland; Togliatti and Longo swiftly issued the order for his execution. The U.S. Army awarded Longo the Bronze Star for his role in the Allied war effort.

After 1945, the PCI, regarded by workers and intellectuals as the only Italian organization to have unequivocally opposed fascism, consolidated its wartime gains and the once small, beleagured Communist Party soon became the largest in western Europe. In 1946, Longo became Deputy Secretary of the PCI and, in national elections held that year, he was elected to the Constituent Assembly, the forerunner of the Chamber of Deputies to which Longo was elected in 1948. Although Togliatti and Longo steered the PCI toward demo-cratic participation in Italian political life and both men rejected much, but not all, of Leninist dogma, they were, nonetheless, "Old Bolsheviks" with close ties to Stalin. Indeed, Western anti-commun-ists called Longo "Il Duro" ("the Hard one"), and regarded him as an intransigent Stalinist prepared to depose the conciliatory Togliatti and lead a communist uprising against the Italian republic. For the next decade and a half, however, Longo and Togliatti worked together to reconcile contradictory political forces; dutifully loyal to the interests and demands of the Soviet State, they nevertheless addressed the realities of Italian society and became the most effective exponents in the Communist-bloc of the concept of "national roads to socialism."

Relations between Moscow and the PCI in the 1950s were marked by extreme caution. When Nikita S. Khrushchev denounced Stalin in 1956, Longo and Togliatti abandoned their Stalinism, but they never accepted Yugoslavian Premier Tito's [q.v.] strict division of Marxist politicians into two categories: those who were Stalinists and those who were "true" communists. Indeed, Longo's response to Tito's harsh condemnation of the Soviet invasion of Hungary was a clever combination of evasion and tact. Longo understood that a power struggle was under way in Russia which pitted moderate adherents of Khrushchev against Kremlin hard-liners, and he, unlike Tito, carefully avoided rhetoric which might undermine the Soviet Premier and force him to adopt more conservative positions. Consequently, Longo affirmed the value of Yugoslavia's individual "path to socialism," but upheld the right of Soviet intervention in eastern European nations to prevent them from embracing capitalism.

Throughout the 1950s and 60s, Longo was the chief defender of PCI policies; although not a theoretician himself, he could adroitly articulate the Marxist catechism. When a vocal group of Maoist intellectuals attacked the PCI leadership as "revisionists" whose naîve emphasis upon democratic challenges to the Italian state had allowed modern monopoly capitalism to develop unimpeded, Longo issued a stern rebuttal. The PCI, he said, believed it possible, and desirable, to establish a nonmonopolistic capitalism as a stage in Italy's progress toward the socialist ideal. Answering the charge of "revisionism," Longo pointed out that even Lenin had granted that a peaceful, gradual transition to socialism was possible. To prevent the creation of a radical splinter party, however, Longo occasionally praised aspects of the Chinese revolution.

In 1964,Togliatti died and Longo was unanimously elected Secretary General of the PCI. Under his leadership, the Party made consistent gains in Italian politics and, in the 1968 elections, drew almost even with the ruling Christian Democrats. Longo effected a rapprochement with the French Communist Party in the mid-1960s when the PCF softened its rigid ideological stance and demonstrated a willingness to establish a united leftist front; in 1968, Longo publicly opposed the Soviet invasion of Czechoslovakia.

Longo retired as party secretary in 1972, relinquishing his power to Enrico Berlinguer and a new generation of Euro-Communists. Although Longo held the title of party President, the position held little political power. Still, he criticized the Euro-Communist strategy of collaboration with the ruling Christian Democrats and, in 1977, after the Soviets had challenged the independent views of Señor Carillo, the head of the Spanish Communist Party, Longo was allowed to publish an article in Pravda which defended the concept of national roads to socialism.   E.T.

Son of peasants. Married: (1) Teresa Noce (div.); (2) Bruna Conti. Children: three sons. Educ: Turin Polytechnic ca. 1915–19. Conscripted into Italian Army 1919; office worker with Fiat, Turin 1920; joined Socialist party 1920; founding member, Italian Communist Party (PCI) 1921; appointed to Secretariat of Young Communist Fedn. and delegate, 4th Congress of Comintern, Moscow 1922; arrested and imprisoned for political activities 1923–24; Ed., L'Avanguardia 1924; Rep., Young Communist Fedn. at 3rd Congress of PCI 1926; Member, Young Communist Intnl., Moscow 1926–27; PCI rep. in France, Switzerland, and Russia ca. 1928–35; Member, Exec. Cttee. and Political Cttee., Comintern since 1935; Inspector Gen., Intnl. Brigades, Spain 1936–39; Pres., Unione Popolaire Italiana, Paris 1939; imprisoned in France 1939–41 and in Italy 1941–43. With Partisan Resistance Movement in Italy 1943–45: PCI rep. for Cttee. of Natl. Liberation for upper Italy; Commandant-Gen., Garibaldi Brigades; Deputy-Comdr., Volunteer Freedom Corps. Deputy Secty.-Gen. 1945–64, Secty.-Gen. 1964–72 and Pres. from 1972, CPI. Deputy, Constituent Assembly 1946; Deputy, Natl. Assembly 1948, 1953, 1958, 1963, 1968; Ed., Via Nuove and Critica Marxista after 1945. Hons: U.S. Bronze Star; Stella D'Oro Garibaldina. *Author:* Un popolo alla macchia, 1948; Sulla via dell'insurrezione nazionale, 1954; Le Brigate Internazional in Spagna, 1956; Revisionismo nuovo ed antico, 1957; Il miracolo economico Italiano e la critica Marxista, 1962; contributed articles to L'Unita and other political jrnls. *Further reading:* article in New York Times Magazine, November 8, 1964; Unity in Diversity by Donald M. Blackmer, 1968.

C(ARL) P(AUL) M(ARIA) ROMME
Dutch statesman
Born Brabant region, The Netherlands, December 21st, 1896
Died Tilburg, The Netherlands, October 16th, 1980

For fifty years C.P.M. Romme served his country as cabinet minister, party leader, diplomatic emissary, and senator. Born of an aristocratic Roman Catholic family in the southern Dutch region of Brabant, Romme studied law in Amsterdam although he never practiced as an attorney. After receiving his doctorate, he taught for several years before joining the Catholic People's Party (KVE), which he led for many years during a period when the KVE held considerable power in the Dutch Parliament. Professor Romme never sought elective office, although he was twice asked to serve as prime minister; he declined, believing he could work more effectively in a less public position. In the 1930s, however, he was appointed Minister for Social Affairs in the Colijn administration and he founded the first Dutch social welfare system. A member of the Dutch government when the Germans invaded Holland in 1940, Romme went underground; he was found and arrested, but later escaped.

After the war, Romme was assigned a diplomatic mission to Holland's major colonial possession, the Dutch East Indies. A three-month tour convinced him that the mother country should divest itself of the colony, and it was largely a result of his efforts that the independent Republic of Indonesia was established in 1949. Romme was also instrumental in gaining admission for the Netherlands in the Benelux customs union with Belgium and Luxembourg in 1947 (which later became the Benelux Economic Union), and he was a founder of the European Economic Community.

In his later years, Romme held a seat in the Dutch Senate. When he reached the age of 75 and was compelled by law to retire, a special title, Minister of State, was created for him by Queen Juliana.   K.B.

Educ: law studies in Amsterdam, doctorate. Teacher; joined Catholic People's Party (KVE); Minister for Social Affairs ca. 1930s; went underground 1940, arrested, and later escaped; diplomatic mission to Holland's colonial possessions, late 1940s; helped in 1949 establishment of Indonesia; a negotiator at formation of Benelux customs union, and a founder of the EEC. Member, Dutch Senate. Hons: created a special Minister of State by Queen Juliana ca. 1971.

EDWIN WAY TEALE
Naturalist, writer, photographer, and illustrator
Born Joliet, Illinois, U.S.A., June 2nd, 1899
Died Norwich, Connecticut, U.S.A., October 18th, 1980

Courtesy Teale estate

A nature photographer and writer of worldwide reputation, Edwin Way Teale has often been ranked on a level with John Bastram and Audubon. In over 30 books and numerous articles, he communicated his belief that nature is "something magical, something that fills a deep need of the human heart."

Teale spent part of his childhood on his grandfather's farm in Illinois, where he became familiar with the outdoors. After attending college at Earlham and earning a master's degree at Columbia University, he worked for several years as a writer in New York. In 1928 Teale became a staff feature writer for *Popular Science Monthly*, a position he held for thirteen years. During this period he did considerable traveling and wrote on all aspects of science for the magazine. His various studies resulted in his first published book, *The Book of Gliders*, in 1930.

While at *Popular Science Monthly* Teale developed his interest in photography, a hobby since childhood. Aroused by the challenge of photographing insects, he discovered that chilling an insect in his icebox would reduce the animal's level of activity so that it could then be photographed in its natural setting. The group of entomological photographs from these experiments led to his first book as a naturalist, *Grassroots Jungles,* published in 1937. Teale soon became known as a nature photographer and displayed his work in many exhibitions, including one-man shows at the American Museum of Natural History in New York, and the Royal Photographic Salon in London. During his career, he built up a valuable photo file of over 30,000 nature negatives.

In 1941, after writing several more books on insects and photography, Teale resigned from his position at *Popular Science Monthly* to devote himself full-time to photographing and writing about nature. Over the next four decades he achieved his lifelong ambition of becoming a distinguished naturalist. In 1943 his *Near Horizons, The Story of an Insect Garden* won the John Burroughs Medal in 1943 for outstanding nature writing. In 1951 *North With the Spring* was published, the first of a four-volume study of the seasons in North America that is perhaps Teale's best-known work. *Autumn Across America* (1956), *Journey Into Summer* (1960) and *Wandering Through Winter* (1965), which won a Pulitzer Prize in 1966, completed the influential series. In preparing each of the books, Teale traveled some 20,000 miles throughout the U.S.

Near the end of his career, Teale visited Britain to see the section of Yorkshire from which his father had emigrated. He expressed his horror at the area's industrialization in *Springtime in Britain,* published in 1970. Teale was contributing editor of *Audubon Magazine* from 1942 until his death and belonged to many nature societies, including the American Ornithologists' Union. His nature studies have been translated into many languages and transcribed into Braille. Orville Prescott of the New York *Times* summed up the naturalist's career when he wrote in a 1960 review of *Journey Into Summer* that Teale was "a man permanently in love with the glory and wonder of life in all its fascinating forms."

J.S.

Born Edwin Alfred Teale. Son of Oliver Cromwell T., railroad mechanic, and Clara Louise Way T., teacher. Married Nellie Imogene Donovan 1923. Son: David Allen, b. 1925 (d. 1945). Methodist. Educ: Earlham Coll., Richmond, Ind., B.A. 1922; Columbia Univ., NYC, M.A. 1926; Earlham Coll., Litt. D. 1957; Indiana Univ., LHD 1970; Univ. of New Haven, Sc.D. 1978. Mil. Service: U.S. Army WWI. Instr. in public speaking, and debating coach, Friends Univ., Wichita, Kans. 1922–24; Editorial Asst. to Dr. Frank Crane and writer of syndicated inspirational editorials, NYC 1925–27; staff feature writer, Popular Science Monthly 1928–41; freelance writer from 1941; Contributing Ed., Audubon Magazine from 1942. Member, and Pres. 1942–43, Baldwin Bird Club; V.P. 1943 and Pres. 1944, N.Y. Entomological Soc.; Pres., American Nature Study Soc. 1947; Pres., Brooklyn Entomological Soc. 1949, 1950, 1953; Pres., Thoreau Soc. 1958; Member. American Ornithologists' Union and Linnean Soc.; Explorers Club; Assoc. Member, Royal Photographic Soc., London and N.Y. Acad. of Science; Fellow, American Assoc. for the Advancement of Science. Hons: John Burroughs Medal 1943; Christopher Award 1957; Indiana Univ. Writers Conference Award 1960; Secondary Educ. Bd., Annual Book Award 1961; Eva L. Gordon Award, American Nature Study Soc. 1965; Sarah Chapman Francis Medal 1965; Pulitzer Prize, non-fiction, (for Wandering Through Winter) 1966; Sarah Josepha Hale Award 1975; Ecology Award, Mass. Horticultural Soc. 1975; Conservation Medal, New England Wildflower Soc. 1975. *Author:* The Book of Gliders, 1930, rev. ed. 1939; Grassroots Jungles, 1937, rev. ed. 1944; The Boys' Book of Insects, 1939; The Boys' Book of Photography, 1939; The Golden Throng, 1940; Byways to Adventure, 1942; Near Horizons, The Story of an Insect Garden, 1942; Dune Boy, The Early Years of a Naturalist, 1943, Armed Services ed., 1944; Insect Life, 1944; The Lost Woods, 1945; Days Without Time, 1948; North with the Spring, 1951; Insect Friends, 1955; Autumn Across America, 1956; Adventures in Nature, 1959; Journey into Summer, 1960; The Lost Dog, 1961; The Bees, 1961; The Strange Lives of Familiar Insects, 1962; Wandering through Winter, 1965; Springtime in Britain, 1970; Photographs of American Nature, 1972; A Naturalist Buys an Old Farm, 1974; A Walk Through the Year, 1978; numerous articles in professional jrnls. *Editor:* Walden by Henry Thoreau, 1946; Green Mansions by W.H. Hudson, 1949; The Insect World of J. Henri Fabre, 1949; Green Treasury, 1952; Circle of the Seasons, 1953; The Life of the Bee by M. Maeterlinck, 1954; The Wilderness World of John Muir, 1955; The Long Island Naturalist: The Thoughts of Thoreau, 1962; Audubon's Wildlife, 1964; The American Seasons, 1976. *Photography exhibition:* one-man shows at American Mus. of Natural History, NYC and Royal Photographic Salon, London; many other natl. and intnl. one-man exhibitions.

LADY ISOBEL (MORAG) BARNETT
British radio and television personality, writer and physician
Born Aberdeen, Scotland, June 30th, 1918
Died Cossington, Leicestershire, England, October 20th, 1980

Lady Isobel Barnett became a well-known radio and television personality through her performances on *What's My Line?*, a popular BBC "quiz" show. At a time when Great Britain had only one

Courtesy BBC Radio Broadcasting House

television channel, Lady Barnett delighted Sunday evening audiences of almost 10 million viewers with her charming, quick-witted "cross examinations" of contestants.

Isobel Marshall was born of a middle class Scottish family in Aberdeen. Her father, a successful neurologist, sent her to a private school south of the scottish border in York and Isobel later studied medicine at Glasgow University. In 1941 she married Geoffrey Barnett, an attorney and business executive in Leicester, where Isobel worked during World War Two as a general medical practitioner.

Through her husband's activities in local government—he was a member of Leicestershire County Council and was elected an alderman in 1945—Isobel became politically involved and was appointed Justice of the Peace in 1948. She subsequently abandoned her medical career and with her dignified bearing, outgoing personality and conversational ease, became an enormously popular public speaker; her husband's election as Lord Mayor of Leicester in 1952 owed considerably to Isobel's campaign efforts. Her natural elegance attracted the attention of a British Broadcasting Corporation representative and, in 1953 when her husband was knighted, Isobel, now Lady Barnett, appeared for the first time as a panel member on television's *What's My Line?*

Attempting to identify the occupations of contestants, Lady Barnett displayed exceptional pwers of intuition. "It was quite incredible how often she guessed the correct occupation," producer Ernest Maxin said, "I doubled the security arrangements but it made no difference. She continued to guess correctly with astonishing frequency." Moreover, Lady Barnett brought prestige to the show with her lively tongue, humor, and what the *London Times* called her personification of the "discreet charm of the bourgeoisie." She starred throughout *What's My Line's?* first run and, when the show was revived in 1963 after a 10-year absence from the screen, she was the only original panelist to reappear. Lady Barnett was a popular speaker and interviewer throughout England; she appeared on the long-running radio program *Any Questions,* starred in television episodes of *Many a Slip* and *Petticoat Line,* and published a popular cookbook in 1966. When Sir Geoffrey Barnett, a former chairman of the Dobson Hardwick business consortium, died in 1970, Lady Barnett, respected in the London financial world for her knowledge of corporate investment, became one of the first women in Britain to serve as director of a unit shares trust.

Lady Barnett died, an apparent suicide, from a drug overdose. Four days earlier, she had been convicted of stealing a carton of milk and a can of tuna fish from a small village store in Rothley, Leicestershire.

M.D.

Born Isobel Marshall. Daughter of Robert McNab M., neurologist. Married Major Geoffrey Morris Barnett, lawyer, Lord Mayor of Leicester, and Alderman of Leicestershire County Council 1941 (knighted 1953, d. 1970). Son: Alastair. Educ: privately, York; Glasgow Univ. M.B., Ch.B. 1940. Gen. medical practitioner, Leicester 1941–48; Justice of the Peace, Leicester Bench 1948–68; Lady Mayoress of Leicester 1952–53; Broadcaster, BBC Radio, London 1947–77; Panelist, BBC Television, London and regional 1953–78; Lectr. and public speaker 1955–79. *Television and radio shows:*

What's My Line; Any Questions; Many a Slip; Petticoat Line. *Author:*
My Life Line (autobiog.), 1956; Lady Barnett's Cookbook, 1966.

VULKO CHERVENKOV
Prime Minister and head of Communist Party of Bulgaria
Born Bulgaria, August 24th, 1900
Died Bulgaria, October 21st, 1980

A leading member of the generation of East European Communist
rulers who rose to power under Stalin, Vulko Chervenkov was both
chief of state and Communist Party leader in Bulgaria during the
1950s. Though he tried to adapt to the changing conditions that
followed Stalin's death, his power declined and he ultimately fell from
office. The son of a non-commissioned officer in the Bulgarian Army,
Chervenkov received a good general education and graduated from
the Sophia gymnasium in 1919. Two years later he joined the
Bulgarian Communist Party. Chervenkov survived an abortive Communist uprising in 1923, but fled to Moscow two years later when the
party was banned following a bomb plot against Czar Boris. In the
Soviet capital he attended the Marx-Engels Institute and apparently
lectured there after graduation. More importantly, he became known
as a loyal Stalinist. During World War Two, Chervenkov was
responsible for much of the Soviet radio's Bulgarian program. He
returned to his native country towards the end of the war with the
Soviet Army. By this time Chervenkov was a protegé of Stalin and
Georgi Dimitrov, his brother-in-law and Bulgaria's first Communist
ruler. With their support he rose quickly, becoming secretary-general
of the Bulgarian Communist Party, and Prime Minister in 1950
following the deaths of Dimitrov and his successor, Kolarov.

Chervenkov ruled in the early 1950s with nearly total dictatorial
powers. Combining the leading posts in state and party, he dominated
practically every aspect of public affairs in a way surpassed only by
Stalin himself in the Soviet bloc. He purged the older Bulgarian
Communists who had not been with him in the Soviet Union and
replaced them either with his supporters from his Moscow days or
with members of the younger generation of home Communists.

But Chervenkov's position began to deteriorate following Stalin's
death in March 1953. Like all the East European states, Bulgaria
followed the Soviet trend towards separation of Party and state
offices. In March 1954 Chervenkov was obliged to yield the Communist Party leadership to Todor Zhivkov. He adjusted to the new
concept of collective leadership and to the limited de-stalinization that
took place in Russia during the mid-1950s. He granted amnesty to
many political prisoners, eased tax and credit policies for collective
farmers, ordered an end to obligatory overtime work for clerical
personnel and lessened restrictions on private artisans and traders.
Chervenkov himself became more accessible to the public and sought
to cultivate the image of final arbitrator and dispenser of justice.

Despite Chervenkov's efforts to keep abreast of developments in
Moscow, the Soviet leader Nikita Khrushchev disliked his formerly
close association with Stalin and viewed him with suspicion. When

Khrushchev attacked Stalin at the twenty-third Soviet Communist Party Congress in February 1956, Chervenkov's opponents within the Bulgarian Communist Party were encouraged to demand his resignation. In April 1956 he gave up the premiership, admitting to cultivating his own "cult of personality."

But Chervenkov remained deputy premier and a member of the Communist Party Politburo, posts that enabled him to take advantage of the turn towards orthodoxy which followed the political unrest in Hungary and Poland of late 1956. After ten months of virtual seclusion, he was appointed Minister of Education in February 1957 and subsequently helped to crush the cultural ferment growing out of the de-stalinization campaign. Chervenkov remained an important figure in Bulgarian politics until Khrushchev's enmity and internal opposition led to Chervenkov's dismissal from the Politburo, the Central Committee and his deputy premiership a month later. In 1962 he was expelled from the Communist Party.

Chervenkov lived in obscurity following his disgrace. Beginning in the late 1960s, however, he was no longer considered a pariah thanks to the rehabilitation of Stalin that followed Khrushchev's 1964 fall from power. Chervenkov's party membership was restored in 1969 and he was given a state funeral upon his death.   T.P.

Married. Educ: Sofia gymnasium 1919; Marx-Engles Inst., Moscow. Member, Bulgarian Communist Party 1921–62 and from 1969; Instr., Marx-Engels Inst. With Bulgarian govt: Cttee. Chmn. on Science, Art and Culture 1946; Secty.-Gen., Bulgarian Communist Party 1950–54; Prime Minister 1950–56; Member, Bulgarian Politburo 1950–61; Bulgarian Deputy Premier 1956–61; Minister of Educ. 1957–61.
Further reading: Bulgaria Under Communist Rule by J.F. Brown.

JESSICA MARMORSTON
Physician, medical researcher, and teacher
Born Kiev, Russia, September 16th, 1900
Died Los Angeles, California, U.S.A., October 21st, 1980

Jessica Marmorston was among the leading medical researchers in the United States, particularly in the fields of heart disease, endocrinology and cancer. Born in Russia, she moved with her family to the United States as a child. She received her medical degree from the University of Buffalo and practiced in the New York City area as an internist and medical researcher until 1943. She subsequently joined the faculty of the University of Southern California where she gained national recognition for her medical research work.

Her research projects, often complex, required surveys of hundreds of patients and involved computerized analytical techniques. In 1959, she found that female hormones, given in doses too small to produce undesirable side effects, could prolong the lives of heart attack victims, especially men. From a study conducted over several years and completed in 1965, she found a link between hormonal change and various forms of cancer. She did not, however, determine the extent to which hormonal changes are a cause of cancer and how much they are a consequence of the disease. Marmorston worked on many health-related projects, including studies of the relationship between aspirin and heart disease, and the relation between aging and arteriosclerosis. S.F.

Daughter of Aaron W. and Ethel Wark M. Married Lawrence Weingarten, movie producer 1945 (d. 1974). Children: Lailee Bakhtiar Mommaerts; Elizabeth Horowitz; Norma Pisar. Brought to USA. Educ: Univ. of Buffalo, B.S., M.D. 1924. With Montefiore Hosp., NYC: Intern and Research Fellow in pathology 1924–25; Assoc. in bacteriology 1925–31. Assoc., bacteriology and experimental pathology, Cornell Univ., Ithaca, N.Y. 1931–38; attending staff, Doctor's Hosp, NYC 1939–43; senior attending staff, Los Angeles County Hosp. 1943; attending staff 1944–48 and research staff 1948, Cedars-Sinai Medical Center, Los Angeles; research staff, Medical Research Inst., Los Angeles 1948. With Univ. of Southern California: Assoc. Prof. medicine 1943–53; Prof., experimental medicine 1953–57; Clinical Prof., medicine 1957–79. Supervising Dir., Calif. Foundn. for Medical Research, Los Angeles, advanced emergency medical care for Los Angeles County 1972–79. Bd.of Dirs., Research Foundn, and St. Joseph Hosp, Burbank, Calif. Member: N.Y. Acad. of Science; American Heart Assoc., Soc. Experimental Biology and Medicine; N.Y. Pathological Soc.; Gerontology Soc.; Reticuloendothelial Soc.; Assoc. Immunology; American Medical Assn.; Medical Soc. of N.Y.; Soc. for History of Medical Science; American Medical Women's Assoc.; Medical Research Assoc. of Calif. Hons: Fellow of American Coll. of Physicians, N.Y. Acad. of Medicine, American Geriatrics Soc., American Coll. of Cardiology, and Royal Soc. *Author:* (with David Perla) Spleen and Resistance, 1935; Natural Resistance and Clinical Medicine, 1941; (with E. Stainbrook) Psychoanalysis and the Human Situation, 1964; (with J. Weiner and M. Allen) Manual of Computer Programs for Preliminary Multivariate Analysis, 1965; (with J. Weiner and P. Geller) Scientific Methods in Clinical Studies, 1940. Contributed numerous articles to medical publications.

CLIFFORD (LEE) LORD
Educational administrator and historian
Born Mount Vernon, New York, U.S.A., September 4th, 1912
Died West Orange, New Jersey, U.S.A., October 22nd, 1980

Clifford Lord, a historian who served as the third President of Hofstra University, was born in Mount Vernon, New York, and attended Amherst College where he received his undergraduate and graduate degrees in history. In 1936, he enrolled in Columbia University's graduate program and taught American history at the school's adult education program, which was then an off-campus extension service. During this time, he also served as consultant for the W.P.A.'s Historical Records Surveys in New York City and New Jersey. When he obtained his doctorate in 1943, Lord decided to forego the academic's traditional teaching career and, instead, he accepted the directorate of the New York State Historical Society at Cooperstown, where he avidly pursued his interest in local history. While serving in the U.S. Navy during World War Two, he co-authored a history of Naval aviation. He returned to civilian life in 1946 and promptly accepted the position of Director of the Wisconsin Historical Society, which he held until 1958. During Lord's tenure, he developed the organization into a model agency for the compilation and assimilation of facts.

Recognized as a superior administrator and as an ardent proponent of adult and community education, Lord was asked in 1958 to become Dean of Columbia University's academically troubled adult education division, the School of General Studies. Although he was instructed to upgrade the school's educational standing, Lord fought successfully for a new admissions policy which did not reflect "geographic distribution, athletic prowess, social standing or Ivy League homgeneity" (he controversially implied that the student bodies of Columbia and Barnard were too uniformly eastern and upper-middle class). In the process, Lord won the loyalty of a rejuvenated faculty and the respect of Columbia's President and its Board of Trustees.

In 1964, Lord was appointed President of Hofstra University, a young but growing institution located on Long Island. During his tenure, Hofstra experienced dramatic expansion; the student body increased to more than 10,000, a school of law was established, and a new library and six large dormitories were constructed on campus. Lord resigned as University Chancellor in 1973 to succeed economist Herman Kahn as President of the Hudson Institute, a position he held for two years.

In 1977, Lord ended a brief period of retirement when he accepted the directorship of the New Jersey State Historical Society. He immediately announced a five-year program for the revitalization of the Society, proposing a massive membership drive and plans for an exhibition which he hoped would make the state's residents aware of their "rich ethnic history." In 1977, Lord was described in a *Time* magazine profile as "a handsome, pipe-smoking historian from Amherst with the restless energy of a traveling salesman" for whom the study of local history was "something of an obsession." In a 1978 interview with the *New York Times,* Lord explained the idealism which informed his lifelong interest in the history of regions, states, and small communities: "If people realize that it is people who make history, they may want to make a little themselves, becoming more involved with their own community and a little less alienated from the systems that govern us."   R.C.

Son of Charles Clifford L. and Bertha Eunice (Lee) L. Married Elizabeth S. Hubbard 1937 (d. 1979). Children: Charles Hubbard, b. 1944; Helen Patricia, b. 1951. Presbyterian. Educ: Amherst Coll., Mass., B.A. 1933, M.A. 1934; Columbia Univ., NYC, Ph.D. 1943. Mil. Service: U.S. Naval Reserve 1943–46; with Naval Aviation History Unit 1944–46, Lt.-Comdr. in charge of Unit 1945–46. Amherst Memorial Fellow in history 1934–36; Instr. in American history, Columbia Univ. Extension Service 1936–41; Consultant, Historical Records Survey, NYC 1936–39 and N.J. 1940–42; Ed., New York History (mag.) 1941–43; Dir., N.Y. State Historical Soc., Cooperstown, N.Y. 1941–46; organized Farmers' Mus., Cooperstown 1942; Ed., Wisconsin Magazine of History 1946–56; Dir., Wisconsin State Historical Soc. 1946–58; advisory council, American History Research Center 1950–59; Dir. 1955–58 and Hon. Dir. from 1958,

Circus World Mus., Baraboo, Wisc.; Dir. and V.P. 1956–63 and Hon. Trustee from 1963, Natl. Railroad Mus; Dean and Prof. of history, Sch. of General Studies, Columbia Univ. 1958–64; Consultant, Western Heritage Center 1960–64, and Natl. Archives, Washington, D.C. 1962–64; Pres. and Prof. of History 1964–72, and Chancellor 1972–73, Hofstra University, Hempstead, N.Y.; Pres., Hudson Inst., Croton-on-Hudson, N.Y. 1973–75; Consultant, N.Y. State Maritime Mus. 1975–76, and Philadelphia Maritime Mus. 1976; Dir., N.J. State Historical Soc. 1977–79. With American Assoc. of Museums: Member since 1943; Councilman 1943–49; Chmn., Cttee. on Territorial Papers 1962–64. With American Assoc. of State and Local History: Member since 1950; Councilman 1950–56, 1960–67; Pres. 1956–70. Member, N.J. Tercentennial Commn. 1961–64; Member, Advisory Bd. of America, History and Life 1964–68; Chmn., Commn. on Independent Colls. 1966–68; Member 1966–72 and Hon. Member since 1972, Smithsonian Inst. Council; Bd. of Dirs., Regional Planning Assoc. 1967–77; Trustee, Rider Coll. since 1977; Chmn., Commn. on Independent Colls. 1966–68; Member: Org. of American Historians; Western N.Y., N.J., and Wisconsin State Historical Assocs.; Newcomen Soc. of North America; Century (NYC). Hons: Hon. LL.D. degrees from Lawrence Coll. 1948, Univ. of Buffalo 1962; Adelphi Univ.; Hon. LHD, Amherst Coll. 1958; Hon. Member, Phi Beta Kappa. *Author:* History of U.S. Naval Aviation, 1949; Teaching History with Community Resources, 1964; Clio's Servant, 1967. *Editor:* Historical Atlas of U.S., 1943 (rev. eds. 1954, 1969); List and Index of Presidential Executive Orders: Unnumbered Series, 1942 (Numbered Series, 1944); Atlas of Congressional Roll Calls, 1st vol., 1943; (with Henry Graff) Ideas in Conflict, 1958; John A. Krout's American Themes, 1963; Localized History Series, 1964–; Keepers of the Past, 1965.

CHARLES ADLER, JR.
Inventor and engineer
Born Baltimore, Maryland, U.S.A., June 20th, 1899
Died Baltimore, Maryland, U.S.A., October 23rd, 1980

Self-described as the "last of the independent inventors," Charles Adler, Jr. patented many automobile, railroad, and aircraft safety devices, which he unselfishly donated to society. Independently wealthy from his family's shoe business, Adler derived no income from his inventions although he sold many of them to the government for $1 to facilitate distribution.

While Adler showed little enthusiasm for formal education—he took five years to complete a four year high school program and later dropped out of Johns Hopkins University—he patented, at the age of 14, electrically operated brakes for automobiles. In 1932, Adler, fascinated by the mechanics of cars and trains but distressed by the inadequacy of existing safety standards, foresaw that increasingly sophisticated safety mechanisms would be needed to accommodate the growth of rail and automobile travel. Thus, he quickly invented a rotating stop-sign, railroad crossing signals, and Adler double-filament incandescent lamps for railroad signals. He also recognized the need to standardize the colored lights of traffic signals and the

Courtesy Amalie Ascher

concomitant need to sharpen the hue and intensity of these colors to facilitate their recognition by color-blind drivers. Convinced that many motorists disobeyed traffic signals because they drove with their windows shut, Adler campaigned for the use of visual warnings in place of audio warning systems.

A pilot himself, Adler also helped improve aviation safety. In 1943 he designed a two-beam light which enabled pilots preparing to land on a dark field to determine the altitude at which to cut the plane's engines. Adler also perfected a sound system which allowed pilots to signal the control tower using Morse Code in the event of radio failure. To offer protection against falling aircraft, he campaigned for the use of warning sirens and invented jet assist bottles, which provided a brief period of lift for falling planes so that pilots could look for an adequate landing location. Adler also engineered airplane tail lights with improved flashing signals, forward lights which could be switched off in clouds to eliminate reflection, and proximity indicators to warn of approaching aircraft.

In the 1950s, Adler campaigned for increased aviation research. Distressed by the curtailment of government air research at the Civil Aeronautics Administration and by a personnel reduction at the Technical Development and Evaluation Center at Indianapolis, he protested: "It's always after plane accidents that we demand corrective measures for things that went wrong. Congress should not try to save money by cutting appropriations for research and development work designed to prevent accidents more costly later on in lives and property." He subsequently invented the blinking navigational lights used by aircraft at night and donated five patents to the Technical Development and Evaluation Center.

Adler's generosity was recognized with a citation for patriotism in 1956 from the Civil Aeronautics Board when he freely turned over his patent on an electronic collision-warning indicator to several manufacturing companies. The American Society of Civil Engineers and the Society of American Military Engineers named him "Engineer of the Year" in 1976.   N.S.

Son of Harry A. and Carolyn Frank A. Married Alene Steiger 1925. Children: Amalie Ascher; Harry 2nd. Jewish. Educ: attended Johns Hopkins Univ., Baltimore 1917–20. Mil. Service: U.S. Army Clerk, WWI. Licensed professional engineer; pilot; inventor. Member: S.A.T.C., 1918; Md. Traffic Safety Commn., 1953–59; Bd. of dirs., Baltimore-Washington Intnl. Airport 1960–66; Life member, Natl. Aerospace Assoc.; Inst. Transp. Engs.; Soc. Automotive Engineers; Airways Engineering Soc.; Aircraft Owners and Pilots Assoc. Hons: Citation for patriotism, C.A.A. 1956; Engineer of the year award, American Soc. of Civil Engineers and Soc. of American Military Engineers 1976; also awards from U.S. Air Force, U.S. Navy, American Legion, Natl. Aeronautics Assn., Aircraft Owners and Pilots. Inventions: rotating stop sign; railroad highway crossing signal; Adler flasher relay; traffic sonic detector; Adler double filament incandescent lamp for railroad signals, traffic signals, and airplane navigation lights; speed-control highway signal system; double reflector aircraft anti-collision strobe light; aircraft flashing position light system; aircraft studded reflector tail light; aircraft reflector lamp; proximity indicator; traffic-activated traffic signal; automobile spaceometer; aircraft height light; many others. Contributor to mags., newspapers; T.V. guest appearances.

FREDERICK GOLDIE
Bishop of Glasgow and Galloway
Born Glasgow, Scotland, September 1st, 1914
Died Glasgow, Scotland, October 23rd, 1980

The Right Reverend Frederick Goldie, Bishop of Glasgow and Galloway since 1974, was born in 1914 in Glasgow. He was educated in Scotland, receiving his B.A. and M.A. from Hatfield College, Durham, and his B.D. from New College and Coates Hall, Edinburgh.

Upon graduating from Durham in 1938, Goldie was appointed Curate at Govan. From 1939 to 1963 he held two consecutive rectorships, the first at Hillington, Glasgow; the second at Dumbarton. In 1940 he became a lecturer at the Theological College, Edinburgh, a position he held for the next twenty-three years. While at the Theological College, Goldie researched and wrote *A History of the Episcopal Church in Scotland,* the first edition appearing in 1950 and a revised edition in 1976. The book is regarded as a thorough and informed treatment of its topic.

From 1963 to 1964 Goldie was concurrently Dean of Glasgow and Galloway and Rector of St. Margaret's, Glasgow. In 1974 he became Bishop of Glasgow and Galloway, a position he held until his death.

E.S.

Son of John G. and Maria G. Married Margaret Baker McCrae 1940. One son; one daughter. Educ: Strathbungo Acad., Glasgow; Hatfield Coll., Durham, B.A. 1938, M.A. 1946; New Coll. and Coates Hall, Edinburgh, B.D. 1939. Curate, Govan 1938; Rector, Hillington, Glasgow 1939–49; Lecr., Theological Coll., Edinburgh 1940–63; Rector, Dumbarton 1949–63; Canon, St. Mary's Cathedral, Glasgow 1956; Dean, Glasgow and Galloway 1963–74; Rector, St. Margaret's, Glasgow 1963–74; Bishop, Glasgow and Galloway, since 1974. Member, Western Club, Glasgow. *Author:* A History of the Episcopal Church in Scotland, 1950, rev. ed. 1976.

INGRI PARIN D'AULAIRE
Writer, illustrator, and artist
Born Kongsberg, Norway, December 27th, 1904
Died Wilton, Connecticut, U.S.A., October 24th, 1980

Ingri Parin d'Aulaire and her husband Edgar Parin d'Aulaire were prominent for almost fifty years as writers and illustrators of children's books. Ingri, who began painting and drawing at an early age, started her formal training in 1923 at the Institute of Arts and Crafts in Oslo, and later studied at the Hans Hofmann School of Art in Munich where she met Edgar Parin d'Aulaire, a fellow student. Political upheavals in that city in 1925 caused the two, along with many other students, to leave and continue their studies in Paris.

From 1925 to 1929, the Parin d'Aulaires (they had married in Norway) studied at the Académie l'Hôte. During this period they traveled extensively on the continent, supporting themselves by their artwork. Ingri, a portraitist, and Edgar, a painter of frescoes and murals, both exhibited their work professionally, with Ingri's show being mounted at the Salon d'Automne in the late 1920s. In 1929 the couple traveled to the United States where they decided to settle permanently and, in 1940, became naturalized citizens.

Although Edgar Parin d'Aulaire had previously illustrated 15 books in Germany, the couple collaborated as writers and illustrators in 1931 to produce *The Magic Rug,* a story based on their winter vacation in Kairawan, Tunisia. Doubtful at first of their ability to combine the different artistic styles of two creative individuals, they quickly managed, as Edgar later said, "to forget the you and I and become one unity with two heads, four hands and one handwriting." Their books were illustrated lithographically, a difficult technique which they mastered by a division of labor: Edgar did the black and white work while Ingri did the color. The Parin d'Aulaires were perfectionists and they once said that each manuscript might be rewritten ten or twelve times before it was submitted for publication. A characteristic feature of their work is its historical accuracy. For *Conquest of the Atlantic* (1933), a non-fiction account of oceangoing voyages from the time of the Vikings to that of Balboa, they conducted research not only at the New York Public Library and the University of Norway but also traveled to Paris to study ship models and costumes in the Louvre.

From the 1930s to the 1970s, the Parin d'Aulaires' produced numerous children's books, several of which received awards. While Edgar is credited with the dramatic element in their stories, Ingri provided the humor. Most of the books are set in Norway or America and are noted for their exceptional illustrations and close attention to historical detail. They produced a series of six biographies of famous American patriotic figures. The first was *George Washington* (1936) for which they made frequent study visits to Virginia; *Abraham Lincoln* (1939), awarded the American Library Association Caldecott Medal, and *Pocahontas* (1946) followed. *Benjamin Franklin* appeared in 1950 and in 1952 the couple researched Buffalo Bill by camping out for six weeks on the midwestern plains. Christopher Columbus (1955) completed the series.

In the 1960s and early 1970s they published several books inspired by Greek and Norse mythology. The Parin d'Aulaires were awarded the Twelfth Annual Regina Medal of the Catholic Library Association in 1970 for their "distinguished contribution to children's literature."

J.S.

Born Ingri Mortenson. Daughter of Per M., govt. official, and Line Sandsmark. Married Edgar Parin d'Aulaire, writer, artist, and illustrator, 1925. Children: Per Ola; Nils Maarten. Emigrated with husband to USA 1929. Naturalized American 1940. Educ: Inst. of Arts and Crafts, Oslo 1923–24; Hans Hofmann Sch. of Art, Munich 1924–25; Académie l'Hôte and with Pola Gauguin and Andre Lhote, Paris 1925–29. Portrait artist 1925–29; writer and illustrator of children's books, with husband, since 1931. Member, Authors' Guild of America and Scandinavian-American Foundn. Hons: (joint recipient with husband) American Library Assoc. Caldecott Medal 1940 and Catholic Library Assoc. Regina Medal 1970. *Author and illustrator:* The Magic Rug, 1931; Ola, 1932; Ola and Blakken and Line, Sine, Trine, 1933 (rev. ed., as The Terrible Troll-Bird, 1976); The Conquest of the Atlantic, 1933; Children of the Northlights, 1935 (London, 1940); George Washington, 1936; Abraham Lincoln, 1939; Animals

Everywhere, 1940 (rev. ed., 1954); Leif the Lucky, 1941; Don't Count Your Chicks, 1943; Wings for Per, 1944; Too Big, 1945; Pocahontas, 1946; Nils, 1948; Foxie, 1949 (rev. ed., as Foxie the Singing Dog, 1969); Benjamin Franklin, 1950; Buffalo Bill, 1952; The Two Cars, and Columbus, 1955; The Magic Meadow, 1958; Book of Greek Myths, 1962; Norse Gods and Giants, 1964; Trolls, 1972.

SIR RICHARD (HAMILTON) GLYN
Conservative MP, author and editor
Born Dorset, England, October 12th, 1907
Died London, England, October 24th, 1980

Colonel Sir Richard Glyn served as Conservative M.P. from North Dorset from 1957 until 1970. Aside from his political interests, Glyn was an authority on the breeding of pedigree dogs and livestock; he published *Bull Terriers and How to Breed Them* (1936), *Champion Dogs of the World* (1967), and *The World's Finest Horses and Ponies* (1971).

Raised on the family estate in Dorset, Glyn graduated from Worcester College, Oxford and he became a barrister in 1935. A member of the Dorset Yeomanry since 1927, Glyn also served his home county as its Deputy Lieutenant and as Deputy Chairman of the Dorset Quarter Sessions. During World War Two, he commanded the 141 Dorset Artillery Regiment, published a history of the Dorset Yeomanry in 1943, and was awarded the Territorial Decoration in 1945. During the Suez crisis, he again commanded a regiment of the Queen's Own Dorset Yeomanry and he was appointed OBE in 1955. As M.P. for Dorset, Colonel Glyn was a member of the Estimates Committee, the Commonwealth War Graves Commission, and served as Parliamentary Private Secretary to Sir David Eccles, president of the Board of Trade.

Glyn's interest in livestock began when he took up the breeding of bull terriers as an Oxford undergraduate and his book on the subject quickly became a standard text. Glyn hoped that his *Champion Dogs of the World*, would become the "most comprehensive dog book ever." Although the book, handsomely illustrated with color photographs by Sally Anne Thompson, was applauded by reviewers and published immediately in Great Britain, the United States, and seven European countries, it did not surpass the American Kennel Club's *Complete Dog Book* (1956) as the most informative work in the field. In 1971, Thompson and Glyn collaborated on the critically acclaimed, *The World's Greatest Horses and Ponies*. Beginning in 1963, Glyn chaired the prestigious Cruft's International Dog Show for 10 years and he became chairman of the English Kennel Club in 1973.   H.S.

Son of Richard Fitzgerald G., 4th and 8th Baronet. Married: (1) Lindsay Mary Baker 1939 (div. 1969, d. 1971); (2) Barbara Henwood 1970. Children: 1st marriage—Amanda Jane, b. 1940; Richard Lindsay, b. 1943; Jeremy George Trion, b. 1946. Educ: Worcester Coll., Oxford, B.A. 1929; called to the bar, Lincoln's Inn 1935. Mil. Service: Joined Queen's Own Dorset Yeomanry (QODY) 1927, 2nd Lt. 1930; Temporary Maj. 1940; Temporary Lt.-Col. 1944; com-

manded 141 Dorset Yeomanry field reg., Royal Artillery, Territorial
Army 1944–45; commanded 294 QODY 1952–55; Col.-deputy com-
mdr., 128 Infantry Brigade 1956–58; A.D.C. to H.M. the Queen
1958–62. Member, and Vice-Chmn., Housing Comm., Chelsea Bor-
ough Council 1948–50; Justice of the Peace, Dorset 1952; Member,
Shaftesbury Rural District Council 1957; M.P. (conservative) North
Dorset 1957–70; Parliamentary Private Secty. to Pres. of Bd. of Trade
1958; Vice-Chmn., Conservative Agriculture Cttee. 1959–65; Deputy
Lt. Dorset 1960; Chmn., Conservative Army Cttee. and Vice-Chmn.
Conservative Defense Cttee. 1961–68; Member, Select Cttee. on
Estimates 1964–70; Commnr., Commonwealth War Graves Commn.
1965–70. Chmn., Crufts Intnl. Dog Show 1963–73; Chmn., Kennel
Club 1973–76; Member, Canine Consultative Council 1974–79. Mem-
ber, United and Cecil Club 1960–64; Pres., Soc. of Dorset Men
1963–70; Pres., Crufts Intnl. Dog Show 1976. Hons: Territorial
Decoration 1945; OBE 1955; Hon. Col., QODY and Somerset
Yeomanry 1961. *Author:* Bull Terriers and How to Breed Them . . . ,
1936 (3rd ed. 1937, 6th rev. ed. 1953); A Short Account of the
Queen's Own Dorset Yeomanry, 1943; ed., Champion Dogs of thfe
World (photos by Sally Anne Thompson), 1967; ed., The World's
Finest Horses and Ponies (photos by Sally Anne Thompson), 1971.

ALEXANDER (MATHEW) PONIATOFF
Founder of Ampex Corporation and development engineer
Born Kazan, Russia, March 25th, 1892
Died Stanford, California, U.S.A., October 24th, 1980

Formerly a loyal subject of the Czar, Alexander Poniatoff emigrated
to the United States where he founded the Ampex Corporation.
Ampex has produced sophisticated tape recording equipment at
reasonable prices since the late 1940s and, by 1980, had achieved
annual sales of $500 million.

Born in Kazan, 400 miles east of Moscow, Poniatoff was the only
boy in his village to attend a high school which was 16 miles from his
home. Instead of working for his father's prosperous timber business,
Poniatoff entered a college in Russia and later received a degree in
mechanical engineering from a technical school in Karlsruhe, Germany. His studies were interrupted in 1914 when Russia declared war
on Germany, and he joined the Imperial Russian Navy, serving as a
military pilot. In the Russian Civil War, Poniatoff fought with the
White Army and, when the Bolsheviks triumphed in 1920, he fled to
safety in Shanghai.

In China he worked for the Shanghai Power Company until
receiving a $2000 bonus which enabled him to move to San Francisco
in 1927. Poniatoff set off on a tour of the country which took him to
Schenectady, New York, where he was hired by General Electric as a
project engineer. He was instructed to design a new type of circuit
breaker and, within one year, he had obtained two patents.

The Pacific Gas and Electric Company recruited Poniatoff in 1930
to develop new products. Ten years later, however, the company was
forced by Depression-era economic conditions to cut back drastically
on its research budget, and Poniatoff lost his job. Casting about for
employment that would make use of his engineering skills, Poniatoff

offered to work for the Dalmo Victor Company, a small electrical appliance development business, on a three month trial basis without pay. He quickly introduced improvements to the company's wave machine, obtained another patent, and was hired immediately. However, Dalmo Victor suffered a financial setback the following year and Poniatoff was released. He worked briefly for Pacific Gas before returning to Dalmo Victor in 1942. The company had obtained a wartime contract to develop radar scanners for the Navy and Poniatoff, working around the clock, built a successful model in 100 days.

In late 1944 Poniatoff independently formed the Ampex Electric and Manufacturing Company (the name was taken from Poniatoff's initials plus "ex" for excellence) with offices located in an abandoned furniture loft in San Carlos, California. Initially founded as a military supplier, the company began to produce high quality motors for furnaces after World War Two.

In the postwar years, Poniatoff was searching for a new product to market when he discovered a Magnetophone tape recorder that had been taken from a German radio station by an American G.I. Poniatoff commissioned Harold Lindsay, an engineer, to design magnetic heads for a new Ampex tape recorder. When the magnetic tapes had been developed, Poniatoff initiated their commercial distribution but, according to an Ampex spokesman, "Everybody was sure it would flop." In 1947, however, Bing Crosby contacted Poniatoff and purchased 20 Model 200 Ampex recorders for $4000 each. Because Crosby refused to do live broadcasts for his program—they interfered with his golf game and public appearances—and the aural quality of his taped transmissions was poor, the ratings for the popular singer's show were slipping. Using the new Ampex tape equipment, the quality of the broadcast was significantly improved and, according to the *Los Angeles Times,* "the market for high-fidelity tape recordings grew from there." When the National Aeronautics and Space Administration and the Defense Department began to use Poniatoff's machine to record data transmitted from rockets and missiles, the success of the Ampex Corporation was assured.

In 1955 Poniatoff became Chairman of the Board of Ampex and, the following year, the company introduced video tape recorders. The video disc recorder was produced in 1976 and became available to consumers four years later. Poniatoff had retired from Ampex in 1970 to become director of the AMP Laboratory, a small engineering research organization owned by Ampex.   N.S.

Married Helen Hess 1932. No children. Russian at birth; escaped to Shanghai in 1920. Emigrated to USA 1927. Naturalized American 1932. Educ: attended coll. in Russia; degree in mechanical engineering from a technical coll. in Karlsruhe. Mil. Service: Pilot, Imperial Russian Navy 1914–17; with White Russian Forces 1917–20. Asst. Engineer, Shanghai Power Co. 1920–27; Project Engineer, General Electric Co., Schenectady, N.Y. 1927–30; Engineer, Pacific Gas and Electric Co. 1930–40; Engineer with Dalmo Victor, Pacific Gas Co., and Westinghouse Co. 1940–44. With Ampex Electric and Manufacturing Co., San Carlos, Calif: Founder 1944; Pres. 1944–55; Chmn. of the Bd. 1955–70. Founder and Dir., Foundn. for Nutrition and Stress. *Patents:* permanent wave machine; magnetic recording tape; home recording equipment; other electronic devices.

HAROLD (WILLIS) DODDS
President of Princeton University
Born Utica, Pennsylvania, U.S.A., June 28th, 1889
Died Hightstown, New Jersey, U.S.A., October 25th, 1980

Harold Dodds served as president of Princeton from 1933 until 1957 and, during his tenure, the university almost doubled in size. Committed to humanitarian ideals and, in education, to a liberal arts curriculum, Dodds oversaw the creation of departments of music, religion, near Eastern studies, and aeronautical engineering, while the number of students increased by 25 percent, and faculty by nearly 100 percent, during his administration. Dodds also served as a trustee of the Danforth and Rockefeller Foundations.

Having received a classical education at Princeton and at the University of Pennsylvania, Dodds taught on the high school level in Pennsylvania for two years before lecturing in economics at Purdue University. He taught politics at Western Reserve before returning to Princeton in 1927 as a political science instructor. Throughout this time Dodds was involved in government work at various levels. He became secretary of the National Municipal League in 1920, a post he held for eight years, and worked as an advisor for the governments of Nicaragua and Cuba on electoral law reform.

As president of the university, Dodds sought to maintain Princeton's scholastic eminence and its academic freedom. When the House Committee on Un-American Activities requested a list of the books used in classes on politics at Princeton, Dodds publicly denounced the Committee's "intrusion" into matters that he believed should remain non-political.

When Alger Hiss, accused of being a communist agent, was invited to speak at Princeton by a student debating society in 1948, many students, faculty members, and alumni protested. Although he personally disapproved of the invitation, Dodds refused to overrule the students' decision, saying, "Education includes the freedom to make mistakes and to learn to accept responsibility for them." He also refused to support, at a time when it was unpopular to do so, the financial support of athletes, maintaining that subsidization was not in the interests of collegiate sports, student-athletes, or higher education in general.

Summarizing his philosophy of education, Dodds once said that he wanted ". . . education for use, not so much for the specific information it gives students, although this is often important, but because in general it teaches those habits of thought and analysis which permit students to absorb, quickly and accurately, new knowledge and apply it with judgment." Although his administration also supported the development of such scientific programs as the Office of Population Research, Dodds primarily emphasized the humanities, which he called "the defenders and advocates of the ideals by which men live."

G.D.

Son of Samuel D. and Alice (Dunn) D. Married Margaret Murray 1917. No children. Educ: Grove City Coll., Phi Beta Kappa, B.A. 1909; Princeton Univ., N.J., M.A. 1914; Univ. of Pennsylvania, Ph.D. 1917. High sch. teacher in Pa. 1909–11; Instr. in economics, Purdue Univ., Ind. 1914–16; Asst. Prof., political science, Western Reserve Univ., Ohio 1916–20; Exec. Secty. for U.S. Food Admin. in Pa. 1917–19; Ed., National Municipal Review 1920–33; Secty., Natl.

Municipal League 1920–28; Prof. of politics, Princeton Univ. 1927–34; Pres. 1933–57 and Pres. emeritus from 1957, Princeton Univ. Trustee: Carnegie Foundn. for Advancement of Teaching 1935; Rockefeller Foundn. 1935–54; Gen. Educ. Bd. 1937; Danforth Foundn. 1957–64. Chairman: American Conference on Refugee Problem, Bermuda 1943; President's Cttee. on Integration of Medical Services of Govt. 1946; Task force on personnel, second Hoover Commn. 1954–55; Council on Foreign Relations. Consultant to Govt. of Nicaragua 1923, 1928 and to Govt. of Cuba. Member, American Acad. of Arts and Science and American Philosophical Soc. Hons: awarded over 30 honorary degrees from many univs., including LL.D. from Yale Univ., Rutgers Univ., Glasgow Univ., Harvard Univ., Columbia Univ. *Author:* Out of this Nettle . . . Danger!, 1943; The Academic President—Educator or Caretaker?, 1962; contributed articles to many jrnls.

VIRGIL (KEEL) FOX
Organist
Born, Princeton, Illinois, U.S.A., May 3rd, 1912
Died West Palm Beach, Florida, U.S.A., October 25th, 1980

According to critic Joseph Kane, organ virtuoso Virgil Fox "did more to popularize his instrument than any other performer in this century." For 19 years the organist of New York City's Riverside Church where he was the acknowledged master of its mighty five-manual, 10,561-pipe Aeolian-Skinner, Fox played the world's most famous models, including the Baroque organ in Leipzig, Germany, once played by Johann Sebastian Bach and the organ in the Cathedral of Notre Dame in Paris. At Carnegie Hall in 1936, Fox gave the first organ concert for which admission was charged and he was a pioneer of the so-called "Heavy Organ" concept in the 1970s.

Fox was born of a musical family in an Illinois farming community where his mother was an alto soloist in the church choir and his father played harmonica at barn dances. A prodigy, Fox was the organist for his hometown church at the age of ten and, seven years later, he won a musical contest that is held every two years by the National Federation of Music Clubs. By 1929, while studying in Chicago with the Bach specialist, Wilhelm Middelschulte, Fox had decided to increase popular appreciation of the organ by expanding its range of emotional expression; very few organists, Middelschulte told him, could "reach the hearts of people" because most musicians were the servants, rather than the masters, of such a technically complex instrument. In 1932 Fox graduated with high honors from the Peabody Conservatory of Music in Baltimore, Maryland. He made his professional debut the following year with performances in New York and London. In the late 1930s and early 1940s, Fox headed the Peabody Conservatory's Organ Department and, from 1946 until 1965, he was the principal organist for the Riverside Church.

To attract larger audiences to organ concerts, Fox combined his impeccable musical skills with flamboyant showmanship. He would embellish performances with chatty, informative discussions of the music and, while playing, his torso would swing and sway as he described elaborate arcs and lines in the air with his hands. In the final decade of his career, during the controversial "Heavy Organ" phase, Fox took to wearing a shimmering paisley sport coat, a black toreador cape, and rhinestone-spangled shoes during concert appearances.

Inspired by the visceral impact of loud rock music and psychedelic light shows, Fox conceived his "Heavy Organ" concept as a way of introducing Bach to young people. In December, 1970, he performed at the Fillmore East rock-emporium; sporting his theatrical attire, he appeared almost iridescent on stage beneath the flashing, multi-colored lights. With his organ amplified to achieve a thunderous volume, Fox boomed out renditions of the Tocatta and the Fugue in D Minor; "J.S. Bach," he announced to an ecstatic crowd of long-haired rock fans, "is delighted you are here." Thereafter, Fox devoted one-half of his 80 annual concerts to young people.

However, classical music critics and such custodians of high culture as William F. Buckley Jr., did not approve of setting Baroque forms to rock music. The amplified organ, they said, was incapable of rendering the subtlety and finely-pitched nuance of classical music. In a *New York Times* interview, Fox responded to the charge that his interpretation of Bach was a vulgarization: "I notice that these Baroquists do not ride in oxcarts. I notice that they do not use outdoor toilets. Yet they continue to grovel in the dung of 200 years ago." What his detractors resented, he said, was the way his "musical expressiveness" conflicted with the desire of critics to keep Bach "under some case in a museum next to a comb some dead queen wore in her hair 3000 years ago."

Fox performed his last concert in Dallas, Texas, on September 26th, 1980. He died of cancer and had been suffering from the disease for four and a half years.   R.C.

Son of Miles S.F. and Birdie E. (Nichols) F. Unmarried. One adopted son. Educ: Peabody Conservatory of Music, Baltimore, Artist's Diploma 1932; private studies with Wilhelm Middelschulte, Chicago 1928–29 and Marcel Dupre, Paris 1932–33. Mil. Service: Staff Sgt., U.S. Army Air Force 1942–46. Church organist: St. Mark's Lutheran Church, Hanover, Pa. 1931; Brown Memorial Church, Baltimore 1938–42; Riverside Church, NYC 1946–65. Concert artist: performing debut, Cincinnati 1926; London debut, Kingsway Hall 1933; NYC debut, Wanamaker Auditorium 1933; recital before American Guild of Organists, Chicago World's Fair 1933; first organ recital for which admission was charged, Carnegie Hall 1936; performed at Library of Congress as guest artist of Elizabeth Sprague Coolidge Found. 1946; dedicated rebuilt organ of Riverside Church with N.Y. Philharmonic 1955; dedicated organ at Philharmonic (now Avery Fisher) Hall, Lincoln Center, NYC; gave first solo recital in Philharmonic Hall 1963; directed organ series, Gall. of Modern Art, NYC 1965–66; dedicated new organ, Carnegie Hall 1974; gave last concert to inaugurate Dallas Symphony's 1980–81 season, Sept. 26, 1980. Performed as solo artist with N.Y. Philharmonic, Philadelphia, Boston, Toronto, Baltimore, Rochester, Detroit, Dallas, Grand Rapids, CBS Symphony and Los Angeles Festival orchestras; was first American organist to play J.S. Bach organ in Thomaskirche, Leipzig, East Germany and Notre Dame de Paris; also played in Westminster Abbey, London and at Marienkirche, Lubeck, West Germany. Head of Organ Dept., Peabody Conservatory 1938–42; Founder of Virgil Fox Intnl. Sch. for Concert Organ. Member: American Guild of Symphony Organists and American Fedn. of Musicians. Hons: Win-

ner, Natl. Fedn. of Music Clubs Biennial Contest 1929; named most
popular organist, Choral and Music Guide Magazine 1952; Mus. D.,
Bucknell Univ. 1963; Distinguished Alumni Award, Peabody Conservatory 1964; most popular organist, Contemporary Keyboard
Magazine 1977–79. *Recordings include:* Virgil Fox Plays Wanamaker,
1964; Here Comes the Bride, 1968; Greatest Hits, 1971; The Fox
Touch, Vol. 1; The Fox Touch, Vol. 2; Into Classics; Organ Book;
many others.

MARCELLO (JOSE DA NEVES ALVES) CAETANO
Lawyer; premier of Portugal
Born Lisbon, Portugal August 7th, 1906
Died Rio de Janeiro, Brazil, October 26th, 1980

A prominent administrative and political figure under Portuguese
dictator Antonio de Oliveira Salazar, Marcello Caetano served as
premier for six years following his mentor's incapacitation. He took
over leadership of a stagnant and backward country, which he
attempted to rule with a combination of cautious reform and fidelity to
Salazar's authoritarian principles. But in the end he failed to satisfy
the contradictory demands of various political groups, and he was
ousted by reformist military officers.

The youngest of five children of a schoolmaster, Caetano studied
law at the University of Lisbon, where he received his doctorate in
1931. His first exposure to politics came during his student years when
he joined the so-called Integralistas, advocates of a fascist state
organized on corporatist lines. In 1929 Caetano began serving as a
legal consultant to the Portuguese government, and he soon attracted
the attention of Salazar, then Finance Minister. Three years later he
became an official of Salazar's newly-founded National Union party.
By the time Salazar took over the government in 1932, Caetano was
well established as his protege. His first important assignment was the
drafting of a constitution for the so-called *Estado Novo,* an authoritarian system modelled on Mussolini's corporate state. The
document served as a theoretical justification for Salazar's rule—
though the dictator, to Caetano's distress, did not hesitate to circum-
vent its provisions at will. Caetano nevertheless remained Salazar's
chief legal adviser, drafting a state administrative code in 1936. He
also taught law at the University of Lisbon.

Caetano served in many posts during the 36 years of Salazar's rule.
Beginning in 1940 he was successively head of the national youth
organization, Minister for Overseas Territories, president of the
National Union party and presiding officer of the Corporate Chamber, the upper house of Portugal's rubber-stamp legislature. In 1955
he was named Minister of State for the Presidency, a position reserved
for Salazar's chief assistant and second-in-command. But Salazar,
more concerned with preserving his own power than with establishing
clear lines of authority, refused to allow the emergence of a single heir
apparent. In 1958 Caetano was obliged to leave government service
for a position as rector of the University of Lisbon. He resigned from
this post too after secret police broke up an on-campus student

demonstration in 1962. But Caetano remained loyal to Salazar in private life and continued to support his government.

When Salazar suffered a crippling stroke in September 1968, Caetano was called from retirement to succeed him as premier. His personal style in office differed sharply from that of his predecessor; less ruthless and more devoted to principle than Salazar, he functioned more as a political mediator than as an absolute dictator. Caetano realized that reform was necessary to lift Portugal from its economic backwardness and isolation, but feared that too rapid change would destroy the authoritarian system which he had helped construct. Initially, he enjoyed broad support in Portuguese society; conservative "ultras" in the military, Catholic Church and business elite expected him to continue Salazar's policies, while reformist groups hoped that he would be open to new ideas.

Caetano soon developed a characteristic mixture of reform and restraint. Women were given the right to vote, press censorship was eased and important political exiles, including socialist leader Mario Soares, were permitted to return to Portugal. At the same time, Caetano reappointed all of Salazar's old ministers to supervise the new policies. In October 1969 he sought to legitimize his rule by holding National Assembly elections in which opposition groups were allowed to participate; but restrictions on campaigning and balloting ensured that the official National Union party took all 130 seats in the new legislature. Shortly after the election, Caetano eliminated the powerful and autonomous secret police organization (PIDE), placing the state security apparatus under the Ministry of the Interior.

On one issue, however, Caetano refused to compromise: the continued existence of Portugal's colonial empire. By the end of Salazar's reign, unrest in Angola, Mozambique and Guinea-Bissau had become a serious drain on the country's meager resources. Fully 40 percent of the Portuguese budget and 150,000 soldiers were committed to fighting guerrilla-led independence movements. The struggle brought Portugal international opprobrium and isolation; domestically it became the focus of a bitter rift between reformists who wanted to abandon the territories and conservatives who viewed the colonial question as a basic test of the government's strength. Since Caetano could not rule without conservative support, he had little room for maneuver on the issue. Though he offered to modify administrative arrangements in the colonies, he drew the line at limited autonomy for the territorial inhabitants.

As the colonial dispute increasingly dominated Portuguese politics, Caetano's inflexibility on this one issue overshadowed his willingness to compromise on others. Ultimately, the impasse cost him his job. In May 1974 he was ousted by reformist officers of the Armed Forces Movement under General Antonio de Spinola. One of the first acts of the new government was to announce a change in colonial policy, and independence for the territories followed quickly. Caetano was exiled to Brazil, where he spent the rest of his life. In his last years he served as director of the Institute of Comparative Law in Rio de Janeiro. He died at 74 of natural causes.   S.L.G.

Son of José Maria Alves C., teacher, and Josepha Maria da Neves Alves C. Married Teresa de Barros 1930. Children: João; José Maria; Miguel; Ana Maria. Roman Catholic. Educ: Univ. of Lisbon, LL.B.

1927; LL.D. 1931; Legal advisor to Ministry of Finance, Lisbon 1929–32; Prof. of law, Univ. of Lisbon 1933–68; completed drafting of State Admin. Code 1936; elected to Council of the Colonial Empire 1936; Natl. Commnr. for Youth 1940; special envoy to Brazil 1941; Minister for Colonies 1944–47; Pres. of Natl. Union Party 1947–49; Pres., Corporate Chamber 1949–55; V.P., Overseas Council 1953–58; Asst. Prime Minister 1955–58; Rector, Univ. of Lisbon 1959–62; Prime Minister 1968–74; deposed and exiled to Brazil 1974; Head, Inst. of Comparative Law, Rio de Janeiro since 1974. Hons: Grand Comdr. (G.C.), Military Order of Christ; G.C., Order of the Empire; G.C., Order of Public Instructors (Portugal): G.C., St. Raymundo de Penafort; G.C., Order of Santiago; G.C., Order of Catholic Queen Isabella; G.C., Order of Alphonse X (Spain); G.C., Order of the Southern Comdr. (Brazil); G.C., Order of the Crown (Belgium); G.C., Order of Merit (West Germany). *Author:* A Depreciacão da Moeda depois da Guerra 1931; Manual de Direito Administrativo, 1936; Tratado Elementar de Direito Administrativo, 1944; Portugal e o direito Colonial Internacional, 1948; Ciência Política e Direito Constitucional, 1955; (Ed.) O Direito (Univ. of Lisbon Law jrnl).

EMANUEL NEUMANN
Political leader, statesman
Born Libau, Latvia, Russia (now Latvian Soviet Socialist Republic, U.S.S.R.), July 2nd, 1893
Died Tel Aviv, Israel, October 26th, 1980

A leader of the Zionist movement, Emanuel Neumann contributed to the unification of world-wide Jewry in the first half of the twentieth century. His diplomacy was in part responsible for the creation of Israel as an independent state in 1948.

Emanuel Neumann was raised in an orthodox Jewish home in Brooklyn, New York, where his immigrant family moved from Russia soon after his birth. His father, a founder of the first modern Hebrew school in America, insisted that the children speak Hebrew at home, and it was perhaps young Neumann's bilingual abilities which led him to study modern languages at Columbia University. He was later awarded a doctor of laws degree from Columbia and worked as an attorney in New York City.

Neumann's concern for the welfare of Jews throughout the world and for the preservation of a sacred homeland in Jerusalem led to his involvement in the establishment of Young Judea, a Zionist youth movement. His dedication to the cause of Zionism was recognized by the World Zionist Organization, which, in 1918, asked him to serve as Educational Director. Throughout the 1920s, Neumann organized several funds in support of a free and unified Jewish Palestine. In 1931, he became a member of the World Zionist Executive and worked with the Jewish Agency for Palestine in Jerusalem, where he devoted himself to the country's economic development. Neumann secretly conducted meetings in 1932 with King Abdullah, the ruler of Transjordan (now Jordan), to arrange the purchase of land even though Jews at that time were forbidden, under the regulations of the British Mandatory Administration, to settle or own land in Transjordan.

In 1940, Neumann returned to America and became increasingly involved in the political affairs of the Zionist movement. He organized the American Palestine Committee and, as its leader, he conducted negotiations with the State Department concerning the partitioning of Palestine. Twice he testified before the Foreign Affairs Committee of the House of Representatives and helped to secure passage by Congress of the Palestine Resolution in 1945. Two years later, as a member of the Jewish Agency delegation to the United Nations, he conferred with representatives of many governments and played a crucial role in the adoption of the U.N. partition resolution of 1947.

During this period, Neumann became interested in the development of hydro-electric power sources in the Jordan Valley and, in 1946, he accompanied two American engineers to Palestine to present the Anglo-American Committee with a proposal for a Jordan Valley Authority project.

Throughout the final two decades of his life, Neumann, serving first as president of the Zionist Organization of America, and later as chairman of the United States section of the World Zionist Organization, worked to enlist political support, particularly among Americans, for the state of Israel. Responding to what he believed were widespread distortions of Zionism's true meaning, Neumann, in his autobiographical memoir, *In the Arena* (1976), defined the term as "an essentially simple and uncomplicated expression of the Jewish *will to live*—a struggle for collective existence and national liberation in the teeth of a none too friendly and at times savagely hostile world."

H.N.P.

Son of Sundel H.N., parochial educator. Married Fannie. Children: Gabriel J.; one daughter. Jewish. Brought to U.S. ca. 1895. Educ: Columbia Univ., B.A.; New York Univ.; Columbia Univ., LL.D. Instr., Boys High School, Brooklyn, N.Y.; practiced law, NYC; Co-founded Young Judea, ca. 1915; ed., Young Judean during WWI; Educational Dir., Zionist Org. of America 1918–20; co-founded, Keren Hayesod (Palestine Foundn. Fund) 1921; co-founder, and Chmn., Exec. Cttee. United Palestine Appeal 1925–27; Pres., Natl. Jewish Fund 1928–30; Member, World Zionist Exec., and Jewish Agency for Palestine, Jerusalem 1931–39, 1946; organized American Palestine Cttee., Washington D.C., 1940; headed Dept. of Public Relations and Political Action, of Emergency Cttee. for Zionist Affairs; organized and headed Commn. on Palestine Surveys 1943; leader, American delegation, World Zionist Congress 1946; delegation to U.N. 1947; Member, Exec. 1951, 1956; Pres., Zionist Org. of America 1954–58; co-established Tarbuth Foundn. for the Advancement of Hebrew Culture 1961; Pres., Theodor Herzl Inst. and Foundn.; Ed., Mainstream (mag.). Member, N.Y. State Bar Assoc.; Chmn. U.S. section, World Zionist Org. 1968–72. Testified as spokesman for American Palestine Cttee. before Foreign Affairs Cttee., U.S. House of Reps., Washington, D.C. 1940; presented Jewish case before Anglo-American Cttee. of Inuiry, Washington, D.C. 1945; Rep., Jewish Agency in negotiations with British Foreign Minister, London 1947. *Author:* In the Arena, 1976; contributed articles to The Reconstitutionist; and other Zionist publications. Addressed numerous Zionist orgs.

JUDY LAMARSH
Canadian cabinet minister, and attorney
Born Chatham, Ontario, Canada, December 20th, 1924
Died, Toronto, Ontario, Canada, October 27th, 1980

Appointed in 1963 as Minister of Health and Welfare in the Liberal government of Prime Minister Lester B. Pearson, Judy LaMarsh became the first woman cabinet member in Canada since the 1950s. LaMarsh had been elected to Parliament in 1960 and, in late 1965, she was named Secretary of State. Noted for her brash, outspoken style, LaMarsh supported liberal domestic legislation and, deeply suspicious of Soviet political intentions, she helped persuade the Liberal Party to adopt aggressive, NATO-oriented, national defense policies.

A descendant of French Protestant refugees, Julia Verlyn (Judy) LaMarsh attended high school in Niagara Falls, Canada. After graduation she tried to join the Women's Division of the Air Force but was turned down because of poor eyesight. However, in 1943, she left the University of Toronto to join the Canadian women's Army Corps. After completing basic training, she studied industrial drafting and was assigned to service with the Royal Canadian Engineers and, later, with Pacific Military Intelligence at Vancouver. In 1945 LaMarsh returned to the University of Toronto and obtained her B.A. degree in 13 months. She subsequently joined the Young Liberal Club and entered Toronto's Law School.

In 1950 LaMarsh returned to Niagara Falls where she began to build both a legal practice with her father and a base of political support within the Liberal Party. She served as president of the Ontario Women's Liberal Association and was a member of the Liberal Party's Advisory Committee before her election to the Canadian Parliament in 1960; LaMarsh held the seat concurrently with her cabinet posts until 1968.

The only female Liberal Party member of Parliament, LaMarsh quickly made her presence felt. Calling for increased defense spending, she characterized the Conservative Party's foreign policy as complacent and naive; in her first session, she addressed the Parliament nearly 100 times on many issues, an accomplishment which prompted the *Christian Science Monitor* to remark, "Remaining unheard is an unheard-of-thing for Judy LaMarsh." As Minister of Health and Welfare, one of her first acts was to announce that she had given up a two-pack-a-day cigarette habit to inaugurate a nationwide anti-smoking campaign. The youngest member of the Pearson cabinet, LaMarsh created a consumers advisory committee which reported to the government on food and drug products. She also helped lay the groundwork for a medical care insurance plan, the Canada Pension Plan, and a federal assistance program for the elderly, unemployed, and the disabled.

LaMarsh's political career came to an abrupt end in 1968 when her description of Prime Minister Pierre Trudeau as "that bastard" was overheard on national television. The remark was made after a Liberal convention in which Trudeau defeated Paul Hellyer, the candidate supported by LaMarsh, for the Party leadership. After leaving politics, she returned to her legal practice and also worked as a writer and radio commentator.   R.S.

Daughter of Wilfrid L., lawyer, and Rhoda (Conibear) L. Educ: Stamford Coll., Hamilton Normal Sch., Univ. of Toronto. Mil.

Service: Canadian Women's Army Corps 1943–45. Lawyer ca. 1950–60; M.P. 1960–69; Minister of Natl. Health and Welfare 1963–65; Secty. of State 1965–69; Member, LaMarsh, MacBeen, Slovak, Sinclair & Nicolette (law firm) 1969–80. V.P., Ontario Assoc. of Rural-Urban Municipalities. Member: Planning Assoc. of Canada; Intnl. Parliament Union; Commonwealth Parliament Assoc. *Author:* Memories of a Bird in a Gilded Cage, 1969.

BERND T(EO) MATTHIAS
Physicist
Born Frankfurt on Main, Germany, June 8th, 1918
Died La Jolla, California, October 27th, 1980

Dr. Bernd T. Matthias, considered to be a leading candidate for a Nobel Prize in either chemistry or physics, made significant contributions to the fields of superconductivity and ferro–electricity. During his career Matthias discovered most of the world's known superconducting materials and was frequently consulted by researchers from other countries in his laboratory at the Institute for Pure and Applied Physical Sciences at the University of California at San Diego.

Born in Frankfurt, Germany in 1918, Matthias moved when the Nazis came to power to Switzerland, where he received his doctorate in physics at the Federal Institute of Technology in Zurich in 1943, studying under the prominent physicist, Wolfgang Pauli. After coming to the United States in 1947, Matthias joined the Bell Laboratories in 1948 and, in 1961, the faculty of the University of California at San Diego.

Perhaps the most significant contribution of Matthias and his co-workers was the discovery in 1954 of a superconducting alloy of niobium and tin which, due to its ability to conduct a current without a loss of energy, has become the basis for considerably improved superconducting generators, magnets, and transmission systems. Superconductivity, the condition of zero resistance to electron flow in certain materials when the temperature becomes sufficiently low, is essential to many new technologies, including the ongoing attempt to use fusion of hydrogen atoms to generate power. Because of Matthias's theoretical and practical work in this area, several materials have been discovered which become superconductive at temperatures slightly higher than the 18.3 degrees centigrade above absolute zero required for Matthias's niobium–tin alloy. One of the aims of Matthias and other physicists has been to reach the highest possible temperature for superconductivity so that superconductors can become even more useful. According to Bell Laboratories, there were only about 30 superconducting materials known when Matthias entered the field; there are now over 1000, many of them discovered with his help.

Matthias also made important contributions to the understanding of the relationship between electric currents and magnetic properties in certain materials.   E.S.

Son of Ludwig M. and Marta Lipman M. Married Joan Trapp 1950. No children. German at birth; naturalized American 1951. Educ:

Federal Inst. of Technology, Zurich, Ph.D. in Physics 1943. Scientific collaborator, Federal Inst. of Technology 1942–47; staff member, div. of industrial cooperative, Mass. Inst. of Technology 1947–48; member of technical staff, Bell Laboratories, Murray Hill, N.J., since 1948; Asst. Prof. of physics, Univ. of Chicago 1949–51; Prof. of Physics since 1961 and Dir., Inst. for Pure and Applied Physical Sciences since 1971, Univ. of Calif. at San Diego. Member: Natl. Acad. of Sciences since 1965; American Assoc. for Advancement of Science since 1965; New York Acad. of Sciences; American Physical Soc.; American Acad. of Arts and Sciences; Swiss Physicists Soc.; Sigma Xi. Hons: Research Corp. Award 1962; John Price Wetherill Medal, Franklin Inst. 1963; Industrial Research Man of the Year 1968; Oliver E. Buckley Solid State Physics Prize 1970; Hon. D.Sc. from Lausanne 1978; American Physical Soc. Intnl. Prize for New Materials 1979. *Discoveries:* numerous elements and compounds with superconducting properties, including alloy of niobium and tin in 1954. *Author:* 300 papers in intnl. and natl. jrnls.

IMRE KOVÁCS
Hungarian nationalist and writer
Born Felsögöböjárás, Hungary, March 19th, 1913
Died New York City, U.S.A., October 28th, 1980

Imre Kovács was born in 1913 in a serf's village on one of the vast estates of Archduke Josef von Habsburg. His parents were peasants who worked 14 hours a day, six days a week, for a bare subsistence living, in a feudal system so well entrenched that it survived even the First World War and the destruction of the Austro-Hungarian empire.

In 1932 Kovács enrolled in Budapest University of Economics, where he joined the radical peasant writers' group, the Village Explorers. Five years later he published *A néma forradalom* (*The Silent Revolution*), a devastating condemnation of Hungarian feudalism and of the postwar governments that supported it. The book described the despair and hunger that were driving the peasantry into apocalyptic religious sects with such grim names as "The Starvers," "The Seedless," and "The Scythe-Cross." "There are two nations in Hungary," Kovács wrote, "the haves and the have-nots. The former have abrogated to themselves the right of nation building. The have-nots are banding together in sects, which have assumed various forms of Utopias, mostly in the Great Beyond. Here they are disdained and hungry; there they will bathe in glory and their stomachs will be full." The pro-Nazi, pro-feudal regime of Admiral Nicholas Horthy banned the book, expelled Kovács from the university, and sentenced him to three months' imprisonment.

Upon his release, Kovács joined the liberal-nationalist March Front, a group formed in opposition to the communist National Front, and continued to press for agrarian and political reform. In 1939 he became a founding member of the progressive National Peasants Party, serving as its secretary-general during the war years and afterwards winning a seat in the first democratically elected Parliament. He resigned his party office in 1946 after Communist infiltrators gained control of the party and led it into a leftist coalition. In the following year, the Soviet Union deposed the elected government and made Hungary one of its satellite nations. Kovács went into exile and lived in Switzerland, France, and England before settling permanently in the United States.

In New York City, Kovács became active in a number of emigré groups, including the Hungarian National Council, the International Association for Social Research, and the Free Europe Committee, for which he served as publications editor and director of special projects. In 1958, as minister of the First Hungarian Reformed Church of New York, he led picketing outside United Nations headquarters to protest Soviet repression in Hungary. A year later he published *Facts About Hungary,* an account of the country's postwar struggle for democracy, its subversion by the Communists, and the brutal suppression by the Soviet Union of the 1956 uprising. "Much stronger than the sense of outrage," he wrote, "is the feeling of no longer being able in the second half of the 20th century to tolerate murders, melodramatic scenes of executions, and exceptionally severe prison terms. If there is any yardstick by which we can measure that delicate distinction between Man and the brute still present in him, I believe this is the test in morality and humanism."

Kovács was fascinated by the Communist regime's willingness to betray its own progressive elements in the name of ideological purity and its machine-like capacity for crushing the slightest manifestation of nonconformity. This was the subject of his second novel, *The Ninety and Nine,* published in an English translation in 1955. Its hero, Leslie Rab, is a peasant who has risen to the second highest position in the Hungarian Communist Party only to fall victim to a purge. With his cellmate, the Jesuit Father Janos, Rab holds a philosophical debate on theoretical questions of church versus state. "If, perhaps, the dialogues between the priest and Number Two demand a trained intellect," wrote Richard Plant in the *New York Times Book Review,* "Mr. Kovács' chronicle of tortures, arrests, betrayals and triple-betrayals is as impressive as it is agonizing. . . . The last chapters paint a terrifying picture of wholesale brainwashing. Here the novel attains the level for which it was striving. . . . It depicts in vivid, ghastly colors how these notorious self-incriminations and confessions are brought about."

Despite his staunch anti-communism, Kovács avoided the more reactionary exile groups, adhering to the progressive nationalism which had first brought him into politics. He took the U.S. to task for underestimating Soviet motivation and discipline and for maintaining a contradictory foreign aid program that strengthened fascism in Spain, Titoism in Yugoslavia, and socialism and capitalism, successively, in England. The U.S., he suggested, should break off relations with the Soviet-controlled puppet regimes of Eastern Europe and recognize governments-in-exile made up of refugees who had been democratically elected to serve in legitimate governments. Assistance to dissident elements in the peasantry and bourgeoisie of Hungary, he added, would at least help the Hungarians to split off from Moscow and form an independent communist regime like that of Tito in Yugoslavia, which could act as a hedge to further Soviet expansion.

Kovács founded *Uj Látóhatár* (Horizons) a journal of Hungarian emigré writing, in Munich in 1958, and was the author of a number of studies of political and agrarian issues in Hungary, the Soviet Union, and Latin America. His memoirs have been published in German, Hungarian, and French.					R.C.

Son of Imre K. and Carola (Kek) K., peasants. Married Edna Harvey Campbell. Daughter: Andrea. Calvinist. Emigrated to U.S. 1949. Educ: Budapest Univ. of Economics (now Karl Marx Univ.) 1932–37. Expelled from univ. and jailed for three months for publication of A néma forradalom 1937. Member, Village Explorers group of radical peasant writers; joined liberal-nationalist March Front 1937; Founding Member 1939–47 and Secty.-Gen. 1939–46, National Peasants Party; M.P. 1945–47; went into exile 1947, subsequently residing in Switzerland, France, and England; writer, minister, and political activist, NYC since 1949. Worked for National Hungarian Council 1951; minister, First Hungarian Reformed Church of New York from ca. 1958; Pres., Intnl. Assn. for Social Research 1962–63; Sr. Ed. of Publications and Special Projects Dir., Free Europe Cttee. from 1963. Founder 1958 and Contributing Ed., Uj Látóhatár (Horizons; literary and political review), Munich. Member, International P.E.N. *Author:* A néma forradalom (The Silent Revolution), 1937; Kivandalos (Emigration), 1938; Kolonto (novel), 1939; A Parasztéletforma Csödje (on the bankruptcy of peasant life), 1940; Magyar Feudalizmus-Magyar Parasztság (Hungarian Feudalism-Hungarian Peasantry), 1941; Szovjet-Oroszország-Agráropolitikaja (Soviet Agricultural Policy), 1943; Elsullyedt Orszag (The Sunken Country), 1945; Agráropolitikai Feladatok (on Hungarian agricultural problems), 1946; The Ninety and Nine (novel), 1955; Facts About Hungary, 1959, rev. ed. 1966. Memoirs published in German as Im Shatten der Sowjets (In the Soviet Shadow), 1948; in Hungarian as Magyarország Megszállása, 1979; enlarged ed. in French as D'une Occupation à l'autre: la tragédie Hongroise (From One Occupation to Another: The Hungarian Tragedy), 1949.

J(OHN) H(ASBROUCK) VAN VLECK
Theoretical physicist
Born Middletown, Connecticut, U.S.A., March 13th, 1899
Died Cambridge, Massachusetts, U.S.A., October 28th, 1980

Professor J.H. Van Vleck, often called the father of modern magnetism, won the 1977 Nobel Prize in Physics for a series of papers during the late 1920s and early 1930s which laid the foundations for contemporary solid-state physics. Using the methods of quantum mechanics, he studied the behavior of atoms within a material in a line of research that was to lead others to the invention of such varied devices as transistors, lasers, computer memories, solar energy converters, and office copying machines. In a long career at the universities of Minnesota, Wisconsin, and finally Harvard, he won international honors and taught many of the nation's leading physicists, including several fellow Nobel Prize winners.

In 1920, the year of Van Vleck's graduation from the university of Wisconsin, his father became Visiting Professor of Mathematics at

Courtesy Dept. of Physics, Harvard University

Harvard. It was there that Van Vleck took his doctorate, with a thesis that was one of the first purely theoretical works accepted by the Harvard physics department. After two more years there, Van Vleck took an assistant professorship at Minnesota, where he started work on his first book, *Quantum Principles and Line Spectra*. While he was working on its galley proof, late in 1925, a great revolution in physics occurred. It was realized that probability theory must be involved in computations on the behavior of electrons within an atom; quantum theory, with its treatment in classical mechanics, was displaced by quantum mechanics.

This revolution began in Europe through the matrix mechanics of Bohr and Heisenberg and the wave mechanics of Schrödinger, but it quickly spread to the United States. The University of Wisconsin had a program of visiting professorships; Van Vleck traveled there to meet Schrödinger, Born, Heisenberg, and Dirac, among others. In 1928 Van Vleck moved to Wisconsin, partly to return to his alma mater but also to be able to spend the whole year with European physicists of such international renown.

Van Vleck's own work at that time was in magnetism. In 1932 his classic book *The Theory of Electric and Magnetic Susceptibilities* covered the quantum-mechanical approach to the ferro-, dia-, and paramagnetism of free atoms and molecules, and simple solids; it laid the foundation for all subsequent work in magnetism. In the same year, Van Vleck published a paper, which he later described as his favorite, giving a consistent explanation of the apparently irregular variations in paramagnetic behavior from one ion to another.

A crystalline material produces an electric field that can affect the behavior of any foreign atom or ion within it, modifying the energy state of the system. Van Vleck pioneered the exploration of crystal fields. In 1935, a year after leaving Wisconsin for Harvard, he showed how crystalline potential theory could be generalized into what was later called ligand field theory. Both crystal and ligand fields theories are now regarded as fundamental to much of the research in physics, chemistry, geology, and biochemistry. They are used to explore such solid-state devices as lasers. Later in the 1930s Van Vleck made another significant contribution when he showed that interrelationships among the electrons in an atom or ion can lead the particles to behave as if they were mini-magnets.

During World War Two, Van Vleck worked at the Radio Research Laboratory in Cambridge, Massachusetts, contributing to solutions of problems in radio-frequency spectroscopy and magnetic resonance theory. After the war he returned to Harvard, where from 1951 to 1957 he served as the first Dean of the School of Engineering and Applied Physics. From 1951 to 1969 he was Hollis Professor of Mathematics and Natural Philosophy, the oldest endowed science chair in North America.

A warm and outgoing man descended from the Dutch settlers of the Hudson valley, Van Vleck made a point of being available to colleagues and graduate students for consultation on scientific or private matters. As a teacher he was the father of the second generation of America's outstanding solid-state physicists, including Walter Brattain and John Bardeen, who won the Nobel Prize for their development of the transistor. Both were honored before their teacher. "I thought the statute of limitations had run out on me," said Van Vleck when he heard that he was to share the 1977 prize.

When not in his offices at Lyman Laboratory, Professor Van Vleck and his wife liked to travel—especially by train. Twice he circumnavigated the globe for the chance it offered to see and ride steam locomotives in other countries. It was said that he knew the timetables for all the major passenger trains in the U.S. and Europe. His many honors included membership in the National Academy of Sciences, the Royal Society, and the Académie des Sciénces; honorary doctorates from the University of Oxford and the University of Paris; election to the Légion d'honneur and the National Medal of Science.

R.W.

Son of Edward Burr, mathematician, and Helen Laurence Raymond Van V. Married Abigail June Pearson 1927. Presbyterian. Educ: Univ. of Wisconsin, Madison, B.S. 1920; Harvard Univ., Cambridge, Mass., M.A. 1921, Ph.D. 1922. Instr. in Physics, Harvard Univ. 1922–23. With Univ. of Minn., St. Paul; Asst. Prof. of Physics 1923–26; Assoc. Prof. 1926–27; Prof. of Theoretical Physics, Univ. of Wisc. 1928–34. With Harvard Univ.: Assoc. Prof. of Math. Physics 1934–35; Prof. 1935–80; head of theory group of Radio Research Lab. 1943–45; Chmn. of Physics Dept. 1945–49; Hollis Prof. of Math. and Natural Philosophy 1951–69; Prof. Emeritus since 1969. Visiting Lectr.: Stanford univ., Palo Alto, Calif. 1927, 1934, 1941; Univ. of Mich., Ann Arbor 1933; Columbia Univ., NYC 1934; Princeton Univ., N.J. 1937. Lorentz Prof., Leiden, Netherlands 1960; Eastman Prof., Oxford Univ., England 1961–62; consultant to Radiation Research Lab., Massachusetts Inst. Technology, Cambridge 1942–45. Assoc. Ed. for various physics jrnls. Member: Nat. Acad. of Science; Intnl. Acad. of Quantum Molecular Science; American Mathematics Soc.; Holland Soc., N.Y.; Sociètè Française de Physique (honorary); Royal Netherlands Acad. of Sciences; Royal Acad. of Sciences, Uppsala, Sweden; Royal Acad. of Sciences; Royal Soc. of London; Académie des Sciénces, Paris; American Soc. of Physics, Councillor 1932–35; Pres. 1952–53; American Assn. for Advancement of Science, Vice-Pres. 1960. Hons: Guggenheim Memorial Foundn. Fellowship 1930; Sc.D.: Wesleyan Univ., Middletown, Conn. 1936; Univ. of Md., College Park, Md., 1955; Rockford Coll., Rockford, Ill. 1961; Univ. of Nancy, France 1961; Univ. of Chicago, 1968; Univ. of Minn., St. Paul 1971; Dr. Honoris Causa, Univ. of Grenoble, France 1950; Univ. of Paris, 1960; Sc.D. Honoris Causa, Oxford Univ., England 1958; Albert A. Michelson Award, case Inst. of Technology 1963; Irving Langmuir award, General electric Foundn. 1965; Natnl. Medal of Science 1966; Distinguished Service Award, Univ. of Wisc. Alumni Assn. 1967; Holland Soc. Medal, New York 1969; Cresson Medal, Franklin Inst. 1971; Lorentz Medal, Netherlands Acad. of Sciences 1974; Chevalier, Legion d'honneur; with Dr. Philip Anderson and Sir Nevill Mott, Nobel Prize for Physics 1977. *Author:* Quantum Principles and Line Spectra, 1926; The Theory of Electric and Magnetic Susceptibilities, 1932 (reissued 1965); Biographical Memoir of Charles Elwood Mendenhall 1872–1935, 1938; The Cherwell-Simon Memorial Lectures 1961 and 1962 (with H.B.G. Casimir), 1962; Thirty Years of Microwave Spectroscopy (Alpheus W. Smith Lecture), 1963. *Major articles:* Contributed nearly 100 articles to various physics jrnls. *Further reading:* "The 1977 Nobel Prize in Physics," in Science, vol. 198, Nov. 18, 1977.

GEORGE BORG OLIVIER
Prime Minister of Malta
Born Valletta, Malta, July 5th, 1911
Died Sliema, Malta, October 29th, 1980

George Borg Olivier, a leader of the Nationalist Party for more than three decades, served twice as Prime Minister of Malta. He was a key figure in the negotiations which led Great Britain to grant the country independence in 1964. Under Borg Olivier's rule, manufacturing and tourist industries were developed and the Maltese economy overcame its dependence upon revenue generated by British military installations on the island. Borg Olivier was a moderate who advocated close ties with the Western Alliance and he obtained associate membership for Malta in the European Economic Community.

Borg Olivier was born of a well-to-do family—his father was an architect and civil engineer—with a tradition of public service in Malta's British-ruled government. Educated at the Royal University of Malta, Borg Olivier served as president of a fervidly nationalist student political organization until it was suppressed by British authorities. He graduated with a Doctorate of Laws in 1937 and, two years later, entered politics by joining the Nationalist Party. Borg Olivier subsequently became a member of the ruling Council of Government and served there continuously until 1947 when he was elected to the newly formed Legislative Assembly, which had been established after the war by a new constitution. In 1950, Borg Olivier became Minister of Works and Reconstruction and Minister of Education in the Nationalist Cabinet of Dr. Enrico Mizzi. Later that year, Mizzi died and Borg Olivier succeeded him as Prime Minister and leader of the Nationalist Party.

As Prime Minister, Borg Olivier, facing opposition in the Assembly from the socialist Malta Labor Party, effected a coalition with the Malta Workers Party. Having solidified his base of power in the Assembly, he began to press the British for increased Maltese autonomy and moved to strengthen the country's ties to the NATO alliance. Borg Olivier's tilt to the West owed both to his support of liberal capitalism and to Malta's reliance upon Western tourist dollars and British defense expenditures. Consequently, Borg Olivier welcomed the establishment of NATO's Headquarters for the Allied Forces in the Mediterranean (HAF-MED) on Malta, but he made no headway in negotiations with the British government on Maltese independence because the island's strategic location provided Westminster with a superior base for naval and air facilities.

In 1955 Borg Olivier's government was defeated in the Assembly by one vote and he was succeeded as Prime Minister by Dom Mintoff, the Labor Party leader. When Mintoff sought Maltese integration with Great Britain, Borg Olivier emerged as the spokesman for an opposition movement which coalesced around the Nationalist Party. In 1958, Mintoff resigned and, when Borg Olivier refused to take over, the British Colonial Office assumed political command of the island. Four years later, a new constitution was drafted and, with Great Britain prepared to re-open negotiations for independence, an election was held pitting Borg Olivier against Mintoff.

The electorate was evenly divided between the two parties. While the Labor Party was backed by urban workers, the Nationalists received support from the Roman Catholic Church and the middle and upper classes. (The Nationalist Party's political base existed primarily in the smaller villages and rural areas where the Church was strong.) Indeed, the Church's role in the campaign was, perhaps, the decisive factor; nightly vigils were held in support of Borg Olivier; the entire executive committee of the Labor Party was interdicted; and church bells were rung to drown out the sound of Labor rallies. In the end, the Nationalist Party won 25 of 50 Assembly seats and Borg Olivier became Prime Minister again. Within a year, he had settled the final terms of Malta's independence. In return for autonomy within the Commonwealth, Great Britain was guaranteed continued use of its military bases on the island; a new constitution, submitted by Borg Olivier to the Assembly, won legislative endorsement and was ratified in a popular referendum held in February, 1964. On September 21, Borg Olivier became the Prime Minister of an independent Malta.

In his second term, Borg Olivier, seeking foreign investment, linked Malta more closely to the Western alliance. In 1971, however, he was defeated in the general election by Mintoff's Labor Party. Borg Olivier was narrowly defeated again in 1976 and he was persuaded to relinquish his control of the Nationalist Party. The election was seen as a popular ratification of Mintoff's socialist domestic programs and his policy of nonalignment in foreign affairs.   T.P.

Son of Oliviero B. O., architect and civil engineer. Married Alexandra Mattei 1943. Two sons; one daughter. Educ: Valletta Lyceum; Royal Univ. of Malta, Doctorate of Laws 1937. Member, Council of Government 1939–45; M.P. and Member, Nationalist Party from 1947; Minister of Education and of Justice 1950–51; Minister of Works and Reconstruction 1950–55; Prime Minister 1950–55, 1962–71; Leader of the Opposition 1955–58, 1971–76; Minister of Economic Planning and Finance 1962–65. Hons: Hon. D. Litt., Royal Univ. of Malta 1964; Order of Pope Pius IX 1964; Knight Grand Cross; Order of St. Sylvester.
Further Reading: Malta and the End of Empire by D. Austin, 1967.

I.M. PARSONS
Publisher and author
Born London, England, May 21st, 1906
Died England, October 29th, 1980

Ian Macnaghten Parsons, as Chairman of Chatto and Windus and as President of the Publisher's Association, was a leading figure in British publishing. Parsons was also a novelist, critical biographer, and editor of poetry anthologies.

Parsons grew up on Pont Street in the Westminster section of central London. He attended Winchester College, and later Trinity College, Cambridge, where he earned a senior scholarship and first class honors in English literature. Having edited *The Granta* and the *Cambridge Review* as an undergraduate, Parsons joined Chatto and Windus in 1928. He began as a typographer, advanced to art editor, and became a partner in 1930. At that time, Chatto and Windus was a relatively small firm, distinguished by a list of authors that included

Courtesy M.T. Parsons

Lytton Strachey and Clive Bell of the Bloomsbury Group. Support of these authors made the firm the major publisher of avant-garde literature in Great Britain and Parsons himself remained associated with Leonard and Virginia Woolf throughout his career. In the 1930s, he published *Night and Day,* a weekly magazine styled as a counterpart to *The New Yorker,* which ceased publication in December 1937 after just six months in print.

During World War Two, Parsons accepted a commission in the Volunteer Reserves of the Royal Air Force, seeing intelligence duty in France before the evacuation, and again after the Normandy invasion. He achieved the rank of wing-commander, and was appointed Officer of the British Empire in 1944.

In 1946, Chatto and Windus changed dramatically as the partnership was dissolved and the firm was reorganized as a limited company. Chatto and Windus absorbed the management of Christophers, and Leonard and Virginia Woolf's Hogarth Press. Parsons served as Chairman and Managing Director of the Board of Directors until 1954, when he replaced the retired Harold Raymond as Chairman and, during these years, the company ambitiously published such contemporary poets and critics as William Empson and F.R. Leavis. Parsons also acted as director of Hunter and Foulis Ltd., the Reprint Society Ltd., the Scottish Academic Press, the Sussex University Press and served as Chairman of Spring Productions Ltd., and as Joint Chairman of Chatto, Bodley Head and Jonathan Cape Ltd. In 1957, Parsons became President of the Publisher's Association and, in 1962, he contributed to the success of an action in Restrictive Practices Court which upheld the trade rights of booksellers and publishers. "Under the leadership of Ian Parsons, Chatto and Windus had without question or doubt one of the most distinctive and typically British imprints," commented Roger Straus of Farrar, Straus and Giroux in New York.

Parsons wrote two books, *Shades of Albany* (1928) (subtitled "A Facetious Phantasy") and, with George Spater, *A Marriage of True Minds: An Intimate Portrait of Leonard and Virginia Woolf* (1977). Parsons also wrote a laudatory introduction to the re-issued version of Leonard Woolf's early novel, *The Wise Virgins* (1979). While Parsons edited an encyclopedia of air warfare, and one of wildlife, he was hailed by critics as a champion of poetry. In addition to five anthologies, he selected and introduced the *Poems of C. Day Lewis* (1977) and the *Collected Works of Isaac Rosenberg* (1979). Rosenberg's work might well have been forgotten after the poet's death in World War One had it not been for Parsons' sponsorship. Parsons was made a Commander of the British Empire in 1971, and awarded an Honorary D. Litt. from the University of St. Andrews in 1975.   L.H.

Son of Edward Percival and Mabel Margret P. Married Marjorie Tulip Ritchie 1934. No children. Educ: Winchester Coll.; Trinity Coll., Cambridge, Senior Scholar (1st Class Hons. English Lit.). With Chatto and Windus: joined 1928; partner 1930–46; Chmn. and Managing Dir. of Bd. of Dirs. 1946–53; Company Chmn. 1954–74. Dir., Hunter and Foulis Ltd.., and the Reprint Soc. Ltd.; Dir., Scottish Academic Press, 1969–76; Dir., Univ. of Sussex Press, 1971–76; Chmn., Sprint Productions Ltd. 1979; Joint Chmn., Chatto, Bodley Head and Jonathan Cape Ltd. 1979; Pres., Publisher's Assn. 1957–59. Court Asst., Stationers' and Newspaper Makers' Co., 1977.

Mil. service: Wing Comdr., Volunteer Reserves, R.A.F., WWII.
Hons: OBE, 1944; CBE, 1971; Hon. D. Litt., Univ. of St. Andrews,
1975. *Editor*—The Poet's Corner: The Hundred Most Popular English
Poems, 1930; The Progress of Poetry: An Anthology of Verse from
Hardy to the Present Day, 1936; Poetry for Pleasure, 8 vols., 1952–56;
Men Who March Away: Poems of the First World War, 1965; (with
Eve Harlow) The Encyclopedia of Wild Life, 1974; The Encyclopedia
of Air Warfare, 1974; Poems of C. Day Lewis, 1977; Collected Works
of Isaac Rosenberg, 1979; Bird, Beast and Flower, 1979. *Author*—
Shades of Albany, 1928; (with George Spater) A Marriage of True
Minds, 1977; (introd.) The Wise Virgins, by Leonard Woolf, rev. ed.
1979.
Further reading—Journey to the Trenches: The Life of Isaac Rosenberg, 1890–1918, 1975; A Century of Writers, 1855–1955: A Cente-
nary Volume, ed. by D.M. Low, 1955.

EDELMIRO FARRELL
Army General and President of Argentina
Born Avellaneda, Buenos Aires, Argentina, 1887
Died Buenos Aires, Argentina, October 31st, 1980

General Edelmiro Farrell ruled Argentina during the final year of
World War Two. Accused by the U.S. government of Nazi sympathies, Farrell was forced to declare war against the Axis powers; he
was also a participant in the rise to power of Colonal Juan Peron.

A 1908 military academy graduate, Farrell had achieved the rank of
Brigadier-General when a coup staged by the United Officers' Group
(GOU) overthrew the government of President Ramon S. Castillo.
The new regime was led by three generals—Rawson, Ramirez and
Farrell—who were sympathetic to the Axis powers, and by Colonel
Juan Peron, who represented the younger generation of officers
within the GOU. Because the generals had to contend with conflicting
forces—Argentine nationalists urged closer ties with the Germans
while the United States withheld recognition of the new government
so long as its leaders refused to declare war against the fascists—the
regime lacked stability. First Rawson served as President but he was
quickly succeeded by Ramirez, who appointed Farrell Vice-President
and Minister of War. When Farrell became President in February,
1944, he elevated Peron to the posts of Minister of War, Secretary of
Labor, and Vice-President. While Peron solidifed and expanded his
base of power with the workers, Farrell attempted to prepare
Argentinian nationalists for the impending fascist defeat. Bowing to
pressure from the U.S. government and Great Britain, Farrell
declared war on the Axis in the spring of 1945. As a result of this
diplomatic gesture, the United States formally recognized Farrell's
government and Argentina was granted a seat in the United Nations,
which was then being formed.

In 1945, senior military officers, wary of the Argentine labor
movement's growing strength, forced Peron into exile. The following
year, however, mass demonstrations returned Peron to the country
and, when he was elected President on June 4, Farrell retired from
political and military life. When Peron was overthrown in 1955,

Farrell requested that a court of inquiry be formed to prove that he was not responsible for the "excesses" of the Peron regime.   L.R.

Educ: Military Acad., grad. 1908. Attended Superior War Coll. 1918–20; served with Mountain Regiments in the Andes; Brig.-Gen. 1943; named Minister of War and V.P. of Argentina 1943; Pres., Feb. 1944, retired 1947. Hons: Golden Condor award.

JAN WERICH
Playwright and actor
Born Prague, Czechoslovakia, 1905
Died Prague, Czechoslovakia, October 31st, 1980

Jan Werich, a well-loved Czechoslovakian actor, singer, producer, director and writer, was the founder of Prague's highly popular Liberated Theater (later known as the Voskovec and Werich—V and W—Theater). A vociferous opponent of fascism, he also made no secret of his dislike for the Soviet-dominated regime of the postwar years.

As a law student in Prague, Werich was fascinated by the many American western films. By juxtaposing the machoism posturings of sheriffs and cowboys with that of the fascists, Werich saw an opportunity to express his political views in a satirical way. In one evening he wrote *Vest Pocket Review* (1927) and that same week presented it to a student gathering; his review achieved overnight success and ran for 208 performances. This was the beginning of the Liberated Theater. Over the next decade Werich and his friend George Voskovec produced, directed and performed in 26 witty and lively theatrical fantasies, many in the tradition of the *Commedia dell'Arte*. Music for the shows was composed by Jaroslav Jezek.

Werich's 1936 production of *The World is Ours,* a comedy satirizing nazi attempts to undermine unity among Czech workers in preparation for the annexing of the Sudetenland, predicted the presence of secret caches of fascist arms in Czech warehouses, factories and churches, and the nazi agitation of labor unions and of the powerful People's Front. Prague critics praised the play but it was faulted by some for its "exaggeration" of fascist activities. Unfortunately the play's thesis proved true all too quickly: in 1938 the Treaty of Munich granted the Sudetenland to Hitler, and the extremely popular V and W Theater was closed; it was sorely missed. A political commentator later wrote that the Theater symbolized the "heart of Czech culture . . . It stood for the whole stubbornly democratic, courageous and freedom-loving philosophy of the ordinary Czech people."

Persecuted and blacklisted by the fascists, Werich and Voskovec fled to the United States in January 1929. They wrote 2,000 war information and political satire programs which were broadcast by the U.S. Office of War Information to Czechoslovakia. Commenting on the problems at home, Werich said: "Czechs have a way of thinking straight . . . they are a patient people. They know when to start a battle and they know when to keep quiet." Werich's anti-Hitler satire, *The Ass and His Shadow* was first produced in Cleveland in 1940; he made his New York stage debut in 1945, playing Stephano in *The Tempest.*

Werich and Voskovec returned to Prague when the war was over, but after the 1948 *coup d'état,* Voskovec went back to America to pursue his acting career. Werich remained in Czechoslovakia and appeared in a few films and on television, but the authorities prevented him from resuming anything along the lines of the V and W Theater. There was some talk of a Voskovec and Werich revival in 1968, but the Soviet invasion intervened. Werich published two extremely popular books—*Italian Holidays,* which was later serialized in *Literárí noviny,* and *Finfárum,* a collection of fairy tales with illustrations by Trnka. He continued to produce plays until the late 1960s when ill health forced him to retire. He had finally been honored by the Czech authorities in 1963 when he was named a *National Artist.*   R.T.

Educ: studied law in Prague. Playwright, actor, and producer since 1927. Founder and Dir. 1927–38, Liberated Theater (also known as Voskovec and Werich Theater); lived in America during WWII, writing radio broadcasts to Czechoslovakia for U.S. Office of War Information, and plays, and acting; returned to Czechoslovakia after the war, continued to write and produce plays; also acted occasionally in films and on television. Hons: National Artist 1963. *Plays*—Vest Pocket Review, 1927; The World is Ours, 1936; The Ass and his Shadow, 1940; The Man who Came to Dinner (adaptation), 1946; (co-author) Fist in the Eye, 1947–48; many others. *Other*—Fimfárum (fairy tales); Italian Holidays.

SIR KENNETH (WILLIAM) BLACKBURNE
British colonial administrator; Governor-General of Jamaica
Born Bristol, England, December 12th, 1907
Died Castletown, Isle of Man, November 4th, 1980

Sir Kenneth Blackburne spent his entire career in Britain's Colonial Office, serving in Africa, the Middle East, and the Caribbean, as well as in London. In his last positions, as Governor and then Governor-General of Jamaica, he represented the British government in the critical period before and after the island's independence.

He was the elder son of a Dean of Bristol. After secondary education at Marlborough College, Blackburne went on to Clare College, Cambridge. At the age of 22 he entered the British Colonial Service, becoming Assistant District Officer in Nigeria. He was transferred to Palestine in 1935 and for three years he held the position of Assistant District Commissioner for the Nazareth district and, for a brief period, acted as Chief District Commissioner of Galilee. With opposing nationalist groups in the area battling for power in what was often open warfare, Blackburne's job was a most difficult, and often dangerous one. He was withdrawn from field duty and returned to London in 1938. The following year he was named to the Order of the British Empire in recognition of his work in Palestine.

For the next three years he worked in various capacities in the Colonial Office, but in 1941 he was sent to West Africa as Colonial Secretary of The Gambia. Two years later he was assigned to the first of three posts he was to hold in the Caribbean. From 1943 to 1947 he served as Administrative Secretary to the Comptroller for Development and Welfare in the British West Indies, and periodically assumed the role of Acting Comptroller. During this tenure he was named Companion to the Order of St. Michael and St. George.

In 1947 Blackburne was again summoned back to London, this time as Director of Information Services in the Colonial Office. It was his task to expand and reorganize the Information Services in the effort to improve diplomatic communication and to foster better understanding of colonial affairs as the British Empire entered the post-war era of decolonization and territorial independence. As part of his drive to encourage public interest in the changing colonial situation and support for government policies, Blackburne initiated a series of "Colonial Weeks" in various parts of Great Britain and had June 1949 named "Colonial Month."

Blackburne returned to the Caribbean in 1950 to become Governor of the Leeward Islands. Composed of over thirty islands but with a land area of only 422 square miles, politically and racially disunited, and with a poor economy, the Leeward Islands were difficult to govern. During Blackburne's term, the Federation of the Lesser Antilles, to which the Leeward Islands had been party, fell apart. Under his leadership, the Leewards joined the wider British West Indies Federation.

When, in 1957, Sir Hugh Foot was transferred to Cyprus from the dual office of Captain-General and Governor-in-Chief of Jamaica, Sir Kenneth Blackburne (he had been knighted in 1952) was chosen to be his successor. He assumed the position at a time of mounting political unrest and agitation for independence from the United Kingdom. After two hundred years as one of Britain's most valuable colonies, Jamaica had by the early part of the 20th century become beset by problems of massive unemployment and racial strife, and large numbers of Jamaicans began to emigrate to Great Britain. Under articles providing increased self-government—enacted the year he became Governor-in-Chief—the Jamaican legislature, which for the first time was composed of more native-born Jamaicans than British, voted in 1958 to join the British West Indies Federation, and to seek independence jointly. But unity was short-lived; a 1961 referendum resulted in Jamaica's secession from the Federation and the island then pursued a policy of separate independence from the United Kingdom. Independence was achieved in August of the following year. A constitution modeled on the British parliamentary system established a republic within the British Commonwealth of Nations. Sir Kenneth Blackburne was asked to stay in Jamaica as the first Governor-General; he agreed to do so for one year, after which time he retired.

He returned to England and his home on the Isle of Man, where he devoted himself to local civic activities and to recreations such as sailing and gardening. In 1976, calling upon his intimate knowledge of the Colonial Service and his many years of experience in the field, he published *Lasting Legacy: A Story of British Colonialism.*   K.B.

Son of Very Rev. H.W.B., clergyman. Married Bridget Senhouse Constant Wilson 1935. One son, one daughter. Educ: Marlborough Coll.; Clare Coll., Cambridge 1926–29. Served in British Colonial Service 1930–63: Asst. District Officer, Nigeria 1930–35; Asst. District Commnr., Nazareth, Palestine 1935–38; Acting District Commnr., Galilee, Palestine 1938; Acting Asst. Principal, then Principal, Colonial Office, London 1938–41; Colonial Secty., The Gambia 1941–43; Administrative Secty. to the Comptroller for Development and Welfare in the West Indies 1943–47 and Acting Comptroller 1944 and 1946; Dir. of Informational Services, Colonial Office, London 1947–50; Governor and Commander-in-Chief of the Leeward Island 1950–56; Captain-General and Governor-in-Chief of Jamaica 1957–62; Governor-General of Jamaica 1962 until retirement 1963. Hons: OBE 1939, CMG 1946; KCMG 1952; Knight of St. John 1952; GBE 1962; GCMG 1962.

NOEL (A.) LANGLEY
Screenwriter, novelist and playwright
Born Durban, South Africa, December 25th, 1911
Died Desert Hot Springs, California, U.S.A., November 4th, 1980

Noel Langley was largely responsible for the script of a fantastically successful movie which millions of adults and children who have seen—and continue to see—would never connect with his name. At the age of 26, Langley wrote the basic screenplay for *The Wizard of Oz*.

Raised and educated in Durban, South Africa, he later attended the University of Natal before leaving for England. Langley, still in his early twenties, had two London plays running in the same year (1934). The first one, *Queer Cargo,* was a potboiler about missing diamonds in a South Seas setting; the other, a trifling romance, *For Ever,* had Dante and Beatrice as the main characters. The following year, Langley published his first novel, *Cage Me a Peacock* set in the Roman period; he later used the story as the basis for a musical.

Hollywood, always eager for fresh talents from Europe, soon attracted Langley; his first film assignment there was to salvage an earlier script for a Jeannette Macdonald-Nelson Eddy musical, and he did it with characteristic speed and skill. That film, *Maytime,* was 1937's most financially successful feature. Next, he was asked to adapt a script for M-G-M's production number 1069 from L. Frank Baum's The Wizard of Oz.

Ten writers were eventually assigned some aspect of the script, if only to add jokes to the dialogue, but Langley's 43 page treatment provided the basic framework for the finished film. It was Langley who amplified the Kansas incidents, sketched in only briefly in the original novel, and argued for the preliminary introduction of the major characters as earthly figures before they reappeared in the Land of Oz. Having already published a children's book, Langley reasoned that the fantasy figures must have realistic surrogates to make them acceptable to young viewers. In the four scripts Langley submitted during the year he worked on the film were such additions as the Cowardly Lion who frightened himself by pulling on his own tail, trees that slap the hands of potential apple pickers, and the bulk of the dialogue between Dorothy and the Good Witch in Munchkin land. The 1930's studios had little respect for writers; Langley was taken off the project and then reassigned, as others were consulted, individually or in teams, sometimes consecutively and often in veiled competition. Characteristically, Langley never saw the completed film until after its commercial release. Believing that it "missed the boat all the way around," Langley said he loathed it. However, upon seeing it many years later, he reversed his opinion and considered it "not a bad picture."

Langley's boyish charm and independent attitudes earned him the title of "pixie nonconformist" on the M-G-M lot. His quick tongue got him blacklisted from the studio for a while when it was reported to Mayer that Langley made the remark that: "every time Mayer smiles at me, I feel a snake has crawled over my foot."

His best known work after *The Wizard of Oz* is the highly successful play, *Edward, My Son* which he wrote in collaboration with Robert Morley; Langley later adapted it for the screen. The majority of his other plays were rather undistinguished. Much of his film work revolved around the adaptation of well-known literary works, including *Tom Brown's School-Days, Ivanhoe, The Prisoner of Zenda, Pickwick Papers,* and the *Vagabond King.* His film version of three Somerset Maugham short stories appeared as *Trio* in 1950. Langley's last film, *Search for Bridey Murphey* which he wrote and directed, appeared in 1957.   L.R./R.T.

Married: (1) Naomi Mary Legate, 1937 (div. 1954); 3 sons, 2 daughters; (2) Pamela Deeming, 1959. Educ: Univ. of Natal, B.A. Mil. service: Royal Canadian Navy, to rank of lieutenant, 1942–45. Member, Writers Guild of America, West. Hon: with Robert Morley, Donaldson Award for Edward My Son, NYC production 1948. *Plays:* Queer Cargo, For Ever, 1934; Farm of Three Echoes, 1935, NYC version 1939; No Regrets, 1937; The Walrus and the Carpenter, 1941; Little Lambs Eat Ivy, (with Robert Morley) Edward My Son, 1947; Cage Me a Peacock (musical), 1959; An Elegance of Rebels, 1960; The Burning Bush, The Land of Green Ginger, 1966; The Snow Queen, 1967. *Screenwriter:* School for Husbands, 1932; Maytime, 1937; The Wizard of Oz, 1938; They Made Me a Fugitive, 1946; Cardboard Cavalier, Adam and Evalyn, 1948; Edward My Son, 1949; Ivanhoe, The Pickwick Papers (also dir.), Married Alive, 1952; Knights of the Round Table, 1953; Our Girl Friday (also dir.), Trilby and Svengali (also dir.), Vagabond King, The Adventures of Sadie, 1955; The Search for Bridey Murphy (also dir.), 1957. *Author:* Cage Me a Peacock, 1935; There's a Porpoise Close Behind Us, 1936, in USA as So Unlike the English, 1937; Land of Green Ginger, 1937, in USA as Tale of the Land of Green Ginger, 1938; Hocus Pocus, 1941; The Music of the Heart, 1946; The Cabbage Patch, 1947; The True and Pathetic Story of Desbarollda the Waltzing Mouse, Nymph in Clover, 1948; The Inconstant Moon, 1949; (with Hazel Pynegar) Somebody's Rocking My Dreamboat, 1949; Tales of Mystery and Revenge, 1950; The Rift in the Lute, (with Hazel Pynegar) Cuckoo in the Dell, 1951; Where Did Everybody Go?, 1960; The Loner, 1967; My Beloved Teck, 1970; A Dream of Dragonflies, 1972; (co-author) There's a Horse in My Tree.

MILDRED ADAMS
Journalist, writer, translator
Born Illinois, U.S.A., 1894
Died New York City, U.S.A., November 5th, 1980

Mildred Adams Kenyon, who wrote under her maiden name, was an expert on literary and political life in Spain and Latin America, and a prolific journalist and translator from the Spanish.

Born in Illinois, Adams attended the University of California at Berkeley, Columbia University, and Yale University. In the 1920s she went to Spain as a freelance journalist for the New York Times and remained there until the outbreak of the Spanish Civil War in 1936, when she returned to New York to head an emergency committee assisting republican refugees.

After the war Adams became a correspondent for the London Economist, a regular contributor to the New York Times Magazine and Book Review, and an advisor to two literary and cultural journals, *Revista de Occidente* in Madrid and *Sur* in Argentina. Hundreds of her essays and articles on the political life of Latin America, Africa, and Europe appeared in print. Her translations from the Spanish included eight volumes by the philosopher José Ortega y Gasset, including *Man and Crisis* and *An Interpretation of Universal History*.

Adams also wrote five books of her own, among them studies of

Courtesy W. Houston Kenyon, Jr.

Latin America, British postwar socialism, and the women's suffrage movement. Her biography of the Spanish poet and playwright Frederico García Lorca, whom she first met in Granada in 1928 (and who was later killed by right-wing assassins), was published in 1977. Critical reaction to the book was mixed. "Adams . . . presents him through such a haze of cliché that her book doesn't record much apart from her own rather pallid good intentions," wrote a critic in the *New York Review of Books*. A reviewer in The Atlantic, however, called the book "a neat, informative, readable and useful piece of work."

Adams, who was married to W. Houston Kenyon, Jr., was a director of the Foreign Policy Association, the Near East Foundation, and the Americas Foundation.   J.S.

Married W. Houston Kenyon, Jr. Educ: Univ. of California at Berkeley; Columbia Univ.; Yale Univ. Freelance journalist for New York Times in Spain from late 1920s to 1936; ran emergency rescue cttee. for loyalist refugees during Spanish Civil War, NYC 1936. Freelance writer, journalist, and translator from the Spanish since 1930s; part-time corresp., The London Economist 1946–75; regular contributor to New York Times Magazine and Book Review and other periodicals; American advisor to Revista de Occidente (jrnl.), Madrid; American advisor to Sur (lit. jrnl.), Argentina. Dir. and Exec. Cttee Member, Foreign Policy Assn.; Dir., Near East Foundn.; Dir., Americas Foundn. *Translator:* Man and Crisis (by José Ortega y Gasset), 1922; Invertebrate Spain (by Ortega y Gasset), 1937; An Interpretation of Universal History (by Ortega y Gasset), 1973; five other works by Ortega y Gasset; Knight of El Dorado (by German Arciniegas), 1942. *Author:* Britain's Road to Recovery, 1949; Latin America: Evolution or Explosion, 1964; The Right to be People, 1967; García Lorca: Playwright and Poet, 1977. Numerous essays and articles in New Republic, National Review, New York Times Magazine, Foreign Policy Bulletin, Foreign Affairs, and other periodicals.

NEVILL (HENRY AYLMER KENDALL) COGHILL
Scholar and popularizer of Middle English literature
Born Castle Townshend, Skibbereen, County Cork, Ireland, April 18th, 1899
Died Oxford, England, November 6th, 1980

Nevill Coghill, for more than 40 years one of the best known and most popular of Oxford dons, was a leading member of the university's theater movement and a specialist in Middle English literature. His lively translation and broadcasts of Geoffrey Chaucer's *The Canterbury Tales,* and his adaptation of the *Tales* for the London musical stage, brought the poet's earthy charm and ribald wit to modern audiences.

Coghill, the son of a baronet, was born Nevill Henry Aylmer Kendall Coghill at Castle Townshend, Skibbereen, County Cork. He grew up in the countryside in the south of Ireland and attended Bitton Grange and the Haileybury School. After serving as a gunner on the Salonika front in 1918, he read history at Exeter College, Oxford, taking Second Class honors, and stayed on to earn a First Class degree in English literature. He was elected a Research Fellow of Exeter in 1924 and was named an Official Fellow, Librarian, and Tutor of the College a year later. As a scholar, he specialized in Elizabethan and Jacobean drama and in Middle English poetry, on which he wrote a number of books and articles.

In 1930 Coghill staged Milton's *Samson Agonistes* in the Exeter College gardens, the beginning of a long association with the theatrical life of the university. As a member of the Oxford University Drama Commission, he assisted in the formulation of recommendations for the future development of the dramatic arts, in whose behalf he founded the Experimental Theatre Club, served as curator of the Oxford University Theatre, and presented numerous plays and operas, many in open-air settings which took full poetic advantage of sunlight and shadow. His productions of *A Midsummer Night's Dream* and *Pilgrim's Progress* were seen on London stages in 1945 and 1951. In 1948 he and Gwynne Windham wrote and produced *The Masque of Hope,* performed at University College in honor of Princess (later Queen) Elizabeth.

During the late 1930s, Coghill made radio broadcasts, some of which were recorded and published, of John Bunyan's *Pilgrim's Progress* and Chaucer's *The Canterbury Tales* and *Troilus and Criseyde.* His 1951 rendering of the *Tales* into modern English was, according to the *Encyclopedia Britannica,* "perhaps the most popular" of 20th-century versions; one critic noted that it "preserves the freshness and racy vitality" of the original. Coghill also translated *Troilus and Criseyde* and William Langland's *The Vision of Piers Plowman.* His critical work *The Pardon of Piers Plowman,* delivered as the Israel Gollancz Memorial Lecture at the British Academy in 1945, was published in book form a year later; *The Poet Chaucer* appeared in 1949.

When F.P. Wilson retired from Merton College in 1957, Coghill was elected to succeed his former tutor in the Merton Chair of English Literature. He delivered the Clark Lecture at Trinity College, Cambridge, in 1959 on *Shakespeare's Professional Skills* and published editions of the plays of T.S. Eliot.

In 1966, the year of his retirement from Oxford, Coghill staged a production of Christopher Marlowe's *Dr. Faustus* that starred Elizabeth Taylor and Coghill's former student, Richard Burton, who had taken up acting partly on Coghill's encouragement. A film version of *Dr. Faustus,* co-directed by Coghill from his own screenplay, was shot in Rome with the same leading players in 1967.

Coghill's musical adaptation of *The Canterbury Tales,* written in collaboration with Martin Starkie and set to music by Richard Hill and John Hawkins, had a five-year run in London and successful productions in New York, Australia, and Europe. *New York Times* critic Clive Barnes thought the choreography sprightly and the acting beguiling, but was unimpressed by Coghill's lyrics. "It is curious," he wrote, "that a man who was such a theatrical academic—his lectures were as good as the old silent movies—should prove such an academic man of the theater."

Coghill also reworked a section of *The Nun's Priest's Tale,* the fable of Chanticleer, as a song text in 1947. It was set to music by Thomas Woods. His readings of several of the *Tales* are available on long-playing records. *Chaucer's Idea of What is Noble* and *A Choice of Chaucer's Verse* appeared in the early 1970s.

Coghill, who was briefly married and had one daughter, was elected a Fellow of the Royal Society of Literature in 1950 and served as president of the Poetry Society and the English Association. On the occasion of his retirement from Oxford he was presented with a collection of essays on Shakespearean theatricals, *To Nevill Coghill from Friends,* compiled by John Lawlor and W.H. Auden.   J.P./J.S.

Son of Sir Egerton Bush C., 5th baronet, and Elizabeth Hildegarde Augusta (Somerville) C. Married Elspeth Nora Harley, author and translator, 1927 (div. 1933). Daughter: Carol Martin. Church of England. Educ: Bitton Grange; Haileybury Sch.; Exeter Coll., Oxford (Stapledon Scholar), B.A. (Second Class Hons. in history) 1922, B.A. (First Class Hons, in English literature) 1923, M.A. 1926; Resident Fellow 1924, Fellow in English literature 1925–57, and Emeritus Fellow since 1957, Exeter Coll.; Professorial Fellow 1957–66 and Emeritus Fellow since 1966, Merton Coll., Oxford. Mil. Service: 2nd Lt., Royal Field Artillery, British Salonika Force 1917–19. With Exeter Coll., Oxford: Tutor 1925–57; Librarian of Coll. 1925; Dean of Degrees 1940; Sub-Rector 1940–45. Teacher, Royal Naval Coll., Dartmouth ca. 1924; Gresham Prof. of Rhetoric, Mercers' Company, London 1948; Merton Prof. of English Literature, Merton Coll., Oxford 1957–66. Producer of plays and operas since 1930s; author, translator, editor, and broadcaster since 1940s; Sir Israel Gollancz Memorial Lectr., British Acad. 1945; Clark Lectr., Trinity Coll., Cambridge 1953. Sr. Member, Oxford Univ. Dramatic Soc. 1934–66; Founder, Oxford Univ. Experimental Theatre Club 1935; Dir., Friends of Oxford Univ. Dramatic Soc. 1940–47; Member, Oxford Univ. Drama Commn. 1945; Gov., Shakespeare Memorial Theatre, Stratford-upon-Avon 1956; Pres., Poetry Soc. 1964–66; Pres., English Assn. 1970–71; Curator, Oxford Univ. Theatre; Member, Travellers' Club. Hons: elected Fellow, Royal Soc. of Literature 1950; Hon. D. Litt., Williams Coll. 1966; Hon. LL.D., St. Andrews Univ. 1971. *Author: Books*—The Pardon of Piers Plowman, 1945; The Poet Chaucer, 1949, 2nd ed. 1967; Geoffrey Chaucer, 1959; Piers Plowman, 1964; Shakespeare's Professional Skills, 1964; Chaucer's Idea of What is Noble, 1971. *Plays*—(with Glynne Wickham) The Masque of Hope, Oxford 1948; (adapter, with Martin Starkie) The Canterbury Tales, London 1968. *Articles*—"The Basis of Shakespearean Comedy: A Study of Medieval Affinities," in English Association Essays and Studies, New Series, Vol. 3, 1950; others. *Translator:* (also adapter) Chanticleer, A Tale for Singing: words derived from The Nun's Priest's Tale (by Geoffrey Chaucer) and set for voices by Thomas Wood, 1947; Visions from Piers Plowman, Taken from the Poem by William Langland, 1949; (with C. Tolkien) The Nun's Priest's Tale (by Chaucer), 1951; The Canterbury Tales (by Chaucer), 1951; (with C. Tolkien) The Pardoner's Tale (by Chaucer), 1958; The Man of Law's Tale (by Chaucer), 1969; Troilus and Criseyde (by Chaucer), 1971. *Editor:* (also author of introduction) The Vision of Piers Plowman (by Langland), 1959; Murder in the Cathedral (by T.S. Eliot), 1965; The Family Reunion (by Eliot,) 1969; The Tragedy of Romeo and Juliet (by Shakespeare), 1971; A Choice of Chaucer's Verse, 1972; The Cocktail Party (by Eliot), 1974. *Producer:* Samson Agonistes, Oxford 1930; Troilus and Criseyde, Oxford 1937; A Midsummer Night's Dream, London 1945; The Winter's Tale, Oxford 1946; The Tempest, Oxford 1949; Pilgrim's Progress, London 1951; Dr. Faustus, Oxford

1966; many others. *Scriptwriter and co-director:* (film version) Dr. Faustus, 1967. *Broadcaster:* The Canterbury Tales, First Series 1946–47, Second Series 1949, rev. ed. 1951; Pilgrim's Progress (by John Bunyan), 1947; Troilus and Criseyde, 1947. *Recordings:* (compiler) Agincourt 1415: The Decline of Chivalry, 1969; The Pardoner's Tale; others.

STEVE MCQUEEN
Film and television actor
Born Indianapolis, Indiana, U.S.A., March 24th, 1930
Died Juarez, Mexico, November 7th, 1980

When Steve McQueen arrived in Hollywood in 1955, he was a former juvenile delinquent, marine, and jack-of-all-trades with a taste for motorcycle racing and some training as an actor. Within a few years he had become one of the most popular and highly paid film actors in the industry, a perennially steely-eyed tough guy who dominated the screen in a succession of cowboy and soldier roles.

McQueen was born in Idianapolis in 1930 to a mother who was still in her teens. His father, a Navy pilot, stuntman, and gambler, deserted the family six months later. Until he was nine, he lived with relatives on a farm in Slater, Missouri, where he milked cows and learned to shoot; then his mother took him back to Indianapolis and the Silver Lake area of Los Angeles, where he quickly fell in with teenage street gangs and became a car thief. At the Junior Boys' Republic in Chino, California, a reform school to which his mother and her new husband had him committed when he was 14, he finished the ninth grade and was persuaded to go straight by a fatherly superintendent. (In later years he set up a scholarship fund for young inmates and often visited the school to give them encouragement.)

Released from the Republic at the age of 15, McQueen headed for New York, lied about his age to get an able-bodied seaman's card, and shipped out to Cuba and the Dominican Republic on a tanker. For the next year and a half he scratched together a living in the States and Canada as a carnival barker, timber worker, and oil rigger before enlisting in the Marines in 1947. He was trained as a tank driver and developed a fascination for all things mechanical, especially vehicles. On one occasion he served 41 days in the brig, the first 21 on bread and water, for going AWOL; on another, he distinguished himself by helping to rescue drowning soldiers whose transport had capsized in Arctic waters.

Back in New York, McQueen settled in a cold-water flat in Greenwich Village, where he hustled his way through a series of odd jobs, including taxi mechanic, bartender, encyclopedia salesman, dockhand, and poker payer, and scrounged meals from a succession of girlfriends. The Village in those years was a congenial place for ex-servicemen. "For the first time in my life," he told an interviewer later, "I was exposed to music, culture, a little kindness, a little sensitivity. It was a way of life where people talked out their problems, instead of punching you." On the advice of a girlfriend, he

auditioned for a drama teacher, Sanford Meisner, who accepted him
as a student and got him a one-line part in a Yiddish play. With the
help of two scholarships and a grant from the G.I. bill, he continued
studying at the Uta Hagen-Herbert Berghof Drama Studio and at Lee
Strasberg's Actors Studio, racing motorcycles in his spare time.

For the next few years, McQueen took minor roles in stock
productions and television shows, including an episode of the CBS
western *Trackdown* in which he played a bounty hunter, Josh
Randall. The episode grew into a successful series called *Wanted,
Dead or Alive.* Years of living by his fists and his wits enabled
McQueen to bring a rare sense of authenticity to the role.

McQueen had already made three low-budget films *(The Blob,
Never Love a Stranger,* and *The Great St. Louis Bank Robbery)* when
director John Sturges cast him as a soldier in a Frank Sinatra vehicle,
Never So Few, in 1959. His next role, as an expert gunman in *The
Magnificent Seven,* caught the attention of the critics, who saw in his
quiet self-confidence and wary machismo an echo of the late James
Dean. He continued to build a box-office following with soldier roles
in *Hell is for Heroes* and *The War Lover.*

The movie that made McQueen a star was *The Great Escape,* the
story of an attempt by 76 Allied soldiers to tunnel their way out of a
German prisoner-of-war camp during World War II. McQueen, as the
rebellious, independent Cooler Kid, decoys the pursuing Germans by
riding a stolen motorcycle to the Swiss frontier, setting off a
spectacular chase scene through the Bavarian mountains. The final,
failed leap across a barbed-wire fence was performed by a stuntman,
but McQueen did most of his own riding and won the Best Actor
Award from the Moscow Film Festival.

After *The Great Escape* came *Love with the Proper Stranger* and
Soldier in the Rain. In *Baby the Rain Must fall* he was a paroled
convict trying to keep his anger and confusion from turning into
violence; in *The Cincinnati Kid* he was an expert poker player who
loses to Edward G. Robinson in a fixed game. Each performance
added to his image as a scrappy, inarticulate, but appealing loner who
showed his inner strength less by what he said than by the squint of his
eyes and the set of his jaw. He was exactly the kind of rough-and-
ready anti-hero the audiences of the mid-1960s were looking for.

By 1965 McQueen was one of the best-paid stars in Hollywood; his
name on the marquee was a guarantee of success for a film. According
to director Robert Wise, he had "that lean and hungry look which
men identify with and which arouses in women their maternal instinct
and their desire to love." One critic called him "a Sphinx without a
secret." Whenever possible, he took part in motorcycle and sportscar
competitions, sometimes under the name of Harvey Mushman, and
placed high in major races, including the Sebring 12-Hour Endurance
Tests and the Elsinore Grand Prix. "Acting," he once said, "is like
racing. You need the same absolute concentration. You have to reach
inside of you and bring forth a lot of broken glass. That's painful."

Despite his popularity, McQueen, who was married and had two
children, did not fit in with the Hollywood social scene. Many of his
friends were mechanics and racers, and his speech combined the
beatnik jargon of his Greenich Village days with the earthy slang of
the Marines. A skin-diving accident had left him deaf in one ear and

hard of hearing in the other, but he refused to wear a hearing aid, preferring to seem aloof rather than compromise his "tough-guy" image.

After 1965 McQueen made one hit film after another, most of them produced or co-produced by his own company, Solar. He won an Academy Award nomination in 1967 for *The Sand Pebbles,* in which he played a ship's engineer on an American gunboat who dies helping to rescue missionaries from wartime China. In *Nevada Smith* he scoured the old West, knife in teeth, on the trail of his parents' killers; in *The Thomas Crown Affair* he was a cool, cynical businessman who masterminds a bank heist to defy "the establishment" and his own boredom. His fame was clinched with *Bullitt,* in which he played a tight-lipped police detective who tracks down an underworld villain after a heart-stopping car chase up and down the hills of San Francisco. Some of the stunts he performed were so dangerous that the cameraman refused to get near enough to film them, and the director, Peter Yates, had to take over the photography himself. *Bullitt* was followed by *The Reivers,* an adaptation of William Faulkner's novel, with McQueen playing a rascally but charming Mississippi farmhand, and *Junior Bonner,* about an aging rodeo champion. *Le Mans,* his attempt to capture the thrills of the 24-hour Grand Prix motor race, was one of his few unsuccessful movies.

In the early 1970s, McQueen joined Paul Newman, Barbra Streisand, Sidney Poitier, and Dustin Hoffman to form First Artists, an independent production company. His first film for the company was *The Getaway,* a bank-robbery shott-'em-up that co-starred Ali MacGraw, whom the recently divorced McQueen married in 1973.

Papillon, about a convict's escape from Devil's Island, and *The Towering Inferno,* a big-budget disaster movie, were the last films in which McQueen was to appear for five years. His main project during this period of semi-retirement was a film adaptation of Henrik Ibsen's *An Enemy of the People,* in which he played Dr. Stockmann, a man whose life is destroyed because he tells the truth about a polluted town spring. Warner Brothers, the distributor for most First Artists films, refused to release it on the grounds that it was uncommercial. In the meantime, McQueen turned down brief roles in *A Bridge Too Far* and *Apocalypse Now* because the fees were too low—he reportedly wanted $3 million for each—and withdrew from *Taipan* when the producers missed a scheduled installment of his $10 million salary. Some $18 million in foreign sales of the picture had already been made on the strength of his name alone.

McQueen returned to the screen in 1980 as a frontiersman in *Tom Horn* and a modern-day bounty hunter in *The Hunter.* Neither was successful at the box office. In the summer of 1980 he confirmed rumors that he was suffering from mesothelioma, a rare lung cancer that had spread to his neck, chest, and stomach. When conventional medical treatment failed to cure him, McQueen, who had recently married for the third time, checked into the Plaza Santa Maria Hospital near Tiajuana, Mexico, for an unorthodox course of therapy that included massive doses of vitramins, injections of animal cells, and laetrile. He died of a heart attack after undergoing surgery to remove a tumor in his neck.

J.P.

Born Terrence Stephen McQueen. Son of William M. and Julia
(Crawford) M. Married: (1) Neile Adams, actress and dancer, 1956
(div. 1972); (2) Ali MacGraw, actress, 1973 (div. 1978); (3) Barbara
Minty, model, 1980. Children: 1st marriage—Terri Leslie, b. 1959;
Chadwick Steven, b. 1960. Baptized Roman Catholic. Educ: Orear-
ville Sch., Slater, Mo.; Junior Boys' Republic, Chino, Calif. (through
ninth grade) ca. 1943–44; Neighborhood Playhouse, NYC ca. 1951;
Uta Hagen-Herbert Berghof Dramatic Sch., NYC 1952–54; Actors
Studio, NYC ca. 1954. Mil. Service: tank driver, 2nd Marine Div.,
Fleet Marine Force 1947–50. In Merchant Marine ca. 1946; odd jobs
in Texas, Ontario, and NYC ca. 1945 and 1950–51. Television and film
actor since 1955, film producer since 1968; also motorcycle and car
racer. Dir., Solar Productions and related businesses since 1961;
Member, Advisory Council for Youth Studies, Univ. of Southern
California; active in work with Navajo Indians in American South-
west. Hons: Best Actor, Moscow Film Festival (for The Great
Escape) 1964; Academy Award nomination (for The Sand Pebbles)
1967; named top box-office star 1967; voted Star of the Year 1969;
placed second in Sebring Endurance Tests 1970; placed tenth in
Elsinore Grand Prix; placed high in other racing contests. *Plays:* Peg
O' My Heart, Fayetteville, N.Y. 1952; Time Out for Ginger, tour
1954; Member of the Wedding, Rochester, N.Y. 1954; The Gap,
NYC ca. 1955; A Hatful of Rain, NYC 1956. *Television: Episodes—*
Goodyear Playhouse, 1955; U.S. Steel Hour, 1956; Studio One, 1957;
West Point, 1957; Climax, 1958; Tales of Wells Fargo, 1958; Track-
down, 1958; Alfred Hitchcock Presents, 1959, 1960. *Series—*Wanted,
Dead or Alive (Josh Randall), 1958–60. *Films:* Somebody Up There
Likes Me (extra), 1956; Never Love a Stranger (Martin Cabell), 1957;
The Great St. Louis Bank Robbery (George Fowler), 1958; The Blob
(Steve), 1958; Never So Few (Bill Ringo), 1959; The Magnificent
Seven (Vin), 1960; The Honeymoon Machine (Lt. Howard), 1961;
Hell is for Heroes (Reese), 1961; The War Lover (Buzz Rickson),
1962; The Great Escape (Virgil Hilts, the Cooler Kid), 1963; Love
with the Proper Stranger (Rocky), 1963; Soldier in the Rain (Eustis
Clay), 1963; Baby the Rain Must Fall (Henry Thomas), 1965; The
Cincinnati Kid (title role), 1965; The Sand Pebbles (Jake Holman),
1966; Nevada Smith (title role), 1966; (also co-producer) The Thomas
Crown Affair (title role), 1968; (also producer) Bullitt (Frank Bullitt),
1968; The Reivers (Boon Hogganbeck), 1969; (also co-producer) Le
Mans (Michael Delaney), 1971; (producer only) On Any Sunday,
1971; (also co-producer) Junior Bonner (title role), 1972; (also
producer) The Getaway (Doc McCoy), 1972; Papillon (title role),
1973; The Towering Inferno (Fire Chief), 1974; (also producer) An
Enemy of the People (Dr. Stockmann), 1978; (also co-producer) Tom
Horn, 1980 (title role); (also co-producer) The Hunter, 1980.
Further reading: Steve McQueen: The Unauthorized Biography by
Malachy McCoy, 1974; Steve McQueen: Star on Wheels by William
Nolan, 1974.

LORD NETHERTHORPE
President of the National Farmers' Union, and company director
Born West Bank, Anston, near Sheffield, England, January 6th, 1908
Died Hertfordshire, England, November 8th, 1980

James Turner, who was created first Baron Netherthorpe in 1959, was
for 15 years President of the National Farmers' Union (NFU) of

England and Wales, during which time the NFU attained a much
greater political influence, though Netherthorpe refused to be publicly
associated with any particular party. He was also a director of
numerous companies and became chairman of Fisons Ltd., a leading
supplier to the agricultural industry.

The son of a smallholder, James Turner gained farming experience
from an early age. When he was 29 he became chairman of the
Nottinghamshire County Branch of the NFU and maintained that post
for six years. Then, in 1943, he served as County Delegate to
Headquarters and the following year assumed the Vice Presidency;
after a year in that office he was elected President at the age of 37. At
that time, with the war over, farming was undergoing great changes
and modernization, and there was a need for more cooperation with
the government. The Annual Price Review had become normal
procedure and the Agriculture Act of 1947 legally required the
Minister of Agriculture to consult the NFU and the farming unions in
Scotland and Northern Ireland. James Turner proved exceptionally
skillful in his negotiations with the government; he always managed to
carefully balance the needs of the farmers and the consumers, and
kept in mind Britain's national agricultural interests. As confidence in
his leadership grew, he came to be respected by all sides.

In 1944–45, Turner led a delegation of U.K. farmers to the
Dominions, and when, in the next year, the International Federation
of Agricultural Producers was formed, he was elected its first
president. His two presidencies took him on official missions to other
European countries and to North America. In 1949 he was awarded a
knighthood.

During this period he was also active on a number of public bodies
including the Agricultural Research Council, the Animal Health
Trust, and the Council of the British Association for the Advancement of Science. He became a director of Lloyd's Bank Ltd., the NFU
Mutual Insurance Society Ltd., and of several other companies.

Lord Netherthorpe received his barony in 1959, and retired from
the presidency of the NFU in 1960. He joined the board of Fisons
Ltd., becoming chairman in 1962, a position he held until 1973. In the
1960s, Netherthorpe chaired the British Productivity Council for a
year; he also served as President of the Royal Association of British
Dairy Farmers and of the Royal Agricultural Society of England. As
well, he had been a member of the National Economic Development
Corporation and of the Pay Board.   R.T./J.S.

Born James Turner. Son of Albert Edward Mann T. and Lucy
Helliwell T. Married Margaret Lucy Mattock 1935. Four sons (one
d.). Educ: sch. in Knaresborough; Leeds Univ., B.Sc. 1928. Farmer.
With Natl. Farmers' Union of England & Wales: Chmn., Not-
tinghamshire County Branch 1939–41; Notts. County Delegate to
NFU Headquarters 1942–44; V.P. 1944; Pres. 1945–60. Dir. 1960–78;
Deputy Chmn. 1961 and Chmn. 1962–73, Fisons Ltd.; Vice-Chmn.,
Unigate since 1976. Director: Lloyds Bank Ltd. 1957–78; Steetley Co.
Ltd. 1965–78; Natl. Bank of New Zealand Ltd. 1976–79; Abbey Natl.
Building Soc.; Film Research and Development Ltd.; J.H. Frennes &
Co. (Holdings) Ltd. Rank Foundn; Rank Group Holdings Ltd.; F.D.
& R. Holdings Ltd. Leader, U.K. Delegations to Dominions and
North America 1944–45. Pres: Intnl. Fedn. of Agricultural Producers
1946–48; Royal Assoc. of British Dairy Farmers 1964; Royal Agri-

cultural Soc. of England 1965. Chmn., British Productivity Council 1963. Member: Commn. of Inquiry into Undustrial Representation 1971–72; Natl. Economic Development Council 1971–75; Pay Bd. 1974; Animal Health Trust. Liveryman, Painter-Stainers Co., and Farmers Co. Hons: knighted 1949; LL.D. Leeds Univ. 1952; created baron 1959; LL.D. Birmingham Univ. 1959.

PATRICK (GORDON) CAMPBELL. (LORD GLENAVY)
Humorous writer and broadcaster
Born Dublin, Ireland, June 6th, 1913
Died London, England, November 9th, 1980

Heads of state and shopkeepers, shoe-shine boys and learned judges—they were all prey to Patrick Campbell's pen; but there was no better prey than himself, a titled dilettante with a peculiar stammer. His avowed indolence and high living might have led one to suppose that he drifted through life as a socialite, dabbling at a bit of light journalism, broadcasting and golf. In a sense that was true; but Patrick Campbell's life enabled him to realize his considerable talents as a humorist and raconteur; his newspaper columns entertained readers of the *Sunday Times* (London) for almost 20 years and his appearances on BBC-TV panel shows—particularly *Call My Bluff*—during the 1960s and 1970s, made him a firm favorite with British audiences.

Patrick Campbell was born in Dublin in 1913, the son of the second Lord Glenavy, to whose title he succeeded in 1963. His wealthy background allowed him, upon leaving Oxford without a degree, to avoid any consistent or gainful employment. A foray into the business world of Germany ended with the start of the Second World War, much to the relief of the young employee and his sponsors. Campbell returned to Ireland and began his journalistic career reporting on Rotary luncheons for the *Irish Times,* for which he soon became the "Parliamentary Sketch Writer." He reported speeches in the local accents of the speakers, and while this delighted some, it hardly endeared him to the politicians.

Under the auspices of family friends, Campbell went to London and engaged in what he called "a brief entanglement" with Lord Beaverbrook at the *Daily Express.* His function there was never clearly defined, and when it appeared that Ireland might be threatened by German forces, Campbell returned to Dublin to join the newly-formed Irish Marine Service. Reinstated at the *Irish Times* before the end of the war, Campbell began a column on life in Dublin. In his efforts to find suitable topics he would pedal round the city on his bicycle; in the process, he asserted, he learned the name of every dog in Dublin.

Campbell developed his facility for translating his encounters with landlords, merchants, and other "perennial bores" into incisive and engaging satire, and this talent led to his being engaged as associate editor of the British magazine *Lilliput* in 1947. He found himself for the first time earning a regular income, which afforded him real independence from his family. Campbell rapidly became involved with London's glamorous "high life," and his presence at *Lilliput* dwindled to the occasional Thursday appearance before lunch at his club. Most of the writer's time was spent on golf courses and at the film studios of the Rank Organization, who contracted and paid Campbell for work on film scripts, few of which were actually ever written. In his autobiography, *My Life and Easy Times* (1967), Campbell wrote that his several incomes and many social contacts secured for him what he considered to be the ideal life, "among famous and notorious people at their ease, drink flowing, with no office to go to, and inside gossip that newspapers would have paid a fortune for."

But Campbell's life of leisure was shortlived; as he failed to fulfill his numerous commissions he was dismissed, first from *Lilliput* and then from the film studios. At middle-age Campbell was without a steady job or a family, having dissolved two marriages. He turned to radio and television which had replaced newspapers and magazines as the prime entertainment medium. Campbell's quick humor was an instant success and he was enlisted for the television shows *Not So Much a Programme, More a Way of Life,* which grew out of the spontaneous and often satirical style of entertainment developing in Britain in the late 1950s and early 60s. Campbell's anecdotal, stammered interruptions were frequently far from the topic of discussion. Having, as his producers alleged, "no opinions of any kind," his contributions lent a hilarious—at times almost sur-realistically bewildering—dimension to the show. As a panel member of *Call My Bluff,* Campbell was required to provide definitions for obscure or archaic words (the opposite team had to guess which of the given meanings was correct), and this proved an excellent device for Campbell's banter. His stammer became part of his style: he would readily deliver most of his definition then would suddenly lose his voice; the silent moments as he grappled to recover it gave a pregnancy to his words and contributed to the idiosyncrasy of his humor.

Campbell's 15 books, including such titles as *A Short Trot with a Cultured Mind, Life in Thin Slices,* and *Come Here Till I Tell You* contain many pieces of fine-crafted writing. Admitting his privilege, Campbell was never an elitist; and his wry observations of people's foibles and eccentricities display a constant delight in his fellow man.

R.T./A.S.

Son of 2nd Lord Glenavy, Secty. of Dept. of Industry and Commerce, Irish Free State, and Beatrice Elvery. Married: (1) Sylvia Willoughby Lee 1941 (div. 1947); (2) Cherry Lowson Monro 1947 (div. 1966); (3) Vivienne Orme 1966. Daughter: Brigid. Protestant.. Educ: Rossall, Fleetwood, Lancs.; Pembroke Coll., Oxford Univ. Mil. Service: Irish Marine Service 1941–44. Reporter and columnist, Irish Times 1944–47; columnist and author, London since 1947; Assoc. Ed., Lilliput (mag.) 1947–53; columnist, *Sunday Dispatch* 1947–59; film script consultant, Rank Org. 1948–55; Panelist for BBC-TV programs Not so Much a Programme, More a Way of Life, and Call My Bluff 1962–79; columnist, *Sunday Times* 1961–80. *Author: essay collections* —A Long Drink of Cold Water, 1950; A Short Trot with a Cultured Mind, 1952; Life in Thin Slices, 1954; Patrick Campbell's Omnibus, 1956; Come Here Till I Tell You, 1960; Constantly in Pursuit, 1962; How to Become a Scratch Golfer, 1963; Brewing Up in the Basement,

1963; Rough Husbandry, 1965; A Bunch of New Roses, 1967; The Coarse of Events, 1968; The High Speed Gas Works, 1970; Fat Tuesday Tails, 1972; 35 Years on the Job, 1973. *Autobiography*—My Life and Easy Times, 1967.

CHARLES B. HOEVEN
Congressman, U.S. House of Representatives
Born Hospers, Iowa, U.S.A., March 30th, 1895
Died Orange City, Iowa, U.S.A., November 9th, 1980

Charles Hoeven of Iowa, a leader of House Republicans during the Eisenhower, Kennedy, and Johnson administrations began his career as an attorney in Sioux County, Iowa. Elected to the Iowa State Senate in 1937, he served as its president pro-tempore until 1941. In the following year Hoeven was elected to the 78th Congress and represented north-west Iowa for 22 years. He served as Deputy Minority Whip from 1957 to 1964, as ranking Republican on the House Committee on Agriculture from 1948 to 1965, and from 1957 to 1962 was chairman of the House Republican Conference.

Mr. Hoeven exercised his most effective leadership from his seat on the Agriculture Committee, where he was a consistent spokesman for both Republican ideology and grain-belt agriculture. Feed-grains were the focus of Kennedy's farm policy; the administration wanted to stem growth of the tremendous stockpiles of government owned surplus grain through supply-management controls of grain production. Republicans considered such controls over-regulation and farmers feared they would constitute manipulation of the grains market, though the existing policy of government buying created a "support level" for grain prices. In March 1961 the administration sponsored a bill which contained the threat that the government would sell surplus grain, and thus undermine grain prices, unless farmers comply with a voluntary program of acreage reduction. The bill barely passed the House, over Hoeven's opposition. However this was a temporary measure and in June 1962 the House voted on a bill which would provide more permanent controls on feed-grain production. In a surprise upset the administration's farm bill was defeated by a coalition of Republicans and Southern Democrats. The defeat, called a "staggering setback" by the administration, was Kennedy's first major defeat in Congress. The bill had been vigorously opposed by the American Farm Bureau. In September a much modified compromise bill passed the House over unanimous Republican opposition.

In 1964 Hoeven led opposition to Johnson's food stamp bill. Republicans maintained that the program would not be used to dispose of surplus commodities but would become a widely used and expensive welfare program. This time, however, the attempted coalition with Southern Democrats failed.

Despite his work on the Committee on Agriculture, Mr. Hoeven's leadership was undermined when, at the outset of the new Congress in 1963, he lost the Republican Conference chairmanship to the much younger Gerald R. Ford of Michigan. Ford was one of a group of rebellious young Republican congressmen intent on changing the party's image which included also Melvin Laird of Wisconsin and Charles Goodell of New York. Though the chairmanship was largely a symbolic post, the ouster of Hoeven, hatched in secrecy and carried out precisely, caught the traditional leadership by surprise and demonstrated the power of the new, less conservative, element in the party. The "Young Turks," as they came to be called, were concerned with the party's image in the wake of losses in the 1962 elections and boasted that there were "no jowls" among them. Their concrete victory was to increase their House Republican Conference membership from five to eight; but Hoeven declared, as did editorial observers, that he was merely a scapegoat and that the real target of the rebellion was House Minority Leader Charles A. Halleck of Indiana. (Halleck was unseated two years later.) The move to oust Hoeven was linked also to an effort by Laird to gain conservative control of the House Rules Committee, which controls the flow of legislation on the House floor. If successful this initiative would have created a convenient procedural obstacle to the Kennedy administration's legislative proposals. Its failure limited the impact of the Young Turks' show of force to a minor victory within the party.

Charles Hoeven retired in 1965.   D.S.

Son of Gerrit H. and Lena Weiland H. Married Velma Ruth Pike 1919. Children: Pauline Ruth Marshall; Charles Pike. Presbyterian. Educ: State Univ. of Iowa, Iowa City, B.A. 1920, LL.B. 1922. Mil. Service: Sergeant, U.S. Army 1917–19. Attorney for Sioux County, Iowa 1925–37; Iowa Sate Senator 1939–41, and Pres. pro tempore 1937–41; Permanent Chmn., Iowa State Judicial Convention 1942. With U.S. House of Representatives: Member from 6th and 8th Congressional Dists., Iowa 1943–65; Chmn., Republican Conference and Member, Republican Policy Cttee. 1957–65; Deputy Republican Whip 1957–65. Congressional Delegate, Food and Agriculture Organization, Rome 1957; U.S. Delegate to Interparliamentary Union, London 1957, Brussels 1961, Belgrade 1963, and Copenhagen 1964; appointed member, Special Advisory Cttee. on Public Opinion, Dept. of State 1970. Dir. and V.P., Alton Savings Bank, Iowa since 1932. Member: 21st Judicial Bar. Assoc.; Iowa County Attorneys Assoc.; Presbytery of Northwest Iowa, Moderator (1967). Hons: LL.D., Westmar Coll. 1956, and Morningside Coll. 1965; Honor Iowans Award 1966 and LL.D. 1968, Buena Vista Coll.

PURAN CHAND(RA) JOSHI
General Secretary, Communist Party of India
Born North India, 1908
Died New Delhi, India, November 9th, 1980

Puran Chand Joshi was the general secretary of the Communist Party of India (CPI) from 1935 to 1948, guiding it through the turbulent time preceeding India's independence and partition, and helping it make the transition to a legal political party. Born in 1908 in North India, he received a college education and became a skilled leader and disseminator of propaganda. He was a prolific writer but not a dynamic speaker, and never developed a personal mass following, although his entire political life was devoted to the CPI.

To Joshi, the CPI was analagous to a large family. Congress was the "elder brother;" the CPI was the "younger brother." The Indian people as a whole were the "real parents." The CPI headquarters staff, which grew from eight to 120 members under Joshi, was "one big joint family" with "one single Mai" (old mother).

Joshi advocated a rightist strategy and attempted to create a united front with Nehru, but leftist factions in the CPI became dissatisfied and began a campaign to discredit Joshi as a deviationist. As 1947 progressed, Joshi remained the nominal leader, but the CPI moved gradually left, and gave its support to Ranadive, who became the effective leader. Joshi was expunged in December 1947 when the CPI aligned itself with Moscow and began to employ terrorist tactics. The last vestige of Joshi's policy was a promise to support the Indian government against the communal riots. Joshi was accused of hypocrisy at this time, and vacillated between confession and denial of deviations and of collaboration with the British for financial gain while in office. (He later denied this, offering confidential account sheets to Gandhi as evidence.)

By March 1948, when the CPI ratified Ranadive's position as general secretary, the organization had become a leftist front working underground against Congress, advocating guerilla warfare, violence, and terrorism.

Ranadive overreacted to unrest in the world, and foresaw a worldwide breakdown of capitalism and imperialism. While Joshi was in disgrace he began to use his intellectual advantage over Ranadive to regain favor at his opponent's expense, accusing him of Titoism and Trotskyism and of separating the CPI from the interests of the Indian government. He published many pamphlets opposing Ranadive (and later Rao) from 1949 to 1951, and appealed to communist parties abroad for support to help the CPI correct its mistakes and rejoin the worldwide communist fold.

When Joshi was expelled from the party along with five percent of the membership (4000–5000) in January 1950, he appealed and was granted a retrial on the grounds that he had worked successfully for the party from 1935 to 1947, and that reformist mistakes were a natural consequence. The official judgment was that the Second Congress had dealt correctly but harshly. All members expelled between the Second Congress and June 1950 were readmitted. Joshi remained outside the Central Committee, but became increasingly influential and edited the unofficial communist monthly, *India To-Day*.

Indian communism was Joshi's whole life. He once explained to Mahatma Gandhi, "We seek to guide, criticize and mould the entire life, both personal and political, of our members"—it was probably attitudes of this kind which caused non-communist Prime Minister Indira Gandhi to lose office. But her subsequent re-election suggests that Joshi's big-brother aims, while still abhorrent to the West, have considerable currency in a country gripped by poverty and disease, a caste system, and an ever-burgeoning birth rate.   N.S./R.T.

With Communist Party of India: Gen. Secty 1935–48; suspended Dec. 1948; expelled Jan. 1950; reinstated to membership June 1950; edited *India To-Day. Author:* Correspondence Between Mahatma Gandhi and P.C. Joshi, 1945; View to Comrades Abroad and B.T. Ranadive, 1950; For a Mass Policy, 1951; Problems of the Mass Movement, 1951; For the Final Bid for Power!; Letters to Foreign Comrades pamphlets. *Major Articles:* "Documents for Discussion" series, 1951; "India— What Now?," World News and Views XXV, #31, Aug. 11, 1945; "Indian Communists and the Congress," #45, Nov. 11, 1945; "The Punjab Riots," Labour Monthly, XXIX, #10, Oct. 1947; "Congress and the Communists," Dec. 1944, and others.

ANDREI (ALEKSEYEVICH) AMALRIK
Soviet historian, writer, and political dissident
Born Moscow, U.S.S.R., May 12th, 1938
Died Guadalajara, Spain, November 11th, 1980

A critic of the Soviet regime throughout his life, Andrei Amalrik was, after Aleksandr Solzhenitsyn, perhaps the most prominent Soviet dissident to live in exile in the West. Amalrik, a scholar, social and political essayist, and playwright, was sentenced three times to a regimen of hard labor in Siberian camps, where he served more than five years. Amalrik constantly risked extreme punishment rather than compromise what he called "the freedom which allows the authorities to do much to a man, but which renders them powerless to deprive him of his moral values."

When Andrei Amalrik was born in 1938, the Stalinist purge trials were at their peak. Andrei's uncle, a state prosecutor, was sentenced to five years in prison during the purges of the late 1930s; at the conclusion of his trial, he exclaimed, "This is not a Soviet court but a fascist torture chamber." Consequently, he was executed rather than taken to a camp. Andrei's father, a talented historian, was twice forced to abandon his formal education, first during the revolution and later when the German army invaded the Soviet Union in 1941. A commissioned officer, the elder Amalrik once casually stated that Stalin's military unpreparedness had contributed to the early successes of the German army; the remark was overheard and he was sentenced to eight years in prison camp. However, the father was released in 1943 to serve in the defense of Stalingrad, where he was severely wounded and officially designated an invalid. In a 1970 interview with the *New York Times,* Amalrik said, "I was against the system when I was a child."

Andrei Amalrik first came to the attention of watchful Soviet authorities as a history student at Moscow University. He wrote an exceptional dissertation on ancient Russian history in which he contended that Viking invaders, rather than Slavs, had made the principal contribution to the formation of the Russian state. The implication that Russians had been incapable of independently developing a civilized culture contradicted the official Soviet mythology of the "people" and Amalrik was told that his dissertation would be accepted only if he altered his conclusion. His refusal resulted in expulsion from the university and forfeiture of a career commensurate with his intellectual abilities and academic training. He attempted to transmit the study to a noted professor of Slavic languages through the Danish Embassy; instead, the KGB was alerted and Amalrik was warned against placing the manuscript in the hands of Western scholars.

Barred from a professional career, Amalrik moved in with his disabled father, who needed constant supervision. Amalrik supported himself by a series of odd jobs and, privately, he began to write experimental, modernist plays such as *Nose! Nose? No-se!* (1973), which show the influence of Samuel Beckett and Eugene Ionesco. He also began to exploit Soviet society's "grey belt" of activities which are theoretically permissible but officially frowned upon in practice; as such, Amalrik began to collect abstract art which had been painted by friends and to meet with foreigners to promote these avant-garde works. However, in May, 1965, the Soviet secret police raided his apartment, confiscating his art collection and plays. Amalrik was charged with "producing, harboring, and disseminating pornographic works" but released when officials in the Union of Writers were unable to concoct a suitable definition of pornography.

On May 24th, 1965, Amalrik was charged with "parasitism," arrested, quickly tried, and sentenced to two and one-half years of labor on a remote collective farm in Siberia. The parasite law, which stated that anyone unemployed for a month could be exiled to do "socially useful work," was often used against nonconformist intellectuals, including poet Joseph Brodsky. Later that year, Andrei received word that his father's condition had worsened. He was allowed to return to Moscow for a visit, but after bureaucratic delays and a long railroad trip home, Amalrik's father died before he arrived. However, while staying in Moscow, Amalrik persuaded Gyusel Makudinova, a painter and full-blooded Tatar whom he barely knew, to marry him. In mid-October, they returned to Siberia where they lived in extreme poverty. In July, 1966, Amalrik's conviction was overturned by the Russian Supreme Court on the grounds that he was not a parasite because he had been the only living relative of an invalid; that the invalid had been dead for nearly a year was a stark irony not lost on Amalrik. He chronicled his capture, arrest, and year of imprisonment in *Involuntary Journey to Siberia* (1970).

Amalrik and Gyusel lived in a small, sunless room in a communal apartment in Moscow for the next four years, sharing kitchen, bath, and telephone facilities with 11 other people, some of whom were Soviet spies. Nevertheless, Amalrik refused to conform; he and his wife entertained guests, many of whom were Westerners who shared their interests in jazz and modern art. The Amalriks, knowing the location of secret microphones planted by the KGB, lowered their voices only to conceal the names of fellow dissidents. Until the secret police stepped up their campaign of harrassment in 1968, Amalrik was allowed to publish articles for small Soviet art and drama journals, and he continued to protest political injustice. In 1969 Amalrik confused even the KGB when he issued a sharp reproach to another dissident, writer Anatoly Kuznetsov, who had been allowed to emigrate to England after pretending to "name names" for the KGB. Amalrik accused the author of moral cowardice and said: "I want to condemn the philosophy of impotence and self-justification which runs through all you have said and written in the West. 'I was given no choice,' you seem to be saying—and this sounds like a justification not only for yourself but also for the whole Soviet creative intelligentsia, or at least for that liberal part of it to which you belong."

By 1969 Amalrik had completed the manuscript for *Involuntary Journey to Siberia* and *Will the Soviet Union Survive Until 1984?* and they were published in the West the following year. *Will the Soviet Union Survive Until 1984?* is a pessimistic account of the possibilities of democratization in the USSR and a prediction that the country will crumble after its expansionist policies provoke a war with China, which will unleash deep, antagonistic forces now gathering strength within the Soviet empire. According to Amalrik, Soviet society is composed of three "classes": a ruling bureaucratic elite, which is too ideologically rigid to institute the reforms necessary for its survival; a weak middle class of technicians and functionaries whose desire for change is undermined by a slavish concern for economic privileges; and a vast peasant-proletariat, which has been systematically suppressed for so many centuries that it cannot grasp the concept of intellectual freedom. Amalrik's analysis is conservative as well as grim; adhering to a cyclical view of history, he suggests that the collapses of pre-revolutionary Russia in 1905 and 1917 are simply reoccurring. Moreover, Amalrik shares no common ground with Aleksandr Solzhenitsyn or such nineteenth-century Russian visionaries as Alexander Herzen and Leo Tolstoy. He made no appeal to the redemptive virtues of Mother Russia and he was unmoved by the mythology of the common "people's" essential goodness, an ancient concept that is preserved in the ideologies of both Soviet Marxists and dissident intellectuals. Indeed, Amalrik wrote that "the Christian ethic, with its concepts of both right and wrong, has been shaken loose and driven out of the popular consciousness. An attempt has been made to replace it with 'class' morality, which can be summarized as follows: Good is what at any given moment is required by authority."

In May 1970, Amalrik was arrested for "disseminating falsehoods derogatory to the Soviet state." The prosecution used five documents against him: His books, his letter to Kuznetsov, and two television interviews he had given to a CBS correspondent. At the trial's conclusion, Amalrik compared the persecution of dissidents to medieval witch hunts; it is believed that the outburst earned him a harsher sentence than the one requested by the state prosecutor. He was given a three year term in an intensive labor camp; while traveling to Siberia, Amalrik, who suffered from a congenital heart disease, contracted meningitis and nearly died in a prison hospital.

Amalrik's prison term expired in May, 1973, but authorities charged him once again with "spreading falsehoods derogatory to the Soviet state," this time among fellow prisoners, and he was sentenced to an additional three years. Despite protest in the West and a 117-day hunger strike by Amalrik, Soviet officials remained intransigent at first. However, when his health began to fail, Amalrik's sentence was commuted to exile and he was released in 1975, returning to Moscow with Gyusel. The Amalriks were subjected to continual harrassment and authorities urged them to accept visas to Israel; the Amalriks, who were not Jewish, refused on principle. In 1976 they finally acquired an exit visa to the Netherlands.

Amalrik taught history in the Netherlands and in the United States before moving to the Haute Savoie region of France, where he wrote articles for expatriate dissident journals. Amalrik was killed in an automobile accident while en route to Madrid with his wife and two other Soviet exiles to participate in a meeting organized by dissident groups.   E.T.

Son of Aleksei Serbeevich A., archaeologist and historian. Married Gyusel Makudinova, artist 1965. No children. Educ: Moscow Univ. 1959–63, expelled without degree. Cartographer, medical lab. asst., construction worker, technical translator, artist's model, and tutor in Russian and mathematics, Moscow 1963–65; arrested on charges of promoting pornography, charges dismissed, rearrested on charges of social parasitism, tried, convicted and sentenced to 3 years hard labor in Siberia, May-June 1965; goatherd, Siberia 1965–66; conviction overturned by Soviet appeals court, July 1966; freelance drama and art critic for Novosti Press Agency, Moscow 1966–68; newspaper deliverer, Moscow Post Office 1968–69; banished to village of Akulino, Ryazan district 1969–70; arrested in Akulino on charges of defaming Soviet Union, tried, convicted and sentenced to 3 years in prison labor camp, May 1970; in prison 1970–73; sentenced to 3 additional years for spreading anti-Soviet propaganda among fellow prisoners 1973; sentence commuted to two years in exile 1973; in exile, Madagan City, Siberia 1973–75; resident in Moscow 1975–76; emigrated to Netherlands 1976; taught, lectured and wrote at Utrecht Univ., Holland, in the U.S. and in France 1976–80. Hons: Human Rights Award of the Intnl. Human Rights League 1976. *Author* (in translation): Will the Soviet Union Survive Until 1984?, 1970; Involuntary Journey to Siberia, 1966; Nose! Nose? No-se! (collection of 5 plays), 1973; Notes of a Revolutionary, 1981.
Further reading: "Andrei Amalrik, Rebel" by Susan Jacoby, New York Times Magazine, July 29th, 1973; "The Bitter Price" by Helen Munchnic, New York Review of Books, Nov. 19, 1970.

ROBERT LEE WOLFF
Historian, author, educator
Born New York City, U.S.A., December 22nd, 1915
Died Cambridge, Massachusetts., U.S.A., November 11th, 1980

Robert Lee Wolff, Coolidge Professor of History at Harvard University, was an expert in Balkan affairs and a scholar of English Victorian literature.

Wolff earned his A.B. in 1936 and his A.M. in 1937 from Harvard University, and spent the next four years as a Teaching Fellow. During World War II, as an expert in Balkan history and politics, he served with the Research and Analysis Branch of the Office of Strategic Services (the forerunner of the CIA) and headed its Balkan Section from 1942 to 1946. In 1944, he conducted a fact-finding mission to Rumania to learn the extent of Soviet influence in that country.

After the war, Wolff returned to Harvard and completed his Ph.D. in history in 1947. After two years on the faculty of the University of Wisconsin, and another year at Brown University on a President's Fellowship, he rejoined the department of history at Harvard and became a full professor in 1955. That year, he collaborated with Clarence Crane Brinton on a two-volume *History of Civilization*.

In 1956 Wolff published *The Balkans in Our Time,* which the *New York Times Book Review* called "a major feat . . . encompassing within one meaty and readable volume the kaleidoscopic history of Yugoslavia, Rumania, Bulgaria and Albania in this century." After lecturing in Geneva, Switzerland, Wolff assumed the chairmanship of the Harvard Department of History from 1960 to 1963. In 1962 he co-edited the second volume of *A History of the Crusades.* His *Civilization in the West* and *Modern Civilization* were both written in collaboration with Clarence Crane Brinton. He was named Archibald Cary Coolidge Professor of History at Harvard in 1965.

Wolff, the son of an English professor at Columbia University, was also interested in Victorian literature and owned an extensive collection of first-edition works, of which he completed the first volume of a projected five-volume catalogue. In 1961 he published *The Golden Key: A Study of the Fiction of George MacDonald,* the first of a series on lesser-known Victorian writers. During the 1970s, despite failing health, he wrote *Strange Stories, and Other Explorations in Victorian Fiction, Gains and Losses: Novels of Faith and Doubt in Victorian England, Sensational Victorian: The Life and Fiction of Mary Elizabeth Braddon,* and *William Carlton, Irish Peasant Novelist.*

Wolff, who was married and had four children, served as a trustee of Harvard University and Radcliffe College and was a member of the Board of Scholars of the Dumbarton Oaks Research Institute.   J.S.

Son of Samuel Lee W., Prof. of English, and Mathilde (Abraham) W. Married Mary Andrews 1937. Children: Rosamund Purcell; Katharine; Robert Lee; James A. Educ: Harvard Univ., A.B. 1936, A.M. 1937, Teaching Fellow 1937–41, Ph.D. 1947; President's Fellowship, Brown Univ. 1949–50. Mil. Service: Asst. to Dir. 1941 and Chief 1942–46, Balkan Sect., Research and Analysis Branch, Office of Strategic Services. Asst. Prof. of History 1947 and Assoc. Prof. 1948–49, Univ. of Wisconsin. With Dept. of History, Harvard Univ.: Assoc. Prof. 1950–55; Prof. 1955–65; Dept. Chmn. 1960–63; Archibald Cary Coolidge Prof. of History since 1965. Visiting Lectr., École universitaire des hautes études internationales, Geneva 1957; Harvard Lectr., Yale Univ. 1961. Trustee: Brooks Sch. from 1962; Trustee and Council Member, Radcliffe Coll. from 1965; Trustee, Harvard Univ. from 1971. Member Bd. of Scholars, Dumbarton Oaks Library and Research Inst. 1955; Exec. Cttee., Russian Research Center; Exec. Cttee., Center for Middle Eastern Studies; American Historical Assn.; Medieval Acad. of America; Knickerbocker Club, NYC; Somerset Tavern, Boston. Hons: Fellowships, Rockefeller and American Council of Learned Socs. 1946–47; Hon. D. Litt., Williams Coll. 1961; Fellow, American Acad. of Arts and Sciences. *Author:* (with Clarence Crane Brinton) A History of Civilization, 1955, 5th ed. 1975; The Balkans in Our Time, 1956; The Golden Key: A Study of the Fiction of George MacDonald, 1961; (co-ed) A History of the Crusades, Vol. II, 1962, 2nd ed. 1969; (with Clarence Crane Brinton) Civilization in the West, 1964; (with Clarence Crane Brinton) Modern Civilization, 1967; Strange Stories, and Other Explorations in Victorian Fiction, 1971; Studies in the Latin Empire of Constantinople, 1976; Gains and Losses: Novels of Faith and Doubt in Victorian England, 1977; Sensational Victorian: The Life and Fiction of Mary Elizabeth Braddon, 1979; William Carlton, Irish Peasant Novelist,

1980; (compiler) catalogue of his own collection of Victorian literature, 1980; (ed.) series of volumes on The Vietnam Experience, 1980.

JOHN (THOMAS) WILKINSON
Theologian and church historian
Born Hull, England, 1894
Died Manchester, England, November 13th, 1980

The Reverend John Thomas Wilkinson, a minister of the Primitive
Presbyterian Church, educator, and noted ecclesiastical historian, was
an authority on the history of nonconformity, on the seventeenth-
century Puritans, and on the Cambridge Platonists. Wilkinson, who
referred to theology as the "Queen of Sciences," believed that many
theological issues might be more effectively resolved by a linguistic
rather than a strictly interpretive approach.

After his ordination in 1917, the Reverend Wilkinson served in
numerous parishes throughout England and pursued his interest in
church history, writing and editing several books on the seventeenth-
century divine Richard Baxter. Beginning in 1946, Wilkinson devoted
much of his energy to education and lecturing. After serving as tutor
in church history at Hartley Victoria College for seven years, he was
appointed principal in 1953, a position he held until his retirement in
1959. During this latter period Wilkinson was also a lecturer on the
history of church doctrine at Manchester University.

Wilkinson made a special study of Anglican liturgies, pursuing the
topic not only through research at St. Augustine's College, Canterbury, and St. George's College, Jerusalem, but also less formally
through interviews with Anglicans from different parts of the world.
Recognizing the need for reform in the Book of Common Prayer but
also the reluctance of the people to accept these changes, Wilkinson
said that it would be "sheer cowardice to cling to a form of worship
which neglected [newly revealed] discoveries." He felt that by
studying the basic principles of the liturgy of the Anglican Church, the
communicants would be able to perceive basic patterns and elements
in the religious service which could be changed or omitted without
damaging the essentials.

While studying in Jerusalem, Wilkinson tried to reconstruct the Last
Supper at or near its site, shocking the participants with the differences between the Holy Communion they knew and the one they
were experiencing at the time. He constructed a liturgy according to
the principles he discovered during the course of his investigation and
wrote several books on the topic.

The Reverend Wilkinson, who will also be remembered as one of
the last great expository preachers, was awarded the rare Doctorate of
Divinity of Manchester University in 1965.   N.S.

Married Marion, 1921 (d. May 1980). Children: Alan; Leonard;
Hettie Dormer. Methodist. Educ: Boulevard Sch.; Hartley Victoria
Coll.; Manchester Univ., BA, BD. Ordained minister of the Primitive
Presbyterian Church 1917; served in Horwich, Kidderminster, Cradley
Heath, Liverpool, Knighton, Scarborough, and Kendal 1917–1946.

Hartley Victoria Coll.: tutor in church hist. 1946–1953; principal
1953–1959. Lecturer in the hist. of church doctrine, Manchester Univ.
1953–1959. Hons: Fellow, Royal Historical Soc.; Doctorate of Divinity of Manchester Univ. 1965. *Author:* Richard Baxter and Margaret
Charlton, 1927; Principles of Biblical Interpretation, 1960; No Apology, 1962; Interpretation and Community, 1963. *Editor:* The Reformed Pastor by Richard Baxter, 1939; The Saints' Everlasting Rest
by Richard Baxter, 1963.

JAMES K(ENNETH) FOREMAN
Chemist
Born Kent, England, April 7th, 1928
Died London, England, November 14th, 1980

Dr. James Kenneth Foreman, Deputy Director of the National
Physical Laboratory, was a specialist in radiochemistry and automated
chemical analysis. He was born in Kent, England in 1928, attended
Ashford Grammar School, and earned a D.Sc. degree with first class
honors from Medway Technical College in 1949.

At the Woolwich Arsenal Chemical Inspectorate, Foreman helped
to devise methods and instrumentation for the detection and analysis
of trace impurities in fissionable materials. He was able to apply these
techniques to further work in the fine chemical analysis of fission and
fusion by-products at the Windscale Works of the U.K. Atomic
Energy Administration, where he headed the production support
research team from 1956 to 1965. His group was among the first in
Britain to isolate significant amounts of the radioactive isotope
Technetium-99 by purely chemical means.

Foreman, who was married and had five children, transferred to the
Research Division of the Laboratory of the Government Chemist as
superintendent in 1966, and became deputy government chemist in
1970. His work here involved the analysis of the suspected carcinogen
N-nitrosamine and of dental silicates. In order to perform the large
number of tests that carcinogen detection requires, Foreman and his
research group developed various kinds of automated analysis equipment, which he and P. B. Stockwell described in their books
Automatic Chemical Analysis and *Topics in Automatic Chemical
Analysis*.

In 1977, Foreman became deputy director of the National Physical
Laboratory, heading the chemical standards, analysis, and computer
sections. He received an honorary D.Sc. from London University in
1976 and a Gold Medal from the Society of Analytic Chemistry in
1977 for his original work in trace chemical isolation and for
establishing a theoretical and practical basis for automated chemical
lab procedures.   R.S.

Son of William James F. and Grace Esther F. Married Celia Christine
Joan Head (div. 1978). Children: three sons; two daughters. Educ:
Ashford Grammar Sch., Ashford, Kent; Medway Technical Coll.,
B.S. (First Class Hons.) 1949. Staff member, Chemical Inspectorate,
Ministry of Supply, Woolwich Arsenal, Woolwich 1949–51; staff
member 1952–56 and Head of Research Production Team 1956–65,

U.K. Atomic Energy Admin., Windscale and Calder Hall Works, Cumberland; Superintendent of Research Div. 1966–70 and Deputy Govt. Chemist 1970–77, Lab. of the Govt. Chemist, London; Deputy Dir., Natl. Physical Lab. since 1977. Council Member and Member of Qualifications and Education Bd., Royal Soc. of Chemistry. Hons: Hon. D.Sc., London Univ. 1976; Gold Medal, Soc. for Analytic Chemistry 1977; Hon. Treas., Analytical Div., Royal Soc. of Chemistry; Fellow, Royal Inst. of Chemistry. *Author:* (with P.B. Stockwell) Automatic Chemical Analysis, 1975; (with Stockwell) Topics in Automatic Chemical Analysis, 1979; papers in chemical jrnls.

ARNOLD (LIONEL) HASKELL
Author, critic, lecturer
Born London, England, July 19th, 1903
Died Bath, England, November 14th, 1980

Arnold Lionel Haskell, an author, dance critic and educator, made numerous contributions to the world of theater and ballet. Among his most noteworthy achievements was his role in establishing the Royal Ballet as the national company of Great Britain and introducing ballet to a much wider audience.

Haskell's attraction to the theater and to dance was already evident in his early school days, when he would cut classes, frequently with his fellow-student John Gielgud, to see performances of Serge Diaghilev's Ballets Russes. Later, while recuperating in Paris from an illness that interrupted his law studies at Cambridge, he became personally acquainted with many members of the Russian ballet world and met a Russian emigré, Vera Saitsova, whom he later married.

After receiving his M.A. from Trinity College in 1926, Haskell joined the editorial staff of the London publishing company William Heinemann Ltd., where he worked until 1932. In 1929 the first of his many books on ballet, *Some Studies in Ballet,* appeared in a privately printed edition. This was soon followed by a series of dance biographies. In 1930 Haskell co-founded the Camargo Society, a ballet-producing organization which provided valuable assistance to British dancers, choreographers and ballet companies. He also established the Royal Ballet Benevolent Fund in 1936 and a decade later became the first director of the Sadler's Wells (now Royal) Ballet School. In 1934 influential *Balletomania: the Story of an Obsession* appeared, a work that introduced the word "balletomane" into the English language and communicated much of Haskell's own enthusiasm for ballet to readers.

Despite his important services for British ballet, Haskell's first love remained the Russian ballet and its performers. England, he wrote in *Balletomania,* was "of local importance, a pleasant colorful backwater, apart from the mainstream of ballet tradition." He intended the Camargo Society as a means of helping the dance world survive the dark period that followed Diaghilev's death in 1929. When a successor company to the Ballets Russes was formed in 1933, he enthusiastically followed it on tour and rated it much more favorably than other critics. New British companies, including those of George Balanchine and Kurt Jooss, left him much cooler. Haskell's biography of Diaghilev, published in 1935, was for many years the most sensitive account of the great impresario and the only one to place him in cultural context.

Haskell continued as a lecturer and advisor on the dance through the 1970s, touring many countries including the Soviet Union and Cuba. He also wrote and edited over two dozen works. Anna Kisselgoff wrote in the *New York Times* that "It is impossible to trace the growth of British ballet without being aware of his authoritative presence." In addition to his great contribution to the understanding of ballet, Haskell devoted much attention to painting and sculpture. In 1932 he completed *The Sculptor Speaks,* a study of Jacob Epstein, whose works he collected; in his last years he worked on a monograph on the little-known sculptor Wlerick. When he died at Bath at the age of 77, Haskell had lived to see the Royal Ballet become world-famous and ballet itself become, as he had wished, an art enjoyed by popular audiences.

Son of Jacob S. H., banker, and Emmy Msritz H. Married: (1) Vera Saitsova 1926 (d. 1968); (2) Vivienne Marks 1970. Children: Francis; Stephen; Helen. Roman Catholic. Educ: Trinity Hall, Cambridge, M.A. (with hons.) 1926. On editorial staff, William Heinemann Ltd., London 1927–32; toured U.S. with Russian Ballet 1933–34; Dance critic, Daily Telegraph, London 1935–38; Guest critic, Melbourne Herald and Sydney Daily Telegraph, Australia 1936–37; Lectr. in Australia 1940–45; Dir., Royal Ballet Sch. 1946–65; Ed., Ballet Annual 1947–63; Lectr., British Council in Europe 1950–51, 1953–55; Gov., Trent Park Training Coll. 1953–58, 1961; Advisor, Dutch govt. on formation of natl. ballet co. 1954; Gov., Royal Ballet since 1957; Lectr. and student of ballet, USSR 1960, 1962; Guest Lectr., Natl. Council of Culture, Cuba 1967, 1968. Co-founder, Camargo Soc. 1930; Founder, Royal Ballet Benevolent Fund 1936; V.P., Catholic Stage Guild; on Council, Royal West of England Acad. 1961; V.P. of jury, Varna Intnl. dance competition 1964–66, 1970; Gov., Royal Ballet Sch. 1966–67; Guest, Youth Org., USSR 1967; Trustee, Holburne Menstrie Mus. 1970; V.P., Bath Preservation Trust; on Council, Bath Univ. 1971–76; Dir., Festival Ballet Trust. Member of jury, Intnl. Ballet contest, Moscow 1969, 1973. Hons: Chevalier de la Légion d'Honneur 1950; CBE 1954; Hon. member, Bath Inst. Medical Engineering 1971; Hon. D. Litt., Bath Univ. 1974; Fellow, Royal Soc. of London 1977. *Author:* Some Studies in Ballet, 1928 (limited, privately printed ed.); Vera Trefilova, 1928; Anton Dolin, 1929 (2nd ed., 1934); Penelope Spencer, and other Studies, 1930; Tamara Karsavina, 1930; The Marie Rambert Ballet, 1930 (3rd ed., 1931); Our Dancers: First Series, 1932; The Sculptor Speaks, 1932; Black on White, 1933; Balletomania: The Story of an Obsession, 1934; (with Walter Nouvel) Diaghileff, 1935; The Balletomane's Scrap-Book, 1936; Prelude to Ballet, 1936; Felicity Dances, 1937 (U.S. ed., 1938); Dancing Round the World, 1937 (U.S. ed., 1938); Ballet, 1938 (rev. ed. 1955); Ballet Panorama, 1938 (2nd ed., 1943); Balletomane's Album, 1939; Waltzing Matilda, 1940 (2nd ed., 1941); Australia, 1941; The Dominions: Partnership or Rift?, 1943; The National Ballet, 1943 (2nd ed., 1947); Australians: The Anglo-Saxondom of the Southern Hemisphere, 1943; British Ballet, 1945; The Making of a Dancer, 1946; Miracle in the Gorbals, 1946; Ballet Since 1939, 1946; Ballet Vignettes, 1948; Going to the Ballet, 1950 (U.S. title, How to Enjoy Ballet, 1951); (autobiog.) In his True

Centre, 1951; Ballet, 1945–50, 1951; Saints Alive, 1953; A Picture
Book of Ballet, 1954 (rev. ed. 1957); The Story of Dance, 1960 (U.S.
title, The Wonderful World of Dance, 1960); The Beauty of Ballet,
1961; The Russian Genius in Ballet, 1963; Ballet Retrospect, 1964
(U.S. ed., 1965); What is Ballet, 1965; Heroes and Roses, 1966; Ballet
Russe, 1968; Infantilia, 1971; (autobiog.) Balletomane at Large, 1972;
Balletomania, Then and Now, 1976 (rev. ed. 1979). *Trans.:* Child of
the Ballet, O. Joyeux, 1953; History of Russian Ballet from Its Origins
to the Present Day, Serge Lifar, 1954. *Editor:* Who's Who in Dancing,
1932; Ballet: To Poland, 1940; Sadler's Wells Ballet Books, 1–4, 1949;
(with Mark Carter and Michael Wood) Gala Performance, 1955;
Ballet Decade, 1956; World Ballet, 1958; Ballet in Colour, 1959 (U.S.
ed., 1960); Ballet Annual, 1947–63. *Contributor:* Ballet in Action,
Merlyn Severn, 1938; Encyclopedia Britannica; Chamber's Encyclopaedia; Annual Register; British Journal of Aesthetics.

BARON COLERAINE OF HALTEMPRICE
British cabinet minister
Born Helensburgh, Scotland, February 27th, 1901
Died London, England, November 15th, 1980

Lord Coleraine, born Richard Law, served in Winston Churchill's
wartime cabinet and spent 22 years in the House of Commons. He was
the son of Andrew Bonar Law, Prime Minister of Great Britain from
1921 to 1923, who left office after accepting an unpopular war debt
settlement negotiated with the United States by Stanley Baldwin, then
Chancellor of the Exchequer. Law attended St. John's College,
Oxford, traveled in India, Asia, and the Americas, and spent two
years as a journalist in London, New York, and Philadelphia before
returning to England in 1930 to take up a political career. The
following year he was elected to Parliament as a Unionist (Conservative) from Southwest Hull in Yorkshire and quickly impressed
his colleagues with a speech in defense of his father, whom he
described as an extremely ill man forced by less principled members of
his own party to accept a settlement he regarded as "monstrously
unjust."

During the 1930s Law served on the Medical Research Council and
the Industrial Health Research Board and gained a reputation as one
of the rising young leaders of the Conservative Party. His opposition
to Conservative Prime Minister Neville Chamberlain's policy of
appeasement towards German aggression helped bring about the
replacement of the Chamberlain government with an all-party coalition headed by Winston Churchill. Law was named Financial Secretary to the War Office and soon moved to the Foreign Office as
Parliamentary Under-Secretary of State, in which post he defended
government policy to the House of Commons, participated in treaty
negotiations with Soviet Foreign Minister V. M. Molotov, and headed
the Parliamentary Delegation to the Food and Agriculture Conference in Hot Springs, Virginia (1943). In September 1943 he was
promoted to cabinet rank as Minister of State and undertook the
coordination of Allied relief efforts in the liberated countries. Speaking to the Foreign Press Association in London, Law explained his

conviction that a spirit of international cooperation would be a postwar necessity: "The world is getting smaller and it is no longer possible for statesmen to advance the interests of their own countries without considering the interests of other countries. . . . Just as there are limits beyond which a man should not go in an effort to enrich himself at the expense of his neighbors, so are there limits—perhaps even more narrowly drawn—in the case of nations."

Law was made Minister of Education in Churchill's caretaker government when the war ended, but lost his portfolio and his seat in the House of Commons when the Labour Party drove the Conservatives from power in 1945. Later that year he was returned to Parliament as the representative from staunchly Conservative South Kensington, but with his party in opposition he could do little more than watch as the Labour government began building the modern British welfare state. Despite his suspicion of state interferences in the private sector, he supported Prime Minister Clement Attlee's 1946 bill giving the government control over the development of nuclear energy, saying, "I would ask the House to believe that the idea of an armaments race, especially in this field, is absolutely repugnant to me, and I am sure it must be abhorrent to the whole House, but if there is one prospect more alarming than the prospect of an armaments race it is the prospect of an armaments race in which we come in last."

In 1950 Law won election from the newly-created Haltemprice Division in Yorkshire, which included parts of his old Hull constituency. In the following year the Tories returned to power under Churchill's leadership, but Law, who was devoting more and more time to his many business interests, was not offered a role in the new government. He was elevated to the peerage in 1954 as the first Baron Coleraine of Haltemprice and took his seat in the House of Lords, serving on committees and councils on transport, civil service, and youth employment, and chairing a Parliamentary delegation to the USSR. He was also chairman of the Marshall Scholarship Commission, the Mansfield House University Settlement, and the Royal Postgraduate Medical School of London, and chairman of the board of Horlicks Ltd. To forestall a conflict-of-interest charge, he resigned three of his business directorships in 1963 before launching an attack on governmental mishandling of the civil nuclear power program, which, he said, had had a catastrophic effect on industry.

Lord Coleraine's belief in conservatism as the route to authentic and lasting social progress was set forth in his book *For Conservatives Only,* published in 1970. "It is his feeling for the fragility of civilization which makes the Conservative distrustful of sudden change," he wrote. "So far from a conservative attitude of mind being an anomaly in a revolutionary age, it is perhaps the condition for survival." He accused modern Conservative leaders from Stanley Baldwin to Edward Heath of having forsaken the party's longstanding ideals in order to achieve a specious political "consensus" in whose name they had ratified the very things they were bound by philosophy and principle to oppose, including the welfare state, controlled markets, and the dissolution of class distinctions. Within a decade of the book's publication, Lord Coleraine saw the party return to stricter standards of conservatism under Prime Minister Margaret Thatcher.

R.C.

Son of Right Hon. Andrew Bonar L., Prime Minister of Great
Britain, and Annie Pitcairn Robley L. Married Mary Virginia Nellis
1929 (d. 1978). Sons: James Martin Bonar L., b. 1931; Andrew Bonar
L., b. 1933. Educ: Shrewsbury Sch.; St. John's Coll., Oxford; Fellow,
Royal Postgrad. Medical Sch., London 1972. Drama critic, Daily
Express, London 1927; ed. staff, Morning Post, London 1927; ed.
staff, New York Herald Tribune 1928–29; ed. staff, Philadelphia
Public Ledger 1929–30. As M.P. for Southwest Hull, Yorkshire
(Unionist) 1931–45, for South Kensington Div., London (Conser-
vative) 1945–50, and for Haltemprice Div. of Kingston-upon-Hull,
Yorkshire (Conservative) 1950–54: Member, Medical Research Coun-
cil 1936–40; Member, Industrial Health Research Bd. 1936–40;
Leader, U.K. Delegation, Conference on Food and Agriculture, Hot
Springs, Va. 1943; Chmn., Council of British Socs. for Relief Abroad
1945, 1949, 1954. Financial Secty., War Office 1940–41; Parliamentary
Under-Secy. of State, Foreign Office 1941–43; Minister of State,
Foreign Office 1943–45; Minister of Educ. 1945. As Member of the
House of Lords since 1954: Leader, All-Party Parliamentary Delega-
tion to USSR 1954; Chmn., Natl. Youth Employment Council
1955–62; Chmn., Central Transport Consultative Cttee. 1955–58;
Chmn., Standing Advisory Cttee. on Pay of Higher Civil Service
1957–61. Chmn., Mansfield House Univ. Settlement 1953–66; Chmn.,
Marshall Scholarship Commn. 1956–65; Chmn., Royal Postgrad.
Medical Sch., London 1958–71. Chmn. of Bd., Horlicks Ltd.; chmn.
and dir. of numerous other companies. Hons: P.C. 1943; Hon. LL.D.,
New Brunswick Univ. 1951; created 1st Baron Coleraine of Hal-
temprice 1954; Hon. Treas., British Sailors' Soc. 1955–74; created
High Steward of City and County of Kingston-upon-Hull 1971.
Author: The Individual and the Community, sect. in The Character of
England (ed. by Ernest Barker), 1947; Return from Utopia, 1950; For
Conservatives Only, 1970.

JOAN (MARGARET) FLEMING
Crime novelist
Born Horwich, Lancashire, England, March 27th, 1908
Died November 15th, 1980

Courtesy David Fleming

Joan Fleming, the author of more than 30 mystery novels and several
historical romances, delighted her devoted reading public with her
varied plots and her witty, humorous, and sympathetic depiction of
characters. Fleming began her writing career in her mid-thirties with a
series of juvenile novels, the first of which was *Dick Brownie and the
Zaga Bog* (1944), followed by several others. After her first crime
novel, *Two Lovers Too Many,* appeared in 1949, she wrote at least
one detective fiction a year for the next 30 years. One of her novels,
The Deeds of Doctor Deadcert (1955), was made into the film *Family
Doctor* in 1957.

Fleming was noted for her personal, idiosyncratic, at times even
zany, style, and for a psychological approach to the genre of crime
fiction that resembled that of Patricia Highsmith. The psychology of
the victims, the incongruent comedy of her situations, and the contrast
between manners and cultures were frequently emphasized. Usually
her characters found themselves reluctant, unconventional heroes
thrust into situations for which they were ill-prepared. Although many
of her settings were domestic British ones, she often used as

background those countries in which she had traveled. Perhaps her best-known character was the Turkish philosopher Nuri Bey, whose amusing passivity and disorganization come into dangerous and at times humorous conflict with a villainous world; the first Nuri Bey novel, *When I Grow Rich,* won the Crime Writers Association Golden Dagger Award in 1962.

In addition to her detective novels Fleming published four historical gothics during the past several years for which she did extensive research at the London Library.   J.N.

Daughter of David and Sarah Elizabeth (Suttcliffe) Gibson. Married Norman Belle Beattie Fleming June 1932 (d. 1968). Children: Penelope; Lalage; David; Rowan Whitfield. Educ: Brighthelmston Sch., Southport, Lancs.; Grand Belle Vue, Lausanne; Lausanne Univ. Doctor's secty. 1928–32; Writer since 1949. Hons: Crime Writers Assn. Critics Award 1962, 1970. *Books: Novels*—Two Lovers Too Many, 1949; A Daisy-Chain for Satan, 1950; The Gallows in My Garden, 1951; The Man Who Looked Back, 1951 (reissued as A Cup of Cold Poison, 1969); Polly Put the Kettle On, 1952; The Good and the Bad, 1953; He Ought to Be Shot, 1955; The Deeds of Dr. Deadcert, 1955; You Can't Believe Your Eyes, 1957; Maiden's Prayer, 1957; Malice Matrimonial, 1959; Miss Bones, 1959; The Man From Nowhere, 1960; In the Red, 1961; When I Grow Rich, 1962; Death of a Sardine, 1963; The Chill and the Kill, 1964; Nothing Is The Number When You Die, 1965; Midnight Hag, 1966; No Bones About It, 1967; Kill or Cure, 1968; Hell's Belle, 1968; Young Man I Think You're Dying, 1970; Screams from a Penny Dreadful, 1971; Grim Death and the Barrow Boys, 1971 (as Be A Good Boy, New York, 1972); Alas Poor Father, 1972; Dirty Butter for Servants, 1972; You Won't Let Me Finish, 1973 (as You Won't Let Me Finnish, New York, 1974); How to Live Dangerously, 1974; Too Late! Too Late! the Maiden Cried: A Gothick Novel, 1975; To Make an Underworld, 1976; Every Inch a Lady, 1977; The Day of the Donkey Derby, 1978. *Uncollected short stories*—Cat on the Trail, 1964; Gone Is Gone, 1966; Still Waters, 1969; The Bore, 1972. *Children's fiction*—Dick Brownie and the Zaga Bog, 1944; Mulberry Hall, 1945; The Riddle in the River, 1946; Button Jugs, 1947; Quonian Quartet (includes four juvenile novels), 1949. *Other*—Shakespeare's Country in Colour, 1960.

BORIS (SOLOMON) ARONSON
Set designer and artist
Born Kiev, Russia, October 15th, 1899
Died Nyack, New York, U.S.A., November 16th, 1980

Stage designer Boris Aronson, a six-time Tony Award winner, was one of ten children born to Solomon Aronson, the Chief Rabbi of Kiev. When he was eight, he drew a fly on a schoolbook with such exactitude that his teacher tried to brush it away. "I learned two things," said Aronson. "First, that it is easy to fool people in art, and second, if you can make a fly look like a fly, you're in."

Aronson's interest in the stage was sparked by a childhood fascination with a painted peacock on the stage curtain of the Kiev opera house. He entered the State Art School of Kiev at the age of 13

and studied in Moscow, Berlin and Paris before emigrating to the U.S. in 1923.

In New York, he began designing sets for Yiddish theater productions, including the experimental Unser Theater and the Yiddish Art Theater, and was working on Broadway by 1930. During the Depression, he designed *Awake and Sing!* and other productions for the Group Theater, a collection of leftist playwrights and artists dedicated to staging social-realist dramas. He went on to create sets and costumes for more than 100 productions, including plays, musicals, ballets, and operas, working in a seemingly infinite variety of styles. According to *New York Times* critic Brooks Atkinson, "His greatest quality is his understanding of the theater and theater scripts and the excitement with which he is able to identify with them. Every design is fresh and original. Like all first-rank artists, Boris never repeats himself." In 1945 he married Lisa Jalowetz, who often assisted him, and with whom he had one son.

Aronson achieved his greatest popular and critical successes with his work for musicals, particularly the Hal Prince-Stephen Sondheim productions of the 1960s and 1970s. Some of his best work was inspired by his childhood in Russia and his travels in pre-war Europe. His brilliantly evocative sets for *Fiddler on the Roof*, which earned him the New York Drama Critics Award, utilized Jewish folk motifs in the style of Marc Chagall. His *Cabaret* set was dominated by a huge mirror that drew the audience into the midst of the decadent Berlin demi-monde.

For *Pacific Overtures*, Aronson took his inspiration from the Japanese popular arts, of which he was a lifelong devotee. His sets captured the delicacy and color of *ukiyo-e* prints. "The appearance of Perry's battleship is the evening's show-stopper," wrote a reviewer in *Newsweek*. "First the prow with two baleful headlights looms in the dusk. Then, in accordian fashion, the rest of the ship spills into being like a black dragon. It is a breathtaking moment. . . . To see his work is like seeing the graph of a sensitive mind in motion."

Aronson's designs for *Company* had the geometric quality of the cityscape. "Movement in New York," he explained, "is vertical, horizontal, angular, never casual. In Versailles, you bow; in New York, you dodge cabs. Finally, I conceived a set that was basically a gymnasium for acting."

Aronson, who received fellowships from the Ford and Guggenheim Foundations, designed sets and costumes for several ballets, including Mikhail Baryshnikov's 1976 production of *The Nutcracker,* and for the Metropolitan Opera House. His sketches and paintings were frequently exhibited in New York galleries; a 1947 show at the Museum of Modern Art featured sets created with light from colored transparencies. He also designed the interiors of two synagogues. A complete retrospective of his paintings and designs was scheduled to open in March 1981 at the Lincoln Center for the Performing Arts in New York City.   A.E.

Son of Solomon A., chief rabbi of Kiev, and Deborah (Turovsky) A. Married Lisa Jalowetz 1945. Son: Marc Henry. Jewish. Emigrated to U.S. 1923. Educ: traditional Jewish schs.; State Art Sch., Kiev 1912–18; Sch. of the Theater, Kiev; Sch. of Modern Painting, Moscow; art studies in Berlin and Paris. Stage designer, costume

designer, and artist since 1924. Member, United Scenic Artists. Hons:
Guggenheim Fellowship 1950; Tony Awards in set design 1951 (for
The Rose Tattoo, The Country Girl, and Season in the Sun), 1967 (for
Cabaret), 1969 (for Zorba), 1971 (for Company), 1972 (for Follies),
1976 (for Pacific Overtures); American Theatre Wing Award 1951;
Ford Foundn. grant 1962; Joseph Maharam Award (for Cabaret)
1967. *Set and/or costume designer: stage*—Day and Night, 1924; The
Final Balance, 1925; Bronx Express, 1925; Tenth Commandment,
1926; Tragedy of Nothing, 1927; $2 \times 2 = 5$, 1927; Stempenyu the
Fiddler, 1929; Jew Süss, 1929; Angels on Earth, 1929; Roaming Stars,
1930; Walk a Little Faster, 1932; Small Miracle, 1934; Ladies' Money,
1934; Battleship Gertie, 1935; Three Men on a Horse, 1935; Awake
and Sing!, 1935; The Body Beautiful, 1935; Weep for the Virgins,
1935; Paradise Lost, 1935; Western Waters, 1937; The Merchant of
Yonkers, 1938; The Gentle People, 1939; Ladies and Gentlemen,
1939; The Unconquered, 1940; Heavenly Express, 1940; Cabin in the
Sky, 1940; The Night Before Christmas, 1941; Clash by Night, 1941;
Cafe Crown, 1942; R.U.R., 1942; The Russian People, 1942; The
Family, 1943; What's Up, 1943; South Pacific, 1943; Sadie Thompson,
1944; The Stranger, 1945; The Desert Song, 1945; The Assassin, 1945;
Truckline Cafe, 1946; The Gypsy Lady, 1946; Sweet Bye and Bye,
1946; The Big People, 1947; Skipper Next to God, 1948; The
Survivors, 1948; Love Life, 1948; Detective Story, 1949; The Bird
Cage, 1950; Season in the Sun, 1950; The Country Girl, 1950; The
Rose Tattoo, 1951; Barefoot in Athens, 1951; I Am a Camera, 1951;
I've Got Sixpence, 1952; The Crucible, 1953; My Three Angels, 1953;
The Frogs of Spring, 1953; Mademoiselle Colombe, 1954; The Master
Builder, 1955; Bus Stop, 1955; Once Upon a Tailor, 1955; A View
from the Bridge, 1955; A Memory of Two Mondays, 1955; The Diary
of Anne Frank, 1955; Dancing in the Chequered Shade, 1955; Girls of
Summer, 1956; Small War on Murray Hill, 1957; A Hole in the Head,
1957; Orpheus Descending, 1957; The Rope Dancers, 1957; This is
Goggle, 1958; The Firstborn, 1958; The Cold Wind and the Warm,
1958; J.B., 1958; Coriolanus, Stratford-upon-Avon 1959; The Flower-
ing Cherry, 1959; A Loss of Roses, 1959; Semi-Detached, 1960; Do
Re Mi, 1960; Garden of Sweets, 1961; A Gift of Time, 1962; Judith,
London 1962; Andorra, 1963; Fiddler on the Roof, 1964; Incident at
Vichy, 1964; Cabaret, 1966; The Price, 1968; Zorba, 1968; Company,
1970; Follies, 1972; The Creation of the World and Other Business,
1972; The Great God Brown, 1972; A Little Night Music, 1973;
Pacific Overtures, 1976. *Ballets*—The Great American Goof, 1940;
The Snow Maiden, 1942; Red Poppy, Cleveland 1943; Pictures at an
Exhibition, 1944; Ballade, 1952; L'Histoire du Soldat, 1965; The
Tzaddik, 1974. *Operas*—Mourning Becomes Electra, 1967; Fidelio,
1970. *Exhibitions:* Anderson Galls., NYC 1927; Paris 1928; New Art
Circle, NYC 1931, 1938; The Guild Art Gall., NYC 1935; Boyer
Gall., NYC 1937; Stendhall Galls., Los Angeles 1941; Nierendorf
Galls., Los Angeles 1945; Mus. of Modern Art, NYC 1947; Bertha
Schaefer, NYC 1958; Saidenberg Gall., NYC 1962; Storm King Art
Center (retrospective), Mountainville, N.Y. 1963; Wright/Hepburn/
Webster Gall., London 1968. *Other:* designed interiors of Temple
Sinai, Washington, D.C. 1959, and Community Center Synagogue,
Sands Points, N.Y. 1959. *Author:* Marc Chagall (in Russian), 1923;
Modern Graphic Art (in Russian), 1924.

WILLIAM H(OWE) M(CELWAIN) TALBOT
Sculptor and teacher
Born Boston, Massachusetts, U.S.A., January 10th, 1918
Died Torrington, Connecticut, U.S.A., November 16th, 1980

Courtesy Mrs. William Talbot

In his career as a kinetic artist and sculptor, William H. M. Talbot worked first with stainless steel in his sculptural and architectural designs; he later moved on to concrete and the mixed media of stained glass with electronic components.

After formal training under Walter Hancock at the Pennsylvania Academy of Fine Arts and private study in 1941 with George Demitrios in Boston, Talbot attended the American Academy in Rome where he was awarded the Prix de Rome. In 1942, while he was serving in the Army, Talbot's work was represented in a group exhibition at the Pennsylvania Academy of Fine Arts. After the war, Talbot continued his studies at the Academie des Beaux-Arts in Paris under Marcel Gaumont, working on several of the pieces that were exhibited in his first one-person show in 1949 in St. Louis.

In the 1950s Talbot, among other projects, designed two fountains. The first, a stainless steel sculpture fountain for a library garden in Massachusetts, was done in collaboration with two other architects in 1950; the other, this one for an office building in St. Louis in 1959, was designed and executed solely by Talbot.

The 1960s was a productive decade for Talbot. He participated in group shows and the New York World's Fair, presented one-person exhibitions, and held several visiting lectureships and the presidency of the New York Sculptors Guild. He remained active in the 1970s, and, in 1975, received the sculpture award of the National Institute of Arts and Letters.   J.S.

Son of John Cleveland T. and Dorothy Howe McElwain T. Married Joan Sangree 1946. Children: Constance; Augusta; John; Peter. Educ: Pa. Acad. of Fine Arts 1936–38; privately with George Demitrios, Boston 1938–39; American Acad. in Rome 1940–41; Academie des Beaux-Arts, Paris, with Marcel Gaumont 1945–46. Mil. Service: U.S. Army, WWII, 1941–45. Sculptor from 1940. Teacher, Birch Wathen Sch. 1947–48; Artist-in-residence, Univ. of Mich. 1949. Visiting Lectr., Earlham Coll., Ind. 1964. Visiting Lectr., St. Lawrence Univ., Canton, N.Y. 1965. Washington Art Assn., Conn.: founder 1952; trustee 1952–58. Sculptors Guild: Pres. 1965–68; Vice-Pres. 1968–72. Member: Fedn. of Modern Painters and Sculptors; Architectural League of N.Y.; Century Assn. Hons: Cresson Fellowship, Pa. Acad. of Fine Arts 1941; Prix de Rome, American Acad. in Rome 1941; Sculpture award, St. Louis Artists Guild 1950; Howard Penrose Prize, Conn. Acad. of Fine Arts 1953; Natl. Inst. of Arts and Letters award 1975. *Exhibitions: One-person*—Carroll-Knight Gall., St. Louis 1949; Andrew-Morris Gall., NYC 1963; Earlham Coll. 1964; Martin Schweig Gall. 1965; St. Lawrence Univ. 1966; Hartford Jewish Community Center 1967; Mattatuck Historical Soc. Mus., Waterbury, Conn. 1967; Rehn Galls. 1968; Martin Schweig Gall. 1969; Rehn Galls. 1971; Arts Club of Chicago 1972. *Group*—Pa. Acad. of Fine Arts 1942, 1949; Philadelphia Mus. Intnl. 1949; DeCordova and Dana, Lincoln, Mass. 1949; Univ. of Mich. 1949; Whitney Mus. of American Art 1950, 1961, 1963; N.Y. World's Fair 1964–65; Pa. Acad. of Fine Arts 1966; Wadsworth, Hartford, Conn. 1966; Stamford Mus. and Nature Center, Conn. 1968; Sculptors Guild 1968, 1969, and Annuals; Fedn. of Modern Painters and Sculptors Annuals;

Fairmont Park Assn., Philadelphia; Sculpture Intnl.; Boston Arts
Festival; many others. *Commissions:* Bryn Mawr Coll., Pa. 1948;
fountain, Fitchburg Youth Library, Mass. 1950; Natl. Council, State
Garden Clubs, St. Louis, Mo. 1959; memorial sculpture and stairwell,
Johnson Rehabilitation Center, Barnes Hosp., St. Louis, Mo. 1964.
Collections: Bryn Mawr Coll.; Earlham Coll., Ind.; The Cambridge
Sch.; Rumsey Hall Sch.; St. Lawrence Univ.; St. John's Church,
Washington, Conn.; Washington Univ., Conn.; Whitney Mus. of
American Art, NYC.

RICHARD (COTTON) CARLINE
Artist
Born Oxford, England, 1896
Died England, November 18th, 1980

Richard Cotton Carline was in every sense a British patron of the arts.
Carline's long career included the roles of author, educator, sponsor
and collector. He was also an artist of distinction himself.

Born into a family of painters, Carline was immersed in art from
birth. At the age of four, he won a prize from the Royal Drawing
Society. The young man received his formal training in Paris, then
later in Hampstead. During the First World War, Carline's talents
were employed in camouflage design. He also served as an official war
artist in Europe and the Middle East.

After the war, Carline completed his education in England, and
went on to teach at the Rossall School, the Ruskin Drawing School,
and the University of London. These years brought an increasing
commitment for Carline to the quality of instruction in the fine arts.
Carline knew that the position of art in public education was
secondary at best. "Perhaps," he wrote, "the art class might gain in
status by a change in name, with 'art' discarded in favour of 'vision.'"
To his mind, the fine arts were integral to any curriculum: "If the
power to think visually is lacking, the pupil will be wholly dependent
on auditory means of study." Carline's book, *Draw They Must,* a
classic in the field of art education, evolved from the years he spent
with his wife Nancy on the Cambridge Examination Syndicate.

Carline's sister Hilda was a successful painter, exhibiting her work
at the Royal Academy and the Tate Gallery. In 1925, she married the
artist Stanley Spencer. The relation played an important part in
Carline's life. He came to champion the work of his brother-in-law,
for whom he was a frequent portrait subject. Carline also served as
president of the Friends of Stanley Spencer Gallery, and in 1978 he
published *Stanley Spencer At War.*

Carline's own work is in the tradition of Brisith Post-Impressionism.
In contrast, though, to the urban English scenes of the London
Group, Carline's subjects were often the exotic encounters of his
travels. Primitive villages, mosquito netting, and shipboard scenes
attracted his eye. Remarkable among his early works is a view of
Jerusalem from the air. Carline's works are collected in the Tate
Gallery, the Bristol Art Gallery, and elsewhere.

Throughout his life, Carline was an avid traveller. Europe, South
America, Asia, and the Pacific were among his destinations. He

travelled for pleasure and inspiration, but also in his official capacities as Art Councillor for UNESCO, chairman of the Artists' International Association, and as a member of the British Council and the Advisory Council for Education in the Colonies. Two unusual books are associated with his travels: *The Arts of West Africa,* among the first studies of indigenous African art, and *Pictures in the Post,* based on Carline's extensive personal collection of postcards.

Carline was also an active sponsor, organizing several exhibitions, and founding the Hampstead Artists' Council. These talents as an organizer made Carline's involvement in the fine arts complete. "The general public's ability to appreciate art was inevitably reduced when machine-based industry replaced old hand-craft culture, thus depriving the people of the need to make and handle works of art in their daily life," wrote Carline. He worked daily to return the arts to this centrality, which they constantly occupied in his own life.   N.S.

Son of George C., painter, and Anne C., painter. Wife: Nancy. Children: Francis; Hermione. Educ: Tudor-Hart Sch. of Art, Paris and Hampstead; Slade Sch. Mil. Service: camouflage artist and official war artist in Europe and the Middle East, WWI; camouflage designer WWII. Active as landscape and figure painter; Teacher of art, Rossall Sch. and Ruskin Drawing Sch., Oxford; Lectr., Univ. of London Extramural Dept. and in U.S.; Art Consultant, UNESCO 1946–47; Examiner, Cambridge Examination Syndicate from 1955. Organized exhibits at Imperial War Mus., Ashmolean, Cookham Festival, Royal Acad.; traveled to China with exhibitions for British Council 1957–63; Founder and Chmn., Hampstead Artists' Council; organized intnl. conference on Training the Artist, London 1965; V.P. and Chmn., Natl. Cttee. for the U.K. of the Intnl. Assoc. of Artists; Pres., Friends of Stanley Spencer Gallery; Advisory Council for educ. in the colonies. Hons: many awards from the Royal Drawing Soc. *Exhibitions:* Tate Gall., London; Imperial War Mus.; Arts Council Collection; Bristol Art Gall.; Carlines and Spencers at Morley Gall.; others. *Author:* Pictures in the Post: The Story of the Picture Postcard, 1929; The Arts of West Africa, 1935; Draw They Must, 1968; Introduction to the Catalogue of Current exhibitions at the Royal Acad.; Stanley Spencer at War, 1978; contributed to Burlington Magazine, Studio Arts Review, and other jrnls.

JOHN R. FISCHETTI
Editorial cartoonist
Born Brooklyn, New York, U.S.A., September 27th, 1916
Died Chicago, Illinois, U.S.A., November 18th, 1980

The American political cartoonist John Fischetti, who won the Pulitzer Prize for his work in 1969, was born in Brooklyn's Little Italy section and left home at the age of 16 to go to sea during the Depression. He studied commercial art at Pratt Institute for three years, worked on animated films for the Walt Disney Studios, and sold his first political cartoon to the *Chicago Sun* in 1941. While serving with the Army Signal Corps in France during World War II he drew cartoons for the Army newspaper *Stars and Stripes;* after the war his work appeared in *Punch, Collier's, Esquire,* and other magazines. He became a syndicated cartoonist for the Newspaper Enterprise Association in 1950 and in 1962 was hired by the *New York Herald-Tribune,* where his colleagues included Bill Mauldin and Dan Dowling. When the *Herald-Tribune* folded in 1967, Fischetti was hired as chief editorial cartoonist with the *Chicago Daily News.* In 1978 the *News* went out of business and Fischetti moved to the *Chicago-Sun Times* and the Field Newspaper Syndicate.

Fischetti's political cartoons, which introduced gray tones and a horizontal format (both now in common use), were notable for their strong, imaginative symbolism and their sympathy for themes of peace and social justice. One, entitled "American Style," showed a skeletal figure draped in an American flag holding a bloody scythe and a list of assassinated leaders. Another, with the satirical caption "Why don't they lift themselves up by their own bootstraps like we did?," showed a black man suspended by his arms from chains labelled "white racism." For these and other pictures Fischetti was awarded the Pulitzer Prize in 1969. He also received awards from the American Civil Liberties Union, the National Cartoonists Society, the National Headliners Club, and other groups. "When I sit down in the morning to begin work on a political cartoon now," Fischetti once wrote, "I am part of all the people I worked with, part close Italian family and part talent. I bring this to my drawing board, and I feel very confident and dream impossible dreams for mankind."

In 1973 Fischetti published an autobiography entitled *Zinga, Zinga Za!.* The title was a stock phrase that one of his cousins used as an answer to every question, and, Fischetti said, made as much sense as the words of most politicians. "For me," he added, "the point of political cartooning is to take some of the zing out of the Zinga Zinga Zas."

Fischetti was married and had two sons. He died of a heart attack in Chicago.

L.H.

Born Giovanni Fischetti. Son of Pietro F. and Emanuela (Navarra) F. Married Karen Mortenson (Christiansen?) 1948. Sons: Peter; Michael. Roman Catholic. Educ: Pratt Inst., NYC 1937–40. Mil. Service: Signal Corps, U.S. Army, France, WWII; also artist and cartoonist, Stars and Stripes (Army newspaper) 1942–46. Freelance artist, Los Angeles, Chicago, San Francisco in 1930s; cartoonist for animated films, Walt Disney Studios, Burbank, Calif; political cartoonist since 1941; illustrator for Coronet, Esquire, Saturday Evening Post, Collier's, New York Times, Punch, other periodicals; syndicated cartoonist, Newspaper Enterprise Assn. 1950–61; staff cartoonist, New York Herald-Tribune 1962–67; chief editorial cartoonist, Chicago Daily News 1967–78; cartoonist, Publishers Newspaper Syndicate; editoral cartoonist, Chicago Sun-Times and Field Newspaper Syndicate since 1978. Hons: awards from Sigma Delta Chi (Soc. of Professional Journalists) 1954, 1956; Front-Page Award, New York Newspaper Guild 1962; Hon. D.F.A., Colby Coll. 1969; Pulitzer Prize 1969; named Best Editorial Cartoonist, Natl. Cartoonist Soc. four consecutive years; James P. McGuire Journalism Award, American Civil Liberties Union 1972; medal, Natl. Headliners Club; first annual Communications Award, Chicago Justinia Soc. of Lawyers. *Books: Illustrator*—Inside Western Union (by Maurice Joseph Rivise), 1952; Waldorf-in-the-Catskills: The Grossinger Legend (by Harold Jaediker Taub), 1952. *Author*—Zinga, Zinga Za! From Little Italy to the Pulitzer Prize (autobiography), 1973.

SOLOMON McCOMBS
Artist
Born Eufaula, Oklahoma, U.S.A., May 17th, 1913
Died Tulsa, Oklahoma, U.S.A., November 18th, 1980

The American Indian artist Solomon McCombs, a vice-chief of the Creek Nation, was born in Oklahoma in 1913. His father, the son of Creek Indians who had been forced to come to Oklahoma along the "Trail of Tears" in the 1830s, was the pastor of the Tuskegee Indian Baptist Church; his mother, who taught him traditional Indian folkways, was the descendant of a Creek chief. McCombs attended rural schools and studied under the traditional artists Princess Ataloa and Acee Blue Eagle at Bacone College, which had been founded by his great-uncle. Later he took classes in art and anatomy at Tulsa Downtown College while he was serving with the U.S. Corps of Engineers.

McCombs first exhibited his paintings in 1936 at the American Indian Exposition in Tulsa. During the next four decades he participated in group and one-person shows at the Museum of Modern Art in New York City, the Smithsonian Institute, the San Francisco Museum of Art, the Corcoran Gallery in Washington, D.C., and numerous other places; his work appeared at the Indian Annual of the Philbrook Art Center in Tulsa every year since 1946. He painted in a two-dimensional, decorative style based on traditional Indian art and using tribal symbols and themes. Among the many awards he received were the Grand Award of the 29th Annual American Indian Exposition, the Waite Phillips Trophy from the Philbrook Art Center, and the Shield Award of the American Indian and Eskimo Cultural Foundation, of which he was a founder and past president. He frequently gave illustrated lectures on Indian art and culture and traveled on a U.S. State Department lecture tour to the Middle East, Africa, and Asia in 1954.

McCombs's commissions included a painting for President Kennedy's inaugural parade in 1961, the design of the North American Indian float used in President Johnson's inaugural parade in 1964, and a mural in the Post Office of Marietta, Oklahoma. His paintings decorate American embassies in Spain, Brazil, and Liberia. The U.S. Bureau of Indian Affairs and the Creek Council House are among the institutions that own collections of his work.

McCombs, who was married to the painter Margarita Sauer, worked as an illustrator, architectural draftsman, and cartographer for various companies and federal agencies before joining the General Services Administration in 1950. From 1956 until his retirement in 1973 he was a graphic designer and illustrator for the U.S. State Department. He died of a stroke following abdominal surgery.

Vice-chief of Creek Indian Nation. Son of James M., Baptist Minister, and Ella McIntosh. Married Margarita Sauer 1961. Educ: rural Okla. schs; Bacone Coll. High Sch., Bacone, Okla., grad. 1937; Bacone Coll. ca. 1937–38; art classes, Tulsa Univ. Downtown Coll. 1944. Illustrator, architectural draftsman, cartographer, and mockup designer: Douglas Aircraft Co., Tulsa 1943; U.S. Corps of Engineers, Tulsa 1944; Clovis, N.M., Air Force Base 1947; Bureau of Reclamation, Neb. 1948; U.S. General Services Admin., Washington, D.C. 1950–56. Illustrative draftsman, later graphic designer and illustrator, Audio-Visual Services Div., U.S. State Dept. 1956–73. Lectr. on

Indian art and culture, Intnl. Educational Exchange Service tour to Middle East, India, Burma, and Africa, U.S. Dept. of State 1954. Finance auditor and Treas. 1956–57, Soc. of Federal Artists and Designers, Washington, D.C.; Co-founder 1960s and Pres., American Indian and Eskimo Cultural Foundn., Washington, D.C.; Member, Foreign Service Reserve Corps. Hons: Waite Phillips Special Indian Artists' Trophy, Philbrook Art Center 1965; Grand Award, 24th Annual American Indian Exposition, Tulsa 1969; Grand Master's Award, Five Civilized Tribes Mus., Muskogee, Okla.; Shield Award, American Indian and Eskimo Cultural Foundn.; awards from Inter-Tribal Indian Ceremonial, Mus. of New Mexico, Scottsdale Indian Art Exhibition, some 10 others. *Exhibitions: Group*—American Indian Exposition, Tulsa 1936 and subsequent years; Philbrook Art Center, Tulsa since 1946; Univ. of Oklahoma Touring Exhib. 1955–57; Howard Univ. 1962; Scottsdale Natl. Indian Art Exhib., 1962; Contemporary American Indian Art, U.S. Dept. of State 1963; 1st Annual North American Indian Art Exposition, Charlotte, N.C. 1964; American Assn. of Univ. Women; Bacone Coll.; Bismarck Natl. Indian Art Show, N.D.; Corcoran Gall., Washington, D.C.; Denver Art Mus.; Gilcrease Mus. of American History and Art, Tulsa; Inter-Tribal Indian Ceremonial, Gallup, N.M.; Joslyn Art Mus., Omaha; James Graham and Sons, NYC; Mus. of Modern Art, NYC; Mus. of New Mexico, Santa Fe; Smithsonian Inst; San Francisco Mus. of Art. *One-person*—Joslyn Art Mus.; Philbrook Art Center; others. *Collections:* U.S. Bureau of Indian Affairs; Creek Indian Council House and Mus.; Denver Art Mus.; Gilcrease Mus. of American History and Art; Joslyn Art Mus.; Mus. of New Mexico; Univ. of Oklahoma Mus. of Art; others. *Other:* Mural, U.S. Post Office, Marietta, Okla.; painting for Pres. Kennedy's inaugural parade, 1961; design for floats for Pres. Johnson's inaugural parade, 1964.

MAURICE BÉVENOT
Jesuit scholar and ecumenist
Born 1897
Died November 19th, 1980

Maurice Bévenot was a British Jesuit scholar and theologian whose studies of St. Cyprian, a bishop and martyr of the early church, helped shape the ecumenical reforms of the Second Vatican Council. A professor of patristics and ecclesiology at Heythrop College in England, Father Bévenot was appointed by Pope John XXIII in 1960 to the Secretariat for Promoting Christian Unity, a planning commission for Vatican II.

Father Bévenot came from an activist Catholic family. His father, who later became the first professor of French at the University of Birmingham in England, served as a Papal Zouave, one of the French forces that fought against Garibaldi at Mentana in 1867 to protect the Papal States against absorption into a newly unified Italy. Two of Father Bévenot's younger brothers became Benedictine priests and one of his sisters a nun.

As a youth, Bévenot attended Mount St. Mary's, a Jesuit boarding school near Sheffield, England. In 1914 he entered the Jesuit novitiate at Roehampton, England, beginning a long, demanding process, which included the study of scholastic philosophy and classics, that eventually led to membership in the Society of Jesus. In 1930 he was ordained a priest in the Society of Jesus and entered the Gregorian University at Rome, where he began the study of Saint Cyprian, the bishop of Carthage from 200 to 258 A.D., which became his life work. Bévenot's first book, *St. Cyprian's De Unitate, Chapter 4 in the Light of the Manuscripts,* was published by the Gregorian University in 1937.

In 1936 Father Bévenot went to Heythrop Pontifical Athenaeum, where he taught and wrote until his death. He specialized in the early Fathers of the Church, and in many aspects of ecclesiology, including the doctrine of the unity of the Catholic Church on which Cyprian himself had written. Publication of *The Tradition of Manuscripts: A Study in the Transmission of St. Cyprian's Treatises* (1961) established Bévenot as an authority on the hermeneutics of manuscript study.

Father Bévenot's background in ecclesiology and in the tradition of the early Church Fathers reinforced his interest in religious toleration and ecumenism. During World War II he participated in "The Sword of the Spirit," a British Catholic—and, later, Christian—movement dedicated to upholding Britain's cause in the war, to combating the evils of totalitarianism, and bringing together all peoples to secure a Christian peace. He later worked assiduously with the Council for Christians and Jews.

Father Bévenot's appointment to the Secretariat for Promoting Christian Unity was the culmination of his service to the cause of ecumenism. The Secretariat, established by Pope John XXIII in 1960 and directed by the Jesuit theologian Cardinal Augustin Bea of Germany, was originally intended as a preparatory commission for the Second Vatican Council, scheduled to begin work in 1962. The Secretariat, however, became an integral part of the Council itself, drafting proposals concerning the unity of the Church and establishing cordial relations with Christians of all faiths. Father Bévenot served as a *peritus,* or non-voting expert, at the Second Vatican Council, his vast knowledge and expertise in ecclesiology used as a resource for the ecumenical mission.

When Heythrop Pontifical Athenaeum was incorporated into London University as Heythrop College in 1970, Father Bévenot remained with it as a Senior Fellow. He continued to teach patristics and ecclesiology and also gave occasional lectures at King's College on Latin paleography, the study of ancient writing and inscriptions. J.N.

Educ: Mount St. Mary's Boarding Sch., Sheffield, England; Jesuit Novitiate, Roehampton; St. Mary's Hall, Stonyhurst; Campion Hall, Univ. Oxford, classics 1920–24; Heythrop Pontifical Athenaeum (from 1970 Heythrop Coll., Univ. of London), Oxfordshire; Gregorian Univ., Rome, doctoral studies. Ordained into Soc. of Jesus 1930. Taught at Beaumont Coll., Old Windsor; Heythrop Coll., Oxfordshire and London, from 1936. Special advisor to Ed., Heythrop Journal from 1960; Secretariat for Promoting Christian Unity; Peritus (non-voting expert), Second Vatican Council. Member: The Sword of the Spirit Movement, during WWII; Council for Christians and Jews. Hon: Arnold Historical Essay Prize, Oxford 1929. *Author:* St. Cyprian's De Unitate, Chapter 4, in the Light of the Manuscripts, 1938; The Tradition of Manuscripts: A Study in the Transmission of St. Cyprian's Treatises, 1961; (critical ed.) De Lapsis and De Unitate of St. Cyprian, 1971, incorporated in the Corpus Christianorum, 1972. *Translator:* The Lapsed, The Unity of the Catholic Church by Saint Cyprian, 1957, rev. ed. 1971; numerous reviews and articles for the Heythrop Journal.

MAURICE M. BOUKSTEIN
Lawyer and American Zionist leader
Born Cohoes, New York, U.S.A., October 24th, 1905
Died Fort Lauderdale, Florida, U.S.A., November 19th, 1980

Maurice M. Boukstein, an American Zionist leader who served as legal counsel to the Jewish Agency and other Israeli cultural and financial organizations, was born in upstate New York in 1905 to a family of Russian immigrants. At the age of seven he moved with his parents to Palestine, where, despite the death of his father and the absence of his mother, who was stranded in Russia during World War I, he studied at the Gymnasia Herzliya in Tel Aviv. He later returned to the United States to attend college and earned two law degrees from St. Lawrence University while serving as secretary and director of the American Economic Committee for Palestine.

During the 1940s, Boukstein undertook legal and administrative work for a number of Zionist organizations, including Hadassah, the American Zionist Economic Committee, and the United Palestine Appeal; he was also a consultant to the U.S. Board of Economic Warfare and represented the Haganah, the Jewish underground defense force of Palestine, in the United States. In 1946 he negotiated on behalf of the Jewish Agency and the World Zionist Organization over the disposition of property stolen by the Nazis from Jews they had killed and recovered by the U.S. armed forces. Among the cargoes at issue was the "Hungarian gold train," which contained jewelry, works of art, and furniture. Boukstein helped to establish the Jewish Restitution Successor Organization to receive such property and to use it for the benefit of impoverished refugees. Later he helped to set up the Conference on Jewish Material Claims against Germany and assisted the Jewish Agency in filing reparations suits. In negotiations with Prime Minister David Ben-Gurion, he secured for the Jewish Agency official responsibility for the resettling of immigrants in the newly-established State of Israel; he also convinced the U.S. Senate Foreign Relations Committee to preserve the agency's tax-exempt status in the United States so that it could continue to collect funds.

Boukstein, who was married and had two daughters, was a principal partner of Guzik and Boukstein in New York City from 1951 to 1973 and a senior partner of Reavis and McGrath thereafter. He was a member of the board of directors of the Jewish National Fund, the Zionist Organization of America, and the United Israel Appeal; general counsel to the Israeli Consulate in New York; a founder of the Memorial Foundation for Jewish Culture; and an executive of the America-Israel Cultural Foundation. During the 1960s he was involved in the case of Yossele Schumacher, an Israeli boy who had been kidnapped to the U.S. by his ultra-Orthodox grandfather, and succeeded in returning him to his parents. In 1976 he was awarded an honorary doctorate from the Weizmann Institute of Science in Rehovot, Israel, an institution he had helped to found in 1949 and which he had served as legal advisor, governor, and chairman of the executive council.

Son of Elias B. and Ida (Fish) B., timber dealers. Married Anna Hornstein 1931. Daughters: Sara Markel; Dina Weisberger. Jewish. Taken to Palestine 1912; later returned to U.S.A. Educ: Gymnasia Herzliya, Tel Aviv; New York Univ. 1929–32; St. Lawrence Univ. Law Sch., Canton, N.Y., LL.B. 1935, LL.M. 1936. Mil. Service: consultant, U.S. Bd. of Economic Warfare 1942. Principal partner, Guzik & Boukstein law firm, NYC 1951–73; sr. partner, Reavis & McGrath law firm, NYC since 1973; counsel for U.S. and foreign corporations. Secty. 1933–37 and Member, Bd. of Dirs. since 1934, American Economic Cttee. for Palestine; Gen. Counsel since 1940, Hadassah; Secty., Palestine Economic Corp. 1940–41; Member, Bd. of Dirs., United Palestine Appeal 1941–45; Member, Bd. of Dirs., Jewish National Fund 1941–45; Member, American Zionist Cttee. 1942–45; Member, Bd. of Dirs., Keren ha-Yesod 1943–45; legal advisor, Jewish Agency for Israel and World Zionist Org. since 1946; Gen. Counsel, Consulate General of Israel, NYC since 1948; Delegate, 23rd World Zionist Conference, Jerusalem 1951; Delegate, Jewish Reparation Claims Conference, The Hague 1952; Founder 1953 and Gen. Counsel since 1953, Conference on Jewish Material Claims Against Germany; co-founder, Gen. Counsel, and Member, Exec. Cttee., Memorial Foundn. for Jewish Culture; Member, Exec. Cttee., World Foundn. for Jewish Culture. With Zionist Org. of America: Member, Admin. Cttee. 1940–45; Member, Exec. Cttee. 1941–45; Chmn., Platform Cttee., American Jewish Conference 1943. With Jewish Restitution Successor Org.: Co-founder 1947; Member, Bd. of Dirs. since 1947; Chmn. of Exec. Cttee. 1962. With Weizmann Inst. of Science, Rehovot, Israel: Co-founder 1949; Member, Bd. of Govs. since 1949; Member, Exec. Council 1970–71; legal advisor. Member, Bd. of Dirs. and Exec. Cttee.: America-Israel Cultural Foundn.; United Jewish Appeal; United Israel Appeal. Member: American Bar Assn.; New York County Lawyers Assn.; American Acad. of Political Science; Putnam Country Club; New York Univ. Club. Hons: hon. doctorate, Weizmann Inst. of Science 1976.

EDMUND (JOHN) BOWEN
Photochemist
Born Worcester, England, April 28th, 1898
Died November 19th, 1980

Edmund John Bowen, Aldrichian Praelector in Chemistry at University College, Oxford, was awarded the Royal Society's Davy Medal for his experimental work in the quantum analysis of photochemical reactions. His 1942 book *The Chemical Aspects of Light* remained the standard text on fluorescence, chemiluminescence, and photochemistry for over a decade.

Bowen, the son of an English schoolmaster, was born in 1898. He attended his father's school and the Royal Grammar School, both in Worcester, and won a Brackenbury Scholarship to Balliol College,

Oxford, during World War I. He soon left Oxford to enlist as a lieutenant in an artillery unit in France, where he saw action in the battles of Ypres and Cambrai and in the retreat of March 1918. After the war, Bowen obtained his B.A. and M.A. from Balliol College, transferring to University College as a Fellow in 1922 and earning his D.Sc. there in 1947. He was elected to the Royal Society in 1935.

In the "underground" laboratories of Balliol, Trinity, and the newer Physical Chemistry Laboratory, Bowen developed methods for the quantum determination of light yields from the decomposition of chlorine and phosphorous oxides. During these and other experiments, he designed the "fluorescent quantum counter," which enabled the first quantitative measurements to be taken of alternative photochemical reaction pathways. He held the position of Aldrichian Praelector in Chemistry from 1952 to 1965, when he became an Honorary Fellow of University College.

Bowen wrote *The Chemical Aspects of Light* and *Luminescence in Chemistry,* co-authored *The Fluorescence of Solutions* with F. Wokes, and edited *Recent Progress in Photobiology.* In addition to his thorough grasp of chemistry, Bowen possessed an expert's knowledge of geology, paleontology, and historical literature. He died on November 19 at the age of 82. N.S.

Son of Edmund Riley B., educator, and Lilias (Kamester) B. Married Edith Moule 1924. Children: Margaret Pinset; Humphrey John. Educ: St. John's Elementary Sch. for Boys, Worcester; Royal Grammar Sch., Worcester; Balliol Coll., Oxford (Brackenbury Scholar), B.A. 1920, M.A. 1922; University Coll., Oxford, D.Sc. 1947; Fellow, Univ. Coll., Oxford 1922–65. Mil. Service: Lt., 13th Siege Battery, Royal Garrison Artillery, France 1917–18. At Oxford Univ.: Jr. Proctor 1935–36 and Domestic Bursar, University Coll.; Aldrichian Praelector in Chemistry 1952–65. V.P., Chemical Soc. of London; V.P., Faraday Soc.; Member, Physical Soc. Hons.: Fellow 1935 and Davy Medal 1963, Royal Soc. of London; Hon. Fellow, University Coll., Oxford 1965; Niels Finsen Medal 1968; Fellow, Pharmaceutical Soc.; Fellow, Chemical Soc.. *Author:* The Chemical Aspects of Light, 1942, 2nd. ed. 1946; (with F. Wokes) The Fluorescence of Solutions, 1953; (ed.) Recent Progress in Photobiology, 1965; Luminescence in Chemistry, 1968; also numerous articles and papers in Journal of the Chemical Soc., Proceedings of the Royal Soc., Transactions of the Faraday Soc., others.

SIR JOHN McEWEN
Australian political leader and cabinet minister
Born Chiltern, Victoria, Australia, March 29th, 1900
Died Melbourne, Victoria, Australia, November 21st, 1980

A member of Australian Federal Cabinets for all but eight years between 1937 and 1971, Sir John McEwen did much to speed the growth of his country's exports. He was leader of the Federal Country Party from 1958 to 1971, during which time he sought to expand the organization's base beyond its rural constituency. Nicknamed "Black Jack" because of his reputation as a tough trade negotiator and

political in-fighter, McEwen was interim Prime Minister in December 1967 and January 1968.

McEwen was orphaned at the age of seven. Subsequently raised by a widowed grandmother, he left school at 13 and began working as a messenger. He continued his studies in night school to qualify for a civil service post. In 1918, as soon as he was eligible, McEwen joined the Australian armed forces, but the First World War ended before he reached the front in Europe. Returning home, he acquired 80 acres of land at Stanhope, Victoria, 150 miles from Melbourne. Building from this base, he became a 3,000-acre wheat farmer and sheep rancher.

McEwen entered politics as a leader of the demobilized soldier-settlers in his district. He went on to win election to the Federal House of Representatives in 1934 as a member of the rural-based Country Party. Three years later, he entered the cabinet as Minister for the Interior in the Australian Party-Country Party governing coalition. He subsequently held a number of government posts, including Minister for External Affairs, Minister for Air and Civil Aviation and membership on the Advisory War Council. During the period of Labor Party rule from 1941 to 1949, McEwen was a prominent member of the Opposition, particularly after he became deputy leader of the Country Party in 1943. When his party returned to power in 1949 as junior partner of the Liberal Party, he was appointed Minister for Commerce and Agriculture.

McEwen remained involved in economic policy-making as Minister for Trade and Minister for Trade and Industry in subsequent governments, seeking with considerable success to expand Australia's exports. In 1957 he negotiated the country's first postwar trade treaty with Japan. By the mid-1960s Australia's exports to Japan, consisting largely of foodstuffs, wool and minerals, nearly equalled exports to Britain. McEwen also negotiated a free trade area between Australia and New Zealand, which went into effect in 1966, and opened up new markets for Australian wheat in the Soviet Union and Communist China. While developing markets in Asia and the Pacific, McEwen opposed British entry into the European Common Market, which he feared would end Australian trade preferences in Britain. During the 1960s he led numerous trade delegations to the General Agreement on Tariffs and Trade (GATT) negotiations in Geneva.

As leader of the Country Party beginning in 1958, McEwen served as Deputy Prime Minister in the Liberal-Country coalition government. During the early 1960s, his chances of becoming Prime Minister seemed excellent despite the handicap of belonging to the junior coalition partner. But he lost the opportunity by his aggressive efforts to expand the Country Party's electorate from its rural base, a course which brought it into conflict with the Liberal Party. In 1963, McEwen rejected a redistricting of parliamentary constituencies that would have benefitted the Liberals at the expense of the Country Party. To win urban support for his Party, he reversed its traditional low tariff stance in favor of protectionism. In 1966 he produced a Country Party platform that went beyond the organization's usual bounds into such apparently Liberal fields as secondary industry and industrial relations. In that year's elections, some prominent Liberals retaliated by backing a rural group opposing the Country Party.

When Prime Minister Harold Holt died in a drowning accident,

McEwen served as interim Prime Minister from December 19, 1967 to January 10, 1968, when the Liberals chose a new leader. But he was able to block Holt's logical successor, Commonwealth Treasurer and Liberal Party Deputy Leader William McMahon, whose views diverged from McEwen's on a number of economic issues. Declaring that neither he nor his party would serve under McMahon, McEwen forced the choice of John Gorton as new Prime Minister.

During the last years of his political life, McEwen faced declining support for his views both outside and inside the Country Party. Full employment made high tariffs seem unnecessary. With the rural sector of the economy in decline, McEwen lost support for his position that agriculture, even when unprofitable, should be subsidized to preserve what he regarded as a superior way of life. After he retired in 1971, the Country Party came out in favor of the rationalization of agriculture.

McEwen continued working his farm until 1976. He died following a long illness.

M.L.

Son of David James M. and Amy Ellen Porter M. Married: (1) Annie Mills McLeod 1921 (d. 1967); (2) Mary Eileen Byrne 1968. No children. Mil. Service: Australian Imperial Forces 1918. Farmer at Stanhope, Victoria 1919–76; Member, Federal House of Representatives 1934–71 (Echuca Div. 1937–49; Murray Div. 1949–71); Minister for the Interior 1937–39; Minister for External Affairs 1940; Minister for Air and Civil Aviation 1940–41; Member, War Cabinet 1940–41; Member, Advisory War Council 1941–45; Deputy Leader, Australian Parliamentary Country Party 1958–71; Minister for Commerce and Agriculture 1949–56; Minister for Trade 1956–63; Leader, Australian Parliamentary Country Party 1958–71; Deputy Prime Minister 1958–67, 1968–71; Minister for Trade and Industry 1963–71; Prime Minister, Dec. 1967-Jan. 1968. Australian delegate, UN Conference on Intnl. Organizations, San Francisco 1945; led numerous delegations to General Agreement on Tariffs and Trade talks, Geneva. Hons: Privy Councillor 1953; Companion of Honour 1969; G.C.M.G. 1971; Order of the Rising Sun 1st Class (Japan) 1973.

A(RTHUR) J(AMES) M(ARSHALL) SMITH
Poet, critic, and anthologist
Born Montreal, Quebec, Canada, November 8th, 1902
Died Canada, November 21st, 1980

From the early 1930s through the 1960s, A.J.M. Smith was a leader of the modern movement in Canadian poetry. As a poet, critic, and anthologist, Smith urged fellow Canadians to reject the old-fashioned pieties of colonialist literature and, like T.S. Eliot and William Butler Yeats, write a modern verse that was neither parochial in theme nor purely local in subject matter.

While studying science at McGill University, Smith also edited the *McGill Literary Supplement* and began writing poetry. In 1925 he and poet F.A. Scott launched the *McGill Fortnightly Review*. The *Review* was the first journal published in Canada wholly dedicated to modern poetry; Scott and Smith hoped to free Canadian poetry of its

colonialist provincialism, and they published young writers whose
poetic voice was both cosmopolitan and distinctively Canadian. *New
Provinces: Poems of Several Authors,* an important anthology edited
by Smith, appeared in 1936. The book contained works by several
pioneers of avant-garde Canadian poetry such as Smith, Scott, E.J.
Pratt, and A.M. Klein; critic George Woodcock said that "the book's
importance, like that of Smith's own poetry, lay in the fact that it
showed how a poetry sensitive to a special environment and a local
tradition could take on a cosmopolitan character, drawing from and
contributing to a wider tradition in a way merely colonial poets have
never been able to do." Smith's later anthologies, *The Book of
Canadian Poetry* (1943) and *Modern Canadian Verse* (1967), contained poets from both the colonial and national eras; as such,
unexpected similarities and continuities between the two traditions are
evident.

Smith's poetry is noted for its emotional intensity, evenness of tone,
and finely honed craftsmanship. In one poem, he stated that the ideal
poetic form was:

> as hard
> And as smooth and as white
> As a brook pebble cold and unmarred. . . .

Although Smith's aesthetic principles were shaped in the 1930s, his
poetry is timeless. His imagist poems are obviously inspired by the
Canadian landscape but they evoke fundamental human emotions and
contain universal themes. Smith used an austere language to suggest
strong and richly nuanced feelings. Reviewing *The Book of Canadian
Poetry,* critic Northrop Frye cited Smith's "The Lonely Land" as the
anthology's best and most representative Canadian poem for its
"evocation of stark terror . . . in a sparsely settled country.":

> This is a beauty
> of dissonance,
> this resonance
> of stony strand,
> curled over a black pine
> and wind-battered branch
> when the wind
> bends the tops of the pines
> and curdles the sky
> from the north.

Thus, Smith's imagism allowed him to abstract from the purely
Canadian to meditate upon the meaning of his experience.

In 1962 Smith published his *Collected Poems,* which was followed
five years later by *Poems: New and Collected.* Although he selected
only 100 poems for the two slender volumes and arranged them
thematically rather than chronologically, Smith's influences are apparent. From the Symbolists, the imagism of Ezra Pound, and John
Donne and the Metaphysical School, Smith established a modern
form in which his intention was:

To hold in a verse as austere
As the spirit of prairie and river,
Lonely, unbuyable, dear,
The North, as a deed, and for ever.

L.G./E.T.

Married Jeannie Dougal Robbins 1927. One son. Educ: McGill Univ.,
Montréal, B.Sc. 1925, M.A. 1926; Univ. of Edinburgh, Ph.D. 1931.
Asst. Prof., Ball State Teachers Coll., Muncie, Ind. 1930–31; Instr.,
Doane Coll., Crete, Neb. 1934–35; Asst. Prof., Univ. of South
Dakota, Vermillion 1935–36. With Michigan State Univ., East Lans-
ing: Instr. 1931–33; Member of the English Dept. since 1936; Prof. of
English and Poet-in-Residence from 1960, now retired. Visiting Prof:
Univ. of Toronto 1944, 1945; Univ. of Washington, Seattle 1949;
Queen's Univ., Kingston, Ontario 1952, 1960; Univ. of British
Columbia, Vancouver 1956; Dalhousie Univ., Halifax, Nova Scotia
1966–67; Sir George Williams Univ., Montreal, summers 1967, 1969;
McGill Univ. 1969–70. Co-founding ed., McGill Fortnightly Review,
Montréal 1925. Hons: Guggenheim Fellowship 1941, 1942; Harriet
Monroe Memorial Prize for poetry 1943; Gov.-Gen.'s Award 1944;
Rockefeller Fellowship 1944; Hon. D. Litt, McGill Univ. 1958;
LL.D., Queen's Univ. 1966; Lorne Pierce Medal 1966; Canada
Centennial Medal 1967; D.C.L., Bishop's Univ. 1967; Canada Coun-
cil Medal 1968. *Books: Poetry*—News of the Phoenix and Other
Poems, 1943; A Sort of Ecstasy: Poems New and Selected, 1954;
Collected Poems, 1962; Poems: New and Collected, 1967; Poets
Between the Wars (with others), 1967. *Editor:* (with F.R. Scott) New
Provinces: Poems of Several Authors, 1936; The Book of Canadian
Poetry, 1943 (new eds. in 1948 and 1957); Seven Centuries of Verse:
Englash and American, from the Early English Lyrics to the Present
Day, 1947 (new eds. 1957 and 1967); The Worldly Muse: An
Anthology of Serious Light Verse, 1951; (with M.L. Rosenthal)
Exploring Poetry, 1955 (rev. ed. 1973); (with F.R. Scott) The Blasted
Pine: An Anthology of Satire, Invective and Disrespectful Verse,
Chiefly by Canadian Writers, 1957 (rev. ed. 1967); The Oxford Book
of Canadian Verse: In English and French, 1960 (rev. ed. 1965);
Masks of Fiction: Canadian Critics on Canadian Prose, 1961; Essays
for College Writing, 1965; The Book of Canadian Prose, 2 vols. 1965,
1973; 100 Poems: Chaucer to Dylan Thomas, 1965; Modern Canadian
Verse: In English and French, 1967; The Collected Poems of Anne
Wilkinson and a Prose Memoir, 1968. *Literary Criticism*—Some
Poems of E.J. Pratt: Aspects of Imagery and Theme, 1969; Towards a
View of Canadian Letters: Selected Essays 1928–72, 1973.
Further reading: Ten Canadian Poets by Desmond Pacey, 1958; "A
Salute to A.J.M. Smith" by various authors, in Canadian Literature,
Winter 1963; Odysseus Ever Returning by George Woodcock, 1970.

JULES LÉGER
Diplomat and government official
Born Saint-Anicet, Quebec, Canada, April 4th, 1913
Died Ottawa, Ontario, Canada, November 22nd, 1980

One of the most experienced and skilled members of Canada's foreign
service, Jules Léger was Undersecretary of State for External Affairs
and served as Ambassador to France during a period of tension

Courtesy Government House, Ottowa, Ontario

between the two nations. He later became Governor-General of Canada, only the second French-Canadian to hold that post.

Son of a village storekeeper, Léger received a B.A. degree in 1933 from the Collège de Valleyfield in Quebec. He studied law at the University of Montreal from 1933 to 1936 and earned a doctorate from the Sorbonne in Paris in 1938. After working as associate editor of the Ottawa French-language newspaper *Le Droit,* Léger moved on to the University of Ottawa in 1940, where for two years he was Professor of Diplomatic History and Current Affairs.

Meanwhile, Léger entered the Canadian External Affairs Department in 1940 as a third secretary, functioning also as a special wartime assistant to William Lyon Mackenzie, Prime Minister and Secretary of State for External Affairs. In 1943 Léger was assigned to the Canadian legation in Santiago, Chile, where he rose by 1946 to first secretary. Sent to London in 1947, Léger served as first secretary in the office of the High Commissioner for Canada. In 1948–49 he advised the Canadian delegation to the United Nations General Assembly in Paris.

Leger returned to Ottawa in 1949 to act as executive assistant to Prime Minister Louis St. Laurent. He was chief of the European Division in the Department of External Affairs in 1950–51 and Assistant Undersecretary of State for External Affairs from 1951 to 1953. In 1953–54, Léger served as Canadian ambassador to Mexico.

In August 1954 Léger was named Undersecretary of State for External Affairs, the senior civil service position in the External Affairs Department. Ranking second only to the External Affairs Minister, he dealt with the 1956 Suez crisis and other critical world events. From 1958 to 1962 Léger was permanent Canadian representative to the NATO Council and to the Organization for European Economic Cooperation.

Following a stint as ambassador to Italy from 1962 to 1964, Léger served for four and a half years as ambassador to France. Relations between the countries were strained because of French President Charles De Gaulle's sympathy for the separatist movement in predominantly French-speaking Quebec. Although extremely knowledgeable concerning French interests and sensitivities, Léger failed to improve Canadian-French relations and was subjected to many diplomatic snubs.

Recalled home in the fall of 1968, Léger was appointed Undersecretary of State in November. As chief civil servant in the Department of State, he was responsible for implementing federal government programs such as bilingualism and biculturalism, for the financing of Indian associations, and for promoting new projects like Opportunities for Youth. In March 1973 Léger returned to diplomatic service as ambassador to Belgium and Luxembourg.

Shortly afterward, Léger was nominated by Prime Minister Trudeau and approved by Britain's Queen Elizabeth II for a five-year term as Governor-General of Canada. On January 14, 1974 he became the 21st Governor-General, the fourth born in Canada and the second from a French-Canadian background. As the representative of the British Crown, Léger had the power to veto legislation, summon and dissolve Parliament and call elections. But by tradition he exercised these powers according to the wishes of the Prime Minister, and his role was essentially ceremonial.

Only six months after beginning his term, Léger suffered a stroke that left him unable to speak. But intensive therapy enabled him to regain the use of his paralyzed left side and to speak again. By the spring of 1976, Léger was able to return to a nine-hour working day and make tours of all the provinces.

Bringing a new sense of informality to his job, Léger invited thousands of children to garden parties and annual Christmas dinners. On the formal level he presided over the elimination of some of the last vestiges of colonial authority, overseeing the transfer from Britain of the power to declare war, sign peace treaties and accredit diplomats abroad. He indicated his support for the Canadianization of the office of Governor-General. Among the important pieces of legislation Léger signed was a 1975 bill establishing Petro-Canada, the first government-owned petroleum corporation, and a 1976 measure abolishing the death penalty for civilians.

Léger's term as Governor-General ended in January 1979. He died less than a week after suffering a second stroke.   M.L.

Son of Ernest L., storekeeper, and Alda Beauvais L. Married Gabrielle Carmel 1938. Daughter: Hélène. Roman Catholic. Educ: Collège de Valleyfield, B.A. 1933; Univ. of Montreal 1933–36 (law); Sorbonne, D.Litt. 1938. Assoc. Ed., Le Droit, Ottawa 1938–39; Prof. of Diplomatic History and Current Affairs, Univ. of Ottawa 1940–42; Third Secty., External Affairs Dept. 1940–43; Third Secty. 1943, Second Secty. 1944, and First Secty. 1946, Canadian Mission to Chile; First Secty., Office of the High Commnr. for Canada, London 1947–48; Adviser, Canadian delegation to UN General Assembly, Paris 1948–49; seconded to Prime Minister's office 1949–50; Chief, European Div., External Affairs Dept. 1950–51; Asst. Undersecty. of State for External Affairs 1951–53; Ambassador to Mexico 1953–54; Undersecty. of State for External Affairs 1954–58; Permanent Representative to NATO Council and to Organization for European Economic Cooperation 1958–62; Ambassador to Italy 1962–64 and to France 1965–68; Undersecty. of State 1968–73; Ambassador to Belgium and Luxembourg 1973–74; Gov.-Gen. of Canada 1974–79. Hons: Chancellor and Principal Companion of the Order of Canada; Chancellor and Commander of the Order of Military Merit; Canadian Forces Decoration; LL.D., McGill Univ., Montreal 1960; Privy Councillor 1979.

JOHN W(ILLIAM) McCORMACK
Speaker of the United States House of Representatives
Born South Boston, Massachusetts, U.S.A., December 21st, 1891
Died Dedham, Massachusetts, U.S.A., November 22nd, 1980

A member of the U.S. House of Representatives for 43 years, John McCormack rose to power in the 1930s and 1940s as the trusted lieutenant of Speaker Sam Rayburn, whom he succeeded as Speaker of the House in 1962. McCormack helped shepherd through Congress most of the great liberal Democratic legislation of this century, from Franklin D. Roosevelt's New Deal to Lyndon B. Johnson's Great Society. McCormack, whose nine year tenure as Speaker was the second longest in history, profited from the House seniority system as

a young Congressman but was criticized in his later years as a symbol of that very system's cumbrousness.

The paternal and maternal grandparents of John W. McCormack immigrated to the United States during the Irish potato famine in the 1840s. John's father was a bricklayer in South Boston with a family of twelve children, nine of whom died at early ages. "We're not proud of it," Edward "Knocko" McCormack, John's brother, once recalled, "but we don't shun the fact that we were the poorest family in South Boston." When the father died, 13-year old John was forced to quit school and support his mother and two younger brothers by running errands for a brokerage firm for $3.50 a week. He soon found work as an office boy with the law firm of William T. Way and moved up to the $4 a week income bracket. However, McCormack also graduated from reading Horatio Alger stories to studying legal texts at night between errands; at the age of 21, without benefit of a formal high school education, he passed the Massachusetts bar examination and soon became a successful Boston trial attorney.

McCormack entered politics as a functionary at the lowest levels of the local Democratic Party apparatus and, in 1917, was elected as a delegate to the Massachusetts Constitutional Convention. The position qualified him for exemption from military service but McCormack, a staunch patriot with an eye on higher elective office, enlisted, serving stateside during World War One and attaining the rank of Sergeant Major. McCormack was elected to the Massachusetts House of Representatives in 1920 where he served one term before being elected to the state Senate in 1923. In 1926 McCormack unsuccessfully challenged incumbent Democratic Congressman James A. Gallivan in South Boston's Twelfth Congressional District; after the election, he worked full time as a partner in the now lucrative law firm of McCormack and Hardy.

In 1928, after Gallivan had died in office, McCormack was elected to Congress. "Where I was brought up the people were poor," McCormack once said, "probably no district in America is more political than mine." Over the next four decades, McCormack kept closely attuned to his constituents' needs; at Thanksgiving and Christmas he walked the district's streets dispensing season's greetings, canned goods, and turkeys. Moreover, the 12th Congressional District, once so predominantly Catholic and Irish-American that it is said to have produced more nuns and priests than any other area of the country, became more and more ethnically diverse as its population swelled to include eastern European immigrants, Italians, Jews and blacks—a natural constituency for a fiercely partisan Democrat who consistently supported liberal domestic legislation.

In an institution where "to get along, you go along" is the unwritten rule of success, McCormack quickly proved himself an able legislator who played by the rules—and played well. He established close friendships with Democratic minority leaders Sam Rayburn, who admired his party loyalty, and John Nance Garner, who admired his skill at poker. When the Democrats took control of the House after Roosevelt's landslide victory in 1932, McCormack became the first Democratic Representative to be named to the powerful Ways and Means Committee after serving in Congress for less than four years; he soon became known as an expert on questions of taxation. In 1936 he supported Rayburn for the position of Democratic majority leader and, four years later, when Rayburn acceded to Speakership of the House, McCormack became majority leader.

McCormack and Rayburn were symbols of the broadly-based New Deal coalition. One was from the urban northeast, the other from the rural south, one was a Catholic, and the other a Protestant; together, they mobilized congressional support for President Roosevelt's legislative program. A skilled parliamentarian and feared debater, McCormack mixed an acid wit with partisan vitriol to intimidate political opponents. In 1941, when the Axis seemed invincible and public opinion was divided between internationalism and isolationism, McCormack played a crucial role winning extension of the military draft. According to the *New York Times,* he roamed the House exhorting Democrats to support the controversial measure and when one Representative explained that his constituents were opposed to the draft, McCormack growled, "You're a member of the Jewish faith. How can you let the draft die while Hitler is killing Jews in Europe?" To another reluctant legislator, he snapped, "You're a Harvard man, you ought to know what this bill means. You're one of Franklin Roosevelt's fair-haired boys. How in hell can you do this to him?" Draft extension carried the House by one vote.

During McCormack's first tenure as House Majority Leader, which lasted from 1940 until the Republicans gained control of the House after the 1946 elections, he regularly supported New Deal and Fair Deal legislation and, in foreign affairs, became known as a passionate anti-Communist. In the 1930s McCormack had characterized Communism as a "Godless" heresy; moreover, he introduced anti-Communist legislation, chaired the House Committee in Un-American Activities during its first investigations of alleged Nazi and Communist acts of subversion, and called for U.S. recognition of the Franco regime in Spain as early as 1939. Thus, as the Cold War intensified in the late 1940s, McCormack readily supported economic and military aid for Greece and Turkey in 1947, and for Korea and Formosa in 1950. When Red China opposed U.N. efforts to arrange a Korean ceasefire in 1951, McCormack introduced a measure asking the U.N. to "immediately act and declare the Chinese Communist authorities an aggressor . . ."

McCormack served as minority whip in the Republican Congress of 1953–55 and as majority leader for the remainder of the Eisenhower Administration. Although partisan Democratic opposition was relatively mute during the Eisenhower presidency, Rayburn and McCormack passed a bill in 1959 which extended by three months the eligibility period for unemployment compensation. McCormack continued to be a bellicose anti-Communist and, in 1954, having announced that Communism had the "mind of a world killer," he voted for the Communist Control Act, which would have made the Communist Party illegal; throughout the 1950s, McCormack attacked the Administration's defense budgets as inadequate.

In late August 1961, House Speaker Rayburn fell and McCormack was elected Speaker Pro Tempore; Rayburn died later that year and, when the 87th Congress convened in 1962, McCormack called in his political IOU's, received the unanimous backing of his Democratic colleagues, and was easily elected to the Speakership. Although McCormack had headed the pro-Kennedy Massachusetts delegation to the 1960 Democratic Convention and consistently supported New

Frontier legislation, there were rumors of friction between him and the President in 1962 when McCormack's nephew, the Massachusetts Attorney-General whom the childless Speaker regarded as a son, ran against Edward M. "Ted" Kennedy in the primary for a U.S. Senate seat. McCormack denied any feud between himself and the President and maintained that his earlier opposition to Kennedy's decision to halt Federal aid to parochial schools derived from his devout Catholicism and close ties to church leaders.

Following Kennedy's assassination in November, 1963, McCormack was a proverbial "heartbeat" away from the Presidency; and, during the early months of the Johnson Administration, many House Democrats who believed the Speaker too old and lacking in leadership ability to govern the country hoped he would resign. "I would rather be Speaker than President," McCormack said, brushing aside suggestions that he step down as Speaker. However, more serious threats to the Speaker's power were generated by the deepening conflict in Vietnam, which McCormack unswervingly supported. To younger liberal Democrats, McCormack was an old cold-warrior who personified the deficiencies of the seniority system, its rigidity and ceremonial procedures which emphasized the process, rather than the content, of legislation. In January, 1969, liberal Representative Morris Udall, who called McCormack an ineffective leader, challenged him in the House Democratic Caucus for the Speakership. However, Udall received support only from anti-war Democrats and McCormack easily defeated him.

In October 1969, a scandal burst over the capital when *Life* Magazine reported that a long-time McCormack aide, Dr. Martin Sweig, and his associate, Nathan Voloshen, had used the Speaker's office for influence-peddling. McCormack immediately denied any involvement in the affair and defiantly stated that he would seek re-election in 1970. However, in May, 1970, Voloshen pleaded guilty and, although the Speaker was cleared of any wrongdoing, McCormack announced that he would retire at the end of his term. Among his final Congressional acts, McCormack oversaw passage of a bill which lowered the legal voting age to 18 and declared his support for the Equal Rights Amendment.   E.T.

Son of Joseph M. McC., bricklayer, and Ellen (O'Brien) McC. Married M. Harriet Joyce, singer, 1920. No children. Educ: John Andrew Grammar Sch. until age 13. Mil. Service: with U.S. Army, WWI. Newsboy 1903; errand boy in brokerage firm; office boy, William T. Way's law office; admitted to Mass. bar 1913; practiced law in Boston; Partner, McCormack and Hardy (law firm); Member, Mass. House of Reps. 1920–22 and State Senate 1923–26. With U.S. House of Reps: Member 1927–71; Majority Leader 1940–47, 1944–53, 1956–61; Minority Whip 1947–48, 1953–55; Speaker Pro Tempore 1961–62; Speaker 1962–71. Chmn., House Cttee. Investigating Un-American Activities; 1st Chmn., House Science and Astronautic Cttee.; Chmn., Democratic Party Platform 1944, 1952, 1956; Chmn., Mass. delegation for Kennedy, Democratic Natl. Convention 1960. Member, South Boston Citizens' Assoc.; American Legion. Hons: Knight Comdr. of the Order of St. Gregory the Great, with star; Rosette, Knights of Malta; 11 hon. degrees including LL.B. from Boston Univ.

MAE WEST
Actress and comedienne
Born Brooklyn, New York, August 17th, 1892
Died Los Angeles, California, November 22nd, 1980

Mae West was born in Brooklyn, New York on August 17th, most likely in 1892, although dates from 1885 through 1893 are quoted. Her father, John Patrick West, was a prizefighter turned livery driver. He later ran a detective agency for 12 years and ultimately entered the real estate business. Mae remembered her father as a cruel and unlikable man.

Her mother, Matilda Delker-Dolger, was born in Bavaria and had been trained as a fashion model and dressmaker. Forbidden by her husband to work, she often took young Mae with her to vaudeville shows. At the age of five Mae began imitating the stars of the day at church socials. At seven she was enrolled in "Professor" Watts' Dancing School (the extent of her formal education). That year she made her debut at the Royal Theatre on Fulton Street in Brooklyn in one of the Professor's regular concerts. Amateur night appearances followed and she joined stock companies playing child parts in such plays as *Little Nell* and *Mrs. Wiggs of the Cabbage Patch*.

At the age of fifteen she joined a vaudeville troupe where she met a good-looking song and dance man named Frank Wallace. They formed an act together and took it on the road in 1910. On April 11, 1911 they were married quietly in Milwaukee. Mae quickly discovered that marriage did not suit her and weeks later she helped Frank get a part in a show just beginning a 40-week tour. That effectively ended their partnership, though the marriage was not officially dissolved until 1943. In subsequent interviews and memoirs Mae denied having ever been married. "I'd have to give up my hobby," she would say.

Mae's first break came with the show, *A la Broadway*, in September 1911. It ran only eight performances but it got Mae some good reviews. It led to parts in two further musical reviews, *Vera Violetta* and *A Winsome Widow*. By 1913 she had developed a vaudeville act with her younger sister Beverly. Her sister did not last, but Mae's experiment with writing comic monologues proved successful. While on tour in Chicago she stopped into a black club and saw people doing a "funny sort of dance" called the "shimmy." She added it to her act along with her ever more stylish and provocative wardrobe. She was starting to cause riots and break house records wherever she played. During this period she would carefully note the effect her material had on the audiences to ensure that she was not driving away the women. "You can't set house records if you don't bring in women too," she explained.

In 1918–19 she starred in a Rudolf Friml musical called *Sometime,* co-starring with Ed Wynn. She brought the shimmy to Broadway and it was a hit. In 1922 she put together a new act with Harry Richman and at the same time began studying the dramatic potential of sexuality. She read Freud, Jung, Adler and Havelock Ellis and wanted to write a play incorporating her findings. Late in 1922 Richman left to form another act freeing Mae from the need to work continuously. This permitted her to investigate her subject firsthand and discover things she could not find in books.

The dramatic result was a play she called *Sex,* which opened in April 1926. The play was produced by Mae's mother and her attorney after it had been rejected by the Shuberts, the producers of her earlier hits. *Sex* did not receive happy reviews: "a crude, inept play" (New York Times), "nasty, infantile, amateurish and vicious" (Variety). Nonetheless, it did very good business for nearly a year before it was raided by the New York Police Department. The play closed a month later and Mae ultimately spent a highly publicized and not unpleasant eight days on Welfare Island.

In 1927 her second play, *The Drag* ("a homosexual comedy drama in three acts") opened in Bridgeport, Connecticut to sell-out crowds. It closed after two weeks under pressure from New York City officials who declared it too "vulgar" for the New York stage. Mae herself said she closed it because the public was "too child-like to face the problems of homosexuality like grownups." In any case she quickly followed it with *The Wicked Age,* another popular success and critic's nightmare. Her next play, *Diamond Lil,* was an unqualified success and even gathered many favorable reviews. The play established for all time the "Mae West" character she was to portray for the rest of her life, "a scarlet woman for whom love was only a pastime but diamonds were a career." The play was set in the Bowery in the 1890s, and the action revolved around Gus Jordan, a saloon keeper and ward boss who enjoyed Diamond Lil's favors. Lil, the dance hall singer and "one of the finest women who ever walked the streets," is surrounded by petty gangsters and thieves trying to horn in on Jordan's saloon and white slave trade. Nonetheless Lil is able to manipulate the men well enough to keep herself in diamonds and champagne. A Salvation Army captain sets up a mission in a vacant building next door to the saloon and attempts to reform Lil. She in turn responds with her most famous line, "Why don't you come up sometime and see me? You know you can be had." Gus Jordan and the other lowlifes fight and kill for their share of the territory. The Salvation Army captain turns out to be an undercover detective who sends the survivors off to jail, preferring to deal with Lil himself. The play ends with Lil in the captain's arms saying to herself, "Is this love? Or just something for the winter season?"

Mae wrote two more plays, *Pleasure Man* and *The Constant Sinner* before accepting an offer from Paramount to go to Hollywood in 1932. When she arrived she moved into a spacious apartment where she would live until her death.

Her first role was in a George Raft [q.v.] film, *Night After Night.* She immediately set to work rewriting her part in the film. (When she first arrives at Raft's speakeasy the hat-check girl remarks, "Goodness, what beautiful diamonds." Mae replies, "Goodness had nothing to do with it dearie.") The success of the film pulled Paramount away from the brink of bankruptcy and they gave Mae a remarkable degree of control over her film projects.

Her next film was an adaptation of *Diamond Lil* retitled *She Done Him Wrong.* In it she introduced as the Salvation Army captain an unknown young actor she had discovered walking down a studio street, Cary Grant.

She became the biggest box-office draw of 1933. By 1935 she was the highest paid woman in the United States and she shrewdly invested her money in land around the Los Angeles area.

Although *She Done Him Wrong* is widely regarded as Mae West's finest picture, it got her into trouble with the Hays Office, a board of censors which had instituted a new Production Code to watch over the morals of Hollywood films. Another direct result of her films was the creation of The Legion of Decency by Bishop Bernard Sheil of Chicago and others to monitor film production.

I'm No Angel (also 1933), however, continued her box office successes. In an effort to get around the strictness of the Production Code Mae West resorted to a style of ambiguous double-entendres that got her message across more by how she spoke rather than what she said. (i.e. Cary Grant: "Do you mind if I get personal?" Mae West: "I don't mind if you get familiar." or "If only I could trust you." Mae: "Hundreds have.") When delivered in her lazy drawl and accompanied by a simultaneous grind of her hips the meaning was clear. After *I'm No Angel* the censors began to have a more critical effect on her films. From 1934 through 1943 she was featured in *Belle of the Nineties, Goin' to Town, Klondike Annie, Go West, Young Man, Every Day's a Holiday, My Little Chickadee* (with W. C. Fields) and *The Heat's On.* By this point her films were so watered down that they had lost much of their vitality and popular appeal. With the minor exceptions of *Myra Breckinridge* (1970) and *Sextette* (1978) her film career was over.

In the late 1930s Mae had been working on a film script based on the life of Catherine the Great of Russia. In 1944 she decided to bring it to the stage instead. *Catherine Was Great* was a lavish and spectacular production. At the final curtain Mae would address the audience: "Catherine was a great empress. She had three hundred lovers. I did the best I could in a couple of hours." It ran for six months on Broadway and then went on tour. She returned in 1947 with a comedy, *Come on Up,* and in 1949 with a revival of *Diamond Lil.* She toured with it on and off until 1952.

In 1954 she put together a Las Vegas night club act that featured nine "musclemen" in loincloths. She continued with this show until 1959. During this period she was more than ever a national legend. She recorded an album and appeared on a number of radio and television programs. In 1959 she published her autobiography, *Goodness Had Nothing To Do With It.*

She never married again and continued to live a quiet existence away from Hollywood parties and nightlife. One of the "musclemen," Paul Novak, became her constant companion and stayed with her until her death. Although she favored outrageous hats and costumes that called attention to her blonde tresses and petite but voluptuous figure, she was never in life like the wild and sinful woman she portrayed. She once told an interviewer, "I'm my own original creation. I concentrate on myself most of the time; that's the only way a person can become a star in the true sense. I never wanted a love that meant surrender of my self-possession. I saw what it did to other people when they loved another person the way I loved myself, and I didn't want that problem. I had to stay in command of my career."

Her "creation" was substantially unchanging throughout her movies and plays. She played a different kind of sex symbol, not the "sexy-but-dumb" blonde, but rather a "sexy-and-smart" woman. Rather than being a sex object for men, she acted as if men were the sex objects. Although she was a classically curvaceous siren, she was not especially beautiful by movie standards. Her sex appeal was not based so much in how she looked as it was in what went on in her head. She was, it should be remembered, 40 years old before she made her first film. As the film critic Pauline Kael remarked, "In her movies Mae West celebrated the victory of experience over innocence, of talent over youth." To her, sex was play and sin was a kind of joke we were all taken in by.   M.M.

Daughter of John Patrick W. and Matilda Delker-Dolger W. Married Frank Wallace 1911 (div. 1943). No children. Privately educated. *Performances: Plays*—Little Nell, The Marchioness, Mrs. Wiggs of the Cabbage Patch, Ten Nights in a Barroom, East Lynne, The Fatal Wedding, all 1897–1903; A la Broadway, New York 1911; Vera Violetta, New York 1911; A Winsome Widow, New York 1912; Such Is Life, San Francisco 1915; Sometime, New York 1918; Demi-Tasse Review, New York 1919; The Mimic World, New York 1921; Sex, New York 1926; The Wicked Age, New York 1927; Diamond Lil, New York 1928; The Constant Sinner, New York 1931; Catherine Was Great, New York 1944; Come On Up, New York 1947; Diamond Lil (revival) 1949–51; Sextette, Chicago 1961. *Vaudeville* as "Vaudeville's Youngest Headliner," 1913–18; night club review, 1954–57. *Films*—Night After Night, 1932; She Done Him Wrong, 1933; I'm No Angel, 1933; Belle of the Nineties, 1934; Goin' to Town, 1935; Klondike Annie, 1936; Go West, Young Man, 1936; Every Day's a Holiday, 1938; My Little Chickadee, 1940; The Heat's On, 1943; Myra Breckinridge, 1970; Sextette, 1978. Also appeared on many radio and television programs. *Phonograph recordings*—The Fabulous Mae West, 1955; Way Out West, 1966; Wild Christmas, 1966. *Author: Plays*—Sex, 1926; The Drag, 1927; The Wicked Age, 1927; Diamond Lil, 1928; Pleasure Man, 1928; The Constant Sinner, 1931; Catherine Was Great, 1944. *Screenplays*—She Done Him Wrong, 1933; I'm No Angel, 1933; Belle of the Nineties, 1934; Goin' to Town, 1935; Klondike Annie, 1936; Go West, Young Man, 1936; Every Day's a Holiday, 1938; My Little Chickadee, 1940 (co-author). *Novels*—The Constant Sinner; Diamond Lil, 1932. *Other*—Goodness Had Nothing to Do With It (autobiography), 1959; On Sex, Health and ESP (non-fiction), 1975.
Further reading: The Crazy Mirror by Raymond Durgnat, 1969.

SANGAD CHALORYOO
Thai admiral and politician
Born Suphan Buri, Thailand, March 4th, 1915
Died Bangkok, Thailand, November 23rd, 1980

Courtesy Khunying Sucon Chaloryoo

Admiral Sangad Chaloryoo, who briefly headed military governments in Thailand in 1976 and 1977, was a professional naval officer for most of his career. He was educated at Thai military colleges and received naval training in the United States. During the Korean War, when Thailand was allied with the U.S., he commanded the Royal Thai Navy Flotilla. He rose through the naval hierarchy, serving as chief of staff of the Anti-Submarine Squadron, the Royal Fleet, and the Supreme Command Headquarters, and was named commander in chief of the Royal Fleet in 1972.

Chaloryoo became Supreme Commander of the Thai Armed Forces in 1975 and retired in September 1976. On October 6, one day after he took office as Minister of Defense, he led a coup by the National Administration Reform Council that restored temporary martial law to Thailand after three years of civilian rule. (Military coups had become routine in Thailand since the first one in 1932.) After serving in the next civilian government as Minister of War and member of the prime minister's advisory council, he led a second coup, this time by the Revolutionary Council, and served as president of the National Policy Council in the military regime until ill health forced his retirement. He died in Bangkok of a heart ailment.   L.R.

Also spelled Chalawyu. Son of Plaek C. and Somlim C. Married: (1) Benjamas Angkinandha 1942 (d. during WWII); (2) Khunying Sucon 1950. Children: 2nd marriage—Thongplew; Nuj. Educ: Ban Sam Chao Deg Phraya Sch.; Royal Naval Acad.; Naval Command and Staff Coll.; Natl. Defense Coll.; Naval War Coll.; naval training in USA; attached to Office of Chief of Staff, Royal Thai Navy 1940; Commanding Officer, HTMS Suraj 1949–51, HTMS Thongplew 1952, and HTMS Tachin 1953; Chief of Staff 1956 and Commanding Officer 1957, Anti-Submarine Squadron; Member, House of Reps. 1957–59 and Constitutional Assembly 1959–63; Chief of Staff, Royal Fleet 1962; Asst. Chief of Staff for Operations, Royal Thai Navy 1964; Member, Senate (first period) 1968–71, (second period) 1971; Deputy Chief of Naval Staff 1969; Deputy Chief of Staff, Supreme Command Headquarters 1971; Comdr.-in-Chief, Royal Fleet 1972; held posts in Natl. Legislatives 1972–73, 1975; Deputy Comdr.-in-Chief, later Comdr.-in-Chief, Royal Thai Navy 1973–76; Supreme Comdr., Armed Forces 1975–76; retired Sept. 1976. Served in several posts in Natl. Assembly 1976; Minister of Defense Oct. 5-6, 1976; led military coup and headed govt. as Chmn., Natl. Admin. Reform Council, Oct. 6-22, 1976; Minister of Defense and Chmn., Prime Minister's Advisory Council 1976–77; led coup as Chmn. of Revolutionary Council 1977; Pres., Natl. Policy Council 1977–79. Hons: Special Officer of 1st Regiment of Royal Guards 1976; Knight Grand Cordon, Special Class, Order of the White Elephant; Knight Grand Cordon, Order of the Crown; Knight Grand Comdr., 2nd Class, Order of Chula Chom Klao; Victory Medal. *Author:* Manual of Anti-submarine Warfare in Royal Thai Navy; When Japanese Attacked Singapore in World War Two; numerous articles on naval topics.

MARIANNE KRIS
Child psychoanalyst and teacher
Born Vienna, Austria, May 27th, 1900
Died London, England, November 23rd, 1980

Dr. Marianne Kris was a psychoanalyst, teacher, and an originator of the study of child psychoanalysis. She was born in Vienna in 1900, the year Sigmund Freud formed the nucleus of what was later to become the Vienna Psychoanalytic Society, and was a childhood playmate of Anna Freud, his youngest daughter. Her father, Dr. Oskar Rie, was the pediatrician for Freud's children and had collaborated with him in a study of childhood cerebral paralysis. Her cousin, Wilhelm Fliess, was Freud's close friend and correspondent.

Kris received her medical degree from the University of Vienna in 1925, and trained at the Psychoanalytic Institute of Berlin. In 1927 she married Dr. Ernst Kris, an art historian and psychoanalyst who was one of Sigmund Freud's early biographers. Their two children, who both grew up to be psychiatrists, were born in 1931 and 1934. During this period, Kris, Anna Freud, Edith Jackson, and Dorothy Burlingame formulated the basic theoretical and clinical elements of child psychoanalysis. Her own specialization became the clinical therapy of children.

In 1938 the Krises left Vienna to escape Nazi persecution and settled for a time in London, where Kris worked with Anna Freud at the Hampstead War Nursery, a center for homeless children that Freud had started during the London blitz. Moving to New York in 1941, the Krises joined the faculty of the New York Psychoanalytic Institute. During a residency of nearly 40 years, Kris gained a reputation as an exceptional teacher. According to a former student, "She didn't let you drift off into theory. She made you stick to the patient and what was good for the patient." She also taught at several other institutions, including the Child Study Center at Yale University (founded by her husband), the Psychoanalytic Training and Research Staff of Columbia University, the Albert Einstein Medical College, and the Western New England Institute for Psychoanalysis.

Kris published pioneering studies on problems in child psychoanalytic treatment and the modulation of family dynamics through individual psychoanalysis of each member. With Anna Freud, she served as managing editor of *The Psychoanalytic Study of the Child,* an annual journal. In 1965 she founded and became the first president of the International Association of Child Psychoanalysis.

In 1961 Kris treated the movie actress Marilyn Monroe for nervous tension and enrolled her as a patient in the Payne-Whitney clinic. Although Monroe was not a patient of Kris's at the time of her death in 1962, she willed the balance of a trust fund "to be used by [Kris] for the furtherance of the work of such psychiatric institutions or groups as she shall elect."

At the time of her own death, Kris had received no funds from the estate, and was involved in litigation with the executor, Aaron Frisch. She bequeathed the Monroe legacy to the Hampstead Child Clinic in London.

Kris died of a heart attack in London where she was attending a scientific conference. Her unfinished works included a new study of sibling relationships. Colleagues at a memorial service recalled her "deep and gentle insight" and her ability to provide practical advice to troubled patients."   J.N.

Daughter of Oskar Rie, pediatrician. Married Ernst K., psychoanalyst and art historian, 1927 (d. 1957). Children: Anna Wolff, psychiatrist, b. 1931; Anton, psychiatrist, b. 1934. Jewish. Escaped from Nazi Germany 1938; emigrated to U.S. ca. 1940. Educ: Univ. of Vienna, M.D. 1925; Berlin Psychoanalytic Inst. late 1920; postgrad. studies at Psychoanalytic Inst., Austria. Private practice in psychoanalysis since 1941; Faculty Member, New York Psychoanalytic Inst. since 1941; Sr. Research Assoc., Child Study Center, Yale Univ. 1960; Sr. Staff Member, Psychoanalysis Clinical Training and Research Center, Columbia Univ. since 1974; Sr. Faculty Member, Western New England Inst. for Psychoanalysis, New Haven, Conn. Consultant in child psychiatry, Albert Einstein Coll. of Medicine 1970; Sr. Consultant, New York Child Development Center; assoc. of faculty, Cornell-New York Hosp. Freud Anniversary Lectr., New York Acad. of Medicine 1972; (with Anna Freud) Managing Ed., The Psychoana-

lytic Study of the Child (jrnl.). Founder 1965 and 1st Pres., Intnl.
Assn. of Child Psychoanalysis; Charter Member, American Acad. of
Child Psychiatry. Member: AMA; American Assn. for Advancement
of Science; American Psychoanalytic Assn.; American Psychosomatic
Assn.; Intnl. Psychoanalytic Assn. Hons: Life Fellow, American
Acad. of Child Psychology. *Author:* "The Use of Prediction in a
Longitudinal Study," in The Psychoanalytic Study of the Child, vol.
12; (with A.J. Solnit) "Trauma and Infantile Experiences: A Long-
itudinal Perspective," in Psychic Trauma (ed. by S.S. Furst), 1967.

HERBERT (SEBASTIAN) AGAR
Historian and editor
Born New Rochelle, New York, U.S.A., September 29th, 1897
Died Sussex, England, November 24th, 1980

A newspaper editor and Pulitzer Prize-winning historian, Herbert
Agar's commitment to the values of democratic liberalism extended
beyond America to include the cause of Britain before and during
World War Two. This vision of an international community dedicated
to safeguarding the essential freedoms informed Agar's many articles,
speeches, and books. In the 1930s, earlier than most of his American
colleagues, Agar recognized the perils of isolationism and spoke out
for cooperation among democratic nations and he constantly emphasized the importance of strong ties between Britain and America,
nations he regarded as bulwarks of the democratic tradition. In *A
Time for Greatness* (1942) Agar wrote, "There is nothing worth
fighting for except an idea, for it alone can last, can provide a basis for
the developing future. Touch the American tradition anywhere, in
any speech or document or song or ritual, and the same 'explosive
idea' emerges, the one force that Hitler fears, the idea of *all* men."

When Agar went to England in 1928 as a correspondent for a St.
Louis newspaper, he already believed devoutly in the American
democratic process and his interest in the Anglo-American tradition
had developed during his service as a Naval reservist in World War I
and as teacher of history and English afterward. After 1928, Agar
spent most of his life in England, except for a short period before the
United States declared war in 1941.

While in London as a correspondent of the Louisville *Times,* Agar
was also a literary editor of the *English Review* and wrote several
literary studies, some with his second wife, Eleanor Carroll Chilton.
However, he soon put aside his work on literature to explore the
historical and political topics on which his reputation became based.
Agar, a typically American combination of the idealist and pragmatist, wrote a popular treatise on the American presidency from George
Washington to Warren Harding, *The People's Choice* (1933), for
which he received the Pulitzer Prize for History.

When Agar returned to the United States in 1934, he joined the
editorial staff of the Louisville *Courier–Journal* and traveled
throughout the country as a lecturer and writer. After becoming
editor of the paper in 1939, Agar devoted much of his time to the
cause of American involvement in the growing European conflict,
reaching a national audience through his articles and speeches on the

controversial issue. Agar's efforts to secure peace through international cooperation continued through the influential agency of Freedom House, Incorporated, an organization of which he was a founder
and first president.

After the United States entered the war, Agar—now a lieutenant–commander in the Naval Reserve—headed the London branch of
the Office of War Information, spending most of his time as special
assistant to Ambassador John G. Winant. In this capacity he traveled
throughout the country to deliver inspirational speeches to British and
American audiences on the need for continuing cooperation between
the two countries, and on America's unavoidable responsibility for
leadership in the modern world.

After the war Agar continued to live in England, although he often
went to the United States and served as Adlai Stevenson's chief
advisor and speechwriter during the 1952 presidential campaign.
Agar, who was president of both a British publishing house and an
independent television station, continued to publish books on history
and politics. *The United States: The Presidents, the Parties, and the
Constitution* (1950) focused on the way in which strong and weak
presidents had brought about major changes in the government of the
United States and the interpretation of the Constitution. Among his
other influential studies were *The Saving Remnant: An Account of
Jewish Survival Since 1914* (1960), which dealt with the efforts of the
American Jewish Joint Distribution Committee in the two world wars,
and his last major work, *The Darkest Year: Britain Alone, June
1940–June 1941* (1973), in which he returned to the subject of the
balance of power between democratic and totalitarian states during
World War Two.   E.S.

Son of John Giraud A. and Agnes Louise A. Educ: Columbia Univ.,
A.B. 1919; Princeton Univ., A.M. 1922, Ph.D. 1924. Married: (1)
Adeline Scott 1918 (div. 1933); (2) Eleanor Carroll Chilton 1933 (div.
1945); (3) Barbara Lutyens Wallace 1945. Mil. Service: seaman, later
chief quartermaster, USNR 1917–18; lt. comdr., USNR 1942. London
corresp., Louisville Courier–Journal, Louisville Times, 1929–34; Ed.,
English Review, London 1930–34; wrote syndicated daily newspaper
column, "Tide and Time," U.S. 1935–39; Ed., Louisville Courier
Journal 1940–42; Dir., British division, Office of War Information,
London 1942–46. U.S. Embassy, London: Special Asst. to Ambass.
1943–45; Counsellor for Public Affairs 1945–46. British Isle Ed.,
Freedom and Union 1947; Dir., Rupert Hart–Davis Ltd., London
1953–64; Dir., T.W.W. Ltd., independent television station, South
Wales and West of England 1957–68. Founder and Pres., Freedom
House, Inc., New York 1941–43. Member: Phi Beta Kappa; Savile;
Natl. Arts; Century. Hons: Pulitzer Prize for History 1933; Hon.
Litt.D., Southwestern Univ., Memphis 1936; Hon. L.L.D., Boston
Univ. 1941. *Author:* (with W. Fisher and E. Chilton) Fire and Sleet
and Candlelight (verse), 1928; Milton and Plato (essay), 1928; (with
E. C. Chilton) The Garment of Praise (essays on poetry), 1929; Bread
and Circuses (essays), 1930; (trans. from French) The Defeat of
Baudelaire, 1930; The People's Choice, 1933; Land of the Free, 1935;
(ed. with Allen Tate) Who Owns America? (symposium), 1936; What
Is America?, 1936; Pursuit of Happiness: Story of American Democ-
racy, 1938; (with Helen Hill) Beyond German Victory, 1940; (with
Committee of 15) The City of Man: A Declaration on World
Democracy, 1940; A Time for Greatness, 1942; (ed.) The Formative

Years: A History of the United States During the Administrations of Jefferson and Madison, 1947; The Price of Union, 1950; The United States: The Presidents, The Parties, The Constitution, 1950; A Declaration of Faith, 1952; Abraham Lincoln, 1952; The Price of Power: America Since 1945, 1957; The Saving Remnant: An Account of Jewish Survival Since 1914, 1960; The Perils of Democracy, 1965; The Darkest Year: Britain Alone, June 1940-June 1941, 1973.

GEORGE RAFT
Screen actor
Born New York City, U.S.A., September 26th, 1895
Died Los Angeles, California, U.S.A., November 24th, 1980

Along with Edward G. Robinson and James Cagney, George Raft was the most famous screen gangster of the 1930s. For his portrayals of raffish tough guys, Raft was believed to be Hollywood's highest paid film star in 1933; unable to overcome his mobster image, Raft's career went into decline and, by the late 1960s, his fortune had been squandered.

Born in the rough and tumble "Hell's Kitchen" section of New York City's West Side, George Raft came naturally to his "tough guy" image. As a young man during the Prohibition Era he was hired by childhood friend Owney Maddon as an escort driver for a convoy of bootlegger's trucks. Raft tried out a number of careers before becoming a successful nightclub dancer, including bantam weight boxing, although he was knocked out seven times in 17 matches, and being a minor league baseball player, although his batting average was never higher than .240. By 1920, Raft was earning a modest wage as a "taxi dancer"—and a somewhat notorious reputation as a gigolo—in such dance halls as the Audubon ballroom.

With his dark, good-looks and his hair plastered down with vaseline to affect the fashionable "patent-leather look," Raft soon caught the attention of Stanley Burns, a talent scout who signed him up with a vaudeville touring company run by Harry and Elsie Pilcer. Following his dance tour, which included several appearances in London, Raft worked at several nightclubs where Fred Astaire remembered him as an "extraordinary dancer who did the fastest, most exciting, Charleston I ever saw." He was earning $150 a week, but there was a seamier side to his stint in Manhattan's night-clubs. "If you were an entertainer on Broadway in those days," Raft once said, "you would have to be blind and lame not to associate with gangsters. Look, they owned the clubs and that's where the work was."

The ambitious and energetic Raft, who was at one time working simultaneously in two theaters and two nightclubs, eventually won a small part in a Hollywood film, *Queen of the Night Clubs* (1929). From 1929 to 1932, he appeared in several minor films, but it was director Howard Hawks who made Raft a star by casting him in the role of Gino Rinaldi for the 1932 feature film *Scarface*.

Through his portrayal of a "classy" gangster who could "make" a fast buck and a beautiful "dame" with equal ease and had a penchant for flashy clothes, snap-brim hats, and "cool" gestures—such as insouciantly flipping a coin in the scene in which he was gunned down by his "boss"—Raft became an overnight sensation. That success, however, was double-edged; Raft could never shake free of the typecast, celluloid image of the mobster; worse yet, it was reinforced by his highly publicized friendships with Madden, "Bugsy" Siegel, and other underworld figures. Still, the gangster role furnished Raft with several critically acclaimed performances, including his portrayal of a loyal, self-sacrificing convict in *Each Dawn I Die* (1939) with Jimmy Cagney; and in the part of a tormented ex-con in *Invisible Stripes* (1939). Along with Edward G. Robinson and Humphrey Bogart, with whom he starred in *They Drive by Night* (1940), Raft made up the "tough-guy" trio upon which Warner Brothers relied for their "assembly line" production of gangland and prison dramas. As a top-ranking, box office star in the late 1930s, Raft commanded the-then princely salary of $5000 a week.

In the 1940s, reluctant to play characters who lived on the wrong side of the law, Raft turned down the lead roles in *The Maltese Falcon, Casablanca, High Sierra,* and *All Through the Night*—parts which catapulted Humphrey Bogart to superstardom. Because he could not judge scripts astutely, Raft, at the age of 55, returned to the night club circuit, eventually working as entertainment director of the Capri Hotel in Havana until Castro's rebel forces took control of the Cuban capital. Raft received a more serious setback in 1965 when he was prosecuted by the Internal Revenue Service for tax evasion. Referring to the $75,000 he reportedly owed in back taxes, Raft said: "When I was doing good, I had three servants, a publicity man, an agent, lawyers, and nine million parasites, bought a dozen suits and four dozen neckties at a time, and bet on a lot of horses. I don't know where it all went . . . I wish the government would leave me something." In 1967, the screen gangster suffered from his underworld associations when the Home Office denied him permission to enter Great Britain, where Raft had been hosting the Colony Club, a gambling casino in London's fashionable Mayfair district. Stating that "his presence in the United Kingdom would not be conducive to the public good," he was also banned from Britain in 1971 and again in 1974.

By the late 1960s, Raft had retired from films and his fortune was gone. He appeared in a popular television commercial in which he led a group of convicts in a cup-banging, dining hall demonstration for Alka Seltzer, and worked as a public relations official for a Las Vegas hotel. Moreover, there was considerable sympathy for the aging film star in America and, in a 1967 *New York Post* article, Pete Hamill wrote: "I for one only wish that someone would give him a long coat and a machine gun, a pair of spats and a blonde, and let him flip a silver dollar in the air, before shooting it out with the cops. George Raft, of all people, should be allowed to go out in style."   L.R.

Born George Ranft (changed name in 1917). Son of Conrad R. and Eva (Glockner) R. Roman Catholic. Bantam-weight boxer, Polo Athletic Club 1911; semi-pro baseball player 1911; dancer, Audubon Ballroom, Churchill's Sunken Galleries, and Manhattan Casino 1917–20. Dance performer: The Lilies of the Fields touring co. 1920; Union Square Theater 1920; night-clubs, El Fey, Parody Club, The Playground; "The City Chap" Liberty Theater 1925; The Rivoli Theater and The Palace 1929–30. *Films:* Queen of the Night Clubs, 1929; Hush Money, Palmy Days, Quick Millions, 1931; Scarface,

Taxi, Dancers in the Dark, Madame Racketeer, Night After Night, Undercover Man, If I had a Million, Night World, Love Is a Racket, 1932; Pick Up, Midnight Club, The Bowery, 1933; All of Me, Bolero, The Trumpet Blows, Limehouse Blues, 1934; Rumba, Stolen Harmony, The Glass Key, Every Night at Eight, She Couldn't Take It, 1935; It Had to Happen, Yours for the Asking, 1936; Souls at Sea, 1937; You and Me, Spawn of the North, 1938; The Lady's from Kentucky, Each Dawn I Die, Invisible Stripes, I Stole a Million, 1939; The House Across the Bay, They Drive by Night, 1940; Manpower, 1941; Broadway, 1942; Stage Door Canteen, Background to Danger, 1943; Follow the Boys, 1944; Nob Hill, Johnny Angel, 1945; Mr. Ace, Nocturne, Whistle Stop, 1946; Intrigue, Christmas Eve, 1947; Race Street, 1948; Johnny Allegro, Red Light, A Dangerous Profession, Outpost in Morocco, Nous irons a Paris, 1949; Lucky Nick Cain, 1951; Loan Shark, 1952; I'll Get You, The Man from Cairo, 1953; Rogue Cop, Black Widow, 1954; A Bullet for Joey, 1955; Around the World in 80 Days, 1956; Some Like It Hot, 1959; Jet over the Atlantic, Ocean's Eleven, 1960; The Ladies' Man, 1961; Two Guys Abroad, For Those Who Think Young, The Patsy, 1964; Five Golden Dragons, The Upper Hand, Casino Royale, 1967; Skidoo, 1968; Deadhead Miles, 1971; Hammersmith is Out, 1972.

Further reading: The George Raft File: The Unauthorized Biography by Robert James Parrish, 1973; George Raft by Lewis Yablonsky, 1974.

HENRIETTA (HILL) SWOPE
Astronomer
Born St. Louis, Missouri, U.S.A., October 26th, 1902
Died Pasadena, California, U.S.A., November 24th, 1980

The development of techniques to measure distances in space was the lifework of the American astronomer Henrietta H. Swope. The daughter of General Electric president Gerard Swope and the niece of journalist Herbert Bayard Swope, she was born in St. Louis and raised in Ossining, New York, where she began stargazing in her backyard. After receiving her A.B. in mathematics from Barnard College and her master's degree in astronomy from Radcliffe, she joined the staff of Dr. Harlow Shapley at the Harvard University Observatory. During the next 14 years she studied some 60,000 photographs to learn more about cepheids, variable stars which have unstable gaseous shells and hence appear to pulsate. Since the periodicity of a cepheid's pulsation is directly related to its intrinsic luminosity, and since luminosity is an indicator of distance, it is possible, as Swope and her colleagues demonstrated, to compute a galaxy's distance from the Milky Way by observing the pulse periods of the cepheids within it.

During the Second World War, Swope worked on radar experiments at the Massachusetts Institute of Technology and at the Navy's Hydrographic Office, where she helped to invent loran (long-range navigation), a method of plotting ship and plane location using radio signals. For the next 16 years she continued to refine the cepheid measuring system at the Mount Wilson and Palomar Observatories in California. In 1962 she announced that the distance between the Milky Way and Andromeda, our nearest galactic neighbor, is 2.2

million light years (or three million billion miles). Previous estimates had ranged from 700,000 to three million light years. "Oh, there is much to be done," Swope told a reporter who asked her what she planned to do next. "I'm going to go right on counting stars. People don't seem to grow old as young as they used to."

Swope did not use direct telescopic observation in her research; instead, she used photometry, the measurement of the starlight recorded on a photographic plate during prolonged exposure to a single region of the sky. In 1969 she donated funds to the Carnegie Institute of Washington towards the construction of the Las Campanas Observatory in Chile, which now contains a 40-inch telescope named in her honor. She was awarded the Annie Jump Cannon Prize from the American Astronomy Society in 1968.

Swope also established the Swope Loan Fund to aid students at Barnard College, where she taught for five years. The College awarded her its Medal of Distinction in 1980.   A.D.

Daughter of Gerard S., pres. of General Electric Co., and Mary (Hill) S. Unmarried. Educ: Barnard Coll., A.B. 1925; Radcliffe Coll., A.M. 1928. Mil. Service: staff member, Radiation Laboratory, Massachusetts Inst. of Technology 1942–43; mathematician, Hydrographic Office, U.S. Dept. of Navy 1943–47. Asst., Harvard Univ. Observatory 1928–42; Assoc. Astronomer, Barnard Coll., Columbia Univ. 1947–52; Resident Fellow, Mount Wilson and Palomar Observatories 1952–78. Founder, Swope Loan Fund, Barnard Coll. Member: American Astronomy Soc. since 1928; Astronomical Soc. of the Pacific since 1954; Royal Astronomical Soc. of Great Britain since 1960. Hons: Annie Jump Cannon Prize, American Astronomy Soc. 1968; Distinguished Alumna Award 1975 and Medal of Distinction 1980, Barnard Coll.; hon. doctorate, Univ. of Basel, 1975; telescope at Las Campanas Observatory, Chile, named in her honor. *Major articles:* Harvard Coll. Observatory Annals, Vol. 9, No. 7, 1936; "The Draco System: A Dwarf Galaxy," in Astronomical Journal, 1961; "Variable Star Field 96' South Preceding Nucleus of Andromeda Galaxy," Astronomical Journal, 1963; (with W. Baade) "Variables in the Andromeda Galaxy, Fields I & III," Astronomical Journal, Vol. 70, 1965; "Thirteen Periodic Variable Stars Brighter than Normal RR Lyraetype Variables in Four Dwarf Galaxies," Astronomical Journal, Vol. 73, No. 10, 1968.

SIR ALAN (KENNETH) SCOTT-MONCRIEFF
Naval officer and civil servant
Born England, September 3rd, 1900
Died England, November 25th, 1980

Admiral Sir Alan Kenneth Scott-Moncrieff, Commander in Chief of the Far East Station from 1955 to 1957, was a member of the Royal Navy during three wars, saw action in two of them, and was honored by the governments of three nations. Scott-Moncrieff's career began in 1917 when he joined the HMS Orion as midshipman. From 1942, when he became captain of the destroyer HMS Faulkner, until 1944 Scott-Moncrieff participated in the Russian convoys which were under frequent submarine and aircraft attack. For his handling of this

dangerous escort he became a Companion of the Distinguished
Service Order in 1942. The next year, after serving as senior officer of
a group of destroyers involved in the conflict in Sicily and Salerno, he
received a bar for this decoration. After World War Two, during
which he saw more action in the Aegean, he became chief of staff to
Sir Charles Lambe, Commander in Chief of the East Indies.

In 1950 he received his admiralty and was made commander of the
Commonwealth Naval Forces in the Korean War during which he was
again under fire. Scott-Moncrieff was awarded several honors for his
characteristically brave and skillful command, including Commander
of the Order of the British Empire in 1953. In 1955 he succeeded
Lambe as Commander in Chief of the Far East Station, a position he
held for two years.

Scott-Moncrieff, who retired in 1958, died at the age of 80.   N.S.

Son of Robert Lawrence S.–M. and Victoria Troutbeck S.M. Married: (1) Norah Doreen Vereker 1923 (d. 1973); (2) Winifred Titley
1974. Children: 1st marriage—one daughter; 2nd marriage—two
stepsons. Educ.: RN Colleges, Osborne, Dartmouth, Mil. Service:
Joined HMS Orion as Midshipman 1917; Comdr., HMS Enchantress
1939–40; duty capt. for admiralty 1941; special duties for U.S. Naval
Forces; Chief Signal Officer to Lord Louis Mountbatten, Combined
Operations Headquarters; Comdr., HMS Faulkner; Capt. "D" 8th
Destroyer Flotilla, Home Fleet 1942–43 (despatches twice); Sr.
Officer, destroyers of Force H. Mediterranean theater; Capt., Signal
Sch., Petersfield; Chief of Staff to Comdr. in Chief, East Indies;
Imperial Defence Coll., 1948; Comdr., HMS Superb 1949; Flag
Officer Comdr., Fifth Cruiser Squadron 1951–52; Korean War (CBE,
despatches); Admiral Command Reserves 1953–55; Comdr. in Chief,
Far East Station 1955–57; retired 1958. Chmn., NATO, Naval
Advisory Cttee 1950. A Younger Brother of Trinity House; Victory
Services Club; Naval and Military; Phyllis Court (Henley-on-
Thames). Hons: DSO 1942, bar 1943; King Haakon Medal, Norway
1945; American Legion of Merit, U.S. 1952; CBE 1952, C.B. 1952;
KCB 1955; Deputy Lt. for Greater London 1962.

KONRAD WACHSMANN
Architect
Born Frankfurt an der Oder, Germany, 1901
Died West Los Angeles, California, U.S.A., November 25th, 1980

Konrad Wachsmann, one of the most influential architects of his time
and a pioneer in the field of prefabricated construction, demonstrated
through his buildings in the United States and Europe the com-
patibility of aesthetics and technology, of beauty and function.
Wachsmann—who, like the more widely known Buckminster Fuller,
believed that one of the solutions to contemporary problems was
technological design—inspired considerable discussion on the place of
the spirit in an industrialized, secular society. In commenting on
Wachsmann's work in 1971, architecture critic John Pestier said that
"because Wachsmann has chosen to subordinate esthetics while
concentrating on more basic design problems, he has been sometimes

pigeonholed as a technician, inventor or engineer. He is, among other things, all of these, but also recognizes and successfully expresses the poetry inherent in good construction."

Born in 1901 in Germany, Wachsmann, trained as a joiner and carpenter, studied at the Arts and Crafts School in Berlin and Dresden under Heinrich Tessenow and at the Berlin Academy of Art under Hans Poelzig. He was active as an architect in Germany and Italy from 1925 until 1941. For a three-year period beginning in 1926 Wachsmann was the chief architect for a company that manufactured the largest number of prefabricated wooden buildings in Europe. In 1928 he custom designed out of local timber a country house for Albert Einstein near Potsdam, Germany, which is now restored and maintained by the East German government. In 1932 he went to Rome where he worked on a covered market project and built blocks of apartments in reinforced concrete.

In 1941, when he had emigrated to the U.S. to escape the growing power of fascism, he collaborated with Walter Gropius with whom he had worked on a project the previous year in Key West, Florida. In 1942 Wachsmann and Gropius developed the building system for the General Panel Corporation of New York which employed standardized building parts in a flexible manner for the first time in prefabricated housing. Although the project—a realization of Wachsmann's commitment to the revolutionary concept of "modular coordination"—received extensive public support and publicity, it was criticized by architects, building unions, and material manufacturers who were not prepared for its radical design and the threat it posed to conventional construction. By 1946 the General Panel Corporation was producing prefabricated houses at the rate of one every 12 minutes in an old Lockheed warehouse in Burbank, California.

Working with Serge Chermayeff in 1946 with a commission from the U.S. Air Force, Wachsmann employed his controversial design in the "Mobilar Structure," a system for the construction of aircraft hangars to any required size. In all his projects for industrial buildings Wachsmann was clear as to the role of the architect. As he said, "It will be the task of the universal planner to combine the requisite technological components by a creative act into a complete whole. The universal planner becomes part of the creative team, combining prefabricated parts and planning with them in the widest sense."

After resigning from the General Panel Corporation in 1949, Wachsmann became a teacher at the Illinois Institute of Technology in Chicago for the next fifteen years, during which time he continued to design buildings and to collaborate on various projects; he was also able to pursue his research on town and country planning in the United States in the form of team-work with his students. With the support of the government, he toured throughout the world to discuss his ideas on contemporary architecture and the manufacture of industrialized building elements, hosting seminars at colleges and universities in Japan, Israel, Austria, and Germany.

In 1964, after joining the faculty of the University of Southern California as Professor of Architecture, he organized its Graduate School of Architecture and inaugurated the Doctor of Building Science degree at its Building Institute. Although he retired in 1971, Wachsmann remained active as a lecturer, seminar leader, and teacher until the day before his death.   E.S.

Emigrated to U.S. 1941; naturalized American 1946. Educ: Arts and Crafts Sch., Berlin and Dresden; Acad. of Art, Berlin. Architect, Germany and Italy 1925–41; Co-founder (with Walter Gropius) and technical dir., General Panel Corp., N.Y. and Calif. 1941–1949; Prof. of Design and Dir., Dept. of Advanced Building Research, Illinois Inst. of Technology, Chicago 1949–64. Univ. of Southern Calif., Los Angeles: Prof. of Architecture, Dir. of Building Research Div., and Chmn. of the Graduate Program on Industrialization 1964–73; Prof. Emeritus since 1973. Hons: Rome Prize, German Acad. in Rome 1932. *Architect:* Rance River Bridge (project), France 1925; standardized panel system for prefabricated housing 1925; prefabricated hotel, Curacao, West Indies 1926; prefabricated tennis court pavilion, Berlin 1927; Albert Einstein Country House, Caputh, near Potsdam, Germ. 1928; Advertising Tower, Intnl. Building Exhibition, Berlin 1931; covered market (project), Rome 1935; office building and recreational complex, Rome 1936; (with Walter Gropius) leisure center (project), Key West, Fla. 1940; (with Walter Gropius) General Panel Corp. Building System 1942; (with Walter Gropius) convalescent home (project), Key West, Fla. 1942; factory, Burbank, Calif. 1945–47; (with Serge Chermayeff) Mobilar Structure Building System Studio, N.Y. 1946; Marshall House, 6643 Lindenhurst, Los Angeles 1948; General Panel House, 2861 Nichols Canyon, Los Angeles 1950; (with Mies van der Rohe) Convention Center (project), Chicago 1954; plan for the center and harbor of Genoa 1961; Italsider Headquarters, Genoa 1963; City Hall, California City 1966. *Exhibitions:* Mobilar Structure, Mus. of Modern Art, NYC 1946; Mus. of Science and Industry, Chicago 1973. *Author: Books*—Holzhausbau: Tecnik und Gestaltung, Berlin 1931; Wendepunkt im Bauen, Wiesbaden 1959, English trans. by Thomas E. Burton as The Turning Point in Building: Structure and Design, 1961; Aspekte (photographs), 1961. *Articles*— "Mobilar Structures," Pencil Points, N.Y., Mar. 1946; "Ein Konstruktionssystem für Hallenbauten," Baukunst und Werkform, Nuremberg, #9, 1954; "Building in Our Time," Architectural Association Journal, London, Apr. 1957; "Das Stadium in Team," Bauen und Wohnen, Zurich, Oct. 1960; "Concetti di Architettura," Casabella, Milan, Oct. 1960; "Research: The Mother of Invention," Arts and Architecture, Los Angeles, Apr. 1967; interview with Walter Menzies, Building Design, London, Aug. 6, 1976.

RACHEL ROBERTS
Actress
Born Llanelly, Wales, September 29th, 1927
Died Los Angeles, California, U.S.A., November 26th, 1980

Rachel Roberts, a versatile dramatic and comic actress, was perhaps best known for her work with the directors of the Free Cinema movement, who made strongly realistic films of working-class life. Roberts, whose father and grandfather were both Baptist ministers, was born in Llanelly, Wales, in 1927 and brought up in strict Baptist tradition. After studying at the University of Wales and the Royal Academy of Dramatic Art, she became a repertory player, appearing variously in musicals, revues, and Shakespearean dramas. In 1956 she spent a season as a leading actress at the Bristol Old Vic and a few years later starred as the villainess of Michael Gilbert's *A Clean Kill*.

In 1960, Roberts, who had already appeared in four films, won the

Courtesy International Creative Management

Best Actress Award from the British Film Academy for her performance as a bored married woman who becomes pregnant by a rebellious young factory worker in *Saturday Night and Sunday Morning,* Karl Reisz's drama of working-class Lancashire. She won the award again in 1963 for *This Sporting Life,* the story of a violent, ambitious rugby player who starts an affair with his unhappy landlady. "As the driven widow with two children," wrote A.H. Weiler in the *New York Times,* "Rachel Roberts . . . contributes a striking delineation of a fading woman torn between the memory of happiness and a yearning for marriage and a love she cannot give." Lindsay Anderson, who directed the film, cast her again as a lascivious businesswoman in *O Lucky Man!* in 1973.

Roberts and her first husband, Alan Dobie, were divorced in 1960. Two years later she became the fourth wife of actor Rex Harrison, with whom she had starred in *Platonov* on the London stage. Harrison was a celebrity, twenty years older than Roberts, and her own career went into eclipse; her few stage credits during the 1960s included *August for the People* (in which Harrison also starred) and the musical *Maggie May.* "I used to be a very good actress," she recalled. "Then I married Rex Harrison and got lost. I just ceased to exist."

They were divorced in 1971, but Roberts, still known as the "ex-Mrs. Harrison," had great difficulty in re-establishing herself as an actress in England. Her career remained in a backwater until she went to Hollywood to make *Doctors' Wives.* During the 1970s she was seen in *Murder on the Orient Express, Foul Play, When a Stranger Calls,* and *Picnic at Hanging Rock,* for which she won the best actress award at the Asian Film Festival. She played a trouble-shooting housekeeper on CBS-TV's *The Tony Randall Show* from 1976 to 1978 and made two television dramas, *A Circle of Children* and *Great Expectations.*

In 1972 Roberts also appeared with Albert Finney, her co-star in *Saturday Night and Sunday Morning,* in the acclaimed play *Alpha Beta,* earning the London Evening Standard's best actress award. Of the film version, made in 1973, Richard Eder wrote in the *New York Times:* "Mr. Finney is wrath, anguish, hesitancy and charm in one spunky, seedy package. Miss Roberts is even better. She makes classic tragedy out of this row-house misery." She played in *Once a Catholic* in 1979 and received the British Academy's Best Actress Award for her role as the dying mother in John Schlesinger's film *Yanks* in 1980.

Roberts was found dead in the garden of her home in West Los Angeles. The death was initially attributed to lye or acid poisoning. The Los Angeles coroner later ruled that she had committed suicide by acute barbiturate intoxication.   J.P./J.N.

Daughter of Richard Rhys R., Baptist minister, and Rachel Ann R. Married: (1) Alan Dobie, actor, 1955 (div. 1960); (2) Rex Harrison, actor, 1962 (div. 1971). No children. Raised a Baptist. Educ: Univ. of Wales, B.A.; Royal Acad. of Dramatic Art, London. Stage, screen, and television actress since 1951, with Old Vic Repertory company 1954; with Bristol Old Vic Repertory Company 1956–57. Hons: British Academy Awards for best actress 1960 (for Saturday Night and Sunday Morning) and 1963 (for This Sporting Life), for best supporting actress 1980 (for Yanks); Clarence Derwent Award for best supporting stage actress (for Platonov) 1960; Academy Award nomination for best actress (for This Sporting Life) 1963; Best Actress

Golden Crown Plaque, Asia Film Festival (for Picnic at Hanging Rock) 1972; Best Actress Award, London Evening Standard (for Alpha Beta) 1972; Athene Seyler Award for Comedy, Royal Acad. of Dramatic Arts. *Performances: Stage*—The Tempest (Ceres), Stratford-upon-Avon 1953; The Buccaneer (Mrs. Winterton), 1953; At the Lyric, later called Going to Town, London 1954; Macbeth (First Witch), London 1954; Othello (Bianca), London 1954; Henry IV, Parts I and II (Mistress Quickly), London 1954; Henvy V (Alice), 1954; Troilus and Cressida, London 1956; Oh My Papa (Iduna), Bristol 1956; The Recruiting Officer (Melinda), Bristol 1956; The Queen and the Rebels (Argia), Bristol 1957; The Sleeping Beauty (Prince Florizel), Bristol 1957; The Dutch Courtesan (Mary Faugh), 1958; A Clean Kill (Ann Patten), London 1959; The Happy Haven (Mrs. Letouzel), 1960; Platonov (Anna Petrovna), London 1960; August for the People (Mrs. Fulton), Edinburgh 1960; Maggie May (title role), London 1961; The Three Musketeers Ride Again (Madame de Winter), 1969; Who's Afraid of Virginia Woolf, London; The Effect of Gamma Rays on Man-in-the-Moon Marigolds (Beatrice), Los Angeles 1971; Alpha Beta (Mrs. Elliot), London 1972; The Visit, New York 1973; Chemin de Fer, New York 1973; The End of Me Old Cigar (Lady Regine), Greenwich, England 1975; Once a Catholic, NYC 1979. *Films*—Valley of Song, 1952; The Weak and the Wicked, 1954; The Good Companions, 1957; Our Man in Havana, 1959; Saturday Night and Sunday Morning (Brenda), 1962; Girl on Approval, 1962; This Sporting Life (Mrs. Hammond), 1963; A Flea in Her Ear (Suzanne), 1968; The Reckoning, 1969; Doctors' Wives, 1971; The Wild Rovers, 1971; O Lucky Man!, 1973; Alpha Beta (Mrs. Elliot), 1973; The Belstone Fox, 1973; Murder on the Orient Express, 1974; Picnic at Hanging Rock, 1976; Foul Play, 1978; When A Stranger Calls, 1979; Yanks, 1980. *Television*—The Young Yvette (Yvette Guilbert); Our Mutual Friend (Lizzie Hexam); Release (Catherine Bailey); Jonathan North; Circus; Time; Sunday Out of Season; Shadow Squad; Great Expectations, 1974; A Circle of Children, 1977; The Tony Randall Show, 1976–78.

JOHN HUBBARD
Theoretical physicist and applied mathematician
Born Teddington, Middlesex, England, 1931
Died California, U.S.A., November 27th, 1980

John Hubbard, a specialist in the atomic theory of metals, attended the Imperial College of London, where he won First Class Honors on a Royal Scholarship and earned his doctorate in mathematics. His thesis outlined a new theoretical model of the behavior of electrons in common metals (the "dialectric approach"). This research formed the basis for his subsequent work in physics, in which he produced elegant solutions to problems ranging from the characteristics of the transition metals such as iron, copper, and silver to practical applications of high-energy plasma physics.

Hubbard joined the Theoretical Physics Division of the Atomic Energy Research Establishment at Harwell in 1955, becoming leader of the Solid State Physics Group and then Deputy Chief Scientific Officer. His research was divided between fundamental and applied areas. Apart from his continuing investigation of metals, he studied neutron-scattering from a variety of liquids and solids, and magnetic and liquid thermodynamics. In applied research, Hubbard developed techniques for isotope separation by centrifuge and tested plasmas for use in fusion reactors. From 1963 to 1966 he presented a well-received series of papers in the *Proceedings of the Royal Society* on magnetic electrons in the transition metals.

Hubbard moved with his wife and three children to California in 1976 to join the IBM Research Laboratory at San Jose, where he studied quasi-one-dimensional systems—thin films of matter—and solved some persistent theoretical difficulties in the description of magnetism in iron. Hubbard died on November 27 after a short illness.   N.S.

Married. Children: two sons, one daughter. Educ: Hampton Grammar Sch.; Imperial Coll., London (Royal Scholar), bachelor's degree (First Class Hons.) 1953, Ph.D. in mathematics ca. 1955. With Theoretical Physics Div., Atomic Energy Research Establishment, Harwell, England: joined 1955; leader, Solid State Physics Group 1961; Deputy Chief Scientific Officer. With staff of Research Laboratory, IBM, San Jose, Calif. since 1976. *Major articles:* series of papers in Proceedings of the Royal Society, 1963–66; contributor to professional jrnls.

LORD BALLANTRAE
Soldier and author; Governor General of New Zealand
Born London, England, May 6th, 1911
Died London, England, November 28th, 1980

The noted military careerist and author Bernard Edward Fergusson who was made a peer—Baron Ballantrae of Auchairne and the Bay of Islands in 1972—was the younger son of General Sir Charles Fergusson, Seventh Baronet of Kilkerran. After attending Eton and the Royal Military College at Sandhurst, Fergusson joined the famous Highlanders—the Black Watch—in 1931, having received from the regiment a dispensation because he did not have the annual independent income of 250 required of officers. Although often financially pressed, Fergusson considered membership in the prestigious regiment more than ample recompense. He once summed up his devotion to duty, using the words of his mentor, General A.P. Wavell: "Never forget, the Regiment is the foundation of everything."

Fergusson first served with Wavell, an old Black Watch officer, in 1935 as the General's aide-de-camp, an assignment he called "the greatest stroke of luck that ever befell me." The cultured and articulate Wavell oversaw Fergusson's military apprenticeship and also encouraged his young protégé to become a writer. Fergusson responded by publishing a total of 14 books—history, biography, verse, and fiction—the first of which, *Eton Portrait*, was brought out at the end of his first tour with Wavell in 1937.

Fergusson next spent a year as an Intelligence Officer in Palestine, matching wits with anti-British elements militarily active in the region during the 1930s. He was reassigned to instructional duty at Sandhurst in 1938, serving with reluctance as a teacher of French to cadets until the outbreak of war and assignment to the 46th Infantry as Brigade Major. Posted first to Anglia with the invasion defense forces, he was transferred upon disappearance of the immediate German threat, to the London staff of the Home Forces Command where his duties, he complained to his chief, could have been done by a "one-legged major." Challenged to find such an officer, Fergusson did exactly that, and for his enterprise was ordered to Turkey in 1941 as part of the British Liaison Staff stationed in the-then neutral country. When Greece fell to the Nazis, he was sent to Cairo to rejoin Wavell, then heading the campaign against the Vichy forces in Syria and Lebanon. After Wavell, who had fallen from favor with Churchill, was reassigned to India, Fergusson begged his chief to return him to his old Battalion, then stationed at Tobruk. Wavell complied, and from Tobruk Fergusson was dispatched in October, 1942 to the command of "irregular" warfare specialist Orde Wingate, an old Palestine hand, for service in Burma.

Fergusson spent the next two years under Wingate, taking part in two of the most notable commando operations of the Asian war—campaigns which he later described in two books, *Beyond the Chindwin* (1945) and *The Wild Green Earth* (1946). In the first of these expeditions behind Japanese lines, Fergusson led a column of 318 men across the Chindwin River. Only 95 returned from the operation, which he later called the "spiritual watershed" of his life. After Wingate's death, he left Burma; referring to Fergusson, the Anglophobic American General "Vinegar Joe" Stilwell once wrote, "He looks like a dude, but I think he's a soldier."

Before his second tour of duty in Palestine, Fergusson spent the remainder of the war in routine staff duties and conducting an unsuccessful campaign for Parliament. Offered the job of heading anti-terrorist activities for the Palestine Police in 1946, he accepted on the condition that, after a two-year tour, he would return to his Regiment as Battalion commander. Although he expected a "thankless and tricky job," he did not anticipate the intensity of postwar Zionist fervor. In addition to anti-British hostility among Jews and Arabs, Fergusson's task was further complicated by intra-force suspicion of him as an outsider and army officer.

These difficulties were heightened by the Roy Farrand case in which a British officer under his command was accused of murdering a Jew suspected of terrorism. Torn between support for a subordinate and the need to avoid the appearance of partiality, Fergusson failed to act at all, losing the respect of both superiors and subordinates. Forced to resign, he later reflected that "far from doing any good, I had inadvertently done great harm." He assumed the promised Battalion Colonelcy in 1948, but only after pressure was applied to the Regimental command to ignore the Farrand affair.

The remainder of Fergusson's military career was spent in the Regiment in Europe and with the Territorial Army in Scotland, except for a brief stint as an intelligence officer during the 1956 Suez Crisis—where the performance of his section was, he admitted, "ludicrously bad." In 1958, having failed to win promotion to General, he retired to concentrate on a writing career. In 1962, however, he received a knighthood and was appointed Governor General of New Zealand, an office held by his father and grandfather before him. He occupied the post until 1967.   R.C.

Son of Gen. Sir Charles F., 7th Baronet of Kilkerran, and Lady Alice
Boyle F. Married Laura Margaret Grenfell 1950 (d. 1979). Son:
George Duncan, b. 1955. Church of Scotland. Educ: Eton; Royal Mil.
Coll., Sandhurst 1931; attended Staff Coll., Camberly 1940. Joined
Black Watch Regiment 1931; Lt. 1934; Aide-de-camp to Maj.-Gen.
A.P. Wavell, 2nd Div., Aldershot 1935–37; in Palestine 1937 (medal
and clasp); instr. in French, Royal Mil. Coll. 1938–39; Capt. 1939;
Brigade Maj., 46th Infantry Brigade 1940; Wavell's staff, Cairo and
New Delhi 1941–42; joined 1st Battalion, Black Watch, Tobruk 1942;
with Wingate's Burmese Expeditionary forces 1942–44 (DSO 1943);
Dir., Combined Mil. Operations, London 1945–46; Asst. Inspector-
Gen., Palestine Police 1946–47; comdr., 1st Battalion, Black Watch
1948–51; Col. of Intelligence, Supreme Headquarters, Allied Powers,
Europe 1951–53; Comdr., 156th Highland Brigade, Territorial Army
1955–56; Intelligence Officer, Allied Headquarters, Port Said Opera-
tions 1956; Comdr., 29th Infantry Brigade 1957–59; retired as Brig.
1958. Appointed Gov.-Gen. and Comdr.-in-Chief, N.Z. 1962–67;
Member, Intnl. Observer Team, Nigeria 1968–69; Chmn., London
Bd., Bank of New Zealand since 1968; Member, Cttee. to Review
1952 Defamation Act 1971–74; Chmn., Scottish Trust for the Phys-
ically Disabled since 1971; Chmn., British Council 1972–76; Lord
High Comnr. to Gen. Assembly, Church of Scotland 1973–74;
Chancellor, Univ. of St. Andrews, Scotland since 1973. Hons: OBE
1950; GCMG 1962; GCVO 1963; DCL, Canterbury Univ. 1965;
D. Univ., Waikato (N.Z.) 1967; Hon. Col., Black Watch 1969–76;
LL.D., Strathclyde Univ. 1971; created Baron of Auchairne 1972;
LL.D., Dundee Univ. 1973; K.T. 1974; D.Litt., St. Andrews Univ.
1974; Registrar, Order of St. Michael and St. George 1979. *Author:*
Eton Portrait, 1937; Beyond the Chindwin, 1945; Lowland Soldier
(verse), 1945; The Wild Green Earth, 1946; The Black Watch and the
King's Enemies, 1950; Rupert of the Rhine, 1952; The Rare Adven-
ture (novel), 1954; The Watery Maze, 1961; Wavell: Portrait of a
Soldier, 1961; Return to Burma, 1962; The Trumpet in the Hall
(autobiog.), 1970; Captain John Niven, 1972; Hubble-Bubble (light
verse), 1978; Travel Warrant, 1979.

DOROTHY DAY
Roman Catholic journalist and social worker
Born Brooklyn, New York, U.S.A., November 8th, 1897
Died New York City, U.S.A., November 29th, 1980

Dorothy Day, founder of the Catholic Worker Movement, was a
major figure in American Catholicism. Both in her own actions on
behalf of the poor and through her influence on such activists as the
Berrigan brothers, she helped form the combination of religious faith
and social commitment which has gained wide acceptance among
contemporary Catholics.

The daughter of a journalist, Day grew up in a non-religious
Protestant home. After attending high school in Chicago, she entered
the University of Illinois at Urbana. There she became familiar with
the writings of Tolstoy, Upton Sinclair, the anarchist Peter Kropotkin
and others who aroused in her a strong sense of social justice. After
two years she left college to move with her family to New York, where
she entered a prolonged period of secular radicalism. She worked for

the socialist daily *The Call,* joined the militant Industrial Workers of the World and became acquainted with such left-wing writers as Max Eastman and Jon Reed. These friendships brought her to the staff of the radical journal *The Masses* and its successor, the *Liberator,* both suppressed for opposing U.S. participation in World War One. Through the writer and activist Mike Gold, with whom she had an extended love affair, Day became part of the literary circle that centered on the Playwrights' Theater in Greenwich Village; here she spent much of her time in discussions with Eugene O'Neill and other aspiring writers. She also participated in pacifist and suffragette protests, incurring the first of her many arrests in 1918 for demonstrating in front of the White House.

During the influenza epidemic of 1918, Day worked as a nurse in Brooklyn. The postwar years were a time of uncertainty for her. She traveled briefly in Europe, loosened her ties with the radical movement and settled into a common-law marriage in New York. A change in her life came in 1927, with the birth of her daughter. Wishing to spare the child the "doubting, undisciplined and amoral" existence she felt she had led, she sought "the gift of faith." She soon had herself baptized in the Roman Catholic Church. The move meant a break with her husband, an uncompromising atheist, and with most of her radical friends. But she did not abandon her social conscience or her desire to help the poor.

At first, Day could reconcile her religious and social beliefs only by writing for the liberal Catholic journal *Commonweal.* But in December 1932 she met Peter Maurin, a French Catholic who advocated an activist program which he called the "Green Revolution." Maurin's ideas inspired Day's own concept of "personalism," which sought in social action the transformation of individuals rather than of economic or political relationships. On May Day 1933, the two collaborators published the first issue of the *Catholic Worker,* a monthly periodical that reached a peak circulation of 150,000 by 1936. When homeless victims of the Depression sought aid at the paper's New York office, Day and Maurin began creating a network of hospices or "hospitality houses" which provided free food and shelter for the destitute. They also sought to settle some of their charges in farming communes, two of which were established near New York.

When Maurin died in 1949, Day carried on by herself with publication of the *Catholic Worker* and management of the hospitality houses. She also became known for her outspoken—and frequently unpopular—stands on current issues. She contradicted widespread Catholic support for Franco in the Spanish Civil War, advocated draft resistance during World War Two and later demonstrated frequently against nuclear armaments. In 1949 she supported a strike of undertakers against the Catholic archdiocese of New York. More recently, her consistent pacifism made her a vigorous opponent of the Vietnam war, and her support for labor causes ensured her participation in Cesar Chavez's efforts to unionize California farm workers. Among the organizations which she influenced or helped establish were the Association of Catholic Trade Unionists and the Association of Catholic Conscientious Objectors.

Day's political positions frequently offended such conservative Church leaders as Cardinal Spellman of New York and Cardinal McIntyre of Los Angeles. Yet she always managed to avoid being

censured or ordered to halt her activities, largely because of her
respect for ecclesiastical authority. "There are many ways to handle a
Cardinal," she once quipped. She never challenged official Catholic
dogma or mingled in theological debates, which she saw as wasteful in
view of the practical work to be done. Her combination of social
radicalism and doctrinal conservatism puzzled many middle-class U.S.
Catholics, who tended to reverse the mixture. But leftists in the
Church, including Trappist philosopher Thomas Merton and the
activist priests Philip and Daniel Berrigan, respected her motives and
drew courage from her example.

Day spent her last years at Maryhouse, a Catholic Worker hospice
on New York's Lower East Side. Her funeral, held in the destitute
surroundings in which she had spent her life, attracted such diverse
figures as Cardinal Cooke of New York, Abbie Hoffman, Cesar
Chavez and sociologist Michael Harrington.   S.L.G.

Daughter of John D. and Grace Satterlee D. Married Forster
Batterham. Daughter: Tamar Teresa Hennessy. Episcopal, later
Roman Catholic. Educ: Univ. of Illinois, Urbana 1914–1916. Re-
porter, The Call 1916–1917; staff member of The Masses 1917 and of
Liberator 1918, 1921; probationary nurse, Kings County Hosp.,
Brooklyn 1918–1919; feature writer, New Orleans Item 1922; script
writer, Pathe Films, Hollywood, Calif.; writer, Commonweal Maga-
zine 1932; co-founder and publisher (with Peter Maurin), The
Catholic Worker 1933; co-founder (with Peter Maurin), numerous
hospices and farms for homeless poor, since 1933. Hons: Laetare
Medal, Notre Dame Univ. 1971; Melcher Book Award 1972. *Author:*
From Union Square to Rome, 1938; House of Hospitality, 1939; On
Pilgrimage, 1948; The Long Loneliness, 1952; Therese, 1960; Loaves
and Fishes, 1963; On Pilgrimage: The Sixties, 1972. *Interview:* with
Colman McCarthy in the New Republic, 168, Feb. 24, 1973.
Further reading: Dorothy Day and the Catholic Worker Movement:
symposium, in America, 127: 378, Nov. 11, 1972.

JOEL HURSTFIELD
Historian
Born November 4th, 1911
Died November 29th, 1980

Professor Joel Hurstfield, a noted authority on British history of the
Tudor period, was best known for his work on the emerging
institutions of the early modern state. Active in both Britain and the
U.S., he was an important link between the academic communities of
the two countries.

After earning his B.A. with First Class Honors at University
College, London, Hurstfield did two years of postgraduate study at
the University of London before becoming a lecturer at University
College, Southampton. His interest in the Tudor period was aroused
by his work under the eminent historian John Neale at the University
of London. But he also devoted much attention to contemporary
issues, and was about to embark on a political career when his plans
were interrupted by the outbreak of World War II. During the war he
served on the National Savings Committee and as official historian in

the Offices of the War Cabinet; in the latter position he contributed a volume to the official history of the war, *Control of Raw Materials* (1953).

In the postwar years, Hurstfield changed his plans and returned to academic life as a lecturer at Queen Mary College, London. In 1951 he joined the faculty of University College, London, where he remained for the rest of his career. He was named Astor Professor of English History in 1962 and one year later became a Fellow of the College. He also served intermittently as Dean of the Faculty of Arts and chairman of the History Department. In addition to his many duties at University College, he helped conduct the influential Tudor seminar at the Institute of Historical Research, where he counted among his colleagues Neale and Professor S.T. Bindoff [q.v.].

Hurstfield's connection with the U.S. began in 1934, when he visited the country as a member of Britain's University Debating Team. In addition to frequent lecture trips, he lived in Washington in 1973 as Senior Research Fellow at the Folger Shakespeare Library. Four years later he was named Senior Research Fellow at the Huntington Library in California, a position he retained after his retirement from University College in 1979.

Hurstfield's published work covered a broad expanse of Tudor studies, including the period's literature and regional history. But he devoted much of his attention to previously obscure government institutions, foremost among them the Court of Wards. This body, responsible for administering property inherited by minors, was described by Hurstfield in *The Queen's Wards* (1958). The Court was unpopular even in its own time for selling wardships to private individuals, who frequently exploited the property of their charges and married them off for profit. Hurstfield acknowledged the corruption of this practice, but pointed out that it fulfilled functions dictated by the weakness of the early modern state; under-the-table payments supplemented the inadequate salaries of government officials, and the institution of wardship provided an indirect means of taxing the otherwise unreachable landed classes. Hurstfield returned to the theme of "legitimate" corruption in *Freedom, Corruption and Government in Elizabethan England* (1973), a collection of previously published articles. Here he argued that such corrupt practices as tax-farming appeared at points of "fundamental weakness" in government, where the state's ambitions exceeded its power. Modern criticism of Tudor-era corruption is often anachronistic, Hurstfield contended, because it relies on values formed under the influence of a strong and centralized state.

Also notable among Hurstfield's works was *Elizabeth I and the Unity of England* (1960), a balanced biographical study of the Tudor queen. The volume praised Elizabeth's flexibility and pragmatism as major influences in preserving national unity, but viewed the end of her reign as a time of stagnation and dissolution. Hurstfield concluded that Elizabeth controlled political opposition in the country but left many problems to her unfortunate successors.   S.L.G.

Married Elizabeth Valmai Walters. One daughter; one son. Educ: Owen's Sch., Manchester; University Coll., London, B.A.; postgrad. studentship, Univ. of London 1935–36. Asst. Lectr. and Lectr., University Coll., Southampton 1937–40; Asst. Commnr., Natl. Savings Cttee. 1940–42; Official Historian, Offices of the War Cabinet 1942–46; Lectr., Queen Mary Coll., London 1946–51. With University Coll., London: Lectr. 1951–53; Reader in Modern History 1953–59; Prof. of Modern History 1959–62; Fellow 1963–69; Hon. Resident Fellow 1979–80. James Ford Special Lectr. in History, Oxford Univ. 1972; Senior Research Fellow, Folger Shakespeare Library 1973; John Coffin Memorial Lectr., Univ. of London 1974; Andrew Mellon Senior Research Fellow, Huntington Library 1977–78; A.H. Dodd Memorial Lectr., University Coll., Bangor 1978; Creighton Lectr., Univ. of London 1978. Hons: Pollard and Gladstone prizes, University Coll., London. *Author:* Control of Raw Materials, 1953; The Queens' Wards, 1958; Elizabeth I and the Unity of England, 1960; (jt. ed.) Elizabethan Government and Society, 1961; Tudor Times (English History in Pictures), 1964; The Elizabethan Nation, 1964; (jt. ed.) Shakespeare's World, 1964; (ed.) The Reformation Crisis, 1965; (jt. ed.) Elizabethan People: State and Society, 1972; Freedom, Corruption and Government in Elizabethan England, 1973; (ed.) Historical Association Book of the Tudors, 1973; The Historian as Moralist; Reflections on the Study of Tudor England, 1975; The Illusion of Power in Tudor Politics, 1980; Man as a Prisoner of his Past: The Elizabethan Experience, 1980.

ELIZABETH SHOUMATOFF
Portraitist
Born Kharkov, Russia, 1888
Died Glen Cove, New York, U.S.A., November 30th, 1980

Well known for her more than 3000 portraits, Elizabeth Shoumatoff was born of an aristocratic Russian family in the late nineteenth century and immigrated to the United States after the October Revolution of 1917. Her most famous paintings are studies of her adopted country's very rich, including duPonts, Fords, Mellons, and Rockefellers, and very powerful, including Presidents Franklin D. Roosevelt and Lyndon B. Johnson.

The daughter of a Russian general, Elizabeth Avinoff was raised in the family's Ukrainian mansion which housed a valuable collection of classical paintings assembled by her grandfather, who had been a page in the court of Catherine the Great. Although much of her youth was spent traveling with her father from one Army post to another throughout Russia, Elizabeth first studied art under the tutelage of an English governess in Samarkand. She then took up painting as an avocation and received more advanced training in St. Petersburg, Kiev, and Moscow.

In 1917, Elizabeth accompanied her husband, Leo Shoumatoff, to the United States, where he had been sent to purchase arms for the faltering Kerensky regime. When the government fell to the Bolsheviks later that year, the Shoumatoffs settled in prosperous Orange County, New York. Following her husband's death in a 1928 drowning accident, Elizabeth Shoumatoff painted her first commissioned portrait for George Innes, Jr., a fellow artist; the work was well received and she soon found herself flooded with offers from the wealthy patrons of Yama Farms, an inn for summer residents of Napponock, New York, located near her home. Shoumatoff's reputation as a first-rate portraitist who worked very quickly was soon established. A typical sitting began with a rapidly executed watercolor sketch followed by a full-sized oil painting which, finished in approximately three weeks, was based on a few sittings for the expression and several photographs which were taken for the pose. So that her subjects might appear "at their absolute best," she usually painted their eyes first; to portray children, Shoumatoff would rivet their attention with stories which she invented as she painted.

In 1945, Shoumatoff, who had earlier painted a small portrait of President Franklin D. Roosevelt, was asked by Lucy Rutherford, a mutual friend, to do a larger one. She traveled to the presidential retreat at Warm Springs, Georgia and, on April 12, while sitting for his portrait, Roosevelt suddenly slumped forward in his chair; he died later that day of a cerebral hemorrhage. Shoumatoff later recalled that, originally, she had not been an admirer of F.D.R. and was unexcited by the prospect of painting him. "But as soon as I began painting his portrait," she explained, "I fell completely under his charm." Indeed, her second, unfinished painting is a frontal study of the President's face and upper torso and, like much "official" art, it is a skillful, but highly idealized likeness; the face reflects little of the war-weary haggardness so evident in photographs of Roosevelt taken during his last months. The portrait was first exhibited in Gimbel's Department Store in New York City on July 23, 1945. Years later, Shoumatoff donated the painting to the Presidential memorial at Warm Springs.

Also impressed by Shoumatoff's work was President Lyndon B. Johnson, who hung her earlier portrait of Roosevelt in his White House office. In 1967, after he had rejected an official portrait by Peter Hurd as "the ugliest thing I've ever seen," Johnson himself sat for Shoumatoff. Johnson announced that he was "very pleased" with her likeness and Shoumatoff was commissioned to do portraits of his wife, Lady Bird, and their two daughters. Her painting was reproduced on the Johnson commemorative postage stamp issued after the former president's death in 1973.

Another widely admired work by Shoumatoff was the portrait of her brother, Andrey Avinoff, who served as Director Emeritus of the Carnegie Museum. The portrait was purchased by the Carnegie Institute and hung in the museum office. At the time of her death, Shoumatoff had lived and worked for over six decades in Locust Valley on New York's Long Island.   A.D.

Daughter of a Russian gen. Married Leo Shoumatoff (d. 1928). Immigrated to U.S. 1917. Portrait artist from 1928. *Portraits:* George Innes Jr.; Franklin D. Roosevelt; Lyndon B. Johnson; Lady Bird Johnson; Andrey Avinoff; members of the duPont, Mellon, Ford and Rockefeller families; many others.

DECEMBER

CHAUDHRI MOHAMAD ALI
Prime Minister of Pakistan
Born Jullundur, Punjab, India, July 15th, 1905
Died Karachi, Sind, Pakistan, December 1st, 1980

In its first decade as an independent state, Pakistan faced staggering geographic, economic and religious problems. It fell to Chaudhri Mohamad Ali, a career civil servant in British-ruled India, to put the country on a reasonably firm financial footing in the early 1950s. During his tenure as prime minister he also implemented the constitutional arrangement that bears his name: the Mohamad Ali formula, providing for parliamentary parity between East and West Pakistan. The consequences of this system would be felt only in the 1970s, when regional conflict tore the state apart.

Born in the Punjab, Mohamad Ali grew up in the village life of turn-of-the-century Muslim India. After adopting the tribal name of Chaudhri, he settled in the major city of the Punjab, Lahore, where he attended Punjab University. After graduating in 1927 he began to teach chemistry at Islamia College in Lahore.

Mohamad Ali's career changed sharply the next year, when he joined the colonial civil service. Between 1928 and 1947 he served in increasingly important government posts, as his ability to handle financial and accounting matters established his reputation as a bureaucrat. In 1936 he was appointed private secretary to India's Finance Minister, Sir James Grigg. He then assumed a higher post in the Finance Department in 1938, moved to the Department of Supply and, by 1945, had become Financial Adviser of War and Supply.

Mohamad Ali was a career bureaucrat rather than a politician. Nevertheless, by the mid-1940s he had gained special prominence as one of India's leading Muslim government officials. Non-Muslims had generally been more active in pressing for independence; as a result, members of the Muslim Pakistan Movement turned to Mohamad Ali for administrative leadership as independence neared. He became a member of the steering committee of the Partition Council that set the terms for the division of India. When Pakistan became a self-governing dominion following partition in 1947, Mohamad Ali was named secretary-general, in which position he supervised the execution of ministerial policy.

In 1951 Mohamad Ali entered the cabinet as Finance Minister. Partition had created an independent Muslim state, but its economic viability remained in doubt. The country included disparate groups of Indians whose only common bond was religion; its two sections were separated by a thousand miles of Indian territory. Moreover, partition had effectively deprived Pakistan of an industrial base and much of its economic infrastructure. Mohamad Ali embarked upon an extensive program of industrial development, and between 1950 and 1955 factory production increased nearly threefold. In order to finance Pakistan's industrialization, Mohamad Ali imposed import controls to limit the outflow of foreign exchange. He also worked closely with the

International Bank for Reconstruction and Development (IBRD) and
the International Monetary Fund (IMF) to gain support for his
industrial projects. He initiated state action to establish new industries, then turned them over to the private sector. In 1953 he chaired
the board of governors of both the IBRD and the IMF.

The success of his economic policies soon thrust Mohamad Ali into
the political limelight. In August 1955 he was chosen president of the
Muslim League party, the leading Muslim party in West Pakistan, and
formed a coalition government in which he served as prime minister
and minister of defense. As head of government he pressed for strong
ties with the West. He participated in the conference at which a
mutual-defense agreement, known as the Baghdad Pact, was concluded among Great Britain, Iraq, Turkey, and Pakistan. He also
concluded an agreement with India, normalizing trading arrangements.

Finally, in 1956, Pakistan abandoned its status as a British dominion
and adopted a new constitution. Mohamad Ali supported a formula
that nominally balanced political power between west and east. In
fact, the consolidation of the western provinces into one unit strengthened the political power of the Punjab and threatened the integrity of
tribes, such as the Baluchis, who roamed across an unstable border
with Afghanistan. The more populous east was underrepresented in
terms of the size of its population.

In the short run, the problems posed by the constitution were
overshadowed by political squabbling among members of the dominant Muslim League party. In September 1956 Mohamad Ali fell from
power as his support in the party dwindled. Two years later General
Ayub Khan seized power, setting aside the constitution altogether.
Mohamad Ali opposed Khan's dictatorship and campaigned against
him in the presidential election of 1965.

In 1967 Mohamad Ali's book *The Emergence of Pakistan* criticizing
the way in which the Indian subcontinent had been divided, was
published. During the 1970s he remained out of view. Often in bad
health in this period, he died in Karachi in December 1980.   M.T.

Son of Chaudhri Khair-ud-din and Ayesha. Married Razia Sultana
1931. Children: four sons, one daughter. Muslim. Educ.: Univ.
Punjab, Lahore, M.Sc. 1927. Lectr. in chemistry, Islamia Coll.,
Lahore 1927–28. Joined Indian Accounts and Audit Service 1928;
Accountant-Gen. Bahawalpur state 1932–36. With Govt. of India:
private secty. to Finance Minister 1936; Under-Secty. Finance Dept.
1938–39; Deputy Financial Adviser 1939–43; Joint Financial Adviser,
Ministry of Supply 1943–45; Financial Adviser War and Supply
1945–47. Member, Lend-Lease Mission 1946. Member, Steering
Cttee. Partition Council 1947; Sect.-Gen. to Govt. of Pakistan
1947–51. Entered Pakistani cabinet: Minister of Finance 1951; Minister of Finance and Econ. Affairs 1954–55. Entered Pakistani electoral
politics: member, Constituent Assembly 1955; Prime Minister and
Defense Minister 1955–56. Leader Nizam-E-Islam Party. Active in
Intnl. Bank for Reconstruction and Devel.: chmn., Bd. of Govs. 1953;
chmn., Bd. of Govs., Intnl. Monetary Fund 1953. *Author:* The
Emergence of Pakistan, 1967.

ROMAIN GARY
Novelist
Born Tbilisi, Georgia, Russia, May 8th, 1914
Died Paris, France, December 2nd, 1980

The suffering that human beings delight in inflicting on each other was the main theme of Romain Gary's fiction, mixed with a black humor born of his own experiences in World War II. "Literary creation," he said, "became for me a matter of survival, a necessity like air and bread, the only escape from the helplessness and infirmity of being human, a manner of yielding up the soul so as to remain alive."

Gary was born Roman Kacewgary in Tbilisi, Russia, in 1914, to parents of Jewish and Tartar stock. His father left the family while he was still a young child; Gary saw him occasionally and later found out that he had died of a heart attack as he was being led to the gas chambers of a Nazi concentration camp. He was raised by his mother, a former actress of extraordinary courage and an equally extraordinary capacity for self-delusion, who devoted her life to helping her adored son realize the greatness that was, she insisted, his destiny. From the time he was eight, when they were living in poverty in Vilna, Poland, she began grooming him to become an Ambassador of France, a country she imagined as "a world of Viennese waltzes and gypsy music, horsemen, camellias, whispers at dawn and tears by candlelight," where diplomats drank champagne, fought duels of honor, and seduced beautiful women in the line of duty. Instead of going to school, Gary had private tutors and took lessons in shooting, fencing, riding and deportment, while Madame Kacew ran a hat and dress business that barely squeaked by on the strength of forged Parisian labels. She was also determined that he would be a great artist of some kind; he took up writing after failing as a violinist and an actor. He was also expected to fight anyone who insulted her and to endure constant humiliation while she boasted about his assured future to everyone she met. "I had always known," he wrote in his autobiography *Promise at Dawn,* "that my mission on earth was one of retribution; that I existed, as it were, only by proxy; that the mysterious force presiding over our destiny had cast me into the scale so as to balance, by the weight of achievement, my mother's life of toil, lovelessness and sacrifice . . . I always saw myself as *her* victory."

In 1927, Gary nearly died of a kidney inflammation and Mme. Kacew bankrupted her dressmaking business to pay for specialists to treat him. After several months in Warsaw, they settled in Nice, where Gary attended the lycée and Mme. Kacew scraped together a living persuading tourists to buy trinkets that she represented as family jewels smuggled out of revolutionary Russia. During this time she went without food in order to be able to serve Gary a beefsteak every day. Eventually she became the manager of a small hotel. Gary (who was ping-pong champion of Nice in his eighteenth year) moved to Aix-en-Provence to study law, supporting himself meantime with such odd jobs as waiter, dishwasher, deliveryman, and hotel clerk, and sold his first short story to a Paris newspaper. Following his mother's plan, he entered the Air Force Academy to train as a pilot, but was refused a commission because he was of foreign (and Jewish) birth and was made a gunnery instructor.

When France surrendered to the Germans in 1940, Gary escaped to England, joined the Free French Air Force, and was posted to Africa as a bomber in the Lorraine Squadron. Most of his friends were killed in combat; Gary himself was wounded three times, survived numerous crashes, nearly died of typhoid in Damascus, and won the Cross of the Liberation, the Croix de Guerre, and the Legion of Honor. During these harrowing years, his morale was boosted by a constant flow of letters from his mother. In 1945 he returned to Nice to discover that she had died three years before; the letters, all written in the months before her death, had been mailed at intervals by a friend, at her request.

By the war's end, Gary was a published novelist in two languages; his *A European Education,* a series of episodes in the lives of two young Parisian partisans, written between bombing patrols, came out in England in 1944 and in France a year later and won the *Prix de critiques.* It was, said an American critic, "a terrible parable for our times." Gary's next seven novels were written while he was a member of the French diplomatic service, which he had unexpectedly been invited to join in 1945. They included the much-praised *The Roots of Heaven,* about an inmate in a Nazi camp for whom freedom is symbolized by the elephant herds of Africa, and who eventually leads a guerilla army to defend the animals against hunters. The novel won the Prix Goncourt in 1958. Another novel, *Lady L,* and Gary's autobiography, *Promise at Dawn,* were later made into movies.

Gary left the Foreign Service in 1960, after five years as Consul-General in Los Angeles. He continued to write short stories, plays, and novels, of which the most notorious was *The Dance of Genghis Cohn,* a macabre tale about a former S.S. officer possessed by the spirit of a Jewish comedian who was one of his victims. As with most of his works, reaction was mixed. André Malraux called the book "one of the rare contributions of our time, both to mythology and to literature." A reviewer in *Newsweek* said: "Gary . . . plunges his brilliant verbal scalpel into the tenderest portions of the human condition and removes a slice of twentieth-century life that is witty, disturbing and, in part, tasteless." Gary also directed two films.

In 1963, Gary married the American actress Jean Seberg, with whom he had a son. He had previously been married to an English writer, and, according to his autobiography, to an African woman who had contracted leprosy; an earlier engagement to a Hungarian woman had been ended by the war. Most of his relationships with women were somewhat overshadowed by the single-minded devotion of his mother. "It is wrong to have been loved so much so young, so early," he wrote in 1959. "Wherever you go, you carry within you the poison of comparisons, and you spend your days waiting for something you have already had and will never have again."

Seberg and Gary, who lived during the 1960s in Hollywood, were attracted to leftist politics and became involved with the Black Panther movement. Eventually, Gary, who had been concerned with issues of social justice since his youth, decided that Hollywood's activists were "phony liberals," and satirized them, and American racism as well, in his 1970 novel *White Dog* (about his and Seberg's efforts to recondition a German Shepherd trained to attack black people). By then, however, the F.B.I. had decided to punish Seberg by planting a rumor in a gossip column that her unborn child had been fathered by a black activist. Seberg miscarried the child, went into a lasting depression, and tried to commit suicide on every anniversary of its death; in September of 1979, she died of a combination of barbiturates and alcohol. Her marriage to Gary had broken up some time before.

Gary, who once wrote that "the greatest effort of my life has always been the effort to give up, to attain despair, and so know peace, at last," died of a self-inflicted gunshot wound fifteen months later. J.P./
S.M.

Born Roman Kacew (originally Kacewgary, Kassevgari). Son of Leibja K. and Mina (Josel) K., actress, haberdasher, and hotel manager. Married: (1) Leslie Blanch, writer (div. 1963); (2) Jean Seberg, actress, 1963 (div.). Children: 2nd marriage—Diego. Jewish. Russian at birth; naturalized French. Educ: private tutors; Polish Sch. of Warsaw; Lycée de Nice; Univ. of Aix-en-Provence, license in law; Univ. of Paris; Univ. of Warsaw, diploma in Slavic languages. Mil. Service: French Air Force Acad. 1937; Instr. and Pilot, French Air Force 1937–40; bomber, Lorraine Squadron, Free French Air Force and RAF, Africa, Palestine, and France 1940–45; awarded Officier de la Legion d'honneur, Compagnon de la Liberation, Croix de guerre. Novelist since 1943. With French Foreign Service 1945–60: served at embassies in London, Bulgaria, and Switzerland; First Secty., French delegation to U.N.; Consul-Gen., Los Angeles 1956–60. Chargé de mission, Ministry of Information 1967–68. Hons: Prix des critiques (for Éducation européene) 1945; Prix Goncourt (for Les racines du ciel) 1956; Book-of-the-Month Club selection (The Gasp) 1973. *Books:* Éducation européene, 1945 (Forest of anger, UK 1949; A European Education, US 1960; Nothing Important Ever Dies, UK 1961); Tulipe, 1946; Le grand vestiaire, 1949 (The Company of Men, 1950); Les couleurs du jour, 1952 (The Colors of the Day, 1953); Les racines du ciel, 1956 (The Roots of Heaven, 1958); La promesse de l'aube, 1959 (Promise at Dawn, 1962); Madame L, 1959 (Lady L., 1959); The Talent Scout, 1961; Hissing Tales (short stories), 1964; The Ski Bum, 1965; Frère Océan, 1965; Pour Sganarelle, 1965; La Danse de Gengis Cohn, 1967 (The Dance of Genghis Cohn, 1968); La tête coupable, 1968 (The Guilty Head, 1969); Le mangeur d'étoiles, and Adieu Gary Cooper, 1969; Chien blanc, 1970 (The White Dog, 1970); Europa, 1972; Les enchanteurs, 1973; The Gasp, 1973; La nuit sera calme, and Les têtes de Stéphanie, 1974; Au delà de cette limite votre ticket n'est plus valable, 1975; (as René Deville) Direct Flight to Allah, 1975; The Way Out, 1977; Charge d'âme, 1978. *Plays:* Johnie Coeur; Gloire à nos illustres pionniers. *Film director:* Les oiseaux vont mourir au Pérou, 1968; Kill, 1971.
Further Reading: Religious Themes in Two Modern Novelists by T.R. Spivey, 1965; French Novelists Today by Henri Peyre, 1967.

LORD GORDON-WALKER OF LEYTON
British Labour Party politician, and cabinet minister
Born Worthing, Sussex, England, April 7th, 1907
Died London, England, December 2nd, 1980

Lord Gordon–Walker—former Labour Minister, Foreign Secretary, and Secretary of State for Foreign Affairs in Great Britain—was a man who rose above political controversy and played a significant role in the establishment of the social democratic policies for the Labour Party during the 1950s and 1960s. If Lord Gordon–Walker had a

reputation for stubbornness and aloofness among some members of
the government and a segment of the British public, he was nonetheless a politician whose loyalty to his party and refusal to resort to
demogoguery or self-serving policy made him in many ways unique.

Born Patrick Chrestien Gordon Walker in 1907 at Worthing,
Sussex, he was brought up in the Punjab where his father, a Fabian,
was a Scottish judge in the Indian Civil Service. Returning to England
for his education, Gordon Walker graduated from Wellington College
with a scholarship to Christ Church, Oxford where he wrote a well-
received thesis on the National Debt. A year of study spent at several
universities in Germany was a formative period in his life for, in
addition to becoming fluent in German, his close observation of the
German political situation gave him a strong dislike and suspicion of
both nazism and communism. He became a fervent supporter of the
cause of political refugees from Germany and throughout his life
remained in close contact with German socialists whose aims and
beliefs he shared.

In 1931, mainly because of the quality of his thesis, Gordon Walker
was elected a Student and History Tutor at Christ Church where, for
the next nine years, he taught, wrote, and was active in the University
Labour Party. While a don, he wrote two of his six books: *History of
Europe in the Sixteenth and Seventeenth Centuries* (1935) and *Outline
of Man's History* (1939). In 1935 he stood for Parliament for Oxford
City and although he was defeated, the Labour vote was increased. At
the start of the Second World War he joined the European Service of
the BBC and did important propaganda work, being especially
successful in gaining the trust of German workers whose situation he
understood well. After a short period as editor of Radio Luxembourg,
he was made assistant director of the German service.

In 1945 Gordon Walker went to the House of Commons, having
won a by-election at Smethwick, an industrial suburb of Birmingham.
Two years later he became Under Secretary of State for Commonwealth Relations and skillfully handled negotiations with India during
its first years as a republic, earning the respect of Nehru at this difficult
time. By 1950 he attained Cabinet rank as Secretary of State for
Commonwealth Relations and became a member of the Privy Council, soon facing his first major difficulty in his management of what
became known as the Seretse Khama affair. Gordon Walker defended
the government's refusal to recognize Seretse Khama, who had
married an English woman, as head of the Bamangwato tribe in South
Africa, maintaining that the government's position was for the well-
being of the tribe. His stand was an unpopular one. Because of his
unwavering policy on this volatile issue, he was accused of indulging in
an untimely obstinacy and suspected of being inordinately swayed by
South African opinion.

When the General Election of 1951 sent Gordon Walker and his
party into opposition, he became closely associated with the Labour
Party leader, Hugh Gaitskell, helping to consolidate Gaitskell's
strength in 1959 and supporting him against the unilateralists in 1960.
He also led the Labour Opposition to the Conservative government's
Commonwealth Immigration Bill of 1962 which restricted the immigration of primarily dark-skinned people to England, a record which
was to prove an insurmountable handicap with the public when he was
to come up for re-election to his seat at Smethwick. When he was

Courtesy Lady Gordon-Walker

offered the nomination for the leadership of the Labour Party, he declined, realizing that to accept would be to involve the party in a drawn-out ballot.

Although Gordon Walker had strongly disagreed with Harold Wilson's approach to the Labour Party during his close association with Gaitskell, Wilson appointed him "shadow" Foreign Secretary in 1963. The appointment was a popular one, since Gordon Walker was respected by his party members for his judiciousness and knowledge of defense matters. However, when he came up for re-election to Smethwick in October, 1964, he lost by 1774 votes, the only member of the Labour Shadow Cabinet to be defeated. The campaign, which Gordon Walker considered the "dirtiest" he could remember, had centered primarily around the immigration issue and had strong racist overtones. The slogan of the opposition was "If You Want A Nigger Neighbour, Vote Labour."

Despite this defeat, Wilson appointed him as Foreign Secretary and had him run, with his and the party's backing, for a traditionally secure seat in the by-election for Leyton so that he would have his necessary place in the Commons. When he lost this election as well, the blow to party morale and to Gordon Walker was heavy. Many factors were cited for the defeat, among them the racial issue and local Labour resentment at having an outside candidate forced on the constituency. Gordon Walker had no alternative. In a dignified manner that gained him considerable respect and admiration he quietly resigned from office. Although he had been Foreign Secretary for only three months, he had gained the respect of foreign leaders and made much progress in the fostering of better international understanding, especially with the West German government.

That there was still confidence in his diplomatic abilities was demonstrated in the spring of 1965 when Harold Wilson appointed him to an important fact-finding mission to South–East Asia during which he was instrumental in persuading various governments to agree to a conference on Cambodia. His significant role in Wilson's government ended with this mission to South–East Asia, although he won a seat at Leyton by more than 8000 votes the second time he stood in 1966 and went on to become Minister without Portfolio in January 1967 and then Secretary of State for Education and Science in August of the same year. However, following a cabinet restructure in April 1968, his resignation was asked for.

Despite his various defeats and the atmosphere of controversy within which he often found himself, Gordon Walker retained the respect of his colleagues. As Lord Peart, another Labour peer, said upon his death, Gordon Walker "made a tremendous contribution to the Labour Movement. He never wavered in his beliefs and was a strong social democrat."   E.S.

Born Patrick Chrestien Gordon Walker. Son of Alan Lachlan G. and Dora Marguerite Chrestien G. Married Audrey Muriel Rudolf 1934. Twin sons; three daughters. Educ: Wellington Coll.; Christ Church, Oxford Univ., M.A., B.Litt. Student and History Tutor, Christ Church 1931–1940; BBC European Service 1940–44; Chief Ed., Radio Luxembourg 1944; Asst. Dir., German Service, BBC 1945; M.P. (Labour) for Smethwick 1945–64 and for Leyton 1966–74; Parliamentary Private Secty. to Herbert Morrison 1946; Parliamentary Under-

Secty. of State for Commonwealth Relations 1950–51; Foreign Secty., Oct. 1964–Jan. 1965; Minister without Portfolio, Jan.–Aug. 1967; Secty. of State for Education and Science 1967–68; Advisor to Initial Teaching Alphabet Foundn. 1965–67; Leader, U.K. Delegation to Council of Europe 1966; Chmn., British Film Inst. 1946; Vice–Chmn., British Council 1947; Chmn., Book Development Council 1965–67. *Author:* History of Europe in the Sixteenth and Seventeenth Centuries, 1935; Outline of Man's History, 1939; The Lid Lifts, 1945; Re-statement of Liberty, 1951; The Commonwealth, 1962; The Cabinet, 1970.

SIR OSWALD MOSLEY
Founder of British Union of Fascists and former Member of Parliament
Born Staffordshire, England, November 16th, 1896
Died Orsay, France, December 2nd, 1980

A British aristocrat regarded in the 1920s as a potential prime minister, Sir Oswald Mosley was the founder of the British Union of Fascists. Mosley was an admirer of Mussolini and Hitler who believed Great Britain was being forced into war with Nazi Germany by an international conspiracy of Jewish financial interests; in the mid 1930s, he led Blackshirt followers on violent rampages through Jewish neighborhoods in the East End of London. Referring to Mosley's great personal magnetism and his racist ideology, critic Kenneth Rose wrote that "no man ever squandered a glittering armory of gifts so wantonly, on so worthless a cause."

Sir Oswald Mosley came from an aristocratic family and, from his father, the fifth baronet of Ancoats, Lancashire and of Rolleston, Staffordshire, he inherited a title which had been created in 1781. Mosley received a conventional upper class education, attending Winchester and, later, the Royal Military College, Sandhurst. During World War One, he served as a cavalry officer with the 16th Lancers in France before transferring to the Royal Flying Corps; he was said to have been a gallant, and somewhat reckless, soldier who was left with a permanent limp after a plane crash.

In 1918 Mosley was elected to Parliament as a Conservative from a middle class constituency in Harrow, Middlesex. Between 1918 and 1922, Mosley's golden future seemed assured; a member of Parliament at age 22, he was young, handsome, intelligent, a gifted speaker, very wealthy and made wealthier still by his marriage in 1920 to Lady Cynthia Curzon. Lady Cynthia was the daughter of the former Viceroy of India, the Marquess Curzon of Kedleston, and the maternal granddaughter of an American multimillionaire; her marriage to Mosley was the social event of the season and was attended by two kings and two queens. However, in 1922, having angered fellow Conservatives with his bitter attacks on such prominent leaders as Winston Churchill, the ambitious and impatient Mosley stood successfully for re-election as an Independent Conservative. But Mosley's ideology was constantly shifting in the 1920s and, in 1924, he joined the Labour Party.

Although Mosley was defeated in the 1924 elections, he was

returned to the House of Commons two years later, as a Labour Candidate from Smethwick, Birmingham. Again Mosley's future seemed promising; a friend and political confederate of Labour leader Ramsay MacDonald, many predicted that Mosley would eventually become Prime Minister. By all accounts, Mosley's political skills flowered in the late 1920s. He was a spellbinding orator whose power to move and sway audiences was second only to Churchill. Yet, after meeting Mosley in 1930, Fabian Socialist Beatrice Webb remarked: "So much perfection argues rottenness somewhere."

When the Labour Party acceded to power in 1929, Mosley was given cabinet status by Prime Minister Ramsay MacDonald. As Chancellor of the Duchy of Lancaster, he was assigned to devise plans for "national reconstruction," but Mosley, whose economic views moved increasingly leftward as the crisis of world depression deepened in Britain, proposed a Keynesian solution for unemployment which was soundly rejected by the Cabinet. On February 28, 1931, with the support of such noted Socialists as John Strachey, Harold Nicholson, and Oliver Baldwin, Mosley founded the New Party. Campaigning on a more or less left-wing platform, the New Party and its slate of candidates, which included Mosley, was crushed in the 1931 elections. Disenchanted with conventional socialism, Mosley declared himself a devotée of political "modernism"; in early 1932, he traveled to Mussolini's Italy to study the modern movement first hand, and, when he returned, he was a committed fascist.

In October 1932, Mosley merged his New Party with the British Fascists, a small group which had been established much earlier, to form the British Union of Fascists. The organization, which adopted the black shirt as a party uniform and the fascist salute as a sign of protocol, was modelled along authoritarian lines; Mosley himself held absolute power and there was a small Directorate to which members were appointed, not elected. The party program was, at first, influenced more by Italian fascism than by the German variety. Mosley imagined the ideal state to be a corporate leviathan; seeking an end to the "rule of the financial gangster"—later identified as Jews—Mosley proposed a National Council of Corporations to direct economic life and dictate policy to a new "technical Parliament" which was to be composed of industrial specialists. The prime minister in Sir Oswald's scheme was to be anointed by the king and a Fascist Grand Council; the fascist state, Mosley said, would "bring not the end of freedom but the beginning of freedom. Real freedom is economic freedom . . . ." Political freedom he did not care to define.

In 1934 the Union of Fascists came increasingly under the influence of the Nazis and Mosley publicly embraced Hitler's anti-Semitism. At an October rally at Albert Hall, Sir Oswald said: "Not on grounds of race or religion, but on the fundamental principle of Fascism, we declare that we will not tolerate an organized community within the state which owes allegiance not to Britain, but to another race in foreign countries . . . We shall not fight Germany again in a Jewish quarrel." According to Mosley "the new German has another mission in the world than to elevate savages," and the Jews, he said, "must put the interests of Britain before those of Jewry, or be deported from Britain . . ." Although membership in the Union of Fascists never exceeded more than 10,000 active members, most of whom were of lower-middle class and working class origin, the party, in the 1937

London County Council election, polled as much as 20 per cent of the vote in some sections of London's working class—and heavily Jewish—East End.

In the mid 1930s the Fascists conducted open-air rallies in the East End which provoked left-wing resistance. While a uniformed Mosley harangued the multitudes, Blackshirts ruthlessly beat, clubbed, and kicked hecklers who interrupted his speeches. After one especially violent confrontation in October 1936, the "Battle of Cable Avenue" which spawned a bloody aftermath, known as the "Mile End Road Pogrom" in which Blackshirts viciously assaulted Jews in the streets, the wearing of political uniforms was forbidden by law. Still, Mosley defiantly wore his black costume, but the authorities refused to be baited; rather than arrest their quarry, they sent policemen to protect him and thus prevent further violence at the rallies.

Mosley continued to agitate in favor of alliance with Hitler. In 1936 he married Lady Diana Mitford in Germany (Lady Cynthia had died in 1933) and Hitler, a friend of Mitford's sister, attended the ceremony. On May 23, 1940, with a German invasion anticipated by the authorities, Mosley, his wife, and eight subordinates were placed under custody; formal charges were never pressed and it was explained that they had been detained "for custodial and not for punitive purposes." As a result, the British Union of Fascists and National Socialists (the name had been changed in 1936) collapsed overnight; in November 1943, Home Secretary Herbert Morrison ordered Mosley's release.

Mosley attempted to revive the Fascists after the war but he received almost no support. To Britons, Mosley's identification with Hitler and extremist violence discredited him. Moreover, political conditions in Britain had never been favorable to totalitarianism; there was no serious threat of Communism against which the Right could react, and the dissolution of the Empire did not provoke intense nationalism. Mosley spent most of the remainder of his life in self-imposed exile in France; he was overwhelmingly defeated in an attempt to be elected to Parliament from North Kensington in 1959 and physically assaulted after a London speech in 1962.   E.T.

Son of Sir Oswald M., 5th Baronet, and Maud Heathcote M. Married: (1) Lady Cynthia Curzon 1920 (d. 1933); (2) Hon. Diana Mitford 1936. Children: 1st marriage—Vivien, b. 1921; Nicholas, Baron Ravensdale, novelist, b. 1923; Michael, b. 1932; 2nd marriage— Oswald Alexander, b. 1928; Max Rufus, b. 1940. Educ: Winchester; Royal Mil. Coll., Sandhurst. Commissioned 16th Lancers, with Royal Flying Corps 1914–15; with regt. in France 1915–16; discharged with injuries 1918. M.P. (Conservative) 1918–22 and M.P. (Independent) 1922–24, Div. of Harrow, Middx; M.P. (Labour), Smethwick 1926–31; Chancellor of Duchy of Lancs. 1929–30; founded New Party 1931; New Party candidate for Div. of Stoke 1931 (defeated); founding Member, British Union of Fascists 1932; interned by British govt. 1940–43; entered publishing business 1946; founded Union Movement (for European unity) 1948; Parliamentary candidate of Union Party 1959, 1966. *Author:* The Greater Britain, 1932; My Answer, 1946; The Alternative, 1947; Europe: Faith and Plan, 1958; Right or Wrong: 300 Questions Answered, 1961; My Life (autobiog.), 1968; numerous pamphlets and articles.
Further reading: The Fascists in Britain by Colin Cross, 1963; "The Problem of Mosley" by Robert Skidelsky, in Encounter, Sept. 1969.

JOHN H(ERMAN) RANDALL, JR.
Philosopher, historian, educator and author
Born Grand Rapids, Michigan, U.S.A., February 14th, 1899
Died New York City, U.S.A., December 2nd, 1980

Within the modern naturalist school of philosophy, John H. Randall, Jr. achieved influence through a synthesis of three intellectual traditions, theology, ethical pragmatism, and cultural realism. Randall was influenced early on by his father, an eminent Baptist clergyman whose studies of theology and the history of ideas were represented in a series of well-received books, including a father-son collaboration, *Religion and the Modern World* (1929). Randall himself was an adherent of John Dewey's conception of philosophy as social criticism and shared Dewey's belief that "to know" obliges one to act. As a student of Columbia's Professor Frederick J.E. Woodbridge, a brilliant teacher whose realist philosophy drew equally from Aristotle, Spinoza, and Locke, Randall came to believe that it is the underlying structure of culture which determines the shape and appearance of reality. From these disparate ideas Randall deduced a philosophy of history in which the ever-changing present is believed to be woven from the cultural traditions of the past.

A Phi Beta Kappa graduate of Columbia College in 1918, Randall began his teaching career there in 1921 and his first important book, *The Making of the Modern Mind,* appeared in 1926. Although he would later reject its periodization of cultural history in favor of a theory of continuous transition, the book established him as a major figure in the field of intellectual history. Between 1920 and 1926, Randall helped Columbia College institute the highly regarded Contemporary Civilization Syllabus, an intensive four semester program which traced cultural development from classical antiquity through the industrial revolution and stressed the continuity of certain intellectual traditions throughout different historical epochs. The famous "C.C." curriculum became a widely imitated model for college liberal arts programs.

During the 1920s, Randall became increasingly concerned about the nature of ethics in contemporary industrial society. Based on observations of both Europe and America, he concluded that "objective" scientific definitions of "truth" had become pervasive in modern culture, threatening to render subjective reason obsolete. The machine, Randall said, had become a socio-political, as well as economic, phenomenon and, rather than existing only as a means of simplifying human labor, the machine had acquired the power to create values. Constructing an ethical code which could reassert the historical primacy of human culture became the focus of Randall's subsequent work. As an intellectual historian, a metaphysician, a philosopher of religion, and a linguist, he consistently cited philosophy as a critical tool capable of reorganizing and redefining cultural experience and institutionalized beliefs.

Randall was deeply committed to an activist ethical philosophy. Having visited Germany on the eve of Hitler's victory, he signed a socialist manifesto in 1933, denouncing the rise of economic nationalism that seemed to be pushing the world toward international war; and, in 1935, when left-wing, pro-communist agitation politicized the American Federation of Teachers, he publicly resigned to protest the undemocratic nature of the takeover. In 1940 he assailed efforts to ban Bertrand Russell, the controversial pacifist and philosopher, from a teaching post at City College of New York; in the postwar era, Randall emerged as an outspoken foe of the anti-communist witch-hunters, both on and off campus.

Randall's most important scholarly work was the two-volume, *The Career of Philosophy in Modern Times,* completed in 1965 and honored with the Ralph Waldo Emerson Award of the Phi Beta Kappa Society. Hailed as the most ambitious history of philosophy undertaken in the English language, Randall summed up in the book his "historical naturalism" by tracing cultural continuities from the time of Europe's discovery of Aristotle in the Middle Ages to the Age of Darwin and the machine. R.C.

Son of John Herman R., clergyman, author, and Minerva I. Ballard R. Married Mercedes Irene Moritz 1922 (d. 1977). Children: John Herman, III, teacher; Frances Ballard. Educ: Columbia Univ., B.A. 1918, M.A. 1919, Ph.D. 1922. With Columbia Univ; Instr., Philosophy Dept. 1921–25; Asst. Prof. 1925–31; Assoc. Prof. 1931–35; Prof. 1935–51; F.J.E. Woodbridge Prof. of Philosophy 1951–67; F.J.E. Woodbridge Prof. Emeritus since 1967. Member and Pres. 1953–57, Renaissance Soc. of America; Member and Pres. 1956, American Philosophical Soc.; Member and Pres. 1966–67, Metaphysical Soc. of America; Member, Ethical Culture Soc. Hons: Nicholas Murray Butler Award in Silver, Columbia Univ. 1947; Litt. D., Ohio Wesleyan Univ. 1961; Hon. Ph.D., Univ. of Padua (Italy) 1967; Ralph Waldo Emerson Award of the Phi Beta Kappa Soc. for volume II of the Career of Philosophy in Modern Times 1967; LL.D., Temple Univ. 1968; L.H.D., Columbia Univ. 1968, and Bard Coll. 1972; Fellow, American Acad. of Arts and Sciences. *Author:* The Problem of Group Responsibility, 1922; The Making of the Modern Mind, 1926 (50th Anniversary ed., 1976); Our Changing Civilization, 1929; The Role of Knowledge in Western Religion, 1958; Nature and Historical Experience, 1958; Aristotle, 1960; The School of Padua and the Emergence of Modern Science, 1961; The Career of Philosophy in Modern Times, vol. I, 1962, vol. II, 1965; How Philosophy Uses Its Past, 1963; The Meaning of Religion for Man, 1968; Plato: Dramatist of the Life of Reason, 1970; Hellenistic Ways of Deliverance and the Making of the Christian Synthesis, 1970; Philosophy After Darwin, 1977. *Co-author:* Introduction to Contemporary Civilization (Syllabus), 1920–26; Introduction to Reflective Thinking, 1923; Studies in the History of Ideas (vol. II), 1925; Religion and the Modern World, 1929; American Philosophy Today and Tomorrow, 1935; The Philosophy of John Dewey, 1939; The Philosopher of the Common Man, 1940; Philosophy: An Introduction, 1942; Naturalism and the Human Spirit, 1944; Preface to Philosophy, 1946; Theory and Practice in Historical Study, 1946; Freedom and Experience, 1947; Wellsprings of the American Spirit, 1948; Organized Religion in the United States, 1948; Renaissance Philosophy of Man, 1948; The Philosophy of Ernst Cassirer, 1949; Freedom and Reason, 1951; The Philosophy of Paul Tillich, 1952; Contemporary American Philosophy, 1970. *Editor:* Journal of the History of Ideas; Aristotle's Vision of Nature (J.E.F. Woodbridge Lectures, 1953). *Joint editor:* Journal of Philosophy.

H(AMILTON) S(HIRLEY) AMERASINGHE
United Nations diplomat
Born Colombo, Ceylon (now Sri Lanka), March 18th, 1913
Died New York City, U.S.A., December 4th, 1980

In the 1970s H.S. Amerasinghe achieved prominence as one of the leading figures in the North-South debate over the control and distribution of the world's natural resources. As president of the third UN Conference on the Law of the Sea, Amerasinghe tried to forge a new international legal code governing fishing rights, exploitation of the mineral resources of the seabed, scientific research, and environmental control of the sea.

Born into a leading Sinhalese family in Colombo, when Ceylon was a British colony, Amerasinghe was educated in the Western classics and graduated in 1934 from the University College of Ceylon. Three years later he entered the Ceylonese civil service and rose through the hierarchy of the colonial administration. In 1953, five years after Ceylon had attained self-governing status, Amerasinghe was named counselor of the Ceylonese Embassy in the USA, his first diplomatic post. From 1955 to 1963 the central focus of his career was the administration of Ceylon's domestic affairs, first with the General Treasury, then with the Central Bank of Ceylon.

Amerasinghe's interest in the status of non-aligned states began to surface in the late 1950s. While serving as Ceylon's High Commissioner to India in the mid-1960s, Amerasinghe participated in several meetings of non-aligned states, including the Second Afro-Asian Conference, held in Jakarta, Indonesia, in 1964. Three years later he was appointed Ceylon's ambassador to the United Nations.

By the time Amerasinghe took his seat in the UN General Assembly, the growing number of Third World states had already begun to affect the kind of issues addressed by the international body. Amerasinghe quickly assumed a leading role as champion of Third World interests. In 1968 he was asked to head an ad hoc committee concerned with the international use of seabeds, a post which grew in importance as its mandate was extended to include a fundamental revision of international law of the sea. In 1969 he headed a controversial committee established to investigate possible violations of human rights by Israel in territories captured in the 1967 Arab-Israeli war. In 1971 Amerasinghe was proposed as a possible successor to retiring UN Secretary-General U Thant, but at the time he was regarded as too pro-Arab and pro-Soviet by the West. He was elected president of the General Assembly, however, in 1976.

Amerasinghe's most notable work involved reshaping the international law of the sea. From 1973 to 1980 he presided over a series of UN committee debates over the new code. The main points in dispute pitted either the superpowers against the smaller states or the West against the Third World. Smaller states wanted to control a 200-mile strip off their coastlines, while the US and the Soviet Union insisted on a 12-mile limit. Third World representatives also proposed creation of an international authority to control exploitation of mineral deposits on the seabed, while Western states viewed this activity as the prerogative of private corporations. Amerasinghe's knowledge of the complex issues involved in the debate won him such respect that, when the Sri Lankan government recalled him from his UN post in 1978, he was given a special appointment as chairman of the UN

Conference on the Law of the Sea. By the time of his death, some of the most important matters of dispute seemed near resolution.   M.T.

Unmarried. Buddhist. Educ: Univ. Coll. of Ceylon 1934. Joined Ceylon Civil Service 1937: Secty. to Minister of Health 1941–46; Resident Manager, Gal Oya Devel. Bd. 1950–52; served with Gen. Treasury: Controller of Establishments 1955–57; Controller of Supply, Cadre, and Finance 1958; Secty. 1961–63. Permanent Secty., Ministry of Nationalised Services 1958; Permanent Secty. Ministry of Finance 1961–63; Dir. Bank of Ceylon 1962–63. Served as Ceylonese diplomat: Counsellor, Washington, D.C. 1953–55; Alternate Delegate to UN 1957; High Commissioner of Ceylon in India 1963–67; Ambassador to Nepal and Afghanistan 1963–67; Permanent Representative from Ceylon (Sri Lanka after 1972) to UN 1967–78. With UN: chaired cttees.: Peaceful Uses of Sea Bed and Ocean Floor Beyond Limits of National Jurisdiction 1968–72; Investigation of Israeli Practices affecting Human Rights of Population of Occupied Territories 1969–73, ad hoc Cttee. on Indian Ocean; Pres. Third UN Law of the Sea Conf. 1973–80; Pres., General Assembly 1976–77.

FRANCISCO SÁ CARNEIRO
Portuguese Prime Minister and lawyer
Born Oporto, Portugal, July 19th, 1934
Died Lisbon, Portugal, December 4th, 1980

The sudden death in a plane crash of Francisco Sá Carneiro, the Prime Minister of Portugal, came near the end of a heated campaign for the Portuguese presidency in which the conservative Sá Carneiro was supporting the opposition candidate—Gen. António Soares Carneiro (no relation)—against President António Ramalho Eanes, the incumbent. It has been feared that his death might weaken and ultimately split the Democratic Alliance Coalition whose main architect he had been and which had been held together mainly through the force of his personality. Known as the "Fighting Cock," as a man who did not retreat from confrontation at any level—whether it was with the Ambassador of the United States at the time, Frank Carlucci, or the president of the Republic—Sá Carneiro had a colorful reputation as a bold, unpredictable gambler in the field of politics. As he said about his controversial campaign against President Eanes, "Until now, I've always bet and I've always won."

In the shifting world of Portuguese politics Sá Carneiro was a rather unconventional figure. Although he first came to prominence as a liberal reformer from 1969 to 1973 under the dictatorship of Marcello Caetano, he gradually moved to the right after the "revolution of the carnations" in 1974 which ended the Caetano regime and gave Portugal a strong leftist orientation. He might have run for president himself instead of supporting the rather unimaginative, undynamic Gen. Carneiro if his own personal life had been more in conformance with the strict Catholic beliefs of his country; however, his protracted divorce proceedings with his wife of over twenty years and his open relationship with the Danish divorcee Snu Bonnier Abecassis—who was killed in the plane crash with him—made such a candidacy inconceivable, even by the daring Sá Carneiro with his reputation for confrontation. Capturing the attention and respect of the Portuguese people, Sá Carneiro had refined into an effective weapon the dramatic tactic of resigning from office if he did not achieve his ends. On two occasions he resigned the party leadership and got himself twice re-elected with even stronger margins, forcing his opponents out in the process. He last threatened to resign if his candidate did not defeat Eanes, and there is every indication he would have done so, most likely to his own advantage. Sá Carneiro's grand design for himself and his nation was to have culminated in the election that would have placed his candidate in the presidency and been the start of those constitutional and military changes to which he was committed.

Sá Carneiro, born in the northern city of Oporto in 1934, received his law degree from Lisbon University and practiced law for several years. After joining the official opposition when Caetano succeeded Salazar in 1968, Sá Carneiro the next year became an independent member of the Portuguese National Assembly and authored eight major legislative proposals until he resigned in 1973. His resignation, the first of several, resulted from his repeated requests for a full-scale inquiry into the activities of the secret police, a holdover from the Salazar regime. When Caetano was ousted from power in the 1974 military coup that ended half a century of dictatorship, Sá Carneiro's position in favor of the restoration of civil liberties and the courage with which he maintained it were remembered, and he quickly began to emerge as a national leader.

At this point Sá Carneiro and several colleagues formed the Popular Democratic Party (PPD), later called the Social Democratic Party (PSD). The PPD declared its backing for the Armed Forces Movement (MFA) that had carried out the leftist coup and within a short time became the strongest party after the Socialists. The PPD, of which Sá Carneiro was first secretary general, then president, defined itself as social democratic and non-Marxist and was represented in all but one of the many provisional governments during Portugal's first years as a democracy. In the first of these provisional governments, which lasted from May to June 1974, Sá Carneiro was a Minister without Portfolio, although the following year he was inactive for health reasons and underwent treatment in London. Despite the growing influence of the PPD, however, when Sá Carneiro sought membership for his party in the Socialist International, Mario Soares—whose regular Socialist organization was already a member—intervened to block the move. What Portugal needed during this period was a stable government, but the opposition between Soares and Sá Carneiro made it impossible for their parties to work together. In fact, when the PPD did well in the elections for the first post revolutionary parliament in 1976, Soares refused to share power with Sá Carneiro's party.

However, in the elections of 1979 Sá Carneiro was able to wrest control from Soares' Socialists after his own party, some of whose members wanted a center–left coalition, had been restructured and renamed the Social Democrats and Sá Carneiro had moved to the right. The time was appropriate for Sá Carneiro's characteristically bold initiatives which succeeded in attracting the disillusioned Catholic peasantry in the north, the conservative middle class, and the traditionalist elements of the Army. Together with Freitas do Amaral's Center Democrats, the Christian Democrats, and the small

Monarchist party, Sá Carneiro's party formed the Democratic Alliance. When this rightist coalition won a six-seat majority in the parliament in the elections of December 1979—a majority increased in the elections of October 1979 which gave the Parliament the power to revise the Constitution—Portugal had its first stable government in over five years.

As Premier, Sá Carneiro formed right-wing cabinets and strongly protested the Soviet military intervention in Afghanistan and supported the U.S. in their economic sanctions against Iran in reaction to the taking of the hostages. During the presidential campaign in late 1980 in which Sá Carneiro backed the conservative Gen. Carneiro, he spoke often of what he called his "National Project"—a President pledged to act in concert with the Premier and a constitution reformed of its Marxist elements. Without question Sá Carneiro was the dynamic, indispensable force behind the little-known, inexperienced Gen. Carneiro. During the campaign he criticized President Eanes more than did Gen. Carneiro, claiming that Eanes would be an obstacle in the revision of the constitution along less leftist lines.

Optimistic about his candidate's chances against the popular Eanes, Sá Carneiro—along with Mrs. Abecassis, the Defense Minister, and five others—died in a plane crash on the way to a political rally in Oporto on December 4, only three days before the crucial election. The acting Prime Minister, Freitas do Amaral, addressed the nation shortly after Sá Carneiro's death and urged the people to remain calm, promising that there would be an official inquiry into the circumstances of the crash. The Social Democratic Party claimed that there was no evidence of sabotage.

Although a postponement of the election was considered by the government, the election took place as scheduled since the laws of Portugal provide for delay only when one of the presidential candidates dies. There was some speculation that Sá Carneiro's death might prove to be of some help to Gen. Carneiro among an unpredictable, emotional electorate. However, Eanes, with the support of the leftist opposition, was re-elected on December 7; among the reasons cited for his victory were his experience and his familiarity to the people during five years of rule. President Eanes chose as Prime Minister the Social Democrat, Francisco Pinto Balsemão. Balsemão and his center-right Cabinet took office on January 9, 1981, pledging to govern for four years and to "liberate civil society" from the Marxist legacy of Portugal's revolution, thus echoing some of the key points of Sá Carneiro's own National Project.   E.S.

Son of José Gualberto S.C. and Maria Francesca S.C. Married Isabel Nunes Matos 1956. Three sons; two daughters. Educ: Law Faculty, Lisbon Univ. Co-founder, Confronto Co-operative, Oporto (dissolved by Govt. 1972); Pres., Revista dos Tribunais; Independent member, Natl. Assembly 1969–73; worked with Expresso and other newspapers; Co-founder and Secty.–Gen., Popular Democratic Party (PPD), later the Social Democratic Party (PSD) 1974–1978; Pres. (re-elected), PSD Natl. Council since Jan. 1978; Minister without Portfolio, first provisional govt. May–June 1974; Chmn., PSD 1975–77; Leader, PSD 1976; Head (re-elected), Democratic Alliance since 1979; Prime Minister of Portugal since Dec. 1979. *Author:* Uma Tentativa de Participação Politica, 1971; Revisão da Constituição

Politica, 1971; As Revisões da Constituição Politica, 1973; Ser ou Não Ser Deputado?, 1973; Por uma Social–Democracia, 1975; Poder Civil, Autoridade Democrática e Social–Democracia, 1975.

THEA HOLME
Actress, writer, and director
Born London, England, December 27th, 1907
Died Northwood, Middlesex, England, December 4th, 1980

Thea Holme was known for her theatrical career as actress and writer as well as director. Her acting was marked by elegance and restraint, her writing and directing by grace and the ability to organize and to present detail.

Before turning to the theater, Holme had studied art. Her first appearance as an actress was with the prestigious Ben Greet Players in 1924, and it was with them that she also made her Paris debut the following year. She returned to the City of Light with the English Players later in 1925 to perform at the Columbia University Theater in 1929.

During the 1930s she played numerous roles opposite her husband, Stanford Holme, at the Oxford Playhouse, where he was the producer. "Hard indeed of heart was the undergraduate who did not fall madly in love with this most elegant beauty with the wondering eyes," wrote the London *Times* of her during this period. Thea was known for the range of her acting ability, which encompassed both classical and modern roles, and was particularly famous in England for her performances as Elizabeth Barrett, Rosalind, and above all, Lady Precious Stream, a part she took very successfully to the West End.

Flexibility was the keynote during Stanford Holme's tenure as producer at the Oxford Playhouse. The previous administration of the theater had insisted on programming "important" plays that the audience did not particularly enjoy. The Holmes, however, were willing to try classical and modern plays by both well-known and unknown authors, and even to put on pantomimes, if they thought their audiences would find them entertaining. They were concerned with the shared emotional experiences of audience and actors, and this preoccupation communicated itself to their public, which reciprocated by offering the couple affection and royalty.

Thea Holme performed frequently in the West End as well as in radio dramas during the 1930s. In 1936–37, she created her most famous radio part in *Prisoner of Zenda*. She joined the then newly-formed BBC repertory company in 1939, and is also known for having performed in London's earliest televised dramatic series. During World War Two she toured with the Council for the Encouragement of Music and the Arts (now known as the Arts Council of Great Britain) and played and directed at the Open Air Theatre in Regent's Park, London.

Beginning to write in 1937, it was not until her husband became the National Trust's curator of the Carlyle's house in Cheyne Row, Chelsea that Mrs. Holme undertook her first book. For *The Carlyles at Home* she culled letters, reminiscences, and various domestic and housekeeping records of Thomas and Jane Welsh Carlyle, making of them a light, entertaining narrative of their married life. This was a far more ambitious project than her earlier modifications of Jane Austen novels, television adaptations, and radio scripts. Holme's writing gifts led to her being named a Fellow of the Royal Society of Literature.

L.R.

Daughter of Philip Mainwaring Johnston (architect and antiquary) and Florence Wynne J. Married Stanford Holme (actor and director). Son: Timothy Philip, b. 1928 (writer). Educ: Dulwich; Slade; Central Sch. for Speech Training and Dramatic Art. Active as an actress, mainly in London, Paris and N.Y. 1924–69; active as writer, 1937–80. Hon: Fellow, Royal Soc. of Lit. *Performances: Plays*—A Midsummer Night's Dream (Hippolyta), 1924; You Never Can Tell (Dolly), 1925; The Importance of Being Earnest (Cecily Cardew), 1925; Rookery Nook (Rhoda Marley), 1927; Much Ado About Nothing (Beatrice), 1929; Leave It To Psmith (Cynthia McTodd), 1930; Oxford Playhouse Repertory Company, performances (leading roles), 1931–38; The School for Scandal (Lady Teazle), 1934; Black Swans (Mary Summers), 1938; Tobias and the Angel (Sara), July 1938; As You Like It (Phebe), 1938; Saint Joan (title role), 1939; BBC Repertory Co. 1939; Toured with Council for the Encouragement of Music and the Arts, ca. 1939; Macbeth (Lady Macduff), 1942; Toured Britain 1942–44. *Directed and played leading roles in*—Open Air Theatre, Regent's Park; Lady Precious Stream (title role), 1944; Twelfth Night (Viola), 1944. *Radio and Television*—Prisoner of Zenda (radio drama), 1936–37; Nicholas Nickleby (television series), 1969. *Author:* Roman Holiday (play), 1937; The Carlyles at Home, 1965; Chelsea (nonfiction), 1972; Prinny's Daughter (Regency biography), 1976; Caroline (Regency biography), 1979; Caroline: A Biography of Caroline of Brunswick, 1980; also numerous television adaptations and scripts for radio serials.

SULTAN I. IBRAIMOV
Premier, Kirghiz S.S.R.
Born 1927
Died Frunze, Kirghiz, USSR, December 4th, 1980

Sultan I. Ibraimov symbolized the political authority and scientific progress brought by Communist modernization programs to the land and people of Kirghizia, one of the central Asian republics that constitute the USSR. Little known to many Europeans and most Americans, the Kirghiz Soviet Socialist Republic is regarded by many in the "Third World" as an example of how a tribal, nomadic culture can be modernized by a state controlled economy.

Born in 1927, Ibraimov was a collective farm worker and tractor driver before graduating from the Tashkent Institute of Irrigation and Agricultural Mechanization. Water supply had long been problematic for the Kirghiz people, since precipitation is uneven in the valleys where most of the Republic's three million people live. Casting about for a solution to this dilemma, the newly formed Kirghiz Academy of Sciences created a special institute in 1955 to study the problem; Ibraimov, a 27-year-old member of the Communist Party, was a member of the Institute's staff.

The Academy's work was successful and Ibraimov was rewarded by being made an instructor in the Party's Central Committee in 1957. Thereafter, Ibraimov rose rapidly in the Kirghiz Party apparatus and he was named as the Committee's Candidate Member in 1961, a non-voting position which he held until 1963, when he became a Full Member. Also during this period, he held high posts in the ministry responsible for land reclamation and water economy.

At a relatively young age by Soviet standards, Ibraimov, not yet forty, was made Secretary of the Central Committee in 1966 and was also named to its Bureau, a prestigious and powerful branch organization. In addition to being chief of the Kirghiz Communist Party in the district of Osh, a major city in the republic, Ibraimov served briefly as its President before becoming Premier in 1978.   L.R.

Educ: Tashkent Inst. of Irrigation and Agricultural Mechanization, grad. 1954. Collective farm worker, tractor driver and hydro-technical specialist 1943–55; joined Communist Party 1954; Staff Member, Inst. of Water and Energy Economy, Acad. of Science, Kirghiz SSR 1955–57. With Central Cttee., Kirghiz Communist Party: Instr.; 2nd Secty., Academic Affairs Cttee. 1957–61; Candidate Member 1961–63; Full Member 1963; with Ministry of Water Economy 1961–66; Secty. 1966–68; Member of the Bureau 1966. 1st Secty., Osh District Cttee. 1968; Pres., and then Premier, Kirghiz SSR since 1978.

STELLA WALSH
Track and field star
Born Wierzchownia, Poland, April 3rd, 1911
Died Cleveland, Ohio, U.S.A., December 4th, 1980

Stella Walsh was the world's premier woman runner in the 1930s and 40s. An Olympic Gold medalist for her native Poland, Walsh held more than 60 world records during her career and was the first woman to run the 100-yard dash in less than 10 seconds. Walsh, however, was buried amid controversial reports that she had been a man.

Christened Stanislawa Walasiewicz, she came to the United States at the age of two when her parents emigrated from Poland, settling in Cleveland, Ohio. In 1928, the 17 year old Stella Walsh—she changed her name to accommodate public school teachers—tried out for the U.S. Olympic team but was disqualified when it was discovered that she was not an American citizen. When she stunned onlookers by sprinting 50 yards in 6.1 seconds at a Madison Square Garden meet in 1930, she was established as a world-class runner. Two years later, she took steps to obtain U.S. citizenship so that she could compete as an American in Los Angeles at the 1932 World Olympic games. However, her position with the New York Central Railroad was abolished and, when she started to accept a job with Cleveland's Municipal Recreation Department, Walsh was told by the Amateur Athletic Union (AAU) that employment in "physical education work" would make her ineligible for Olympic competition. Finally, Walsh accepted work in the Polish consul's office in New York City and participated in the Olympics as a Pole, winning a gold medal and setting an Olympic record when she ran the 100-meter dash in 11.9 seconds.

Between 1932 and the 1936 Olympic games in Berlin, Walsh competed in meets throughout Europe and the United States. She set the world mark for the 60 meter run with a 7.3 second effort and established the 100 meter record the following year at Warsaw with an 11.7 second run; in 1935, Walsh broke two more world records by clocking 23.6 seconds in the 200 meter event at Warsaw, and 24.3 seconds in a 220 meter run at Cleveland. Later that year, after competing in Germany, Walsh expressed concern over anti-Semitic outbursts directed toward a teammate, Mary Friewald, a Polish hurdles champion; the event, which deeply angered Walsh, was a portent of the Nazi-inspired politicization of the 1936 Olympics in which she won a silver medal for the 100 meter run and placed sixth in the women's discus event.

Walsh continued to be one of the world's dominant women runners throughout the 1940s and early 1950s and, at one time, she held more than 60 world records; in 1954, at the age of 43, she won her fifth U.S. pentathlon championship. An avowed anti-communist, Walsh asserted in 1955 that the Polish government she had hitherto represented "does not exist" and declared her intention of competing with the U.S. team in the 1956 Olympic games. When U.S. officials subsequently declared her ineligible on the grounds that she had represented Poland in 1932 and 1936, Walsh married Harry Olson, a U.S. citizen, thus assuring her eligibility. Just weeks after the marriage, however, she placed third in a 200 meter run at American University in Washington, D.C., and failed to make the team. Walsh then retired and moved to California.

In 1964, Walsh, who had left her husband, returned to Cleveland where she became active in Polish-American organizations. She was shot to death in the parking lot of a department store where she had gone to purchase ribbons for medals that were to be awarded to a visiting women's basketball team from Poland. Because she was the victim of a violent crime, Walsh's body was taken to the Cuyahoga County coroner's office where it was discovered that she had male organs and further tests have been ordered to see if she also had male hormones. Stella Walsh, who struggled as an athlete to establish her national identity, was buried amid confusion over her true sexual identity and under the threat of having her medals revoked by the International Olympic Committee if Walsh were proven to have been a man.   A.D.

Born Stanislawa Walasiewicz. Married Harry Olson, draftsman, 1956, estranged. No children. Brought to U.S. 1913. Naturalized American 1947. Worked with N.Y. Central Railroad and in office of Polish Consul Gen., NYC; track and field athlete from 1930. Hons: Grand Natl. Sports Prize of Poland 1935; Cross of Merit, Poland 1980; Member, Citizens Savings (Helms) Hall of Fame. *Records: Outdoor*—100-yards (10.8 seconds), 1930; 200-meters (24.1 seconds), 1932, 1934; 220-yards (24.3 seconds), 1935; 100-meters (11.6 seconds), 1943. *Indoor*—40-yards (5.2 seconds), 1930; 50-yards (6.0 seconds), 1930; 220-yards (25.8 seconds), 1941; 200-meters (25.8 seconds), 1941. *World*—60-meters (7.3 seconds), 1933; 100-meters (11.7 seconds), 1934; 200-meters (23.6 seconds), 1935; 220-yards (24.3 seconds), 1935; 100-meters (11.6 seconds), 1937.

MARGOT BENNETT
Mystery writer
Born Lenzie, Scotland, 1912
Died London, England, December 6th, 1980

Margot Bennett's contributions to crime fiction are characterized by a stylistic originality, a humor, and a sensitivity to character development and the complexities of society that frequently transcend the genre. As the critic Melvyn Barnes has said of her novels they "may be enjoyed as much by the reader who is fascinated by the puzzle as by the reader whose interest mainly lies in the examination of human relationships."

After working as an advertising copywriter in Australia and England and a volunteer nurse for the International Brigade in Spain, Margot Bennett wrote her first murder mystery, *Time To Change Hats* (1945), a contemporary tale set in England that perceptively conveys the chaos that war creates in the patterns of everyday life. Without lightening the grimness of her story, Bennett employed humor at various points. As she said thirty years later, "I tried the novelty of combining comedy with the obligatory murder. This gave me a good start—but the book was too long." Despite its length, however, the novel was well-received by both the public and the critics, being favorably compared by Graham Greene to Evelyn Waugh's *Put Out More Flags*. Her second book, *Away Went The Little Fish* (1945)—similar in setting and style to her first—was praised for its intricate plot, sophisticated wit, and true-to-life characters, a combination of elements that became one of her trademarks.

After *The Golden Pebble* (1948)—in which Bennett departed from the crime story genre with a tale of a sophisticated intellectual who finds a spiritual home in a provincial country village—she wrote what was the most popular book of her career, *The Widow of Bath* (1952). This depiction of the pervasive lure of crime in the seaside resort, is a fascinating study of greed, deception, and betrayal in which Bennett's talent for keen observation and psychological complexity is in high form.

Bennet's second novel outside the crime genre was *The Long Way Back* (1954). Set in the distant future, many centuries after atomic warfare has devastated Europe, it is an ironic parable about civilization and its dual capacity for survival and self-destruction. This work—and *The Golden Pebble*—were signs that Bennett was becoming somewhat impatient with the crime genre that she soon abandoned.

However, before she abandoned it, she wrote two more novels in the genre. *The Man Who Didn't Fly* (1955), a classic mystery that is also a masterly psychological study, was in Bennett's own estimation and that of the critics her finest work. After *Someone From The Past* was published in 1958, Bennett said she was putting aside the genre because it was no longer a relevant form for the complexities of modern life. There was considerable disappointment among her public and the critics who were eager for more of her well-crafted stories. As Julian Symons said of her crime novels from the 1950s, they were "the only English crime stories that bear comparison with Raymond Chandler in the continual crackle of her wit, and their downbeat cynicism."

Bennett, however, remained firm in her decision. Thereafter, she wrote numerous television plays, several screenplays, and a non-fiction book, *The Intelligent Woman's Guide to Atomic Radiation* (1964), but no more crime novels. When she did return to novel-writing, it was to write two books about the inequalities of society that display little of the wit and cleverness of her earlier work.   K.B.

Married Richard Bennett 1938. One daughter; three sons. Educ: primary sch., Scotland; secondary sch., Australia. Advertising copywriter: Sydney, Australia early 1930s; London, England mid-1930s. Volunteer nurse, Intnl. Brigade, Spain 1936–38. *Author: Novels*—Time To Change Hats, 1945; Away Went The Little Fish, 1946; The Golden Pebble, 1948; The Widow of Bath, 1952; Farewell Crown and Goodbye King, 1953; The Long Way Back, 1954; The Man Who Didn't Fly, 1956; Someone From The Past, 1958; That Summer's Earthquake, 1964; The Furious Masters, 1968. *Short stories (uncollected):* "An Old-Fashioned Poker For My Uncle's Head," 1946; "No Bath For the Browns," 1965. *Television plays*—20 episodes of Emergency Ward Ten, 1956; The Sun Divorce, 1956; The Widow of Bath, 1959; 2 episodes of The Third Man, 1960; 8 episodes of Maigret, 1960–64; 1 episode of They Met in a City, 1961; Killer in the Band, 1962; 1 episode of The Flying Swan, 1965; The Big Spender, 1965; The Tungsten Ring, 1966; 7 episodes of Honey Lane, 1968. *Screenplays*—The Crowning Touch, 1959; The Man Who Liked Funerals, 1959. *Other*—The Intelligent Woman's Guide to Atomic Radiation, 1964.

SIR RODERICK McLEOD
Military commander
Born Great Britain, January 15th, 1905
Died Great Britain, December 6th, 1980

Born of a long line of soldiers, Roderick McLeod served in the military for forty years and commanded what many consider the toughest and most elite troops in the British Army, the parachutists and the men of the Special Air Service Brigade. A veteran of duty in India's "north-west frontier" region in the early 1930s, McLeod was appointed to the Royal Horse Artillery in 1932, the same branch in which his father had served as an officer. Upon his return to England in 1938, he attended the Staff College before assuming general staff duties with the 4th Infantry Division and the War Office. Appointed first commander of the 1st Air-Landing Light Regiment, McLeod accompanied that unit to North Africa in mid-1943; he was subsequently made commander of the 1st Airborne Division and deputy commander of the 1st Parachute Brigade.

Assigned in 1944 the task of forming and leading a commando squad called the Special Air Service Brigade, McLeod's duties involved diplomatic acumen as well as tactical military expertise. This group, designed to attack enemy communication lines, headquarters, and airfields behind the battle front, was made up of battle-hardened English, French and Belgian soldiers who not infrequently engaged in off-duty brawls and were known to use hand-grenades in place of rod and reel on fishing expeditions. Brigadier McLeod often had to wage administrative battles on several fronts with superior officers to ensure proper combat deployment of the SAS troops.

After the war, McLeod served in India as Director of Military Operations until his appointment to the Imperial Defence College as assistant commander in 1947. During the 1950s, his numerous assignments included several years with the British occupation army in Germany, four years as Director of Military Operations in the War Office—a post he considered "most exacting"—and a return to the Imperial Defence College as Chief Army Instructor in 1957. Later that year, he was promoted to Lieutenant-General and appointed Deputy Chief of Staff to the Ministry of Defence. In 1960 he returned to the Far East as Commandant of Hong Kong. From 1963 until 1965, General McLeod was chief officer of the Eastern Command as well as Aide-de-Camp to the Queen.   L.R.

Born Roderick William McLeod. Son of Col. Reginald George McQueen M. and Cicely Knightley (Boyd) M. Married: (1) Camilla Rachel Hunter (d. 1942); (2) Mary Vavasour Lloyd Thomas Driver 1946. Children: 1st marriage—one daughter. Educ: Wellington Coll., Berks.; Royal Military Acad., Woolwich. Commissioned 1925; at Northwest frontier, India 1931–32; attended Staff Coll., 1938; Comdr., Special Air Service Brigade 1944–45; Dir. Military Operations, India 1945–46; Asst. Comdr., Staff Coll. 1948–49; Commander, Royal Artillery, 7th Armoured Div. 1950; Dir. Military Operations, War Office 1951–54; Gen. Officer Commanding, 6th Armoured Div., 1955–56; Chief Army Instr., Imperial Defence Coll., Jan.-Dec. 1957; Deputy Chief of Defence Staff 1957–60; Comdr. and Gen., British Forces, Hong Kong 1960–61; Gen. Officer Commanding-in-Chief, Eastern Command 1962–65; Aide-de-Camp (Gen.) to the Queen, 1963–65. Colonel Commandant, Royal Artillery, 1958; Deputy Lieutenant for Surrey, 1967. Hons: CBE, 1945; Chevalier Legion of Honor, 1945; Croix de Guerre avec Palme, 1945; Comdr. Order of Leopold II, 1946; CB, 1952; GBE, 1964.

JOHN LENNON
Songwriter, singer, musician
Born Liverpool, England, October 9th, 1940
Died New York City, U.S.A., December 8th, 1980

The canonization of John Lennon as a contemporary prophet began in 1964 when the Beatles first toured America, continued through the years of drug visions and apocalyptic politics, was kept alive by a small but devoted following while he retired to raise his son, and burst into full force when he was murdered. The hundreds of thousands of people who attended his memorials were simultaneously mourning for the legendary Beatle and his world-changing music, the collective dream of the Sixties and its betrayal in the Seventies, and the intelligent, loving, and talented man who had been an influential part of their cultural and emotional landscapes for more than 15 years.

The role of prophet, with its overtones of self-sacrifice, was courted by Lennon for a long time, especially in his post-Beatle years: it lent a public significance to the inner torment that he had suffered since childhood, when he was abandoned by his mother and father. He was able to write lines like "The way things are going, they're gonna crucify me" with tongue only partially in cheek, and likewise to declare himself a genius because "Genius is pain." His fans, on the whole, were happy to acquiesce in this myth as they had acquiesced in the other myths of the Beatles, from innocent sexuality to transcendent wisdom.

More recently, Lennon, secure at last in his family and creativity and looking forward to many more years of both, repudiated all such claims and the willingness of people to accept them. "What happens," he said in a 1980 interview, "is that somebody comes along with a good piece of the truth. Instead of the truth's being looked at, the person who brought it is looked at. The messenger is worshipped, instead of the message. . . . Well, you make your own dream. . . . That's what I'm saying now." A few months after he made these remarks, a deranged follower, obsessed with the Lennon persona of the past, shot him to death in the gateway of his home.

The mythical progress of John Lennon (for his life and myth have long since become inseparable) began in 1940 in the English port city of Liverpool, where he was born during an air raid. His father, a merchant seaman, jumped ship 18 months later and was little heard from afterwards; his mother moved in with another man and left the five-year-old John to be raised by her married sister, Mimi Smith. He was a constant reader and daydreamer from an early age, but was afflicted with a sense of being different, of seeing more acutely than everyone else. "I always was so psychic or intuitive or poetic or whatever you want to call it, that I was always seeing things in a hallucinatory way. . . . Neither my auntie nor my friends nor anybody could ever see what I did. It was very, very scary. . . . It caused me always to be a rebel."

By the time he entered Quarry Bank High School he was a gang leader and troublemaker with a caustic wit and a low tolerance for teachers and school rules; he quickly sank to the bottom of the class and failed his crucial O-level examinations. A sympathetic headmaster, noting his talent as a cartoonist, helped him to get into the Liverpool College of Art.

By then, however, it was far too late for a conventional life; Lennon, like thousands of other British teenagers, had lost his head to the rock'n'roll music that was being imported from the United States and was spending most of his time playing the guitar and singing with his own band, the Quarrymen. His moodiness, cynicism, and black humor were made worse by the sudden death of his mother, who had re-entered his life a few years earlier; still, he was a natural leader for whose attention the other band members competed. He and Paul McCartney began writing elementary rock songs together in 1957; George Harrison joined in 1958.

During the next few years, the Beatles, as they came to call themselves, played hundreds of dates in coffee clubs, ballrooms, and the seamy nightclubs of Hamburg's Reeperbahn, where they put together a roaring, energetic, amphetamine-charged act that attracted an enormous teenage following. Their talent was matched by their ambition. In 1962, with their rough Teddy-boy image prettied up by manager Brian Epstein and a new member, Ringo Starr, on drums, they put out the first of many hit records and set out on the first of their chaotic concert tours. Wherever they played—and nowhere more than in America—their audiences, mostly female, fell into a communal hysteria. By 1965 an extraordinary conjunction of social and cultural forces, not least the emotional potency of rock music and

The Beatles

its challenge to authoritarian values, had made them the focus of mass youth movements on two continents.

An American fan who was 15 in 1963 described a typical obsession with Lennon in Hunter Davies's 1968 biography *The Beatles*. "John was the most important person in my life. . . . When absolutely nothing else in life was good, I'd go to my room and have the Beatles, especially my darling John. They all furnished something I desperately needed. . . . I didn't like school and I didn't like home. They gave me something to live for when everything was black and depressing."

Lennon and the others, while continuing to turn out records, play concerts, and caper through two antic films, protected themselves from the weight of their fans' collective fantasies (from which they and their growing business network derived huge profits) by living together in an insulated world of drugs, groupies, and hangers-on, often to the exclusion of their wives and children. (Lennon had married his girlfriend, Cynthia Powell, in 1962 when she was pregnant with their son Julian.) A youth subculture based on rock music and marijuana was beginning to coalesce around them; England in particular was experiencing a resurgence of vitality as businessmen eager to exploit their success scoured Liverpool and the newly Swingin' London for rock bands to export.

As their public personas became better defined, John emerged as a sensitive but intellectually aggressive man whose relentless candor and pointed wit undermined the Beatles' commercially acceptable cuteness. By 1966 he had published two bestselling books of stories, poems, and cartoons in a surrealist vein, had starred in Dick Lester's film *How I Won The War,* and had shocked the American Bible Belt with his remark that the Beatles were "bigger than Jesus Christ." He was also consuming large quantities of LSD, like nearly everyone else in the rock music world, and was about to become the leading visionary of a culture awash in visions.

The romance between the Beatles and their fans, as it evolved during the 1960s, had come to be predicated on the shared understanding that conventional notions of reality form only a small part of an infinitely complex truth and that conventional mores and values are likewise open to question. The subculture owed this discovery to chemicals, but the Beatles were soon exploring other routes to awakened perception; their interest in meditation and mystical religion were logical steps in that direction. Lennon and McCartney, who had started out writing simple rockers with attractive harmonies, were now producing songs of a musical and lyrical complexity unprecedented in popular music; one critic called them "the greatest songwriters since Schubert."

Their composition process, as described in Davies's book and other places, involved the two of them trading ideas and toying with sound effects until the song emerged and was realized instrumentally with the assistance of the other Beatles and George Martin, their producer, whose training in classical music compensated for their own inability to read and write musical notation. The appeal of their songs was due in large part to the tension between McCartney's sentimentality and Lennon's abrasiveness. On the later albums, particularly *Revolver* and *Sgt. Pepper,* his lyrics became increasingly ambiguous, open to as many interpretations as his listeners, avid for enlightenment, could read into them. Even at their most surrealistic, when the lyrics were a montage of dislocated images and the music full of disturbing, inviting nuances (as in *Strawberry Fields Forever* or *I Am the Walrus),* his songs had extraordinary imaginative power and emotional intensity.

By 1966 the Beatles' studio-created music was too complex to perform on stage and the Beatles themselves, after four years of incessant touring, were desperate to resume more normal lives. As soon as they retired from touring, however, they lost the interdependence necessary to keep them together as a group and began to drift apart, although they continued to put out one brilliant and vastly influential album after another until 1970. The process of disintegration was accelerated by the business fiascoes that followed after the death of their manager, Brian Epstein, in 1967, and the group finally collapsed in a welter of personal feuds and lawsuits.

John Lennon and wife Yoko Ono

Lennon had long since divorced himself from the group and was completely absorbed in his relationship with Yoko Ono, a conceptual artist and avant-garde singer who had become a combination of muse, mother, and wife to him. To disillusioned rock fans it appeared that he had thrown away a charmed life, but he made it clear afterwards that she had rescued him from emotional and spiritual chaos when everyone else was content to let him destroy himself.

During the first six years of their marriage, Lennon and Ono experimented incessantly with art forms, music, and political philosophies, turning their lives into a series of absurd media events as if they could shock the world into righting itself by the force of their audacious example. For a time they were dedicated pacifists, holding a public "Bed Peace" in lieu of a honeymoon, sending symbolic acorns to world leaders, buying billboard space in twelve cities to declare that "War is over if you want it," and returning Lennon's MBE to the Queen as an antiwar gesture (he had received it in 1965 for services to Britain's economy). Later on they indulged in a flirtation with radical politics in New York City, where they had settled, and helped to organize antiwar demonstrations at the 1972 Republican National Convention. They produced a number of short films, did benefit concerts for political prisoners and retarded children, gave press conferences from inside large bags, and underwent primal scream therapy. Their music varied from random noises and old-fashioned rock (of which Lennon was still a peerless exponent) to the rhythmic chanting of *Give Peace a Chance* and the spare, haunting loveliness of *Imagine,* Lennon's dream of a society released from its own violence. "It is the most violent people who go for love and peace," he said. "I am a violent man who has learned not to be violent and regrets his violence."

Lennon's nonconformist stance was not appreciated by the Nixon government, which moved to deport him as a criminal (based on a 1969 conviction for possession of cannabis) when his visa expired in 1972. While he was fighting the deportation order and the lawsuit stemming from the Beatles' dissolution, Ono's former husband disappeared with their five-year-old daughter, Kyoko, after she was awarded legal custody of the child. There followed an 18-month separation during which Lennon went through one of his more self-destructive rages; after their reconciliation in 1975 they moved into the Dakota, a fortress-like apartment house in New York, and entered a long period of seclusion. On Lennon's birthday in 1975 an appeals judge overturned the deportation case and Yoko, who had previously suffered three miscarriages, bore a son, Sean.

For the next five years Lennon and Ono worked on their longest and most fruitful experiment: the creation of a harmonious, mutually interdependent married life carried on as a constant exchange of strengths between equal partners. Lennon, who had been too over-worked to experience the childhood of his son Julian, and too crippled by sexual stereotypes to participate in raising him, willingly gave up his career to be a full-time mother to Sean, while Ono, a strong-minded businesswoman for all her mysticism, directed their financial interests and real estate holdings, which included a dairy ranch. "I like it to be known," said Lennon, "that, yes, I looked after the baby and I made bread and I was a househusband and I am proud of it. It's the wave of the future and I'm glad to be in on the forefront of that, too."

They also had strong ideas about the responsibility that the members of a society bear toward one another. Ten percent of their annual income was set aside for donations to charities; among their 1980 contributions was a gift of $1,000 towards the purchase of bullet-proof vests for New York City policemen. In an open letter to the public, printed in newspapers in May 1979, they wrote, "All people who come to us are angels in disguise, carrying messages and gifts to us from the Universe."

By the summer of 1980, Lennon and Ono, their creativity re-freshed, were ready to start recording again. *Double Fantasy,* containing seven songs by each, all in celebration of love and family life, was released in November. "Lennon seems calm, confident, and content," wrote Stephen Holden in *Rolling Stone.* "For the first time in ages, he doesn't appear driven to deliver a major statement—so, naturally he does." "He's reaching out to me, the woman," said Ono of their single *Starting Over/Kiss Kiss Kiss.* "Reaching out after all that's happened, over the battlefield of dead families. . . . Altogether, both sides are a prayer to change the Eighties."

A month later Lennon was shot to death in the gateway of his apartment building by a man who had been stalking him for three days. On the following Sunday, thousands of mourners joined together to observe ten minutes of silent prayer in his memory, as Yoko Ono had requested. In New York's Central Park the crowd numbered more than 100,000. Until that day it had been unthinkable that a man of John Lennon's survival power and mythical stature could be removed from the world so easily; he had seemed as indestructible as his music.   J.P.

Born John Winston Lennon; changed name to John Ono Lennon 1969. Son of Fred L., merchant sailor and dishwasher, and Julia (Stanley) L. Married: (1) Cynthia Powell, art student, 1962 (div. 1968); (2) Yoko Ono, conceptual artist, 1969. Sons: 1st marriage—Julian, b. 1963; 2nd marriage—Sean, b. 1975. Raised as a Christian; later a pantheist. British citizen; settled in U.S. ca. 1971 and successfully fought deportation orders issued in 1973 and 1974; permanent resident of U.S. since 1976. Educ: Dovedale Primary Sch., Liverpool; Quarry Bank High Sch., Liverpool 1952–57; Liverpool Coll. of Art ca. 1957–60. Rock composer, lyricist, singer, and guitarist since 1950s; led rock group since 1956. Group known as The Beatles since 1961, played clubs in Liverpool and Hamburg and toured U.K. 1959–62; toured worldwide 1963–66; made records, appeared in films, and served as guiding spirits of youth movement in Britain and USA 1961–70. Lennon also writer, actor, cartoonist, record producer, avant-garde film producer, co-dir. of Apple Corp., and cultural and

political activist; recorded and played concerts with Yoko Ono, Plastic Ono Band, Elephant's Memory band, and others 1968–74; full-time father and husband 1975–80; returned to recording 1980. Founder, Spirit Foundn. Hons: Foyle's Literary Prize 1964 (for In His Own Write); MBE 1965 (returned 1969). With Beatles—New Musical Express poll winners 1961, 1965, 1966; Top Group, Merseybeat poll 1962; Show Business Personalities of the Year, Variety Club of Great Britain 1964; four Grammy Awards (for Sgt. Pepper) 1968; numerous gold records. With Paul McCartney—named outstanding English composers of 1963 by the London Times; multiple Ivor Novello Awards 1964, 1965, 1966, 1967, 1969; Grammy Award (for Michelle) 1967; others. *Partial discography:* Please Please Me, 1963; With the Beatles, 1963; Meet the Beatles!, 1964; The Beatles' Second Album, 1964; A Hard Day's Night, 1964; Something New, 1964; Beatles for Sale, 1964 (in U.S. as Beatles '65); The Early Beatles, 1965; Beatles VI, 1965; Help!, 1965; Rubber Soul, 1965; "Yesterday" . . . and Today, 1966; Revolver, 1966; A Collection of Beatles Oldies, 1966; Sgt. Pepper's Lonely Hearts Club Band, 1967; Magical Mystery Tour, 1967; Unfinished Music No. 1: Two Virgins, 1968; Yellow Submarine, 1969; Unfinished Music No. 2: Life with the Lions, 1969; Abbey Road, 1969; Wedding Album, 1969; The Plastic Ono Band: Live Peace in Toronto, 1969; Hey Jude, 1970; Let It Be, 1970; John Lennon/Plastic Ono Band, 1970; Imagine, 1971; Some Time in New York City, 1972; Mind Games, 1973; Walls and Bridges, 1974; Rock'n'Roll, 1975; Shaved Fish, 1975; Double Fantasy, 1980; also numerous singles, EPs, reissues, miscellaneous live albums, bootlegs. *Films: Performer*—A Hard Day's Night, 1964; Help!, 1965; How I Won the War, 1967; Magical Mystery Tour, 1967; Yellow Submarine, 1968; Rock'n'Roll Circus (unreleased), 1968; Let It Be, 1970; also numerous TV films, promotional films, and taped concerts. *Co-Producer*—Rape, 1969; Apotheosis (Balloon), Cannes Film Festival 1971; Fly, 1971; Imagine, 1972; Up Your Legs Forever; others. *Television appearances*—Thank Your Lucky Stars, 1963; Juke Box Jury, 1963; Sunday Night at the London Palladium, 1963; Royal Variety Show, London 1963; Ed Sullivan Show, NYC 1964; Ready Steady Go, 1964; Top of the Pops, 1964, 1966, 1967; One World: All You Need is Love (special), 1967; David Frost Show, 1967, 1972, 1975; Dick Cavett Show, 1970, 1972; many others. *Exhibitions:* (with Yoko Ono) Robert Fraser Gall., London, 1968; Covent Garden, 1968; London Art Gall. (lithographs), 1970; others. *Author: Books*—In His Own Write, 1964; A Spaniard in the Works, 1965. *Plays*—In His Own Write, London 1968; episode in Oh! Calcutta!, 1969. *Interviews:* Lennon Remembers: The Rolling Stone Interviews (compiled by Jann Wenner), 1971; Beatles in Their Own Words (compiled by Barry Miles); Newsweek Mag., Sept. 1980; Playboy Magazine, Jan. 1981; many others.
Further reading: A Cellarful of Noise by Brian Epstein, 1964; The True Story of the Beatles by Billy Shepherd, 1964; The Beatles by Hunter Davies, 1968; Apple to the Core by Peter McCabe and Robert Schonfeld, 1972; We Love You Beatles by M. Sutton, 1972; The Lennon Factor by P. Young, 1972; Twilight of the Gods by Wilfred Mellers, 1975; Love Me Do by Michael Braun, 1977; Mersey Beat: The Beginning of the Beatles by Barry Miles, 1978; The Beatles Forever by Nicholas Schaffner, 1978.

MARCELLO PAGLIERO
Film director and actor
Born London, England, January 15th, 1907
Died Paris, France, December 9th, 1980

Marcello Pagliero was one of the leading figures of the post–World War Two neo-realist school of Italian filmmaking. Born in London of a Genoese father and a French mother, he lived in Italy as a child, graduated from law school, and became a literary, art, and film critic.

Because he was fluent in English, he was hired in the late 1930s to dub voices for British and American films. He began writing film scripts in 1941 and collaborated on a number of set designs with Giulio Del Torre. His first film as a director, *07, Tassi,* begun in 1943, was interrupted by World War II and not finished until 1946.

In 1943 Pagliero met the famed director Roberto Rossellini, who took him on as co-director of *Desiderio.* Rossellini also offered him an acting job as the resistance leader Manfredi in his celebrated film *Roma, Città aperta (Open City),* which was shot in the streets of Rome in 1944 while it was still under occupation by the Nazis. The film won international acclaim, and Pagliero became known as an efficient, serious actor. The following year, Rossellini and Pagliero, along with Alfred Hayes, Klaus Mann, Federico Fellini, and Sergeo Amidici, collaborated on the script of *Paisà,* in which Pagliero also acted. "Like its predecessor," wrote critic Pierre Leprohon, "it presents (with a marvelously adroit mixture of tragedy, humour, subtlety, cruelty, and human knowledge) a significant selection of episodes from the reconquest of Italy. . . . Both [films] mark the flowering of a genre which was to give the Italian cinema a unique position for several years. . . . It was to set up its cameras in the streets and in the fields, demolishing the studio walls, and restoring contact with life as it is really lived."

In 1946 Pagliero directed *Fosse Ardeatine,* a documentary about a massacre of Roman citizens by the Nazis, and his best work, *Roma, Città libera,* "a highly distinctive tale of strange nocturnal happenings in Rome" (according to Leprohon). He moved to France in 1947, where he became popular as an actor in such films as *Les Jeux sont faits* and *Dedée d'Anvers.* His later films, made in both France and Italy, included *Un Homme marche dans la ville, Les Amants de Bras-Morts,* and *La Putain respectueuse,* an adaptation of the Sartre play which Pagliero co-directed with Charles Brabant. After directing a version of Jules Verne's *20,000 Leagues Under the Sea* in the Soviet Union in 1960, he became a writer and director for French television.

S.F.

Studied law, Italy. Art, literary, and film critic 1930s; translated and dubbed dialogue from American and British films into Italian, late 1930s; screenwriter and set designer 1941–43; film director and actor, Italy and France since 1943; television scriptwriter, France since 1964. *Director:* 07, Tassi (Taxi), 1943; (co-dir.) Giorni di Gloria, 1945; (with Roberto Rossellini) Desiderio, 1945; Roma, Città libera, 1945; (co-dir.) Fosse Ardeatine, 1946; Un Homme marche dans la ville, 1950; La Rose rouge, 1950; Les Amants de Bras-Morts, 1951; (with Charles Brabant) La Putain respectueuse, 1952; Destinées, 1953; Vergine Moderna, ca. 1954; Vestire gli Ignudi, 1954; Cheri-Bibi, 1955; L'Odyssée de Capitaine Steve/La Vallée du Paradis, 1956; Il Tesoro Nero, 1956; Vingt Mille Lieues sur la Terre (20,000 Leagues Under the Sea), 1960. *Actor:* Roma, Città aperta (Open City, Manfredi), 1945; (also co-scenarist) Paisà, 1946; L'Altra, 1947; Les Jeux sont faits, 1947; Dedée d'Anvers, 1948; Tourbillon, 1952; Seven Thunders, 1957; Le Bel Age, 1958; Les Mauvais Coups, 1961; Ton Ombre est la mienne, 1962; Je vous alue Mafia, 1965; Les Gauloises bleues, 1966.

HIS BEATITUDE BENEDICTOS I
Patriarch of Jerusalem
Born Brusa, Asia Minor, 1892
Died Jerusalem, Israel, December 10th, 1980

As Abbot of the Church of the Holy Sepulchre in Jerusalem, Benedictos I was the spiritual leader of approximately 160,000 members of the Greek Orthodox Church in Israel and Jordan. Because each regional patriarch of the Greek Orthodox Church is autonomous, he wielded considerable power. Known for his interests in history, law and ecumenical principles, Patriarch Benedictos I sought to unify the Eastern Orthodox Patriarch of Constantinople with the Roman Catholic Papacy. In 1964, Patriarch Athenagoras and Pope Paul V met, the first occasion on which the spiritual heads of these churches had spoken together in 500 years.

After graduating from the Patriarchal Academy in Jerusalem, Vasilios Papadopoulos became a monk, taking the name Benedictos. He was then ordained a Deacon in the Chapel of Calvary in the Church of the Holy Sepulchre. During World War One, he followed Damianos, the Patriarch of Jerusalem, into exile in Damascus. In the course of his studies in both Jerusalem and Athens, Benedictos became fluent in Greek, French, English and Arabic—knowledge which he put to use when he was named Patriarchal representative in 1927. Benedictos's rise to Patriarch began with his ordination as priest and subsequent elevation to the rank of Archimandrite in October, 1929. When he returned to Jerusalem in early February, 1946, Benedictos was immediately made a member of the Holy Synod of the Patriarchate and, in March 1951, received the title Archbishop of Tiberias.

His Beatitude Benedictos (right) greeting Dr. Arthur Ramsey, Archbishop of Centerbury in London

Benedictos I was a compromise candidate for Patriarch. After two weeks of deadlock, the feuding Arab and Greek factions with the Jerusalem Patriarchate's Holy Synod had reached a stalemate. The lower echelons of the Patriarchate were Arabs and the upper positions remained in the hands of the Greeks. Each faction wanted one of its members elected Patriarch, but both realized their opponents would not give in. At last they decided unanimously that Turkish-born Benedictos was the ideal choice for Patriarch.

On March 1st, 1957, Benedictos I was enthroned, thereby becoming the leader of the oldest and largest Christian community in Jerusalem and custodian of some 100 holy sites such as the Tomb of Christ in Jerusalem and the Grotto of the Nativity in Bethlehem. His full, formal title was "His Beatitude and Holiness Benedictos, Holy Father and Patriarch of the Holy City of Jerusalem and all Palestine, Syria, Arabia, Beyond the Jordan, Cana of Galilee and Saint Sion." He is perhaps best known in the United States for his visit in 1961 to such cities as New York, Chicago, Boston, Detroit, Pittsburgh, Los

Angeles, San Francisco, New Orleans, and Washington, D.C. At the White House, Patriarch Benedictos presented President John F. Kennedy with the Grand Cross and Insignia of the Order of the Holy Sepulchre, the highest honor the Greek Orthodox Patriarchate of Jerusalem can confer. The medal is said to contain within it a fragment of the true Cross.   L.R.

Born Vasilios Papadopoulos. Unmarried. Greek Orthodox. Lived in Jerusalem since 1906. Turkish citizen. Educ: Greek Orthodox Patriarchal Acad., Jerusalem 1906–14; Univ. of Athens, degrees in law, economics, political science and Greek Orthodox Theology 1921–25. Secty. in offices of Jerusalem Patriarchate 1914; ordained Deacon 1914; Rep., Jerusalem Patriarchate at World Christian Conference of Faith and Order, Geneva 1927; Exarch (Patriarchal Rep.) of the Holy Sepulchre in Athens 1929–46; ordained priest and Archimandrite 1929; named member of Holy Synod of Jerusalem 1946; appointed Chmn., Pending Property Cttee. and Legal Advisor to Patriarchate 1947; Chmn., Financial Cttee. 1950; Rep., Patriarch of Jerusalem at Trusteeship Conference on the Internationalization of Jerusalem 1950; Archbishop of Tiberias 1951; Greek Orthodox Patriarch of Jerusalem from 1957. Hons: Grand Cross of King George of Greece; Grand Cross and Cordon of the Patriarchate of Damascus; Order of St. Dionysios of the Island of Zakynthos of Greece; Order of St. Sergios.

CHARLES PARKER
BBC Radio features producer and creator of the Radio Ballads
Born Bournemouth, England, 1919
Died England, December 10th, 1980

Today, British radio documentaries enjoy a usually deserved reputation for excellence and innovation. Program-makers are well aware of the dramatic impact inherent in letting ordinary people tell their own stories in their own voices, and of the effective technique of combining these voices with music and songs, to underline and comment on the points being made. So widely accepted is this technique, that it is hard to believe it was virtually unknown until the late 1950s, and derives largely from the work of one man: Charles Parker, creator of the Radio Ballads.

Born in Bournemouth in 1919, Parker in his early career was typical of the many "bright young men" who joined the BBC after the Second World War. In many ways he was 'classic' BBC material—a graduate of Queen's College, Cambridge, where he had involved himself in the university's theatrical life, followed by war service with the Royal Navy, he had obtained the rank of Lieutenant-Commander of submarines and been decorated with a DSO before embarking on an initially conventional, but finally stormy career with the BBC.

Parker was working for the features department at BBC Birmingham when, in 1958, he was asked to make a program about a Stockport railwayman who had died heroically in a runaway train accident. Several things combined to make this program out of the ordinary. Parker had become increasingly interested in folk music and through this had met Ewan McColl, the socialist folk singer, and his collaborator Peggy Seeger, and Parker hired them to assist him on the program. McColl had worked for the BBC during the 1930s under the legendary Manchester controller Archie Harding, another socialist, who had encouraged programs which featured working people. McColl also brought with him an enthusiasm for the newly developed portable tape recorder—an enthusiasm which Parker quickly shared. At this time 'ordinary' people were rarely heard on radio; their words would be recorded, and then 'properly spoken' by actors. Within a week Parker had exhausted the entire Midlands region tape stock, recording some 70 to 80 hours of conversations with the train driver's family and work-mates, which he then edited into an hour-long program of narrative interwoven with songs composed by McColl, Seeger and others. *The Ballad of John Axon* (1958) was not only a fine tribute to an heroic man, but also conveyed with unprecedented vividness what it was like to be a railwayman.

Over the next eight years, Parker and his team completed eight more Radio Ballads, despite growing opposition both within the BBC and outside it. *Song of the Road* (1959), a celebration of the workers who built the M1, Britain's first motorway, was criticized for being 'biased in favor of the working class.' *Singing the Fishing* (1960), perhaps the finest of the Ballads, dealt with the North Sea herring industry, and won an Italia prize for the BBC. Among Parker's other Ballads were: *The Big Hewer* (coalminers); *The Fight Game* (boxers); *On the Edge* (teenagers); and *The Travelling People* (gypsies). These programs led to profound and radical changes in the style and techniques of British broadcasting, and were influential in many other countries; they also had a lasting effect on Parker himself.

Originally a conventional Anglican Tory (Conservative) Parker now became, through his work, a convinced socialist, increasingly identifying with the lives and aspirations of the people whose words he recorded. Contact with the gypsies while making *The Travelling People,* for example, led to him becoming Chairman of the Gypsy Liaison Committee in Birmingham. But his committed stance caused growing unease within certain factions at the BBC. The closing down of the once prestigious Features Department, and the curtailed independence of the regions, served to narrow Parker's scope, and he found it ever more difficult to make the programs he wanted. In 1973 he was forced to accept an 'early retirement.'

From then, until his death seven years later from a stroke, he continued his work in other forms, as a writer and lecturer (especially to schools), and in particular through the Banner Theatre of Actuality in Birmingham, which he founded, although he was evidently frustrated at being exiled from his chosen medium. But despite the overt rejection he suffered, his work has had a deep and irreversible effect on both radio and television documentaries.   T.F.

Married Phyllis Norman 1944. One son and one daughter. Educ: grad., Queen's Coll., Cambridge. Mil. Service: Lt.-Comdr. of submarines, Royal Navy. Awarded DSO 1945. Joined the BBC; composed first of his ballads while working for Features Dept., BBC Birmingham 1958; retired 1973. Chmn., Gypsy Liaison Cttee., Birmingham. Founder, Banner Theatre of Actuality, Birmingham. Hons: Italia prize for the BBC (for Singing the Fishing) 1960. *Compositions include:* The Ballad of John Axon, 1958; Song of the Road, 1959;

Singing the Fishing, 1960; The Big Hewer; The Fight Game; On the Edge; The Travelling People.

JEAN LESAGE
Canadian politician and Premier of Quebec
Born Montreal, Canada, June 10th, 1912
Died Quebec, Canada, December 11th, 1980

As Premier of Quebec from 1960 to 1966, Jean Lesage launched a sweeping overhaul of that province's social, economic, and administrative structure. Lesage had been a leader of the Liberal Party since the late 1940s.

An attorney by profession, Lesage entered Canadian politics in 1945 when he was elected to a seat in the House of Commons. In 1953 he was appointed Minister of Natural Resources in the Liberal administration of Prime Minister Louis S. St. Laurent. Five years later, he resigned his seat to become head of the Quebec Liberal party and, in 1960, after the Liberals had been out of power for 14 years, Lesage was elected Premier of Quebec.

After years of conservative rule in the heavily Catholic, French-speaking province, Lesage instituted a seemingly radical modernization program. His government tripled welfare spending, raised the health department budget six times over what it had been, and assumed responsibility for education, which had hitherto been administered exclusively by the Roman Catholic Church. Lesage also increased government's administrative role by nationalizing almost all of the province's hydroelectric resources and private utilities. The Liberals were defeated in the 1966 election; Lesage continued to lead the Liberal Party until his retirement in 1970.

Although not a separatist himself, Lesage's Energy Minister had been Rene Levesque, who abandoned the Liberal Party in 1968 when Lesage refused to support his call for the province to secede from the Canadian federal system. Levesque subsequently formed the Parti Quebecois, which won provincial elections in 1976, elevating Levesque to the position of Premier. T.P.

Son of Xavier L. and Cecile Cote L. Married Corinne Lagarde 1938. Children: Jules; René; Marie; Raymond. Roman Catholic. Educ: Laval Univ., B.A., LL.L.; Univ. of Western Ontario, D.C.L. 1963. Crown Attorney, Quebec District 1939–44; Member, Canada's Natl. Parliament 1945–58; Canadian delegate to the U.N. 1950–51; Asst. to the Minister of External Affairs 1951; Asst. to the Minister of Finance 1952; Minister of Natural Resources 1953–57; head of the Liberal Party of Quebec 1958–70; Premier of Quebec 1960–66. Hons: French Language Medal, Académie Française 1963.

SIR JULES THORN
Founder of Thorn Electrical Industries
Born Austria, February 1899
Died England, December 12th, 1980

Sir Jules Thorn was founder, chairman, managing director, and president of Thorn Electrical Industries, leading it through a series of postwar acquisitions to conglomerate status with more than 150 subsidiaries employing over 70,000 people.

Born in Austria in 1899, Thorn studied business management at the University of Vienna before traveling to England in the 1920s as a sales representative for an Austrian gas mantle firm. He soon settled in England as an importer of light bulbs and radio valves and then opened a shop which specialized in radio rentals. He proceeded to purchase a company which manufactured electric lamps. In 1936 the newly purchased Ferguson Radio Corporation became Thorn Electrical Industries.

After World War Two Thorn began expansion through acquisition from the base he had created in consumer electronics. He purchased domestic appliance and tool companies and opened the world's largest radio and television rental facility. He began to enter engineering and research, and was responsible for a variety of brand names including Bendix, Mazda, Kenwood, Parkinson Cowan, Multi Broadcast, Clarkson, Towler, and Ferguson.

Driven by an instinct for profit, Thorn was not afraid to speculate and to reinvest even his personal fortune in experimental markets, but had keen intuition for good and bad economic opportunities, rewarded by ever-burgeoning profits. Enthusiastic and affable, he inspired confidence in both investors and employees.

Thorn personally and meticulously controlled all of the corporation's projects. Naively astonished that not everyone shared his totally-consuming commitment to business, he delighted in his self-imposed reputation as a rebel. Functioning from day to day with boundless energy, he expected similar performance from his employees and colleagues; his dedication and concern engendered loyalty and efficiency.

Knighted in 1964, Thorn participated in professional associations. The small, private sector of his life was kept strictly segregated from business; he enjoyed traveling, music, and reading. Although part of Sir Jules Thorn's success in running an empire of such vast magnitude as Thorn Electrical Industries depended on his ability to delegate responsibility, he found it extremely difficult to choose his own successor. He died at the age of 81, a pioneer in the mass production of high-quality consumer goods.   J.S.

Educ: Univ. of Vienna, studies in business management. Emigrated to England ca. 1920s. Naturalized British citizen. Sales rep., Austrian gas mantle co., England; sold imported light bulbs and radio valves, England; with Electric Lamp Service Co. 1928; opened rental shop for radios, Twickenham 1931; with electric factory, Edmonton 1932; acquired Ferguson Radio Corp. Ltd. 1936 (renamed Thorn Electrical Industries). With Thorn Electrical Industries: Managing Dir. 1937–69; Chmn. 1937–76; Pres. 1976–80. Business acquisitions: Ecko-Ensign Electric Co. 1950; Tricity Cookers 1951; Ultra Radio and TV 1961; Metal Industries 1967; Radio Rentals (merger) 1968; Kenwood 1968; KMT Holdings 1968; Parkinson Cowan 1971; Clarkson Intl. Tools

1974; J. and F. Stone Retail 1975; Cleveland Twist Drill 1976. Opened lighting lab 1975. Member, British Radio Equipment Manufacturing Assoc. 1964–68; Chmn. and Pres., Radio Industrial Council 1966; Pres., Conference of Electronics Industry 1971; Member, Sch. Council, Univ. Coll. of London Medical Sch. Hons: knighted 1964; Hon. Master of the Bench, Middle Temple 1969; Fellow, Royal Soc. of Arts; Hon. Fellow, Illuminating Engineering Soc.

DUKE OF PORTLAND
SIR FERDINAND CAVENDISH-BENTINCK
Speaker of Kenya's Legislative Council
Born England, July 4th, 1889
Died Nairobi, Kenya, December 13th, 1980

Sir Ferdinand Cavendish-Bentinck, an Englishman who spent most of his life in East Africa and died at the age of 91 in Nairobi, Kenya, was a key political figure whose considerable influence in the affairs declined as self-determination for African blacks was achieved in the late 1950s. Cavendish-Bentinck, the eighth Duke of Portland and one of Britain's biggest landowners, ended his career by attempting to safeguard minority rights for the European community in Kenya. After a brief military and engineering career, Cavendish-Bentinck went to Uganda in 1925, serving for two years as private secretary to the Governor. Relocating in East Africa in 1930, he became honorary secretary of the Convention of Associations, the political organization of resident Europeans. Soon active in the politics of neighboring Kenya, then a British colony with a self-ruling white colonial government, Cavendish-Bentinck was elected to its Legislative Council two years later. Active in many public capacities during World War II, he devoted his energies in subsequent years to the development of Kenyan agriculture, still the country's chief economic enterprise at the time of Cavendish-Bentinck's death—though only about 15 percent of its total land is truly arable.

Minister of Agriculture from 1954 to 1962, "C-B," as he was affectionately known throughout Kenya, was appointed Speaker of the Legislative Council in 1955. He resigned that office in 1960 when it became certain that the Council would have an African majority. Always ardent in his endeavors to persuade young Europeans to settle in Kenya, Cavendish-Bentinck was persuaded to lead the Kenya Coalition, an organization to secure the civil rights of the European community. His attempt to re-enter elective politics failed when he was defeated in 1961 by his white opponent who enjoyed strong African support. He then accepted a controversial assignment to London in the face of declining support from the Europeans who had lost confidence in his ability to maintain their position of influence. Leaving 26 years of service in the Legislative Council behind him, C-B slowly faded out of Kenya's politics. He succeeded his cousin as Duke of Portland in 1977.   A.C.

Earl of Portland, Viscount Woodstock, Baron Cirencester, Marquess of Titchfield, Baron Bolsover. Known as C-B. Son of William George Frederick C.-B. and Ruth Mary St. Maur C.-B. Married: (1) Went-

worth Frances Hope-Johnstone 1912 (dissolved); (2) Gwyneth 1950.
Educ: Eton; Royal Military Coll., Sandhurst; and in Germany. Mil.
Service: 60th Rifles, King's Royal Rifle Corps, served in Malta, India,
and Europe, 1914–18; Gen. Staff Officer, War Office; Co. Comdr.,
later Asst. Adjutant, Royal Military Coll., Sandhurst. Worked for
Vickers Ltd., Brussels, 1923–24; Private Secty. to Gov. of Uganda,
1925–27; founder and chmn. Kenya Assn., 1932; member, Legislative
Council, and Exec. Council, Kenya, 1934–60; chmn., Tanganyika
League and African Defence Fedn., 1938; chmn., Agricultural Pro-
duction and Settlement Bd., Kenya, 1939–45; Timber Controller for
E. Africa, 1940–45; member, E. African Civil Defence and Supply
Council, 1940–45; Delegate, Delhi Conference, 1940; Member to
Agricultural and Natural Resources in Kenya Govt., 1945–55;
Speaker of Kenya Legislative Council, 1955–60; Head, Kenya Coali-
tion; Member, E. African Advisory Council on Agriculture, Animal
Industry and Forestry; E. African Agricultural, Forestry, and Veterin-
ary Research Organisations Cttee. Hons: Officier de la Couronne
Hon. Secty. of the Convention of Assocs.; CMG 1941; KBE 1956; 8th
Duke of Portland 1977. Author of major articles on African subjects.

SIR (RONALD) MARK (CUNLIFFE) TURNER
Merchant banker and business executive
Born London, England, 1906
Died London, England, December 13th, 1980

Sir Mark Turner, a merchant banker for most of his career, became
chairman of the Rio Tinto-Zinc Corporation, a mining and industrial
conglomerate which he had helped to form in 1962.

Educated at Wellington College, Turner joined the merchant
banking firm of M. Samuel & Co. in 1924 and moved to Robert
Benson & Co. Ltd. ten years later. In 1939, at the beginning of the
Second World War, he joined the Ministry of Economic Warfare,
where he remained until 1944 when he entered the Foreign Office.
Turner served as under-secretary in the Allied Control Office from
1945 until 1947, and, for his work in the post-war administration of
economic affairs in Germany and Austria, he was knighted in 1946.

Returning to London in 1947, Turner became a managing director
of the merchant banking firm of Benson-Lonsdale. He also accepted
positions as non-executive director and then managing director of the
Rio Tinto Company. Retaining the former position after leaving
managerial duties to Sir Val Duncan, Turner was instrumental in
bringing about a merger, in 1962, of Rio Tinto with the Consolidated
Zinc Corporation. Turner served as deputy chairman of Rio Tinto
Zinc (RTZ) from 1966 until 1975, when he became chairman and chief
executive; he also served as the company's finance director beginning
in 1973. The combined interests of RTZ include mining and manufacturing concerns related to the production of aluminium, copper, gold,
iron ore, lead, silver, uranium, zinc and alloy metals; it also has
holdings in coal and oil production and in chemicals and chemical
products, including borax.

In addition to his activities at RTZ, Turner held a number of
directorships in banking firms and mining companies.   J.S.

Son of Christopher R.T. and Jill H.P. (Cunliffe) T. Married: (1)
Elizabeth Mary Sutton 1931 (div. 1936); (2) Margaret Wake 1939.
Three sons; three daughters. With M. Samuel & Co. 1924–34; with
Robert Benson & Co. 1934–39; with Ministry of Economic Warfare
1939–44; Foreign Office 1944–45; Under-secty., Control Office for
Germany and Austria 1945–47; Managing Dir., Benson Lonsdale
1947–71; Chmn., Mercantile Credit Co. 1957–72; Deputy Chmn.,
Leinwort, Benson Co. 1966–71, Kleinwort Benson Lonsdale 1969–77;
Deputy Chmn. 1966–75 and Chmn. and Chief Exec. from 1975, Rio
Tinto Zinc; Chmn., British Home Stores 1968–76 and Bank of
America Intnl. Ltd. 1971–76. Dir: Rio Algon; Whitbread Investment
Co. Ltd.; Brinco Ltd.; Conzinc Rio Tinto of Australia; Hamilton
Brothers Oil Co. (Great Britain) Ltd. Chmn., Anglesey Aluminum.
Hons: knighted 1946.

SIR (THOMAS) HUGH (WILLIAM) BEADLE
Chief Justice of Rhodesia
Born Salisbury, Rhodesia, February 6th, 1905
Died Johannesburg, South Africa, December 14th, 1980

The Right Hon. Sir Hugh Beadle, as chief justice of Rhodesia, was a
prominent intermediary between the regime of Ian Smith and the
British government during the Rhodesian independence crisis of the
1960s. Beadle, born in Salisbury, was educated at Cape Town
University in South Africa and won a Rhodes Scholarship to Queens
College, Oxford, where he earned a B.C.L. degree. Beginning in
1930, he practiced law in Bulawayo and served with the Royal West
African Frontier Force in 1939. He sat in Parliament as a member of
the United Party from 1939 to 1950 and was Parliamentary Secretary
to the Prime Minister and Deputy Judge Advocate-General to the
Southern Rhodesian Forces from 1940 to 1946. After the Second
World War he held several ministerial posts, including Minister of
Justice, in Rhodesian cabinets. He was appointed a judge of the High
Court in 1950 and Chief Justice in 1961, three months after he was
created a knight, and was named to the Privy Council in 1964.

During the 1960s, when the white-minority-ruled government of
Rhodesia declared itself independent from Britain in order to avoid a
planned transition to black majority rule, Beadle, a close friend of
British colonial governor Sir Humphrey Gibbs, played a significant
role in negotiations between the estranged nations. In 1965 he was
named to head a royal commission to determine whether independence was genuinely desired by the Rhodesian population. In November of that year, the Prime Minister of Rhodesia, Ian Smith,
proclaimed a state of emergency and announced a Unilateral Declaration of Independence that was not recognized by Britain, which
moved to institute economic sanctions through the United Nations.
Beadle nonetheless traveled to London to try to effect a reconciliation, although Smith declared that Beadle was not authorized to
represent his regime. He acted as an advisor to Smith during the 1968
negotiations with Wilson aboard the H.M.S. Tiger at Gibraltar,
where, much to the irritation of Wilson, he counseled Smith to keep

the British proposals secret from the Rhodesian public until they had been discussed by the cabinet.

In 1968, after the Rhodesian government had executed several African political prisoners in defiance of a royal reprieve, the High Court ruled that the Unilateral Declaration of Independence, which had come under legal challenge, was indeed valid, and that the Smith regime was both the *de facto* and the *de jure* government of the country. "I'm satisfied that few well informed persons living in Rhodesia at the moment would disagree with the statement that the territory has been effectively governed during the past two years," Beadle said. "It had to be accepted that the present Government was in effective control." The British announced that Beadle would no longer be recognized as deputy to its colonial governor. A year later, when he ruled that the British could not legally take control from the firmly established Smith regime, he was nearly stripped of his honorary fellowship from Queen's College, Oxford, which had been awarded him for his upholding of the 1961 constitution.

In a celebrated case in 1973, Beadle reversed the conviction of Peter Niesewand, a journalist who had been sentenced to two years in prison for violating the Official Secrets Act, ruling that his publications had not been prejudicial to the security of the state. Another landmark decision was his 1977 release of two Botswanan nationals who had been captured on Botswanan soil and charged with illegal possession of arms. (At the time, Botswana was granting political asylum to Rhodesian political refugees.) Beadle, declaring that to hear the case would be to condone the illegal abduction of non-Rhodesian nations, declared that the court had no jurisdiction. "To allow states not at war with each other to . . . invade each other's territory and capture each other's nationals . . . is not conducive to preserving law and order."

Beadle, an avid sportsman who was once nearly killed by a bull elephant he had wounded, retired from the court in 1977. He was married three times and had two daughters by his first wife.   N.S.

Son of A. W. B., Secty. to Southern Rhodesian Treasury. Married: (1) Leonie Barry 1934 (d. 1953); (2) Olive Staley Jackson 1954 (d. 1974); (3) Pleasance Johnson 1976. Children: 1st marriage—two daughters. Church of England. Educ: Salisbury Boys' High Sch.; Diocesan Coll., Rondebosch; Univ. of Cape Town, South Africa, B.A. with hons. in Dutch Roman law and LL.B.; Queen's Coll., Oxford (Rhodes Scholarship), B.C.L. ca. 1928. Mil. Service: seconded Royal West African Frontier Force, Gold Coast 1939–40. Advocate, Bulawayo 1930–39; Member of Parliament from Bulawayo North (United Party) 1939–50; Deputy Judge Advocate-Gen., Southern Rhodesian Forces 1940–46; Parliamentary Secty. to Prime Minister 1940–46; Minister of Justice, Internal Affairs, Health, and Education 1946–50; Judge 1950–61 and Chief Justice 1961–77, High Court. Member: Bulawayo Club; Salisbury Club. Hons: Q.C. 1946; OBE 1946; Cross of the Grand Comdr., Royal Hellenic Order of the Phoenix, Greece 1950; CMG 1957; knighted 1961; P.C. 1964; Hon. Fellow, Queen's Coll., Oxford 1966.

LORD ERSKINE OF RERRICK
Banker and solicitor; Governor of Northern Ireland
Born Scotland, December 14th, 1893
Died Great Britain, December 14th, 1980

Lord Erskine of Rerrick—born John Maxwell Erskine—a notable Scottish banker and business executive, spent almost 60 years with the Commercial Bank of Scotland (which was later assumed into the Royal Bank of Scotland). He also served on numerous Scottish and British public bodies, and for four years in the 1960s, was Governor of the troubled province of Northern Ireland.

After his graduation from Edinburgh University, Erskine joined the legal staff of the Commercial Bank of Scotland at their head office in Edinburgh. During his early years with the bank he qualified as a solicitor, and in 1924 was appointed an inspector of branches. A year later he was promoted to the post of Assistant Manager of the bank's main London office. Early in the 1930s he returned to Edinburgh as Assistant General Manager and in 1932, at only 38 years of age, he became General Manager, a position he held until 1953. In 1937 he was elected to the presidency of the Institute of Bankers in Scotland, and served for three years.

Active in public affairs, Erskine was appointed a Deputy Lieutenant and Justice of the Peace for the County of the City of Edinburgh in 1932, and from 1939 until 1945 he served as the Chairman of the King George and Queen Elizabeth Officers' club, Edinburgh, for Overseas Personnel under the Empire Societies War Hospital Committee.

Erskine served as President of the Edinburgh Chamber of Commerce and Manufacturers from 1941–44, and became first Chairman of the Central Committee of the Scottish Chambers of Commerce from 1942–44. He also joined the Postmaster General's Advisory Council and served in the War Works Commission. His work with the Scottish Savings Committee as Chairman and later President, earned Erskine a CBE in 1946; he was knighted in 1949.

Lord Erskine was also involved in the improvement of Scottish medical and social services during the 1940s, sitting on the Hetherington Departmental Committee on Hospital Policy in Scotland and on the Committee of Management, the Royal Victoria Hospital Tuberculosis Trust. Also involved in social service and education, Erskine served as Chairman and then President of the Scottish Council of Social Services. In addition he found time to be a trustee of the Carnegie Trust for Scottish Universities, and president of the Edinburgh Union of Boys' Clubs. An advocate of the use of hydro-electric power, Erskine was a member of the North of Scotland Hydro-Electric Board for 11 years and was the Board's Department Chairman in 1960–61.

Two years before his retirement as General Manager of the Commercial Bank of Scotland, Erskine was named a Director and continued in that capacity until 1969. Erskine's continuing concern with the related fields of energy use and transportation led him to the Chairmanship of the Transportation Users' Consultative Committee, 1954–57, membership in the Scottish Transportation Council, 1955–56, and membership in the National Referral Tribunal for the Coal Mining Industry, 1956–59.

A change of direction for Erskine occurred in 1964 when he became Governor of Northern Ireland, the first Presbyterian to hold that

position. Lord Erskine wholeheartedly assumed the role of peacemaker, both between Protestants and Catholics in Northern Ireland
and between Northern Ireland and the Irish Republic. He managed to
persuade the Cardinal to break a tradition built from hostility, of not
attending any functions at the government house, and braved the
insults of Protestant extremists (whose effrontery caused Lady
Erskine to suffer a heart attack). Lord Erskine retired as Governor in
1968. Erskine was honored many times. Most notably, he was
knighted in 1956, made a Baronet in 1961 and a Baron in 1964.   J.S.

Son of John E. Married: Henrietta Dunnett 1922. Children: Major
Hon. Iain Maxwell Erskine; one daughter. Presbyterian. Educ:
Kirkcudbright Acad.; Edinburgh Univ., c. 1905–10. Joined Commer-
cial Bank of Scotland Ltd. (now part of Royal Bank of Scotland),
1910: Member, Law Dept., head office 1910; Solicitor, c. 1910–20;
Inspector of branches 1924; Asst. Mgr. in London 1925–30; Asst.
General Mgr. 1930–32; Gen. Mgr. 1932–53; Dir. 1951–69. Gov. of
Northern Ireland 1964–68. Chmn., Securicor (Scotland) Ltd.; Dir.,
Caledonian Insurance Co., Guardian Assurance Co.; Vice Pres.,
Trustee Savings Bank Assn. Appointed Justice of the Peace 1932;
Pres., Inst. of Bankers in Scotland 1937–40; Chmn., King George and
Queen Elizabeth Officers' Club, Edinburgh, for Overseas Personnel
under Empire Societies War Hosp. Cttee., 1939–45; Pres., Edinburgh
Chamber of Commerce and Manufacturers, 1941–44; First Chmn.,
Central Cttee., Scottish Chambers of Commerce (now Scottish
Chamber of Commerce), 1942–44; Member, Hetherington Depart-
mental Cttee. on Hospital Policy in Scotland, 1942; Trustee and
Member, Exec. Cttee., Carnegie Trust for Scottish Univs., 1944–57;
Member, Cttee. of Management, Royal Victoria Hosp. Tuberculosis
Trust, 1944–56; Member, Postmaster General's Advisory Council,
1945–49; Chmn. 1945–58 and Pres. 1958–72, Scottish Savings Cttee.;
Edinburgh Union of Boys' Clubs, 1945–56; Member, War Works
Commn., 1945–59; Member 1948–59 and Deputy Chmn. 1960–61,
North of Scotland Hydro-Electric Bd.; Pres. 1949–57 and Chmn.
1945–49, Scottish Council of Social Service; Member, Scottish Cttee.
on Scottish Financial and Trade Statistics (Catto Cttee.) 1950–52;
Chmn., Scottish Hosp. Endowments Research Trust 1953–71; Chmn.,
Transportation Users' Consultative Cttee. for Scotland, 1954–57;
Member, Scottish Transportation Council, 1955–56; Member, Natl.
Referral Tribunal for Coal Mining Industry, 1956–59; Founding
Member, Thistle Foundn. Member, Queen's Body Guard for Scot-
land (Royal Co. of Archers), 1935–80. Hons: F.R.S.E. 1933; D.L.,
Edinburgh Univ. 1940; C.B.E. 1946; knighted 1949; G.B.E. 1956;
Baronet 1960; Hon. L.L.D., Glasgow Univ., 1962; created Baron
1964; elected a Knight of St. John 1965; Freeman, Royal Burgh of
Kirkcudbright 1967; Hon. L.L.D., Queen's Univ., Belfast 1968; Hon.
Life Member, Edinburgh Chamber of Commerce and Manufacturers,
1968, and Northern Ireland Chamber of Commerce and Industry,
1968; Hon. Member, Co. of Merchants of City of Edinburgh, 1970;
Hon. F.R.C.P.E., 1972; Hon. Life Member, Caledonian Club,
Edinburgh.

ELSTON (GENE) HOWARD
Baseball player and coach
Born St. Louis, Missouri, U.S.A., February 23rd, 1929
Died New York City, U.S.A., December 14th 1980

Elston Howard's talent as a baseball player enabled him to contribute stability and leadership to one of the most successful teams in professional sports. Between 1955, when he joined the New York Yankees, and 1964, when the Yankees completed a string of nine American League pennants and four world championships, Howard played a vital role.

While serving as catcher, outfielder, and first baseman, Howard emerged as a respected and trusted teammate among such notables as Mickey Mantle, Whitey Ford, and Yogi Berra and compiled a career batting average of .274. His brilliance during the 1958 World Series earned him the Babe Ruth Award as the Series' outstanding performer, and five years later Howard, who represented the American League in nine all-star games, was recognized as the League's Most Valuable Player.

Acquired by the Boston Red Sox in 1967, primarily for his leadership qualities, Howard confirmed the Red Sox' faith in his judgment and his rapport with fellow players by helping to coax the Bostonians to their upset pennant victory of that year. Finishing his playing career with the Red Sox after the 1968 season, he returned to the Yankees to become the American League's first black coach.

Howard's major league statistics might have been even more impressive were it not for two factors. Because there was still some reluctance among baseball executives to sign black players during the early 1950s, Howard's early career was spent as an employee of the Kansas City Monarchs of the Negro League. When Howard's talents as an athlete finally inspired recognition from major league clubs, he found himself on the talent-laden Yankees, who could boast all-star performers at most positions and Hall-of-Fame candidates at others. In order to secure a playing position, Howard was obliged to perform behind the plate, at first base, and in the outfield; he did not catch more than one hundred games in a single season until 1961, when he was 32 years old.

Howard participated in many activities for charitable organizations and frequently represented the Yankee organization as a speaker. In 1980 he served in a front office capacity with the Yankees.   S.T.

Son of Wayman H. and Emmaline H. Married Arlene Henley 1954. Employee, Kansas City Monarchs of the Negro League ca. 1950; played with New York Yankees 1955–1967; Boston Red Sox 1967–68; Coach, New York Yankees; Officer, New York Yankees 1980. Hons: Babe Ruth Award 1958; American League Most Valuable Player 1963; Golden Glove Award 1963–64.

JOËL LE THEULE
French cabinet minister
Born Sable-sur-Sarthe, Sarthe, France, March 22nd, 1930
Died Sable-sur-Sarthe, Sarthe, France, December 14th, 1980

Although he began his career as a geography teacher at Saint Cyr, the French military academy, French Cabinet Minister Joël Le Theule turned to a political career at the age of 28. In 1958 he was elected to the French National Assembly from the district of Sable-sur-Sarthe in Western France and was returned to office in every subsequent legislative election; moreover, he won on the first ballot in each electoral contest. Le Theule was also active in local and regional politics and had served as mayor of Sable-sur-Sarthe since 1959.

Le Theule was part of the new generation of political leaders who were elected in 1958, with the return of General Charles de Gaulle to power during the Franco-Algerian conflict. Regarded as an expert in military affairs, Le Theule served as Deputy Chairman, and later Chairman, of the Defense Committee of the National Assembly. Le Theule also held four ministerial positions. He was Minister of the Overseas Departments and Territories in the government of Georges Pompidou in 1968; Secretary of State for Information under Prime Minister Maurice Couve de Murville from 1978 to 1980 and Minister of Defense in 1980 in the cabinet of Prime Minister Raymond Barre.

As Minister of Transportation, Le Theule achieved notoriety for his handling of a fishermen's blockade of French ports in 1980. The fishermen had been complaining of high fuel costs and other economic dislocations affecting the fishing industry and their strike halted sea traffic to major French ports for several weeks, threatening to cut off the country's supply of imported oil. Le Theule used the French navy to break the blockade and, consequently, came under strong criticism from trade unions for his actions. As Transportation Minister, he had been applauded for his settlement of an air controllers' job action which had been disrupting air traffic.

Le Theule had served as Defense Minister for only two months when he was stricken with a heart attack in April. He had been suffering from heart trouble since 1978.   H.L.

Son of Francois Le T. and Germaine Le T. Unmarried. Educ: Inst. Saint-Julien-Martin, Angers; Univ. of Angers; Univ. of Paris, agrégation in geography. Geography teacher, Military Sch. of La Flèche, Saint Cyr 1955–58; elected to Natl. Assembly from Sarthe district 1958; Mayor of Sable-sur-Sarthe 1959–80; Deputy Chmn. 1967 and Chmn. 1967–68, Cttee. of Natl. Defense; Minister of Overseas Depts. and Territories 1968; Secty. of State in charge of Information 1968–69; Minister of Transportation 1979–80; Minister of Defense, Oct.-Dec. 1980; Chmn., Cttee. for the Economic Expansion of La Sarthe and Member, General Council of Sable-sur-Sarthe 1973–80. Member, parliamentary study group for problems of industrial cinematography 1975; V.P., European Movement group 1977; Member, Rassemblement pour la République.

(ALBERT) ANGUS CAMPBELL
Social psychologist and Director of the Institute for Social Research
Born Leiters, Indiana, U.S.A., August 10th, 1919
Died Ann Arbor, Michigan, U.S.A., December 15th, 1980

Angus Campbell was a pioneer in the use of sample survey techniques for studying attitudes and complex behavior in different population groups. He also helped establish the Institute for Social Research at the University of Michigan.

Born in Indiana, Angus Campbell was raised in Portland, Oregon, and received his B.A. and M.A. degrees in psychology from the University of Oregon. His doctoral studies were undertaken at Stanford University where he worked as research assistant for E.R. Hilgard, a professor of experimental psychology. In 1936, Campbell became a professor of social psychology at Northwestern University.

During World War Two Campbell was among the several social scientists who worked with Dr. Rensir Likert in Washington, D.C., to provide government agencies with anticipatory studies of postwar trends in American social and economic life. Likert's research group was attached to the U.S. Department of Agriculture and, in 1946, when federal funding ran out, he moved the organization to the University of Michigan where it was named the Institute for Social Research.

Campbell served as director of the institute's Survey Research Center until 1970, when he succeeded Likert as director of the Institute for Social Research. During this time, he also lectured at the university in psychology and sociology.

In 1954, Campbell co-authored *The Voter Decides,* an empirical study of the multifarious factors which influence voting behavior. The book was hailed by the noted political scientist J.O. Key, Jr., as "the most impressive analysis yet made of a national election by the survey method." In the late 1960s, following the outbreak of riots in 15 major American cities, the National Commission on Civil Disorders asked the Survey Research Center to undertake an investigation of racial conflict. The initial study was conducted by Campbell and Harry Schuman, a sociology professor at Michigan, and the institute's work on racial relations has continued.

In the 1970s, Campbell attempted to gauge the contemporary American attitude toward the quality of life which resulted in publication of *The Sense of Well Being in America* (1980). After conducting extensive interviews on work, marriage, family structure, the standard of living, and the neighborhood, Campbell concluded that "there appear to be a growing number of people in this country for whom values other than those of economic character have become important enough that they are prepared to trade off economic return in order to achieve them." A prolific author, Campbell published many articles in such journals as the *American Journal of Psychology, Public Opinion Quarterly, American Political Science Review,* and *Scientific American.* H.L.

Son of Albert Alexis C. and Orpha C. Married Jean Winter 1940. Children: Carol; Joan; Bruce. Educ: Univ. of Oregon, B.A. 1931, M.A. 1932; Stanford Univ., Stanford, Calif., Ph.D. 1936. Instr., Dept. of Psychology, Northwestern Univ., Evanston, Ill. 1936–39; Postdoctoral Fellow, Social Science Research Council 1939–40; Asst. Prof. of Psychology, Northwestern Univ. 1940–42; Asst. Head, Div.

of Program Surveys, U.S. Dept. of Agriculture, Washington, D.C.
1942–46. With Univ. of Michigan, Ann Arbor: Assoc. Prof., psychol-
ogy and sociology 1946–49; Prof. from 1949; Asst. Dir. 1946–48 and
Dir. 1948–70, Survey Research Center; Assoc. Dir. 1948–70, Dir.
1970–75, and Program Dir. from 1975, Inst. for Social Research.
Member: American Psychological Assoc.; American Sociological
Assoc.; American Assoc. of Public Opinion Research; Soc. for the
Study of Social Issues. Hons: Fulbright Research Fellow, Norway
1958–59; American Psychological Assoc. Award for Distinguished
Scientific Contributions 1974; Fellow, American Acad. of Arts and
Science. *Author: Books*—(with G. Gurin and W.E. Miller) The Voter
Decides, 1954; (with P.E. Converse, W.E. Miller, and D.E. Stokes)
The American Voter, 1960; (with P.E. Converse, W.E. Miller, and
D.E. Stokes) Elections and the Political Order, 1966; White Attitudes
Toward Black People, 1971; (with P.E. Converse) The Human
Meaning of Social Change, 1972; (joint author) The Quality of
American Life: Perceptions, Evaluations, and Satisfactions, 1976; The
Sense of Well Being in America, 1980. *Major articles*—(with W.E.
Miller) "The Motivational Basis of Straight and Split Ticket Voting,"
American Political Science Review, June 1957; "Surge and Decline: A
Study of Electoral Change," Public Opinion Quarterly, Fall, 1960.

ALVIN (WARD) GOULDNER
Sociologist
Born New York City, U.S.A., July 29th, 1920
Died Madrid, Spain, December 15th, 1980

A controversial radical sociologist, Alvin W. Gouldner renounced
scholarly objectivity and detachment and argued that sociology should
be a vehicle for social change. He criticized both the functionalist and
Marxist schools of sociology and predicted growing political power in
both the West and the Soviet bloc for a "New Class" of intellectuals
and technical experts.

While completing his graduate work at Columbia University,
Gouldner served as resident sociologist for the American Jewish
Committee and taught sociology at the University of Buffalo. He then
held teaching positions at Antioch College and the University of
Illinois in Urbana before making his permanent academic home at
Washington University in St. Louis in 1959. In 1951 Gouldner edited
Studies in Leadership: Leadership and Democratic Action, a collection
of 33 papers by social scientists. Three years later he published
Patterns of Industrial Bureaucracy and *Wildcat Strike,* the latter based
on a study of a gypsum plant near the Great Lakes. He used his
observations of change in the plant's management to modify Max
Weber's theory of bureaucracy. These studies earned him a reputation
as an independent-minded sociologist capable both of original field
studies and high-level theoretical discussion.

As founder of *Trans-Action* magazine in 1963 and its first editor-in-
chief Gouldner demonstrated his concern with social actions. In a
statement of purpose in the journal's first issue, he wrote that "the
main public function of social science is to help men understand and
solve the problem of modern societies." The goal of *Trans-Action,*
therefore, would be "to speed the flow of social science findings and

ideas into the larger community, facilitating their use in everyday life."

Gouldner surprised his colleagues with his next work, *Enter Plato: Classical Greece and the Origins of Social Theory* (1966). Concentrating on a relatively remote period, he presented a rough sociological account of ancient Athens up to the fourth century B.C. and then analyzed the social philosophy of Plato, the West's first major theorist. Believing that the social theorist's values must be known before his work can be properly understood or criticized, Gouldner sought to describe Plato's ideas in their historical and social context. The book suggested Gouldner's views regarding the sources and purposes of modern sociology. He saw Plato's social theory as an attempt to deal with the conflicts caused by the rationalization and secularization of Athenian society since the sixth century B.C., and he indicated that all major theoretical systems have been attempts to diagnose and prescribe remedies for social instability. Under these circumstances, Gouldner claimed, sociologists defeat themselves if they reduce their knowledge to technical expertise.

Many sociologists regarded Gouldner's *The Coming Crisis in Western Sociology* (1970) as his most important work. In large measure a critique of prevailing Western sociology, the book rebutted the claims of Talcott Parsons and other functionalists that their analysis was value-free. By substituting utility and considerations of effectiveness for moral criteria, Gouldner argued, modern sociology seeks to manipulate individuals in order to preserve the status quo. He called for a radical "reflexive sociology" that would work for a new, less alienating society to replace the decadent bourgeois order. This new sociology would eschew detachment and state its goals, for Gouldner believed that the quality of social science depended greatly on the rigor and comprehensiveness with which its purposes were articulated. Though not elaborating extensively upon his reflexive sociology, he indicated that it would emerge from the New Left and the psychedelic counterculture, which counterpoised communitarianism, freedom, and spontaneity to impersonal, consumer-oriented social attitudes. In *For Sociology* (1973), a collection of essays, Gouldner responded to criticism of his previous book. Since he believed in assessing sociology by its values and purposes, stated or hidden, Gouldner's rebuttals often seemed to be personal attacks upon the motives of his critics.

In *The Future of Intellectuals and the Rise of the New Class* (1979), Gouldner foresaw the displacement of the bourgeoisie by a rapidly expanding New Class of university-educated administrators, teachers, publicists, professionals and scientists. Marx, having failed in Gouldner's estimate to see that cultural accumulation would replace the accumulation of capital as the driving force of history, had erroneously predicted that the proletariat would become the new ruling class. Gouldner acknowledged that the New Class valued money, power, and status. But since its common culture was founded on critical thinking, he wrote, it would be impelled by its nature to adopt a new politics rejecting hierarchy, authority and all orthodoxies. Gouldner predicted a similar development in the Soviet bloc.

In his last book, *The Two Marxisms: Contradictions and Anomalies in the Development of Theory* (1980), Gouldner claimed that a fundamental contradiction ran through Marx's work. He argued that

while Marx claimed to offer a science that saw social actions as
controlled by external social forces, he often merely denied the
Hegelian notion of ideas as the driving force of history. This muddle,
Gouldner wrote, has confused Marx's followers ever since.

Gouldner died during a lecture tour in Europe.   M.L.

Son of Louis G. and Estelle (Fetbrandt) G. Married: (1) . . .;
(2) Janet Lee Walker 1966. Children: 1st marriage—Richard; Alan;
Andrew; 2nd marriage—Alessandra. Educ: Bernard Baruch Coll.,
City Coll. of New York (now City Coll. of the City Univ. of N.Y.),
BBA 1941; Columbia Univ., NYC, M.A. 1945, Ph.D. 1953. Resident
sociologist, American Jewish Cttee. 1945–47; Asst. Prof., sociology,
Univ. of Buffalo (now State Univ. of New York at Buffalo) 1947–51;
Consulting sociologist, Standard Oil Co. of N.J. 1951–52; Assoc.
Prof., sociology, Antioch Coll., Ohio 1952–54; Assoc. Prof. 1954–57
and Prof., sociology 1959–67, Univ. of Illinois, Urbana. With Wash-
ington Univ., St. Louis, Mo: Chmn., Dept. of Sociology 1959–64;
Prof. of sociology 1959–67; Max Weber Prof. of Social Theory
1967–80. Lectr: Free Univ., Berlin 1965; Stockholm Sch. of Econom-
ics, 1965, 1977; Hebrew Univ., Jerusalem 1966; Warsaw Univ. 1966;
Goldsmith's Coll., London 1977. Prof. Univ. of Amsterdam 1972–76.
Founder, and Ed.-in-Chief, Trans-Action 1963–66; Co-founder, and
Ed., Theory and Society, Amsterdam 1974–80; Ed.-in-Chief, New
Critics Press 1969–80; Ed., Bobbs-Merrill Reprint Series 1960–80;
Consulting Ed., Penguin Books, London 1969–74. Member, and Pres.
1962, Soc. for the Study of Social Problems. Member: American
Sociological Assoc.; Soc. for the Psychological Study of Social Issues;
Sociological Research Assoc. Hons: awards and fellowships from
Social Science Research Council; Fellow, Center for Advanced Study
in the Behavioral Sciences, Stanford Univ. 1961–62. *Author:* (ed.)
Studies in Leadership: Leadership and Democratic Action, 1950;
Patterns of Industrial Bureaucracy, 1954; Wildcat Strike, 1954; (ed.)
Emile Durkheim, Socialism and Saint-Simon, 1958, (with R.A.
Peterson) Notes on Technology and the Moral Order, 1962; (with
H.P. Gouldner) Modern Sociology, 1963; Enter Plato: Classical
Greece and the Origins of Social Theory, 1965; (ed. with S.M. Miller)
Applied Sociology: Opportunities and Problems, 1965; The Coming
Crisis of Western Sociology, 1970; For Sociology, 1973; The Dialectic
of Ideology and Technology: The Origins, Grammar, and Future of
Ideology, 1976; The Future of Intellectuals and the Rise of the New
Class, 1979; The Two Marxisms: Contradictions and Anomalies in the
Development of Theory, 1980.

GILBERT HOLLIDAY
Diplomat
Born Wigton, Cumberland, England, April 10th, 1910
Died December 15th, 1980

For over three decades a career diplomat, Gilbert Leonard Holliday
represented Great Britain in ten countries on five continents. Holliday
served as ambassador to the Kingdom of Laos during the mid-1950s
when that nation was wracked by near civil war after the French
withdrawal from Indo-China in 1954.

A Laming Travelling Fellow at Oxford in 1931, Holliday served the consular and diplomatic services in the political and commercial capitals of Latin America, the United States and Europe, before his appointment as ambassador to Laos in 1956. Upon his return to London in 1958, he worked in the Foreign Office for several years before being named ambassador to Bolivia. Familiar with Latin America because he had served as consular official in Buenos Aires, Santiago and Valparaiso earlier in his career, Holliday remained in La Paz four years. His last foreign posting was Morocco, where he served, again as ambassador, from 1956 until his retirement four years later.   L.R.

Son of Rev. Andrew Barnes H. and Violet H. (White) H. Married: (1) Anita Lopez 1934 (d. 1952); (2) Jane Mary Wilkinson 1958. Children: 1st marriage—two sons; 2nd marriage—one son; two daughters. Educ: Rydal Sch.; Queen's Coll., Oxford. Laming Travelling Fellow, Queen's Coll. 1931–32. Consular and Diplomatic service in Buenos Aires, Valparaiso, Santiago, Katowice, Los Angeles, N.Y., Warsaw, Paris, Berne and Stockholm; Ambassador, Laos 1956–58; Foreign Office 1958–60; Ambassador to Bolivia 1960–64, to Morocco 1965–69. Hons: Companion, Order of St. Michael and St. George 1954.

PETER COLLINSON
Motion picture director
Born Lincolnshire, England, 1936
Died Los Angeles, California, U.S.A., December 16th, 1980

The collapse of the British film industry at the beginning of the 1970s—from which it has yet to recover—impelled many talented film-makers into drastic changes of career, not always for the better. Well-established figures, such as John Schlesinger and Karel Reisz, were able to move toward the Hollywood studios. Others chose the comparative security of television. And a number of young directors, just embarking on potentially interesting careers, were forced (if they wanted to stay in films) into making the best of whatever they could get. One such director was Peter Collinson.

Collinson was born in Lincolnshire, into a theatrical family. His parents split up, and the boy spent most of his childhood at the Actors' Orphanage in Surrey. President of the Orphanage was Noel Coward, who helped Collinson get a start in show business, first at the Empire Music Hall at New Cross in London, and then at the Arts Theatre in London making his first public stage appearance as the back half of a pantomime horse.

After National Service in Malaya, Collinson returned to the theatre, then moved into commercial television. His first chance to direct came when he joined the newly-established Northern Ireland TV station; within a year he had become Senior Drama Director, and his work won several awards. Returning to London, he directed for ATV and Rediffusion, before making his first film, *The Penthouse* (1967), an adaptation of a school-of-Pinter stage play; completed on a budget of £36,000, the film attracted considerable attention at the Cannes festival.

Collinson rapidly followed up with two more small-budget features: *Up The Junction* (1967), a late entry in the tradition of British working-class 'realism'; and *The Long Day's Dying* (1968), an explicitly violent anti-war film, scripted by playwright Charles Wood, which won 'Best Picture' award at the 1968 San Sebastian festival. On the strength of this success, he was offered his first big-budget assignment, *The Italian Job* (1969), an undemandingly enjoyable 'caper' movie in which the stars (Michael Caine and Noel Coward) were largely upstaged by the cars, a fleet of amazingly acrobatic red Minis.

Despite a weakness for mannered direction, Collinson had now shown himself a fluent, versatile, and potentially significant director, who could well have benefited from the discipline of working within a secure cinematic tradition. Unfortunately, this was just what Britain in 1970 could not offer. Over the next ten years, Collinson's talent was wasted on a depressing series of films which were at best mediocre— and, at worst, abysmally bad. They consisted mainly of 'action adventures', international co-productions with perfunctory plots and incompetent scripts: *Open Season* (1974); *The Sellout* (1975); *Tigers Don't Cry* (1976). There was also a Spaghetti-style Western: *The Man Called Noon* (1973); and a couple of ill-advised re-makes: *And Then There Were None* (1974), third and worst version of Agatha Christie's *Ten Little Niggers* (in US: Ten Little Indians), and *The Spiral Staircase* (1975), a re-make of Siodmak's classic 1946 *film noir*.

Collinson's last film, completed before his death from cancer, was *The Earthling;* this is scheduled for release early in 1981.   P.K.

Son of a violinist and conductor, and an actress. Parents divorced; sent to Actors' Orphanage, Surrey. Married Hazel—. Two sons. Mil. Service: two years in National Service, Malaya. Stage hand, Empire Music Hall, New Cross and Arts Theatre. Toured with 'nudie' shows. Began working in commercial television; joined Northern Ireland TV station, rose to Senior Drama Director. Dir., ATV and Rediffusion, London. Originator and producer (with Ian Hendry), The Informer, TV series. Hons: The Long Day's Dying official entry to 1968 Cannes film festival; Best Picture and Best Director awards (for The Long Day's Dying) 1968 San Sebastian film festival; Catholic Church Humanitarian award (for The Long Day's Dying). *Director: films*— The Penthouse, 1967; Up the Junction, 1967; The Long Day's Dying, 1968; The Italian Job, 1969; You Can't Win 'Em All, 1970; Fright, 1971; Innocent Bystanders, 1972; The Man Called Noon, 1973; Straight on Till Morning, 1974; Open Season, 1974; The Spiral Staircase, 1975; And Then There Were None (also known as Ten Little Indians), 1974; The Spiral Staircase, 1975; The Sellout, 1975; Tigers Don't Cry, 1976; Tomorrow Never Comes, 1977; The Earthling, 1981. *TV includes*—(series) Love Story; Wednesday Night Play; The Power Game; Drama '64; Blackmail; (film) The House on Garibaldi Street, 1980.

COLONEL HARLAND SANDERS
Founder, Kentucky Fried Chicken Corp.
Born near Henryville, Indiana, U.S.A., September 9th, 1890
Died Shelbyville, Kentucky, U.S.A., December 16th, 1980

Colonel Harland Sanders, the founder and symbol of Kentucky Fried Chicken, was a self-made millionaire who traveled the world in the distinctive white suit and black string tie of a Southern gentleman to promote his inimitable product.

Sanders was born in 1890 to a poor farm family in Indiana. From the age of six, when his father died, he scavenged food and cooked for his two younger siblings while his mother scraped a living together by sewing and peeling tomatoes. When his mother remarried, Sanders left home to work as a farmhand, and began a 28-year succession of low-paying jobs, including railroad fireman, plowman, buggy painter, midwife, ferryboat operator, and insurance salesman. Sometime during this period he spent a year in Cuba with the U.S. Army and earned a Doctor of Law degree through a correspondence course from Southern University.

In 1929, when he was 39, Sanders opened a gas station in Corbin, Kentucky, where he served his own home cooking to his family and occasional travelers. His reputation spread, and he soon converted the gas station into Sanders' Cafe and took an eight-week course in restaurant and hotel management from Cornell University to learn "things like how many potatoes to cook." In 1936 Governor Ruby Laffoon awarded him the honorary title of Kentucky Colonel.

By 1939, using the newly-invented pressure cooker and his "secret blend of eleven herbs and spices," Sanders had perfected his "finger-lickin' good" fried chicken recipe, which soon made Sanders' Cafe a most successful business. After 35 years, however, the cafe was bypassed by a new superhighway and Sanders was forced to sell at a loss and live on his Social Security check.

Sanders, who had once sold his fried chicken recipe to another restaurant, now decided to try a franchise arrangement on a wider scale. He and his second wife traveled by car throughout the U.S. and Canada preparing chicken for restaurant owners and convincing them to use the blend (the recipe remained secret) at a cost of four cents per chicken. After two years they had signed up a mere five restaurants; four years later they had more than 600 customers and an annual income of more than $300,000 a year. He and his wife split the administrative chores to keep costs down. They were soon swamped by the demands of the rapidly growing company, however, and in 1964 sold the firm (with the exception of its Canada branch) to businessmen John Y. Brown Jr. and Jack Massey for $2 million and an annual salary of $40,000 (later raised to $70,000). By 1971, when the corporation merged with Heublein, Inc., it was worth $185 million a year. Eventually it comprised 6,000 outlets in 48 countries. In 1974 Sanders sued the new owners for compromising his good name by introducing an unproven novelty called "extra crispy chicken;" the suit was settled out of court for $1 million.

The Colonel, whose smiling face adorned restaurant signs and chicken packages worldwide, traveled some 200,000 miles yearly on behalf of the franchise and appeared on commercials and talk shows. He donated the entire income from Kentucky Fried Chicken Canada, of which he retained ownership, to the Harland Sanders Foundation, which distributes funds to charitable and educational organizations. He also adopted more than 70 orphans, but left his entire estate to charity, preferring his children to make their own way, as he had done. He was given the Horatio Alger Award by Norman Vincent Peale in 1965.

Sanders was worth an estimated $3.5 million when he died at the age of 90. John Y. Brown Jr., now Governor of Kentucky, called him "the spirit of the American Dream" and permitted his body to lie in state in the rotunda of the state capitol. Flags in Louisville were flown at half-staff in his memory.   J.N.

Married: (1) Josephine King 1908 (div. 1947); (2) Claudia Ledington 1948. Children: 1st marriage—Margaret; Mildred Ruggles; Harland Jr. (d.). Adopted over 70 orphans. Protestant. Educ: Indiana grammar schs. to seventh grade; correspondence course leading to Doctor of Law degree, Southern Univ.; course in restaurant and hotel management, Cornell Univ. during 1930s. Mil. Service: U.S. Army, Cuba. Various jobs 1901–29, including farmhand, midwife, plowman, ferryboat operator, insurance salesman, and railroad fireman; owner, gas station, then Sanders' Cafe, Corbin, Ky. 1929–56. With Kentucky Fried Chicken Corp.: Owner 1956–64; Member, Bd. of Dirs. 1964–70; goodwill ambassador and figurehead since 1964. Owner, Kentucky Fried Chicken Canada since 1956. Founder, Harland Sanders Foundn. Hons: named Hon. Kentucky Colonel 1936; Horatio Alger Award 1965.

PRINCESS VIKTORIA (LUISE)
Princess of Germany and Prussia
Born Potsdam, Germany, September 13th, 1892
Died Brunswick, Germany, December 16th, 1980

The life of Princess Viktoria Luise possessed the charm and moral resolution of the best fairy tales. After the most indulged childhood, she witnessed the collapse of family and nation, becoming a refugee herself, and arriving at a sense of gratitude and commitment to the suffering.

Born at Marmor Palace in Potsdam, the Princess was a most welcome arrival after six brothers. Her parents, Kaiser Wilhelm II of Germany, King of Prussia, and the Kaiserin, Auguste-Viktoria (Dona) felt that their "small but very strong little daughter" had been a gift from God. She was christened Viktoria after her grandmother, the Empress Frederick, who was the daughter of Queen Victoria.

As a child Viktoria enjoyed all the privileges that royalty and a loving family confer. At the age of 18, she was confirmed at the Church of St. Nicholas in Berlin and on this birthday she was named Colonel-in-Chief of the Second Guards Hussar Regiment. Her grandmother had been in charge of this regiment, and she proudly marched her soldiers past her father. In 1911, the Princess's fascination with air travel was rewarded by a namesake—zeppelin "Viktoria Luise," the first to fly over the ocean. A new and very large ocean liner was also named in her honor—the "Kaiserin."

Although royal matches had been suggested, the Princess was free to choose her own husband. Overcoming political difficulties and royal feuds, she announced her engagement in 1912 to His Royal Highness Ernst August, Duke of Brunswick, son of the Duke of Cumberland. It was not until a year later that family intervention on both sides broke down the last obstacles, ending the discord between the Houses of Hohenzollern and Brunswick. The wedding day, May 24th, 1913, was an historical event, full of pomp and circumstance, with 1,100 guests in attendance. The number of wedding gifts was so tremendous that several furniture vans were required to transport them. Among those in attendance was King George V of England. This was to be the last British Royal visit to Germany for more than 50 years. Shortly afterwards the Duke of Cumberland relinquished the throne to his son. Ernst August, the couple's first child, was born in March 1914, followed by Georg Wilhelm in 1915, their daughter Friederike in 1917, Christian in 1919, and Welf-Heinrich in 1923.

World War One brought the downfall of the Princess's hero, her father. His abdication as Kaiser and King of Prussia marked the end of royal power. Final hopes for a royal future dissolved with the spread of social discontent.

Princess Viktoria first met Hitler in 1933 when he invited her and her husband to confer with him in Berlin on the subject of Anglo-German relations. She described him as "polite, correct, and friendly," but when Hitler demanded that a marriage be arranged between Friederike and Edward Prince of Wales, Viktoria's opinion of him began to change. Although one of her brothers allied himself with Hitler, her father would not associate himself in any way with the dictator and begged Viktoria to do the same. Nevertheless, Viktoria and her husband worked intensively to maintain amicable relations between England and Germany.

By the summer of 1939 war was a reality. Princess Viktoria knew that three of her sons would be mobilized; Georg Wilhelm and Christian were already in active service. Instructing them to send her a coded message if and when they received marching orders, she hoarded gasoline to insure that a shortage would not preclude a final visit to them. But her family was forced into another role. Welf-Heinrich was dismissed by Hitler and Christian was turned down for the Knight's Cross of Iron. Viktoria wrote to Hitler asking for reasons. At length the Führer replied that the princess had acted against the National Socialist State. The royal family was no longer useful to Hitler's designs. The Gestapo arrested the younger Ernst August and the prince and princess were forced to flee from their home. They found refuge in Blankenburg, where they laid out a makeshift Red Cross flag in the castle courtyard. Scrounging for food, the princess and her husband began to aid the suffering. As American troops drew nearer, Blankenburg fell. The Americans lifted the ban on movement so that Ernst August and his sons could scour the hills for resistors and offer them a chance to surrender.

After World War Two, Princess Viktoria looked upon her ravaged homeland with deep sorrow. Distraught over the division between East and West, she turned to charitable work. She founded and actively chaired a children's charity foundation: "I travelled thousands of kilometers each year in search of funds and everywhere I found willingness on the part of others to help. It was a wonderful feeling to be able to aid all those needy children." Working actively until 1955, she lived to see the Duchess Viktoria Luise Association grow into a nationwide charity.

Personal loss came to Viktoria in 1953 with the death of Prince Ernst August. She revelled, though, in her family of sixteen grandchildren and greatgrandchildren, including her granddaughter Friederike, Queen of Greece, and her greatgrandson, King Constantine. There was a public celebration of the Princess's 80th birthday. The subject of many interviews, she did not take her fame for granted, and was very moved to see so many people "patiently trying for hours either to have a friendly word with me or just wanting to shake my hand."

Born to the greatest riches, then exposed to harsh changes, Princess Viktoria was never bitter; she rose, rather, with the downfall of her family and her nation. "My life has been fulfilled and it has been a richly eventful one," she concluded.   N.S.

Born Viktoria Luise Adelheid Mathilde Charlotte. Daughter of Kaiser Wilhelm II of Germany, King of Prussia, and Auguste-Viktoria (Dona), Princess of Schleswig-Holstein-Sonderburg-Augustenburg. Married Ernst August, Duke of Brunswick 1913. Children: Ernst August; Georg Wilhelm; Friederike; Christian. Catholic. Privately educated. Named Col.-in-chief, 2nd Guards Hussar Regt. 1910. Established a children's charity foundn. and The Duchess Viktoria Luise Assoc. *Author:* Memoirs of H.R.H. Viktoria Luise, Duchess of Runswick and Luneburg, Princess of Prussia, 1965, English ed., 1977.

CONRAD AHLERS
Journalist and member of Bundestag
Born Hamburg, Germany, November 8th, 1922
Died Bonn, West Germany, December 18th, 1980

Conrad Ahlers, a German army paratroop veteran of World War Two and a journalist with more than two decades experience in West Germany and with the BBC in London, helped topple the government of Chancellor Konrad Adenauer. As executive editor of the German news weekly, *Der Spiegel,* Ahlers published an article critical of both the West German army's military preparedness and the policies of Defense Minister Franz Joseph Strauss. The wave of arrests ordered by Strauss, and supported by Adenauer, resulted in a political crisis known as the *"Spiegel* affair."

Following the 1962 NATO military exercises, Fallex '62, Ahlers wrote an article describing the very poor performance of the *Bundeswehr* (German army) forces. Although the story contained little information that was officially classified, the Defense Ministry immediately issued ominous statements about treason and the divulgence of military secrets. Action by the Security Group of the Federal Police soon followed; *Der Spiegel's* offices were sealed, searched, and occupied by the authorities while its editors and publishers were arrested by the police in a series of evening raids. Ahlers, on holiday in Torremolinos, was eventually placed under custody by Spanish police through the initiative of Interpol. While Ahlers and his colleagues spent two months in prison, heated debate over Strauss's actions, the status of press freedom in the Federal Republic, and the actual condition of the *Bundeswehr,* was fueled by widespread demonstrations against the Adenauer government.

Chancellor Adenauer, the "old man" of postwar German politics, was himself drawn into the widening controversy; when he described *Der Spiegel* as a "sheet which has a circulation of 500,000 copies and systematically commits treason for money" in a parliamentary debate the opposition members of the Bundestag booed and whistled. Reaction to the affair outside the government was equally strong; neither German nor foreign newspapers could resist comparisons between Strauss's actions and the police state practices of Hitler's Germany. Eventually a Federal High Court dismissed all charges against the *Spiegel* staff for lack of evidence, but the incident's political repercussions were significant: Strauss resigned and Adenauer pledged to retire within the year.

Ironically, the *"Spiegel* affair" launched a career in government for Ahlers when he was appointed Deputy Director of the West German Press and Information Service by Chancellor Willy Brandt in 1969. Ahlers held the post until his election to the Bundestag three years later as a Social Democrat. He had returned to professional journalism in 1980 as head of the German Radio's foreign broadcast section.

L.R.

Son of Adolf A. and Gertrud (Krancke) A. Married Heilwig von der Mehden 1949. One son; two daughters. Educ: Gymnasium; Univ. of Hamburg. Mil. Service: Paratrooper in WWII. Ed., German lang. service of the BBC, London 1948–49; Ed., Sonntagsblatt 1949–51; Duty Information Officer, Ministry of Defense, Federal Republic 1951–53; Foreign policy Ed., Die Welt 1953–56; Head of Bonn office of Der Spiegel 1956–59; Domestic policy Ed., Frankfurter Rundschau 1959–62; Exec. Ed., Der Spiegel 1962–66; Deputy Chief 1966–69 and State Secty., Govt. spokesman, and Head 1969–72, Press and Information Office, Federal Republic; Member of the Bundestag 1972; Head of Publications, Friedrich-Krupp Stiftung since 1973; Head of foreign broadcast section, German Radio since 1980. *Author:* Die Vorkapitalistichen Produktionsweisen, Erlangen, 1973; Stationen einer Republik, 1979.

FRANCES FULLER
Actress and executive
Born Charleston, South Carolina, U.S.A., October 4th, 1907
Died New York City, New York, U.S.A., December 18th, 1980

Frances Fuller Miner, the former president, director, and chairman of the board of the American Academy of Dramatic Arts, was noted for her portrayals of a variety of roles ranging from wistful ingenues to Aunt Carrie of television's *Love of Life.*

Fuller, born into a prominent South Carolina family, appeared on the stage for the first time at the age of five in the children's play *Racketty-Packetty House* and played Portia in a school production of *The Merchant of Venice* when she was 12. After graduating from the Academy of the Sacred Heart in Manhattanville, New York, in 1925, she studied at the American Academy of Dramatic Arts for two years, supporting herself with part-time jobs as a typist and doctor's assistant.

Fuller had been with a stock company in Chester, Pennsylvania, for only three weeks in 1928 when she won the role of Peggy Grant in *The Front Page,* the Ben Hecht and Charles MacArthur melodrama of Chicago reporters. The play was a triumphant Broadway success, and Fuller's name was made. She went on to play ingenue roles in *Café* and another journalistic melodrama, *Five Star Final.* In 1932 she played Leslie Howard's compassionate mistress in *The Animal Kingdom* and appeared opposite Humphrey Bogart as a flirtatious dancer in *I Love You Wednesday;* the following year she appeared in *Her Master's Voice.*

Fuller's Broadway successes led to her first motion picture role, co-starring with Gary Cooper in a light romantic comedy, *One Sunday Afternoon,* which premiered in 1933. She returned to Broadway in 1936 as Kaye Hamilton, the aspiring actress of the George S. Kaufman and Edna Ferber comedy classic *Stage Door,* and appeared in *Excursion* a year later.

In 1948 Fuller joined the teaching staff of the American Academy of Dramatic Arts, where she taught such pupils as Anne Bancroft, Grace Kelly, and Don Murray that good actors require "strong determination, spirit of competition, sensitivity and imagination, physical assets, well adjusted personality and generosity." During the 1950s and 1960s, while she served as president and director of the Academy, she appeared in *Home Is the Hero* and was standby for Helen Hayes and Betty Field in *A Touch of the Poet.* Her last Broadway role was in the 1963 drama *Lady of the Camellias.* She was also active in television productions, including *Studio One, Play of the Week, U.S. Steel Hour, Suspense Theater, Kraft Television Theater,* and the religious drama program *Lamp Unto My Feet,* and was best known to viewers of daytime serials as Aunt Carrie on *Love of Life.* Her later films were *The Girl in the Red Velvet Swing, They Might be Giants,* and the satirical mystery *Homebodies.*

Fuller and her husband, the director and producer Worthington Miner, served as co-chairmen of the board of the Academy since 1974. They had three children.   J.S.

Born Frances Leonore Fuller. Daughter of Wallace Watt F., electrical engineer, and Leonore (Byrnes) F., federal govt. exec. Married: Worthington C. Miner, producer and dir., 1929. Children: Peter, television dir.; Margaret Rawson; Mary Elizabeth. Educ: Acad. of the Sacred Heart, Manhattanville, N.Y., grad. 1925; American Acad. of Dramatic Arts, NYC 1926–28. Actress in theater, films, and television since 1930. With American Acad. of Dramatic Arts: Teacher 1948–50, 1954–74; Pres. 1954–64; Dir. 1954–74; Co-chairman of the Bd. since 1974. Member: Actors Equity Assn.; Stage Actors Guild; American Fedn. of Television and Radio Artists; Authors League of America; Broadcast Music Inc. Hons: Hon. L.H.D., Pace Univ. 1974. *Performances: Plays*—The Front Page (Peggy Grant), 1928; Café (Jane Geddis), 1930; Five Star Final (Jenny Townsend), 1930; The Animal Kingdom (Daisy Sage), 1932; I Love You Wednesday (Victoria Meredith), 1932; Her Master's Voice (Queena Farrar), 1933; The Country Wife, 1935; The Coward, 1935; Stage Door (Kaye Hamilton), 1936; Excursion (Lollie), 1937; Home Is the Hero (Mrs.

Green), 1954; A Touch of the Poet, 1958; Lady of the Camellias (Nanine), 1963. *Films*—One Sunday Afternoon, 1933; Elmer and Elsie, 1934; The Girl in the Red Velvet Swing (Mrs. Stanford White), 1955; They Might Be Giants, 1971; Homebodies, 1974. *Television*— Love of Life (Aunt Carrie), 1966–69; Studio One; Play of the Week; U.S. Steel Hour; Suspense Theater; Kraft Television Theater; Lamp Unto My Feet; Today Show.

ALEKSEI N(IKOLAEVICH) KOSYGIN
Soviet Prime Minister
Born St. Petersburg (now Leningrad), Russia, February 21st, 1904
Died Moscow, USSR, December 18th, 1980

In 1904, the year Kosygin was born, Lenin gained control of the Russian Social Democratic Workers Party and thus gave up his thoughts about emigrating to America. Trotsky was quick to warn of the dangers inherent in Lenin's tight centralization of the party's power, and with amazing prescience anticipated the rise of Stalin: "the party organization replaces the party itself; then, the Central Committee replaces the organization, and finally, the dictator replaces the Central Committee."

Sixty years later, when Aleksei Kosygin together with Leonid Brezhnev assumed the leadership of the Soviet Union, Lenin had been dead for 40 years, the brutal and paranoid reign of Joseph Stalin was over, and for the last eleven years the country had been led by Nikita Khrushchev, a man whose undoubted courage and vision was frequently marred by erratic and autocratic behavior. Adopting very little of the styles and methods of any of their predecessors, Brezhnev and Kosygin—at first a studiously restrained and almost faceless duo—ruled the Soviet Union by consensus. Later, Brezhnev's personality blossomed, but Kosygin remained a sober, publicity-shy politician throughout his long political career.

Kremlinologists confidently predicted that the Brezhnev-Kosygin collective leadership would quickly fall apart, and, as had happened before, power would concentrate in one leader, thus confirming the essentially dictatorial nature of the system. As first secretary of the Communist party, Brezhnev, from the start, was considered to be the slightly more powerful figure, but it was by no means certain that he would, or could, consolidate his position. Prime minister Kosygin, considered one of the toughest and most intelligent of modern Soviet leaders, seemed more interested in making the system operate efficiently than in pursuing the ideology that created the system. A reserved man, with strong family ties, it is arguable that the acquisition of personal power was never Kosygin's motivating force. It was, perhaps, survival—his own and the system's—which impelled him to work with such fortitude and dedication.

The son of a lathe worker, Aleksei Nikolaevich Kosygin was born on February 21st, 1904, in one of the poorest districts of St. Petersburg. Twelve days before his birth, the Imperial Russian Navy was severely beaten by the Japanese at Port Arthur. The mighty tsarist regime was beginning to look a little tarnished: by the time

Kosygin was a year old, the Russian Minister of the Interior had been assassinated and in Kosygin's native city, the "Bloody Sunday" slayings of peaceful demonstrators by Imperial Guards at the Winter Palace had strengthened the resolve of workers to overthrow the monarchy. Joseph Dzhugashvili, a young Georgian who had not yet adopted his Russian name of Stalin ("steely"), had just joined the Bolshevik party and was in hiding from the authorities. But ten-year-old Nikita Khrushchev knew little of Bolshevik revolution; he was still peacefully tending cattle in the Kursk countryside. Unlike Khrushchev and Brezhnev, Kosygin was committed to the socialist cause at an early age; however, surprisingly little is known about his boyhood in St. Petersburg.

The Revolution broke out when Kosygin was 13, and two years later he volunteered for the Red Army. When the White Army of anti-Bolsheviks was defeated in 1921, Kosygin, then 17, was demobilized. He enrolled at the Training School for Cooperatives in Petrograd (formerly St. Petersburg) and studied there until 1924—the year that Lenin died and Petrograd was renamed Leningrad. Then, as a qualified instructor and manager in the cooperative movement, Kosygin was sent to Siberia.

The assignment was a difficult one: the cooperative movement had developed in Russia during the 19th century and was particularly strong in Siberia where its administration was still in the hands of noncommunists, including many Social Democrats. Kosygin and his fellow communist youth league (Komsomol) members had to penetrate the cooperative groups, reorganize them along party lines and bring them into the new government-controlled economic system. Starting as an instructor in the Irkutsk regional cooperative, Kosygin was later promoted to manager of the planning department in the Siberian Territorial Union of Cooperatives. While serving in Siberia, he met his future wife Klavdiya who was working there as a teacher, and in 1927—a year before Stalin gained control of the Soviet leadership—Kosygin left the Komsomol to become a full party member. In 1929 Kosygin returned to Leningrad where he entered the Kirov Textile Institute to pursue a five-year course in textile engineering.

Graduating in 1934, Kosygin became foreman and shop superintendent at the Zhelyabov textile plant, one of the largest such concerns in Leningrad. In the same year, Sergei Kirov, the Leningrad party chief, was assassinated, apparently on orders from Stalin. Andrei Zhdanov, a communist ideologue who was also at that time a Stalin henchman, became the new Leningrad leader. The continuing liquidation of communist members created a shortage of party officials with expertise in industrial fields; thus Kosygin, a loyal party member, well educated and with experience as a local technocrat, was in an excellent position for advancement. By 1935 he had joined the committee of Leningrad's Vyborg Borough, and a year later, at only 32 years of age, he was named director of the large October Textile Mill, where he won the esteem of workers for his efficiency and fair-minded attitudes. When Kosygin was 34, Zhdanov put him in charge of organizing the city's industrial transport system. Rising rapidly, Kosygin became chairman of Leningrad city council—a position equivalent to that of mayor—in October of 1938, and early the following year, he was elected as a Deputy to the country's legislative

assembly, becoming a cabinet minister or "people's commissar." Respected as a no-nonsense but humane manager, Kosygin was named to the newly created position of chief of the Soviet textile industry. After years of inept management and neglect, there was a dire shortage of fabrics and clothing, and this was causing vigorous protest throughout the USSR. At the 18th Party Congress in March 1939, Kosygin, at Stalin's behest, attacked the policies of other commissars, which, he said, were responsible for the textile industry's worsening condition; but he was careful to praise Soviet progress in general, stating that their successes to date had "shown up the capitalist nations in all their rottenness." Kosygin outlined a 16-point modernization plan for the industry and got himself elected to the 62-member commission led by Stalin to revise the third five-year plan.

In 1940, at the age of 36, Kosygin was again promoted. This time he was named a member of the Council of Ministers—effectively a deputy premier—initially working under prime minister Vyacheslav Molotov; he also joined Molotov's Economic Council and began to take control of all Soviet industrial planning. While serving in these capacities, Hitler invaded the Soviet Union (June 1941). Early in the USSR's involvement in the Second World War—which the Soviets refer to as the "Great Patriotic War"—Kosygin joined Anastas Mikoyan on the Council for Evacuation. He organized the movement of industry from the path of the German forces to the Urals and beyond, and helped to establish munitions factories in the east. Then in January 1942, Kosygin was given the massive, crucial task of evacuating half a million people from Leningrad—moving them across the frozen lake Ladoga to avoid the German and Finnish siege; he stayed in the starving, blockaded city for six months. In 1943, Kosygin was appointed prime minister of the war-torn Russian Republic (the largest of the 15 Soviet republics, covering nearly 80 percent of the USSR land area, and containing well over half of the Soviet population).

When the Germans retreated after the battle of Stalingrad in February 1943, Kosygin's major concerns were the rebuilding and repairing of the nation's industries and ruined cities, and the rationing of food. At the Tenth Session of the Supreme Soviet in 1944, he described the nation's plans to restore and improve services. Considering the Soviet Union's desperate position after the war, Kosygin's program was ambitious and surprisingly welfare-oriented. He described the massive reconstruction programs, the special provisions and accommodation for the million-plus war orphans, and outlined improvements in public health and reforms in education, including compulsory schooling for all children seven years of age and over. Perhaps because Kosygin knew his social concerns would not impress Stalin, he took pains to speak glowingly of Stalin's "great leadership." Later in 1944, Kosygin announced increased agricultural and industrial investment in order to improve productivity.

Stalin certainly was impressed by Kosygin's abilities as a planner, and in March 1946, when Kosygin was 42, he was selected as a candidate (non-voting) member of the ruling Politburo; by virtue of this position, Kosygin became one of Stalin's eight deputy premiers. Worried by massive corruption and inefficiency within the Finance Ministry and by the plight of the Soviet currency, Stalin drastically devalued the ruble, raised Kosygin to full (voting) membership of the

Politburo, and put him in temporary charge of the ministry (1948).
Hundreds of officials were found guilty of falsifying records and
embezzling funds. By December, Kosygin had effected a number of
improvements and restored calm. He was then named head of the
Ministry of Light Industry (later the Ministry of Food and Light
Industry)—another "trouble-shooting" position. The Ministry now
encompassed the textile industry in which postwar reconstruction had
been badly neglected.

Kosygin's reputation as a highly-competent bureaucrat may explain
why he remained unscathed by Stalin's purges; but his survival was
probably assured by his clever diplomacy in dealing with Stalin and his
aides, and particularly, his apparent loyalty and lack of political
ambition. However, Khrushchev was amazed by Kosygin's survival;
many of those arrested had denounced Kosygin, and Khrushchev
could only surmise that he "must have drawn a lottery ticket."

Whether or not Stalin believed those who, under duress, had
informed against Kosygin, he was certainly suspicious of him, if for no
other reason than that Kosygin was from Leningrad. Aided and
abetted by his closest confidant Malenkov, Stalin became convinced
that a group of Leningraders was hatching plots against his regime
with Yugoslavia's Marshall Tito [q.v.], but both Malenkov and
Mikoyan assured Stalin that Kosygin was not party to the collusion.
Officially, Kosygin did remain loyal to Stalin (he reaffirmed his loyalty
at the 1952 Party Congress), but a Soviet defector—and an anti-
communist with no reason to be biased in favor of Kosygin—later
claimed that at a birthday party held in Leningrad in the late 1940s,
Kosygin drunkenly referred to Stalin as a "pockmarked bastard," and
said that if Stalin was removed from office, real socialism could make
the Soviet Union a great country. Some Kremlin-watchers believed
that Kosygin finally got onto Stalin's "hit list" in 1953 and that he was
saved from death only because Stalin died before the order could be
effected.

Kosygin's Leningrad mentor, Zhdanov, had no such luck. He died
in 1948, ostensibly of a heart attack, but in somewhat obscure
circumstances. However, no doubts surrounded the deaths of
Leningrad politicians Alexander Kuznetsov and Nikolai Voznesensky.
They were liquidated on instructions from Malenkov, the man widely
expected to become Stalin's successor.

The first of several setbacks in Kosygin's career occurred at the
Party Congress in 1952 (Stalin had last convened a Congress in 1939,
and this one was believed to be in preparation for another purge). The
Politburo, which then consisted of ten full members and four alternate
members, was reorganized into a Presidium with 25 regular members
and 11 candidate members. Despite Kosygin's affirmation of loyalty,
he was given only a candidate membership, although he did retain his
positions as Deputy Chairman of the Council of Ministers (a deputy
prime minister) and as Minister of Food and Light Industry.

When Stalin died in March 1953, Khrushchev became party leader,
Malenkov took over as Prime Minister and the Politburo was reduced
to ten members. This time Kosygin was excluded from the Politburo,
but kept his ministry, which under Premier Malenkov's control,
became the Ministry of Industrial Consumer Goods Production. By
the fall, when the rivalries between Khrushchev and Malenkov were
becoming increasingly bitter, Kosygin was once again made a deputy

prime minister. He relinquished his ministerial duties in 1954, when he was 50 years old, to concentrate on the improvement of material conditions for the Soviet people. His responsibilities ranged over a number of industries, and one of his major tasks was to supervise changes in the notoriously inadequate system of food distribution. The following year Khrushchev emerged as victor of the power struggle, and Kosygin's boss, Malenkov, was demoted.

At the 20th Party Congress in February 1956, Kosygin explained how disparities between immediate and long-term planning were creating serious dangers for the economy. Thus, in December, he was appointed First Deputy Chairman of the State Economic Planning Committee (Gosplan), and was again relieved of his deputy premiership so that he could work exclusively on implementing his remedies. By diminishing party control of the economy, the government hoped that Khrushchev's increasing power could be restrained. But when, the following year, the so-called "anti-party" group led by Malenkov and Molotov tried to topple Khrushchev during a Central Committee struggle, they failed. Kosygin, who had never shown much interest in party affairs, was forceful in his defense of Khrushchev, and was rewarded by being readmitted as a candidate member of the Politburo. This was an upturn in Kosygin's political fortunes; in the preceding five years he had lost ground in the central power structure of the party and government despite his continuing reputation as a tough and practical planner.

Within a few months (in March 1958) he was once again named a deputy prime minister, and a year later he became Director of Gosplan. Kosygin began to liberalize and decentralize economic controls and instituted incentives for workers and managers. Despite Kosygin's earlier efforts, availability of consumer goods had rarely been a high priority issue, but now there was a concentrated effort to improve the material well-being of the population.

At the 22nd Party Congress (1960), Kosygin delivered one of the major political speeches of his career. He attacked Molotov and his associates for their interference in economic affairs, charging that they "created conditions in which it was impossible to work," and his denunciation of Stalin was the severest condemnation of the former leader at the Congress: "We must and shall do all we can to purge the cult of personality from our party and our society, to cut off its shoots and dig up its roots." Those who had already noted the considerable power of Khrushchev's personality might have found irony in Kosygin's speech, but it is extremely doubtful that Kosygin intended even a veiled criticism of the way his leader exercized power. Indeed, Kosygin seemed at this time to be hand-in-glove with Khrushchev, and in a major shake-up, Khrushchev further improved Kosygin's position by restoring him to full membership of the Politburo and naming him a first deputy prime minister—a post shared with Mikoyan. However, although Khrushchev and Kosygin were political allies at this time, their personal friendship appeared to be rather tepid.

As a major Khrushchev deputy, Kosygin was a frequent official visitor, and member of Soviet economic missions to European, Asian and Latin American countries. He accompanied Khrushchev on his trip to France, and in 1961 visited India to negotiate an economic cooperation agreement. He also attended meetings of the Council for

Mutual Economic Aid in various Soviet satellite countries. In November 1962, shortly after the Cuban missile crisis had been resolved, a conciliatory Kosygin said that the concessions made by both the Soviet Union and the USA had established that "it was possible to eliminate the threat of thermonuclear world war."

Early in 1963, Khrushchev appointed Kosygin and Mikoyan to his newly-formed Supreme National Council, responsible for running the Soviet economy. In April of that year, Khrushchev named Kosygin as a possible successor to the premiership, and three months later, when Mikoyan was appointed Chairman of the Presidium of the Supreme Soviet, Kosygin, now the only first deputy premier, ranked next to Khrushchev in the government hierarchy.

The harvest that year was particularly bad and the Soviet Union had to dip into its emergency war supplies. The government also found it necessary to purchase large quantities of grain from the West, thus decreasing its precious gold and currency reserves and exacerbating the difficulties of its already-ailing economy. The growth rate target had been missed year after year and real annual growth had steadily fallen. Khrushchev's often simplistic remedies to complex problems only made matters worse. His attempts to raise the "socialist consciousness" of farmers by severely restricting privately-owned livestock and crops (he banned individual ownership of cows) led to a serious shortage of many staple foods. The widespread dissatisfaction occasionally boiled over into public outrage and even violence.

Discontent was by no means restricted to the public; some of Khrushchev's ministers were extremely unhappy about Khrushchev, and Kosygin in particular—a hard-working, level-headed economic planner—had every reason to be angered by the erratic, almost flippant, actions of his leader. With a secrecy born of fear, various ministers discussed the possibility of overthrowing Khrushchev, and he probably sealed his own fate by his accommodating overtures to West Germany in preparation for his controversial trip to Bonn. His total disregard for official policy, which was to support the German Democratic Republic and pursue a hard line against Western Germany, convinced the waverers that he should go. At a plenary meeting of the Central Committee held on October 14th 1964, Khrushchev was voted out of office. The official version, given out two days later, stated that the Committee had granted "Khrushchev's request to be relieved of his duties . . . in view of his advanced age and deterioration of health." It was further announced that the Presidium had selected Leonid Brezhnev as First Secretary of the Party, and Aleksei Kosygin had been unanimously elected as Chairman of the Council of Ministers, or Prime Minister. The two men who had been at the center of Khrushchev's ouster, first appeared in public as the new leaders at a Red Square rally held on October 19th to honor three cosmonauts.

Thus Kosygin became the first person to assume the Soviet premiership having risen through government—not party—ranks. His appointment may come to be viewed as a significant shift in Soviet policies as it may indicate a willingness within the powerful party hierarchy to soften its ideological approach to the economy and allow its development to be influenced by government pragmatists more responsive to the vicissitudes of daily life and more interested in incentives for growth than in sacrifice for strict ideals.

Brezhnev, as the new party chief, directed all party politics and relations with other communist states, while Kosygin, the Prime Minister, managed the government and affairs with the non-communist world. The suddenness of Khrushchev's departure surprised the Western powers and they were, at first, apprehensive of the new administration. But there was general satisfaction with Kosygin's appointment because he was seen as the Kremlin politician most likely to pursue a non-belligerent foreign policy. Indeed, within days of taking office, Kosygin and Brezhnev assured Foy D. Kohler, the US ambassador in the USSR, that Moscow would stress peaceful coexistence. The new leaders also called for communist solidarity with China and promised Wladyslaw Gomulka, First Secretary of the Polish Communist Party, that the Kremlin would not rescind the agreements which had given greater freedom to the East European communist nations in the later Khrushchev years. The UN Secretary General U Thant spoke warmly of Kosygin's "unostentatious" manner, and called him one of the Soviet Union's "most respected leaders."

From the start, Kosygin was known as the "Chief Engineer," confirming the view that he was the administrator, technician and planner rather than the ideologist or party politician. With grim memories of the Stalin regime, and Khrushchev's erratic leadership fresh in their minds, Brezhnev and Kosygin instituted the so-called "age of the faceless managers." The two men spent most of their time working quietly on the serious problems before them. They greatly reduced the number of public appearances and pronouncements and eschewed the grand state occasions which had been so popular in recent years. Both men kept their personal lives strictly private, and Kosygin's wife, son and daughter were quite unknown to the Russian people.

The new leaders lost no time in implementing changes to improve agriculture, social services and economic and industrial management. A much needed substantial increase in agricultural investment and some reduction in the command planning of farming so that natural market forces could come into play, enabled the expansion of private plots and allowed collective farmers to increase their livestock. This reduced food shortages and helped to restore people's faith in the government. The collective farmers were helped by being paid at shorter intervals instead of only once a year, and peasant farmers were appeased by the introduction of old age pensions and sickness benefits which had been denied them during the first 45 years of communist rule. However, agriculture was by no means freed from rigid central control and many limitations on private enterprise continued. These constraints, together with inclement weather and old-fashioned farming methods, were major factors in the country's continuing failure to achieve its food production goals.

Reforms in the administration of the economy were just as swift as those in agriculture. A centralized plan for the economy replaced Khrushchev's cumbersome regional system, and the dismantling of the party's agricultural and industrial policy organizations, gave the government a freer hand in carrying out its reforms. Kosygin was thus able to concentrate on material rather than ideological standards, and announced in March 1965, the "Twin Aims" of better wages and greater availability of consumer goods. Kosygin's undoubted talents as an organizer were quickly noticed, and for a while, he appeared to be making headway at Brezhnev's expense. Confidently, in his five-year plan for 1966–70, Kosygin announced the government's intention, previously prohibited by Khrushchev, to develop mass car production. He then proposed reduction of controls on factory managers and workers through bonuses paid out of the profits. This idea, originally advanced by a Pole, Oskar Lange, in 1956, was undoubtedly the most radical economic reform since the very early years of the Soviet state when hunger and increasing unruliness had obliged the government to support the survival of limited private enterprise.

Unfortunately for Kosygin, his plans for agriculture and economy were never properly implemented. To a large extent they were thwarted by the entrenched bureaucracies of both the party and the government and by groups with vested interests in the status quo, such as those in the higher echelons of the military-industrial complex. Exasperated, Kosygin spoke out against their refusal to face the realities of a modern economy. In 1970, admitting that the five-year-plan's economic goals had not been met—the national income had grown only four percent instead of the projected six percent—Kosygin cited the continuing problems of poor harvests and inefficient management. By this time, Brezhnev had clearly emerged as the more powerful figure, and there was a serious move afoot to elect a new prime minister. But Kosygin survived—mainly because the Politburo could not agree on an alternative premier. Kosygin had been resigned to his own departure, and it is thought that he had taken comfort in the fact that he would no longer be Brezhnev's whipping boy. Nevertheless he agreed to stay on, and continued to apply himself diligently to the problems. Five years later, Kosygin had better economic news. He proudly announced to the 25th Party Congress in 1975 that the USSR was now the world's largest producer of several vital commodities, including pig iron, steel, cement and oil; but he added a warning that ways must be found to further improve productivity as the labor force was growing at a slower rate than anticipated and could no longer be relied upon to expand enough to continue the upward trend in industrial output.

During the 1970s, Kosygin spearheaded the Soviet Union's efforts to improve its industries with the help of Western technology and expertise. This stimulation, together with improvements in management techniques and further modernization of the economic system, helped to make the lot of the Soviet people a little easier. Nevertheless, Kosygin was aware that their advancement still fell short of Japanese and Western achievements in many areas, and with the continuing problem of poor grain harvests, manpower shortages, and massive defense spending, the standard of living remained well below that of the Western world. Many observers wondered if the cold, unenthusiastic thanks Brezhnev extended to Kosygin on his retirement in October 1980, suggested that the party was unhappy with Kosygin's achievements on the economic front, and some speculated that he was being made the scapegoat for the failure to meet recent five-year-plan goals.

When Kosygin became Prime Minister he did not feel that Soviet foreign policy required the radical overhauling that had become imperative on the economic and industrial fronts. Rather, as with the basic party and government systems of operation, he was content to maintain the status quo. But ever a pragmatist, he tried to avoid

ideological confrontation and sought peaceful coexistence—despite
his occasionally bellicose rhetoric—with the capitalist world. He also
sought a peaceful solution to the Sino-Soviet border disputes, and
devoted much of his time to developing Soviet relations with Third
World countries. However, as with the economy, his good intentions
were often thwarted by problems within the communist movement.
The Soviet invasion of Czechoslovakia, at a time when the world was
forgetting Moscow's crushing of the Hungarian revolution, was a
major blow to Soviet relations with the outside world; and the policy
of detente with Western Europe and America which blossomed during
Nixon's later years in the White House, was seriously weakened when
Soviet tanks entered Afghanistan in December 1979.

The increase in US military activities on behalf of the anti-
communist Vietnamese government foiled Kosygin's early efforts to
improve relations with America and expand trade between the two
countries. In his 1965 New Year's message, Kosygin attempted to
enhance the USSR's image as a peacemaker and at the same time
embarrass America, by calling for an end to foreign intervention in
the internal affairs of other countries. He also stressed the need for
general disarmament and the banning of nuclear weapons. Shortly
thereafter he visited Mao Tse-tung in Peking, but their icy meeting
produced nothing more than a hardening of position on both sides. He
had gone to Peking from Hanoi, where, in response to President
Johnson's announcement that the US would renew bombing of North
Vietnamese military targets, he promised Hanoi the USSR's full
support. With apparent reluctance, the Soviet Union abandoned its
intention of reducing its military budget and instead, increased it by
five percent. Kosygin evaded foreign efforts to reconvene the Geneva
Conference and refused to discuss ways of ending the war, declaring
that any peace initiatives would have to come from Hanoi.

In January 1966, Kosygin adroitly mediated at the Tashkent
conference and increased his international prestige when his efforts
led to the ending of the India-Pakistan war. A few months later in
Helsinki, Kosygin suggested a solely European conference on European security. By excluding the USA, he hoped to strengthen the
Soviet bloc's ties with its Western neighbors. When General de Gaulle
later visited Moscow, the two men found themselves in general
agreement on inter-European relations, and in order to cement Soviet
friendship with France, Kosygin gave de Gaulle direct teleprinter
access to the Kremlin, thus providing him with a "hotline" facility
previously restricted to one Western leader—the US President.
However, Kosygin made little effort to improve the tense relations
existing between the Soviet Union and Western Germany, and when
he returned de Gaulle's visit by going to Paris in December 1966, he
took the opportunity to censure both Bonn and Washington.

In London the following year, Kosygin made friendly gestures
toward the British by proposing an Anglo-Soviet peace pact. He
called for the dismantling of Nato and Warsaw Pact forces, and noting
the tension in Sino-Soviet relations, he maintained that the Chinese
were entirely in the wrong. Also while in London, he added his weight
to the Hanoi peace initiative which promised to discuss the possibility
of negotiations if the USA would call an unconditional halt to
bombing raids on North Vietnam. The Americans agreed to comply
on the condition that Hanoi would agree to cease its infiltration of

South Vietnam; when Hanoi rejected this counter demand, the peace effort failed.

Vehemently opposed to American incursions in South East Asia (he had referred to American intentions as "Hitlerite"), Kosygin refused President Johnson's invitation to visit Washington, but he did agree to Soviet-American talks on the limitation of both defensive and offensive nuclear weapons. However, the stunning Israeli victory over the Arabs in the Six-Day War of June 1967 brought Kosygin to the UN General Assembly in New York to debate the issue of the captured territories, and while there, he agreed to meet with Johnson at Glassboro State College in New Jersey. No agreements were made at either of their two meetings at Glassboro, and although their talks were cordial, Kosygin's antipathy toward the Americans—at least on the issue of Vietnam—remained as strong as ever. In a later interview he declared: "The Soviet people cannot approve of a policy developing friendship with the United States while American troops kill totally innocent people, and conduct an illegal war and seize foreign territories." On his way back from the UN, Kosygin visited Castro in Havana, and also paid another visit to General de Gaulle in Paris.

While little is known of the politicking behind the USSR's momentous decision to eradicate the Dubcek government's "socialism with a human face" in Czechoslovakia, it is widely supposed that Kosygin was against the move, and such a stance would accord with his reputation as a "dove." Press reports suggested that Kosygin wanted to restore Czechoslovakia's loyalty to the USSR through negotiation and a mixture of economic rewards and punishments. Apparently Brezhnev favored Kosygin's approach, but as the crisis deepened, he was swayed by the arguments of his military advisors.

Kosygin attended Ho Chi Minh's funeral in Hanoi in September 1969, and while he was there, US President Nixon ordered a resumption of the bombing of North Vietnam. Despite widespread angry reactions to this, Kosygin's criticism of it, coming only 13 months after the Soviet invasion of Czechoslovakia, had a somewhat hollow ring. Still incensed by Chinese activities on its borders with the USSR (fighting had flared up on the Ussuri River with scores of casualties on both sides), Kosygin went from Hanoi to Peking to try to work out a solution with Zhao Enlai. But as before, nothing was resolved and although talks were restarted, the rancor continued unabated.

In 1971, Kosygin visited Canada, repaying Prime Minister Trudeau's visit to Moscow in May of that year. Kosygin reiterated the USSR's desire for peaceful coexistence and discussed closer trading relations between the two countries. He then went on to Cuba where his friendly reception quickly scotched rumors of a breach in Soviet-Cuban relations. The talks resulted in a reaffirmation of Soviet support and another censure of the American blockade of Cuba. Soon thereafter, Kosygin visited Baghdad and signed a 15-year friendship treaty with the Iraqis. Previously, Egypt had been the Soviet Union's major Middle Eastern ally, and when Egyptian President Sadat later dismissed the Russians, the Soviets could console themselves by their strengthening influence in Iraq.

With Nixon's pledge to end American military involvement in Vietnam, and with the Soviets' continuing assertion of peaceful intentions, a meaningful detente between East and West could at last

be discussed. In 1972, during President Nixon's first visit to Moscow (he paid a second visit in 1974), Kosygin signed agreements for Soviet-American cooperation in space, scientific and technical programs. It was now quite apparent to Western observers that Brezhnev was firmly in charge of the Soviet side of the negotiations and Kosygin served more as a government figurehead than as a policy-maker.

In 1973, Kosygin visited President Tito in Yugoslavia. The two men had a lot in common: both were sons of poor craftsmen and fought in the Red Army; both men served in the Kremlin in its early days and came to loathe Stalin; and both were tough, surviving pragmatists seeking to strengthen their respective economies without too much regard for ideology. But there were also important differences: Tito was ruthless, imaginative and unorthodox—a showman with a warm personality, a lively humor and expensive tastes. Kosygin was dour and virtually humorless, with a charm so quiet, it was often imperceptible. But above all, he was a staunch supporter of the Soviet status quo, and even if he had learned to forget Tito's early purges and forgive his delight in material possessions, he would find it impossible to ignore Tito's deviation from the Soviet system. It is therefore not surprising that Tito expressed anger at Kosygin's "condescending" attitude during his visit. The Russian leader appeared to be more relaxed on his trip to Cairo that year, after the renewed hostilities between Israel and the Arab countries. He probably found the discussion of ceasefire plans and weapons supplies much more to his liking.

Until his retirement, Kosygin was a regular traveler, visiting countries where a little diplomacy might strengthen Soviet ties, and also going to capitals such as Bucharest, Belgrade and Tripoli where his presence might discourage leaders from erring too far from the Soviet sphere of influence. One of his last major diplomatic missions was to India in March 1979, where he tried, to no avail, to elicit support for the Cambodian regime imposed by Vietnam after its recent capture of Phnom Penh.

Ill health was given as the reason for Kosygin's retirement on October 23rd 1980. As there had been rumors for some time that he would retire because of his heart ailment, observers thought it unlikely that he had been forced from office. Kosygin's colleagues were more generous in their praise of him when he died than they had been on his retirement eight weeks earlier. However the announcement of his death was delayed for more than a day so that the news would not interfere with the celebration of Brezhnev's birthday. Kosygin is survived by his son, who is in the Soviet Army, and by his daughter, who runs the Library of Foreign Literature. His wife died in 1967. Kosygin collected six Orders of Lenin during his long government career and in 1964 he was named a Hero of Socialist Labor, the USSR's highest honor. At his state funeral which followed two days of official mourning, the new Prime Minister, Nikolai Tikhonov, eulogized Kosygin as a man "who dedicated his entire life to serving the people" and whose life "was inseparably linked with the struggle for the realization of the ideals of communism."

An heir of a great socialist revolution, Kosygin like millions of other Russians, must have had visions of a future free of tyranny. But the promise was short-lived; as Trotsky had feared, the people's will was substituted by a self-perpetuating central power structure. Kosygin's real inheritance was a system in desperate need of democratization. But rather than try to reform the system, Kosygin was apparently content to become a bureaucrat within it. Perhaps inevitably, like the other members of the Politburo, he ended up an old and sombre Kremlin conformist clinging warily to power. But unlike most of his elitist comrades, Kosygin significantly improved the efficiency of his government, and earned at least a tenuous respect within the Soviet Union for his genuine desire to improve living standards and to find peaceful solutions to problems with other nations.   R.T.

Son of a lathe worker. Wife: Klavdiya, d. 1967. One son; one daughter. Educ: Training Sch. for Cooperatives, Petrograd (formerly St. Petersburg, later Leningrad) 1929–34, grad. in textile engineering. Volunteer in Red Army 1919–21. Joined Komsomol (youth league) 1920s; Instr., Irkutsk Regional Cooperative, and subsequently Mgr. of Planning Dept., Siberian Territorial Union of Cooperatives 1924–29; joined Communist Party 1927; Foreman and Shop Superintendent, Zhelyabov Textile Plant, Leningrad 1934–36; joined Cttee. of Vyborg Council, Leningrad 1935; Dir., October Textile Mill, Leningrad 1936–38; in charge of Leningrad Industrial Transport System 1938; Chmn. (Mayor) Leningrad City Council 1938–39; elected a Deputy of Supreme Soviet legislative assembly and named a People's Commissar (cabinet minister) 1939; Commissar of Soviet Textile Industry 1939–40; appointed a Member of USSR Council of Ministers (effectively a deputy prime minister) and of USSR Economic Council 1940; joined wartime Council of Evacuation 1941, in charge of Leningrad evacuation 1942; appointed Prime Minister of Russian Republic 1943; Soviet Finance Minister 1948; Minister of Light Industry (later, of Food and Light Industry, and then, of Industrial Consumer Goods Production) 1948–54; reappointed to Council of Ministers 1953–54, in charge of improvement of material conditions of Soviet people 1954–56; First Deputy Chmn. 1956–59 and Dir. 1959–60, State Economic Planning Cttee. (Gosplan); again appointed to Council of Ministers 1958; appointed a First Deputy Prime Minister 1960; Member, National Council for Soviet Economy 1963; Prime Minister of the USSR 1964 until retirement 1980. With Politburo: Candidate Member 1946–48, 1952–53, 1957–60 and Member 1948–52, 1960–80. Hons: Order of Lenin (six times); Order of Red Banner; Hero of Socialist Labor 1964; Order of October Revolution 1978; ashes placed in Kremlin wall.
*Further reading:*Men Versus Systems: Agriculture in the U.S.S.R., Poland, and Czechoslovakia by A. E. Adams and J. S. Adams, 1971; The Communist Party of the Soviet Union by Leonard Schapiro, 1971; Brezhnev: The Masks of Power by John Dornberg, 1974.

ALBERT (MICHAEL) MARGAI
Prime Minister of Sierra Leone
Born Sierra Leone, October 10th, 1910
Died Washington, D.C., U.S.A., December 18th, 1980

Albert Margai was a leading figure in the political life of Sierra Leone from the late 1940s until being ousted from power by the military in 1967. Having succeeded his brother as Prime Minister in 1964, Margai unsuccessfully attempted to introduce one-party rule to Sierra Leone.

Educated in Roman Catholic schools in Bonthe and Freetown, Albert Margai, the son of a physician, began training in 1931 to become a male nurse. He later was certified as a druggist, but, in 1944, Margai moved to London to study law and he was admitted to the bar three years later. After establishing a successful private practice in Sierra Leone, Margai and his brother, Milton, formed the Sierra Leone People's Party (SLPP) in 1951. Also that year, Albert was elected to the Legislative Council and given a portfolio of education and welfare; when a ministerial system of government was introduced, Margai became Minister of Education, Local Government and Social Welfare. Elections held in 1957 produced a large legislative majority for the SLPP, but Margai, who had become increasingly radicalized, abandoned the party to form the People's National Party (PNP) with Siaka Stevens.

In 1960, however, a reconciliation was effected between the Margai brothers and Albert rejoined the SLPP. Two years later, he was appointed Minister of Finance and, when his brother died in 1964, succeeded him as Prime Minister. During his tenure, Margai attempted to transform Sierra Leone's political structure to accommodate one-party rule under a strong presidency with executive, rather than merely ceremonial, powers. In late 1966, on the eve of national elections, Margai proposed a new constitution which would have made the country a republic; however, the document received little support and the Prime Minister was forced to retract it. In a desperate bid to retain his position, Margai subsequently ordered the arrest of several military officers, accusing them of conspiring to overthrow the government. The British Governor-General, Sir Henry Lightfoot-Boston, then intervened in the election and declared Margai's opponent, Siaka Stevens, to be the new Prime Minister. The appointment, however, was quickly vetoed by the Sierra Leone army commander, a Margai supporter, but he was immediately removed from power by other officers who established a military government in March 1967. They ruled the country until 1968 when Stevens assumed power. Ironically, Stevens accomplished legally what Margai, who spent the remainder of his life in exile in London, could not by means of subterfuge; in 1971, Stevens became President of the Republic of Sierra Leone and, seven years later, one party rule was officially established.   T.P.

Son of Ndaneh M., and M.E.S. M. Wife: Esther 1949. Ten children. Educ: St. Patrick's Roman Catholic Sch., Bonthe, Sierra Leone; St. Edward's Secondary Sch., Freetown, Sierra Leone; Middle Temple, London 1944; called to the bar 1947. Nurse and pharmacist 1932–44; Member, Sierra Leone Protectorate Assembly 1949; Sierra Leone Legislative Council 1951; Minister of Educ. and Welfare and Local Govt. 1951–57; Member, Sierra Leone People's Party (SLPP) 1951–58; Founding Member, People's Natl. Party ca. 1958; rejoined SLPP 1960; Minister of Finance 1962–64; Prime Minister of Sierra Leone 1964–67. Hons: Knight of the Grand Cross of St. Gregory the Great.

NIKOLAI (VASILEVICH) MELNIKOV
Mining and energy expert
Born Sarapul, Udmurt, U.S.S.R., February 28th, 1909
Died U.S.S.R., December 18th, 1980

Nikolai V. Melnikov was an authority on mining and an expert on energy resource management. After graduating from the Sverdlovsk Mining Institute in 1933, he gained practical experience in engineering and administrative jobs in open-cast mining, a method in which terraces are cut into the terrain to form a network of roads for the easy extraction and transportation of ore. In 1944, the year he joined the Communist Party, Melnikov was appointed to his first official post as Deputy Minister of Coal Industries in the East Region. After teaching at the Academy of Fuel Industries and directing the Skochinskii Mining Institute during the 1950s and early 1960s, he served as a deputy in the Supreme Soviet and headed the State Committe on Fuel Industries. He also chaired a number of councils and committees on mining, energy, and natural resources for the government and for the Academy of Sciences, to whose Presidium he was elected in 1967. In recent years he was rector of the Academy of the National Economy and director of the Institute on Complex Use of Resources.

Melnikov wrote over 100 books and articles on mining and energy management, most on open-cast methods; several of his books have become standard government reference texts. For his contributions to the mining industry, he received the State Prize, the Order of Lenin, two Orders of the Red Badge of Labor, and several other medals and awards. N.S.

Educ: Sverdlovsk Mining Inst., grad. 1933. Engineer and Admin., mining and coal industries 1934–45; Member, Communist Party since 1944; Deputy Minister of Coal Industry, East Region 1944–48; Chmn., State Cttee. for Fuel Industry, Gosplan 1961–65; Deputy, Supreme Soviet 1962–66; Chmn., Commn. for Research on Production of Energy and Natural Resources from 1966, and Chmn., Council for Physical and Engineering Problems of Exploitation of Mineral Resources, Inst. of Earth Physics from 1967, Acad. of Sciences; Head of Commn., State Science and Technical Cttee., Council of Mining; Member, Council of Ministers, Bureau for Fuel and Metallurgy Industries. Prof., Acad. of Fuel Industries 1950–56; Deputy Dir. 1955–64 and Dir. since 1964, A.A. Skochinskii Laboratory of Open-Cast Mining, Acad. of Sciences; Member, Certification Commn., Ministry of Higher and Special Secondary Education; Rector, Acad. of National Economy; Dir., Inst. on Complex Use of Resources. Member, Cttee. for Lenin Prizes. With Acad. of Sciences: Corresponding Member 1953–62; Member since 1962; Member of Presidium since 1966. Hons: jt. State Prize for fundamental improvement in open-cast mining 1946; Stalin Prize 1946; Merited Scientist of the Russian Soviet Federated Socialist Republic; Order of Lenin; Order of Red Banner of Labor (twice); Miner's Glory Badge of Honor, Class 1. *Author:* Open-Cast Mineral Mining, 1948; Drilling Wells and Blast Holes at Open-Cast Workings, 1953; Mechanization of Works in Open-Cast Mining, 1954; Development of Science in the Field of Open-Cast Mining in the USSR, 1957; Fundamentals of Line Technology in Open-Cast Mining, 1962; numerous other books and papers on mining technology and resource management.

A playwright, novelist, and author of screenplays, Ben Travers was ranked with Arthur Wing Pinero and Georges Feydeau as one of the three great modern writers of farce. Travers eschewed Feydeau's mechanical contrivances of both plot and character to produce farce that began under reasonable circumstances and was inhabited by universally believable, recognizable character types. According to critic J.C. Trewin, no comic writer knew better than Travers the necessity of a "cracking pace, a fuming last-act rally . . . and dialogue that, though it snows down in whirling flakes of nonsense, never freezes into the cold glitter of epigrams."

Born into the Victorian era, Travers once said he was fascinated by theater in childhood, despite parental and social disapproval of stage performers. After schooling at Charterhouse, he entered the wholesale grocery firm of Joseph Travers and Sons; quickly growing bored, he requested a transfer to the company's Malayan branch where one of his few pleasures was the reading of Pinero's farces. In 1938 Travers drew on his memories of Asia for a play set in Malaya, *Banana Ridge,* in which Travers himself played the part of a Chinese servant.

Travers returned to England in 1911 with plans of becoming a dramatist. He took a job with the publishing house of John Lane and, during World War One, served as a pilot and aviation instructor. After the war he wrote a series of comic novels, including *A Cukoo in the Nest* (1922), and *Rookery Nook* (1923). However, in 1925, Travers's relatively late start in writing for the stage got under way when he adapted *A Cukoo in the Nest* for Aldwych Theatre actors Ralph Lynn and Tom Walls. Established as the Aldwych's informal house dramatist, Travers wrote nine plays, now known as the "Aldwych farces," between 1925 and 1933 upon which his critical reputation rests.

The Aldwych players composed a virtual stock company, ideally suited to Travers's verbal fireworks and ability to visualize the comic mise-en-scène; by the late 1920s, he was the most prosperous playwright in Britain and, in 1933, his plays had been produced almost 2,700 times. The settings included a haunted house cared for by a sinister butler named Death in the 1927 play, *Thark;* a Scotland Yard murder investigation in *Plunder* (1928); a cab lost in a London fog in 1930's *A Night Like This;* and the misadventures of an English cricket team in Australia in *A Bit of a Test* (1933). Travers's only excursion into serious drama was a 1936 play based on the life of St. Paul, *Chastity, My Brother,* which suffered critically when the real identity of its author became known. Travers may have had this set-back in mind when he remarked in *Theatre World* two years later: "The only trouble with writing farces is that some of the critics are inclined to be such snobs. They never think that a man who writes funny stuff can ranked with the great ones of literature."

When World War Two began in Europe, Travers once more served his country as an intelligence officer with the Royal Air Force, rising to the rank of Squadron Leader and becoming Air Advisor to the Ministry of Information's censorship department. Ironically, several of Travers's early plays had been censored for their bawdy language.

In the postwar years, he continued to write plays, screenplays, and wrote occasionally for television.

The popularity of Travers's plays endured well into the 1970s. His last work, *The Bed Before Yesterday,* was a considerable success in the London theater season of 1975 and the-then 89-year-old writer had the pleasant opportunity of seeing the premiere of his new comedy at one theater and then attending the revival of his 1928 play, *Plunder,* at another. Travers also wrote a whimsical, two-volume autobiography, *Vale of Laughter* (1957), and *A-sitting on a Gate* (1978). A past president of the Dramatists Club, he was made a Commander, Order of the British Empire in 1976.   L.R.

Son of W.F.T. Married Violet Mouncey 1916 (d. 1951). Two sons; one daughter. Educ: Abbey Sch., Beckenham, Surrey; Charterhouse, Surrey. Mil. Service: Pilot instr., Royal Naval Air Service 1914; Squadron Comdr. 1917; transferred as Maj. to Royal Air Force (RAF) 1918; received Air Force Cross 1920; rejoined RAF as Intelligence Officer 1939; Squadron Leader 1940; Air Advisor, Ministry of Information 1941–45. With Joseph Travers and Sons. ca. 1908–11; with John Lane Publishing ca. 1911–14; professional writer from 1920. Prime Warden of the Fishermongers Co. 1946; Pres., Dramatists Club 1956–60. Hons: Evening Standard award 1976; CBE 1976. *Author: Novels*—The Dippers, 1920; A Cukoo in the Nest, 1922; Rookery Nook, 1923; Mischief, 1924; The Dippers, together with Game and Rubber and The Dunkum Jane, 1932; Hyde Side Up, 1933. *Plays*—The Dippers, 1922; The Three Graces (adaptation), 1924; A Cukoo in the Nest, 1925; Rookery Nook, 1926; Thark, 1927; Mischief, 1928; Plunder, 1928; A Cup of Kindness, 1929; A Night Like This, 1930; Turkey Time, 1931; Dirty Work, 1932; A Bit of a Test, 1933; Chastity, My Brother, 1936; Nun's Veiling, (as O Mistress Mine, 1936), 1953; Banana Ridge, 1938; Spotted Dick, 1939; She Follows Me About, 1943; Outrageous Fortune, 1947; Runaway Victory, 1949; Wild Horses, 1952; Corker's End, 1968; The Bed Before Yesterday, 1975. *Screenplays*—Rookery Nook, 1930; A Chance of a Night-time, 1931; Mischief, 1931; Plunder, 1931; A Cukoo in the Nest, 1932; Thark, 1932; A Night Like This, 1932; Just My Luck, 1933; Turkey Time, 1933; Lady in Danger, 1934; A Cup of Kindness, 1934; Fighting Stock, 1935; Stormy Weather, 1935; Foreign Affairs, 1935; Pot Luck, 1936; Dishonour Bright, 1936; For Valour, 1937; Second Best Bed, 1937; Old Iron, 1938; Up to the Neck, 1938; Uncle Silas, 1947. *Television plays*—Potter, 1948; Picture Page, 1949. *Short stories*—The Collection Today, 1929; *Other*—Vale of Laughter (autobiog.), 1957; A-sitting on a Gate, 1978; The Leacock Book (editor), 1930; Pretty Pictures: Being a Selection of the Best American Pictorial Humour, 1932.

HECTOR CÁMPORA
President of Argentina and Ambassador to Mexico
Born San Andres de Giles, Buenos Aires, Argentina
Died Mexico City, Mexico, December 19th, 1980

Self-described as the "obsequious servant" of Argentine dictator Juan D. Peron, Dr. Hector Cámpora served briefly as President of Argentina in 1973. Cámpora's 49-day caretaker rule prepared the way

for Peron's return to power from exile and, as Peron's stand-in, he angered the military junta which rules Argentina and was himself later exiled to Mexico.

Hector J. Cámpora was born in the small town of San Andres de Giles, located in the Buenos Aires province. A dentist by profession, Cámpora entered politics in 1946 when he was elected to the Chamber of Deputies on the Peronist ticket. Cámpora was a dedicated supporter of Peron; he served continuously in the Argentine parliament and was for seven years its president. However, in 1955, after Peron was unseated by a military coup, exiled to Spain, and the Peronist party was outlawed, Cámpora was imprisoned although he escaped two years later, making his way to Chile.

Having returned from exile, Peron was barred from running in the 1973 election by residence requirements which he failed to meet. Instead, he chose as his surrogate Cámpora, who campaigned under the slogan, "Cámpora in government, Peron in power." Cámpora took office in May and quickly incurred the wrath of Argentina's military establishment by freeing more than 500 leftist political prisoners, legalizing the Communist Party, recognizing Fidel Castro's Cuban regime, and nationalizing bank deposits. In July he resigned, forcing a new election, in which Peron and his wife, Isabel Martinez de Peron, were installed as President and Vice-President, having won 61 percent of the vote. Peron then rewarded Cámpora by appointing him Ambassador to Mexico.

Before his death in office less than a year after assuming the Presidency, Peron fired Cámpora for his associations with leftists while serving as ambassador. In 1974 Isabel Peron became President of a country increasingly wracked by terrorism, interparty political strife, declining productivity and escalating inflation; two years later, she was removed from power by the military. Cámpora, who had been expelled from the Peronist party, had returned to Argentina in 1975.

Declaring himself the victim of political harrassment, Cámpora sought refuge in the Mexican Embassy in Buenos Aires, and lived there for three and one half years. In November 1979, after numerous appeals by the Mexican government, the military regime provided Cámpora with safe conduct to Mexico where he died of cancer. A.C.

Active as dentist. Elected to Chamber of Deputies 1946–55, served as Pres.; in prison during outlaw of Peronist party 1955, escaped to Chile 1957. Elected Pres. of Argentina, May 1973, resigned June 1973; Ambassador to Mexico 1973–74; expelled from Peronist Party 1974; returned to Argentina 1975, issued safe conduct to Mexico, Nov. 1979.

JOHN D(AVID) B(AWDEN) MITCHELL
Layer and educator
Born England, May 28th, 1917
Died Edinburgh, Scotland, December 19th, 1980

John D. B. Mitchell, an outstanding lawyer and professor of law, began his studies at the London School of Economics and Political Science, from which he graduated in 1938 with First Class Honours in law. Commissioned into the North Staffs Regiment in 1939, Mitchell served with the British Expeditionary Forces in France in 1940, where he was severely wounded and taken prisoner in the same year. He was repatriated in 1943, and until 1946 he served as Staff Officer, with the rank of Major.

At the end of World War Two, Mitchell returned to the law and in 1947 became a solicitor. Following a year's lectureship in law at the University College of Wales, Aberystwyth, he was offered a lectureship at the Law Society School in London. This led in turn to his returning to the University of London in 1949 as Lecturer in English Law, and in 1952, as Reader in English Law.

In 1954 Mitchell published his highly acclaimed *The Contracts of Public Authorities,* in which he compared the laws of government contracts in the United States, France, and his native England, and criticized English Common Law in comparison to American Constitutional Law and the Administrative Law of France. That same year Mitchell was appointed as Professor to the Chair of Constitutional Law at the University of Edinburgh, the first English lawyer to hold that post.

During his tenure at the University of Edinburgh, Mitchell widened the scope of his studies of constitutional law, investigating the Institutions and Rules of Scotland. In 1964 he published *Constitutional Law,* a penetrating examination of local and international aspects of Constitutional Law.

Mitchell's study of French Public Law, together with his interest in international economics, and the overview of politics he obtained during the war, led to his investigation of the European Economic Community, and to the establishment of the Centre of European Governmental Studies at the University of Edinburgh in the late 1960s, which he directed in 1968. That year the Salvesen Chair of European Institutions was created at the University of Edinburgh; Mitchell held the Chair, as well as the directorship of the Centre, until his death.

Throughout the 1970s, Mitchell contributed many thought provoking, highly original articles to legal publications and to books and magazines. He also established a high reputation as a lecturer both in Great Britain and on the Continent. In addition to his scholastic activities, he served on a number of important committees and commissions including the Douglas-Hume Committee on the Future Government of Scotland, 1968–69, the Vedel Committee of the European Economic Community, 1971–72, and the Hansard Society Commission on Electoral Reform, 1975–76. Mitchell also held a seat on the University of Edinburgh Court from 1958–62 and again from 1976–79 and additional posts with such organizations as the United Kingdom Association for European law, for which he was joint secretary, and the United Kingdom Committee on Comparative Law, of which he was chairman.

At the time of Mitchell's death after only a brief illness, the third edition of his *Constitutional Law* was in preparation; the written evidence he submitted to the House of Lords Select Committee concerning the European Economic Community is scheduled to be published shortly. The contributions he made to the study of the laws of Britain, relating them realistically to the judicial foundations of Europe and the United States, are unrivaled.   J.S.

Son of A.M. Married Jeanne Rosamund Nickerson 1945. Two
daughters. Educ: Colfe's Grammar Sch.; London Sch. of Economics
and Political Science, Univ. of London, Ph.D., L.L.B. (1st Class
Hons. in Law 1938, Whittuck Scholar). Mil. Service: WWII, commn,
N. Staffs Regiment 1939; with British Expeditionary Forces, France
1940; P.O.W. 1940–43, repatriated 1943; Staff Officer, Major,
1943–46. Admitted as Solicitor, 1947. Lectr. in Law, Univ. Coll. of
Wales at Aberystwyth, 1947–48; Lectr., Law Soc.'s Sch., London,
1948–49; Lectr., English Law, 1949–52, Reader in English Law,
1952–54, Univ. of London; With Univ. of Edinburgh: Prof., Chair of
Constitutional Law, 1954–68, Dir., Centre of European Governmen-
tal Studies, from 1968, and Holder, Salvesen Chair of European
Instns., from 1968. Member: Douglas-Hume Cttee. on Future govt. of
Scotland, 1968–69; Vedel Cttee., E.E.C., 1971–72; Hansard Soc.
Commn. on Electoral Reform, 1975–76; Political Science and Intnl.
Relations Cttee., Social Science Rsearch Council, 1975–79; Univ. of
Edinburgh Court, 1958–62, 1976–79; joint secty., United Kingdom
Assn. for European Law; chmn., United Kingdom Natnl. Cttee. on
Comparative Law; chmn. and Hon. pres, Universities Assn. of
Contemporary European Studies. Hons: L.L.D., Univ. of Edinburgh
1964; Docteur de l'Université, Univ. of Lille, 1965; C.B.E. 1973;
L.L.D., Univ. of Amsterdam 1975. *Author*—Contracts of Public
Authorities, 1954; Constitutional Law, 1964 (2nd ed. 1968, 3rd ed. in
preparation). *Major articles:* writings submitted to House of Lords
Select Cttee. on the E.E.C., to be published; contributions to various
legal publications.

GEOFFREY (TREMAYNE) SAMBELL
Archbishop of Perth and Metropolitan of Western Australia
Born Violet Town, Victoria, Australia, October 28th, 1914
Died Perth, Western Australia, December 19th, 1980

The Most Reverend Geoffrey Tremayne Sambell, Archbishop of
Perth and Metropolitan of Western Australia during the 1970s, was
noted for his emphasis on practical Christianity and his efforts to make
the Australian church more aware of the Christian experience as a
world phenomenon. He was born in 1914, educated at the University
of Melbourne, and ordained in 1941, in time to serve as chaplain to
the Australian Military Forces during the Second World War. From
1947 to 1962 he was director of the Melbourne Diocesan Centre, an
organization concerned with bringing the church into the lives of poor
people on the fringes of society; he also directed the Home Mission
and served as Archdeacon of Essendon and Melbourne. He continued
his domestic missionary work as Bishop Co-adjutor of Melbourne
from 1962 to 1969 and as Archbishop of Perth and Metropolitan since
1969, steering the church into a pioneering involvement with such
social problems as housing and aboriginal rights. He was president of
the Victorian Council for Social Services and chairman of the Social
Responsibilities Commission of the Australian Church.

Sambell, who led the Church's Mutual Responsibility and Interdependence Programme for seven years, also played a prominent role in
strengthening the Church's ties to its Anglican counterparts in the
East Asian countries and in fostering greater exchange within the

Anglican Church as a whole through its Partners in Mission policy. He
was instrumental in the establishment of the Anglican Consultative
Council by the Synods of the Anglican Communion and the Lambeth
Conference of 1968 and was made an episcopal member of the
Council in 1971; later he was elected to its standing committee and
chaired its Church and Society section. He died in Perth after a year's
illness.   G.D.

Son of E. S. Unmarried. Church of England. Educ: Melbourne High
Sch.; Melbourne Univ., Theological Lic. 1939, B.A. 1946; Fellow,
Australian Coll. of Theology 1962. Mil. Service: Chaplain 1942–46
and Sr. Chaplain 1949–58, Australian Army. Ordained deacon 1940,
priest 1941. Dir., Melbourne Diocesan Centre 1947–62, also Dir. of
Home Mission; Archdeacon of Essendon 1955–62; Bishop Co-adjutor,
Diocese of Melbourne 1961–69; Archdeacon of Melbourne 1962–69;
Archbishop of Perth and Metropolitan of Western Australia since
1969. With Anglican Consultative Council: Member since 1971;
elected to standing cttee.; Chmn., sect. on Church and Society 1976.
Dir., Brotherhood of St. Lawrence 1956–58; Head, Mutual Respon-
sibility and Interdependence Programme of the Australian Church
1963–69; Chmn., Social Responsibilities Commn., Australian Church.
Pres., Victorian Council of Social Services 1956–58; Chmn., Natl.
Consultative Council on Social Welfare since 1976. Member:
Melbourne Club; Royal Automobile Club of Victoria; West Australia
Club, Perth; Weld Club, Perth; Lake Karrinyup Club, Perth.

MARC CONNELLY
Playwright
Born McKeesport, Pennsylvania, U.S.A., December 13th, 1890
Died New York City, New York, U.S.A., December 21st, 1980

Marc Connelly, the prize-winning playwright of *The Green Pastures*
and a mainstay of the American theater for seventy years, was born in
1890 in McKeesport, Pennsylvania, where his parents, both former
actors, ran a hotel that was frequented by traveling performers. After
leaving Trinity Hall, a private school, to help support his widowed
mother, the 17-year-old Connelly went to work collecting money for
the classified advertising department of the *Pittsburgh Press*. For the
next few years he worked as a reporter in Pittsburgh, turning out skits
for little theater groups in his spare time. In 1915 he went to New
York, where he supported himself by writing jokes and song lyrics
until he was hired as a theater reporter by the *Morning Telegraph*. He
and George S. Kaufman, his counterpart on the *New York Times,*
soon began a collaboration that resulted in seven plays produced in
New York between 1921 and 1924. Their first success, *Dulcy,* was a
light, fast-paced comedy that starred the up-and-coming Lynn Fontaine. Most of their work was in a similar vein, but they could also be
innovative: *Merton of the Movies* was one of the first plays to use rapid
scene changes in imitation of cinematic pacing, and *Beggar on
Horseback*, based on Paul Apel's play *Hans Sonnenstoessors Holen-
fahrt,* combined an expressionistic style with social satire. Connelly

next wrote *The Wisdom Tooth* and, with Herman J. Mankiewicz, *The Wild Man of Borneo,* after which he went to Hollywood to write screenplays, including *The Cradle Song, Captains Courageous,* and *I Married a Witch.*

Green Pastures, the work that made Connelly famous, grew out of his reading *Ol' Man Adam an' his Chillun,* Roark Bradford's retelling of Old Testament stories in the idiom of rural Southern blacks. Connelly visited Bradford in Louisiana to study black religion, culture, and speech patterns; his finished play was filled with the living poetry of a folk culture of which most New Yorkers were ignorant. Production was delayed for two years because of the cowardice of financial backers, who feared that the play's all-black cast might alienate white theatergoers and that it might be construed as sacrilegious (its angels hold a fish fry and its main character declares, "Even bein' God ain't no bed of roses"). Indeed, the play was banned in England by the Lord High Chamberlain.

In the United States, however, the play, which Connelly directed himself, turned out to be a resounding success, not only on Broadway, where it ran for five years, but on national tours. Brooks Atkinson, in an ecstatic *New York Times* review, called it "a play of surpassing beauty. . . . Marc Connelly has lifted his fable of the Lord walking on the earth to those exalted heights where utter simplicity in religious conception produces a play of great emotional depth and spiritual exaltation—in fact the divine comedy of the modern theatre." Connelly was awarded the Pulitzer Prize for the play in 1930 and directed a film version in 1936. It was later presented on television and was revived in 1951, but met with opposition from blacks who felt that it perpetuated outmoded stereotypes.

American theater tastes began to change after 1930, and none of Connelly's later plays reached the same heights as *The Green Pastures.* He continued to write movie scripts and produced, directed, and acted in numerous plays, some of them his own. He championed *Our Town,* now a stage classic, when Thornton Wilder was still unknown, and played the role of the stage manager in its New York and London productions in the mid-1940s; later he appeared in films and television dramas, including *The Defenders.* "Every playwright should act," he once said. "It is a way of improving his own craft."

Connelly also taught playwriting at the Yale Drama School, served as president of the Authors League and the National Institute of Arts and Letters, and was a member of the executive committee of the U.S. National Commission for UNESCO. In 1965 he published a novel of comic suspense, *A Souvenir from Qam,* and in 1968 a book of memoirs entitled *Voices Off-Stage.* His last play, *A Stitch in Time,* was written for Helen Hayes, who had starred in his *To the Ladies!* some 55 years before.

The high-spirited Connelly, who was known to whisk his friends off to Europe on a whim, was one of the most beloved figures of the New York literary and theater worlds since the 1920s, when he helped to found the *New Yorker* magazine and was one of the legendary circle of pundits at the Algonquin Hotel. (Asked recently whether table talk now is as fascinating as it was in that golden era, he replied, "Mine is.") His friends, who were reputed to number in the hundreds, included the humorist Robert Benchley, the violinist Jascha Heifetz, the critic Alexander Woollcott, and hosts of writers, poets, artists, and

royalty, who appreciated his talents as a wit, mimic, and master
raconteur. At his funeral, the playwright Garson Kanin said: "Mr.
Connelly leaves one of the largest immediate families of any man who
ever lived. He leaves the whole theater community."   J.P./A.E.

Born Marcus Cook Connelly. Son of Patrick Joseph C. and Mabel
Fowler (Cook) C., actors and hotel proprietors. Married Madeline
Hurlock, comedienne, 1930 (div. 1935). No children. Educ: Trinity
Hall, Washington, Pa. 1902–07. Reporter, Associated Press and
Pittsburgh Gazette-Times ca. 1910–14, also author of skits for Pitts-
burgh Athletic Assn. and little theater groups; freelance lyricist and
joke writer, NYC 1914–17; theater reporter, Morning Telegraph,
NYC 1917. Playwright, director, actor, and screenwriter since ca.
1920; Prof. of Playwriting, Yale Sch. of Drama 1946–50; lectr. since
1948. Council Member, Dramatists Guild since 1920; Pres., Exec.
Cttee., U.S. Natl. Commn. to UNESCO 1951; Pres. 1953–56 and
Member, Natl. Inst. of Arts and Letters; Advisor, Equity Theater
Library 1960; Pres., Authors League of America. Member: Actors
Equity Assn.; American Fedn. of Television and Radio Artists;
Screen Actors Guild; The Players Club; Savage Club, London; Coffee
House Club; Thanatopsis Inside Straight Literary and Chowder Club
and Algonquin Round Table, 1920s. Hons: Pulitzer Prize (for The
Green Pastures) 1930; O. Henry Award (for short story Coroner's
Inquest) 1930; Hon. Litt.D., Bowdoin Coll. 1952; Hon. Litt. D.,
Baldwin-Wallace Coll. 1962; certificate of appreciation, City of New
York 1980. *Playwright:* $2.50, Pittsburgh 1913; (lyricist only) The
Lady of Luzon, Pittsburgh 1914; (lyricist only) Follow the Girl, NYC
1915; (lyricist only) The Amber Express, NYC 1916; (with George S.
Kaufman) Dulcy, NYC 1921, London 1923; Erminie (rev. version of
play by Henry Paulton), NYC 1921; (with Kaufman) To the Ladies!,
NYC 1922, London 1932; (sketches only) No Sirree!, NYC 1922;
(sketches only) The Forty-Niners, NYC 1922; (with Kaufman) West
of Pittsburgh, NYC 1922, rev. version as The Deep Tangled Wild-
wood, NYC 1923; (with Kaufman) Merton of the Movies, NYC 1922,
London 1923; (with Kaufman) A Christmas Carol, in The Bookman,
Dec. 1922; (with Kaufman) Helen of Troy, New York, NY 1923;
(with Kaufman) Beggar on Horseback, NYC 1924, London 1925;
(with Kaufman) Be Yourself, NYC 1924; The Wisdom Tooth, NYC
1926; (with Herman J. Mankiewicz; also. dir.) The Wild Man of
Borneo, NYC 1927; How's the King?, NYC 1927; (also dir.) The
Green Pastures, NYC 1930, also television version 1957; The Survey,
in The New Yorker mag., 1934; (with Frank B. Elser) The Farmer
Takes a Wife, NYC 1934, abridged version in Best Plays of 1934–35;
Little David . . . An Unproduced Scene from The Green Pastures, in
The Best One-Act Plays of 1937; (with Arnold Sundgaard; also dir.
and co-producer) Everywhere I Roam, 1938; The Traveler, 1939; The
Mole on Lincoln's Cheek (radio play), 1941, also in The Free
Company Presents (ed. by James Boyd), 1941; (also dir.) The Flowers
of Virtue, NYC 1942; (also dir.) A Story for Strangers, NYC 1948;
(also dir.) Hunter's Moon, London 1958; (also dir.) The Portable
Yenberry, Lafayette, Ind. 1962; A Stitch in Time, 1977. *Screenwriter:*
Whispers, 1920; The Bridegroom, The Burglar, The Suitor, and The
Uncle (shorts), 1929; The Unemployed Ghost (short), 1931; The
Cradle Song, 1933; The Little Duchess (short), 1934; The Green
Pastures, 1936; The Farmer Takes a Wife, 1937; Captains Coura-
geous, 1937; I Married a Witch, 1942; Reunion, 1942; The Imposter,
1944; Fabiola, 1951; Crowded Paradise, 1956; Exit Smiling. *Director:
Plays*—Overture, New Haven, Conn. 1930, Berkeley Square, NYC

1930; (with Gabriel Beer-Hofmann) Anatol, NYC 1930; Acropolis, London 1933; Till the Cows Come Home, London 1936; (also co-producer) Having a Wonderful Time, NYC 1937; The Two Bouquets, NYC 1938; The Happiest Days, NYC 1939; (also co-producer) Hope for the Best, NYC 1945. *Films*—The Green Pastures, 1936. *Actor: Plays*—No Sirree!, NYC 1922; The Forty-Niners (Compère), NYC 1922; Our Town (Stage Manager), NYC 1944, London 1946; The Tall Story (Charles Osman), NYC 1959; The Portable Yenberry (Dr. Bingham), Lafayette, Ind. 1962. *Films*—The Bridegroom, The Burglar, The Suitor, The Uncle (shorts), 1929; The Unemployed Ghost, 1934; The Spirit of St. Louis (Father Hussman), 1957; The Tall Story (Charles Osman), 1959. *Television*—The Defenders series, 1963; The Borgia Stick (Davenport), 1967; New York Illustrated; The Trials of O'Brien; Today Show; Merv Griffin Show. *Author:* Coroner's Inquest, 1930, and other short stories; A Souvenir from Qam (novel), 1965; Voices Off-Stage: A Book of Memoirs, 1968; travel and humor for The New Yorker and other magazines. Manuscript collection at the Univ. of Wisconsin, Madison.
Further reading: Marc Connelly by Paul Nolan, 1969.

FRANCIS (RALPH) TUBBS
Horticulturalist
Born England, October 8th, 1907
Died Norwich, England, December 21st, 1980

Dr. Francis Tubbs made many contributions to the field of horticulture through his own research and as director of the large East Malling Research Station.

After graduating from the Royal College of Science, he did postgraduate research at Rothamsted Experimental Station. Then in 1930, he became a plant physiologist at the Tea Research Institute of Ceylon. There, he gained prominence in the field by cloning selections of tea, thus increasing productivity of that country's tea.

Because of the success of his tea research and extensive research with a perennial tree crop, Tubbs was appointed director of the East Malling Fruit Research Station in 1949. During his period as director, many developments were made: New apple rootstocks were introduced, worldwide links were made with other research institutes to further the study of woody plants, and healthy, virus-free plant material was discovered. Tubbs also made many improvements to the station by renovating many buildings and modernizing and refurbishing laboratories. Tubbs was made a CBE in 1960.

After retiring in 1969, he continued research as a Leverhulme Research Fellow at the John Innes Institute, Norwich. Active throughout his life in the Royal Horticultural Society's Fruit and Vegetable and Fruit Group's Committees, he was given their most prestigious award, the Victoria Medal of Honour in Horticulture, in 1973. Tubbs remained active in this society and the International Society for Horticultural Science until the late 1970s.   S.F.

Son of William Edward T. and Elizabeth Clara T. Married Helen Beatrice Alice Green 1939. Educ: Hackney Downs Sch.; Imperial Coll. of Science, M.Sc. 1928; research at Rothamsted, Ph.D. 1930.

Mil. Service: Lieut. Col. RARO, The Durham Light Infantry, 1939–45 (Croix de Guerre); Officer Order of Orange Nassau, 1946 (Chevalier Order of Leopold II avec Palme, Croix de Guerre avec Palme). Plant physiologist, Tea Research Inst. of Ceylon, 1930–48. Dir., East Malling Research Station, 1949–69. Member, Royal Horticultural Soc., and Intnl. Soc. for Horticultural Science. *Author:* Frequent contributor to many scientific journals.

KARL DÖNITZ
German admiral
Born Berlin-Grünau, Germany, September 16th, 1891
Died Aumühle, West Germany, December 22nd, 1980

A brilliant naval strategist, Karl Dönitz directed the submarine campaign which was one of Germany's greatest threats to the Allies during World War Two. He successively organized and commanded the German submarine fleet, served as head of the German Navy and, in the war's final days, followed Adolf Hitler as chief of state, in which post he arranged for Germany's surrender. Despite his fanatical devotion to the Nazi cause, he was widely respected on the Allied side as a superb professional soldier and leader of men.

The son of a prosperous engineer, Dönitz grew up in a family with a long tradition of government service. After graduating from a Realgymnasium (or technical high school) in Weimar, he entered the Imperial Navy Training School in April 1910. He began active service as a sub-lieutenant on the light cruiser *Breslau,* which fought under the Turkish flag in 1914. Dönitz then returned to Germany for submarine training and was appointed watch officer on an attack submarine. In 1918 he was given command of a coastal submarine, the UB68; in October his boat was sunk by an Allied convoy, and he became a British prisoner of war.

Returning to Germany in July 1919, Dönitz resumed his naval career. But opportunities for command were limited in the country's severely curtailed armed forces. While holding a series of posts on the Baltic coast, Dönitz apparently prepared secret plans and specifications for the rebuilding of the German submarine fleet. Like many of his fellow-officers, he disliked the Weimar Republic and hoped for a restoration of authoritarian rule. Yet Dönitz went further in expressing his political convictions: in the early 1920s he joined the fledgling Nazi party. When Hitler took power in January 1933, Dönitz was away on a tour of the Indian Ocean. He returned to Germany in July and was shortly afterwards made captain of the training cruiser *Emden.*

Dönitz's great opportunity came in 1935, when the London Naval Agreement permitted Germany again to build submarines. Promoted from captain to commodore (later rear admiral), Dönitz was placed in command of the new submarine force. In the following years he created a rigorously trained and technically advanced service, equipped with such devices as magnetic mines and torpedoes that followed the sound of propellers. But he also had to contend with low priority in the military pecking order; Hitler showed greater interest in more obvious symbols of power, such as airplanes, armored vehicles and capital ships. By the start of World War Two, only 25 of the 70 submarines allowed by the London treaty were in service.

The war at sea began slowly, subordinated to political considerations and developments on land. But submarine production increased as it became obvious that Britain would not conclude a compromise peace; by March 1943 the rate of construction had risen to 40 vessels a month. The first and most daring German strike came on October 14, 1939, when the submarine U47, on Dönitz's orders, penetrated the British naval base at Scapa Flow in the Orkney Islands to sink the battleship *Royal Oak*. All constraints on sea warfare fell with the German invasion of Western Europe in May 1940. The next month, German submarines sank some 289,000 tons of Allied shipping. The effort to isolate and paralyze Britain by blocking its sea lanes came dangerously close to success. The British lost 640,000 tons of shipping in April 1941 alone, but could replace just one million tons for the entire year. Only the enormous industrial capacity of the U.S. sustained Britain at this time. Yet American shipping losses also exceeded the country's replacement rate in April and May 1942.

Much of the effectiveness of Germany's underwater campaign resulted from new tactics introduced by Dönitz. German submarines had operated individually in World War One, but the fate of the UB68 taught Dönitz the vulnerability of the single vessel. Instead he developed the concept of the "wolf pack," a group of submarines fighting together. Supported by aircraft, submarines in the pack cooperated in tasks of reconnaissance, attack and defense. "Milk cow" submarines refueled the boats at sea, giving them greater range and flexibility. German submarine crews trained in these tactics before the war and applied them with devastating impact in the North Atlantic and on the Arctic shipping route to Russia.

By the end of 1942, the performance of the German submarine force stood in sharp contrast to the failure of the surface fleet to challenge Allied naval superiority. In January 1943 Hitler, who favored scrapping Germany's remaining surface warships, removed Grand Admiral Erich Raeder as naval commander in chief. Dönitz, architect of perhaps the most successful aspect of the German war effort, was given the position. But his promotion came at a time when the conditions of submarine warfare were becoming increasingly difficult. Britain and the U.S. met the challenge of the wolf pack by forming armed merchant ship convoys, coordinating the actions of air and sea forces and improving submarine detection with radar and other devices. Dönitz attempted to counter these developments with technical innovations, including the Schnorkel and improved batteries that allowed submarines to remain underwater over longer distances. But his efforts were not enough to overcome the Allied advantage in industrial production. Fighting on the sea lanes peaked in the first half of 1943. Thereafter, Germany's failure to cut the lines of communication between Britain, Russia and the U.S. meant Allied victory in the Battle of the Atlantic.

Of the 1,168 German submarines that operated in the course of the war, 630 were sunk; only 12,000 of their 39,000 crew members survived. But these appalling casualties did not shake Dönitz's devotion to the war effort or his confidence in Hitler. Towards the end of the war he spent much of his time guarding the German coast against possible invasion and evacuating Germans threatened by

Soviet forces in northeastern Europe. As late as early April 1945 he declared, "At the latest next year, perhaps even this year, Europe will recognize that Adolf Hitler is the only statesman of stature in Europe."

Dönitz was not the only high official who followed Hitler to the end, but he was one of the few whose military reputation survived intact. Generally absent from Berlin, he also avoided the degrading factional struggles fought among members of Hitler's immediate entourage. Perhaps these were the considerations that motivated Hitler, who committed suicide on April 30th, to name Dönitz his successor as Reich President and head of government. Operating from Flensburg in northwestern Germany, Dönitz could only attempt to obtain the most advantageous surrender terms possible. He first offered to negotiate a separate surrender to the Western Allies, hoping to give German forces in the East more time to flee the Russians. But after Allied leaders reiterated their demand for unconditional surrender, he signed final orders for capitulation on May 9, 1945.

Dönitz was arrested on May 23 and later tried as a war criminal before the International Military Tribunal in Nuremberg. The charges against him centered on his refusal to permit German submarines to rescue the crews of torpedoed Allied ships. Dönitz based his defense on the need to protect German vessels endangered by such operations, and on the claim that Allied commanders had issued similar orders. The IMT essentially accepted these arguments but convicted Dönitz, as the last Nazi chief of state, of complicity in the regime's atrocities—an accusation he steadfastly denied. Still, his sentence of ten years' imprisonment was the lightest imposed on any former German official convicted of major war crimes.

Following his release from Berlin's Spandau prison in October 1956, Dönitz retired on a government pension. His two sons had been killed in the war, and following his wife's death in 1962 he lived withdrawn from public view in the Hamburg suburb of Aumühle. His funeral aroused controversy because of the West German government's refusal to send an official representative or permit officers to attend in uniform. The liberal newspaper *Süddeutsche Zeitung,* defending the decision, argued that the country's "citizen in uniform must be different from the very type which Dönitz so perfectly and so fatefully embodied—the pure military specialist."   L.H./S.L.G.

Married (wife d. 1962). Two sons (both d. in WWII). Lutheran. Educ: Realgymnasium, Weimar; Imperial Navy Training Sch. Officer on Breslau 1914; submarine training 1915; submarine watch officer, later capt. 1916–18; torpedo boat comdr. 1920–23; Comdr., torpedo boat flotilla, Kiel 1923–27; navigation officer, flagship of Comdr. of German Baltic Sea fleet 1927–29; Sr. Staff Officer, Baltic Station 1930–34; Capt., training cruiser Emden 1933–35; Comdr., German submarine fleet 1935–45; Grand Admiral and Comdr.-in-Chief, Germany Navy 1943–45; Reich Pres. 1945. Hons: Clasp to the Iron Cross 1st Class 1939; Knight's Cross 1940; Oak Leaves to Knight's Cross 1943; Golden (Nazi) Party Badge 1944. *Author:* Die Fahrten der Breslau im Schwarzen Meer, 1917; Die U-bootswaffe, 1939; Memoirs: Ten Years and Twenty Days, 1958; Mein wechselvolles Leben, 1968; Deutsche Strategie zur See im Zweiten Weltkrieg, 1970.
Further reading: Spandau: The Secret Diaries by Albert Speer, 1976; Capitulation 1945 by Marlis G. Steinert, 1969.

THOMAS (CECIL) HUNT
Gastroenterologist
Born England, June 5th, 1901
Died England, December 22nd, 1980

Dr. Thomas Cecil Hunt, a prominent authority on gastroenterology, began his professional studies at Magdalen College, Oxford, where he obtained a First Class Honours degree. He continued his education at St. Mary's Medical School, Paddington, in 1922. Hunt served as Demonstrator and Tutor of Physiology in 1924, but interrupted his stay at St. Mary's Medical School for two years of study in Germany, from 1924–26, as the recipient of the Radcliffe Travelling Fellowship in Pharmacology. Upon his return to England, Hunt graduated from Oxford in 1926, B.M., B.Ch. and later D.M.

Hunt's career officially began in 1927 when he became an Assistant in the Medical Unit of St. Mary's Hospital. In 1928 he was elected a member of the Royal College of Physicians, and was advanced to the position of Medical Registrar at St. Mary's Hospital, a post he held until 1930, when he became a Mackenzie Mackinnon Resident Fellow. Active in the medical community, Hunt became a member of the Association of Physicians, Great Britain and Ireland in 1931.

A fascination with gastroenterology, with the diseases and treatments of the digestive tract, was kindled by Sir Arthur Hurst. A founder of Hurst's British Association of Gastroenterology in 1937, Dr. Hunt soon became an international expert on the subject.

During World War Two Hunt served with the Royal Army Medical Corps from 1940–1944 as an officer in West Africa, North Africa, and the Middle East, where he was mentioned in dispatches, and from 1944–45 as a Brigadier and a Consultant to the Persia Iraq Command.

At the end of the war, Hunt returned to St. Mary's Hospital, retaining his affiliation for the rest of his career, as well as serving as consulting physician at the Royal Masonic Hospital and at the King Edward VII Hospital for Officers.

Hunt served as the presiding member of the London Congress of the European and Mediterranean Society of Gastroenterology in 1956, as the president of the British Society of Gastro-enterology, and as the senior censor, Examiner in Medicine and vice-president of the Royal College of Physicians. He was one of the forces behind the establishment of the new Regent's Park College. As President of the World Organization of Gastroenterology from 1962–66, and chairman of the research committee, he organized important studies on the impact of environmental factors in different parts of the world as a cause of alimentary cancer. Hunt was honored for his work in Britain in 1964 as Commander of the British Empire, and throughout the world by honorary fellowships in societies of gastroenterology. He was also a Fellow of the Royal Society of Medicine, past president of that society's Clinical Section, and a member of the Oxford Graduate Medical Club.

Hunt continued to be active in the medical world during the 1970s. He was always aware of the pressing need for financial backing for research into gastroenterological disorders and founded the British Digestive Foundation in 1970. An accomplished speaker and writer, he was Harveian Orator in 1972, and wrote prolifically for medical journals including *Gut,* for which he was primarily responsible, and for the *British Encyclopedia of Medical Practice.*   J.S.

Son of Rev. A.T.G. H. Married Barbara Todd 1930. Children: one son; two daughters. Educ: St. Paul's Sch.; Magdalen Coll., Oxford (Demy), (1st class hons. Physiology 1922); at St. Mary's Medical Sch., St. Mary's Hosp.: Theodore Williams Scholarship, Anatomy 1922, Pathology 1924; Univ. Scholar, Radcliffe Prize, Pharmacology; and Travelling Fellowship, 1924–26 in Germany; graduated from Oxford, B.M., B.Ch. 1926, D.M. Mil. Service: with Royal Army Medical Corps during WWII: Lt.-Col., Col.-in-charge, in W. Africa, N. Africa, Middle East 1940–44, and Brig., 1944–45; Consultant, Persia Iraq Command. Worked as demonstrator and tutor, Physiology, Oxford, 1924. With St. Mary's Hosp.: Asst., Medical Unit 1927–28, Medical Registrar 1928–30, Mackenzie Mackinnon Resident Fellow 1930–31; Sr. Censor, Royal Coll. of Physicians 1967; Consulting physician, St. Mary's Hosp. (Royal Masonic Hosp.), King Edward VII Hosp. for Officers, Paddington Hosp.; Examiner in Medicine, Royal College of Physicians, and London Univ. Co-founded Regent's Park Coll. Member, Assn. of Physicians, Great Britain and Ireland 1931; Fellow, Royal Soc. of Medicine (pres., Clinical Section); founder 1932, pres. 1956, British Soc. of Gastro-enterology; Member, Medical Soc. London; Pres. 1962–66, chmn. of research cttee., World Org. of Gastro-enterology; Oxford Graduate Medical Club; founder 1970, chmn., British Digestive Foundn.; chmn., Medical Sickness Annuity and Life Assurance Soc. from 1974. Hons: elected Member, Royal Coll. of Physicians 1928; CBE 1964; hon. Member, Soc. of Gastro-enterology, in France, Belgium, Switzerland, Sweden, Mexico, and Nigeria; Fellow, Royal Coll. of Physicians 1972; Harveian Orator 1972. Contributor to numerous medical jrnls.

ETHEL WILSON
Canadian novelist
Born Port Elizabeth, South Africa, January 20th, 1888
Died Vancouver, British Columbia, Canada, December 22nd, 1980

Ethel Wilson was a Canadian novelist whose strength was in her simplicity. One of the first winners of the prestigious Canada Council Medal, she wrote of her adopted British Columbia, creating characters who can be appreciated in universal terms.

Ethel Davis Bryant was born in Port Elizabeth, South Africa on Janary 20, 1888. She was the daughter of a British Methodist missionary. Soon after her birth, the Bryant family returned to England where Ethel spent her early childhood. When she was eight years old, Ethel Bryant was orphaned and was sent to Canada to live with her relatives in Vancouver, British Columbia. She was educated in England, however, at Trinity Hall boarding school in Lancashire.

Ethel Bryant returned to Vancouver to finish her education and became a public school teacher there. In 1920 she married Dr. Wallace Wilson, a physician.

As a public school teacher, Ethel Wilson developed her narrative style by making up stories to entertain her students. Her first published short story "I Just Love Dogs" appeared in 1937. Other stories followed, later collected and reprinted in *Mrs. Golightly and Other Stories* (1961). Her first novel *Hetty Dorval*, the story of an adventuress who tries to escape the consequences of her actions, was published in 1947. Two years later Ethel Wilson produced a second novel, *The Innocent Traveller,* a series of sketches about a family that moves from England to Vancouver, grasping tightly at its English way of life. *Equations of Love* (1952) consists of two novelettes: "Tuesday and Wednesday" and "Lilly's Story," stories in which characters who are basically innocents find peace in their various "equations of love"—love between the sexes, love within the family, the love of animate and inanimate nature. *Swamp Angel* (1954) and *Love and Salt Water* (1956) are both novels about women who must build lives for themselves despite the misfortunes they suffer.

Hetty Dorval, Ethel Wilson's first novel, is prefaced with a quotation from John Donne: "No man is an Island . . . I am involved in all mankind." The spirit of this belief pervades all Ethel Wilson's writing. Human relationships are the central theme of her work, and she sees the "equations of love" as the foundation of all happiness, all conflict, all peace. The mountains, sea, lakes, rivers, and animals of British Columbia play their roles in these equations of love, interacting with the human characters to provide solace as well as struggle.

Ethel Wilson has been called an artist of high quality although of limited quantity. Her work is traditional but its accent is highly individual. The disarming simplicity of her writing belies its sophistication; she writes of human action and motivation in a manner that is quietly right. However, some of Ethel Wilson's critics have found her narrative style to be abrupt and point out "an uncertainty in point of view" in her work. But for many, her simplicity and sense of comedy and irony make her characters endearing as well as enduring.   J.N.

Born Ethel Davis Bryant. Daughter of Rev. Bryant, Methodist missionary. Married Wallace Wilson, physician, 1920. Educ: Trinity Hall, Southport, Lancs.; Univ. of British Columbia, Vancouver, D. Litt. 1955. Teacher in Vancouver; writer from 1937. Hons: Canada Council Medal 1962; Lorne Pierce Medal 1964; Medal of Service, Order of Canada 1970. *Books: Novels*—Hetty Dorval, 1947; The Innocent Traveller, 1949; The Equations of Love, with Tuesday and Wednesday, and Lilly's Story, 1952; Lilly's Story, 1952; Swamp Angel, 1954; Love and Salt Water, 1956. *Short stories*—Mrs. Golightly and Other Stories, 1961.
Further reading: Ethel Wilson by Desmond Pacey, 1967.

S(TANLEY) T(HOMAS) BINDOFF
Historian
Born Brighton, England, April 8th, 1908
Died December 23rd, 1980

Professor Stanley Thomas Bindoff, one of Britain's best-known historians of the Tudor period, helped train several generations of students in three decades of teaching at the University of London. He was respected not only as a meticulous scholar but also as a devoted teacher and administrator who gave unstintingly of his time to the institutions of his profession.

Bindoff worked his way through London's University College as a part-time journalist and tutor, numbering among his pupils Prince

Farouk of Egypt. After earning his B.A. with History Honors and his
M.A. with distinction, he worked briefly for the Netherlands Information Bureau before accepting a teaching position at his alma mater.
He spent most of World War Two in the Naval Intelligence Division
of the British Admiralty, returning to University College in 1945. Six
years later he was appointed professor of history at Queen Mary
College in London, where he taught until his retirement in 1975. He
soon became absorbed in teaching and administrative duties, so that
his published output was fairly small. But his influence on students
and colleagues was considerable and widely attested. Among the
organizations which he served was the University of London's
Institute of Historical Research, where he conducted the Tudor
seminar togeher wih the eminent historians Sir John Neale and
Professor Joel Hurstfield [q.v.]. He also carried out many tasks for the
English Historical Association and sat on the advisory committee of
the University College of Rhodesia. In addition to his activities in
England, Bindoff spent much time in the U.S. as visiting professor at a
number of colleges and universities, including Columbia, Wellesley,
Harvard and Swarthmore.

Bindoff's original academic interest was modern Dutch history, but
he shifted to English history of the Tudor period under Sir John
Neale's influence. His first book, *The Scheldt Question to 1839* (1945),
reflected his early studies, tracing the use and legal status of the
Scheldt River, an important trade artery of the Low Countries. In
1950 his *Tudor England,* a highly-praised survey of the field, was
published as part of the Penguin History of England series. A decade
later he helped organize and edit *Elizabethan Government and
Society,* a volume of essays dedicated to Sir John Neale. Bindoff also
collaborated closely with his wife, Marjorie, a medieval historian; he
spent much of his last years helping her complete her book, *The Court
of King's Bench, 1450 to 1550.* Shortly before his death he finished a
volume on the British Parliament in the early Tudor period, part of
the official *History of Parliament* series.   S.L.G.

Son of Thomas H. B. and Mary B. Married Marjorie Blatcher
(d. 1979). One son; one daughter. Educ: Brighton Grammar Sch.;
University Coll., London, B.A. 1929, M.A. 1933. Research Asst.,
Inst. of Historical Research 1930–33; with Netherlands Information
Bureau 1933–34. With University Coll., London: Asst. Lectr. and
Lectr. 1935–45; Reader in Modern History 1945–51; Fellow from
1958. Service in Naval Intelligence Div., British Admiralty 1942–45;
Prof. of history, Queen Mary Coll. 1951–75; Visiting Prof. of history:
Columbia Univ., NYC 1960; Claremont Grad. Sch. 1966; Wellesley
Coll. and Harvard Univ. 1968; Swarthmore Coll. 1973. Member:
Utrecht Historical Soc.; Royal Dutch Soc. of Literature; Univ. of
London Senate. Hons: Alexander Medallist of the Royal Historical
Soc. 1935; Fellow, Royal Historical Soc. 1946. *Author:* (jt. author)
British Diplomatic Representatives, 1789–1852, 1934; The Scheldt
Question to 1839, 1945; Ket's Rebellion (Historical Assoc. Pamphlet),
1949; Tudor England, 1950; (jt. ed.) Elizabethan Government and
Society, 1961. *Editor:* (with J.T. Boulton) Research in Progress in
English and Historical Studies in the British Isles, 1974.

(RICHARD) AMBROSE REEVES
Anglican bishop, and anti-apartheid crusader
Born Norwich, Norfolk, England, December 6th, 1899
Died England, December 23rd, 1980

The Anglican bishop Ambrose Reeves was an outspoken critic of the South African government's policy of apartheid. His views led to his deportation from South Africa where he had served as Bishop of Johannesburg from 1949 to 1961. He continued in his crusade against apartheid as president of the British Anti-Apartheid Movement from 1970 until his death in 1980.

Richard Ambrose Reeves was born in Norwich, England in 1899. He attended Yarmouth Grammar School and from there went up to Cambridge University, to Sidney Sussex College. While at Cambridge he became involved with the Student Christian Movement. From Cambridge he went on to the College of the Resurrection at Mirfield to prepare to receive orders in the Anglican (Episcopal) Church. He also studied at the General Theological Seminary in New York City.

After being ordained in the Church of England, Ambrose Reeves served as a curate at St. Alban's Church in Golders Green, London; as Rector of St. Margaret's Church, Leven; and as Vicar of St. James, Haydock.

In 1942, Reeves became a rector in the city of Liverpool which had suffered heavily from nazi bombing. Reeves arranged for a hut to be erected joining the still-standing church tower of Our Lady and St. Nicholas and drew together the remains of the congregation.

Reeves worked closely with other religious groups in Liverpool, and in 1948, went to Amsterdam as a delegate to the founding session of the World Council of Churches. He suggested setting up the ecumenical conference that would be known as "Amsterdam in Liverpool."

In 1949 Ambrose Reeves was consecrated as Bishop of Johannesburg, South Africa. This was one of the most demanding jobs in all of Africa. The population of South Africa was growing rapidly as a result of increasing industrial development. New church buildings were needed and new ministers to serve the growing congregations. Reeves's predecessor, Archbishop Geoffrey Clayton, had encouraged white South Africans to enter the ministry. Reeves continued that work, and saw to it that the standards for training were raised and the number of ordained ministers increased.

Reeves worked to integrate his Church's work in South Africa and turned what had been missions into parishes. He was outspoken in his opposition to apartheid, the South African policy of racial separation. He became involved in organizations and with individuals who were fiercely critical of the government and its racial policies. The government as well as the press turned on him and used him as a target of abuse. Bishop Reeves was a man of strongly held convictions who was not afraid to fight for his beliefs, and he could be impatient with those who did not view the world in the same way he did. In diocesan administration he was sometimes accused of being dictatorial.

The shooting at Sharpeville brought the situation between Bishop Reeves and the South African government to a head. In March 1960, South African police killed 67 people and wounded 186 others during a demonstration against the "pass laws" that were used to control the movement of the blacks. Bishop Reeves spoke out vociferously against the police, charging that they had used the lethal dum-dum bullets. They had not. Bishop Reeves and his family became subjected to threats and pressures both subtle and overt during the days that followed the Sharpeville shootings. They fled the country, at first to Swaziland, later to Britain. Bishop Reeves returned to South Africa in September 1960 and on September 12th, he was officially deported. Six months later he resigned from his episcopate in Johannesburg.

After his resignation, Reeves became General Secretary of the Student Christian Movement, the group he had first become involved with as an undergraduate at Cambridge. While holding this office, he also served as Assistant Bishop of London. From 1966 to 1972 he was Rector at St. Michael's Church in Lewes and, in 1966 he was also named Assistant Bishop in the diocese of Chichester.

Bishop Reeves continued as a voice against apartheid after his deportation. He wrote *The Shooting at Sharpeville: The Agony of South Africa* (1960) and *South Africa—Yesterday and Tomorrow: A Challenge to Christians* (1962). He became president of the Anti-Apartheid Movement in England, a post he held until his death at the age of 81.   J.N.

Son of Richard R. Married A. Margaret van Ryssen 1931. Two sons (one d.); two daughters. Educ: Yarmouth Grammar Sch.; Sidney Sussex Coll., Cambridge; Coll. of the Resurrection, Mirfield; General Theological Seminary, N.Y. Secty., Theological Coll. Dept. of Student Christian Movement; Curate, St. Albans, Golders Green, London 1926–31; Rector, St. Margaret's Church, Leven, Fife 1931–45; Secty., World's Student Christian Fedn., Geneva 1935–37; Vicar, St. James Church, Haydock 1937–42; Rector of Liverpool 1942–49; Bishop of Johannesburg, South Africa 1949–61; deported from South Africa 1960; Secty., Student Christian Movement 1962–65; Asst. Bishop, London 1962–66; Priest in charge, then Rector, St. Michael's Church, Lewes 1966–72; Asst. Bishop of Chichester 1966–80. Hons: Prelate order of St. John of Jerusalem 1953; Hon. Fellow, Sidney Sussex Coll., Cambridge Univ. 1960; Hon. D. Litt., Sussex Univ. 1975. *Author:* The Shooting at Sharpeville: The Agony of South Africa, 1960; South Africa—Yesterday and Tomorrow: A Challenge to Christians, 1962; Let the Facts Speak, 1962; Calvary Now, 1965.

ROBERT E(DMONDS) KINTNER
Journalist and television executive
Born Stroudsburg, Pennsylvania, U.S.A., September 12th, 1909
Died Washington, D.C., U.S.A., December 23rd, 1980

Robert E. Kintner was the only man to have been president of two major broadcasting companies, the American Broadcasting Corporation and the National Broadcasting Corporation. A former newspaperman, Kintner is credited with having helped revolutionize television journalism. He alone among television executives elected to broadcast the Army-McCarthy hearings of 1954, an event which contributed to the downfall of the demagogic Senator Joseph McCarthy.

After taking his B.A. degree from Swarthmore College in 1931, Robert Kintner joined the staff of the New York *Herald Tribune*

where he covered Wall Street financial news. In 1933, with profound changes being made in Federal economic and fiscal policy, the paper sent Kintner to Washington, D.C., to report on the Treasury Department. Kintner quickly became friends with such powerful New Deal "insiders" as Joseph P. Kennedy; moreover, his coverage of the Treasury was so inordinately thorough and accurate that Joseph Alsop, Jr. invited him to collaborate on a nationally syndicated column called "The Capital Parade." Kintner and Alsop also jointly published two well-received books, *Men Around the President* (1939), and *American White Paper: The Story of American Diplomacy and the Second World War* (1940). However, the Kintner-Alsop partnership ended in 1941 when they joined the Army. Kintner was stationed both overseas and in Washington with the War Department's Bureau of Public Relations; he had attained the rank of Lieutenant Colonel at the time of his medical discharge in 1944 after a plane crash.

In 1944 Edward Noble, an old friend and former Undersecretary of Commerce, hired Kintner as Vice-President in charge of public relations for the-then lowly ABC; by 1949, Kintner had risen to the network Presidency. Kintner wasted little time in garnering large budgets for news operations and expanding radio and television news coverage. Although programming in the broadcast industry is strictly ruled by the profit margin—most of which derives from "entertainment" shows—ABC ranked so far behind NBC and CBS that Kintner could afford to experiment with increased news coverage. Thus, in 1954 Kintner televised Senator Joseph McCarthy's congressional hearings on communist infiltration in the U.S. Army without fear of pre-empting lucrative programs.

McCarthy was then perceived by much of the public as a knight attempting to slay the invisible communist dragon which had seemingly insinuated itself into every vestige of American life. His method of operation had been to hold press conferences in which he made reckless charges which were dutifully printed beneath shrill headlines in newspapers from coast to coast. On television, however, the Senator came across as a ploddingly dull bully and, when he was sharply rebuked by Army counsel Joseph Welch, McCarthy's high-handed tactics were exposed and he was publicly discredited. ABC coverage of the event was, according to the *Washington Post,* a "landmark" in television news; less than three years later, Kintner was hired as president of NBC, then second only to CBS, the perennial industry leader.

Until Kintner took over at NBC, CBS had ruled supreme over network news since the days of Edward R. Murrow. Kintner, whose strategy was to strengthen NBC's overall programming schedule by first shoring up its news department, had been impressed with Chet Huntley and David Brinkley's coverage of the 1956 Democratic National Convention and he teamed the two as anchormen for the network's evening news show; by 1960 the Huntley-Brinkley report was number one in the ratings and Walter Cronkite on CBS had fallen to second place. Kintner also introduced other innovations: He moved the evening news broadcast from 6:30 PM to 7:00 PM when more people were home; in an effort to infuse the news with drama, he initiated the practice of interrupting regularly scheduled programming with sudden news bulletins; he broadcast the funeral of former Secretary of State John Foster Dulles, a network first, and he ordered round-the-clock coverage of President Kennedy's funeral to be shown without commercial advertisements. At NBC, where he was called "the managing editor," Kintner's policy was "CBS plus 30," meaning that NBC equalled CBS newstime—plus 30 minutes more.

During Kintner's tenure, NBC became increasingly competitive with CBS in all areas. In 1966, however, he resigned from the network after an administrative shakeup. Having been a close friend of both the Kennedys and President Lyndon B. Johnson, Kintner immediately accepted a position of liaison between Johnson and the Cabinet. He resigned after a year, however, and journalist David Halberstam in *The Powers That Be* (1979), described Kintner's Washington experience as an "unsuccessful and unhappy" one.

Reporting Kintner's departure from NBC, *Newsweek* magazine said that "he has been as responsible as any one man for the worst and the best in television." Although he helped elevate network news reporting to the highest standards of print journalism, he also spawned some of television's most mindless westerns, insipid situation comedies, and formula-ridden dramas.   E.T./M.B.

Son of Albert H.K. and Lillian M. (Stofflet) K. Married Jean Rodney 1940. Children: Susan; Michael. Educ: Swarthmore Coll., B.A. 1931. Mil. Service: with U.S. Army during WWII, Legion of Merit. Financial news reporter, Herald Tribune 1933–37; Columnist, Herald Tribune and North American Newspaper Alliance 1937–41; V.P., Public Relations 1944–50 and Pres. 1950–56, American Broadcasting Corp. (ABC); Pres., Natl. Broadcasting Corp. (NBC) 1956–66; Cabinet liaison, Johnson admin. 1966–67. *Author:* (with Joseph Alsop) Men around the President, 1939; American White Paper: The Story of American Diplomacy and the Second World War, 1940.

FRANK NORMAN
Playwright and author
Born Bristol, England, June 9th, 1930
Died London, England, December 23rd, 1980

John Frank Norman, who spent his childhood in an orphanage and much of young adulthood in prison, overcame those obstacles to become a prize-winning playwright and an accomplished author.

Norman entered the orphanage, one of Dr. Barnardo's Homes, in 1937, and received his education there and at St. Mary's Church School in Kingston, Surrey. He left the orphanage in 1946 as an apprentice in a tomato nursery, but ran away to London, where he spent the following years at small jobs, becoming, as Norman later put it, "an accomplished layabout." During the late 1940s and 1950s he served at least six prison sentences at such institutions as Wandsworth and Pentonville, culminating in a three-year term for burglary at Camp Hill Prison, on the Isle of Wight, from 1954 to 1957.

Upon his release, Norman determined to write about his prison experiences. That year he began his career as an author, sitting on a bench in Hyde Park, writing in a sixpenny exercise book. The manuscript became *Bang to Rights: An Account of Prison Life,* a grim denunciation of the British penal system, published in 1958 with an enthusiastic foreword by Raymond Chandler. That same year, an essay by Norman on London slang, together with excerpts from his book, appeared in the magazine *Encounter*. The magazine's co-editor, Stephen Spender, suggested that Norman try writing a play as dramatic dialogue seemed the obvious vehicle for his talents. The idea appealed to Norman even though, as he later admitted, "I knew nothing whatever about the theatre . . . I was vaguely aware that a straight play was in three acts, and that was the format in which I laid out my . . . dialogue."

At the suggestion of a friend, Norman sent the outline of his play, a cockney comedy set in a Soho gambling den, to Joan Littlewood, producer of the Theatre Workshop, Stratford East. To his amazement, she accepted it. In its finished form, as a musical with songs by Lionel Bart, *Fings Ain't Wot They Used T'Be* opened at the Theatre Royal in 1959. It captivated audiences and critics alike, running for over two years. Norman won the praises of V.S. Pritchett, who called him "a born comic," and of Richard McLaughlin, who wrote of Norman's "natural skill in bringing everything alive." In 1960 the musical earned Norman the Drama Award of the London *Evening Standard*.

Norman wrote busily for stage and television during the next decades. His one motion picture screenplay, *In the Nick,* appeared in 1960, and in 1964 Joan Littlewood and the Theatre Workshop produced Norman's second musical, *A Kayf Up West,* with music by Stanley Myers. Although Norman himself considered it a better play than his first, it was not a commercial success. Not discouraged, he went on to create two plays for television, *Just Call Me Lucky,* and *The Sufferings of Peter Obnizov.* A stage drama, *Insideout,* had been commissioned by The Royal Shakespeare Company in the mid-1960s, but they did not produce it. Norman sent a revised edition to the Royal Court, where it was staged in 1969 and published in *Plays and Players* in 1970. Norman returned to the musical comedy field in 1972 with *Costa Packet.* With songs by Lionel Bart and Alan Klein, the plot unfolded the adventures and misadventures of the members of a package tour. It was received by the public with delight. Norman's last play, written for television and entitled *Incorrigible Rogue,* appeared in 1976.

In addition to his work as a playwright, Norman actively explored the fields of fiction and non-fiction. His first novel, *The Monkey Pulled His Hair,* was published in 1967, appearing in the United States two years later as *Only the Rich.* It was followed at regular intervals by such titles as *Barney Snip: Artist, Much Ado About Nuffink,* and his last novel, *Down and Out in High Society,* which appeared in 1975. Norman married twice, and with his second wife Geraldine, Sale Room Correspondent of *The Times,* wrote *The Fake's Progress,* composed of excerpts from a taped interview with artist and forger Tom Keating.

Though Norman's plays and much of his fiction are marked by humor—in the case of *Costa Packet,* with low comedy—most of his works of non-fiction are serious books, reflecting the starkness of his early days and calling to the public's attention the "so-called criminals: the hopelessly deprived, the misunderstood and the overpunished." This sense of sympathy marks the social concerns underlying Norman's comedy. His gifts of laughter and the commonplace, reminiscent of the works of Nelson Algren and Damon Runyan, found comic form for his early misfortunes, and assured his stature as a popular, accomplished writer.   J.S.

Married: (1). . . ; (2) Geraldine N., (correspondent, The Times) 1971. 1st marriage—one daughter. Educ: St. Mary's Church Sch., Kingston, Surrey; Dr. Barnardo's Homes, 1937–46. Mil. Service: 2 years British Army. Various jobs, ca. 1946–54: farm laborer; with travelling fair. Served various prison terms, burglary; 3 yrs., Camp Hill Prison, Isle of Wight, 1954–57. Van driver, 1957–58. Author, playwright, 1958–80. Member: P.E.N. Hon.: Drama Award, London Evening Standard, 1960. *Author: Stage Plays*—Fings Ain't Wot They Used T'Be (songs by Lionel Bart), 1959 (published, 1960; U.S. ed., 1962); A Kayf Up West (music, Stanley Myers), 1964; Insideout, 1969 (published in Plays and Players, 1970); Costa Packet (songs by Lionel Bart and Alan Klein), 1972. *Screenplay*—In the Nick, 1960. *Television Plays*—Just Call Me Lucky, 1965; The Sufferings of Peter Obnizov, 1967; Incorrigible Rogue, 1976. *Novels*—The Monkey Pulled His Hair, 1967 (U.S. ed., as Only the Rich, 1969); Barney Snip: Artist, 1968; Dogem-Greaser, 1971; One of Our Own, 1973; Much Ado about Nuffink, 1974; Down and Out in High Society, 1975. *Other*—Bang to Rights: An Account of Prison Life, 1958; Stand On Me: A True Story of Soho (autobiog.), 1960 (U.S. ed., 1961); The Gunz (autobiog.), 1962; Soho Night and Day, 1966; Banana Boy (autobiog.), 1969; Norman's London, 1969; Lock 'em Up and Count 'em (penal reform), 1971; The Lives of Frank Norman (anthology), 1972; Why Fings Went West, 1975; (with Geraldine Norman) The Fake's Progress. Represented in Manuscript Collection, Univ. of Indiana, Bloomington.

ALEC WILDER
Composer
Born Rochester, New York, U.S.A., February 16th, 1907
Died Gainesville, Florida, U.S.A., December 23rd, 1980

The American composer Alec Wilder, whose work combined jazz and classical idioms, was born in Rochester, New York, in 1907, the youngest of four children. "They lived that whole ambience of voting Republican and hating Jews," he recalled in a 1973 *New Yorker* interview. "They just maintained the proper prejudices." His father died when he was six.

Wilder, who was educated in private schools, was a shy, book-loving child who often played the clown with other people. His family planned to send him to Princeton University, but he failed his high school Regents examinations and instead returned to Rochester to study music at the Eastman School, much to their dismay. At Eastman he took private lessons in counterpoint from Herbert Inch and in composition from Edward Royce.

His first popular song, *All the King's Horses,* appeared in the 1930 revue *Three's a Crowd.* From then on he composed several hundred songs, including *Who Can I Turn To, I'll Be Around,* and *While We're Young,* which were made famous by such eminent singers as Mabel Mercer, Frank Sinatra, Bing Crosby, and Mildred Bailey. Critic Whitney Balliet said of his songs, "The melodic lines flicker and turn unexpectedly, moving through surprising intervals and using rhythm in a purposeful, agile, jazz-based manner."

"My criteria," Wilder told Balliet in a *New Yorker* interview, "are limited to the singing (melodic) line and include the elements of intensity, unexpectedness, originality, sinuosity of phrase, clarity, naturalness, control, unclutteredness, sophistication, and honest sentiment. Melodrama, cleverness, contrivance, imitativeness, pretentiousness, aggressiveness, calculatedness, and shallowness may be elements that result in a hit song but never in a great song."

Wilder brought his innovative combination of classicism and jazz to a series of works he wrote for Mitch Miller's woodwind octet in the 1940s. "They were gunned down by the jazz boys because they had a classical flavor," he recalled, "and they were gunned down by the classical boys because they had a jazz flavor." During the 1950s, when the field of popular music was taken over by rock songwriters, Wilder, with the encouragement of the French horn player John Barrows, began writing chamber music. He often wrote with particular performers in mind and was once taken to task by other composers for writing a work for the virtuoso double bass player Gary Karr which they feared would be too difficult for anyone else to play. Wilder also received commissions for movie scores, including *Daddy Long-Legs,* a film that was never completed. It was, said the disappointed Wilder, "the best score I ever wrote." His other compositions included cantatas, piano and orchestral pieces, and operas.

Said one critic of Wilder's unorthodox work: "He writes mainly for wood instruments, and the academic community tends accordingly to look at his pieces as divertissements, as entertainments. They also regard him as frivolous because he is primarily a melodist, a composer who thinks in terms of timbres and coloristic things. You see, he had little formal training, and his gods have always been Bach and Debussy and Fauré and Ravel. But if he is wholly outside the academic community, he is revered by the great performers, like John Barrows and Harvey Phillips and Bernard Garfield. He is a major figure to them."

In 1968 Wilder and James T. Maher collaborated on the book *American Popular Song,* an examination of the genre's development in the first half of the century. (His own songs were modestly excluded from the first edition.) He later accepted an invitation from National Public Radio to host a weekly series on the subject. His second book, *Letters I Never Mailed,* was a collection of imaginary letters to real people.

Wilder, who kept his possessions in three suitcases, lived for more than 50 years at the Algonquin Hotel in New York City and the Sheraton Hotel in Rochester. He strenuously avoided all publicity. "Years ago I solved the problem of publicity by playing the buffoon whenever I was interviewed," he said, "and by means of hyperbole I gave the writers what they wanted—the label of eccentricity. . . . But I never told them much because I knew they were only half listening and would be exasperated and possibly angry if I persisted in presenting my true self." A memoir of his life at the Algonquin remains unpublished.

Wilder's last songs, *The Long Night* and *One More Road,* were written for Frank Sinatra. He died of lung cancer in Florida. L.R./J.P.

Born Alexander Lafayette Chew Wilder. Son of George W., bank
president, and Lillian (Chew) W. Unmarried. Educ: St. Paul's Sch.,
Garden City, N.Y.; Collegiate Sch., NYC; studied privately at the
Eastman Sch. of Music, Rochester, N.Y. Active as composer since
1930. Host, radio show on popular music, Natl. Public Radio 1976.
Member, American Soc. of Composers, Authors, and Publishers.
Principal Compositions: Songs—All the King's Horses, 1930; It's So
Peaceful in the Country; Stop That Dancin' Up There; Who Can I
Turn To; J.P. Dooley III; Soft as Spring; Moon and Sand; At the
Swing Shift Ball; I'll be Around; While We're Young; The Long
Night; One More Road; several hundred others. *Sonatas*—Horn
Sonata No. 3; Tuba Sonata No. 1; Flute Sonata No. 2; Bassoon
Sonata No. 2; Viola Sonata. *Chamber and ensemble works*—Concerto
for Saxophone and Chamber Orch., 1967; Brass Quintet No. 3; Wind
Quintets Nos. 3, 4, 6, 10; Concerto (for wind quintet with baritone
saxophone); Trio (for clarinet, flute, piano); Trio (for clarinet, horn,
piano); Theme and Variations; Slow Dance; The Children Met the
Train; Jack, This Is my Husband; The House Detective Registers; A
Debutante's Diary; Neurotic Goldfish; Sea Fugue Mama; Octet for
Winds. *Piano works*—Seldom the Sun; Such a Tender Night; She'll be
Seven in May; Walking Home in the Spring. *Movie scores*—Sand
Castle; Albert Schweitzer; Daddy Long-Legs (unfinished).*Operas*—
The Lowland Sea, 1951; Sunday Excursion, 1953; Ellen, 1955;
Kihiwake Island, 1955. *Other*—Miss Chicken Little (operetta), 1953;
A Child's Introduction to the Orchestra, 1954; Carl Sandburg Suite
(for orchestra), 1960; Entertainment No. 1 (for band); Children's Plea
for Peace (for narrator, children's chorus, orch.); Juke Box (ballet).
Author: American Popular Song: The Great Innovators 1900–1950,
1972; Letters I Never Mailed, 1975; memoir of life at the Algonquin
Hotel (unpublished).
Further reading: "The President of the Derriere-Garde," in the New
Yorker, July 9, 1973.

(PERCIVAL) ARLAND USSHER
Irish author, essayist, and translator
Born London, England, September 9th, 1899
Died Dublin, Ireland, December 24th, 1980

Arland Ussher was an Irish translator, author, and essayist who had
been called by the Irish press "Ireland's grand old man of letters." He
defined the essential Irish quality as "a combination of mysticism and
irony" and claimed that quality for his own.

Percival Arland Ussher was born in Battersea, London on September 9, 1899 to a family that had long lived in Ireland. They were part
of the "Protestant Ascendancy," a group Ussher would later satirize
as "the Colonels," those Anglo-Irishmen who held the power and the
land in Ireland, often as absentee landlords during the centuries of
English domination, whose loyalties and social ties were to England,
whose circumstances were often greatly reduced after the Irish
famines of the late 19th century and more particularly after Irish
independence. His family was distinguished not only by its ancestry
but also by its accomplishments. He was the son of Beverly G. Ussher,
Inspector of Schools for the Board of Education and grandson of R.J.
Ussher, a noted ornithologist. His mother, Emily Jebb, came from a

half-Irish Shropshire family and had two sisters who founded the Save the Children Fund. Ussher himself later boasted of early ancestors who published the first book printed in Gaelic in 1571, a translation of the Protestant Catechism, and were responsible for the first Irish version of the New Testament, published in 1602.

Arland Ussher's first love was Ireland and the Gaelic language. "Although an offspring of the former Ascendancy," he wrote, "I never felt any sentimental ties to that class when it was in the ascendant." At an early age he objected to—and later dropped—his first name "Percival" because "Percy" is the name usually given to the fool in Irish folklore. Even as a child in school in England he subscribed to Irish patriotic and separatist journals. This appreciation of all things Irish got him in trouble with the British forces that occupied Ireland when he was a young man. He was removed from a train by British regulars after a baggage search had revealed a book of 17th century Gaelic poetry in his luggage. He was taken to the camp, questioned, abused, and threatened for an hour and a half by two officers. He was finally released, as he told the story later, saved by his accent and appearance as a "Protestant gentleman." He distressed his elders by not staying long at either Trinity College, Dublin, or St. John's College, Cambridge, preferring instead to live in Ireland and take Irish language courses at Ring College in Waterford County.

Ussher's first publication was a translation from the Gaelic of Merriman's *The Midnight Court,* described by W.B. Yeats as "that vital, extravagant, immoral, preposterous poem." Yeats wrote the introduction to Ussher's translation.

The Irish folktales that he had delighted in from his early childhood fascinated Ussher and he eventually published two volumes of them. He used Tom Murray, the plowman at the Ussher estate at Cappagh, as his principal source, taking copious notes as he followed the old man and his plow. Murray's portrait appears as the frontispiece to one of these volumes, *Cainnt an tSean Shaoghail* ("Old World Speech") (1942).

Ussher's later writings fall under the category of philosophical belles-lettres. He described his feeling as reflecting "different facets of a private philosophy—especially in relation to national characters, cultures, and languages." He wrote several books about the Irish, including *The Face and Mind of Ireland* (1949) and *Three Great Irishmen* (1953). Ussher also wrote on modern philosophy: *Postscript on Existentialism and Other Essays* (1946) and *Journey Through Dread* (1955). He traveled much abroad and wrote about the peoples he met, including the Jews, in *The Magic People* (1951), and the Spanish, in *Spanish Mercy* (1959).

Although Arland Ussher received critical acclaim, popular acclaim and the money that follows it did not come his way. Several of his earlier works were published by the "Sandymount Press," a fictitious name that disguised the support he was given from private subscriptions. His style was ornate, one critic describing it as prose that seems to "obfuscate rather than illuminate his thought." He is remembered, however, for such pithy epigrams as "the Irishman treats sex as the Englishman treats death."

Arland Ussher died in Dublin where he had lived for many years and where he had conducted a weekly salon for many of his friends in artistic and literary circles.   J.N.

Son of Beverly G. U. and Emily Jebb U. Married: (1) Emily
Whitehead, 1925; (2) Margaret Keith, 1976. Children: 1st marriage—
Henrietta Owen. Educ: Abbotsholme Sch., Derbyshire; Trinity Coll.,
Dublin; St. John's Coll., Cambridge; took Irish language courses,
Ring Coll., Waterford County, Ireland. Hons: Gregory Medal of the
Academy of Letters; bronze bust in Royal Dublin Soc.'s library,
Ballsbridge, Ireland. *Writings:* (translated in verse from Gaelic) The
Midnight Court, preface by W.B. Yeats, 1926; Cainnt an tSean
Shaoghail (Old World Speech), 1942; Postscript on Existentialism and
Other Essays, 1946; The Twilight of Ideas, and Other Essays, 1948;
The Face and Mind of Ireland, 1949 (U.S. ed., 1950); The Magic
People, 1952 (U.S. ed., 1952); Three Great Irishmen, 1952 (U.S. ed.,
1953); An Alphabet of Aphorisms, 1953; (with Carl von Metzradt)
Enter These Enchanted Woods, an Interpretation of Grimm's Fairy
Tales, 1954, 1957; Journey Through Dread, 1955 (U.S. ed., 1956);
The Thoughts of Wi Wong, 1956; The XXII Keys of Tarot, 1957,
1969; Spanish Mercy, 1959; Sages and Schoolmen, 1967; Eros and
Psyche, 1977; From a Dead Lantern, a Journal (ed. by Robert Nyle
Parisious), 1978. Contributor to New English Weekly, Adelphi,
Dublin, and other periodicals.

GREGORY BATTCOCK
Art critic and professor of art history
Born New York City, U.S.A., July 2nd, 1941
Died San Juan, Puerto Rico, December 25th, 1980

Gregory Battcock, an art critic and educator, always supported new
ideas and experimentation in art. His career began at Michigan State
University where he studied under the well-known artist Abraham
Rattner. Battcock exhibited at many local art shows, and in 1959, an
abstract in oils won first place in the Southern Michigan Annual
Exhibit.

After graduation, he spent a few years touring Europe and the
Middle East. He studied at L'Accademia di Belle Art in Rome for a
year. In Athens, he assisted M. Jean Tsarouchis with the design of
costumes and sets for the Greek Royal Theatre. Later, he assisted
Tsarouchis at the Royal Opera, Covent Garden, in London, with the
famous Media production of *Alexis Mitosis* for Maria Callas.

Upon his return to the United States in 1961, he had his first one-
man exhibit at the Schainen Stern Galleries in New York City. His art,
which was in the Abstract Expressionist or action style, won high
praise from critics. Martin Reis, director of the Hudson River
Museum in New York, said Battcock "paints rough blocks of color
that move and tilt slowly through the canvas. Working in the avant-
garde tradition, his colors are strong but subtle combinations of neon
yellows and electric greens on white areas that reflect the temper and
aspects of New York City."

In 1964, he entered Hunter College in New York City to obtain a
masters degree. At this time Battcock began to concentrate on his
career as an educator and art critic.

In 1973, he was made the editor of *Arts Magazine* to which he had
frequently contributed since 1968. Publisher Alvin Demick said the
magazine was entering "the most energetic period of editorial expan-

sion. . . . The appointment reflected determination to remain the most authoritative source interested in new ideas in contemporary art." Battcock was also the New York correspondent for *Arts and Artists;* his critical essays were also frequently published in *Art in America, Domus* and *The Art Journal.*

He was very interested in the training of young artists and felt that many standard procedures and goals in art education had to be re-examined. Because many changes had taken place in the art-making process, he felt that education must also change. In his book *New Ideas in Art Education,* Battcock said, "Today's artist, art educator, and critic will find aesthetic stimulation, not in art but outside of it. The subject of art will cease to be art."

He became more involved in art education when in 1970, he became a professor of art history at William Paterson College in Wayne, New Jersey. Five years later he became an adjunct professor at New York University. He obtained his doctorate degree in art history from New York University in 1979.

Continuously, Battcock pushed for new frontiers in art. In his book *The New Art,* he said, "Art should, to a much greater extent than it does now, involve the popular imagination and help determine cultural destiny and the identification and refinement of the ordinary."

A man of relatively modest means, but a bon vivant, Gregory Battcock managed to indulge his expensive tastes and became an authority on wines and a frequent passenger on luxury ocean liners. When time permitted he went to stay at his condominium in Puerto Rico, and it was there, on Christmas Day 1980, that he was found murdered by an intruder.   S.F.

Son of Gregory J.B. and Elizabeth B. Unmarried. Roman Catholic. Educ: Michigan State Univ., East Lansing, B.A. 1958; Acad. di Belle Arte, Rome, cert. 1960; Hunter Coll., New York, M.A. 1965; New York Univ., Ph.D. 1979. Active as artist 1957–70; New York corresp., Domus 1967–80; American corresp., Art and Artists 1968–80; Prof. of Art History, William Paterson Coll., Wayne, N.J. 1970–80; Ed., Arts Magazine 1973–75; General Ed., Dutton series of Documents in Modern Art 1973–76; Adjunct Assoc. Prof., New York Univ. 1975–80. *Author:* The New Art, 1964; New American Cinema, 1967; Minimal Art, 1968; Idea Art, 1973; Super Realism (ed.), 1975; Why Art, 1976; New Ideas in Art Education, (ed.), 1970; New Artist's Video, 1978; Beyond Appearance, 1980; The New Music, 1980. Frequent contributor to art journals and magazines, and to various New York periodicals.

AHMED (TAIBI) BENHIMA
Moroccan politician and diplomat
Born Safi, Morocco, November 13th, 1927
Died Rabat, Morocco, December 25th, 1980

As a student in Paris during the late 1940s, Ahmed Benhima and his older brother Mohammed were members of the nationalistic North African Students Association, a connection which ultimately led them

into the Istiqual Party, founded in 1944 to press for Moroccan freedom from French colonial dominion. With the coming of independence in 1956, Ahmed entered his country's diplomatic corps in the Istiqual Party-backed government of King Mohammed. He won a series of important assignments, serving as Chargé d'Affaires at Paris in 1956–57, ambassador to Italy in 1957–59, and as Secretary General to the Ministry of Foreign Affairs in Rabat during 1959–61. In this latter capacity Benhima played a significant role in negotiations with the United States over the fate of air bases established in Morocco during the war under the "Free French" colonial regime.

When Benhima was awarded Morocco's critical joint portfolio in the United Nations and the United States in August 1961, the handsome French-educated diplomat proved an immediate success. Profiled by *Vogue* in 1964 as one of the U.N.'s rising young men, Benhima was singled out in that style-conscious magazine for "a quick decisive intelligence, immense influence and more charm than any one man deserves." Among his more delicate assignments during this first of two tenures at the U.N. was defending his country's invasion of Algeria in October, 1963, in a dispute over territory.

In 1964, not yet 40 years old, he was called home to become Foreign Minister and oversaw the sensitive 1965 negotiations with the De Gaulle government regarding the nationalization of French interests in Morocco. Benhima maintained a delicate course between the radical demands for immediate expropriation without compensation and the need to uphold Moroccan nationalism without damaging its reputation in the west. Benhima remained at the Ministry until February, 1966, when he was shifted to the office of Director of the Royal Cabinet in the cabinet shuffle following charges that agents of Morocco had seized and forcibly repatriated exiled Opposition leader, Medhi Ben Barka, in violation of French sovereignty.

In early 1967 he returned as Morocco's Permanent Representative to the U.N. to represent his nation's generally moderate, pro-western position during the difficult period of the "Six Day War" and its aftermath—a task complicated by pressures from the Arab world to maintain a united anti-Israel front. Recalled in 1972 to serve as Foreign Minister again, Benhima was involved in the continuing effort to maintain western ties without offending the Arab bloc; he served with the Foreign Ministers of Kuwait, Saudi Arabia, and Algeria, on a four nation delegation that carried to President Nixon a plan for ending renewed Israel-Egypt hostilities in October, 1973.

In his last official post as Minister of Information (1974–77), his considerable diplomatic skills were frequently on display.   R.C.

Son of Tayeb B. and Ben Hida B. Educ: Univ. of Nancy, France; Univ. of Paris. Chargé d'Affaires, Paris 1956–57; Ambassador to Rome 1957–59; Secty.-Gen. to the Ministry of Foreign Affairs 1959–61; Permanent Rep. to U.N. 1961–64 and 1967–71; Minister of Foreign Affairs 1964–66; Dir. of the Royal Cabinet 1966–67; Minister of Foreign Affairs 1972–74; Minister of Information 1974–77.

FRED EMNEY
Comedian and actor
Born London, England, February 12th, 1900
Died London, England, December 25th, 1980

Fred Emney belonged to the stage "by nature more even than by training," wrote the London *Times,* so much a part of his comic persona was his vast size and girth. His training, however, was extensive, beginning practically at birth, for he was born into a theatrical family; his father, Fred Emney Sr., was a popular star of the British variety stage and music hall.

Fred Emney Jr. made his first appearance on the stage at age 15, playing a page boy in *Romance;* it is said that Emney outgrew his costume so quickly that it became easier to replace the actor than the costume. He took part in a pantomime, *Puss In Boots,* in Drury Lane in 1916, and then toured the British Isles for three years with a musical comedy troupe. In 1920 he went to the United States, where for eleven years he was a popular performer on the vaudeville circuits.

After returning to Great Britain in 1931, Emney established his reputation in musical comedy, and within a few seasons he had proved himself the master of a variety of characters and genres. Good actors use the body to achieve maximum theatrical expression and Emney was no exception: his body was less the object of humor than the instrument of high comedy. Emney's thoughts were transformed into physical expressions, gestures, and movements for in spite of his size, he moved easily, indeed lightly. But Emney was not merely a rolly-polly jokester; his comedy was intelligent, imaginative, and often inspired. His obvious self-esteem made degeneration to the pathetic or the grotesque impossible.

After appearing in *The Schoolmistress* and *Goody Two Shoes* in London in the early 30s, Emney formed a comedy team with Leslie Henson and Richard Hearne that played the Gaity Theatre from 1935 until 1938, in association with impresario Frith Banbury. Among the other notable actors and actresses with whom he played were Beatrice Lillie, in *Big Top* at His Majesty's Theatre in 1942, and Elsie Randolph and Jack Buchanon, with both in *It's Time To Dance* in the last years of the war. Several of his most successful roles were ones he had written for himself. Among these were the title roles in *Big Boy,* which was presented at the Saville Theatre in 1945, and in *Happy As A King,* which played the Prince's Theatre in 1953. Emney's penchant for complicated plots and confused identities was given full rein in the latter piece, in which he played a king forced to assume the guise of an imposter masquerading as himself. The most enduring image of Emney will be that of the enormous man in tweeds, a monocle in his eye, a cup of tea in one hand and a fat cigar in the other, as he appeared in *Blue For A Boy* (1950).

Beginning in 1957 with *Emney Enterprises,* he appeared on television frequently but to disappointing effect. Emney's colossal frame demanded a setting appropriate to his dimensions and the television box seemed unable to contain the full range of his talent. Flattened perspective, close-ups, and unfixed camera views missed the body language that Emney employed so skillfully in his acting. His last stage engagement was in *When We Are Married* at the Strand Theatre in 1970.   K.B.

Son of Fred E., comedian. Educ: Cranleigh Sch. Comedian and actor
from 1915; on tour 1916–19; acted in vaudeville in U.S. 1920–31; with
Gaity Theatre, London 1935–38; acted in England until 1970.
Performances include: (all in London) Romance (page boy), 1915;
Puss in Boots (squire), 1916; The Schoolmistress (rear admiral);
Goody Two Shoes (Lord Georgous); Big Top; It's Time to Dance; Big
Boy, 1945; Blue for a Boy, 1950; Ring Round the Moon; Happy as a
King; A Sister to Assist Her; When we are Married, 1970; television
performances on Emney Enterprises.

ARTHUR (JACOB) MARDER
Historian
Born Boston, Massachusetts, U.S.A., March 8th, 1910
Died Santa Barbara, California, U.S.A., December 25th, 1980

One of America's leading naval historians, Arthur Marder was an
authority on the development of British sea power in the twentieth
century. His work, known for its broad scope and scrupulous attention
to detail, brought him many honors and wide recognition within his
profession.

After obtaining his doctorate from Harvard in 1936, Marder taught
briefly at the University of Oregon and served as a research fellow at
Harvard before going to work for the Office of Strategic Services at
the start of World War Two. In 1942 he left the OSS to study
Japanese. Though he intended to return to government service as an
official historian, a severe sinus condition made it impossible for him
to live in Washington. Instead he taught briefly at Hamilton College
before becoming a professor of history at the University of Hawaii, his
academic home for the next 20 years. He finished his career as
professor at the University of California in Irvine.

Marder first became interested in British naval history as a Harvard
undergraduate, when the diplomatic historian William Langer directed his attention to the Anglo-German naval negotiations that
preceded World War One. His first book, *The Anatomy of British Sea
Power* (1940), was a monographic study of British naval policy in the
Edwardian era which set the stage for his later work. In 1952 he
completed *Portrait of an Admiral,* a study of Admiral Sir Herbert
Richmond, one of the Royal Navy's most important strategists and the
driving force behind creation of the British Naval Staff in 1912. By this
time Marder was also well along in the project of collecting and
organizing the correspondence of Lord Fisher, Britain's First Sea Lord
from 1904 to 1910. The material, with Marder's commentary, appeared in three volumes under the title *Fear God and Dread Nought.*

Marder's work on Fisher, architect of the naval policy that deter-
mined the size and character of the British fleet to the end of World
War One, prepared him for his most extensive and best-known work.
This was *From the Dreadnought to Scapa Flow: the Royal Navy in the
Fisher Era.* Published in five volumes between 1961 and 1970, the
magisterial study traced the course of British naval policy from
Fisher's advent as First Sea Lord to the aftermath of World War One.
It was generally a triumphant story, beginning with the naval building
program with which Fisher saved the Royal Navy from decrepitude

and ending with the surrender of Germany's High Seas Fleet, the main challenge to British naval supremacy. But Marder found much to criticize in the Royal Navy, including slipshod staff work, poorly designed and built ships, inadequate strategic and tactical training of officers and an outmoded offensive mentality that delayed adoption of the convoy system as a response to German submarine warfare. Still, Marder concluded that the British fleet performed its wartime function well: despite the lack of a decisive naval battle, it successfully protected the sea lanes and denied their use to the enemy. Marder's exhaustive research in previously unopened archives gave special weight to his judgments; most experts concluded that his work was unlikely to be amended or surpassed.

After virtually exhausting the naval history of the early twentieth century, Marder turned to other subjects in his next book, *From the Dardanelles to Oran* (1974). This was a collection of previously published articles, including an analysis of why the naval lessons of World War One were misconstrued in the interwar period, the first scholarly account of the Royal Navy's role in the Abyssinian crisis of 1935–36 and a description of the British attack on the French fleet at Oran in July 1940. Marder's last book, *Operation Menace* (1976), recounted the unsuccessful attempt of an Anglo-Free French expedition to occupy Dakar, French West Africa in September 1940. At the time of his death he was engaged in a study of Anglo-Japanese naval relations before and during World War Two, an interest aroused by his wartime work for the OSS.   S.L.G.

Son of Maxwell M. and Ida (Greenstein) M. Married Jan North. One daughter; one son. Educ: Harvard Univ., B.A. 1931, M.A. 1934, Ph.D. 1936. Asst. Prof., Univ. of Oregon 1936–38; Research assoc. Harvard Univ. and Radcliffe Coll. 1939–41; Research Analyst, Office of Strategic Services 1941–42; Rockefeller Foundation Fellow 1942–43; Assoc. Prof., Hamilton Coll. 1943–44; Assoc. Prof. and Prof. 1944–64, Univ. of Hawaii; Prof., Univ. of California, Irvine 1964–77; George Eastman Prof., Oxford Univ. 1969–70; Fellow, Royal United Services Inst. for Defence Studies 1977; Fellow, Natl. Endowment for the Humanities 1978–79. Member: American Historical Assoc.; Conference on British Studies; British Acad.; American Acad. of Arts and Sciences. Hons: Beer Prize, American Historical Assoc. 1941; Chesney Memorial Gold Medal, Royal United Services Inst. 1968; Comdr., Order of the British Empire 1970; D. Litt., Oxford Univ. 1971; Distinguished Faculty Lectureship Award, Univ. of California, Irvine 1977; Distinguished Visitor Award, Australian-American Educational Foundation 1979. *Author:* Anatomy of British Sea Power, 1940; Portrait of an Admiral, 1952; Fear God and Dread Nought, three volumes, 1952–59; From the Dreadnought to Scapa Flow, five volumes, 1961–70; From the Dardanelles to Oran, 1974; Operation Menace, 1976.

COLLIER YOUNG
Movie and television writer, and producer
Born Indianapolis, Indiana, U.S.A., 1908
Died Santa Monica, California, U.S.A., December 25th, 1980

Collier Young brought to the early years of American television the imagination and story-telling ability that he had developed as a scriptwriter and publicist for the giant Hollywood studios. As creator and producer of such television series as "The Rogues" and "Ironside" he earned popular as well as critical acclaim. His third wife, the actress Joan Fontaine, characterized him as "a perennial Peter Pan, a wit and a wag whose avocation was writing and producing. Give him a lampshade and he'd wear it."

Collier Young graduated in 1930 from Dartmouth College in Hanover, New Hampshire, and began his career as an advertising copywriter. He later became a literary agent, and then, in 1940, a story editor for RKO studios in Hollywood. His Hollywood career was interrupted by the Second World War, during which, as a lieutenant commander in the U.S. Navy, he made documentary films of several naval battles in the South Pacific.

Young married four times. In 1948, after a first marriage had ended in divorce, he married the Hollywood actress Ida Lupino. Under an agreement with Howard Hughes, then head of RKO, Young and Lupino formed an independent production company, Emerald Productions which was later called Film Makers. Their purpose was to make high-quality, low-budget independent films on bold themes that would show how America lived. Collier Young produced; Ida Lupino directed. Their films included: "Not Wanted" (1949) about unwed mothers, "Outrage" (1950) about rape, and "The Hitchhiker" (1953) which depicted a confrontation with a psychopathic killer. The production company lasted longer than the Young-Lupino marriage, which he later described as "an adventure in celluloid." In an admittedly audacious move in 1953, he starred his ex-wife, Ida Lupino, with his third and then current wife, Joan Fontaine, in a movie he conceived of and produced called "The Bigamist," the story of a man who is married to two women at the same time. Collier Young's marriage to Joan Fontaine lasted from 1952 to 1961.

Collier Young was a creative force in the early years of television. He produced the series "Alcoa Presents," a dramatic series that became the hit series "One Step Beyond." He created the TV series "Mr. Adams and Eve," about two movie stars with enlarged egos who are married to each other. The stars in this series were Ida Lupino and her new husband Howard Duff. His series "The Rogues" starred Gig Young, David Niven, and Charles Boyer as a family of sophisticated con artists. "The Rogues" was very well received by the critics but didn't receive the ratings needed to keep it on the airwaves.

It was with the series "Ironside" that Collier Young gained popular as well as critical acclaim. Young created the character of Ironside, the detective confined to his wheelchair, played by Raymond Burr, wrote the first several episodes and produced the series. "Ironside" appeared on U.S. television from 1967 through 1975 and is still being shown in reruns.

As is demonstrated by his casting of "The Bigamist" and "Mr. Adams and Eve," Mr. Young's tongue was often in his cheek. He loved a good joke, especially when it was on him. He often told the story of the time he dressed up in the full regalia of a Civil War officer and walked into a New York bar. The bartender was so entertained by this apparition that he let Young pay for his drinks in Confederate money. The New York Police Department was not so amused. When Young left the bar he found a ticket on his horse for illegal parking.

Collier Young died at the age of 72, from injuries he had suffered in an automobile accident a few weeks earlier.   J.N.

Married: (1) . . . (div.); (2) Ida Lupino, actress, 1948 (div. 1950); (3) Joan Fontaine, actress, 1952 (div. 1961); (4) Meg Marsh. Educ: Dartmouth Coll., 1930. Mil. Service: Lieutenant Comdr., U.S. Navy, WWII. Worked as advertising copywriter; literary agent; story editor, RKO Studios, Hollywood 1940; writer and publicist for Myron Selznick, Sam Goldwyn, Louis B. Mayer, Jack Warner, and Howard Hughes. Formed independent prod. co., with Ida Lupino, Emerald Productions (later Film Makers). *Producer: Films*—Not Wanted, 1949; Outrage, 1950; Beware My Lovely, 1952; The Hitchhiker, 1953; The Bigamist, 1953; Mad at the World, 1955; Huk, 1956. *Television series*—Alcoa Presents (later called One Step Beyond), 1959–61; Mr. Adams and Eve, 1956–58; The Rogues, 1964–65; Ironside, 1967–75. *Author:* The Todd Dossier, 1969.

C(HARLES) H(ENRY) DOBINSON
Professor of education
Born London, England, October 7th, 1903
Died Sonning Common, Berkshire, England, December 26th, 1980

Professor C.H. Dobinson, an academician of international reputation, avoided the conventional "ivory towers" of his profession to become a policy-shaping participant in British education. In the course of his long career, his combination of a thoroughgoing comprehension of the politics of education with a global vision laid the foundations for countless education programs between England and developing countries.

Dobinson's start in the field was modest. Following his graduation from Oxford, where he earned a first class honors degree in natural science (geology) and a diploma in education, in 1927 he accepted a post as biology master at the Mill Hill School in Birmingham. His tenure there was peaceful and uninterrupted until the early years of World War II when he was forced to evacuate the school to Monmouthshire. Though the remaining years of the war were taxing, Dobinson employed every means of organization, improvisation, and cunning to keep the school afloat.

When the war ended, Dobinson's ascent up the academic ladder was rapid. After a six-year position as Reader in Education at the University of Oxford, he held two simultaneous posts at Reading: Head of the Department of Education—responsible for postgraduate teacher training and research—and Director of the Institute of Education. Occupied though he was by these posts, Dobinson's commitment to service often carried him away from the Oxford and Reading campuses. He held a number of visiting professorships throughout the United States and Canada, served on various committees and commissions—including the Banjo Commission on Education in the Western Region of Nigeria—and was an advisor to the United Kingdom's first delegation to Unesco.

These offices enlarged Dobinson's views on education, and he became severely critical of the attitudes of successive English governments toward foreign students studying in England. His dedication was rewarded by what has become a steady flow of personnel from developing countries into courses at Reading as well as the Agricultural Extension and Rural Development Center. His services to overseas education were recognized when he was made a Companion of the Order of St. Michael and St. George (CMG) in 1969, one year after he retired from Reading. G.H.

Son of Henry Mark D. and Florence Gertrude D. Married Dorothy Maude Shooter 1929. One son; one daughter. Educ: Brockley County Grammar Sch., London. Wadham Coll., Oxford: Moderations in Mathematics; 1st class honours in Natural Science (Geology), Diploma in Educ. London B.Sc. Biology Master, Mill Hill Sch. 1927–33; Headmaster, King Edward VI Grammar Sch., Five Ways, Birmingham 1933–45; Reader in Educ., Oxford Univ., 1945–51; Advisor, UK first delegation to Unesco 1946; Reading Univ. 1951–1968: Prof. of Educ.; Head, Dept. of Educ.; Dir., Inst. of Educ. Visiting Prof.: Syracuse 1950, 1955, 1957; Arkansas 1950, 1952, 1967; Cornell 1959; Alberta 1960; Missouri 1961, 1963, 1964, 1966, 1968, 1970, 1973; Calgary 1969. Chmn., Educ. Cttee. of Natl. Fedn. of Community Associations 1949–62; Gov., Unesco Intnl. Inst. of Educ., Hamburg 1949–62; Banjo Commn. on Educ. in Western Nigeria 1960–61; Advisory Commn. on Higher Teaching in the Sudan 1964. Hons: Fellow, Geological Soc. Companion of St. Michael and St. George 1969. *Author:* (ed.) Education in a Changing World, 1950; Technical Education for Adolescents, 1951; Schooling 1963–1970, 1963; Jean-Jacques Rousseau, 1969; (ed.) Comenius, 1970; various school textbooks between 1929 and 1966; articles in UK press since 1970 on technical education in France and Germany; articles in education press of UK, USA, France and Sweden.

SHOTARO KAMIYA
Businessman
Born Aichi, Japan, July 9th, 1898
Died Tokyo, Japan, December 26th, 1980

A pioneer of the Japanese automobile industry, Shotaro Kamiya played a major role in making Toyota one of the world's largest-selling cars. His most important contribution to Toyota was his work in establishing and developing a separate marketing arm of the company.

Like many Japanese businessmen of his generation, Kamiya did not receive a college education. After graduating from the Nagoya Commercial School in 1917, he worked in England and the United States for Mitsui and Co., the giant Japanese trading firm. In 1926 he began working for America's General Motors Co. in Japan; he left in 1935 to work at the Toyota Automatic Weaving Machine Manufacturing Co. where he remained until 1944 when he became a director of the Toyota Motor Car Co.

Kamiya believed that profits could be increased by dividing the Toyota Motor Car Co. into separate manufacturing and marketing arms. Implementation of his idea was delayed by the priorities of World War Two, during which Toyota stressed truck production and delayed its plans to produce a popularly priced commercial car. The chaos of the postwar years caused further delay; however, in 1950, the Toyota Motor Sales Co. was established, and Kamiya became its first president.

In his new post, Kamiya laid the groundwork for the creation of a nationwide network of dealerships that ultimately expanded to 319 franchised dealers and over 3,300 outlets selling Toyota products. Under his leadership, Toyota began steady penetration of European and U.S. markets. By 1969, Toyota had become the third largest automobile producer in the world behind General Motors and Ford. Much of this success was attributed to Kamiya's motto which became the company's guiding philosophy: "First the customer, then the dealers, then the manufacturer."

Kamiya attracted international attention in 1970 when he dedicated a Buddhist shrine at Tateshina to the souls of auto accident victims. He was among the contributors to the $440,000 shrine, and at the dedication, he prayed that the shrine's statue of Kwannon—Buddhist goddess of mercy—"will protect the automobile from disaster."

In 1975 Kamiya was appointed chairman of Toyota Motor Sales, and he became honorary chairman in 1979.   M.T.

Married. Children: Shoichi; Hiroshi; Akie. Buddhist. Educ: Nagoya Commercial Sch., grad. 1917. Executive, Mitsui and Co., in England and U.S.; Japan General Motors Co. 1926–35; Toyota Automatic Weaving Machine Manufacturing Co. 1935–44; Dir., Toyota Motor Car Co. 1944–79. With Toyota Motor Sales Co.: Pres. 1950–75; Chmn. 1975–79; Hon. Chmn. since 1979. Hons: Hon. Advisor, Japanese Automobile Assoc.; decorations from the Emperor 1960, 1962, 1968, 1973; Prime Minister's Export Promotion Award 1967. *Author:* My Life with Toyota, 1976.

TONY SMITH
Sculptor
Born South Orange, New Jersey, U.S.A., 1912
Died New York City, U.S.A., December 26th, 1980

Tony Smith, a sculptor associated with the Minimalist movement of the late 1960s and early 1970s, created imposing black polyhedral structures on a monumental scale. A friend of Jackson Pollock, Mark Rothko, and Ad Reinhart, and "one of the best-known unknowns in American art" (according to the organizer of his first show), Smith was born in New Jersey in 1912. He contracted tuberculosis as a child and was isolated in a small building on the family grounds where he amused himself by constructing sculptures—"pueblo villages"—with cardboard medicine boxes. His early instruction was by private tutor; later he attended Georgetown University and took night classes from 1933 to 1936 with George Grosz, George Bridgman and others at the Art Students League. At the New Bauhaus in Chicago, where he studied architecture in 1937, he "enjoyed Moholy and Archipenko as personalities," but was disappointed in "how little benefit I received from the school." He withdrew the next year to work as Frank Lloyd Wright's assistant on a project to develop inexpensive housing for the U.S. Government. Smith began his own architectural practice in 1940, and from 1946 onward taught architecture and design at New York University, Cooper Union, and a succession of other schools. During this period, he became friends with Barnett Newman, Rothko, Pollock and other artists of the New York School as he tried unsuccessfully to establish a painting career; he also delivered the Friday evening lectures at the famous Eighth Street Studio.

For W.A., 1969, by Tony Smith
Courtesy Solomon R. Guggenheim Museum

By 1960 Smith had begun making cardboard and wooden sculpture maquettes, and in 1962 fabricated his first steel piece, *The Black Box,* which was inspired by an index-card file. Smith's concepts were architectonic in form and grand in scale from the outset: his *Cigarette* of 1961 is 26 feet wide by 18 feet long by 15 feet high. "I have always admired very simple, very authoritative, very enduring things," he said. "In my studio, they [his sculpture] remind me of Stonehenge." Although he first executed his large works in inexpensive plywood mockups, he soon began to commission fabrication shops, notably the Industrial Welding Co. of Newark, New Jersey, to contruct steel or bronze versions.

Smith's structures occupy a middle ground between an older tradition of massive monuments and the new, rigorous, ahistorical purity of Minimalist theoreticians such as Robert Morris and Robert Smithson. "Smith does not think of these works as traditional, intimate sculpture," wrote a critic in *Dictionary of American Sculptors,* "nor as monuments, but rather as objects whose rhythmically controlled forms unfold within a continuous flow of space that includes both object and spectator. Thus, despite their size they are not self-contained and symbolic, like older public sculptures, but man-sized spatial organizers and, although abstract, seem to push and pull within themselves as if possessing certain anthropological tensions."

Smith's first show, at the Wadsworth Atheneum in Hartford, Connecticut in 1964, was a critical success. After exhibiting in the influential "Primary Structures" show at the Jewish Museum in New York City, along with Robert Morris, Donald Judd, Carl Andre and other Minimal artists, Smith found an unexpectedly large demand for his work. In 1967 alone he participated in 15 one-person or group shows in the United States and Europe. Since many of his large sculptures, such as *Amaryllis, One Two Three,* and *Throwback,* were finding permanent homes on the grounds of the world's major modern-art museums, Smith crafted smaller maquettes for galleries and devised schemes for earthworks the size of mountains. "They are, of course, distinctly of our time," wrote critic John Russell of Smith's works in 1976, ". . . but they also manifest an unrestrained Romanticism: it is as if he set himself, in the time that is left to him, to rebuild the Pyramids, duplicate Valhalla, and drag Angkor Wat into the age of cybernetics."

Smith, who was married and had three daughters, died of heart failure in New York City at the age of 68.   S.A./D.S.

Born Anthony Peter Smith. Son of Peter S., machinery manufacturer. Married Jane Lanier Brotherton. Daughters: Chiara; Anne; Beatrice.

Roman Catholic. Educ: private tutors; Jesuit sch.; Georgetown Univ.;
Art Students League, NYC 1933–36; New Bauhaus, Chicago 1937–38;
architectural apprentice with Frank Lloyd Wright 1938–39. Tool-
maker, draftsman, and purchasing agent, NYC 1933–36; practicing
architect 1940–60; sculptor since 1960. Prof. since 1962 and prof.
emeritus, Hunter Coll., NYC. Teacher: Sch. of Education, NYC
1946–50; Cooper Union, NYC 1950–53; Pratt Inst., NYC 1950–53 and
1957–58; Bennington Coll., Bennington, Vt. 1958–61. Member,
American Acad. of Arts and Letters 1978. Hons: Longview Foundn.
Art Award 1966; Natl. Council for the Arts Award 1966; Guggenheim
Foundn. Fellowship 1968; Fine Arts Medal, American Inst. of
Architects 1971; Distinguished Teaching of Art Award, College Art
Assn. 1974; Creative Arts Award for Sculpture, Brandeis Univ. 1974.
Exhibitions: One-person—Wadsworth Atheneum, Hartford, Conn.
1964; Inst. for Contemporary Art, Univ. of Pennsylvania, Phila-
delphia 1966; Walker Art Center, Minneapolis 1967; Galerie Muller,
Stuttgart 1967; Bryant Park (outdoor show), NYC 1967; Galerie Rene
Ziegler, Zurich 1968; Galerie Yvon Lambert, Paris 1968; Donald
Morris Gall., Detroit 1968; Fischbach Gall., NYC 1968; Mus. of
Modern Art (traveling show), 1968; Univ. of Hawaii, Honolulu 1969;
Newark Mus., N.J. 1970; Montclair Art Mus., N.J. 1970; Princeton
Univ. Art Mus., N.J. 1970; New Jersey State Mus., Trenton 1971;
Knoedler & Co., NYC 1971; Mus. of Modern Art, NYC 1972; Univ.
of Maryland Art Gall., College Park 1974; Fourcade, Droll Gall.,
NYC 1976; Hilberry Gall., Birmingham, Mich. 1977; Pace Gall.,
NYC 1979. *Group*—Black, White and Grey, Wadsworth Atheneum,
Hartford, Conn. 1964; Annuals, Whitney Mus. of Art, NYC 1966,
1971, 1973; Primary Structure Sculpture, Jewish Mus., NYC 1966;
Sculpture in Environment, NYC Dept. of Parks 1967; Color, Image
and Form, Detroit Inst. of Arts 1967; A Generation of Innovation,
Art Inst. of Chicago 1967; Amer. Sculptors of the 60s, Los Angeles
County Mus. of Art 1967; Philadelphia Mus. of Art 1967; Intnl.
Exhib., Carnegie Inst., Pittsburgh 1967; Scale as Content, Corcoran
Gall., Washington, D.C. 1967; Schemata 7, Finch Coll., NYC 1967;
5th Intnl. Exhib., Guggenheim Mus., NYC 1967; Dwan Gall., NYC
1967; Rejective Art, American Fedn. of Arts, NYC 1967; Art in
Embassies, Mus. of Modern Art, Prague 1967; Documenta IV,
Kassel, West Germany 1968; 34th Venice Biennale 1968; Plus by
Minus, Albright/Knox Gall., Buffalo, N.Y. 1968; Martin Luther King
Memorial, Mus. of Modern Art, NYC 1968; Minimal Art, Gemeent-
museum, The Hague 1968; Hemisfair, San Antonio, Texas 1968; The
Art of the Real (traveling exhib.), Mus. of Modern Art, NYC, Tate
Gall., London, Centre National d'Art Contemporain, Paris 1968;
Brooklyn Mus., NYC 1968; Galerie Simone Stern, New Orleans 1968;
Newark Mus., N.J. 1968; Seattle Art Mus., Wash. 1968; Mayor Daly
Protest, Richard Feigen Gall., Chicago 1968; N.Y. Painting and
Sculpture 1940–1970, Mus. of Modern Art, NYC 1969–70; Minimal
Art, Akademie der Kunst, Berlin 1969; 1st Invitational Exhib. of
Modern Sculpture, Hakone Open-Air Mus., Japan 1969; Expo 70,
Osaka, Japan 1970; Boston Univ., Mass. 1970; Sheldon Memorial Art
Gall., Univ. of Nebraska, Lincoln 1970; Rijksmuseum Kroller-
Muller, Otterlo, Netherlands 1970; Monumental Art, Contemporary
Arts Center, Cincinnati 1970; American Sculpture, Univ. of Nebras-
ka, Lincoln 1970; Art and Technology, Los Angeles County Mus.,
Calif. 1971; L'Art Vivant Americain, Foundn. Maeght, St. Paul de
Vence, France 1971; Sonsbeek '71, Arnheim 1971; 11th Intnl.
Biennial of Outdoor Sculpture, Middleheim Mus., Antwerp 1971;
Natl. Welfare Rights Benefit Show, Washington, D.C. 1971; San
Francisco Mus. of Art 1971; Indianapolis Mus. of Art 1974; Contem-
porary Arts Center, Cincinnati 1974; Walker Art Center, Minneapolis

1974; Art Inst. of Chicago, 1974; New Orleans Mus. of Art, 1976; Meadow Brook Art Gall., Oakland Univ., Rochester, Mich. 1977; New York State Mus., Albany, N.Y. 1977; American Acad. of Arts and Letters, NYC 1978. *Collections:* Wadsworth Atheneum, Hartford, Conn.; Walker Art Center, Minneapolis, Minn.; Mus. of Modern Art, NYC; Corcoran Gall., Washington, D.C.; Detroit Inst. of Arts, Natl. Gall. of Canada, Ottowa;Rijksmuseum Kroller-Muller, Otterlo, Netherlands; Albright-Knox Gall., Buffalo, N.Y.; other public and private collections. *Author:* "Remarks on Modules," in Two Exhibitions of Sculpture (ed. by Samuel Wagstaff), 1966; statement in "Homage to the Square," Art in America, 1967; contribution to "Who Was Jackson Pollock?," Art in America, 1967; "The Maze," Aspen, 1967; "Die," Art Now, 1969; statement in Design Quarterly, 1970.

Further reading: Tony Smith: Two Exhibitions of Sculpture (ed. by Samuel Wagstaff), 1966; "Old Master of the New Frontier" in Art News, Dec. 1966; "Talking with Tony Smith" in Artforum, Dec. 1966; "Tony Smith: the Ineluctable Modality of the Visible" in Art International 1967; Oct. 1967; "Tony Smith" in Artforum, April 1968; Tony Smith (catalogue by Renee Sabatello) 1968; "Tony Smith's Lunar Ammo Dump" in Art Scene, May 1968; "Tony Smith: Talk About Sculpture" in Art News, April 1971; Tony Smith: Recent Sculpture (catalogue by Martin Friedman and Lucy Lippard) 1971; Lucy Lippard, Tony Smith, 1972; "The Morphology of Tony Smith's Work" in Artforum, April 1974.

EGIDIO VAGNOZZI
Roman Catholic cardinal, and Vatican diplomat
Born Rome, Italy, February 2nd, 1906
Died Rome, Italy, December 26th, 1980

Egidio Cardinal Vagnozzi served as Apostolic Delegate to the United States from 1959 until 1967, a period when sweeping reforms were introduced to Roman Catholicism by the Second Vatican Council. Vagnozzi was viewed by many liberal Catholics as an opponent of the spirit of Vatican II.

Born in a working class district of Rome, Egidio Vagnozzi decided, when he was an eight-year-old altar boy, to become a priest. He entered the seminary four years later and progressed so rapidly in his educational training that he earned dispensation from the usual ordination age of 24, and was admitted to the priesthood two years early. His request for an Asian mission was denied and Vagnozzi was ordered instead to continue his studies. In 1930, having earned the last of his three doctorates—they were in philosophy, theology and canon law—Vagnozzi was assigned to the staff of the Vatican Secretariat of State; he was raised to the rank of monsignor in 1932 and appointed to an advisory role on the staff of the Apostolic Delegate to the United States, where he remained for ten years.

During his first American tour, Vagnozzi's duties became increasingly important and he adapted to American customs with such alacrity that, upon recall to the Vatican in 1942, he became known among his colleagues as "the American." After the war, he was

posted to serve as counselor to the Parisian Papal Nuncio, Archbishop Angelo Roncalli, who later became Pope John XXIII. His longing for an Asian ministry was finally realized in 1948 when he was sent as Papal emissary to India and, after his elevation to Archbishop, Vagnozzi worked in the Philippines from 1949 until 1958. As the first Papal Nuncio to the island nation, he became known as a strong and efficacious opponent of the pro-communist Hukhabalup insurgents, and also emerged as the spokesman for a strengthened native clergy. In 1958 Vice-President Richard M. Nixon, on a tour of the Far East, described Vagnozzi as one of the most knowledgeable men on Asian affairs that he had met. Thus, when Pope John XXIII needed a replacement for Cardinal-designate Cicognani in the critical office of Apostolic Delegate to the United States, he immediately called upon Vagnozzi, a former subordinate with considerable experience in America and the acknowledged respect of its political leaders.

A theological conservative whose values had been shaped during the Papacy of Pius XII, Vagnozzi was unprepared for the progressive reforms of Vatican II and troubled by the enthusiasm with which they were embraced by much of the American episcopacy. He publicly discouraged pastoral discussion of such liberal theologians as Tielhard de Chardin and Hans Kung. In 1960, Vagnozzi criticized what he perceived to be the extreme liberalism of many lay Catholics, saying, "The Church cannot have a change of thought—it is inspired by the Holy Spirit. But every age can make a contribution to its perennial philosophy." Moreover, he expressed reservations about conducting mass in English and his vigorous defense of Pius XII's reluctance to condemn Nazi anti-Semitism seemed too exculpatory for many progressive Catholics.

Although he claimed not to be out of step with the reformist spirit of the Vatican, many liberal members of the Church regarded Vagnozzi as an enemy of the ecumenical movement. In 1965 he circulated a "confidential" directive which purportedly contained orders from the Holy See instructing American church leaders to refrain from participation in ecumenical services until a Councilor Commission established the official forms of joint worship. When a group of liberal churchmen made the letter public, the Holy See expressed surprise, and suspicions were aroused that Vagnozzi had acted in concert with anti-liberal members of the Curial bureaucracy, headed by the archconservative Cardinal Ottavini, in an attempt to undermine Vatican II reforms.

In 1967, when Pope Paul made Vagnozzi a Cardinal and recalled him to Rome to head the Sacred College's Prefecture for Economic Affairs of the Holy See, his increasingly troubled relations with leaders in the American church hierarchy came to an end. Because Vagnozzi sought consideration as a candidate for the Papacy, and had therefore hoped to obtain a major office in the Curia, some observers interpreted his appointment to the Sacred College, which gave him salary and title but little real power, as a setback.   R.C.

Son of Francesco V., fireman, and Pasqua Iachetti V. Educ: Pontifical Roman Seminary 1918–21; Pontifical Universitas Lateranensis, Ph.L. 1923, Ph.D. 1924, Reader of Sacred Theology 1927, STD 1928, JCL 1929, JCD 1930. On staff, Vatican Secretariat of State 1930–32; named monsignor 1932; with Apostolic Delegation to U.S. as secty.,

auditor and counselor, Washington, D.C. 1932–42; Counselor, Lisbon 1942; Secretariat of State, Vatican, Rome 1942–46; Counselor to Papal Nuncio, Paris 1946–48; sent to India as chargé d'affaires and counselor to newly established Papal Nunciature 1948–49; promoted to Archbishopric and appointed to Titular Bishopric of Myra in Asia Minor 1949; appointed Apostolic Delegate to U.S. Territory of the Philippines 1949; Papal Nuncio to the Philippines 1951–58; Apostolic Delegate to U.S. 1959–67; elevated to Sacred Coll. of Cardinals 1967; head of Prefecture for Economic Affairs for Holy See from 1967. Member: Council on Public Ecclesiastical Affairs and Congregation for Eastern Churches from 1968; Congregation for the Evangelicalization of Peoples from 1957; Vatican Court's Supreme Tribunal of the Apostolic Signature from 1972. Hons: Comdr., French Legion of Honor; Order of Sikatunan, Grand Cross of the Order of the Holy Sepulchre; 23 hon. degrees from various colls. and univs.
Further reading: The Inner Elite by G. MacEoin, 1978.

LORD ST. HELENS
Military officer and politician
Born October 28th, 1912
Died December 27th, 1980

Lord St. Helens rose to political prominence during the late 1950s and early 1960s, a period of ascendancy for the British Conservative Party. It was during this period that he assumed several parliamentary and governmental posts that placed him in the second rank of Conservative Party officials.

Lord St. Helens' venture into politics, however, was his second career: his first was a military one. His father, Brigadier-General Henry G. Young, had served with the British Army in India, and directed his son toward the military. Michael Hughes-Young, as he was known until 1964, attended public school at Harrow, then entered the Royal Military College at Sandhurst. He received his first commission with the Black Watch, a Scottish regiment, in 1932. During the 1930s he held a number of overseas commissions; in 1934 he was attached to the French Army and in 1935 he was temporarily transferred to the King's African Rifles. In 1940 he served under General Wavell in the campaign that ousted Italian forces from Abyssinia (now Ethiopia). He also saw action in the European theater of operations, and participated in the Allied invasion of France in 1944. Wounded twice during the war, he received the Military Cross.

In 1947, while still in his mid-thirties, Hughes-Young retired from military service with the rank of lieutenant-colonel. Turning to politics, he began working for the British Conservative Party's Central Office in 1947. He ran for the parliamentary seat from St. Helens in 1951, but the Conservative sweep into power did not bring him victory. Four years later, though, Hughes-Young was successful in his bid for Parliament. From 1955 until 1964 he represented Central Wandsworth, and gradually advanced within the party's parliamentary ranks under the leadership of Harold Macmillan and Sir Alec Douglas Home. He briefly held the post of Parliamentary Private Secretary to the Minister of State, Board of Trade, in the spring of 1956; he was then appointed Assistant Whip, a post he held for the next two years.

From the late 1950s until 1964 Hughes-Young served as Lord Commissioner of the Treasury and as Treasurer of Her Majesty's Household. By the early 1960s the Conservative ascendancy had begun to weaken; in 1964 the party lost its majority in Parliament, and Hughes-Young lost his seat. In his last official act as prime minister in December 1964, Sir Alec Douglas Home elevated eight individuals to peerages. Among them was Hughes-Young, who received the title of first baron of St. Helens.   S.L.G.

Son of Brig. Henry G. Young. Married Elizabeth Agnes Blakiston-Houston 1939 (d. 1956). Two sons (elder d. 1970); three daughters. Educ: Harrow; Royal Military Coll., Sandhurst. Mil. Service: Lt., Black Watch 1932; attached to French Army 1934; temporarily assigned to King's African Rifles 1935; fought in Abyssinian War 1940; participated in invasion of France 1944. Member, British Conservative Party Central Office 1948–55; M.P. from Central Wandsworth 1955–64; Private Parliamentary Secty., Minister of State, Bd. of Trade 1956; Asst. Govt. Whip 1956–58; Lord Comnr. of the Treasury 1958–62; Deputy Govt. Chief Whip 1959–64; Treasurer of Her Majesty's Household 1962–64. Hons: M.C. 1944; created first Baron of St. Helens 1964.

SAM LEVENE
Stage and screen actor
Born Russia, August 28th, 1905
Died New York City, U.S.A., December 28th, 1980

If it had not been for the young Sam Levene's Yiddish accent and lack of poise, which he felt were interfering with his salesmanship in the family garment business, he might never have become one of the leading character actors of the United States. Several years after graduating from high school in 1923, Levene enrolled in the American Academy of Dramatic Arts in order to improve his diction and gain self-confidence. After several private lessons, the head of the Academy suggested that Levene enroll full-time and offered him a full scholarship.

The early years were lean ones. At one point he appeared in sixteen straight flops, never working more than eight weeks in succession and on several occasions taking menial jobs at Adirondack resorts to make ends meet. His youthful enthusiasm for the theater carried him along, however, until 1932 when he got the part of Finklestein in "Dinner at Eight." After this success, followed by three years of steady work culminating in the role of Patsy in "Three Men on a Horse" in 1935, Levene's career was made.

Levene soon was a much sought-after character actor. However, known mainly for typecast roles—hustling, fast-talking, street-wise ethnics, as typified by the Nathan Detroit role he originated in "Guys and Dolls"—it seemed, to Levene's increasing annoyance, that he was unable to broaden his range. Although he conceded that he was as much responsible for this as the casting directors, Levene became somewhat embittered in his later years because of this failure to develop as an actor. "I don't think I've studied hard enough," he said in an interview in 1974; "I don't think I have the range of a [George C.] Scott." He felt that, for anyone less gifted than a Scott or an Olivier, the theater had a built-in insecurity that weighed ever more heavily on him as the years passed. Although a star in Neil Simon's 1972 hit "The Sunshine Boys," he nonetheless observed: "If you don't have a stage, you're out of business. There's no continuity in the theater. No matter how long you run, you have to close. If this play runs fifty years, it would close." He was also disappointed about never having achieved the level of stardom at which an actor can translate his stage successes into movie parts; two of his choicest roles—Nathan Detroit and Al in "The Sunshine Boys"—went to better-known actors in the film versions.

Despite his self-criticism and disenchantment with his career, however, Levene knew the strength of his talent and never lacked for critical acclaim. No matter how weak the vehicle, his acting was always singled out for praise. In an article on his 35th anniversary in show business, *Newsweek* credited Levene with doing for the shrug "what Nijinsky did with the *grand jeté*": "Woe pushes down on him, pressing on his brow, his cheek lines, the corners of his mouth. What do they want from his life anyway? But then the gloom reaches his shoulders, and Levene can cope. So sue him! He sighs, he shrugs, he will endure."

R.C.

Son of Harry L. and Beth Weiner L. Married Constance Hoffman 1953 (div.). Son: Joseph Kenneth, b. 1955. Jewish. Brought to USA 1907. Naturalized American 1937. Educ: Stuyvesant High Sch., NYC, grad. 1923; American Acad. of Dramatic Arts, NYC 1925–27. Pres., Deauville Costume Co. 1923–25; actor since 1927. *Performances: Plays*—Wall Street (first theatrical appearance), 1927; Jarnegan, 1928; Street Scene, 1929; This Man's Town, 1930; Wonder Boy, 1931; Dinner at Eight, 1932; Yellow Jack, 1934; Spring Song, 1934; Three Men on a Horse, 1935; Room Service, 1937; Margin for Error, 1939; Guys and Dolls, 1940; Grand Guignol Plays, 1943; The Sound of Hunting, 1945; Light Up the Sky, 1948, 1970, 1974, 1975; The Matchmaker (London), 1954; Hot Corner, 1956; Fair Game, 1957; Make a Million, 1958; Heartbreak House, 1959; The Good Soup, 1959; The Devil's Advocate, 1961; Let it Ride, 1961; Seidman and Son, 1962; Cafe Crown, 1964; Last Analysis, 1965; Nathan Weinstein's Daughter, 1966; The Impossible Years, 1966; Don't Drink the Water, 1968; Paris is Out, 1970; A Dream Out of Time, 1970; The Sunshine Boys, 1972–74; Dreyfuss, 1976; The Royal Family, 1976–77; The Merchant, 1977; The Prince of Grand Street, 1978; The Goodbye People, 1978; Goodnight Grandpa, 1979. *Films*—roles in over 30 films including Three Men on a Horse, Yellow Jack, Shopworn Angel, Act One, Shadow of the Thin Man, and The Babe Ruth Story.

SHLOMO RAVITZ
Cantor, composer, and teacher
Born Novogrudok, Russia, ca. 1885
Died Tel Aviv, Israel, December 28th, 1980

Shlomo Ravitz—cantor, composer, conductor—was, to a generation of cantors, a mentor of remarkable influence. Born midway between the towns of Vilna and Bernowitz, Ravitz began singing traditional liturgical music at the age of eight. Four years later he penned what was to be the first of countless compositions for cantors and choirs, and at the age of 15 he was enrolled at the cantorial school of Kiev under the tutelage of Pinchas Minkowski. He completed his cantorial apprenticeship in Vienna, studying with two premiere composers of liturgical music, Professors Otto Waldemere and Karl Shefftman.

Having already earned a reputation as a man of tireless industry, Ravitz left Vienna in 1902 to accept the cantorship of Shalvi in Lithuania. Possessing what seems to have been an insatiable appetite for travel, he left after less than a year and spent the next 30 years as cantor of Lublin and Bardichev in Poland, and of Charkov, Karantchug, and Riga in Russia. Although he never stayed long at any one of his posts, word of his cantorial virtuosity and of his inspiring compositions prompted invitations from every major center of cantorial music in Eastern Europe, including Moscow, Kiev, Odessa, and Petrograd. Ravitz rejected these prestigious offers and accepted instead an invitation in 1928 from the Synagogue of Johannesburg, which was the home of a sizeable and aristocratic Jewish community. After two years in this rarefied environment he felt too far removed from his origins and returned to Riga.

Ravitz resumed his duties as Riga's cantor for two years until he was persuaded by his son Levi to join him in Palestine, where the Great Synagogue of Tel Aviv had just been completed. Shortly thereafter, Ravitz accepted the cantorship of the Great Synagogue; his son was appointed the conductor of its choir.

The years 1932–39 witnessed the so-called Golden Era of Cantorial Music, during which Ravitz and Joseph Rosenblatt established themselves as luminaries. Through his participation in Oneg Shabbat Choir ceremonies, he met and formed a close friendship with the Israeli poet Chaim Nachman Bialik. He set several of the poet's works to music—most notably "To the Bird" *(El-Hatzippor)* and "The Song of Work" *(Shir ha' Avodah v'han'laha)*. Although Ravitz spent most of his time meeting the obligations that his position at the Great Synagogue demanded, he was nonetheless absorbed in creating in his compositions a distinctly Israeli style of cantorial music. Well-known as an innovator, he tried to fuse the monotonous Sephardic mode of pronunciation with European musical themes. It is generally believed, however, that the results proved that he was working with incompatible traditions.

Since Ravitz's voice could no longer fill the Great Synagogue's immense space, he resigned his position in 1939. The remaining years of his life were dedicated to the foundation and prosperity of the Bilu Elementary School in Tel Aviv where he bestowed his passionate love of song and prayer upon the students. He also published a two-volume anthology of synagogue liturgy. In 1978, Ravitz's status as an Israeli cultural giant was confirmed when he was awarded the Yakir of Tel Aviv—an honor usually reserved for statesmen. To Ravitz, the greatest reward came from the reverent love he received from his students, who fondly remember their beloved pedagogue briskly walking along, humming his music. His talent and dedication transcended barriers of time and space, bringing the traditions of European and Israeli, cantorial music together. G.H.

Married. Children: two sons; two daughters. Jewish. Emigrated to Vienna to study; to Johannesburg, South Africa 1928–30; to Palestine 1932, Israeli citizen. Educ: Cantorial Sch., Kiev. Active as Cantor: to Shalvi 1902; to Lublin 1903–06; to Bardichev 1907; to Karantchug 1908–12; to Charkov 1909–21; to Riga 1922–28, 1930–32; to Johannesburg 1928–30; to Tel Aviv 1932–39. Conducted Oneg Shabbat Choir. Founded Bilu Sch. 1939. Awarded Yakir (key) of Tel Aviv 1978. *Author:* The Voice of Israel, 1964.

JAMES GILLULY
Geologist
Born Seattle, Washington, U.S.A., June 24th, 1896
Died Denver, Colorado, U.S.A., December 29th, 1980

A U.S. Geological Survey scientist for much of his career, James Gilluly won high regard within his profession for his precise geologic mapping of many areas of the United States. But he was best known for his maverick views on the process of mountain formation.

After receiving his B.S. degree at the University of Washington in 1920, Gilluly did graduate work at Yale leading to a Ph.D. in geology in 1926. As a graduate student, he performed an important demonstration showing that petrographic study of well cuttings provided information on the arrangement of rock strata useful in oil exploration.

Gilluly worked for the U.S. Geological Survey from 1921 to 1938, then served as professor of geology at the University of California at Los Angeles until 1950 before returning to the Survey in various senior-level positions. He was primarily a structural geologist, and among the areas mapped by Gilluly were parts of California, Oregon, Arizona, Alaska, Nevada, New York and the Panama Canal Zone. He also advanced the understanding of metaphoric and igneous rocks, geomorphology, and the relation between magmatic injection and the formation of copper deposits.

Gilluly's most noted contribution came in his 1948 presidential address to the Geological Society of America. Here he challenged the widely held theory that mountain ranges are created by short bursts of great crustal mobility interrupting long periods of quiescence. Gilluly argued that mountain-building, or orogenic, activity results from slow but persistent movement within the earth's crust. The crustal activity of the past, he believed, was probably no different from that of today.

In his address, Gilluly noted that the northwestern area of the Baldwin Hills in California was rising three feet per century and that an area between San Bernardino and Victorville was rising 20 inches per century. Extended through geologic time, Gilluly stated, these rates could account for any extant mountains. He also examined the record of sediments deposited among hills in the Nevada-Idaho region during the Cretaceous Period. Had the uplift occurred in a brief spurt, the early sediment layer would have reflected the erosion of high mountains and would have therefore contained large pieces of rock. As the mountains were worn down, the sediment deposited by streams and other currents would have consisted of increasingly finer particles. Therefore, upper layer sediments would be finer than those of lower layers. In fact, Gilluly reported, the Cretaceous sediment layers are uniform, indicating that the uplift occurred in small spurts. W.T. Pecora, in presenting the Geological Society of America's Penrose Medal for 1958 to Gilluly, observed that "His analysis, often quoted, both in North America and abroad, has had profound effect on geological thought."

Gilluly received the Distinguished Service Medal from the U.S. Department of the Interior in 1959 and the Bucher Medal from the American Geophysical Union in 1969 as well as an honorary Doctor of Science degree from Princeton in 1959.

He retired in 1966.   M.L.

Son of Charles E.G. and Louisa (Briegel) G. Married Enid Adelaide Frazier 1925. Children: Molly Shaw; Wally Jones. Educ: Univ. of Washington, B.S. 1920; Yale Univ., Sc.D. 1926. Mil. Service: with U.S. Navy 1917–19; Geological consultant to chief engineer, South West Pacific War Theatre 1943–44. Junior Geologist, Natl. Refining Co. 1921. With U.S. Geological Survey: Geologist 1921–38, 1950–54; Chief of General Geology Branch 1954–57; Chief of Fuels Branch 1957–59. Prof. of geology 1938–50 and Faculty Research Lectr. 1948, Univ. of California, Los Angeles; Bownocker Lectr., Ohio State Univ. 1951. Member and Council Member 1938–40, Soc. of Economic Geologists; Member, V.P. 1947, and Pres. 1948, Geological Soc. of America; also Member of Natl. Acad. of Sciences, American Acad. of Arts and Sciences, Mineralogical Soc. of America, American Assoc. of Petroleum Geologists, Soc. of Economic Paleontologists and Mineralogists, American Geophysical Union, Seismological Soc. of America, Geochemical Soc., Colorado Scientific Soc., Geological Soc. of London, Geologische Vereinigung (Bonn). Hons: Penrose Medal, Geological Soc. of America 1958; Distinguished Service Medal, U.S. Dept. of the Interior 1959; Hon. D.Sc., Princeton Univ. 1959; Alumnus summa Laude dignatus, Univ. of Washington 1963; Mucher Medal, American Geophysical Union 1969. *Author:* (with Aaron C. Waters and A.O. Woodford) Principles of Geology, 1951, rev. eds. 1959, 1968, 1975.

TIM HARDIN
Songwriter and singer
Born Eugene, Oregon, U.S.A., 1940
Died Los Angeles, California, U.S.A., December 29th, 1980

Remembered chiefly as the writer of a cornucopia of love songs popularized by other singers in the 1960s and 70s, Tim Hardin was also the largely-unrecognized originator of the "laid-back" vocal style and soft arrangement, which became one of the dominant sounds in the popular music of the time.

Hardin was raised in a musical family: his father, who held a master's degree in music, played bass in amateur and semi-professional jazz bands; his mother, Molly Small Hardin, maintained her celebrated career as a concert violinist throughout Tim's childhood. Tim started to sing and play guitar while a high school student. Upon dropping out of school before his senior year, he enlisted in the United States Marine Corps, which stationed him in Southeast Asia for two years. After his discharge in 1961, he enrolled in the American Academy of Dramatic Arts in New York City, but decided after two weeks to pursue a career in music rather than in the theater.

After roaming the East Coast for a while, Hardin came to settle in Cambridge, Massachusetts, at a time when Cambridge was at the center of the folk music movement that burgeoned nationwide in the late 1950s and early 60s. Joining in free-for-all hootenannies around town, Hardin's distinctive musical style was recognized, and he was soon performing in coffee-houses throughout the Boston area, sharing the stage with such soon-to-be famous young folk singers as Bob Dylan, Joan Baez, Jim McGuinn, and Mimi and Richard Farina. Hardin's early repertoire consisted mainly of the songs of Southern black blues singers such as Leadbelly and Robert Johnson, some of whom—Mississippi John Hurt, Bukka White, and Brownie McGhee—were enjoying revived popularity on the East Coast coffee-house circuit, where Hardin came to know them in person. Although his voice lacked the strength and dynamism of those he emulated, it was full of a plaintive, rough-edged expressiveness that lent itself effectively to singing the blues. Lillian Roxon has called Hardin "one of the very best of the white blues singers."

In 1963 Hardin left Cambridge and his local following for New York City. There he formed a band with a drummer, a pianist, a bassist, and an electric guitarist—unusual instrumentation for a folk singer in those days—and performed regularly at the Night Owl Cafe in Greenwich Village. In spite of the instrumentation, his sound was soft and subdued, the band providing a pale wash of harmony over which he floated his voice, the heavier tone of his Cambridge blues now buoyed by a light jazz feeling and only the slightest touch of rock 'n' roll. It was a sound that, two or three years later, was to become almost the sine qua non of the so-called "folk-rock" of The Mamas & The Papas, The Lovin' Spoonful (two groups which originated in the Greenwich Village folk music circles that formed around Hardin) and others such as Donovan, The Buffalo Springfield, Simon & Garfunkel, and Jesse Colin Young.

Having created his distinctive sound, Hardin began writing his own songs—wistful, romantic odes to elusive love, set to gently pretty melodies—which won him the enthusiastic attention of the music profession long before the public caught on. Before his recordings were on the market, Hardin compositions were being sung by both unknown and well-known singers. Bobby Darin was able to resuscitate his career with "If I Were A Carpenter," borrowing from Hardin not only his song but also his vocal style (much to Hardin's embitterment), having heard a demonstration recording of Hardin's own rendition. Audiences outside of New York did not hear the songwriter sing until 1966, when he appeared at the Newport Folk Festival and released his first record album after two years in the studio. It was a decided critical success and a fair commercial success; a second volume released early the following year fared equally well. Songs such as "Don't Make Promises," "Green Rocky Road," "Reason To Believe," "Misty Roses," "Lady Came From Baltimore," and "You Upset The Grace of Living When You Lie" became standards in the repertoires of many of the most prominent interpretive singers of the time, including Joan Baez, Rod Stewart, Peter, Paul & Mary, and Joel Grey, not to mention every college student with a guitar. "If I Were A Carpenter" (which appeared on Hardin's second album) proved to be an especially durable vehicle, providing hits for The Four Tops and for Johnny Cash and June Carter as well as for Darin; the song is most often recalled now as the theme song of countless weddings of the blissful decade between 1966 and 1976. As a performer, Hardin had only one record on the hit charts during his career, "Simple Song of Freedom" in 1969, written, ironically, by Bobby Darin.

Hardin's third album, released in 1967, was culled from tapes he had recorded in Cambridge in 1963 but had never intended to publish. The agitated blues of that period startled his gentler new fans but illustrated a versatility most had not suspected. With the 1968 release of a live concert album featuring his best-known songs, a 1969 album which included only a few new Hardin originals, and the publication of *The Best of Tim Hardin* the same year, it seemed that he was running out of inspiration. But before 1969 was over he had recorded the most ambitious work of his career, *Suite For Susan Moore and Damion—We Are—One, One, All In One*. Dedicated to his wife and son, the album combined his thematically-connected songs with instrumental selections and spoken poetry.

By this time Hardin was living in rural Woodstock, New York, where his neighbors were Bob Dylan and members of The Band. Hardin has been credited with inspiring the relaxed, pastoral mood of Dylan's 1968 album, *John Wesley Hardin,* which was named after an ancestor of Hardin's, a nineteenth-century Western outlaw.

The 1970s were difficult years for Hardin. A heroin addict for years, his health broke down and had to be painfully rehabilitated with increasing frequency, putting an end to his concert tours. After recording *Bird On The Wire,* an album entirely of other writers' material, in 1971, he moved to England, living in London for most of the decade. During that time he recorded only two albums, *Painted Head* in 1973, on which, aided by English rock guitarist Peter Frampton, he tried unsuccessfully to invigorate his sound with rock 'n' roll, and *Nine* in 1974, an altogether lackluster jumble of ill-fitting styles. That same year his first two albums were repackaged; his early songs retained their popularity, and royalties from ever-new cover versions sustained him financially. In 1978 he returned to the United States, settling in Los Angeles, where he died in uncertain but apparently natural circumstances.   K.B.

Son of a real estate salesman and Molly Small H., musician. Educ: public sch. until 1959. Mil. Service: U.S. Marine Corps 1959–61. Married Susan Moore. Son: Damion. Singer and guitarist in Cambridge, Mass. 1961–63; in NYC 1963–67, in Woodstock, N.Y. 1967–71, in London 1971–78, in Los Angeles 1978–80. *Records: Albums*—Tim Hardin, 1966; Tim Hardin Vol. II, 1967; This is Tim Hardin, 1967; Tim Hardin 3 Live in Concert, 1968; Tim Hardin 4, 1969; Tim Hardin, Suite for Susan Moore and Damion—We Are— One, One, All in One, 1969; Bird on the Wire, 1971; Painted Head, 1973; Tim Hardin Nine, 1974; Tim Hardin Vols. I & II (repackaged),

1974. *Singles*—Green Rocky Road/Never Too Far, 1967; Black Sheep Boy/Misty Roses, 1967; Tribute to Hank Williams/You Upset the Grace of Living when you Lie, 1967; Simple Song of Freedom, 1969.

NADEZHDA (YAKOVLEVNA KHAZINA) MANDELSTAM
Author
Born Saratov, Russia, October 31st, 1889
Died Moscow, U.S.S.R., December 29th, 1980

Nadezhda Mandelstam, widow of the Russian poet Osip Mandelstam, was the author of a two-volume memoir, *Hope Against Hope* (1970) and *Hope Abandoned* (1974), that details the systematic persecution of her husband, herself, and a generation of intellectuals during the rule of Stalin. As such, her books are important historical documents of the terror of those years, about which official Soviet accounts are so conspicuously silent. More personally, she recorded her years with Mandelstam—as friend, lover, and wife—before his banishment and death in a forced labor camp in 1938. In the face of arrest and confiscation of his papers, Nadezhda functioned as archivist for her husband's work; she memorized many of his poems, secreted letters with friends, provided background on obscure references in his writings, and offered insight into the poetic processes of his mind. Largely because of her Homeric memory and strategies of survival, Osip Mandelstam is now recognized as one of the great poets of this century.

Born in Saratov, Nadezhda Yakovlevna Khazina spent most of her youth in Kiev. Her parents were, she said, "nice, highly educated people," who provided their two daughters and one son with a comfortable environment that included wide travel and tutelage by a series of English governesses. From them Nadezhda Yakovlevna gained familiarity with European languages and culture—a knowledge that later assured her survival as an English teacher and translator who was banished to provincial Russian towns after her husband's death.

In 1919 she met Mandelstam, a poet already famous for his association with a group of writers, which included Anna Akhmatova, Boris Pasternak and Nikolai Gumilev, who published in the Journal *Apollon*. Called the Acmeists, their poetry was radically imagistic, allusive, and thematically hostile to the revolutionary enthusiasm of the time. Mandelstam's second book, published in 1923, is dedicated to Nadezhda and, in 1924, after a protracted romance, they married.

During the hard years of the late 1920s, Nedezhda worked as an English translator on such projects as Upton Sinclair's *Machine* and the novels of Captain Mayne Reid. Although the marriage was happy, Osip Mandelstam was at odds with the authorities throughout the decade. Without reluctance, Nadezhda assumed the role of protector, soothing his fears, and guarding against strangers. However, on May 30th, 1934, despite repeated warnings, Mandelstam was arrested for writing these lines in a poem about Stalin:

We live, deaf to the land beneath us,
Ten steps away no one hears our speeches.

All we hear is the Kremlin mountaineer,
The murderer and peasant-slayer.

Through the intervention of Nikolai Bukharin, a member of the Central Committee of the Soviet communist Party and himself a victim of the Stalin purges later on, the first arrest was commuted to exile in the provincial town of Voronezh. These years before Mandelstam's second arrest in 1938 are described in *Hope Against Hope* as a period of deprivation, fear, and illness, but also of great creativity; in three years, the husband and wife changed living quarters five times, and as new poems were hurriedly copied in notebooks, Nadezhda would immediately commit them to memory. On May 1st, 1938, Osip Mandelstam was arrested again; the precise date and circumstance of his death remain unclear, and Nadezhda was not told that he had died until many years later.

Until her return to Moscow in 1964, after teaching English in a succession of small schools and colleges and preparing her memoirs, Nadezhda returned to Moscow from banishment in 1964. Upon publication in the West in 1969, *Hope Against Hope*—translated, Nadezhda means hope—was hailed as a masterpiece for its vivid portraits of the many writers she had known, especially those of Pasternak and Akhmatova, who had been her loyal friends. In reviewing the book, critic George Steiner stressed the resilience of her mind: "She experienced what Orwell imagined: the methodical reduction of human beings to the status of non-persons." *Hope Abandoned* (1974), a later, less cohesive book, was also well-received, although her peremptory assessments of fellow Russian intellectuals angered many of her friends. The voice behind this book is that of one who, as Simon Karlinsky says, "sits in judgment not only over Mandelstam's enemies and persecutors, but over the whole of Russian 20th Century culture. . . . The condemnation is sweeping and the verdict grim indeed."

In her later years, Nadezhda's small apartment in Moscow became a meeting place for young Soviet intellectuals and Western visitors eager to hear her stories of a vanished literary era. She was happy to compare unfavorably the poetry of anyone, with the exception of T.S. Eliot, to that of her husband. Described by her English translator, Max Hayward, as a "vinegary, Brechtian, steel-hard woman of great intelligence, limitless courage, no illusions, permanent convictions and a wild sense of the absurdity of life," Nadezhda Mandelstam could charm unsuspecting visitors in her role as "Poet's Widow" and then shock them with a sudden torrent of profanities.

Though she was born a Jew, Nadezhda worshipped in the faith of the Russian Orthodox Church. Her apartment was filled with icons, and during the last year of her illness, she was visited regularly by a priest. She died of a heart ailment, one of the last survivors of a brilliant literary generation.   R.W.

Daughter of Yakov Khazin, physician. Married Osip Emilievich Mandelstam 1924 (d. 1938). Russian Orthodox (born Jewish). Educ: studied painting in Kiev ca. 1920–21; earned "Kandidat nauk" degree in English philology 1956. Translator in 1920s and 30s; worked occasionally in textile factories; English teacher in provincial towns 1939–63; writer in Moscow since 1964. *Author:* Functions of the Accusative Case on the Basis of Materials Drawn from Anglo-Saxon

Poetic Monuments, 1956; Hope Against Hope, 1970; Mozart and Salieri, 1973; Chapter 42 of Hope Against Hope, 1973; Hope Abandoned, 1974; contributed foreword to Osip Mandelstam: Poems, 1978; translated and edited numerous books and articles during 1920s and 30s, usually anonymously.

Further reading: Reviews of Hope Abandoned by Joseph Brodsky in New York Review of Books, Feb. 7, 1974, and by George Steiner in The New Yorker, Feb. 18, 1974; Mandelstam. The Complete Critical Prose and Letters by Jane Gary Harris (editor), 1978.

PAUL MORRISON
Theater set designer
Born Altoona, Pennsylvania, U.S.A., July 9th, 1906
Died New York City, U.S.A., December 29th, 1980

One of the American theater's most prolific scenic, lighting and costume designers, Paul Morrison was associated for much of his career with New York's Neighborhood Playhouse, whose theater school he directed for 17 years.

Raised amid his family's hotel business in Altoona, Pennsylvania, Morrison graduated from Lafayette College, where he remained for five years as instructor in the Drama Department before moving to New York in 1932. After a successful start as actor and stage manager with the Theater Guild and Group Theater, he spent two years in Chicago as technical director and design supervisor for the Federal Theater Project, part of the New Deal's Works Project Administration. During World War Two he served as head of the design department for the United Service Organization's overseas productions.

Morrison's experience as a Broadway stage designer began during the five years before the war that he spent as chairman of the Theater Department at Bard College. To his credit are the sets, lighting and costumes for more than 60 plays spanning 25 years. He also created the lighting for the Leonard Bernstein-Lillian Hellman musical version of *Candide* (1956) and for the City Center productions of *South Pacific* and *Porgy and Bess* (both in 1961). More recently, Morrison directed and designed the National Performing Arts tour of *A Man for All Seasons* (1963) and was production supervisor for *Conduct Unbecoming* (1970).

Morrison relished the occasional opportunity to return to acting. He appeared in Clifford Odets' *Paradise Lost* and in *The Member of the Wedding*, both under the direction of Harold Clurman [q.v.]. He played the role of stage manager in Thornton Wilder's comedy *The Skin of Our Teeth*, with Helen Hayes and Leif Erickson. When the Theater Guild Repertory Company took the same play to Europe in 1961, Morrison was also technical director and designed the scenery, lighting and costumes.

In 1965 Morrison again collaborated with Harold Clurman as part of a coaching team that worked with members of the Kumo Gekidan in Tokyo, Japan, on an informal presentation of Eugene O'Neill's *Long Day's Journey into Night*. The performance was sponsored by the U.S. State Department.

Since 1942 Morrison taught at the Neighborhood Playhouse School of the Theater, one of the country's leading centers for training young stage performers. On May 5, 1963, he became executive director of the school, a position he held until his death.   L.M.

Son of Patrick M. and Catherine (Murphy) M. Educ: Lafayette Coll, B.A. 1927. Drama Instr., Lafayette Coll. 1927–32; technical dir. and design supervisor, Chicago Div., Federal Theater Project 1935–36; Chmn., Theater Dept., Bard Coll. 1936–41; Dir. of design dept. for overseas production, United Services Org. 1942–45; Exec. Dir., Neighborhood Playhouse Sch. of the Theater 1963–80. Member: Actors Equity Assn.; United Scenic Artists Local 829. *Sets designed:* include: Hedda Gabbler, 1942; I'll Take the High Road, 1943; Affairs of State, 1950; Arms and the Man, 1950; The Cellar and the Well, 1950; Billy Budd, 1951; Golden Boy, 1952; Four Saints in Three Acts, 1952; On Borrowed Time, 1953; Cyrano de Bergerac, 1953; The Confidential Clerk, 1954; Bus Stop, 1955; Tamburlaine, 1956; Separate Tables, 1956; Ziegfeld Follies, 1957; The Visit, 1958; Much Ado about Nothing, 1959; Duel of the Angels, 1960; The Cat and the Canary, 1965.

HAROLD TITTMAN, JR.
U.S. diplomat
Born St. Louis, Missouri, U.S.A., January 8th, 1893
Died Manchester, New Hampshire, U.S.A., December 29th, 1980

A career Foreign Service officer and U.S. Ambassador to Haiti and Peru, Harold Tittman, Jr., held numerous diplomatic posts in Europe and South America between 1920 and 1958. During the early years of the Second World War, he was the only official link between President Roosevelt and Pope Pius XII.

A 1916 graduate of Yale, Tittman served as a pilot in the squadron of Captain Eddie Rickenbacker, the famous American "ace." Tittman, who lost a leg when his plane was shot down over France, was decorated for bravery by both the French and American governments. Tittman's foreign service career actively began in 1921 when he was posted to service with the American embassy in Paris. He was assigned to the embassy in Rome in 1925 and, five years later, he became First Secretary.

In 1940 Tittman was appointed assistant to Myron C. Taylor, President Roosevelt's representative to the Vatican. When the United States declared war on the Axis powers in late 1941, Tittman was barred from living in Rome, and, along with other Allied envoys to the Holy See, he moved to a palazzo within Vatican City; thereafter, Tittman was F.D.R.'s diplomatic representative to the Pope. Granted a special audience in January, 1943, Tittman relayed to Pope Pius XII Roosevelt's dismay over the Pope's failure to condemn Nazi barbarism in his Christmas message. The Pope replied that such an indictment would ultimately have been an embarrassment to the allies—to speak of German evil, he told Tittman, would have also required him to castigate Soviet iniquities.

When Mussolini fell from power later in 1943, the Pope acted as an intermediary in the new government's effort to forge a peace settlement with the allies; according to the *New York Times*, "Tittman became a key figure in those backstage negotiations." When the U.S. Fifth Army liberated Rome, Tittman regained his freedom.

After the war, Tittman served as U.S. Ambassador to Haiti and Peru. After heading the Intergovernmental Committee for European Migration for three years, Tittman retired from diplomatic service in 1958.

T.P.

Son of Harold T. and Emma Copelin T. Married Eleanora Barclay 1928. Two sons. Educ: Yale Univ. 1916. Mil. Service: pilot in Capt. Eddie Rickenbacker's WWI squadron 1917–20. With U.S. Foreign Service: Secty. of embassy in Paris 1921–25 and in Rome 1925–36; named First Secty. 1930; Asst. Chief, Div. of European Affairs, Dept. of State 1936–39; Consul Gen., Geneva 1939–40; Asst. to Pres.'s personal rep. to the Vatican, Rome 1940–46; Ambassador to Haiti 1946–48; Ambassador to Peru 1948–55; Dir., Intergovernmental Cttee. for European Migration 1955–58. Hons: Distinguished Service Cross; Order of the Purple Heart; Victory Cross; Croix de Guerre.

IRVIN F. WESTHEIMER
Businessman, philanthropist and founder of Big Brothers
Born Newark, New Jersey, U.S.A., September 19th, 1879
Died Cincinnati, Ohio, U.S.A., December 29th, 1980

Irvin F. Westheimer, the founder of Big Brothers, was the son of a whiskey distiller in St. Joseph, Missouri, whose business he joined when he was 21. In 1901 he opened a branch office of the Westheimer Distillery in Cincinnati, Ohio, and it was there, two years later, that he founded Big Brothers. On the Fourth of July, 1903, he went to his office, hoping to catch up on work. Work was forgotten, however, when, as he recalled many years later: "I glanced out the window and saw a boy rummaging in a garbage can for food for himself and his scruffy-looking dog." Westheimer left his office, went into the alley, and introduced himself to the boy. Although frightened at first, the boy, whose name was Tom, accepted Westheimer's invitation to lunch. Tom later took Westheimer home, where he met Tom's mother and five fatherless siblings. Through Westheimer's assistance, Tom's mother was able to find steady work, but that seemed to Westheimer to be insufficient: A job cannot make up for the loss of a father. After soliciting the support of friends and colleagues in the Cincinnati business community, he established the first chapter of Big Brothers.

The guiding idea behind Big Brothers was that each member might "adopt" a fatherless boy as a foster-brother and provide the child with friendship, moral and perhaps financial support, and brotherly guidance. As the organization grew, recreational facilities, summer camps, cultural centers, and scholarship funds were established. Within a few years, chapters had formed around the country. While the original Cincinnati chapter was predominantly Jewish, others were highly Protestant or Catholic; Westheimer, however, was emphatically non-sectarian. "I am as opposed as I could possibly be to segregation," he said. "I am not a Jew first. I am an American of the Jewish faith." By the time Congress chartered Big Brothers of America in 1958, the organization was entirely interfaith and interracial. In 1977 Big Brothers merged with Big Sisters, which had been formed in the first decade of the century by Mrs. Cornelius Vanderbilt. At the time of Westheimer's death, Big Brothers-Big Sisters of America operated 360 agencies nationwide in the service of 168,000 children.

Aside from his philanthropic work, Westheimer was a successful businessman who amassed a fortune as a liquor manufacturer and distributor, a banker, and a stockbroker. He headed Westheimer Investment Brokers until 1963, when his company merged with Hayden, Stone and he went into semi-retirement; Westheimer remained active in Big Brothers for the rest of his life. In his later years Westheimer received many honors in recognition of his dedication and generosity to the underprivileged; one such honor was the Governor's Award, presented him by Governor James A. Rhodes of Ohio in 1977.   K.B.

Son of a whiskey distiller. Joined Westheimer Distillery and opened branch in Cincinnati 1901; established first chapter, Big Brothers ca. 1903; businessman, stockbroker, banker, and Head, Westheimer Investment Brokers. Hons: Gov.'s award from Ohio 1977.

MAURICE CORNFORTH
Philosopher
Born London, England, October 28th, 1909
Died England, December 31st, 1980

The foremost English Marxist philosopher of his era and an active communist, Maurice Cornforth was known for his critical analyses of empiricism, logical positivism, and linguistic philosophy. He was also the author of intoductory works on Marxism for general readers.

After receiving a B.A. degree from University College, London, in 1929, Cornforth attended Trinity College, Cambridge. There he specialized in logic, studying Bertrand Russell's *Principia Mathematica* and attending seminars given by Ludwig Wittgenstein. While Cornforth was at Cambridge, a friend introduced him to Lenin's *Materialism and Empirio-Criticism.* Upon passing his final logic examinations and receiving a second B.A. in 1931, he joined Maurice Dobb and others to form the first Communist Party organization at Cambridge. From 1933 to 1945 Cornforth worked full-time for the Party in East Anglia, where he was a farm laborer.

During the early postwar years Cornforth served as assistant editor of *Soviet Weekly,* published in London. In 1951 he became managing director at the London publishing firm of Lawrence and Wishart. There he was responsible for a general list and had a major hand in the publication of an English-language *Collected Works* of Marx and Engels, of which 14 volumes appeared during his lifetime.

In his first book, *Science Versus Idealism,* Cornforth argued that British empiricism and logical positivism, by narrowing the range of rational knowledge to subjective sensations or linguistic conventions, paradoxically encouraged mystical thought as a means of escape from the limits imposed on reason. As a rationalist and a dialectical materialist, he affirmed the existence of a material world not merely composed of sense data. The ability of the sciences to alter the environment, Cornforth argued, both demonstrated the reality of the material world and gainsayed those philosophers who argued that the sciences were primarily linguistic devices.

In his three-volume *Dialectical Materialism* (1952–54) and *The Theory of Knowledge,* Cornforth offered a primer on Marxism. His *Marxism and the Linguistic Philosophy* (1965) presented the answers of a dialectical materialist to the questions which have interested linguistic philosophers. *The Open Philosophy and the Open Society* (1968) was a defense of Marxism against the criticism of liberals, and particularly of philosopher Karl Popper. Cornforth insisted on the scientific nature of Marxism. He acknowledged the erroneous efforts of Communists in the time of Stalin to turn Marxism into a rigid, unchanging orthodoxy but insisted that socialism had been successfully established in the Soviet Union. In his final book, *Communism and Philosophy* (1980), he criticized many of his former views.   M.L.

Son of Luke Wiseman C. and Violet (Drucquer) C. Married: (1) Kitty Klugmann 1931; (2) Kathleen Elliott. Educ: Univ. Coll., Univ. of London, B.A. 1929; Trinity Coll., Cambridge Univ., B.A. 1931, M.A. 1934. Eastern district organizer, Communist Party of Great Britain 1933–45; Asst. Ed., Soviet Weekly, London 1945–51; Managing Dir., Lawrence and Wishart Ltd. 1951–75. Member, Assoc. of Scientific Workers. *Author:* Science Versus Materialism, 1946; Dialectical Materialism, 3 vols., 1952–54; Philosophy for Socialists, 1959; Marxism and the Linguistic Philosophy, 1965; The Open Philosophy and the Open Society, 1968; Communism and Philosophy, 1980.

(HERBERT) MARSHALL McLUHAN
Communications theorist
Born Edmonton, Alberta, Canada, July 21st, 1911
Died Toronto, Ontario, Canada, December 31st, 1980

Marshall McLuhan, the communications theorist whose aphorisms became stock phrases of the media-conscious 1960s, was one of the first cultural critics to examine the ways in which rapidly developing information technologies are altering Western societies and to address his findings to the general public rather than to other scholars. The ideas he generated, though provocative, were rarely well thought out, but served as a stimulus to other, more capable students of culture. According to Arthur M. Schlesinger Jr., his work was "a chaotic combination of bland assertion, astute guesswork, fake analogy, dazzling insight, hopeless nonsense, shockmanship, showmanship, wisecracks, and oracular mystification," which nonetheless contains one "deeply serious argument . . . that the emergence of electronic technology is confronting modern man with a crisis of consciousness."

McLuhan was born in Edmonton, in the Canadian West, to parents of Scotch-Irish descent, and grew up in Winnipeg. His father was a real estate and insurance salesman, his mother an actress. He entered

the University of Manitoba as an engineering student, switched to English literature, and graduated with a B.A. in 1933 and an M.A. the year after. At Trinity Hall, Cambridge, where he earned a second B.A. (and eventually a Ph.D. in Elizabethan literature), he studied under I.A. Richards and F.R. Leavis, from whom he picked up an interest in popular culture.

In 1937, McLuhan, who was teaching at the University of Wisconsin, was converted to Roman Catholicism. (His parents were Baptist and Methodist; one of his brothers became an Episcopalian priest.) "My conversion was so sudden," he said later, "that I never took instruction." He married Corinne Keller Lewis, a drama student, with whom he had six children, and became well known as a Tennyson specialist at St. Louis University and Assumption College. He joined the faculty of St. Michael's College, the Catholic division of the University of Toronto, in 1946.

McLuhan's first essay into the field of culture hermeneutics was his 1951 book *The Mechanical Bride,* an attack on "the pressures set up around us today by the mechanical agencies of the press, radio, movies, and advertising." Between 1953 and 1960 he chaired a seminar on culture and communications under a Ford Foundation grant, founded and edited the magazine *Explorations* together with anthropologist Edmund Carpenter, and directed media studies for the U.S. Office of Education and the National Association of Education Broadcasters.

With *The Gutenberg Galaxy,* McLuhan began to develop the public following that was to reach cult proportions in the mid-1960s. The book, which won the Canadian Governor-General's prize for critical prose in 1963, examined the changes wrought by the invention of movable type on societies previously based in oral communication. Linear printing, McLuhan claimed, with its use of an abstract serial alphabet, fostered an overdependence on linear, sequential thinking to the exclusion of other modes of perception, destroyed the unity of the senses with its overemphasis on vision, and separated thought from action. The resulting fragmentation in human consciousness and in society, he said, would be resolved by the advent of electronic communications, which would heighten, rather than deaden, sensory awareness, and which would recreate the tribal community on a worldwide scale (the "global village").

McLuhan elaborated on this theory in *Understanding Media* (1967), in which he argued that electronic devices, such as telephones and typewriters, are extensions of the human central nervous system and are therefore powerful transformers of human perception. Television, for example, involves its viewers in the mental completion of the image (which is formed by the eye from patterns of dots); it is absorbing where print is alienating and fosters a vastly different sense of reality—hence the famous aphorism "the medium is the message."

McLuhan's timely realization that the form of a society is determined by its technology was welcomed by the critics, but he was taken to task for his jargon, his excursions into pop psychology, and his fuzzy thinking. (Richard Nixon, he said, failed to project himself well on television because he was a "hot" performer in a "cool" medium; books—a "hot" medium because of their "low definition"—he pronounced doomed to obsolescence.) Dwight MacDonald called him "an ingenious, imaginative, and (above all) fertile thinker" whose book was "impure nonsense, nonsense adulterated by sense."

The controversy over McLuhan's theories intensified with the publication of *The Medium is the Massage* in 1967. The title, a pun on his own aphorism, was intended to alert the public to the idea that "a medium is not something neutral," but an active force in changing human consciousness. The book was a collection of slogans, captions, and pithy texts by McLuhan, with cartoons, photographs, and supergraphics selected by Quentin Fiore, and packaged together in an imitation of television (or, as McLuhan put it, as "a collido-scope of interfaced situations."). Tom Nairn, writing in *New Statesman,* said: "[McLuhan] is a monomaniac who happens to be hooked on something extremely important. . . . But the colossal evasiveness, the slipshod reasoning and weak-kneed glibness accompanying the mania make him dangerous going. . . . Capable of the most brilliant and stimulating insight into relationships other historians and social theorists have ignored, he systematically fails to develop this insight critically. Consequently, his view of the connection between media and society is an unbelievable shambles."

By the late 1960s, media students and advertising experts had adopted McLuhan as nothing less than the prophet of the electronic age (he was known as "the high priest of Madison Avenue"), while more scholarly critics of Western culture accused him of being a charlatan. McLuhan was at pains to point out that he made no value judgments on the culture he described; his was entirely an exploratory mission, designed to call attention to society's technological determinants so that their power might be perceived, acknowledged and, perhaps, transcended. Jonathan Miller, in an essay on McLuhan, suggested that his work was intended "to find a new form of iconic symbolism through which the redemptive mysteries of God can be experienced."

From 1963 on, McLuhan directed Toronto University's McLuhan Centre for Culture and Technology, which had been established (as the result of a bequest made specifically in his name) to study "the psychic and social consequences of technology and the media." He took a leave of absence in 1966 to take the Albert Schweitzer Chair in the Humanities at Fordham University. His lectures, here and elsewhere, were said to be unusually wide-ranging and convoluted.

During the 1970s, McLuhan continued to write provocative books, made a film and an album to illustrate his ideas, served as a consultant to clients ranging from big business to the Vatican, and collected awards from organizations and governments in Germany, Italy, Great Britain, the United States, and Canada. He played a cameo role, as himself, in Woody Allen's film *Annie Hall* and saw the word McLuhanism enshrined in the Oxford English Dictionary.

McLuhan underwent surgery in 1967 for removal of a benign brain tumor. He retired from teaching in September 1979 following a stroke and died of a second stroke a year later.   J.P.

Son of Herbert Ernest M., real estate and insurance salesman, and Elsie Naomi (Hall) M., actress. Married Corinne Keller Lewis, actress, 1939. Children: Eric; Mary Colton; Teresa; Stephanie; Elizabeth O'Sullivan; Michael. Born Protestant; Roman Catholic since 1937. Educ: Univ. of Manitoba, B.A. 1932, M.A. 1934; Trinity Hall, Cambridge, B.A. 1936; M.A. 1939; Ph.D. 1942. Faculty member, Univ. of Wisconsin 1936–37; Instr. in English, St. Louis

Univ. 1937–44; Assoc. Prof. of English, Assumption Univ., Windsor, Ontario 1944–46; Albert Schweitzer Prof. in the Humanities, Fordham Univ., NYC 1967–68; Eugene McDermott Prof., Univ. of Dallas 1975. With Univ. of Toronto: Assoc. Prof. of English 1946–79 and Prof. of English 1952–79, St. Michael's Coll.; Dir., McLuhan Centre for Culture and Technology since 1963. With Explorations (jrnl.): Co-founder 1954; Co-ed. 1954–59; Ed. since 1964. Chmn., Ford Foundn. seminar on culture and communication 1953–55; Dir., media project for U.S. Office of Education and Assn. of Educational Broadcasters 1959–60; Consultant, Vatican Pontifical Commn. for Social Communications 1973; also consultant to business and organizations; Pound Lectr. 1978, many other lectures. Hons: Governor-General's Award for critical prose (for The Gutenberg Galaxy), Canada 1963; FRSC 1964; award in culture and communications, Niagara Univ. 1967; Molson Award in Social Sciences, Canada Council 1967; Carl Einstein Prize, Young German Art Critics, West Germany 1967; C.C. 1970; President's Award, Inst. of Public Relations, Great Britain 1970; Christian Culture Award, Assumption Univ. 1971; Gold Medal of the Italian Republic 1971; President's Cabinet Award, Univ. of Detroit 1972. Hon. D.Litt. from Univ. of Windsor 1965, Assumption Univ. 1966, Univ. of Manitoba 1967, Simon Fraser Univ. 1967, Grinnel Coll. 1967, St. John Fisher Coll. 1969, Univ of Western Ontario 1972, Univ. of Toronto 1977; Hon. LL.D. from Univ. of Alberta 1971, Niagara Univ. 1978. *Books:* The Mechanical Bride: Folklore of Industrial Man, 1951; Selected Poetry of Tennyson, 1956; (ed., with Edmund S. Carpenter) Explorations in Communications, 1960; The Gutenberg Galaxy: The Making of Typographic Man, 1962; Understanding Media: The Extensions of Man, 1964; (with R.J. Schoeck) Voices of Literature, Vols. I–III, 1964, 1965, 1970; (with Quentin Fiore) The Medium is the Massage: An Inventory of Effects, 1967; War and Peace in the Global Village, 1968; (with Harley Parker) Through the Vanishing Point: Space in Poetry and Painting, 1968; The Interior Landscape: Selected Literary Criticism (ed. by E. McNamara), 1969; Counterblast, 1969; Culture is Our Business, 1970; (with Wilfred Watson) From Cliché to Archetype, 1970; (with B. Nevitt) Take Today: The Executive as Dropout, 1972; (with Eric McLuhan and Kathy Hutchon) The City as Classroom, 1977; D'oeil à oreille, 1977; (with P. Babin) Autre homme, autre chrétien à l'âge électronique, 1977; Wolin steuert die Welt?, 1978. *Film:* This is Marshall McLuhan, 1968. *Recordings:* The Medium is the Message, 1967. Many articles in scholarly and popular journals and magazines. *Further reading:* McLuhan: Hot and Cool by Gerald Emanuel Stearns (ed.), 1967; McLuhan: Pro and Con by Raymond Rosenthal (ed.), 1968; Master Minds by Richard Kostelanetz, 1969; Marshall McLuhan by Jonathan Miller, 1971.

BOB SHAWKEY
Pitcher and manager of the New York Yankees
Born Brookville, Pennsylvania, U.S.A., December 4th, 1890
Died Syracuse, New York, U.S.A., December 31st, 1980

Bob Shawkey, former pitcher for the New York Yankees, was born in Pennsylvania in 1890. He was working as a fireman on the Pennsylvania Railroad when Harry Truman, a local shopkeeper and former semi-pro pitcher, decided that the young man had a future in baseball and began grooming him for the major leagues. By 1911 he was ready to join the Harrisburg team of the Tri-State League, where his right-handed fastball caught the notice of the legendary Connie Mack, founder, owner, and manager of the Philadelphia Athletics, who took him on as a regular in 1913. Two years later he was picked up on waivers for $2,500 by the Yankees, for whom he played for the next 13 years (with time out for service in the Navy). During his career he played a total of 498 games, won 198 and lost 150, and achieved a lifetime ERA of 3.09, with 1,135 strikeouts and 1,025 walks; his 1920 ERA of 2.46 was the best in the American League that year. He won 20 or more games in four of his pitching years and ten or more games in five other years; the best was a 24–14 record in 1916. He also pitched five World Series, compiling a 1-3-1 mark in eight appearances.

Although not a pitcher of Hall of Fame caliber, Shawkey (nicknamed "Bob the Gob") achieved some memorable moments. He was the pitcher of record in the only tie game ever recorded in World Series history, the second game of the Yankee-Giant contest on October 5, 1922. Shawkey had pitched ten innings and was deadlocked 3–3 with Giant hurler Joe Barnes when the umpires decided to call the game on account of darkness. The furious crowd rained bottles and seat cushions on the Polo Grounds in protest; Commissioner Landis, who was present, responded by declaring the game tied and ordering the gate receipts donated to charity, thus preventing the rowdy fans from receiving refunds. (The game was replayed the next day and was won by the Giants 3–0). Another high point came in 1923 when manager Miller Huggins asked Shawkey to pitch the opening game in the newly built Yankee Stadium. In 1927, his last season, he was a part of the "Murderer's Row" championship team that defeated the Pittsburgh Pirates in four straight games.

Shawkey left the team in 1928. According to the *New York Telegram,* he pleaded with Huggins for a coaching job but was hired only after the Yankee manager decided that one of his bright young prospects needed the tutoring of an old veteran. When Huggins died suddenly in 1930, Shawkey was invited to take over as manager after coach Arthur Fletcher refused the job. His appointment was greeted with surprise in the sporting press; the *Telegram* called him the "happy subject of one of the luckiest strokes in the annals of the sport." He found himself heading baseball's proudest organization, the boss of such great players as Ruth, Gehrig, and Lazzeri, but was dismissed after one season when he steered the defending champions to a third-place finish and a mediocre 86–68 mark.

With the exception of several later part-time jobs as a pitching coach, this was Shawkey's last major league experience. He continued in the Yankee farm system as manager with the Jersey City, Scranton, and Newark clubs before becoming coach at Dartmouth College in 1950. In 1976 he was honored with an invitation to throw out the first ball of the season in the newly remodeled Yankee stadium. R.C./J.P.

Born James Robert Shawkey. Married. Children. Mil. Service: U.S. Navy 1917–18. Pitcher, Tri-State League team, Harrisburg, Pa. 1911–12; pitcher, Philadelphia Athletics, American League 1913–15. With New York Yankees, American League: obtained on waivers 1915; pitcher 1915–27; pitching coaching 1929; manager 1930. Pitcher,

Montreal team, International League 1928; manager, Yankee farm clubs at Jersey City, N.J., and Scranton, Pa. 1931–35, and at Newark, N.J. 1947–49; pitching coach and instr., various major league teams; baseball coach, Dartmouth Coll. 1950–55. Hons: named to Pennsylvania Sports Hall of Fame.

RAOUL WALSH
Motion picture director
Born New York City, U.S.A., March 11th, 1887
Died Simi Valley, California, U.S.A., December 31st, 1980

Raoul Walsh began directing in 1912, a year before films were first made in Hollywood. He directed his last film in 1964, with Hollywood's Golden Years long past, and the studio system in decline. During the intervening 52 years, Walsh directed over 120 films, and quite possibly a lot more than that. The only source of information for much of Walsh's early career was Walsh himself, and he was a ready, vivid, and cheerfully unreliable raconteur.

He was born in Manhattan. His father was an Irish immigrant who had built up a successful tailoring business, and his mother was half-Irish and half-Spanish. Walsh attended college at Seton Hall in New York, but interrupted his studies to take ship on a cargo schooner owned by his uncle. The vessel, bound for Cuba, ran into a hurricane and had to be towed to Mexico; there Walsh disembarked, learned to ride and to rope steers, and joined a trail herd heading north. From Texas he drifted up to Butte, Montana, where he acted as assistant anaesthetist to a local surgeon, and succeeded in killing at least one patient. ("He had no chance anyhow.") Back in Texas, he fell in with a travelling theatrical company in San Antonio, who needed someone who could ride a horse on a treadmill.

In 1912, after two years on the stage, Walsh moved into film acting, first for the Pathé brothers, then for D. W. Griffith at Biograph, who gave him his first directorial assignment. Sent down to Mexico to make a film about Pancho Villa, Walsh succeeded through blatant flattery in persuading the revolutionary general to play himself in a series of heroic scenes, while Walsh played Villa as a young man. *The Life of General Villa,* co-directed with Griffith's assistant Christy Cabanne, was released in 1914.

Walsh continued to direct for Griffith, making a series of two-reelers, as well as acting and writing scenarios (sometimes combining all three activities on the same picture). His most notable acting role of the period was as John Wilkes Booth, assassin of Lincoln, in Griffith's classic *Birth of a Nation* (1915). Also in 1915, he joined William Fox, and directed his first solo full-length feature, *The Regeneration*. He was to stay with Fox's company for twenty years, and gradually gave up acting to concentrate on directing.

Among the fifty or so films Walsh made for Fox were comedies, melodramas, outdoor adventures, period pieces, Westerns, war films and gangster movies. To all of them he brought a vigorous professionalism, and a knack for direct, uncluttered narrative. The best-remembered of his silent films include *The Thief of Baghdad* (1924), a dazzling spectacular vehicle for Douglas Fairbanks; *What Price Glory?*

(1926), a rambunctious blend of bawdy comedy and war picture, which was so successful that it generated three sequels, all directed by Walsh with the same two leads (Victor McLaglen and Edmund Lowe); and *Sadie Thompson,* first of several versions of Somerset Maugham's story *Rain,* with Gloria Swanson in the title role, and Walsh, in what was to be his last acting appearance, as Sergeant O'Hara.

Walsh reacted to the arrival of sound with typical insouciance; he immediately set out for Utah to shoot a Western talkie on location. *In Old Arizona* (1929) was to have starred Walsh himself as the Cisco Kid. But, with two reels shot, he was driving through the desert one night when a jackrabbit, presumably confused by the headlights, jumped through his windscreen. Walsh was badly cut by the glass, and had to have his right eye removed. Refusing a glass eye ("No, I'd get drunk and lose it") he adopted a black eye-patch, which he wore with buccaneering panache. The film was completed by Irving Cummings, with Warner Baxter taking over the starring role.

The next year Walsh directed another pioneering Western, also shot on exterior location. *The Big Trail* (1930) was the first film ever made in a 70mm wide-screen process, a system known as 'Fox Grandeur'; it also starred a young unknown called John Wayne. The film failed, largely as a result of the cumbersome Grandeur process, and Wayne returned to 'B' movies for another eight years, until John Ford rediscovered him.

After leaving Fox in 1935, Walsh freelanced for a few years, making films for MGM, Paramount and RKO, and handling a couple of assignments in Britain, before joining Warner Brothers in 1939. During his twelve years at Warners he made what are generally reckoned to be his finest films, among them his first assignment, *The Roaring Twenties* (1939). Starring Cagney and Bogart as rival mobsters in the Prohibition era, it comes across with raw energy and exhilarating pace, a fitting culmination to the great decade of Warners gangster movies.

The first half of *They Drive by Night* (1940) was also well up to standard, with Raft and Bogart as long-distance truck drivers; thereafter it collapsed into overheated courtroom melodrama. There was no such weakness, though, in *High Sierra* (1941), perhaps the best film Walsh ever made. Tightly scripted by John Huston, it gave Bogart his breakthrough into top-billing as 'Mad Dog' Earle, a doomed gangster on the run. Walsh later re-made the film as a western, *Colorado Territory* (1949), with Joel McCrea. Also in 1941, in a very different vein, he made *Strawberry Blonde,* a charming piece of period nostalgia, starring Cagney as a small-town dentist. This, too, he later re-made, as a musical, *One Sunday Afternoon* (1948).

That same year, a vintage one for Walsh, he directed *Manpower* (1941), a tough drama in the classic Warners style, about high-tension linesmen; and the first of his films with Errol Flynn, *They Died With Their Boots On* (1941), a sympathetic portrayal of General Custer at Little Big Horn. He was to make seven more movies starring Flynn, including the notorious *Objective Burma* (1945). This was the film in which Flynn 'took Burma single-handed', and its alleged slighting of British wartime achievements caused it to be banned in Britain until 1952.

Of the other films Walsh made for Warners, the most notable are *Pursued* (1947), a moody, haunted work with a good claim to be the first of the 'psychological Westerns' which were to become fashionable in the 50s; and *White Heat* (1949), the last of the great traditional gangster movies, with Cagney in magnificent form as the psychotic, mother-fixated gunman. After his contract expired in 1951, Walsh worked for most of the major studios, making some enjoyable movies, but nothing to equal his best work of the 1940s. His last film was an elegiac Western, *A Distant Trumpet* (1964). With the sight in his remaining eye beginning to fail, he retired to his ranch in Southern California, to raise horses and cattle, and enjoy the outdoor life.

During his active career, Walsh had never attracted much 'serious' critical attention; but towards the end of the 60s he was discovered as a subject worthy of cinematic study. He took this in his stride as he had most other events, welcoming his visitors with a fine repertoire of colorful anecdote, and avoiding any but the most factual commentary on his films. He once remarked, in characteristically laconic summary: "I made some hits, I made some near-hits, and I made a lot of turkeys. And I don't want to play any favorites. Let it go, you know."   P.K.

Son of Thomas W., men's clothing designer, and Elizabeth (Brough) W. Married: (1) Miriam Cooper, actress, 1916–27; (2) Lorraine Welles; (3) Mary Simpson. Children: Robert (foster son). Educ: public sch., NYC; Seton Hall Univ., NYC. Worked as cattle hand, Mexico and Texas. Actor 1909–28: toured with acting co.; actor in Westerns for Pathé brothers; actor and asst. dir. to D.W. Griffith, Biograph Studios 1912. Dir: with Fox Studios 1915–20 and 1926–35; with Paramount Studios 1925–26; mainly with Warner Brothers 1939–51; freelanced for several studios, including M-G-M and RKO. Formed Raoul Walsh Enterprises. Hons: three-month film retrospective, Mus. of Modern Art 1974. *Actor:* The Life of General Villa (also co-dir. and scenarist), 1912; The Little Country Mouse, 1913; Sands of Fate, 1914; The Availing Prayer, 1914; Lest We Forget, 1914; The Great Leap, 1914; The Dishonored Medal, 1914; Sierra Jim's Reformation, 1914; For His Master, 1914; The Birth of a Nation (also co-dir.), 1915; The Smuggler, 1915. *Director:* The Double Knot (also actor), 1914; The Mystery of the Hindu Image (also actor), 1914; The Gunman, 1914; The Final Verdict (also actor), 1914; The Death Dice, 1915; His Return (also actor), 1915; The Greaser (also actor), 1915; The Fencing Master, 1915; A Man For All That (also actor), 1915; Eleven-Thirty, 1915; The Buried Hand, 1915; The Celestial Code, 1915; A Bad Man and Others, 1915; The Regeneration (also scenarist), 1915; Carmen (also scenarist and producer), 1915; Pillars of Society, 1916; The Serpent (also co-scenarist and producer), 1916; Blue Blood and Red (also scenarist and producer), 1916; The Honor System (also actor, scenarist and producer), 1917; The Conqueror, 1917; Betrayed (also scenarist and producer), 1917; This is the Life (also co-scenarist), 1917; The Pride of New York, 1917; The Silent Lie, 1917; The Innocent Sinner (also scenarist), 1917; The Woman and the Law (also scenarist), 1918; The Prussian Cur (also scenarist), 1918; On the Jump (also scenarist), 1918; Every Mother's Son (also scenarist), 1918; I'll Say So, 1918; Evangeline (also scenarist and producer), 1919; The Strongest (also scenarist), 1919; Should A Husband Forgive (also scenarist), 1920; From Now On (also scenarist), 1920; The Deep Purple, 1920; The Oath (also producer), 1921; Serenade (also producer), 1921; Lost and Found on a South Sea Island (in Great Britain as Lost and Found), 1922; Kindred of the Dust (also producer), 1922; The Thief of Baghdad, 1924; East of Suez, 1925; The Spaniard (in Great Britain as Spanish Lore), 1925;

The Wanderer, 1925; The Lucky Lady (also producer), 1926; The
Lady of the Harem, 1926; What Price Glory?, 1926; The Monkey
Talks (also producer), 1927; The Loves of Carmen, 1927; Sadie
Thompson (also actor and scenarist), 1928; The Red Dance (in Great
Britain as The Red Dance of Moscow; also producer), 1928; Me,
Gangster, 1928; Hot For Paris (also author), 1929; In Old Arizona
(co-dir.), 1929; The Cock-Eyed World (also scenarist), 1929; The Big
Trail, 1930; The Man Who Came Back, 1931; Women of All Nations,
1931; Yellow Ticket (in Great Britain as The Yellow Passport; also
producer), 1931; Wild Girl (in Great Britain as Salomy Jane), 1932;
Me and My Gal (also known as Pier 13), 1932; Sailor's Luck, 1933;
The Bowery, 1933; Going Hollywood, 1933; Under Pressure, 1935;
Baby-Face Harrington, 1935; Every Night at Eight, 1935; Klondike
Annie, 1936; Big Brown Eyes (also co-scenarist), 1936; Spendthrift
(also co-scenarist), 1936; O.H.M.S. (in USA as You're in the Army
Now), 1937; Jump for Glory (in USA as When Thief Meets Thief),
1937; Artists and Models, 1937; Hitting a New High, 1937; College
Swing (in Great Britain as Swing, Teacher, Swing), 1938; St. Louis
Blues, 1939; The Roaring Twenties, 1939; Dark Command, 1940;
They Drive By Night (in Great Britain as Road To Frisco), 1940; High
Sierra, 1941; The Strawberry Blonde, 1941; Manpower, 1941; They
Died With Their Boots On, 1941; Desperate Journey, 1942; Gentle-
man Jim, 1942; Background to Danger, 1943; Northern Pursuit, 1943;
Uncertain Glory, 1944; Objective Burma, 1945; Salty O'Rourke,
1945; The Horn Blows at Midnight, 1945; The Man I Love, 1946;
Pursued, 1947; Cheyenne, 1947; Silver River, 1948; Fighter Squadron,
1948; One Sunday Afternoon, 1948; Colorado Territory, 1949; White
Heat, 1949; Murder Inc. (in Great Britain as The Enforcer), 1951;
Along the Great Divide, 1951; Captain Horatio Hornblower, 1951;
Distant Drums, 1951; Glory Alley, 1952; the World in His Arms,
1952; The Lawless Breed, 1952; Blackbeard the Pirate, 1952; Sea
Devils, 1953; A Lion is in the Streets, 1953; Gun Fury, 1953;
Saskatchewan (in Great Britain as O'Rourke of the Royal Mounted),
1954; Battle Cry, 1955; The Tall Men, 1955; The Revolt of Mamie
Stover, 1956; The King and Four Queens, 1956; Band of Angels,
1957; The Naked and the Dead, 1958; The Sheriff of Fractured Jaw,
1958; A Private's Affair, 1959; Esther and the King (in Italy as Esther
E Il Re; also co-scenarist and producer), 1960; Marines, Let's Go
(also author and producer), 1961; A Distant Trumpet, 1964. *Author:*
Each Man in His Time (autobiog.), 1974.

ADDENDUM

SHALOM OF SAFED
Israeli "naive" painter
Born Safed, Palestine, ca. 1887
Died Safed, Israel, January 16th, 1980

For over sixty years Shalom Moskowitz, a devout Hasidic Jew, lived in the small, isolated city of Safed, earning his living as a watchmaker until, at the urging of Israeli artist Yosl Bergner, he began to paint in 1957. Bergner, one of a number of Israeli artists who had recently moved to the picturesque city in Galilee, traditionally a great center of Kabbalah or Jewish mysticism, encouraged Shalom to paint after seeing the brightly colored wooden toys which Shalom occasionally made and sold in the town.

The paintings Shalom made were innocent of the illusionistic pictorial conventions of perspective and modeling. He produced perfectly flat paintings populated by stereotypic figures which appeal visually through their balanced design and strong yet well controlled color. Though visually his work recalls the "behind glass" paintings of the nineteenth century folk artists of Palestine (in whom there has been a resurgence of interest due, in part, to Shalom's own success), it is not clear whether he had any but the most fleeting contact with such work, and this only in his childhood. Of the western art tradition he was completely unaware.

Shalom's subject matter was the stories of the Old Testament; the setting of the stories he made his native Safed. His paintings usually consisted of a narrative sequence of scenes which "read," like written Hebrew, from right to left and from top to bottom, except when the action leads to Jerusalem, and the composition ascends the page.

If the individual works can be seen not as cluttered series of illustrations but as whole compositions with pictorial unity, it is because of Shalom's sense for the right open space, and the rhythmic repetition of stylized detail. Though the paintings have a spontaneous, direct, and playful quality, Shalom claimed he conceived the whole composition before execution: "From the beginning, I see the whole story in front of my eyes, clear as a dream."

Mindful of the Biblical injunction against the creation of graven images, Shalom considered himself not an artist but a story teller: "I do not make images. I retell the stories of the Bible in color and line." It is with regard to the spirit of this stated intention that some Israeli critics have seen in Shalom a truly Jewish artist and a possible model for more conventional Israeli artists. Not only is his work independent of the western art tradition in visual terms, but his intention is fundamentally different from that of most western art in that he desires neither to imitate nor to give form to reality. Writes one critic: "To Shalom as to . . . Talmudic interpreters the Second Commandment did not forbid all forms of representation, but only those that imitate nature by creating illusions of idealized, perfect images; images that by outdoing God's creations and placing man at the center of the universe lead to idolatry."

Shalom's admirers resist the terms "naive," "primitive," or "folk" art, citing his intuitive visual sophistication and especially the force of his imagination, which brings his subjects alive by convincingly compressing time and space. If most naive art is the untutored depiction of the immediate local environment, Shalom's work is, by contrast, the subjective, imaginative expression of one for whom the Biblical story has a local habitation.   D.S.

Worked in Safed, Israel as watchmaker, stonemaker, and silversmith, until about age 70. Ashkenazic Jew. One-man museum exhibitions: The Jewish Museum, New York 1961, 1964; The Israel Museum, Jerusalem 1967; Stedelijk Museum, Amsterdam 1967; Moderna Museet, Stockholm 1967; Kunsthaus Museum, Zurich 1968; Palais des Beaux Arts, Brussels 1968; Whitechapel Galleries, London 1969; Pennsylvania Academy of Fine Arts, Philadelphia 1971; The Detroit Institute of Arts 1971. Represented in the collections of: The Museum of Modern Art, New York; The National Museum of Modern Art, Paris; The Philadelphia Museum of Art; and museums listed under one-man exhibitions. Gallery shows in: Tel Aviv; New York; Paris; Detroit; Chicago; Bern; Zurich. Numerous group shows.

DIEGO FABBRI
Playwright
Born Forli, Italy, July 2nd, 1911
Died Riccione, Italy, August 14th, 1980

Diego Fabbri, an Italian playwright of the postwar years, examined the pursuit of a "tragic Christianity" in the modern world where temptations and traps abound and where truth is often only a vague notion. At first a deeply sober and somewhat pessimistic dramatist, Fabbri's later works are lighter and more irreverent. But he never abandoned his faith, believing that religion, though often painful to practice, offered hope and inspiration.

Raised by devoutly Catholic parents in Forli, Fabbri's love of the theater was realized at an early age. By the time he was eight, Diego was a regular performer in local productions. As a young man, he wrote several plays for his parish theater group; the earliest of which, *I fiori del dolore* (Flowers of Grief) was written when he was seventeen.

While studying law at the University of Bologna, Fabbri wrote a number of plays for an all-male amateur acting troupe. After completing his degree in 1936 he attempted to mount his play *Il nodo* (The Knot), but the fascist government banned it, ostensibly because of its "extreme pessimism."

Fabbri took up a position with the Catholic press and was soon transferred to Rome. In 1940 he became secretary-general of the Catholic Film Center and did much to liberalize the church's attitude to the theater and the cinema. The following year, his tenth play, *Orbite* (Orbits) was produced in Rome, and a few months later this was followed by *Paludi* (Marshes), a revised version of the censored *Il nodo*. The deeply pessimistic vein of Fabbri's early work did not appeal to a wide public, but nevertheless his reputation as a playwright grew.

During the Second World War Fabbri became an active Christian
Democrat, and in the nine-month occupation of Rome by the German
army, he delivered a number of lectures, one of which, "Christ
Betrayed," caused controversy because of its sympathetic attitude
toward Marxism. After the war, Fabbri wrote screenplays and
produced a series of religious films. For a time he also edited and
contributed to the magazines *La fiera litteraria* and *Il dramma*. His
series of critical essays on contemporary dramatists Cesare Ludovici,
Rosso di San Secondo and Ugo Betti in *La fiera litteraria* were widely
acclaimed.

Fabbri returned to playwriting late in the 1940s and with his play
Inquisizione (Inquisition), performed in 1950, his reputation soared.
The play, which won the National Prize that year, portrayed a young
priest's crisis of faith. An elderly priest gently exposes the hypocrisy
and selfishness behind his young colleague's counselling of a couple
who are about to split up. The old priest, who has always wished to
see a miracle, achieves his ambition as the young priest begins to
understand true compassion and humility, and the couple are reunited. The Catholic hierarchy took a dim view of Fabbri's portrayal
of the church, and a year later, his *Il seduttore* (The Seducer), so
incensed the Vatican that he was forced to revise the original ending,
in which the protagonist, rather than choose between his three lovers,
commits suicide (considered an heretical act by the church). In
Processo di famiglia (Family Trial), produced in 1953, Fabbri explored
the destructiveness of the Christian/Communist controversy within
Italian society. A child's mother, father, kindly foster parents, and
priest all fight for his custody. Caught between irreconcilable forces,
the boy kills himself.

Fabbri's next play, (1955), *Processo a Gesù* (literally, Trial of Jesus,
but the English version appeared as *Between Two Thieves)* marked a
change in his style. The dark pessimism and bitterness of Fabbri's
youth gave way to irony and wry humor, and the play won international acclaim. A traveling family of German-Jewish actors enact a
trial of Jesus to determine his innocence or guilt and to name those
responsible for his death. The family draws lots to decide who will
portray the various characters. One of the characters, Elias, whose
son died at the hands of anti-Semites, plays the part of the judge; the
witnesses include Mary and Joseph, Mary Magdalene, Judas Iscariot,
Pontius Pilate and Caiaphas. After the court's jurisdiction is defined,
Christ's personality is scrutinized, and Pilate is found guilty of his
murder. Then members of the troupe seated in the audience stand up
to comment; a prostitute and a blind man express their need for Jesus,
but an intellectual denounces him. The lover of Daniel's widow, in an
emotional interruption, confesses that he is partly responsible for
Daniel's death, thus adding a twist to the court's deliberations on
guilt, racism and atonement.

Continuing in his less-reverent vein, Fabbri's 1956 play *Vegli d'armi*
(Vigil of Arms), portrays some Jesuits discussing modern Christianity
while St. Ignatius, in the guise of a butler, attends them. Fabbri again
came under fire from the Vatican for *La bugiarda* (The Liar), in which
a woman strings along both her husband and her lover by skillful lies.
Originally censored, the play was well-received at London's World
Theatre Season. Fabbri's next play *Figli d'art* (Sons of Art), written in
1959 and directed by Luchino Visconti, won a prize at the Paris
Theatre of the Nations Festival.

In the last decade,Fabbri wrote mainly for television. But a recent stage play, *Incontro al parco delle terme*, was scheduled for production late in 1980. During his long writing career, Fabbri also wrote adaptations of French authors and works by Dostoyevsky.

Like many postwar Italian dramatists, Fabbri was influenced by the works of Pirandello, but his plays also demonstrate his interest in the styles and themes of Ugo Betti, Ibsen and Chekhov. A moralist, and a lyrical writer with the ability to tell a good story, Fabbri carefully created a dialectic between the perfect (God) and the imperfect (man). Man's moral dilemmas and search for a state of grace were his constant themes and gained him a wide following with Catholic audiences around the world.   R.T./H.S.

Son of devout Catholics. Educ: Univ. of Bologna, D. Jur. 1936; worked for Catholic publ. 1936–40; Secty.-Gen., Catholic Film Center 1940–50; Ed. and contributor La Fiera Litteraria and Il Dramma. Playwright, screenwriter 1936–80. Hons: Natl. theatre prize for Inquisizione 1950; Marzotto Intl. Prize for Portrait of a Young Man; Theatre of the Nations Prize, Paris, for Figli d'Art. *Stage Plays*—I fiori del dolore (Flowers of Grief) 1931, rev. 1933; Ritorno (Return) 1933; I loro peccati (Their Sins) 1935; Il Fanciu Do sconosciuto (The Unknown Child) 1935; Il nodo (The Knot) 1936; Ricordo (Memory) 1937, produced 1940; Rifiorirà la terra (The Earth Will Bloom Again) 1937; Miraggi (Mirages) 1937; Orbite (Orbits) 1941; Paludi (The Marshes), rev. version of Il nodo 1942; La libreria del sole (The Bookshop of the Sun) 1943; Rancore (Rancor) ca. 1946, produced 1950; Inquisizione (Inquisition) 1950; Il seduttore (The Seducer) 1951; Processo di famiglia (Family Trial) 1953; Processo a Gesù (Between Two Thieves) 1955; La bugiarda (The Liar) 1956; Veglia d'armi (Vigil of Arms) 1956; Delirio (Delirium) 1958; Figli d'arte (Sons of Art) 1959; Lo scoiattolo, 1961; Ritratto d'ignoto (Portrait of an Unknown Person) 1962; A tavola non si parla d'amore, 1963; Qualcuno fra voi, 1963; Il Confidente, 1964; L'avvenimento, 1967; Lascio alle mie dinne, 1969; Non è per scherzo de ti ho amato, 1971. *Radio play*—Il prato (The Meadows) 1941; Divertimento; Delirio; Contemplazione; Trasmissione interotta; Il Bosco incantato (children's theater). *Films* —La Porta del Cielo (story and screenplay, in collaboration) 1945; Un Giorno nella vita (story in collaboration) 1946; Il Testimone (screenplay, in collaboration) 1946; Daniele Cortis (screenplay, in collaboration) 1947; Guerra alla guerra (story) 1948; Fabiola (screenplay) 1950; La Bellezza del diavolo (screenplay) 1950; Verginita (screenplay) 1952; I Sette peccati capitali (consulting artist) 1952; Processo alla città (screenplay) 1952; Europa '51 (screenplay) 1952; Il Mondo le Condanna (story) 1953; La Passeggiata (screenplay) 1953; I Venti (screenplay) 1953; Il Seduttore (screenplay) 1954. *Articles* (in Revista del Dramma italiano) Drammatica di Ugo Betti, Mar. 15, 1940; Il teatro de Cesare Vico Ludovici, Mar. 15, 1941; Il Teatro de Rosso di San Secondo, Sept. 15, 1941. *Adaptations*—I demoni (from Dostoyevsky) 1957; Processo Karamozov (from Dostoyevsky) 1960; Teresa Desqueyroux (from Mauriac) 1961.

ELIZEBETH (SMITH) FRIEDMAN
American cryptographer
Born Huntington, Indiana, U.S.A., August 26th, 1892
Died Washington, D.C., U.S.A., October 31st, 1980

According to David Kahn, the author of *The Code-Breakers* (1967), Elizebeth and William Friedman were "the most famous husband-and-wife team in the history of cryptology." Working for the U.S. government, they helped break the secret codes of German spies, rum-runners, and heroin smugglers; during the Second World War, they deciphered complex Japanese diplomatic codes.

After graduating from Hillsdale College in Michigan and a short period of employment with Chicago's Newberry Library, Elizebeth Smith soon found work in "Colonel" George Fabyan's "think-tank," the Riverbank Laboratories. A wealthy eccentric, attempting to unlock the codes and ciphers in William Shakespeare's plays to prove that Francis Bacon was their real author, Fabyan hired Smith to direct the work of 12 people, one of whom was William Friedman. As the only organized group with experience in ciphers, the Riverbank Laboratory cryptographers were engaged to work for the War Department when the United States entered the First World War. At about this time, Elizebeth and "Bill" Friedman married and, having discovered no evidence to support Fabyan's literary theories, they left the Riverbank Laboratories in 1920 to work explicitly for the federal government.

While her husband helped establish, and then head, the Army's Signal Intelligence Service, Elizebeth became a part of the Treasury Department's war against rum-runners and heroin smugglers. Although she reported that their codes "were of a complexity never even attempted by any government," Smith deciphered 12,000 messages in three years of work for the department's Prohibition Bureau, and she also testified as a key witness in a case involving international law and U.S. relations with Canada.

Prior to American entrance into the Second World War, Lt. Colonel William Friedman, then serving as chief of the Army's Crypt-analysis Bureau, laboriously attempted to break Japanese diplomatic codes, also known as the "Purple Codes." By 1940, he had cracked the secret codes but the wages of his success were high: Friedman suffered a nervous breakdown. It is reported that Elizebeth took over many of her husband's duties during his period of convalescence but little is currently known of the full range of her activities during the wartime years. However, she was responsible in 1944 for cracking the Japanese "Doll Woman Case" code, which helped solve intelligence mysteries concerning the strategic deployment of allied warships. After the war, the Friedmans returned to the cryptographic study of Shakespearean drama and collaborated on *The Shakespearean Ciphers Examined* (1957), which used cryptanalytic methods to prove that Shakespeare had not been the literary pseudonym of Francis Bacon. Elizebeth Friedman's last reported cryptographic accomplishment was the establishment of a coding system for the International Monetary Fund. L.R.

Born Elizebeth Smith. Daughter of John Murphy S. and Sopha Strock S. Married William Frederick Friedman 1917 (d. 1969). Children: John Ramsay; Barbara. Educ: Hillsdale Coll., Michigan 1915; postgrad.

study, American Univ. 1921–23. Worked in Cipher Dept., Riverbank Laboratories 1916–20; communications specialist in War Dept. 1921–22 and in Navy Dept. 1923; Chief Cryptopgraphy Secty., Treasury Dept. 1924–42; Research Analyst, Navy Dept. 1942–46; Communications Consultant, Intnl. Monetary Fund 1946–49; independent research and writing since 1950. Member, Natl. Bd. of League of Women Voters 1934. Hons: co-recipient with husband, Folger Shakespeare Library Prize 1955; American Shakespeare Theatre award 1958. *Author:* (with husband) The Shakespearean Ciphers Examined, 1957.

Index of Obituary Writers

S.A.	Steve Anzovin	T. Smith
D.B.	David Buckley	H. Cook
K.B.	Kenneth Braun	M. Bennett, B. Bigard, K. Blackburne, H. Byrd, F. Emney, B. Evans, T. Hardin, M. Marini, P. Masherov, C.P.M. Romme, I. Westheimer
L.B.	Leslie Bernstein	G. Patrick
M.B.	Michael Binder	R.E. Kintner
R.B.	Rick Black	D. Burpee, G. Pickering
T.B.	Tom Bulmer	P.E. Haggerty, S. Kuffler
A.C.	Alan Crawford	W.J. Baroody, Sr., H. Cámpora, G. Champion, N. Erim, I. Gosnjak, J.B. Longley, A. Lowenstein, J. McDonnell, F. Cavendish-Bentinck, A. Somoza, K. Tynan
K.C.	Kathy Callaway	W.O. Douglas
J.C.	Jody Cohen	A.E. Scheflen
J.C.	Judy Cooke	O. Manning
R.C.	Richard Calhoun	E. Arnold, Lord Ballantrae, G. Bateson, A.T. Benhima, R. Bonelli, J. Bonham, M. Boukstein, A. Burns, H. Clurman, Lord Coleraine, J. Dollard, J.J. Fouché, V. Fox, H. Harrison, E. Hass, R. Hayden, R. Hurley, H.M. Jones, D. Kenney, Y. Khan, I. Kovács, L. Kronenberger, S. Levene, S. Levenson, B. Loden, C. Lord, H. Morgenthau, C. McWilliams, L. Muñoz Marín, W.A. Patterson, S. Pignedoli, J. Randall, G. Russell, D. Schary, B. Shawkey, C.P. Snow, J.L. Talmon, E. Vagnozzi
A.D.	Arthur Daniels	E. Shoumatoff, H. Swope, S. Walsh
D.D.	David Dan	P. Brovka
G.D.	Garry Dobbins	R. Cross, H.W. Dodds, G.T. Sambell
M.D.	Michael Deaves	T. Adams, A.J. Arkell, Lord Armstrong, S.J. Bailey, G.H. Baker, M. Ballinger, Lady Barnett, C. Beaton, M. Boussac, Lord Brock, M. Brosio, E.C. Bullard, B. Butlin, E.R. Campbell, R. Carpenter, J.T. Christie, J. Collier, C. Curran, D. Dean, C. Ebert, G.P. Elliott, C. Ellis, P. Etchebaster, P. Farb, J. Fontanet, Lord Godber, I. Gosnjak, H. Griffith, K. Grubb, L. Guttman, K. Hammond, R. Hawkins, P. Hendy, S. Holmes, G.W. Johnson, D. Joseph, S. Kapwepwe, C. Kleinwort, J. Laurie, W. Lewin, A.R. Longworth, E. Lyons, W. Mallalieu, J. Methven, G. Oliver, J. Paleckis, Lord Pannell, E. Payne, C.H. Pearson, G. Pirie, H.H. Plaskett, W. Prager, A. Renshaw, R. Roberts, W.A. Robson, F. Ronne, J.D. Scott, J. Silverheels, R.A. Smith, M. Stone, M. Sullivan, Baroness Summerskill, G. Sutherland, R. Symonette, W.M.W. Thomas, I. Ward, H. Watt, R. Williams, E. Wyndham White
A.E.	Alan Ellenzweig	B. Aronson, M. Connelly, E. Croft-Murray
L.F.	Louise Forsyth	J. Adamson, A. Andersch, D. Bryceson, L. Dagover, Baroness Emmet, R. Glyn, I. Kaminska, G. Meany, P. Nenni, A. Pettersson, A. Ross, W. Tatarkiewicz, H.E. Wendel
S.F.	Susan Froetschel	G. Battcock, S.W. Cheney, J. Marmorston, W. Midgley, M. Pagliero, F. Tubbs
T.F.	Theresa Fitzgerald	C. Parker, W. Gaunt
J.G.	Julie Garriott	J. Dragonette, W. Susskind
L.G.	Lise Goett	A.J.M. Smith
L.G.	Leon Goldstein	R.L. Dennison
R.G.	Ron Givens	G.M. Burnett
S.L.G.	Steven L. Goulden	S.T. Bindoff, M. Caetano, W.D. Crittenberger, D. Day, W.R. Dornberger, K. Dönitz, H.G. Douglas, V. Gruen, J. Hurstfield, A. Marder, A.A. Tabatabai
G.H.	George Hill	C.H. Dobinson, S. Ravitz
L.H.	Langdon Hammer	K. Dönitz, J. Fischetti, I.M. Parsons
C.J.	Clark Judge	Y. Allon, A. Okun
I.J.	Ian Johnson	J. Gillot, R. Imru, Prince Peter
S.J.	Steve Jakubowski	T. Aderemi, S.A. al-Bitar, A. Deutsch, T.K. Finletter, S. Gandhi, S. Khama, A.C. Nielsen, Sr., C. Orde, M. Spychalski, S. Warren
J.K.	Judy Kass	T. Avery, G. Pitot
L.K.	Leslie Koppelman	S. McCombs
P.K.	Philip Kemp	P. Collinson, Z. Dan, T. Fisher, A. Hitchcock, H. Käutner, L. Milestone, G. Pal, R. Walsh
C.L.	Chris Larson	H. Gantt
H.L.	Herbert Levine	A. Campbell, J. Le Theule
M.L.	Michael Levine	M. Cornforth, J. Gilluly, A. Gouldner, S. Kamiya, J. Léger, J. McEwen

L.M.	Linda Moot	P. Morrison
M.M.	Michael McDonnell	A. Bell, L. Sutherland, M. West
S.M.	Sandra McGowan	W.F. Libby, G. Shakespeare, R. Gary
B.N.	Byron Nelson	D. Mercer, M. Rukeyser
J.N.	Joan Naper	M. Bévenot, J. Fleming, V. Kirkus, M. Kris, M. McLuhan, A. Reeves, Rachel Roberts, H. Sanders, A. Ussher, E. Wilson, C. Young
A.B.P.	Ann Byrd Platt	R.F. Brown, E.C. Clark, P. Guston, F. Ingelfinger, B. Kaufman, M.M. Peshkin, R.B. Stevens
D.P.	David Podell	J. Piaget
H.N.P.	Howard N. Portnoy	M. O'Hara, E. Neumann
J.P.	Janet Podell	H.R. Abramson, J. Adamson, Y. Allon, R. Ardrey, M. Ballinger, C. Beaton, S.D. Berger, A. Brook, M. Brosio, E. Bullard, R. Carpenter, G. Champion, N. Coghill, J. Collier, M. Connelly, C. Curran, A. Deutsch, C. Ellis, P. Etchebaster, J. Fontanet, G.S. Fraser, S. Gandhi, H. Gantt, J.M. Gil-Robles, V.V. Giri, M. Hatta, D. Joseph, S. Kapwepwe, W. Kaufmann, S. Khama, A. Kostelanetz, C. Laye, J. Lennon, W. Lewin, Y. Malik, S. McQueen, M. McLuhan, G. Meany, K. Medford, D. Mercer, M. Monroney, H. Morgenthau, L. Muñoz Marín, P. Nenni, J.J. Niles, M. Ohira, A. Okun, J. Owens, R. Paasio, E. Payne, C.H. Pearson, G. Pirie, D. Partsalides, W.L. Patterson, J. Piaget, H.H. Plaskett, K.A. Porter, W. Roberts, F. Ronne, D. Schary, P. Sellers, Shah of Iran, A. Shukairy, C.P. Snow, A. Somoza, W. Stein, C. Still, Baroness Summerskill, G. Sutherland, W. Tatarkiewicz, M. Tauber, W. Tolbert, K. Tynan, R. Valli, H. Watt, R. Williams, E. Wyndham White, M.I. Yacoub III
S.P.	Sybil Pincus	R. Ardrey, J. Durante, G.S. Fraser, J. Iturbi, A. Kostelanetz, C. Laye, L. Ngoyi, A.P. Mantovani, A. Sjöberg, R. Valli
T.P.	Thomas Parker	G. Borg Olivier, V. Chervenkov, W. Colmer, A. Demichelli, W.J. Gallman, J.M. Gil-Robles, S. Grayzel, M. Ja'abri, J. Lesage, H.L. Lindo, A. Margai, J. Paleckis, A. Sanguinetti, S.F. Reed, A.H. Sharaf, M.G. Sullivan, H. Tittman
L.R.	Leonard Rubenstein	H.A. Abramson, C. Ahlers, E. Bastyan, S. Chaloryoo, E. Farrell, G. Holliday, I. Ibraimov, N. Langley, M.A. Lavrentyev, R. McLeod, G. Raft, F. von Schlabrendorff, B. Travers, M. Valin
L.R.	Léonie Rosenstiel	Benedictos I, T. Holme, A. Wilder
S.R.	Sandi Resnick	M. Burrows
A.G.S.	Anthony G. Seaton	H. Jacques
A.S.	Amy Slaton	P. Campbell, M. Martinez, W. Roberts
B.S.	Betty Scharf	W. Stein
D.S.	David Sassian	C. Hoeven, S. of Safed, M.F. Tauber
D.S.	Drew Silver	A. Brook, W.A. Kienbusch, T. Smith, C. Still
E.A.S.	Emily A. Schaeffer	A. Kleiner
E.S.	Edward Singer	E.H.S. Burhop
E.S.	Edward Sklepowich	H. Agar, F. Sá Carneiro, A. Carpentier, F. Goldie, Lord Gordon-Walker, P.E. Gorman, B. Matthias, K. Wachsmann
H.S.	Howard Stein	Viscount Dilhorne, R. Duvoisin, J. Krumgold
J.S.	Julie Schwartzman	Lord Netherthorpe
J.S.	Jeff Sherman	J. Mauchly
J.S.	Josepha Sherman	M. Adams, D. Banks, R. Brackman, N. Coghill, Lord Erskine, F. Fuller, A. Haskell, T. Hunt, R. Kellar, E. Lampman, M. Martenot, J. Mitchell, F.V. Morley, F. Norman, I. Parin d'Aulaire, W. Talbot, E.W. Teale, R.L. Wolff
J.S.	John Simmons	J. Thorn, M. Turner
L.C.S.	L.C. Suddarth	S.D. Berger, M. Monroney
M.S.	Martin Sokolinsky	G. Amendola, O. Romero.
M. S.	Michael Solinsky	R. Baxter
N.S.	Nancy Stoff	C. Adler, H. Beadle, E.J. Bowen, R. Carline, J. Hubbard, P.C. Joshi, N. Melnikov, A.M. Poniatoff, A. Scott-Moncrieff, Princess Viktoria, J. Wilkinson
R.S.	Russell Shane	R. Pascal, J.K. Foreman, J. LaMarsh
S.S.	Stephanie Szakal	D. Brennan
E.T.	Edward Tallman	A. Amalrik, R. Barthes, Prince Boun Oum, M. Cole, C. Courtneidge, E. Gerö, R.E. Kintner, L. Longo, J. McCormack, H. Miller, O. Mosley, J.-P. Sartre, A. Shternfeld, A.J.M. Smith, A. White, A. Zimin
E.T.	Elisa Turner	J. Beecher, J.H. Griffin, D.O. Stewart

M.T.	**Michael Turk**	Chandhri M. Ali, H.S. Amerasinghe, S. Kamiya, Lord St. Helens
R.T.	**Roland Turner**	A. Andersch, A.J. Arkell, G. Bateson, P. Blanshard, E.R. Campbell, P. Campbell, Viscount Dilhorne, R. Duvoisin, Lord Godber, D. Haymes, D. Janssen, W.R. Keeton, O. Kokoschka, A. Kosygin, S. Lesser, N. Lloyd, M. Marini, K. Mendelssohn, Lord Netherthorpe, A. Ross, O.D. Schreiner, J. Tito, Ton Duc Thang, J. Werich
S.T.	**Susan Tannen**	R. Gardiner
S.T.	**Steve Tischler**	T. Barry, E. Howard, R.W. Marquard, J. Owens, O.D. Schreiner
A.W.	**Ann Weiss**	L. Guilloux, J. Iwaszkiewicz, P. Robert, H.N. Sherrill
H.W.	**Harry Waldman**	Abū Salmā, J. Kotelawala
M.W.	**Mark Winchell**	H. Miller, K.A. Porter
R.W.	**Robin Wagner**	E. Fromm
R.W.	**Richard Woodward**	L.C. Bates, J. Bélehrádek, A. Diop, H.R. Hays, W. Kaufmann, N. Mandelstam, P. Sellers, J.H. Van Vleck

Abbreviations Index

A.A. Associate in Arts
ABC American Broadcasting Company; Australian Broadcasting Commission
ACT Australian Capital Territory
ADC Aide-de-Camp
Admin. Administration; Administrative; Administrator
AEA Actor's Equity Association
AFB Air Force Base
AFC Air Force Cross; Australian Flying Corps
AFD Doctor of Fine Arts
AFL-CIO American Federation of Labor and Congress of Industrial Organizations
AFTRA American Federation of TV and Radio Artists
AIA American Institute of Architects
AID Agency for International Development (US)
Ala. Alabama
Alta. Alberta
A.M. Master of Arts
ANZUS Australia-New Zealand-United States
Apr. April
Ariz. Arizona
Ark. Arkansas
Arts D. Doctor of Fine Arts
Assn. Association
Assoc. Associate
Asst. Assistant
Aug. August
Autobiog. Autobiography
Ave. Avenue
b. born
B.A. Bachelor of Arts
BAC Bachelor of Art of Obstetrics
BBA Bachelor of Business Administration
BBC British Broadcasting Corporation
B.C. British Columbia
B.Ch. Bachelor of Surgery
B.Comm. Bachelor of Commerce
Bd. Board
B. Bachelor of Dental Surgery
B.D.Sc. Bachelor of Dental Science
Beds. Bedfordshire
BEE Bachelor of Electrical Engineering
Berks. Berkshire
BFA Bachelor of Fine Arts
BFPO British Forces Post Office
BHL Bachelor of Hebrew Letters
Biochem. Biochemistry
Biog. Biography
Biol. Biological, Biology
Bldg. Building
B.Litt. Bachelor of Letters
Blvd. Boulevard
B.M. Bachelor of Medicine
Brig. Brigadier
Bros. Brothers
B.S. Bachelor of Science; Bachelor of Surgery
B.Sc. (Dent.) Bachelor of Science in Dentistry
BSE Bachelor of Didactic Science
BST Bachelor of Sacred Theology
Bucks. Buckinghamshire
Bus. Business
c. *or* **ca.** circa
Calif. California
Cambs. Cambridgeshire

Capt. Captain
CARE Cooperative for American Relief Everywhere (formerly: Cooperative for American Remittances to Europe; Cooperative for American Remittances Everywhere)
Carms. Carmarthenshire
C.B. Companion, Order of Bath
CBC Canadian Broadcasting Corporation
CBE Commander, Order of the British Empire
CBS Columbia Broadcasting System
C.C. Companion, Order of Canada
C.D. Canadian Forces Decoration
CENTO Central Treaty Organization
CFC Congregation of Christian Brothers
C.H. Companion of Honour
Ch.B. Bachelor of Surgery
Ch.D. Doctor of Chemistry
Ch.M. Master of Surgery
Chmn. Chairman
C.I. Imperial Order of the Crown of India
Cia. Company
CIA Central Intelligence Agency
Cie. Company
CIE Companion, Order of the Indian Empire
CLD Doctor of Civil Law
C.M. Mastery in Surgery
CMG Companion, Order of St. Michael and St. George
Co. Company
Co-ed. Co-editor
Col. Colonel
Coll. College
Colo. Colorado
Comdg. Commanding
Comdr. Commander
Commn. Commission
Conn. Connecticut
Coop. Cooperative
Corp. Corporation
Corresp. Correspondent
CPA Certified Public Accountant
CSD Doctor of Christian Science
CSI Companion, Order of the Star of India
CSIRO Commonwealth Scientific and Industrial Research Organization
Ct. Court
Cttee. Committee
CVO Companion, Royal Victorian Order
d. deceased
D.Arch. Doctor of Architecture
D.A.Sc. Doctor of Agricultural Science
DBE Dame Commander, Order of the British Empire
D.C. District of Columbia
DCE Doctor of Civil Engineering
D.Ch. Doctor of Surgery
DCL Doctor of Civil Law
DCMG Dame Commander, Order of St. Michael and St. George
D.Cn.L. Doctor of Canon Law
D.Comm. Doctor of Commerce
DCS Doctor of Commercial Science
DCT Doctor of Christian Theology
DCVO Dame Commander, Royal Victorian Order
D.D. Doctor of Divinity

D.D.Sc. Doctor of Dental Science
D.E. Doctor of Engineering
Dec. December
D.Econ. Doctor of Economics
D.Econ.Sc. Doctor of Economic Science
D.Ed. Doctor of Education
Def. Defense
Del. Delaware
D.en.D. Doctor of Law
D.Eng. Doctor of Engineering
D.en.Med. Doctor of Medicine
Dept. Department
D.es L. Doctor of Letters
D. es S. Doctor of Science
D. es Sc.Pol. Doctor of Political Science
Devel. Development, Developing
DFA Doctor of Fine Arts
DFC Distinguished Flying Cross
D.H. Doctor of Humanities
DHL Doctor of Hebrew Letters; Doctor of Humane Letters
DHS Doctor of Health Science
Dir. Director
D.Iur. Doctor of Law
D.Iur.Utr. Doctor of Civil and Canon Law
Div. Division
div. divorced
D.Jur. Doctor of Jurisprudence
DLES Doctor of Letters in Economic Studies
D.Lit. Doctor of Literature; Doctor of Letters
D.Litt. Doctor of Literature; Doctor of Letters
DLS Doctor of Library Science
D.M. Doctor of Medicine
DMD Doctor of Medical Dentistry
D.Med. Doctor of Medicine
D.Mus. Doctor of Music
D.O. Doctor of Ophthalmology; Doctor of Osteopathy
Doc.Eng. Doctor of Engineering
Doc.rer.pol. Doctor of Political Science
DOL Doctor of Oriental Learning
DPA Doctor of Public Administration
D.Paed. Doctor of Pedagogy
D.P.Ec. Doctor of Political Economy
D.Ped. Doctor of Pedagogy
D.Ph. Doctor of Philosophy
DPH Doctor of Public Health
D.Phil. Doctor of Philosophy
DPM Doctor of Psychiatric Medicine
D.Pol.Sci. Doctor of Political Science
Dr. Drive
Dr.Bus.Admin. Doctor of Business Administration
Dr.Rel.Ed. Doctor of Religious Education
Dr.en Fil.y Let. Doctor of Philosophy and Letters
Dr.Eng. Doctor of Engineering
Dr.Ing. Doctor of Engineering
Dr.Iur. Doctor of Law
Dr.Med. Doctor of Medicine
Dr.Nat.Sc. Doctor of Natural Science
Dr.Oec. (Publ.) Doctor of Public Economy
Dr.P.H. Doctor of Public Health
Dr.Phil. Doctor of Philosophy
Dr.Pol.Sc. Doctor of Political Science
Dr.Theol. Doctor of Theology
D.S. Doctor of Science

DSAO Diplomatic Service Administration Office (U.K.)
D.Sc. Doctor of Science
DSC Distinguished Service Cross
DSE Doctor of Science in Economics
DSO Distinguished Service Order
D.Soc.S. Doctor of Social Science
D.Soc.Sci. Doctor of Social Science
DSS Doctor of Sacred Scripture
D.S.Sc. Doctor of Social Science
DST Doctor of Sacred Theology
D.Tech. Doctor of Technology
D.Theol. Doctor of Theology
DUP Doctor of the University of Paris
DVM Doctor of Veterinary Medicine
E. East
Econ(s). Economics
Ed. Editor
ed. edition;Editor
E.D. Doctor of Engineering
Ed.D. Doctor of Education
Educ. Educated
EEC European Economic Community
EFTA European Free Trade Association
Elem. Elementary
Eng.D. Doctor of Engineering
Eng.Sc.D. Doctor of Engineering Science
Exec. Executive
FBI Federal Bureau of Investigation
Feb. February
Fed. Federal
Fedn. Federation
Fla. Florida
Foundn. Foundation
FPO Fleet Post Office
FRCP Fellow Royal College of Physicians
FRS Fellow of the Royal Society
FRSC Fellow of the Royal Society of Canada
FRSE Fellow of the Royal Society of Edinburgh
FRSL Fellow of the Royal Society of Literature
FRSM Fellow of the Royal Society of Medicine
FRSNZ Fellow of the Royal Society of New Zealand
FSIAD Fellow of the Society of Industrial Artists and Designers
Ft. Fort
Ga. Georgia
Gall. Gallery
GATT General Agreement on Tariffs and Trade
GBE Knight/Dame Grand Cross, Order of the British Empire
G.C. George Cross
GCB Knight Grand Cross, Order of the Bath
GCIE Knight Grand Commander, Order of the Indian Empire
GCMG Knight/Dame Grand Cross, Order of St. Michael and St. George
GCSI Knight/Grand Commander, Order of the Star of India
GVCO Knight/Dame Grand Cross, Royal Victorian Order
Gen. General
Geog. Geographical, Geography
Geol. Geological, Geology
Glam. Glamorgan

GLC Greater London Council
Glos. Gloucestershire
Gov. Governor
Govt. Government
GPO General Post Office
Grad. Graduate
Hants. Hampshire
H.E. His Eminence; His/Her Excellency
Herts. Hertfordshire
Hist. History
H.H. His Holiness
H.M. His/Her Majesty (or Majesty's)
HMAS His/Her Majesty's Australian Ship
HMS His/Her Majesty's Ship; His/Her Majesty's
Service
Hon. Honorable; Honorary
Hosp. Hospital
HRH His/Her Royal Highness
IBM International Business Machines
ICI Imperial Chemical Industries
ILEA Inner London Education Authority
Ill. Illinois
illus. illustrated, illustration
Inc. Incorporated
Ind. Indiana
Inst. Institute
Instn. Institution
Instr. Instructor
Intnl. International
ITA Independent Television Authority (U.K.)
ITV Independent Television (U.K.)
Jan. January
J.B. Jurum Baccalaureus
JCB Juris Canonici Bachelor
JCD Doctor of Canon Law
JCL Juris Canonici Lector
J.D. Doctor of Jurisprudence
Jr. Junior
JSD Doctor of Juristic Science
Jt. Joint
Ju.D. Doctor of Law
JUD Doctor of Civil and Canon Law
Jul. July
Jun. June
Kans. Kansas
KBE Knight Commander, Order of the British Empire
K.C. King's Counsel
KCB Knight Commander, Order of the Bath
KCIE Knight Commander, Order of the Indian Empire
KCMG Knight Commander, Order St. Michael and St.
George
KCSI Knight Commander, Order of the Star of India
KCVO Knight Commander, Royal Victorian Order
K.G. Knight, Order of the Garter
K.T. Knight, Order of the Thistle
Ky. Kentucky
L.A. Los Angeles
La. Louisiana
Lab. Laboratory
Lancs. Lancashire
Lang. Language
LCC London County Council (England)
LDS Licentiate in Dental Surgery
Lectr. Lecturer

Leics. Leicestershire
LHD Doctor of Humane Letters
L.I. Long Island
Lincs. Lincolnshire
Lit. Literature
Lit.D. Doctor of Literature; Doctor of Letters
Litt.D. Doctor of Literature; Doctor of Letters
LL.B. Bachelor of Laws
LL.M. Master of Laws
LMCC Licentiate of the Medical Council of Canada
LRCP Licentiate of the Royal College of Physicians
LRCPE Licentiate of the Royal College of Physicians
of Edinburgh
LRCS Licentiate of the Royal College of Surgeons
LRCSE Licentiate of the Royal College of Surgeons of
Edinburgh
Lt. Lieutenant
Ltd. Limited
Ltee. Limited
Mag. Magazine
Maj. Major
Man. Manitoba
Mar. March
Mass. Massachusetts
Math(s). Mathematic(s)
M.B. Bachelor of Medicine
MBA Master of Business Administration
MBE Member, Order of the British Empire
M.C. Military Cross
MCE Master of Civil Engineering
M.Ch. Master in Surgery
M.Ch.D. Master in Dental Surgery
MDV Master of Veterinary Medicine
Me. Maine
Med.Sc.D. Doctor of Medical Science
Mfg. Manufacturing
Mgr. Manager
MHL Master of Hebrew Letters
Mich. Michigan
Mil. Military
Middx. Middlesex
Minn. Minnesota
misc. miscellaneous
Miss. Mississippi
M.L. Master of Laws
MLD Magister Legum Diplomaticarus
MLS Master of Library Science
Mo. Missouri
Mon. Monmouthshire
Mont. Montana
M.P. Member of Parliament
MPH Master of Public Health
ms(s). manuscript(s)
M.S. Master of Surgery
M.Sc.D. Master of Dental Science
MSW Master of Social Work
Mt. Mount
Mus. Museum
Mus.D. Doctor of Music
Mus.Doc. Doctor of Music
MVO Member, Royal Victorian Order
N. North
NAACP National Association for the Advancement of
Colored People

NASA National Aeronautics and Space Administration (U.S.)
NATO North Atlantic Treaty Organization
N.B. New Brunswick
NBC National Broadcasting Company
N.C. North Carolina
N.Dak. North Dakota
N.E. North-East
Nebr. Nebraska
Nev. Nevada
Nfld. Newfoundland
N.H. New Hampshire
N.Ire. Northern Ireland
N.J. New Jersey
N.M. New Mexico
No. Number
Northants. Northamptonshire
Notts. Nottinghamshire
Nov. November
N.S. Nova Scotia
NSW New South Wales
N.T. Northern Territory
N.V. Naamloze Vennootschap (limited liability company)
N.W. North-West
N.Y. New York (state)
NYC New York City
N.Z. New Zealand
OBE Officer, Order of the British Empire
O.C. Officer, Order of Canada
Oct. October
O.D. Doctor of Ophthalmology; Doctor of Osteopathy
OECD Organization for Economic Cooperation and Development
OEEC Organization for European Economic Cooperation
Okla. Oklahoma
O.M. Order of Merit
Ont. Ontario
O.P. Dominican Order
Orch. Orchestra
Ore. Oregon
Org. Organization
orig. original, originally
OSB Benedictine Order
Oxon. Oxfordshire
Pa. Pennsylvania
P.C. Privy Councillor
Pd.D. Doctor of Pedagogy
PEI Prince Edward Island
Pembs. Pembrokeshire
PEN Poets, Playwrights, Essayists, Editors and Novelists
Pharm.D. Doctor of Pharmacy
Ph.B. Bachelor of Philosophy
Ph.D. Doctor of Philosophy
Pl. Place
PLO Palestine Liberation Organization
P.O. Post Office
POB Post Office Box
Polytech. Polytechnical
Postgrad. Postgraduate
POW Prisoner of War
P.R. Puerto Rico
Prep. Preparatory

Pres. President
Prof. Professor
Pty. Proprietary
Q.C. Queen's Counsel
QHP Queen's Honorary Physician
QHS Queen's Honorary Surgeon
Qld. Queensland
Que. Quebec
Rt. Route
RAAF Royal Australian Air Force
RAF Royal Air Force
RCA Radio Corporation of America
Rd. Road
R.D. Rural Delivery
Rep. Representative
Rev. Reverend
rev.ed. revised edition
RFD Rural Free Delivery
R.I. Rhode Island
RIBA Royal Institute of British Architects
Rm. Room
R.N. Registered Nurse
R.R. Rural Route
S. South
S.A. South Australia
Salop. Shropshire
Sask. Saskatchewan
S.C. South Carolina; Senior Counsel (Ireland)
Sc.D. Doctor of Science
Sch. School
S.Dak. South Dakota
S.E. South-East
SEATO South-East Treaty Organization
Secty. Secretary
Sept. September
Sgt. Sergeant
SHAPE Supreme Headquarters, Allied Powers, Europe
S.J. Society of Jesus (Jesuit Order)
SJD Doctor of Juristic Science
So. South
Soc. Society
Sq. Square
Sr. Senior
St. Saint; Street
Staffs. Staffordshire
STD Doctor of Sacred Theology
Ste. Sainte
Supt. Superintendent
S.W. South-West
Tenn. Tennessee
Tex. Texas
Th.D. Doctor of Theology
trans. translation; translator
Treas. Treasurer
TUC Trades Union Congress
UAR United Arab Republic
UJD Doctor of Canon and Civil Law
U.K. United Kingdom
U.N. United Nations
Unesco United Nations Educational Scientific and Cultural Organization
Unicef United Nations Childrens' Emergency Fund
Univ. University, Université, Universitat
UPI United Press International
U.S. United States

USA United States of America
USAID United States Agency for International
    Development
USAEUR United States Army in Europe
USNR United States Naval Reserve
USS United States Ship; United States Service
USSR Union of Soviet Socialist Republics
Va. Virginia
V.A. Royal Order of Victoria and Albert
V.C. Victoria Cross
Vic. Victoria
VMD Doctor of Veterinary Medicine
vol. volume
V.P. Vice President

Vt. Vermont
W. West
W.A. Western Australia
Wash. Washington (state)
WHO World Health Organization
Wilts. Wiltshire
Wisc. Wisconsin
Worcs. Worcestershire
W.Va. West Virginia
W.W. World War
Wyo. Wyoming
YMCA Young Men's Christian Association
YMHA Young Men's Hebrew Association
YWCA Young Women's Christian Association

DATE DUE
